BARRON'S
FINANCIAL TABLES
FOR BETTER
MONEY MANAGEMENT

Canadian Mortgage Payments

Second Edition

Stephen S. Solomon
M.S., Applied Mathematics

Clifford W. Marshall
Ph.D., Applied Mathematics
Professor of Mathematics
Polytechnic Institute of New York

Martin Pepper
Principal, Coopers & Lybrand
Fellow, Society of Actuaries

BARRON'S

Great effort has been made to develop accurate tables; however, no warranty of absolute accuracy is given.

All inquiries should be addressed to:
Barron's Educational Series, Inc.
250 Wireless Boulevard
Hauppauge, New York 11788

Library of Congress Catalog Card No. 92-35744

International Standard Book No. 0-8120-1617-3

Library of Congress Cataloging-in-Publication Data

Solomon, Steven S.
Canadian mortgage payments / Stephen S. Solomon, Clifford W. Marshall, Martin Pepper. — 2nd ed.
p. cm. — (Barron's financial guides)
ISBN 0-8120-1617-3
1. Interest—Canada—Tables. 2. Mortgage loans—Canada—Tables. I. Marshall, Clifford W., 1928– II. Pepper, Martin. III. Title. IV. Series.
HG1634.S654 1993
332.8'2'0212—dc20 92-35744
CIP

PRINTED IN THE UNITED STATES OF AMERICA

456 977 9876543

Contents

All tables are computed on the basis of nominal annual rates compounded semi-annually.

Introduction

The idea behind *Barron's Financial Tables for Better Money Management* is to provide assistance to anyone who invests, makes purchases, or borrows money. Since these guides require no financial or mathematical expertise, they can be used easily by the average investor or mortgage seeker. The tables are easy to read and are preceded by sample situations that show the nature and scope of the tables. Following each sample situation a short explanation tells how to use a particular table to find the desired answer and how to locate data on the table. After reading the situation and explanation you should be able to apply the same procedure to answer questions regarding your particular situation. If you spend time "walking through" all the situations given, you will better understand how to use the tables.

Because these tables are designed for the non-professional, no formulas or mathematical derivations are shown. Such derivations are not required for proper use of the tables.

Monthly Mortgage Payment Tables

Prospective home buyers must consider many important factors when purchasing a home. For most, the purchase of a home is the largest investment of their lives, and the financial arrangements are uppermost in their minds. Therefore, understanding the basis for mortgage financing is the most important factor in the entire undertaking.

The most common source of financing among home buyers is the conventional mortgage. A mortgage is an agreement between a buyer and a lender, usually a bank. Under the terms of the typical mortgage, in return for a loan the buyer agrees to make monthly payments to the lender for a specific number of years. Part of the monthly payment goes for repayment of a portion of the original loan principal and part goes for payment of an interest charge at a specified rate.

Several types of mortgage loans are available today. The tables in this book are for the type used most often by home buyers, under which monthly payments are constant over a fixed repayment period.

The tables that follow cover mortgage loans with interest rates between 5% and 24% and show the required monthly payment for loan amounts ranging from $100 to $250,000 with repayment periods of 1 to 40 years. Here are some illustrative situations to help you understand and use the tables:

Situation 1

Mr. Smith wants to buy a house that costs $60,000.00. He has a down payment of $10,000.00 and now seeks a 30-year conventional mortgage of $50,000.00 (after paying separately all required fees, service charges, etc.). If the stipulated interest rate is 13%, he can determine the required monthly mortgage payment by (1) locating the 13% pages of the monthly mortgage payment tables, (2) finding the vertical column that shows 30 years, (3) looking down the left column on the same page until he finds $50,000.00, and (4) looking across to the 30-year column, which shows a monthly payment of $539.89.

Situation 2

Ms. Green wishes to purchase a house for $110,000.00 and has a down payment of $30,000.00. A bank will give her an $80,000.00 mortgage for 25 years at 12¾%. Ms. Green can determine the monthly mortgage payment by locating the 12¾% pages and the 25-year column on the top of the appropriate page. After looking down the left side of the page for the loan amount of $80,000.00, she then must look across the line to the 25-year column, where she will find a monthly payment of $867.75.

5.00 % Monthly Payments

LOAN AMOUNT	YEARS 1	2	3	4	5	6	7
100	8.56	4.38	2.99	2.30	1.88	1.61	1.41
200	17.12	8.77	5.99	4.60	3.77	3.22	2.82
500	42.79	21.92	14.97	11.50	9.42	8.04	7.05
1000	85.58	43.85	29.95	23.01	18.85	16.08	14.11
2000	171.17	87.70	59.90	46.01	37.70	32.16	28.22
5000	427.92	219.24	149.74	115.03	94.24	80.41	70.55
6000	513.50	263.09	179.69	138.04	113.09	96.49	84.66
7000	599.09	306.94	209.64	161.04	131.93	112.57	98.77
8000	684.67	350.79	239.58	184.05	150.78	128.65	112.88
9000	770.26	394.64	269.53	207.05	169.63	144.73	126.99
10000	855.84	438.48	299.48	230.06	188.48	160.81	141.10
12000	1027.01	526.18	359.37	276.07	226.17	192.97	169.32
15000	1283.76	657.73	449.22	345.09	282.72	241.22	211.65
20000	1711.68	876.97	598.96	460.12	376.95	321.62	282.20
25000	2139.60	1096.21	748.70	575.15	471.19	402.03	352.75
30000	2567.52	1315.45	898.44	690.18	565.43	482.43	423.29
31000	2653.10	1359.30	928.38	713.19	584.28	498.52	437.40
32000	2738.69	1403.15	958.33	736.19	603.13	514.60	451.51
33000	2824.27	1447.00	988.28	759.20	621.98	530.68	465.62
34000	2909.86	1490.85	1018.23	782.21	640.82	546.76	479.73
35000	2995.44	1534.69	1048.18	805.21	659.67	562.84	493.84
36000	3081.02	1578.54	1078.12	828.22	678.52	578.92	507.95
37000	3166.61	1622.39	1108.07	851.22	697.37	595.00	522.06
38000	3252.19	1666.24	1138.02	874.23	716.21	611.08	536.17
39000	3337.77	1710.09	1167.97	897.24	735.06	627.16	550.28
40000	3423.36	1753.94	1197.91	920.24	753.91	643.25	564.39
41000	3508.94	1797.79	1227.86	943.25	772.76	659.33	578.50
42000	3594.53	1841.63	1257.81	966.25	791.61	675.41	592.61
43000	3680.11	1885.48	1287.76	989.26	810.45	691.49	606.72
44000	3765.69	1929.33	1317.71	1012.27	829.30	707.57	620.83
45000	3851.28	1973.18	1347.65	1035.27	848.15	723.65	634.94
46000	3936.86	2017.03	1377.60	1058.28	867.00	739.73	649.05
47000	4022.45	2060.88	1407.55	1081.28	885.84	755.81	663.16
48000	4108.03	2104.72	1437.50	1104.29	904.69	771.90	677.27
49000	4193.61	2148.57	1467.45	1127.30	923.54	787.98	691.38
50000	4279.20	2192.42	1497.39	1150.30	942.39	804.06	705.49
51000	4364.78	2236.27	1527.34	1173.31	961.23	820.14	719.60
52000	4450.37	2280.12	1557.29	1196.32	980.08	836.22	733.71
53000	4535.95	2323.97	1587.24	1219.32	998.93	852.30	747.82
54000	4621.53	2367.81	1617.18	1242.33	1017.78	868.38	761.93
55000	4707.12	2411.66	1647.13	1265.33	1036.63	884.46	776.04
56000	4792.70	2455.51	1677.08	1288.34	1055.47	900.54	790.15
57000	4878.29	2499.36	1707.03	1311.35	1074.32	916.63	804.26
58000	4963.87	2543.21	1736.98	1334.35	1093.17	932.71	818.37
59000	5049.45	2587.06	1766.92	1357.36	1112.02	948.79	832.48
60000	5135.04	2630.91	1796.87	1380.36	1130.86	964.87	846.59
65000	5562.96	2850.15	1946.61	1495.39	1225.10	1045.27	917.14
70000	5990.88	3069.39	2096.35	1610.42	1319.34	1125.68	987.69
75000	6418.80	3288.63	2246.09	1725.45	1413.58	1206.09	1058.24
80000	6846.72	3507.87	2395.83	1840.48	1507.82	1286.49	1128.79
85000	7274.64	3727.12	2545.57	1955.52	1602.06	1366.90	1199.33
90000	7702.56	3946.36	2695.31	2070.55	1696.30	1447.30	1269.88
95000	8130.48	4165.60	2845.05	2185.58	1790.54	1527.71	1340.43
100000	8558.40	4384.84	2994.79	2300.61	1884.77	1608.11	1410.98
105000	8986.32	4604.08	3144.53	2415.64	1979.01	1688.52	1481.53
110000	9414.24	4823.33	3294.27	2530.67	2073.25	1768.93	1552.08
120000	10270.08	5261.81	3593.74	2760.73	2261.73	1929.74	1693.18
130000	11125.92	5700.29	3893.22	2990.79	2450.21	2090.55	1834.28
140000	11981.76	6138.78	4192.70	3220.85	2638.68	2251.36	1975.37
150000	12837.60	6577.26	4492.18	3450.91	2827.16	2412.17	2116.47
160000	13693.44	7015.75	4791.66	3680.97	3015.64	2572.98	2257.57
170000	14549.28	7454.23	5091.14	3911.03	3204.12	2733.79	2398.67
180000	15405.12	7892.72	5390.62	4141.09	3392.59	2894.61	2539.77
190000	16260.96	8331.20	5690.10	4371.15	3581.07	3055.42	2680.87
200000	17116.79	8769.68	5989.57	4601.21	3769.55	3216.23	2821.96
210000	17972.63	9208.17	6289.05	4831.27	3958.03	3377.04	2963.06
220000	18828.47	9646.65	6588.53	5061.33	4146.50	3537.85	3104.16
230000	19684.31	10085.14	6888.01	5291.39	4334.98	3698.66	3245.26
240000	20540.15	10523.62	7187.49	5521.45	4523.46	3859.48	3386.36
250000	21395.99	10962.10	7486.97	5751.52	4711.93	4020.29	3527.45

Monthly Payments 5.00 %

LOAN AMOUNT	8	9	10	11	12	13	14
				YEARS			
100	1.26	1.15	1.06	0.98	0.92	0.87	0.83
200	2.53	2.30	2.12	1.97	1.84	1.74	1.65
500	6.32	5.75	5.29	4.92	4.61	4.35	4.13
1000	12.64	11.49	10.58	9.84	9.22	8.70	8.26
2000	25.27	22.99	21.16	19.68	18.45	17.41	16.52
5000	63.18	57.46	52.91	49.20	46.12	43.52	41.31
6000	75.81	68.96	63.49	59.03	55.34	52.23	49.57
7000	88.45	80.45	74.07	68.87	64.56	60.93	57.84
8000	101.08	91.94	84.65	78.71	73.79	69.64	66.10
9000	113.72	103.43	95.23	88.55	83.01	78.34	74.36
10000	126.36	114.93	105.81	98.39	92.23	87.05	82.62
12000	151.63	137.91	126.98	118.07	110.68	104.45	99.15
15000	189.53	172.39	158.72	147.59	138.35	130.57	123.94
20000	252.71	229.85	211.63	196.78	184.46	174.09	165.25
25000	315.89	287.31	264.54	245.98	230.58	217.61	206.56
30000	379.07	344.78	317.44	295.17	276.70	261.14	247.87
31000	391.70	356.27	328.03	305.01	285.92	269.84	256.13
32000	404.34	367.76	338.61	314.85	295.14	278.55	264.39
33000	416.97	379.25	349.19	324.69	304.37	287.25	272.66
34000	429.61	390.75	359.77	334.53	313.59	295.95	280.92
35000	442.24	402.24	370.35	344.37	322.81	304.66	289.18
36000	454.88	413.73	380.93	354.21	332.03	313.36	297.44
37000	467.51	425.22	391.52	364.05	341.26	322.07	305.71
38000	480.15	436.72	402.10	373.89	350.48	330.77	313.97
39000	492.78	448.21	412.68	383.72	359.70	339.48	322.23
40000	505.42	459.70	423.26	393.56	368.93	348.18	330.49
41000	518.06	471.19	433.84	403.40	378.15	356.89	338.76
42000	530.69	482.69	444.42	413.24	387.37	365.59	347.02
43000	543.33	494.18	455.00	423.08	396.60	374.30	355.28
44000	555.96	505.67	465.59	432.92	405.82	383.00	363.54
45000	568.60	517.16	476.17	442.76	415.04	391.70	371.81
46000	581.23	528.66	486.75	452.60	424.27	400.41	380.07
47000	593.87	540.15	497.33	462.44	433.49	409.11	388.33
48000	606.50	551.64	507.91	472.28	442.71	417.82	396.59
49000	619.14	563.13	518.49	482.12	451.94	426.52	404.85
50000	631.78	574.63	529.07	491.96	461.16	435.23	413.12
51000	644.41	586.12	539.66	501.79	470.38	443.93	421.38
52000	657.05	597.61	550.24	511.63	479.61	452.64	429.64
53000	669.68	609.10	560.82	521.47	488.83	461.34	437.90
54000	682.32	620.60	571.40	531.31	498.05	470.05	446.17
55000	694.95	632.09	581.98	541.15	507.28	478.75	454.43
56000	707.59	643.58	592.56	550.99	516.50	487.46	462.69
57000	720.22	655.07	603.15	560.83	525.72	496.16	470.95
58000	732.86	666.57	613.73	570.67	534.95	504.86	479.22
59000	745.50	678.06	624.31	580.51	544.17	513.57	487.48
60000	758.13	689.55	634.89	590.35	553.39	522.27	495.74
65000	821.31	747.02	687.80	639.54	599.51	565.80	537.05
70000	884.49	804.48	740.70	688.74	645.62	609.32	578.36
75000	947.66	861.94	793.61	737.93	691.74	652.84	619.68
80000	1010.84	919.40	846.52	787.13	737.86	696.36	660.99
85000	1074.02	976.87	899.43	836.32	783.97	739.89	702.30
90000	1137.20	1034.33	952.33	885.52	830.09	783.41	743.61
95000	1200.37	1091.79	1005.24	934.71	876.20	826.93	784.92
100000	1263.55	1149.25	1058.15	983.91	922.32	870.46	826.23
105000	1326.73	1206.72	1111.06	1033.11	968.43	913.98	867.55
110000	1389.91	1264.18	1163.96	1082.30	1014.55	957.50	908.86
120000	1516.26	1379.10	1269.78	1180.69	1106.78	1044.55	991.48
130000	1642.62	1494.03	1375.59	1279.08	1199.01	1131.59	1074.10
140000	1768.97	1608.96	1481.41	1377.47	1291.25	1218.64	1156.73
150000	1895.33	1723.88	1587.22	1475.87	1383.48	1305.68	1239.35
160000	2021.68	1838.81	1693.04	1574.26	1475.71	1392.73	1321.97
170000	2148.04	1953.73	1798.85	1672.65	1567.94	1479.77	1404.60
180000	2274.39	2068.66	1904.67	1771.04	1660.17	1566.82	1487.22
190000	2400.75	2183.58	2010.48	1869.43	1752.41	1653.87	1569.84
200000	2527.10	2298.51	2116.30	1967.82	1844.64	1740.91	1652.47
210000	2653.46	2413.43	2222.11	2066.21	1936.87	1827.96	1735.09
220000	2779.81	2528.36	2327.93	2164.60	2029.10	1915.00	1817.71
230000	2906.17	2643.28	2433.74	2262.99	2121.33	2002.05	1900.34
240000	3032.52	2758.21	2539.56	2361.38	2213.57	2089.09	1982.96
250000	3158.88	2873.14	2645.37	2459.78	2305.80	2176.14	2065.58

5.00 % Monthly Payments

LOAN AMOUNT	15	16	17	18	19	20	21
				YEARS			
100	0.79	0.75	0.73	0.70	0.68	0.66	0.64
200	1.58	1.51	1.45	1.40	1.35	1.31	1.28
500	3.94	3.77	3.63	3.50	3.39	3.29	3.19
1000	7.88	7.55	7.26	7.00	6.77	6.57	6.39
2000	15.76	15.10	14.52	14.01	13.55	13.14	12.78
5000	39.41	37.75	36.30	35.01	33.87	32.86	31.94
6000	47.29	45.30	43.56	42.02	40.65	39.43	38.33
7000	55.17	52.85	50.81	49.02	47.42	46.00	44.72
8000	63.05	60.40	58.07	56.02	54.20	52.57	51.11
9000	70.93	67.95	65.33	63.02	60.97	59.14	57.50
10000	78.81	75.50	72.59	70.03	67.75	65.71	63.89
12000	94.57	90.60	87.11	84.03	81.30	78.86	76.66
15000	118.22	113.25	108.89	105.04	101.62	98.57	95.83
20000	157.62	151.00	145.18	140.05	135.50	131.43	127.77
25000	197.03	188.74	181.48	175.07	169.37	164.28	159.71
30000	236.44	226.49	217.78	210.08	203.24	197.14	191.66
31000	244.32	234.04	225.04	217.08	210.02	203.71	198.05
32000	252.20	241.59	232.29	224.09	216.79	210.28	204.43
33000	260.08	249.14	239.55	231.09	223.57	216.85	210.82
34000	267.96	256.69	246.81	238.09	230.34	223.42	217.21
35000	275.84	264.24	254.07	245.09	237.12	229.99	223.60
36000	283.72	271.79	261.33	252.10	243.89	236.57	229.99
37000	291.61	279.34	268.59	259.10	250.67	243.14	236.38
38000	299.49	286.89	275.85	266.10	257.44	249.71	242.77
39000	307.37	294.44	283.11	273.10	264.22	256.28	249.15
40000	315.25	301.99	290.37	280.11	270.99	262.85	255.54
41000	323.13	309.54	297.63	287.11	277.77	269.42	261.93
42000	331.01	317.09	304.89	294.11	284.54	275.99	268.32
43000	338.89	324.64	312.15	301.11	291.32	282.56	274.71
44000	346.77	332.19	319.41	308.12	298.09	289.14	281.10
45000	354.66	339.74	326.66	315.12	304.87	295.71	287.49
46000	362.54	347.29	333.92	322.12	311.64	302.28	293.87
47000	370.42	354.84	341.18	329.13	318.42	308.85	300.26
48000	378.30	362.39	348.44	336.13	325.19	315.42	306.65
49000	386.18	369.94	355.70	343.13	331.96	321.99	313.04
50000	394.06	377.49	362.96	350.13	338.74	328.56	319.43
51000	401.94	385.04	370.22	357.14	345.51	335.13	325.82
52000	409.82	392.59	377.48	364.14	352.29	341.71	332.21
53000	417.71	400.14	384.74	371.14	359.06	348.28	338.59
54000	425.59	407.69	392.00	378.14	365.84	354.85	344.98
55000	433.47	415.24	399.26	385.15	372.61	361.42	351.37
56000	441.35	422.79	406.52	392.15	379.39	367.99	357.76
57000	449.23	430.34	413.77	399.15	386.16	374.56	364.15
58000	457.11	437.89	421.03	406.15	392.94	381.13	370.54
59000	464.99	445.44	428.29	413.16	399.71	387.70	376.93
60000	472.87	452.99	435.55	420.16	406.49	394.28	383.31
65000	512.28	490.74	471.85	455.17	440.36	427.13	415.26
70000	551.69	528.49	508.14	490.19	474.24	459.99	447.20
75000	591.09	566.23	544.44	525.20	508.11	492.84	479.14
80000	630.50	603.98	580.74	560.21	541.98	525.70	511.09
85000	669.91	641.73	617.03	595.23	575.86	558.56	543.03
90000	709.31	679.48	653.33	630.24	609.73	591.41	574.97
95000	748.72	717.23	689.62	665.25	643.60	624.27	606.91
100000	788.12	754.98	725.92	700.27	677.48	657.13	638.86
105000	827.53	792.73	762.22	735.28	711.35	689.98	670.80
110000	866.94	830.48	798.51	770.29	745.23	722.84	702.74
120000	945.75	905.97	871.10	840.32	812.97	788.55	766.63
130000	1024.56	981.47	943.70	910.35	880.72	854.26	830.51
140000	1103.37	1056.97	1016.29	980.37	948.47	919.98	894.40
150000	1182.19	1132.47	1088.88	1050.40	1016.22	985.69	958.28
160000	1261.00	1207.97	1161.47	1120.43	1083.97	1051.40	1022.17
170000	1339.81	1283.46	1234.06	1190.45	1151.71	1117.11	1086.06
180000	1418.62	1358.96	1306.66	1260.48	1219.46	1182.83	1149.94
190000	1497.44	1434.46	1379.25	1330.51	1287.21	1248.54	1213.83
200000	1576.25	1509.96	1451.84	1400.53	1354.96	1314.25	1277.71
210000	1655.06	1585.46	1524.43	1470.56	1422.71	1379.96	1341.60
220000	1733.87	1660.95	1597.03	1540.59	1490.45	1445.68	1405.48
230000	1812.68	1736.45	1669.62	1610.61	1558.20	1511.39	1469.37
240000	1891.50	1811.95	1742.21	1680.64	1625.95	1577.10	1533.26
250000	1970.31	1887.45	1814.80	1750.67	1693.70	1642.81	1597.14

Monthly Payments 5.00 %

LOAN AMOUNT	22	23	24	25	30	35	40
				YEARS			
100	0.62	0.61	0.59	0.58	0.53	0.50	0.48
200	1.24	1.21	1.19	1.16	1.07	1.00	0.96
500	3.11	3.04	2.97	2.91	2.67	2.51	2.39
1000	6.22	6.07	5.94	5.82	5.34	5.01	4.79
2000	12.45	12.15	11.88	11.63	10.67	10.03	9.58
5000	31.12	30.37	29.70	29.08	26.68	25.07	23.94
6000	37.34	36.45	35.64	34.90	32.02	30.09	28.73
7000	43.57	42.52	41.58	40.71	37.36	35.10	33.52
8000	49.79	48.60	47.52	46.53	42.70	40.11	38.30
9000	56.01	54.67	53.45	52.34	48.03	45.13	43.09
10000	62.24	60.75	59.39	58.16	53.37	50.14	47.88
12000	74.69	72.90	71.27	69.79	64.04	60.17	57.46
15000	93.36	91.12	89.09	87.24	80.05	75.21	71.82
20000	124.48	121.50	118.79	116.32	106.74	100.28	95.76
25000	155.60	151.87	148.49	145.40	133.42	125.36	119.70
30000	186.72	182.24	178.18	174.48	160.11	150.43	143.64
31000	192.94	188.32	184.12	180.30	165.44	155.44	148.43
32000	199.16	194.39	190.06	186.11	170.78	160.45	153.22
33000	205.39	200.47	196.00	191.93	176.12	165.47	158.01
34000	211.61	206.54	201.94	197.75	181.45	170.48	162.79
35000	217.84	212.62	207.88	203.56	186.79	175.50	167.58
36000	224.06	218.69	213.82	209.38	192.13	180.51	172.37
37000	230.28	224.77	219.76	215.19	197.47	185.53	177.16
38000	236.51	230.84	225.70	221.01	202.80	190.54	181.95
39000	242.73	236.92	231.64	226.83	208.14	195.55	186.73
40000	248.95	242.99	237.58	232.64	213.48	200.57	191.52
41000	255.18	249.07	243.52	238.46	218.81	205.58	196.31
42000	261.40	255.14	249.46	244.27	224.15	210.60	201.10
43000	267.63	261.22	255.40	250.09	229.49	215.61	205.89
44000	273.85	267.29	261.33	255.91	234.82	220.63	210.67
45000	280.07	273.37	267.27	261.72	240.16	225.64	215.46
46000	286.30	279.44	273.21	267.54	245.50	230.65	220.25
47000	292.52	285.52	279.15	273.35	250.83	235.67	225.04
48000	298.75	291.59	285.09	279.17	256.17	240.68	229.83
49000	304.97	297.67	291.03	284.99	261.51	245.70	234.61
50000	311.19	303.74	296.97	290.80	266.85	250.71	239.40
51000	317.42	309.82	302.91	296.62	272.18	255.72	244.19
52000	323.64	315.89	308.85	302.43	277.52	260.74	248.98
53000	329.87	321.97	314.79	308.25	282.86	265.75	253.77
54000	336.09	328.04	320.73	314.07	288.19	270.77	258.55
55000	342.31	334.11	326.67	319.88	293.53	275.78	263.34
56000	348.54	340.19	332.61	325.70	298.87	280.80	268.13
57000	354.76	346.26	338.55	331.51	304.20	285.81	272.92
58000	360.98	352.34	344.49	337.33	309.54	290.82	277.71
59000	367.21	358.41	350.43	343.15	314.88	295.84	282.49
60000	373.43	364.49	356.37	348.96	320.21	300.85	287.28
65000	404.55	394.86	386.06	378.04	346.90	325.92	311.22
70000	435.67	425.24	415.76	407.12	373.58	350.99	335.16
75000	466.79	455.61	445.46	436.20	400.27	376.07	359.10
80000	497.91	485.99	475.15	465.28	426.95	401.14	383.04
85000	529.03	516.36	504.85	494.36	453.64	426.21	406.98
90000	560.15	546.73	534.55	523.44	480.32	451.28	430.92
95000	591.27	577.11	564.25	552.52	507.01	476.35	454.86
100000	622.39	607.48	593.94	581.60	533.69	501.42	478.80
105000	653.51	637.86	623.64	610.69	560.38	526.49	502.74
110000	684.63	668.23	653.34	639.77	587.06	551.56	526.68
120000	746.86	728.98	712.73	697.93	640.43	601.70	574.56
130000	809.10	789.73	772.13	756.09	693.80	651.85	622.44
140000	871.34	850.47	831.52	814.25	747.17	701.99	670.33
150000	933.58	911.22	890.91	872.41	800.54	752.13	718.21
160000	995.82	971.97	950.31	930.57	853.91	802.27	766.09
170000	1058.06	1032.72	1009.70	988.73	907.27	852.41	813.97
180000	1120.30	1093.47	1069.10	1046.89	960.64	902.56	861.85
190000	1182.54	1154.22	1128.49	1105.05	1014.01	952.70	909.73
200000	1244.77	1214.96	1187.89	1163.21	1067.38	1002.84	957.61
210000	1307.01	1275.71	1247.28	1221.37	1120.75	1052.98	1005.49
220000	1369.25	1336.46	1306.67	1279.53	1174.12	1103.13	1053.37
230000	1431.49	1397.21	1366.07	1337.69	1227.49	1153.27	1101.25
240000	1493.73	1457.96	1425.46	1395.85	1280.86	1203.41	1149.13
250000	1555.97	1518.70	1484.86	1454.01	1334.23	1253.55	1197.01

5.25 % Monthly Payments

LOAN AMOUNT	YEARS 1	2	3	4	5	6	7
100	8.57	4.40	3.01	2.31	1.90	1.62	1.42
200	17.14	8.79	6.01	4.62	3.79	3.24	2.85
500	42.85	21.98	15.03	11.56	9.48	8.10	7.11
1000	85.70	43.96	30.06	23.12	18.96	16.19	14.23
2000	171.39	87.92	60.12	46.23	37.92	32.39	28.45
5000	428.48	219.79	150.29	115.59	94.80	80.97	71.13
6000	514.18	263.75	180.35	138.70	113.76	97.17	85.35
7000	599.87	307.71	210.40	161.82	132.72	113.36	99.58
8000	685.57	351.66	240.46	184.94	151.68	129.56	113.80
9000	771.27	395.62	270.52	208.05	170.64	145.75	128.03
10000	856.96	439.58	300.58	231.17	189.60	161.95	142.25
12000	1028.35	527.50	360.69	277.40	227.52	194.34	170.70
15000	1285.44	659.37	450.87	346.76	284.40	242.92	213.38
20000	1713.92	879.16	601.16	462.34	379.20	323.90	284.50
25000	2142.40	1098.95	751.45	577.93	474.00	404.87	355.63
30000	2570.89	1318.74	901.74	693.51	568.80	485.85	426.75
31000	2656.58	1362.70	931.79	716.63	587.76	502.04	440.98
32000	2742.28	1406.66	961.85	739.75	606.72	518.23	455.20
33000	2827.97	1450.62	991.91	762.86	625.68	534.43	469.43
34000	2913.67	1494.58	1021.97	785.98	644.64	550.62	483.65
35000	2999.37	1538.53	1052.02	809.10	663.60	566.82	497.88
36000	3085.06	1582.49	1082.08	832.21	682.56	583.01	512.10
37000	3170.76	1626.45	1112.14	855.33	701.52	599.21	526.33
38000	3256.45	1670.41	1142.20	878.45	720.48	615.40	540.55
39000	3342.15	1714.37	1172.26	901.56	739.44	631.60	554.78
40000	3427.85	1758.32	1202.31	924.68	758.40	647.79	569.00
41000	3513.54	1802.28	1232.37	947.80	777.36	663.99	583.23
42000	3599.24	1846.24	1262.43	970.92	796.32	680.18	597.45
43000	3684.94	1890.20	1292.49	994.03	815.28	696.38	611.68
44000	3770.63	1934.16	1322.55	1017.15	834.24	712.57	625.90
45000	3856.33	1978.11	1352.60	1040.27	853.20	728.77	640.13
46000	3942.02	2022.07	1382.66	1063.38	872.16	744.96	654.35
47000	4027.72	2066.03	1412.72	1086.50	891.12	761.16	668.58
48000	4113.42	2109.99	1442.78	1109.62	910.08	777.35	682.80
49000	4199.11	2153.95	1472.83	1132.74	929.04	793.55	697.03
50000	4284.81	2197.90	1502.89	1155.85	948.00	809.74	711.25
51000	4370.50	2241.86	1532.95	1178.97	966.96	825.94	725.48
52000	4456.20	2285.82	1563.01	1202.09	985.92	842.13	739.70
53000	4541.90	2329.78	1593.07	1225.20	1004.88	858.33	753.93
54000	4627.59	2373.74	1623.12	1248.32	1023.84	874.52	768.15
55000	4713.29	2417.70	1653.18	1271.44	1042.80	890.72	782.38
56000	4798.99	2461.65	1683.24	1294.55	1061.76	906.91	796.60
57000	4884.68	2505.61	1713.30	1317.67	1080.72	923.11	810.83
58000	4970.38	2549.57	1743.35	1340.79	1099.68	939.30	825.05
59000	5056.07	2593.53	1773.41	1363.91	1118.64	955.50	839.28
60000	5141.77	2637.49	1803.47	1387.02	1137.60	971.69	853.50
65000	5570.25	2857.28	1953.76	1502.61	1232.40	1052.66	924.63
70000	5998.73	3077.07	2104.05	1618.19	1327.20	1133.64	995.75
75000	6427.21	3296.86	2254.34	1733.78	1422.00	1214.61	1066.88
80000	6855.69	3516.65	2404.63	1849.36	1516.80	1295.59	1138.00
85000	7284.17	3736.44	2554.92	1964.95	1611.60	1376.56	1209.13
90000	7712.66	3956.23	2705.21	2080.53	1706.40	1457.54	1280.25
95000	8141.14	4176.02	2855.50	2196.12	1801.20	1538.51	1351.38
100000	8569.62	4395.81	3005.78	2311.70	1896.00	1619.48	1422.50
105000	8998.10	4615.60	3156.07	2427.29	1990.80	1700.46	1493.63
110000	9426.58	4835.39	3306.36	2542.87	2085.60	1781.43	1564.75
120000	10283.54	5274.97	3606.94	2774.05	2275.20	1943.38	1707.00
130000	11140.50	5714.55	3907.52	3005.22	2464.80	2105.33	1849.25
140000	11997.46	6154.13	4208.10	3236.39	2654.40	2267.28	1991.50
150000	12854.43	6593.71	4508.68	3467.56	2844.00	2429.23	2133.75
160000	13711.39	7033.29	4809.25	3698.73	3033.60	2591.17	2276.00
170000	14568.35	7472.88	5109.83	3929.90	3223.20	2753.12	2418.25
180000	15425.31	7912.46	5410.41	4161.07	3412.80	2915.07	2560.50
190000	16282.27	8352.04	5710.99	4392.24	3602.40	3077.02	2702.75
200000	17139.23	8791.62	6011.57	4623.41	3792.00	3238.97	2845.00
210000	17996.20	9231.20	6312.15	4854.58	3981.60	3400.92	2987.25
220000	18853.16	9670.78	6612.73	5085.75	4171.20	3562.86	3129.50
230000	19710.12	10110.36	6913.30	5316.92	4360.80	3724.81	3271.75
240000	20567.08	10549.94	7213.88	5548.09	4550.40	3886.76	3414.00
250000	21424.04	10989.52	7514.46	5779.26	4740.00	4048.71	3556.25

Monthly Payments 5.25 %

LOAN AMOUNT	8	9	10	11	12	13	14
100	1.28	1.16	1.07	1.00	0.93	0.88	0.84
200	2.55	2.32	2.14	1.99	1.87	1.77	1.68
500	6.38	5.81	5.35	4.98	4.67	4.41	4.19
1000	12.75	11.61	10.70	9.96	9.35	8.83	8.39
2000	25.50	23.22	21.40	19.92	18.69	17.66	16.78
5000	63.76	58.05	53.51	49.80	46.73	44.15	41.94
6000	76.51	69.67	64.21	59.76	56.08	52.98	50.33
7000	89.27	81.28	74.91	69.72	65.42	61.80	58.72
8000	102.02	92.89	85.61	79.68	74.77	70.63	67.11
9000	114.77	104.50	96.31	89.65	84.12	79.46	75.50
10000	127.52	116.11	107.01	99.61	93.46	88.29	83.89
12000	153.03	139.33	128.42	119.53	112.16	105.95	100.66
15000	191.28	174.16	160.52	149.41	140.19	132.44	125.83
20000	255.04	232.22	214.03	199.21	186.93	176.58	167.77
25000	318.81	290.27	267.53	249.01	233.66	220.73	209.72
30000	382.57	348.33	321.04	298.82	280.39	264.88	251.66
31000	395.32	359.94	331.74	308.78	289.73	273.71	260.05
32000	408.07	371.55	342.44	318.74	299.08	282.54	268.44
33000	420.82	383.16	353.15	328.70	308.43	291.36	276.82
34000	433.58	394.77	363.85	338.66	317.77	300.19	285.21
35000	446.33	406.38	374.55	348.62	327.12	309.02	293.60
36000	459.08	417.99	385.25	358.58	336.47	317.85	301.99
37000	471.83	429.60	395.95	368.54	345.81	326.68	310.38
38000	484.59	441.21	406.65	378.50	355.16	335.51	318.77
39000	497.34	452.82	417.35	388.46	364.50	344.34	327.16
40000	510.09	464.43	428.06	398.42	373.85	353.17	335.54
41000	522.84	476.04	438.76	408.38	383.20	362.00	343.93
42000	535.59	487.66	449.46	418.34	392.54	370.83	352.32
43000	548.35	499.27	460.16	428.30	401.89	379.66	360.71
44000	561.10	510.88	470.86	438.27	411.24	388.49	369.10
45000	573.85	522.49	481.56	448.23	420.58	397.32	377.49
46000	586.60	534.10	492.26	458.19	429.93	406.14	385.88
47000	599.36	545.71	502.96	468.15	439.27	414.97	394.26
48000	612.11	557.32	513.67	478.11	448.62	423.80	402.65
49000	624.86	568.93	524.37	488.07	457.97	432.63	411.04
50000	637.61	580.54	535.07	498.03	467.31	441.46	419.43
51000	650.36	592.15	545.77	507.99	476.66	450.29	427.82
52000	663.12	603.76	556.47	517.95	486.01	459.12	436.21
53000	675.87	615.37	567.17	527.91	495.35	467.95	444.60
54000	688.62	626.99	577.87	537.87	504.70	476.78	452.98
55000	701.37	638.60	588.58	547.83	514.04	485.61	461.37
56000	714.13	650.21	599.28	557.79	523.39	494.44	469.76
57000	726.88	661.82	609.98	567.75	532.74	503.27	478.15
58000	739.63	673.43	620.68	577.71	542.08	512.10	486.54
59000	752.38	685.04	631.38	587.67	551.43	520.92	494.93
60000	765.13	696.65	642.08	597.63	560.78	529.75	503.32
65000	828.90	754.70	695.59	647.44	607.51	573.90	545.26
70000	892.66	812.76	749.10	697.24	654.24	618.05	587.20
75000	956.42	870.81	802.60	747.04	700.97	662.19	629.15
80000	1020.18	928.87	856.11	796.85	747.70	706.34	671.09
85000	1083.94	986.92	909.62	846.65	794.43	750.48	713.03
90000	1147.70	1044.98	963.12	896.45	841.16	794.63	754.97
95000	1211.46	1103.03	1016.63	946.26	887.90	838.78	796.92
100000	1275.22	1161.08	1070.14	996.06	934.63	882.92	838.86
105000	1338.99	1219.14	1123.64	1045.86	981.36	927.07	880.80
110000	1402.75	1277.19	1177.15	1095.66	1028.09	971.21	922.75
120000	1530.27	1393.30	1284.17	1195.27	1121.55	1059.51	1006.63
130000	1657.79	1509.41	1391.18	1294.88	1215.01	1147.80	1090.52
140000	1785.31	1625.52	1498.19	1394.48	1308.48	1236.09	1174.40
150000	1912.84	1741.63	1605.21	1494.09	1401.94	1324.38	1258.29
160000	2040.36	1857.73	1712.22	1593.69	1495.40	1412.68	1342.18
170000	2167.88	1973.84	1819.23	1693.30	1588.86	1500.97	1426.06
180000	2295.40	2089.95	1926.25	1792.90	1682.33	1589.26	1509.95
190000	2422.93	2206.06	2033.26	1892.51	1775.79	1677.55	1593.83
200000	2550.45	2322.17	2140.28	1992.12	1869.25	1765.84	1677.72
210000	2677.97	2438.28	2247.29	2091.72	1962.72	1854.14	1761.61
220000	2805.49	2554.38	2354.30	2191.33	2056.18	1942.43	1845.49
230000	2933.01	2670.49	2461.32	2290.93	2149.64	2030.72	1929.38
240000	3060.54	2786.60	2568.33	2390.54	2243.10	2119.01	2013.26
250000	3188.06	2902.71	2675.34	2490.14	2336.57	2207.31	2097.15

The column heads 8–14 are in YEARS.

5.25 %			**Monthly Payments**				
LOAN			YEARS				
AMOUNT	15	16	17	18	19	20	21
100	0.80	0.77	0.74	0.71	0.69	0.67	0.6
200	1.60	1.54	1.48	1.43	1.38	1.34	1.3
500	4.00	3.84	3.70	3.57	3.45	3.35	3.2
1000	8.01	7.68	7.39	7.14	6.91	6.71	6.5
2000	16.02	15.36	14.78	14.27	13.82	13.41	13.0
5000	40.05	38.40	36.95	35.68	34.54	33.53	32.6
6000	48.05	46.08	44.34	42.81	41.45	40.24	39.1
7000	56.06	53.75	51.73	49.95	48.36	46.95	45.6
8000	64.07	61.43	59.12	57.08	55.27	53.66	52.2
9000	72.08	69.11	66.51	64.22	62.18	60.36	58.7
10000	80.09	76.79	73.90	71.35	69.09	67.07	65.2
12000	96.11	92.15	88.68	85.62	82.91	80.48	78.3
15000	120.14	115.19	110.85	107.03	103.63	100.60	97.8
20000	160.18	153.58	147.80	142.70	138.18	134.14	130.5
25000	200.23	191.98	184.76	178.38	172.72	167.67	163.1
30000	240.27	230.38	221.71	214.06	207.27	201.21	195.7
31000	248.28	238.06	229.10	221.19	214.18	207.91	202.3
32000	256.29	245.74	236.49	228.33	221.09	214.62	208.8
33000	264.30	253.41	243.88	235.46	227.99	221.33	215.3
34000	272.31	261.09	251.27	242.60	234.90	228.03	221.8
35000	280.32	268.77	258.66	249.73	241.81	234.74	228.4
36000	288.33	276.45	266.05	256.87	248.72	241.45	234.9
37000	296.34	284.13	273.44	264.00	255.63	248.16	241.4
38000	304.35	291.81	280.83	271.14	262.54	254.86	247.9
39000	312.35	299.49	288.22	278.27	269.45	261.57	254.5
40000	320.36	307.17	295.61	285.41	276.36	268.28	261.0
41000	328.37	314.85	303.00	292.54	283.27	274.98	267.5
42000	336.38	322.53	310.39	299.68	290.17	281.69	274.0
43000	344.39	330.21	317.78	306.82	297.08	288.40	280.6
44000	352.40	337.89	325.17	313.95	303.99	295.10	287.1
45000	360.41	345.56	332.56	321.09	310.90	301.81	293.6
46000	368.42	353.24	339.95	328.22	317.81	308.52	300.1
47000	376.43	360.92	347.34	335.36	324.72	315.22	306.7
48000	384.44	368.60	354.73	342.49	331.63	321.93	313.2
49000	392.45	376.28	362.12	349.63	338.54	328.64	319.7
50000	400.45	383.96	369.51	356.76	345.45	335.35	326.2
51000	408.46	391.64	376.90	363.90	352.35	342.05	332.8
52000	416.47	399.32	384.29	371.03	359.26	348.76	339.3
53000	424.48	407.00	391.68	378.17	366.17	355.47	345.8
54000	432.49	414.68	399.07	385.30	373.08	362.17	352.3
55000	440.50	422.36	406.46	392.44	379.99	368.88	358.9
56000	448.51	430.04	413.85	399.57	386.90	375.59	365.4
57000	456.52	437.72	421.24	406.71	393.81	382.29	371.9
58000	464.53	445.39	428.63	413.84	400.72	389.00	378.4
59000	472.54	453.07	436.02	420.98	407.63	395.71	385.0
60000	480.55	460.75	443.41	428.11	414.53	402.41	391.5
65000	520.59	499.15	480.36	463.79	449.08	435.95	424.1
70000	560.64	537.55	517.31	499.47	483.62	469.48	456.8
75000	600.68	575.94	554.27	535.14	518.17	503.02	489.4
80000	640.73	614.34	591.22	570.82	552.71	536.55	522.0
85000	680.77	652.73	628.17	606.50	587.26	570.09	554.6
90000	720.82	691.13	665.12	642.17	621.80	603.62	587.3
95000	760.86	729.53	702.07	677.85	656.35	637.16	619.9
100000	800.91	767.92	739.02	713.52	690.89	670.69	652.5
105000	840.95	806.32	775.97	749.20	725.44	704.23	685.2
110000	881.00	844.71	812.92	784.88	759.98	737.76	717.8
120000	961.09	921.51	886.83	856.23	829.07	804.83	783.0
130000	1041.18	998.30	960.73	927.58	898.16	871.90	848.3
140000	1121.27	1075.09	1034.63	998.93	967.25	938.97	913.6
150000	1201.36	1151.88	1108.53	1070.29	1036.34	1006.04	978.8
160000	1281.45	1228.68	1182.43	1141.64	1105.43	1073.11	1044.1
170000	1361.55	1305.47	1256.34	1212.99	1174.51	1140.17	1109.3
180000	1441.64	1382.26	1330.24	1284.34	1243.60	1207.24	1174.6
190000	1521.73	1459.05	1404.14	1355.70	1312.69	1274.31	1239.8
200000	1601.82	1535.84	1478.04	1427.05	1381.78	1341.38	1305.1
210000	1681.91	1612.64	1551.94	1498.40	1450.87	1408.45	1370.4
220000	1762.00	1689.43	1625.85	1569.75	1519.96	1475.52	1435.6
230000	1842.09	1766.22	1699.75	1641.10	1589.05	1542.59	1500.9
240000	1922.18	1843.01	1773.65	1712.46	1658.14	1609.66	1566.1
250000	2002.27	1919.81	1847.55	1783.81	1727.23	1676.73	1631.4

Monthly Payments 5.25 %

LOAN AMOUNT	22	23	24	25	30	35	40
100	0.64	0.62	0.61	0.60	0.55	0.52	0.50
200	1.27	1.24	1.22	1.19	1.10	1.03	0.99
500	3.18	3.11	3.04	2.98	2.74	2.59	2.48
1000	6.36	6.22	6.08	5.96	5.49	5.17	4.95
2000	12.73	12.43	12.16	11.92	10.97	10.34	9.90
5000	31.81	31.08	30.41	29.80	27.44	25.85	24.75
6000	38.18	37.29	36.49	35.76	32.92	31.03	29.70
7000	44.54	43.51	42.57	41.71	38.41	36.20	34.66
8000	50.90	49.72	48.65	47.67	43.90	41.37	39.61
9000	57.26	55.94	54.73	53.63	49.38	46.54	44.56
10000	63.63	62.15	60.81	59.59	54.87	51.71	49.51
12000	76.35	74.58	72.97	71.51	65.84	62.05	59.41
15000	95.44	93.23	91.22	89.39	82.31	77.56	74.26
20000	127.25	124.30	121.62	119.18	109.74	103.42	99.02
25000	159.06	155.38	152.03	148.98	137.18	129.27	123.77
30000	190.88	186.45	182.43	178.78	164.61	155.13	148.52
31000	197.24	192.67	188.51	184.73	170.10	160.30	153.48
32000	203.60	198.88	194.60	190.69	175.59	165.47	158.43
33000	209.96	205.10	200.68	196.65	181.07	170.64	163.38
34000	216.33	211.31	206.76	202.61	186.56	175.81	168.33
35000	222.69	217.53	212.84	208.57	192.05	180.98	173.28
36000	229.05	223.74	218.92	214.53	197.53	186.15	178.23
37000	235.41	229.96	225.00	220.49	203.02	191.32	183.18
38000	241.78	236.17	231.08	226.45	208.51	196.50	188.13
39000	248.14	242.39	237.16	232.41	214.00	201.67	193.08
40000	254.50	248.60	243.24	238.37	219.48	206.84	198.03
41000	260.87	254.82	249.32	244.33	224.97	212.01	202.98
42000	267.23	261.03	255.41	250.29	230.46	217.18	207.93
43000	273.59	267.25	261.49	256.24	235.94	222.35	212.88
44000	279.95	273.46	267.57	262.20	241.43	227.52	217.84
45000	286.32	279.68	273.65	268.16	246.92	232.69	222.79
46000	292.68	285.89	279.73	274.12	252.41	237.86	227.74
47000	299.04	292.11	285.81	280.08	257.89	243.03	232.69
48000	305.40	298.32	291.89	286.04	263.38	248.21	237.64
49000	311.77	304.54	297.97	292.00	268.87	253.38	242.59
50000	318.13	310.75	304.05	297.96	274.35	258.55	247.54
51000	324.49	316.97	310.14	303.92	279.84	263.72	252.49
52000	330.85	323.18	316.22	309.88	285.33	268.89	257.44
53000	337.22	329.40	322.30	315.84	290.82	274.06	262.39
54000	343.58	335.61	328.38	321.80	296.30	279.23	267.34
55000	349.94	341.83	334.46	327.75	301.79	284.40	272.29
56000	356.30	348.04	340.54	333.71	307.28	289.57	277.25
57000	362.67	354.26	346.62	339.67	312.76	294.74	282.20
58000	369.03	360.47	352.70	345.63	318.25	299.91	287.15
59000	375.39	366.69	358.78	351.59	323.74	305.09	292.10
60000	381.75	372.90	364.87	357.55	329.22	310.26	297.05
65000	413.57	403.98	395.27	387.35	356.66	336.11	321.80
70000	445.38	435.05	425.68	417.14	384.10	361.97	346.56
75000	477.19	466.13	456.08	446.94	411.53	387.82	371.31
80000	509.01	497.20	486.49	476.73	438.97	413.68	396.06
85000	540.82	528.28	516.89	506.53	466.40	439.53	420.82
90000	572.63	559.35	547.30	536.33	493.84	465.38	445.57
95000	604.44	590.43	577.70	566.12	521.27	491.24	470.33
100000	636.26	621.50	608.11	595.92	548.71	517.09	495.08
105000	668.07	652.58	638.51	625.71	576.14	542.95	519.83
110000	699.88	683.65	668.92	655.51	603.58	568.80	544.59
120000	763.51	745.80	729.73	715.10	658.45	620.51	594.10
130000	827.13	807.95	790.54	774.69	713.32	672.22	643.61
140000	890.76	870.10	851.35	834.29	768.19	723.93	693.11
150000	954.39	932.25	912.16	893.88	823.06	775.64	742.62
160000	1018.01	994.40	972.98	953.47	877.93	827.35	792.13
170000	1081.64	1056.55	1033.79	1013.06	932.80	879.06	841.64
180000	1145.26	1118.70	1094.60	1072.65	987.67	930.77	891.15
190000	1208.89	1180.85	1155.41	1132.24	1042.55	982.48	940.65
200000	1272.51	1243.00	1216.22	1191.84	1097.42	1034.19	990.16
210000	1336.14	1305.15	1277.03	1251.43	1152.29	1085.90	1039.67
220000	1399.76	1367.30	1337.84	1311.02	1207.16	1137.61	1089.18
230000	1463.39	1429.45	1398.65	1370.61	1262.03	1189.32	1138.69
240000	1527.02	1491.60	1459.46	1430.20	1316.90	1241.03	1188.19
250000	1590.64	1553.75	1520.27	1489.80	1371.77	1292.74	1237.70

5.50 % Monthly Payments

LOAN	YEARS						
AMOUNT	1	2	3	4	5	6	7
100	8.58	4.41	3.02	2.32	1.91	1.63	1.43
200	17.16	8.81	6.03	4.65	3.81	3.26	2.87
500	42.90	22.03	15.08	11.61	9.54	8.15	7.17
1000	85.81	44.07	30.17	23.23	19.07	16.31	14.34
2000	171.62	88.14	60.34	46.46	38.15	32.62	28.68
5000	429.04	220.34	150.84	116.14	95.36	81.54	71.70
6000	514.85	264.41	181.01	139.37	114.44	97.85	86.04
7000	600.66	308.47	211.18	162.60	133.51	114.16	100.38
8000	686.47	352.54	241.34	185.83	152.58	130.47	114.73
9000	772.28	396.61	271.51	209.05	171.65	146.78	129.07
10000	858.08	440.68	301.68	232.28	190.73	163.09	143.41
12000	1029.70	528.81	362.02	278.74	228.87	195.71	172.09
15000	1287.13	661.02	452.52	348.42	286.09	244.63	215.11
20000	1716.17	881.36	603.36	464.56	381.45	326.18	286.81
25000	2145.21	1101.70	754.20	580.71	476.81	407.72	358.52
30000	2574.25	1322.03	905.04	696.85	572.18	489.27	430.22
31000	2660.06	1366.10	935.21	720.08	591.25	505.58	444.56
32000	2745.87	1410.17	965.37	743.30	610.32	521.88	458.90
33000	2831.68	1454.24	995.54	766.53	629.39	538.19	473.24
34000	2917.48	1498.31	1025.71	789.76	648.47	554.50	487.58
35000	3003.29	1542.37	1055.88	812.99	667.54	570.81	501.92
36000	3089.10	1586.44	1086.05	836.22	686.61	587.12	516.26
37000	3174.91	1630.51	1116.21	859.44	705.68	603.43	530.60
38000	3260.72	1674.58	1146.38	882.67	724.76	619.74	544.94
39000	3346.53	1718.64	1176.55	905.90	743.83	636.05	559.29
40000	3432.33	1762.71	1206.72	929.13	762.90	652.36	573.63
41000	3518.14	1806.78	1236.89	952.36	781.98	668.66	587.97
42000	3603.95	1850.85	1267.05	975.59	801.05	684.97	602.31
43000	3689.76	1894.92	1297.22	998.81	820.12	701.28	616.65
44000	3775.57	1938.98	1327.39	1022.04	839.19	717.59	630.99
45000	3861.38	1983.05	1357.56	1045.27	858.27	733.90	645.33
46000	3947.18	2027.12	1387.73	1068.50	877.34	750.21	659.67
47000	4032.99	2071.19	1417.89	1091.73	896.41	766.52	674.01
48000	4118.80	2115.26	1448.06	1114.96	915.48	782.83	688.35
49000	4204.61	2159.32	1478.23	1138.18	934.56	799.14	702.69
50000	4290.42	2203.39	1508.40	1161.41	953.63	815.44	717.03
51000	4376.23	2247.46	1538.57	1184.64	972.70	831.75	731.37
52000	4462.03	2291.53	1568.73	1207.87	991.77	848.06	745.71
53000	4547.84	2335.59	1598.90	1231.10	1010.85	864.37	760.05
54000	4633.65	2379.66	1629.07	1254.32	1029.92	880.68	774.39
55000	4719.46	2423.73	1659.24	1277.55	1048.99	896.99	788.74
56000	4805.27	2467.80	1689.41	1300.78	1068.06	913.30	803.08
57000	4891.08	2511.87	1719.57	1324.01	1087.14	929.61	817.42
58000	4976.88	2555.93	1749.74	1347.24	1106.21	945.92	831.76
59000	5062.69	2600.00	1779.91	1370.47	1125.28	962.22	846.10
60000	5148.50	2644.07	1810.08	1393.69	1144.35	978.53	860.44
65000	5577.54	2864.41	1960.92	1509.84	1239.72	1060.08	932.14
70000	6006.58	3084.75	2111.76	1625.98	1335.08	1141.62	1003.84
75000	6435.63	3305.09	2262.60	1742.12	1430.44	1223.17	1075.55
80000	6864.67	3525.43	2413.44	1858.26	1525.81	1304.71	1147.25
85000	7293.71	3745.76	2564.28	1974.40	1621.17	1386.26	1218.95
90000	7722.75	3966.10	2715.12	2090.54	1716.53	1467.80	1290.66
95000	8151.79	4186.44	2865.96	2206.68	1811.89	1549.35	1362.36
100000	8580.83	4406.78	3016.80	2322.82	1907.26	1630.89	1434.06
105000	9009.88	4627.12	3167.64	2438.97	2002.62	1712.43	1505.77
110000	9438.92	4847.46	3318.47	2555.11	2097.98	1793.98	1577.47
120000	10297.00	5288.14	3620.15	2787.39	2288.71	1957.07	1720.88
130000	11155.08	5728.82	3921.83	3019.67	2479.43	2120.16	1864.28
140000	12013.17	6169.49	4223.51	3251.95	2670.16	2283.25	2007.69
150000	12871.25	6610.17	4525.19	3484.24	2860.88	2446.33	2151.10
160000	13729.33	7050.85	4826.87	3716.52	3051.61	2609.42	2294.50
170000	14587.42	7491.53	5128.55	3948.80	3242.34	2772.51	2437.91
180000	15445.50	7932.21	5430.23	4181.08	3433.06	2935.60	2581.32
190000	16303.58	8372.89	5731.91	4413.37	3623.79	3098.69	2724.72
200000	17161.67	8813.56	6033.59	4645.65	3814.51	3261.78	2868.13
210000	18019.75	9254.24	6335.27	4877.93	4005.24	3424.87	3011.53
220000	18877.83	9694.92	6636.95	5110.21	4195.96	3587.96	3154.94
230000	19735.92	10135.60	6938.63	5342.49	4386.69	3751.05	3298.35
240000	20594.00	10576.28	7240.31	5574.78	4577.42	3914.14	3441.75
250000	21452.09	11016.95	7541.99	5807.06	4768.14	4077.22	3585.16

Monthly Payments 5.50 %

LOAN AMOUNT	8	9	10	11	12	13	14
100	1.29	1.17	1.08	1.01	0.95	0.90	0.85
200	2.57	2.35	2.16	2.02	1.89	1.79	1.70
500	6.43	5.86	5.41	5.04	4.74	4.48	4.26
1000	12.87	11.73	10.82	10.08	9.47	8.95	8.52
2000	25.74	23.46	21.64	20.17	18.94	17.91	17.03
5000	64.35	58.65	54.11	50.41	47.35	44.77	42.58
6000	77.22	70.38	64.93	60.50	56.82	53.73	51.10
7000	90.09	82.11	75.75	70.58	66.29	62.68	59.61
8000	102.96	93.84	86.58	80.66	75.76	71.64	68.13
9000	115.83	105.57	97.40	90.75	85.23	80.59	76.64
10000	128.69	117.30	108.22	100.83	94.70	89.55	85.16
12000	154.43	140.76	129.86	120.99	113.64	107.46	102.19
15000	193.04	175.95	162.33	151.24	142.05	134.32	127.74
20000	257.39	234.59	216.44	201.66	189.40	179.10	170.32
25000	321.74	293.24	270.55	252.07	236.75	223.87	212.90
30000	386.08	351.89	324.66	302.48	284.10	268.64	255.48
31000	398.95	363.62	335.48	312.57	293.58	277.60	263.99
32000	411.82	375.35	346.30	322.65	303.05	286.55	272.51
33000	424.69	387.08	357.12	332.73	312.52	295.51	281.02
34000	437.56	398.81	367.95	342.82	321.99	304.46	289.54
35000	450.43	410.54	378.77	352.90	331.46	313.42	298.05
36000	463.30	422.27	389.59	362.98	340.93	322.37	306.57
37000	476.17	434.00	400.41	373.06	350.40	331.33	315.09
38000	489.04	445.73	411.23	383.15	359.87	340.28	323.60
39000	501.91	457.46	422.06	393.23	369.34	349.24	332.12
40000	514.78	469.19	432.88	403.31	378.81	358.19	340.63
41000	527.65	480.92	443.70	413.40	388.28	367.15	349.15
42000	540.52	492.65	454.52	423.48	397.75	376.10	357.67
43000	553.39	504.38	465.34	433.56	407.22	385.06	366.18
44000	566.26	516.11	476.17	443.64	416.69	394.01	374.70
45000	579.13	527.84	486.99	453.73	426.16	402.97	383.21
46000	592.00	539.57	497.81	463.81	435.63	411.92	391.73
47000	604.87	551.30	508.63	473.89	445.10	420.88	400.24
48000	617.74	563.03	519.45	483.97	454.57	429.83	408.76
49000	630.61	574.76	530.28	494.06	464.04	438.78	417.28
50000	643.47	586.49	541.10	504.14	473.51	447.74	425.79
51000	656.34	598.22	551.92	514.22	482.98	456.69	434.31
52000	669.21	609.95	562.74	524.31	492.45	465.65	442.82
53000	682.08	621.68	573.56	534.39	501.92	474.60	451.34
54000	694.95	633.41	584.38	544.47	511.39	483.56	459.86
55000	707.82	645.14	595.21	554.55	520.86	492.51	468.37
56000	720.69	656.87	606.03	564.64	530.33	501.47	476.89
57000	733.56	668.60	616.85	574.72	539.80	510.42	485.40
58000	746.43	680.33	627.67	584.80	549.27	519.38	493.92
59000	759.30	692.05	638.49	594.89	558.74	528.33	502.43
60000	772.17	703.78	649.32	604.97	568.21	537.29	510.95
65000	836.52	762.43	703.43	655.38	615.56	582.06	553.53
70000	900.86	821.08	757.54	705.80	662.91	626.84	596.11
75000	965.21	879.73	811.65	756.21	710.26	671.61	638.69
80000	1029.56	938.38	865.76	806.62	757.61	716.38	681.27
85000	1093.91	997.03	919.86	857.04	804.96	761.16	723.85
90000	1158.25	1055.68	973.97	907.45	852.31	805.93	766.43
95000	1222.60	1114.33	1028.08	957.87	899.67	850.71	809.00
100000	1286.95	1172.97	1082.19	1008.28	947.02	895.48	851.58
105000	1351.30	1231.62	1136.30	1058.70	994.37	940.25	894.16
110000	1415.64	1290.27	1190.41	1109.11	1041.72	985.03	936.74
120000	1544.34	1407.57	1298.63	1209.94	1136.42	1074.58	1021.90
130000	1673.03	1524.87	1406.85	1310.77	1231.12	1164.12	1107.06
140000	1801.73	1642.16	1515.07	1411.59	1325.82	1253.67	1192.22
150000	1930.42	1759.46	1623.29	1512.42	1420.52	1343.22	1277.38
160000	2059.12	1876.76	1731.51	1613.25	1515.23	1432.77	1362.53
170000	2187.81	1994.06	1839.73	1714.08	1609.93	1522.32	1447.69
180000	2316.51	2111.35	1947.95	1814.91	1704.63	1611.86	1532.85
190000	2445.20	2228.65	2056.17	1915.73	1799.33	1701.41	1618.01
200000	2573.90	2345.95	2164.39	2016.56	1894.03	1790.96	1703.17
210000	2702.59	2463.25	2272.61	2117.39	1988.73	1880.51	1788.33
220000	2831.29	2580.54	2380.83	2218.22	2083.44	1970.05	1873.48
230000	2959.98	2697.84	2489.05	2319.05	2178.14	2059.60	1958.64
240000	3088.68	2815.14	2597.27	2419.87	2272.84	2149.15	2043.80
250000	3217.37	2932.44	2705.49	2520.70	2367.54	2238.70	2128.96

5.50 % Monthly Payments

LOAN AMOUNT	15	16	17	18	19	20	21
100	0.81	0.78	0.75	0.73	0.70	0.68	0.67
200	1.63	1.56	1.50	1.45	1.41	1.37	1.33
500	4.07	3.90	3.76	3.63	3.52	3.42	3.33
1000	8.14	7.81	7.52	7.27	7.04	6.84	6.66
2000	16.28	15.62	15.04	14.54	14.09	13.69	13.33
5000	40.69	39.05	37.61	36.35	35.22	34.22	33.32
6000	48.83	46.86	45.13	43.61	42.27	41.06	39.99
7000	56.97	54.67	52.66	50.88	49.31	47.91	46.65
8000	65.10	62.48	60.18	58.15	56.35	54.75	53.31
9000	73.24	70.29	67.70	65.42	63.40	61.60	59.98
10000	81.38	78.10	75.22	72.69	70.44	68.44	66.64
12000	97.66	93.72	90.27	87.23	84.53	82.13	79.97
15000	122.07	117.15	112.84	109.04	105.66	102.66	99.96
20000	162.76	156.20	150.45	145.38	140.89	136.88	133.29
25000	203.45	195.24	188.06	181.73	176.11	171.10	166.61
30000	244.14	234.29	225.67	218.07	211.33	205.32	199.93
31000	252.28	242.10	233.19	225.34	218.37	212.16	206.59
32000	260.42	249.91	240.72	232.61	225.42	219.01	213.26
33000	268.55	257.72	248.24	239.88	232.46	225.85	219.92
34000	276.69	265.53	255.76	247.15	239.51	232.69	226.59
35000	284.83	273.34	263.28	254.42	246.55	239.54	233.25
36000	292.97	281.15	270.81	261.69	253.60	246.38	239.92
37000	301.11	288.96	278.33	268.95	260.64	253.22	246.58
38000	309.24	296.77	285.85	276.22	267.68	260.07	253.24
39000	317.38	304.58	293.37	283.49	274.73	266.91	259.91
40000	325.52	312.39	300.90	290.76	281.77	273.76	266.57
41000	333.66	320.20	308.42	298.03	288.82	280.60	273.24
42000	341.80	328.01	315.94	305.30	295.86	287.44	279.90
43000	349.93	335.82	323.46	312.57	302.91	294.29	286.57
44000	358.07	343.63	330.98	319.84	309.95	301.13	293.23
45000	366.21	351.44	338.51	327.11	316.99	307.98	299.89
46000	374.35	359.25	346.03	334.38	324.04	314.82	306.56
47000	382.49	367.06	353.55	341.64	331.08	321.66	313.22
48000	390.62	374.87	361.07	348.91	338.13	328.51	319.89
49000	398.76	382.68	368.60	356.18	345.17	335.35	326.55
50000	406.90	390.49	376.12	363.45	352.22	342.20	333.22
51000	415.04	398.30	383.64	370.72	359.26	349.04	339.88
52000	423.18	406.11	391.16	377.99	366.30	355.88	346.55
53000	431.31	413.92	398.69	385.26	373.35	362.73	353.21
54000	439.45	421.73	406.21	392.53	380.39	369.57	359.87
55000	447.59	429.54	413.73	399.80	387.44	376.42	366.54
56000	455.73	437.35	421.25	407.07	394.48	383.26	373.20
57000	463.86	445.16	428.78	414.34	401.53	390.10	379.87
58000	472.00	452.97	436.30	421.60	408.57	396.95	386.5
59000	480.14	460.78	443.82	428.87	415.61	403.79	393.20
60000	488.28	468.59	451.34	436.14	422.66	410.63	399.86
65000	528.97	507.63	488.96	472.49	457.88	444.85	433.18
70000	569.66	546.68	526.57	508.83	493.10	479.07	466.5
75000	610.35	585.73	564.18	545.18	528.32	513.29	499.82
80000	651.04	624.78	601.79	581.52	563.55	547.51	533.15
85000	691.73	663.83	639.40	617.87	598.77	581.73	566.47
90000	732.42	702.88	677.01	654.21	633.99	615.95	599.79
95000	773.11	741.93	714.63	690.56	669.21	650.17	633.11
100000	813.80	780.98	752.24	726.90	704.43	684.39	666.43
105000	854.49	820.02	789.85	763.25	739.65	718.61	699.75
110000	895.18	859.07	827.46	799.59	774.87	752.83	733.08
120000	976.56	937.17	902.69	872.28	845.32	821.27	799.72
130000	1057.94	1015.27	977.91	944.97	915.76	889.71	866.36
140000	1139.32	1093.37	1053.13	1017.66	986.20	958.15	933.01
150000	1220.70	1171.46	1128.36	1090.36	1056.65	1026.59	999.65
160000	1302.08	1249.56	1203.58	1163.05	1127.09	1095.03	1066.29
170000	1383.46	1327.66	1278.81	1235.74	1197.53	1163.47	1132.94
180000	1464.84	1405.76	1354.03	1308.43	1267.98	1231.90	1199.58
190000	1546.22	1483.85	1429.25	1381.12	1338.42	1300.34	1266.21
200000	1627.60	1561.95	1504.48	1453.81	1408.86	1368.78	1332.8
210000	1708.98	1640.05	1579.70	1526.50	1479.31	1437.22	1399.5
220000	1790.36	1718.15	1654.92	1599.19	1549.75	1505.66	1466.15
230000	1871.74	1796.24	1730.15	1671.88	1620.19	1574.10	1532.80
240000	1953.12	1874.34	1805.37	1744.57	1690.64	1642.54	1599.44
250000	2034.50	1952.44	1880.60	1817.26	1761.08	1710.98	1666.08

Monthly Payments 5.50 %

LOAN AMOUNT	YEARS 22	23	24	25	30	35	40
100	0.65	0.64	0.62	0.61	0.56	0.53	0.51
200	1.30	1.27	1.24	1.22	1.13	1.07	1.02
500	3.25	3.18	3.11	3.05	2.82	2.66	2.56
1000	6.50	6.36	6.22	6.10	5.64	5.33	5.12
2000	13.01	12.71	12.45	12.21	11.28	10.66	10.23
5000	32.51	31.78	31.12	30.52	28.20	26.65	25.58
6000	39.02	38.14	37.35	36.62	33.83	31.98	30.69
7000	45.52	44.50	43.57	42.73	39.47	37.31	35.81
8000	52.02	50.85	49.79	48.83	45.11	42.64	40.92
9000	58.52	57.21	56.02	54.94	50.75	47.97	46.04
10000	65.03	63.57	62.24	61.04	56.39	53.30	51.16
12000	78.03	76.28	74.69	73.25	67.67	63.96	61.39
15000	97.54	95.35	93.36	91.56	84.59	79.94	76.73
20000	130.05	127.13	124.49	122.08	112.78	106.59	102.31
25000	162.57	158.92	155.61	152.60	140.98	133.24	127.89
30000	195.08	190.70	186.73	183.12	169.17	159.89	153.47
31000	201.58	197.06	192.95	189.22	174.81	165.22	158.58
32000	208.09	203.41	199.18	195.33	180.45	170.55	163.70
33000	214.59	209.77	205.40	201.43	186.09	175.88	168.81
34000	221.09	216.13	211.63	207.53	191.73	181.21	173.93
35000	227.60	222.48	217.85	213.64	197.37	186.54	179.05
36000	234.10	228.84	224.08	219.74	203.01	191.87	184.16
37000	240.60	235.20	230.30	225.84	208.65	197.20	189.28
38000	247.10	241.55	236.52	231.95	214.28	202.53	194.39
39000	253.61	247.91	242.75	238.05	219.92	207.86	199.51
40000	260.11	254.27	248.97	244.16	225.56	213.18	204.62
41000	266.61	260.62	255.20	250.26	231.20	218.51	209.74
42000	273.11	266.98	261.42	256.36	236.84	223.84	214.86
43000	279.62	273.34	267.65	262.47	242.48	229.17	219.97
44000	286.12	279.69	273.87	268.57	248.12	234.50	225.09
45000	292.62	286.05	280.09	274.68	253.76	239.83	230.20
46000	299.12	292.41	286.32	280.78	259.40	245.16	235.32
47000	305.63	298.76	292.54	286.88	265.04	250.49	240.43
48000	312.13	305.12	298.77	292.99	270.68	255.82	245.55
49000	318.63	311.48	304.99	299.09	276.31	261.15	250.66
50000	325.14	317.84	311.22	305.20	281.95	266.48	255.78
51000	331.64	324.19	317.44	311.30	287.59	271.81	260.90
52000	338.14	330.55	323.66	317.40	293.23	277.14	266.01
53000	344.64	336.91	329.89	323.51	298.87	282.47	271.13
54000	351.15	343.26	336.11	329.61	304.51	287.80	276.24
55000	357.65	349.62	342.34	335.72	310.15	293.13	281.36
56000	364.15	355.98	348.56	341.82	315.79	298.46	286.47
57000	370.65	362.33	354.79	347.92	321.43	303.79	291.59
58000	377.16	368.69	361.01	354.03	327.07	309.12	296.70
59000	383.66	375.05	367.23	360.13	332.70	314.45	301.82
60000	390.16	381.40	373.46	366.23	338.34	319.78	306.94
65000	422.68	413.19	404.58	396.75	366.54	346.43	332.51
70000	455.19	444.97	435.70	427.27	394.73	373.07	358.09
75000	487.70	476.75	466.82	457.79	422.93	399.72	383.67
80000	520.22	508.54	497.95	488.31	451.13	426.37	409.25
85000	552.73	540.32	529.07	518.83	479.32	453.02	434.83
90000	585.24	572.10	560.19	549.35	507.52	479.67	460.40
95000	617.76	603.89	591.31	579.87	535.71	506.31	485.98
100000	650.27	635.67	622.43	610.39	563.91	532.96	511.56
105000	682.79	667.45	653.55	640.91	592.10	559.61	537.14
110000	715.30	699.24	684.68	671.43	620.30	586.26	562.72
120000	780.33	762.80	746.92	732.47	676.69	639.55	613.87
130000	845.35	826.37	809.16	793.51	733.08	692.85	665.03
140000	910.38	889.94	871.40	854.55	789.47	746.15	716.18
150000	975.41	953.51	933.65	915.59	845.86	799.44	767.34
160000	1040.43	1017.07	995.89	976.63	902.25	852.74	818.50
170000	1105.46	1080.64	1058.13	1037.67	958.64	906.03	869.65
180000	1170.49	1144.21	1120.38	1098.70	1015.03	959.33	920.81
190000	1235.52	1207.77	1182.62	1159.74	1071.42	1012.63	971.96
200000	1300.54	1271.34	1244.86	1220.78	1127.81	1065.92	1023.12
210000	1365.57	1334.91	1307.11	1281.82	1184.20	1119.22	1074.28
220000	1430.60	1398.47	1369.35	1342.86	1240.59	1172.52	1125.43
230000	1495.62	1462.04	1431.59	1403.90	1296.98	1225.81	1176.59
240000	1560.65	1525.61	1493.84	1464.94	1353.38	1279.11	1227.74
250000	1625.68	1589.18	1556.08	1525.98	1409.77	1332.40	1278.90

5.75 % Monthly Payments

LOAN AMOUNT	YEARS 1	2	3	4	5	6	7
100	8.59	4.42	3.03	2.33	1.92	1.64	1.45
200	17.18	8.84	6.06	4.67	3.84	3.28	2.89
500	42.96	22.09	15.14	11.67	9.59	8.21	7.23
1000	85.92	44.18	30.28	23.34	19.19	16.42	14.46
2000	171.84	88.36	60.56	46.68	38.37	32.85	28.91
5000	429.60	220.89	151.39	116.70	95.93	82.12	72.28
6000	515.52	265.07	181.67	140.04	115.11	98.54	86.74
7000	601.44	309.24	211.95	163.38	134.30	114.96	101.20
8000	687.36	353.42	242.23	186.72	153.48	131.39	115.65
9000	773.28	397.60	272.50	210.06	172.67	147.81	130.11
10000	859.20	441.78	302.78	233.40	191.85	164.23	144.57
12000	1031.05	530.13	363.34	280.08	230.23	197.08	173.48
15000	1288.81	662.66	454.17	350.09	287.78	246.35	216.85
20000	1718.41	883.55	605.56	466.79	383.71	328.47	289.13
25000	2148.01	1104.44	756.95	583.49	479.64	410.58	361.42
30000	2577.61	1325.33	908.35	700.19	575.56	492.70	433.70
31000	2663.53	1369.51	938.62	723.53	594.75	509.12	448.16
32000	2749.46	1413.68	968.90	746.87	613.93	525.55	462.62
33000	2835.38	1457.86	999.18	770.21	633.12	541.97	477.07
34000	2921.30	1502.04	1029.46	793.55	652.30	558.39	491.53
35000	3007.22	1546.22	1059.74	816.89	671.49	574.82	505.99
36000	3093.14	1590.39	1090.02	840.23	690.68	591.24	520.44
37000	3179.06	1634.57	1120.29	863.57	709.86	607.66	534.90
38000	3264.98	1678.75	1150.57	886.91	729.05	624.09	549.36
39000	3350.90	1722.93	1180.85	910.25	748.23	640.51	563.81
40000	3436.82	1767.10	1211.13	933.59	767.42	656.93	578.27
41000	3522.74	1811.28	1241.41	956.93	786.60	673.36	592.73
42000	3608.66	1855.46	1271.68	980.27	805.79	689.78	607.18
43000	3694.58	1899.64	1301.96	1003.60	824.97	706.20	621.64
44000	3780.50	1943.81	1332.24	1026.94	844.16	722.63	636.10
45000	3866.42	1987.99	1362.52	1050.28	863.34	739.05	650.55
46000	3952.34	2032.17	1392.80	1073.62	882.53	755.47	665.01
47000	4038.26	2076.35	1423.08	1096.96	901.71	771.90	679.47
48000	4124.18	2120.52	1453.35	1120.30	920.90	788.32	693.92
49000	4210.10	2164.70	1483.63	1143.64	940.09	804.74	708.38
50000	4296.02	2208.88	1513.91	1166.98	959.27	821.17	722.84
51000	4381.94	2253.06	1544.19	1190.32	978.46	837.59	737.29
52000	4467.86	2297.24	1574.47	1213.66	997.64	854.01	751.75
53000	4553.79	2341.41	1604.74	1237.00	1016.83	870.44	766.21
54000	4639.71	2385.59	1635.02	1260.34	1036.01	886.86	780.66
55000	4725.63	2429.77	1665.30	1283.68	1055.20	903.28	795.12
56000	4811.55	2473.95	1695.58	1307.02	1074.38	919.71	809.58
57000	4897.47	2518.12	1725.86	1330.36	1093.57	936.13	824.03
58000	4983.39	2562.30	1756.14	1353.70	1112.75	952.55	838.49
59000	5069.31	2606.48	1786.41	1377.04	1131.94	968.98	852.95
60000	5155.23	2650.66	1816.69	1400.38	1151.13	985.40	867.40
65000	5584.83	2871.54	1968.08	1517.08	1247.05	1067.52	939.69
70000	6014.43	3092.43	2119.47	1633.78	1342.98	1149.63	1011.97
75000	6444.04	3313.32	2270.86	1750.47	1438.91	1231.75	1084.25
80000	6873.64	3534.21	2422.26	1867.17	1534.83	1313.87	1156.54
85000	7303.24	3755.10	2573.65	1983.87	1630.76	1395.98	1228.82
90000	7732.84	3975.98	2725.04	2100.57	1726.69	1478.10	1301.11
95000	8162.45	4196.87	2876.43	2217.27	1822.62	1560.22	1373.39
100000	8592.05	4417.76	3027.82	2333.96	1918.54	1642.33	1445.67
105000	9021.65	4638.65	3179.21	2450.66	2014.47	1724.45	1517.96
110000	9451.25	4859.54	3330.60	2567.36	2110.40	1806.57	1590.24
120000	10310.46	5301.31	3633.38	2800.76	2302.25	1970.80	1734.81
130000	11169.66	5743.09	3936.17	3034.15	2494.10	2135.03	1879.38
140000	12028.87	6184.86	4238.95	3267.55	2685.96	2299.27	2023.94
150000	12888.07	6626.64	4541.73	3500.95	2877.81	2463.50	2168.51
160000	13747.28	7068.42	4844.51	3734.34	3069.67	2627.73	2313.08
170000	14606.48	7510.19	5147.29	3967.74	3261.52	2791.97	2457.64
180000	15465.69	7951.97	5450.08	4201.14	3453.38	2956.20	2602.21
190000	16324.89	8393.74	5752.86	4434.53	3645.23	3120.43	2746.78
200000	17184.10	8835.52	6055.64	4667.93	3837.08	3284.67	2891.35
210000	18043.30	9277.30	6358.42	4901.33	4028.94	3448.90	3035.91
220000	18902.50	9719.07	6661.20	5134.72	4220.79	3613.13	3180.48
230000	19761.71	10160.85	6963.99	5368.12	4412.65	3777.37	3325.05
240000	20620.91	10602.62	7266.77	5601.52	4604.50	3941.60	3469.62
250000	21480.12	11044.40	7569.55	5834.91	4796.36	4105.83	3614.18

Monthly Payments 5.75 %

LOAN AMOUNT	8	9	10	11	12	13	14
100	1.30	1.18	1.09	1.02	0.96	0.91	0.86
200	2.60	2.37	2.19	2.04	1.92	1.82	1.73
500	6.49	5.92	5.47	5.10	4.80	4.54	4.32
1000	12.99	11.85	10.94	10.21	9.59	9.08	8.64
2000	25.97	23.70	21.89	20.41	19.19	18.16	17.29
5000	64.94	59.25	54.72	51.03	47.97	45.41	43.22
6000	77.92	71.10	65.66	61.23	57.57	54.49	51.86
7000	90.91	82.94	76.60	71.44	67.16	63.57	60.51
8000	103.90	94.79	87.55	81.65	76.76	72.65	69.15
9000	116.89	106.64	98.49	91.85	86.35	81.73	77.80
10000	129.87	118.49	109.43	102.06	95.95	90.81	86.44
12000	155.85	142.19	131.32	122.47	115.14	108.98	103.73
15000	194.81	177.74	164.15	153.09	143.92	136.22	129.66
20000	259.75	236.99	218.86	204.12	191.90	181.63	172.88
25000	324.68	296.23	273.58	255.14	239.87	227.03	216.10
30000	389.62	355.48	328.30	306.17	287.85	272.44	259.32
31000	402.61	367.33	339.24	316.38	297.44	281.52	267.96
32000	415.59	379.18	350.18	326.59	307.04	290.60	276.61
33000	428.58	391.03	361.13	336.79	316.63	299.68	285.25
34000	441.57	402.87	372.07	347.00	326.23	308.76	293.90
35000	454.55	414.72	383.01	357.20	335.82	317.84	302.54
36000	467.54	426.57	393.95	367.41	345.42	326.93	311.18
37000	480.53	438.42	404.90	377.61	355.01	336.01	319.83
38000	493.52	450.27	415.84	387.82	364.61	345.09	328.47
39000	506.50	462.12	426.78	398.03	374.20	354.17	337.12
40000	519.49	473.97	437.73	408.23	383.80	363.25	345.76
41000	532.48	485.82	448.67	418.44	393.39	372.33	354.41
42000	545.47	497.67	459.61	428.64	402.99	381.41	363.05
43000	558.45	509.52	470.56	438.85	412.58	390.49	371.69
44000	571.44	521.37	481.50	449.05	422.18	399.58	380.34
45000	584.43	533.22	492.44	459.26	431.77	408.66	388.98
46000	597.42	545.07	503.39	469.47	441.36	417.74	397.63
47000	610.40	556.91	514.33	479.67	450.96	426.82	406.27
48000	623.39	568.76	525.27	489.88	460.55	435.90	414.91
49000	636.38	580.61	536.22	500.08	470.15	444.98	423.56
50000	649.36	592.46	547.16	510.29	479.74	454.06	432.20
51000	662.35	604.31	558.10	520.50	489.34	463.14	440.85
52000	675.34	616.16	569.05	530.70	498.93	472.23	449.49
53000	688.33	628.01	579.99	540.91	508.53	481.31	458.13
54000	701.31	639.86	590.93	551.11	518.12	490.39	466.78
55000	714.30	651.71	601.88	561.32	527.72	499.47	475.42
56000	727.29	663.56	612.82	571.52	537.31	508.55	484.07
57000	740.28	675.41	623.76	581.73	546.91	517.63	492.71
58000	753.26	687.26	634.70	591.94	556.50	526.71	501.35
59000	766.25	699.11	645.65	602.14	566.10	535.79	510.00
60000	779.24	710.96	656.59	612.35	575.69	544.88	518.64
65000	844.17	770.20	711.31	663.38	623.67	590.28	561.86
70000	909.11	829.45	766.02	714.41	671.64	635.69	605.08
75000	974.05	888.69	820.74	765.43	719.62	681.09	648.30
80000	1038.98	947.94	875.45	816.46	767.59	726.50	691.52
85000	1103.92	1007.19	930.17	867.49	815.57	771.91	734.74
90000	1168.86	1066.43	984.89	918.52	863.54	817.31	777.96
95000	1233.79	1125.68	1039.60	969.55	911.51	862.72	821.18
100000	1298.73	1184.93	1094.32	1020.58	959.49	908.13	864.40
105000	1363.66	1244.17	1149.03	1071.61	1007.46	953.53	907.62
110000	1428.60	1303.42	1203.75	1122.64	1055.44	998.94	950.84
120000	1558.47	1421.91	1313.18	1224.70	1151.39	1089.75	1037.28
130000	1688.35	1540.40	1422.61	1326.75	1247.34	1180.56	1123.72
140000	1818.22	1658.90	1532.05	1428.81	1343.28	1271.38	1210.16
150000	1948.09	1777.39	1641.48	1530.87	1439.23	1362.19	1296.60
160000	2077.97	1895.88	1750.91	1632.93	1535.18	1453.00	1383.04
170000	2207.84	2014.37	1860.34	1734.99	1631.13	1543.81	1469.48
180000	2337.71	2132.87	1969.77	1837.04	1727.08	1634.63	1555.92
190000	2467.58	2251.36	2079.20	1939.10	1823.03	1725.44	1642.37
200000	2597.46	2369.85	2188.64	2041.16	1918.98	1816.25	1728.81
210000	2727.33	2488.34	2298.07	2143.22	2014.93	1907.06	1815.25
220000	2857.20	2606.84	2407.50	2245.27	2110.88	1997.88	1901.69
230000	2987.08	2725.33	2516.93	2347.33	2206.82	2088.69	1988.13
240000	3116.95	2843.82	2626.36	2449.39	2302.77	2179.50	2074.57
250000	3246.82	2962.31	2735.80	2551.45	2398.72	2270.31	2161.01

5.75 % Monthly Payments

LOAN AMOUNT	15	16	17	18	19	20	21
100	0.83	0.79	0.77	0.74	0.72	0.70	0.6
200	1.65	1.59	1.53	1.48	1.44	1.40	1.3
500	4.13	3.97	3.83	3.70	3.59	3.49	3.4
1000	8.27	7.94	7.66	7.40	7.18	6.98	6.8
2000	16.54	15.88	15.31	14.81	14.36	13.96	13.6
5000	41.34	39.71	38.28	37.02	35.90	34.91	34.0
6000	49.61	47.65	45.93	44.42	43.09	41.89	40.8
7000	57.88	55.59	53.59	51.83	50.27	48.88	47.6
8000	66.14	63.53	61.25	59.23	57.45	55.86	54.4
9000	74.41	71.47	68.90	66.64	64.63	62.84	61.2
10000	82.68	79.41	76.56	74.04	71.81	69.82	68.
12000	99.21	95.30	91.87	88.85	86.17	83.79	81.6
15000	124.02	119.12	114.84	111.06	107.71	104.73	102.0
20000	165.36	158.83	153.11	148.08	143.62	139.64	136.0
25000	206.70	198.53	191.39	185.10	179.52	174.56	170.1
30000	248.04	238.24	229.67	222.12	215.43	209.47	204.1
31000	256.30	246.18	237.33	229.53	222.61	216.45	210.9
32000	264.57	254.12	244.98	236.93	229.79	223.43	217.7
33000	272.84	262.07	252.64	244.33	236.97	230.41	224.5
34000	281.11	270.01	260.29	251.74	244.15	237.40	231.3
35000	289.38	277.95	267.95	259.14	251.33	244.38	238.1
36000	297.64	285.89	275.61	266.55	258.52	251.36	244.9
37000	305.91	293.83	283.26	273.95	265.70	258.34	251.7
38000	314.18	301.77	290.92	281.35	272.88	265.33	258.5
39000	322.45	309.71	298.57	288.76	280.06	272.31	265.3
40000	330.72	317.66	306.23	296.16	287.24	279.29	272.1
41000	338.98	325.60	313.88	303.57	294.42	286.27	278.9
42000	347.25	333.54	321.54	310.97	301.60	293.25	285.7
43000	355.52	341.48	329.20	318.37	308.78	300.24	292.5
44000	363.79	349.42	336.85	325.78	315.96	307.22	299.3
45000	372.06	357.36	344.51	333.18	323.14	314.20	306.1
46000	380.32	365.30	352.16	340.59	330.33	321.18	313.
47000	388.59	373.25	359.82	347.99	337.51	328.17	319.
48000	396.86	381.19	367.47	355.39	344.69	335.15	326.
49000	405.13	389.13	375.13	362.80	351.87	342.13	333.
50000	413.39	397.07	382.79	370.20	359.05	349.11	340.
51000	421.66	405.01	390.44	377.61	366.23	356.09	347.
52000	429.93	412.95	398.10	385.01	373.41	363.08	353.
53000	438.20	420.89	405.75	392.41	380.59	370.06	360.
54000	446.47	428.83	413.41	399.82	387.77	377.04	367.
55000	454.73	436.78	421.06	407.22	394.95	384.02	374.
56000	463.00	444.72	428.72	414.63	402.14	391.01	381.
57000	471.27	452.66	436.38	422.03	409.32	397.99	387.
58000	479.54	460.60	444.03	429.43	416.50	404.97	394.
59000	487.81	468.54	451.69	436.84	423.68	411.95	401.
60000	496.07	476.48	459.34	444.24	430.86	418.93	408.
65000	537.41	516.19	497.62	481.26	466.76	453.85	442.
70000	578.75	555.90	535.90	518.28	502.67	488.76	476.
75000	620.09	595.60	574.18	555.30	538.57	523.67	510.
80000	661.43	635.31	612.46	592.32	574.48	558.58	544.
85000	702.77	675.02	650.74	629.34	610.38	593.49	578.
90000	744.11	714.72	689.01	666.36	646.29	628.40	612.
95000	785.45	754.43	727.29	703.38	682.19	663.31	646.
100000	826.79	794.14	765.57	740.40	718.10	698.22	680.
105000	868.13	833.85	803.85	777.42	754.00	733.14	714.
110000	909.47	873.55	842.13	814.45	789.91	768.05	748.
120000	992.15	952.97	918.69	888.49	861.72	837.87	816.
130000	1074.83	1032.38	995.24	962.53	933.53	907.69	884.
140000	1157.51	1111.79	1071.80	1036.57	1005.34	977.51	952.
150000	1240.18	1191.21	1148.36	1110.61	1077.15	1047.34	1020.
160000	1322.86	1270.62	1224.91	1184.65	1148.96	1117.16	1088.
170000	1405.54	1350.04	1301.47	1258.69	1220.77	1186.98	1156.
180000	1488.22	1429.45	1378.03	1332.73	1292.58	1256.80	1224.
190000	1570.90	1508.86	1454.59	1406.77	1364.39	1326.63	1292.
200000	1653.58	1588.28	1531.14	1480.81	1436.20	1396.45	1360.
210000	1736.26	1667.69	1607.70	1554.85	1508.01	1466.27	1428.
220000	1818.94	1747.10	1684.26	1628.89	1579.82	1536.09	1496.
230000	1901.62	1826.52	1760.81	1702.93	1651.63	1605.92	1564.
240000	1984.30	1905.93	1837.37	1776.97	1723.44	1675.74	1633.
250000	2066.97	1985.35	1913.93	1851.01	1795.25	1745.56	1701.

Monthly Payments 5.75 %

LOAN AMOUNT	22	23	24	25	30	35	40
100	0.66	0.65	0.64	0.63	0.58	0.55	0.53
200	1.33	1.30	1.27	1.25	1.16	1.10	1.06
500	3.32	3.25	3.18	3.13	2.90	2.75	2.64
1000	6.64	6.50	6.37	6.25	5.79	5.49	5.28
2000	13.29	13.00	12.74	12.50	11.59	10.98	10.56
5000	33.22	32.50	31.85	31.25	28.96	27.45	26.41
6000	39.87	39.00	38.21	37.50	34.76	32.94	31.69
7000	46.51	45.50	44.58	43.75	40.55	38.43	36.98
8000	53.15	52.00	50.95	50.00	46.34	43.92	42.26
9000	59.80	58.50	57.32	56.25	52.14	49.41	47.54
10000	66.44	65.00	63.69	62.50	57.93	54.90	52.82
12000	79.73	78.00	76.43	75.00	69.51	65.88	63.39
15000	99.66	97.50	95.54	93.75	86.89	82.35	79.23
20000	132.89	130.00	127.38	125.00	115.86	109.80	105.65
25000	166.11	162.50	159.23	156.26	144.82	137.25	132.06
30000	199.33	195.00	191.07	187.51	173.78	164.70	158.47
31000	205.97	201.50	197.44	193.76	179.58	170.20	163.75
32000	212.62	208.00	203.81	200.01	185.37	175.69	169.03
33000	219.26	214.50	210.18	206.26	191.16	181.18	174.32
34000	225.91	221.00	216.55	212.51	196.96	186.67	179.60
35000	232.55	227.50	222.92	218.76	202.75	192.16	184.88
36000	239.19	234.00	229.29	225.01	208.54	197.65	190.16
37000	245.84	240.50	235.66	231.26	214.33	203.14	195.45
38000	252.48	247.00	242.02	237.51	220.13	208.63	200.73
39000	259.13	253.50	248.39	243.76	225.92	214.12	206.01
40000	265.77	260.00	254.76	250.01	231.71	219.61	211.29
41000	272.42	266.50	261.13	256.26	237.50	225.10	216.57
42000	279.06	272.99	267.50	262.51	243.30	230.59	221.86
43000	285.70	279.49	273.87	268.76	249.09	236.08	227.14
44000	292.35	285.99	280.24	275.01	254.88	241.57	232.42
45000	298.99	292.49	286.61	281.26	260.68	247.06	237.70
46000	305.64	298.99	292.98	287.51	266.47	252.55	242.99
47000	312.28	305.49	299.35	293.76	272.26	258.04	248.27
48000	318.93	311.99	305.72	300.01	278.05	263.53	253.55
49000	325.57	318.49	312.08	306.26	283.85	269.02	258.83
50000	332.21	324.99	318.45	312.51	289.64	274.51	264.12
51000	338.86	331.49	324.82	318.76	295.43	280.00	269.40
52000	345.50	337.99	331.19	325.01	301.23	285.49	274.68
53000	352.15	344.49	337.56	331.26	307.02	290.98	279.96
54000	358.79	350.99	343.93	337.51	312.81	296.47	285.25
55000	365.44	357.49	350.30	343.76	318.60	301.96	290.53
56000	372.08	363.99	356.67	350.01	324.40	307.45	295.81
57000	378.73	370.49	363.04	356.26	330.19	312.94	301.09
58000	385.37	376.99	369.41	362.51	335.98	318.43	306.37
59000	392.01	383.49	375.78	368.76	341.77	323.92	311.66
60000	398.66	389.99	382.14	375.01	347.57	329.41	316.94
65000	431.88	422.49	413.99	406.26	376.53	356.86	343.35
70000	465.10	454.99	445.84	437.52	405.50	384.31	369.76
75000	498.32	487.49	477.68	468.77	434.46	411.76	396.17
80000	531.54	519.99	509.53	500.02	463.42	439.21	422.59
85000	564.77	552.49	541.37	531.27	492.39	466.66	449.00
90000	597.99	584.99	573.22	562.52	521.35	494.11	475.41
95000	631.21	617.49	605.06	593.77	550.32	521.57	501.82
100000	664.43	649.99	636.91	625.02	579.28	549.02	528.23
105000	697.65	682.49	668.75	656.27	608.24	576.47	554.64
110000	730.87	714.99	700.60	687.52	637.21	603.92	581.05
120000	797.32	779.99	764.29	750.03	695.14	658.82	633.88
130000	863.76	844.98	827.98	812.53	753.06	713.72	686.70
140000	930.20	909.98	891.67	875.03	810.99	768.62	739.52
150000	996.64	974.98	955.36	937.53	868.92	823.52	792.35
160000	1063.09	1039.98	1019.05	1000.04	926.85	878.43	845.17
170000	1129.53	1104.98	1082.74	1062.54	984.78	933.33	897.99
180000	1195.97	1169.98	1146.43	1125.04	1042.70	988.23	950.82
190000	1262.42	1234.98	1210.12	1187.54	1100.63	1043.13	1003.64
200000	1328.86	1299.98	1273.81	1250.04	1158.56	1098.03	1056.46
210000	1395.30	1364.97	1337.51	1312.55	1216.49	1152.93	1109.29
220000	1461.75	1429.97	1401.20	1375.05	1274.42	1207.84	1162.11
230000	1528.19	1494.97	1464.89	1437.55	1332.34	1262.74	1214.93
240000	1594.63	1559.97	1528.58	1500.05	1390.27	1317.64	1267.76
250000	1661.07	1624.97	1592.27	1562.56	1448.20	1372.54	1320.58

6.00 % Monthly Payments

LOAN AMOUNT	YEARS 1	2	3	4	5	6	7
100	8.60	4.43	3.04	2.35	1.93	1.65	1.46
200	17.21	8.86	6.08	4.69	3.86	3.31	2.91
500	43.02	22.14	15.19	11.73	9.65	8.27	7.29
1000	86.03	44.29	30.39	23.45	19.30	16.54	14.57
2000	172.07	88.57	60.78	46.90	38.60	33.08	29.15
5000	430.16	221.44	151.94	117.26	96.49	82.69	72.87
6000	516.20	265.72	182.33	140.71	115.79	99.23	87.44
7000	602.23	310.01	212.72	164.16	135.09	115.77	102.01
8000	688.26	354.30	243.11	187.61	154.39	132.31	116.59
9000	774.29	398.59	273.50	211.06	173.69	148.84	131.16
10000	860.33	442.87	303.89	234.51	192.99	165.38	145.73
12000	1032.39	531.45	364.66	281.42	231.58	198.46	174.88
15000	1290.49	664.31	455.83	351.77	289.48	248.07	218.60
20000	1720.65	885.75	607.77	469.03	385.97	330.76	291.47
25000	2150.81	1107.19	759.71	586.28	482.46	413.45	364.33
30000	2580.98	1328.62	911.66	703.54	578.96	496.14	437.20
31000	2667.01	1372.91	942.05	726.99	598.26	512.68	451.77
32000	2753.04	1417.20	972.43	750.44	617.55	529.22	466.34
33000	2839.08	1461.49	1002.82	773.89	636.85	545.76	480.92
34000	2925.11	1505.77	1033.21	797.34	656.15	562.30	495.49
35000	3011.14	1550.06	1063.60	820.79	675.45	578.83	510.06
36000	3097.17	1594.35	1093.99	844.25	694.75	595.37	524.64
37000	3183.21	1638.63	1124.38	867.70	714.05	611.91	539.21
38000	3269.24	1682.92	1154.77	891.15	733.35	628.45	553.78
39000	3355.27	1727.21	1185.15	914.60	752.64	644.99	568.36
40000	3441.30	1771.50	1215.54	938.05	771.94	661.53	582.93
41000	3527.34	1815.78	1245.93	961.50	791.24	678.06	597.50
42000	3613.37	1860.07	1276.32	984.95	810.54	694.60	612.08
43000	3699.40	1904.36	1306.71	1008.40	829.84	711.14	626.65
44000	3785.43	1948.65	1337.10	1031.86	849.14	727.68	641.22
45000	3871.47	1992.93	1367.49	1055.31	868.44	744.22	655.80
46000	3957.50	2037.22	1397.87	1078.76	887.73	760.75	670.37
47000	4043.53	2081.51	1428.26	1102.21	907.03	777.29	684.94
48000	4129.56	2125.80	1458.65	1125.66	926.33	793.83	699.52
49000	4215.60	2170.08	1489.04	1149.11	945.63	810.37	714.09
50000	4301.63	2214.37	1519.43	1172.56	964.93	826.91	728.66
51000	4387.66	2258.66	1549.82	1196.02	984.23	843.45	743.24
52000	4473.69	2302.95	1580.21	1219.47	1003.53	859.98	757.81
53000	4559.73	2347.23	1610.59	1242.92	1022.82	876.52	772.38
54000	4645.76	2391.52	1640.98	1266.37	1042.12	893.06	786.96
55000	4731.79	2435.81	1671.37	1289.82	1061.42	909.60	801.53
56000	4817.82	2480.10	1701.76	1313.27	1080.72	926.14	816.10
57000	4903.86	2524.38	1732.15	1336.72	1100.02	942.67	830.68
58000	4989.89	2568.67	1762.54	1360.17	1119.32	959.21	845.25
59000	5075.92	2612.96	1792.93	1383.63	1138.62	975.75	859.82
60000	5161.95	2657.25	1823.31	1407.08	1157.91	992.29	874.40
65000	5592.12	2878.68	1975.26	1524.33	1254.41	1074.98	947.26
70000	6022.28	3100.12	2127.20	1641.59	1350.90	1157.67	1020.13
75000	6452.44	3321.56	2279.14	1758.85	1447.39	1240.36	1093.00
80000	6882.61	3542.99	2431.09	1876.10	1543.89	1323.05	1165.86
85000	7312.77	3764.43	2583.03	1993.36	1640.38	1405.74	1238.73
90000	7742.93	3985.87	2734.97	2110.61	1736.87	1488.43	1311.59
95000	8173.10	4207.31	2886.91	2227.87	1833.36	1571.12	1384.46
100000	8603.26	4428.74	3038.86	2345.13	1929.86	1653.81	1457.33
105000	9033.42	4650.18	3190.80	2462.38	2026.35	1736.50	1530.19
110000	9463.58	4871.62	3342.74	2579.64	2122.84	1819.20	1603.06
120000	10323.91	5314.49	3646.63	2814.15	2315.83	1984.58	1748.79
130000	11184.24	5757.37	3950.51	3048.67	2508.81	2149.96	1894.53
140000	12044.56	6200.24	4254.40	3283.18	2701.80	2315.34	2040.26
150000	12904.89	6643.11	4558.29	3517.69	2894.79	2480.72	2185.99
160000	13765.21	7085.99	4862.17	3752.20	3087.77	2646.10	2331.72
170000	14625.54	7528.86	5166.06	3986.72	3280.76	2811.48	2477.46
180000	15485.86	7971.74	5469.94	4221.23	3473.74	2976.87	2623.19
190000	16346.19	8414.61	5773.83	4455.74	3666.73	3142.25	2768.92
200000	17206.52	8857.49	6077.72	4690.26	3859.71	3307.63	2914.65
210000	18066.84	9300.36	6381.60	4924.77	4052.70	3473.01	3060.39
220000	18927.17	9743.23	6685.49	5159.28	4245.69	3638.39	3206.12
230000	19787.49	10186.11	6989.37	5393.79	4438.67	3803.77	3351.85
240000	20647.82	10628.98	7293.26	5628.31	4631.66	3969.15	3497.59
250000	21508.14	11071.86	7597.14	5862.82	4824.64	4134.54	3643.32

Monthly Payments 6.00 %

LOAN AMOUNT	8	9	10	11	12	13	14
	YEARS						
100	1.31	1.20	1.11	1.03	0.97	0.92	0.88
200	2.62	2.39	2.21	2.07	1.94	1.84	1.75
500	6.55	5.98	5.53	5.16	4.86	4.60	4.39
1000	13.11	11.97	11.07	10.33	9.72	9.21	8.77
2000	26.21	23.94	22.13	20.66	19.44	18.42	17.55
5000	65.53	59.85	55.33	51.65	48.60	46.04	43.87
6000	78.63	71.82	66.39	61.98	58.32	55.25	52.64
7000	91.74	83.79	77.46	72.31	68.04	64.46	61.41
8000	104.84	95.75	88.52	82.64	77.76	73.67	70.19
9000	117.95	107.72	99.59	92.97	87.48	82.88	78.96
10000	131.06	119.69	110.65	103.30	97.20	92.09	87.73
12000	157.27	143.63	132.78	123.95	116.65	110.50	105.28
15000	196.58	179.54	165.98	154.94	145.81	138.13	131.60
20000	262.11	239.39	221.30	206.59	194.41	184.17	175.46
25000	327.64	299.23	276.63	258.24	243.01	230.22	219.33
30000	393.17	359.08	331.95	309.89	291.61	276.26	263.20
31000	406.27	371.05	343.02	320.22	301.33	285.47	271.97
32000	419.38	383.02	354.08	330.54	311.05	294.68	280.74
33000	432.48	394.99	365.15	340.87	320.77	303.88	289.51
34000	445.59	406.96	376.21	351.20	330.49	313.09	298.29
35000	458.70	418.93	387.28	361.53	340.22	322.30	307.06
36000	471.80	430.90	398.34	371.86	349.94	331.51	315.83
37000	484.91	442.87	409.41	382.19	359.66	340.72	324.61
38000	498.01	454.84	420.47	392.52	369.38	349.93	333.38
39000	511.12	466.80	431.54	402.85	379.10	359.14	342.15
40000	524.22	478.77	442.60	413.18	388.82	368.34	350.93
41000	537.33	490.74	453.67	423.51	398.54	377.55	359.70
42000	550.44	502.71	464.73	433.84	408.26	386.76	368.47
43000	563.54	514.68	475.80	444.17	417.98	395.97	377.25
44000	576.65	526.65	486.86	454.50	427.70	405.18	386.02
45000	589.75	538.62	497.93	464.83	437.42	414.39	394.79
46000	602.86	550.59	508.99	475.16	447.14	423.60	403.57
47000	615.96	562.56	520.06	485.49	456.86	432.80	412.34
48000	629.07	574.53	531.12	495.82	466.58	442.01	421.11
49000	642.17	586.50	542.19	506.15	476.30	451.22	429.89
50000	655.28	598.47	553.25	516.48	486.02	460.43	438.66
51000	668.39	610.44	564.32	526.81	495.74	469.64	447.43
52000	681.49	622.41	575.39	537.14	505.46	478.85	456.20
53000	694.60	634.38	586.45	547.46	515.18	488.06	464.98
54000	707.70	646.35	597.52	557.79	524.90	497.26	473.75
55000	720.81	658.31	608.58	568.12	534.62	506.47	482.52
56000	733.91	670.28	619.65	578.45	544.34	515.68	491.30
57000	747.02	682.25	630.71	588.78	554.06	524.89	500.07
58000	760.12	694.22	641.78	599.11	563.78	534.10	508.84
59000	773.23	706.19	652.84	609.44	573.51	543.31	517.62
60000	786.34	718.16	663.91	619.77	583.23	552.52	526.39
65000	851.86	778.01	719.23	671.42	631.83	598.56	570.26
70000	917.39	837.86	774.56	723.07	680.43	644.60	614.12
75000	982.92	897.70	829.88	774.71	729.03	690.65	657.99
80000	1048.45	957.55	885.21	826.36	777.63	736.69	701.85
85000	1113.98	1017.40	940.53	878.01	826.24	782.73	745.72
90000	1179.50	1077.24	995.86	929.66	874.84	828.77	789.59
95000	1245.03	1137.09	1051.18	981.30	923.44	874.82	833.45
100000	1310.56	1196.94	1106.51	1032.95	972.04	920.86	877.32
105000	1376.09	1256.78	1161.84	1084.60	1020.65	966.90	921.18
110000	1441.62	1316.63	1217.16	1136.25	1069.25	1012.95	965.05
120000	1572.67	1436.32	1327.81	1239.54	1166.45	1105.03	1052.78
130000	1703.73	1556.02	1438.46	1342.84	1263.66	1197.12	1140.51
140000	1834.78	1675.71	1549.11	1446.13	1360.86	1289.20	1228.24
150000	1965.84	1795.40	1659.76	1549.43	1458.06	1381.29	1315.98
160000	2096.90	1915.10	1770.42	1652.72	1555.27	1473.38	1403.71
170000	2227.95	2034.79	1881.07	1756.02	1652.47	1565.46	1491.44
180000	2359.01	2154.48	1991.72	1859.31	1749.68	1657.55	1579.17
190000	2490.06	2274.18	2102.37	1962.61	1846.88	1749.63	1666.90
200000	2621.12	2393.87	2213.02	2065.90	1944.09	1841.72	1754.63
210000	2752.18	2513.57	2323.67	2169.20	2041.29	1933.81	1842.37
220000	2883.23	2633.26	2434.32	2272.49	2138.49	2025.89	1930.10
230000	3014.29	2752.95	2544.97	2375.79	2235.70	2117.98	2017.83
240000	3145.34	2872.65	2655.62	2479.09	2332.90	2210.06	2105.56
250000	3276.40	2992.34	2766.27	2582.38	2430.11	2302.15	2193.29

6.00 % Monthly Payments

LOAN AMOUNT	15	16	17	18	19	20	21
100	0.84	0.81	0.78	0.75	0.73	0.71	0.69
200	1.68	1.61	1.56	1.51	1.46	1.42	1.39
500	4.20	4.04	3.90	3.77	3.66	3.56	3.47
1000	8.40	8.07	7.79	7.54	7.32	7.12	6.95
2000	16.80	16.15	15.58	15.08	14.64	14.24	13.89
5000	41.99	40.37	38.95	37.70	36.59	35.61	34.73
6000	50.39	48.44	46.74	45.24	43.91	42.73	41.67
7000	58.79	56.52	54.53	52.78	51.23	49.85	48.62
8000	67.19	64.59	62.32	60.32	58.55	56.98	55.56
9000	75.59	72.67	70.11	67.86	65.87	64.10	62.51
10000	83.99	80.74	77.90	75.40	73.19	71.22	69.46
12000	100.79	96.89	93.48	90.48	87.83	85.46	83.35
15000	125.98	121.11	116.85	113.10	109.78	106.83	104.18
20000	167.98	161.48	155.80	150.81	146.38	142.44	138.91
25000	209.97	201.85	194.75	188.51	182.97	178.05	173.64
30000	251.96	242.22	233.71	226.21	219.57	213.66	208.37
31000	260.36	250.30	241.50	233.75	226.89	220.78	215.31
32000	268.76	258.37	249.29	241.29	234.21	227.90	222.26
33000	277.16	266.44	257.08	248.83	241.52	235.02	229.21
34000	285.56	274.52	264.87	256.37	248.84	242.14	236.15
35000	293.96	282.59	272.66	263.91	256.16	249.27	243.10
36000	302.36	290.67	280.45	271.45	263.48	256.39	250.04
37000	310.76	298.74	288.24	278.99	270.80	263.51	256.99
38000	319.16	306.82	296.03	286.53	278.12	270.63	263.93
39000	327.55	314.89	303.82	294.07	285.44	277.75	270.88
40000	335.95	322.96	311.61	301.61	292.76	284.88	277.82
41000	344.35	331.04	319.40	309.15	300.08	292.00	284.77
42000	352.75	339.11	327.19	316.69	307.40	299.12	291.72
43000	361.15	347.19	334.98	324.23	314.71	306.24	298.66
44000	369.55	355.26	342.77	331.77	322.03	313.36	305.61
45000	377.95	363.33	350.56	339.31	329.35	320.48	312.55
46000	386.35	371.41	358.35	346.85	336.67	327.61	319.50
47000	394.74	379.48	366.14	354.39	343.99	334.73	326.44
48000	403.14	387.56	373.93	361.93	351.31	341.85	333.39
49000	411.54	395.63	381.72	369.47	358.63	348.97	340.34
50000	419.94	403.70	389.51	377.01	365.95	356.09	347.28
51000	428.34	411.78	397.30	384.55	373.27	363.22	354.23
52000	436.74	419.85	405.09	392.09	380.58	370.34	361.17
53000	445.14	427.93	412.88	399.63	387.90	377.46	368.12
54000	453.54	436.00	420.67	407.17	395.22	384.58	375.06
55000	461.94	444.07	428.46	414.71	402.54	391.70	382.01
56000	470.33	452.15	436.25	422.25	409.86	398.83	388.95
57000	478.73	460.22	444.04	429.79	417.18	405.95	395.90
58000	487.13	468.30	451.83	437.33	424.50	413.07	402.85
59000	495.53	476.37	459.62	444.87	431.82	420.19	409.79
60000	503.93	484.45	467.41	452.42	439.14	427.31	416.74
65000	545.92	524.82	506.36	490.12	475.73	462.92	451.47
70000	587.92	565.19	545.31	527.82	512.33	498.53	486.19
75000	629.91	605.56	584.26	565.52	548.92	534.14	520.92
80000	671.91	645.93	623.21	603.22	585.51	569.75	555.65
85000	713.90	686.30	662.16	640.92	622.11	605.36	590.38
90000	755.89	726.67	701.12	678.62	658.70	640.97	625.11
95000	797.89	767.04	740.07	716.32	695.30	676.58	659.83
100000	839.88	807.41	779.02	754.03	731.89	712.19	694.56
105000	881.88	847.78	817.97	791.73	768.49	747.80	729.29
110000	923.87	888.15	856.92	829.43	805.08	783.41	764.02
120000	1007.86	968.89	934.82	904.83	878.27	854.63	833.47
130000	1091.85	1049.63	1012.72	980.23	951.46	925.84	902.93
140000	1175.84	1130.37	1090.62	1055.64	1024.65	997.06	972.39
150000	1259.82	1211.11	1168.53	1131.04	1097.84	1068.28	1041.84
160000	1343.81	1291.85	1246.43	1206.44	1171.03	1139.50	1111.30
170000	1427.80	1372.60	1324.33	1281.84	1244.22	1210.72	1180.76
180000	1511.79	1453.34	1402.23	1357.25	1317.41	1281.94	1250.21
190000	1595.78	1534.08	1480.13	1432.65	1390.60	1353.16	1319.67
200000	1679.77	1614.82	1558.04	1508.05	1463.79	1424.38	1389.12
210000	1763.75	1695.56	1635.94	1583.45	1536.98	1495.60	1458.58
220000	1847.74	1776.30	1713.84	1658.86	1610.16	1566.81	1528.04
230000	1931.73	1857.04	1791.74	1734.26	1683.35	1638.03	1597.49
240000	2015.72	1937.78	1869.64	1809.66	1756.54	1709.25	1666.95
250000	2099.71	2018.52	1947.54	1885.06	1829.73	1780.47	1736.41

Monthly Payments 6.00 %

LOAN AMOUNT	22	23	24	25	30	35	40
100	0.68	0.66	0.65	0.64	0.59	0.57	0.55
200	1.36	1.33	1.30	1.28	1.19	1.13	1.09
500	3.39	3.32	3.26	3.20	2.97	2.83	2.73
1000	6.79	6.64	6.52	6.40	5.95	5.65	5.45
2000	13.57	13.29	13.03	12.80	11.90	11.31	10.90
5000	33.94	33.22	32.58	31.99	29.74	28.26	27.25
6000	40.72	39.87	39.09	38.39	35.69	33.92	32.71
7000	47.51	46.51	45.61	44.79	41.64	39.57	38.16
8000	54.30	53.16	52.12	51.18	47.59	45.22	43.61
9000	61.09	59.80	58.64	57.58	53.53	50.87	49.06
10000	67.87	66.45	65.15	63.98	59.48	56.53	54.51
12000	81.45	79.73	78.18	76.78	71.38	67.83	65.41
15000	101.81	99.67	97.73	95.97	89.22	84.79	81.76
20000	135.75	132.89	130.31	127.96	118.96	113.05	109.02
25000	169.68	166.11	162.88	159.95	148.71	141.31	136.27
30000	203.62	199.34	195.46	191.94	178.45	169.58	163.53
31000	210.41	205.98	201.97	198.34	184.40	175.23	168.98
32000	217.19	212.62	208.49	204.74	190.34	180.88	174.43
33000	223.98	219.27	215.01	211.14	196.29	186.53	179.88
34000	230.77	225.91	221.52	217.53	202.24	192.19	185.33
35000	237.56	232.56	228.04	223.93	208.19	197.84	190.78
36000	244.34	239.20	234.55	230.33	214.14	203.49	196.23
37000	251.13	245.85	241.07	236.73	220.08	209.14	201.68
38000	257.92	252.49	247.58	243.13	226.03	214.80	207.13
39000	264.70	259.14	254.10	249.52	231.98	220.45	212.58
40000	271.49	265.78	260.61	255.92	237.93	226.10	218.04
41000	278.28	272.42	267.13	262.32	243.88	231.75	223.49
42000	285.07	279.07	273.64	268.72	249.83	237.41	228.94
43000	291.85	285.71	280.16	275.12	255.77	243.06	234.39
44000	298.64	292.36	286.67	281.51	261.72	248.71	239.84
45000	305.43	299.00	293.19	287.91	267.67	254.36	245.29
46000	312.22	305.65	299.70	294.31	273.62	260.02	250.74
47000	319.00	312.29	306.22	300.71	279.57	265.67	256.19
48000	325.79	318.94	312.74	307.11	285.52	271.32	261.64
49000	332.58	325.58	319.25	313.51	291.46	276.97	267.09
50000	339.36	332.23	325.77	319.90	297.41	282.63	272.54
51000	346.15	338.87	332.28	326.30	303.36	288.28	277.99
52000	352.94	345.51	338.80	332.70	309.31	293.93	283.45
53000	359.73	352.16	345.31	339.10	315.26	299.58	288.90
54000	366.51	358.80	351.83	345.50	321.20	305.24	294.35
55000	373.30	365.45	358.34	351.89	327.15	310.89	299.80
56000	380.09	372.09	364.86	358.29	333.10	316.54	305.25
57000	386.88	378.74	371.37	364.69	339.05	322.19	310.70
58000	393.66	385.38	377.89	371.09	345.00	327.85	316.15
59000	400.45	392.03	384.40	377.49	350.95	333.50	321.60
60000	407.24	398.67	390.92	383.88	356.89	339.15	327.05
65000	441.17	431.89	423.50	415.87	386.64	367.41	354.31
70000	475.11	465.12	456.07	447.86	416.38	395.68	381.56
75000	509.05	498.34	488.65	479.85	446.12	423.94	408.82
80000	542.98	531.56	521.23	511.85	475.86	452.20	436.07
85000	576.92	564.78	553.80	543.84	505.60	480.46	463.32
90000	610.86	598.01	586.38	575.83	535.34	508.73	490.58
95000	644.79	631.23	618.96	607.82	565.08	536.99	517.83
100000	678.73	664.45	651.53	639.81	594.82	565.25	545.09
105000	712.67	697.67	684.11	671.80	624.56	593.51	572.34
110000	746.60	730.90	716.69	703.79	654.31	621.78	599.60
120000	814.47	797.34	781.84	767.77	713.79	678.30	654.11
130000	882.35	863.79	846.99	831.75	773.27	734.83	708.61
140000	950.22	930.23	912.15	895.73	832.75	791.35	763.12
150000	1018.09	996.68	977.30	959.71	892.24	847.88	.817.63
160000	1085.97	1063.12	1042.45	1023.69	951.72	904.40	872.14
170000	1153.84	1129.57	1107.60	1087.67	1011.20	960.93	926.65
180000	1221.71	1196.01	1172.76	1151.65	1070.68	1017.45	981.16
190000	1289.58	1262.46	1237.91	1215.63	1130.16	1073.98	1035.67
200000	1357.46	1328.90	1303.06	1279.61	1189.65	1130.50	1090.18
210000	1425.33	1395.35	1368.22	1343.59	1249.13	1187.03	1144.68
220000	1493.20	1461.79	1433.37	1407.57	1308.61	1243.55	1199.19
230000	1561.08	1528.24	1498.52	1471.56	1368.09	1300.08	1253.70
240000	1628.95	1594.68	1563.68	1535.54	1427.58	1356.60	1308.21
250000	1696.82	1661.13	1628.83	1599.52	1487.06	1413.13	1362.72

6.25 % Monthly Payments

LOAN AMOUNT	YEARS 1	2	3	4	5	6	7
100	8.61	4.44	3.05	2.36	1.94	1.67	1.47
200	17.23	8.88	6.10	4.71	3.88	3.33	2.94
500	43.07	22.20	15.25	11.78	9.71	8.33	7.35
1000	86.14	44.40	30.50	23.56	19.41	16.65	14.69
2000	172.29	88.79	61.00	47.13	38.82	33.31	29.38
5000	430.72	221.99	152.50	117.82	97.06	83.27	73.45
6000	516.87	266.38	182.99	141.38	116.47	99.92	88.14
7000	603.01	310.78	213.49	164.94	135.88	116.57	102.83
8000	689.16	355.18	243.99	188.50	155.30	133.23	117.52
9000	775.30	399.58	274.49	212.07	174.71	149.88	132.21
10000	861.45	443.97	304.99	235.63	194.12	166.53	146.90
12000	1033.74	532.77	365.99	282.76	232.94	199.84	176.28
15000	1292.17	665.96	457.49	353.45	291.18	249.80	220.35
20000	1722.89	887.95	609.98	471.26	388.24	333.07	293.81
25000	2153.62	1109.93	762.48	589.08	485.30	416.33	367.26
30000	2584.34	1331.92	914.97	706.89	582.36	499.60	440.71
31000	2670.48	1376.32	945.47	730.46	601.77	516.25	455.40
32000	2756.63	1420.71	975.97	754.02	621.18	532.91	470.09
33000	2842.77	1465.11	1006.47	777.58	640.60	549.56	484.78
34000	2928.92	1509.51	1036.97	801.15	660.01	566.21	499.47
35000	3015.06	1553.91	1067.47	824.71	679.42	582.87	514.16
36000	3101.21	1598.30	1097.97	848.27	698.83	599.52	528.85
37000	3187.35	1642.70	1128.47	871.84	718.24	616.17	543.54
38000	3273.50	1687.10	1158.97	895.40	737.66	632.83	558.23
39000	3359.64	1731.50	1189.46	918.96	757.07	649.48	572.92
40000	3445.79	1775.89	1219.96	942.52	776.48	666.13	587.61
41000	3531.93	1820.29	1250.46	966.09	795.89	682.79	602.30
42000	3618.08	1864.69	1280.96	989.65	815.30	699.44	616.99
43000	3704.22	1909.08	1311.46	1013.21	834.72	716.09	631.68
44000	3790.36	1953.48	1341.96	1036.78	854.13	732.75	646.37
45000	3876.51	1997.88	1372.46	1060.34	873.54	749.40	661.06
46000	3962.65	2042.28	1402.96	1083.90	892.95	766.05	675.75
47000	4048.80	2086.67	1433.46	1107.47	912.36	782.71	690.44
48000	4134.94	2131.07	1463.96	1131.03	931.78	799.36	705.13
49000	4221.09	2175.47	1494.46	1154.59	951.19	816.01	719.82
50000	4307.23	2219.87	1524.95	1178.16	970.60	832.67	734.51
51000	4393.38	2264.26	1555.45	1201.72	990.01	849.32	749.20
52000	4479.52	2308.66	1585.95	1225.28	1009.42	865.97	763.89
53000	4565.67	2353.06	1616.45	1248.85	1028.84	882.63	778.58
54000	4651.81	2397.45	1646.95	1272.41	1048.25	899.28	793.27
55000	4737.96	2441.85	1677.45	1295.97	1067.66	915.93	807.96
56000	4824.10	2486.25	1707.95	1319.53	1087.07	932.59	822.65
57000	4910.25	2530.65	1738.45	1343.10	1106.48	949.24	837.34
58000	4996.39	2575.04	1768.95	1366.66	1125.90	965.89	852.03
59000	5082.53	2619.44	1799.45	1390.22	1145.31	982.55	866.73
60000	5168.68	2663.84	1829.95	1413.79	1164.72	999.20	881.42
65000	5599.40	2885.83	1982.44	1531.60	1261.78	1082.47	954.87
70000	6030.13	3107.81	2134.94	1649.42	1358.84	1165.73	1028.32
75000	6460.85	3329.80	2287.43	1767.23	1455.90	1249.00	1101.77
80000	6891.57	3551.79	2439.93	1885.05	1552.96	1332.27	1175.22
85000	7322.30	3773.77	2592.42	2002.86	1650.02	1415.53	1248.67
90000	7753.02	3995.76	2744.92	2120.68	1747.08	1498.80	1322.12
95000	8183.74	4217.74	2897.41	2238.50	1844.14	1582.07	1395.57
100000	8614.47	4439.73	3049.91	2356.31	1941.20	1665.33	1469.03
105000	9045.19	4661.72	3202.40	2474.13	2038.26	1748.60	1542.48
110000	9475.91	4883.70	3354.90	2591.94	2135.32	1831.87	1615.93
120000	10337.36	5327.68	3659.89	2827.57	2329.44	1998.40	1762.83
130000	11198.80	5771.65	3964.88	3063.20	2523.56	2164.93	1909.73
140000	12060.25	6215.62	4269.87	3298.84	2717.68	2331.46	2056.64
150000	12921.70	6659.60	4574.86	3534.47	2911.80	2498.00	2203.54
160000	13783.14	7103.57	4879.85	3770.10	3105.92	2664.53	2350.44
170000	14644.59	7547.54	5184.84	4005.73	3300.04	2831.06	2497.34
180000	15506.04	7991.52	5489.84	4241.36	3494.16	2997.60	2644.25
190000	16367.48	8435.49	5794.83	4476.99	3688.28	3164.13	2791.15
200000	17228.93	8879.46	6099.82	4712.62	3882.40	3330.66	2938.05
210000	18090.38	9323.44	6404.81	4948.25	4076.52	3497.20	3084.95
220000	18951.82	9767.41	6709.80	5183.89	4270.64	3663.73	3231.86
230000	19813.27	10211.38	7014.79	5419.52	4464.76	3830.26	3378.76
240000	20674.72	10655.36	7319.78	5655.15	4658.88	3996.80	3525.66
250000	21536.16	11099.33	7624.77	5890.78	4853.00	4163.33	3672.56

Monthly Payments 6.25 %

LOAN AMOUNT	8	9	10	11	12	13	14
			YEARS				
100	1.32	1.21	1.12	1.05	0.98	0.93	0.89
200	2.64	2.42	2.24	2.09	1.97	1.87	1.78
500	6.61	6.05	5.59	5.23	4.92	4.67	4.45
1000	13.22	12.09	11.19	10.45	9.85	9.34	8.90
2000	26.45	24.18	22.38	20.91	19.69	18.67	17.81
5000	66.12	60.45	55.94	52.27	49.23	46.68	44.52
6000	79.35	72.54	67.13	62.72	59.08	56.02	53.42
7000	92.57	84.63	78.31	73.18	68.93	65.36	62.32
8000	105.80	96.72	89.50	83.63	78.77	74.69	71.23
9000	119.02	108.81	100.69	94.09	88.62	84.03	80.13
10000	132.24	120.90	111.88	104.54	98.47	93.37	89.03
12000	158.69	145.08	134.25	125.45	118.16	112.04	106.84
15000	198.37	181.35	167.82	156.81	147.70	140.05	133.55
20000	264.49	241.80	223.75	209.08	196.94	186.74	178.07
25000	330.61	302.25	279.69	261.35	246.17	233.42	222.58
30000	396.73	362.70	335.63	313.62	295.40	280.10	267.10
31000	409.96	374.79	346.82	324.07	305.25	289.44	276.00
32000	423.18	386.88	358.01	334.53	315.10	298.78	284.90
33000	436.41	398.97	369.19	344.98	324.94	308.12	293.81
34000	449.63	411.06	380.38	355.44	334.79	317.45	302.71
35000	462.86	423.15	391.57	365.89	344.64	326.79	311.61
36000	476.08	435.24	402.76	376.34	354.48	336.13	320.52
37000	489.30	447.33	413.94	386.80	364.33	345.46	329.42
38000	502.53	459.42	425.13	397.25	374.18	354.80	338.32
39000	515.75	471.51	436.32	407.71	384.02	364.14	347.23
40000	528.98	483.60	447.51	418.16	393.87	373.47	356.13
41000	542.20	495.69	458.70	428.61	403.72	382.81	365.03
42000	555.43	507.78	469.88	439.07	413.56	392.15	373.94
43000	568.65	519.87	481.07	449.52	423.41	401.48	382.84
44000	581.87	531.96	492.26	459.98	433.26	410.82	391.74
45000	595.10	544.05	503.45	470.43	443.10	420.16	400.65
46000	608.32	556.14	514.63	480.88	452.95	429.49	409.55
47000	621.55	568.23	525.82	491.34	462.80	438.83	418.45
48000	634.77	580.32	537.01	501.79	472.65	448.17	427.36
49000	648.00	592.41	548.20	512.25	482.49	457.50	436.26
50000	661.22	604.50	559.38	522.70	492.34	466.84	445.16
51000	674.45	616.59	570.57	533.15	502.19	476.18	454.07
52000	687.67	628.68	581.76	543.61	512.03	485.51	462.97
53000	700.89	640.77	592.95	554.06	521.88	494.85	471.87
54000	714.12	652.86	604.13	564.52	531.73	504.19	480.78
55000	727.34	664.95	615.32	574.97	541.57	513.53	489.68
56000	740.57	677.04	626.51	585.42	551.42	522.86	498.58
57000	753.79	689.13	637.70	595.88	561.27	532.20	507.49
58000	767.02	701.22	648.89	606.33	571.11	541.54	516.39
59000	780.24	713.31	660.07	616.79	580.96	550.87	525.29
60000	793.47	725.40	671.26	627.24	590.81	560.21	534.20
65000	859.59	785.85	727.20	679.51	640.04	606.89	578.71
70000	925.71	846.30	783.14	731.78	689.27	653.58	623.23
75000	991.83	906.75	839.08	784.05	738.51	700.26	667.74
80000	1057.95	967.20	895.01	836.32	787.74	746.95	712.26
85000	1124.08	1027.66	950.95	888.59	836.98	793.63	756.78
90000	1190.20	1088.11	1006.89	940.86	886.21	840.31	801.29
95000	1256.32	1148.56	1062.83	993.13	935.44	887.00	845.81
100000	1322.44	1209.01	1118.77	1045.40	984.68	933.68	890.33
105000	1388.57	1269.46	1174.71	1097.67	1033.91	980.37	934.84
110000	1454.69	1329.91	1230.65	1149.94	1083.15	1027.05	979.36
120000	1586.93	1450.81	1342.52	1254.48	1181.61	1120.42	1068.39
130000	1719.18	1571.71	1454.40	1359.02	1280.08	1213.79	1157.42
140000	1851.42	1692.61	1566.28	1463.56	1378.55	1307.16	1246.46
150000	1983.66	1813.51	1678.15	1568.10	1477.02	1400.52	1335.49
160000	2115.91	1934.41	1790.03	1672.64	1575.48	1493.89	1424.52
170000	2248.15	2055.31	1901.91	1777.18	1673.95	1587.26	1513.55
180000	2380.40	2176.21	2013.78	1881.72	1772.42	1680.63	1602.59
190000	2512.64	2297.11	2125.66	1986.26	1870.89	1774.00	1691.62
200000	2644.89	2418.01	2237.54	2090.80	1969.36	1867.36	1780.65
210000	2777.13	2538.91	2349.41	2195.34	2067.82	1960.73	1869.68
220000	2909.37	2659.81	2461.29	2299.88	2166.29	2054.10	1958.72
230000	3041.62	2780.71	2573.17	2404.42	2264.76	2147.47	2047.75
240000	3173.86	2901.61	2685.04	2508.96	2363.23	2240.84	2136.78
250000	3306.11	3022.52	2796.92	2613.50	2461.69	2334.21	2225.81

6.25 % Monthly Payments

LOAN AMOUNT	15	16	17	18	19	20	21
100	0.85	0.82	0.79	0.77	0.75	0.73	0.71
200	1.71	1.64	1.59	1.54	1.49	1.45	1.42
500	4.27	4.10	3.96	3.84	3.73	3.63	3.54
1000	8.53	8.21	7.93	7.68	7.46	7.26	7.09
2000	17.06	16.42	15.85	15.36	14.92	14.53	14.18
5000	42.65	41.04	39.63	38.39	37.29	36.31	35.44
6000	51.18	49.25	47.55	46.07	44.75	43.58	42.53
7000	59.72	57.46	55.48	53.74	52.21	50.84	49.62
8000	68.25	65.66	63.41	61.42	59.66	58.10	56.71
9000	76.78	73.87	71.33	69.10	67.12	65.37	63.79
10000	85.31	82.08	79.26	76.78	74.58	72.63	70.88
12000	102.37	98.49	95.11	92.13	89.50	87.15	85.06
15000	127.96	123.12	118.89	115.16	111.87	108.94	106.32
20000	170.62	164.16	158.52	153.55	149.16	145.26	141.77
25000	213.27	205.20	198.14	191.94	186.45	181.57	177.21
30000	255.92	246.24	237.77	230.33	223.74	217.88	212.65
31000	264.45	254.44	245.70	238.01	231.20	225.15	219.74
32000	272.98	262.65	253.62	245.68	238.66	232.41	226.83
33000	281.52	270.86	261.55	253.36	246.12	239.67	233.91
34000	290.05	279.07	269.48	261.04	253.58	246.94	241.00
35000	298.58	287.28	277.40	268.72	261.03	254.20	248.09
36000	307.11	295.48	285.33	276.40	268.49	261.46	255.18
37000	315.64	303.69	293.25	284.07	275.95	268.72	262.27
38000	324.17	311.90	301.18	291.75	283.41	275.99	269.35
39000	332.70	320.11	309.10	299.43	290.87	283.25	276.44
40000	341.23	328.31	317.03	307.11	298.32	290.51	283.53
41000	349.76	336.52	324.96	314.78	305.78	297.78	290.62
42000	358.29	344.73	332.88	322.46	313.24	305.04	297.71
43000	366.82	352.94	340.81	330.14	320.70	312.30	304.80
44000	375.35	361.15	348.73	337.82	328.16	319.56	311.88
45000	383.88	369.35	356.66	345.49	335.61	326.83	318.97
46000	392.42	377.56	364.59	353.17	343.07	334.09	326.06
47000	400.95	385.77	372.51	360.85	350.53	341.35	333.15
48000	409.48	393.98	380.44	368.53	357.99	348.61	340.24
49000	418.01	402.19	388.36	376.20	365.45	355.88	347.33
50000	426.54	410.39	396.29	383.88	372.90	363.14	354.4
51000	435.07	418.60	404.21	391.56	380.36	370.40	361.50
52000	443.60	426.81	412.14	399.24	387.82	377.67	368.59
53000	452.13	435.02	420.07	406.92	395.28	384.93	375.68
54000	460.66	443.22	427.99	414.59	402.74	392.19	382.77
55000	469.19	451.43	435.92	422.27	410.20	399.45	389.8
56000	477.72	459.64	443.84	429.95	417.65	406.72	396.9
57000	486.25	467.85	451.77	437.63	425.11	413.98	404.0
58000	494.78	476.06	459.69	445.30	432.57	421.24	411.1
59000	503.32	484.26	467.62	452.98	440.03	428.51	418.2
60000	511.85	492.47	475.55	460.66	447.49	435.77	425.3
65000	554.50	533.51	515.17	499.05	484.78	472.08	460.7
70000	597.15	574.55	554.80	537.44	522.07	508.40	496.1
75000	639.81	615.59	594.43	575.82	559.36	544.71	531.6
80000	682.46	656.63	634.06	614.21	596.65	581.02	567.0
85000	725.11	697.67	673.69	652.60	633.94	617.34	602.5
90000	767.77	738.71	713.32	690.99	671.23	653.65	637.9
95000	810.42	779.75	752.95	729.38	708.52	689.97	673.3
100000	853.08	820.79	792.58	767.76	745.81	726.28	708.8
105000	895.73	861.83	832.21	806.15	783.10	762.60	744.2
110000	938.38	902.86	871.83	844.54	820.39	798.91	779.7
120000	1023.69	984.94	951.09	921.32	894.97	871.54	850.5
130000	1109.00	1067.02	1030.35	998.09	969.55	944.17	921.4
140000	1194.31	1149.10	1109.61	1074.87	1044.13	1016.79	992.3
150000	1279.61	1231.18	1188.87	1151.65	1118.71	1089.42	1063.2
160000	1364.92	1313.26	1268.12	1228.42	1193.30	1162.05	1134.1
170000	1450.23	1395.34	1347.38	1305.20	1267.88	1234.68	1205.0
180000	1535.54	1477.42	1426.64	1381.98	1342.46	1307.31	1275.8
190000	1620.85	1559.49	1505.90	1458.75	1417.04	1379.93	1346.7
200000	1706.15	1641.57	1585.15	1535.53	1491.62	1452.56	1417.6
210000	1791.46	1723.65	1664.41	1612.31	1566.20	1525.19	1488.5
220000	1876.77	1805.73	1743.67	1689.08	1640.78	1597.82	1559.4
230000	1962.08	1887.81	1822.93	1765.86	1715.36	1670.45	1630.3
240000	2047.38	1969.89	1902.18	1842.63	1789.94	1743.07	1701.1
250000	2132.69	2051.97	1981.44	1919.41	1864.52	1815.70	1772.0

(YEARS: 15–21)

Monthly Payments 6.25 %

LOAN AMOUNT	22	23	24	25	30	35	40
100	0.69	0.68	0.67	0.65	0.61	0.58	0.56
200	1.39	1.36	1.33	1.31	1.22	1.16	1.12
500	3.47	3.40	3.33	3.27	3.05	2.91	2.81
1000	6.93	6.79	6.66	6.55	6.11	5.82	5.62
2000	13.86	13.58	13.33	13.09	12.21	11.63	11.24
5000	34.66	33.95	33.32	32.74	30.53	29.08	28.11
6000	41.59	40.74	39.98	39.28	36.63	34.90	33.73
7000	48.52	47.53	46.64	45.83	42.74	40.72	39.35
8000	55.45	54.32	53.30	52.38	48.84	46.53	44.97
9000	62.38	61.12	59.97	58.93	54.95	52.35	50.59
10000	69.32	67.91	66.63	65.47	61.05	58.17	56.21
12000	83.18	81.49	79.96	78.57	73.26	69.80	67.45
15000	103.97	101.86	99.95	98.21	91.58	87.25	84.32
20000	138.63	135.81	133.26	130.95	122.11	116.33	112.42
25000	173.29	169.76	166.58	163.69	152.63	145.42	140.53
30000	207.95	203.72	199.89	196.42	183.16	174.50	168.64
31000	214.88	210.51	206.55	202.97	189.27	180.31	174.26
32000	221.81	217.30	213.22	209.52	195.37	186.13	179.88
33000	228.74	224.09	219.88	216.06	201.48	191.95	185.50
34000	235.68	230.88	226.54	222.61	207.58	197.76	191.12
35000	242.61	237.67	233.21	229.16	213.69	203.58	196.74
36000	249.54	244.46	239.87	235.71	219.79	209.40	202.36
37000	256.47	251.25	246.53	242.25	225.90	215.21	207.98
38000	263.40	258.04	253.20	248.80	232.00	221.03	213.61
39000	270.33	264.83	259.86	255.35	238.11	226.85	219.23
40000	277.27	271.62	266.52	261.90	244.21	232.66	224.85
41000	284.20	278.41	273.18	268.44	250.32	238.48	230.47
42000	291.13	285.20	279.85	274.99	256.42	244.30	236.09
43000	298.06	291.99	286.51	281.54	262.53	250.11	241.71
44000	304.99	298.78	293.17	288.09	268.63	255.93	247.33
45000	311.92	305.58	299.84	294.63	274.74	261.75	252.95
46000	318.86	312.37	306.50	301.18	280.85	267.56	258.58
47000	325.79	319.16	313.16	307.73	286.95	273.38	264.20
48000	332.72	325.95	319.83	314.28	293.06	279.20	269.82
49000	339.65	332.74	326.49	320.82	299.16	285.01	275.44
50000	346.58	339.53	333.15	327.37	305.27	290.83	281.06
51000	353.51	346.32	339.82	333.92	311.37	296.65	286.68
52000	360.45	353.11	346.48	340.47	317.48	302.46	292.30
53000	367.38	359.90	353.14	347.01	323.58	308.28	297.92
54000	374.31	366.69	359.80	353.56	329.69	314.10	303.54
55000	381.24	373.48	366.47	360.11	335.79	319.91	309.17
56000	388.17	380.27	373.13	366.66	341.90	325.73	314.79
57000	395.10	387.06	379.79	373.20	348.00	331.55	320.41
58000	402.04	393.85	386.46	379.75	354.11	337.36	326.03
59000	408.97	400.64	393.12	386.30	360.21	343.18	331.65
60000	415.90	407.43	399.78	392.84	366.32	349.00	337.27
65000	450.56	441.39	433.10	425.58	396.85	378.08	365.38
70000	485.22	475.34	466.41	458.32	427.37	407.16	393.48
75000	519.87	509.29	499.73	491.06	457.90	436.25	421.59
80000	554.53	543.25	533.04	523.79	488.43	465.33	449.70
85000	589.19	577.20	566.36	556.53	518.95	494.41	477.80
90000	623.85	611.15	599.67	589.27	549.48	523.49	505.91
95000	658.51	645.10	632.99	622.00	580.01	552.58	534.01
100000	693.17	679.06	666.30	654.74	610.53	581.66	562.12
105000	727.82	713.01	699.62	687.48	641.06	610.74	590.23
110000	762.48	746.96	732.93	720.22	671.59	639.83	618.33
120000	831.80	814.87	799.56	785.69	732.64	697.99	674.54
130000	901.12	882.77	866.20	851.16	793.69	756.16	730.76
140000	970.43	950.68	932.83	916.64	854.75	814.33	786.97
150000	1039.75	1018.59	999.46	982.11	915.80	872.49	843.18
160000	1109.07	1086.49	1066.09	1047.59	976.85	930.66	899.39
170000	1178.38	1154.40	1132.72	1113.06	1037.91	988.82	955.60
180000	1247.70	1222.30	1199.35	1178.53	1098.96	1046.99	1011.82
190000	1317.02	1290.21	1265.98	1244.01	1160.01	1105.16	1068.03
200000	1386.33	1358.11	1332.61	1309.48	1221.07	1163.32	1124.24
210000	1455.65	1426.02	1399.24	1374.96	1282.12	1221.49	1180.45
220000	1524.97	1493.92	1465.87	1440.43	1343.17	1279.65	1236.66
230000	1594.28	1561.83	1532.50	1505.91	1404.23	1337.82	1292.88
240000	1663.60	1629.74	1599.13	1571.38	1465.28	1395.99	1349.09
250000	1732.91	1697.64	1665.76	1636.85	1526.33	1454.15	1405.30

6.50 % Monthly Payments

LOAN AMOUNT	1	2	3	4	5	6	7
			YEARS				
100	8.63	4.45	3.06	2.37	1.95	1.68	1.48
200	17.25	8.90	6.12	4.74	3.91	3.35	2.96
500	43.13	22.25	15.30	11.84	9.76	8.38	7.40
1000	86.26	44.51	30.61	23.68	19.53	16.77	14.81
2000	172.51	89.01	61.22	47.35	39.05	33.54	29.62
5000	431.28	222.54	153.05	118.38	97.63	83.84	74.04
6000	517.54	267.04	183.66	142.05	117.15	100.61	88.85
7000	603.80	311.55	214.27	165.73	136.68	117.38	103.65
8000	690.05	356.06	244.88	189.40	156.21	134.15	118.46
9000	776.31	400.57	275.49	213.08	175.73	150.92	133.27
10000	862.57	445.07	306.10	236.75	195.26	167.69	148.08
12000	1035.08	534.09	367.32	284.10	234.31	201.23	177.69
15000	1293.85	667.61	459.15	355.13	292.89	251.53	222.12
20000	1725.13	890.15	612.19	473.50	390.51	335.38	296.15
25000	2156.42	1112.68	765.24	591.88	488.14	419.22	370.19
30000	2587.70	1335.22	918.29	710.25	585.77	503.07	444.23
31000	2673.96	1379.72	948.90	733.93	605.30	519.83	459.04
32000	2760.21	1424.23	979.51	757.61	624.82	536.60	473.85
33000	2846.47	1468.74	1010.12	781.28	644.35	553.37	488.65
34000	2932.73	1513.25	1040.73	804.96	663.88	570.14	503.46
35000	3018.98	1557.75	1071.34	828.63	683.40	586.91	518.27
36000	3105.24	1602.26	1101.95	852.31	702.93	603.68	533.08
37000	3191.50	1646.77	1132.56	875.98	722.45	620.45	547.88
38000	3277.75	1691.28	1163.17	899.66	741.98	637.22	562.69
39000	3364.01	1735.78	1193.78	923.33	761.50	653.99	577.50
40000	3450.27	1780.29	1224.39	947.01	781.03	670.75	592.31
41000	3536.52	1824.80	1255.00	970.68	800.56	687.52	607.12
42000	3622.78	1869.30	1285.61	994.36	820.08	704.29	621.92
43000	3709.04	1913.81	1316.22	1018.03	839.61	721.06	636.73
44000	3795.29	1958.32	1346.83	1041.71	859.13	737.83	651.54
45000	3881.55	2002.83	1377.44	1065.38	878.66	754.60	666.35
46000	3967.81	2047.33	1408.05	1089.06	898.18	771.37	681.15
47000	4054.06	2091.84	1438.66	1112.73	917.71	788.14	695.96
48000	4140.32	2136.35	1469.27	1136.41	937.24	804.91	710.77
49000	4226.58	2180.86	1499.88	1160.08	956.76	821.67	725.58
50000	4312.83	2225.36	1530.49	1183.76	976.29	838.44	740.38
51000	4399.09	2269.87	1561.10	1207.43	995.81	855.21	755.19
52000	4485.35	2314.38	1591.71	1231.11	1015.34	871.98	770.00
53000	4571.60	2358.88	1622.32	1254.78	1034.86	888.75	784.81
54000	4657.86	2403.39	1652.93	1278.46	1054.39	905.52	799.62
55000	4744.12	2447.90	1683.54	1302.13	1073.92	922.29	814.42
56000	4830.37	2492.41	1714.15	1325.81	1093.44	939.06	829.23
57000	4916.63	2536.91	1744.75	1349.48	1112.97	955.83	844.04
58000	5002.89	2581.42	1775.36	1373.16	1132.49	972.59	858.85
59000	5089.14	2625.93	1805.97	1396.83	1152.02	989.36	873.65
60000	5175.40	2670.44	1836.58	1420.51	1171.54	1006.13	888.46
65000	5606.68	2892.97	1989.63	1538.89	1269.17	1089.98	962.50
70000	6037.97	3115.51	2142.68	1657.26	1366.80	1173.82	1036.54
75000	6469.25	3338.04	2295.73	1775.64	1464.43	1257.66	1110.58
80000	6900.54	3560.58	2448.78	1894.01	1562.06	1341.51	1184.61
85000	7331.82	3783.12	2601.83	2012.39	1659.69	1425.35	1258.65
90000	7763.10	4005.65	2754.88	2130.76	1757.32	1509.20	1332.69
95000	8194.39	4228.19	2907.92	2249.14	1854.95	1593.04	1406.73
100000	8625.67	4450.73	3060.97	2367.52	1952.57	1676.89	1480.77
105000	9056.95	4673.26	3214.02	2485.89	2050.20	1760.73	1554.81
110000	9488.24	4895.80	3367.07	2604.27	2147.83	1844.58	1628.85
120000	10350.80	5340.87	3673.17	2841.02	2343.09	2012.26	1776.92
130000	11213.37	5785.94	3979.27	3077.77	2538.35	2179.95	1925.00
140000	12075.94	6231.02	4285.36	3314.52	2733.60	2347.64	2073.08
150000	12938.50	6676.09	4591.46	3551.27	2928.86	2515.33	2221.15
160000	13801.07	7121.16	4897.56	3788.03	3124.12	2683.02	2369.23
170000	14663.64	7566.23	5203.65	4024.78	3319.38	2850.71	2517.31
180000	15526.20	8011.31	5509.75	4261.53	3514.63	3018.40	2665.38
190000	16388.77	8456.38	5815.85	4498.28	3709.89	3186.08	2813.46
200000	17251.34	8901.45	6121.95	4735.03	3905.15	3353.77	2961.54
210000	18113.91	9346.52	6428.04	4971.78	4100.41	3521.46	3109.61
220000	18976.47	9791.60	6734.14	5208.54	4295.66	3689.15	3257.69
230000	19839.04	10236.67	7040.24	5445.29	4490.92	3856.84	3405.77
240000	20701.61	10681.74	7346.34	5682.04	4686.18	4024.53	3553.84
250000	21564.17	11126.81	7652.43	5918.79	4881.44	4192.22	3701.92

Monthly Payments 6.50 %

LOAN AMOUNT	8	9	10	11	12	13	14
			YEARS				
100	1.33	1.22	1.13	1.06	1.00	0.95	0.90
200	2.67	2.44	2.26	2.12	1.99	1.89	1.81
500	6.67	6.11	5.66	5.29	4.99	4.73	4.52
1000	13.34	12.21	11.31	10.58	9.97	9.47	9.03
2000	26.69	24.42	22.62	21.16	19.95	18.93	18.07
5000	66.72	61.06	56.55	52.90	49.87	47.33	45.17
6000	80.06	73.27	67.87	63.48	59.84	56.80	54.21
7000	93.41	85.48	79.18	74.05	69.82	66.26	63.24
8000	106.75	97.69	90.49	84.63	79.79	75.73	72.27
9000	120.09	109.90	101.80	95.21	89.77	85.19	81.31
10000	133.44	122.11	113.11	105.79	99.74	94.66	90.34
12000	160.13	146.54	135.73	126.95	119.69	113.59	108.41
15000	200.16	183.17	169.66	158.69	149.61	141.99	135.51
20000	266.88	244.23	226.22	211.58	199.48	189.32	180.69
25000	333.59	305.28	282.77	264.48	249.35	236.65	225.86
30000	400.31	366.34	339.33	317.38	299.22	283.98	271.03
31000	413.66	378.55	350.64	327.95	309.19	293.44	280.06
32000	427.00	390.76	361.95	338.53	319.17	302.91	289.10
33000	440.34	402.97	373.26	349.11	329.14	312.38	298.13
34000	453.69	415.19	384.57	359.69	339.11	321.84	307.17
35000	467.03	427.40	395.88	370.27	349.09	331.31	316.20
36000	480.38	439.61	407.19	380.85	359.06	340.77	325.23
37000	493.72	451.82	418.50	391.43	369.04	350.24	334.27
38000	507.06	464.03	429.82	402.01	379.01	359.70	343.30
39000	520.41	476.24	441.13	412.59	388.98	369.17	352.34
40000	533.75	488.45	452.44	423.17	398.96	378.64	361.37
41000	547.10	500.67	463.75	433.75	408.93	388.10	370.41
42000	560.44	512.88	475.06	444.33	418.90	397.57	379.44
43000	573.78	525.09	486.37	454.91	428.88	407.03	388.47
44000	587.13	537.30	497.68	465.48	438.85	416.50	397.51
45000	600.47	549.51	508.99	476.06	448.83	425.97	406.54
46000	613.81	561.72	520.30	486.64	458.80	435.43	415.58
47000	627.16	573.93	531.61	497.22	468.77	444.90	424.61
48000	640.50	586.15	542.92	507.80	478.75	454.36	433.65
49000	653.85	598.36	554.24	518.38	488.72	463.83	442.68
50000	667.19	610.57	565.55	528.96	498.70	473.30	451.71
51000	680.53	622.78	576.86	539.54	508.67	482.76	460.75
52000	693.88	634.99	588.17	550.12	518.64	492.23	469.78
53000	707.22	647.20	599.48	560.70	528.62	501.69	478.82
54000	720.56	659.41	610.79	571.28	538.59	511.16	487.85
55000	733.91	671.62	622.10	581.86	548.57	520.63	496.89
56000	747.25	683.84	633.41	592.43	558.54	530.09	505.92
57000	760.60	696.05	644.72	603.01	568.51	539.56	514.95
58000	773.94	708.26	656.03	613.59	578.49	549.02	523.99
59000	787.28	720.47	667.34	624.17	588.46	558.49	533.02
60000	800.63	732.68	678.66	634.75	598.44	567.95	542.06
65000	867.35	793.74	735.21	687.65	648.31	615.28	587.23
70000	934.06	854.80	791.77	740.54	698.17	662.61	632.40
75000	1000.78	915.85	848.32	793.44	748.04	709.94	677.57
80000	1067.50	976.91	904.87	846.34	797.91	757.27	722.74
85000	1134.22	1037.97	961.43	899.23	847.78	804.60	767.91
90000	1200.94	1099.02	1017.98	952.13	897.65	851.93	813.08
95000	1267.66	1160.08	1074.54	1005.02	947.52	899.26	858.26
100000	1334.38	1221.14	1131.09	1057.92	997.39	946.59	903.43
105000	1401.10	1282.19	1187.65	1110.82	1047.26	993.92	948.60
110000	1467.82	1343.25	1244.20	1163.71	1097.13	1041.25	993.77
120000	1601.25	1465.36	1357.31	1269.50	1196.87	1135.91	1084.11
130000	1734.69	1587.48	1470.42	1375.29	1296.61	1230.57	1174.46
140000	1868.13	1709.59	1583.53	1481.09	1396.35	1325.23	1264.80
150000	2001.57	1831.70	1696.64	1586.88	1496.09	1419.89	1355.14
160000	2135.01	1953.82	1809.75	1692.67	1595.83	1514.55	1445.48
170000	2268.44	2075.93	1922.86	1798.46	1695.57	1609.21	1535.83
180000	2401.88	2198.04	2035.97	1904.25	1795.31	1703.86	1626.17
190000	2535.32	2320.16	2149.08	2010.05	1895.05	1798.52	1716.51
200000	2668.76	2442.27	2262.19	2115.84	1994.79	1893.18	1806.85
210000	2802.19	2564.39	2375.30	2221.63	2094.52	1987.84	1897.20
220000	2935.63	2686.50	2488.40	2327.42	2194.26	2082.50	1987.54
230000	3069.07	2808.61	2601.51	2433.21	2294.00	2177.16	2077.88
240000	3202.51	2930.73	2714.62	2539.01	2393.74	2271.82	2168.23
250000	3335.95	3052.84	2827.73	2644.80	2493.48	2366.48	2258.57

6.50 % Monthly Payments

LOAN AMOUNT	15	16	17	18	19	20	21
100	0.87	0.83	0.81	0.78	0.76	0.74	0.72
200	1.73	1.67	1.61	1.56	1.52	1.48	1.45
500	4.33	4.17	4.03	3.91	3.80	3.70	3.62
1000	8.66	8.34	8.06	7.82	7.60	7.41	7.23
2000	17.33	16.69	16.12	15.63	15.20	14.81	14.46
5000	43.32	41.71	40.31	39.08	37.99	37.03	36.16
6000	51.98	50.06	48.37	46.90	45.59	44.43	43.39
7000	60.65	58.40	56.44	54.71	53.19	51.84	50.63
8000	69.31	66.74	64.50	62.53	60.79	59.24	57.86
9000	77.97	75.08	72.56	70.35	68.39	66.65	65.09
10000	86.64	83.43	80.62	78.16	75.98	74.05	72.32
12000	103.96	100.11	96.75	93.79	91.18	88.86	86.79
15000	129.96	125.14	120.94	117.24	113.98	111.08	108.48
20000	173.27	166.85	161.25	156.32	151.97	148.10	144.65
25000	216.59	208.57	201.56	195.40	189.96	185.13	180.81
30000	259.91	250.28	241.87	234.49	227.95	222.15	216.97
31000	268.57	258.62	249.94	242.30	235.55	229.56	224.20
32000	277.24	266.97	258.00	250.12	243.15	236.96	231.43
33000	285.90	275.31	266.06	257.93	250.75	244.37	238.66
34000	294.57	283.65	274.12	265.75	258.35	251.77	245.90
35000	303.23	291.99	282.19	273.57	265.95	259.18	253.13
36000	311.89	300.34	290.25	281.38	273.55	266.58	260.36
37000	320.56	308.68	298.31	289.20	281.14	273.99	267.59
38000	329.22	317.02	306.37	297.02	288.74	281.39	274.83
39000	337.88	325.36	314.44	304.83	296.34	288.80	282.06
40000	346.55	333.71	322.50	312.65	303.94	296.20	289.29
41000	355.21	342.05	330.56	320.46	311.54	303.61	296.52
42000	363.88	350.39	338.62	328.28	319.14	311.01	303.75
43000	372.54	358.74	346.69	336.10	326.73	318.42	310.99
44000	381.20	367.08	354.75	343.91	334.33	325.82	318.22
45000	389.87	375.42	362.81	351.73	341.93	333.23	325.45
46000	398.53	383.76	370.87	359.55	349.53	340.63	332.68
47000	407.19	392.11	378.94	367.36	357.13	348.04	339.92
48000	415.86	400.45	387.00	375.18	364.73	355.44	347.15
49000	424.52	408.79	395.06	382.99	372.33	362.85	354.38
50000	433.18	417.13	403.12	390.81	379.92	370.25	361.61
51000	441.85	425.48	411.19	398.63	387.52	377.66	368.85
52000	450.51	433.82	419.25	406.44	395.12	385.06	376.08
53000	459.18	442.16	427.31	414.26	402.72	392.47	383.31
54000	467.84	450.51	435.37	422.07	410.32	399.87	390.54
55000	476.50	458.85	443.44	429.89	417.92	407.28	397.77
56000	485.17	467.19	451.50	437.71	425.52	414.68	405.01
57000	493.83	475.53	459.56	445.52	433.11	422.09	412.24
58000	502.49	483.88	467.62	453.34	440.71	429.49	419.47
59000	511.16	492.22	475.69	461.16	448.31	436.90	426.70
60000	519.82	500.56	483.75	468.97	455.91	444.30	433.94
65000	563.14	542.27	524.06	508.05	493.90	481.33	470.10
70000	606.46	583.99	564.37	547.13	531.89	518.35	506.26
75000	649.78	625.70	604.69	586.21	569.89	555.38	542.42
80000	693.10	667.42	645.00	625.30	607.88	592.40	578.58
85000	736.41	709.13	685.31	664.38	645.87	629.43	614.74
90000	779.73	750.84	725.62	703.46	683.86	666.45	650.90
95000	823.05	792.56	765.93	742.54	721.86	703.48	687.06
100000	866.37	834.27	806.25	781.62	759.85	740.50	723.23
105000	909.69	875.98	846.56	820.70	797.84	777.53	759.39
110000	953.01	917.70	886.87	859.78	835.83	814.55	795.55
120000	1039.64	1001.12	967.50	937.94	911.82	888.60	867.87
130000	1126.28	1084.55	1048.12	1016.11	987.80	962.65	940.19
140000	1212.92	1167.98	1128.75	1094.27	1063.79	1036.70	1012.52
150000	1299.55	1251.40	1209.37	1172.43	1139.77	1110.75	1084.84
160000	1386.19	1334.83	1289.99	1250.59	1215.76	1184.80	1157.16
170000	1472.83	1418.26	1370.62	1328.75	1291.74	1258.85	1229.48
180000	1559.47	1501.68	1451.24	1406.92	1367.73	1332.90	1301.81
190000	1646.10	1585.11	1531.87	1485.08	1443.71	1406.95	1374.13
200000	1732.74	1668.54	1612.49	1563.24	1519.70	1481.00	1446.45
210000	1819.38	1751.96	1693.12	1641.40	1595.68	1555.05	1518.77
220000	1906.01	1835.39	1773.74	1719.56	1671.67	1629.10	1591.10
230000	1992.65	1918.82	1854.37	1797.73	1747.65	1703.15	1663.42
240000	2079.29	2002.25	1934.99	1875.89	1823.64	1777.20	1735.74
250000	2165.92	2085.67	2015.62	1954.05	1899.62	1851.25	1808.06

Monthly Payments 6.50 %

LOAN AMOUNT	YEARS 22	23	24	25	30	35	40
100	0.71	0.69	0.68	0.67	0.63	0.60	0.58
200	1.42	1.39	1.36	1.34	1.25	1.20	1.16
500	3.54	3.47	3.41	3.35	3.13	2.99	2.90
1000	7.08	6.94	6.81	6.70	6.26	5.98	5.79
2000	14.15	13.88	13.62	13.40	12.53	11.96	11.59
5000	35.39	34.69	34.06	33.49	31.32	29.91	28.97
6000	42.46	41.63	40.87	40.19	37.58	35.89	34.76
7000	49.54	48.57	47.69	46.89	43.85	41.88	40.55
8000	56.62	55.50	54.50	53.59	50.11	47.86	46.35
9000	63.70	62.44	61.31	60.28	56.38	53.84	52.14
10000	70.77	69.38	68.12	66.98	62.64	59.82	57.93
12000	84.93	83.26	81.75	80.38	75.17	71.79	69.52
15000	106.16	104.07	102.18	100.47	93.96	89.74	86.90
20000	141.55	138.76	136.24	133.96	125.28	119.65	115.86
25000	176.93	173.45	170.30	167.46	156.60	149.56	144.83
30000	212.32	208.14	204.37	200.95	187.92	179.47	173.80
31000	219.40	215.08	211.18	207.65	194.18	185.45	179.59
32000	226.48	222.02	217.99	214.34	200.45	191.44	185.38
33000	233.55	228.95	224.80	221.04	206.71	197.42	191.18
34000	240.63	235.89	231.61	227.74	212.98	203.40	196.97
35000	247.71	242.83	238.43	234.44	219.24	209.38	202.76
36000	254.79	249.77	245.24	241.14	225.50	215.37	208.55
37000	261.86	256.71	252.05	247.83	231.77	221.35	214.35
38000	268.94	263.64	258.86	254.53	238.03	227.33	220.14
39000	276.02	270.58	265.68	261.23	244.30	233.31	225.93
40000	283.10	277.52	272.49	267.93	250.56	239.29	231.73
41000	290.17	284.46	279.30	274.63	256.82	245.28	237.52
42000	297.25	291.40	286.11	281.33	263.09	251.26	243.31
43000	304.33	298.34	292.92	288.02	269.35	257.24	249.11
44000	311.41	305.27	299.74	294.72	275.62	263.22	254.90
45000	318.48	312.21	306.55	301.42	281.88	269.21	260.69
46000	325.56	319.15	313.36	308.12	288.15	275.19	266.49
47000	332.64	326.09	320.17	314.82	294.41	281.17	272.28
48000	339.71	333.03	326.99	321.52	300.67	287.15	278.07
49000	346.79	339.96	333.80	328.21	306.94	293.14	283.87
50000	353.87	346.90	340.61	334.91	313.20	299.12	289.66
51000	360.95	353.84	347.42	341.61	319.47	305.10	295.45
52000	368.02	360.78	354.23	348.31	325.73	311.08	301.25
53000	375.10	367.72	361.05	355.01	331.99	317.07	307.04
54000	382.18	374.65	367.86	361.70	338.26	323.05	312.83
55000	389.26	381.59	374.67	368.40	344.52	329.03	318.63
56000	396.33	388.53	381.48	375.10	350.79	335.01	324.42
57000	403.41	395.47	388.29	381.80	357.05	341.00	330.21
58000	410.49	402.41	395.11	388.50	363.31	346.98	336.00
59000	417.57	409.34	401.92	395.20	369.58	352.96	341.80
60000	424.64	416.28	408.73	401.89	375.84	358.94	347.59
65000	460.03	450.97	442.79	435.39	407.16	388.85	376.56
70000	495.42	485.66	476.85	468.88	438.48	418.77	405.52
75000	530.80	520.35	510.91	502.37	469.80	448.68	434.49
80000	566.19	555.04	544.98	535.86	501.12	478.59	463.46
85000	601.58	589.73	579.04	569.35	532.44	508.50	492.42
90000	636.96	624.42	613.10	602.84	563.76	538.41	521.39
95000	672.35	659.11	647.16	636.33	595.08	568.33	550.35
100000	707.74	693.80	681.22	669.82	626.40	598.24	579.32
105000	743.13	728.49	715.28	703.31	657.72	628.15	608.28
110000	778.51	763.18	749.34	736.81	689.04	658.06	637.25
120000	849.29	832.56	817.46	803.79	751.68	717.88	695.18
130000	920.06	901.94	885.59	870.77	814.32	777.71	753.11
140000	990.83	971.32	953.71	937.75	876.96	837.53	811.05
150000	1061.61	1040.70	1021.83	1004.74	939.60	897.36	868.98
160000	1132.38	1110.08	1089.95	1071.72	1002.24	957.18	926.91
170000	1203.16	1179.46	1158.07	1138.70	1064.88	1017.00	984.84
180000	1273.93	1248.84	1226.19	1205.68	1127.52	1076.83	1042.77
190000	1344.70	1318.22	1294.32	1272.67	1190.16	1136.65	1100.71
200000	1415.48	1387.60	1362.44	1339.65	1252.80	1196.47	1158.64
210000	1486.25	1456.98	1430.56	1406.63	1315.45	1256.30	1216.57
220000	1557.03	1526.37	1498.68	1473.61	1378.09	1316.12	1274.50
230000	1627.80	1595.75	1566.80	1540.59	1440.73	1375.95	1332.43
240000	1698.57	1665.13	1634.93	1607.58	1503.37	1435.77	1390.37
250000	1769.35	1734.51	1703.05	1674.56	1566.01	1495.59	1448.30

6.75 % Monthly Payments

LOAN AMOUNT	1	2	3	4	5	6	7
				YEARS			
100	8.64	4.46	3.07	2.38	1.96	1.69	1.49
200	17.27	8.92	6.14	4.76	3.93	3.38	2.99
500	43.18	22.31	15.36	11.89	9.82	8.44	7.46
1000	86.37	44.62	30.72	23.79	19.64	16.88	14.93
2000	172.74	89.23	61.44	47.57	39.28	33.77	29.85
5000	431.84	223.09	153.60	118.94	98.20	84.42	74.63
6000	518.21	267.70	184.32	142.72	117.84	101.31	89.55
7000	604.58	312.32	215.04	166.51	137.48	118.19	104.48
8000	690.95	356.94	245.76	190.30	157.12	135.08	119.40
9000	777.32	401.56	276.48	214.09	176.76	151.96	134.33
10000	863.69	446.17	307.21	237.87	196.40	168.85	149.26
12000	1036.42	535.41	368.65	285.45	235.68	202.62	179.11
15000	1295.53	669.26	460.81	356.81	294.60	253.27	223.88
20000	1727.37	892.34	614.41	475.75	392.80	337.70	298.51
25000	2159.22	1115.43	768.01	594.69	490.99	422.12	373.14
30000	2591.06	1338.52	921.62	713.62	589.19	506.54	447.77
31000	2677.43	1383.13	952.34	737.41	608.83	523.43	462.69
32000	2763.80	1427.75	983.06	761.20	628.47	540.31	477.62
33000	2850.17	1472.37	1013.78	784.99	648.11	557.20	492.54
34000	2936.54	1516.99	1044.50	808.77	667.75	574.08	507.47
35000	3022.90	1561.60	1075.22	832.56	687.39	590.97	522.39
36000	3109.27	1606.22	1105.94	856.35	707.03	607.85	537.32
37000	3195.64	1650.84	1136.66	880.13	726.67	624.74	552.25
38000	3282.01	1695.46	1167.38	903.92	746.31	641.62	567.17
39000	3368.38	1740.07	1198.10	927.71	765.95	658.51	582.10
40000	3454.75	1784.69	1228.82	951.50	785.59	675.39	597.02
41000	3541.12	1829.31	1259.54	975.28	805.23	692.28	611.95
42000	3627.49	1873.92	1290.26	999.07	824.87	709.16	626.87
43000	3713.85	1918.54	1320.98	1022.86	844.51	726.05	641.80
44000	3800.22	1963.16	1351.70	1046.65	864.15	742.93	656.72
45000	3886.59	2007.78	1382.42	1070.43	883.79	759.81	671.65
46000	3972.96	2052.39	1413.14	1094.22	903.43	776.70	686.58
47000	4059.33	2097.01	1443.86	1118.01	923.07	793.58	701.50
48000	4145.70	2141.63	1474.58	1141.80	942.71	810.47	716.43
49000	4232.07	2186.24	1505.30	1165.58	962.35	827.35	731.35
50000	4318.43	2230.86	1536.03	1189.37	981.99	844.24	746.28
51000	4404.80	2275.48	1566.75	1213.16	1001.63	861.12	761.20
52000	4491.17	2320.10	1597.47	1236.95	1021.27	878.01	776.13
53000	4577.54	2364.71	1628.19	1260.73	1040.91	894.89	791.05
54000	4663.91	2409.33	1658.91	1284.52	1060.55	911.78	805.98
55000	4750.28	2453.95	1689.63	1308.31	1080.19	928.66	820.91
56000	4836.65	2498.57	1720.35	1332.10	1099.83	945.55	835.83
57000	4923.02	2543.18	1751.07	1355.88	1119.47	962.43	850.76
58000	5009.38	2587.80	1781.79	1379.67	1139.11	979.32	865.68
59000	5095.75	2632.42	1812.51	1403.46	1158.75	996.20	880.61
60000	5182.12	2677.03	1843.23	1427.25	1178.39	1013.09	895.53
65000	5613.97	2900.12	1996.83	1546.18	1276.58	1097.51	970.16
70000	6045.81	3123.21	2150.44	1665.12	1374.78	1181.93	1044.79
75000	6477.65	3346.29	2304.04	1784.06	1472.98	1266.36	1119.42
80000	6909.50	3569.38	2457.64	1902.99	1571.18	1350.78	1194.04
85000	7341.34	3792.47	2611.24	2021.93	1669.38	1435.21	1268.67
90000	7773.18	4015.55	2764.85	2140.87	1767.58	1519.63	1343.30
95000	8205.03	4238.64	2918.45	2259.81	1865.78	1604.05	1417.93
100000	8636.87	4461.72	3072.05	2378.74	1963.98	1688.48	1492.56
105000	9068.71	4684.81	3225.65	2497.68	2062.18	1772.90	1567.18
110000	9500.56	4907.90	3379.26	2616.62	2160.37	1857.33	1641.81
120000	10364.24	5354.07	3686.46	2854.49	2356.77	2026.17	1791.07
130000	11227.93	5800.24	3993.67	3092.37	2553.17	2195.02	1940.32
140000	12091.62	6246.41	4300.87	3330.24	2749.57	2363.87	2089.58
150000	12955.30	6692.59	4608.08	3568.11	2945.96	2532.72	2238.83
160000	13818.99	7138.76	4915.28	3805.99	3142.36	2701.56	2388.09
170000	14682.68	7584.93	5222.49	4043.86	3338.76	2870.41	2537.34
180000	15546.37	8031.10	5529.69	4281.74	3535.16	3039.26	2686.60
190000	16410.05	8477.28	5836.90	4519.61	3731.56	3208.11	2835.86
200000	17273.74	8923.45	6144.10	4757.49	3927.95	3376.96	2985.11
210000	18137.43	9369.62	6451.31	4995.36	4124.35	3545.80	3134.37
220000	19001.11	9815.79	6758.51	5233.23	4320.75	3714.65	3283.62
230000	19864.80	10261.97	7065.72	5471.11	4517.15	3883.50	3432.88
240000	20728.49	10708.14	7372.92	5708.98	4713.54	4052.35	3582.13
250000	21592.17	11154.31	7680.13	5946.86	4909.94	4221.19	3731.39

Monthly Payments 6.75 %

LOAN AMOUNT	8	9	10	11	12	13	14
100	1.35	1.23	1.14	1.07	1.01	0.96	0.92
200	2.69	2.47	2.29	2.14	2.02	1.92	1.83
500	6.73	6.17	5.72	5.35	5.05	4.80	4.58
1000	13.46	12.33	11.43	10.71	10.10	9.60	9.17
2000	26.93	24.67	22.87	21.41	20.20	19.19	18.33
5000	67.32	61.67	57.17	53.53	50.51	47.98	45.83
6000	80.78	74.00	68.61	64.23	60.61	57.58	55.00
7000	94.25	86.33	80.04	74.94	70.71	67.17	64.16
8000	107.71	98.67	91.48	85.64	80.81	76.77	73.33
9000	121.17	111.00	102.91	96.35	90.92	86.36	82.50
10000	134.64	123.33	114.35	107.05	101.02	95.96	91.66
12000	161.56	148.00	137.22	128.46	121.22	115.15	109.99
15000	201.95	185.00	171.52	160.58	151.53	143.94	137.49
20000	269.27	246.66	228.70	214.10	202.04	191.92	183.32
25000	336.59	308.33	285.87	267.63	252.55	239.90	229.16
30000	403.91	370.00	343.05	321.15	303.06	287.88	274.99
31000	417.37	382.33	354.48	331.86	313.16	297.47	284.15
32000	430.84	394.66	365.91	342.56	323.26	307.07	293.32
33000	444.30	407.00	377.35	353.27	333.36	316.66	302.49
34000	457.76	419.33	388.78	363.97	343.46	326.26	311.65
35000	471.23	431.66	400.22	374.68	353.57	335.86	320.82
36000	484.69	444.00	411.65	385.38	363.67	345.45	329.98
37000	498.16	456.33	423.09	396.09	373.77	355.05	339.15
38000	511.62	468.66	434.52	406.79	383.87	364.64	348.32
39000	525.08	481.00	445.96	417.50	393.97	374.24	357.48
40000	538.55	493.33	457.39	428.20	404.07	383.83	366.65
41000	552.01	505.66	468.83	438.91	414.18	393.43	375.81
42000	565.47	518.00	480.26	449.62	424.28	403.03	384.98
43000	578.94	530.33	491.70	460.32	434.38	412.62	394.15
44000	592.40	542.66	503.13	471.03	444.48	422.22	403.31
45000	605.86	555.00	514.57	481.73	454.58	431.81	412.48
46000	619.33	567.33	526.00	492.44	464.69	441.41	421.65
47000	632.79	579.66	537.44	503.14	474.79	451.01	430.81
48000	646.26	592.00	548.87	513.85	484.89	460.60	439.98
49000	659.72	604.33	560.31	524.55	494.99	470.20	449.14
50000	673.18	616.66	571.74	535.26	505.09	479.79	458.31
51000	686.65	629.00	583.18	545.96	515.20	489.39	467.48
52000	700.11	641.33	594.61	556.67	525.30	498.98	476.64
53000	713.57	653.66	606.05	567.37	535.40	508.58	485.81
54000	727.04	666.00	617.48	578.08	545.50	518.18	494.98
55000	740.50	678.33	628.92	588.78	555.60	527.77	504.14
56000	753.96	690.66	640.35	599.49	565.70	537.37	513.31
57000	767.43	702.99	651.79	610.19	575.81	546.96	522.47
58000	780.89	715.33	663.22	620.90	585.91	556.56	531.64
59000	794.36	727.66	674.66	631.60	596.01	566.16	540.81
60000	807.82	739.99	686.09	642.31	606.11	575.75	549.97
65000	875.14	801.66	743.26	695.83	656.62	623.73	595.80
70000	942.46	863.33	800.44	749.36	707.13	671.71	641.64
75000	1009.77	924.99	857.61	802.88	757.64	719.69	687.47
80000	1077.09	986.66	914.79	856.41	808.15	767.67	733.30
85000	1144.41	1048.33	971.96	909.94	858.66	815.65	779.13
90000	1211.73	1109.99	1029.14	963.46	909.17	863.63	824.96
95000	1279.05	1171.66	1086.31	1016.99	959.68	911.61	870.79
100000	1346.36	1233.32	1143.48	1070.51	1010.19	959.59	916.62
105000	1413.68	1294.99	1200.66	1124.04	1060.70	1007.57	962.45
110000	1481.00	1356.66	1257.83	1177.56	1111.21	1055.55	1008.28
120000	1615.64	1479.99	1372.18	1284.61	1212.22	1151.50	1099.95
130000	1750.27	1603.32	1486.53	1391.67	1313.24	1247.46	1191.61
140000	1884.91	1726.65	1600.88	1498.72	1414.26	1343.42	1283.27
150000	2019.55	1849.99	1715.23	1605.77	1515.28	1439.38	1374.93
160000	2154.18	1973.32	1829.57	1712.82	1616.30	1535.34	1466.59
170000	2288.82	2096.65	1943.92	1819.87	1717.32	1631.30	1558.26
180000	2423.46	2219.98	2058.27	1926.92	1818.34	1727.26	1649.92
190000	2558.09	2343.32	2172.62	2033.97	1919.36	1823.21	1741.58
200000	2692.73	2466.65	2286.97	2141.02	2020.37	1919.17	1833.24
210000	2827.37	2589.98	2401.32	2248.08	2121.39	2015.13	1924.91
220000	2962.00	2713.31	2515.66	2355.13	2222.41	2111.09	2016.57
230000	3096.64	2836.65	2630.01	2462.18	2323.43	2207.05	2108.23
240000	3231.28	2959.98	2744.36	2569.23	2424.45	2303.01	2199.89
250000	3365.91	3083.31	2858.71	2676.28	2525.47	2398.97	2291.55

6.75 % Monthly Payments

LOAN AMOUNT	15	16	17	18	19	20	21
				YEARS			
100	0.88	0.85	0.82	0.80	0.77	0.75	0.74
200	1.76	1.70	1.64	1.59	1.55	1.51	1.48
500	4.40	4.24	4.10	3.98	3.87	3.77	3.69
1000	8.80	8.48	8.20	7.96	7.74	7.55	7.38
2000	17.60	16.96	16.40	15.91	15.48	15.10	14.76
5000	43.99	42.39	41.00	39.78	38.70	37.74	36.89
6000	52.79	50.87	49.20	47.74	46.44	45.29	44.27
7000	61.58	59.35	57.40	55.69	54.18	52.84	51.64
8000	70.38	67.83	65.60	63.65	61.92	60.39	59.02
9000	79.18	76.31	73.80	71.60	69.66	67.94	66.40
10000	87.98	84.79	82.00	79.56	77.40	75.48	73.78
12000	105.57	101.74	98.40	95.47	92.88	90.58	88.53
15000	131.96	127.18	123.00	119.34	116.10	113.23	110.66
20000	175.95	169.57	164.01	159.12	154.80	150.97	147.55
25000	219.94	211.96	205.01	198.90	193.50	188.71	184.44
30000	263.93	254.36	246.01	238.68	232.20	226.45	221.33
31000	272.73	262.84	254.21	246.63	239.94	234.00	228.70
32000	281.52	271.31	262.41	254.59	247.68	241.55	236.08
33000	290.32	279.79	270.61	262.54	255.42	249.10	243.46
34000	299.12	288.27	278.81	270.50	263.16	256.65	250.84
35000	307.92	296.75	287.01	278.46	270.90	264.20	258.21
36000	316.71	305.23	295.21	286.41	278.64	271.74	265.59
37000	325.51	313.71	303.41	294.37	286.38	279.29	272.97
38000	334.31	322.19	311.61	302.32	294.12	286.84	280.35
39000	343.11	330.66	319.81	310.28	301.86	294.39	287.72
40000	351.90	339.14	328.01	318.24	309.60	301.94	295.10
41000	360.70	347.62	336.21	326.19	317.34	309.49	302.48
42000	369.50	356.10	344.41	334.15	325.08	317.03	309.86
43000	378.30	364.58	352.61	342.10	332.82	324.58	317.23
44000	387.09	373.06	360.81	350.06	340.56	332.13	324.61
45000	395.89	381.53	369.01	358.02	348.30	339.68	331.99
46000	404.69	390.01	377.21	365.97	356.04	347.23	339.37
47000	413.49	398.49	385.41	373.93	363.78	354.78	346.74
48000	422.29	406.97	393.61	381.88	371.52	362.33	354.12
49000	431.08	415.45	401.81	389.84	379.26	369.87	361.50
50000	439.88	423.93	410.01	397.80	387.00	377.42	368.88
51000	448.68	432.41	418.21	405.75	394.74	384.97	376.25
52000	457.48	440.88	426.41	413.71	402.48	392.52	383.63
53000	466.27	449.36	434.61	421.66	410.22	400.07	391.01
54000	475.07	457.84	442.81	429.62	417.96	407.62	398.39
55000	483.87	466.32	451.01	437.57	425.70	415.16	405.76
56000	492.67	474.80	459.21	445.53	433.44	422.71	413.14
57000	501.46	483.28	467.42	453.49	441.18	430.26	420.52
58000	510.26	491.76	475.62	461.44	448.92	437.81	427.90
59000	519.06	500.23	483.82	469.40	456.66	445.36	435.27
60000	527.86	508.71	492.02	477.35	464.40	452.91	442.65
65000	571.84	551.11	533.02	517.13	503.10	490.65	479.54
70000	615.83	593.50	574.02	556.91	541.80	528.39	516.43
75000	659.82	635.89	615.02	596.69	580.51	566.13	553.31
80000	703.81	678.28	656.02	636.47	619.21	603.88	590.20
85000	747.80	720.68	697.02	676.25	657.91	641.62	627.09
90000	791.78	763.07	738.02	716.03	696.61	679.36	663.98
95000	835.77	805.46	779.03	755.81	735.31	717.10	700.86
100000	879.76	847.86	820.03	795.59	774.01	754.84	737.75
105000	923.75	890.25	861.03	835.37	812.71	792.59	774.64
110000	967.74	932.64	902.03	875.15	851.41	830.33	811.53
120000	1055.71	1017.43	984.03	954.71	928.81	905.81	885.30
130000	1143.69	1102.21	1066.03	1034.27	1006.21	981.30	959.08
140000	1231.67	1187.00	1148.04	1113.83	1083.61	1056.78	1032.85
150000	1319.64	1271.78	1230.04	1193.39	1161.01	1132.27	1106.63
160000	1407.62	1356.57	1312.04	1272.94	1238.41	1207.75	1180.40
170000	1495.59	1441.35	1394.05	1352.50	1315.81	1283.24	1254.18
180000	1583.57	1526.14	1476.05	1432.06	1393.21	1358.72	1327.95
190000	1671.55	1610.93	1558.05	1511.62	1470.61	1434.20	1401.73
200000	1759.52	1695.71	1640.05	1591.18	1548.01	1509.69	1475.50
210000	1847.50	1780.50	1722.06	1670.74	1625.41	1585.17	1549.28
220000	1935.47	1865.28	1804.06	1750.30	1702.82	1660.66	1623.06
230000	2023.45	1950.07	1886.06	1829.86	1780.22	1736.14	1696.83
240000	2111.43	2034.85	1968.06	1909.42	1857.62	1811.63	1770.61
250000	2199.40	2119.64	2050.07	1988.98	1935.02	1887.11	1844.38

Monthly Payments 6.75 %

LOAN AMOUNT	22	23	24	25	30	35	40
				YEARS			
100	0.72	0.71	0.70	0.69	0.64	0.61	0.60
200	1.44	1.42	1.39	1.37	1.28	1.23	1.19
500	3.61	3.54	3.48	3.43	3.21	3.07	2.98
1000	7.22	7.09	6.96	6.85	6.42	6.15	5.97
2000	14.45	14.17	13.93	13.70	12.85	12.30	11.93
5000	36.12	35.43	34.81	34.25	32.12	30.75	29.83
6000	43.35	42.52	41.78	41.10	38.55	36.90	35.80
7000	50.57	49.61	48.74	47.95	44.97	43.05	41.77
8000	57.80	56.69	55.70	54.80	51.39	49.20	47.73
9000	65.02	63.78	62.66	61.65	57.82	55.35	53.70
10000	72.24	70.87	69.63	68.50	64.24	61.50	59.67
12000	86.69	85.04	83.55	82.21	77.09	73.80	71.60
15000	108.37	106.30	104.44	102.76	96.36	92.25	89.50
20000	144.49	141.74	139.26	137.01	128.49	122.99	119.34
25000	180.61	177.17	174.07	171.26	160.61	153.74	149.17
30000	216.73	212.61	208.88	205.51	192.73	184.49	179.00
31000	223.96	219.69	215.85	212.37	199.15	190.64	184.97
32000	231.18	226.78	222.81	219.22	205.58	196.79	190.94
33000	238.41	233.87	229.77	226.07	212.00	202.94	196.90
34000	245.63	240.95	236.73	232.92	218.43	209.09	202.87
35000	252.86	248.04	243.70	239.77	224.85	215.24	208.84
36000	260.08	255.13	250.66	246.62	231.27	221.39	214.80
37000	267.30	262.21	257.62	253.47	237.70	227.54	220.77
38000	274.53	269.30	264.58	260.32	244.12	233.69	226.74
39000	281.75	276.39	271.55	267.17	250.55	239.84	232.70
40000	288.98	283.47	278.51	274.02	256.97	245.99	238.67
41000	296.20	290.56	285.47	280.87	263.40	252.14	244.64
42000	303.43	297.65	292.44	287.72	269.82	258.29	250.60
43000	310.65	304.73	299.40	294.57	276.24	264.44	256.57
44000	317.88	311.82	306.36	301.42	282.67	270.59	262.54
45000	325.10	318.91	313.32	308.27	289.09	276.74	268.50
46000	332.32	326.00	320.29	315.12	295.52	282.89	274.47
47000	339.55	333.08	327.25	321.97	301.94	289.04	280.44
48000	346.77	340.17	334.21	328.82	308.37	295.19	286.40
49000	354.00	347.26	341.17	335.67	314.79	301.34	292.37
50000	361.22	354.34	348.14	342.52	321.21	307.49	298.34
51000	368.45	361.43	355.10	349.38	327.64	313.64	304.31
52000	375.67	368.52	362.06	356.23	334.06	319.79	310.27
53000	382.90	375.60	369.03	363.08	340.49	325.94	316.24
54000	390.12	382.69	375.99	369.93	346.91	332.09	322.21
55000	397.34	389.78	382.95	376.78	353.34	338.24	328.17
56000	404.57	396.86	389.91	383.63	359.76	344.38	334.14
57000	411.79	403.95	396.88	390.48	366.18	350.53	340.11
58000	419.02	411.04	403.84	397.33	372.61	356.68	346.07
59000	426.24	418.12	410.80	404.18	379.03	362.83	352.04
60000	433.47	425.21	417.77	411.03	385.46	368.98	358.01
65000	469.59	460.65	452.58	445.28	417.58	399.73	387.84
70000	505.71	496.08	487.39	479.53	449.70	430.48	417.67
75000	541.83	531.51	522.21	513.79	481.82	461.23	447.51
80000	577.96	566.95	557.02	548.04	513.94	491.98	477.34
85000	614.08	602.38	591.83	582.29	546.06	522.73	507.18
90000	650.20	637.82	626.65	616.54	578.18	553.48	537.01
95000	686.32	673.25	661.46	650.80	610.31	584.22	566.84
100000	722.44	708.68	696.28	685.05	642.43	614.97	596.68
105000	758.57	744.12	731.09	719.30	674.55	645.72	626.51
110000	794.69	779.55	765.90	753.55	706.67	676.47	656.34
120000	866.93	850.42	835.53	822.06	770.91	737.97	716.01
130000	939.18	921.29	905.16	890.56	835.16	799.47	775.68
140000	1011.42	992.16	974.79	959.07	899.40	860.96	835.35
150000	1083.67	1063.03	1044.41	1027.57	963.64	922.46	895.01
160000	1155.91	1133.90	1114.04	1096.08	1027.88	983.96	954.68
170000	1228.16	1204.76	1183.67	1164.58	1092.13	1045.45	1014.35
180000	1300.40	1275.63	1253.30	1233.09	1156.37	1106.95	1074.02
190000	1372.65	1346.50	1322.92	1301.59	1220.61	1168.45	1133.69
200000	1444.89	1417.37	1392.55	1370.10	1284.86	1229.95	1193.35
210000	1517.13	1488.24	1462.18	1438.60	1349.10	1291.44	1253.02
220000	1589.38	1559.11	1531.81	1507.11	1413.34	1352.94	1312.69
230000	1661.62	1629.98	1601.43	1575.61	1477.58	1414.44	1372.36
240000	1733.87	1700.84	1671.06	1644.12	1541.83	1475.94	1432.02
250000	1806.11	1771.71	1740.69	1712.62	1606.07	1537.43	1491.69

7.00 % Monthly Payments

LOAN AMOUNT	YEARS 1	2	3	4	5	6	7
100	8.65	4.47	3.08	2.39	1.98	1.70	1.50
200	17.30	8.95	6.17	4.78	3.95	3.40	3.01
500	43.24	22.36	15.42	11.95	9.88	8.50	7.52
1000	86.48	44.73	30.83	23.90	19.75	17.00	15.04
2000	172.96	89.45	61.66	47.80	39.51	34.00	30.09
5000	432.40	223.64	154.16	119.50	98.77	85.01	75.22
6000	518.88	268.36	184.99	143.40	118.52	102.01	90.26
7000	605.36	313.09	215.82	167.30	138.28	119.01	105.31
8000	691.85	357.82	246.65	191.20	158.03	136.01	120.35
9000	778.33	402.55	277.48	215.10	177.79	153.01	135.39
10000	864.81	447.27	308.31	239.00	197.54	170.01	150.44
12000	1037.77	536.73	369.98	286.80	237.05	204.01	180.53
15000	1297.21	670.91	462.47	358.50	296.31	255.02	225.66
20000	1729.61	894.55	616.63	478.00	395.08	340.02	300.88
25000	2162.02	1118.18	770.79	597.50	493.85	425.03	376.10
30000	2594.42	1341.82	924.94	717.00	592.62	510.03	451.32
31000	2680.90	1386.55	955.77	740.90	612.38	527.03	466.36
32000	2767.38	1431.27	986.61	764.80	632.13	544.03	481.40
33000	2853.86	1476.00	1017.44	788.70	651.88	561.03	496.45
34000	2940.34	1520.73	1048.27	812.60	671.64	578.04	511.49
35000	3026.82	1565.45	1079.10	836.50	691.39	595.04	526.54
36000	3113.30	1610.18	1109.93	860.40	711.15	612.04	541.58
37000	3199.78	1654.91	1140.76	884.30	730.90	629.04	556.62
38000	3286.27	1699.64	1171.59	908.20	750.65	646.04	571.67
39000	3372.75	1744.36	1202.43	932.10	770.41	663.04	586.71
40000	3459.23	1789.09	1233.26	956.00	790.16	680.04	601.75
41000	3545.71	1833.82	1264.09	979.90	809.92	697.04	616.80
42000	3632.19	1878.55	1294.92	1003.80	829.67	714.04	631.84
43000	3718.67	1923.27	1325.75	1027.70	849.43	731.05	646.89
44000	3805.15	1968.00	1356.58	1051.60	869.18	748.05	661.93
45000	3891.63	2012.73	1387.41	1075.50	888.93	765.05	676.97
46000	3978.11	2057.45	1418.25	1099.40	908.69	782.05	692.02
47000	4064.59	2102.18	1449.08	1123.30	928.44	799.05	707.06
48000	4151.07	2146.91	1479.91	1147.20	948.20	816.05	722.11
49000	4237.55	2191.64	1510.74	1171.10	967.95	833.05	737.15
50000	4324.03	2236.36	1541.57	1194.99	987.70	850.05	752.19
51000	4410.51	2281.09	1572.40	1218.89	1007.46	867.05	767.24
52000	4497.00	2325.82	1603.23	1242.79	1027.21	884.05	782.28
53000	4583.48	2370.55	1634.07	1266.69	1046.97	901.06	797.32
54000	4669.96	2415.27	1664.90	1290.59	1066.72	918.06	812.37
55000	4756.44	2460.00	1695.73	1314.49	1086.47	935.06	827.41
56000	4842.92	2504.73	1726.56	1338.39	1106.23	952.06	842.46
57000	4929.40	2549.45	1757.39	1362.29	1125.98	969.06	857.50
58000	5015.88	2594.18	1788.22	1386.19	1145.74	986.06	872.54
59000	5102.36	2638.91	1819.05	1410.09	1165.49	1003.06	887.59
60000	5188.84	2683.64	1849.89	1433.99	1185.24	1020.06	902.63
65000	5621.24	2907.27	2004.04	1553.49	1284.01	1105.07	977.85
70000	6053.65	3130.91	2158.20	1672.99	1382.79	1190.07	1053.07
75000	6486.05	3354.55	2312.36	1792.49	1481.56	1275.08	1128.29
80000	6918.45	3578.18	2466.51	1911.99	1580.33	1360.08	1203.51
85000	7350.86	3801.82	2620.67	2031.49	1679.10	1445.09	1278.73
90000	7783.26	4025.46	2774.83	2150.99	1777.87	1530.09	1353.95
95000	8215.66	4249.09	2928.98	2270.49	1876.64	1615.10	1429.17
100000	8648.07	4472.73	3083.14	2389.99	1975.41	1700.11	1504.39
105000	9080.47	4696.36	3237.30	2509.49	2074.18	1785.11	1579.61
110000	9512.87	4920.00	3391.46	2628.99	2172.95	1870.12	1654.83
120000	10377.68	5367.27	3699.77	2867.99	2370.49	2040.13	1805.26
130000	11242.49	5814.55	4008.08	3106.99	2568.03	2210.14	1955.70
140000	12107.29	6261.82	4316.40	3345.99	2765.57	2380.15	2106.14
150000	12972.10	6709.09	4624.71	3584.98	2963.11	2550.16	2256.58
160000	13836.91	7156.36	4933.03	3823.98	3160.65	2720.17	2407.02
170000	14701.71	7603.64	5241.34	4062.98	3358.19	2890.18	2557.46
180000	15566.52	8050.91	5549.66	4301.98	3555.73	3060.19	2707.90
190000	16431.33	8498.18	5857.97	4540.98	3753.27	3230.20	2858.33
200000	17296.13	8945.46	6166.28	4779.98	3950.81	3400.21	3008.77
210000	18160.94	9392.73	6474.60	5018.98	4148.36	3570.22	3159.21
220000	19025.75	9840.00	6782.91	5257.98	4345.90	3740.23	3309.65
230000	19890.56	10287.27	7091.23	5496.98	4543.44	3910.24	3460.09
240000	20755.36	10734.55	7399.54	5735.98	4740.98	4080.25	3610.53
250000	21620.17	11181.82	7707.85	5974.97	4938.52	4250.26	3760.97

Monthly Payments 7.00 %

LOAN AMOUNT	YEARS 8	9	10	11	12	13	14
100	1.36	1.25	1.16	1.08	1.02	0.97	0.93
200	2.72	2.49	2.31	2.17	2.05	1.95	1.86
500	6.79	6.23	5.78	5.42	5.12	4.86	4.65
1000	13.58	12.46	11.56	10.83	10.23	9.73	9.30
2000	27.17	24.91	23.12	21.66	20.46	19.45	18.60
5000	67.92	62.28	57.80	54.16	51.15	48.63	46.50
6000	81.50	74.73	69.36	64.99	61.38	58.36	55.79
7000	95.09	87.19	80.92	75.82	71.61	68.09	65.09
8000	108.67	99.65	92.48	86.65	81.84	77.81	74.39
9000	122.26	112.10	104.03	97.49	92.08	87.54	83.69
10000	135.84	124.56	115.59	108.32	102.31	97.27	92.99
12000	163.01	149.47	138.71	129.98	122.77	116.72	111.59
15000	203.76	186.84	173.39	162.48	153.46	145.90	139.49
20000	271.68	249.11	231.19	216.64	204.61	194.53	185.98
25000	339.60	311.39	288.98	270.79	255.77	243.17	232.48
30000	407.52	373.67	346.78	324.95	306.92	291.80	278.97
31000	421.10	386.13	358.34	335.78	317.15	301.53	288.27
32000	434.69	398.58	369.90	346.62	327.38	311.25	297.57
33000	448.27	411.04	381.46	357.45	337.61	320.98	306.87
34000	461.86	423.49	393.02	368.28	347.84	330.71	316.17
35000	475.44	435.95	404.58	379.11	358.07	340.43	325.47
36000	489.03	448.41	416.14	389.94	368.30	350.16	334.77
37000	502.61	460.86	427.70	400.78	378.53	359.89	344.07
38000	516.19	473.32	439.26	411.61	388.76	369.61	353.36
39000	529.78	485.77	450.82	422.44	398.99	379.34	362.66
40000	543.36	498.23	462.38	433.27	409.22	389.07	371.96
41000	556.95	510.68	473.94	444.10	419.45	398.79	381.26
42000	570.53	523.14	485.49	454.93	429.69	408.52	390.56
43000	584.11	535.60	497.05	465.77	439.92	418.25	399.86
44000	597.70	548.05	508.61	476.60	450.15	427.97	409.16
45000	611.28	560.51	520.17	487.43	460.38	437.70	418.46
46000	624.87	572.96	531.73	498.26	470.61	447.43	427.76
47000	638.45	585.42	543.29	509.09	480.84	457.15	437.06
48000	652.03	597.87	554.85	519.93	491.07	466.88	446.36
49000	665.62	610.33	566.41	530.76	501.30	476.61	455.65
50000	679.20	622.79	577.97	541.59	511.53	486.33	464.95
51000	692.79	635.24	589.53	552.42	521.76	496.06	474.25
52000	706.37	647.70	601.09	563.25	531.99	505.79	483.55
53000	719.95	660.15	612.65	574.08	542.22	515.51	492.85
54000	733.54	672.61	624.21	584.92	552.45	525.24	502.15
55000	747.12	685.06	635.77	595.75	562.68	534.97	511.45
56000	760.71	697.52	647.33	606.58	572.91	544.69	520.75
57000	774.29	709.98	658.89	617.41	583.14	554.42	530.05
58000	787.87	722.43	670.45	628.24	593.38	564.15	539.35
59000	801.46	734.89	682.00	639.07	603.61	573.87	548.65
60000	815.04	747.34	693.56	649.91	613.84	583.60	557.94
65000	882.96	809.62	751.36	704.07	664.99	632.23	604.44
70000	950.88	871.90	809.16	758.22	716.14	680.87	650.93
75000	1018.80	934.18	866.95	812.38	767.30	729.50	697.43
80000	1086.72	996.46	924.75	866.54	818.45	778.13	743.93
85000	1154.64	1058.74	982.55	920.70	869.60	826.77	790.42
90000	1222.56	1121.01	1040.35	974.86	920.75	875.40	836.92
95000	1290.48	1183.29	1098.14	1029.02	971.91	924.03	883.41
100000	1358.40	1245.57	1155.94	1083.18	1023.06	972.67	929.91
105000	1426.32	1307.85	1213.74	1137.34	1074.21	1021.30	976.40
110000	1494.24	1370.13	1271.53	1191.49	1125.37	1069.93	1022.90
120000	1630.08	1494.69	1387.13	1299.81	1227.67	1167.20	1115.89
130000	1765.92	1619.24	1502.72	1408.13	1329.98	1264.47	1208.88
140000	1901.76	1743.80	1618.32	1516.45	1432.28	1361.73	1301.87
150000	2037.60	1868.36	1733.91	1624.77	1534.59	1459.00	1394.86
160000	2173.44	1992.91	1849.50	1733.08	1636.90	1556.27	1487.85
170000	2309.29	2117.47	1965.10	1841.40	1739.20	1653.53	1580.84
180000	2445.13	2242.03	2080.69	1949.72	1841.51	1750.80	1673.83
190000	2580.97	2366.58	2196.29	2058.04	1943.82	1848.07	1766.82
200000	2716.81	2491.14	2311.88	2166.35	2046.12	1945.33	1859.81
210000	2852.65	2615.70	2427.47	2274.67	2148.43	2042.60	1952.80
220000	2988.49	2740.26	2543.07	2382.99	2250.73	2139.87	2045.80
230000	3124.33	2864.81	2658.66	2491.31	2353.04	2237.13	2138.79
240000	3260.17	2989.37	2774.26	2599.63	2455.35	2334.40	2231.78
250000	3396.01	3113.93	2889.85	2707.94	2557.65	2431.67	2324.77

7.00 % Monthly Payments

LOAN AMOUNT	15	16	17	18	19	20	21
100	0.89	0.86	0.83	0.81	0.79	0.77	0.75
200	1.79	1.72	1.67	1.62	1.58	1.54	1.50
500	4.47	4.31	4.17	4.05	3.94	3.85	3.76
1000	8.93	8.62	8.34	8.10	7.88	7.69	7.52
2000	17.86	17.23	16.68	16.19	15.77	15.39	15.05
5000	44.66	43.08	41.70	40.48	39.41	38.47	37.62
6000	53.59	51.69	50.03	48.58	47.30	46.16	45.14
7000	62.53	60.31	58.37	56.68	55.18	53.85	52.67
8000	71.46	68.92	66.71	64.77	63.06	61.54	60.19
9000	80.39	77.54	75.05	72.87	70.95	69.24	67.72
10000	89.32	86.15	83.39	80.97	78.83	76.93	75.24
12000	107.19	103.39	100.07	97.16	94.59	92.32	90.29
15000	133.99	129.23	125.09	121.45	118.24	115.40	112.86
20000	178.65	172.31	166.78	161.93	157.66	153.86	150.48
25000	223.31	215.39	208.48	202.42	197.07	192.33	188.10
30000	267.97	258.46	250.17	242.90	236.49	230.79	225.72
31000	276.91	267.08	258.51	251.00	244.37	238.49	233.25
32000	285.84	275.69	266.85	259.10	252.25	246.18	240.77
33000	294.77	284.31	275.19	267.19	260.13	253.87	248.29
34000	303.70	292.93	283.53	275.29	268.02	261.57	255.82
35000	312.64	301.54	291.87	283.39	275.90	269.26	263.34
36000	321.57	310.16	300.21	291.48	283.78	276.95	270.87
37000	330.50	318.77	308.55	299.58	291.66	284.64	278.39
38000	339.43	327.39	316.89	307.68	299.55	292.34	285.91
39000	348.37	336.00	325.23	315.77	307.43	300.03	293.44
40000	357.30	344.62	333.57	323.87	315.31	307.72	300.96
41000	366.23	353.23	341.90	331.97	323.20	315.42	308.49
42000	375.16	361.85	350.24	340.06	331.08	323.11	316.01
43000	384.10	370.46	358.58	348.16	338.96	330.80	323.53
44000	393.03	379.08	366.92	356.26	346.84	338.50	331.06
45000	401.96	387.70	375.26	364.35	354.73	346.19	338.58
46000	410.89	396.31	383.60	372.45	362.61	353.88	346.11
47000	419.83	404.93	391.94	380.55	370.49	361.58	353.63
48000	428.76	413.54	400.28	388.64	378.38	369.27	361.15
49000	437.69	422.16	408.62	396.74	386.26	376.96	368.68
50000	446.62	430.77	416.96	404.84	394.14	384.66	376.20
51000	455.56	439.39	425.30	412.93	402.02	392.35	383.73
52000	464.49	448.00	433.64	421.03	409.91	400.04	391.25
53000	473.42	456.62	441.97	429.13	417.79	407.73	398.77
54000	482.35	465.23	450.31	437.22	425.67	415.43	406.30
55000	491.29	473.85	458.65	445.32	433.56	423.12	413.82
56000	500.22	482.47	466.99	453.42	441.44	430.81	421.35
57000	509.15	491.08	475.33	461.51	449.32	438.51	428.87
58000	518.08	499.70	483.67	469.61	457.20	446.20	436.40
59000	527.02	508.31	492.01	477.71	465.09	453.89	443.92
60000	535.95	516.93	500.35	485.80	472.97	461.59	451.44
65000	580.61	560.00	542.04	526.29	512.38	500.05	489.06
70000	625.27	603.08	583.74	566.77	551.80	538.52	526.68
75000	669.94	646.16	625.44	607.26	591.21	576.98	564.30
80000	714.60	689.24	667.13	647.74	630.63	615.45	601.92
85000	759.26	732.31	708.83	688.22	670.04	653.91	639.54
90000	803.92	775.39	750.52	728.71	709.46	692.38	677.16
95000	848.59	818.47	792.22	769.19	748.87	730.85	714.79
100000	893.25	861.54	833.91	809.67	788.28	769.31	752.41
105000	937.91	904.62	875.61	850.16	827.70	807.78	790.03
110000	982.57	947.70	917.31	890.64	867.11	846.24	827.65
120000	1071.90	1033.85	1000.70	971.61	945.94	923.17	902.89
130000	1161.22	1120.01	1084.09	1052.58	1024.77	1000.10	978.13
140000	1250.55	1206.16	1167.48	1133.54	1103.60	1077.03	1053.37
150000	1339.87	1292.32	1250.87	1214.51	1182.43	1153.97	1128.61
160000	1429.20	1378.47	1334.26	1295.48	1261.25	1230.90	1203.85
170000	1518.52	1464.63	1417.65	1376.45	1340.08	1307.83	1279.09
180000	1607.85	1550.78	1501.05	1457.41	1418.91	1384.76	1354.33
190000	1697.17	1636.94	1584.44	1538.38	1497.74	1461.69	1429.57
200000	1786.50	1723.09	1667.83	1619.35	1576.57	1538.62	1504.81
210000	1875.82	1809.24	1751.22	1700.32	1655.40	1615.55	1580.05
220000	1965.15	1895.40	1834.61	1781.28	1734.22	1692.48	1655.29
230000	2054.47	1981.55	1918.00	1862.25	1813.05	1769.41	1730.53
240000	2143.80	2067.71	2001.39	1943.22	1891.88	1846.35	1805.77
250000	2233.12	2153.86	2084.79	2024.18	1970.71	1923.28	1881.01

Monthly Payments 7.00 %

LOAN AMOUNT	22	23	24	25	30	35	40
100	0.74	0.72	0.71	0.70	0.66	0.63	0.61
200	1.47	1.45	1.42	1.40	1.32	1.26	1.23
500	3.69	3.62	3.56	3.50	3.29	3.16	3.07
1000	7.37	7.24	7.11	7.00	6.59	6.32	6.14
2000	14.75	14.47	14.23	14.01	13.17	12.64	12.28
5000	36.86	36.19	35.57	35.02	32.93	31.59	30.71
6000	44.24	43.42	42.69	42.02	39.52	37.91	36.85
7000	51.61	50.66	49.80	49.03	46.10	44.23	42.99
8000	58.98	57.90	56.92	56.03	52.69	50.55	49.13
9000	66.36	65.13	64.03	63.04	59.27	56.87	55.28
10000	73.73	72.37	71.15	70.04	65.86	63.19	61.42
12000	88.47	86.84	85.38	84.05	79.03	75.82	73.70
15000	110.59	108.56	106.72	105.06	98.79	94.78	92.13
20000	147.46	144.74	142.29	140.08	131.72	126.37	122.84
25000	184.32	180.93	177.87	175.10	164.65	157.97	153.55
30000	221.18	217.11	213.44	210.12	197.58	189.56	184.26
31000	228.56	224.35	220.56	217.13	204.17	195.88	190.40
32000	235.93	231.58	227.67	224.13	210.75	202.20	196.54
33000	243.30	238.82	234.78	231.14	217.34	208.51	202.68
34000	250.68	246.06	241.90	238.14	223.93	214.83	208.82
35000	258.05	253.30	249.01	245.15	230.51	221.15	214.96
36000	265.42	260.53	256.13	252.15	237.10	227.47	221.11
37000	272.79	267.77	263.24	259.15	243.68	233.79	227.25
38000	280.17	275.01	270.36	266.16	250.27	240.11	233.39
39000	287.54	282.24	277.47	273.16	256.86	246.43	239.53
40000	294.91	289.48	284.59	280.17	263.44	252.75	245.67
41000	302.29	296.72	291.70	287.17	270.03	259.06	251.82
42000	309.66	303.95	298.82	294.17	276.61	265.38	257.96
43000	317.03	311.19	305.93	301.18	283.20	271.70	264.10
44000	324.40	318.43	313.05	308.18	289.79	278.02	270.24
45000	331.78	325.67	320.16	315.19	296.37	284.34	276.38
46000	339.15	332.90	327.28	322.19	302.96	290.66	282.52
47000	346.52	340.14	334.39	329.20	309.54	296.98	288.67
48000	353.90	347.38	341.50	336.20	316.13	303.29	294.81
49000	361.27	354.61	348.62	343.20	322.72	309.61	300.95
50000	368.64	361.85	355.73	350.21	329.30	315.93	307.09
51000	376.01	369.09	362.85	357.21	335.89	322.25	313.23
52000	383.39	376.32	369.96	364.22	342.47	328.57	319.38
53000	390.76	383.56	377.08	371.22	349.06	334.89	325.52
54000	398.13	390.80	384.19	378.22	355.65	341.21	331.66
55000	405.50	398.04	391.31	385.23	362.23	347.52	337.80
56000	412.88	405.27	398.42	392.23	368.82	353.84	343.94
57000	420.25	412.51	405.54	399.24	375.40	360.16	350.09
58000	427.62	419.75	412.65	406.24	381.99	366.48	356.23
59000	435.00	426.98	419.77	413.25	388.58	372.80	362.37
60000	442.37	434.22	426.88	420.25	395.16	379.12	368.51
65000	479.23	470.41	462.45	455.27	428.09	410.71	399.22
70000	516.10	506.59	498.03	490.29	461.02	442.30	429.93
75000	552.96	542.78	533.60	525.31	493.95	473.90	460.64
80000	589.83	578.96	569.17	560.33	526.88	505.49	491.35
85000	626.69	615.15	604.75	595.35	559.81	537.08	522.06
90000	663.55	651.33	640.32	630.37	592.74	568.68	552.77
95000	700.42	687.52	675.89	665.39	625.67	600.27	583.48
100000	737.28	723.70	711.47	700.42	658.60	631.86	614.18
105000	774.15	759.89	747.04	735.44	691.53	663.46	644.89
110000	811.01	796.07	782.61	770.46	724.46	695.05	675.60
120000	884.74	868.44	853.76	840.50	790.32	758.24	737.02
130000	958.47	940.81	924.91	910.54	856.18	821.42	798.44
140000	1032.19	1013.18	996.06	980.58	922.04	884.61	859.86
150000	1105.92	1085.55	1067.20	1050.62	987.90	947.79	921.28
160000	1179.65	1157.92	1138.35	1120.67	1053.77	1010.98	982.70
170000	1253.38	1230.29	1209.50	1190.71	1119.63	1074.17	1044.11
180000	1327.11	1302.66	1280.64	1260.75	1185.49	1137.35	1105.53
190000	1400.83	1375.03	1351.79	1330.79	1251.35	1200.54	1166.95
200000	1474.56	1447.40	1422.94	1400.83	1317.21	1263.73	1228.37
210000	1548.29	1519.77	1494.08	1470.87	1383.07	1326.91	1289.79
220000	1622.02	1592.14	1565.23	1540.91	1448.93	1390.10	1351.21
230000	1695.75	1664.51	1636.38	1610.96	1514.79	1453.28	1412.62
240000	1769.48	1736.88	1707.52	1681.00	1580.65	1516.47	1474.04
250000	1843.20	1809.25	1778.67	1751.04	1646.51	1579.66	1535.46

7.25 % Monthly Payments

LOAN AMOUNT	1	2	3	4	5	6	7
				YEARS			
100	8.66	4.48	3.09	2.40	1.99	1.71	1.52
200	17.32	8.97	6.19	4.80	3.97	3.42	3.03
500	43.30	22.42	15.47	12.01	9.93	8.56	7.58
1000	86.59	44.84	30.94	24.01	19.87	17.12	15.16
2000	173.19	89.67	61.88	48.03	39.74	34.24	30.33
5000	432.96	224.19	154.71	120.06	99.34	85.59	75.81
6000	519.56	269.02	185.65	144.08	119.21	102.71	90.98
7000	606.15	313.86	216.60	168.09	139.08	119.82	106.14
8000	692.74	358.70	247.54	192.10	158.95	136.94	121.30
9000	779.33	403.54	278.48	216.11	178.82	154.06	136.46
10000	865.93	448.37	309.42	240.13	198.69	171.18	151.63
12000	1039.11	538.05	371.31	288.15	238.42	205.41	181.95
15000	1298.89	672.56	464.14	360.19	298.03	256.77	227.44
20000	1731.85	896.75	618.85	480.25	397.37	342.35	303.25
25000	2164.82	1120.93	773.56	600.31	496.72	427.94	379.07
30000	2597.78	1345.12	928.27	720.38	596.06	513.53	454.88
31000	2684.37	1389.96	959.22	744.39	615.93	530.65	470.04
32000	2770.96	1434.80	990.16	768.40	635.80	547.77	485.20
33000	2857.56	1479.63	1021.10	792.42	655.67	564.88	500.37
34000	2944.15	1524.47	1052.04	816.43	675.53	582.00	515.53
35000	3030.74	1569.31	1082.99	840.44	695.40	599.12	530.69
36000	3117.33	1614.15	1113.93	864.45	715.27	616.24	545.85
37000	3203.93	1658.98	1144.87	888.47	735.14	633.35	561.02
38000	3290.52	1703.82	1175.81	912.48	755.01	650.47	576.18
39000	3377.11	1748.66	1206.76	936.49	774.88	667.59	591.34
40000	3463.70	1793.49	1237.70	960.50	794.75	684.71	606.50
41000	3550.30	1838.33	1268.64	984.52	814.62	701.83	621.67
42000	3636.89	1883.17	1299.58	1008.53	834.48	718.94	636.83
43000	3723.48	1928.01	1330.53	1032.54	854.35	736.06	651.99
44000	3810.08	1972.84	1361.47	1056.55	874.22	753.18	667.15
45000	3896.67	2017.68	1392.41	1080.57	894.09	770.30	682.32
46000	3983.26	2062.52	1423.35	1104.58	913.96	787.41	697.48
47000	4069.85	2107.36	1454.30	1128.59	933.83	804.53	712.64
48000	4156.45	2152.19	1485.24	1152.60	953.70	821.65	727.81
49000	4243.04	2197.03	1516.18	1176.62	973.56	838.77	742.97
50000	4329.63	2241.87	1547.12	1200.63	993.43	855.88	758.13
51000	4416.22	2286.71	1578.07	1224.64	1013.30	873.00	773.29
52000	4502.82	2331.54	1609.01	1248.65	1033.17	890.12	788.46
53000	4589.41	2376.38	1639.95	1272.67	1053.04	907.24	803.62
54000	4676.00	2421.22	1670.89	1296.68	1072.91	924.36	818.78
55000	4762.59	2466.06	1701.84	1320.69	1092.78	941.47	833.94
56000	4849.19	2510.89	1732.78	1344.70	1112.65	958.59	849.11
57000	4935.78	2555.73	1763.72	1368.72	1132.51	975.71	864.27
58000	5022.37	2600.57	1794.66	1392.73	1152.38	992.83	879.43
59000	5108.96	2645.40	1825.60	1416.74	1172.25	1009.94	894.59
60000	5195.56	2690.24	1856.55	1440.75	1192.12	1027.06	909.76
65000	5628.52	2914.43	2011.26	1560.82	1291.46	1112.65	985.57
70000	6061.48	3138.62	2165.97	1680.88	1390.81	1198.24	1061.38
75000	6494.45	3362.80	2320.68	1800.94	1490.15	1283.83	1137.20
80000	6927.41	3586.99	2475.40	1921.01	1589.49	1369.42	1213.01
85000	7360.37	3811.18	2630.11	2041.07	1688.84	1455.00	1288.82
90000	7793.34	4035.36	2784.82	2161.13	1788.18	1540.59	1364.64
95000	8226.30	4259.55	2939.53	2281.20	1887.52	1626.18	1440.45
100000	8659.26	4483.74	3094.25	2401.26	1986.87	1711.77	1516.26
105000	9092.22	4707.92	3248.96	2521.32	2086.21	1797.36	1592.07
110000	9525.19	4932.11	3403.67	2641.38	2185.55	1882.95	1667.89
120000	10391.11	5380.48	3713.09	2881.51	2384.24	2054.12	1819.51
130000	11257.04	5828.86	4022.52	3121.64	2582.93	2225.30	1971.14
140000	12122.97	6277.23	4331.94	3361.76	2781.61	2396.48	2122.77
150000	12988.89	6725.61	4641.37	3601.89	2980.30	2567.65	2274.39
160000	13854.82	7173.98	4950.79	3842.01	3178.99	2738.83	2426.02
170000	14720.75	7622.35	5260.22	4082.14	3377.67	2910.01	2577.64
180000	15586.67	8070.73	5569.64	4322.26	3576.36	3081.18	2729.27
190000	16452.60	8519.10	5879.07	4562.39	3775.05	3252.36	2880.90
200000	17318.52	8967.47	6188.49	4802.52	3973.73	3423.54	3032.52
210000	18184.45	9415.85	6497.92	5042.64	4172.42	3594.71	3184.15
220000	19050.38	9864.22	6807.34	5282.77	4371.11	3765.89	3335.77
230000	19916.30	10312.60	7116.77	5522.89	4569.79	3937.07	3487.40
240000	20782.23	10760.97	7426.19	5763.02	4768.48	4108.25	3639.03
250000	21648.15	11209.34	7735.61	6003.15	4967.17	4279.42	3790.65

Monthly Payments 7.25 %

LOAN AMOUNT	8	9	10	11	12	13	14
100	1.37	1.26	1.17	1.10	1.04	0.99	0.94
200	2.74	2.52	2.34	2.19	2.07	1.97	1.89
500	6.85	6.29	5.84	5.48	5.18	4.93	4.72
1000	13.70	12.58	11.68	10.96	10.36	9.86	9.43
2000	27.41	25.16	23.37	21.92	20.72	19.72	18.87
5000	68.52	62.89	58.42	54.80	51.80	49.29	47.16
6000	82.23	75.47	70.11	65.75	62.16	59.15	56.60
7000	95.93	88.05	81.79	76.71	72.52	69.01	66.03
8000	109.64	100.63	93.48	87.67	82.88	78.87	75.46
9000	123.34	113.21	105.16	98.63	93.24	88.72	84.90
10000	137.05	125.79	116.85	109.59	103.60	98.58	94.33
12000	164.46	150.95	140.22	131.51	124.32	118.30	113.19
15000	205.57	188.68	175.27	164.39	155.40	147.87	141.49
20000	274.10	251.58	233.69	219.18	207.20	197.17	188.66
25000	342.62	314.47	292.12	273.98	259.00	246.46	235.82
30000	411.15	377.36	350.54	328.77	310.80	295.75	282.98
31000	424.85	389.94	362.22	339.73	321.16	305.61	292.42
32000	438.56	402.52	373.91	350.69	331.52	315.47	301.85
33000	452.26	415.10	385.59	361.65	341.88	325.32	311.28
34000	465.97	427.68	397.28	372.61	352.24	335.18	320.72
35000	479.67	440.26	408.96	383.57	362.60	345.04	330.15
36000	493.38	452.84	420.65	394.53	372.96	354.90	339.58
37000	507.08	465.41	432.33	405.49	383.32	364.76	349.01
38000	520.79	477.99	444.02	416.45	393.68	374.62	358.45
39000	534.49	490.57	455.70	427.41	404.04	384.47	367.88
40000	548.20	503.15	467.38	438.37	414.40	394.33	377.31
41000	561.90	515.73	479.07	449.32	424.76	404.19	386.75
42000	575.61	528.31	490.75	460.28	435.13	414.05	396.18
43000	589.31	540.89	502.44	471.24	445.49	423.91	405.61
44000	603.02	553.47	514.12	482.20	455.85	433.77	415.04
45000	616.72	566.04	525.81	493.16	466.21	443.62	424.48
46000	630.43	578.62	537.49	504.12	476.57	453.48	433.91
47000	644.13	591.20	549.18	515.08	486.93	463.34	443.34
48000	657.84	603.78	560.86	526.04	497.29	473.20	452.78
49000	671.54	616.36	572.55	537.00	507.65	483.06	462.21
50000	685.25	628.94	584.23	547.96	518.01	492.92	471.64
51000	698.95	641.52	595.92	558.92	528.37	502.77	481.07
52000	712.66	654.10	607.60	569.88	538.73	512.63	490.51
53000	726.36	666.67	619.28	580.83	549.09	522.49	499.94
54000	740.07	679.25	630.97	591.79	559.45	532.35	509.37
55000	753.77	691.83	642.65	602.75	569.81	542.21	518.81
56000	767.48	704.41	654.34	613.71	580.17	552.07	528.24
57000	781.18	716.99	666.02	624.67	590.53	561.92	537.67
58000	794.89	729.57	677.71	635.63	600.89	571.78	547.10
59000	808.59	742.15	689.39	646.59	611.25	581.64	556.54
60000	822.30	754.73	701.08	657.55	621.61	591.50	565.97
65000	890.82	817.62	759.50	712.34	673.41	640.79	613.13
70000	959.34	880.51	817.92	767.14	725.21	690.08	660.30
75000	1027.87	943.41	876.35	821.94	777.01	739.37	707.46
80000	1096.39	1006.30	934.77	876.73	828.81	788.67	754.63
85000	1164.92	1069.19	993.19	931.53	880.61	837.96	801.79
90000	1233.44	1132.09	1051.61	986.32	932.41	887.25	848.95
95000	1301.97	1194.98	1110.04	1041.12	984.21	936.54	896.12
100000	1370.49	1257.88	1168.46	1095.91	1036.01	985.83	943.28
105000	1439.02	1320.77	1226.88	1150.71	1087.81	1035.12	990.45
110000	1507.54	1383.66	1285.31	1205.51	1139.61	1084.41	1037.61
120000	1644.59	1509.45	1402.15	1315.10	1243.21	1183.00	1131.94
130000	1781.64	1635.24	1519.00	1424.69	1346.82	1281.58	1226.27
140000	1918.69	1761.03	1635.85	1534.28	1450.42	1380.16	1320.60
150000	2055.74	1886.81	1752.69	1643.87	1554.02	1478.75	1414.92
160000	2192.79	2012.60	1869.54	1753.46	1657.62	1577.33	1509.25
170000	2329.84	2138.39	1986.38	1863.05	1761.22	1675.91	1603.58
180000	2466.89	2264.18	2103.23	1972.65	1864.82	1774.50	1697.91
190000	2603.93	2389.96	2220.08	2082.24	1968.42	1873.08	1792.24
200000	2740.98	2515.75	2336.92	2191.83	2072.02	1971.66	1886.57
210000	2878.03	2641.54	2453.77	2301.42	2175.63	2070.25	1980.89
220000	3015.08	2767.33	2570.61	2411.01	2279.23	2168.83	2075.22
230000	3152.13	2893.11	2687.46	2520.60	2382.83	2267.41	2169.55
240000	3289.18	3018.90	2804.31	2630.19	2486.43	2366.00	2263.88
250000	3426.23	3144.69	2921.15	2739.79	2590.03	2464.58	2358.21

7.25 % Monthly Payments

LOAN AMOUNT	YEARS 15	16	17	18	19	20	21
100	0.91	0.88	0.85	0.82	0.80	0.78	0.7
200	1.81	1.75	1.70	1.65	1.61	1.57	1.5
500	4.53	4.38	4.24	4.12	4.01	3.92	3.8
1000	9.07	8.75	8.48	8.24	8.03	7.84	7.6
2000	18.14	17.51	16.96	16.48	16.05	15.68	15.3
5000	45.34	43.77	42.40	41.19	40.13	39.19	38.3
6000	54.41	52.52	50.87	49.43	48.16	47.03	46.0
7000	63.48	61.27	59.35	57.67	56.19	54.87	53.7
8000	72.55	70.03	67.83	65.91	64.21	62.71	61.3
9000	81.62	78.78	76.31	74.15	72.24	70.55	69.0
10000	90.68	87.53	84.79	82.39	80.27	78.39	76.7
12000	108.82	105.04	101.75	98.86	96.32	94.07	92.0
15000	136.03	131.30	127.19	123.58	120.40	117.58	115.0
20000	181.37	175.07	169.58	164.77	160.54	156.78	153.4
25000	226.71	218.83	211.98	205.97	200.67	195.97	191.8
30000	272.05	262.60	254.37	247.16	240.80	235.17	230.1
31000	281.12	271.35	262.85	255.40	248.83	243.01	237.8
32000	290.19	280.11	271.33	263.64	256.86	250.85	245.5
33000	299.26	288.86	279.81	271.88	264.88	258.69	253.1
34000	308.32	297.61	288.29	280.12	272.91	266.53	260.8
35000	317.39	306.37	296.77	288.35	280.94	274.36	268.5
36000	326.46	315.12	305.25	296.59	288.96	282.20	276.1
37000	335.53	323.87	313.73	304.83	296.99	290.04	283.8
38000	344.60	332.63	322.21	313.07	305.02	297.88	291.5
39000	353.67	341.38	330.68	321.31	313.04	305.72	299.2
40000	362.73	350.13	339.16	329.55	321.07	313.56	306.8
41000	371.80	358.89	347.64	337.79	329.10	321.40	314.5
42000	380.87	367.64	356.12	346.03	337.12	329.24	322.2
43000	389.94	376.39	364.60	354.26	345.15	337.08	329.8
44000	399.01	385.15	373.08	362.50	353.18	344.91	337.5
45000	408.08	393.90	381.56	370.74	361.20	352.75	345.2
46000	417.14	402.65	390.04	378.98	369.23	360.59	352.9
47000	426.21	411.41	398.52	387.22	377.26	368.43	360.5
48000	435.28	420.16	407.00	395.46	385.28	376.27	368.2
49000	444.35	428.91	415.48	403.70	393.31	384.11	375.9
50000	453.42	437.67	423.95	411.93	401.34	391.95	383.5
51000	462.49	446.42	432.43	420.17	409.36	399.79	391.2
52000	471.55	455.17	440.91	428.41	417.39	407.63	398.9
53000	480.62	463.93	449.39	436.65	425.42	415.47	406.6
54000	489.69	472.68	457.87	444.89	433.45	423.30	414.2
55000	498.76	481.43	466.35	453.13	441.47	431.14	421.9
56000	507.83	490.19	474.83	461.37	449.50	438.98	429.6
57000	516.90	498.94	483.31	469.61	457.53	446.82	437.2
58000	525.96	507.69	491.79	477.84	465.55	454.66	444.9
59000	535.03	516.45	500.27	486.08	473.58	462.50	452.6
60000	544.10	525.20	508.75	494.32	481.61	470.34	460.3
65000	589.44	568.97	551.14	535.51	521.74	509.53	498.6
70000	634.78	612.74	593.54	576.71	561.87	548.73	537.0
75000	680.13	656.50	635.93	617.90	602.01	587.92	575.3
80000	725.47	700.27	678.33	659.10	642.14	627.12	613.7
85000	770.81	744.04	720.72	700.29	682.27	666.31	652.1
90000	816.15	787.80	763.12	741.48	722.41	705.51	690.4
95000	861.49	831.57	805.51	782.68	762.54	744.70	728.8
100000	906.83	875.34	847.91	823.87	802.68	783.90	767.1
105000	952.18	919.10	890.30	865.06	842.81	823.09	805.5
110000	997.52	962.87	932.70	906.26	882.94	862.29	843.9
120000	1088.20	1050.40	1017.49	988.64	963.21	940.68	920.6
130000	1178.88	1137.94	1102.28	1071.03	1043.48	1019.07	997.3
140000	1269.57	1225.47	1187.07	1153.42	1123.75	1097.46	1074.0
150000	1360.25	1313.00	1271.86	1235.80	1204.01	1175.85	1150.7
160000	1450.93	1400.54	1356.65	1318.19	1284.28	1254.24	1227.4
170000	1541.62	1488.07	1441.45	1400.58	1364.55	1332.63	1304.2
180000	1632.30	1575.60	1526.24	1482.96	1444.82	1411.02	1380.9
190000	1722.98	1663.14	1611.03	1565.35	1525.08	1489.40	1457.6
200000	1813.67	1750.67	1695.82	1647.74	1605.35	1567.79	1534.3
210000	1904.35	1838.21	1780.61	1730.13	1685.62	1646.18	1611.0
220000	1995.03	1925.74	1865.40	1812.51	1765.89	1724.57	1687.8
230000	2085.72	2013.27	1950.19	1894.90	1846.15	1802.96	1764.5
240000	2176.40	2100.81	2034.98	1977.29	1926.42	1881.35	1841.2
250000	2267.09	2188.34	2119.77	2059.67	2006.69	1959.74	1917.9

Monthly Payments 7.25 %

LOAN AMOUNT	22	23	24	25	30	35	40
100	0.75	0.74	0.73	0.72	0.67	0.65	0.63
200	1.50	1.48	1.45	1.43	1.35	1.30	1.26
500	3.76	3.69	3.63	3.58	3.37	3.24	3.16
1000	7.52	7.39	7.27	7.16	6.75	6.49	6.32
2000	15.04	14.78	14.54	14.32	13.50	12.98	12.64
5000	37.61	36.94	36.34	35.80	33.75	32.44	31.59
6000	45.13	44.33	43.61	42.96	40.50	38.93	37.91
7000	52.66	51.72	50.88	50.11	47.24	45.42	44.23
8000	60.18	59.11	58.14	57.27	53.99	51.91	50.55
9000	67.70	66.50	65.41	64.43	60.74	58.40	56.87
10000	75.22	73.88	72.68	71.59	67.49	64.89	63.18
12000	90.27	88.66	87.22	85.91	80.99	77.87	75.82
15000	112.84	110.83	109.02	107.39	101.24	97.33	94.78
20000	150.45	147.77	145.36	143.18	134.98	129.78	126.37
25000	188.06	184.71	181.70	178.98	168.73	162.22	157.96
30000	225.67	221.65	218.04	214.78	202.48	194.67	189.55
31000	233.20	229.04	225.31	221.93	209.23	201.16	195.87
32000	240.72	236.43	232.57	229.09	215.98	207.65	202.19
33000	248.24	243.82	239.84	236.25	222.73	214.14	208.51
34000	255.76	251.21	247.11	243.41	229.47	220.63	214.82
35000	263.29	258.60	254.38	250.57	236.22	227.11	221.14
36000	270.81	265.99	261.65	257.73	242.97	233.60	227.46
37000	278.33	273.37	268.91	264.89	249.72	240.09	233.78
38000	285.85	280.76	276.18	272.05	256.47	246.58	240.10
39000	293.38	288.15	283.45	279.21	263.22	253.07	246.42
40000	300.90	295.54	290.72	286.37	269.97	259.56	252.73
41000	308.42	302.93	297.99	293.53	276.72	266.05	259.05
42000	315.94	310.32	305.25	300.69	283.47	272.54	265.37
43000	323.47	317.71	312.52	307.85	290.22	279.03	271.69
44000	330.99	325.09	319.79	315.00	296.97	285.52	278.01
45000	338.51	332.48	327.06	322.16	303.72	292.00	284.33
46000	346.03	339.87	334.33	329.32	310.47	298.49	290.64
47000	353.56	347.26	341.59	336.48	317.21	304.98	296.96
48000	361.08	354.65	348.86	343.64	323.96	311.47	303.28
49000	368.60	362.04	356.13	350.80	330.71	317.96	309.60
50000	376.12	369.42	363.40	357.96	337.46	324.45	315.92
51000	383.65	376.81	370.67	365.12	344.21	330.94	322.24
52000	391.17	384.20	377.93	372.28	350.96	337.43	328.55
53000	398.69	391.59	385.20	379.44	357.71	343.92	334.87
54000	406.21	398.98	392.47	386.60	364.46	350.41	341.19
55000	413.74	406.37	399.74	393.76	371.21	356.89	347.51
56000	421.26	413.76	407.01	400.91	377.96	363.38	353.83
57000	428.78	421.14	414.27	408.07	384.71	369.87	360.15
58000	436.30	428.53	421.54	415.23	391.46	376.36	366.46
59000	443.82	435.92	428.81	422.39	398.21	382.85	372.78
60000	451.35	443.31	436.08	429.55	404.95	389.34	379.10
65000	488.96	480.25	472.42	465.35	438.70	421.78	410.69
70000	526.57	517.19	508.76	501.14	472.45	454.23	442.28
75000	564.18	554.14	545.10	536.94	506.19	486.67	473.88
80000	601.80	591.08	581.44	572.73	539.94	519.12	505.47
85000	639.41	628.02	617.78	608.53	573.69	551.56	537.06
90000	677.02	664.96	654.12	644.33	607.43	584.01	568.65
95000	714.63	701.91	690.46	680.12	641.18	616.45	600.24
100000	752.25	738.85	726.80	715.92	674.92	648.90	631.83
105000	789.86	775.79	763.14	751.71	708.67	681.34	663.43
110000	827.47	812.73	799.47	787.51	742.42	713.79	695.02
120000	902.69	886.62	872.15	859.10	809.91	778.68	758.20
130000	977.92	960.50	944.83	930.69	877.40	843.57	821.39
140000	1053.14	1034.39	1017.51	1002.29	944.89	908.46	884.57
150000	1128.37	1108.27	1090.19	1073.88	1012.39	973.35	947.75
160000	1203.59	1182.16	1162.87	1145.47	1079.88	1038.24	1010.94
170000	1278.82	1256.04	1235.55	1217.06	1147.37	1103.13	1074.12
180000	1354.04	1329.93	1308.23	1288.65	1214.86	1168.02	1137.30
190000	1429.27	1403.81	1380.91	1360.25	1282.36	1232.91	1200.49
200000	1504.49	1477.70	1453.59	1431.84	1349.85	1297.80	1263.67
210000	1579.72	1551.58	1526.27	1503.43	1417.34	1362.69	1326.85
220000	1654.94	1625.47	1598.95	1575.02	1484.83	1427.58	1390.04
230000	1730.16	1699.35	1671.63	1646.61	1552.33	1492.47	1453.22
240000	1805.39	1773.24	1744.31	1718.20	1619.82	1557.36	1516.40
250000	1880.61	1847.12	1816.99	1789.80	1687.31	1622.25	1579.59

7.50 % Monthly Payments

LOAN AMOUNT	YEARS 1	2	3	4	5	6	7
100	8.67	4.49	3.11	2.41	2.00	1.72	1.53
200	17.34	8.99	6.21	4.83	4.00	3.45	3.06
500	43.35	22.47	15.53	12.06	9.99	8.62	7.64
1000	86.70	44.95	31.05	24.13	19.98	17.23	15.28
2000	173.41	89.90	62.11	48.25	39.97	34.47	30.56
5000	433.52	224.74	155.27	120.63	99.92	86.17	76.41
6000	520.23	269.69	186.32	144.75	119.90	103.41	91.69
7000	606.93	314.63	217.38	168.88	139.88	120.64	106.97
8000	693.64	359.58	248.43	193.00	159.87	137.88	122.25
9000	780.34	404.53	279.48	217.13	179.85	155.11	137.54
10000	867.05	449.48	310.54	241.25	199.84	172.35	152.82
12000	1040.45	539.37	372.64	289.51	239.80	206.82	183.38
15000	1300.57	674.21	465.80	361.88	299.75	258.52	229.23
20000	1734.09	898.95	621.07	482.51	399.67	344.69	305.64
25000	2167.61	1123.69	776.34	603.14	499.59	430.87	382.04
30000	2601.14	1348.43	931.61	723.76	599.51	517.04	458.45
31000	2687.84	1393.37	962.66	747.89	619.49	534.28	473.74
32000	2774.54	1438.32	993.72	772.02	639.47	551.51	489.02
33000	2861.25	1483.27	1024.77	796.14	659.46	568.74	504.30
34000	2947.95	1528.22	1055.82	820.27	679.44	585.98	519.58
35000	3034.66	1573.16	1086.88	844.39	699.42	603.21	534.86
36000	3121.36	1618.11	1117.93	868.52	719.41	620.45	550.14
37000	3208.07	1663.06	1148.98	892.64	739.39	637.68	565.43
38000	3294.77	1708.01	1180.04	916.77	759.37	654.92	580.71
39000	3381.48	1752.95	1211.09	940.89	779.36	672.15	595.99
40000	3468.18	1797.90	1242.15	965.02	799.34	689.39	611.27
41000	3554.89	1842.85	1273.20	989.14	819.33	706.62	626.55
42000	3641.59	1887.80	1304.25	1013.27	839.31	723.86	641.84
43000	3728.29	1932.74	1335.31	1037.40	859.29	741.09	657.12
44000	3815.00	1977.69	1366.36	1061.52	879.28	758.33	672.40
45000	3901.70	2022.64	1397.41	1085.65	899.26	775.56	687.68
46000	3988.41	2067.59	1428.47	1109.77	919.24	792.80	702.96
47000	4075.11	2112.53	1459.52	1133.90	939.23	810.03	718.24
48000	4161.82	2157.48	1490.57	1158.02	959.21	827.26	733.53
49000	4248.52	2202.43	1521.63	1182.15	979.19	844.50	748.81
50000	4335.23	2247.38	1552.68	1206.27	999.18	861.73	764.09
51000	4421.93	2292.32	1583.73	1230.40	1019.16	878.97	779.37
52000	4508.64	2337.27	1614.79	1254.52	1039.14	896.20	794.65
53000	4595.34	2382.22	1645.84	1278.65	1059.13	913.44	809.93
54000	4682.04	2427.17	1676.90	1302.78	1079.11	930.67	825.22
55000	4768.75	2472.11	1707.95	1326.90	1099.10	947.91	840.50
56000	4855.45	2517.06	1739.00	1351.03	1119.08	965.14	855.78
57000	4942.16	2562.01	1770.06	1375.15	1139.06	982.38	871.06
58000	5028.86	2606.96	1801.11	1399.28	1159.05	999.61	886.34
59000	5115.57	2651.90	1832.16	1423.40	1179.03	1016.85	901.63
60000	5202.27	2696.85	1863.22	1447.53	1199.01	1034.08	916.91
65000	5635.79	2921.59	2018.49	1568.16	1298.93	1120.25	993.32
70000	6069.32	3146.33	2173.75	1688.78	1398.85	1206.43	1069.73
75000	6502.84	3371.06	2329.02	1809.41	1498.77	1292.60	1146.13
80000	6936.36	3595.80	2484.29	1930.04	1598.68	1378.77	1222.54
85000	7369.89	3820.54	2639.56	2050.66	1698.60	1464.95	1298.95
90000	7803.41	4045.28	2794.83	2171.29	1798.52	1551.12	1375.36
95000	8236.93	4270.01	2950.09	2291.92	1898.44	1637.30	1451.77
100000	8670.45	4494.75	3105.36	2412.55	1998.35	1723.47	1528.18
105000	9103.98	4719.49	3260.63	2533.17	2098.27	1809.64	1604.59
110000	9537.50	4944.23	3415.90	2653.80	2198.19	1895.82	1681.00
120000	10404.54	5393.70	3726.44	2895.06	2398.03	2068.16	1833.82
130000	11271.59	5843.18	4036.97	3136.31	2597.86	2240.51	1986.63
140000	12138.63	6292.65	4347.51	3377.57	2797.70	2412.86	2139.45
150000	13005.68	6742.13	4658.04	3618.82	2997.53	2585.20	2292.27
160000	13872.72	7191.60	4968.58	3860.08	3197.37	2757.55	2445.09
170000	14739.77	7641.08	5279.12	4101.33	3397.20	2929.90	2597.90
180000	15606.82	8090.55	5589.65	4342.58	3597.04	3102.24	2750.72
190000	16473.86	8540.03	5900.19	4583.84	3796.87	3274.59	2903.54
200000	17340.91	8989.50	6210.73	4825.09	3996.71	3446.94	3056.36
210000	18207.95	9438.98	6521.26	5066.35	4196.55	3619.28	3209.18
220000	19075.00	9888.45	6831.80	5307.60	4396.38	3791.63	3361.99
230000	19942.04	10337.93	7142.33	5548.86	4596.22	3963.98	3514.81
240000	20809.09	10787.40	7452.87	5790.11	4796.05	4136.32	3667.63
250000	21676.13	11236.88	7763.41	6031.37	4995.89	4308.67	3820.45

Monthly Payments 7.50 %

LOAN AMOUNT	8	9	10	11	12	13	14
			YEARS				
100	1.38	1.27	1.18	1.11	1.05	1.00	0.96
200	2.77	2.54	2.36	2.22	2.10	2.00	1.91
500	6.91	6.35	5.91	5.54	5.25	5.00	4.78
1000	13.83	12.70	11.81	11.09	10.49	9.99	9.57
2000	27.65	25.40	23.62	22.17	20.98	19.98	19.13
5000	69.13	63.51	59.05	55.44	52.45	49.95	47.84
6000	82.96	76.21	70.86	66.52	62.94	59.94	57.40
7000	96.78	88.92	82.67	77.61	73.43	69.94	66.97
8000	110.61	101.62	94.48	88.70	83.92	79.93	76.54
9000	124.44	114.32	106.29	99.78	94.41	89.92	86.11
10000	138.26	127.02	118.10	110.87	104.90	99.91	95.67
12000	165.92	152.43	141.73	133.05	125.88	119.89	114.81
15000	207.39	190.54	177.16	166.31	157.36	149.86	143.51
20000	276.53	254.05	236.21	221.74	209.81	199.82	191.35
25000	345.66	317.56	295.26	277.18	262.26	249.77	239.19
30000	414.79	381.07	354.31	332.62	314.71	299.72	287.02
31000	428.62	393.77	366.12	343.70	325.20	309.71	296.59
32000	442.44	406.48	377.93	354.79	335.69	319.71	306.16
33000	456.27	419.18	389.75	365.88	346.18	329.70	315.73
34000	470.09	431.88	401.56	376.97	356.67	339.69	325.29
35000	483.92	444.58	413.37	388.05	367.16	349.68	334.86
36000	497.75	457.29	425.18	399.14	377.65	359.67	344.43
37000	511.57	469.99	436.99	410.23	388.15	369.66	354.00
38000	525.40	482.69	448.80	421.31	398.64	379.65	363.56
39000	539.23	495.39	460.61	432.40	409.13	389.64	373.13
40000	553.05	508.10	472.42	443.49	419.62	399.63	382.70
41000	566.88	520.80	484.23	454.58	430.11	409.62	392.27
42000	580.71	533.50	496.04	465.66	440.60	419.61	401.83
43000	594.53	546.20	507.85	476.75	451.09	429.60	411.40
44000	608.36	558.90	519.66	487.84	461.58	439.59	420.97
45000	622.18	571.61	531.47	498.92	472.07	449.59	430.54
46000	636.01	584.31	543.28	510.01	482.56	459.58	440.10
47000	649.84	597.01	555.09	521.10	493.05	469.57	449.67
48000	663.66	609.71	566.90	532.19	503.54	479.56	459.24
49000	677.49	622.42	578.71	543.27	514.03	489.55	468.81
50000	691.32	635.12	590.52	554.36	524.52	499.54	478.37
51000	705.14	647.82	602.33	565.45	535.01	509.53	487.94
52000	718.97	660.52	614.14	576.54	545.50	519.52	497.51
53000	732.79	673.23	625.95	587.62	555.99	529.51	507.08
54000	746.62	685.93	637.77	598.71	566.48	539.50	516.64
55000	760.45	698.63	649.58	609.80	576.97	549.49	526.21
56000	774.27	711.33	661.39	620.88	587.46	559.48	535.78
57000	788.10	724.04	673.20	631.97	597.95	569.48	545.35
58000	801.93	736.74	685.01	643.06	608.44	579.47	554.91
59000	815.75	749.44	696.82	654.15	618.93	589.46	564.48
60000	829.58	762.14	708.63	665.23	629.42	599.45	574.05
65000	898.71	825.65	767.68	720.67	681.88	649.40	621.89
70000	967.84	889.17	826.73	776.11	734.33	699.36	669.72
75000	1036.97	952.68	885.78	831.54	786.78	749.31	717.56
80000	1106.11	1016.19	944.84	886.98	839.23	799.26	765.40
85000	1175.24	1079.70	1003.89	942.41	891.68	849.22	813.24
90000	1244.37	1143.21	1062.94	997.85	944.14	899.17	861.07
95000	1313.50	1206.73	1121.99	1053.29	996.59	949.13	908.91
100000	1382.63	1270.24	1181.05	1108.72	1049.04	999.08	956.75
105000	1451.76	1333.75	1240.10	1164.16	1101.49	1049.03	1004.59
110000	1520.89	1397.26	1299.15	1219.59	1153.95	1098.99	1052.42
120000	1659.16	1524.29	1417.26	1330.47	1258.85	1198.90	1148.10
130000	1797.42	1651.31	1535.36	1441.34	1363.75	1298.80	1243.77
140000	1935.68	1778.33	1653.47	1552.21	1468.66	1398.71	1339.45
150000	2073.95	1905.36	1771.57	1663.08	1573.56	1498.62	1435.12
160000	2212.21	2032.38	1889.67	1773.96	1678.47	1598.53	1530.80
170000	2350.47	2159.41	2007.78	1884.83	1783.37	1698.44	1626.47
180000	2488.74	2286.43	2125.88	1995.70	1888.27	1798.34	1722.15
190000	2627.00	2413.45	2243.99	2106.57	1993.18	1898.25	1817.82
200000	2765.26	2540.48	2362.09	2217.44	2098.08	1998.16	1913.50
210000	2903.53	2667.50	2480.20	2328.32	2202.99	2098.07	2009.17
220000	3041.79	2794.52	2598.30	2439.19	2307.89	2197.97	2104.85
230000	3180.05	2921.55	2716.41	2550.06	2412.79	2297.88	2200.52
240000	3318.32	3048.57	2834.51	2660.93	2517.70	2397.79	2296.19
250000	3456.58	3175.60	2952.62	2771.80	2622.60	2497.70	2391.87

7.50 % Monthly Payments

LOAN AMOUNT	15	16	17	18	19	20	21
100	0.92	0.89	0.86	0.84	0.82	0.80	0.78
200	1.84	1.78	1.72	1.68	1.63	1.60	1.56
500	4.60	4.45	4.31	4.19	4.09	3.99	3.91
1000	9.21	8.89	8.62	8.38	8.17	7.99	7.82
2000	18.41	17.78	17.24	16.76	16.34	15.97	15.64
5000	46.03	44.46	43.10	41.91	40.86	39.93	39.10
6000	55.23	53.35	51.72	50.29	49.03	47.92	46.92
7000	64.44	62.25	60.34	58.67	57.20	55.90	54.75
8000	73.64	71.14	68.96	67.05	65.37	63.89	62.57
9000	82.85	80.03	77.58	75.44	73.55	71.87	70.39
10000	92.05	88.92	86.20	83.82	81.72	79.86	78.21
12000	110.46	106.71	103.44	100.58	98.06	95.83	93.85
15000	138.08	133.38	129.30	125.73	122.58	119.79	117.31
20000	184.10	177.85	172.40	167.63	163.44	159.72	156.42
25000	230.13	222.31	215.50	209.54	204.30	199.65	195.52
30000	276.15	266.77	258.60	251.45	245.15	239.58	234.62
31000	285.36	275.66	267.22	259.83	253.33	247.57	242.45
32000	294.56	284.55	275.84	268.22	261.50	255.55	250.27
33000	303.77	293.44	284.46	276.60	269.67	263.54	258.09
34000	312.97	302.34	293.08	284.98	277.84	271.52	265.91
35000	322.18	311.23	301.70	293.36	286.01	279.51	273.73
36000	331.38	320.12	310.32	301.74	294.19	287.50	281.55
37000	340.59	329.01	318.94	310.12	302.36	295.48	289.37
38000	349.80	337.91	327.56	318.51	310.53	303.47	297.19
39000	359.00	346.80	336.18	326.89	318.70	311.45	305.01
40000	368.21	355.69	344.80	335.27	326.87	319.44	312.83
41000	377.41	364.58	353.42	343.65	335.04	327.43	320.65
42000	386.62	373.48	362.04	352.03	343.22	335.41	328.47
43000	395.82	382.37	370.66	360.41	351.39	343.40	336.30
44000	405.03	391.26	379.28	368.80	359.56	351.38	344.12
45000	414.23	400.15	387.90	377.18	367.73	359.37	351.94
46000	423.44	409.04	396.52	385.56	375.90	367.36	359.76
47000	432.64	417.94	405.14	393.94	384.08	375.34	367.58
48000	441.85	426.83	413.76	402.32	392.25	383.33	375.40
49000	451.05	435.72	422.38	410.71	400.42	391.32	383.22
50000	460.26	444.61	431.00	419.09	408.59	399.30	391.04
51000	469.46	453.51	439.62	427.47	416.76	407.29	398.86
52000	478.67	462.40	448.24	435.85	424.94	415.27	406.68
53000	487.87	471.29	456.86	444.23	433.11	423.26	414.50
54000	497.08	480.18	465.48	452.61	441.28	431.25	422.32
55000	506.28	489.07	474.10	461.00	449.45	439.23	430.15
56000	515.49	497.97	482.72	469.38	457.62	447.22	437.97
57000	524.69	506.86	491.34	477.76	465.79	455.20	445.79
58000	533.90	515.75	499.97	486.14	473.97	463.19	453.61
59000	543.10	524.64	508.59	494.52	482.14	471.18	461.43
60000	552.31	533.54	517.21	502.90	490.31	479.16	469.25
65000	598.33	578.00	560.31	544.81	531.17	519.09	508.35
70000	644.36	622.46	603.41	586.72	572.03	559.02	547.46
75000	690.39	666.92	646.51	628.63	612.89	598.95	586.56
80000	736.41	711.38	689.61	670.54	653.75	638.88	625.67
85000	782.44	755.84	732.71	712.45	694.61	678.81	664.77
90000	828.46	800.30	775.81	754.36	735.46	718.74	703.87
95000	874.49	844.77	818.91	796.27	776.32	758.67	742.98
100000	920.51	889.23	862.01	838.17	817.18	798.60	782.08
105000	966.54	933.69	905.11	880.08	858.04	838.53	821.19
110000	1012.57	978.15	948.21	921.99	898.90	878.46	860.29
120000	1104.62	1067.07	1034.41	1005.81	980.62	958.32	938.50
130000	1196.67	1156.00	1120.61	1089.63	1062.34	1038.18	1016.71
140000	1288.72	1244.92	1206.81	1173.44	1144.06	1118.04	1094.91
150000	1380.77	1333.84	1293.01	1257.26	1225.77	1197.90	1173.12
160000	1472.82	1422.76	1379.21	1341.08	1307.49	1277.76	1251.33
170000	1564.87	1511.69	1465.41	1424.90	1389.21	1357.62	1329.54
180000	1656.92	1600.61	1551.62	1508.71	1470.93	1437.48	1407.75
190000	1748.98	1689.53	1637.82	1592.53	1552.65	1517.34	1485.96
200000	1841.03	1778.45	1724.02	1676.35	1634.37	1597.20	1564.16
210000	1933.08	1867.38	1810.22	1760.17	1716.08	1677.06	1642.37
220000	2025.13	1956.30	1896.42	1843.98	1797.80	1756.92	1720.58
230000	2117.18	2045.22	1982.62	1927.80	1879.52	1836.78	1798.79
240000	2209.23	2134.15	2068.82	2011.62	1961.24	1916.65	1877.00
250000	2301.28	2223.07	2155.02	2095.44	2042.96	1996.51	1955.20

Years: 15–21

Monthly Payments 7.50 %

LOAN AMOUNT	YEARS 22	23	24	25	30	35	40
100	0.77	0.75	0.74	0.73	0.69	0.67	0.65
200	1.53	1.51	1.48	1.46	1.38	1.33	1.30
500	3.84	3.77	3.71	3.66	3.46	3.33	3.25
1000	7.67	7.54	7.42	7.32	6.91	6.66	6.50
2000	15.35	15.08	14.85	14.63	13.83	13.32	12.99
5000	38.37	37.71	37.11	36.58	34.57	33.30	32.48
6000	46.04	45.25	44.54	43.89	41.48	39.96	38.98
7000	53.71	52.79	51.96	51.21	48.40	46.63	45.47
8000	61.39	60.33	59.38	58.52	55.31	53.29	51.97
9000	69.06	67.87	66.80	65.84	62.22	59.95	58.47
10000	76.73	75.41	74.23	73.16	69.14	66.61	64.96
12000	92.08	90.49	89.07	87.79	82.97	79.93	77.95
15000	115.10	113.12	111.34	109.73	103.71	99.91	97.44
20000	153.47	150.82	148.45	146.31	138.28	133.22	129.92
25000	191.83	188.53	185.56	182.89	172.85	166.52	162.40
30000	230.20	226.24	222.68	219.47	207.42	199.82	194.89
31000	237.87	233.78	230.10	226.78	214.33	206.48	201.38
32000	245.55	241.32	237.52	234.10	221.24	213.14	207.88
33000	253.22	248.86	244.94	241.41	228.16	219.81	214.37
34000	260.89	256.40	252.37	248.73	235.07	226.47	220.87
35000	268.57	263.94	259.79	256.04	241.99	233.13	227.37
36000	276.24	271.48	267.21	263.36	248.90	239.79	233.86
37000	283.91	279.03	274.63	270.68	255.81	246.45	240.36
38000	291.59	286.57	282.06	277.99	262.73	253.11	246.86
39000	299.26	294.11	289.48	285.31	269.64	259.77	253.35
40000	306.93	301.65	296.90	292.62	276.55	266.43	259.85
41000	314.61	309.19	304.32	299.94	283.47	273.09	266.34
42000	322.28	316.73	311.75	307.25	290.38	279.75	272.84
43000	329.95	324.27	319.17	314.57	297.30	286.41	279.34
44000	337.63	331.81	326.59	321.88	304.21	293.07	285.83
45000	345.30	339.36	334.01	329.20	311.12	299.73	292.33
46000	352.97	346.90	341.44	336.52	318.04	306.40	298.83
47000	360.65	354.44	348.86	343.83	324.95	313.06	305.32
48000	368.32	361.98	356.28	351.15	331.87	319.72	311.82
49000	375.99	369.52	363.70	358.46	338.78	326.38	318.31
50000	383.67	377.06	371.13	365.78	345.69	333.04	324.81
51000	391.34	384.60	378.55	373.09	352.61	339.70	331.31
52000	399.01	392.14	385.97	380.41	359.52	346.36	337.80
53000	406.69	399.69	393.39	387.72	366.43	353.02	344.30
54000	414.36	407.23	400.82	395.04	373.35	359.68	350.79
55000	422.03	414.77	408.24	402.36	380.26	366.34	357.29
56000	429.71	422.31	415.66	409.67	387.18	373.00	363.79
57000	437.38	429.85	423.08	416.99	394.09	379.66	370.28
58000	445.05	437.39	430.51	424.30	401.00	386.32	376.78
59000	452.73	444.93	437.93	431.62	407.92	392.99	383.28
60000	460.40	452.47	445.35	438.93	414.83	399.65	389.77
65000	498.77	490.18	482.46	475.51	449.40	432.95	422.25
70000	537.13	527.89	519.58	512.09	483.97	466.25	454.73
75000	575.50	565.59	556.69	548.67	518.54	499.56	487.21
80000	613.87	603.30	593.80	585.24	553.11	532.86	519.70
85000	652.23	641.01	630.92	621.82	587.68	566.16	552.18
90000	690.60	678.71	668.03	658.40	622.25	599.47	584.66
95000	728.97	716.42	705.14	694.98	656.82	632.77	617.14
100000	767.34	754.12	742.25	731.55	691.39	666.08	649.62
105000	805.70	791.83	779.37	768.13	725.96	699.38	682.10
110000	844.07	829.54	816.48	804.71	760.52	732.68	714.58
120000	920.80	904.95	890.70	877.87	829.66	799.29	779.54
130000	997.54	980.36	964.93	951.02	898.80	865.90	844.51
140000	1074.27	1055.77	1039.15	1024.18	967.94	932.51	909.47
150000	1151.00	1131.19	1113.38	1097.33	1037.08	999.11	974.43
160000	1227.74	1206.60	1187.61	1170.49	1106.22	1065.72	1039.39
170000	1304.47	1282.01	1261.83	1243.64	1175.36	1132.33	1104.35
180000	1381.20	1357.42	1336.06	1316.80	1244.49	1198.94	1169.32
190000	1457.94	1432.84	1410.28	1389.95	1313.63	1265.55	1234.28
200000	1534.67	1508.25	1484.51	1463.11	1382.77	1332.15	1299.24
210000	1611.40	1583.66	1558.73	1536.27	1451.91	1398.76	1364.20
220000	1688.14	1659.07	1632.96	1609.42	1521.05	1465.37	1429.16
230000	1764.87	1734.49	1707.18	1682.58	1590.19	1531.98	1494.13
240000	1841.60	1809.90	1781.41	1755.73	1659.33	1598.58	1559.09
250000	1918.34	1885.31	1855.63	1828.89	1728.47	1665.19	1624.05

7.75 % Monthly Payments

LOAN AMOUNT	YEARS 1	2	3	4	5	6	7
100	8.68	4.51	3.12	2.42	2.01	1.74	1.54
200	17.36	9.01	6.23	4.85	4.02	3.47	3.08
500	43.41	22.53	15.58	12.12	10.05	8.68	7.70
1000	86.82	45.06	31.16	24.24	20.10	17.35	15.40
2000	173.63	90.12	62.33	48.48	40.20	34.70	30.80
5000	434.08	225.29	155.82	121.19	100.49	86.76	77.01
6000	520.90	270.35	186.99	145.43	120.59	104.11	92.41
7000	607.71	315.40	218.15	169.67	140.69	121.46	107.81
8000	694.53	360.46	249.32	193.91	160.79	138.82	123.21
9000	781.35	405.52	280.48	218.15	180.89	156.17	138.61
10000	868.16	450.58	311.65	242.39	200.99	173.52	154.01
12000	1041.80	540.69	373.98	290.86	241.18	208.22	184.82
15000	1302.25	675.87	467.47	363.58	301.48	260.28	231.02
20000	1736.33	901.15	623.30	484.77	401.97	347.04	308.03
25000	2170.41	1126.44	779.12	605.96	502.47	433.80	385.04
30000	2604.49	1351.73	934.95	727.16	602.96	520.56	462.04
31000	2691.31	1396.79	966.11	751.40	623.06	537.91	477.44
32000	2778.13	1441.85	997.28	775.63	643.16	555.27	492.84
33000	2864.94	1486.90	1028.44	799.87	663.26	572.62	508.25
34000	2951.76	1531.96	1059.61	824.11	683.36	589.97	523.65
35000	3038.57	1577.02	1090.77	848.35	703.45	607.32	539.05
36000	3125.39	1622.08	1121.94	872.59	723.55	624.67	554.45
37000	3212.21	1667.14	1153.10	896.83	743.65	642.03	569.85
38000	3299.02	1712.19	1184.27	921.07	763.75	659.38	585.25
39000	3385.84	1757.25	1215.43	945.30	783.85	676.73	600.65
40000	3472.66	1802.31	1246.60	969.54	803.95	694.08	616.06
41000	3559.47	1847.37	1277.76	993.78	824.05	711.43	631.46
42000	3646.29	1892.42	1308.93	1018.02	844.15	728.79	646.86
43000	3733.11	1937.48	1340.09	1042.26	864.24	746.14	662.26
44000	3819.92	1982.54	1371.26	1066.50	884.34	763.49	677.66
45000	3906.74	2027.60	1402.42	1090.74	904.44	780.84	693.06
46000	3993.55	2072.65	1433.59	1114.97	924.54	798.19	708.46
47000	4080.37	2117.71	1464.75	1139.21	944.64	815.55	723.87
48000	4167.19	2162.77	1495.92	1163.45	964.74	832.90	739.27
49000	4254.00	2207.83	1527.08	1187.69	984.84	850.25	754.67
50000	4340.82	2252.89	1558.25	1211.93	1004.94	867.60	770.07
51000	4427.64	2297.94	1589.41	1236.17	1025.03	884.95	785.47
52000	4514.45	2343.00	1620.58	1260.41	1045.13	902.31	800.87
53000	4601.27	2388.06	1651.74	1284.64	1065.23	919.66	816.27
54000	4688.09	2433.12	1682.91	1308.88	1085.33	937.01	831.68
55000	4774.90	2478.17	1714.07	1333.12	1105.43	954.36	847.08
56000	4861.72	2523.23	1745.24	1357.36	1125.53	971.71	862.48
57000	4948.54	2568.29	1776.40	1381.60	1145.63	989.07	877.88
58000	5035.35	2613.35	1807.57	1405.84	1165.73	1006.42	893.28
59000	5122.17	2658.40	1838.73	1430.08	1185.82	1023.77	908.68
60000	5208.98	2703.46	1869.90	1454.31	1205.92	1041.12	924.08
65000	5643.07	2928.75	2025.72	1575.51	1306.42	1127.88	1001.09
70000	6077.15	3154.04	2181.54	1696.70	1406.91	1214.64	1078.10
75000	6511.23	3379.33	2337.37	1817.89	1507.40	1301.40	1155.11
80000	6945.31	3604.62	2493.19	1939.09	1607.90	1388.16	1232.11
85000	7379.39	3829.91	2649.02	2060.28	1708.39	1474.92	1309.12
90000	7813.48	4055.19	2804.84	2181.47	1808.88	1561.68	1386.13
95000	8247.56	4280.48	2960.67	2302.66	1909.38	1648.44	1463.13
100000	8681.64	4505.77	3116.49	2423.86	2009.87	1735.20	1540.14
105000	9115.72	4731.06	3272.32	2545.05	2110.36	1821.96	1617.15
110000	9549.81	4956.35	3428.14	2666.24	2210.86	1908.72	1694.15
120000	10417.97	5406.92	3739.79	2908.63	2411.85	2082.24	1848.17
130000	11286.13	5857.50	4051.44	3151.01	2612.83	2255.77	2002.18
140000	12154.30	6308.08	4363.09	3393.40	2813.82	2429.29	2156.20
150000	13022.46	6758.66	4674.74	3635.78	3014.81	2602.81	2310.21
160000	13890.63	7209.23	4986.39	3878.17	3215.79	2776.33	2464.22
170000	14758.79	7659.81	5298.04	4120.56	3416.78	2949.85	2618.24
180000	15626.95	8110.39	5609.69	4362.94	3617.77	3123.37	2772.25
190000	16495.12	8560.96	5921.34	4605.33	3818.76	3296.89	2926.27
200000	17363.28	9011.54	6232.99	4847.71	4019.74	3470.41	3080.28
210000	18231.45	9462.12	6544.63	5090.10	4220.73	3643.93	3234.29
220000	19099.61	9912.70	6856.28	5332.48	4421.72	3817.45	3388.31
230000	19967.77	10363.27	7167.93	5574.87	4622.70	3990.97	3542.32
240000	20835.94	10813.85	7479.58	5817.26	4823.69	4164.49	3696.34
250000	21704.10	11264.43	7791.23	6059.64	5024.68	4338.01	3850.35

Monthly Payments 7.75 %

LOAN AMOUNT	8	9	10	11	12	13	14
			YEARS				
100	1.39	1.28	1.19	1.12	1.06	1.01	0.97
200	2.79	2.57	2.39	2.24	2.12	2.02	1.94
500	6.97	6.41	5.97	5.61	5.31	5.06	4.85
1000	13.95	12.83	11.94	11.22	10.62	10.12	9.70
2000	27.90	25.65	23.87	22.43	21.24	20.25	19.41
5000	69.74	64.13	59.68	56.08	53.11	50.62	48.52
6000	83.69	76.96	71.62	67.30	63.73	60.74	58.22
7000	97.64	89.79	83.56	78.51	74.35	70.87	67.92
8000	111.59	102.61	95.50	89.73	84.97	80.99	77.62
9000	125.53	115.44	107.43	100.94	95.59	91.12	87.33
10000	139.48	128.27	119.37	112.16	106.21	101.24	97.03
12000	167.38	153.92	143.24	134.59	127.46	121.49	116.44
15000	209.22	192.40	179.05	168.24	159.32	151.86	145.55
20000	278.96	256.53	238.74	224.32	212.43	202.48	194.06
25000	348.71	320.66	298.42	280.40	265.54	253.10	242.58
30000	418.45	384.80	358.11	336.48	318.64	303.72	291.09
31000	432.39	397.62	370.05	347.70	329.27	313.85	300.79
32000	446.34	410.45	381.98	358.91	339.89	323.97	310.50
33000	460.29	423.28	393.92	370.13	350.51	334.10	320.20
34000	474.24	436.10	405.86	381.34	361.13	344.22	329.90
35000	488.19	448.93	417.79	392.56	371.75	354.34	339.61
36000	502.14	461.76	429.73	403.78	382.37	364.47	349.31
37000	516.08	474.58	441.67	414.99	392.99	374.59	359.01
38000	530.03	487.41	453.60	426.21	403.62	384.72	368.71
39000	543.98	500.24	465.54	437.42	414.24	394.84	378.42
40000	557.93	513.06	477.48	448.64	424.86	404.96	388.12
41000	571.88	525.89	489.42	459.86	435.48	415.09	397.82
42000	585.82	538.72	501.35	471.07	446.10	425.21	407.53
43000	599.77	551.54	513.29	482.29	456.72	435.34	417.23
44000	613.72	564.37	525.23	493.50	467.34	445.46	426.93
45000	627.67	577.20	537.16	504.72	477.97	455.58	436.64
46000	641.62	590.02	549.10	515.94	488.59	465.71	446.34
47000	655.57	602.85	561.04	527.15	499.21	475.83	456.04
48000	669.51	615.68	572.97	538.37	509.83	485.96	465.74
49000	683.46	628.50	584.91	549.58	520.45	496.08	475.45
50000	697.41	641.33	596.85	560.80	531.07	506.21	485.15
51000	711.36	654.16	608.78	572.02	541.69	516.33	494.85
52000	725.31	666.98	620.72	583.23	552.32	526.45	504.56
53000	739.26	679.81	632.66	594.45	562.94	536.58	514.26
54000	753.20	692.64	644.60	605.66	573.56	546.70	523.96
55000	767.15	705.46	656.53	616.88	584.18	556.83	533.67
56000	781.10	718.29	668.47	628.10	594.80	566.95	543.37
57000	795.05	731.12	680.41	639.31	605.42	577.07	553.07
58000	809.00	743.94	692.34	650.53	616.05	587.20	562.77
59000	822.94	756.77	704.28	661.74	626.67	597.32	572.48
60000	836.89	769.59	716.22	672.96	637.29	607.45	582.18
65000	906.63	833.73	775.90	729.04	690.40	658.07	630.70
70000	976.37	897.86	835.59	785.12	743.50	708.69	679.21
75000	1046.12	961.99	895.27	841.20	796.61	759.31	727.73
80000	1115.86	1026.13	954.96	897.28	849.72	809.93	776.24
85000	1185.60	1090.26	1014.64	953.36	902.82	860.55	824.76
90000	1255.34	1154.39	1074.33	1009.44	955.93	911.17	873.27
95000	1325.08	1218.53	1134.01	1065.52	1009.04	961.79	921.79
100000	1394.82	1282.66	1193.70	1121.60	1062.15	1012.41	970.30
105000	1464.56	1346.79	1253.38	1177.68	1115.25	1063.03	1018.82
110000	1534.30	1410.92	1313.07	1233.76	1168.36	1113.65	1067.33
120000	1673.79	1539.19	1432.44	1345.92	1274.58	1214.89	1164.36
130000	1813.27	1667.46	1551.80	1458.08	1380.79	1316.13	1261.39
140000	1952.75	1795.72	1671.17	1570.24	1487.01	1417.37	1358.42
150000	2092.23	1923.99	1790.54	1682.40	1593.22	1518.62	1455.45
160000	2231.71	2052.25	1909.91	1794.56	1699.43	1619.86	1552.48
170000	2371.20	2180.52	2029.28	1906.72	1805.65	1721.10	1649.51
180000	2510.68	2308.78	2148.65	2018.88	1911.86	1822.34	1746.54
190000	2650.16	2437.05	2268.02	2131.04	2018.08	1923.58	1843.57
200000	2789.64	2565.32	2387.39	2243.20	2124.29	2024.82	1940.60
210000	2929.12	2693.58	2506.76	2355.36	2230.51	2126.06	2037.63
220000	3068.61	2821.85	2626.13	2467.52	2336.72	2227.30	2134.66
230000	3208.09	2950.11	2745.50	2579.68	2442.94	2328.54	2231.69
240000	3347.57	3078.38	2864.87	2691.84	2549.15	2429.78	2328.72
250000	3487.05	3206.64	2984.24	2804.00	2655.37	2531.03	2425.75

7.75 % Monthly Payments

LOAN AMOUNT	15	16	17	18	19	20	21
				YEARS			
100	0.93	0.90	0.88	0.85	0.83	0.81	0.80
200	1.87	1.81	1.75	1.71	1.66	1.63	1.59
500	4.67	4.52	4.38	4.26	4.16	4.07	3.99
1000	9.34	9.03	8.76	8.53	8.32	8.13	7.97
2000	18.69	18.06	17.52	17.05	16.64	16.27	15.94
5000	46.71	45.16	43.81	42.63	41.59	40.67	39.86
6000	56.06	54.19	52.57	51.16	49.91	48.81	47.83
7000	65.40	63.23	61.33	59.68	58.23	56.94	55.80
8000	74.74	72.26	70.10	68.21	66.54	65.07	63.77
9000	84.09	81.29	78.86	76.73	74.86	73.21	71.74
10000	93.43	90.32	87.62	85.26	83.18	81.34	79.71
12000	112.11	108.39	105.15	102.31	99.82	97.61	95.65
15000	140.14	135.48	131.43	127.89	124.77	122.01	119.57
20000	186.86	180.64	175.24	170.52	166.36	162.68	159.42
25000	233.57	225.80	219.05	213.15	207.95	203.36	199.28
30000	280.29	270.97	262.86	255.78	249.54	244.03	239.13
31000	289.63	280.00	271.63	264.30	257.86	252.16	247.10
32000	298.97	289.03	280.39	272.83	266.18	260.30	255.07
33000	308.31	298.06	289.15	281.35	274.49	268.43	263.04
34000	317.66	307.09	297.91	289.88	282.81	276.56	271.01
35000	327.00	316.13	306.67	298.41	291.13	284.70	278.99
36000	336.34	325.16	315.44	306.93	299.45	292.83	286.96
37000	345.69	334.19	324.20	315.46	307.77	300.97	294.93
38000	355.03	343.22	332.96	323.98	316.08	309.10	302.90
39000	364.37	352.25	341.72	332.51	324.40	317.23	310.87
40000	373.71	361.29	350.48	341.03	332.72	325.37	318.84
41000	383.06	370.32	359.25	349.56	341.04	333.50	326.81
42000	392.40	379.35	368.01	358.09	349.36	341.64	334.78
43000	401.74	388.38	376.77	366.61	357.67	349.77	342.75
44000	411.09	397.42	385.53	375.14	365.99	357.91	350.72
45000	420.43	406.45	394.30	383.66	374.31	366.04	358.70
46000	429.77	415.48	403.06	392.19	382.63	374.17	366.67
47000	439.11	424.51	411.82	400.72	390.95	382.31	374.64
48000	448.46	433.54	420.58	409.24	399.26	390.44	382.61
49000	457.80	442.58	429.34	417.77	407.58	398.58	390.58
50000	467.14	451.61	438.11	426.29	415.90	406.71	398.55
51000	476.49	460.64	446.87	434.82	424.22	414.85	406.52
52000	485.83	469.67	455.63	443.35	432.54	422.98	414.49
53000	495.17	478.71	464.39	451.87	440.85	431.11	422.46
54000	504.51	487.74	473.15	460.40	449.17	439.25	430.43
55000	513.86	496.77	481.92	468.92	457.49	447.38	438.41
56000	523.20	505.80	490.68	477.45	465.81	455.52	446.38
57000	532.54	514.83	499.44	485.97	474.13	463.65	454.35
58000	541.89	523.87	508.20	494.50	482.44	471.79	462.32
59000	551.23	532.90	516.97	503.03	490.76	479.92	470.29
60000	560.57	541.93	525.73	511.55	499.08	488.05	478.26
65000	607.29	587.09	569.54	554.18	540.67	528.72	518.12
70000	654.00	632.25	613.35	596.81	582.26	569.40	557.97
75000	700.72	677.41	657.16	639.44	623.85	610.07	597.83
80000	747.43	722.57	700.97	682.07	665.44	650.74	637.68
85000	794.14	767.73	744.78	724.70	707.03	691.41	677.54
90000	840.86	812.90	788.59	767.33	748.62	732.08	717.39
95000	887.57	858.06	832.40	809.96	790.21	772.75	757.25
100000	934.29	903.22	876.21	852.59	831.80	813.42	797.10
105000	981.00	948.38	920.02	895.22	873.39	854.09	836.96
110000	1027.72	993.54	963.83	937.85	914.98	894.77	876.81
120000	1121.14	1083.86	1051.45	1023.10	998.16	976.11	956.52
130000	1214.57	1174.18	1139.08	1108.36	1081.34	1057.45	1036.23
140000	1308.00	1264.50	1226.70	1193.62	1164.52	1138.79	1115.94
150000	1401.43	1354.83	1314.32	1278.88	1247.70	1220.13	1195.65
160000	1494.86	1445.15	1401.94	1364.14	1330.88	1301.48	1275.36
170000	1588.29	1535.47	1489.56	1449.40	1414.06	1382.82	1355.07
180000	1681.72	1625.79	1577.18	1534.66	1497.24	1464.16	1434.78
190000	1775.15	1716.11	1664.80	1619.92	1580.42	1545.50	1514.49
200000	1868.57	1806.43	1752.42	1705.17	1663.60	1626.85	1594.20
210000	1962.00	1896.76	1840.05	1790.43	1746.78	1708.19	1673.91
220000	2055.43	1987.08	1927.67	1875.69	1829.96	1789.53	1753.62
230000	2148.86	2077.40	2015.29	1960.95	1913.14	1870.87	1833.33
240000	2242.29	2167.72	2102.91	2046.21	1996.32	1952.21	1913.04
250000	2335.72	2258.04	2190.53	2131.47	2079.50	2033.56	1992.75

Monthly Payments 7.75 %

LOAN AMOUNT	YEARS 22	23	24	25	30	35	40
100	0.78	0.77	0.76	0.75	0.71	0.68	0.67
200	1.57	1.54	1.52	1.49	1.42	1.37	1.34
500	3.91	3.85	3.79	3.74	3.54	3.42	3.34
1000	7.83	7.70	7.58	7.47	7.08	6.83	6.68
2000	15.65	15.39	15.16	14.95	14.16	13.67	13.35
5000	39.13	38.48	37.89	37.37	35.40	34.17	33.38
6000	46.95	46.17	45.47	44.84	42.48	41.00	40.05
7000	54.78	53.87	53.05	52.31	49.56	47.84	46.73
8000	62.60	61.56	60.63	59.79	56.64	54.67	53.40
9000	70.43	69.26	68.21	67.26	63.72	61.50	60.08
10000	78.25	76.95	75.78	74.73	70.80	68.34	66.75
12000	93.91	92.34	90.94	89.68	84.96	82.01	80.10
15000	117.38	115.43	113.68	112.10	106.20	102.51	100.13
20000	156.51	153.91	151.57	149.46	141.60	136.68	133.51
25000	195.64	192.38	189.46	186.83	177.00	170.85	166.88
30000	234.76	230.86	227.35	224.20	212.39	205.02	200.26
31000	242.59	238.55	234.93	231.67	219.47	211.85	206.93
32000	250.42	246.25	242.51	239.14	226.55	218.68	213.61
33000	258.24	253.94	250.09	246.62	233.63	225.52	220.29
34000	266.07	261.64	257.67	254.09	240.71	232.35	226.96
35000	273.89	269.33	265.24	261.56	247.79	239.19	233.64
36000	281.72	277.03	272.82	269.04	254.87	246.02	240.31
37000	289.54	284.72	280.40	276.51	261.95	252.85	246.99
38000	297.37	292.42	287.98	283.98	269.03	259.69	253.66
39000	305.19	300.12	295.56	291.46	276.11	266.52	260.34
40000	313.02	307.81	303.14	298.93	283.19	273.35	267.01
41000	320.84	315.51	310.71	306.40	290.27	280.19	273.69
42000	328.67	323.20	318.29	313.87	297.35	287.02	280.36
43000	336.50	330.90	325.87	321.35	304.43	293.86	287.04
44000	344.32	338.59	333.45	328.82	311.51	300.69	293.71
45000	352.15	346.29	341.03	336.29	318.59	307.52	300.39
46000	359.97	353.98	348.61	343.77	325.67	314.36	307.06
47000	367.80	361.68	356.18	351.24	332.75	321.19	313.74
48000	375.62	369.37	363.76	358.71	339.83	328.03	320.42
49000	383.45	377.07	371.34	366.19	346.91	334.86	327.09
50000	391.27	384.76	378.92	373.66	353.99	341.69	333.77
51000	399.10	392.46	386.50	381.13	361.07	348.53	340.44
52000	406.92	400.15	394.08	388.61	368.15	355.36	347.12
53000	414.75	407.85	401.65	396.08	375.23	362.20	353.79
54000	422.58	415.54	409.23	403.55	382.31	369.03	360.47
55000	430.40	423.24	416.81	411.03	389.39	375.86	367.14
56000	438.23	430.93	424.39	418.50	396.47	382.70	373.82
57000	446.05	438.63	431.97	425.97	403.55	389.53	380.49
58000	453.88	446.33	439.55	433.45	410.63	396.36	387.17
59000	461.70	454.02	447.13	440.92	417.71	403.20	393.84
60000	469.53	461.72	454.70	448.39	424.79	410.03	400.52
65000	508.66	500.19	492.60	485.76	460.19	444.20	433.90
70000	547.78	538.67	530.49	523.12	495.59	478.37	467.27
75000	586.91	577.14	568.38	560.49	530.99	512.54	500.65
80000	626.04	615.62	606.27	597.86	566.39	546.71	534.03
85000	665.17	654.10	644.16	635.22	601.79	580.88	567.40
90000	704.29	692.57	682.06	672.59	637.18	615.05	600.78
95000	743.42	731.05	719.95	709.95	672.58	649.22	634.15
100000	782.55	769.53	757.84	747.32	707.98	683.39	667.53
105000	821.67	808.00	795.73	784.69	743.38	717.56	700.91
110000	860.80	846.48	833.62	822.05	778.78	751.73	734.28
120000	939.06	923.43	909.41	896.79	849.58	820.06	801.04
130000	1017.31	1000.38	985.19	971.52	920.38	888.40	867.79
140000	1095.57	1077.34	1060.98	1046.25	991.18	956.74	934.54
150000	1173.82	1154.29	1136.76	1120.98	1061.97	1025.08	1001.30
160000	1252.08	1231.24	1212.54	1195.71	1132.77	1093.42	1068.05
170000	1330.33	1308.19	1288.33	1270.45	1203.57	1161.76	1134.80
180000	1408.59	1385.15	1364.11	1345.18	1274.37	1230.10	1201.56
190000	1486.84	1462.10	1439.90	1419.91	1345.17	1298.44	1268.31
200000	1565.09	1539.05	1515.68	1494.64	1415.97	1366.77	1335.06
210000	1643.35	1616.00	1591.46	1569.37	1486.76	1435.11	1401.82
220000	1721.60	1692.96	1667.25	1644.11	1557.56	1503.45	1468.57
230000	1799.86	1769.91	1743.03	1718.84	1628.36	1571.79	1535.32
240000	1878.11	1846.86	1818.81	1793.57	1699.16	1640.13	1602.08
250000	1956.37	1923.82	1894.60	1868.30	1769.96	1708.47	1668.83

8.00 % Monthly Payments

LOAN AMOUNT	YEARS 1	2	3	4	5	6	7
100	8.69	4.52	3.13	2.44	2.02	1.75	1.55
200	17.39	9.03	6.26	4.87	4.04	3.49	3.10
500	43.46	22.58	15.64	12.18	10.11	8.73	7.76
1000	86.93	45.17	31.28	24.35	20.21	17.47	15.52
2000	173.86	90.34	62.55	48.70	40.43	34.94	31.04
5000	434.64	225.84	156.38	121.76	101.07	87.35	77.61
6000	521.57	271.01	187.66	146.11	121.28	104.82	93.13
7000	608.50	316.18	218.93	170.46	141.50	122.29	108.65
8000	695.43	361.34	250.21	194.81	161.71	139.76	124.17
9000	782.35	406.51	281.49	219.17	181.93	157.23	139.69
10000	869.28	451.68	312.76	243.52	202.14	174.70	155.21
12000	1043.14	542.02	375.32	292.22	242.57	209.64	186.26
15000	1303.92	677.52	469.15	365.28	303.21	262.05	232.82
20000	1738.57	903.36	625.53	487.04	404.28	349.40	310.43
25000	2173.21	1129.20	781.91	608.80	505.35	436.74	388.04
30000	2607.85	1355.04	938.29	730.56	606.42	524.09	465.64
31000	2694.78	1400.21	969.57	754.91	626.64	541.56	481.16
32000	2781.70	1445.37	1000.84	779.26	646.85	559.03	496.69
33000	2868.63	1490.54	1032.12	803.61	667.07	576.50	512.21
34000	2955.56	1535.71	1063.40	827.96	687.28	593.97	527.73
35000	3042.49	1580.88	1094.67	852.32	707.50	611.44	543.25
36000	3129.42	1626.05	1125.95	876.67	727.71	628.91	558.77
37000	3216.35	1671.21	1157.23	901.02	747.92	646.38	574.29
38000	3303.27	1716.38	1188.50	925.37	768.14	663.85	589.81
39000	3390.20	1761.55	1219.78	949.72	788.35	681.32	605.34
40000	3477.13	1806.72	1251.05	974.07	808.57	698.79	620.86
41000	3564.06	1851.89	1282.33	998.43	828.78	716.26	636.38
42000	3650.99	1897.05	1313.61	1022.78	848.99	733.73	651.90
43000	3737.92	1942.22	1344.88	1047.13	869.21	751.20	667.42
44000	3824.84	1987.39	1376.16	1071.48	889.42	768.67	682.94
45000	3911.77	2032.56	1407.44	1095.83	909.64	786.14	698.46
46000	3998.70	2077.73	1438.71	1120.19	929.85	803.61	713.99
47000	4085.63	2122.89	1469.99	1144.54	950.07	821.08	729.51
48000	4172.56	2168.06	1501.26	1168.89	970.28	838.55	745.03
49000	4259.48	2213.23	1532.54	1193.24	990.49	856.02	760.55
50000	4346.41	2258.40	1563.82	1217.59	1010.71	873.49	776.07
51000	4433.34	2303.57	1595.09	1241.95	1030.92	890.96	791.59
52000	4520.27	2348.73	1626.37	1266.30	1051.14	908.43	807.12
53000	4607.20	2393.90	1657.65	1290.65	1071.35	925.90	822.64
54000	4694.13	2439.07	1688.92	1315.00	1091.56	943.37	838.16
55000	4781.05	2484.24	1720.20	1339.35	1111.78	960.84	853.68
56000	4867.98	2529.41	1751.48	1363.70	1131.99	978.31	869.20
57000	4954.91	2574.57	1782.75	1388.06	1152.21	995.78	884.72
58000	5041.84	2619.74	1814.03	1412.41	1172.42	1013.25	900.24
59000	5128.77	2664.91	1845.30	1436.76	1192.64	1030.72	915.77
60000	5215.70	2710.08	1876.58	1461.11	1212.85	1048.19	931.29
65000	5650.34	2935.92	2032.96	1582.87	1313.92	1135.53	1008.89
70000	6084.98	3161.76	2189.34	1704.63	1414.99	1222.88	1086.50
75000	6519.62	3387.60	2345.73	1826.39	1516.06	1310.23	1164.11
80000	6954.26	3613.44	2502.11	1948.15	1617.13	1397.58	1241.72
85000	7388.90	3839.28	2658.49	2069.91	1718.20	1484.93	1319.32
90000	7823.54	4065.12	2814.87	2191.67	1819.27	1572.28	1396.93
95000	8258.18	4290.96	2971.25	2313.43	1920.34	1659.63	1474.54
100000	8692.83	4516.79	3127.64	2435.19	2021.42	1746.98	1552.14
105000	9127.47	4742.63	3284.02	2556.95	2122.49	1834.32	1629.75
110000	9562.11	4968.47	3440.40	2678.71	2223.56	1921.67	1707.36
120000	10431.39	5420.15	3753.16	2922.22	2425.70	2096.37	1862.57
130000	11300.67	5871.83	4065.93	3165.74	2627.84	2271.07	2017.79
140000	12169.96	6323.51	4378.69	3409.26	2829.98	2445.77	2173.00
150000	13039.24	6775.19	4691.45	3652.78	3032.12	2620.46	2328.22
160000	13908.52	7226.87	5004.22	3896.30	3234.27	2795.16	2483.43
170000	14777.80	7678.55	5316.98	4139.82	3436.41	2969.86	2638.65
180000	15647.09	8130.23	5629.74	4383.34	3638.55	3144.56	2793.86
190000	16516.37	8581.91	5942.51	4626.86	3840.69	3319.25	2949.07
200000	17385.65	9033.59	6255.27	4870.37	4042.83	3493.95	3104.29
210000	18254.93	9485.27	6568.03	5113.89	4244.97	3668.65	3259.50
220000	19124.22	9936.95	6880.80	5357.41	4447.11	3843.35	3414.72
230000	19993.50	10388.63	7193.56	5600.93	4649.26	4018.04	3569.93
240000	20862.78	10840.31	7506.32	5844.45	4851.40	4192.74	3725.15
250000	21732.06	11291.99	7819.09	6087.97	5053.54	4367.44	3880.36

Monthly Payments 8.00 %

LOAN AMOUNT	8	9	10	11	12	13	14
				YEARS			
100	1.41	1.30	1.21	1.13	1.08	1.03	0.98
200	2.81	2.59	2.41	2.27	2.15	2.05	1.97
500	7.04	6.48	6.03	5.67	5.38	5.13	4.92
1000	14.07	12.95	12.06	11.35	10.75	10.26	9.84
2000	28.14	25.90	24.13	22.69	21.51	20.52	19.68
5000	70.35	64.76	60.32	56.73	53.77	51.29	49.20
6000	84.42	77.71	72.38	68.07	64.52	61.55	59.04
7000	98.49	90.66	84.45	79.42	75.27	71.81	68.88
8000	112.56	103.61	96.51	90.76	86.03	82.07	78.72
9000	126.64	116.56	108.58	102.11	96.78	92.32	88.55
10000	140.71	129.51	120.64	113.45	107.53	102.58	98.39
12000	168.85	155.42	144.77	136.15	129.04	123.10	118.07
15000	211.06	194.27	180.96	170.18	161.30	153.87	147.59
20000	281.41	259.03	241.28	226.91	215.07	205.16	196.79
25000	351.77	323.78	301.60	283.64	268.83	256.46	245.99
30000	422.12	388.54	361.92	340.36	322.60	307.75	295.18
31000	436.19	401.49	373.99	351.71	333.35	318.01	305.02
32000	450.26	414.44	386.05	363.06	344.11	328.26	314.86
33000	464.33	427.39	398.11	374.40	354.86	338.52	324.70
34000	478.40	440.35	410.18	385.75	365.61	348.78	334.54
35000	492.47	453.30	422.24	397.09	376.36	359.04	344.38
36000	506.54	466.25	434.31	408.44	387.12	369.30	354.22
37000	520.61	479.20	446.37	419.78	397.87	379.55	364.06
38000	534.68	492.15	458.44	431.13	408.62	389.81	373.90
39000	548.75	505.10	470.50	442.47	419.38	400.07	383.74
40000	562.82	518.05	482.56	453.82	430.13	410.33	393.58
41000	576.90	531.01	494.63	465.16	440.88	420.59	403.42
42000	590.97	543.96	506.69	476.51	451.64	430.85	413.26
43000	605.04	556.91	518.76	487.86	462.39	441.10	423.10
44000	619.11	569.86	530.82	499.20	473.14	451.36	432.93
45000	633.18	582.81	542.88	510.55	483.90	461.62	442.77
46000	647.25	595.76	554.95	521.89	494.65	471.88	452.61
47000	661.32	608.71	567.01	533.24	505.40	482.14	462.45
48000	675.39	621.66	579.08	544.58	516.16	492.40	472.29
49000	689.46	634.62	591.14	555.93	526.91	502.65	482.13
50000	703.53	647.57	603.20	567.27	537.66	512.91	491.97
51000	717.60	660.52	615.27	578.62	548.42	523.17	501.81
52000	731.67	673.47	627.33	589.97	559.17	533.43	511.65
53000	745.74	686.42	639.40	601.31	569.92	543.69	521.49
54000	759.81	699.37	651.46	612.66	580.68	553.94	531.33
55000	773.88	712.32	663.52	624.00	591.43	564.20	541.17
56000	787.95	725.28	675.59	635.35	602.18	574.46	551.01
57000	802.02	738.23	687.65	646.69	612.94	584.72	560.85
58000	816.10	751.18	699.72	658.04	623.69	594.98	570.69
59000	830.17	764.13	711.78	669.38	634.44	605.24	580.53
60000	844.24	777.08	723.85	680.73	645.20	615.49	590.37
65000	914.59	841.84	784.17	737.46	698.96	666.78	639.56
70000	984.94	906.59	844.49	794.18	752.73	718.08	688.76
75000	1055.30	971.35	904.81	850.91	806.50	769.37	737.96
80000	1125.65	1036.11	965.13	907.64	860.26	820.66	787.15
85000	1196.00	1100.86	1025.45	964.37	914.03	871.95	836.35
90000	1266.36	1165.62	1085.77	1021.09	967.80	923.24	885.55
95000	1336.71	1230.38	1146.09	1077.82	1021.56	974.53	934.75
100000	1407.06	1295.13	1206.41	1134.55	1075.33	1025.82	983.94
105000	1477.41	1359.89	1266.73	1191.28	1129.09	1077.11	1033.14
110000	1547.77	1424.65	1327.05	1248.00	1182.86	1128.41	1082.34
120000	1688.47	1554.16	1447.69	1361.46	1290.39	1230.99	1180.73
130000	1829.18	1683.67	1568.33	1474.91	1397.93	1333.57	1279.12
140000	1969.89	1813.19	1688.97	1588.37	1505.46	1436.15	1377.52
150000	2110.59	1942.70	1809.61	1701.82	1612.99	1538.73	1475.91
160000	2251.30	2072.22	1930.25	1815.28	1720.53	1641.32	1574.31
170000	2392.00	2201.73	2050.90	1928.73	1828.06	1743.90	1672.70
180000	2532.71	2331.24	2171.54	2042.19	1935.59	1846.48	1771.10
190000	2673.42	2460.76	2292.18	2155.64	2043.12	1949.06	1869.49
200000	2814.12	2590.27	2412.82	2269.10	2150.66	2051.65	1967.88
210000	2954.83	2719.78	2533.46	2382.55	2258.19	2154.23	2066.28
220000	3095.53	2849.30	2654.10	2496.01	2365.72	2256.81	2164.67
230000	3236.24	2978.81	2774.74	2609.46	2473.26	2359.39	2263.07
240000	3376.95	3108.32	2895.38	2722.92	2580.79	2461.98	2361.46
250000	3517.65	3237.84	3016.02	2836.37	2688.32	2564.56	2459.86

8.00 % Monthly Payments

LOAN AMOUNT	15	16	17	18	19	20	21
100	0.95	0.92	0.89	0.87	0.85	0.83	0.81
200	1.90	1.83	1.78	1.73	1.69	1.66	1.62
500	4.74	4.59	4.45	4.34	4.23	4.14	4.06
1000	9.48	9.17	8.91	8.67	8.47	8.28	8.12
2000	18.96	18.35	17.81	17.34	16.93	16.57	16.24
5000	47.41	45.87	44.53	43.36	42.33	41.42	40.61
6000	56.89	55.04	53.43	52.03	50.79	49.70	48.73
7000	66.37	64.21	62.34	60.70	59.26	57.99	56.86
8000	75.85	73.38	71.24	69.37	67.72	66.27	64.98
9000	85.33	82.56	80.15	78.04	76.19	74.55	73.10
10000	94.82	91.73	89.05	86.71	84.65	82.84	81.22
12000	113.78	110.08	106.86	104.05	101.58	99.40	97.47
15000	142.22	137.60	133.58	130.07	126.98	124.25	121.84
20000	189.63	183.46	178.10	173.42	169.31	165.67	162.45
25000	237.04	229.33	222.63	216.78	211.63	207.09	203.06
30000	284.45	275.19	267.16	260.13	253.96	248.51	243.67
31000	293.93	284.36	276.06	268.80	262.42	256.79	251.79
32000	303.41	293.54	284.97	277.47	270.89	265.07	259.92
33000	312.89	302.71	293.87	286.15	279.36	273.36	268.04
34000	322.37	311.88	302.78	294.82	287.82	281.64	276.16
35000	331.85	321.06	311.68	303.49	296.29	289.93	284.28
36000	341.34	330.23	320.59	312.16	304.75	298.21	292.40
37000	350.82	339.40	329.49	320.83	313.22	306.49	300.53
38000	360.30	348.58	338.40	329.50	321.68	314.78	308.65
39000	369.78	357.75	347.30	338.17	330.15	323.06	316.77
40000	379.26	366.92	356.21	346.84	338.61	331.34	324.89
41000	388.74	376.09	365.11	355.51	347.08	339.63	333.02
42000	398.22	385.27	374.02	364.18	355.54	347.91	341.14
43000	407.71	394.44	382.92	372.86	364.01	356.19	349.26
44000	417.19	403.61	391.83	381.53	372.47	364.48	357.38
45000	426.67	412.79	400.73	390.20	380.94	372.76	365.51
46000	436.15	421.96	409.64	398.87	389.40	381.04	373.63
47000	445.63	431.13	418.54	407.54	397.87	389.33	381.75
48000	455.11	440.31	427.45	416.21	406.33	397.61	389.87
49000	464.59	449.48	436.35	424.88	414.80	405.90	398.00
50000	474.08	458.65	445.26	433.55	423.27	414.18	406.12
51000	483.56	467.83	454.16	442.22	431.73	422.46	414.24
52000	493.04	477.00	463.07	450.90	440.20	430.75	422.36
53000	502.52	486.17	471.97	459.57	448.66	439.03	430.49
54000	512.00	495.34	480.88	468.24	457.13	447.31	438.61
55000	521.48	504.52	489.78	476.91	465.59	455.60	446.73
56000	530.97	513.69	498.69	485.58	474.06	463.88	454.85
57000	540.45	522.86	507.59	494.25	482.52	472.16	462.97
58000	549.93	532.04	516.50	502.92	490.99	480.45	471.10
59000	559.41	541.21	525.41	511.59	499.45	488.73	479.22
60000	568.89	550.38	534.31	520.26	507.92	497.01	487.34
65000	616.30	596.25	578.84	563.62	550.24	538.43	527.95
70000	663.71	642.11	623.36	606.97	592.57	579.85	568.57
75000	711.11	687.98	667.89	650.33	634.90	621.27	609.18
80000	758.52	733.84	712.41	693.69	677.22	662.69	649.79
85000	805.93	779.71	756.94	737.04	719.55	704.10	690.40
90000	853.34	825.57	801.47	780.40	761.88	745.52	731.01
95000	900.75	871.44	845.99	823.75	804.20	786.94	771.62
100000	948.15	917.30	890.52	867.11	846.53	828.36	812.24
105000	995.56	963.17	935.04	910.46	888.86	869.78	852.85
110000	1042.97	1009.04	979.57	953.82	931.18	911.19	893.46
120000	1137.78	1100.77	1068.62	1040.53	1015.84	994.03	974.68
130000	1232.60	1192.50	1157.67	1127.24	1100.49	1076.86	1055.91
140000	1327.41	1284.23	1246.72	1213.95	1185.14	1159.70	1137.13
150000	1422.23	1375.96	1335.78	1300.66	1269.80	1242.54	1218.35
160000	1517.04	1467.69	1424.83	1387.37	1354.45	1325.37	1299.58
170000	1611.86	1559.42	1513.88	1474.08	1439.10	1408.21	1380.80
180000	1706.68	1651.15	1602.93	1560.79	1523.76	1491.04	1462.02
190000	1801.49	1742.88	1691.98	1647.50	1608.41	1573.88	1543.25
200000	1896.31	1834.61	1781.03	1734.21	1693.06	1656.71	1624.47
210000	1991.12	1926.34	1870.09	1820.92	1777.71	1739.55	1705.70
220000	2085.94	2018.07	1959.14	1907.63	1862.37	1822.39	1786.92
230000	2180.75	2109.80	2048.19	1994.34	1947.02	1905.22	1868.14
240000	2275.57	2201.53	2137.24	2081.06	2031.67	1988.06	1949.37
250000	2370.38	2293.26	2226.29	2167.77	2116.33	2070.89	2030.59

Monthly Payments 8.00 %

LOAN AMOUNT	22	23	24	25	30	35	40
100	0.80	0.79	0.77	0.76	0.72	0.70	0.69
200	1.60	1.57	1.55	1.53	1.45	1.40	1.37
500	3.99	3.93	3.87	3.82	3.62	3.50	3.43
1000	7.98	7.85	7.74	7.63	7.25	7.01	6.86
2000	15.96	15.70	15.47	15.26	14.49	14.02	13.71
5000	39.89	39.25	38.68	38.16	36.24	35.04	34.28
6000	47.87	47.10	46.41	45.79	43.48	42.05	41.13
7000	55.85	54.95	54.15	53.42	50.73	49.06	47.99
8000	63.83	62.80	61.88	61.06	57.98	56.07	54.84
9000	71.81	70.65	69.62	68.69	65.22	63.07	61.70
10000	79.79	78.50	77.35	76.32	72.47	70.08	68.56
12000	95.75	94.21	92.83	91.59	86.97	84.10	82.27
15000	119.68	117.76	116.03	114.48	108.71	105.12	102.83
20000	159.58	157.01	154.71	152.64	144.94	140.17	137.11
25000	199.47	196.26	193.39	190.80	181.18	175.21	171.39
30000	239.36	235.51	232.06	228.96	217.41	210.25	205.67
31000	247.34	243.37	239.80	236.60	224.66	217.26	212.52
32000	255.32	251.22	247.54	244.23	231.91	224.26	219.38
33000	263.30	259.07	255.27	251.86	239.15	231.27	226.24
34000	271.28	266.92	263.01	259.49	246.40	238.28	233.09
35000	279.26	274.77	270.74	267.12	253.65	245.29	239.95
36000	287.24	282.62	278.48	274.76	260.90	252.30	246.80
37000	295.22	290.47	286.21	282.39	268.14	259.31	253.66
38000	303.19	298.32	293.95	290.02	275.39	266.31	260.51
39000	311.17	306.17	301.68	297.65	282.64	273.32	267.37
40000	319.15	314.02	309.42	305.29	289.88	280.33	274.22
41000	327.13	321.87	317.16	312.92	297.13	287.34	281.08
42000	335.11	329.72	324.89	320.55	304.38	294.35	287.94
43000	343.09	337.57	332.63	328.18	311.63	301.36	294.79
44000	351.07	345.42	340.36	335.81	318.87	308.36	301.65
45000	359.05	353.27	348.10	343.45	326.12	315.37	308.50
46000	367.02	361.12	355.83	351.08	333.37	322.38	315.36
47000	375.00	368.97	363.57	358.71	340.61	329.39	322.21
48000	382.98	376.82	371.30	366.34	347.86	336.40	329.07
49000	390.96	384.67	379.04	373.97	355.11	343.40	335.93
50000	398.94	392.52	386.77	381.61	362.36	350.41	342.78
51000	406.92	400.38	394.51	389.24	369.60	357.42	349.64
52000	414.90	408.23	402.25	396.87	376.85	364.43	356.49
53000	422.88	416.08	409.98	404.50	384.10	371.44	363.35
54000	430.85	423.93	417.72	412.14	391.34	378.45	370.20
55000	438.83	431.78	425.45	419.77	398.59	385.45	377.06
56000	446.81	439.63	433.19	427.40	405.84	392.46	383.91
57000	454.79	447.48	440.92	435.03	413.09	399.47	390.77
58000	462.77	455.33	448.66	442.66	420.33	406.48	397.63
59000	470.75	463.18	456.39	450.30	427.58	413.49	404.48
60000	478.73	471.03	464.13	457.93	434.83	420.50	411.34
65000	518.62	510.28	502.81	496.09	471.06	455.54	445.62
70000	558.52	549.53	541.48	534.25	507.30	490.58	479.89
75000	598.41	588.79	580.16	572.41	543.53	525.62	514.17
80000	638.30	628.04	618.84	610.57	579.77	560.66	548.45
85000	678.20	667.29	657.52	648.73	616.00	595.70	582.73
90000	718.09	706.54	696.19	686.89	652.24	630.74	617.01
95000	757.99	745.80	734.87	725.05	688.48	665.79	651.28
100000	797.88	785.05	773.55	763.21	724.71	700.83	685.56
105000	837.77	824.30	812.23	801.37	760.95	735.87	719.84
110000	877.67	863.55	850.90	839.53	797.18	770.91	754.12
120000	957.45	942.06	928.26	915.86	869.65	840.99	822.67
130000	1037.24	1020.56	1005.61	992.18	942.12	911.07	891.23
140000	1117.03	1099.07	1082.97	1068.50	1014.60	981.16	959.79
150000	1196.82	1177.57	1160.32	1144.82	1087.07	1051.24	1028.34
160000	1276.61	1256.08	1237.68	1221.14	1159.54	1121.32	1096.90
170000	1356.39	1334.58	1315.03	1297.46	1232.01	1191.40	1165.46
180000	1436.18	1413.09	1392.39	1373.78	1304.48	1261.49	1234.01
190000	1515.97	1491.59	1469.74	1450.11	1376.95	1331.57	1302.57
200000	1595.76	1570.10	1547.10	1526.43	1449.42	1401.65	1371.12
210000	1675.55	1648.60	1624.45	1602.75	1521.89	1471.74	1439.68
220000	1755.33	1727.11	1701.81	1679.07	1594.36	1541.82	1508.24
230000	1835.12	1805.61	1779.16	1755.39	1666.84	1611.90	1576.79
240000	1914.91	1884.12	1856.52	1831.71	1739.31	1681.98	1645.35
250000	1994.70	1962.62	1933.87	1908.03	1811.78	1752.07	1713.91

Columns 22–40: YEARS

8.25 % Monthly Payments

LOAN AMOUNT	YEARS 1	2	3	4	5	6	7
100	8.70	4.53	3.14	2.45	2.03	1.76	1.56
200	17.41	9.06	6.28	4.89	4.07	3.52	3.13
500	43.52	22.64	15.69	12.23	10.16	8.79	7.82
1000	87.04	45.28	31.39	24.47	20.33	17.59	15.64
2000	174.08	90.56	62.78	48.93	40.66	35.18	31.28
5000	435.20	226.39	156.94	122.33	101.65	87.94	78.21
6000	522.24	271.67	188.33	146.79	121.98	105.53	93.85
7000	609.28	316.95	219.72	171.26	142.31	123.11	109.49
8000	696.32	362.23	251.10	195.72	162.64	140.70	125.14
9000	783.36	407.50	282.49	220.19	182.97	158.29	140.78
10000	870.40	452.78	313.88	244.65	203.30	175.88	156.42
12000	1044.48	543.34	376.65	293.58	243.96	211.05	187.70
15000	1305.60	679.17	470.82	366.98	304.95	263.82	234.63
20000	1740.80	905.56	627.76	489.31	406.60	351.76	312.84
25000	2176.00	1131.96	784.70	611.63	508.25	439.70	391.05
30000	2611.20	1358.35	941.64	733.96	609.90	527.63	469.26
31000	2698.24	1403.63	973.03	758.43	630.23	545.22	484.90
32000	2785.28	1448.90	1004.41	782.89	650.56	562.81	500.54
33000	2872.32	1494.18	1035.80	807.36	670.89	580.40	516.18
34000	2959.36	1539.46	1067.19	831.82	691.22	597.99	531.82
35000	3046.40	1584.74	1098.58	856.29	711.55	615.57	547.47
36000	3133.44	1630.02	1129.96	880.75	731.88	633.16	563.11
37000	3220.48	1675.29	1161.35	905.22	752.21	650.75	578.75
38000	3307.52	1720.57	1192.74	929.68	772.54	668.34	594.39
39000	3394.56	1765.85	1224.13	954.15	792.87	685.92	610.03
40000	3481.60	1811.13	1255.52	978.62	813.20	703.51	625.68
41000	3568.64	1856.41	1286.90	1003.08	833.53	721.10	641.32
42000	3655.68	1901.69	1318.29	1027.55	853.86	738.69	656.96
43000	3742.72	1946.96	1349.68	1052.01	874.18	756.28	672.60
44000	3829.76	1992.24	1381.07	1076.48	894.51	773.86	688.24
45000	3916.80	2037.52	1412.46	1100.94	914.84	791.45	703.89
46000	4003.84	2082.80	1443.84	1125.41	935.17	809.04	719.53
47000	4090.88	2128.08	1475.23	1149.87	955.50	826.63	735.17
48000	4177.92	2173.36	1506.62	1174.34	975.83	844.22	750.81
49000	4264.96	2218.63	1538.01	1198.80	996.16	861.80	766.45
50000	4352.00	2263.91	1569.40	1223.27	1016.49	879.39	782.10
51000	4439.04	2309.19	1600.78	1247.73	1036.82	896.98	797.74
52000	4526.08	2354.47	1632.17	1272.20	1057.15	914.57	813.38
53000	4613.12	2399.75	1663.56	1296.67	1077.48	932.15	829.02
54000	4700.16	2445.03	1694.95	1321.13	1097.81	949.74	844.66
55000	4787.20	2490.30	1726.34	1345.60	1118.14	967.33	860.31
56000	4874.24	2535.58	1757.72	1370.06	1138.47	984.92	875.95
57000	4961.28	2580.86	1789.11	1394.53	1158.80	1002.51	891.59
58000	5048.32	2626.14	1820.50	1418.99	1179.13	1020.09	907.23
59000	5135.36	2671.42	1851.89	1443.46	1199.46	1037.68	922.87
60000	5222.40	2716.69	1883.27	1467.92	1219.79	1055.27	938.51
65000	5657.60	2943.09	2040.21	1590.25	1321.44	1143.21	1016.72
70000	6092.81	3169.48	2197.15	1712.58	1423.09	1231.15	1094.93
75000	6528.01	3395.87	2354.09	1834.90	1524.74	1319.09	1173.14
80000	6963.21	3622.26	2511.03	1957.23	1626.39	1407.03	1251.35
85000	7398.41	3848.65	2667.97	2079.56	1728.04	1494.96	1329.56
90000	7833.61	4075.04	2824.91	2201.88	1829.69	1582.90	1407.77
95000	8268.81	4301.43	2981.85	2324.21	1931.34	1670.84	1485.98
100000	8704.01	4527.82	3138.79	2446.54	2032.99	1758.78	1564.19
105000	9139.21	4754.22	3295.73	2568.86	2134.64	1846.72	1642.40
110000	9574.41	4980.61	3452.67	2691.19	2236.29	1934.66	1720.61
120000	10444.81	5433.39	3766.55	2935.85	2439.59	2110.54	1877.03
130000	11315.21	5886.17	4080.43	3180.50	2642.88	2286.42	2033.45
140000	12185.61	6338.95	4394.31	3425.15	2846.18	2462.29	2189.87
150000	13056.01	6791.74	4708.19	3669.81	3049.48	2638.17	2346.29
160000	13926.41	7244.52	5022.07	3914.46	3252.78	2814.05	2502.71
170000	14796.81	7697.30	5335.94	4159.11	3456.08	2989.93	2659.12
180000	15667.21	8150.08	5649.82	4403.77	3659.38	3165.81	2815.54
190000	16537.61	8602.87	5963.70	4648.42	3862.68	3341.69	2971.96
200000	17408.01	9055.65	6277.58	4893.08	4065.98	3517.56	3128.38
210000	18278.42	9508.43	6591.46	5137.73	4269.28	3693.44	3284.80
220000	19148.82	9961.21	6905.34	5382.38	4472.57	3869.32	3441.22
230000	20019.22	10414.00	7219.22	5627.04	4675.87	4045.20	3597.64
240000	20889.62	10866.78	7533.10	5871.69	4879.17	4221.08	3754.06
250000	21760.02	11319.56	7846.98	6116.34	5082.47	4396.95	3910.48

Monthly Payments 8.25 %

LOAN AMOUNT	8	9	10	11	12	13	14
				YEARS			
100	1.42	1.31	1.22	1.15	1.09	1.04	1.00
200	2.84	2.62	2.44	2.30	2.18	2.08	2.00
500	7.10	6.54	6.10	5.74	5.44	5.20	4.99
1000	14.19	13.08	12.19	11.48	10.89	10.39	9.98
2000	28.39	26.15	24.38	22.95	21.77	20.79	19.95
5000	70.97	65.38	60.96	57.38	54.43	51.97	49.88
6000	85.16	78.46	73.15	68.85	65.32	62.36	59.86
7000	99.35	91.54	85.34	80.33	76.20	72.75	69.84
8000	113.55	104.61	97.53	91.81	87.09	83.15	79.81
9000	127.74	117.69	109.73	103.28	97.97	93.54	89.79
10000	141.94	130.77	121.92	114.76	108.86	103.93	99.77
12000	170.32	156.92	146.30	137.71	130.63	124.72	119.72
15000	212.90	196.15	182.88	172.13	163.29	155.90	149.65
20000	283.87	261.53	243.84	229.51	217.72	207.86	199.53
25000	354.84	326.92	304.80	286.89	272.15	259.83	249.42
30000	425.81	392.30	365.76	344.27	326.58	311.79	299.30
31000	440.00	405.38	377.95	355.75	337.46	322.19	309.28
32000	454.19	418.45	390.14	367.22	348.35	332.58	319.25
33000	468.39	431.53	402.33	378.70	359.23	342.97	329.23
34000	482.58	444.61	414.52	390.17	370.12	353.37	339.21
35000	496.77	457.68	426.71	401.65	381.00	363.76	349.18
36000	510.97	470.76	438.91	413.12	391.89	374.15	359.16
37000	525.16	483.84	451.10	424.60	402.78	384.55	369.14
38000	539.35	496.91	463.29	436.08	413.66	394.94	379.11
39000	553.55	509.99	475.48	447.55	424.55	405.33	389.09
40000	567.74	523.07	487.67	459.03	435.43	415.73	399.07
41000	581.93	536.14	499.87	470.50	446.32	426.12	409.04
42000	596.13	549.22	512.06	481.98	457.21	436.51	419.02
43000	610.32	562.30	524.25	493.45	468.09	446.91	429.00
44000	624.51	575.37	536.44	504.93	478.98	457.30	438.97
45000	638.71	588.45	548.63	516.40	489.86	467.69	448.95
46000	652.90	601.53	560.83	527.88	500.75	478.09	458.93
47000	667.09	614.60	573.02	539.36	511.64	488.48	468.90
48000	681.29	627.68	585.21	550.83	522.52	498.87	478.88
49000	695.48	640.76	597.40	562.31	533.41	509.27	488.86
50000	709.68	653.83	609.59	573.78	544.29	519.66	498.83
51000	723.87	666.91	621.78	585.26	555.18	530.05	508.81
52000	738.06	679.99	633.98	596.73	566.06	540.44	518.79
53000	752.26	693.06	646.17	608.21	576.95	550.84	528.76
54000	766.45	706.14	658.36	619.69	587.84	561.23	538.74
55000	780.64	719.22	670.55	631.16	598.72	571.62	548.72
56000	794.84	732.29	682.74	642.64	609.61	582.02	558.69
57000	809.03	745.37	694.94	654.11	620.49	592.41	568.67
58000	823.22	758.45	707.13	665.59	631.38	602.80	578.65
59000	837.42	771.52	719.32	677.06	642.27	613.20	588.63
60000	851.61	784.60	731.51	688.54	653.15	623.59	598.60
65000	922.58	849.98	792.47	745.92	707.58	675.56	648.49
70000	993.55	915.37	853.43	803.30	762.01	727.52	698.37
75000	1064.51	980.75	914.39	860.67	816.44	779.49	748.25
80000	1135.48	1046.13	975.35	918.05	870.87	831.45	798.14
85000	1206.45	1111.52	1036.31	975.43	925.30	883.42	848.02
90000	1277.42	1176.90	1097.27	1032.81	979.73	935.38	897.90
95000	1348.38	1242.28	1158.23	1090.19	1034.16	987.35	947.79
100000	1419.35	1307.67	1219.18	1147.57	1088.59	1039.32	997.67
105000	1490.32	1373.05	1280.14	1204.94	1143.01	1091.28	1047.55
110000	1561.29	1438.43	1341.10	1262.32	1197.44	1143.25	1097.44
120000	1703.22	1569.20	1463.02	1377.08	1306.30	1247.18	1197.20
130000	1845.16	1699.97	1584.94	1491.84	1415.16	1351.11	1296.97
140000	1987.09	1830.73	1706.86	1606.59	1524.02	1455.04	1396.74
150000	2129.03	1961.50	1828.78	1721.35	1632.88	1558.97	1496.50
160000	2270.96	2092.27	1950.70	1836.11	1741.74	1662.91	1596.27
170000	2412.90	2223.03	2072.61	1950.86	1850.59	1766.84	1696.04
180000	2554.83	2353.80	2194.53	2065.62	1959.45	1870.77	1795.81
190000	2696.77	2484.57	2316.45	2180.38	2068.31	1974.70	1895.57
200000	2838.70	2615.33	2438.37	2295.13	2177.17	2078.63	1995.34
210000	2980.64	2746.10	2560.29	2409.89	2286.03	2182.56	2095.11
220000	3122.57	2876.87	2682.21	2524.65	2394.89	2286.50	2194.87
230000	3264.51	3007.64	2804.13	2639.40	2503.75	2390.43	2294.64
240000	3406.44	3138.40	2926.04	2754.16	2612.60	2494.36	2394.41
250000	3548.38	3269.17	3047.96	2868.92	2721.46	2598.29	2494.17

8.25 % Monthly Payments

LOAN AMOUNT	YEARS 15	16	17	18	19	20	21
100	0.96	0.93	0.90	0.88	0.86	0.84	0.83
200	1.92	1.86	1.81	1.76	1.72	1.69	1.65
500	4.81	4.66	4.52	4.41	4.31	4.22	4.14
1000	9.62	9.31	9.05	8.82	8.61	8.43	8.27
2000	19.24	18.63	18.10	17.63	17.23	16.87	16.55
5000	48.11	46.57	45.25	44.09	43.07	42.17	41.37
6000	57.73	55.89	54.30	52.90	51.68	50.60	49.65
7000	67.35	65.20	63.34	61.72	60.30	59.04	57.92
8000	76.97	74.52	72.39	70.54	68.91	67.47	66.2
9000	86.59	83.83	81.44	79.36	77.52	75.91	74.47
10000	96.21	93.15	90.49	88.17	86.14	84.34	82.75
12000	115.45	111.78	108.59	105.81	103.36	101.21	99.3
15000	144.32	139.72	135.74	132.26	129.21	126.51	124.1
20000	192.42	186.30	180.98	176.35	172.27	168.68	165.5
25000	240.53	232.87	226.23	220.43	215.34	210.85	206.87
30000	288.63	279.45	271.48	264.52	258.41	253.02	248.25
31000	298.25	288.76	280.53	273.34	267.02	261.46	256.5
32000	307.88	298.08	289.58	282.15	275.64	269.89	264.8
33000	317.50	307.39	298.62	290.97	284.25	278.32	273.07
34000	327.12	316.71	307.67	299.79	292.87	286.76	281.35
35000	336.74	326.02	316.72	308.61	301.48	295.19	289.62
36000	346.36	335.34	325.77	317.42	310.09	303.63	297.89
37000	355.98	344.65	334.82	326.24	318.71	312.06	306.17
38000	365.60	353.97	343.87	335.06	327.32	320.49	314.4
39000	375.22	363.28	352.92	343.87	335.93	328.93	322.72
40000	384.84	372.60	361.97	352.69	344.55	337.36	330.9
41000	394.47	381.91	371.02	361.51	353.16	345.80	339.27
42000	404.09	391.23	380.07	370.33	361.77	354.23	347.5
43000	413.71	400.54	389.12	379.14	370.39	362.66	355.8
44000	423.33	409.85	398.17	387.96	379.00	371.10	364.0
45000	432.95	419.17	407.22	396.78	387.62	379.53	372.37
46000	442.57	428.48	416.26	405.60	396.23	387.97	380.6
47000	452.19	437.80	425.31	414.41	404.84	396.40	388.9
48000	461.81	447.11	434.36	423.23	413.46	404.83	397.1
49000	471.43	456.43	443.41	432.05	422.07	413.27	405.4
50000	481.06	465.74	452.46	440.87	430.68	421.70	413.7
51000	490.68	475.06	461.51	449.68	439.30	430.14	422.0
52000	500.30	484.37	470.56	458.50	447.91	438.57	430.2
53000	509.92	493.69	479.61	467.32	456.53	447.00	438.57
54000	519.54	503.00	488.66	476.13	465.14	455.44	446.8
55000	529.16	512.32	497.71	484.95	473.75	463.87	455.1
56000	538.78	521.63	506.76	493.77	482.37	472.31	463.3
57000	548.40	530.95	515.81	502.59	490.98	480.74	471.6
58000	558.02	540.26	524.86	511.40	499.59	489.17	479.9
59000	567.65	549.58	533.90	520.22	508.21	497.61	488.2
60000	577.27	558.89	542.95	529.04	516.82	506.04	496.4
65000	625.37	605.47	588.20	573.12	559.89	548.21	537.8
70000	673.48	652.04	633.45	617.21	602.96	590.38	579.2
75000	721.58	698.62	678.69	661.30	646.03	632.55	620.6
80000	769.69	745.19	723.94	705.38	689.09	674.72	661.9
85000	817.79	791.77	769.18	749.47	732.16	716.89	703.3
90000	865.90	838.34	814.43	793.56	775.23	759.06	744.7
95000	914.00	884.91	859.68	837.64	818.30	801.23	786.1
100000	962.11	931.49	904.92	881.73	861.37	843.40	827.4
105000	1010.22	978.06	950.17	925.82	904.44	885.57	868.8
110000	1058.32	1024.64	995.42	969.90	947.50	927.74	910.2
120000	1154.53	1117.79	1085.91	1058.08	1033.64	1012.08	992.9
130000	1250.74	1210.93	1176.40	1146.25	1119.78	1096.42	1075.7
140000	1346.95	1304.08	1266.89	1234.42	1205.92	1180.77	1158.4
150000	1443.17	1397.23	1357.39	1322.60	1292.05	1265.11	1241.2
160000	1539.38	1490.38	1447.88	1410.77	1378.19	1349.45	1323.9
170000	1635.59	1583.53	1538.37	1498.94	1464.33	1433.79	1406.7
180000	1731.80	1676.68	1628.86	1587.11	1550.46	1518.13	1489.4
190000	1828.01	1769.83	1719.35	1675.29	1636.60	1602.47	1572.2
200000	1924.22	1862.98	1809.85	1763.46	1722.74	1686.81	1654.9
210000	2020.43	1956.13	1900.34	1851.63	1808.87	1771.15	1737.7
220000	2116.64	2049.27	1990.83	1939.81	1895.01	1855.49	1820.4
230000	2212.85	2142.42	2081.32	2027.98	1981.15	1939.83	1903.2
240000	2309.06	2235.57	2171.82	2116.15	2067.28	2024.17	1985.9
250000	2405.28	2328.72	2262.31	2204.33	2153.42	2108.51	2068.7

Monthly Payments 8.25 %

LOAN AMOUNT	22	23	24	25	30	35	40
				YEARS			
100	0.81	0.80	0.79	0.78	0.74	0.72	0.70
200	1.63	1.60	1.58	1.56	1.48	1.44	1.41
500	4.07	4.00	3.95	3.90	3.71	3.59	3.52
1000	8.13	8.01	7.89	7.79	7.42	7.18	7.04
2000	16.27	16.01	15.79	15.58	14.83	14.37	14.07
5000	40.67	40.03	39.47	38.96	37.08	35.92	35.19
6000	48.80	48.04	47.36	46.75	44.49	43.10	42.22
7000	56.93	56.05	55.26	54.55	51.91	50.29	49.26
8000	65.07	64.06	63.15	62.34	59.33	57.47	56.30
9000	73.20	72.06	71.04	70.13	66.74	64.65	63.33
10000	81.33	80.07	78.94	77.92	74.16	71.84	70.37
12000	97.60	96.08	94.73	93.51	88.99	86.21	84.44
15000	122.00	120.10	118.41	116.88	111.23	107.76	105.56
20000	162.67	160.14	157.88	155.85	148.31	143.68	140.74
25000	203.33	200.17	197.35	194.81	185.39	179.60	175.93
30000	244.00	240.21	236.81	233.77	222.47	215.52	211.11
31000	252.13	248.21	244.71	241.56	229.89	222.70	218.15
32000	260.27	256.22	252.60	249.35	237.30	229.88	225.19
33000	268.40	264.23	260.50	257.15	244.72	237.07	232.22
34000	276.53	272.24	268.39	264.94	252.13	244.25	239.26
35000	284.66	280.24	276.28	272.73	259.55	251.44	246.30
36000	292.80	288.25	284.18	280.52	266.96	258.62	253.33
37000	300.93	296.26	292.07	288.31	274.38	265.80	260.37
38000	309.06	304.26	299.97	296.11	281.79	272.99	267.41
39000	317.20	312.27	307.86	303.90	289.21	280.17	274.45
40000	325.33	320.28	315.75	311.69	296.63	287.35	281.48
41000	333.46	328.28	323.65	319.48	304.04	294.54	288.52
42000	341.60	336.29	331.54	327.28	311.46	301.72	295.56
43000	349.73	344.30	339.43	335.07	318.87	308.91	302.59
44000	357.86	352.30	347.33	342.86	326.29	316.09	309.63
45000	366.00	360.31	355.22	350.65	333.70	323.27	316.67
46000	374.13	368.32	363.12	358.45	341.12	330.46	323.70
47000	382.26	376.33	371.01	366.24	348.54	337.64	330.74
48000	390.40	384.33	378.90	374.03	355.95	344.83	337.78
49000	398.53	392.34	386.80	381.82	363.37	352.01	344.82
50000	406.66	400.35	394.69	389.61	370.78	359.19	351.85
51000	414.80	408.35	402.58	397.41	378.20	366.38	358.89
52000	422.93	416.36	410.48	405.20	385.61	373.56	365.93
53000	431.06	424.37	418.37	412.99	393.03	380.75	372.96
54000	439.20	432.37	426.27	420.78	400.44	387.93	380.00
55000	447.33	440.38	434.16	428.58	407.86	395.11	387.04
56000	455.46	448.39	442.05	436.37	415.28	402.30	394.08
57000	463.60	456.39	449.95	444.16	422.69	409.48	401.11
58000	471.73	464.40	457.84	451.95	430.11	416.66	408.15
59000	479.86	472.41	465.74	459.74	437.52	423.85	415.19
60000	488.00	480.42	473.63	467.54	444.94	431.03	422.22
65000	528.66	520.45	513.10	506.50	482.02	466.95	457.41
70000	569.33	560.48	552.57	545.46	519.10	502.87	492.59
75000	610.00	600.52	592.04	584.42	556.17	538.79	527.78
80000	650.66	640.55	631.51	623.38	593.25	574.71	562.96
85000	691.33	680.59	670.97	662.34	630.33	610.63	598.15
90000	732.00	720.62	710.44	701.31	667.41	646.55	633.34
95000	772.66	760.66	749.91	740.27	704.49	682.47	668.52
100000	813.33	800.69	789.38	779.23	741.56	718.39	703.71
105000	853.99	840.73	828.85	818.19	778.64	754.31	738.89
110000	894.66	880.76	868.32	857.15	815.72	790.23	774.08
120000	975.99	960.83	947.26	935.07	889.88	862.06	844.45
130000	1057.33	1040.90	1026.20	1013.00	964.03	933.90	914.82
140000	1138.66	1120.97	1105.13	1090.92	1038.19	1005.74	985.19
150000	1219.99	1201.04	1184.07	1168.84	1112.35	1077.58	1055.56
160000	1301.33	1281.11	1263.01	1246.77	1186.50	1149.42	1125.93
170000	1382.66	1361.18	1341.95	1324.69	1260.66	1221.26	1196.30
180000	1463.99	1441.25	1420.89	1402.61	1334.82	1293.10	1266.67
190000	1545.32	1521.32	1499.83	1480.53	1408.97	1364.94	1337.04
200000	1626.66	1601.39	1578.76	1558.46	1483.13	1436.77	1407.41
210000	1707.99	1681.45	1657.70	1636.38	1557.29	1508.61	1477.78
220000	1789.32	1761.52	1736.64	1714.30	1631.44	1580.45	1548.15
230000	1870.66	1841.59	1815.58	1792.23	1705.60	1652.29	1618.52
240000	1951.99	1921.66	1894.52	1870.15	1779.76	1724.13	1688.89
250000	2033.32	2001.73	1973.45	1948.07	1853.91	1795.97	1759.26

8.50 % Monthly Payments

LOAN AMOUNT	YEARS 1	2	3	4	5	6	7
100	8.72	4.54	3.15	2.46	2.04	1.77	1.58
200	17.43	9.08	6.30	4.92	4.09	3.54	3.15
500	43.58	22.69	15.75	12.29	10.22	8.85	7.88
1000	87.15	45.39	31.50	24.58	20.45	17.71	15.76
2000	174.30	90.78	63.00	49.16	40.89	35.41	31.53
5000	435.76	226.94	157.50	122.90	102.23	88.53	78.81
6000	522.91	272.33	189.00	147.47	122.68	106.24	94.58
7000	610.06	317.72	220.50	172.05	143.12	123.94	110.34
8000	697.21	363.11	252.00	196.63	163.57	141.65	126.10
9000	784.37	408.50	283.50	221.21	184.01	159.36	141.87
10000	871.52	453.89	315.00	245.79	204.46	177.06	157.63
12000	1045.82	544.66	378.00	294.95	245.35	212.47	189.15
15000	1307.28	680.83	472.49	368.69	306.69	265.59	236.44
20000	1743.04	907.77	629.99	491.58	408.92	354.12	315.26
25000	2178.80	1134.71	787.49	614.48	511.15	442.66	394.07
30000	2614.56	1361.66	944.99	737.37	613.38	531.19	472.88
31000	2701.71	1407.05	976.49	761.95	633.82	548.89	488.65
32000	2788.86	1452.43	1007.99	786.53	654.27	566.60	504.41
33000	2876.01	1497.82	1039.49	811.11	674.71	584.31	520.17
34000	2963.16	1543.21	1070.99	835.69	695.16	602.01	535.94
35000	3050.31	1588.60	1102.49	860.27	715.61	619.72	551.70
36000	3137.47	1633.99	1133.99	884.85	736.05	637.42	567.46
37000	3224.62	1679.38	1165.48	909.43	756.50	655.13	583.22
38000	3311.77	1724.77	1196.98	934.01	776.94	672.84	598.99
39000	3398.92	1770.15	1228.48	958.58	797.39	690.54	614.75
40000	3486.07	1815.54	1259.98	983.16	817.84	708.25	630.51
41000	3573.23	1860.93	1291.48	1007.74	838.28	725.96	646.27
42000	3660.38	1906.32	1322.98	1032.32	858.73	743.66	662.04
43000	3747.53	1951.71	1354.48	1056.90	879.17	761.37	677.80
44000	3834.68	1997.10	1385.98	1081.48	899.62	779.07	693.56
45000	3921.83	2042.49	1417.48	1106.06	920.06	796.78	709.33
46000	4008.99	2087.87	1448.98	1130.64	940.51	814.49	725.09
47000	4096.14	2133.26	1480.48	1155.22	960.96	832.19	740.85
48000	4183.29	2178.65	1511.98	1179.80	981.40	849.90	756.61
49000	4270.44	2224.04	1543.48	1204.38	1001.85	867.61	772.38
50000	4357.59	2269.43	1574.98	1228.95	1022.29	885.31	788.14
51000	4444.74	2314.82	1606.48	1253.53	1042.74	903.02	803.90
52000	4531.90	2360.21	1637.98	1278.11	1063.19	920.72	819.67
53000	4619.05	2405.59	1669.48	1302.69	1083.63	938.43	835.43
54000	4706.20	2450.98	1700.98	1327.27	1104.08	956.14	851.19
55000	4793.35	2496.37	1732.48	1351.85	1124.52	973.84	866.95
56000	4880.50	2541.76	1763.98	1376.43	1144.97	991.55	882.72
57000	4967.66	2587.15	1795.48	1401.01	1165.42	1009.26	898.48
58000	5054.81	2632.54	1826.98	1425.59	1185.86	1026.96	914.24
59000	5141.96	2677.93	1858.48	1450.17	1206.31	1044.67	930.01
60000	5229.11	2723.32	1889.98	1474.75	1226.75	1062.37	945.77
65000	5664.87	2950.26	2047.47	1597.64	1328.98	1150.91	1024.58
70000	6100.63	3177.20	2204.97	1720.54	1431.21	1239.44	1103.40
75000	6536.39	3404.14	2362.47	1843.43	1533.44	1327.97	1182.21
80000	6972.15	3631.09	2519.97	1966.33	1635.67	1416.50	1261.02
85000	7407.91	3858.03	2677.47	2089.22	1737.90	1505.03	1339.84
90000	7843.67	4084.97	2834.96	2212.12	1840.13	1593.56	1418.65
95000	8279.43	4311.92	2992.46	2335.01	1942.36	1682.09	1497.47
100000	8715.19	4538.86	3149.96	2457.91	2044.59	1770.62	1576.28
105000	9150.94	4765.80	3307.46	2580.80	2146.82	1859.16	1655.09
110000	9586.70	4992.74	3464.96	2703.70	2249.05	1947.69	1733.91
120000	10458.22	5446.63	3779.95	2949.49	2453.51	2124.75	1891.54
130000	11329.74	5900.52	4094.95	3195.28	2657.97	2301.81	2049.16
140000	12201.26	6354.40	4409.94	3441.07	2862.42	2478.87	2206.79
150000	13072.78	6808.29	4724.94	3686.86	3066.88	2655.94	2364.42
160000	13944.30	7262.17	5039.93	3932.65	3271.34	2833.00	2522.05
170000	14815.82	7716.06	5354.93	4178.45	3475.80	3010.06	2679.68
180000	15687.33	8169.95	5669.93	4424.24	3680.26	3187.12	2837.30
190000	16558.85	8623.83	5984.92	4670.03	3884.72	3364.19	2994.93
200000	17430.37	9077.72	6299.92	4915.82	4089.18	3541.25	3152.56
210000	18301.89	9531.60	6614.91	5161.61	4293.64	3718.31	3310.19
220000	19173.41	9985.49	6929.91	5407.40	4498.10	3895.37	3467.82
230000	20044.93	10439.37	7244.91	5653.19	4702.55	4072.43	3625.44
240000	20916.45	10893.26	7559.90	5898.98	4907.01	4249.50	3783.07
250000	21787.96	11347.15	7874.90	6144.77	5111.47	4426.56	3940.70

Monthly Payments 8.50 %

LOAN AMOUNT	8	9	10	11	12	13	14
			YEARS				
100	1.43	1.32	1.23	1.16	1.10	1.05	1.01
200	2.86	2.64	2.46	2.32	2.20	2.11	2.02
500	7.16	6.60	6.16	5.80	5.51	5.26	5.06
1000	14.32	13.20	12.32	11.61	11.02	10.53	10.11
2000	28.63	26.41	24.64	23.21	22.04	21.06	20.23
5000	71.58	66.01	61.60	58.03	55.10	52.64	50.57
6000	85.90	79.22	73.92	69.64	66.11	63.17	60.69
7000	100.22	92.42	86.24	81.25	77.13	73.70	70.80
8000	114.54	105.62	98.56	92.85	88.15	84.23	80.92
9000	128.85	118.82	110.88	104.46	99.17	94.76	91.03
10000	143.17	132.03	123.20	116.07	110.19	105.29	101.15
12000	171.80	158.43	147.84	139.28	132.23	126.35	121.38
15000	214.75	198.04	184.80	174.10	165.29	157.93	151.72
20000	286.34	264.05	246.40	232.13	220.38	210.58	202.30
25000	357.92	330.06	308.01	290.16	275.48	263.22	252.87
30000	429.51	396.08	369.61	348.20	330.57	315.87	303.44
31000	443.82	409.28	381.93	359.80	341.59	326.40	313.56
32000	458.14	422.48	394.25	371.41	352.61	336.92	323.67
33000	472.46	435.68	406.57	383.02	363.63	347.45	333.79
34000	486.77	448.89	418.89	394.62	374.65	357.98	343.90
35000	501.09	462.09	431.21	406.23	385.67	368.51	354.02
36000	515.41	475.29	443.53	417.83	396.69	379.04	364.13
37000	529.73	488.49	455.85	429.44	407.71	389.57	374.25
38000	544.04	501.70	468.17	441.05	418.73	400.10	384.36
39000	558.36	514.90	480.49	452.65	429.75	410.63	394.48
40000	572.68	528.10	492.81	464.26	440.77	421.16	404.59
41000	586.99	541.31	505.13	475.87	451.79	431.69	414.71
42000	601.31	554.51	517.45	487.47	462.80	442.21	424.82
43000	615.63	567.71	529.77	499.08	473.82	452.74	434.94
44000	629.94	580.91	542.09	510.69	484.84	463.27	445.05
45000	644.26	594.12	554.41	522.29	495.86	473.80	455.17
46000	658.58	607.32	566.73	533.90	506.88	484.33	465.28
47000	672.89	620.52	579.05	545.51	517.90	494.86	475.40
48000	687.21	633.72	591.37	557.11	528.92	505.39	485.51
49000	701.53	646.93	603.69	568.72	539.94	515.92	495.63
50000	715.84	660.13	616.01	580.33	550.96	526.45	505.74
51000	730.16	673.33	628.33	591.93	561.98	536.97	515.86
52000	744.48	686.53	640.65	603.54	573.00	547.50	525.97
53000	758.80	699.74	652.97	615.15	584.02	558.03	536.09
54000	773.11	712.94	665.29	626.75	595.03	568.56	546.20
55000	787.43	726.14	677.61	638.36	606.05	579.09	556.32
56000	801.75	739.34	689.93	649.97	617.07	589.62	566.43
57000	816.06	752.55	702.25	661.57	628.09	600.15	576.54
58000	830.38	765.75	714.57	673.18	639.11	610.68	586.66
59000	844.70	778.95	726.89	684.78	650.13	621.21	596.77
60000	859.01	792.15	739.21	696.39	661.15	631.73	606.89
65000	930.60	858.17	800.82	754.42	716.25	684.38	657.46
70000	1002.18	924.18	862.42	812.46	771.34	737.02	708.04
75000	1073.77	990.19	924.02	870.49	826.44	789.67	758.61
80000	1145.35	1056.21	985.62	928.52	881.53	842.31	809.19
85000	1216.94	1122.22	1047.22	986.55	936.63	894.96	859.76
90000	1288.52	1188.23	1108.82	1044.59	991.72	947.60	910.33
95000	1360.10	1254.24	1170.42	1102.62	1046.82	1000.25	960.91
100000	1431.69	1320.26	1232.02	1160.65	1101.92	1052.89	1011.48
105000	1503.27	1386.27	1293.62	1218.68	1157.01	1105.53	1062.06
110000	1574.86	1452.28	1355.23	1276.72	1212.11	1158.18	1112.63
120000	1718.03	1584.31	1478.43	1392.78	1322.30	1263.47	1213.78
130000	1861.20	1716.33	1601.63	1508.85	1432.49	1368.76	1314.93
140000	2004.37	1848.36	1724.83	1624.91	1542.68	1474.05	1416.07
150000	2147.53	1980.38	1848.04	1740.98	1652.87	1579.34	1517.22
160000	2290.70	2112.41	1971.24	1857.04	1763.07	1684.62	1618.37
170000	2433.87	2244.44	2094.44	1973.11	1873.26	1789.91	1719.52
180000	2577.04	2376.46	2217.64	2089.17	1983.45	1895.20	1820.67
190000	2720.21	2508.49	2340.84	2205.24	2093.64	2000.49	1921.82
200000	2863.38	2640.51	2464.05	2321.30	2203.83	2105.78	2022.96
210000	3006.55	2772.54	2587.25	2437.37	2314.02	2211.07	2124.11
220000	3149.72	2904.56	2710.45	2553.43	2424.22	2316.36	2225.26
230000	3292.89	3036.59	2833.65	2669.50	2534.41	2421.65	2326.41
240000	3436.05	3168.62	2956.86	2785.57	2644.60	2526.94	2427.56
250000	3579.22	3300.64	3080.06	2901.63	2754.79	2632.23	2528.71

8.50 % Monthly Payments

LOAN AMOUNT	YEARS 15	16	17	18	19	20	21
100	0.98	0.95	0.92	0.90	0.88	0.86	0.84
200	1.95	1.89	1.84	1.79	1.75	1.72	1.69
500	4.88	4.73	4.60	4.48	4.38	4.29	4.21
1000	9.76	9.46	9.19	8.96	8.76	8.59	8.43
2000	19.52	18.92	18.39	17.93	17.53	17.17	16.86
5000	48.81	47.29	45.97	44.82	43.82	42.93	42.14
6000	58.57	56.75	55.17	53.79	52.58	51.51	50.57
7000	68.33	66.20	64.36	62.75	61.34	60.10	59.00
8000	78.09	75.66	73.55	71.72	70.10	68.68	67.43
9000	87.85	85.12	82.75	80.68	78.87	77.27	75.86
10000	97.62	94.58	91.94	89.65	87.63	85.86	84.28
12000	117.14	113.49	110.33	107.57	105.16	103.03	101.14
15000	146.42	141.87	137.91	134.47	131.45	128.78	126.43
20000	195.23	189.15	183.89	179.29	175.26	171.71	168.57
25000	244.04	236.44	229.86	224.11	219.08	214.64	210.71
30000	292.85	283.73	275.83	268.94	262.89	257.57	252.85
31000	302.61	293.19	285.02	277.90	271.66	266.15	261.28
32000	312.37	302.65	294.22	286.87	280.42	274.74	269.71
33000	322.13	312.10	303.41	295.83	289.18	283.32	278.14
34000	331.89	321.56	312.61	304.80	297.95	291.91	286.57
35000	341.66	331.02	321.80	313.76	306.71	300.50	295.00
36000	351.42	340.48	330.99	322.72	315.47	309.08	303.43
37000	361.18	349.93	340.19	331.69	324.24	317.67	311.85
38000	370.94	359.39	349.38	340.65	333.00	326.25	320.28
39000	380.70	368.85	358.58	349.62	341.76	334.84	328.71
40000	390.46	378.31	367.77	358.58	350.52	343.42	337.14
41000	400.22	387.76	376.97	367.55	359.29	352.01	345.57
42000	409.99	397.22	386.16	376.51	368.05	360.59	354.00
43000	419.75	406.68	395.35	385.48	376.81	369.18	362.42
44000	429.51	416.14	404.55	394.44	385.58	377.77	370.85
45000	439.27	425.60	413.74	403.41	394.34	386.35	379.28
46000	449.03	435.05	422.94	412.37	403.10	394.94	387.71
47000	458.79	444.51	432.13	421.33	411.87	403.52	396.14
48000	468.56	453.97	441.33	430.30	420.63	412.11	404.57
49000	478.32	463.43	450.52	439.26	429.39	420.69	413.00
50000	488.08	472.88	459.71	448.23	438.16	429.28	421.42
51000	497.84	482.34	468.91	457.19	446.92	437.87	429.85
52000	507.60	491.80	478.10	466.16	455.68	446.45	438.28
53000	517.36	501.26	487.30	475.12	464.45	455.04	446.71
54000	527.13	510.71	496.49	484.09	473.21	463.62	455.14
55000	536.89	520.17	505.69	493.05	481.97	472.21	463.57
56000	546.65	529.63	514.88	502.02	490.73	480.79	472.00
57000	556.41	539.09	524.07	510.98	499.50	489.38	480.42
58000	566.17	548.54	533.27	519.95	508.26	497.96	488.85
59000	575.93	558.00	542.46	528.91	517.02	506.55	497.28
60000	585.69	567.46	551.66	537.87	525.79	515.14	505.71
65000	634.50	614.75	597.63	582.70	569.60	558.06	547.85
70000	683.31	662.04	643.60	627.52	613.42	600.99	589.99
75000	732.12	709.33	689.57	672.34	657.23	643.92	632.14
80000	780.93	756.61	735.54	717.17	701.05	686.85	674.28
85000	829.73	803.90	781.51	761.99	744.87	729.78	716.42
90000	878.54	851.19	827.49	806.81	788.68	772.70	758.56
95000	927.35	898.48	873.46	851.63	832.50	815.63	800.71
100000	976.16	945.77	919.43	896.46	876.31	858.56	842.85
105000	1024.97	993.06	965.40	941.28	920.13	901.49	884.99
110000	1073.77	1040.34	1011.37	986.10	963.94	944.42	927.13
120000	1171.39	1134.92	1103.31	1075.75	1051.57	1030.27	1011.42
130000	1269.01	1229.50	1195.26	1165.39	1139.21	1116.13	1095.70
140000	1366.62	1324.07	1287.20	1255.04	1226.84	1201.98	1179.99
150000	1464.24	1418.65	1379.14	1344.69	1314.47	1287.84	1264.27
160000	1561.85	1513.23	1471.09	1434.33	1402.10	1373.69	1348.56
170000	1659.47	1607.80	1563.03	1523.98	1489.73	1459.55	1432.84
180000	1757.08	1702.38	1654.97	1613.62	1577.36	1545.41	1517.13
190000	1854.70	1796.96	1746.91	1703.27	1664.99	1631.26	1601.41
200000	1952.32	1891.53	1838.86	1792.91	1752.62	1717.12	1685.70
210000	2049.93	1986.11	1930.80	1882.56	1840.25	1802.97	1769.98
220000	2147.55	2080.69	2022.74	1972.21	1927.89	1888.83	1854.27
230000	2245.16	2175.26	2114.69	2061.85	2015.52	1974.69	1938.55
240000	2342.78	2269.84	2206.63	2151.50	2103.15	2060.54	2022.84
250000	2440.39	2364.42	2298.57	2241.14	2190.78	2146.40	2107.12

Monthly Payments 8.50 %

LOAN AMOUNT	22	23	24	25	30	35	40
100	0.83	0.82	0.81	0.80	0.76	0.74	0.72
200	1.66	1.63	1.61	1.59	1.52	1.47	1.44
500	4.14	4.08	4.03	3.98	3.79	3.68	3.61
1000	8.29	8.16	8.05	7.95	7.59	7.36	7.22
2000	16.58	16.33	16.11	15.91	15.17	14.72	14.44
5000	41.44	40.82	40.27	39.77	37.93	36.80	36.10
6000	49.73	48.99	48.32	47.72	45.51	44.16	43.32
7000	58.02	57.15	56.37	55.68	53.10	51.52	50.54
8000	66.31	65.32	64.43	63.63	60.68	58.89	57.76
9000	74.60	73.48	72.48	71.58	68.27	66.25	64.98
10000	82.89	81.65	80.53	79.54	75.85	73.61	72.20
12000	99.47	97.97	96.64	95.44	91.02	88.33	86.63
15000	124.33	122.47	120.80	119.30	113.78	110.41	108.29
20000	165.78	163.29	161.07	159.07	151.71	147.21	144.39
25000	207.22	204.11	201.33	198.84	189.63	184.02	180.49
30000	248.67	244.94	241.60	238.61	227.56	220.82	216.59
31000	256.96	253.10	249.65	246.56	235.15	228.18	223.81
32000	265.25	261.26	257.71	254.52	242.73	235.54	231.03
33000	273.53	269.43	265.76	262.47	250.32	242.90	238.24
34000	281.82	277.59	273.81	270.42	257.90	250.26	245.46
35000	290.11	285.76	281.87	278.38	265.49	257.62	252.68
36000	298.40	293.92	289.92	286.33	273.07	264.98	259.90
37000	306.69	302.09	297.97	294.28	280.66	272.34	267.12
38000	314.98	310.25	306.03	302.24	288.24	279.70	274.34
39000	323.27	318.42	314.08	310.19	295.83	287.06	281.56
40000	331.56	326.58	322.13	318.15	303.42	294.43	288.78
41000	339.85	334.75	330.19	326.10	311.00	301.79	296.00
42000	348.13	342.91	338.24	334.05	318.59	309.15	303.22
43000	356.42	351.07	346.29	342.01	326.17	316.51	310.44
44000	364.71	359.24	354.35	349.96	333.76	323.87	317.66
45000	373.00	367.40	362.40	357.91	341.34	331.23	324.88
46000	381.29	375.57	370.45	365.87	348.93	338.59	332.10
47000	389.58	383.73	378.51	373.82	356.51	345.95	339.32
48000	397.87	391.90	386.56	381.77	364.10	353.31	346.54
49000	406.16	400.06	394.61	389.73	371.68	360.67	353.76
50000	414.45	408.23	402.67	397.68	379.27	368.03	360.98
51000	422.73	416.39	410.72	405.64	386.85	375.39	368.20
52000	431.02	424.56	418.77	413.59	394.44	382.75	375.42
53000	439.31	432.72	426.83	421.54	402.03	390.11	382.64
54000	447.60	440.88	434.88	429.50	409.61	397.47	389.86
55000	455.89	449.05	442.93	437.45	417.20	404.83	397.07
56000	464.18	457.21	450.99	445.40	424.78	412.20	404.29
57000	472.47	465.38	459.04	453.36	432.37	419.56	411.51
58000	480.76	473.54	467.09	461.31	439.95	426.92	418.73
59000	489.05	481.71	475.15	469.26	447.54	434.28	425.95
60000	497.34	489.87	483.20	477.22	455.12	441.64	433.17
65000	538.78	530.69	523.47	516.99	493.05	478.44	469.27
70000	580.22	571.52	563.73	556.75	530.98	515.24	505.37
75000	621.67	612.34	604.00	596.52	568.90	552.05	541.47
80000	663.11	653.16	644.27	636.29	606.83	588.85	577.56
85000	704.56	693.98	684.53	676.06	644.76	625.65	613.66
90000	746.00	734.81	724.80	715.83	682.69	662.46	649.76
95000	787.45	775.63	765.07	755.60	720.61	699.26	685.86
100000	828.89	816.45	805.33	795.36	758.54	736.06	721.95
105000	870.34	857.27	845.60	835.13	796.47	772.87	758.05
110000	911.78	898.10	885.86	874.90	834.39	809.67	794.15
120000	994.67	979.74	966.40	954.44	910.25	883.28	866.34
130000	1077.56	1061.39	1046.93	1033.97	986.10	956.88	938.54
140000	1160.45	1143.03	1127.46	1113.51	1061.95	1030.49	1010.74
150000	1243.34	1224.68	1208.00	1193.05	1137.81	1104.09	1082.93
160000	1326.23	1306.32	1288.53	1272.58	1213.66	1177.70	1155.13
170000	1409.12	1387.97	1369.06	1352.12	1289.52	1251.31	1227.32
180000	1492.01	1469.61	1449.60	1431.65	1365.37	1324.91	1299.52
190000	1574.89	1551.26	1530.13	1511.19	1441.22	1398.52	1371.71
200000	1657.78	1632.90	1610.66	1590.73	1517.08	1472.13	1443.91
210000	1740.67	1714.55	1691.20	1670.26	1592.93	1545.73	1516.10
220000	1823.56	1796.19	1771.73	1749.80	1668.79	1619.34	1588.30
230000	1906.45	1877.84	1852.26	1829.34	1744.64	1692.94	1660.49
240000	1989.34	1959.49	1932.80	1908.87	1820.49	1766.55	1732.69
250000	2072.23	2041.13	2013.33	1988.41	1896.35	1840.16	1804.89

8.75 % Monthly Payments

LOAN AMOUNT	1	2	3	4	5	6	7
			YEARS				
100	8.73	4.55	3.16	2.47	2.06	1.78	1.59
200	17.45	9.10	6.32	4.94	4.11	3.57	3.18
500	43.63	22.75	15.81	12.35	10.28	8.91	7.94
1000	87.26	45.50	31.61	24.69	20.56	17.83	15.88
2000	174.53	91.00	63.22	49.39	41.12	35.65	31.77
5000	436.32	227.49	158.06	123.47	102.81	89.13	79.42
6000	523.58	272.99	189.67	148.16	123.37	106.95	95.30
7000	610.85	318.49	221.28	172.85	143.94	124.78	111.19
8000	698.11	363.99	252.89	197.54	164.50	142.60	127.07
9000	785.37	409.49	284.50	222.24	185.06	160.43	142.96
10000	872.64	454.99	316.11	246.93	205.62	178.25	158.84
12000	1047.16	545.99	379.34	296.32	246.75	213.90	190.61
15000	1308.95	682.48	474.17	370.40	308.43	267.38	238.26
20000	1745.27	909.98	632.23	493.86	411.24	356.50	317.68
25000	2181.59	1137.47	790.29	617.33	514.05	445.63	397.10
30000	2617.91	1364.97	948.34	740.79	616.87	534.75	476.52
31000	2705.17	1410.47	979.95	765.48	637.43	552.58	492.41
32000	2792.44	1455.97	1011.56	790.18	657.99	570.40	508.29
33000	2879.70	1501.47	1043.18	814.87	678.55	588.23	524.18
34000	2966.96	1546.97	1074.79	839.56	699.11	606.05	540.06
35000	3054.23	1592.46	1106.40	864.26	719.68	623.88	555.94
36000	3141.49	1637.96	1138.01	888.95	740.24	641.70	571.83
37000	3228.75	1683.46	1169.62	913.64	760.80	659.53	587.71
38000	3316.02	1728.96	1201.23	938.33	781.36	677.35	603.60
39000	3403.28	1774.46	1232.84	963.03	801.92	695.18	619.48
40000	3490.54	1819.96	1264.46	987.72	822.49	713.00	635.36
41000	3577.81	1865.46	1296.07	1012.41	843.05	730.83	651.25
42000	3665.07	1910.96	1327.68	1037.11	863.61	748.65	667.13
43000	3752.34	1956.46	1359.29	1061.80	884.17	766.48	683.02
44000	3839.60	2001.95	1390.90	1086.49	904.74	784.30	698.90
45000	3926.86	2047.45	1422.51	1111.19	925.30	802.13	714.79
46000	4014.13	2092.95	1454.12	1135.88	945.86	819.95	730.67
47000	4101.39	2138.45	1485.74	1160.57	966.42	837.78	746.55
48000	4188.65	2183.95	1517.35	1185.26	986.98	855.60	762.44
49000	4275.92	2229.45	1548.96	1209.96	1007.55	873.43	778.32
50000	4363.18	2274.95	1580.57	1234.65	1028.11	891.25	794.21
51000	4450.44	2320.45	1612.18	1259.34	1048.67	909.08	810.09
52000	4537.71	2365.95	1643.79	1284.04	1069.23	926.90	825.97
53000	4624.97	2411.45	1675.40	1308.73	1089.80	944.73	841.86
54000	4712.23	2456.94	1707.02	1333.42	1110.36	962.55	857.74
55000	4799.50	2502.44	1738.63	1358.12	1130.92	980.38	873.63
56000	4886.76	2547.94	1770.24	1382.81	1151.48	998.20	889.51
57000	4974.03	2593.44	1801.85	1407.50	1172.04	1016.03	905.39
58000	5061.29	2638.94	1833.46	1432.19	1192.61	1033.85	921.28
59000	5148.55	2684.44	1865.07	1456.89	1213.17	1051.68	937.16
60000	5235.82	2729.94	1896.68	1481.58	1233.73	1069.50	953.05
65000	5672.13	2957.43	2054.74	1605.05	1336.54	1158.63	1032.47
70000	6108.45	3184.93	2212.80	1728.51	1439.35	1247.75	1111.89
75000	6544.77	3412.42	2370.86	1851.98	1542.16	1336.88	1191.31
80000	6981.09	3639.92	2528.91	1975.44	1644.97	1426.00	1270.73
85000	7417.41	3867.41	2686.97	2098.91	1747.78	1515.13	1350.15
90000	7853.72	4094.91	2845.03	2222.37	1850.60	1604.25	1429.57
95000	8290.04	4322.40	3003.08	2345.84	1953.41	1693.38	1508.99
100000	8726.36	4549.90	3161.14	2469.30	2056.22	1782.50	1588.41
105000	9162.68	4777.39	3319.20	2592.77	2159.03	1871.63	1667.83
110000	9599.00	5004.89	3477.25	2716.23	2261.84	1960.75	1747.25
120000	10471.63	5459.88	3793.37	2963.16	2467.46	2139.00	1906.09
130000	11344.27	5914.87	4109.48	3210.09	2673.08	2317.25	2064.93
140000	12216.91	6369.86	4425.60	3457.02	2878.70	2495.50	2223.78
150000	13089.54	6824.85	4741.71	3703.95	3084.33	2673.75	2382.62
160000	13962.18	7279.84	5057.82	3950.88	3289.95	2852.00	2541.46
170000	14834.81	7734.83	5373.94	4197.81	3495.57	3030.25	2700.30
180000	15707.45	8189.82	5690.05	4444.74	3701.19	3208.50	2859.14
190000	16580.09	8644.81	6006.17	4691.67	3906.81	3386.75	3017.98
200000	17452.72	9099.80	6322.28	4938.60	4112.43	3565.00	3176.82
210000	18325.36	9554.79	6638.40	5185.53	4318.06	3743.25	3335.66
220000	19197.99	10009.77	6954.51	5432.46	4523.68	3921.50	3494.51
230000	20070.63	10464.76	7270.62	5679.39	4729.30	4099.75	3653.35
240000	20943.27	10919.75	7586.74	5926.32	4934.92	4278.00	3812.19
250000	21815.90	11374.74	7902.85	6173.25	5140.54	4456.25	3971.03

Monthly Payments 8.75 %

LOAN AMOUNT	8	9	10	11	12	13	14
	YEARS						
100	1.44	1.33	1.24	1.17	1.12	1.07	1.03
200	2.89	2.67	2.49	2.35	2.23	2.13	2.05
500	7.22	6.66	6.22	5.87	5.58	5.33	5.13
1000	14.44	13.33	12.45	11.74	11.15	10.67	10.25
2000	28.88	26.66	24.90	23.48	22.31	21.33	20.51
5000	72.20	66.65	62.25	58.69	55.77	53.33	51.27
6000	86.64	79.97	74.70	70.43	66.92	63.99	61.52
7000	101.09	93.30	87.14	82.17	78.07	74.66	71.78
8000	115.53	106.63	99.59	93.90	89.23	85.32	82.03
9000	129.97	119.96	112.04	105.64	100.38	95.99	92.28
10000	144.41	133.29	124.49	117.38	111.53	106.65	102.54
12000	173.29	159.95	149.39	140.86	133.84	127.99	123.05
15000	216.61	199.94	186.74	176.07	167.30	159.98	153.81
20000	288.82	266.58	248.98	234.76	223.06	213.31	205.08
25000	361.02	333.23	311.23	293.45	278.83	266.64	256.34
30000	433.22	399.87	373.48	352.14	334.60	319.96	307.61
31000	447.66	413.20	385.93	363.88	345.75	330.63	317.87
32000	462.10	426.53	398.38	375.62	356.90	341.29	328.12
33000	476.55	439.86	410.82	387.36	368.06	351.96	338.38
34000	490.99	453.19	423.27	399.09	379.21	362.62	348.63
35000	505.43	466.52	435.72	410.83	390.36	373.29	358.88
36000	519.87	479.84	448.17	422.57	401.52	383.96	369.14
37000	534.31	493.17	460.62	434.31	412.67	394.62	379.39
38000	548.75	506.50	473.07	446.05	423.82	405.29	389.64
39000	563.19	519.83	485.52	457.78	434.98	415.95	399.90
40000	577.63	533.16	497.97	469.52	446.13	426.62	410.15
41000	592.07	546.49	510.42	481.26	457.28	437.28	420.41
42000	606.51	559.82	522.87	493.00	468.44	447.95	430.66
43000	620.95	573.15	535.32	504.74	479.59	458.61	440.91
44000	635.39	586.48	547.77	516.47	490.74	469.28	451.17
45000	649.83	599.81	560.22	528.21	501.89	479.94	461.42
46000	664.28	613.13	572.66	539.95	513.05	490.61	471.67
47000	678.72	626.46	585.11	551.69	524.20	501.28	481.93
48000	693.16	639.79	597.56	563.43	535.35	511.94	492.18
49000	707.60	653.12	610.01	575.17	546.51	522.61	502.44
50000	722.04	666.45	622.46	586.90	557.66	533.27	512.69
51000	736.48	679.78	634.91	598.64	568.81	543.94	522.94
52000	750.92	693.11	647.36	610.38	579.97	554.60	533.20
53000	765.36	706.44	659.81	622.12	591.12	565.27	543.45
54000	779.80	719.77	672.26	633.86	602.27	575.93	553.70
55000	794.24	733.10	684.71	645.59	613.43	586.60	563.96
56000	808.68	746.42	697.16	657.33	624.58	597.26	574.21
57000	823.12	759.75	709.61	669.07	635.73	607.93	584.47
58000	837.56	773.08	722.06	680.81	646.89	618.60	594.72
59000	852.01	786.41	734.51	692.55	658.04	629.26	604.97
60000	866.45	799.74	746.95	704.28	669.19	639.93	615.23
65000	938.65	866.39	809.20	762.97	724.96	693.25	666.50
70000	1010.85	933.03	871.45	821.66	780.73	746.58	717.77
75000	1083.06	999.68	933.69	880.35	836.49	799.91	769.03
80000	1155.26	1066.32	995.94	939.05	892.26	853.23	820.30
85000	1227.47	1132.97	1058.19	997.74	948.02	906.56	871.57
90000	1299.67	1199.61	1120.43	1056.43	1003.79	959.89	922.84
95000	1371.87	1266.26	1182.68	1115.12	1059.56	1013.22	974.11
100000	1444.08	1332.90	1244.92	1173.81	1115.32	1066.54	1025.38
105000	1516.28	1399.55	1307.17	1232.50	1171.09	1119.87	1076.65
110000	1588.48	1466.19	1369.42	1291.19	1226.85	1173.20	1127.92
120000	1732.89	1599.48	1493.91	1408.57	1338.39	1279.85	1230.45
130000	1877.30	1732.77	1618.40	1525.95	1449.92	1386.51	1332.99
140000	2021.71	1866.06	1742.89	1643.33	1561.45	1493.16	1435.53
150000	2166.12	1999.35	1867.39	1760.71	1672.98	1599.81	1538.07
160000	2310.52	2132.64	1991.88	1878.09	1784.51	1706.47	1640.61
170000	2454.93	2265.93	2116.37	1995.47	1896.05	1813.12	1743.14
180000	2599.34	2399.22	2240.86	2112.85	2007.58	1919.78	1845.68
190000	2743.75	2532.51	2365.36	2230.23	2119.11	2026.43	1948.22
200000	2888.15	2665.80	2489.85	2347.61	2230.64	2133.09	2050.76
210000	3032.56	2799.09	2614.34	2464.99	2342.18	2239.74	2153.30
220000	3176.97	2932.38	2738.83	2582.37	2453.71	2346.39	2255.83
230000	3321.38	3065.67	2863.32	2699.75	2565.24	2453.05	2358.37
240000	3465.79	3198.96	2987.82	2817.14	2676.77	2559.70	2460.91
250000	3610.19	3332.25	3112.31	2934.52	2788.30	2666.36	2563.45

8.75 % Monthly Payments

LOAN AMOUNT	15	16	17	18	19	20	21
100	0.99	0.96	0.93	0.91	0.89	0.87	0.8
200	1.98	1.92	1.87	1.82	1.78	1.75	1.7
500	4.95	4.80	4.67	4.56	4.46	4.37	4.2
1000	9.90	9.60	9.34	9.11	8.91	8.74	8.5
2000	19.81	19.20	18.68	18.23	17.83	17.48	17.1
5000	49.51	48.01	46.70	45.56	44.57	43.69	42.9
6000	59.42	57.61	56.04	54.68	53.48	52.43	51.5
7000	69.32	67.21	65.38	63.79	62.40	61.17	60.0
8000	79.22	76.81	74.72	72.90	71.31	69.91	68.6
9000	89.13	86.41	84.06	82.02	80.22	78.64	77.2
10000	99.03	96.01	93.40	91.13	89.14	87.38	85.8
12000	118.84	115.22	112.08	109.35	106.96	104.86	103.0
15000	148.54	144.02	140.10	136.69	133.70	131.07	128.7
20000	198.06	192.03	186.81	182.26	178.27	174.76	171.6
25000	247.57	240.03	233.51	227.82	222.84	218.46	214.5
30000	297.09	288.04	280.21	273.39	267.41	262.15	257.5
31000	306.99	297.64	289.55	282.50	276.32	270.88	266.0
32000	316.89	307.24	298.89	291.61	285.24	279.62	274.6
33000	326.80	316.85	308.23	300.72	294.15	288.36	283.2
34000	336.70	326.45	317.57	309.84	303.06	297.10	291.8
35000	346.60	336.05	326.91	318.95	311.98	305.84	300.4
36000	356.51	345.65	336.25	328.06	320.89	314.58	309.0
37000	366.41	355.25	345.59	337.18	329.80	323.31	317.5
38000	376.31	364.85	354.93	346.29	338.72	332.05	326.1
39000	386.21	374.45	364.27	355.40	347.63	340.79	334.7
40000	396.12	384.06	373.61	364.51	356.54	349.53	343.3
41000	406.02	393.66	382.95	373.63	365.46	358.27	351.9
42000	415.92	403.26	392.29	382.74	374.37	367.01	360.4
43000	425.83	412.86	401.63	391.85	383.28	375.74	369.0
44000	435.73	422.46	410.97	400.97	392.20	384.48	377.6
45000	445.63	432.06	420.31	410.08	401.11	393.22	386.2
46000	455.54	441.66	429.65	419.19	410.03	401.96	394.8
47000	465.44	451.27	438.99	428.30	418.94	410.70	403.4
48000	475.34	460.87	448.33	437.42	427.85	419.43	411.9
49000	485.24	470.47	457.68	446.53	436.77	428.17	420.5
50000	495.15	480.07	467.02	455.64	445.68	436.91	429.1
51000	505.05	489.67	476.36	464.76	454.59	445.65	437.7
52000	514.95	499.27	485.70	473.87	463.51	454.39	446.3
53000	524.86	508.87	495.04	482.98	472.42	463.13	454.9
54000	534.76	518.47	504.38	492.09	481.33	471.86	463.4
55000	544.66	528.08	513.72	501.21	490.25	480.60	472.0
56000	554.56	537.68	523.06	510.32	499.16	489.34	480.6
57000	564.47	547.28	532.40	519.43	508.08	498.08	489.2
58000	574.37	556.88	541.74	528.55	516.99	506.82	497.8
59000	584.27	566.48	551.08	537.66	525.90	515.55	506.4
60000	594.18	576.08	560.42	546.77	534.82	524.29	514.9
65000	643.69	624.09	607.12	592.34	579.38	567.98	557.9
70000	693.21	672.10	653.82	637.90	623.95	611.68	600.8
75000	742.72	720.10	700.52	683.46	668.52	655.37	643.7
80000	792.24	768.11	747.22	729.03	713.09	699.06	686.6
85000	841.75	816.12	793.93	774.59	757.66	742.75	729.5
90000	891.27	864.12	840.63	820.16	802.22	786.44	772.4
95000	940.78	912.13	887.33	865.72	846.79	830.13	815.4
100000	990.29	960.14	934.03	911.28	891.36	873.82	858.3
105000	1039.81	1008.15	980.73	956.85	935.93	917.51	901.2
110000	1089.32	1056.15	1027.43	1002.41	980.50	961.20	944.1
120000	1188.35	1152.17	1120.84	1093.54	1069.63	1048.59	1029.9
130000	1287.38	1248.18	1214.24	1184.67	1158.77	1135.97	1115.8
140000	1386.41	1344.19	1307.64	1275.80	1247.90	1223.35	1201.6
150000	1485.44	1440.21	1401.05	1366.93	1337.04	1310.73	1287.4
160000	1584.47	1536.22	1494.45	1458.06	1426.18	1398.12	1373.3
170000	1683.50	1632.24	1587.85	1549.18	1515.31	1485.50	1459.1
180000	1782.53	1728.25	1681.26	1640.31	1604.45	1572.88	1544.9
190000	1881.56	1824.26	1774.66	1731.44	1693.58	1660.26	1630.8
200000	1980.59	1920.28	1868.06	1822.57	1782.72	1747.64	1716.6
210000	2079.62	2016.29	1961.46	1913.70	1871.86	1835.03	1802.4
220000	2178.65	2112.31	2054.87	2004.83	1960.99	1922.41	1888.3
230000	2277.68	2208.32	2148.27	2095.96	2050.13	2009.79	1974.1
240000	2376.71	2304.33	2241.67	2187.08	2139.26	2097.17	2059.9
250000	2475.74	2400.35	2335.08	2278.21	2228.40	2184.55	2145.8

Monthly Payments 8.75 %

LOAN AMOUNT	YEARS 22	23	24	25	30	35	40
100	0.84	0.83	0.82	0.81	0.78	0.75	0.74
200	1.69	1.66	1.64	1.62	1.55	1.51	1.48
500	4.22	4.16	4.11	4.06	3.88	3.77	3.70
1000	8.45	8.32	8.21	8.12	7.76	7.54	7.40
2000	16.89	16.65	16.43	16.23	15.51	15.08	14.81
5000	42.23	41.62	41.07	40.58	38.78	37.69	37.02
6000	50.67	49.94	49.28	48.70	46.54	45.23	44.42
7000	59.12	58.26	57.50	56.81	54.29	52.77	51.82
8000	67.57	66.59	65.71	64.93	62.05	60.31	59.22
9000	76.01	74.91	73.93	73.05	69.81	67.85	66.63
10000	84.46	83.23	82.14	81.16	77.56	75.38	74.03
12000	101.35	99.88	98.57	97.39	93.08	90.46	88.84
15000	126.69	124.85	123.21	121.74	116.34	113.08	111.05
20000	168.91	166.47	164.28	162.32	155.13	150.77	148.06
25000	211.14	208.08	205.35	202.90	193.91	188.46	185.08
30000	253.37	249.70	246.42	243.48	232.69	226.15	222.09
31000	261.82	258.02	254.63	251.60	240.45	233.69	229.49
32000	270.26	266.34	262.85	259.72	248.20	241.23	236.90
33000	278.71	274.67	271.06	267.83	255.96	248.77	244.30
34000	287.15	282.99	279.27	275.95	263.71	256.31	251.70
35000	295.60	291.31	287.49	284.06	271.47	263.85	259.11
36000	304.04	299.64	295.70	292.18	279.23	271.39	266.51
37000	312.49	307.96	303.92	300.30	286.98	278.92	273.91
38000	320.94	316.28	312.13	308.41	294.74	286.46	281.31
39000	329.38	324.61	320.34	316.53	302.50	294.00	288.72
40000	337.83	332.93	328.56	324.65	310.25	301.54	296.12
41000	346.27	341.25	336.77	332.76	318.01	309.08	303.52
42000	354.72	349.58	344.99	340.88	325.76	316.62	310.93
43000	363.16	357.90	353.20	348.99	333.52	324.16	318.33
44000	371.61	366.22	361.41	357.11	341.28	331.69	325.73
45000	380.06	374.55	369.63	365.23	349.03	339.23	333.14
46000	388.50	382.87	377.84	373.34	356.79	346.77	340.54
47000	396.95	391.19	386.06	381.46	364.55	354.31	347.94
48000	405.39	399.52	394.27	389.57	372.30	361.85	355.34
49000	413.84	407.84	402.48	397.69	380.06	369.39	362.75
50000	422.28	416.16	410.70	405.81	387.82	376.92	370.15
51000	430.73	424.49	418.91	413.92	395.57	384.46	377.55
52000	439.17	432.81	427.13	422.04	403.33	392.00	384.96
53000	447.62	441.13	435.34	430.16	411.08	399.54	392.36
54000	456.07	449.46	443.55	438.27	418.84	407.08	399.76
55000	464.51	457.78	451.77	446.39	426.60	414.62	407.17
56000	472.96	466.10	459.98	454.50	434.35	422.16	414.57
57000	481.40	474.43	468.20	462.62	442.11	429.69	421.97
58000	489.85	482.75	476.41	470.74	449.87	437.23	429.37
59000	498.29	491.07	484.62	478.85	457.62	444.77	436.78
60000	506.74	499.40	492.84	486.97	465.38	452.31	444.18
65000	548.97	541.01	533.91	527.55	504.16	490.00	481.20
70000	591.20	582.63	574.98	568.13	542.94	527.69	518.21
75000	633.43	624.24	616.05	608.71	581.72	565.39	555.23
80000	675.65	665.86	657.12	649.29	620.50	603.08	592.24
85000	717.88	707.48	698.19	689.87	659.29	640.77	629.26
90000	760.11	749.09	739.26	730.45	698.07	678.46	666.27
95000	802.34	790.71	780.33	771.03	736.85	716.16	703.29
100000	844.57	832.33	821.40	811.61	775.63	753.85	740.30
105000	886.80	873.94	862.47	852.19	814.41	791.54	777.32
110000	929.02	915.56	903.54	892.78	853.19	829.23	814.33
120000	1013.48	998.79	985.68	973.94	930.76	904.62	888.36
130000	1097.94	1082.02	1067.82	1055.10	1008.32	980.00	962.39
140000	1182.39	1165.26	1149.96	1136.26	1085.88	1055.39	1036.42
150000	1266.85	1248.49	1232.09	1217.42	1163.45	1130.77	1110.45
160000	1351.31	1331.72	1314.23	1298.58	1241.01	1206.16	1184.48
170000	1435.76	1414.95	1396.37	1379.74	1318.57	1281.54	1258.51
180000	1520.22	1498.19	1478.51	1460.91	1396.13	1356.93	1332.54
190000	1604.68	1581.42	1560.65	1542.07	1473.70	1432.31	1406.57
200000	1689.13	1664.65	1642.79	1623.23	1551.26	1507.70	1480.60
210000	1773.59	1747.88	1724.93	1704.39	1628.82	1583.08	1554.63
220000	1858.05	1831.12	1807.07	1785.55	1706.39	1658.47	1628.66
230000	1942.50	1914.35	1889.21	1866.71	1783.95	1733.85	1702.69
240000	2026.96	1997.58	1971.35	1947.87	1861.51	1809.24	1776.72
250000	2111.42	2080.81	2053.49	2029.04	1939.08	1884.62	1850.75

9.00 % Monthly Payments

LOAN AMOUNT	YEARS 1	2	3	4	5	6	7
100	8.74	4.56	3.17	2.48	2.07	1.79	1.60
200	17.48	9.12	6.34	4.96	4.14	3.59	3.20
500	43.69	22.80	15.86	12.40	10.34	8.97	8.00
1000	87.38	45.61	31.72	24.81	20.68	17.94	16.01
2000	174.75	91.22	63.45	49.61	41.36	35.89	32.01
5000	436.88	228.05	158.62	124.04	103.39	89.72	80.03
6000	524.25	273.66	190.34	148.84	124.07	107.66	96.04
7000	611.63	319.27	222.06	173.65	144.75	125.61	112.04
8000	699.00	364.88	253.79	198.46	165.43	143.55	128.05
9000	786.38	410.48	285.51	223.26	186.11	161.50	144.05
10000	873.75	456.09	317.23	248.07	206.79	179.44	160.06
12000	1048.50	547.31	380.68	297.69	248.14	215.33	192.07
15000	1310.63	684.14	475.85	372.11	310.18	269.16	240.09
20000	1747.51	912.19	634.47	496.14	413.57	358.88	320.12
25000	2184.38	1140.24	793.08	620.18	516.97	448.60	400.15
30000	2621.26	1368.28	951.70	744.21	620.36	538.32	480.18
31000	2708.64	1413.89	983.42	769.02	641.04	556.27	496.18
32000	2796.01	1459.50	1015.15	793.83	661.72	574.21	512.19
33000	2883.39	1505.11	1046.87	818.64	682.40	592.16	528.19
34000	2970.76	1550.72	1078.59	843.44	703.08	610.10	544.20
35000	3058.14	1596.33	1110.32	868.25	723.76	628.04	560.20
36000	3145.51	1641.94	1142.04	893.06	744.43	645.99	576.21
37000	3232.89	1687.55	1173.76	917.86	765.11	663.93	592.22
38000	3320.26	1733.16	1205.49	942.67	785.79	681.88	608.22
39000	3407.64	1778.77	1237.21	967.48	806.47	699.82	624.23
40000	3495.01	1824.38	1268.93	992.28	827.15	717.77	640.23
41000	3582.39	1869.99	1300.66	1017.09	847.83	735.71	656.24
42000	3669.76	1915.60	1332.38	1041.90	868.51	753.65	672.25
43000	3757.14	1961.20	1364.10	1066.71	889.19	771.60	688.25
44000	3844.51	2006.81	1395.83	1091.51	909.86	789.54	704.26
45000	3931.89	2052.42	1427.55	1116.32	930.54	807.49	720.26
46000	4019.27	2098.03	1459.27	1141.13	951.22	825.43	736.27
47000	4106.64	2143.64	1491.00	1165.93	971.90	843.37	752.27
48000	4194.02	2189.25	1522.72	1190.74	992.58	861.32	768.28
49000	4281.39	2234.86	1554.44	1215.55	1013.26	879.26	784.29
50000	4368.77	2280.47	1586.17	1240.36	1033.94	897.21	800.29
51000	4456.14	2326.08	1617.89	1265.16	1054.62	915.15	816.30
52000	4543.52	2371.69	1649.61	1289.97	1075.29	933.09	832.30
53000	4630.89	2417.30	1681.34	1314.78	1095.97	951.04	848.31
54000	4718.27	2462.91	1713.06	1339.58	1116.65	968.98	864.32
55000	4805.64	2508.52	1744.78	1364.39	1137.33	986.93	880.32
56000	4893.02	2554.13	1776.51	1389.20	1158.01	1004.87	896.33
57000	4980.39	2599.74	1808.23	1414.01	1178.69	1022.82	912.33
58000	5067.77	2645.35	1839.95	1438.81	1199.37	1040.76	928.34
59000	5155.14	2690.96	1871.68	1463.62	1220.05	1058.70	944.34
60000	5242.52	2736.57	1903.40	1488.43	1240.72	1076.65	960.35
65000	5679.40	2964.61	2062.02	1612.46	1344.12	1166.37	1040.38
70000	6116.27	3192.66	2220.63	1736.50	1447.51	1256.09	1120.41
75000	6553.15	3420.71	2379.25	1860.53	1550.90	1345.81	1200.44
80000	6990.03	3648.75	2537.87	1984.57	1654.30	1435.53	1280.47
85000	7426.90	3876.80	2696.48	2108.61	1757.69	1525.25	1360.50
90000	7863.78	4104.85	2855.10	2232.64	1861.09	1614.97	1440.53
95000	8300.66	4332.89	3013.72	2356.68	1964.48	1704.69	1520.56
100000	8737.53	4560.94	3172.33	2480.71	2067.87	1794.41	1600.58
105000	9174.41	4788.99	3330.95	2604.75	2171.27	1884.13	1680.61
110000	9611.29	5017.04	3489.57	2728.78	2274.66	1973.85	1760.64
120000	10485.04	5473.13	3806.80	2976.85	2481.45	2153.30	1920.70
130000	11358.79	5929.22	4124.03	3224.93	2688.23	2332.74	2080.76
140000	12232.55	6385.32	4441.27	3473.00	2895.02	2512.18	2240.82
150000	13106.30	6841.41	4758.50	3721.07	3101.81	2691.62	2400.88
160000	13980.05	7297.51	5075.73	3969.14	3308.60	2871.06	2560.94
170000	14853.81	7753.60	5392.97	4217.21	3515.38	3050.50	2720.99
180000	15727.56	8209.70	5710.20	4465.28	3722.17	3229.94	2881.05
190000	16601.31	8665.79	6027.44	4713.35	3928.96	3409.38	3041.11
200000	17475.07	9121.88	6344.67	4961.42	4135.75	3588.83	3201.17
210000	18348.82	9577.98	6661.90	5209.50	4342.53	3768.27	3361.23
220000	19222.57	10034.07	6979.14	5457.57	4549.32	3947.71	3521.29
230000	20096.33	10490.17	7296.37	5705.64	4756.11	4127.15	3681.34
240000	20970.08	10946.26	7613.60	5953.71	4962.89	4306.59	3841.40
250000	21843.83	11402.35	7930.84	6201.78	5169.68	4486.03	4001.46

Monthly Payments 9.00 %

LOAN AMOUNT	8	9	10	11	12	13	14
				YEARS			
100	1.46	1.35	1.26	1.19	1.13	1.08	1.04
200	2.91	2.69	2.52	2.37	2.26	2.16	2.08
500	7.28	6.73	6.29	5.94	5.64	5.40	5.20
1000	14.57	13.46	12.58	11.87	11.29	10.80	10.39
2000	29.13	26.91	25.16	23.74	22.58	21.61	20.79
5000	72.83	67.28	62.89	59.35	56.44	54.01	51.97
6000	87.39	80.74	75.47	71.22	67.73	64.82	62.36
7000	101.96	94.19	88.05	83.09	79.02	75.62	72.76
8000	116.52	107.65	100.63	94.96	90.30	86.42	83.15
9000	131.09	121.10	113.21	106.83	101.59	97.22	93.54
10000	145.65	134.56	125.79	118.70	112.88	108.03	103.94
12000	174.78	161.47	150.95	142.44	135.46	129.63	124.72
15000	218.48	201.84	188.68	178.05	169.32	162.04	155.90
20000	291.30	269.12	251.58	237.41	225.76	216.05	207.87
25000	364.13	336.40	314.47	296.76	282.20	270.07	259.84
30000	436.95	403.68	377.37	356.11	338.64	324.08	311.81
31000	451.52	417.14	389.94	367.98	349.93	334.89	322.20
32000	466.08	430.59	402.52	379.85	361.22	345.69	332.59
33000	480.65	444.05	415.10	391.72	372.50	356.49	342.99
34000	495.21	457.50	427.68	403.59	383.79	367.29	353.38
35000	509.78	470.96	440.26	415.46	395.08	378.10	363.78
36000	524.34	484.42	452.84	427.33	406.37	388.90	374.17
37000	538.91	497.87	465.42	439.20	417.66	399.70	384.56
38000	553.48	511.33	478.00	451.07	428.94	410.50	394.96
39000	568.04	524.78	490.58	462.94	440.23	421.31	405.35
40000	582.61	538.24	503.15	474.81	451.52	432.11	415.74
41000	597.17	551.70	515.73	486.68	462.81	442.91	426.14
42000	611.74	565.15	528.31	498.55	474.10	453.72	436.53
43000	626.30	578.61	540.89	510.42	485.38	464.52	446.92
44000	640.87	592.06	553.47	522.29	496.67	475.32	457.32
45000	655.43	605.52	566.05	534.16	507.96	486.12	467.71
46000	670.00	618.98	578.63	546.03	519.25	496.93	478.11
47000	684.56	632.43	591.21	557.90	530.54	507.73	488.50
48000	699.13	645.89	603.79	569.77	541.82	518.53	498.89
49000	713.69	659.34	616.36	581.64	553.11	529.33	509.29
50000	728.26	672.80	628.94	593.51	564.40	540.14	519.68
51000	742.82	686.26	641.52	605.38	575.69	550.94	530.07
52000	757.39	699.71	654.10	617.25	586.98	561.74	540.47
53000	771.95	713.17	666.68	629.12	598.26	572.55	550.86
54000	786.52	726.62	679.26	641.00	609.55	583.35	561.25
55000	801.08	740.08	691.84	652.87	620.84	594.15	571.65
56000	815.65	753.54	704.42	664.74	632.13	604.95	582.04
57000	830.21	766.99	716.99	676.61	643.42	615.76	592.43
58000	844.78	780.45	729.57	688.48	654.70	626.56	602.83
59000	859.34	793.90	742.15	700.35	665.99	637.36	613.22
60000	873.91	807.36	754.73	712.22	677.28	648.16	623.62
65000	946.73	874.64	817.63	771.57	733.72	702.18	675.58
70000	1019.56	941.92	880.52	830.92	790.16	756.19	727.55
75000	1092.39	1009.20	943.41	890.27	846.60	810.21	779.52
80000	1165.21	1076.48	1006.31	949.62	903.04	864.22	831.49
85000	1238.04	1143.76	1069.20	1008.97	959.48	918.23	883.46
90000	1310.86	1211.04	1132.10	1068.33	1015.92	972.25	935.42
95000	1383.69	1278.32	1194.99	1127.68	1072.36	1026.26	987.39
100000	1456.51	1345.60	1257.89	1187.03	1128.80	1080.27	1039.36
105000	1529.34	1412.88	1320.78	1246.38	1185.24	1134.29	1091.33
110000	1602.16	1480.16	1383.67	1305.73	1241.68	1188.30	1143.29
120000	1747.82	1614.72	1509.46	1424.43	1354.56	1296.33	1247.23
130000	1893.47	1749.28	1635.25	1543.14	1467.44	1404.36	1351.17
140000	2039.12	1883.84	1761.04	1661.84	1580.32	1512.38	1455.10
150000	2184.77	2018.40	1886.83	1780.54	1693.20	1620.41	1559.04
160000	2330.42	2152.96	2012.62	1899.24	1806.08	1728.44	1662.97
170000	2476.07	2287.52	2138.41	2017.95	1918.96	1836.47	1766.91
180000	2621.72	2422.08	2264.19	2136.65	2031.84	1944.49	1870.85
190000	2767.38	2556.64	2389.98	2255.35	2144.72	2052.52	1974.78
200000	2913.03	2691.20	2515.77	2374.06	2257.60	2160.55	2078.72
210000	3058.68	2825.76	2641.56	2492.76	2370.48	2268.58	2182.65
220000	3204.33	2960.32	2767.35	2611.46	2483.36	2376.60	2286.59
230000	3349.98	3094.88	2893.14	2730.16	2596.24	2484.63	2390.53
240000	3495.63	3229.44	3018.93	2848.87	2709.12	2592.66	2494.46
250000	3641.28	3364.00	3144.71	2967.57	2822.00	2700.69	2598.40

9.00 % Monthly Payments

LOAN AMOUNT	15	16	17	18	19	20	21
				YEARS			
100	1.00	0.97	0.95	0.93	0.91	0.89	0.87
200	2.01	1.95	1.90	1.85	1.81	1.78	1.75
500	5.02	4.87	4.74	4.63	4.53	4.45	4.37
1000	10.05	9.75	9.49	9.26	9.07	8.89	8.74
2000	20.09	19.49	18.97	18.52	18.13	17.78	17.48
5000	50.23	48.73	47.44	46.31	45.33	44.46	43.69
6000	60.27	58.48	56.92	55.57	54.39	53.35	52.43
7000	70.32	68.22	66.41	64.83	63.46	62.24	61.17
8000	80.36	77.97	75.90	74.10	72.52	71.14	69.91
9000	90.41	87.71	85.39	83.36	81.59	80.03	78.65
10000	100.45	97.46	94.87	92.62	90.65	88.92	87.39
12000	120.54	116.95	113.85	111.15	108.78	106.70	104.87
15000	150.68	146.19	142.31	138.93	135.98	133.38	131.08
20000	200.90	194.92	189.75	185.24	181.30	177.84	174.78
25000	251.13	243.65	237.18	231.55	226.63	222.30	218.47
30000	301.36	292.38	284.62	277.86	271.95	266.76	262.17
31000	311.40	302.13	294.11	287.13	281.02	275.65	270.91
32000	321.45	311.87	303.59	296.39	290.08	284.54	279.65
33000	331.49	321.62	313.08	305.65	299.15	293.43	288.39
34000	341.54	331.36	322.57	314.91	308.21	302.32	297.13
35000	351.58	341.11	332.06	324.17	317.28	311.22	305.86
36000	361.63	350.86	341.54	333.44	326.34	320.11	314.60
37000	371.67	360.60	351.03	342.70	335.41	329.00	323.34
38000	381.72	370.35	360.52	351.96	344.47	337.89	332.08
39000	391.76	380.09	370.00	361.22	353.54	346.78	340.82
40000	401.81	389.84	379.49	370.48	362.60	355.68	349.56
41000	411.85	399.59	388.98	379.75	371.67	364.57	358.30
42000	421.90	409.33	398.47	389.01	380.73	373.46	367.04
43000	431.94	419.08	407.95	398.27	389.80	382.35	375.78
44000	441.99	428.83	417.44	407.53	398.86	391.24	384.52
45000	452.03	438.57	426.93	416.80	407.93	400.14	393.25
46000	462.08	448.32	436.42	426.06	416.99	409.03	401.99
47000	472.12	458.06	445.90	435.32	426.06	417.92	410.73
48000	482.17	467.81	455.39	444.58	435.12	426.81	419.47
49000	492.21	477.56	464.88	453.84	444.19	435.70	428.21
50000	502.26	487.30	474.36	463.11	453.25	444.59	436.95
51000	512.30	497.05	483.85	472.37	462.32	453.49	445.69
52000	522.35	506.79	493.34	481.63	471.39	462.38	454.43
53000	532.39	516.54	502.83	490.89	480.45	471.27	463.17
54000	542.44	526.29	512.31	500.15	489.52	480.16	471.91
55000	552.49	536.03	521.80	509.42	498.58	489.05	480.64
56000	562.53	545.78	531.29	518.68	507.65	497.95	489.38
57000	572.58	555.52	540.78	527.94	516.71	506.84	498.12
58000	582.62	565.27	550.26	537.20	525.78	515.73	506.86
59000	592.67	575.02	559.75	546.46	534.84	524.62	515.60
60000	602.71	584.76	569.24	555.73	543.91	533.51	524.34
65000	652.94	633.49	616.67	602.04	589.23	577.97	568.03
70000	703.16	682.22	664.11	648.35	634.56	622.43	611.73
75000	753.39	730.95	711.55	694.66	679.88	666.89	655.42
80000	803.62	779.68	758.98	740.97	725.21	711.35	699.12
85000	853.84	828.41	806.42	787.28	770.53	755.81	742.81
90000	904.07	877.14	853.86	833.59	815.86	800.27	786.51
95000	954.29	925.87	901.29	879.90	861.18	844.73	830.20
100000	1004.52	974.60	948.73	926.21	906.51	889.19	873.90
105000	1054.74	1023.33	996.17	972.52	951.84	933.65	917.59
110000	1104.97	1072.06	1043.60	1018.83	997.16	978.11	961.29
120000	1205.42	1169.52	1138.47	1111.45	1087.81	1067.03	1048.68
130000	1305.87	1266.98	1233.35	1204.08	1178.46	1155.95	1136.07
140000	1406.33	1364.44	1328.22	1296.70	1269.11	1244.87	1223.46
150000	1506.78	1461.90	1423.09	1389.32	1359.76	1333.78	1310.85
160000	1607.23	1559.36	1517.97	1481.94	1450.42	1422.70	1398.24
170000	1707.68	1656.82	1612.84	1574.56	1541.07	1511.62	1485.63
180000	1808.13	1754.28	1707.71	1667.18	1631.72	1600.54	1573.02
190000	1908.59	1851.74	1802.58	1759.80	1722.37	1689.46	1660.41
200000	2009.04	1949.21	1897.46	1852.42	1813.02	1778.38	1747.80
210000	2109.49	2046.67	1992.33	1945.04	1903.67	1867.30	1835.19
220000	2209.94	2144.13	2087.20	2037.67	1994.32	1956.22	1922.58
230000	2310.39	2241.59	2182.08	2130.29	2084.97	2045.14	2009.97
240000	2410.85	2339.05	2276.95	2222.91	2175.62	2134.05	2097.36
250000	2511.30	2436.51	2371.82	2315.53	2266.27	2222.97	2184.75

Monthly Payments 9.00 %

LOAN AMOUNT	22	23	24	25	30	35	40
	YEARS						
100	0.86	0.85	0.84	0.83	0.79	0.77	0.76
200	1.72	1.70	1.68	1.66	1.59	1.54	1.52
500	4.30	4.24	4.19	4.14	3.96	3.86	3.79
1000	8.60	8.48	8.38	8.28	7.93	7.72	7.59
2000	17.21	16.97	16.75	16.56	15.86	15.43	15.17
5000	43.02	42.42	41.88	41.40	39.64	38.59	37.94
6000	51.62	50.90	50.25	49.68	47.57	46.30	45.52
7000	60.22	59.38	58.63	57.96	55.50	54.02	53.11
8000	68.83	67.86	67.01	66.24	63.43	61.74	60.70
9000	77.43	76.35	75.38	74.52	71.35	69.46	68.29
10000	86.04	84.83	83.76	82.80	79.28	77.17	75.87
12000	103.24	101.80	100.51	99.36	95.14	92.61	91.05
15000	129.05	127.25	125.64	124.20	118.92	115.76	113.81
20000	172.07	169.66	167.51	165.60	158.57	154.35	151.75
25000	215.09	212.08	209.39	206.99	198.21	192.93	189.69
30000	258.11	254.49	251.27	248.39	237.85	231.52	227.62
31000	266.71	262.98	259.65	256.67	245.78	239.24	235.21
32000	275.31	271.46	268.02	264.95	253.71	246.96	242.80
33000	283.92	279.94	276.40	273.23	261.63	254.67	250.38
34000	292.52	288.43	284.77	281.51	269.56	262.39	257.97
35000	301.12	296.91	293.15	289.79	277.49	270.11	265.56
36000	309.73	305.39	301.53	298.07	285.42	277.83	273.15
37000	318.33	313.87	309.90	306.35	293.35	285.54	280.73
38000	326.93	322.36	318.28	314.63	301.28	293.26	288.32
39000	335.54	330.84	326.65	322.91	309.20	300.98	295.91
40000	344.14	339.32	335.03	331.19	317.13	308.70	303.50
41000	352.74	347.81	343.40	339.47	325.06	316.41	311.08
42000	361.35	356.29	351.78	347.75	332.99	324.13	318.67
43000	369.95	364.77	360.16	356.03	340.92	331.85	326.26
44000	378.55	373.26	368.53	364.31	348.85	339.57	333.85
45000	387.16	381.74	376.91	372.59	356.77	347.28	341.43
46000	395.76	390.22	385.28	380.87	364.70	355.00	349.02
47000	404.37	398.71	393.66	389.15	372.63	362.72	356.61
48000	412.97	407.19	402.04	397.43	380.56	370.43	364.20
49000	421.57	415.67	410.41	405.71	388.49	378.15	371.78
50000	430.18	424.15	418.79	413.99	396.42	385.87	379.37
51000	438.78	432.64	427.16	422.27	404.34	393.59	386.96
52000	447.38	441.12	435.54	430.55	412.27	401.30	394.54
53000	455.99	449.60	443.91	438.83	420.20	409.02	402.13
54000	464.59	458.09	452.29	447.11	428.13	416.74	409.72
55000	473.19	466.57	460.67	455.39	436.06	424.46	417.31
56000	481.80	475.05	469.04	463.67	443.99	432.17	424.89
57000	490.40	483.54	477.42	471.95	451.91	439.89	432.48
58000	499.00	492.02	485.79	480.23	459.84	447.61	440.07
59000	507.61	500.50	494.17	488.51	467.77	455.33	447.66
60000	516.21	508.99	502.54	496.79	475.70	463.04	455.24
65000	559.23	551.40	544.42	538.19	515.34	501.63	493.18
70000	602.25	593.82	586.30	579.58	554.98	540.22	531.12
75000	645.26	636.23	628.18	620.98	594.62	578.80	569.06
80000	688.28	678.65	670.06	662.38	634.27	617.39	606.99
85000	731.30	721.06	711.94	703.78	673.91	655.98	644.93
90000	774.32	763.48	753.82	745.18	713.55	694.57	682.87
95000	817.33	805.89	795.69	786.58	753.19	733.15	720.80
100000	860.35	848.31	837.57	827.98	792.83	771.74	758.74
105000	903.37	890.72	879.45	869.38	832.47	810.33	796.68
110000	946.39	933.14	921.33	910.78	872.12	848.91	834.61
120000	1032.42	1017.97	1005.09	993.57	951.40	926.09	910.49
130000	1118.46	1102.80	1088.84	1076.37	1030.68	1003.26	986.36
140000	1204.49	1187.63	1172.60	1159.17	1109.97	1080.43	1062.24
150000	1290.53	1272.46	1256.36	1241.97	1189.25	1157.61	1138.11
160000	1376.56	1357.29	1340.12	1324.76	1268.53	1234.78	1213.98
170000	1462.60	1442.13	1423.87	1407.56	1347.82	1311.96	1289.86
180000	1548.63	1526.96	1507.63	1490.36	1427.10	1389.13	1365.73
190000	1634.67	1611.79	1591.39	1573.16	1506.38	1466.30	1441.61
200000	1720.70	1696.62	1675.15	1655.95	1585.67	1543.48	1517.48
210000	1806.74	1781.45	1758.90	1738.75	1664.95	1620.65	1593.35
220000	1892.77	1866.28	1842.66	1821.55	1744.23	1697.83	1669.23
230000	1978.81	1951.11	1926.42	1904.35	1823.51	1775.00	1745.10
240000	2064.84	2035.94	2010.18	1987.15	1902.80	1852.17	1820.98
250000	2150.88	2120.77	2093.93	2069.94	1982.08	1929.35	1896.85

9.25 % Monthly Payments

LOAN AMOUNT	YEARS 1	2	3	4	5	6	7
100	8.75	4.57	3.18	2.49	2.08	1.81	1.61
200	17.50	9.14	6.37	4.98	4.16	3.61	3.23
500	43.74	22.86	15.92	12.46	10.40	9.03	8.06
1000	87.49	45.72	31.84	24.92	20.80	18.06	16.13
2000	174.97	91.44	63.67	49.84	41.59	36.13	32.26
5000	437.44	228.60	159.18	124.61	103.98	90.32	80.64
6000	524.92	274.32	191.01	149.53	124.77	108.38	96.77
7000	612.41	320.04	222.85	174.45	145.57	126.45	112.90
8000	699.90	365.76	254.68	199.37	166.36	144.51	129.02
9000	787.38	411.48	286.52	224.29	187.16	162.57	145.15
10000	874.87	457.20	318.35	249.21	207.96	180.64	161.28
12000	1049.84	548.64	382.02	299.06	249.55	216.76	193.54
15000	1312.31	685.80	477.53	373.82	311.93	270.95	241.92
20000	1749.74	914.40	636.71	498.43	415.91	361.27	322.56
25000	2187.18	1143.00	795.89	623.04	519.89	451.59	403.20
30000	2624.61	1371.60	955.06	747.64	623.87	541.91	483.84
31000	2712.10	1417.32	986.90	772.56	644.66	559.97	499.97
32000	2799.58	1463.04	1018.73	797.49	665.46	578.03	516.10
33000	2887.07	1508.76	1050.57	822.41	686.25	596.10	532.22
34000	2974.56	1554.48	1082.40	847.33	707.05	614.16	548.35
35000	3062.05	1600.20	1114.24	872.25	727.84	632.23	564.48
36000	3149.53	1645.92	1146.07	897.17	748.64	650.29	580.61
37000	3237.02	1691.64	1177.91	922.09	769.44	668.35	596.74
38000	3324.51	1737.36	1209.75	947.01	790.23	686.42	612.86
39000	3411.99	1783.08	1241.58	971.94	811.03	704.48	628.99
40000	3499.48	1828.80	1273.42	996.86	831.82	722.54	645.12
41000	3586.97	1874.52	1305.25	1021.78	852.62	740.61	661.25
42000	3674.45	1920.24	1337.09	1046.70	873.41	758.67	677.38
43000	3761.94	1965.96	1368.92	1071.62	894.21	776.73	693.50
44000	3849.43	2011.68	1400.76	1096.54	915.00	794.80	709.63
45000	3936.92	2057.40	1432.59	1121.46	935.80	812.86	725.76
46000	4024.40	2103.12	1464.43	1146.39	956.60	830.93	741.89
47000	4111.89	2148.84	1496.26	1171.31	977.39	848.99	758.02
48000	4199.38	2194.56	1528.10	1196.23	998.19	867.05	774.14
49000	4286.86	2240.28	1559.93	1221.15	1018.98	885.12	790.27
50000	4374.35	2286.00	1591.77	1246.07	1039.78	903.18	806.40
51000	4461.84	2331.72	1623.61	1270.99	1060.57	921.24	822.53
52000	4549.32	2377.44	1655.44	1295.91	1081.37	939.31	838.66
53000	4636.81	2423.16	1687.28	1320.84	1102.16	957.37	854.78
54000	4724.30	2468.87	1719.11	1345.76	1122.96	975.43	870.91
55000	4811.79	2514.59	1750.95	1370.68	1143.76	993.50	887.04
56000	4899.27	2560.31	1782.78	1395.60	1164.55	1011.56	903.17
57000	4986.76	2606.03	1814.62	1420.52	1185.35	1029.62	919.30
58000	5074.25	2651.75	1846.45	1445.44	1206.14	1047.69	935.42
59000	5161.73	2697.47	1878.29	1470.37	1226.94	1065.75	951.55
60000	5249.22	2743.19	1910.12	1495.29	1247.73	1083.82	967.68
65000	5686.66	2971.79	2069.30	1619.89	1351.71	1174.13	1048.32
70000	6124.09	3200.39	2228.48	1744.50	1455.69	1264.45	1128.96
75000	6561.53	3428.99	2387.66	1869.11	1559.67	1354.77	1209.60
80000	6998.96	3657.59	2546.83	1993.72	1663.65	1445.09	1290.24
85000	7436.40	3886.19	2706.01	2118.32	1767.62	1535.41	1370.88
90000	7873.83	4114.79	2865.19	2242.93	1871.60	1625.72	1451.52
95000	8311.27	4343.39	3024.36	2367.54	1975.58	1716.04	1532.16
100000	8748.70	4571.99	3183.54	2492.14	2079.56	1806.36	1612.80
105000	9186.14	4800.59	3342.72	2616.75	2183.53	1896.68	1693.44
110000	9623.57	5029.19	3501.89	2741.36	2287.51	1986.99	1774.08
120000	10498.44	5486.39	3820.25	2990.57	2495.47	2167.63	1935.36
130000	11373.31	5943.59	4138.60	3239.79	2703.42	2348.27	2096.64
140000	12248.18	6400.79	4456.96	3489.00	2911.38	2528.90	2257.92
150000	13123.05	6857.99	4775.31	3738.22	3119.33	2709.54	2419.20
160000	13997.92	7315.19	5093.66	3987.43	3327.29	2890.17	2580.48
170000	14872.79	7772.38	5412.02	4236.65	3535.25	3070.81	2741.76
180000	15747.66	8229.58	5730.37	4485.86	3743.20	3251.45	2903.04
190000	16622.53	8686.78	6048.73	4735.07	3951.16	3432.08	3064.32
200000	17497.40	9143.98	6367.08	4984.29	4159.11	3612.72	3225.60
210000	18372.27	9601.18	6685.44	5233.50	4367.07	3793.35	3386.88
220000	19247.14	10058.38	7003.79	5482.72	4575.02	3973.99	3548.16
230000	20122.01	10515.58	7322.14	5731.93	4782.98	4154.63	3709.44
240000	20996.88	10972.78	7640.50	5981.15	4990.94	4335.26	3870.72
250000	21871.75	11429.98	7958.85	6230.36	5198.89	4515.90	4032.00

Monthly Payments 9.25 %

LOAN AMOUNT	8	9	10	11	12	13	14
			YEARS				
100	1.47	1.36	1.27	1.20	1.14	1.09	1.05
200	2.94	2.72	2.54	2.40	2.28	2.19	2.11
500	7.34	6.79	6.35	6.00	5.71	5.47	5.27
1000	14.69	13.58	12.71	12.00	11.42	10.94	10.53
2000	29.38	27.17	25.42	24.01	22.85	21.88	21.07
5000	73.45	67.92	63.55	60.02	57.12	54.70	52.67
6000	88.14	81.50	76.25	72.02	68.54	65.64	63.21
7000	102.83	95.08	88.96	84.02	79.96	76.59	73.74
8000	117.52	108.67	101.67	96.03	91.39	87.53	84.27
9000	132.21	122.25	114.38	108.03	102.81	98.47	94.81
10000	146.90	135.84	127.09	120.03	114.24	109.41	105.34
12000	176.28	163.00	152.51	144.04	137.08	131.29	126.41
15000	220.35	203.75	190.64	180.05	171.35	164.11	158.01
20000	293.80	271.67	254.18	240.06	228.47	218.82	210.68
25000	367.25	339.59	317.73	300.08	285.59	273.52	263.36
30000	440.70	407.51	381.27	360.09	342.71	328.22	316.03
31000	455.39	421.09	393.98	372.10	354.13	339.17	326.56
32000	470.08	434.67	406.69	384.10	365.55	350.11	337.09
33000	484.77	448.26	419.40	396.10	376.98	361.05	347.63
34000	499.46	461.84	432.11	408.11	388.40	371.99	358.16
35000	514.15	475.42	444.82	420.11	399.82	382.93	368.70
36000	528.84	489.01	457.53	432.11	411.25	393.87	379.23
37000	543.53	502.59	470.24	444.12	422.67	404.81	389.77
38000	558.22	516.18	482.95	456.12	434.09	415.75	400.30
39000	572.91	529.76	495.65	468.12	445.52	426.69	410.83
40000	587.60	543.34	508.36	480.13	456.94	437.63	421.37
41000	602.29	556.93	521.07	492.13	468.36	448.57	431.90
42000	616.98	570.51	533.78	504.13	479.79	459.51	442.44
43000	631.67	584.09	546.49	516.14	491.21	470.46	452.97
44000	646.36	597.68	559.20	528.14	502.63	481.40	463.51
45000	661.05	611.26	571.91	540.14	514.06	492.34	474.04
46000	675.74	624.84	584.62	552.15	525.48	503.28	484.57
47000	690.43	638.43	597.33	564.15	536.90	514.22	495.11
48000	705.12	652.01	610.04	576.15	548.33	525.16	505.64
49000	719.81	665.59	622.75	588.15	559.75	536.10	516.18
50000	734.50	679.18	635.45	600.16	571.18	547.04	526.71
51000	749.19	692.76	648.16	612.16	582.60	557.98	537.24
52000	763.88	706.34	660.87	624.16	594.02	568.92	547.78
53000	778.57	719.93	673.58	636.17	605.45	579.86	558.31
54000	793.26	733.51	686.29	648.17	616.87	590.80	568.85
55000	807.95	747.10	699.00	660.17	628.29	601.75	579.38
56000	822.64	760.68	711.71	672.18	639.72	612.69	589.92
57000	837.33	774.26	724.42	684.18	651.14	623.63	600.45
58000	852.02	787.85	737.13	696.18	662.56	634.57	610.98
59000	866.71	801.43	749.84	708.19	673.99	645.51	621.52
60000	881.40	815.01	762.54	720.19	685.41	656.45	632.05
65000	954.85	882.93	826.09	780.21	742.53	711.15	684.72
70000	1028.30	950.85	889.64	840.22	799.65	765.86	737.39
75000	1101.75	1018.77	953.18	900.24	856.76	820.56	790.07
80000	1175.20	1086.68	1016.73	960.25	913.88	875.27	842.74
85000	1248.65	1154.60	1080.27	1020.27	971.00	929.97	895.41
90000	1322.10	1222.52	1143.82	1080.28	1028.12	984.67	948.08
95000	1395.55	1290.44	1207.36	1140.30	1085.23	1039.38	1000.75
100000	1469.00	1358.36	1270.91	1200.32	1142.35	1094.08	1053.42
105000	1542.45	1426.27	1334.45	1260.33	1199.47	1148.79	1106.09
110000	1615.90	1494.19	1398.00	1320.35	1256.59	1203.49	1158.76
120000	1762.80	1630.03	1525.09	1440.38	1370.82	1312.90	1264.11
130000	1909.70	1765.86	1652.18	1560.41	1485.06	1422.31	1369.45
140000	2056.60	1901.70	1779.27	1680.44	1599.29	1531.72	1474.79
150000	2203.50	2037.53	1906.36	1800.47	1713.53	1641.12	1580.13
160000	2350.40	2173.37	2033.45	1920.51	1827.76	1750.53	1685.47
170000	2497.30	2309.20	2160.54	2040.54	1942.00	1859.94	1790.82
180000	2644.20	2445.04	2287.63	2160.57	2056.23	1969.35	1896.16
190000	2791.10	2580.88	2414.73	2280.60	2170.47	2078.76	2001.50
200000	2938.00	2716.71	2541.82	2400.63	2284.70	2188.17	2106.84
210000	3084.90	2852.55	2668.91	2520.66	2398.94	2297.57	2212.18
220000	3231.80	2988.38	2796.00	2640.70	2513.17	2406.98	2317.53
230000	3378.70	3124.22	2923.09	2760.73	2627.41	2516.39	2422.87
240000	3525.60	3260.05	3050.18	2880.76	2741.64	2625.80	2528.21
250000	3672.50	3395.89	3177.27	3000.79	2855.88	2735.21	2633.55

9.25 % Monthly Payments

LOAN AMOUNT	15	16	17	18	19	20	21
				YEARS			
100	1.02	0.99	0.96	0.94	0.92	0.90	0.89
200	2.04	1.98	1.93	1.88	1.84	1.81	1.78
500	5.09	4.95	4.82	4.71	4.61	4.52	4.45
1000	10.19	9.89	9.64	9.41	9.22	9.05	8.90
2000	20.38	19.78	19.27	18.82	18.44	18.09	17.79
5000	50.94	49.46	48.18	47.06	46.09	45.23	44.48
6000	61.13	59.35	57.81	56.47	55.31	54.28	53.37
7000	71.32	69.24	67.45	65.89	64.52	63.33	62.27
8000	81.51	79.13	77.08	75.30	73.74	72.37	71.17
9000	91.69	89.02	86.72	84.71	82.96	81.42	80.06
10000	101.88	98.92	96.35	94.12	92.18	90.47	88.96
12000	122.26	118.70	115.62	112.95	110.61	108.56	106.75
15000	152.82	148.37	144.53	141.19	138.26	135.70	133.44
20000	203.77	197.83	192.70	188.25	184.35	180.93	177.92
25000	254.71	247.29	240.88	235.31	230.44	226.16	222.40
30000	305.65	296.75	289.06	282.37	276.53	271.40	266.87
31000	315.84	306.64	298.69	291.78	285.75	280.44	275.77
32000	326.03	316.53	308.33	301.20	294.96	289.49	284.67
33000	336.21	326.42	317.96	310.61	304.18	298.54	293.56
34000	346.40	336.31	327.60	320.02	313.40	307.58	302.46
35000	356.59	346.20	337.23	329.43	322.62	316.63	311.35
36000	366.78	356.10	346.87	338.85	331.83	325.68	320.25
37000	376.97	365.99	356.50	348.26	341.05	334.72	329.15
38000	387.16	375.88	366.14	357.67	350.27	343.77	338.04
39000	397.34	385.77	375.77	367.08	359.49	352.82	346.94
40000	407.53	395.66	385.41	376.49	368.70	361.86	355.83
41000	417.72	405.55	395.04	385.91	377.92	370.91	364.73
42000	427.91	415.45	404.68	395.32	387.14	379.96	373.62
43000	438.10	425.34	414.31	404.73	396.36	389.00	382.52
44000	448.29	435.23	423.95	414.14	405.57	398.05	391.42
45000	458.47	445.12	433.58	423.56	414.79	407.10	400.31
46000	468.66	455.01	443.22	432.97	424.01	416.14	409.21
47000	478.85	464.90	452.85	442.38	433.23	425.19	418.10
48000	489.04	474.80	462.49	451.79	442.44	434.24	427.00
49000	499.23	484.69	472.13	461.21	451.66	443.28	435.90
50000	509.41	494.58	481.76	470.62	460.88	452.33	444.79
51000	519.60	504.47	491.40	480.03	470.10	461.38	453.69
52000	529.79	514.36	501.03	489.44	479.32	470.42	462.58
53000	539.98	524.25	510.67	498.86	488.53	479.47	471.48
54000	550.17	534.14	520.30	508.27	497.75	488.52	480.37
55000	560.36	544.04	529.94	517.68	506.97	497.56	489.27
56000	570.54	553.93	539.57	527.09	516.19	506.61	498.17
57000	580.73	563.82	549.21	536.50	525.40	515.66	507.06
58000	590.92	573.71	558.84	545.92	534.62	524.70	515.96
59000	601.11	583.60	568.48	555.33	543.84	533.75	524.85
60000	611.30	593.49	578.11	564.74	553.06	542.80	533.75
65000	662.24	642.95	626.29	611.80	599.14	588.03	578.23
70000	713.18	692.41	674.46	658.87	645.23	633.26	622.71
75000	764.12	741.87	722.64	705.93	691.32	678.49	667.19
80000	815.06	791.33	770.82	752.99	737.41	723.73	711.67
85000	866.01	840.78	818.99	800.05	783.50	768.96	756.15
90000	916.95	890.24	867.17	847.11	829.58	814.19	800.62
95000	967.89	939.70	915.35	894.17	875.67	859.43	845.10
100000	1018.83	989.16	963.52	941.24	921.76	904.66	889.58
105000	1069.77	1038.61	1011.70	988.30	967.85	949.89	934.06
110000	1120.71	1088.07	1059.87	1035.36	1013.94	995.13	978.54
120000	1222.60	1186.99	1156.23	1129.48	1106.11	1085.59	1067.50
130000	1324.48	1285.90	1252.58	1223.61	1198.29	1176.06	1156.46
140000	1426.36	1384.82	1348.93	1317.73	1290.46	1266.52	1245.42
150000	1528.24	1483.74	1445.28	1411.85	1382.64	1356.99	1334.37
160000	1630.13	1582.65	1541.63	1505.98	1474.82	1447.46	1423.33
170000	1732.01	1681.57	1637.99	1600.10	1566.99	1537.92	1512.29
180000	1833.89	1780.48	1734.34	1694.23	1659.17	1628.39	1601.25
190000	1935.78	1879.40	1830.69	1788.35	1751.34	1718.85	1690.21
200000	2037.66	1978.31	1927.04	1882.47	1843.52	1809.32	1779.17
210000	2139.54	2077.23	2023.39	1976.60	1935.70	1899.79	1868.12
220000	2241.43	2176.15	2119.75	2070.72	2027.87	1990.25	1957.08
230000	2343.31	2275.06	2216.10	2164.84	2120.05	2080.72	2046.04
240000	2445.19	2373.98	2312.45	2258.97	2212.22	2171.18	2135.00
250000	2547.07	2472.89	2408.80	2353.09	2304.40	2261.65	2223.96

Monthly Payments 9.25 %

LOAN AMOUNT	22	23	24	25	30	35	40
				YEARS			
100	0.88	0.86	0.85	0.84	0.81	0.79	0.78
200	1.75	1.73	1.71	1.69	1.62	1.58	1.55
500	4.38	4.32	4.27	4.22	4.05	3.95	3.89
1000	8.76	8.64	8.54	8.44	8.10	7.90	7.77
2000	17.52	17.29	17.08	16.89	16.20	15.79	15.55
5000	43.81	43.22	42.69	42.22	40.51	39.49	38.86
6000	52.57	51.86	51.23	50.67	48.61	47.38	46.64
7000	61.34	60.51	59.77	59.11	56.71	55.28	54.41
8000	70.10	69.15	68.31	67.56	64.81	63.18	62.18
9000	78.86	77.80	76.85	76.00	72.91	71.08	69.95
10000	87.62	86.44	85.39	84.44	81.01	78.97	77.73
12000	105.15	103.73	102.46	101.33	97.22	94.77	93.27
15000	131.44	129.66	128.08	126.67	121.52	118.46	116.59
20000	175.25	172.88	170.77	168.89	162.03	157.95	155.45
25000	219.06	216.10	213.46	211.11	202.54	197.43	194.32
30000	262.87	259.32	256.16	253.33	243.04	236.92	233.18
31000	271.64	267.96	264.70	261.78	251.14	244.82	240.95
32000	280.40	276.61	273.23	270.22	259.25	252.71	248.72
33000	289.16	285.25	281.77	278.67	267.35	260.61	256.50
34000	297.92	293.90	290.31	287.11	275.45	268.51	264.27
35000	306.68	302.54	298.85	295.56	283.55	276.40	272.04
36000	315.45	311.18	307.39	304.00	291.65	284.30	279.82
37000	324.21	319.83	315.93	312.45	299.75	292.20	287.59
38000	332.97	328.47	324.47	320.89	307.85	300.10	295.36
39000	341.73	337.12	333.00	329.34	315.96	307.99	303.13
40000	350.50	345.76	341.54	337.78	324.06	315.89	310.91
41000	359.26	354.40	350.08	346.22	332.16	323.79	318.68
42000	368.02	363.05	358.62	354.67	340.26	331.69	326.45
43000	376.78	371.69	367.16	363.11	348.36	339.58	334.22
44000	385.55	380.34	375.70	371.56	356.46	347.48	342.00
45000	394.31	388.98	384.24	380.00	364.56	355.38	349.77
46000	403.07	397.62	392.77	388.45	372.67	363.27	357.54
47000	411.83	406.27	401.31	396.89	380.77	371.17	365.31
48000	420.60	414.91	409.85	405.34	388.87	379.07	373.09
49000	429.36	423.56	418.39	413.78	396.97	386.97	380.86
50000	438.12	432.20	426.93	422.22	405.07	394.86	388.63
51000	446.88	440.84	435.47	430.67	413.17	402.76	396.41
52000	455.65	449.49	444.01	439.11	421.27	410.66	404.18
53000	464.41	458.13	452.54	447.56	429.38	418.56	411.95
54000	473.17	466.78	461.08	456.00	437.48	426.45	419.72
55000	481.93	475.42	469.62	464.45	445.58	434.35	427.50
56000	490.70	484.06	478.16	472.89	453.68	442.25	435.27
57000	499.46	492.71	486.70	481.34	461.78	450.14	443.04
58000	508.22	501.35	495.24	489.78	469.88	458.04	450.81
59000	516.98	510.00	503.78	498.23	477.98	465.94	458.59
60000	525.75	518.64	512.31	506.67	486.09	473.84	466.36
65000	569.56	561.86	555.01	548.89	526.59	513.32	505.22
70000	613.37	605.08	597.70	591.11	567.10	552.81	544.09
75000	657.18	648.30	640.39	633.34	607.61	592.30	582.95
80000	700.99	691.52	683.09	675.56	648.11	631.78	621.81
85000	744.81	734.74	725.78	717.78	688.62	671.27	660.68
90000	788.62	777.96	768.47	760.00	729.13	710.75	699.54
95000	832.43	821.18	811.17	802.23	769.63	750.24	738.40
100000	876.24	864.40	853.86	844.45	810.14	789.73	777.27
105000	920.05	907.62	896.55	886.67	850.65	829.21	816.13
110000	963.87	950.84	939.24	928.89	891.16	868.70	854.99
120000	1051.49	1037.28	1024.63	1013.34	972.17	947.67	932.72
130000	1139.12	1123.72	1110.02	1097.78	1053.18	1026.65	1010.44
140000	1226.74	1210.16	1195.40	1182.23	1134.20	1105.62	1088.17
150000	1314.36	1296.60	1280.79	1266.67	1215.21	1184.59	1165.90
160000	1401.99	1383.04	1366.17	1351.12	1296.23	1263.56	1243.62
170000	1489.61	1469.48	1451.56	1435.56	1377.24	1342.54	1321.35
180000	1577.24	1555.92	1536.94	1520.01	1458.26	1421.51	1399.08
190000	1664.86	1642.36	1622.33	1604.45	1539.27	1500.48	1476.80
200000	1752.48	1728.80	1707.72	1688.90	1620.28	1579.46	1554.53
210000	1840.11	1815.24	1793.10	1773.34	1701.30	1658.43	1632.26
220000	1927.73	1901.68	1878.49	1857.79	1782.31	1737.40	1709.98
230000	2015.36	1988.12	1963.87	1942.23	1863.33	1816.37	1787.71
240000	2102.98	2074.56	2049.26	2026.68	1944.34	1895.35	1865.44
250000	2190.61	2161.00	2134.65	2111.12	2025.36	1974.32	1943.16

9.50 % Monthly Payments

LOAN AMOUNT	1	2	3	4	5	6	7
				YEARS			
100	8.76	4.58	3.19	2.50	2.09	1.82	1.63
200	17.52	9.17	6.39	5.01	4.18	3.64	3.25
500	43.80	22.92	15.97	12.52	10.46	9.09	8.13
1000	87.60	45.83	31.95	25.04	20.91	18.18	16.25
2000	175.20	91.66	63.90	50.07	41.83	36.37	32.50
5000	437.99	229.15	159.74	125.18	104.56	90.92	81.25
6000	525.59	274.98	191.69	150.22	125.48	109.10	97.50
7000	613.19	320.81	223.63	175.25	146.39	127.28	113.75
8000	700.79	366.64	255.58	200.29	167.30	145.47	130.00
9000	788.39	412.47	287.53	225.32	188.21	163.65	146.25
10000	875.99	458.30	319.48	250.36	209.13	181.83	162.51
12000	1051.18	549.97	383.37	300.43	250.95	218.20	195.01
15000	1313.98	687.46	479.21	375.54	313.69	272.75	243.76
20000	1751.97	916.61	638.95	500.72	418.25	363.67	325.01
25000	2189.97	1145.76	798.69	625.90	522.82	454.58	406.26
30000	2627.96	1374.91	958.43	751.08	627.38	545.50	487.52
31000	2715.56	1420.74	990.38	776.11	648.29	563.69	503.77
32000	2803.16	1466.57	1022.32	801.15	669.21	581.87	520.02
33000	2890.76	1512.40	1054.27	826.19	690.12	600.05	536.27
34000	2978.35	1558.24	1086.22	851.22	711.03	618.24	552.52
35000	3065.95	1604.07	1118.17	876.26	731.94	636.42	568.77
36000	3153.55	1649.90	1150.11	901.29	752.86	654.60	585.02
37000	3241.15	1695.73	1182.06	926.33	773.77	672.79	601.27
38000	3328.75	1741.56	1214.01	951.37	794.68	690.97	617.52
39000	3416.35	1787.39	1245.96	976.40	815.59	709.15	633.77
40000	3503.95	1833.22	1277.90	1001.44	836.51	727.34	650.02
41000	3591.55	1879.05	1309.85	1026.47	857.42	745.52	666.27
42000	3679.14	1924.88	1341.80	1051.51	878.33	763.70	682.52
43000	3766.74	1970.71	1373.75	1076.55	899.24	781.89	698.77
44000	3854.34	2016.54	1405.69	1101.58	920.16	800.07	715.02
45000	3941.94	2062.37	1437.64	1126.62	941.07	818.25	731.27
46000	4029.54	2108.20	1469.59	1151.65	961.98	836.44	747.53
47000	4117.14	2154.03	1501.54	1176.69	982.90	854.62	763.78
48000	4204.74	2199.86	1533.48	1201.73	1003.81	872.80	780.03
49000	4292.33	2245.69	1565.43	1226.76	1024.72	890.99	796.28
50000	4379.93	2291.52	1597.38	1251.80	1045.63	909.17	812.53
51000	4467.53	2337.35	1629.33	1276.83	1066.55	927.35	828.78
52000	4555.13	2383.18	1661.27	1301.87	1087.46	945.54	845.03
53000	4642.73	2429.01	1693.22	1326.91	1108.37	963.72	861.28
54000	4730.33	2474.84	1725.17	1351.94	1129.28	981.90	877.53
55000	4817.93	2520.67	1757.12	1376.98	1150.20	1000.09	893.78
56000	4905.53	2566.50	1789.07	1402.01	1171.11	1018.27	910.03
57000	4993.12	2612.34	1821.01	1427.05	1192.02	1036.45	926.28
58000	5080.72	2658.17	1852.96	1452.09	1212.93	1054.64	942.53
59000	5168.32	2704.00	1884.91	1477.12	1233.85	1072.82	958.78
60000	5255.92	2749.83	1916.86	1502.16	1254.76	1091.00	975.03
65000	5693.91	2978.98	2076.59	1627.34	1359.32	1181.92	1056.29
70000	6131.91	3208.13	2236.33	1752.52	1463.89	1272.84	1137.54
75000	6569.90	3437.28	2396.07	1877.70	1568.45	1363.75	1218.79
80000	7007.89	3666.44	2555.81	2002.88	1673.01	1454.67	1300.04
85000	7445.89	3895.59	2715.55	2128.06	1777.58	1545.59	1381.30
90000	7883.88	4124.74	2875.28	2253.24	1882.14	1636.51	1462.55
95000	8321.87	4353.89	3035.02	2378.42	1986.70	1727.42	1543.80
100000	8759.87	4583.04	3194.76	2503.60	2091.27	1818.34	1625.06
105000	9197.86	4812.20	3354.50	2628.78	2195.83	1909.26	1706.31
110000	9635.85	5041.35	3514.24	2753.96	2300.39	2000.17	1787.56
120000	10511.84	5499.65	3833.71	3004.32	2509.52	2182.01	1950.07
130000	11387.83	5957.96	4153.19	3254.67	2718.65	2363.84	2112.57
140000	12263.81	6416.26	4472.66	3505.03	2927.77	2545.68	2275.08
150000	13139.80	6874.57	4792.14	3755.39	3136.90	2727.51	2437.58
160000	14015.79	7332.87	5111.62	4005.75	3346.03	2909.34	2600.09
170000	14891.77	7791.18	5431.09	4256.11	3555.15	3091.18	2762.59
180000	15767.76	8249.48	5750.57	4506.47	3764.28	3273.01	2925.10
190000	16643.75	8707.78	6070.04	4756.83	3973.41	3454.85	3087.60
200000	17519.73	9166.09	6389.52	5007.19	4182.53	3636.68	3250.11
210000	18395.72	9624.39	6708.99	5257.55	4391.66	3818.51	3412.62
220000	19271.71	10082.70	7028.47	5507.91	4600.79	4000.35	3575.12
230000	20147.69	10541.00	7347.95	5758.27	4809.91	4182.18	3737.63
240000	21023.68	10999.31	7667.42	6008.63	5019.04	4364.02	3900.13
250000	21899.67	11457.61	7986.90	6258.99	5228.17	4545.85	4062.64

Monthly Payments 9.50 %

LOAN AMOUNT	8	9	10	11	12	13	14
				YEARS			
100	1.48	1.37	1.28	1.21	1.16	1.11	1.07
200	2.96	2.74	2.57	2.43	2.31	2.22	2.14
500	7.41	6.86	6.42	6.07	5.78	5.54	5.34
1000	14.82	13.71	12.84	12.14	11.56	11.08	10.68
2000	29.63	27.42	25.68	24.27	23.12	22.16	21.35
5000	74.08	68.56	64.20	60.68	57.80	55.40	53.38
6000	88.89	82.27	77.04	72.82	69.36	66.48	64.05
7000	103.71	95.98	89.88	84.96	80.92	77.56	74.73
8000	118.52	109.69	102.72	97.09	92.48	88.64	85.41
9000	133.34	123.40	115.56	109.23	104.04	99.72	96.08
10000	148.15	137.12	128.40	121.37	115.60	110.80	106.76
12000	177.78	164.54	154.08	145.64	138.72	132.96	128.11
15000	222.23	205.67	192.60	182.05	173.40	166.20	160.13
20000	296.31	274.23	256.80	242.73	231.19	221.59	213.51
25000	370.38	342.79	321.00	303.42	288.99	276.99	266.89
30000	444.46	411.35	385.20	364.10	346.79	332.39	320.27
31000	459.27	425.06	398.04	376.24	358.35	343.47	330.94
32000	474.09	438.77	410.88	388.37	369.91	354.55	341.62
33000	488.91	452.48	423.72	400.51	381.47	365.63	352.30
34000	503.72	466.20	436.56	412.65	393.03	376.71	362.97
35000	518.54	479.91	449.40	424.78	404.59	387.79	373.65
36000	533.35	493.62	462.24	436.92	416.15	398.87	384.32
37000	548.17	507.33	475.08	449.06	427.71	409.95	395.00
38000	562.98	521.04	487.92	461.19	439.27	421.03	405.67
39000	577.80	534.75	500.76	473.33	450.83	432.11	416.35
40000	592.61	548.47	513.60	485.47	462.39	443.19	427.03
41000	607.43	562.18	526.44	497.60	473.95	454.27	437.70
42000	622.24	575.89	539.28	509.74	485.51	465.35	448.38
43000	637.06	589.60	552.12	521.88	497.07	476.43	459.05
44000	651.87	603.31	564.96	534.02	508.63	487.51	469.73
45000	666.69	617.02	577.80	546.15	520.19	498.59	480.40
46000	681.50	630.74	590.64	558.29	531.75	509.67	491.08
47000	696.32	644.45	603.48	570.43	543.31	520.74	501.76
48000	711.13	658.16	616.32	582.56	554.87	531.82	512.43
49000	725.95	671.87	629.16	594.70	566.43	542.90	523.11
50000	740.77	685.58	642.00	606.84	577.99	553.98	533.78
51000	755.58	699.29	654.84	618.97	589.55	565.06	544.46
52000	770.40	713.01	667.68	631.11	601.11	576.14	555.13
53000	785.21	726.72	680.52	643.25	612.67	587.22	565.81
54000	800.03	740.43	693.36	655.38	624.23	598.30	576.48
55000	814.84	754.14	706.20	667.52	635.78	609.38	587.16
56000	829.66	767.85	719.04	679.66	647.34	620.46	597.84
57000	844.47	781.56	731.88	691.79	658.90	631.54	608.51
58000	859.29	795.28	744.72	703.93	670.46	642.62	619.19
59000	874.10	808.99	757.55	716.07	682.02	653.70	629.86
60000	888.92	822.70	770.39	728.20	693.58	664.78	640.54
65000	963.00	891.26	834.59	788.89	751.38	720.18	693.92
70000	1037.07	959.82	898.79	849.57	809.18	775.58	747.30
75000	1111.15	1028.37	962.99	910.25	866.98	830.98	800.67
80000	1185.22	1096.93	1027.19	970.94	924.78	886.37	854.05
85000	1259.30	1165.49	1091.39	1031.62	982.58	941.77	907.43
90000	1333.38	1234.05	1155.59	1092.30	1040.38	997.17	960.81
95000	1407.45	1302.61	1219.79	1152.99	1098.17	1052.57	1014.19
100000	1481.53	1371.16	1283.99	1213.67	1155.97	1107.97	1067.56
105000	1555.61	1439.72	1348.19	1274.35	1213.77	1163.37	1120.94
110000	1629.68	1508.28	1412.39	1335.04	1271.57	1218.76	1174.32
120000	1777.84	1645.40	1540.79	1456.40	1387.17	1329.56	1281.08
130000	1925.99	1782.51	1669.19	1577.77	1502.76	1440.36	1387.83
140000	2074.14	1919.63	1797.59	1699.14	1618.36	1551.16	1494.59
150000	2222.30	2056.75	1925.99	1820.51	1733.96	1661.95	1601.35
160000	2370.45	2193.86	2054.39	1941.87	1849.56	1772.75	1708.10
170000	2518.60	2330.98	2182.79	2063.24	1965.15	1883.55	1814.86
180000	2666.76	2468.10	2311.18	2184.61	2080.75	1994.34	1921.62
190000	2814.91	2605.21	2439.58	2305.97	2196.35	2105.14	2028.37
200000	2963.06	2742.33	2567.98	2427.34	2311.94	2215.94	2135.13
210000	3111.22	2879.45	2696.38	2548.71	2427.54	2326.73	2241.89
220000	3259.37	3016.56	2824.78	2670.08	2543.14	2437.53	2348.64
230000	3407.52	3153.68	2953.18	2791.44	2658.74	2548.33	2455.40
240000	3555.67	3290.79	3081.58	2912.81	2774.33	2659.12	2562.15
250000	3703.83	3427.91	3209.98	3034.18	2889.93	2769.92	2668.91

9.50 % Monthly Payments

LOAN AMOUNT	15	16	17	18	19	20	21
100	1.03	1.00	0.98	0.96	0.94	0.92	0.91
200	2.07	2.01	1.96	1.91	1.87	1.84	1.81
500	5.17	5.02	4.89	4.78	4.69	4.60	4.53
1000	10.33	10.04	9.78	9.56	9.37	9.20	9.05
2000	20.66	20.08	19.57	19.13	18.74	18.40	18.11
5000	51.66	50.19	48.92	47.82	46.86	46.01	45.27
6000	61.99	60.23	58.70	57.38	56.23	55.21	54.32
7000	72.33	70.27	68.49	66.94	65.60	64.42	63.38
8000	82.66	80.30	78.27	76.51	74.97	73.62	72.43
9000	92.99	90.34	88.06	86.07	84.34	82.82	81.48
10000	103.32	100.38	97.84	95.64	93.71	92.02	90.54
12000	123.99	120.46	117.41	114.76	112.45	110.43	108.64
15000	154.98	150.57	146.76	143.45	140.57	138.03	135.81
20000	206.65	200.76	195.68	191.27	187.42	184.05	181.07
25000	258.31	250.95	244.60	239.09	234.28	230.06	226.34
30000	309.97	301.14	293.52	286.91	281.13	276.07	271.61
31000	320.30	311.18	303.31	296.47	290.50	285.27	280.66
32000	330.63	321.22	313.09	306.03	299.87	294.47	289.72
33000	340.96	331.25	322.87	315.60	309.25	303.68	298.77
34000	351.30	341.29	332.66	325.16	318.62	312.88	307.83
35000	361.63	351.33	342.44	334.72	327.99	322.08	316.88
36000	371.96	361.37	352.23	344.29	337.36	331.28	325.93
37000	382.29	371.41	362.01	353.85	346.73	340.49	334.99
38000	392.63	381.44	371.79	363.42	356.10	349.69	344.04
39000	402.96	391.48	381.58	372.98	365.47	358.89	353.09
40000	413.29	401.52	391.36	382.54	374.84	368.09	362.15
41000	423.62	411.56	401.15	392.11	384.21	377.29	371.20
42000	433.95	421.60	410.93	401.67	393.59	386.50	380.25
43000	444.29	431.63	420.71	411.23	402.96	395.70	389.31
44000	454.62	441.67	430.50	420.80	412.33	404.90	398.36
45000	464.95	451.71	440.28	430.36	421.70	414.10	407.42
46000	475.28	461.75	450.07	439.92	431.07	423.31	416.47
47000	485.62	471.79	459.85	449.49	440.44	432.51	425.52
48000	495.95	481.82	469.63	459.05	449.81	441.71	434.58
49000	506.28	491.86	479.42	468.61	459.18	450.91	443.63
50000	516.61	501.90	489.20	478.18	468.55	460.12	452.68
51000	526.95	511.94	498.99	487.74	477.93	469.32	461.74
52000	537.28	521.98	508.77	497.31	487.30	478.52	470.79
53000	547.61	532.01	518.56	506.87	496.67	487.72	479.85
54000	557.94	542.05	528.34	516.43	506.04	496.92	488.90
55000	568.27	552.09	538.12	526.00	515.41	506.13	497.95
56000	578.61	562.13	547.91	535.56	524.78	515.33	507.01
57000	588.94	572.17	557.69	545.12	534.15	524.53	516.06
58000	599.27	582.20	567.48	554.69	543.52	533.73	525.11
59000	609.60	592.24	577.26	564.25	552.89	542.94	534.17
60000	619.94	602.28	587.04	573.81	562.27	552.14	543.22
65000	671.60	652.47	635.96	621.63	609.12	598.15	588.49
70000	723.26	702.66	684.88	669.45	655.98	644.16	633.76
75000	774.92	752.85	733.80	717.27	702.83	690.17	679.03
80000	826.58	803.04	782.72	765.09	749.69	736.18	724.30
85000	878.24	853.23	831.65	812.90	796.54	782.20	769.56
90000	929.90	903.42	880.57	860.72	843.40	828.21	814.83
95000	981.56	953.61	929.49	908.54	890.25	874.22	860.10
100000	1033.23	1003.80	978.41	956.36	937.11	920.23	905.37
105000	1084.89	1053.99	1027.33	1004.17	983.96	966.24	950.64
110000	1136.55	1104.18	1076.25	1051.99	1030.82	1012.25	995.91
120000	1239.87	1204.56	1174.09	1147.63	1124.53	1104.28	1086.44
130000	1343.19	1304.94	1271.93	1243.26	1218.24	1196.30	1176.98
140000	1446.52	1405.32	1369.77	1338.90	1311.95	1288.32	1267.52
150000	1549.84	1505.70	1467.61	1434.53	1405.66	1380.35	1358.05
160000	1653.16	1606.08	1565.45	1530.17	1499.37	1472.37	1448.59
170000	1756.48	1706.46	1663.29	1625.81	1593.09	1564.39	1539.13
180000	1859.81	1806.84	1761.13	1721.44	1686.80	1656.41	1629.66
190000	1963.13	1907.22	1858.97	1817.08	1780.51	1748.44	1720.20
200000	2066.45	2007.60	1956.81	1912.71	1874.22	1840.46	1810.74
210000	2169.77	2107.98	2054.65	2008.35	1967.93	1932.48	1901.27
220000	2273.10	2208.36	2152.49	2103.98	2061.64	2024.51	1991.81
230000	2376.42	2308.74	2250.33	2199.62	2155.35	2116.53	2082.35
240000	2479.74	2409.12	2348.17	2295.26	2249.06	2208.55	2172.89
250000	2583.07	2509.50	2446.02	2390.89	2342.77	2300.58	2263.42

(Years: 15–21)

Monthly Payments 9.50 %

LOAN AMOUNT	YEARS 22	23	24	25	30	35	40
100	0.89	0.88	0.87	0.86	0.83	0.81	0.80
200	1.78	1.76	1.74	1.72	1.66	1.62	1.59
500	4.46	4.40	4.35	4.31	4.14	4.04	3.98
1000	8.92	8.81	8.70	8.61	8.28	8.08	7.96
2000	17.84	17.61	17.40	17.22	16.55	16.16	15.92
5000	44.61	44.03	43.51	43.05	41.38	40.39	39.79
6000	53.53	52.84	52.21	51.66	49.65	48.47	47.75
7000	62.46	61.64	60.92	60.27	57.93	56.55	55.71
8000	71.38	70.45	69.62	68.88	66.20	64.62	63.67
9000	80.30	79.25	78.32	77.49	74.48	72.70	71.63
10000	89.22	88.06	87.02	86.10	82.76	80.78	79.59
12000	107.07	105.67	104.43	103.32	99.31	96.94	95.50
15000	133.84	132.09	130.54	129.15	124.13	121.17	119.38
20000	178.45	176.12	174.05	172.21	165.51	161.56	159.17
25000	223.06	220.15	217.56	215.26	206.89	201.95	198.97
30000	267.67	264.18	261.07	258.31	248.27	242.34	238.76
31000	276.59	272.98	269.78	266.92	256.54	250.42	246.72
32000	285.52	281.79	278.48	275.53	264.82	258.50	254.68
33000	294.44	290.60	287.18	284.14	273.09	266.58	262.64
34000	303.36	299.40	295.88	292.75	281.37	274.66	270.60
35000	312.28	308.21	304.59	301.36	289.64	282.73	278.55
36000	321.21	317.01	313.29	309.97	297.92	290.81	286.51
37000	330.13	325.82	321.99	318.58	306.19	298.89	294.47
38000	339.05	334.63	330.69	327.19	314.47	306.97	302.43
39000	347.97	343.43	339.40	335.80	322.75	315.05	310.39
40000	356.89	352.24	348.10	344.41	331.02	323.12	318.35
41000	365.82	361.04	356.80	353.02	339.30	331.20	326.31
42000	374.74	369.85	365.50	361.63	347.57	339.28	334.27
43000	383.66	378.66	374.21	370.24	355.85	347.36	342.22
44000	392.58	387.46	382.91	378.85	364.12	355.44	350.18
45000	401.51	396.27	391.61	387.46	372.40	363.51	358.14
46000	410.43	405.07	400.31	396.07	380.67	371.59	366.10
47000	419.35	413.88	409.02	404.68	388.95	379.67	374.06
48000	428.27	422.69	417.72	413.29	397.23	387.75	382.02
49000	437.20	431.49	426.42	421.90	405.50	395.83	389.98
50000	446.12	440.30	435.12	430.51	413.78	403.90	397.94
51000	455.04	449.10	443.83	439.12	422.05	411.98	405.89
52000	463.96	457.91	452.53	447.73	430.33	420.06	413.85
53000	472.89	466.72	461.23	456.34	438.60	428.14	421.81
54000	481.81	475.52	469.93	464.95	446.88	436.22	429.77
55000	490.73	484.33	478.64	473.57	455.15	444.30	437.73
56000	499.65	493.13	487.34	482.18	463.43	452.37	445.69
57000	508.57	501.94	496.04	490.79	471.71	460.45	453.65
58000	517.50	510.75	504.74	499.40	479.98	468.53	461.60
59000	526.42	519.55	513.45	508.01	488.26	476.61	469.56
60000	535.34	528.36	522.15	516.62	496.53	484.69	477.52
65000	579.95	572.39	565.66	559.67	537.91	525.08	517.32
70000	624.57	616.42	609.17	602.72	579.29	565.47	557.11
75000	669.18	660.45	652.69	645.77	620.67	605.86	596.90
80000	713.79	704.48	696.20	688.82	662.04	646.25	636.70
85000	758.40	748.51	739.71	731.87	703.42	686.64	676.49
90000	803.01	792.54	783.22	774.92	744.80	727.03	716.28
95000	847.62	836.57	826.74	817.98	786.18	767.42	756.08
100000	892.24	880.60	870.25	861.03	827.55	807.81	795.87
105000	936.85	924.63	913.76	904.08	868.93	848.20	835.66
110000	981.46	968.66	957.27	947.13	910.31	888.59	875.46
120000	1070.68	1056.72	1044.30	1033.23	993.06	969.37	955.04
130000	1159.91	1144.77	1131.32	1119.34	1075.82	1050.15	1034.63
140000	1249.13	1232.83	1218.35	1205.44	1158.58	1130.93	1114.22
150000	1338.36	1320.89	1305.37	1291.54	1241.33	1211.71	1193.81
160000	1427.58	1408.95	1392.40	1377.64	1324.09	1292.49	1273.39
170000	1516.80	1497.01	1479.42	1463.75	1406.84	1373.28	1352.98
180000	1606.03	1585.07	1566.45	1549.85	1489.60	1454.06	1432.57
190000	1695.25	1673.13	1653.47	1635.95	1572.35	1534.84	1512.15
200000	1784.47	1761.19	1740.50	1722.06	1655.11	1615.62	1591.74
210000	1873.70	1849.25	1827.52	1808.16	1737.86	1696.40	1671.33
220000	1962.92	1937.31	1914.55	1894.26	1820.62	1777.18	1750.91
230000	2052.14	2025.37	2001.57	1980.36	1903.37	1857.96	1830.50
240000	2141.37	2113.43	2088.60	2066.47	1986.13	1938.74	1910.09
250000	2230.59	2201.49	2175.62	2152.57	2068.89	2019.52	1989.68

9.75 % Monthly Payments

LOAN AMOUNT	YEARS 1	2	3	4	5	6	7
100	8.77	4.59	3.21	2.52	2.10	1.83	1.64
200	17.54	9.19	6.41	5.03	4.21	3.66	3.27
500	43.86	22.97	16.03	12.58	10.52	9.15	8.19
1000	87.71	45.94	32.06	25.15	21.03	18.30	16.37
2000	175.42	91.88	64.12	50.30	42.06	36.61	32.75
5000	438.55	229.71	160.30	125.75	105.15	91.52	81.87
6000	526.26	275.65	192.36	150.90	126.18	109.82	98.24
7000	613.97	321.59	224.42	176.05	147.21	128.12	114.61
8000	701.68	367.53	256.48	201.21	168.24	146.43	130.99
9000	789.39	413.47	288.54	226.36	189.27	164.73	147.36
10000	877.10	459.41	320.60	251.51	210.30	183.04	163.74
12000	1052.52	551.29	384.72	301.81	252.36	219.64	196.48
15000	1315.65	689.12	480.90	377.26	315.45	274.55	245.60
20000	1754.21	918.82	641.20	503.01	420.60	366.07	327.47
25000	2192.76	1148.53	801.50	628.77	525.75	457.59	409.34
30000	2631.31	1378.23	961.80	754.52	630.90	549.11	491.21
31000	2719.02	1424.17	993.86	779.67	651.93	567.41	507.58
32000	2806.73	1470.11	1025.92	804.82	672.96	585.71	523.95
33000	2894.44	1516.05	1057.98	829.97	693.99	604.02	540.33
34000	2982.15	1562.00	1090.04	855.12	715.02	622.32	556.70
35000	3069.86	1607.94	1122.10	880.27	736.05	640.62	573.07
36000	3157.57	1653.88	1154.16	905.42	757.08	658.93	589.45
37000	3245.28	1699.82	1186.22	930.58	778.11	677.23	605.82
38000	3332.99	1745.76	1218.28	955.73	799.14	695.53	622.19
39000	3420.70	1791.70	1250.34	980.88	820.17	713.84	638.57
40000	3508.41	1837.64	1282.40	1006.03	841.20	732.14	654.94
41000	3596.12	1883.58	1314.46	1031.18	862.23	750.45	671.31
42000	3683.83	1929.52	1346.52	1056.33	883.26	768.75	687.69
43000	3771.54	1975.46	1378.58	1081.48	904.29	787.05	704.06
44000	3859.25	2021.41	1410.64	1106.63	925.32	805.36	720.44
45000	3946.96	2067.35	1442.70	1131.78	946.35	823.66	736.81
46000	4034.67	2113.29	1474.76	1156.93	967.38	841.96	753.18
47000	4122.38	2159.23	1506.82	1182.08	988.41	860.27	769.56
48000	4210.09	2205.17	1538.88	1207.23	1009.44	878.57	785.93
49000	4297.80	2251.11	1570.94	1232.38	1030.47	896.87	802.30
50000	4385.51	2297.05	1603.00	1257.53	1051.50	915.18	818.68
51000	4473.22	2342.99	1635.06	1282.68	1072.53	933.48	835.05
52000	4560.94	2388.93	1667.12	1307.84	1093.56	951.78	851.42
53000	4648.65	2434.87	1699.18	1332.99	1114.59	970.09	867.80
54000	4736.36	2480.82	1731.24	1358.14	1135.62	988.39	884.17
55000	4824.07	2526.76	1763.29	1383.29	1156.65	1006.70	900.54
56000	4911.78	2572.70	1795.35	1408.44	1177.68	1025.00	916.92
57000	4999.49	2618.64	1827.41	1433.59	1198.71	1043.30	933.29
58000	5087.20	2664.58	1859.47	1458.74	1219.74	1061.61	949.66
59000	5174.91	2710.52	1891.53	1483.89	1240.77	1079.91	966.04
60000	5262.62	2756.46	1923.59	1509.04	1261.80	1098.21	982.41
65000	5701.17	2986.17	2083.89	1634.79	1366.95	1189.73	1064.28
70000	6139.72	3215.87	2244.19	1760.55	1472.10	1281.25	1146.15
75000	6578.27	3445.58	2404.49	1886.30	1577.25	1372.77	1228.01
80000	7016.82	3675.28	2564.79	2012.05	1682.40	1464.28	1309.88
85000	7455.37	3904.99	2725.09	2137.81	1787.55	1555.80	1391.75
90000	7893.93	4134.69	2885.39	2263.56	1892.70	1647.32	1473.62
95000	8332.48	4364.40	3045.69	2389.31	1997.85	1738.84	1555.48
100000	8771.03	4594.10	3205.99	2515.07	2103.00	1830.35	1637.35
105000	9209.58	4823.81	3366.29	2640.82	2208.16	1921.87	1719.22
110000	9648.13	5053.51	3526.59	2766.57	2313.31	2013.39	1801.09
120000	10525.23	5512.92	3847.19	3018.08	2523.61	2196.43	1964.82
130000	11402.34	5972.33	4167.79	3269.59	2733.91	2379.46	2128.56
140000	12279.44	6431.74	4488.39	3521.10	2944.21	2562.50	2292.29
150000	13156.54	6891.15	4808.99	3772.60	3154.51	2745.53	2456.03
160000	14033.65	7350.56	5129.59	4024.11	3364.81	2928.57	2619.76
170000	14910.75	7809.98	5450.18	4275.62	3575.11	3111.60	2783.50
180000	15787.85	8269.39	5770.78	4527.12	3785.41	3294.64	2947.23
190000	16664.96	8728.80	6091.38	4778.63	3995.71	3477.67	3110.97
200000	17542.06	9188.21	6411.98	5030.14	4206.01	3660.71	3274.70
210000	18419.16	9647.62	6732.58	5281.64	4416.31	3843.75	3438.44
220000	19296.26	10107.03	7053.18	5533.15	4626.61	4026.78	3602.18
230000	20173.37	10566.44	7373.78	5784.66	4836.91	4209.82	3765.91
240000	21050.47	11025.85	7694.38	6036.16	5047.21	4392.85	3929.65
250000	21927.57	11485.26	8014.98	6287.67	5257.51	4575.89	4093.38

Monthly Payments 9.75 %

LOAN AMOUNT	8	9	10	11	12	13	14
			YEARS				
100	1.49	1.38	1.30	1.23	1.17	1.12	1.08
200	2.99	2.77	2.59	2.45	2.34	2.24	2.16
500	7.47	6.92	6.49	6.14	5.85	5.61	5.41
1000	14.94	13.84	12.97	12.27	11.70	11.22	10.82
2000	29.88	27.68	25.94	24.54	23.39	22.44	21.64
5000	74.71	69.20	64.86	61.35	58.48	56.10	54.09
6000	89.65	83.04	77.83	73.63	70.18	67.32	64.91
7000	104.59	96.88	90.80	85.90	81.88	78.54	75.73
8000	119.53	110.72	103.77	98.17	93.57	89.75	86.54
9000	134.47	124.56	116.74	110.44	105.27	100.97	97.36
10000	149.41	138.40	129.71	122.71	116.97	112.19	108.18
12000	179.29	166.08	155.66	147.25	140.36	134.63	129.81
15000	224.12	207.60	194.57	184.06	175.45	168.29	162.27
20000	298.82	276.81	259.43	245.42	233.93	224.39	216.36
25000	373.53	346.01	324.28	306.77	292.42	280.48	270.45
30000	448.23	415.21	389.14	368.13	350.90	336.58	324.54
31000	463.17	429.05	402.11	380.40	362.60	347.80	335.35
32000	478.12	442.89	415.08	392.67	374.29	359.02	346.17
33000	493.06	456.73	428.05	404.94	385.99	370.24	356.99
34000	508.00	470.57	441.03	417.21	397.69	381.46	367.81
35000	522.94	484.41	454.00	429.48	409.38	392.68	378.63
36000	537.88	498.25	466.97	441.75	421.08	403.89	389.44
37000	552.82	512.09	479.94	454.02	432.78	415.11	400.26
38000	567.76	525.93	492.91	466.29	444.47	426.33	411.08
39000	582.70	539.77	505.88	478.57	456.17	437.55	421.90
40000	597.64	553.61	518.85	490.84	467.87	448.77	432.72
41000	612.59	567.45	531.83	503.11	479.56	459.99	443.53
42000	627.53	581.29	544.80	515.38	491.26	471.21	454.35
43000	642.47	595.13	557.77	527.65	502.96	482.43	465.17
44000	657.41	608.97	570.74	539.92	514.65	493.65	475.99
45000	672.35	622.81	583.71	552.19	526.35	504.87	486.80
46000	687.29	636.65	596.68	564.46	538.05	516.09	497.62
47000	702.23	650.49	609.65	576.73	549.74	527.31	508.44
48000	717.17	664.33	622.62	589.00	561.44	538.53	519.26
49000	732.11	678.17	635.60	601.27	573.14	549.75	530.08
50000	747.06	692.01	648.57	613.55	584.83	560.96	540.89
51000	762.00	705.85	661.54	625.82	596.53	572.18	551.71
52000	776.94	719.69	674.51	638.09	608.23	583.40	562.53
53000	791.88	733.53	687.48	650.36	619.92	594.62	573.35
54000	806.82	747.37	700.45	662.63	631.62	605.84	584.17
55000	821.76	761.21	713.42	674.90	643.32	617.06	594.98
56000	836.70	775.06	726.40	687.17	655.01	628.28	605.80
57000	851.64	788.90	739.37	699.44	666.71	639.50	616.62
58000	866.58	802.74	752.34	711.71	678.41	650.72	627.44
59000	881.53	816.58	765.31	723.98	690.10	661.94	638.25
60000	896.47	830.42	778.28	736.25	701.80	673.16	649.07
65000	971.17	899.62	843.14	797.61	760.28	729.25	703.16
70000	1045.88	968.82	907.99	858.96	818.77	785.35	757.25
75000	1120.58	1038.02	972.85	920.32	877.25	841.45	811.34
80000	1195.29	1107.22	1037.71	981.67	935.73	897.54	865.43
85000	1269.99	1176.42	1102.56	1043.03	994.22	953.64	919.52
90000	1344.70	1245.62	1167.42	1104.38	1052.70	1009.74	973.61
95000	1419.41	1314.83	1232.28	1165.74	1111.18	1065.83	1027.70
100000	1494.11	1384.03	1297.13	1227.09	1169.66	1121.93	1081.79
105000	1568.82	1453.23	1361.99	1288.44	1228.15	1178.03	1135.88
110000	1643.52	1522.43	1426.85	1349.80	1286.63	1234.12	1189.97
120000	1792.93	1660.83	1556.56	1472.51	1403.60	1346.31	1298.15
130000	1942.34	1799.24	1686.27	1595.22	1520.56	1458.51	1406.32
140000	2091.76	1937.64	1815.99	1717.93	1637.53	1570.70	1514.50
150000	2241.17	2076.04	1945.70	1840.64	1754.50	1682.89	1622.68
160000	2390.58	2214.44	2075.42	1963.34	1871.46	1795.09	1730.86
170000	2539.99	2352.85	2205.13	2086.05	1988.43	1907.28	1839.04
180000	2689.40	2491.25	2334.84	2208.76	2105.40	2019.47	1947.22
190000	2838.81	2629.65	2464.56	2331.47	2222.36	2131.66	2055.40
200000	2988.22	2768.05	2594.27	2454.18	2339.33	2243.86	2163.58
210000	3137.63	2906.46	2723.98	2576.89	2456.30	2356.05	2271.75
220000	3287.05	3044.86	2853.70	2699.60	2573.26	2468.24	2379.93
230000	3436.46	3183.26	2983.41	2822.31	2690.23	2580.44	2488.11
240000	3585.87	3321.67	3113.12	2945.02	2807.20	2692.63	2596.29
250000	3735.28	3460.07	3242.84	3067.73	2924.16	2804.82	2704.47

9.75 % Monthly Payments

LOAN AMOUNT	15	16	17	18	19	20	21
				YEARS			
100	1.05	1.02	0.99	0.97	0.95	0.94	0.92
200	2.10	2.04	1.99	1.94	1.91	1.87	1.84
500	5.24	5.09	4.97	4.86	4.76	4.68	4.61
1000	10.48	10.19	9.93	9.72	9.53	9.36	9.21
2000	20.95	20.37	19.87	19.43	19.05	18.72	18.43
5000	52.39	50.93	49.67	48.58	47.63	46.79	46.06
6000	62.86	61.11	59.60	58.29	57.15	56.15	55.28
7000	73.34	71.30	69.54	68.01	66.68	65.51	64.49
8000	83.82	81.48	79.47	77.73	76.20	74.87	73.70
9000	94.29	91.67	89.40	87.44	85.73	84.23	82.91
10000	104.77	101.85	99.34	97.16	95.26	93.59	92.13
12000	125.72	122.22	119.21	116.59	114.31	112.31	110.55
15000	157.16	152.78	149.01	145.74	142.88	140.38	138.19
20000	209.54	203.71	198.68	194.31	190.51	187.18	184.25
25000	261.93	254.63	248.35	242.89	238.14	233.97	230.31
30000	314.31	305.56	298.01	291.47	285.77	280.77	276.38
31000	324.79	315.74	307.95	301.19	295.29	290.13	285.59
32000	335.27	325.93	317.88	310.90	304.82	299.49	294.80
33000	345.74	336.12	327.82	320.62	314.34	308.85	304.01
34000	356.22	346.30	337.75	330.33	323.87	318.21	313.23
35000	366.70	356.49	347.68	340.05	333.39	327.56	322.44
36000	377.17	366.67	357.62	349.77	342.92	336.92	331.65
37000	387.65	376.86	367.55	359.48	352.44	346.28	340.86
38000	398.13	387.04	377.49	369.20	361.97	355.64	350.08
39000	408.61	397.23	387.42	378.91	371.50	365.00	359.29
40000	419.08	407.41	397.35	388.63	381.02	374.36	368.50
41000	429.56	417.60	407.29	398.34	390.55	383.72	377.71
42000	440.04	427.78	417.22	408.06	400.07	393.08	386.93
43000	450.51	437.97	427.15	417.78	409.60	402.44	396.14
44000	460.99	448.15	437.09	427.49	419.12	411.80	405.35
45000	471.47	458.34	447.02	437.21	428.65	421.15	414.56
46000	481.95	468.52	456.96	446.92	438.17	430.51	423.78
47000	492.42	478.71	466.89	456.64	447.70	439.87	432.99
48000	502.90	488.90	476.82	466.35	457.23	449.23	442.20
49000	513.38	499.08	486.76	476.07	466.75	458.59	451.41
50000	523.85	509.27	496.69	485.79	476.28	467.95	460.63
51000	534.33	519.45	506.62	495.50	485.80	477.31	469.84
52000	544.81	529.64	516.56	505.22	495.33	486.67	479.05
53000	555.28	539.82	526.49	514.93	504.85	496.03	488.27
54000	565.76	550.01	536.43	524.65	514.38	505.39	497.48
55000	576.24	560.19	546.36	534.36	523.90	514.74	506.69
56000	586.72	570.38	556.29	544.08	533.43	524.10	515.90
57000	597.19	580.56	566.23	553.80	542.96	533.46	525.12
58000	607.67	590.75	576.16	563.51	552.48	542.82	534.33
59000	618.15	600.93	586.10	573.23	562.01	552.18	543.54
60000	628.62	611.12	596.03	582.94	571.53	561.54	552.75
65000	681.01	662.05	645.70	631.52	619.16	608.33	598.82
70000	733.39	712.97	695.37	680.10	666.79	655.13	644.88
75000	785.78	763.90	745.04	728.68	714.42	701.92	690.94
80000	838.17	814.83	794.71	777.26	762.04	748.72	737.00
85000	890.55	865.75	844.37	825.83	809.67	795.51	783.07
90000	942.94	916.68	894.04	874.41	857.30	842.31	829.13
95000	995.32	967.61	943.71	922.99	904.93	889.10	875.19
100000	1047.71	1018.53	993.38	971.57	952.55	935.90	921.25
105000	1100.09	1069.46	1043.05	1020.15	1000.18	982.69	967.32
110000	1152.48	1120.39	1092.72	1068.73	1047.81	1029.49	1013.38
120000	1257.25	1222.24	1192.06	1165.88	1143.06	1123.08	1105.51
130000	1362.02	1324.09	1291.40	1263.04	1238.32	1216.67	1197.63
140000	1466.79	1425.94	1390.73	1360.20	1333.58	1310.26	1289.76
150000	1571.56	1527.80	1490.07	1457.36	1428.83	1403.85	1381.88
160000	1676.33	1629.65	1589.41	1554.51	1524.09	1497.44	1474.01
170000	1781.10	1731.50	1688.75	1651.67	1619.34	1591.03	1566.13
180000	1885.87	1833.36	1788.09	1748.83	1714.60	1684.62	1658.26
190000	1990.64	1935.21	1887.43	1845.98	1809.85	1778.21	1750.38
200000	2095.41	2037.06	1986.76	1943.14	1905.11	1871.80	1842.51
210000	2200.18	2138.92	2086.10	2040.30	2000.36	1965.39	1934.64
220000	2304.95	2240.77	2185.44	2137.45	2095.62	2058.98	2026.76
230000	2409.73	2342.62	2284.78	2234.61	2190.87	2152.57	2118.89
240000	2514.50	2444.48	2384.12	2331.77	2286.13	2246.16	2211.01
250000	2619.27	2546.33	2483.46	2428.93	2381.39	2339.75	2303.14

Monthly Payments 9.75 %

LOAN AMOUNT	22	23	24	25	30	35	40
				YEARS			
100	0.91	0.90	0.89	0.88	0.85	0.83	0.81
200	1.82	1.79	1.77	1.76	1.69	1.65	1.63
500	4.54	4.48	4.43	4.39	4.23	4.13	4.07
1000	9.08	8.97	8.87	8.78	8.45	8.26	8.15
2000	18.17	17.94	17.73	17.55	16.90	16.52	16.29
5000	45.42	44.84	44.34	43.89	42.25	41.30	40.73
6000	54.50	53.81	53.20	52.66	50.70	49.56	48.87
7000	63.58	62.78	62.07	61.44	59.15	57.82	57.02
8000	72.67	71.75	70.94	70.22	67.61	66.08	65.16
9000	81.75	80.72	79.81	78.99	76.06	74.34	73.31
10000	90.83	89.69	88.67	87.77	84.51	82.60	81.45
12000	109.00	107.63	106.41	105.32	101.41	99.12	97.75
15000	136.25	134.53	133.01	131.66	126.76	123.90	122.18
20000	181.67	179.38	177.35	175.54	169.01	165.20	162.91
25000	227.08	224.22	221.69	219.43	211.27	206.49	203.64
30000	272.50	269.07	266.02	263.31	253.52	247.79	244.36
31000	281.58	278.04	274.89	272.09	261.97	256.05	252.51
32000	290.67	287.01	283.76	280.87	270.42	264.31	260.66
33000	299.75	295.97	292.62	289.64	278.87	272.57	268.80
34000	308.83	304.94	301.49	298.42	287.32	280.83	276.95
35000	317.92	313.91	310.36	307.20	295.77	289.09	285.09
36000	327.00	322.88	319.23	315.97	304.22	297.35	293.24
37000	336.08	331.85	328.09	324.75	312.67	305.61	301.38
38000	345.17	340.82	336.96	333.53	321.12	313.87	309.53
39000	354.25	349.79	345.83	342.31	329.58	322.13	317.67
40000	363.33	358.76	354.70	351.08	338.03	330.39	325.82
41000	372.42	367.73	363.56	359.86	346.48	338.65	333.97
42000	381.50	376.70	372.43	368.64	354.93	346.91	342.11
43000	390.58	385.66	381.30	377.41	363.38	355.17	350.26
44000	399.67	394.63	390.17	386.19	371.83	363.43	358.40
45000	408.75	403.60	399.03	394.97	380.28	371.69	366.55
46000	417.83	412.57	407.90	403.75	388.73	379.95	374.69
47000	426.92	421.54	416.77	412.52	397.18	388.21	382.84
48000	436.00	430.51	425.64	421.30	405.63	396.47	390.98
49000	445.08	439.48	434.50	430.08	414.08	404.73	399.13
50000	454.17	448.45	443.37	438.85	422.53	412.99	407.27
51000	463.25	457.42	452.24	447.63	430.98	421.25	415.42
52000	472.33	466.38	461.11	456.41	439.43	429.51	423.57
53000	481.42	475.35	469.97	465.19	447.88	437.77	431.71
54000	490.50	484.32	478.84	473.96	456.33	446.03	439.86
55000	499.58	493.29	487.71	482.74	464.79	454.29	448.00
56000	508.67	502.26	496.58	491.52	473.24	462.55	456.15
57000	517.75	511.23	505.44	500.29	481.69	470.81	464.29
58000	526.83	520.20	514.31	509.07	490.14	479.07	472.44
59000	535.92	529.17	523.18	517.85	498.59	487.33	480.58
60000	545.00	538.14	532.04	526.62	507.04	495.59	488.73
65000	590.42	582.98	576.38	570.51	549.29	536.89	529.46
70000	635.83	627.83	620.72	614.40	591.54	578.19	570.18
75000	681.25	672.67	665.06	658.28	633.80	619.48	610.91
80000	726.67	717.51	709.39	702.17	676.05	660.78	651.64
85000	772.08	762.36	753.73	746.05	718.30	702.08	692.37
90000	817.50	807.20	798.07	789.94	760.56	743.38	733.09
95000	862.92	852.05	842.40	833.82	802.81	784.68	773.82
100000	908.33	896.89	886.74	877.71	845.06	825.98	814.55
105000	953.75	941.74	931.08	921.59	887.32	867.28	855.28
110000	999.17	986.58	975.42	965.48	929.57	908.58	896.00
120000	1090.00	1076.27	1064.09	1053.25	1014.08	991.17	977.46
130000	1180.83	1165.96	1152.76	1141.02	1098.58	1073.77	1058.91
140000	1271.67	1255.65	1241.44	1228.79	1183.09	1156.37	1140.37
150000	1362.50	1345.34	1330.11	1316.56	1267.60	1238.97	1221.82
160000	1453.33	1435.03	1418.79	1404.33	1352.10	1321.57	1303.28
170000	1544.16	1524.72	1507.46	1492.10	1436.61	1404.16	1384.73
180000	1635.00	1614.41	1596.13	1579.87	1521.12	1486.76	1466.19
190000	1725.83	1704.10	1684.81	1667.65	1605.62	1569.36	1547.64
200000	1816.66	1793.79	1773.48	1755.42	1690.13	1651.96	1629.10
210000	1907.50	1883.48	1862.16	1843.19	1774.63	1734.56	1710.55
220000	1998.33	1973.17	1950.83	1930.96	1859.14	1817.15	1792.01
230000	2089.16	2062.86	2039.50	2018.73	1943.65	1899.75	1873.46
240000	2180.00	2152.54	2128.18	2106.50	2028.15	1982.35	1954.92
250000	2270.83	2242.23	2216.85	2194.27	2112.66	2064.95	2036.37

10.00 % Monthly Payments

LOAN AMOUNT	YEARS 1	2	3	4	5	6	7
100	8.78	4.61	3.22	2.53	2.11	1.84	1.65
200	17.56	9.21	6.43	5.05	4.23	3.68	3.30
500	43.91	23.03	16.09	12.63	10.57	9.21	8.25
1000	87.82	46.05	32.17	25.27	21.15	18.42	16.50
2000	175.64	92.10	64.34	50.53	42.30	36.85	32.99
5000	439.11	230.26	160.86	126.33	105.74	92.12	82.48
6000	526.93	276.31	193.03	151.59	126.89	110.54	98.98
7000	614.75	322.36	225.21	176.86	148.03	128.97	115.48
8000	702.58	368.41	257.38	202.12	169.18	147.39	131.98
9000	790.40	414.46	289.55	227.39	190.33	165.82	148.47
10000	878.22	460.52	321.72	252.66	211.48	184.24	164.97
12000	1053.86	552.62	386.07	303.19	253.77	221.09	197.96
15000	1317.33	690.77	482.59	378.98	317.22	276.36	247.45
20000	1756.44	921.03	643.45	505.31	422.95	368.48	329.94
25000	2195.55	1151.29	804.31	631.64	528.69	460.60	412.42
30000	2634.66	1381.55	965.17	757.97	634.43	552.72	494.91
31000	2722.48	1427.60	997.34	783.23	655.58	571.15	511.40
32000	2810.30	1473.65	1029.52	808.50	676.73	589.57	527.90
33000	2898.12	1519.70	1061.69	833.76	697.87	607.99	544.40
34000	2985.94	1565.76	1093.86	859.03	719.02	626.42	560.89
35000	3073.77	1611.81	1126.03	884.30	740.17	644.84	577.39
36000	3161.59	1657.86	1158.20	909.56	761.32	663.27	593.89
37000	3249.41	1703.91	1190.38	934.83	782.46	681.69	610.39
38000	3337.23	1749.96	1222.55	960.09	803.61	700.11	626.88
39000	3425.05	1796.01	1254.72	985.36	824.76	718.54	643.38
40000	3512.88	1842.07	1286.89	1010.62	845.91	736.96	659.88
41000	3600.70	1888.12	1319.07	1035.89	867.06	755.39	676.37
42000	3688.52	1934.17	1351.24	1061.16	888.20	773.81	692.87
43000	3776.34	1980.22	1383.41	1086.42	909.35	792.23	709.37
44000	3864.16	2026.27	1415.58	1111.69	930.50	810.66	725.86
45000	3951.98	2072.32	1447.76	1136.95	951.65	829.08	742.36
46000	4039.81	2118.38	1479.93	1162.22	972.79	847.51	758.86
47000	4127.63	2164.43	1512.10	1187.48	993.94	865.93	775.35
48000	4215.45	2210.48	1544.27	1212.75	1015.09	884.35	791.85
49000	4303.27	2256.53	1576.44	1238.01	1036.24	902.78	808.35
50000	4391.09	2302.58	1608.62	1263.28	1057.38	921.20	824.85
51000	4478.92	2348.63	1640.79	1288.55	1078.53	939.63	841.34
52000	4566.74	2394.69	1672.96	1313.81	1099.68	958.05	857.84
53000	4654.56	2440.74	1705.13	1339.08	1120.83	976.47	874.34
54000	4742.38	2486.79	1737.31	1364.34	1141.98	994.90	890.8
55000	4830.20	2532.84	1769.48	1389.61	1163.12	1013.32	907.3
56000	4918.03	2578.89	1801.65	1414.87	1184.27	1031.75	923.8
57000	5005.85	2624.94	1833.82	1440.14	1205.42	1050.17	940.3
58000	5093.67	2671.00	1866.00	1465.40	1226.57	1068.59	956.8
59000	5181.49	2717.05	1898.17	1490.67	1247.71	1087.02	973.3
60000	5269.31	2763.10	1930.34	1515.94	1268.86	1105.44	989.8
65000	5708.42	2993.36	2091.20	1642.26	1374.60	1197.56	1072.3
70000	6147.53	3223.62	2252.06	1768.59	1480.34	1289.68	1154.7
75000	6586.64	3453.87	2412.93	1894.92	1586.08	1381.80	1237.2
80000	7025.75	3684.13	2573.79	2021.25	1691.82	1473.92	1319.7
85000	7464.86	3914.39	2734.65	2147.58	1797.55	1566.04	1402.2
90000	7903.97	4144.65	2895.51	2273.90	1903.29	1658.16	1484.7
95000	8343.08	4374.91	3056.37	2400.23	2009.03	1750.28	1567.2
100000	8782.19	4605.17	3217.23	2526.56	2114.77	1842.40	1649.6
105000	9221.30	4835.42	3378.10	2652.89	2220.51	1934.52	1732.1
110000	9660.41	5065.68	3538.96	2779.22	2326.25	2026.64	1814.6
120000	10538.63	5526.20	3860.68	3031.87	2537.72	2210.89	1979.6
130000	11416.84	5986.72	4182.40	3284.53	2749.20	2395.13	2144.6
140000	12295.06	6447.23	4504.13	3537.18	2960.68	2579.37	2309.5
150000	13173.28	6907.75	4825.85	3789.84	3172.15	2763.61	2474.5
160000	14051.50	7368.27	5147.58	4042.50	3383.63	2947.85	2639.5
170000	14929.72	7828.78	5469.30	4295.15	3595.11	3132.09	2804.4
180000	15807.94	8289.30	5791.02	4547.81	3806.59	3316.33	2969.4
190000	16686.16	8749.82	6112.75	4800.46	4018.06	3500.57	3134.4
200000	17564.38	9210.33	6434.47	5053.12	4229.54	3684.81	3299.3
210000	18442.59	9670.85	6756.19	5305.78	4441.02	3869.05	3464.3
220000	19320.81	10131.37	7077.92	5558.43	4652.49	4053.29	3629.3
230000	20199.03	10591.88	7399.64	5811.09	4863.97	4237.53	3794.2
240000	21077.25	11052.40	7721.36	6063.74	5075.45	4421.77	3959.2
250000	21955.47	11512.92	8043.09	6316.40	5286.92	4606.01	4124.2

Monthly Payments 10.00 %

LOAN AMOUNT	8	9	10	11	12	13	14
100	1.51	1.40	1.31	1.24	1.18	1.14	1.10
200	3.01	2.79	2.62	2.48	2.37	2.27	2.19
500	7.53	6.98	6.55	6.20	5.92	5.68	5.48
1000	15.07	13.97	13.10	12.41	11.83	11.36	10.96
2000	30.13	27.94	26.21	24.81	23.67	22.72	21.92
5000	75.34	69.85	65.52	62.03	59.17	56.80	54.80
6000	90.40	83.82	78.62	74.43	71.01	68.16	65.77
7000	105.47	97.79	91.72	86.84	82.84	79.52	76.73
8000	120.54	111.76	104.83	99.25	94.67	90.88	87.69
9000	135.61	125.72	117.93	111.65	106.51	102.24	98.65
10000	150.67	139.69	131.03	124.06	118.34	113.60	109.61
12000	180.81	167.63	157.24	148.87	142.01	136.32	131.53
15000	226.01	209.54	196.55	186.09	177.51	170.39	164.41
20000	301.35	279.39	262.07	248.12	236.69	227.19	219.22
25000	376.68	349.24	327.58	310.14	295.86	283.99	274.02
30000	452.02	419.08	393.10	372.17	355.03	340.79	328.83
31000	467.09	433.05	406.20	384.58	366.86	352.15	339.79
32000	482.16	447.02	419.31	396.98	378.70	363.51	350.75
33000	497.22	460.99	432.41	409.39	390.53	374.87	361.71
34000	512.29	474.96	445.51	421.80	402.37	386.23	372.67
35000	527.36	488.93	458.62	434.20	414.20	397.59	383.63
36000	542.43	502.90	471.72	446.61	426.03	408.95	394.59
37000	557.49	516.87	484.82	459.01	437.87	420.31	405.55
38000	572.56	530.84	497.93	471.42	449.70	431.67	416.51
39000	587.63	544.81	511.03	483.82	461.54	443.03	427.48
40000	602.70	558.78	524.13	496.23	473.37	454.39	438.44
41000	617.76	572.75	537.24	508.64	485.21	465.75	449.40
42000	632.83	586.72	550.34	521.04	497.04	477.10	460.36
43000	647.90	600.69	563.44	533.45	508.87	488.46	471.32
44000	662.97	614.66	576.55	545.85	520.71	499.82	482.28
45000	678.03	628.62	589.65	558.26	532.54	511.18	493.24
46000	693.10	642.59	602.75	570.66	544.38	522.54	504.20
47000	708.17	656.56	615.86	583.07	556.21	533.90	515.16
48000	723.23	670.53	628.96	595.48	568.05	545.26	526.12
49000	738.30	684.50	642.07	607.88	579.88	556.62	537.08
50000	753.37	698.47	655.17	620.29	591.71	567.98	548.05
51000	768.44	712.44	668.27	632.69	603.55	579.34	559.01
52000	783.50	726.41	681.38	645.10	615.38	590.70	569.97
53000	798.57	740.38	694.48	657.50	627.22	602.06	580.93
54000	813.64	754.35	707.58	669.91	639.05	613.42	591.89
55000	828.71	768.32	720.69	682.32	650.89	624.78	602.85
56000	843.77	782.29	733.79	694.72	662.72	636.14	613.81
57000	858.84	796.26	746.89	707.13	674.55	647.50	624.77
58000	873.91	810.23	760.00	719.53	686.39	658.86	635.73
59000	888.98	824.20	773.10	731.94	698.22	670.22	646.69
60000	904.04	838.17	786.20	744.35	710.06	681.58	657.65
65000	979.38	908.01	851.72	806.37	769.23	738.38	712.46
70000	1054.72	977.86	917.24	868.40	828.40	795.17	767.26
75000	1130.05	1047.71	982.75	930.43	887.57	851.97	822.07
80000	1205.39	1117.55	1048.27	992.46	946.74	908.77	876.87
85000	1280.73	1187.40	1113.79	1054.49	1005.91	965.57	931.68
90000	1356.07	1257.25	1179.30	1116.52	1065.08	1022.37	986.48
95000	1431.40	1327.10	1244.82	1178.55	1124.26	1079.17	1041.29
100000	1506.74	1396.94	1310.34	1240.58	1183.43	1135.96	1096.09
105000	1582.08	1466.79	1375.85	1302.60	1242.60	1192.76	1150.89
110000	1657.41	1536.64	1441.37	1364.63	1301.77	1249.56	1205.70
120000	1808.09	1676.33	1572.40	1488.69	1420.11	1363.16	1315.31
130000	1958.76	1816.03	1703.44	1612.75	1538.46	1476.75	1424.92
140000	2109.43	1955.72	1834.47	1736.81	1656.80	1590.35	1534.53
150000	2260.11	2095.42	1965.51	1860.86	1775.14	1703.95	1644.14
160000	2410.78	2235.11	2096.54	1984.92	1893.48	1817.54	1753.74
170000	2561.46	2374.80	2227.57	2108.98	2011.83	1931.14	1863.35
180000	2712.13	2514.50	2358.61	2233.04	2130.17	2044.74	1972.96
190000	2862.80	2654.19	2489.64	2357.09	2248.51	2158.33	2082.57
200000	3013.48	2793.89	2620.67	2481.15	2366.85	2271.93	2192.18
210000	3164.15	2933.58	2751.71	2605.21	2485.20	2385.52	2301.79
220000	3314.83	3073.28	2882.74	2729.27	2603.54	2499.12	2411.40
230000	3465.50	3212.97	3013.77	2853.32	2721.88	2612.72	2521.01
240000	3616.17	3352.66	3144.81	2977.38	2840.23	2726.31	2630.62
250000	3766.85	3492.36	3275.84	3101.44	2958.57	2839.91	2740.23

10.00 % Monthly Payments

LOAN AMOUNT	15	16	17	18	19	20	21
100	1.06	1.03	1.01	0.99	0.97	0.95	0.94
200	2.12	2.07	2.02	1.97	1.94	1.90	1.87
500	5.31	5.17	5.04	4.93	4.84	4.76	4.69
1000	10.62	10.33	10.08	9.87	9.68	9.52	9.37
2000	21.25	20.67	20.17	19.74	19.36	19.03	18.74
5000	53.11	51.67	50.42	49.34	48.40	47.58	46.86
6000	63.74	62.00	60.51	59.21	58.09	57.10	56.23
7000	74.36	72.33	70.59	69.08	67.77	66.62	65.61
8000	84.98	82.67	80.68	78.95	77.45	76.13	74.98
9000	95.60	93.00	90.76	88.82	87.13	85.65	84.35
10000	106.23	103.33	100.84	98.69	96.81	95.17	93.72
12000	127.47	124.00	121.01	118.43	116.17	114.20	112.47
15000	159.34	155.00	151.27	148.03	145.21	142.75	140.59
20000	212.45	206.67	201.69	197.38	193.62	190.33	187.45
25000	265.57	258.34	252.11	246.72	242.02	237.92	234.31
30000	318.68	310.00	302.53	296.06	290.43	285.50	281.17
31000	329.30	320.34	312.62	305.93	300.11	295.02	290.54
32000	339.93	330.67	322.70	315.80	309.79	304.53	299.92
33000	350.55	341.01	332.79	325.67	319.47	314.05	309.29
34000	361.17	351.34	342.87	335.54	329.15	323.57	318.66
35000	371.79	361.67	352.96	345.41	338.83	333.08	328.03
36000	382.42	372.01	363.04	355.28	348.51	342.60	337.41
37000	393.04	382.34	373.13	365.14	358.19	352.12	346.78
38000	403.66	392.67	383.21	375.01	367.88	361.63	356.15
39000	414.29	403.01	393.29	384.88	377.56	371.15	365.52
40000	424.91	413.34	403.38	394.75	387.24	380.67	374.90
41000	435.53	423.67	413.46	404.62	396.92	390.18	384.27
42000	446.15	434.01	423.55	414.49	406.60	399.70	393.64
43000	456.78	444.34	433.63	424.36	416.28	409.22	403.01
44000	467.40	454.67	443.72	434.23	425.96	418.73	412.38
45000	478.02	465.01	453.80	444.09	435.64	428.25	421.76
46000	488.64	475.34	463.89	453.96	445.32	437.77	431.13
47000	499.27	485.67	473.97	463.83	455.00	447.28	440.50
48000	509.89	496.01	484.05	473.70	464.68	456.80	449.87
49000	520.51	506.34	494.14	483.57	474.37	466.32	459.25
50000	531.13	516.67	504.22	493.44	484.05	475.83	468.62
51000	541.76	527.01	514.31	503.31	493.73	485.35	477.99
52000	552.38	537.34	524.39	513.18	503.41	494.87	487.36
53000	563.00	547.68	534.48	523.04	513.09	504.38	496.74
54000	573.63	558.01	544.56	532.91	522.77	513.90	506.11
55000	584.25	568.34	554.65	542.78	532.45	523.42	515.48
56000	594.87	578.68	564.73	552.65	542.13	532.93	524.85
57000	605.49	589.01	574.82	562.52	551.81	542.45	534.23
58000	616.12	599.34	584.90	572.39	561.49	551.97	543.60
59000	626.74	609.68	594.98	582.26	571.17	561.48	552.97
60000	637.36	620.01	605.07	592.13	580.86	571.00	562.34
65000	690.48	671.68	655.49	641.47	629.26	618.58	609.20
70000	743.59	723.34	705.91	690.81	677.67	666.17	656.07
75000	796.70	775.01	756.34	740.16	726.07	713.75	702.93
80000	849.82	826.68	806.76	789.50	774.47	761.33	749.79
85000	902.93	878.35	857.18	838.84	822.88	808.91	796.65
90000	956.04	930.01	907.60	888.19	871.28	856.50	843.51
95000	1009.16	981.68	958.03	937.53	919.69	904.08	890.38
100000	1062.27	1033.35	1008.45	986.88	968.09	951.66	937.24
105000	1115.38	1085.02	1058.87	1036.22	1016.50	999.25	984.10
110000	1168.50	1136.68	1109.29	1085.56	1064.90	1046.83	1030.96
120000	1274.72	1240.02	1210.14	1184.25	1161.71	1142.00	1124.69
130000	1380.95	1343.35	1310.98	1282.94	1258.52	1237.16	1218.41
140000	1487.18	1446.69	1411.83	1381.63	1355.33	1332.33	1312.13
150000	1593.40	1550.02	1512.67	1480.31	1452.14	1427.50	1405.86
160000	1699.63	1653.36	1613.52	1579.00	1548.95	1522.66	1499.58
170000	1805.86	1756.69	1714.36	1677.69	1645.76	1617.83	1593.30
180000	1912.09	1860.03	1815.21	1776.38	1742.57	1713.00	1687.03
190000	2018.31	1963.36	1916.05	1875.06	1839.38	1808.16	1780.75
200000	2124.54	2066.70	2016.89	1973.75	1936.19	1903.33	1874.48
210000	2230.77	2170.03	2117.74	2072.44	2033.00	1998.50	1968.20
220000	2336.99	2273.37	2218.58	2171.13	2129.81	2093.66	2061.92
230000	2443.22	2376.70	2319.43	2269.81	2226.61	2188.83	2155.65
240000	2549.45	2480.04	2420.27	2368.50	2323.42	2283.99	2249.37
250000	2655.67	2583.37	2521.12	2467.19	2420.23	2379.16	2343.09

Monthly Payments 10.00 %

LOAN AMOUNT	22	23	24	25	30	35	40
				YEARS			
100	0.92	0.91	0.90	0.89	0.86	0.84	0.83
200	1.85	1.83	1.81	1.79	1.73	1.69	1.67
500	4.62	4.57	4.52	4.47	4.31	4.22	4.17
1000	9.25	9.13	9.03	8.94	8.63	8.44	8.33
2000	18.49	18.27	18.07	17.89	17.25	16.88	16.67
5000	46.23	45.66	45.17	44.72	43.13	42.21	41.66
6000	55.47	54.80	54.20	53.67	51.76	50.65	50.00
7000	64.72	63.93	63.23	62.61	60.39	59.10	58.33
8000	73.96	73.06	72.27	71.56	69.01	67.54	66.66
9000	83.21	82.20	81.30	80.50	77.64	75.98	75.00
10000	92.45	91.33	90.33	89.45	86.27	84.42	83.33
12000	110.94	109.59	108.40	107.34	103.52	101.31	100.00
15000	138.68	136.99	135.50	134.17	129.40	126.63	124.99
20000	184.91	182.66	180.67	178.90	172.53	168.85	166.66
25000	231.13	228.32	225.83	223.62	215.67	211.06	208.32
30000	277.36	273.99	271.00	268.35	258.80	253.27	249.99
31000	286.60	283.12	280.03	277.29	267.43	261.71	258.32
32000	295.85	292.25	289.07	286.24	276.05	270.15	266.66
33000	305.09	301.39	298.10	295.18	284.68	278.60	274.99
34000	314.34	310.52	307.13	304.13	293.31	287.04	283.32
35000	323.58	319.65	316.17	313.07	301.93	295.48	291.65
36000	332.83	328.78	325.20	322.02	310.56	303.92	299.99
37000	342.07	337.92	334.23	330.96	319.19	312.37	308.32
38000	351.32	347.05	343.27	339.91	327.81	320.81	316.65
39000	360.57	356.18	352.30	348.85	336.44	329.25	324.99
40000	369.81	365.32	361.33	357.79	345.07	337.69	333.32
41000	379.06	374.45	370.37	366.74	353.69	346.13	341.65
42000	388.30	383.58	379.40	375.68	362.32	354.58	349.99
43000	397.55	392.71	388.43	384.63	370.95	363.02	358.32
44000	406.79	401.85	397.47	393.57	379.57	371.46	366.65
45000	416.04	410.98	406.50	402.52	388.20	379.90	374.98
46000	425.28	420.11	415.53	411.46	396.83	388.35	383.32
47000	434.53	429.25	424.57	420.41	405.45	396.79	391.65
48000	443.77	438.38	433.60	429.35	414.08	405.23	399.98
49000	453.02	447.51	442.63	438.30	422.71	413.67	408.32
50000	462.26	456.65	451.67	447.24	431.33	422.12	416.65
51000	471.51	465.78	460.70	456.19	439.96	430.56	424.98
52000	480.75	474.91	469.73	465.13	448.59	439.00	433.31
53000	490.00	484.04	478.77	474.08	457.21	447.44	441.65
54000	499.24	493.18	487.80	483.02	465.84	455.88	449.98
55000	508.49	502.31	496.83	491.97	474.47	464.33	458.31
56000	517.73	511.44	505.87	500.91	483.09	472.77	466.65
57000	526.98	520.58	514.90	509.86	491.72	481.21	474.98
58000	536.23	529.71	523.93	518.80	500.35	489.65	483.31
59000	545.47	538.84	532.97	527.75	508.97	498.10	491.65
60000	554.72	547.97	542.00	536.69	517.60	506.54	499.98
65000	600.94	593.64	587.17	581.42	560.73	548.75	541.64
70000	647.17	639.30	632.33	626.14	603.87	590.96	583.31
75000	693.39	684.97	677.50	670.87	647.00	633.17	624.97
80000	739.62	730.63	722.67	715.59	690.13	675.39	666.64
85000	785.85	776.30	767.83	760.31	733.27	717.60	708.30
90000	832.07	821.96	813.00	805.04	776.40	759.81	749.97
95000	878.30	867.63	858.17	849.76	819.53	802.02	791.63
100000	924.53	913.29	903.33	894.49	862.67	844.23	833.30
105000	970.75	958.95	948.50	939.21	905.80	886.44	874.96
110000	1016.98	1004.62	993.67	983.94	948.93	928.65	916.63
120000	1109.43	1095.95	1084.00	1073.38	1035.20	1013.08	999.96
130000	1201.88	1187.28	1174.33	1162.83	1121.47	1097.50	1083.29
140000	1294.34	1278.61	1264.67	1252.28	1207.74	1181.92	1166.62
150000	1386.79	1369.94	1355.00	1341.73	1294.00	1266.35	1249.95
160000	1479.24	1461.26	1445.33	1431.18	1380.27	1350.77	1333.28
170000	1571.69	1552.59	1535.67	1520.63	1466.54	1435.19	1416.61
180000	1664.15	1643.92	1626.00	1610.08	1552.80	1519.62	1499.94
190000	1756.60	1735.25	1716.33	1699.53	1639.07	1604.04	1583.27
200000	1849.05	1826.58	1806.67	1788.97	1725.34	1688.46	1666.60
210000	1941.50	1917.91	1897.00	1878.42	1811.60	1772.89	1749.93
220000	2033.96	2009.24	1987.33	1967.87	1897.87	1857.31	1833.26
230000	2126.41	2100.57	2077.67	2057.32	1984.14	1941.73	1916.59
240000	2218.86	2191.90	2168.00	2146.77	2070.40	2026.16	1999.92
250000	2311.31	2283.23	2258.33	2236.22	2156.67	2110.58	2083.25

10.25 % Monthly Payments

LOAN AMOUNT	YEARS 1	2	3	4	5	6	7
100	8.79	4.62	3.23	2.54	2.13	1.85	1.66
200	17.59	9.23	6.46	5.08	4.25	3.71	3.32
500	43.97	23.08	16.14	12.69	10.63	9.27	8.31
1000	87.93	46.16	32.28	25.38	21.27	18.54	16.62
2000	175.87	92.32	64.57	50.76	42.53	37.09	33.24
5000	439.67	230.81	161.42	126.90	106.33	92.72	83.10
6000	527.60	276.97	193.71	152.28	127.59	111.27	99.72
7000	615.53	323.14	225.99	177.66	148.86	129.81	116.34
8000	703.47	369.30	258.28	203.05	170.12	148.36	132.97
9000	791.40	415.46	290.56	228.43	191.39	166.90	149.59
10000	879.33	461.62	322.85	253.81	212.66	185.45	166.21
12000	1055.20	553.95	387.42	304.57	255.19	222.54	199.45
15000	1319.00	692.44	484.27	380.71	318.98	278.17	249.31
20000	1758.67	923.25	645.70	507.61	425.31	370.90	332.41
25000	2198.34	1154.06	807.12	634.52	531.64	463.62	415.52
30000	2638.00	1384.87	968.55	761.42	637.97	556.35	498.62
31000	2725.94	1431.03	1000.83	786.80	659.23	574.89	515.24
32000	2813.87	1477.20	1033.12	812.18	680.50	593.44	531.86
33000	2901.80	1523.36	1065.40	837.56	701.77	611.98	548.48
34000	2989.74	1569.52	1097.69	862.94	723.03	630.53	565.10
35000	3077.67	1615.68	1129.97	888.32	744.30	649.07	581.72
36000	3165.60	1661.84	1162.26	913.71	765.56	667.62	598.34
37000	3253.54	1708.01	1194.54	939.09	786.83	686.16	614.97
38000	3341.47	1754.17	1226.83	964.47	808.09	704.71	631.59
39000	3429.40	1800.33	1259.11	989.85	829.36	723.25	648.21
40000	3517.34	1846.49	1291.40	1015.23	850.62	741.79	664.83
41000	3605.27	1892.66	1323.68	1040.61	871.89	760.34	681.45
42000	3693.20	1938.82	1355.97	1065.99	893.16	778.88	698.07
43000	3781.14	1984.98	1388.25	1091.37	914.42	797.43	714.69
44000	3869.07	2031.14	1420.54	1116.75	935.69	815.97	731.31
45000	3957.00	2077.31	1452.82	1142.13	956.95	834.52	747.93
46000	4044.94	2123.47	1485.11	1167.51	978.22	853.06	764.55
47000	4132.87	2169.63	1517.39	1192.89	999.48	871.61	781.17
48000	4220.81	2215.79	1549.68	1218.27	1020.75	890.15	797.79
49000	4308.74	2261.95	1581.96	1243.65	1042.02	908.70	814.41
50000	4396.67	2308.12	1614.25	1269.04	1063.28	927.24	831.03
51000	4484.61	2354.28	1646.53	1294.42	1084.55	945.79	847.66
52000	4572.54	2400.44	1678.82	1319.80	1105.81	964.33	864.28
53000	4660.47	2446.60	1711.10	1345.18	1127.08	982.88	880.90
54000	4748.41	2492.77	1743.38	1370.56	1148.34	1001.42	897.52
55000	4836.34	2538.93	1775.67	1395.94	1169.61	1019.97	914.14
56000	4924.27	2585.09	1807.95	1421.32	1190.87	1038.51	930.76
57000	5012.21	2631.25	1840.24	1446.70	1212.14	1057.06	947.38
58000	5100.14	2677.42	1872.52	1472.08	1233.41	1075.60	964.00
59000	5188.07	2723.58	1904.81	1497.46	1254.67	1094.15	980.62
60000	5276.01	2769.74	1937.09	1522.84	1275.94	1112.69	997.24
65000	5715.67	3000.55	2098.52	1649.75	1382.27	1205.42	1080.34
70000	6155.34	3231.36	2259.94	1776.65	1488.59	1298.14	1163.45
75000	6595.01	3462.18	2421.37	1903.55	1594.92	1390.87	1246.55
80000	7034.68	3692.99	2582.79	2030.46	1701.25	1483.59	1329.66
85000	7474.34	3923.80	2744.22	2157.36	1807.58	1576.31	1412.76
90000	7914.01	4154.61	2905.64	2284.26	1913.91	1669.04	1495.86
95000	8353.68	4385.42	3067.07	2411.17	2020.23	1761.76	1578.97
100000	8793.34	4616.23	3228.49	2538.07	2126.56	1854.49	1662.07
105000	9233.01	4847.05	3389.92	2664.97	2232.89	1947.21	1745.17
110000	9672.68	5077.86	3551.34	2791.88	2339.22	2039.94	1828.28
120000	10552.01	5539.48	3874.19	3045.69	2551.87	2225.38	1994.48
130000	11431.35	6001.10	4197.04	3299.49	2764.53	2410.83	2160.69
140000	12310.68	6462.73	4519.89	3553.30	2977.19	2596.28	2326.90
150000	13190.02	6924.35	4842.74	3807.11	3189.84	2781.73	2493.10
160000	14069.35	7385.98	5165.59	4060.91	3402.50	2967.18	2659.31
170000	14948.68	7847.60	5488.43	4314.72	3615.15	3152.63	2825.52
180000	15828.02	8309.22	5811.28	4568.53	3827.81	3338.08	2991.72
190000	16707.35	8770.85	6134.13	4822.33	4040.47	3523.53	3157.93
200000	17586.69	9232.47	6456.98	5076.14	4253.12	3708.97	3324.14
210000	18466.02	9694.09	6779.83	5329.95	4465.78	3894.42	3490.34
220000	19345.36	10155.72	7102.68	5583.76	4678.44	4079.87	3656.55
230000	20224.69	10617.34	7425.53	5837.56	4891.09	4265.32	3822.76
240000	21104.03	11078.96	7748.38	6091.37	5103.75	4450.77	3988.97
250000	21983.36	11540.59	8071.23	6345.18	5316.40	4636.22	4155.17

Monthly Payments 10.25 %

LOAN AMOUNT	8	9	10	11	12	13	14
100	1.52	1.41	1.32	1.25	1.20	1.15	1.11
200	3.04	2.82	2.65	2.51	2.39	2.30	2.22
500	7.60	7.05	6.62	6.27	5.99	5.75	5.55
1000	15.19	14.10	13.24	12.54	11.97	11.50	11.10
2000	30.39	28.20	26.47	25.08	23.95	23.00	22.21
5000	75.97	70.50	66.18	62.71	59.86	57.50	55.52
6000	91.16	84.59	79.42	75.25	71.84	69.00	66.63
7000	106.36	98.69	92.65	87.79	83.81	80.51	77.73
8000	121.55	112.79	105.89	100.33	95.78	92.01	88.84
9000	136.75	126.89	119.12	112.87	107.75	103.51	99.94
10000	151.94	140.99	132.36	125.41	119.73	115.01	111.05
12000	182.33	169.19	158.83	150.49	143.67	138.01	133.26
15000	227.91	211.49	198.54	188.12	179.59	172.51	166.57
20000	303.88	281.98	264.72	250.82	239.45	230.01	222.09
25000	379.85	352.48	330.90	313.53	299.31	287.52	277.62
30000	455.82	422.97	397.08	376.24	359.18	345.02	333.14
31000	471.02	437.07	410.32	388.78	371.15	356.52	344.25
32000	486.21	451.17	423.55	401.32	383.12	368.02	355.35
33000	501.41	465.27	436.79	413.86	395.10	379.52	366.46
34000	516.60	479.37	450.02	426.40	407.07	391.02	377.56
35000	531.79	493.47	463.26	438.94	419.04	402.53	388.66
36000	546.99	507.57	476.50	451.48	431.01	414.03	399.77
37000	562.18	521.67	489.73	464.03	442.99	425.53	410.87
38000	577.38	535.77	502.97	476.57	454.96	437.03	421.98
39000	592.57	549.87	516.20	489.11	466.93	448.53	433.08
40000	607.77	563.97	529.44	501.65	478.90	460.03	444.19
41000	622.96	578.06	542.68	514.19	490.88	471.53	455.29
42000	638.15	592.16	555.91	526.73	502.85	483.03	466.40
43000	653.35	606.26	569.15	539.27	514.82	494.53	477.50
44000	668.54	620.36	582.38	551.81	526.79	506.03	488.61
45000	683.74	634.46	595.62	564.36	538.77	517.53	499.71
46000	698.93	648.56	608.86	576.90	550.74	529.03	510.82
47000	714.12	662.66	622.09	589.44	562.71	540.53	521.92
48000	729.32	676.76	635.33	601.98	574.68	552.04	533.03
49000	744.51	690.86	648.56	614.52	586.66	563.54	544.13
50000	759.71	704.96	661.80	627.06	598.63	575.04	555.24
51000	774.90	719.06	675.03	639.60	610.60	586.54	566.34
52000	790.10	733.15	688.27	652.14	622.57	598.04	577.44
53000	805.29	747.25	701.51	664.69	634.55	609.54	588.55
54000	820.48	761.35	714.74	677.23	646.52	621.04	599.65
55000	835.68	775.45	727.98	689.77	658.49	632.54	610.76
56000	850.87	789.55	741.21	702.31	670.47	644.04	621.86
57000	866.07	803.65	754.45	714.85	682.44	655.54	632.97
58000	881.26	817.75	767.69	727.39	694.41	667.04	644.07
59000	896.45	831.85	780.92	739.93	706.38	678.54	655.18
60000	911.65	845.95	794.16	752.47	718.36	690.04	666.28
65000	987.62	916.44	860.34	815.18	778.22	747.55	721.81
70000	1063.59	986.94	926.52	877.89	838.08	805.05	777.33
75000	1139.56	1057.43	992.70	940.59	897.94	862.55	832.85
80000	1215.53	1127.93	1058.88	1003.30	957.81	920.06	888.38
85000	1291.50	1198.43	1125.06	1066.01	1017.67	977.56	943.90
90000	1367.47	1268.92	1191.24	1128.71	1077.53	1035.07	999.42
95000	1443.44	1339.42	1257.42	1191.42	1137.40	1092.57	1054.95
100000	1519.41	1409.91	1323.60	1254.12	1197.26	1150.07	1110.47
105000	1595.38	1480.41	1389.78	1316.83	1257.12	1207.58	1165.99
110000	1671.36	1550.90	1455.96	1379.54	1316.99	1265.08	1221.52
120000	1823.30	1691.90	1588.32	1504.95	1436.71	1380.09	1332.56
130000	1975.24	1832.89	1720.68	1630.36	1556.44	1495.09	1443.61
140000	2127.18	1973.88	1853.04	1755.77	1676.16	1610.10	1554.66
150000	2279.12	2114.87	1985.40	1881.19	1795.89	1725.11	1665.71
160000	2431.06	2255.86	2117.76	2006.60	1915.61	1840.12	1776.75
170000	2583.00	2396.85	2250.12	2132.01	2035.34	1955.12	1887.80
180000	2734.94	2537.84	2382.48	2257.42	2155.07	2070.13	1998.85
190000	2886.89	2678.83	2514.84	2382.84	2274.79	2185.14	2109.89
200000	3038.83	2819.83	2647.20	2508.25	2394.52	2300.15	2220.94
210000	3190.77	2960.82	2779.56	2633.66	2514.24	2415.15	2331.99
220000	3342.71	3101.81	2911.92	2759.07	2633.97	2530.16	2443.04
230000	3494.65	3242.80	3044.28	2884.48	2753.70	2645.17	2554.08
240000	3646.59	3383.79	3176.63	3009.90	2873.42	2760.18	2665.13
250000	3798.53	3524.78	3308.99	3135.31	2993.15	2875.18	2776.18

10.25 % Monthly Payments

LOAN AMOUNT	15	16	17	18	19	20	21
	YEARS						
100	1.08	1.05	1.02	1.00	0.98	0.97	0.95
200	2.15	2.10	2.05	2.00	1.97	1.94	1.91
500	5.38	5.24	5.12	5.01	4.92	4.84	4.77
1000	10.77	10.48	10.24	10.02	9.84	9.68	9.53
2000	21.54	20.97	20.47	20.05	19.67	19.35	19.07
5000	53.85	52.41	51.18	50.11	49.19	48.38	47.67
6000	64.61	62.90	61.42	60.14	59.02	58.05	57.20
7000	75.38	73.38	71.65	70.16	68.86	67.73	66.73
8000	86.15	83.86	81.89	80.18	78.70	77.40	76.27
9000	96.92	94.34	92.12	90.20	88.54	87.08	85.80
10000	107.69	104.83	102.36	100.23	98.37	96.75	95.33
12000	129.23	125.79	122.83	120.27	118.05	116.10	114.40
15000	161.54	157.24	153.54	150.34	147.56	145.13	143.00
20000	215.38	209.65	204.72	200.45	196.74	193.50	190.66
25000	269.23	262.06	255.90	250.57	245.93	241.88	238.33
30000	323.07	314.48	307.08	300.68	295.12	290.26	285.99
31000	333.84	324.96	317.32	310.70	304.95	299.93	295.53
32000	344.61	335.44	327.55	320.73	314.79	309.61	305.06
33000	355.38	345.92	337.79	330.75	324.63	319.28	314.59
34000	366.15	356.41	348.02	340.77	334.47	328.96	324.13
35000	376.92	366.89	358.26	350.80	344.30	338.63	333.66
36000	387.69	377.37	368.50	360.82	354.14	348.31	343.19
37000	398.46	387.85	378.73	370.84	363.98	357.98	352.73
38000	409.23	398.34	388.97	380.86	373.82	367.66	362.26
39000	420.00	408.82	399.20	390.89	383.65	377.33	371.79
40000	430.77	419.30	409.44	400.91	393.49	387.01	381.33
41000	441.54	429.78	419.68	410.93	403.33	396.68	390.86
42000	452.30	440.27	429.91	420.95	413.16	406.36	400.39
43000	463.07	450.75	440.15	430.98	423.00	416.03	409.93
44000	473.84	461.23	450.38	441.00	432.84	425.71	419.46
45000	484.61	471.71	460.62	451.02	442.68	435.39	428.99
46000	495.38	482.20	470.86	461.05	452.51	445.06	438.53
47000	506.15	492.68	481.09	471.07	462.35	454.74	448.06
48000	516.92	503.16	491.33	481.09	472.19	464.41	457.59
49000	527.69	513.64	501.56	491.11	482.03	474.09	467.12
50000	538.46	524.13	511.80	501.14	491.86	483.76	476.66
51000	549.23	534.61	522.04	511.16	501.70	493.44	486.19
52000	560.00	545.09	532.27	521.18	511.54	503.11	495.72
53000	570.76	555.57	542.51	531.20	521.37	512.79	505.26
54000	581.53	566.06	552.74	541.23	531.21	522.46	514.79
55000	592.30	576.54	562.98	551.25	541.05	532.14	524.32
56000	603.07	587.02	573.22	561.27	550.89	541.81	533.86
57000	613.84	597.50	583.45	571.30	560.72	551.49	543.39
58000	624.61	607.99	593.69	581.32	570.56	561.16	552.92
59000	635.38	618.47	603.92	591.34	580.40	570.84	562.46
60000	646.15	628.95	614.16	601.36	590.23	580.51	571.99
65000	699.99	681.36	665.34	651.48	639.42	628.89	619.66
70000	753.84	733.78	716.52	701.59	688.61	677.27	667.32
75000	807.69	786.19	767.70	751.70	737.79	725.64	714.99
80000	861.53	838.60	818.88	801.82	786.98	774.02	762.65
85000	915.38	891.01	870.06	851.93	836.17	822.39	810.32
90000	969.22	943.43	921.24	902.04	885.35	870.77	857.98
95000	1023.07	995.84	972.42	952.16	934.54	919.15	905.65
100000	1076.91	1048.25	1023.60	1002.27	983.72	967.52	953.32
105000	1130.76	1100.67	1074.78	1052.39	1032.91	1015.90	1000.98
110000	1184.61	1153.08	1125.96	1102.50	1082.10	1064.28	1048.65
120000	1292.30	1257.90	1228.32	1202.73	1180.47	1161.03	1143.98
130000	1399.99	1362.73	1330.68	1302.95	1278.84	1257.78	1239.31
140000	1507.68	1467.55	1433.04	1403.18	1377.21	1354.53	1334.64
150000	1615.37	1572.38	1535.40	1503.41	1475.59	1451.28	1429.97
160000	1723.06	1677.20	1637.76	1603.64	1573.96	1548.04	1525.31
170000	1830.76	1782.03	1740.12	1703.86	1672.33	1644.79	1620.64
180000	1938.45	1886.85	1842.48	1804.09	1770.70	1741.54	1715.97
190000	2046.14	1991.68	1944.84	1904.32	1869.08	1838.29	1811.30
200000	2153.83	2096.50	2047.20	2004.54	1967.45	1935.05	1906.63
210000	2261.52	2201.33	2149.56	2104.77	2065.82	2031.80	2001.96
220000	2369.21	2306.16	2251.92	2205.00	2164.19	2128.55	2097.30
230000	2476.90	2410.98	2354.28	2305.23	2262.57	2225.30	2192.63
240000	2584.60	2515.81	2456.64	2405.45	2360.94	2322.06	2287.96
250000	2692.29	2620.63	2559.00	2505.68	2459.31	2418.81	2383.29

Monthly Payments 10.25 %

LOAN AMOUNT	22	23	24	25	30	35	40
100	0.94	0.93	0.92	0.91	0.88	0.86	0.85
200	1.88	1.86	1.84	1.82	1.76	1.73	1.70
500	4.70	4.65	4.60	4.56	4.40	4.31	4.26
1000	9.41	9.30	9.20	9.11	8.80	8.63	8.52
2000	18.82	18.60	18.40	18.23	17.61	17.25	17.04
5000	47.04	46.49	46.00	45.57	44.02	43.13	42.61
6000	56.45	55.79	55.20	54.68	52.82	51.75	51.13
7000	65.86	65.08	64.40	63.80	61.63	60.38	59.65
8000	75.27	74.38	73.60	72.91	70.43	69.00	68.17
9000	84.67	83.68	82.80	82.02	79.23	77.63	76.69
10000	94.08	92.98	92.00	91.14	88.04	86.26	85.21
12000	112.90	111.57	110.40	109.36	105.64	103.51	102.25
15000	141.12	139.47	138.00	136.70	132.05	129.38	127.82
20000	188.16	185.96	184.00	182.27	176.07	172.51	170.42
25000	235.20	232.45	230.01	227.84	220.09	215.64	213.03
30000	282.24	278.93	276.01	273.41	264.11	258.77	255.63
31000	291.65	288.23	285.21	282.52	272.91	267.39	264.15
32000	301.06	297.53	294.41	291.64	281.72	276.02	272.68
33000	310.47	306.83	303.61	300.75	290.52	284.65	281.20
34000	319.88	316.13	312.81	309.86	299.32	293.27	289.72
35000	329.29	325.42	322.01	318.98	308.13	301.90	298.24
36000	338.69	334.72	331.21	328.09	316.93	310.52	306.76
37000	348.10	344.02	340.41	337.20	325.73	319.15	315.28
38000	357.51	353.32	349.61	346.32	334.54	327.77	323.80
39000	366.92	362.62	358.81	355.43	343.34	336.40	332.32
40000	376.33	371.91	368.01	364.54	352.14	345.02	340.84
41000	385.73	381.21	377.21	373.66	360.95	353.65	349.37
42000	395.14	390.51	386.41	382.77	369.75	362.28	357.89
43000	404.55	399.81	395.61	391.89	378.56	370.90	366.41
44000	413.96	409.10	404.81	401.00	387.36	379.53	374.93
45000	423.37	418.40	414.01	410.11	396.16	388.15	383.45
46000	432.78	427.70	423.21	419.23	404.97	396.78	391.97
47000	442.18	437.00	432.41	428.34	413.77	405.40	400.49
48000	451.59	446.30	441.61	437.45	422.57	414.03	409.01
49000	461.00	455.59	450.81	446.57	431.38	422.66	417.53
50000	470.41	464.89	460.01	455.68	440.18	431.28	426.05
51000	479.82	474.19	469.21	464.79	448.98	439.91	434.58
52000	489.22	483.49	478.41	473.91	457.79	448.53	443.10
53000	498.63	492.79	487.61	483.02	466.59	457.16	451.62
54000	508.04	502.08	496.81	492.14	475.40	465.78	460.14
55000	517.45	511.38	506.01	501.25	484.20	474.41	468.66
56000	526.86	520.68	515.21	510.36	493.00	483.03	477.18
57000	536.26	529.98	524.41	519.48	501.81	491.66	485.70
58000	545.67	539.27	533.61	528.59	510.61	500.29	494.22
59000	555.08	548.57	542.81	537.70	519.41	508.91	502.74
60000	564.49	557.87	552.01	546.82	528.22	517.54	511.27
65000	611.53	604.36	598.01	592.39	572.23	560.67	553.87
70000	658.57	650.85	644.01	637.95	616.25	603.79	596.48
75000	705.61	697.34	690.02	683.52	660.27	646.92	639.08
80000	752.65	743.83	736.02	729.09	704.29	690.05	681.69
85000	799.69	790.32	782.02	774.66	748.31	733.18	724.29
90000	846.73	836.80	828.02	820.23	792.33	776.31	766.90
95000	893.77	883.29	874.02	865.79	836.34	819.43	809.50
100000	940.82	929.78	920.02	911.36	880.36	862.56	852.11
105000	987.86	976.27	966.02	956.93	924.38	905.69	894.72
110000	1034.90	1022.76	1012.02	1002.50	968.40	948.82	937.32
120000	1128.98	1115.74	1104.02	1093.63	1056.43	1035.07	1022.53
130000	1223.06	1208.72	1196.03	1184.77	1144.47	1121.33	1107.74
140000	1317.14	1301.70	1288.03	1275.91	1232.51	1207.59	1192.95
150000	1411.22	1394.67	1380.03	1367.04	1320.54	1293.84	1278.16
160000	1505.30	1487.65	1472.03	1458.18	1408.58	1380.10	1363.38
170000	1599.39	1580.63	1564.04	1549.32	1496.61	1466.35	1448.59
180000	1693.47	1673.61	1656.04	1640.45	1584.65	1552.61	1533.80
190000	1787.55	1766.59	1748.04	1731.59	1672.69	1638.87	1619.01
200000	1881.63	1859.57	1840.04	1822.72	1760.72	1725.12	1704.22
210000	1975.71	1952.54	1932.04	1913.86	1848.76	1811.38	1789.43
220000	2069.79	2045.52	2024.05	2005.00	1936.80	1897.64	1874.64
230000	2163.88	2138.50	2116.05	2096.13	2024.83	1983.89	1959.85
240000	2257.96	2231.48	2208.05	2187.27	2112.87	2070.15	2045.06
250000	2352.04	2324.46	2300.05	2278.41	2200.90	2156.40	2130.27

10.50 % Monthly Payments

LOAN AMOUNT	1	2	3	4	5	6	7
	YEARS						
100	8.80	4.63	3.24	2.55	2.14	1.87	1.67
200	17.61	9.25	6.48	5.10	4.28	3.73	3.35
500	44.02	23.14	16.20	12.75	10.69	9.33	8.37
1000	88.04	46.27	32.40	25.50	21.38	18.67	16.74
2000	176.09	92.55	64.80	50.99	42.77	37.33	33.49
5000	440.22	231.37	161.99	127.48	106.92	93.33	83.72
6000	528.27	277.64	194.39	152.98	128.30	112.00	100.47
7000	616.31	323.91	226.78	178.47	149.69	130.66	117.21
8000	704.36	370.18	259.18	203.97	171.07	149.33	133.96
9000	792.40	416.46	291.58	229.46	192.45	167.99	150.70
10000	880.45	462.73	323.98	254.96	213.84	186.66	167.45
12000	1056.54	555.28	388.77	305.95	256.61	223.99	200.94
15000	1320.67	694.10	485.96	382.44	320.76	279.99	251.17
20000	1760.90	925.46	647.95	509.92	427.68	373.32	334.90
25000	2201.12	1156.83	809.94	637.40	534.60	466.65	418.62
30000	2641.35	1388.19	971.93	764.88	641.51	559.98	502.35
31000	2729.39	1434.47	1004.33	790.38	662.90	578.65	519.09
32000	2817.44	1480.74	1036.72	815.87	684.28	597.31	535.84
33000	2905.48	1527.01	1069.12	841.37	705.67	615.98	552.58
34000	2993.53	1573.28	1101.52	866.86	727.05	634.65	569.33
35000	3081.57	1619.56	1133.92	892.36	748.43	653.31	586.07
36000	3169.62	1665.83	1166.31	917.86	769.82	671.98	602.82
37000	3257.66	1712.10	1198.71	943.35	791.20	690.64	619.56
38000	3345.71	1758.38	1231.11	968.85	812.58	709.31	636.31
39000	3433.75	1804.65	1263.51	994.34	833.97	727.98	653.05
40000	3521.80	1850.92	1295.90	1019.84	855.35	746.64	669.80
41000	3609.84	1897.20	1328.30	1045.34	876.74	765.31	686.54
42000	3697.89	1943.47	1360.70	1070.83	898.12	783.97	703.28
43000	3785.93	1989.74	1393.10	1096.33	919.50	802.64	720.03
44000	3873.98	2036.02	1425.49	1121.82	940.89	821.31	736.77
45000	3962.02	2082.29	1457.89	1147.32	962.27	839.97	753.52
46000	4050.07	2128.56	1490.29	1172.82	983.65	858.64	770.26
47000	4138.11	2174.83	1522.69	1198.31	1005.04	877.30	787.01
48000	4226.16	2221.11	1555.08	1223.81	1026.42	895.97	803.75
49000	4314.20	2267.38	1587.48	1249.30	1047.81	914.64	820.50
50000	4402.25	2313.65	1619.88	1274.80	1069.19	933.30	837.24
51000	4490.29	2359.93	1652.28	1300.30	1090.57	951.97	853.99
52000	4578.34	2406.20	1684.67	1325.79	1111.96	970.63	870.73
53000	4666.38	2452.47	1717.07	1351.29	1133.34	989.30	887.48
54000	4754.43	2498.75	1749.47	1376.79	1154.73	1007.97	904.22
55000	4842.47	2545.02	1781.87	1402.28	1176.11	1026.63	920.97
56000	4930.52	2591.29	1814.27	1427.78	1197.49	1045.30	937.71
57000	5018.56	2637.57	1846.66	1453.27	1218.88	1063.96	954.46
58000	5106.61	2683.84	1879.06	1478.77	1240.26	1082.63	971.20
59000	5194.65	2730.11	1911.46	1504.27	1261.64	1101.30	987.95
60000	5282.70	2776.38	1943.86	1529.76	1283.03	1119.96	1004.69
65000	5722.92	3007.75	2105.84	1657.24	1389.95	1213.29	1088.42
70000	6163.15	3239.12	2267.83	1784.72	1496.87	1306.62	1172.14
75000	6603.37	3470.48	2429.82	1912.20	1603.79	1399.95	1255.87
80000	7043.60	3701.85	2591.81	2039.68	1710.70	1493.28	1339.59
85000	7483.82	3933.21	2753.80	2167.16	1817.62	1586.61	1423.31
90000	7924.05	4164.58	2915.78	2294.64	1924.54	1679.94	1507.04
95000	8364.27	4395.94	3077.77	2422.12	2031.46	1773.27	1590.76
100000	8804.50	4627.31	3239.76	2549.60	2138.38	1866.60	1674.49
105000	9244.72	4858.67	3401.75	2677.08	2245.30	1959.93	1758.21
110000	9684.95	5090.04	3563.73	2804.56	2352.22	2053.26	1841.94
120000	10565.40	5552.77	3887.71	3059.52	2566.06	2239.92	2009.39
130000	11445.85	6015.50	4211.69	3314.48	2779.89	2426.59	2176.83
140000	12326.30	6478.23	4535.66	3569.44	2993.73	2613.25	2344.28
150000	13206.74	6940.96	4859.64	3824.40	3207.57	2799.91	2511.73
160000	14087.19	7403.69	5183.61	4079.36	3421.41	2986.57	2679.18
170000	14967.64	7866.42	5507.59	4334.32	3635.25	3173.23	2846.63
180000	15848.09	8329.15	5831.57	4589.28	3849.08	3359.89	3014.08
190000	16728.54	8791.88	6155.54	4844.24	4062.92	3546.55	3181.53
200000	17608.99	9254.61	6479.52	5099.20	4276.76	3733.21	3348.98
210000	18489.44	9717.35	6803.49	5354.16	4490.60	3919.87	3516.42
220000	19369.89	10180.08	7127.47	5609.12	4704.44	4106.53	3683.87
230000	20250.34	10642.81	7451.45	5864.08	4918.27	4293.19	3851.32
240000	21130.79	11105.54	7775.42	6119.04	5132.11	4479.85	4018.77
250000	22011.24	11568.27	8099.40	6374.00	5345.95	4666.51	4186.22

Monthly Payments 10.50 %

LOAN AMOUNT	8	9	10	11	12	13	14
100	1.53	1.42	1.34	1.27	1.21	1.16	1.12
200	3.06	2.85	2.67	2.54	2.42	2.33	2.25
500	7.66	7.11	6.68	6.34	6.06	5.82	5.62
1000	15.32	14.23	13.37	12.68	12.11	11.64	11.25
2000	30.64	28.46	26.74	25.35	24.22	23.29	22.50
5000	76.61	71.15	66.85	63.39	60.56	58.21	56.25
6000	91.93	85.38	80.22	76.06	72.67	69.86	67.50
7000	107.25	99.61	93.58	88.74	84.78	81.50	78.74
8000	122.57	113.83	106.95	101.42	96.89	93.14	89.99
9000	137.89	128.06	120.32	114.10	109.00	104.78	101.24
10000	153.21	142.29	133.69	126.77	121.12	116.43	112.49
12000	183.86	170.75	160.43	152.13	145.34	139.71	134.99
15000	229.82	213.44	200.54	190.16	181.67	174.64	168.74
20000	306.43	284.59	267.38	253.55	242.23	232.85	224.99
25000	383.03	355.73	334.23	316.93	302.79	291.06	281.23
30000	459.64	426.88	401.08	380.32	363.35	349.28	337.48
31000	474.96	441.11	414.44	393.00	375.46	360.92	348.73
32000	490.28	455.34	427.81	405.68	387.57	372.56	359.98
33000	505.60	469.57	441.18	418.35	399.68	384.20	371.23
34000	520.93	483.80	454.55	431.03	411.79	395.85	382.48
35000	536.25	498.03	467.92	443.71	423.91	407.49	393.72
36000	551.57	512.26	481.29	456.39	436.02	419.13	404.97
37000	566.89	526.49	494.66	469.06	448.13	430.77	416.22
38000	582.21	540.72	508.03	481.74	460.24	442.42	427.47
39000	597.53	554.94	521.40	494.42	472.35	454.06	438.72
40000	612.85	569.17	534.77	507.09	484.46	465.70	449.97
41000	628.18	583.40	548.14	519.77	496.58	477.34	461.22
42000	643.50	597.63	561.51	532.45	508.69	488.99	472.47
43000	658.82	611.86	574.87	545.13	520.80	500.63	483.72
44000	674.14	626.09	588.24	557.80	532.91	512.27	494.97
45000	689.46	640.32	601.61	570.48	545.02	523.91	506.22
46000	704.78	654.55	614.98	583.16	557.13	535.56	517.47
47000	720.10	668.78	628.35	595.84	569.24	547.20	528.72
48000	735.42	683.01	641.72	608.51	581.36	558.84	539.97
49000	750.75	697.24	655.09	621.19	593.47	570.48	551.21
50000	766.07	711.47	668.46	633.87	605.58	582.13	562.46
51000	781.39	725.70	681.83	646.55	617.69	593.77	573.71
52000	796.71	739.93	695.20	659.22	629.80	605.41	584.96
53000	812.03	754.16	708.57	671.90	641.91	617.06	596.21
54000	827.35	768.38	721.94	684.58	654.03	628.70	607.46
55000	842.67	782.61	735.30	697.25	666.14	640.34	618.71
56000	858.00	796.84	748.67	709.93	678.25	651.98	629.96
57000	873.32	811.07	762.04	722.61	690.36	663.63	641.21
58000	888.64	825.30	775.41	735.29	702.47	675.27	652.46
59000	903.96	839.53	788.78	747.96	714.58	686.91	663.71
60000	919.28	853.76	802.15	760.64	726.70	698.55	674.96
65000	995.89	924.91	869.00	824.03	787.25	756.77	731.20
70000	1072.49	996.05	935.84	887.42	847.81	814.98	787.45
75000	1149.10	1067.20	1002.69	950.80	908.37	873.19	843.70
80000	1225.71	1138.35	1069.53	1014.19	968.93	931.40	899.94
85000	1302.31	1209.49	1136.38	1077.58	1029.49	989.62	956.19
90000	1378.92	1280.64	1203.23	1140.96	1090.04	1047.83	1012.43
95000	1455.53	1351.79	1270.07	1204.35	1150.60	1106.04	1068.68
100000	1532.14	1422.93	1336.92	1267.74	1211.16	1164.25	1124.93
105000	1608.74	1494.08	1403.76	1331.12	1271.72	1222.47	1181.17
110000	1685.35	1565.23	1470.61	1394.51	1332.28	1280.68	1237.42
120000	1838.56	1707.52	1604.30	1521.28	1453.39	1397.11	1349.91
130000	1991.78	1849.82	1737.99	1648.06	1574.51	1513.53	1462.41
140000	2144.99	1992.11	1871.68	1774.83	1695.62	1629.96	1574.90
150000	2298.20	2134.40	2005.38	1901.60	1816.74	1746.38	1687.39
160000	2451.42	2276.70	2139.07	2028.38	1937.85	1862.81	1799.88
170000	2604.63	2418.99	2272.76	2155.15	2058.97	1979.23	1912.38
180000	2757.84	2561.28	2406.45	2281.93	2180.09	2095.66	2024.87
190000	2911.06	2703.58	2540.14	2408.70	2301.20	2212.08	2137.36
200000	3064.27	2845.87	2673.83	2535.47	2422.32	2328.51	2249.86
210000	3217.48	2988.16	2807.53	2662.25	2543.43	2444.94	2362.35
220000	3370.70	3130.46	2941.22	2789.02	2664.55	2561.36	2474.84
230000	3523.91	3272.75	3074.91	2915.79	2785.67	2677.79	2587.33
240000	3677.12	3415.04	3208.60	3042.57	2906.78	2794.21	2699.83
250000	3830.34	3557.34	3342.29	3169.34	3027.90	2910.64	2812.32

10.50 % Monthly Payments

LOAN AMOUNT	15	16	17	18	19	20	21
				YEARS			
100	1.09	1.06	1.04	1.02	1.00	0.98	0.97
200	2.18	2.13	2.08	2.04	2.00	1.97	1.94
500	5.46	5.32	5.19	5.09	5.00	4.92	4.85
1000	10.92	10.63	10.39	10.18	9.99	9.83	9.69
2000	21.83	21.26	20.78	20.36	19.99	19.67	19.39
5000	54.58	53.16	51.94	50.89	49.97	49.17	48.47
6000	65.50	63.79	62.33	61.07	59.97	59.01	58.17
7000	76.41	74.43	72.72	71.24	69.96	68.84	67.86
8000	87.33	85.06	83.11	81.42	79.96	78.68	77.56
9000	98.25	95.69	93.50	91.60	89.95	88.51	87.25
10000	109.16	106.32	103.88	101.78	99.94	98.35	96.95
12000	131.00	127.59	124.66	122.13	119.93	118.02	116.34
15000	163.75	159.49	155.83	152.66	149.92	147.52	145.42
20000	218.33	212.65	207.77	203.55	199.89	196.69	193.90
25000	272.91	265.81	259.71	254.44	249.86	245.87	242.37
30000	327.49	318.97	311.65	305.33	299.83	295.04	290.85
31000	338.41	329.60	322.04	315.50	309.83	304.88	300.54
32000	349.32	340.24	332.43	325.68	319.82	314.71	310.24
33000	360.24	350.87	342.82	335.86	329.82	324.55	319.93
34000	371.16	361.50	353.21	346.04	339.81	334.38	329.63
35000	382.07	372.13	363.59	356.21	349.81	344.22	339.32
36000	392.99	382.77	373.98	366.39	359.80	354.05	349.02
37000	403.91	393.40	384.37	376.57	369.80	363.89	358.71
38000	414.82	404.03	394.76	386.75	379.79	373.72	368.40
39000	425.74	414.66	405.15	396.93	389.78	383.55	378.10
40000	436.66	425.30	415.54	407.10	399.78	393.39	387.79
41000	447.57	435.93	425.92	417.28	409.77	403.22	397.49
42000	458.49	446.56	436.31	427.46	419.77	413.06	407.18
43000	469.41	457.19	446.70	437.64	429.76	422.89	416.88
44000	480.32	467.82	457.09	447.81	439.76	432.73	426.57
45000	491.24	478.46	467.48	457.99	449.75	442.56	436.27
46000	502.15	489.09	477.87	468.17	459.75	452.40	445.96
47000	513.07	499.72	488.25	478.35	469.74	462.23	455.66
48000	523.99	510.35	498.64	488.52	479.73	472.07	465.35
49000	534.90	520.99	509.03	498.70	489.73	481.90	475.05
50000	545.82	531.62	519.42	508.88	499.72	491.74	484.74
51000	556.74	542.25	529.81	519.06	509.72	501.57	494.44
52000	567.65	552.88	540.20	529.23	519.71	511.41	504.13
53000	578.57	563.52	550.59	539.41	529.71	521.24	513.83
54000	589.49	574.15	560.97	549.59	539.70	531.08	523.52
55000	600.40	584.78	571.36	559.77	549.70	540.91	533.22
56000	611.32	595.41	581.75	569.94	559.69	550.75	542.91
57000	622.23	606.05	592.14	580.12	569.68	560.58	552.61
58000	633.15	616.68	602.53	590.30	579.68	570.41	562.30
59000	644.07	627.31	612.92	600.48	589.67	580.25	572.00
60000	654.98	637.94	623.30	610.65	599.67	590.08	581.69
65000	709.57	691.11	675.25	661.54	649.64	639.26	630.17
70000	764.15	744.27	727.19	712.43	699.61	688.43	678.64
75000	818.73	797.43	779.13	763.32	749.58	737.61	727.11
80000	873.31	850.59	831.07	814.21	799.56	786.78	775.59
85000	927.89	903.75	883.01	865.09	849.53	835.95	824.06
90000	982.48	956.91	934.96	915.98	899.50	885.13	872.54
95000	1037.06	1010.08	986.90	966.87	949.47	934.30	921.01
100000	1091.64	1063.24	1038.84	1017.76	999.45	983.47	969.49
105000	1146.22	1116.40	1090.78	1068.64	1049.42	1032.65	1017.96
110000	1200.80	1169.56	1142.72	1119.53	1099.39	1081.82	1066.44
120000	1309.97	1275.89	1246.61	1221.31	1199.34	1180.17	1163.38
130000	1419.13	1382.21	1350.49	1323.08	1299.28	1278.52	1260.33
140000	1528.30	1488.53	1454.38	1424.86	1399.22	1376.86	1357.28
150000	1637.46	1594.86	1558.26	1526.63	1499.17	1475.21	1454.23
160000	1746.62	1701.18	1662.14	1628.41	1599.11	1573.56	1551.18
170000	1855.79	1807.51	1766.03	1730.19	1699.06	1671.90	1648.13
180000	1964.95	1913.83	1869.91	1831.96	1799.00	1770.25	1745.08
190000	2074.12	2020.15	1973.80	1933.74	1898.95	1868.60	1842.02
200000	2183.28	2126.48	2077.68	2035.51	1998.89	1966.95	1938.97
210000	2292.44	2232.80	2181.56	2137.29	2098.84	2065.29	2035.92
220000	2401.61	2339.12	2285.45	2239.06	2198.78	2163.64	2132.87
230000	2510.77	2445.45	2389.33	2340.84	2298.73	2261.99	2229.82
240000	2619.94	2551.77	2493.22	2442.62	2398.67	2360.34	2326.77
250000	2729.10	2658.10	2597.10	2544.39	2498.62	2458.68	2423.72

Monthly Payments 10.50 %

LOAN AMOUNT	22	23	24	25	30	35	40
				YEARS			
100	0.96	0.95	0.94	0.93	0.90	0.88	0.87
200	1.91	1.89	1.87	1.86	1.80	1.76	1.74
500	4.79	4.73	4.68	4.64	4.49	4.40	4.35
1000	9.57	9.46	9.37	9.28	8.98	8.81	8.71
2000	19.14	18.93	18.74	18.57	17.96	17.62	17.42
5000	47.86	47.32	46.84	46.42	44.91	44.05	43.55
6000	57.43	56.78	56.21	55.70	53.89	52.86	52.26
7000	67.00	66.25	65.58	64.98	62.87	61.67	60.97
8000	76.58	75.71	74.94	74.27	71.85	70.48	69.68
9000	86.15	85.17	84.31	83.55	80.83	79.29	78.39
10000	95.72	94.64	93.68	92.83	89.81	88.10	87.10
12000	114.86	113.56	112.42	111.40	107.78	105.72	104.52
15000	143.58	141.96	140.52	139.25	134.72	132.14	130.65
20000	191.44	189.27	187.36	185.67	179.63	176.19	174.20
25000	239.30	236.59	234.20	232.08	224.54	220.24	217.75
30000	287.16	283.91	281.04	278.50	269.44	264.29	261.29
31000	296.73	293.37	290.41	287.78	278.42	273.10	270.00
32000	306.30	302.84	299.78	297.07	287.40	281.91	278.71
33000	315.88	312.30	309.14	306.35	296.39	290.72	287.42
34000	325.45	321.77	318.51	315.63	305.37	299.53	296.13
35000	335.02	331.23	327.88	324.92	314.35	308.34	304.84
36000	344.59	340.69	337.25	334.20	323.33	317.15	313.55
37000	354.16	350.16	346.62	343.48	332.31	325.96	322.26
38000	363.74	359.62	355.98	352.77	341.29	334.77	330.97
39000	373.31	369.08	365.35	362.05	350.27	343.58	339.68
40000	382.88	378.55	374.72	371.33	359.26	352.39	348.39
41000	392.45	388.01	384.09	380.62	368.24	361.20	357.10
42000	402.02	397.47	393.46	389.90	377.22	370.01	365.81
43000	411.60	406.94	402.82	399.18	386.20	378.82	374.52
44000	421.17	416.40	412.19	408.47	395.18	387.62	383.23
45000	430.74	425.87	421.56	417.75	404.16	396.43	391.94
46000	440.31	435.33	430.93	427.03	413.14	405.24	400.65
47000	449.88	444.79	440.30	436.31	422.13	414.05	409.36
48000	459.45	454.26	449.66	445.60	431.11	422.86	418.07
49000	469.03	463.72	459.03	454.88	440.09	431.67	426.78
50000	478.60	473.18	468.40	464.16	449.07	440.48	435.49
51000	488.17	482.65	477.77	473.45	458.05	449.29	444.20
52000	497.74	492.11	487.14	482.73	467.03	458.10	452.91
53000	507.31	501.58	496.50	492.01	476.01	466.91	461.62
54000	516.89	511.04	505.87	501.30	485.00	475.72	470.33
55000	526.46	520.50	515.24	510.58	493.98	484.53	479.04
56000	536.03	529.97	524.61	519.86	502.96	493.34	487.75
57000	545.60	539.43	533.98	529.15	511.94	502.15	496.46
58000	555.17	548.89	543.34	538.43	520.92	510.96	505.17
59000	564.75	558.36	552.71	547.71	529.90	519.77	513.88
60000	574.32	567.82	562.08	557.00	538.88	528.58	522.59
65000	622.18	615.14	608.92	603.41	583.79	572.63	566.14
70000	670.04	662.46	655.76	649.83	628.70	616.68	609.69
75000	717.90	709.78	702.60	696.25	673.61	660.72	653.24
80000	765.76	757.10	749.44	742.66	718.51	704.77	696.78
85000	813.62	804.41	796.28	789.08	763.42	748.82	740.33
90000	861.48	851.73	843.12	835.50	808.33	792.87	783.88
95000	909.34	899.05	889.96	881.91	853.23	836.92	827.43
100000	957.20	946.37	936.80	928.33	898.14	880.97	870.98
105000	1005.06	993.69	983.64	974.75	943.05	925.01	914.53
110000	1052.92	1041.01	1030.48	1021.16	987.95	969.06	958.08
120000	1148.64	1135.64	1124.16	1114.00	1077.77	1057.16	1045.18
130000	1244.36	1230.28	1217.84	1206.83	1167.58	1145.25	1132.27
140000	1340.08	1324.92	1311.52	1299.66	1257.40	1233.35	1219.37
150000	1435.80	1419.55	1405.20	1392.49	1347.21	1321.45	1306.47
160000	1531.52	1514.19	1498.88	1485.33	1437.02	1409.54	1393.57
170000	1627.24	1608.83	1592.56	1578.16	1526.84	1497.64	1480.67
180000	1722.96	1703.46	1686.24	1670.99	1616.65	1585.74	1567.77
190000	1818.68	1798.10	1779.92	1763.83	1706.47	1673.83	1654.86
200000	1914.40	1892.74	1873.60	1856.66	1796.28	1761.93	1741.96
210000	2010.12	1987.37	1967.28	1949.49	1886.09	1850.03	1829.06
220000	2105.84	2082.01	2060.96	2042.33	1975.91	1938.12	1916.16
230000	2201.55	2176.65	2154.64	2135.16	2065.72	2026.22	2003.26
240000	2297.27	2271.29	2248.32	2227.99	2155.54	2114.32	2090.35
250000	2392.99	2365.92	2342.00	2320.82	2245.35	2202.41	2177.45

10.75 % Monthly Payments

LOAN AMOUNT	1	2	3	4	5	6	7
				YEARS			
100	8.82	4.64	3.25	2.56	2.15	1.88	1.69
200	17.63	9.28	6.50	5.12	4.30	3.76	3.37
500	44.08	23.19	16.26	12.81	10.75	9.39	8.43
1000	88.16	46.38	32.51	25.61	21.50	18.79	16.87
2000	176.31	92.77	65.02	51.22	43.00	37.58	33.74
5000	440.78	231.92	162.55	128.06	107.51	93.94	84.35
6000	528.94	278.30	195.06	153.67	129.01	112.73	101.22
7000	617.10	324.69	227.57	179.28	150.52	131.51	118.09
8000	705.25	371.07	260.08	204.89	172.02	150.30	134.96
9000	793.41	417.45	292.59	230.50	193.52	169.09	151.83
10000	881.56	463.84	325.10	256.12	215.02	187.88	168.69
12000	1057.88	556.61	390.12	307.34	258.03	225.45	202.43
15000	1322.35	695.76	487.66	384.17	322.53	281.81	253.04
20000	1763.13	927.68	650.21	512.23	430.05	375.75	337.39
25000	2203.91	1159.60	812.76	640.29	537.56	469.69	421.74
30000	2644.69	1391.52	975.31	768.35	645.07	563.63	506.08
31000	2732.85	1437.90	1007.82	793.96	666.57	582.41	522.95
32000	2821.01	1484.28	1040.33	819.57	688.07	601.20	539.82
33000	2909.16	1530.67	1072.84	845.18	709.57	619.99	556.69
34000	2997.32	1577.05	1105.35	870.79	731.08	638.78	573.56
35000	3085.48	1623.43	1137.86	896.40	752.58	657.56	590.43
36000	3173.63	1669.82	1170.37	922.01	774.08	676.35	607.30
37000	3261.79	1716.20	1202.88	947.63	795.58	695.14	624.17
38000	3349.95	1762.59	1235.40	973.24	817.09	713.93	641.04
39000	3438.10	1808.97	1267.91	998.85	838.59	732.71	657.91
40000	3526.26	1855.35	1300.42	1024.46	860.09	751.50	674.78
41000	3614.41	1901.74	1332.93	1050.07	881.59	770.29	691.65
42000	3702.57	1948.12	1365.44	1075.68	903.09	789.08	708.52
43000	3790.73	1994.51	1397.95	1101.30	924.60	807.86	725.39
44000	3878.88	2040.89	1430.46	1126.91	946.10	826.65	742.26
45000	3967.04	2087.27	1462.97	1152.52	967.60	845.44	759.13
46000	4055.20	2133.66	1495.48	1178.13	989.10	864.23	776.00
47000	4143.35	2180.04	1527.99	1203.74	1010.61	883.01	792.86
48000	4231.51	2226.42	1560.50	1229.35	1032.11	901.80	809.73
49000	4319.67	2272.81	1593.01	1254.96	1053.61	920.59	826.60
50000	4407.82	2319.19	1625.52	1280.58	1075.11	939.38	843.47
51000	4495.98	2365.58	1658.03	1306.19	1096.62	958.16	860.34
52000	4584.14	2411.96	1690.54	1331.80	1118.12	976.95	877.21
53000	4672.29	2458.34	1723.05	1357.41	1139.62	995.74	894.08
54000	4760.45	2504.73	1755.56	1383.02	1161.12	1014.53	910.95
55000	4848.61	2551.11	1788.07	1408.63	1182.62	1033.31	927.82
56000	4936.76	2597.50	1820.58	1434.25	1204.13	1052.10	944.69
57000	5024.92	2643.88	1853.09	1459.86	1225.63	1070.89	961.56
58000	5113.07	2690.26	1885.60	1485.47	1247.13	1089.68	978.43
59000	5201.23	2736.65	1918.11	1511.08	1268.63	1108.46	995.30
60000	5289.39	2783.03	1950.62	1536.69	1290.14	1127.25	1012.17
65000	5730.17	3014.95	2113.18	1664.75	1397.65	1221.19	1096.52
70000	6170.95	3246.87	2275.73	1792.81	1505.16	1315.13	1180.86
75000	6611.73	3478.79	2438.28	1920.86	1612.67	1409.07	1265.21
80000	7052.52	3710.71	2600.83	2048.92	1720.18	1503.00	1349.56
85000	7493.30	3942.63	2763.38	2176.98	1827.69	1596.94	1433.90
90000	7934.08	4174.55	2925.94	2305.04	1935.20	1690.88	1518.25
95000	8374.86	4406.47	3088.49	2433.09	2042.71	1784.82	1602.60
100000	8815.65	4638.38	3251.04	2561.15	2150.23	1878.75	1686.95
105000	9256.43	4870.30	3413.59	2689.21	2257.74	1972.69	1771.29
110000	9697.21	5102.22	3576.14	2817.27	2365.25	2066.63	1855.64
120000	10578.77	5566.06	3901.25	3073.38	2580.27	2254.51	2024.34
130000	11460.34	6029.90	4226.35	3329.50	2795.29	2442.38	2193.03
140000	12341.90	6493.74	4551.46	3585.61	3010.32	2630.26	2361.73
150000	13223.47	6957.58	4876.56	3841.73	3225.34	2818.13	2530.42
160000	14105.03	7421.42	5201.66	4097.84	3440.36	3006.01	2699.11
170000	14986.60	7885.25	5526.77	4353.96	3655.38	3193.88	2867.81
180000	15868.16	8349.09	5851.87	4610.07	3870.41	3381.76	3036.50
190000	16749.73	8812.93	6176.98	4866.19	4085.43	3569.63	3205.20
200000	17631.29	9276.77	6502.08	5122.30	4300.45	3757.51	3373.89
210000	18512.86	9740.61	6827.18	5378.42	4515.47	3945.38	3542.59
220000	19394.42	10204.45	7152.29	5634.54	4730.50	4133.26	3711.28
230000	20275.99	10668.29	7477.39	5890.65	4945.52	4321.13	3879.98
240000	21157.55	11132.12	7802.50	6146.77	5160.54	4509.01	4048.67
250000	22039.11	11595.96	8127.60	6402.88	5375.56	4696.89	4217.37

Monthly Payments 10.75 %

LOAN AMOUNT	YEARS 8	9	10	11	12	13	14
100	1.54	1.44	1.35	1.28	1.23	1.18	1.14
200	3.09	2.87	2.70	2.56	2.45	2.36	2.28
500	7.72	7.18	6.75	6.41	6.13	5.89	5.70
1000	15.45	14.36	13.50	12.81	12.25	11.79	11.39
2000	30.90	28.72	27.01	25.63	24.50	23.57	22.79
5000	77.25	71.80	67.51	64.07	61.26	58.93	56.97
6000	92.69	86.16	81.02	76.88	73.51	70.71	68.37
7000	108.14	100.52	94.52	89.70	85.76	82.50	79.76
8000	123.59	114.88	108.02	102.51	98.01	94.28	91.16
9000	139.04	129.24	121.53	115.33	110.26	106.07	102.55
10000	154.49	143.60	135.03	128.14	122.51	117.85	113.95
12000	185.39	172.32	162.04	153.77	147.02	141.42	136.74
15000	231.74	215.40	202.54	192.21	183.77	176.78	170.92
20000	308.98	287.20	270.06	256.28	245.03	235.70	227.89
25000	386.23	359.00	337.57	320.35	306.28	294.63	284.87
30000	463.47	430.80	405.09	384.42	367.54	353.55	341.84
31000	478.92	445.16	418.59	397.24	379.79	365.34	353.23
32000	494.37	459.52	432.09	410.05	392.04	377.12	364.63
33000	509.82	473.88	445.60	422.87	404.29	388.91	376.02
34000	525.27	488.24	459.10	435.68	416.54	400.69	387.42
35000	540.72	502.60	472.60	448.49	428.79	412.48	398.81
36000	556.16	516.96	486.11	461.31	441.05	424.26	410.21
37000	571.61	531.32	499.61	474.12	453.30	436.05	421.60
38000	587.06	545.68	513.11	486.94	465.55	447.83	432.99
39000	602.51	560.04	526.61	499.75	477.80	459.62	444.39
40000	617.96	574.40	540.12	512.56	490.05	471.40	455.78
41000	633.41	588.76	553.62	525.38	502.30	483.19	467.18
42000	648.86	603.12	567.12	538.19	514.55	494.97	478.57
43000	664.31	617.48	580.63	551.01	526.80	506.76	489.97
44000	679.76	631.84	594.13	563.82	539.06	518.54	501.36
45000	695.21	646.20	607.63	576.64	551.31	530.33	512.76
46000	710.66	660.56	621.14	589.45	563.56	542.11	524.15
47000	726.10	674.92	634.64	602.26	575.81	553.90	535.55
48000	741.55	689.28	648.14	615.08	588.06	565.68	546.94
49000	757.00	703.64	661.64	627.89	600.31	577.47	558.34
50000	772.45	718.00	675.15	640.71	612.56	589.25	569.73
51000	787.90	732.36	688.65	653.52	624.81	601.04	581.12
52000	803.35	746.72	702.15	666.33	637.07	612.82	592.52
53000	818.80	761.08	715.66	679.15	649.32	624.61	603.91
54000	834.25	775.44	729.16	691.96	661.57	636.39	615.31
55000	849.70	789.80	742.66	704.78	673.82	648.18	626.70
56000	865.15	804.17	756.16	717.59	686.07	659.96	638.10
57000	880.59	818.53	769.67	730.40	698.32	671.75	649.49
58000	896.04	832.89	783.17	743.22	710.57	683.54	660.89
59000	911.49	847.25	796.67	756.03	722.82	695.32	672.28
60000	926.94	861.61	810.18	768.85	735.08	707.11	683.68
65000	1004.19	933.41	877.69	832.92	796.33	766.03	740.65
70000	1081.43	1005.21	945.21	896.99	857.59	824.96	797.62
75000	1158.68	1077.01	1012.72	961.06	918.85	883.88	854.60
80000	1235.92	1148.81	1080.24	1025.13	980.10	942.81	911.57
85000	1313.17	1220.61	1147.75	1089.20	1041.36	1001.73	968.54
90000	1390.41	1292.41	1215.26	1153.27	1102.61	1060.66	1025.51
95000	1467.66	1364.21	1282.78	1217.34	1163.87	1119.58	1082.49
100000	1544.90	1436.01	1350.29	1281.41	1225.13	1178.51	1139.46
105000	1622.15	1507.81	1417.81	1345.48	1286.38	1237.43	1196.43
110000	1699.39	1579.61	1485.32	1409.55	1347.64	1296.36	1253.41
120000	1853.88	1723.21	1620.35	1537.69	1470.15	1414.21	1367.35
130000	2008.37	1866.81	1755.38	1665.84	1592.67	1532.06	1481.30
140000	2162.86	2010.41	1890.41	1793.98	1715.18	1649.91	1595.24
150000	2317.35	2154.01	2025.44	1922.12	1837.69	1767.76	1709.19
160000	2471.84	2297.61	2160.47	2050.26	1960.20	1885.61	1823.14
170000	2626.33	2441.22	2295.50	2178.40	2082.72	2003.46	1937.08
180000	2780.82	2584.82	2430.53	2306.54	2205.23	2121.32	2051.03
190000	2935.32	2728.42	2565.56	2434.68	2327.74	2239.17	2164.97
200000	3089.81	2872.02	2700.59	2562.82	2450.25	2357.02	2278.92
210000	3244.30	3015.62	2835.62	2690.96	2572.77	2474.87	2392.87
220000	3398.79	3159.22	2970.65	2819.11	2695.28	2592.72	2506.81
230000	3553.28	3302.82	3105.68	2947.25	2817.79	2710.57	2620.76
240000	3707.77	3446.42	3240.71	3075.39	2940.30	2828.42	2734.71
250000	3862.26	3590.02	3375.74	3203.53	3062.82	2946.27	2848.65

10.75 % Monthly Payments

LOAN AMOUNT	15	16	17	18	19	20	21
				YEARS			
100	1.11	1.08	1.05	1.03	1.02	1.00	0.99
200	2.21	2.16	2.11	2.07	2.03	2.00	1.97
500	5.53	5.39	5.27	5.17	5.08	5.00	4.93
1000	11.06	10.78	10.54	10.33	10.15	10.00	9.86
2000	22.13	21.57	21.08	20.67	20.31	19.99	19.71
5000	55.32	53.92	52.71	51.67	50.76	49.98	49.29
6000	66.39	64.70	63.25	62.00	60.92	59.97	59.14
7000	77.45	75.48	73.79	72.33	71.07	69.97	69.00
8000	88.52	86.26	84.33	82.67	81.22	79.96	78.86
9000	99.58	97.05	94.87	93.00	91.37	89.96	88.72
10000	110.64	107.83	105.42	103.33	101.53	99.95	98.57
12000	132.77	129.40	126.50	124.00	121.83	119.94	118.29
15000	165.97	161.75	158.12	155.00	152.29	149.93	147.86
20000	221.29	215.66	210.83	206.67	203.05	199.90	197.15
25000	276.61	269.58	263.54	258.33	253.81	249.88	246.44
30000	331.93	323.49	316.25	310.00	304.58	299.85	295.72
31000	343.00	334.28	326.79	320.33	314.73	309.85	305.58
32000	354.06	345.06	337.33	330.66	324.88	319.84	315.44
33000	365.13	355.84	347.87	341.00	335.03	329.84	325.30
34000	376.19	366.62	358.42	351.33	345.19	339.83	335.15
35000	387.26	377.41	368.96	361.66	355.34	349.83	345.01
36000	398.32	388.19	379.50	372.00	365.49	359.82	354.87
37000	409.38	398.97	390.04	382.33	375.64	369.82	364.73
38000	420.45	409.76	400.58	392.66	385.80	379.81	374.58
39000	431.51	420.54	411.12	403.00	395.95	389.81	384.44
40000	442.58	431.32	421.67	413.33	406.10	399.81	394.30
41000	453.64	442.11	432.21	423.66	416.25	409.80	404.16
42000	464.71	452.89	442.75	434.00	426.41	419.80	414.01
43000	475.77	463.67	453.29	444.33	436.56	429.79	423.87
44000	486.84	474.45	463.83	454.66	446.71	439.79	433.73
45000	497.90	485.24	474.37	465.00	456.87	449.78	443.59
46000	508.96	496.02	484.92	475.33	467.02	459.78	453.44
47000	520.03	506.80	495.46	485.66	477.17	469.77	463.30
48000	531.09	517.59	506.00	496.00	487.32	479.77	473.16
49000	542.16	528.37	516.54	506.33	497.48	489.76	483.02
50000	553.22	539.15	527.08	516.66	507.63	499.76	492.87
51000	564.29	549.94	537.62	527.00	517.78	509.75	502.73
52000	575.35	560.72	548.17	537.33	527.93	519.75	512.59
53000	586.42	571.50	558.71	547.66	538.09	529.74	522.45
54000	597.48	582.29	569.25	558.00	548.24	539.74	532.30
55000	608.54	593.07	579.79	568.33	558.39	549.73	542.16
56000	619.61	603.85	590.33	578.66	568.54	559.73	552.02
57000	630.67	614.63	600.87	589.00	578.70	569.72	561.88
58000	641.74	625.42	611.41	599.33	588.85	579.72	571.73
59000	652.80	636.20	621.96	609.66	599.00	589.71	581.59
60000	663.87	646.98	632.50	620.00	609.15	599.71	591.45
65000	719.19	700.90	685.21	671.66	659.92	649.68	640.74
70000	774.51	754.81	737.91	723.33	710.68	699.66	690.02
75000	829.83	808.73	790.62	775.00	761.44	749.63	739.31
80000	885.16	862.65	843.33	826.66	812.20	799.61	788.60
85000	940.48	916.56	896.04	878.33	862.97	849.59	837.89
90000	995.80	970.48	948.75	929.99	913.73	899.56	887.17
95000	1051.12	1024.39	1001.46	981.66	964.49	949.54	936.46
100000	1106.44	1078.31	1054.16	1033.33	1015.26	999.51	985.75
105000	1161.77	1132.22	1106.87	1084.99	1066.02	1049.49	1035.03
110000	1217.09	1186.14	1159.58	1136.66	1116.78	1099.46	1084.32
120000	1327.73	1293.97	1265.00	1239.99	1218.31	1199.42	1182.90
130000	1438.38	1401.80	1370.41	1343.33	1319.83	1299.37	1281.47
140000	1549.02	1509.63	1475.83	1446.66	1421.36	1399.32	1380.05
150000	1659.67	1617.46	1581.25	1549.99	1522.88	1499.27	1478.62
160000	1770.31	1725.29	1686.66	1653.32	1624.41	1599.22	1577.20
170000	1880.96	1833.12	1792.08	1756.66	1725.93	1699.17	1675.77
180000	1991.60	1940.95	1897.49	1859.99	1827.46	1799.12	1774.35
190000	2102.24	2048.78	2002.91	1963.32	1928.99	1899.07	1872.92
200000	2212.89	2156.61	2108.33	2066.66	2030.51	1999.03	1971.49
210000	2323.53	2264.44	2213.74	2169.99	2132.04	2098.98	2070.07
220000	2434.18	2372.27	2319.16	2273.32	2233.56	2198.93	2168.64
230000	2544.82	2480.11	2424.58	2376.65	2335.09	2298.88	2267.22
240000	2655.47	2587.94	2529.99	2479.99	2436.61	2398.83	2365.79
250000	2766.11	2695.77	2635.41	2583.32	2538.14	2498.78	2464.37

Monthly Payments 10.75 %

LOAN AMOUNT	22	23	24	25	30	35	40
100	0.97	0.96	0.95	0.95	0.92	0.90	0.89
200	1.95	1.93	1.91	1.89	1.83	1.80	1.78
500	4.87	4.82	4.77	4.73	4.58	4.50	4.45
1000	9.74	9.63	9.54	9.45	9.16	8.99	8.90
2000	19.47	19.26	19.07	18.91	18.32	17.99	17.80
5000	48.68	48.15	47.68	47.27	45.80	44.97	44.50
6000	58.42	57.78	57.22	56.72	54.96	53.97	53.39
7000	68.16	67.41	66.76	66.18	64.12	62.96	62.29
8000	77.89	77.04	76.29	75.63	73.28	71.96	71.19
9000	87.63	86.67	85.83	85.08	82.44	80.95	80.09
10000	97.37	96.30	95.37	94.54	91.60	89.94	88.99
12000	116.84	115.57	114.44	113.45	109.92	107.93	106.79
15000	146.05	144.46	143.05	141.81	137.40	134.92	133.49
20000	194.73	192.61	190.73	189.08	183.20	179.89	177.98
25000	243.42	240.76	238.42	236.35	229.00	224.86	222.48
30000	292.10	288.91	286.10	283.62	274.80	269.83	266.97
31000	301.84	298.54	295.64	293.07	283.96	278.83	275.87
32000	311.57	308.17	305.18	302.52	293.12	287.82	284.77
33000	321.31	317.80	314.71	311.98	302.28	296.81	293.67
34000	331.05	327.44	324.25	321.43	311.44	305.81	302.57
35000	340.78	337.07	333.79	330.89	320.60	314.80	311.47
36000	350.52	346.70	343.32	340.34	329.76	323.80	320.37
37000	360.26	356.33	352.86	349.79	338.92	332.79	329.27
38000	369.99	365.96	362.40	359.25	348.08	341.79	338.16
39000	379.73	375.59	371.93	368.70	357.24	350.78	347.06
40000	389.47	385.22	381.47	378.15	366.40	359.78	355.96
41000	399.20	394.85	391.01	387.61	375.56	368.77	364.86
42000	408.94	404.48	400.54	397.06	384.72	377.76	373.76
43000	418.68	414.11	410.08	406.52	393.88	386.76	382.66
44000	428.42	423.74	419.62	415.97	403.04	395.75	391.56
45000	438.15	433.37	429.15	425.42	412.20	404.75	400.46
46000	447.89	443.00	438.69	434.88	421.36	413.74	409.36
47000	457.63	452.63	448.23	444.33	430.52	422.74	418.26
48000	467.36	462.26	457.76	453.79	439.68	431.73	427.15
49000	477.10	471.89	467.30	463.24	448.84	440.72	436.05
50000	486.84	481.52	476.84	472.69	458.00	449.72	444.95
51000	496.57	491.15	486.37	482.15	467.16	458.71	453.85
52000	506.31	500.78	495.91	491.60	476.32	467.71	462.75
53000	516.05	510.41	505.45	501.05	485.48	476.70	471.65
54000	525.78	520.04	514.98	510.51	494.64	485.70	480.55
55000	535.52	529.67	524.52	519.96	503.80	494.69	489.45
56000	545.26	539.31	534.06	529.42	512.96	503.69	498.35
57000	554.99	548.94	543.59	538.87	522.12	512.68	507.25
58000	564.73	558.57	553.13	548.32	531.28	521.67	516.15
59000	574.47	568.20	562.67	557.78	540.44	530.67	525.04
60000	584.20	577.83	572.20	567.23	549.60	539.66	533.94
65000	632.89	625.98	619.89	614.50	595.40	584.63	578.44
70000	681.57	674.13	667.57	661.77	641.20	629.61	622.93
75000	730.25	722.28	715.25	709.04	687.00	674.58	667.43
80000	778.94	770.44	762.94	756.31	732.80	719.55	711.92
85000	827.62	818.59	810.62	803.58	778.60	764.52	756.42
90000	876.30	866.74	858.31	850.85	824.40	809.49	800.91
95000	924.99	914.89	905.99	898.12	870.20	854.47	845.41
100000	973.67	963.05	953.67	945.39	916.00	899.44	889.91
105000	1022.35	1011.20	1001.36	992.66	961.80	944.41	934.40
110000	1071.04	1059.35	1049.04	1039.93	1007.60	989.38	978.90
120000	1168.40	1155.65	1144.41	1134.46	1099.20	1079.33	1067.89
130000	1265.77	1251.96	1239.77	1229.00	1190.80	1169.27	1156.88
140000	1363.14	1348.26	1335.14	1323.54	1282.40	1259.21	1245.87
150000	1460.51	1444.57	1430.51	1418.08	1374.00	1349.16	1334.86
160000	1557.87	1540.87	1525.88	1512.62	1465.60	1439.10	1423.85
170000	1655.24	1637.18	1621.24	1607.16	1557.20	1529.04	1512.84
180000	1752.61	1733.48	1716.61	1701.70	1648.80	1618.99	1601.83
190000	1849.97	1829.79	1811.98	1796.23	1740.40	1708.93	1690.82
200000	1947.34	1926.09	1907.34	1890.77	1832.00	1798.88	1779.81
210000	2044.71	2022.39	2002.71	1985.31	1923.60	1888.82	1868.80
220000	2142.08	2118.70	2098.08	2079.85	2015.20	1978.76	1957.79
230000	2239.44	2215.00	2193.45	2174.39	2106.80	2068.71	2046.78
240000	2336.81	2311.31	2288.81	2268.93	2198.40	2158.65	2135.77
250000	2434.18	2407.61	2384.18	2363.47	2290.00	2248.59	2224.76

11.00 % Monthly Payments

LOAN AMOUNT	YEARS 1	2	3	4	5	6	7
100	8.83	4.65	3.26	2.57	2.16	1.89	1.70
200	17.65	9.30	6.52	5.15	4.32	3.78	3.40
500	44.13	23.25	16.31	12.86	10.81	9.45	8.50
1000	88.27	46.49	32.62	25.73	21.62	18.91	16.99
2000	176.54	92.99	65.25	51.45	43.24	37.82	33.99
5000	441.34	232.47	163.12	128.64	108.10	94.55	84.97
6000	529.61	278.97	195.74	154.36	129.73	113.46	101.97
7000	617.88	325.46	228.36	180.09	151.35	132.37	118.96
8000	706.14	371.96	260.99	205.82	172.97	151.28	135.96
9000	794.41	418.45	293.61	231.55	194.59	170.18	152.95
10000	882.68	464.95	326.23	257.27	216.21	189.09	169.94
12000	1059.22	557.94	391.48	308.73	259.45	226.91	203.93
15000	1324.02	697.42	489.35	385.91	324.31	283.64	254.92
20000	1765.36	929.89	652.47	514.54	432.42	378.19	339.89
25000	2206.70	1162.37	815.58	643.18	540.52	472.73	424.86
30000	2648.04	1394.84	978.70	771.82	648.63	567.28	509.83
31000	2736.31	1441.33	1011.32	797.54	670.25	586.19	526.83
32000	2824.57	1487.83	1043.95	823.27	691.87	605.10	543.82
33000	2912.84	1534.32	1076.57	849.00	713.49	624.01	560.82
34000	3001.11	1580.82	1109.19	874.73	735.11	642.92	577.81
35000	3089.38	1627.31	1141.82	900.45	756.73	661.83	594.81
36000	3177.65	1673.81	1174.44	926.18	778.35	680.74	611.80
37000	3265.91	1720.30	1207.06	951.91	799.98	699.65	628.79
38000	3354.18	1766.80	1239.69	977.63	821.60	718.56	645.79
39000	3442.45	1813.29	1272.31	1003.36	843.22	737.47	662.78
40000	3530.72	1859.79	1304.93	1029.09	864.84	756.38	679.78
41000	3618.98	1906.28	1337.56	1054.82	886.46	775.28	696.77
42000	3707.25	1952.78	1370.18	1080.54	908.08	794.19	713.77
43000	3795.52	1999.27	1402.80	1106.27	929.70	813.10	730.76
44000	3883.79	2045.77	1435.43	1132.00	951.32	832.01	747.76
45000	3972.06	2092.26	1468.05	1157.73	972.94	850.92	764.75
46000	4060.32	2138.75	1500.67	1183.45	994.56	869.83	781.74
47000	4148.59	2185.25	1533.30	1209.18	1016.19	888.74	798.74
48000	4236.86	2231.74	1565.92	1234.91	1037.81	907.65	815.73
49000	4325.13	2278.24	1598.54	1260.63	1059.43	926.56	832.73
50000	4413.40	2324.73	1631.17	1286.36	1081.05	945.47	849.72
51000	4501.66	2371.23	1663.79	1312.09	1102.67	964.38	866.72
52000	4589.93	2417.72	1696.41	1337.82	1124.29	983.29	883.71
53000	4678.20	2464.22	1729.04	1363.54	1145.91	1002.20	900.71
54000	4766.47	2510.71	1761.66	1389.27	1167.53	1021.11	917.70
55000	4854.74	2557.21	1794.28	1415.00	1189.15	1040.02	934.69
56000	4943.00	2603.70	1826.91	1440.72	1210.77	1058.93	951.69
57000	5031.27	2650.20	1859.53	1466.45	1232.40	1077.83	968.68
58000	5119.54	2696.69	1892.15	1492.18	1254.02	1096.74	985.68
59000	5207.81	2743.19	1924.78	1517.91	1275.64	1115.65	1002.67
60000	5296.08	2789.68	1957.40	1543.63	1297.26	1134.56	1019.67
65000	5737.41	3022.15	2120.52	1672.27	1405.36	1229.11	1104.64
70000	6178.75	3254.63	2283.63	1800.91	1513.47	1323.66	1189.61
75000	6620.09	3487.10	2446.75	1929.54	1621.57	1418.20	1274.58
80000	7061.43	3719.57	2609.87	2058.18	1729.68	1512.75	1359.56
85000	7502.77	3952.05	2772.98	2186.81	1837.78	1607.30	1444.53
90000	7944.11	4184.52	2936.10	2315.45	1945.89	1701.84	1529.50
95000	8385.45	4416.99	3099.22	2444.09	2053.99	1796.39	1614.47
100000	8826.79	4649.47	3262.33	2572.72	2162.10	1890.94	1699.45
105000	9268.13	4881.94	3425.45	2701.36	2270.20	1985.48	1784.42
110000	9709.47	5114.41	3588.57	2829.99	2378.31	2080.03	1869.39
120000	10592.15	5579.36	3914.80	3087.27	2594.52	2269.13	2039.33
130000	11474.83	6044.31	4241.03	3344.54	2810.73	2458.22	2209.28
140000	12357.51	6509.25	4567.27	3601.81	3026.94	2647.31	2379.22
150000	13240.19	6974.20	4893.50	3859.08	3243.15	2836.41	2549.17
160000	14122.87	7439.15	5219.73	4116.36	3459.36	3025.50	2719.11
170000	15005.55	7904.09	5545.96	4373.63	3675.57	3214.59	2889.06
180000	15888.23	8369.04	5872.20	4630.90	3891.77	3403.69	3059.00
190000	16770.90	8833.99	6198.43	4888.17	4107.98	3592.78	3228.95
200000	17653.58	9298.93	6524.66	5145.44	4324.19	3781.88	3398.89
210000	18536.26	9763.88	6850.90	5402.72	4540.40	3970.97	3568.83
220000	19418.94	10228.83	7177.13	5659.99	4756.61	4160.06	3738.78
230000	20301.62	10693.77	7503.36	5917.26	4972.82	4349.16	3908.72
240000	21184.30	11158.72	7829.60	6174.53	5189.03	4538.25	4078.67
250000	22066.98	11623.67	8155.83	6431.81	5405.24	4727.34	4248.61

Monthly Payments 11.00 %

LOAN AMOUNT	8	9	10	11	12	13	14
100	1.56	1.45	1.36	1.30	1.24	1.19	1.15
200	3.12	2.90	2.73	2.59	2.48	2.39	2.31
500	7.79	7.25	6.82	6.48	6.20	5.96	5.77
1000	15.58	14.49	13.64	12.95	12.39	11.93	11.54
2000	31.15	28.98	27.27	25.90	24.78	23.86	23.08
5000	77.89	72.46	68.19	64.76	61.96	59.64	57.70
6000	93.46	86.95	81.82	77.71	74.35	71.57	69.24
7000	109.04	101.44	95.46	90.66	86.74	83.50	80.78
8000	124.62	115.93	109.10	103.61	99.13	95.43	92.33
9000	140.19	130.42	122.74	116.56	111.52	107.35	103.87
10000	155.77	144.91	136.37	129.51	123.92	119.28	115.41
12000	186.93	173.90	163.65	155.42	148.70	143.14	138.49
15000	233.66	217.37	204.56	194.27	185.87	178.92	173.11
20000	311.54	289.83	272.75	259.03	247.83	238.57	230.81
25000	389.43	362.28	340.93	323.79	309.79	298.21	288.52
30000	467.31	434.74	409.12	388.54	371.75	357.85	346.22
31000	482.89	449.23	422.76	401.50	384.14	369.78	357.76
32000	498.47	463.72	436.39	414.45	396.53	381.71	369.30
33000	514.05	478.21	450.03	427.40	408.92	393.63	380.84
34000	529.62	492.71	463.67	440.35	421.31	405.56	392.38
35000	545.20	507.20	477.31	453.30	433.71	417.49	403.92
36000	560.78	521.69	490.94	466.25	446.10	429.42	415.46
37000	576.36	536.18	504.58	479.21	458.49	441.35	427.01
38000	591.93	550.67	518.22	492.16	470.88	453.28	438.55
39000	607.51	565.16	531.85	505.11	483.27	465.20	450.09
40000	623.09	579.65	545.49	518.06	495.66	477.13	461.63
41000	638.66	594.15	559.13	531.01	508.06	489.06	473.17
42000	654.24	608.64	572.77	543.96	520.45	500.99	484.71
43000	669.82	623.13	586.40	556.91	532.84	512.92	496.25
44000	685.40	637.62	600.04	569.87	545.23	524.85	507.79
45000	700.97	652.11	613.68	582.82	557.62	536.77	519.33
46000	716.55	666.60	627.32	595.77	570.01	548.70	530.87
47000	732.13	681.09	640.95	608.72	582.41	560.63	542.41
48000	747.70	695.58	654.59	621.67	594.80	572.56	553.95
49000	763.28	710.08	668.23	634.62	607.19	584.49	565.49
50000	778.86	724.57	681.86	647.57	619.58	596.42	577.03
51000	794.44	739.06	695.50	660.53	631.97	608.34	588.57
52000	810.01	753.55	709.14	673.48	644.36	620.27	600.12
53000	825.59	768.04	722.78	686.43	656.76	632.20	611.66
54000	841.17	782.53	736.41	699.38	669.15	644.13	623.20
55000	856.74	797.02	750.05	712.33	681.54	656.06	634.74
56000	872.32	811.52	763.69	725.28	693.93	667.99	646.28
57000	887.90	826.01	777.33	738.23	706.32	679.91	657.82
58000	903.48	840.50	790.96	751.19	718.71	691.84	669.36
59000	919.05	854.99	804.60	764.14	731.11	703.77	680.90
60000	934.63	869.48	818.24	777.09	743.50	715.70	692.44
65000	1012.52	941.94	886.42	841.85	805.46	775.34	750.14
70000	1090.40	1014.39	954.61	906.60	867.41	834.98	807.85
75000	1168.29	1086.85	1022.80	971.36	929.37	894.62	865.55
80000	1246.17	1159.31	1090.98	1036.12	991.33	954.27	923.25
85000	1324.06	1231.76	1159.17	1100.88	1053.29	1013.91	980.96
90000	1401.94	1304.22	1227.36	1165.63	1115.25	1073.55	1038.66
95000	1479.83	1376.68	1295.54	1230.39	1177.20	1133.19	1096.36
100000	1557.72	1449.13	1363.73	1295.15	1239.16	1192.83	1154.07
105000	1635.60	1521.59	1431.92	1359.91	1301.12	1252.47	1211.77
110000	1713.49	1594.05	1500.10	1424.66	1363.08	1312.12	1269.47
120000	1869.26	1738.96	1636.47	1554.18	1486.99	1431.40	1384.88
130000	2025.03	1883.88	1772.85	1683.69	1610.91	1550.68	1500.29
140000	2180.80	2028.79	1909.22	1813.21	1734.83	1669.97	1615.70
150000	2336.57	2173.70	2045.59	1942.72	1858.74	1789.25	1731.10
160000	2492.35	2318.62	2181.97	2072.24	1982.66	1908.53	1846.51
170000	2648.12	2463.53	2318.34	2201.75	2106.57	2027.82	1961.92
180000	2803.89	2608.44	2454.71	2331.27	2230.49	2147.10	2077.32
190000	2959.66	2753.36	2591.08	2460.78	2354.41	2266.38	2192.73
200000	3115.43	2898.27	2727.46	2590.30	2478.32	2385.67	2308.14
210000	3271.20	3043.18	2863.83	2719.81	2602.24	2504.95	2423.54
220000	3426.98	3188.10	3000.20	2849.33	2726.16	2624.23	2538.95
230000	3582.75	3333.01	3136.58	2978.84	2850.07	2743.52	2654.36
240000	3738.52	3477.92	3272.95	3108.36	2973.99	2862.80	2769.76
250000	3894.29	3622.84	3409.32	3237.87	3097.90	2982.08	2885.17

Column headings 8–14: YEARS

11.00 % Monthly Payments

LOAN AMOUNT	15	16	17	18	19	20	21
100	1.12	1.09	1.07	1.05	1.03	1.02	1.00
200	2.24	2.19	2.14	2.10	2.06	2.03	2.00
500	5.61	5.47	5.35	5.24	5.16	5.08	5.01
1000	11.21	10.93	10.70	10.49	10.31	10.16	10.02
2000	22.43	21.87	21.39	20.98	20.62	20.31	20.04
5000	56.07	54.67	53.48	52.45	51.56	50.78	50.10
6000	67.28	65.61	64.17	62.94	61.87	60.94	60.13
7000	78.49	76.54	74.87	73.43	72.18	71.09	70.15
8000	89.71	87.48	85.57	83.92	82.49	81.25	80.17
9000	100.92	98.41	96.26	94.41	92.80	91.41	90.19
10000	112.13	109.35	106.96	104.90	103.12	101.56	100.21
12000	134.56	131.21	128.35	125.88	123.74	121.88	120.25
15000	168.20	164.02	160.44	157.35	154.67	152.35	150.31
20000	224.27	218.69	213.91	209.80	206.23	203.13	200.42
25000	280.33	273.36	267.39	262.25	257.79	253.91	250.52
30000	336.40	328.04	320.87	314.70	309.35	304.69	300.63
31000	347.61	338.97	331.57	325.18	319.66	314.85	310.65
32000	358.82	349.91	342.26	335.67	329.97	325.00	320.67
33000	370.04	360.84	352.96	346.16	340.28	335.16	330.69
34000	381.25	371.77	363.65	356.65	350.59	345.32	340.71
35000	392.46	382.71	374.35	367.14	360.90	355.47	350.73
36000	403.68	393.64	385.05	377.63	371.21	365.63	360.75
37000	414.89	404.58	395.74	388.12	381.53	375.79	370.78
38000	426.10	415.51	406.44	398.61	391.84	385.94	380.80
39000	437.32	426.45	417.13	409.10	402.15	396.10	390.82
40000	448.53	437.38	427.83	419.59	412.46	406.26	400.84
41000	459.74	448.32	438.52	430.08	422.77	416.41	410.86
42000	470.96	459.25	449.22	440.57	433.08	426.57	420.88
43000	482.17	470.19	459.92	451.06	443.40	436.73	430.90
44000	493.38	481.12	470.61	461.55	453.71	446.88	440.92
45000	504.60	492.06	481.31	472.04	464.02	457.04	450.94
46000	515.81	502.99	492.00	482.53	474.33	467.19	460.96
47000	527.02	513.92	502.70	493.02	484.64	477.35	470.98
48000	538.24	524.86	513.39	503.51	494.95	487.51	481.01
49000	549.45	535.79	524.09	514.00	505.26	497.66	491.03
50000	560.66	546.73	534.79	524.49	515.58	507.82	501.05
51000	571.88	557.66	545.48	534.98	525.89	517.98	511.07
52000	583.09	568.60	556.18	545.47	536.20	528.13	521.09
53000	594.30	579.53	566.87	555.96	546.51	538.29	531.11
54000	605.52	590.47	577.57	566.45	556.82	548.45	541.13
55000	616.73	601.40	588.26	576.94	567.13	558.60	551.15
56000	627.94	612.34	598.96	587.43	577.44	568.76	561.17
57000	639.16	623.27	609.66	597.92	587.76	578.91	571.19
58000	650.37	634.20	620.35	608.41	598.07	589.07	581.22
59000	661.58	645.14	631.05	618.90	608.38	599.23	591.24
60000	672.80	656.07	641.74	629.39	618.69	609.38	601.26
65000	728.86	710.75	695.22	681.84	670.25	660.17	651.36
70000	784.93	765.42	748.70	734.29	721.81	710.95	701.47
75000	841.00	820.09	802.18	786.74	773.36	761.73	751.57
80000	897.06	874.76	855.66	839.19	824.92	812.51	801.68
85000	953.13	929.44	909.13	891.64	876.48	863.29	851.78
90000	1009.19	984.11	962.61	944.09	928.04	914.08	901.89
95000	1065.26	1038.78	1016.09	996.53	979.59	964.86	951.99
100000	1121.33	1093.46	1069.57	1048.98	1031.15	1015.64	1002.10
105000	1177.39	1148.13	1123.05	1101.43	1082.71	1066.42	1052.20
110000	1233.46	1202.80	1176.53	1153.88	1134.27	1117.20	1102.31
120000	1345.59	1312.15	1283.48	1258.78	1237.38	1218.77	1202.51
130000	1457.73	1421.49	1390.44	1363.68	1340.50	1320.33	1302.72
140000	1569.86	1530.84	1497.40	1468.58	1443.61	1421.90	1402.93
150000	1681.99	1640.18	1604.36	1573.48	1546.73	1523.46	1503.14
160000	1794.12	1749.53	1711.31	1678.37	1649.84	1625.02	1603.35
170000	1906.26	1858.87	1818.27	1783.27	1752.96	1726.59	1703.56
180000	2018.39	1968.22	1925.23	1888.17	1856.07	1828.15	1803.77
190000	2130.52	2077.57	2032.18	1993.07	1959.19	1929.72	1903.98
200000	2242.65	2186.91	2139.14	2097.97	2062.30	2031.28	2004.19
210000	2354.79	2296.26	2246.10	2202.87	2165.42	2132.84	2104.40
220000	2466.92	2405.60	2353.06	2307.76	2268.53	2234.41	2204.61
230000	2579.05	2514.95	2460.01	2412.66	2371.65	2335.97	2304.82
240000	2691.18	2624.29	2566.97	2517.56	2474.76	2437.54	2405.03
250000	2803.32	2733.64	2673.93	2622.46	2577.88	2539.10	2505.24

Monthly Payments 11.00 %

LOAN AMOUNT	22	23	24	25	30	35	40
				YEARS			
100	0.99	0.98	0.97	0.96	0.93	0.92	0.91
200	1.98	1.96	1.94	1.93	1.87	1.84	1.82
500	4.95	4.90	4.85	4.81	4.67	4.59	4.54
1000	9.90	9.80	9.71	9.63	9.34	9.18	9.09
2000	19.80	19.60	19.41	19.25	18.68	18.36	18.18
5000	49.51	48.99	48.53	48.13	46.70	45.90	45.44
6000	59.41	58.79	58.24	57.75	56.04	55.08	54.53
7000	69.32	68.59	67.94	67.38	65.38	64.26	63.62
8000	79.22	78.38	77.65	77.00	74.72	73.44	72.71
9000	89.12	88.18	87.36	86.63	84.05	82.62	81.80
10000	99.02	97.98	97.06	96.25	93.39	91.80	90.89
12000	118.83	117.58	116.48	115.50	112.07	110.16	109.07
15000	148.53	146.97	145.59	144.38	140.09	137.70	136.33
20000	198.05	195.96	194.13	192.51	186.79	183.59	181.78
25000	247.56	244.95	242.66	240.63	233.48	229.49	227.22
30000	297.07	293.94	291.19	288.76	280.18	275.39	272.66
31000	306.97	303.74	300.90	298.38	289.52	284.57	281.75
32000	316.87	313.54	310.60	308.01	298.86	293.75	290.84
33000	326.78	323.34	320.31	317.63	308.20	302.93	299.93
34000	336.68	333.14	330.01	327.26	317.54	312.11	309.02
35000	346.58	342.93	339.72	336.89	326.88	321.29	318.11
36000	356.48	352.73	349.43	346.51	336.22	330.47	327.20
37000	366.39	362.53	359.13	356.14	345.56	339.65	336.29
38000	376.29	372.33	368.84	365.76	354.90	348.83	345.37
39000	386.19	382.13	378.55	375.39	364.24	358.01	354.46
40000	396.09	391.92	388.25	385.01	373.58	367.19	363.55
41000	405.99	401.72	397.96	394.64	382.91	376.37	372.64
42000	415.90	411.52	407.66	404.26	392.25	385.55	381.73
43000	425.80	421.32	417.37	413.89	401.59	394.73	390.82
44000	435.70	431.12	427.08	423.51	410.93	403.91	399.91
45000	445.60	440.91	436.78	433.14	420.27	413.09	409.00
46000	455.51	450.71	446.49	442.76	429.61	422.27	418.08
47000	465.41	460.51	456.20	452.39	438.95	431.45	427.17
48000	475.31	470.31	465.90	462.01	448.29	440.63	436.26
49000	485.21	480.11	475.61	471.64	457.63	449.81	445.35
50000	495.12	489.90	485.32	481.26	466.97	458.99	454.44
51000	505.02	499.70	495.02	490.89	476.31	468.17	463.53
52000	514.92	509.50	504.73	500.52	485.65	477.35	472.62
53000	524.82	519.30	514.43	510.14	494.99	486.53	481.71
54000	534.72	529.10	524.14	519.77	504.33	495.71	490.80
55000	544.63	538.89	533.85	529.39	513.67	504.89	499.88
56000	554.53	548.69	543.55	539.02	523.01	514.07	508.97
57000	564.43	558.49	553.26	548.64	532.34	523.25	518.06
58000	574.33	568.29	562.97	558.27	541.68	532.43	527.15
59000	584.24	578.09	572.67	567.89	551.02	541.60	536.24
60000	594.14	587.89	582.38	577.52	560.36	550.78	545.33
65000	643.65	636.88	630.91	625.64	607.06	596.68	590.77
70000	693.16	685.87	679.44	673.77	653.76	642.58	636.22
75000	742.67	734.86	727.97	721.90	700.45	688.48	681.66
80000	792.19	783.85	776.50	770.02	747.15	734.38	727.10
85000	841.70	832.84	825.04	818.15	793.85	780.28	772.55
90000	891.21	881.83	873.57	866.28	840.54	826.18	817.99
95000	940.72	930.82	922.10	914.40	887.24	872.08	863.44
100000	990.23	979.81	970.63	962.53	933.94	917.97	908.88
105000	1039.74	1028.80	1019.16	1010.66	980.63	963.87	954.32
110000	1089.25	1077.79	1067.69	1058.78	1027.33	1009.77	999.77
120000	1188.28	1175.77	1164.76	1155.04	1120.73	1101.57	1090.66
130000	1287.30	1273.75	1261.82	1251.29	1214.12	1193.37	1181.54
140000	1386.32	1371.73	1358.88	1347.54	1307.51	1285.16	1272.43
150000	1485.35	1469.71	1455.95	1443.79	1400.91	1376.96	1363.32
160000	1584.37	1567.69	1553.01	1540.05	1494.30	1468.76	1454.21
170000	1683.39	1665.68	1650.07	1636.30	1587.69	1560.56	1545.10
180000	1782.42	1763.66	1747.13	1732.55	1681.09	1652.35	1635.98
190000	1881.44	1861.64	1844.20	1828.81	1774.48	1744.15	1726.87
200000	1980.46	1959.62	1941.26	1925.06	1867.88	1835.95	1817.76
210000	2079.49	2057.60	2038.32	2021.31	1961.27	1927.75	1908.65
220000	2178.51	2155.58	2135.39	2117.56	2054.66	2019.54	1999.54
230000	2277.53	2253.56	2232.45	2213.82	2148.06	2111.34	2090.42
240000	2376.56	2351.54	2329.51	2310.07	2241.45	2203.14	2181.31
250000	2475.58	2449.52	2426.58	2406.32	2334.84	2294.94	2272.20

11.25 % Monthly Payments

LOAN AMOUNT	YEARS 1	2	3	4	5	6	7
100	8.84	4.66	3.27	2.58	2.17	1.90	1.71
200	17.68	9.32	6.55	5.17	4.35	3.81	3.42
500	44.19	23.30	16.37	12.92	10.87	9.52	8.56
1000	88.38	46.61	32.74	25.84	21.74	19.03	17.12
2000	176.76	93.21	65.47	51.69	43.48	38.06	34.24
5000	441.90	233.03	163.68	129.22	108.70	95.16	85.60
6000	530.28	279.63	196.42	155.06	130.44	114.19	102.72
7000	618.66	326.24	229.15	180.90	152.18	133.22	119.84
8000	707.03	372.84	261.89	206.74	173.92	152.25	136.96
9000	795.41	419.45	294.63	232.59	195.66	171.28	154.08
10000	883.79	466.06	327.36	258.43	217.40	190.32	171.20
12000	1060.55	559.27	392.84	310.12	260.88	228.38	205.44
15000	1325.69	699.08	491.05	387.65	326.10	285.47	256.80
20000	1767.59	932.11	654.73	516.86	434.80	380.63	342.40
25000	2209.48	1165.14	818.41	646.08	543.50	475.79	428.00
30000	2651.38	1398.17	982.09	775.29	652.20	570.95	513.59
31000	2739.76	1444.77	1014.83	801.14	673.94	589.98	530.71
32000	2828.14	1491.38	1047.56	826.98	695.68	609.01	547.83
33000	2916.52	1537.98	1080.30	852.82	717.42	628.04	564.95
34000	3004.90	1584.59	1113.04	878.67	739.16	647.07	582.07
35000	3093.28	1631.19	1145.77	904.51	760.90	666.10	599.19
36000	3181.66	1677.80	1178.51	930.35	782.64	685.14	616.31
37000	3270.04	1724.40	1211.25	956.20	804.38	704.17	633.43
38000	3358.42	1771.01	1243.98	982.04	826.12	723.20	650.55
39000	3446.79	1817.62	1276.72	1007.88	847.86	742.23	667.67
40000	3535.17	1864.22	1309.45	1033.72	869.60	761.26	684.79
41000	3623.55	1910.83	1342.19	1059.57	891.34	780.29	701.91
42000	3711.93	1957.43	1374.93	1085.41	913.08	799.32	719.03
43000	3800.31	2004.04	1407.66	1111.25	934.82	818.36	736.15
44000	3888.69	2050.64	1440.40	1137.10	956.56	837.39	753.27
45000	3977.07	2097.25	1473.14	1162.94	978.30	856.42	770.39
46000	4065.45	2143.85	1505.87	1188.78	1000.04	875.45	787.51
47000	4153.83	2190.46	1538.61	1214.63	1021.78	894.48	804.63
48000	4242.21	2237.07	1571.35	1240.47	1043.52	913.51	821.75
49000	4330.59	2283.67	1604.08	1266.31	1065.26	932.55	838.87
50000	4418.97	2330.28	1636.82	1292.16	1087.00	951.58	855.99
51000	4507.35	2376.88	1669.55	1318.00	1108.74	970.61	873.11
52000	4595.73	2423.49	1702.29	1343.84	1130.48	989.64	890.23
53000	4684.11	2470.09	1735.03	1369.69	1152.22	1008.67	907.35
54000	4772.48	2516.70	1767.76	1395.53	1173.96	1027.70	924.47
55000	4860.86	2563.30	1800.50	1421.37	1195.70	1046.73	941.59
56000	4949.24	2609.91	1833.24	1447.21	1217.44	1065.77	958.71
57000	5037.62	2656.52	1865.97	1473.06	1239.18	1084.80	975.83
58000	5126.00	2703.12	1898.71	1498.90	1260.92	1103.83	992.95
59000	5214.38	2749.73	1931.45	1524.74	1282.66	1122.86	1010.07
60000	5302.76	2796.33	1964.18	1550.59	1304.40	1141.89	1027.19
65000	5744.66	3029.36	2127.86	1679.80	1413.10	1237.05	1112.79
70000	6186.55	3262.39	2291.55	1809.02	1521.80	1332.21	1198.39
75000	6628.45	3495.42	2455.23	1938.23	1630.50	1427.37	1283.99
80000	7070.35	3728.44	2618.91	2067.45	1739.20	1522.52	1369.59
85000	7512.24	3961.47	2782.59	2196.66	1847.90	1617.68	1455.19
90000	7954.14	4194.50	2946.27	2325.88	1956.60	1712.84	1540.78
95000	8396.04	4427.53	3109.96	2455.10	2065.30	1808.00	1626.38
100000	8837.93	4660.55	3273.64	2584.31	2174.00	1903.15	1711.98
105000	9279.83	4893.58	3437.32	2713.53	2282.69	1998.31	1797.58
110000	9721.73	5126.61	3601.00	2842.74	2391.39	2093.47	1883.18
120000	10605.52	5592.66	3928.36	3101.17	2608.79	2283.78	2054.38
130000	11489.32	6058.72	4255.73	3359.61	2826.19	2474.10	2225.58
140000	12373.11	6524.78	4583.09	3618.04	3043.59	2664.42	2396.78
150000	13256.90	6990.83	4910.46	3876.47	3260.99	2854.73	2567.97
160000	14140.70	7456.89	5237.82	4134.90	3478.39	3045.05	2739.17
170000	15024.49	7922.94	5565.18	4393.33	3695.79	3235.36	2910.37
180000	15908.28	8389.00	5892.55	4651.76	3913.19	3425.68	3081.57
190000	16792.08	8855.05	6219.91	4910.19	4130.59	3615.99	3252.77
200000	17675.87	9321.11	6547.27	5168.62	4347.99	3806.31	3423.97
210000	18559.66	9787.16	6874.64	5427.05	4565.39	3996.62	3595.16
220000	19443.46	10253.22	7202.00	5685.49	4782.79	4186.94	3766.36
230000	20327.25	10719.27	7529.37	5943.92	5000.19	4377.25	3937.56
240000	21211.04	11185.33	7856.73	6202.35	5217.59	4567.57	4108.76
250000	22094.84	11651.38	8184.09	6460.78	5434.99	4757.89	4279.96

Monthly Payments 11.25 %

LOAN AMOUNT	8	9	10	11	12	13	14
				YEARS			
100	1.57	1.46	1.38	1.31	1.25	1.21	1.17
200	3.14	2.92	2.75	2.62	2.51	2.41	2.34
500	7.85	7.31	6.89	6.54	6.27	6.04	5.84
1000	15.71	14.62	13.77	13.09	12.53	12.07	11.69
2000	31.41	29.25	27.54	26.18	25.07	24.14	23.37
5000	78.53	73.12	68.86	65.45	62.66	60.36	58.44
6000	94.23	87.74	82.63	78.54	75.20	72.43	70.12
7000	109.94	102.36	96.41	91.63	87.73	84.51	81.81
8000	125.65	116.98	110.18	104.72	100.26	96.58	93.50
9000	141.35	131.61	123.95	117.81	112.79	108.65	105.19
10000	157.06	146.23	137.72	130.89	125.33	120.72	116.87
12000	188.47	175.48	165.27	157.07	150.39	144.87	140.25
15000	235.59	219.35	206.58	196.34	187.99	181.08	175.31
20000	314.12	292.46	275.44	261.79	250.65	241.45	233.75
25000	392.64	365.58	344.30	327.24	313.32	301.81	292.19
30000	471.17	438.69	413.17	392.68	375.98	362.17	350.62
31000	486.88	453.32	426.94	405.77	388.51	374.24	362.31
32000	502.58	467.94	440.71	418.86	401.04	386.31	374.00
33000	518.29	482.56	454.48	431.95	413.58	398.39	385.69
34000	534.00	497.19	468.25	445.04	426.11	410.46	397.37
35000	549.70	511.81	482.03	458.13	438.64	422.53	409.06
36000	565.41	526.43	495.80	471.22	451.17	434.60	420.75
37000	581.11	541.06	509.57	484.31	463.71	446.67	432.44
38000	596.82	555.68	523.34	497.40	476.24	458.75	444.12
39000	612.52	570.30	537.12	510.49	488.77	470.82	455.81
40000	628.23	584.92	550.89	523.58	501.30	482.89	467.50
41000	643.94	599.55	564.66	536.67	513.84	494.96	479.19
42000	659.64	614.17	578.43	549.76	526.37	507.04	490.87
43000	675.35	628.79	592.20	562.85	538.90	519.11	502.56
44000	691.05	643.42	605.98	575.94	551.44	531.18	514.25
45000	706.76	658.04	619.75	589.03	563.97	543.25	525.94
46000	722.46	672.66	633.52	602.12	576.50	555.32	537.62
47000	738.17	687.29	647.29	615.21	589.03	567.40	549.31
48000	753.88	701.91	661.07	628.30	601.57	579.47	561.00
49000	769.58	716.53	674.84	641.38	614.10	591.54	572.69
50000	785.29	731.16	688.61	654.47	626.63	603.61	584.37
51000	800.99	745.78	702.38	667.56	639.16	615.69	596.06
52000	816.70	760.40	716.15	680.65	651.70	627.76	607.75
53000	832.40	775.03	729.93	693.74	664.23	639.83	619.44
54000	848.11	789.65	743.70	706.83	676.76	651.90	631.12
55000	863.82	804.27	757.47	719.92	689.29	663.98	642.81
56000	879.52	818.89	771.24	733.01	701.83	676.05	654.50
57000	895.23	833.52	785.02	746.10	714.36	688.12	666.19
58000	910.93	848.14	798.79	759.19	726.89	700.19	677.87
59000	926.64	862.76	812.56	772.28	739.42	712.26	689.56
60000	942.35	877.39	826.33	785.37	751.96	724.34	701.25
65000	1020.87	950.50	895.19	850.82	814.62	784.70	759.69
70000	1099.40	1023.62	964.05	916.26	877.28	845.06	818.12
75000	1177.93	1096.73	1032.91	981.71	939.95	905.42	876.56
80000	1256.46	1169.85	1101.78	1047.16	1002.61	965.78	935.00
85000	1334.99	1242.97	1170.64	1112.61	1065.27	1026.14	993.44
90000	1413.52	1316.08	1239.50	1178.05	1127.94	1086.51	1051.87
95000	1492.05	1389.20	1308.36	1243.50	1190.60	1146.87	1110.31
100000	1570.58	1462.31	1377.22	1308.95	1253.26	1207.23	1168.75
105000	1649.10	1535.43	1446.08	1374.40	1315.93	1267.59	1227.19
110000	1727.63	1608.54	1514.94	1439.84	1378.59	1327.95	1285.62
120000	1884.69	1754.77	1652.66	1570.74	1503.91	1448.67	1402.50
130000	2041.75	1901.01	1790.39	1701.63	1629.24	1569.40	1519.37
140000	2198.81	2047.24	1928.11	1832.53	1754.57	1690.12	1636.25
150000	2355.86	2193.47	2065.83	1963.42	1879.89	1810.84	1753.12
160000	2512.92	2339.70	2203.55	2094.32	2005.22	1931.56	1870.00
170000	2669.98	2485.93	2341.27	2225.21	2130.55	2052.29	1986.87
180000	2827.04	2632.16	2479.00	2356.11	2255.87	2173.01	2103.75
190000	2984.09	2778.39	2616.72	2487.00	2381.20	2293.73	2220.62
200000	3141.15	2924.62	2754.44	2617.90	2506.52	2414.46	2337.50
210000	3298.21	3070.86	2892.16	2748.79	2631.85	2535.18	2454.37
220000	3455.27	3217.09	3029.88	2879.69	2757.18	2655.90	2571.25
230000	3612.32	3363.32	3167.61	3010.58	2882.50	2776.62	2688.12
240000	3769.38	3509.55	3305.33	3141.48	3007.83	2897.35	2805.00
250000	3926.44	3655.78	3443.05	3272.37	3133.16	3018.07	2921.87

11.25 % Monthly Payments

LOAN AMOUNT	15	16	17	18	19	20	21
				YEARS			
100	1.14	1.11	1.09	1.06	1.05	1.03	1.02
200	2.27	2.22	2.17	2.13	2.09	2.06	2.04
500	5.68	5.54	5.43	5.32	5.24	5.16	5.09
1000	11.36	11.09	10.85	10.65	10.47	10.32	10.19
2000	22.73	22.17	21.70	21.29	20.94	20.64	20.37
5000	56.81	55.43	54.25	53.24	52.36	51.59	50.93
6000	68.18	66.52	65.10	63.88	62.83	61.91	61.11
7000	79.54	77.61	75.95	74.53	73.30	72.23	71.30
8000	90.90	88.69	86.80	85.18	83.77	82.55	81.48
9000	102.27	99.78	97.66	95.83	94.24	92.87	91.67
10000	113.63	110.87	108.51	106.47	104.71	103.19	101.85
12000	136.35	133.04	130.21	127.77	125.66	123.82	122.22
15000	170.44	166.30	162.76	159.71	157.07	154.78	152.78
20000	227.26	221.74	217.01	212.94	209.43	206.37	203.71
25000	284.07	277.17	271.26	266.18	261.78	257.96	254.63
30000	340.89	332.61	325.52	319.42	314.14	309.56	305.56
31000	352.25	343.69	336.37	330.06	324.61	319.87	315.74
32000	363.61	354.78	347.22	340.71	335.08	330.19	325.93
33000	374.97	365.87	358.07	351.36	345.55	340.51	336.11
34000	386.34	376.95	368.92	362.01	356.02	350.83	346.30
35000	397.70	388.04	379.77	372.65	366.50	361.15	356.49
36000	409.06	399.13	390.62	383.30	376.97	371.47	366.67
37000	420.43	410.21	401.47	393.95	387.44	381.78	376.86
38000	431.79	421.30	412.32	404.59	397.91	392.10	387.04
39000	443.15	432.39	423.17	415.24	408.38	402.42	397.23
40000	454.51	443.47	434.02	425.89	418.85	412.74	407.41
41000	465.88	454.56	444.87	436.54	429.32	423.06	417.60
42000	477.24	465.65	455.72	447.18	439.80	433.38	427.78
43000	488.60	476.73	466.58	457.83	450.27	443.70	437.97
44000	499.97	487.82	477.43	468.48	460.74	454.01	448.15
45000	511.33	498.91	488.28	479.13	471.21	464.33	458.34
46000	522.69	509.99	499.13	489.77	481.68	474.65	468.52
47000	534.05	521.08	509.98	500.42	492.15	484.97	478.71
48000	545.42	532.17	520.83	511.07	502.62	495.29	488.89
49000	556.78	543.26	531.68	521.71	513.09	505.61	499.08
50000	568.14	554.34	542.53	532.36	523.57	515.93	509.26
51000	579.51	565.43	553.38	543.01	534.04	526.24	519.45
52000	590.87	576.52	564.23	553.66	544.51	536.56	529.64
53000	602.23	587.60	575.08	564.30	554.98	546.88	539.82
54000	613.59	598.69	585.93	574.95	565.45	557.20	550.01
55000	624.96	609.78	596.78	585.60	575.92	567.52	560.19
56000	636.32	620.86	607.63	596.24	586.39	577.84	570.38
57000	647.68	631.95	618.48	606.89	596.86	588.16	580.56
58000	659.05	643.04	629.33	617.54	607.34	598.47	590.75
59000	670.41	654.12	640.18	628.19	617.81	608.79	600.93
60000	681.77	665.21	651.04	638.83	628.28	619.11	611.1
65000	738.59	720.64	705.29	692.07	680.64	670.70	662.04
70000	795.40	776.08	759.54	745.31	732.99	722.30	712.97
75000	852.21	831.51	813.79	798.54	785.35	773.89	763.9
80000	909.03	886.95	868.05	851.78	837.71	825.48	814.8
85000	965.84	942.38	922.30	905.01	890.06	877.07	865.7
90000	1022.66	997.82	976.55	958.25	942.42	928.67	916.6
95000	1079.47	1053.25	1030.81	1011.49	994.77	980.26	967.6
100000	1136.29	1108.68	1085.06	1064.72	1047.13	1031.85	1018.5
105000	1193.10	1164.12	1139.31	1117.96	1099.49	1083.44	1069.4
110000	1249.91	1219.55	1193.56	1171.19	1151.84	1135.04	1120.3
120000	1363.54	1330.42	1302.07	1277.67	1256.56	1238.22	1222.2
130000	1477.17	1441.29	1410.58	1384.14	1361.27	1341.41	1324.0
140000	1590.80	1552.16	1519.08	1490.61	1465.98	1444.59	1425.9
150000	1704.43	1663.03	1627.59	1597.08	1570.70	1547.78	1527.7
160000	1818.06	1773.89	1736.09	1703.56	1675.41	1650.96	1629.6
170000	1931.69	1884.76	1844.60	1810.03	1780.12	1754.15	1731.5
180000	2045.31	1995.63	1953.11	1916.50	1884.84	1857.33	1833.3
190000	2158.94	2106.50	2061.61	2022.97	1989.55	1960.52	1935.2
200000	2272.57	2217.37	2170.12	2129.44	2094.26	2063.70	2037.0
210000	2386.20	2328.24	2278.62	2235.92	2198.98	2166.89	2138.9
220000	2499.83	2439.10	2387.13	2342.39	2303.69	2270.07	2240.7
230000	2613.46	2549.97	2495.63	2448.86	2408.40	2373.26	2342.6
240000	2727.09	2660.84	2604.14	2555.33	2513.12	2476.44	2444.4
250000	2840.71	2771.71	2712.65	2661.81	2617.83	2579.63	2546.3

Monthly Payments 11.25 %

LOAN AMOUNT	22	23	24	25	30	35	40
				YEARS			
100	1.01	1.00	0.99	0.98	0.95	0.94	0.93
200	2.01	1.99	1.98	1.96	1.90	1.87	1.86
500	5.03	4.98	4.94	4.90	4.76	4.68	4.64
1000	10.07	9.97	9.88	9.80	9.52	9.37	9.28
2000	20.14	19.93	19.75	19.60	19.04	18.73	18.56
5000	50.34	49.83	49.38	48.99	47.60	46.83	46.39
6000	60.41	59.80	59.26	58.79	57.12	56.19	55.67
7000	70.48	69.77	69.14	68.58	66.64	65.56	64.95
8000	80.55	79.73	79.01	78.38	76.16	74.93	74.23
9000	90.62	89.70	88.89	88.18	85.68	84.29	83.51
10000	100.69	99.67	98.77	97.98	95.19	93.66	92.79
12000	120.83	119.60	118.52	117.57	114.23	112.39	111.35
15000	151.03	149.50	148.15	146.96	142.79	140.49	139.18
20000	201.38	199.33	197.53	195.95	190.39	187.31	185.58
25000	251.72	249.16	246.92	244.94	237.99	234.14	231.97
30000	302.06	299.00	296.30	293.93	285.58	280.97	278.37
31000	312.13	308.96	306.18	303.72	295.10	290.34	287.65
32000	322.20	318.93	316.06	313.52	304.62	299.70	296.93
33000	332.27	328.90	325.93	323.32	314.14	309.07	306.21
34000	342.34	338.86	335.81	333.12	323.66	318.43	315.49
35000	352.41	348.83	345.69	342.91	333.18	327.80	324.76
36000	362.48	358.80	355.56	352.71	342.70	337.17	334.04
37000	372.54	368.76	365.44	362.51	352.22	346.53	343.32
38000	382.61	378.73	375.32	372.31	361.74	355.90	352.60
39000	392.68	388.70	385.19	382.10	371.26	365.26	361.88
40000	402.75	398.66	395.07	391.90	380.78	374.63	371.16
41000	412.82	408.63	404.95	401.70	390.30	383.99	380.44
42000	422.89	418.60	414.82	411.50	399.82	393.36	389.72
43000	432.96	428.56	424.70	421.29	409.34	402.73	399.00
44000	443.03	438.53	434.58	431.09	418.86	412.09	408.28
45000	453.09	448.50	444.45	440.89	428.38	421.46	417.55
46000	463.16	458.46	454.33	450.69	437.90	430.82	426.83
47000	473.23	468.43	464.21	460.48	447.42	440.19	436.11
48000	483.30	478.40	474.08	470.28	456.94	449.55	445.39
49000	493.37	488.36	483.96	480.08	466.46	458.92	454.67
50000	503.44	498.33	493.84	489.88	475.97	468.29	463.95
51000	513.51	508.30	503.71	499.68	485.49	477.65	473.23
52000	523.58	518.26	513.59	509.47	495.01	487.02	482.51
53000	533.64	528.23	523.47	519.27	504.53	496.38	491.79
54000	543.71	538.20	533.34	529.07	514.05	505.75	501.07
55000	553.78	548.16	543.22	538.87	523.57	515.11	510.34
56000	563.85	558.13	553.10	548.66	533.09	524.48	519.62
57000	573.92	568.09	562.97	558.46	542.61	533.85	528.90
58000	583.99	578.06	572.85	568.26	552.13	543.21	538.18
59000	594.06	588.03	582.73	578.06	561.65	552.58	547.46
60000	604.13	597.99	592.60	587.85	571.17	561.94	556.74
65000	654.47	647.83	641.99	636.84	618.77	608.77	603.13
70000	704.81	697.66	691.37	685.83	666.36	655.60	649.53
75000	755.16	747.49	740.75	734.82	713.96	702.43	695.92
80000	805.50	797.33	790.14	783.80	761.56	749.26	742.32
85000	855.85	847.16	839.52	832.79	809.16	796.09	788.71
90000	906.19	896.99	888.90	881.78	856.75	842.91	835.11
95000	956.53	946.82	938.29	930.77	904.35	889.74	881.50
100000	1006.88	996.66	987.67	979.75	951.95	936.57	927.90
105000	1057.22	1046.49	1037.06	1028.74	999.55	983.40	974.29
110000	1107.57	1096.32	1086.44	1077.73	1047.14	1030.23	1020.69
120000	1208.25	1195.99	1185.21	1175.71	1142.34	1123.89	1113.48
130000	1308.94	1295.65	1283.97	1273.68	1237.53	1217.54	1206.27
140000	1409.63	1395.32	1382.74	1371.66	1332.73	1311.20	1299.06
150000	1510.32	1494.99	1481.51	1469.63	1427.92	1404.86	1391.85
160000	1611.00	1594.65	1580.28	1567.61	1523.12	1498.51	1484.64
170000	1711.69	1694.32	1679.04	1665.58	1618.31	1592.17	1577.43
180000	1812.38	1793.98	1777.81	1763.56	1713.51	1685.83	1670.22
190000	1913.07	1893.65	1876.58	1861.53	1808.70	1779.49	1763.01
200000	2013.75	1993.32	1975.34	1959.51	1903.90	1873.14	1855.80
210000	2114.44	2092.98	2074.11	2057.49	1999.09	1966.80	1948.59
220000	2215.13	2192.65	2172.88	2155.46	2094.29	2060.46	2041.38
230000	2315.82	2292.31	2271.65	2253.44	2189.48	2154.11	2134.17
240000	2416.51	2391.98	2370.41	2351.41	2284.68	2247.77	2226.96
250000	2517.19	2491.64	2469.18	2449.39	2379.87	2341.43	2319.75

11.50 % Monthly Payments

LOAN AMOUNT	1	2	3	4	5	6	7
				YEARS			
100	8.85	4.67	3.28	2.60	2.19	1.92	1.7
200	17.70	9.34	6.57	5.19	4.37	3.83	3.4
500	44.25	23.36	16.42	12.98	10.93	9.58	8.6
1000	88.49	46.72	32.85	25.96	21.86	19.15	17.2
2000	176.98	93.43	65.70	51.92	43.72	38.31	34.4
5000	442.45	233.58	164.25	129.80	109.30	95.77	86.2
6000	530.94	280.30	197.10	155.76	131.16	114.92	103.4
7000	619.44	327.02	229.95	181.71	153.01	134.08	120.7
8000	707.93	373.73	262.80	207.67	174.87	153.23	137.9
9000	796.42	420.45	295.65	233.63	196.73	172.39	155.2
10000	884.91	467.16	328.50	259.59	218.59	191.54	172.4
12000	1061.89	560.60	394.19	311.51	262.31	229.85	206.9
15000	1327.36	700.75	492.74	389.39	327.89	287.31	258.6
20000	1769.81	934.33	656.99	519.18	437.18	383.08	344.9
25000	2212.27	1167.91	821.24	648.98	546.48	478.85	431.1
30000	2654.72	1401.49	985.49	778.78	655.78	574.62	517.3
31000	2743.21	1448.21	1018.34	804.74	677.64	593.78	534.6
32000	2831.70	1494.93	1051.19	830.69	699.49	612.93	551.8
33000	2920.19	1541.64	1084.03	856.65	721.35	632.08	569.1
34000	3008.69	1588.36	1116.88	882.61	743.21	651.24	586.3
35000	3097.18	1635.08	1149.73	908.57	765.07	670.39	603.6
36000	3185.67	1681.79	1182.58	934.53	786.93	689.55	620.8
37000	3274.16	1728.51	1215.43	960.49	808.79	708.70	638.0
38000	3362.65	1775.23	1248.28	986.45	830.65	727.85	655.3
39000	3451.14	1821.94	1281.13	1012.41	852.51	747.01	672.5
40000	3539.63	1868.66	1313.98	1038.37	874.37	766.16	689.8
41000	3628.12	1915.37	1346.83	1064.33	896.23	785.32	707.0
42000	3716.61	1962.09	1379.68	1090.29	918.09	804.47	724.3
43000	3805.10	2008.81	1412.53	1116.25	939.95	823.62	741.5
44000	3893.59	2055.52	1445.38	1142.20	961.80	842.78	758.8
45000	3982.08	2102.24	1478.23	1168.16	983.66	861.93	776.0
46000	4070.57	2148.96	1511.08	1194.12	1005.52	881.09	793.3
47000	4159.06	2195.67	1543.93	1220.08	1027.38	900.24	810.5
48000	4247.56	2242.39	1576.78	1246.04	1049.24	919.39	827.7
49000	4336.05	2289.11	1609.63	1272.00	1071.10	938.55	845.0
50000	4424.54	2335.82	1642.48	1297.96	1092.96	957.70	862.2
51000	4513.03	2382.54	1675.33	1323.92	1114.82	976.86	879.5
52000	4601.52	2429.26	1708.18	1349.88	1136.68	996.01	896.7
53000	4690.01	2475.97	1741.03	1375.84	1158.54	1015.16	914.0
54000	4778.50	2522.69	1773.88	1401.80	1180.40	1034.32	931.2
55000	4866.99	2569.40	1806.72	1427.76	1202.26	1053.47	948.5
56000	4955.48	2616.12	1839.57	1453.72	1224.11	1072.63	965.7
57000	5043.97	2662.84	1872.42	1479.67	1245.97	1091.78	983.0
58000	5132.46	2709.55	1905.27	1505.63	1267.83	1110.93	1000.2
59000	5220.95	2756.27	1938.12	1531.59	1289.69	1130.09	1017.4
60000	5309.44	2802.99	1970.97	1557.55	1311.55	1149.24	1034.7
65000	5751.90	3036.57	2135.22	1687.35	1420.85	1245.01	1120.9
70000	6194.35	3270.15	2299.47	1817.14	1530.14	1340.78	1207.1
75000	6636.81	3503.73	2463.72	1946.94	1639.44	1436.55	1293.4
80000	7079.26	3737.32	2627.96	2076.74	1748.74	1532.32	1379.6
85000	7521.71	3970.90	2792.21	2206.53	1858.03	1628.09	1465.8
90000	7964.17	4204.48	2956.46	2336.33	1967.33	1723.86	1552.1
95000	8406.62	4438.06	3120.71	2466.12	2076.62	1819.63	1638.3
100000	8849.07	4671.65	3284.95	2595.92	2185.92	1915.40	1724.5
105000	9291.53	4905.23	3449.20	2725.72	2295.22	2011.17	1810.7
110000	9733.98	5138.81	3613.45	2855.51	2404.51	2106.94	1897.0
120000	10618.89	5605.97	3941.94	3115.10	2623.10	2298.48	2069.4
130000	11503.80	6073.14	4270.44	3374.70	2841.70	2490.02	2241.9
140000	12388.70	6540.30	4598.94	3634.29	3060.29	2681.56	2414.3
150000	13273.61	7007.47	4927.43	3893.88	3278.88	2873.11	2586.8
160000	14158.52	7474.63	5255.93	4153.47	3497.47	3064.65	2759.3
170000	15043.43	7941.80	5584.42	4413.06	3716.06	3256.19	2931.7
180000	15928.33	8408.96	5912.92	4672.66	3934.65	3447.73	3104.2
190000	16813.24	8876.13	6241.41	4932.25	4153.25	3639.27	3276.6
200000	17698.15	9343.29	6569.91	5191.84	4371.84	3830.81	3449.1
210000	18583.06	9810.45	6898.40	5451.43	4590.43	4022.35	3621.5
220000	19467.96	10277.62	7226.90	5711.02	4809.02	4213.89	3794.0
230000	20352.87	10744.78	7555.39	5970.62	5027.61	4405.43	3966.4
240000	21237.78	11211.95	7883.89	6230.21	5246.21	4596.97	4138.9
250000	22122.69	11679.11	8212.38	6489.80	5464.80	4788.51	4311.4

Monthly Payments 11.50 %

LOAN AMOUNT	8	9	10	11	12	13	14
	YEARS						
100	1.58	1.48	1.39	1.32	1.27	1.22	1.18
200	3.17	2.95	2.78	2.65	2.53	2.44	2.37
500	7.92	7.38	6.95	6.61	6.34	6.11	5.92
1000	15.83	14.76	13.91	13.23	12.67	12.22	11.84
2000	31.67	29.51	27.82	26.46	25.35	24.43	23.67
5000	79.17	73.78	69.54	66.14	63.37	61.08	59.18
6000	95.01	88.53	83.45	79.37	76.05	73.30	71.01
7000	110.84	103.29	97.35	92.60	88.72	85.52	82.85
8000	126.68	118.04	111.26	105.82	101.39	97.74	94.68
9000	142.51	132.80	125.17	119.05	114.07	109.95	106.52
10000	158.35	147.55	139.08	132.28	126.74	122.17	118.35
12000	190.02	177.06	166.89	158.74	152.09	146.60	142.02
15000	237.52	221.33	208.62	198.42	190.11	183.25	177.53
20000	316.70	295.11	278.15	264.56	253.49	244.34	236.70
25000	395.87	368.89	347.69	330.70	316.86	305.42	295.88
30000	475.04	442.66	417.23	396.84	380.23	366.51	355.05
31000	490.88	457.42	431.14	410.07	392.90	378.72	366.89
32000	506.71	472.17	445.05	423.30	405.58	390.94	378.72
33000	522.55	486.93	458.95	436.53	418.25	403.16	390.56
34000	538.38	501.68	472.86	449.75	430.93	415.38	402.39
35000	554.22	516.44	486.77	462.98	443.60	427.59	414.23
36000	570.05	531.19	500.68	476.21	456.27	439.81	426.06
37000	585.89	545.95	514.58	489.44	468.95	452.03	437.90
38000	601.72	560.71	528.49	502.67	481.62	464.24	449.73
39000	617.56	575.46	542.40	515.90	494.30	476.46	461.57
40000	633.39	590.22	556.31	529.12	506.97	488.68	473.40
41000	649.23	604.97	570.21	542.35	519.65	500.89	485.24
42000	665.06	619.73	584.12	555.58	532.32	513.11	497.07
43000	680.90	634.48	598.03	568.81	544.99	525.33	508.91
44000	696.73	649.24	611.94	582.04	557.67	537.54	520.74
45000	712.57	663.99	625.85	595.26	570.34	549.76	532.58
46000	728.40	678.75	639.75	608.49	583.02	561.98	544.41
47000	744.24	693.50	653.66	621.72	595.69	574.20	556.25
48000	760.07	708.26	667.57	634.95	608.37	586.41	568.08
49000	775.91	723.01	681.48	648.18	621.04	598.63	579.92
50000	791.74	737.77	695.38	661.40	633.71	610.85	591.75
51000	807.57	752.53	709.29	674.63	646.39	623.06	603.59
52000	823.41	767.28	723.20	687.86	659.06	635.28	615.42
53000	839.24	782.04	737.11	701.09	671.74	647.50	627.26
54000	855.08	796.79	751.01	714.32	684.41	659.71	639.09
55000	870.91	811.55	764.92	727.54	697.09	671.93	650.93
56000	886.75	826.30	778.83	740.77	709.76	684.15	662.76
57000	902.58	841.06	792.74	754.00	722.43	696.36	674.60
58000	918.42	855.81	806.64	767.23	735.11	708.58	686.43
59000	934.25	870.57	820.55	780.46	747.78	720.80	698.27
60000	950.09	885.32	834.46	793.68	760.46	733.02	710.10
65000	1029.26	959.10	904.00	859.83	823.83	794.10	769.28
70000	1108.44	1032.88	973.54	925.97	887.20	855.18	828.45
75000	1187.61	1106.66	1043.08	992.11	950.57	916.27	887.63
80000	1266.78	1180.43	1112.61	1058.25	1013.94	977.35	946.80
85000	1345.96	1254.21	1182.15	1124.39	1077.31	1038.44	1005.98
90000	1425.13	1327.99	1251.69	1190.53	1140.69	1099.52	1065.15
95000	1504.31	1401.76	1321.23	1256.67	1204.06	1160.61	1124.33
100000	1583.48	1475.54	1390.77	1322.81	1267.43	1221.69	1183.50
105000	1662.65	1549.32	1460.31	1388.95	1330.80	1282.78	1242.68
110000	1741.83	1623.09	1529.84	1455.09	1394.17	1343.86	1301.85
120000	1900.18	1770.65	1668.92	1587.37	1520.91	1466.03	1420.20
130000	2058.52	1918.20	1808.00	1719.65	1647.66	1588.20	1538.55
140000	2216.87	2065.76	1947.07	1851.93	1774.40	1710.37	1656.90
150000	2375.22	2213.31	2086.15	1984.21	1901.14	1832.54	1775.25
160000	2533.57	2360.86	2225.23	2116.49	2027.88	1954.71	1893.60
170000	2691.92	2508.42	2364.30	2248.77	2154.63	2076.88	2011.95
180000	2850.26	2655.97	2503.38	2381.05	2281.37	2199.05	2130.30
190000	3008.61	2803.53	2642.46	2513.34	2408.11	2321.21	2248.65
200000	3166.96	2951.08	2781.53	2645.62	2534.86	2443.38	2367.00
210000	3325.31	3098.63	2920.61	2777.90	2661.60	2565.55	2485.36
220000	3483.66	3246.19	3059.69	2910.18	2788.34	2687.72	2603.71
230000	3642.00	3393.74	3198.76	3042.46	2915.08	2809.89	2722.06
240000	3800.35	3541.30	3337.84	3174.74	3041.83	2932.06	2840.41
250000	3958.70	3688.85	3476.92	3307.02	3168.57	3054.23	2958.76

11.50 % Monthly Payments

LOAN AMOUNT	15	16	17	18	19	20	21
				YEARS			
100	1.15	1.12	1.10	1.08	1.06	1.05	1.04
200	2.30	2.25	2.20	2.16	2.13	2.10	2.07
500	5.76	5.62	5.50	5.40	5.32	5.24	5.18
1000	11.51	11.24	11.01	10.81	10.63	10.48	10.35
2000	23.03	22.48	22.01	21.61	21.26	20.96	20.70
5000	57.57	56.20	55.03	54.03	53.16	52.41	51.75
6000	69.08	67.44	66.04	64.83	63.79	62.89	62.10
7000	80.59	78.68	77.04	75.64	74.42	73.37	72.45
8000	92.11	89.92	88.05	86.44	85.06	83.85	82.80
9000	103.62	101.16	99.06	97.25	95.69	94.33	93.15
10000	115.13	112.40	110.06	108.05	106.32	104.81	103.50
12000	138.16	134.88	132.08	129.67	127.58	125.78	124.21
15000	172.70	168.60	165.09	162.08	159.48	157.22	155.26
20000	230.26	224.80	220.13	216.11	212.64	209.63	207.01
25000	287.83	281.00	275.16	270.14	265.80	262.04	258.76
30000	345.40	337.20	330.19	324.16	318.96	314.44	310.51
31000	356.91	348.44	341.19	334.97	329.59	324.93	320.86
32000	368.42	359.68	352.20	345.77	340.22	335.41	331.21
33000	379.94	370.92	363.21	356.58	350.85	345.89	341.57
34000	391.45	382.16	374.21	367.38	361.49	356.37	351.92
35000	402.96	393.40	385.22	378.19	372.12	366.85	362.27
36000	414.48	404.64	396.23	389.00	382.75	377.33	372.62
37000	425.99	415.88	407.23	399.80	393.38	387.81	382.97
38000	437.50	427.12	418.24	410.61	404.01	398.30	393.32
39000	449.01	438.36	429.24	421.41	414.65	408.78	403.67
40000	460.53	449.60	440.25	432.22	425.28	419.26	414.02
41000	472.04	460.84	451.26	443.02	435.91	429.74	424.37
42000	483.55	472.08	462.26	453.83	446.54	440.22	434.72
43000	495.07	483.32	473.27	464.63	457.17	450.70	445.07
44000	506.58	494.56	484.28	475.44	467.81	461.18	455.42
45000	518.09	505.80	495.28	486.24	478.44	471.67	465.77
46000	529.61	517.04	506.29	497.05	489.07	482.15	476.12
47000	541.12	528.28	517.29	507.85	499.70	492.63	486.47
48000	552.63	539.51	528.30	518.66	510.33	503.11	496.82
49000	564.15	550.75	539.31	529.47	520.96	513.59	507.17
50000	575.66	561.99	550.31	540.27	531.60	524.07	517.52
51000	587.17	573.23	561.32	551.08	542.23	534.55	527.87
52000	598.69	584.47	572.33	561.88	552.86	545.04	538.22
53000	610.20	595.71	583.33	572.69	563.49	555.52	548.57
54000	621.71	606.95	594.34	583.49	574.12	566.00	558.92
55000	633.23	618.19	605.34	594.30	584.76	576.48	569.28
56000	644.74	629.43	616.35	605.10	595.39	586.96	579.63
57000	656.25	640.67	627.36	615.91	606.02	597.44	589.98
58000	667.77	651.91	638.36	626.71	616.65	607.92	600.33
59000	679.28	663.15	649.37	637.52	627.28	618.41	610.68
60000	690.79	674.39	660.38	648.33	637.92	628.89	621.03
65000	748.36	730.59	715.41	702.35	691.08	681.29	672.78
70000	805.92	786.79	770.44	756.38	744.24	733.70	724.53
75000	863.49	842.99	825.47	810.41	797.40	786.11	776.28
80000	921.06	899.19	880.50	864.43	850.55	838.52	828.04
85000	978.62	955.39	935.53	918.46	903.71	890.92	879.79
90000	1036.19	1011.59	990.56	972.49	956.87	943.33	931.54
95000	1093.75	1067.79	1045.59	1026.52	1010.03	995.74	983.29
100000	1151.32	1123.99	1100.63	1080.54	1063.19	1048.15	1035.05
105000	1208.89	1180.19	1155.66	1134.57	1116.35	1100.55	1086.80
110000	1266.45	1236.39	1210.69	1188.60	1169.51	1152.96	1138.55
120000	1381.58	1348.79	1320.75	1296.65	1275.83	1257.77	1242.05
130000	1496.72	1461.19	1430.81	1404.70	1382.15	1362.59	1345.56
140000	1611.85	1573.59	1540.88	1512.76	1488.47	1467.40	1449.06
150000	1726.98	1685.98	1650.94	1620.81	1594.79	1572.22	1552.57
160000	1842.11	1798.38	1761.00	1728.87	1701.11	1677.03	1656.07
170000	1957.24	1910.78	1871.06	1836.92	1807.43	1781.85	1759.58
180000	2072.38	2023.18	1981.13	1944.98	1913.75	1886.66	1863.08
190000	2187.51	2135.58	2091.19	2053.03	2020.07	1991.48	1966.59
200000	2302.64	2247.98	2201.25	2161.08	2126.39	2096.29	2070.09
210000	2417.77	2360.38	2311.32	2269.14	2232.71	2201.11	2173.60
220000	2532.90	2472.78	2421.38	2377.19	2339.03	2305.92	2277.10
230000	2648.04	2585.18	2531.44	2485.25	2445.35	2410.73	2380.61
240000	2763.17	2697.57	2641.50	2593.30	2551.66	2515.55	2484.11
250000	2878.30	2809.97	2751.57	2701.36	2657.98	2620.36	2587.61

Monthly Payments 11.50 %

LOAN AMOUNT	22	23	24	25	30	35	40
100	1.02	1.01	1.00	1.00	0.97	0.96	0.95
200	2.05	2.03	2.01	1.99	1.94	1.91	1.89
500	5.12	5.07	5.02	4.99	4.85	4.78	4.73
1000	10.24	10.14	10.05	9.97	9.70	9.55	9.47
2000	20.47	20.27	20.10	19.94	19.40	19.10	18.94
5000	51.18	50.68	50.24	49.85	48.50	47.76	47.35
6000	61.42	60.82	60.29	59.82	58.20	57.31	56.82
7000	71.65	70.95	70.34	69.79	67.90	66.87	66.29
8000	81.89	81.09	80.38	79.76	77.60	76.42	75.76
9000	92.12	91.22	90.43	89.74	87.30	85.97	85.23
10000	102.36	101.36	100.48	99.71	97.00	95.52	94.70
12000	122.83	121.63	120.58	119.65	116.40	114.63	113.64
15000	153.54	152.04	150.72	149.56	145.50	143.28	142.04
20000	204.72	202.72	200.96	199.41	194.01	191.04	189.39
25000	255.90	253.40	251.20	249.27	242.51	238.81	236.74
30000	307.08	304.08	301.44	299.12	291.01	286.57	284.09
31000	317.32	314.21	311.49	309.09	300.71	296.12	293.56
32000	327.55	324.35	321.53	319.06	310.41	305.67	303.03
33000	337.79	334.48	331.58	329.03	320.11	315.22	312.50
34000	348.03	344.62	341.63	339.00	329.81	324.78	321.97
35000	358.26	354.76	351.68	348.97	339.51	334.33	331.44
36000	368.50	364.89	361.73	358.94	349.21	343.88	340.91
37000	378.73	375.03	371.77	368.91	358.91	353.43	350.38
38000	388.97	385.16	381.82	378.88	368.61	362.99	359.84
39000	399.21	395.30	391.87	388.85	378.31	372.54	369.31
40000	409.44	405.44	401.92	398.82	388.01	382.09	378.78
41000	419.68	415.57	411.97	408.79	397.71	391.64	388.25
42000	429.91	425.71	422.01	418.77	407.41	401.19	397.72
43000	440.15	435.84	432.06	428.74	417.11	410.75	407.19
44000	450.39	445.98	442.11	438.71	426.81	420.30	416.66
45000	460.62	456.11	452.16	448.68	436.51	429.85	426.13
46000	470.86	466.25	462.21	458.65	446.21	439.40	435.60
47000	481.09	476.39	472.25	468.62	455.91	448.96	445.07
48000	491.33	486.52	482.30	478.59	465.61	458.51	454.54
49000	501.57	496.66	492.35	488.56	475.31	468.06	464.01
50000	511.80	506.79	502.40	498.53	485.02	477.61	473.48
51000	522.04	516.93	512.45	508.50	494.72	487.16	482.95
52000	532.28	527.07	522.49	518.47	504.42	496.72	492.42
53000	542.51	537.20	532.54	528.44	514.12	506.27	501.89
54000	552.75	547.34	542.59	538.41	523.82	515.82	511.36
55000	562.98	557.47	552.64	548.38	533.52	525.37	520.83
56000	573.22	567.61	562.69	558.35	543.22	534.93	530.30
57000	583.46	577.75	572.73	568.32	552.92	544.48	539.77
58000	593.69	587.88	582.78	578.30	562.62	554.03	549.24
59000	603.93	598.02	592.83	588.27	572.32	563.58	558.71
60000	614.16	608.15	602.88	598.24	582.02	573.13	568.18
65000	665.34	658.83	653.12	648.09	630.52	620.90	615.52
70000	716.52	709.51	703.36	697.94	679.02	668.66	662.87
75000	767.70	760.19	753.60	747.80	727.52	716.42	710.22
80000	818.88	810.87	803.84	797.65	776.02	764.18	757.57
85000	870.07	861.55	854.08	847.50	824.53	811.94	804.92
90000	921.25	912.23	904.32	897.35	873.03	859.70	852.26
95000	972.43	962.91	954.56	947.21	921.53	907.46	899.61
100000	1023.61	1013.59	1004.80	997.06	970.03	955.22	946.96
105000	1074.79	1064.27	1055.04	1046.91	1018.53	1002.99	994.31
110000	1125.97	1114.95	1105.27	1096.77	1067.03	1050.75	1041.66
120000	1228.33	1216.31	1205.75	1196.47	1164.04	1146.27	1136.35
130000	1330.69	1317.66	1306.23	1296.18	1261.04	1241.79	1231.05
140000	1433.05	1419.02	1406.71	1395.88	1358.04	1337.31	1325.74
150000	1535.41	1520.38	1507.19	1495.59	1455.05	1432.84	1420.44
160000	1637.77	1621.74	1607.67	1595.30	1552.05	1528.36	1515.14
170000	1740.13	1723.10	1708.15	1695.00	1649.05	1623.88	1609.83
180000	1842.49	1824.46	1808.63	1794.71	1746.05	1719.40	1704.53
190000	1944.85	1925.82	1909.11	1894.42	1843.06	1814.93	1799.22
200000	2047.21	2027.18	2009.59	1994.12	1940.06	1910.45	1893.92
210000	2149.57	2128.54	2110.07	2093.83	2037.06	2005.97	1988.62
220000	2251.93	2229.89	2210.55	2193.53	2134.07	2101.49	2083.31
230000	2354.29	2331.25	2311.03	2293.24	2231.07	2197.02	2178.01
240000	2456.65	2432.61	2411.51	2392.95	2328.07	2292.54	2272.71
250000	2559.01	2533.97	2511.99	2492.65	2425.08	2388.06	2367.40

11.75 % Monthly Payments

LOAN AMOUNT	1	2	3	4	5	6	7
				YEARS			
100	8.86	4.68	3.30	2.61	2.20	1.93	1.74
200	17.72	9.37	6.59	5.22	4.40	3.86	3.47
500	44.30	23.41	16.48	13.04	10.99	9.64	8.69
1000	88.60	46.83	32.96	26.08	21.98	19.28	17.37
2000	177.20	93.65	65.93	52.15	43.96	38.55	34.74
5000	443.01	234.14	164.81	130.38	109.89	96.38	86.86
6000	531.61	280.96	197.78	156.45	131.87	115.66	104.23
7000	620.21	327.79	230.74	182.53	153.85	134.94	121.60
8000	708.82	374.62	263.70	208.60	175.83	154.21	138.97
9000	797.42	421.45	296.67	234.68	197.81	173.49	156.35
10000	886.02	468.27	329.63	260.75	219.79	192.77	173.72
12000	1063.23	561.93	395.55	312.91	263.74	231.32	208.46
15000	1329.03	702.41	494.44	391.13	329.68	289.15	260.58
20000	1772.04	936.55	659.26	521.51	439.57	385.54	347.44
25000	2215.05	1170.69	824.07	651.89	549.47	481.92	434.29
30000	2658.06	1404.82	988.88	782.26	659.36	578.31	521.15
31000	2746.67	1451.65	1021.85	808.34	681.34	597.58	538.52
32000	2835.27	1498.48	1054.81	834.42	703.32	616.86	555.90
33000	2923.87	1545.30	1087.77	860.49	725.30	636.14	573.27
34000	3012.47	1592.13	1120.74	886.57	747.28	655.41	590.64
35000	3101.07	1638.96	1153.70	912.64	769.25	674.69	608.01
36000	3189.68	1685.79	1186.66	938.72	791.23	693.97	625.38
37000	3278.28	1732.61	1219.62	964.79	813.21	713.24	642.76
38000	3366.88	1779.44	1252.59	990.87	835.19	732.52	660.13
39000	3455.48	1826.27	1285.55	1016.94	857.17	751.80	677.50
40000	3544.08	1873.10	1318.51	1043.02	879.15	771.07	694.87
41000	3632.69	1919.92	1351.48	1069.09	901.13	790.35	712.24
42000	3721.29	1966.75	1384.44	1095.17	923.11	809.63	729.61
43000	3809.89	2013.58	1417.40	1121.25	945.08	828.90	746.99
44000	3898.49	2060.41	1450.36	1147.32	967.06	848.18	764.36
45000	3987.09	2107.23	1483.33	1173.40	989.04	867.46	781.73
46000	4075.70	2154.06	1516.29	1199.47	1011.02	886.74	799.10
47000	4164.30	2200.89	1549.25	1225.55	1033.00	906.01	816.47
48000	4252.90	2247.72	1582.22	1251.62	1054.98	925.29	833.84
49000	4341.50	2294.54	1615.18	1277.70	1076.96	944.57	851.22
50000	4430.11	2341.37	1648.14	1303.77	1098.93	963.84	868.59
51000	4518.71	2388.20	1681.10	1329.85	1120.91	983.12	885.96
52000	4607.31	2435.03	1714.07	1355.92	1142.89	1002.40	903.33
53000	4695.91	2481.85	1747.03	1382.00	1164.87	1021.67	920.70
54000	4784.51	2528.68	1779.99	1408.08	1186.85	1040.95	938.08
55000	4873.12	2575.51	1812.96	1434.15	1208.83	1060.23	955.45
56000	4961.72	2622.34	1845.92	1460.23	1230.81	1079.50	972.82
57000	5050.32	2669.16	1878.88	1486.30	1252.79	1098.78	990.19
58000	5138.92	2715.99	1911.84	1512.38	1274.76	1118.06	1007.56
59000	5227.52	2762.82	1944.81	1538.45	1296.74	1137.33	1024.93
60000	5316.13	2809.64	1977.77	1564.53	1318.72	1156.61	1042.31
65000	5759.14	3043.78	2142.58	1694.91	1428.62	1253.00	1129.16
70000	6202.15	3277.92	2307.40	1825.28	1538.51	1349.38	1216.02
75000	6645.16	3512.06	2472.21	1955.66	1648.40	1445.76	1302.88
80000	7088.17	3746.19	2637.03	2086.04	1758.30	1542.15	1389.74
85000	7531.18	3980.33	2801.84	2216.42	1868.19	1638.53	1476.60
90000	7974.19	4214.47	2966.65	2346.79	1978.08	1734.92	1563.46
95000	8417.20	4448.60	3131.47	2477.17	2087.98	1831.30	1650.32
100000	8860.21	4682.74	3296.28	2607.55	2197.87	1927.69	1737.18
105000	9303.22	4916.88	3461.10	2737.93	2307.76	2024.07	1824.04
110000	9746.23	5151.02	3625.91	2868.30	2417.66	2120.45	1910.89
120000	10632.25	5619.29	3955.54	3129.06	2637.44	2313.22	2084.61
130000	11518.27	6087.56	4285.17	3389.81	2857.23	2505.99	2258.33
140000	12404.30	6555.84	4614.80	3650.57	3077.02	2698.76	2432.05
150000	13290.32	7024.11	4944.42	3911.32	3296.80	2891.53	2605.77
160000	14176.34	7492.39	5274.05	4172.08	3516.59	3084.30	2779.48
170000	15062.36	7960.66	5603.68	4432.83	3736.38	3277.07	2953.20
180000	15948.38	8428.93	5933.31	4693.59	3956.17	3469.83	3126.92
190000	16834.40	8897.21	6262.94	4954.34	4175.95	3662.60	3300.64
200000	17720.42	9365.48	6592.57	5215.10	4395.74	3855.37	3474.35
210000	18606.44	9833.76	6922.19	5475.85	4615.53	4048.14	3648.07
220000	19492.46	10302.03	7251.82	5736.61	4835.31	4240.91	3821.79
230000	20378.48	10770.30	7581.45	5997.36	5055.10	4433.68	3995.51
240000	21264.51	11238.58	7911.08	6258.11	5274.89	4626.45	4169.22
250000	22150.53	11706.85	8240.71	6518.87	5494.67	4819.21	4342.94

Monthly Payments 11.75 %

LOAN AMOUNT	8	9	10	11	12	13	14
100	1.60	1.49	1.40	1.34	1.28	1.24	1.20
200	3.19	2.98	2.81	2.67	2.56	2.47	2.40
500	7.98	7.44	7.02	6.68	6.41	6.18	5.99
1000	15.96	14.89	14.04	13.37	12.82	12.36	11.98
2000	31.93	29.78	28.09	26.73	25.63	24.72	23.97
5000	79.82	74.44	70.22	66.84	64.08	61.81	59.92
6000	95.79	89.33	84.26	80.20	76.90	74.17	71.90
7000	111.75	104.22	98.31	93.57	89.72	86.54	83.88
8000	127.71	119.11	112.35	106.94	102.53	98.90	95.87
9000	143.68	133.99	126.39	120.31	115.35	111.26	107.85
10000	159.64	148.88	140.44	133.67	128.17	123.62	119.83
12000	191.57	178.66	168.52	160.41	153.80	148.35	143.80
15000	239.46	223.32	210.66	200.51	192.25	185.43	179.75
20000	319.29	297.76	280.87	267.35	256.33	247.24	239.67
25000	399.11	372.20	351.09	334.18	320.41	309.06	299.58
30000	478.93	446.65	421.31	401.02	384.50	370.87	359.50
31000	494.89	461.53	435.35	414.39	397.31	383.23	371.48
32000	510.86	476.42	449.40	427.75	410.13	395.59	383.46
33000	526.82	491.31	463.44	441.12	422.95	407.95	395.45
34000	542.79	506.20	477.49	454.49	435.76	420.32	407.43
35000	558.75	521.09	491.53	467.85	448.58	432.68	419.41
36000	574.71	535.97	505.57	481.22	461.40	445.04	431.40
37000	590.68	550.86	519.62	494.59	474.21	457.40	443.38
38000	606.64	565.75	533.66	507.96	487.03	469.77	455.36
39000	622.61	580.64	547.70	521.32	499.85	482.13	467.35
40000	638.57	595.53	561.75	534.69	512.66	494.49	479.33
41000	654.54	610.42	575.79	548.06	525.48	506.85	491.31
42000	670.50	625.30	589.84	561.43	538.30	519.21	503.30
43000	686.46	640.19	603.88	574.79	551.11	531.58	515.28
44000	702.43	655.08	617.92	588.16	563.93	543.94	527.26
45000	718.39	669.97	631.97	601.53	576.75	556.30	539.25
46000	734.36	684.86	646.01	614.89	589.56	568.66	551.23
47000	750.32	699.74	660.05	628.26	602.38	581.03	563.21
48000	766.29	714.63	674.10	641.63	615.20	593.39	575.20
49000	782.25	729.52	688.14	655.00	628.01	605.75	587.18
50000	798.21	744.41	702.18	668.36	640.83	618.11	599.16
51000	814.18	759.30	716.23	681.73	653.65	630.47	611.15
52000	830.14	774.19	730.27	695.10	666.46	642.84	623.13
53000	846.11	789.07	744.32	708.47	679.28	655.20	635.11
54000	862.07	803.96	758.36	721.83	692.10	667.56	647.10
55000	878.04	818.85	772.40	735.20	704.91	679.92	659.08
56000	894.00	833.74	786.45	748.57	717.73	692.29	671.06
57000	909.96	848.63	800.49	761.93	730.55	704.65	683.05
58000	925.93	863.51	814.53	775.30	743.36	717.01	695.03
59000	941.89	878.40	828.58	788.67	756.18	729.37	707.01
60000	957.86	893.29	842.62	802.04	768.99	741.73	719.00
65000	1037.68	967.73	912.84	868.87	833.08	803.55	778.91
70000	1117.50	1042.17	983.06	935.71	897.16	865.36	838.83
75000	1197.32	1116.61	1053.28	1002.55	961.24	927.17	898.75
80000	1277.14	1191.06	1123.50	1069.38	1025.33	988.98	958.66
85000	1356.96	1265.50	1193.71	1136.22	1089.41	1050.79	1018.58
90000	1436.79	1339.94	1263.93	1203.06	1153.49	1112.60	1078.49
95000	1516.61	1414.38	1334.15	1269.89	1217.58	1174.41	1138.41
100000	1596.43	1488.82	1404.37	1336.73	1281.66	1236.22	1198.33
105000	1676.25	1563.26	1474.59	1403.56	1345.74	1298.03	1258.24
110000	1756.07	1637.70	1544.81	1470.40	1409.82	1359.85	1318.16
120000	1915.71	1786.58	1685.24	1604.07	1537.99	1483.47	1437.99
130000	2075.36	1935.46	1825.68	1737.75	1666.16	1607.09	1557.83
140000	2235.00	2084.35	1966.12	1871.42	1794.32	1730.71	1677.66
150000	2394.64	2233.23	2106.55	2005.09	1922.49	1854.34	1797.49
160000	2554.29	2382.11	2246.99	2138.76	2050.65	1977.96	1917.32
170000	2713.93	2530.99	2387.43	2272.44	2178.82	2101.58	2037.16
180000	2873.57	2679.87	2527.86	2406.11	2306.98	2225.20	2156.99
190000	3033.21	2828.76	2668.30	2539.78	2435.15	2348.83	2276.82
200000	3192.86	2977.64	2808.74	2673.46	2563.32	2472.45	2396.65
210000	3352.50	3126.52	2949.18	2807.13	2691.48	2596.07	2516.49
220000	3512.14	3275.40	3089.61	2940.80	2819.65	2719.69	2636.32
230000	3671.79	3424.28	3230.05	3074.47	2947.81	2843.31	2756.15
240000	3831.43	3573.17	3370.49	3208.15	3075.98	2966.94	2875.99
250000	3991.07	3722.05	3510.92	3341.82	3204.14	3090.56	2995.82

11.75 % Monthly Payments

LOAN AMOUNT	15	16	17	18	19	20	21
				YEARS			
100	1.17	1.14	1.12	1.10	1.08	1.06	1.05
200	2.33	2.28	2.23	2.19	2.16	2.13	2.10
500	5.83	5.70	5.58	5.48	5.40	5.32	5.26
1000	11.66	11.39	11.16	10.96	10.79	10.65	10.52
2000	23.33	22.79	22.33	21.93	21.59	21.29	21.03
5000	58.32	56.97	55.81	54.82	53.97	53.23	52.58
6000	69.99	68.36	66.98	65.79	64.76	63.87	63.10
7000	81.65	79.76	78.14	76.75	75.55	74.52	73.61
8000	93.31	91.15	89.30	87.72	86.35	85.16	84.13
9000	104.98	102.54	100.46	98.68	97.14	95.81	94.65
10000	116.64	113.94	111.63	109.64	107.93	106.45	105.16
12000	139.97	136.72	133.95	131.57	129.52	127.74	126.20
15000	174.96	170.91	167.44	164.47	161.90	159.68	157.75
20000	233.29	227.87	223.25	219.29	215.87	212.90	210.33
25000	291.61	284.84	279.07	274.11	269.83	266.13	262.91
30000	349.93	341.81	334.88	328.93	323.80	319.36	315.49
31000	361.59	353.21	346.04	339.90	334.59	330.00	326.01
32000	373.26	364.60	357.21	350.86	345.39	340.65	336.53
33000	384.92	375.99	368.37	361.83	356.18	351.29	347.04
34000	396.59	387.39	379.53	372.79	366.97	361.94	357.56
35000	408.25	398.78	390.70	383.75	377.77	372.58	368.07
36000	419.91	410.17	401.86	394.72	388.56	383.23	378.59
37000	431.58	421.57	413.02	405.68	399.35	393.87	389.11
38000	443.24	432.96	424.18	416.65	410.15	404.52	399.62
39000	454.91	444.35	435.35	427.61	420.94	415.16	410.14
40000	466.57	455.75	446.51	438.58	431.73	425.81	420.66
41000	478.24	467.14	457.67	449.54	442.53	436.45	431.17
42000	489.90	478.54	468.83	460.51	453.32	447.10	441.69
43000	501.56	489.93	480.00	471.47	464.11	457.74	452.21
44000	513.23	501.32	491.16	482.43	474.91	468.39	462.72
45000	524.89	512.72	502.32	493.40	485.70	479.03	473.24
46000	536.56	524.11	513.49	504.36	496.49	489.68	483.76
47000	548.22	535.50	524.65	515.33	507.29	500.32	494.27
48000	559.89	546.90	535.81	526.29	518.08	510.97	504.79
49000	571.55	558.29	546.97	537.26	528.87	521.62	515.30
50000	583.21	569.69	558.14	548.22	539.67	532.26	525.82
51000	594.88	581.08	569.30	559.19	550.46	542.91	536.34
52000	606.54	592.47	580.46	570.15	561.25	553.55	546.85
53000	618.21	603.87	591.62	581.11	572.05	564.20	557.37
54000	629.87	615.26	602.79	592.08	582.84	574.84	567.89
55000	641.54	626.65	613.95	603.04	593.63	585.49	578.40
56000	653.20	638.05	625.11	614.01	604.43	596.13	588.92
57000	664.86	649.44	636.28	624.97	615.22	606.78	599.44
58000	676.53	660.84	647.44	635.94	626.01	617.42	609.95
59000	688.19	672.23	658.60	646.90	636.81	628.07	620.47
60000	699.86	683.62	669.76	657.86	647.60	638.71	630.99
65000	758.18	740.59	725.58	712.69	701.57	691.94	683.57
70000	816.50	797.56	781.39	767.51	755.54	745.16	736.15
75000	874.82	854.53	837.20	822.33	809.50	798.39	788.73
80000	933.14	911.50	893.02	877.15	863.47	851.62	841.31
85000	991.46	968.47	948.83	931.98	917.44	904.84	893.90
90000	1049.79	1025.43	1004.64	986.80	971.40	958.07	946.48
95000	1108.11	1082.40	1060.46	1041.62	1025.37	1011.29	999.06
100000	1166.43	1139.37	1116.27	1096.44	1079.34	1064.52	1051.64
105000	1224.75	1196.34	1172.09	1151.26	1133.30	1117.75	1104.22
110000	1283.07	1253.31	1227.90	1206.09	1187.27	1170.97	1156.81
120000	1399.71	1367.25	1339.53	1315.73	1295.20	1277.42	1261.97
130000	1516.36	1481.18	1451.15	1425.37	1403.14	1383.88	1367.14
140000	1633.00	1595.12	1562.78	1535.02	1511.07	1490.33	1472.30
150000	1749.64	1709.06	1674.41	1644.66	1619.00	1596.78	1577.46
160000	1866.29	1822.99	1786.04	1754.31	1726.94	1703.23	1682.63
170000	1982.93	1936.93	1897.66	1863.95	1834.87	1809.69	1787.79
180000	2099.57	2050.87	2009.29	1973.59	1942.81	1916.14	1892.96
190000	2216.21	2164.81	2120.92	2083.24	2050.74	2022.59	1998.12
200000	2332.86	2278.74	2232.54	2192.88	2158.67	2129.04	2103.29
210000	2449.50	2392.68	2344.17	2302.53	2266.61	2235.49	2208.45
220000	2566.14	2506.62	2455.80	2412.17	2374.54	2341.95	2313.61
230000	2682.79	2620.55	2567.43	2521.82	2482.47	2448.40	2418.78
240000	2799.43	2734.49	2679.05	2631.46	2590.41	2554.85	2523.94
250000	2916.07	2848.43	2790.68	2741.10	2698.34	2661.30	2629.11

Monthly Payments 11.75 %

LOAN AMOUNT	22	23	24	25	30	35	40
				YEARS			
100	1.04	1.03	1.02	1.01	0.99	0.97	0.97
200	2.08	2.06	2.04	2.03	1.98	1.95	1.93
500	5.20	5.15	5.11	5.07	4.94	4.87	4.83
1000	10.40	10.31	10.22	10.14	9.88	9.74	9.66
2000	20.81	20.61	20.44	20.29	19.76	19.48	19.32
5000	52.02	51.53	51.10	50.72	49.41	48.70	48.30
6000	62.42	61.84	61.32	60.87	59.29	58.44	57.96
7000	72.83	72.14	71.54	71.01	69.17	68.18	67.62
8000	83.23	82.45	81.76	81.16	79.05	77.91	77.28
9000	93.64	92.75	91.98	91.30	88.94	87.65	86.95
10000	104.04	103.06	102.20	101.44	98.82	97.39	96.61
12000	124.85	123.67	122.64	121.73	118.58	116.87	115.93
15000	156.06	154.59	153.30	152.17	148.23	146.09	144.91
20000	208.08	206.12	204.40	202.89	197.64	194.79	193.21
25000	260.10	257.65	255.50	253.61	247.04	243.48	241.51
30000	312.12	309.18	306.60	304.33	296.45	292.18	289.82
31000	322.53	319.49	316.82	314.48	306.33	301.92	299.48
32000	332.93	329.79	327.04	324.62	316.22	311.66	309.14
33000	343.34	340.10	337.26	334.77	326.10	321.40	318.80
34000	353.74	350.40	347.48	344.91	335.98	331.14	328.46
35000	364.15	360.71	357.70	355.06	345.86	340.88	338.12
36000	374.55	371.02	367.92	365.20	355.74	350.61	347.78
37000	384.95	381.32	378.14	375.34	365.63	360.35	357.44
38000	395.36	391.63	388.36	385.49	375.51	370.09	367.10
39000	405.76	401.93	398.58	395.63	385.39	379.83	376.76
40000	416.17	412.24	408.80	405.78	395.27	389.57	386.42
41000	426.57	422.55	419.02	415.92	405.15	399.31	396.08
42000	436.97	432.85	429.24	426.07	415.03	409.05	405.74
43000	447.38	443.16	439.46	436.21	424.92	418.79	415.41
44000	457.78	453.46	449.68	446.35	434.80	428.53	425.07
45000	468.19	463.77	459.90	456.50	444.68	438.27	434.73
46000	478.59	474.08	470.12	466.64	454.56	448.01	444.39
47000	488.99	484.38	480.34	476.79	464.44	457.75	454.05
48000	499.40	494.69	490.56	486.93	474.33	467.49	463.71
49000	509.80	504.99	500.78	497.08	484.21	477.23	473.37
50000	520.21	515.30	511.00	507.22	494.09	486.96	483.03
51000	530.61	525.61	521.22	517.37	503.97	496.70	492.69
52000	541.02	535.91	531.44	527.51	513.85	506.44	502.35
53000	551.42	546.22	541.66	537.65	523.73	516.18	512.01
54000	561.82	556.52	551.88	547.80	533.62	525.92	521.67
55000	572.23	566.83	562.10	557.94	543.50	535.66	531.33
56000	582.63	577.14	572.32	568.09	553.38	545.40	540.99
57000	593.04	587.44	582.54	578.23	563.26	555.14	550.65
58000	603.44	597.75	592.76	588.38	573.14	564.88	560.31
59000	613.84	608.05	602.98	598.52	583.02	574.62	569.97
60000	624.25	618.36	613.20	608.67	592.91	584.36	579.64
65000	676.27	669.89	664.30	659.39	642.32	633.05	627.94
70000	728.29	721.42	715.40	710.11	691.72	681.75	676.24
75000	780.31	772.95	766.50	760.83	741.13	730.45	724.54
80000	832.33	824.48	817.60	811.55	790.54	779.14	772.85
85000	884.35	876.01	868.70	862.28	839.95	827.84	821.15
90000	936.37	927.54	919.80	913.00	889.36	876.54	869.45
95000	988.39	979.07	970.90	963.72	938.77	925.23	917.76
100000	1040.41	1030.60	1022.00	1014.44	988.18	973.93	966.06
105000	1092.44	1082.13	1073.10	1065.17	1037.59	1022.63	1014.36
110000	1144.46	1133.66	1124.20	1115.89	1087.00	1071.32	1062.66
120000	1248.50	1236.72	1226.40	1217.33	1185.81	1168.72	1159.27
130000	1352.54	1339.78	1328.60	1318.78	1284.63	1266.11	1255.88
140000	1456.58	1442.84	1430.80	1420.22	1383.45	1363.50	1352.48
150000	1560.62	1545.90	1532.99	1521.66	1482.27	1460.89	1449.09
160000	1664.66	1648.96	1635.19	1623.11	1581.08	1558.29	1545.69
170000	1768.71	1752.02	1737.39	1724.55	1679.90	1655.68	1642.30
180000	1872.75	1855.08	1839.59	1826.00	1778.72	1753.07	1738.91
190000	1976.79	1958.14	1941.79	1927.44	1877.54	1850.47	1835.51
200000	2080.83	2061.20	2043.99	2028.89	1976.35	1947.86	1932.12
210000	2184.87	2164.26	2146.19	2130.33	2075.17	2045.25	2028.72
220000	2288.91	2267.32	2248.39	2231.77	2173.99	2142.64	2125.33
230000	2392.95	2370.38	2350.59	2333.22	2272.81	2240.04	2221.94
240000	2497.00	2473.44	2452.79	2434.66	2371.63	2337.43	2318.54
250000	2601.04	2576.50	2554.99	2536.11	2470.44	2434.82	2415.15

12.00 %   Monthly Payments

LOAN AMOUNT	YEARS 1	2	3	4	5	6	7
100	8.87	4.69	3.31	2.62	2.21	1.94	1.75
200	17.74	9.39	6.62	5.24	4.42	3.88	3.50
500	44.36	23.47	16.54	13.10	11.05	9.70	8.75
1000	88.71	46.94	33.08	26.19	22.10	19.40	17.50
2000	177.43	93.88	66.15	52.38	44.20	38.80	35.00
5000	443.57	234.69	165.38	130.96	110.49	97.00	87.49
6000	532.28	281.63	198.46	157.15	132.59	116.40	104.99
7000	620.99	328.57	231.53	183.34	154.69	135.80	122.49
8000	709.71	375.51	264.61	209.54	176.79	155.20	139.99
9000	798.42	422.45	297.69	235.73	198.89	174.60	157.48
10000	887.13	469.38	330.76	261.92	220.98	194.00	174.98
12000	1064.56	563.26	396.91	314.30	265.18	232.80	209.98
15000	1330.70	704.08	496.14	392.88	331.48	291.00	262.47
20000	1774.27	938.77	661.52	523.84	441.97	388.00	349.97
25000	2217.84	1173.46	826.91	654.80	552.46	485.00	437.46
30000	2661.40	1408.15	992.29	785.76	662.95	582.00	524.95
31000	2750.12	1455.09	1025.36	811.95	685.05	601.40	542.45
32000	2838.83	1502.03	1058.44	838.14	707.15	620.80	559.95
33000	2927.54	1548.97	1091.52	864.33	729.25	640.20	577.44
34000	3016.26	1595.91	1124.59	890.53	751.35	659.60	594.94
35000	3104.97	1642.84	1157.67	916.72	773.45	679.00	612.44
36000	3193.68	1689.78	1190.74	942.91	795.54	698.40	629.94
37000	3282.40	1736.72	1223.82	969.10	817.64	717.80	647.44
38000	3371.11	1783.66	1256.90	995.29	839.74	737.20	664.94
39000	3459.82	1830.60	1289.97	1021.49	861.84	756.60	682.43
40000	3548.54	1877.54	1323.05	1047.68	883.94	776.00	699.93
41000	3637.25	1924.48	1356.13	1073.87	906.04	795.40	717.43
42000	3725.96	1971.41	1389.20	1100.06	928.14	814.80	734.93
43000	3814.68	2018.35	1422.28	1126.25	950.23	834.20	752.43
44000	3903.39	2065.29	1455.35	1152.45	972.33	853.60	769.93
45000	3992.10	2112.23	1488.43	1178.64	994.43	873.00	787.42
46000	4080.82	2159.17	1521.51	1204.83	1016.53	892.40	804.92
47000	4169.53	2206.11	1554.58	1231.02	1038.63	911.80	822.42
48000	4258.25	2253.04	1587.66	1257.21	1060.73	931.20	839.92
49000	4346.96	2299.98	1620.74	1283.41	1082.82	950.60	857.42
50000	4435.67	2346.92	1653.81	1309.60	1104.92	970.00	874.92
51000	4524.39	2393.86	1686.89	1335.79	1127.02	989.40	892.41
52000	4613.10	2440.80	1719.96	1361.98	1149.12	1008.80	909.91
53000	4701.81	2487.74	1753.04	1388.17	1171.22	1028.20	927.41
54000	4790.53	2534.67	1786.12	1414.36	1193.32	1047.60	944.91
55000	4879.24	2581.61	1819.19	1440.56	1215.42	1067.00	962.41
56000	4967.95	2628.55	1852.27	1466.75	1237.51	1086.40	979.91
57000	5056.67	2675.49	1885.35	1492.94	1259.61	1105.80	997.40
58000	5145.38	2722.43	1918.42	1519.13	1281.71	1125.20	1014.90
59000	5234.09	2769.37	1951.50	1545.32	1303.81	1144.60	1032.40
60000	5322.81	2816.30	1984.57	1571.52	1325.91	1164.00	1049.90
65000	5766.37	3051.00	2149.96	1702.48	1436.40	1261.00	1137.39
70000	6209.94	3285.69	2315.34	1833.44	1546.89	1358.00	1224.88
75000	6653.51	3520.38	2480.72	1964.40	1657.38	1455.00	1312.37
80000	7097.08	3755.07	2646.10	2095.36	1767.88	1552.00	1399.87
85000	7540.64	3989.77	2811.48	2226.32	1878.37	1649.00	1487.36
90000	7984.21	4224.46	2976.86	2357.27	1988.86	1746.00	1574.85
95000	8427.78	4459.15	3142.24	2488.23	2099.35	1843.00	1662.34
100000	8871.34	4693.84	3307.62	2619.19	2209.85	1940.00	1749.83
105000	9314.91	4928.53	3473.00	2750.15	2320.34	2037.00	1837.32
110000	9758.48	5163.23	3638.39	2881.11	2430.83	2134.00	1924.81
120000	10645.61	5632.61	3969.15	3143.03	2651.81	2328.00	2099.80
130000	11532.75	6101.99	4299.91	3404.95	2872.80	2522.00	2274.78
140000	12419.88	6571.38	4630.67	3666.87	3093.78	2716.00	2449.76
150000	13307.02	7040.76	4961.44	3928.79	3314.77	2910.00	2624.75
160000	14194.15	7510.15	5292.20	4190.71	3535.75	3104.00	2799.73
170000	15081.28	7979.53	5622.96	4452.63	3756.74	3298.00	2974.71
180000	15968.42	8448.91	5953.72	4714.55	3977.72	3492.00	3149.70
190000	16855.55	8918.30	6284.48	4976.47	4198.71	3686.00	3324.68
200000	17742.69	9387.68	6615.25	5238.39	4419.69	3880.00	3499.66
210000	18629.82	9857.07	6946.01	5500.31	4640.68	4074.00	3674.65
220000	19516.96	10326.45	7276.77	5762.23	4861.66	4268.00	3849.63
230000	20404.09	10795.84	7607.53	6024.15	5082.65	4462.00	4024.61
240000	21291.23	11265.22	7938.30	6286.07	5303.63	4656.00	4199.60
250000	22178.36	11734.60	8269.06	6547.99	5524.61	4850.00	4374.58

Monthly Payments 12.00 %

LOAN AMOUNT	8	9	10	11	12	13	14
			YEARS				
100	1.61	1.50	1.42	1.35	1.30	1.25	1.21
200	3.22	3.00	2.84	2.70	2.59	2.50	2.43
500	8.05	7.51	7.09	6.75	6.48	6.25	6.07
1000	16.09	15.02	14.18	13.51	12.96	12.51	12.13
2000	32.19	30.04	28.36	27.01	25.92	25.02	24.26
5000	80.47	75.11	70.90	67.54	64.80	62.54	60.66
6000	96.57	90.13	85.08	81.04	77.76	75.05	72.79
7000	112.66	105.15	99.26	94.55	90.72	87.56	84.93
8000	128.75	120.17	113.44	108.06	103.68	100.07	97.06
9000	144.85	135.19	127.62	121.56	116.64	112.57	109.19
10000	160.94	150.21	141.80	135.07	129.60	125.08	121.32
12000	193.13	180.26	170.16	162.08	155.51	150.10	145.59
15000	241.41	225.32	212.70	202.61	194.39	187.62	181.98
20000	321.88	300.43	283.61	270.14	259.19	250.16	242.64
25000	402.36	375.54	354.51	337.68	323.99	312.71	303.31
30000	482.83	450.64	425.41	405.21	388.79	375.25	363.97
31000	498.92	465.67	439.59	418.72	401.75	387.76	376.10
32000	515.02	480.69	453.77	432.23	414.70	400.26	388.23
33000	531.11	495.71	467.95	445.73	427.66	412.77	400.36
34000	547.20	510.73	482.13	459.24	440.62	425.28	412.50
35000	563.30	525.75	496.31	472.75	453.58	437.79	424.63
36000	579.39	540.77	510.49	486.25	466.54	450.30	436.76
37000	595.49	555.79	524.67	499.76	479.50	462.80	448.89
38000	611.58	570.82	538.85	513.27	492.46	475.31	461.02
39000	627.67	585.84	553.03	526.78	505.42	487.82	473.16
40000	643.77	600.86	567.21	540.28	518.38	500.33	485.29
41000	659.86	615.88	581.39	553.79	531.34	512.84	497.42
42000	675.96	630.90	595.57	567.30	544.30	525.35	509.55
43000	692.05	645.92	609.75	580.80	557.26	537.85	521.69
44000	708.15	660.94	623.93	594.31	570.22	550.36	533.82
45000	724.24	675.97	638.11	607.82	583.18	562.87	545.95
46000	740.33	690.99	652.29	621.33	596.14	575.38	558.08
47000	756.43	706.01	666.47	634.83	609.10	587.89	570.21
48000	772.52	721.03	680.65	648.34	622.06	600.39	582.35
49000	788.62	736.05	694.83	661.85	635.02	612.90	594.48
50000	804.71	751.07	709.01	675.35	647.98	625.41	606.61
51000	820.81	766.10	723.19	688.86	660.94	637.92	618.74
52000	836.90	781.12	737.37	702.37	673.89	650.43	630.88
53000	852.99	796.14	751.55	715.88	686.85	662.94	643.01
54000	869.09	811.16	765.73	729.38	699.81	675.44	655.14
55000	885.18	826.18	779.91	742.89	712.77	687.95	667.27
56000	901.28	841.20	794.10	756.40	725.73	700.46	679.40
57000	917.37	856.22	808.28	769.90	738.69	712.97	691.54
58000	933.47	871.25	822.46	783.41	751.65	725.48	703.67
59000	949.56	886.27	836.64	796.92	764.61	737.99	715.80
60000	965.65	901.29	850.82	810.42	777.57	750.49	727.93
65000	1046.12	976.40	921.72	877.96	842.37	813.03	788.59
70000	1126.60	1051.50	992.62	945.50	907.17	875.58	849.26
75000	1207.07	1126.61	1063.52	1013.03	971.96	938.12	909.92
80000	1287.54	1201.72	1134.42	1080.57	1036.76	1000.66	970.58
85000	1368.01	1276.83	1205.32	1148.10	1101.56	1063.20	1031.24
90000	1448.48	1351.93	1276.22	1215.64	1166.36	1125.74	1091.90
95000	1528.95	1427.04	1347.13	1283.17	1231.15	1188.28	1152.56
100000	1609.42	1502.15	1418.03	1350.71	1295.95	1250.82	1213.22
105000	1689.89	1577.25	1488.93	1418.24	1360.75	1313.36	1273.88
110000	1770.36	1652.36	1559.83	1485.78	1425.55	1375.91	1334.54
120000	1931.31	1802.58	1701.63	1620.85	1555.14	1500.99	1455.87
130000	2092.25	1952.79	1843.43	1755.92	1684.74	1626.07	1577.19
140000	2253.19	2103.01	1985.24	1890.99	1814.33	1751.15	1698.51
150000	2414.13	2253.22	2127.04	2026.06	1943.93	1876.23	1819.83
160000	2575.08	2403.44	2268.84	2161.13	2073.52	2001.32	1941.16
170000	2736.02	2553.65	2410.65	2296.20	2203.12	2126.40	2062.48
180000	2896.96	2703.87	2552.45	2431.27	2332.71	2251.48	2183.80
190000	3057.90	2854.08	2694.25	2566.34	2462.31	2376.56	2305.12
200000	3218.85	3004.29	2836.05	2701.42	2591.90	2501.65	2426.44
210000	3379.79	3154.51	2977.86	2836.49	2721.50	2626.73	2547.77
220000	3540.73	3304.72	3119.66	2971.56	2851.09	2751.81	2669.09
230000	3701.67	3454.94	3261.46	3106.63	2980.69	2876.89	2790.41
240000	3862.61	3605.15	3403.26	3241.70	3110.28	3001.97	2911.73
250000	4023.56	3755.37	3545.07	3376.77	3239.88	3127.06	3033.06

12.00 % Monthly Payments

LOAN AMOUNT	YEARS 15	16	17	18	19	20	21
100	1.18	1.15	1.13	1.11	1.10	1.08	1.07
200	2.36	2.31	2.26	2.22	2.19	2.16	2.14
500	5.91	5.77	5.66	5.56	5.48	5.40	5.34
1000	11.82	11.55	11.32	11.12	10.96	10.81	10.68
2000	23.63	23.10	22.64	22.25	21.91	21.62	21.37
5000	59.08	57.74	56.60	55.62	54.78	54.05	53.42
6000	70.90	69.29	67.92	66.75	65.73	64.86	64.10
7000	82.71	80.84	79.24	77.87	76.69	75.67	74.78
8000	94.53	92.39	90.56	88.99	87.64	86.48	85.47
9000	106.34	103.93	101.88	100.12	98.60	97.29	96.15
10000	118.16	115.48	113.20	111.24	109.56	108.10	106.83
12000	141.79	138.58	135.84	133.49	131.47	129.72	128.20
15000	177.24	173.22	169.80	166.86	164.33	162.15	160.25
20000	236.32	230.97	226.40	222.48	219.11	216.19	213.66
25000	295.40	288.71	283.00	278.10	273.89	270.24	267.08
30000	354.48	346.45	339.60	333.73	328.67	324.29	320.50
31000	366.30	358.00	350.92	344.85	339.62	335.10	331.18
32000	378.12	369.55	362.24	355.97	350.58	345.91	341.86
33000	389.93	381.09	373.56	367.10	361.53	356.72	352.55
34000	401.75	392.64	384.88	378.22	372.49	367.53	363.23
35000	413.56	404.19	396.20	389.35	383.44	378.34	373.91
36000	425.38	415.74	407.52	400.47	394.40	389.15	384.59
37000	437.20	427.29	418.84	411.59	405.36	399.96	395.28
38000	449.01	438.83	430.16	422.72	416.31	410.77	405.96
39000	460.83	450.38	441.48	433.84	427.27	421.58	416.64
40000	472.64	461.93	452.80	444.97	438.22	432.39	427.33
41000	484.46	473.48	464.12	456.09	449.18	443.20	438.01
42000	496.28	485.03	475.44	467.22	460.13	454.01	448.69
43000	508.09	496.58	486.76	478.34	471.09	464.82	459.38
44000	519.91	508.12	498.08	489.46	482.04	475.63	470.06
45000	531.72	519.67	509.40	500.59	493.00	486.44	480.74
46000	543.54	531.22	520.72	511.71	503.96	497.25	491.43
47000	555.36	542.77	532.04	522.84	514.91	508.06	502.11
48000	567.17	554.32	543.36	533.96	525.87	518.87	512.79
49000	578.99	565.87	554.68	545.09	536.82	529.68	523.48
50000	590.80	577.41	566.00	556.21	547.78	540.49	534.16
51000	602.62	588.96	577.32	567.33	558.73	551.30	544.84
52000	614.44	600.51	588.64	578.46	569.69	562.11	555.53
53000	626.25	612.06	599.96	589.58	580.65	572.92	566.21
54000	638.07	623.61	611.28	600.71	591.60	583.73	576.89
55000	649.89	635.16	622.60	611.83	602.56	594.54	587.58
56000	661.70	646.70	633.92	622.95	613.51	605.35	598.26
57000	673.52	658.25	645.24	634.08	624.47	616.16	608.94
58000	685.33	669.80	656.56	645.20	635.42	626.96	619.62
59000	697.15	681.35	667.88	656.33	646.38	637.77	630.31
60000	708.97	692.90	679.20	667.45	657.33	648.58	640.99
65000	768.05	750.64	735.80	723.07	712.11	702.63	694.41
70000	827.13	808.38	792.40	778.69	766.89	756.68	747.82
75000	886.21	866.12	849.00	834.31	821.67	810.73	801.24
80000	945.29	923.86	905.60	889.93	876.45	864.78	854.65
85000	1004.37	981.60	962.20	945.56	931.22	918.83	908.07
90000	1063.45	1039.35	1018.80	1001.18	986.00	972.88	961.49
95000	1122.53	1097.09	1075.39	1056.80	1040.78	1026.93	1014.90
100000	1181.61	1154.83	1131.99	1112.42	1095.56	1080.97	1068.32
105000	1240.69	1212.57	1188.59	1168.04	1150.33	1135.02	1121.73
110000	1299.77	1270.31	1245.19	1223.66	1205.11	1189.07	1175.15
120000	1417.93	1385.79	1358.39	1334.90	1314.67	1297.17	1281.98
130000	1536.09	1501.28	1471.59	1446.14	1424.22	1405.27	1388.81
140000	1654.25	1616.76	1584.79	1557.39	1533.78	1513.36	1495.65
150000	1772.41	1732.24	1697.99	1668.63	1643.34	1621.46	1602.48
160000	1890.58	1847.73	1811.19	1779.87	1752.89	1729.56	1709.31
170000	2008.74	1963.21	1924.39	1891.11	1862.45	1837.66	1816.14
180000	2126.90	2078.69	2037.59	2002.35	1972.00	1945.75	1922.97
190000	2245.06	2194.17	2150.79	2113.60	2081.56	2053.85	2029.80
200000	2363.22	2309.66	2263.99	2224.84	2191.11	2161.95	2136.64
210000	2481.38	2425.14	2377.19	2336.08	2300.67	2270.05	2243.47
220000	2599.54	2540.62	2490.39	2447.32	2410.22	2378.14	2350.30
230000	2717.70	2656.11	2603.59	2558.56	2519.78	2486.24	2457.13
240000	2835.86	2771.59	2716.79	2669.80	2629.34	2594.34	2563.96
250000	2954.02	2887.07	2829.99	2781.05	2738.89	2702.44	2670.80

Monthly Payments 12.00 %

LOAN AMOUNT	22	23	24	25	30	35	40
			YEARS				
100	1.06	1.05	1.04	1.03	1.01	0.99	0.99
200	2.11	2.10	2.08	2.06	2.01	1.99	1.97
500	5.29	5.24	5.20	5.16	5.03	4.96	4.93
1000	10.57	10.48	10.39	10.32	10.06	9.93	9.85
2000	21.15	20.95	20.79	20.64	20.13	19.85	19.70
5000	52.87	52.38	51.96	51.59	50.32	49.63	49.26
6000	63.44	62.86	62.36	61.91	60.38	59.56	59.11
7000	74.01	73.34	72.75	72.23	70.45	69.49	68.96
8000	84.58	83.81	83.14	82.55	80.51	79.41	78.82
9000	95.16	94.29	93.53	92.87	90.57	89.34	88.67
10000	105.73	104.77	103.93	103.19	100.64	99.27	98.52
12000	126.88	125.72	124.71	123.83	120.77	119.12	118.22
15000	158.60	157.15	155.89	154.78	150.96	148.90	147.78
20000	211.46	209.54	207.85	206.38	201.28	198.54	197.04
25000	264.33	261.92	259.82	257.97	251.60	248.17	246.30
30000	317.19	314.31	311.78	309.57	301.92	297.80	295.56
31000	327.76	324.78	322.17	319.89	311.98	307.73	305.41
32000	338.34	335.26	332.57	330.21	322.04	317.66	315.26
33000	348.91	345.74	342.96	340.53	332.11	327.59	325.11
34000	359.48	356.21	353.35	350.85	342.17	337.51	334.97
35000	370.06	366.69	363.75	361.16	352.24	347.44	344.82
36000	380.63	377.17	374.14	371.48	362.30	357.37	354.67
37000	391.20	387.64	384.53	381.80	372.36	367.29	364.52
38000	401.77	398.12	394.92	392.12	382.43	377.22	374.37
39000	412.35	408.60	405.32	402.44	392.49	387.15	384.22
40000	422.92	419.07	415.71	412.76	402.55	397.07	394.08
41000	433.49	429.55	426.10	423.08	412.62	407.00	403.93
42000	444.07	440.03	436.49	433.40	422.68	416.93	413.78
43000	454.64	450.50	446.89	443.72	432.75	426.85	423.63
44000	465.21	460.98	457.28	454.04	442.81	436.78	433.48
45000	475.79	471.46	467.67	464.35	452.87	446.71	443.34
46000	486.36	481.94	478.07	474.67	462.94	456.63	453.19
47000	496.93	492.41	488.46	484.99	473.00	466.56	463.04
48000	507.50	502.89	498.85	495.31	483.07	476.49	472.89
49000	518.08	513.37	509.24	505.63	493.13	486.41	482.74
50000	528.65	523.84	519.64	515.95	503.19	496.34	492.60
51000	539.22	534.32	530.03	526.27	513.26	506.27	502.45
52000	549.80	544.80	540.42	536.59	523.32	516.20	512.30
53000	560.37	555.27	550.81	546.91	533.39	526.12	522.15
54000	570.94	565.75	561.21	557.23	543.45	536.05	532.00
55000	581.52	576.23	571.60	567.54	553.51	545.98	541.86
56000	592.09	586.70	581.99	577.86	563.58	555.90	551.71
57000	602.66	597.18	592.39	588.18	573.64	565.83	561.56
58000	613.23	607.66	602.78	598.50	583.70	575.76	571.41
59000	623.81	618.13	613.17	608.82	593.77	585.68	581.26
60000	634.38	628.61	623.56	619.14	603.83	595.61	591.11
65000	687.25	681.00	675.53	670.73	654.15	645.24	640.37
70000	740.11	733.38	727.49	722.33	704.47	694.88	689.63
75000	792.98	785.76	779.46	773.92	754.79	744.51	738.89
80000	845.84	838.15	831.42	825.52	805.11	794.15	788.15
85000	898.71	890.53	883.38	877.11	855.43	843.78	837.41
90000	951.57	942.92	935.35	928.71	905.75	893.41	886.67
95000	1004.44	995.30	987.31	980.30	956.07	943.05	935.93
100000	1057.30	1047.69	1039.27	1031.90	1006.39	992.68	985.19
105000	1110.17	1100.07	1091.24	1083.49	1056.71	1042.32	1034.45
110000	1163.03	1152.45	1143.20	1135.09	1107.03	1091.95	1083.71
120000	1268.76	1257.22	1247.13	1238.28	1207.66	1191.22	1182.23
130000	1374.49	1361.99	1351.06	1341.47	1308.30	1290.49	1280.75
140000	1480.22	1466.76	1454.98	1444.66	1408.94	1389.76	1379.27
150000	1585.95	1571.53	1558.91	1547.85	1509.58	1489.02	1477.79
160000	1691.68	1676.30	1662.84	1651.04	1610.22	1588.29	1576.31
170000	1797.41	1781.07	1766.76	1754.23	1710.86	1687.56	1674.83
180000	1903.14	1885.83	1870.69	1857.42	1811.50	1786.83	1773.34
190000	2008.87	1990.60	1974.62	1960.61	1912.14	1886.10	1871.86
200000	2114.60	2095.37	2078.55	2063.80	2012.77	1985.37	1970.38
210000	2220.33	2200.14	2182.47	2166.99	2113.41	2084.63	2068.90
220000	2326.06	2304.91	2286.40	2270.18	2214.05	2183.90	2167.42
230000	2431.79	2409.68	2390.33	2373.37	2314.69	2283.17	2265.94
240000	2537.52	2514.45	2494.26	2476.56	2415.33	2382.44	2364.46
250000	2643.25	2619.21	2598.18	2579.75	2515.97	2481.71	2462.98

12.25 % Monthly Payments

LOAN AMOUNT	1	2	3	4	5	6	7
100	8.88	4.70	3.32	2.63	2.22	1.95	1.76
200	17.76	9.41	6.64	5.26	4.44	3.90	3.53
500	44.41	23.52	16.59	13.15	11.11	9.76	8.81
1000	88.82	47.05	33.19	26.31	22.22	19.52	17.63
2000	177.65	94.10	66.38	52.62	44.44	39.05	35.25
5000	444.12	235.25	165.95	131.54	111.09	97.62	88.13
6000	532.95	282.30	199.14	157.85	133.31	117.14	105.75
7000	621.77	329.35	232.33	184.16	155.53	136.66	123.38
8000	710.60	376.40	265.52	210.47	177.75	156.19	141.00
9000	799.42	423.45	298.71	236.78	199.97	175.71	158.63
10000	888.25	470.49	331.90	263.09	222.18	195.23	176.25
12000	1065.90	564.59	398.28	315.70	266.62	234.28	211.50
15000	1332.37	705.74	497.85	394.63	333.28	292.85	264.38
20000	1776.49	940.99	663.80	526.17	444.37	390.47	352.50
25000	2220.62	1176.24	829.74	657.71	555.46	488.09	440.63
30000	2664.74	1411.48	995.69	789.26	666.55	585.70	528.76
31000	2753.57	1458.53	1028.88	815.57	688.77	605.23	546.38
32000	2842.39	1505.58	1062.07	841.88	710.99	624.75	564.01
33000	2931.22	1552.63	1095.26	868.18	733.21	644.27	581.63
34000	3020.04	1599.68	1128.45	894.49	755.43	663.80	599.26
35000	3108.87	1646.73	1161.64	920.80	777.65	683.32	616.88
36000	3197.69	1693.78	1194.83	947.11	799.87	702.84	634.51
37000	3286.52	1740.83	1228.02	973.42	822.08	722.37	652.13
38000	3375.34	1787.88	1261.21	999.73	844.30	741.89	669.76
39000	3464.16	1834.93	1294.40	1026.04	866.52	761.42	687.38
40000	3552.99	1881.98	1327.59	1052.34	888.74	780.94	705.01
41000	3641.81	1929.03	1360.78	1078.65	910.96	800.46	722.64
42000	3730.64	1976.08	1393.97	1104.96	933.18	819.99	740.26
43000	3819.46	2023.13	1427.16	1131.27	955.39	839.51	757.89
44000	3908.29	2070.18	1460.35	1157.58	977.61	859.03	775.51
45000	3997.11	2117.23	1493.54	1183.89	999.83	878.56	793.14
46000	4085.94	2164.28	1526.73	1210.20	1022.05	898.08	810.76
47000	4174.76	2211.32	1559.92	1236.50	1044.27	917.60	828.39
48000	4263.59	2258.37	1593.11	1262.81	1066.49	937.13	846.01
49000	4352.41	2305.42	1626.30	1289.12	1088.71	956.65	863.64
50000	4441.24	2352.47	1659.49	1315.43	1110.92	976.17	881.26
51000	4530.06	2399.52	1692.68	1341.74	1133.14	995.70	898.89
52000	4618.89	2446.57	1725.87	1368.05	1155.36	1015.22	916.51
53000	4707.71	2493.62	1759.06	1394.36	1177.58	1034.74	934.14
54000	4796.54	2540.67	1792.25	1420.66	1199.80	1054.27	951.76
55000	4885.36	2587.72	1825.44	1446.97	1222.02	1073.79	969.39
56000	4974.19	2634.77	1858.63	1473.28	1244.23	1093.31	987.01
57000	5063.01	2681.82	1891.82	1499.59	1266.45	1112.84	1004.64
58000	5151.83	2728.87	1925.01	1525.90	1288.67	1132.36	1022.26
59000	5240.66	2775.92	1958.20	1552.21	1310.89	1151.88	1039.89
60000	5329.48	2822.97	1991.39	1578.52	1333.11	1171.41	1057.51
65000	5773.61	3058.22	2157.33	1710.06	1444.20	1269.03	1145.64
70000	6217.73	3293.46	2323.28	1841.60	1555.29	1366.64	1233.77
75000	6661.86	3528.71	2489.23	1973.14	1666.39	1464.26	1321.89
80000	7105.98	3763.96	2655.18	2104.69	1777.48	1561.88	1410.02
85000	7550.10	3999.20	2821.13	2236.23	1888.57	1659.49	1498.15
90000	7994.23	4234.45	2987.08	2367.77	1999.66	1757.11	1586.27
95000	8438.35	4469.70	3153.03	2499.32	2110.76	1854.73	1674.40
100000	8882.47	4704.95	3318.98	2630.86	2221.85	1952.35	1762.52
105000	9326.60	4940.19	3484.92	2762.40	2332.94	2049.96	1850.65
110000	9770.72	5175.44	3650.87	2893.95	2444.03	2147.58	1938.78
120000	10658.97	5645.94	3982.77	3157.03	2666.22	2342.82	2115.03
130000	11547.22	6116.43	4314.67	3420.12	2888.40	2538.05	2291.28
140000	12435.46	6586.93	4646.57	3683.20	3110.59	2733.29	2467.53
150000	13323.71	7057.42	4978.46	3946.29	3332.77	2928.52	2643.79
160000	14211.96	7527.91	5310.36	4209.38	3554.96	3123.75	2820.04
170000	15100.21	7998.41	5642.26	4472.46	3777.14	3318.99	2996.29
180000	15988.45	8468.90	5974.16	4735.55	3999.33	3514.22	3172.54
190000	16876.70	8939.40	6306.05	4998.63	4221.51	3709.46	3348.80
200000	17764.95	9409.89	6637.95	5261.72	4443.70	3904.69	3525.05
210000	18653.20	9880.39	6969.85	5524.81	4665.88	4099.93	3701.30
220000	19541.44	10350.88	7301.75	5787.89	4888.06	4295.16	3877.55
230000	20429.69	10821.38	7633.64	6050.98	5110.25	4490.40	4053.81
240000	21317.94	11291.87	7965.54	6314.06	5332.43	4685.63	4230.06
250000	22206.18	11762.37	8297.44	6577.15	5554.62	4880.87	4406.31

Monthly Payments 12.25 %

LOAN AMOUNT	YEARS 8	9	10	11	12	13	14
100	1.62	1.52	1.43	1.36	1.31	1.27	1.23
200	3.24	3.03	2.86	2.73	2.62	2.53	2.46
500	8.11	7.58	7.16	6.82	6.55	6.33	6.14
1000	16.22	15.16	14.32	13.65	13.10	12.65	12.28
2000	32.45	30.31	28.63	27.29	26.21	25.31	24.56
5000	81.12	75.78	71.59	68.24	65.52	63.27	61.41
6000	97.35	90.93	85.90	81.88	78.62	75.93	73.69
7000	113.57	106.09	100.22	95.53	91.72	88.58	85.97
8000	129.80	121.24	114.54	109.18	104.82	101.24	98.25
9000	146.02	136.40	128.86	122.83	117.93	113.89	110.54
10000	162.25	151.55	143.17	136.47	131.03	126.55	122.82
12000	194.70	181.86	171.81	163.77	157.24	151.86	147.38
15000	243.37	227.33	214.76	204.71	196.55	189.82	184.23
20000	324.49	303.11	286.35	272.95	262.06	253.10	245.64
25000	405.62	378.88	357.93	341.19	327.58	316.37	307.05
30000	486.74	454.66	429.52	409.42	393.09	379.65	368.46
31000	502.96	469.81	443.84	423.07	406.20	392.30	380.74
32000	519.19	484.97	458.16	436.72	419.30	404.96	393.02
33000	535.41	500.12	472.47	450.37	432.40	417.61	405.30
34000	551.64	515.28	486.79	464.01	445.50	430.27	417.58
35000	567.86	530.43	501.11	477.66	458.61	442.92	429.87
36000	584.09	545.59	515.43	491.31	471.71	455.58	442.15
37000	600.31	560.74	529.74	504.96	484.81	468.23	454.43
38000	616.54	575.90	544.06	518.60	497.92	480.89	466.71
39000	632.76	591.05	558.38	532.25	511.02	493.54	478.99
40000	648.98	606.21	572.70	545.90	524.12	506.20	491.27
41000	665.21	621.37	587.01	559.55	537.23	518.85	503.56
42000	681.43	636.52	601.33	573.19	550.33	531.51	515.84
43000	697.66	651.68	615.65	586.84	563.43	544.16	528.12
44000	713.88	666.83	629.97	600.49	576.54	556.81	540.40
45000	730.11	681.99	644.28	614.14	589.64	569.47	552.68
46000	746.33	697.14	658.60	627.78	602.74	582.12	564.97
47000	762.56	712.30	672.92	641.43	615.84	594.78	577.25
48000	778.78	727.45	687.23	655.08	628.95	607.43	589.53
49000	795.01	742.61	701.55	668.73	642.05	620.09	601.81
50000	811.23	757.76	715.87	682.37	655.15	632.74	614.09
51000	827.45	772.92	730.19	696.02	668.26	645.40	626.38
52000	843.68	788.07	744.50	709.67	681.36	658.05	638.66
53000	859.90	803.23	758.82	723.32	694.46	670.71	650.94
54000	876.13	818.38	773.14	736.96	707.57	683.36	663.22
55000	892.35	833.54	787.46	750.61	720.67	696.02	675.50
56000	908.58	848.69	801.77	764.26	733.77	708.67	687.78
57000	924.80	863.85	816.09	777.91	746.88	721.33	700.07
58000	941.03	879.00	830.41	791.55	759.98	733.98	712.35
59000	957.25	894.16	844.73	805.20	773.08	746.64	724.63
60000	973.48	909.32	859.04	818.85	786.18	759.29	736.91
65000	1054.60	985.09	930.63	887.09	851.70	822.57	798.32
70000	1135.72	1060.87	1002.22	955.32	917.22	885.84	859.73
75000	1216.85	1136.64	1073.80	1023.56	982.73	949.12	921.14
80000	1297.97	1212.42	1145.39	1091.80	1048.25	1012.39	982.55
85000	1379.09	1288.20	1216.98	1160.03	1113.76	1075.66	1043.96
90000	1460.21	1363.97	1288.57	1228.27	1179.28	1138.94	1105.37
95000	1541.34	1439.75	1360.15	1296.51	1244.79	1202.21	1166.78
100000	1622.46	1515.53	1431.74	1364.75	1310.31	1265.49	1228.19
105000	1703.58	1591.30	1503.33	1432.98	1375.82	1328.76	1289.60
110000	1784.71	1667.08	1574.91	1501.22	1441.34	1392.04	1351.01
120000	1946.95	1818.63	1718.09	1637.70	1572.37	1518.59	1473.82
130000	2109.20	1970.18	1861.26	1774.17	1703.40	1645.13	1596.64
140000	2271.44	2121.74	2004.43	1910.64	1834.43	1771.68	1719.46
150000	2433.69	2273.29	2147.61	2047.12	1965.46	1898.23	1842.28
160000	2595.94	2424.84	2290.78	2183.59	2096.49	2024.78	1965.10
170000	2758.18	2576.39	2433.96	2320.07	2227.52	2151.33	2087.92
180000	2920.43	2727.95	2577.13	2456.54	2358.55	2277.88	2210.74
190000	3082.68	2879.50	2720.30	2593.02	2489.59	2404.43	2333.55
200000	3244.92	3031.05	2863.48	2729.49	2620.62	2530.98	2456.37
210000	3407.17	3182.60	3006.65	2865.97	2751.65	2657.53	2579.19
220000	3569.41	3334.16	3149.83	3002.44	2882.68	2784.07	2702.01
230000	3731.66	3485.71	3293.00	3138.92	3013.71	2910.62	2824.83
240000	3893.91	3637.26	3436.17	3275.39	3144.74	3037.17	2947.65
250000	4056.15	3788.81	3579.35	3411.87	3275.77	3163.72	3070.47

12.25 % Monthly Payments

LOAN AMOUNT	15	16	17	18	19	20	21
				YEARS			
100	1.20	1.17	1.15	1.13	1.11	1.10	1.09
200	2.39	2.34	2.30	2.26	2.22	2.20	2.17
500	5.98	5.85	5.74	5.64	5.56	5.49	5.43
1000	11.97	11.70	11.48	11.28	11.12	10.98	10.85
2000	23.94	23.41	22.96	22.57	22.24	21.95	21.70
5000	59.84	58.52	57.39	56.42	55.59	54.88	54.25
6000	71.81	70.22	68.87	67.71	66.71	65.85	65.10
7000	83.78	81.93	80.35	78.99	77.83	76.83	75.95
8000	95.75	93.63	91.82	90.28	88.95	87.80	86.81
9000	107.72	105.33	103.30	101.56	100.07	98.78	97.66
10000	119.69	117.04	114.78	112.85	111.19	109.75	108.51
12000	143.62	140.44	137.74	135.42	133.42	131.70	130.21
15000	179.53	175.55	172.17	169.27	166.78	164.63	162.76
20000	239.37	234.07	229.56	225.69	222.37	219.50	217.01
25000	299.22	292.59	286.95	282.12	277.96	274.38	271.27
30000	359.06	351.11	344.34	338.54	333.56	329.25	325.52
31000	371.03	362.81	355.82	349.83	344.67	340.23	336.37
32000	383.00	374.51	367.29	361.11	355.79	351.20	347.22
33000	394.96	386.22	378.77	372.40	366.91	362.18	358.07
34000	406.93	397.92	390.25	383.68	378.03	373.15	368.92
35000	418.90	409.63	401.73	394.96	389.15	384.13	379.77
36000	430.87	421.33	413.21	406.25	400.27	395.10	390.63
37000	442.84	433.03	424.68	417.53	411.39	406.08	401.48
38000	454.81	444.74	436.16	428.82	422.50	417.05	412.33
39000	466.78	456.44	447.64	440.10	433.62	428.03	423.18
40000	478.74	468.14	459.12	451.39	444.74	439.00	434.03
41000	490.71	479.85	470.59	462.67	455.86	449.98	444.88
42000	502.68	491.55	482.07	473.96	466.98	460.95	455.73
43000	514.65	503.25	493.55	485.24	478.10	471.93	466.58
44000	526.62	514.96	505.03	496.53	489.22	482.90	477.43
45000	538.59	526.66	516.51	507.81	500.33	493.88	488.28
46000	550.56	538.37	527.98	519.10	511.45	504.85	499.13
47000	562.53	550.07	539.46	530.38	522.57	515.83	509.98
48000	574.49	561.77	550.94	541.67	533.69	526.80	520.83
49000	586.46	573.48	562.42	552.95	544.81	537.78	531.68
50000	598.43	585.18	573.90	564.24	555.93	548.75	542.53
51000	610.40	596.88	585.37	575.52	567.05	559.73	553.39
52000	622.37	608.59	596.85	586.81	578.16	570.70	564.24
53000	634.34	620.29	608.33	598.09	589.28	581.68	575.09
54000	646.31	631.99	619.81	609.37	600.40	592.65	585.94
55000	658.27	643.70	631.29	620.66	611.52	603.63	596.79
56000	670.24	655.40	642.76	631.94	622.64	614.60	607.64
57000	682.21	667.10	654.24	643.23	633.76	625.58	618.49
58000	694.18	678.81	665.72	654.51	644.88	636.55	629.34
59000	706.15	690.51	677.20	665.80	655.99	647.53	640.19
60000	718.12	702.22	688.68	677.08	667.11	658.50	651.04
65000	777.96	760.73	746.06	733.51	722.70	713.38	705.30
70000	837.80	819.25	803.45	789.93	778.30	768.25	759.55
75000	897.65	877.77	860.84	846.35	833.89	823.13	813.80
80000	957.49	936.29	918.23	902.78	889.48	878.00	868.06
85000	1017.33	994.81	975.62	959.20	945.08	932.88	922.31
90000	1077.18	1053.32	1033.01	1015.62	1000.67	987.75	976.56
95000	1137.02	1111.84	1090.40	1072.05	1056.26	1042.63	1030.82
100000	1196.86	1170.36	1147.79	1128.47	1111.85	1097.50	1085.07
105000	1256.71	1228.88	1205.18	1184.89	1167.45	1152.38	1139.32
110000	1316.55	1287.40	1262.57	1241.32	1223.04	1207.25	1193.58
120000	1436.23	1404.43	1377.35	1354.17	1334.22	1317.00	1302.08
130000	1555.92	1521.47	1492.13	1467.01	1445.41	1426.76	1410.59
140000	1675.61	1638.50	1606.91	1579.86	1556.60	1536.51	1519.10
150000	1795.29	1755.54	1721.69	1692.71	1667.78	1646.26	1627.60
160000	1914.98	1872.57	1836.47	1805.55	1778.97	1756.01	1736.11
170000	2034.67	1989.61	1951.25	1918.40	1890.15	1865.76	1844.62
180000	2154.35	2106.65	2066.03	2031.25	2001.34	1975.51	1953.13
190000	2274.04	2223.68	2180.80	2144.10	2112.52	2085.26	2061.63
200000	2393.72	2340.72	2295.58	2256.94	2223.71	2195.01	2170.14
210000	2513.41	2457.75	2410.36	2369.79	2334.89	2304.76	2278.65
220000	2633.10	2574.79	2525.14	2482.64	2446.08	2414.51	2387.15
230000	2752.78	2691.83	2639.92	2595.48	2557.26	2524.26	2495.66
240000	2872.47	2808.86	2754.70	2708.33	2668.45	2634.01	2604.17
250000	2992.16	2925.90	2869.48	2821.18	2779.63	2743.76	2712.67

Monthly Payments 12.25 %

LOAN AMOUNT	22	23	24	25	30	35	40
				YEARS			
100	1.07	1.06	1.06	1.05	1.02	1.01	1.00
200	2.15	2.13	2.11	2.10	2.05	2.02	2.01
500	5.37	5.32	5.28	5.25	5.12	5.06	5.02
1000	10.74	10.65	10.57	10.49	10.25	10.11	10.04
2000	21.49	21.30	21.13	20.99	20.49	20.23	20.09
5000	53.71	53.24	52.83	52.47	51.23	50.57	50.22
6000	64.46	63.89	63.40	62.97	61.48	60.69	60.26
7000	75.20	74.54	73.96	73.46	71.73	70.80	70.30
8000	85.94	85.19	84.53	83.95	81.97	80.92	80.35
9000	96.68	95.84	95.10	94.45	92.22	91.03	90.39
10000	107.43	106.48	105.66	104.94	102.47	101.15	100.44
12000	128.91	127.78	126.79	125.93	122.96	121.38	120.52
15000	161.14	159.73	158.49	157.41	153.70	151.72	150.65
20000	214.85	212.97	211.32	209.89	204.93	202.30	200.87
25000	268.57	266.21	264.16	262.36	256.16	252.87	251.09
30000	322.28	319.45	316.99	314.83	307.40	303.44	301.31
31000	333.02	330.10	327.55	325.32	317.64	313.56	311.35
32000	343.76	340.75	338.12	335.82	327.89	323.67	321.39
33000	354.51	351.40	348.69	346.31	338.14	333.79	331.44
34000	365.25	362.05	359.25	356.81	348.38	343.90	341.48
35000	375.99	372.70	369.82	367.30	358.63	354.02	351.52
36000	386.73	383.34	380.38	377.79	368.88	364.13	361.57
37000	397.48	393.99	390.95	388.29	379.12	374.25	371.61
38000	408.22	404.64	401.52	398.78	389.37	384.36	381.65
39000	418.96	415.29	412.08	409.28	399.62	394.48	391.70
40000	429.71	425.94	422.65	419.77	409.86	404.59	401.74
41000	440.45	436.59	433.22	430.27	420.11	414.71	411.79
42000	451.19	447.24	443.78	440.76	430.36	424.82	421.83
43000	461.93	457.88	454.35	451.25	440.60	434.94	431.87
44000	472.68	468.53	464.91	461.75	450.85	445.05	441.92
45000	483.42	479.18	475.48	472.24	461.10	455.17	451.96
46000	494.16	489.83	486.05	482.74	471.34	465.28	462.00
47000	504.90	500.48	496.61	493.23	481.59	475.40	472.05
48000	515.65	511.13	507.18	503.72	491.84	485.51	482.09
49000	526.39	521.77	517.75	514.22	502.08	495.63	492.13
50000	537.13	532.42	528.31	524.71	512.33	505.74	502.18
51000	547.87	543.07	538.88	535.21	522.57	515.86	512.22
52000	558.62	553.72	549.44	545.70	532.82	525.97	522.26
53000	569.36	564.37	560.01	556.20	543.07	536.09	532.31
54000	580.10	575.02	570.58	566.69	553.31	546.20	542.35
55000	590.84	585.67	581.14	577.18	563.56	556.31	552.40
56000	601.59	596.31	591.71	587.68	573.81	566.43	562.44
57000	612.33	606.96	602.28	598.17	584.05	576.54	572.48
58000	623.07	617.61	612.84	608.67	594.30	586.66	582.53
59000	633.82	628.26	623.41	619.16	604.55	596.77	592.57
60000	644.56	638.91	633.97	629.66	614.79	606.89	602.61
65000	698.27	692.15	686.80	682.13	666.03	657.46	652.83
70000	751.98	745.39	739.64	734.60	717.26	708.04	703.05
75000	805.70	798.63	792.47	787.07	768.49	758.61	753.27
80000	859.41	851.88	845.30	839.54	819.73	809.19	803.48
85000	913.12	905.12	898.13	892.01	870.96	859.76	853.70
90000	966.84	958.36	950.96	944.48	922.19	910.33	903.92
95000	1020.55	1011.60	1003.79	996.96	973.42	960.91	954.14
100000	1074.26	1064.85	1056.62	1049.43	1024.66	1011.48	1004.35
105000	1127.98	1118.09	1109.45	1101.90	1075.89	1062.06	1054.57
110000	1181.69	1171.33	1162.29	1154.37	1127.12	1112.63	1104.79
120000	1289.12	1277.82	1267.95	1259.31	1229.59	1213.78	1205.23
130000	1396.54	1384.30	1373.61	1364.26	1332.05	1314.93	1305.66
140000	1503.97	1490.79	1479.27	1469.20	1434.52	1416.07	1406.10
150000	1611.39	1597.27	1584.93	1574.14	1536.99	1517.22	1506.53
160000	1718.82	1703.75	1690.60	1679.08	1639.45	1618.37	1606.97
170000	1826.25	1810.24	1796.26	1784.03	1741.92	1719.52	1707.40
180000	1933.67	1916.72	1901.92	1888.97	1844.38	1820.67	1807.84
190000	2041.10	2023.21	2007.58	1993.91	1946.85	1921.81	1908.27
200000	2148.53	2129.69	2113.25	2098.85	2049.31	2022.96	2008.71
210000	2255.95	2236.18	2218.91	2203.80	2151.78	2124.11	2109.14
220000	2363.38	2342.66	2324.57	2308.74	2254.24	2225.26	2209.58
230000	2470.80	2449.15	2430.23	2413.68	2356.71	2326.41	2310.02
240000	2578.23	2555.63	2535.90	2518.62	2459.18	2427.56	2410.45
250000	2685.66	2662.12	2641.56	2623.57	2561.64	2528.70	2510.89

12.50 % Monthly Payments

LOAN AMOUNT	YEARS 1	2	3	4	5	6	7
100	8.89	4.72	3.33	2.64	2.23	1.96	1.78
200	17.79	9.43	6.66	5.29	4.47	3.93	3.55
500	44.47	23.58	16.65	13.21	11.17	9.82	8.88
1000	88.94	47.16	33.30	26.43	22.34	19.65	17.75
2000	177.87	94.32	66.61	52.85	44.68	39.29	35.51
5000	444.68	235.80	166.52	132.13	111.69	98.24	88.76
6000	533.62	282.96	199.82	158.55	134.03	117.88	106.52
7000	622.55	330.12	233.12	184.98	156.37	137.53	124.27
8000	711.49	377.28	266.43	211.40	178.71	157.18	142.02
9000	800.42	424.45	299.73	237.83	201.05	176.83	159.77
10000	889.36	471.61	333.03	264.25	223.39	196.47	177.53
12000	1067.23	565.93	399.64	317.11	268.06	235.77	213.03
15000	1334.04	707.41	499.55	396.38	335.08	294.71	266.29
20000	1778.72	943.21	666.07	528.51	446.77	392.95	355.05
25000	2223.40	1179.01	832.59	660.64	558.47	491.18	443.81
30000	2668.08	1414.82	999.10	792.76	670.16	589.42	532.58
31000	2757.02	1461.98	1032.41	819.19	692.50	609.06	550.33
32000	2845.95	1509.14	1065.71	845.61	714.84	628.71	568.08
33000	2934.89	1556.30	1099.01	872.04	737.18	648.36	585.83
34000	3023.82	1603.46	1132.32	898.47	759.52	668.01	603.59
35000	3112.76	1650.62	1165.62	924.89	781.86	687.65	621.34
36000	3201.70	1697.78	1198.92	951.32	804.19	707.30	639.09
37000	3290.63	1744.94	1232.23	977.74	826.53	726.95	656.84
38000	3379.57	1792.10	1265.53	1004.17	848.87	746.60	674.60
39000	3468.50	1839.26	1298.83	1030.59	871.21	766.24	692.35
40000	3557.44	1886.42	1332.14	1057.02	893.55	785.89	710.10
41000	3646.38	1933.58	1365.44	1083.44	915.89	805.54	727.86
42000	3735.31	1980.74	1398.74	1109.87	938.23	825.18	745.61
43000	3824.25	2027.90	1432.05	1136.29	960.57	844.83	763.36
44000	3913.18	2075.06	1465.35	1162.72	982.90	864.48	781.11
45000	4002.12	2122.23	1498.65	1189.14	1005.24	884.13	798.87
46000	4091.06	2169.39	1531.96	1215.57	1027.58	903.77	816.62
47000	4179.99	2216.55	1565.26	1242.00	1049.92	923.42	834.37
48000	4268.93	2263.71	1598.56	1268.42	1072.26	943.07	852.12
49000	4357.86	2310.87	1631.87	1294.85	1094.60	962.72	869.88
50000	4446.80	2358.03	1665.17	1321.27	1116.94	982.36	887.63
51000	4535.74	2405.19	1698.47	1347.70	1139.28	1002.01	905.38
52000	4624.67	2452.35	1731.78	1374.12	1161.61	1021.66	923.13
53000	4713.61	2499.51	1765.08	1400.55	1183.95	1041.30	940.89
54000	4802.54	2546.67	1798.38	1426.97	1206.29	1060.95	958.64
55000	4891.48	2593.83	1831.69	1453.40	1228.63	1080.60	976.39
56000	4980.42	2640.99	1864.99	1479.82	1250.97	1100.25	994.14
57000	5069.35	2688.15	1898.29	1506.25	1273.31	1119.89	1011.90
58000	5158.29	2735.31	1931.60	1532.68	1295.65	1139.54	1029.65
59000	5247.22	2782.47	1964.90	1559.10	1317.99	1159.19	1047.40
60000	5336.16	2829.63	1998.20	1585.53	1340.32	1178.84	1065.15
65000	5780.84	3065.44	2164.72	1717.65	1452.02	1277.07	1153.92
70000	6225.52	3301.24	2331.24	1849.78	1563.71	1375.31	1242.68
75000	6670.20	3537.04	2497.76	1981.91	1675.41	1473.54	1331.44
80000	7114.88	3772.84	2664.27	2114.04	1787.10	1571.78	1420.21
85000	7559.56	4008.65	2830.79	2246.16	1898.79	1670.02	1508.97
90000	8004.24	4244.45	2997.31	2378.29	2010.49	1768.25	1597.73
95000	8448.92	4480.25	3163.82	2510.42	2122.18	1866.49	1686.49
100000	8893.60	4716.06	3330.34	2642.54	2233.87	1964.73	1775.26
105000	9338.28	4951.86	3496.86	2774.67	2345.57	2062.96	1864.02
110000	9782.96	5187.66	3663.37	2906.80	2457.26	2161.20	1952.78
120000	10672.32	5659.27	3996.41	3171.05	2680.65	2357.67	2130.31
130000	11561.68	6130.87	4329.44	3435.31	2904.04	2554.14	2307.83
140000	12451.04	6602.48	4662.48	3699.56	3127.42	2750.62	2485.36
150000	13340.40	7074.08	4995.51	3963.82	3350.81	2947.09	2662.88
160000	14229.76	7545.69	5328.54	4228.07	3574.20	3143.56	2840.41
170000	15119.12	8017.30	5661.58	4492.33	3797.59	3340.03	3017.94
180000	16008.48	8488.90	5994.61	4756.58	4020.97	3536.51	3195.46
190000	16897.84	8960.51	6327.65	5020.83	4244.36	3732.98	3372.99
200000	17787.20	9432.11	6660.68	5285.09	4467.75	3929.45	3550.51
210000	18676.56	9903.72	6993.71	5549.34	4691.14	4125.92	3728.04
220000	19565.92	10375.32	7326.75	5813.60	4914.52	4322.40	3905.56
230000	20455.28	10846.93	7659.78	6077.85	5137.91	4518.87	4083.09
240000	21344.64	11318.53	7992.82	6342.11	5361.30	4715.34	4260.62
250000	22234.00	11790.14	8325.85	6606.36	5584.69	4911.81	4438.14

Monthly Payments 12.50 %

LOAN AMOUNT	YEARS 8	9	10	11	12	13	14
100	1.64	1.53	1.45	1.38	1.32	1.28	1.24
200	3.27	3.06	2.89	2.76	2.65	2.56	2.49
500	8.18	7.64	7.23	6.89	6.62	6.40	6.22
1000	16.36	15.29	14.46	13.79	13.25	12.80	12.43
2000	32.71	30.58	28.91	27.58	26.49	25.60	24.86
5000	81.78	76.45	72.28	68.94	66.24	64.01	62.16
6000	98.13	91.74	86.73	82.73	79.48	76.81	74.59
7000	114.49	107.03	101.19	96.52	92.73	89.62	87.03
8000	130.84	122.32	115.64	110.31	105.98	102.42	99.46
9000	147.20	137.61	130.10	124.10	119.23	115.22	111.89
10000	163.55	152.90	144.55	137.88	132.47	128.02	124.32
12000	196.27	183.47	173.46	165.46	158.97	153.63	149.19
15000	245.33	229.34	216.83	206.83	198.71	192.03	186.48
20000	327.11	305.79	289.10	275.77	264.95	256.04	248.64
25000	408.89	382.24	361.38	344.71	331.18	320.05	310.80
30000	490.66	458.69	433.65	413.65	397.42	384.07	372.97
31000	507.02	473.98	448.11	427.44	410.67	396.87	385.40
32000	523.37	489.26	462.56	441.23	423.91	409.67	397.83
33000	539.73	504.55	477.02	455.02	437.16	422.47	410.26
34000	556.08	519.84	491.47	468.81	450.41	435.27	422.69
35000	572.44	535.13	505.93	482.60	463.65	448.08	435.13
36000	588.80	550.42	520.38	496.38	476.90	460.88	447.56
37000	605.15	565.71	534.84	510.17	490.15	473.68	459.99
38000	621.51	581.00	549.29	523.96	503.40	486.48	472.42
39000	637.86	596.29	563.75	537.75	516.64	499.29	484.86
40000	654.22	611.58	578.20	551.54	529.89	512.09	497.29
41000	670.57	626.87	592.66	565.33	543.14	524.89	509.72
42000	686.93	642.16	607.11	579.11	556.39	537.69	522.15
43000	703.28	657.45	621.57	592.90	569.63	550.49	534.58
44000	719.64	672.74	636.02	606.69	582.88	563.30	547.02
45000	735.99	688.03	650.48	620.48	596.13	576.10	559.45
46000	752.35	703.32	664.93	634.27	609.37	588.90	571.88
47000	768.70	718.61	679.39	648.06	622.62	601.70	584.31
48000	785.06	733.90	693.84	661.84	635.87	614.50	596.74
49000	801.42	749.19	708.30	675.63	649.12	627.31	609.18
50000	817.77	764.48	722.75	689.42	662.36	640.11	621.61
51000	834.13	779.77	737.21	703.21	675.61	652.91	634.04
52000	850.48	795.06	751.66	717.00	688.86	665.71	646.47
53000	866.84	810.34	766.12	730.79	702.11	678.52	658.91
54000	883.19	825.63	780.57	744.58	715.35	691.32	671.34
55000	899.55	840.92	795.03	758.36	728.60	704.12	683.77
56000	915.90	856.21	809.48	772.15	741.85	716.92	696.20
57000	932.26	871.50	823.94	785.94	755.09	729.72	708.63
58000	948.61	886.79	838.39	799.73	768.34	742.53	721.07
59000	964.97	902.08	852.85	813.52	781.59	755.33	733.50
60000	981.33	917.37	867.30	827.31	794.84	768.13	745.93
65000	1063.10	993.82	939.58	896.25	861.07	832.14	808.09
70000	1144.88	1070.27	1011.85	965.19	927.31	896.15	870.25
75000	1226.66	1146.71	1084.13	1034.13	993.55	960.16	932.41
80000	1308.43	1223.16	1156.40	1103.07	1059.78	1024.17	994.57
85000	1390.21	1299.61	1228.68	1172.02	1126.02	1088.19	1056.74
90000	1471.99	1376.06	1300.95	1240.96	1192.25	1152.20	1118.90
95000	1553.77	1452.51	1373.23	1309.90	1258.49	1216.21	1181.06
100000	1635.54	1528.95	1445.50	1378.84	1324.73	1280.22	1243.22
105000	1717.32	1605.40	1517.78	1447.79	1390.96	1344.23	1305.38
110000	1799.10	1681.85	1590.06	1516.73	1457.20	1408.24	1367.54
120000	1962.65	1834.74	1734.61	1654.61	1589.67	1536.26	1491.86
130000	2126.21	1987.64	1879.16	1792.50	1722.14	1664.28	1616.18
140000	2289.76	2140.53	2023.71	1930.38	1854.62	1792.31	1740.51
150000	2453.31	2293.43	2168.26	2068.26	1987.09	1920.33	1864.83
160000	2616.87	2446.32	2312.81	2206.15	2119.56	2048.35	1989.15
170000	2780.42	2599.22	2457.36	2344.03	2252.04	2176.37	2113.47
180000	2943.98	2752.11	2601.91	2481.92	2384.51	2304.39	2237.79
190000	3107.53	2905.01	2746.46	2619.80	2516.98	2432.42	2362.12
200000	3271.08	3057.91	2891.01	2757.69	2649.45	2560.44	2486.44
210000	3434.64	3210.80	3035.56	2895.57	2781.93	2688.46	2610.76
220000	3598.19	3363.70	3180.11	3033.45	2914.40	2816.48	2735.08
230000	3761.75	3516.59	3324.66	3171.34	3046.87	2944.50	2859.40
240000	3925.30	3669.49	3469.21	3309.22	3179.34	3072.52	2983.72
250000	4088.86	3822.38	3613.76	3447.11	3311.82	3200.55	3108.05

12.50 % Monthly Payments

LOAN AMOUNT	15	16	17	18	19	20	21
	YEARS						
100	1.21	1.19	1.16	1.14	1.13	1.11	1.10
200	2.42	2.37	2.33	2.29	2.26	2.23	2.20
500	6.06	5.93	5.82	5.72	5.64	5.57	5.51
1000	12.12	11.86	11.64	11.45	11.28	11.14	11.02
2000	24.24	23.72	23.27	22.89	22.56	22.28	22.04
5000	60.61	59.30	58.18	57.23	56.41	55.71	55.09
6000	72.73	71.16	69.82	68.68	67.69	66.85	66.11
7000	84.85	83.02	81.46	80.12	78.98	77.99	77.13
8000	96.97	94.88	93.09	91.57	90.26	89.13	88.15
9000	109.10	106.74	104.73	103.01	101.54	100.27	99.17
10000	121.22	118.60	116.37	114.46	112.82	111.41	110.19
12000	145.46	142.32	139.64	137.35	135.39	133.69	132.23
15000	181.83	177.89	174.55	171.69	169.23	167.12	165.28
20000	242.44	237.19	232.73	228.92	225.65	222.82	220.38
25000	303.05	296.49	290.92	286.15	282.06	278.53	275.47
30000	363.66	355.79	349.10	343.38	338.47	334.23	330.57
31000	375.78	367.65	360.74	354.83	349.75	345.37	341.59
32000	387.90	379.51	372.37	366.27	361.03	356.51	352.61
33000	400.02	391.37	384.01	377.72	372.31	367.66	363.63
34000	412.14	403.23	395.65	389.16	383.60	378.80	374.64
35000	424.26	415.09	407.28	400.61	394.88	389.94	385.66
36000	436.39	426.95	418.92	412.06	406.16	401.08	396.68
37000	448.51	438.81	430.56	423.50	417.44	412.22	407.70
38000	460.63	450.67	442.19	434.95	428.73	423.36	418.72
39000	472.75	462.53	453.83	446.39	440.01	434.50	429.74
40000	484.87	474.38	465.46	457.84	451.29	445.64	440.76
41000	497.00	486.24	477.10	469.29	462.57	456.78	451.78
42000	509.12	498.10	488.74	480.73	473.85	467.93	462.80
43000	521.24	509.96	500.37	492.18	485.14	479.07	473.81
44000	533.36	521.82	512.01	503.62	496.42	490.21	484.83
45000	545.48	533.68	523.65	515.07	507.70	501.35	495.85
46000	557.61	545.54	535.28	526.52	518.98	512.49	506.87
47000	569.73	557.40	546.92	537.96	530.27	523.63	517.89
48000	581.85	569.26	558.56	549.41	541.55	534.77	528.91
49000	593.97	581.12	570.19	560.85	552.83	545.91	539.93
50000	606.09	592.98	581.83	572.30	564.11	557.05	550.95
51000	618.21	604.84	593.47	583.75	575.39	568.20	561.97
52000	630.34	616.70	605.10	595.19	586.68	579.34	572.99
53000	642.46	628.56	616.74	606.64	597.96	590.48	584.00
54000	654.58	640.42	628.38	618.08	609.24	601.62	595.02
55000	666.70	652.28	640.01	629.53	620.52	612.76	606.04
56000	678.82	664.14	651.65	640.97	631.81	623.90	617.06
57000	690.95	676.00	663.29	652.42	643.09	635.04	628.08
58000	703.07	687.86	674.92	663.87	654.37	646.18	639.10
59000	715.19	699.72	686.56	675.31	665.65	657.32	650.12
60000	727.31	711.58	698.20	686.76	676.94	668.46	661.14
65000	787.92	770.88	756.38	743.99	733.35	724.17	716.23
70000	848.53	830.17	814.56	801.22	789.76	779.88	771.33
75000	909.14	889.47	872.75	858.45	846.17	835.58	826.42
80000	969.75	948.77	930.93	915.68	902.58	891.29	881.52
85000	1030.36	1008.07	989.11	972.91	958.99	946.99	936.61
90000	1090.97	1067.37	1047.30	1030.14	1015.40	1002.70	991.71
95000	1151.58	1126.66	1105.48	1087.37	1071.81	1058.40	1046.80
100000	1212.19	1185.96	1163.66	1144.60	1128.23	1114.11	1101.89
105000	1272.79	1245.26	1221.85	1201.83	1184.64	1169.81	1156.99
110000	1333.40	1304.56	1280.03	1259.06	1241.05	1225.52	1212.08
120000	1454.62	1423.15	1396.39	1373.52	1353.87	1336.93	1322.27
130000	1575.84	1541.75	1512.76	1487.98	1466.69	1448.34	1432.46
140000	1697.06	1660.35	1629.13	1602.44	1579.52	1559.75	1542.65
150000	1818.28	1778.94	1745.49	1716.90	1692.34	1671.16	1652.84
160000	1939.50	1897.54	1861.86	1831.36	1805.16	1782.57	1763.03
170000	2060.72	2016.13	1978.23	1945.82	1917.98	1893.98	1873.22
180000	2181.93	2134.73	2094.59	2060.28	2030.81	2005.39	1983.41
190000	2303.15	2253.33	2210.96	2174.74	2143.63	2116.81	2093.60
200000	2424.37	2371.92	2327.32	2289.20	2256.45	2228.22	2203.79
210000	2545.59	2490.52	2443.69	2403.66	2369.27	2339.63	2313.98
220000	2666.81	2609.12	2560.06	2518.12	2482.10	2451.04	2424.17
230000	2788.03	2727.71	2676.42	2632.58	2594.92	2562.45	2534.36
240000	2909.24	2846.31	2792.79	2747.04	2707.74	2673.86	2644.55
250000	3030.46	2964.90	2909.16	2861.50	2820.56	2785.27	2754.74

Monthly Payments 12.50 %

LOAN AMOUNT	22	23	24	25	30	35	40
			YEARS				
100	1.09	1.08	1.07	1.07	1.04	1.03	1.02
200	2.18	2.16	2.15	2.13	2.09	2.06	2.05
500	5.46	5.41	5.37	5.34	5.21	5.15	5.12
1000	10.91	10.82	10.74	10.67	10.43	10.30	10.24
2000	21.83	21.64	21.48	21.34	20.86	20.61	20.47
5000	54.56	54.10	53.70	53.35	52.15	51.52	51.18
6000	65.48	64.92	64.44	64.02	62.58	61.82	61.41
7000	76.39	75.75	75.18	74.69	73.01	72.12	71.65
8000	87.30	86.57	85.92	85.36	83.44	82.43	81.88
9000	98.22	97.39	96.66	96.03	93.87	92.73	92.12
10000	109.13	108.21	107.40	106.70	104.30	103.03	102.35
12000	130.96	129.85	128.89	128.04	125.16	123.64	122.83
15000	163.69	162.31	161.11	160.05	156.45	154.55	153.53
20000	218.26	216.42	214.81	213.40	208.60	206.06	204.71
25000	272.82	270.52	268.51	266.76	260.75	257.58	255.89
30000	327.39	324.62	322.21	320.11	312.89	309.10	307.06
31000	338.30	335.44	332.95	330.78	323.32	319.40	317.30
32000	349.22	346.27	343.69	341.45	333.75	329.70	327.53
33000	360.13	357.09	354.43	352.12	344.18	340.01	337.77
34000	371.04	367.91	365.17	362.79	354.61	350.31	348.01
35000	381.95	378.73	375.91	373.46	365.04	360.61	358.24
36000	392.87	389.55	386.66	384.13	375.47	370.92	368.48
37000	403.78	400.37	397.40	394.80	385.90	381.22	378.71
38000	414.69	411.19	408.14	405.47	396.33	391.52	388.95
39000	425.61	422.01	418.88	416.14	406.76	401.83	399.18
40000	436.52	432.83	429.62	426.81	417.19	412.13	409.42
41000	447.43	443.65	440.36	437.48	427.62	422.43	419.65
42000	458.34	454.47	451.10	448.15	438.05	432.74	429.89
43000	469.26	465.29	461.84	458.82	448.48	443.04	440.12
44000	480.17	476.11	472.58	469.49	458.91	453.34	450.36
45000	491.08	486.94	483.32	480.16	469.34	463.64	460.60
46000	502.00	497.76	494.06	490.83	479.77	473.95	470.83
47000	512.91	508.58	504.80	501.50	490.20	484.25	481.07
48000	523.82	519.40	515.54	512.17	500.63	494.55	491.30
49000	534.74	530.22	526.28	522.84	511.06	504.86	501.54
50000	545.65	541.04	537.02	533.51	521.49	515.16	511.77
51000	556.56	551.86	547.76	544.18	531.92	525.46	522.01
52000	567.47	562.68	558.50	554.85	542.35	535.77	532.24
53000	578.39	573.50	569.24	565.52	552.78	546.07	542.48
54000	589.30	584.32	579.98	576.19	563.21	556.37	552.71
55000	600.21	595.14	590.72	586.86	573.64	566.68	562.95
56000	611.13	605.96	601.46	597.53	584.07	576.98	573.19
57000	622.04	616.79	612.20	608.20	594.50	587.28	583.42
58000	632.95	627.61	622.94	618.87	604.93	597.59	593.66
59000	643.87	638.43	633.69	629.54	615.36	607.89	603.89
60000	654.78	649.25	644.43	640.21	625.79	618.19	614.13
65000	709.34	703.35	698.13	693.56	677.94	669.71	665.30
70000	763.91	757.46	751.83	746.92	730.09	721.23	716.48
75000	818.47	811.56	805.53	800.27	782.24	772.74	767.66
80000	873.04	865.66	859.23	853.62	834.39	824.26	818.84
85000	927.60	919.77	912.94	906.97	886.53	875.77	870.01
90000	982.17	973.87	966.64	960.32	938.68	927.29	921.19
95000	1036.73	1027.98	1020.34	1013.67	990.83	978.81	972.37
100000	1091.30	1082.08	1074.04	1067.02	1042.98	1030.32	1023.55
105000	1145.86	1136.18	1127.74	1120.37	1095.13	1081.84	1074.72
110000	1200.43	1190.29	1181.45	1173.72	1147.28	1133.35	1125.90
120000	1309.56	1298.49	1288.85	1280.43	1251.58	1236.39	1228.25
130000	1418.69	1406.70	1396.26	1387.13	1355.88	1339.42	1330.61
140000	1527.82	1514.91	1503.66	1493.83	1460.17	1442.45	1432.96
150000	1636.95	1623.12	1611.06	1600.53	1564.47	1545.48	1535.32
160000	1746.08	1731.33	1718.47	1707.24	1668.77	1648.51	1637.67
170000	1855.21	1839.53	1825.87	1813.94	1773.07	1751.55	1740.03
180000	1964.34	1947.74	1933.28	1920.64	1877.37	1854.58	1842.38
190000	2073.47	2055.95	2040.68	2027.34	1981.67	1957.61	1944.74
200000	2182.59	2164.16	2148.09	2134.05	2085.96	2060.64	2047.09
210000	2291.72	2272.37	2255.49	2240.75	2190.26	2163.68	2149.44
220000	2400.85	2380.57	2362.89	2347.45	2294.56	2266.71	2251.80
230000	2509.98	2488.78	2470.30	2454.15	2398.86	2369.74	2354.15
240000	2619.11	2596.99	2577.70	2560.85	2503.16	2472.77	2456.51
250000	2728.24	2705.20	2685.11	2667.56	2607.46	2575.80	2558.86

12.75 % Monthly Payments

LOAN AMOUNT	YEARS 1	2	3	4	5	6	7
100	8.90	4.73	3.34	2.65	2.25	1.98	1.79
200	17.81	9.45	6.68	5.31	4.49	3.95	3.58
500	44.52	23.64	16.71	13.27	11.23	9.89	8.94
1000	89.05	47.27	33.42	26.54	22.46	19.77	17.88
2000	178.09	94.54	66.83	53.08	44.92	39.54	35.76
5000	445.24	236.36	167.09	132.71	112.30	98.86	89.40
6000	534.28	283.63	200.50	159.25	134.76	118.63	107.28
7000	623.33	330.90	233.92	185.80	157.21	138.40	125.16
8000	712.38	378.17	267.34	212.34	179.67	158.17	143.04
9000	801.43	425.45	300.75	238.88	202.13	177.94	160.92
10000	890.47	472.72	334.17	265.42	224.59	197.71	178.80
12000	1068.57	567.26	401.01	318.51	269.51	237.26	214.56
15000	1335.71	709.08	501.26	398.14	336.89	296.57	268.20
20000	1780.94	945.43	668.34	530.85	449.19	395.43	357.61
25000	2226.18	1181.79	835.43	663.56	561.48	494.28	447.01
30000	2671.42	1418.15	1002.51	796.27	673.78	593.14	536.41
31000	2760.46	1465.42	1035.93	822.82	696.24	612.91	554.29
32000	2849.51	1512.69	1069.35	849.36	718.70	632.68	572.17
33000	2938.56	1559.97	1102.77	875.90	741.16	652.45	590.05
34000	3027.61	1607.24	1136.18	902.44	763.62	672.23	607.93
35000	3116.65	1654.51	1169.60	928.99	786.07	692.00	625.81
36000	3205.70	1701.78	1203.02	955.53	808.53	711.77	643.69
37000	3294.75	1749.05	1236.44	982.07	830.99	731.54	661.57
38000	3383.80	1796.32	1269.85	1008.61	853.45	751.31	679.45
39000	3472.84	1843.60	1303.27	1035.16	875.91	771.08	697.33
40000	3561.89	1890.87	1336.69	1061.70	898.37	790.85	715.21
41000	3650.94	1938.14	1370.10	1088.24	920.83	810.63	733.09
42000	3739.98	1985.41	1403.52	1114.78	943.29	830.40	750.97
43000	3829.03	2032.68	1436.94	1141.33	965.75	850.17	768.85
44000	3918.08	2079.95	1470.36	1167.87	988.21	869.94	786.73
45000	4007.13	2127.23	1503.77	1194.41	1010.67	889.71	804.61
46000	4096.17	2174.50	1537.19	1220.95	1033.13	909.48	822.49
47000	4185.22	2221.77	1570.61	1247.50	1055.59	929.25	840.37
48000	4274.27	2269.04	1604.02	1274.04	1078.05	949.03	858.25
49000	4363.31	2316.31	1637.44	1300.58	1100.50	968.80	876.13
50000	4452.36	2363.58	1670.86	1327.12	1122.96	988.57	894.01
51000	4541.41	2410.86	1704.28	1353.67	1145.42	1008.34	911.89
52000	4630.46	2458.13	1737.69	1380.21	1167.88	1028.11	929.77
53000	4719.50	2505.40	1771.11	1406.75	1190.34	1047.88	947.65
54000	4808.55	2552.67	1804.53	1433.29	1212.80	1067.65	965.53
55000	4897.60	2599.94	1837.94	1459.84	1235.26	1087.42	983.41
56000	4986.65	2647.22	1871.36	1486.38	1257.72	1107.20	1001.29
57000	5075.69	2694.49	1904.78	1512.92	1280.18	1126.97	1019.17
58000	5164.74	2741.76	1938.20	1539.46	1302.64	1146.74	1037.05
59000	5253.79	2789.03	1971.61	1566.01	1325.10	1166.51	1054.94
60000	5342.83	2836.30	2005.03	1592.55	1347.56	1186.28	1072.82
65000	5788.07	3072.66	2172.12	1725.26	1459.85	1285.14	1162.22
70000	6233.31	3309.02	2339.20	1857.97	1572.15	1384.00	1251.62
75000	6678.54	3545.38	2506.29	1990.69	1684.45	1482.85	1341.02
80000	7123.78	3781.74	2673.37	2123.40	1796.74	1581.71	1430.42
85000	7569.02	4018.09	2840.46	2256.11	1909.04	1680.57	1519.82
90000	8014.25	4254.45	3007.54	2388.82	2021.34	1779.42	1609.22
95000	8459.49	4490.81	3174.63	2521.53	2133.63	1878.28	1698.62
100000	8904.72	4727.17	3341.72	2654.25	2245.93	1977.14	1788.03
105000	9349.96	4963.53	3508.80	2786.96	2358.22	2075.99	1877.43
110000	9795.20	5199.89	3675.89	2919.67	2470.52	2174.85	1966.83
120000	10685.67	5672.60	4010.06	3185.10	2695.11	2372.56	2145.63
130000	11576.14	6145.32	4344.23	3450.52	2919.71	2570.28	2324.43
140000	12466.61	6618.04	4678.40	3715.95	3144.30	2767.99	2503.24
150000	13357.09	7090.75	5012.57	3981.37	3368.89	2965.70	2682.04
160000	14247.56	7563.47	5346.75	4246.80	3593.48	3163.42	2860.84
170000	15138.03	8036.19	5680.92	4512.22	3818.08	3361.13	3039.64
180000	16028.50	8508.91	6015.09	4777.65	4042.67	3558.84	3218.45
190000	16918.98	8981.62	6349.26	5043.07	4267.26	3756.56	3397.25
200000	17809.45	9454.34	6683.43	5308.49	4491.86	3954.27	3576.05
210000	18699.92	9927.06	7017.60	5573.92	4716.45	4151.99	3754.85
220000	19590.39	10399.77	7351.78	5839.34	4941.04	4349.70	3933.66
230000	20480.87	10872.49	7685.95	6104.77	5165.63	4547.41	4112.46
240000	21371.34	11345.21	8020.12	6370.19	5390.23	4745.13	4291.26
250000	22261.81	11817.92	8354.29	6635.62	5614.82	4942.84	4470.06

Monthly Payments 12.75 %

LOAN AMOUNT	YEARS 8	9	10	11	12	13	14
100	1.65	1.54	1.46	1.39	1.34	1.30	1.26
200	3.30	3.08	2.92	2.79	2.68	2.59	2.52
500	8.24	7.71	7.30	6.96	6.70	6.48	6.29
1000	16.49	15.42	14.59	13.93	13.39	12.95	12.58
2000	32.97	30.85	29.19	27.86	26.78	25.90	25.17
5000	82.43	77.12	72.97	69.65	66.96	64.75	62.92
6000	98.92	92.55	87.56	83.58	80.35	77.70	75.50
7000	115.41	107.97	102.15	97.51	93.74	90.65	88.08
8000	131.89	123.39	116.75	111.44	107.14	103.60	100.67
9000	148.38	138.82	131.34	125.37	120.53	116.55	113.25
10000	164.87	154.24	145.93	139.30	133.92	129.50	125.83
12000	197.84	185.09	175.12	167.16	160.70	155.40	151.00
15000	247.30	231.36	218.90	208.95	200.88	194.25	188.75
20000	329.73	308.49	291.86	278.60	267.84	259.00	251.66
25000	412.17	385.61	364.83	348.25	334.80	323.75	314.58
30000	494.60	462.73	437.80	417.90	401.76	388.50	377.50
31000	511.09	478.15	452.39	431.83	415.15	401.45	390.08
32000	527.57	493.58	466.98	445.76	428.55	414.40	402.66
33000	544.06	509.00	481.58	459.69	441.94	427.35	415.24
34000	560.55	524.43	496.17	473.62	455.33	440.30	427.83
35000	577.03	539.85	510.76	487.55	468.72	453.25	440.41
36000	593.52	555.27	525.36	501.48	482.11	466.20	452.99
37000	610.01	570.70	539.95	515.41	495.51	479.16	465.58
38000	626.49	586.12	554.54	529.34	508.90	492.11	478.16
39000	642.98	601.55	569.14	543.27	522.29	505.06	490.74
40000	659.47	616.97	583.73	557.20	535.68	518.01	503.33
41000	675.95	632.40	598.32	571.13	549.07	530.96	515.91
42000	692.44	647.82	612.92	585.06	562.47	543.91	528.49
43000	708.93	663.24	627.51	598.99	575.86	556.86	541.08
44000	725.41	678.67	642.10	612.92	589.25	569.81	553.66
45000	741.90	694.09	656.70	626.85	602.64	582.76	566.24
46000	758.39	709.52	671.29	640.78	616.03	595.71	578.83
47000	774.87	724.94	685.88	654.71	629.43	608.66	591.41
48000	791.36	740.37	700.48	668.64	642.82	621.61	603.99
49000	807.85	755.79	715.07	682.57	656.21	634.56	616.58
50000	824.33	771.21	729.66	696.50	669.60	647.51	629.16
51000	840.82	786.64	744.26	710.43	683.00	660.46	641.74
52000	857.31	802.06	758.85	724.36	696.39	673.41	654.33
53000	873.79	817.49	773.44	738.29	709.78	686.36	666.91
54000	890.28	832.91	788.03	752.22	723.17	699.31	679.49
55000	906.77	848.34	802.63	766.15	736.56	712.26	692.07
56000	923.25	863.76	817.22	780.08	749.96	725.21	704.66
57000	939.74	879.18	831.81	794.01	763.35	738.16	717.24
58000	956.23	894.61	846.41	807.94	776.74	751.11	729.82
59000	972.71	910.03	861.00	821.87	790.13	764.06	742.41
60000	989.20	925.46	875.59	835.80	803.52	777.01	754.99
65000	1071.63	1002.58	948.56	905.45	870.48	841.76	817.91
70000	1154.07	1079.70	1021.53	975.10	937.44	906.51	880.82
75000	1236.50	1156.82	1094.49	1044.75	1004.40	971.26	943.74
80000	1318.93	1233.94	1167.46	1114.40	1071.37	1036.01	1006.65
85000	1401.37	1311.06	1240.43	1184.05	1138.33	1100.76	1069.57
90000	1483.80	1388.19	1313.39	1253.70	1205.29	1165.51	1132.49
95000	1566.23	1465.31	1386.36	1323.35	1272.25	1230.26	1195.40
100000	1648.67	1542.43	1459.32	1393.00	1339.21	1295.01	1258.32
105000	1731.10	1619.55	1532.29	1462.65	1406.17	1359.76	1321.23
110000	1813.53	1696.67	1605.26	1532.30	1473.13	1424.52	1384.15
120000	1978.40	1850.91	1751.19	1671.60	1607.05	1554.02	1509.98
130000	2143.27	2005.16	1897.12	1810.90	1740.97	1683.52	1635.81
140000	2308.13	2159.40	2043.05	1950.20	1874.89	1813.02	1761.65
150000	2473.00	2313.64	2188.99	2089.50	2008.81	1942.52	1887.48
160000	2637.87	2467.89	2334.92	2228.80	2142.73	2072.02	2013.31
170000	2802.73	2622.13	2480.85	2368.10	2276.65	2201.52	2139.14
180000	2967.60	2776.37	2626.78	2507.39	2410.57	2331.02	2264.97
190000	3132.47	2930.61	2772.72	2646.69	2544.49	2460.53	2390.80
200000	3297.34	3084.86	2918.65	2785.99	2678.41	2590.03	2516.64
210000	3462.20	3239.10	3064.58	2925.29	2812.33	2719.53	2642.47
220000	3627.07	3393.34	3210.51	3064.59	2946.25	2849.03	2768.30
230000	3791.94	3547.59	3356.45	3203.89	3080.17	2978.53	2894.13
240000	3956.80	3701.83	3502.38	3343.19	3214.10	3108.03	3019.96
250000	4121.67	3856.07	3648.31	3482.49	3348.02	3237.53	3145.79

12.75 % Monthly Payments

LOAN AMOUNT	15	16	17	18	19	20	21
				YEARS			
100	1.23	1.20	1.18	1.16	1.14	1.13	1.12
200	2.46	2.40	2.36	2.32	2.29	2.26	2.24
500	6.14	6.01	5.90	5.80	5.72	5.65	5.59
1000	12.28	12.02	11.80	11.61	11.45	11.31	11.19
2000	24.55	24.03	23.59	23.22	22.89	22.62	22.38
5000	61.38	60.08	58.98	58.04	57.23	56.54	55.94
6000	73.65	72.10	70.78	69.65	68.68	67.85	67.13
7000	85.93	84.11	82.57	81.26	80.13	79.15	78.32
8000	98.21	96.13	94.37	92.86	91.57	90.46	89.50
9000	110.48	108.15	106.16	104.47	103.02	101.77	100.69
10000	122.76	120.16	117.96	116.08	114.47	113.08	111.88
12000	147.31	144.20	141.55	139.30	137.36	135.69	134.25
15000	184.14	180.25	176.94	174.12	171.70	169.62	167.82
20000	245.52	240.33	235.92	232.16	228.93	226.16	223.76
25000	306.89	300.41	294.90	290.20	286.17	282.70	279.70
30000	368.27	360.49	353.88	348.24	343.40	339.24	335.64
31000	380.55	372.51	365.68	359.85	354.85	350.54	346.83
32000	392.82	384.52	377.47	371.46	366.29	361.85	358.01
33000	405.10	396.54	389.27	383.06	377.74	373.16	369.20
34000	417.38	408.56	401.07	394.67	389.19	384.47	380.39
35000	429.65	420.57	412.86	406.28	400.63	395.77	391.58
36000	441.93	432.59	424.66	417.89	412.08	407.08	402.76
37000	454.20	444.60	436.45	429.49	423.53	418.39	413.95
38000	466.48	456.62	448.25	441.10	434.97	429.70	425.14
39000	478.76	468.64	460.05	452.71	446.42	441.01	436.33
40000	491.03	480.65	471.84	464.32	457.87	452.31	447.52
41000	503.31	492.67	483.64	475.93	469.31	463.62	458.70
42000	515.58	504.69	495.43	487.53	480.76	474.93	469.89
43000	527.86	516.70	507.23	499.14	492.21	486.24	481.08
44000	540.13	528.72	519.03	510.75	503.65	497.54	492.27
45000	552.41	540.74	530.82	522.36	515.10	508.85	503.46
46000	564.69	552.75	542.62	533.97	526.55	520.16	514.64
47000	576.96	564.77	554.41	545.57	537.99	531.47	525.83
48000	589.24	576.78	566.21	557.18	549.44	542.78	537.02
49000	601.51	588.80	578.01	568.79	560.89	554.08	548.21
50000	613.79	600.82	589.80	580.40	572.33	565.39	559.40
51000	626.06	612.83	601.60	592.01	583.78	576.70	570.58
52000	638.34	624.85	613.39	603.61	595.23	588.01	581.77
53000	650.62	636.87	625.19	615.22	606.67	599.32	592.96
54000	662.89	648.88	636.99	626.83	618.12	610.62	604.15
55000	675.17	660.90	648.78	638.44	629.57	621.93	615.34
56000	687.44	672.92	660.58	650.05	641.01	633.24	626.52
57000	699.72	684.93	672.37	661.65	652.46	644.55	637.71
58000	711.99	696.95	684.17	673.26	663.91	655.85	648.90
59000	724.27	708.96	695.97	684.87	675.35	667.16	660.09
60000	736.55	720.98	707.76	696.48	686.80	678.47	671.27
65000	797.93	781.06	766.74	754.52	744.03	735.01	727.21
70000	859.30	841.14	825.72	812.56	801.27	791.55	783.15
75000	920.68	901.23	884.70	870.60	858.50	848.09	839.09
80000	982.06	961.31	943.68	928.64	915.73	904.63	895.03
85000	1043.44	1021.39	1002.66	986.68	972.97	961.17	950.97
90000	1104.82	1081.47	1061.64	1044.72	1030.20	1017.71	1006.91
95000	1166.20	1141.55	1120.62	1102.76	1087.44	1074.24	1062.85
100000	1227.58	1201.63	1179.60	1160.80	1144.67	1130.78	1118.79
105000	1288.96	1261.72	1238.58	1218.84	1201.90	1187.32	1174.73
110000	1350.34	1321.80	1297.56	1276.88	1259.14	1243.86	1230.67
120000	1473.09	1441.96	1415.53	1392.96	1373.60	1356.94	1342.55
130000	1595.85	1562.13	1533.49	1509.04	1488.07	1470.02	1454.43
140000	1718.61	1682.29	1651.45	1625.12	1602.54	1583.10	1566.31
150000	1841.37	1802.45	1769.41	1741.20	1717.00	1696.18	1678.19
160000	1964.12	1922.62	1887.37	1857.28	1831.47	1809.25	1790.07
170000	2086.88	2042.78	2005.33	1973.36	1945.94	1922.33	1901.94
180000	2209.64	2162.94	2123.29	2089.43	2060.40	2035.41	2013.82
190000	2332.40	2283.11	2241.25	2205.51	2174.87	2148.49	2125.70
200000	2455.15	2403.27	2359.21	2321.59	2289.34	2261.57	2237.58
210000	2577.91	2523.43	2477.17	2437.67	2403.80	2374.65	2349.46
220000	2700.67	2643.60	2595.13	2553.75	2518.27	2487.72	2461.34
230000	2823.43	2763.76	2713.09	2669.83	2632.74	2600.80	2573.22
240000	2946.19	2883.92	2831.05	2785.91	2747.20	2713.88	2685.10
250000	3068.94	3004.09	2949.01	2901.99	2861.67	2826.96	2796.98

Monthly Payments 12.75 %

LOAN AMOUNT	22	23	24	25	30	35	40
	YEARS						
100	1.11	1.10	1.09	1.08	1.06	1.05	1.04
200	2.22	2.20	2.18	2.17	2.12	2.10	2.09
500	5.54	5.50	5.46	5.42	5.31	5.25	5.21
1000	11.08	10.99	10.92	10.85	10.61	10.49	10.43
2000	22.17	21.99	21.83	21.69	21.23	20.98	20.86
5000	55.42	54.97	54.58	54.23	53.07	52.46	52.14
6000	66.50	65.96	65.49	65.08	63.68	62.95	62.57
7000	77.59	76.96	76.41	75.93	74.30	73.44	72.99
8000	88.67	87.95	87.32	86.77	84.91	83.94	83.42
9000	99.76	98.94	98.24	97.62	95.52	94.43	93.85
10000	110.84	109.94	109.15	108.47	106.14	104.92	104.28
12000	133.01	131.93	130.98	130.16	127.36	125.90	125.13
15000	166.26	164.91	163.73	162.70	159.20	157.38	156.41
20000	221.68	219.88	218.31	216.94	212.27	209.84	208.55
25000	277.10	274.85	272.88	271.17	265.34	262.30	260.69
30000	332.52	329.81	327.46	325.41	318.41	314.76	312.83
31000	343.60	340.81	338.37	336.25	329.02	325.25	323.26
32000	354.69	351.80	349.29	347.10	339.64	335.74	333.68
33000	365.77	362.80	360.20	357.95	350.25	346.24	344.11
34000	376.86	373.79	371.12	368.79	360.86	356.73	354.54
35000	387.94	384.78	382.04	379.64	371.48	367.22	364.97
36000	399.02	395.78	392.95	390.49	382.09	377.71	375.39
37000	410.11	406.77	403.87	401.33	392.70	388.20	385.82
38000	421.19	417.76	414.78	412.18	403.32	398.70	396.25
39000	432.28	428.76	425.70	423.03	413.93	409.19	406.68
40000	443.36	439.75	436.61	433.87	424.54	419.68	417.10
41000	454.44	450.75	447.53	444.72	435.16	430.17	427.53
42000	465.53	461.74	458.44	455.57	445.77	440.66	437.96
43000	476.61	472.73	469.36	466.41	456.38	451.16	448.39
44000	487.70	483.73	480.27	477.26	467.00	461.65	458.81
45000	498.78	494.72	491.19	488.11	477.61	472.14	469.24
46000	509.87	505.72	502.10	498.95	488.23	482.63	479.67
47000	520.95	516.71	513.02	509.80	498.84	493.12	490.10
48000	532.03	527.70	523.93	520.65	509.45	503.62	500.52
49000	543.12	538.70	534.85	531.50	520.07	514.11	510.95
50000	554.20	549.69	545.76	542.34	530.68	524.60	521.38
51000	565.29	560.68	556.68	553.19	541.29	535.09	531.81
52000	576.37	571.68	567.60	564.04	551.91	545.58	542.24
53000	587.45	582.67	578.51	574.88	562.52	556.08	552.66
54000	598.54	593.67	589.43	585.73	573.13	566.57	563.09
55000	609.62	604.66	600.34	596.58	583.75	577.06	573.52
56000	620.71	615.65	611.26	607.42	594.36	587.55	583.95
57000	631.79	626.65	622.17	618.27	604.98	598.04	594.37
58000	642.87	637.64	633.09	629.12	615.59	608.54	604.80
59000	653.96	648.63	644.00	639.96	626.20	619.03	615.23
60000	665.04	659.63	654.92	650.81	636.82	629.52	625.66
65000	720.46	714.60	709.49	705.04	689.88	681.98	677.79
70000	775.88	769.57	764.07	759.28	742.95	734.44	729.93
75000	831.30	824.54	818.65	813.51	796.02	786.90	782.07
80000	886.72	879.50	873.22	867.75	849.09	839.36	834.21
85000	942.14	934.47	927.80	921.98	902.16	891.82	886.35
90000	997.56	989.44	982.38	976.22	955.22	944.28	938.48
95000	1052.98	1044.41	1036.95	1030.45	1008.29	996.74	990.62
100000	1108.40	1099.38	1091.53	1084.68	1061.36	1049.20	1042.76
105000	1163.82	1154.35	1146.11	1138.92	1114.43	1101.66	1094.90
110000	1219.24	1209.32	1200.68	1193.15	1167.50	1154.12	1147.04
120000	1330.08	1319.26	1309.84	1301.62	1273.63	1259.04	1251.31
130000	1440.92	1429.20	1418.99	1410.09	1379.77	1363.96	1355.59
140000	1551.76	1539.13	1528.14	1518.56	1485.90	1468.88	1459.86
150000	1662.60	1649.07	1637.29	1627.03	1592.04	1573.80	1564.14
160000	1773.44	1759.01	1746.45	1735.49	1698.18	1678.72	1668.42
170000	1884.28	1868.95	1855.60	1843.96	1804.31	1783.64	1772.69
180000	1995.12	1978.89	1964.75	1952.43	1910.45	1888.56	1876.97
190000	2105.96	2088.82	2073.91	2060.90	2016.58	1993.48	1981.24
200000	2216.80	2198.76	2183.06	2169.37	2122.72	2098.40	2085.52
210000	2327.65	2308.70	2292.21	2277.84	2228.86	2203.32	2189.80
220000	2438.49	2418.64	2401.36	2386.30	2334.99	2308.24	2294.07
230000	2549.33	2528.58	2510.52	2494.77	2441.13	2413.16	2398.35
240000	2660.17	2638.51	2619.67	2603.24	2547.26	2518.08	2502.62
250000	2771.01	2748.45	2728.82	2711.71	2653.40	2623.00	2606.90

13.00 % Monthly Payments

LOAN AMOUNT	YEARS 1	2	3	4	5	6	7
100	8.92	4.74	3.35	2.67	2.26	1.99	1.80
200	17.83	9.48	6.71	5.33	4.52	3.98	3.60
500	44.58	23.69	16.77	13.33	11.29	9.95	9.00
1000	89.16	47.38	33.53	26.66	22.58	19.90	18.01
2000	178.32	94.77	67.06	53.32	45.16	39.79	36.02
5000	445.79	236.91	167.66	133.30	112.90	99.48	90.04
6000	534.95	284.30	201.19	159.96	135.48	119.37	108.05
7000	624.11	331.68	234.72	186.62	158.06	139.27	126.06
8000	713.27	379.06	268.25	213.28	180.64	159.17	144.07
9000	802.43	426.45	301.78	239.94	203.22	179.06	162.07
10000	891.58	473.83	335.31	266.60	225.80	198.96	180.08
12000	1069.90	568.59	402.37	319.92	270.96	238.75	216.10
15000	1337.38	710.74	502.97	399.90	338.70	298.44	270.12
20000	1783.17	947.66	670.62	533.19	451.60	397.92	360.17
25000	2228.96	1184.57	838.28	666.49	564.50	497.39	450.21
30000	2674.75	1421.49	1005.93	799.79	677.40	596.87	540.25
31000	2763.91	1468.87	1039.46	826.45	699.98	616.77	558.26
32000	2853.07	1516.25	1072.99	853.11	722.56	636.67	576.27
33000	2942.23	1563.64	1106.52	879.77	745.14	656.56	594.27
34000	3031.39	1611.02	1140.06	906.43	767.72	676.46	612.28
35000	3120.55	1658.40	1173.59	933.09	790.30	696.35	630.29
36000	3209.70	1705.78	1207.12	959.75	812.88	716.25	648.30
37000	3298.86	1753.17	1240.65	986.41	835.46	736.14	666.31
38000	3388.02	1800.55	1274.18	1013.07	858.04	756.04	684.32
39000	3477.18	1847.93	1307.71	1039.73	880.62	775.94	702.32
40000	3566.34	1895.32	1341.24	1066.39	903.20	795.83	720.33
41000	3655.50	1942.70	1374.77	1093.05	925.78	815.73	738.34
42000	3744.65	1990.08	1408.30	1119.71	948.36	835.62	756.35
43000	3833.81	2037.46	1441.83	1146.37	970.94	855.52	774.36
44000	3922.97	2084.85	1475.37	1173.03	993.52	875.41	792.37
45000	4012.13	2132.23	1508.90	1199.69	1016.10	895.31	810.37
46000	4101.29	2179.61	1542.43	1226.35	1038.68	915.21	828.38
47000	4190.45	2227.00	1575.96	1253.01	1061.26	935.10	846.39
48000	4279.61	2274.38	1609.49	1279.67	1083.84	955.00	864.40
49000	4368.76	2321.76	1643.02	1306.32	1106.42	974.89	882.41
50000	4457.92	2369.14	1676.55	1332.98	1129.00	994.79	900.42
51000	4547.08	2416.53	1710.08	1359.64	1151.58	1014.68	918.42
52000	4636.24	2463.91	1743.61	1386.30	1174.16	1034.58	936.43
53000	4725.40	2511.29	1777.15	1412.96	1196.74	1054.48	954.44
54000	4814.56	2558.68	1810.68	1439.62	1219.32	1074.37	972.45
55000	4903.71	2606.06	1844.21	1466.28	1241.90	1094.27	990.46
56000	4992.87	2653.44	1877.74	1492.94	1264.48	1114.16	1008.47
57000	5082.03	2700.82	1911.27	1519.60	1287.06	1134.06	1026.47
58000	5171.19	2748.21	1944.80	1546.26	1309.64	1153.96	1044.48
59000	5260.35	2795.59	1978.33	1572.92	1332.22	1173.85	1062.49
60000	5349.51	2842.97	2011.86	1599.58	1354.80	1193.75	1080.50
65000	5795.30	3079.89	2179.52	1732.88	1467.70	1293.23	1170.54
70000	6241.09	3316.80	2347.17	1866.18	1580.60	1392.70	1260.58
75000	6686.88	3553.72	2514.83	1999.48	1693.50	1492.18	1350.62
80000	7132.68	3790.63	2682.48	2132.78	1806.40	1591.66	1440.67
85000	7578.47	4027.55	2850.14	2266.07	1919.31	1691.14	1530.71
90000	8024.26	4264.46	3017.79	2399.37	2032.21	1790.62	1620.75
95000	8470.05	4501.37	3185.45	2532.67	2145.11	1890.10	1710.79
100000	8915.84	4738.29	3353.10	2665.97	2258.01	1989.58	1800.83
105000	9361.64	4975.20	3520.76	2799.27	2370.91	2089.06	1890.87
110000	9807.43	5212.12	3688.41	2932.57	2483.81	2188.54	1980.92
120000	10699.01	5685.95	4023.72	3199.16	2709.61	2387.49	2161.00
130000	11590.60	6159.77	4359.04	3465.76	2935.41	2586.45	2341.08
140000	12482.18	6633.60	4694.35	3732.36	3161.21	2785.41	2521.17
150000	13373.77	7107.43	5029.66	3998.95	3387.01	2984.37	2701.25
160000	14265.35	7581.26	5364.97	4265.55	3612.81	3183.33	2881.33
170000	15156.94	8055.09	5700.28	4532.15	3838.61	3382.28	3061.42
180000	16048.52	8528.92	6035.59	4798.74	4064.41	3581.24	3241.50
190000	16940.10	9002.75	6370.90	5065.34	4290.21	3780.20	3421.58
200000	17831.69	9476.58	6706.21	5331.94	4516.01	3979.16	3601.67
210000	18723.27	9950.41	7041.52	5598.53	4741.81	4178.11	3781.75
220000	19614.86	10424.23	7376.83	5865.13	4967.61	4377.07	3961.83
230000	20506.44	10898.06	7712.14	6131.73	5193.41	4576.03	4141.92
240000	21398.03	11371.89	8047.45	6398.33	5419.21	4774.99	4322.00
250000	22289.61	11845.72	8382.76	6664.92	5645.01	4973.95	4502.08

Monthly Payments 13.00 %

LOAN AMOUNT	8	9	10	11	12	13	14
100	1.66	1.56	1.47	1.41	1.35	1.31	1.27
200	3.32	3.11	2.95	2.81	2.71	2.62	2.55
500	8.31	7.78	7.37	7.04	6.77	6.55	6.37
1000	16.62	15.56	14.73	14.07	13.54	13.10	12.73
2000	33.24	31.12	29.46	28.14	27.07	26.20	25.47
5000	83.09	77.80	73.66	70.36	67.69	65.49	63.67
6000	99.71	93.36	88.39	84.43	81.22	78.59	76.41
7000	116.33	108.92	103.12	98.50	94.76	91.69	89.14
8000	132.95	124.48	117.86	112.58	108.30	104.79	101.88
9000	149.57	140.04	132.59	126.65	121.84	117.89	114.61
10000	166.18	155.60	147.32	140.72	135.37	130.99	127.35
12000	199.42	186.71	176.78	168.86	162.45	157.18	152.82
15000	249.28	233.39	220.98	211.08	203.06	196.48	191.02
20000	332.37	311.19	294.64	281.44	270.75	261.97	254.70
25000	415.46	388.99	368.30	351.80	338.44	327.47	318.37
30000	498.55	466.79	441.96	422.16	406.12	392.96	382.04
31000	515.17	482.35	456.69	436.23	419.66	406.06	394.78
32000	531.79	497.90	471.42	450.31	433.20	419.16	407.51
33000	548.41	513.46	486.15	464.38	446.74	432.26	420.25
34000	565.02	529.02	500.89	478.45	460.27	445.36	432.98
35000	581.64	544.58	515.62	492.52	473.81	458.46	445.72
36000	598.26	560.14	530.35	506.59	487.35	471.55	458.45
37000	614.88	575.70	545.08	520.67	500.89	484.65	471.19
38000	631.50	591.26	559.81	534.74	514.42	497.75	483.92
39000	648.12	606.82	574.55	548.81	527.96	510.85	496.66
40000	664.73	622.38	589.28	562.88	541.50	523.95	509.39
41000	681.35	637.94	604.01	576.96	555.04	537.05	522.13
42000	697.97	653.50	618.74	591.03	568.57	550.15	534.86
43000	714.59	669.06	633.47	605.10	582.11	563.24	547.60
44000	731.21	684.62	648.21	619.17	595.65	576.34	560.33
45000	747.83	700.18	662.94	633.24	609.19	589.44	573.07
46000	764.44	715.74	677.67	647.32	622.72	602.54	585.80
47000	781.06	731.30	692.40	661.39	636.26	615.64	598.54
48000	797.68	746.86	707.13	675.46	649.80	628.74	611.27
49000	814.30	762.42	721.87	689.53	663.34	641.84	624.01
50000	830.92	777.98	736.60	703.60	676.87	654.94	636.74
51000	847.54	793.54	751.33	717.68	690.41	668.03	649.48
52000	864.15	809.10	766.06	731.75	703.95	681.13	662.21
53000	880.77	824.65	780.79	745.82	717.49	694.23	674.95
54000	897.39	840.21	795.53	759.89	731.02	707.33	687.68
55000	914.01	855.77	810.26	773.96	744.56	720.43	700.42
56000	930.63	871.33	824.99	788.04	758.10	733.53	713.15
57000	947.25	886.89	839.72	802.11	771.64	746.63	725.89
58000	963.86	902.45	854.45	816.18	785.17	759.73	738.62
59000	980.48	918.01	869.19	830.25	798.71	772.82	751.35
60000	997.10	933.57	883.92	844.32	812.25	785.92	764.09
65000	1080.19	1011.37	957.58	914.69	879.94	851.42	827.76
70000	1163.29	1089.17	1031.24	985.05	947.62	916.91	891.44
75000	1246.38	1166.96	1104.90	1055.41	1015.31	982.40	955.11
80000	1329.47	1244.76	1178.56	1125.77	1083.00	1047.90	1018.79
85000	1412.56	1322.56	1252.22	1196.13	1150.68	1113.39	1082.46
90000	1495.65	1400.36	1325.88	1266.49	1218.37	1178.88	1146.13
95000	1578.74	1478.15	1399.54	1336.85	1286.06	1244.38	1209.81
100000	1661.84	1555.95	1473.20	1407.21	1353.75	1309.87	1273.48
105000	1744.93	1633.75	1546.86	1477.57	1421.43	1375.37	1337.16
110000	1828.02	1711.55	1620.52	1547.93	1489.12	1440.86	1400.83
120000	1994.20	1867.14	1767.84	1688.65	1624.50	1571.85	1528.18
130000	2160.39	2022.74	1915.15	1829.37	1759.87	1702.83	1655.53
140000	2326.57	2178.33	2062.47	1970.09	1895.25	1833.82	1782.88
150000	2492.75	2333.93	2209.79	2110.81	2030.62	1964.81	1910.22
160000	2658.94	2489.52	2357.11	2251.53	2165.99	2095.80	2037.57
170000	2825.12	2645.12	2504.43	2392.25	2301.37	2226.78	2164.92
180000	2991.30	2800.71	2651.75	2532.97	2436.74	2357.77	2292.27
190000	3157.49	2956.31	2799.07	2673.70	2572.12	2488.76	2419.62
200000	3323.67	3111.90	2946.39	2814.42	2707.49	2619.74	2546.97
210000	3489.86	3267.50	3093.71	2955.14	2842.87	2750.73	2674.31
220000	3656.04	3423.10	3241.03	3095.86	2978.24	2881.72	2801.66
230000	3822.22	3578.69	3388.35	3236.58	3113.62	3012.71	2929.01
240000	3988.41	3734.29	3535.67	3377.30	3248.99	3143.69	3056.36
250000	4154.59	3889.88	3682.99	3518.02	3384.37	3274.68	3183.71

13.00 % Monthly Payments

LOAN AMOUNT	15	16	17	18	19	20	21
100	1.24	1.22	1.20	1.18	1.16	1.15	1.14
200	2.49	2.43	2.39	2.35	2.32	2.30	2.27
500	6.22	6.09	5.98	5.89	5.81	5.74	5.68
1000	12.43	12.17	11.96	11.77	11.61	11.48	11.36
2000	24.86	24.35	23.91	23.54	23.22	22.95	22.72
5000	62.15	60.87	59.78	58.85	58.06	57.38	56.79
6000	74.58	73.04	71.74	70.62	69.67	68.85	68.15
7000	87.01	85.22	83.69	82.39	81.28	80.33	79.50
8000	99.44	97.39	95.65	94.17	92.89	91.80	90.86
9000	111.87	109.56	107.61	105.94	104.51	103.28	102.22
10000	124.30	121.74	119.56	117.71	116.12	114.75	113.58
12000	149.16	146.09	143.47	141.25	139.34	137.70	136.29
15000	186.46	182.61	179.34	176.56	174.18	172.13	170.36
20000	248.61	243.48	239.12	235.41	232.24	229.51	227.15
25000	310.76	304.34	298.90	294.27	290.30	286.88	283.94
30000	372.91	365.21	358.69	353.12	348.35	344.26	340.73
31000	385.34	377.39	370.64	364.89	359.97	355.73	352.08
32000	397.77	389.56	382.60	376.66	371.58	367.21	363.44
33000	410.20	401.73	394.55	388.43	383.19	378.69	374.80
34000	422.63	413.91	406.51	400.20	394.80	390.16	386.16
35000	435.06	426.08	418.47	411.97	406.41	401.64	397.51
36000	447.49	438.26	430.42	423.74	418.03	413.11	408.87
37000	459.92	450.43	442.38	435.51	429.64	424.59	420.23
38000	472.35	462.60	454.33	447.29	441.25	436.06	431.59
39000	484.78	474.78	466.29	459.06	452.86	447.54	442.95
40000	497.21	486.95	478.25	470.83	464.47	459.01	454.30
41000	509.65	499.12	490.20	482.60	476.09	470.49	465.66
42000	522.08	511.30	502.16	494.37	487.70	481.96	477.02
43000	534.51	523.47	514.12	506.14	499.31	493.44	488.38
44000	546.94	535.65	526.07	517.91	510.92	504.91	499.73
45000	559.37	547.82	538.03	529.68	522.53	516.39	511.09
46000	571.80	559.99	549.98	541.45	534.14	527.86	522.45
47000	584.23	572.17	561.94	553.22	545.76	539.34	533.81
48000	596.66	584.34	573.90	564.99	557.37	550.81	545.16
49000	609.09	596.51	585.85	576.76	568.98	562.29	556.52
50000	621.52	608.69	597.81	588.53	580.59	573.77	567.88
51000	633.95	620.86	609.76	600.30	592.20	585.24	579.24
52000	646.38	633.04	621.72	612.07	603.82	596.72	590.59
53000	658.81	645.21	633.68	623.85	615.43	608.19	601.95
54000	671.24	657.38	645.63	635.62	627.04	619.67	613.31
55000	683.67	669.56	657.59	647.39	638.65	631.14	624.67
56000	696.10	681.73	669.55	659.16	650.26	642.62	636.02
57000	708.53	693.91	681.50	670.93	661.87	654.09	647.38
58000	720.96	706.08	693.46	682.70	673.49	665.57	658.74
59000	733.39	718.25	705.41	694.47	685.10	677.04	670.10
60000	745.82	730.43	717.37	706.24	696.71	688.52	681.45
65000	807.97	791.30	777.15	765.09	754.77	745.89	738.24
70000	870.13	852.16	836.93	823.95	812.83	803.27	795.03
75000	932.28	913.03	896.71	882.80	870.89	860.65	851.82
80000	994.43	973.90	956.49	941.65	928.95	918.02	908.61
85000	1056.58	1034.77	1016.27	1000.51	987.01	975.40	965.39
90000	1118.73	1095.64	1076.06	1059.36	1045.06	1032.78	1022.18
95000	1180.89	1156.51	1135.84	1118.21	1103.12	1090.15	1078.97
100000	1243.04	1217.38	1195.62	1177.07	1161.18	1147.53	1135.76
105000	1305.19	1278.25	1255.40	1235.92	1219.24	1204.91	1192.54
110000	1367.34	1339.11	1315.18	1294.77	1277.30	1262.28	1249.33
120000	1491.64	1460.85	1434.74	1412.48	1393.42	1377.04	1362.91
130000	1615.95	1582.59	1554.30	1530.19	1509.54	1491.79	1476.48
140000	1740.25	1704.33	1673.86	1647.89	1625.66	1606.54	1590.06
150000	1864.56	1826.07	1793.43	1765.60	1741.77	1721.30	1703.64
160000	1988.86	1947.80	1912.99	1883.31	1857.89	1836.05	1817.21
170000	2113.16	2069.54	2032.55	2001.01	1974.01	1950.80	1930.79
180000	2237.47	2191.28	2152.11	2118.72	2090.13	2065.55	2044.36
190000	2361.77	2313.02	2271.67	2236.43	2206.25	2180.31	2157.94
200000	2486.07	2434.75	2391.23	2354.13	2322.37	2295.06	2271.51
210000	2610.38	2556.49	2510.80	2471.84	2438.48	2409.81	2385.09
220000	2734.68	2678.23	2630.36	2589.55	2554.60	2524.57	2498.67
230000	2858.99	2799.97	2749.92	2707.25	2670.72	2639.32	2612.24
240000	2983.29	2921.71	2869.48	2824.96	2786.84	2754.07	2725.82
250000	3107.59	3043.44	2989.04	2942.67	2902.96	2868.83	2839.39

Monthly Payments 13.00 %

LOAN AMOUNT	22	23	24	25	30	35	40
100	1.13	1.12	1.11	1.10	1.08	1.07	1.06
200	2.25	2.23	2.22	2.20	2.16	2.14	2.12
500	5.63	5.58	5.55	5.51	5.40	5.34	5.31
1000	11.26	11.17	11.09	11.02	10.80	10.68	10.62
2000	22.51	22.33	22.18	22.05	21.60	21.36	21.24
5000	56.28	55.84	55.45	55.12	53.99	53.41	53.10
6000	67.53	67.00	66.54	66.14	64.79	64.09	63.72
7000	78.79	78.17	77.64	77.17	75.59	74.77	74.34
8000	90.05	89.34	88.73	88.19	86.38	85.45	84.96
9000	101.30	100.51	99.82	99.22	97.18	96.13	95.58
10000	112.56	111.67	110.91	110.24	107.98	106.81	106.20
12000	135.07	134.01	133.09	132.29	129.57	128.17	127.44
15000	168.84	167.51	166.36	165.36	161.97	160.22	159.30
20000	225.12	223.35	221.82	220.48	215.96	213.62	212.40
25000	281.39	279.19	277.27	275.60	269.95	267.03	265.50
30000	337.67	335.02	332.72	330.72	323.94	320.43	318.60
31000	348.93	346.19	343.82	341.75	334.73	331.12	329.22
32000	360.18	357.36	354.91	352.77	345.53	341.80	339.84
33000	371.44	368.53	366.00	363.79	356.33	352.48	350.46
34000	382.70	379.69	377.09	374.82	367.13	363.16	361.08
35000	393.95	390.86	388.18	385.84	377.93	373.84	371.70
36000	405.21	402.03	399.27	396.87	388.72	384.52	382.32
37000	416.46	413.20	410.36	407.89	399.52	395.20	392.94
38000	427.72	424.36	421.45	418.91	410.32	405.88	403.56
39000	438.97	435.53	432.54	429.94	421.12	416.56	414.18
40000	450.23	446.70	443.63	440.96	431.92	427.25	424.80
41000	461.49	457.87	454.72	451.99	442.71	437.93	435.42
42000	472.74	469.03	465.81	463.01	453.51	448.61	446.04
43000	484.00	480.20	476.90	474.04	464.31	459.29	456.66
44000	495.25	491.37	488.00	485.06	475.11	469.97	467.28
45000	506.51	502.54	499.09	496.08	485.90	480.65	477.90
46000	517.76	513.70	510.18	507.11	496.70	491.33	488.52
47000	529.02	524.87	521.27	518.13	507.50	502.01	499.14
48000	540.28	536.04	532.36	529.16	518.30	512.69	509.76
49000	551.53	547.21	543.45	540.18	529.10	523.38	520.38
50000	562.79	558.37	554.54	551.20	539.89	534.06	531.00
51000	574.04	569.54	565.63	562.23	550.69	544.74	541.62
52000	585.30	580.71	576.72	573.25	561.49	555.42	552.24
53000	596.55	591.88	587.81	584.28	572.29	566.10	562.86
54000	607.81	603.04	598.90	595.30	583.09	576.78	573.48
55000	619.07	614.21	609.99	606.32	593.88	587.46	584.10
56000	630.32	625.38	621.09	617.35	604.68	598.14	594.72
57000	641.58	636.55	632.18	628.37	615.48	608.82	605.34
58000	652.83	647.71	643.27	639.40	626.28	619.51	615.96
59000	664.09	658.88	654.36	650.42	637.08	630.19	626.58
60000	675.35	670.05	665.45	661.44	647.87	640.87	637.20
65000	731.62	725.89	720.90	716.56	701.86	694.27	690.30
70000	787.90	781.72	776.36	771.69	755.85	747.68	743.40
75000	844.18	837.56	831.81	826.81	809.84	801.09	796.50
80000	900.46	893.40	887.26	881.93	863.83	854.49	849.60
85000	956.74	949.24	942.72	937.05	917.82	907.90	902.70
90000	1013.02	1005.07	998.17	992.17	971.81	961.30	955.80
95000	1069.30	1060.91	1053.63	1047.29	1025.80	1014.71	1008.90
100000	1125.58	1116.75	1109.08	1102.41	1079.79	1068.11	1062.00
105000	1181.85	1172.59	1164.54	1157.53	1133.78	1121.52	1115.10
110000	1238.13	1228.42	1219.99	1212.65	1187.77	1174.92	1168.20
120000	1350.69	1340.10	1330.90	1322.89	1295.75	1281.74	1274.40
130000	1463.25	1451.77	1441.81	1433.13	1403.72	1388.55	1380.60
140000	1575.81	1563.45	1552.71	1543.37	1511.70	1495.36	1486.79
150000	1688.36	1675.12	1663.62	1653.61	1619.68	1602.17	1592.99
160000	1800.92	1786.80	1774.53	1763.85	1727.66	1708.98	1699.19
170000	1913.48	1898.47	1885.44	1874.09	1835.64	1815.79	1805.39
180000	2026.04	2010.15	1996.35	1984.33	1943.62	1922.60	1911.59
190000	2138.59	2121.82	2107.25	2094.57	2051.60	2029.42	2017.79
200000	2251.15	2233.50	2218.16	2204.81	2159.58	2136.23	2123.99
210000	2363.71	2345.17	2329.07	2315.06	2267.56	2243.04	2230.19
220000	2476.27	2456.85	2439.98	2425.30	2375.53	2349.85	2336.39
230000	2588.82	2568.52	2550.89	2535.54	2483.51	2456.66	2442.59
240000	2701.38	2680.20	2661.79	2645.78	2591.49	2563.47	2548.79
250000	2813.94	2791.87	2772.70	2756.02	2699.47	2670.28	2654.99

13.25 % Monthly Payments

LOAN AMOUNT	YEARS 1	2	3	4	5	6	7
100	8.93	4.75	3.36	2.68	2.27	2.00	1.81
200	17.85	9.50	6.73	5.36	4.54	4.00	3.63
500	44.63	23.75	16.82	13.39	11.35	10.01	9.07
1000	89.27	47.49	33.65	26.78	22.70	20.02	18.14
2000	178.54	94.99	67.29	53.55	45.40	40.04	36.27
5000	446.35	237.47	168.23	133.89	113.51	100.10	90.68
6000	535.62	284.96	201.87	160.66	136.21	120.12	108.82
7000	624.89	332.46	235.52	187.44	158.91	140.14	126.96
8000	714.16	379.95	269.16	214.22	181.61	160.16	145.09
9000	803.43	427.45	302.81	240.99	204.31	180.18	163.23
10000	892.70	474.94	336.45	267.77	227.01	200.21	181.37
12000	1071.24	569.93	403.74	321.33	272.41	240.25	217.64
15000	1339.04	712.41	504.68	401.66	340.52	300.31	272.05
20000	1785.39	949.88	672.90	535.54	454.02	400.41	362.74
25000	2231.74	1187.35	841.13	669.43	567.53	500.51	453.42
30000	2678.09	1424.82	1009.35	803.31	681.03	600.62	544.10
31000	2767.36	1472.32	1043.00	830.09	703.73	620.64	562.24
32000	2856.63	1519.81	1076.64	856.87	726.43	640.66	580.38
33000	2945.90	1567.31	1110.29	883.64	749.14	660.68	598.51
34000	3035.17	1614.80	1143.93	910.42	771.84	680.70	616.65
35000	3124.44	1662.29	1177.58	937.20	794.54	700.72	634.79
36000	3213.71	1709.79	1211.22	963.98	817.24	720.74	652.92
37000	3302.98	1757.28	1244.87	990.75	839.94	740.76	671.06
38000	3392.25	1804.78	1278.51	1017.53	862.64	760.78	689.20
39000	3481.51	1852.27	1312.16	1044.31	885.34	780.80	707.33
40000	3570.78	1899.76	1345.80	1071.08	908.04	800.82	725.47
41000	3660.05	1947.26	1379.45	1097.86	930.74	820.84	743.61
42000	3749.32	1994.75	1413.09	1124.64	953.45	840.86	761.74
43000	3838.59	2042.25	1446.74	1151.41	976.15	860.88	779.88
44000	3927.86	2089.74	1480.38	1178.19	998.85	880.90	798.02
45000	4017.13	2137.23	1514.03	1204.97	1021.55	900.92	816.15
46000	4106.40	2184.73	1547.67	1231.75	1044.25	920.94	834.29
47000	4195.67	2232.22	1581.32	1258.52	1066.95	940.96	852.43
48000	4284.94	2279.72	1614.96	1285.30	1089.65	960.98	870.56
49000	4374.21	2327.21	1648.61	1312.08	1112.35	981.01	888.70
50000	4463.48	2374.71	1682.25	1338.85	1135.05	1001.03	906.84
51000	4552.75	2422.20	1715.90	1365.63	1157.76	1021.05	924.98
52000	4642.02	2469.69	1749.54	1392.41	1180.46	1041.07	943.11
53000	4731.29	2517.19	1783.19	1419.19	1203.16	1061.09	961.25
54000	4820.56	2564.68	1816.83	1445.96	1225.86	1081.11	979.39
55000	4909.83	2612.18	1850.48	1472.74	1248.56	1101.13	997.52
56000	4999.10	2659.67	1884.12	1499.52	1271.26	1121.15	1015.66
57000	5088.37	2707.16	1917.77	1526.29	1293.96	1141.17	1033.80
58000	5177.64	2754.66	1951.41	1553.07	1316.66	1161.19	1051.93
59000	5266.91	2802.15	1985.06	1579.85	1339.36	1181.21	1070.07
60000	5356.18	2849.65	2018.70	1606.63	1362.07	1201.23	1088.21
65000	5802.52	3087.12	2186.93	1740.51	1475.57	1301.33	1178.89
70000	6248.87	3324.59	2355.15	1874.40	1589.08	1401.44	1269.57
75000	6695.22	3562.06	2523.38	2008.28	1702.58	1501.54	1360.26
80000	7141.57	3799.53	2691.60	2142.17	1816.09	1601.64	1450.94
85000	7587.92	4037.00	2859.83	2276.05	1929.59	1701.74	1541.63
90000	8034.27	4274.47	3028.05	2409.94	2043.10	1801.85	1632.31
95000	8480.61	4511.94	3196.28	2543.82	2156.60	1901.95	1722.99
100000	8926.96	4749.41	3364.50	2677.71	2270.11	2002.05	1813.68
105000	9373.31	4986.88	3532.73	2811.59	2383.61	2102.15	1904.36
110000	9819.66	5224.35	3700.95	2945.48	2497.12	2202.26	1995.04
120000	10712.35	5699.29	4037.40	3213.25	2724.13	2402.46	2176.41
130000	11605.05	6174.23	4373.85	3481.02	2951.14	2602.67	2357.78
140000	12497.75	6649.18	4710.30	3748.79	3178.15	2802.87	2539.15
150000	13390.44	7124.12	5046.75	4016.56	3405.16	3003.08	2720.52
160000	14283.14	7599.06	5383.21	4284.33	3632.17	3203.28	2901.88
170000	15175.83	8074.00	5719.66	4552.11	3859.19	3403.49	3083.25
180000	16068.53	8548.94	6056.11	4819.88	4086.20	3603.69	3264.62
190000	16961.23	9023.88	6392.56	5087.65	4313.21	3803.90	3445.99
200000	17853.92	9498.82	6729.01	5355.42	4540.22	4004.10	3627.35
210000	18746.62	9973.76	7065.46	5623.19	4767.23	4204.31	3808.72
220000	19639.31	10448.70	7401.91	5890.96	4994.24	4404.51	3990.09
230000	20532.01	10923.65	7738.36	6158.73	5221.25	4604.72	4171.46
240000	21424.71	11398.59	8074.81	6426.50	5448.26	4804.92	4352.82
250000	22317.40	11873.53	8411.26	6694.27	5675.27	5005.13	4534.19

Monthly Payments 13.25 %

LOAN AMOUNT	8	9	10	11	12	13	14
100	1.68	1.57	1.49	1.42	1.37	1.32	1.29
200	3.35	3.14	2.97	2.84	2.74	2.65	2.58
500	8.38	7.85	7.44	7.11	6.84	6.62	6.44
1000	16.75	15.70	14.87	14.21	13.68	13.25	12.89
2000	33.50	31.39	29.74	28.43	27.37	26.50	25.77
5000	83.75	78.48	74.36	71.07	68.42	66.24	64.44
6000	100.50	94.17	89.23	85.29	82.10	79.49	77.32
7000	117.25	109.87	104.10	99.50	95.78	92.74	90.21
8000	134.00	125.56	118.97	113.72	109.47	105.98	103.10
9000	150.75	141.26	133.84	127.93	123.15	119.23	115.98
10000	167.50	156.95	148.71	142.15	136.83	132.48	128.87
12000	201.01	188.34	178.45	170.58	164.20	158.98	154.65
15000	251.26	235.43	223.07	213.22	205.25	198.72	193.31
20000	335.01	313.90	297.42	284.30	273.67	264.96	257.74
25000	418.76	392.38	371.78	355.37	342.09	331.20	322.18
30000	502.51	470.86	446.14	426.44	410.50	397.44	386.61
31000	519.26	486.55	461.01	440.66	424.19	410.69	399.50
32000	536.02	502.25	475.88	454.87	437.87	423.93	412.39
33000	552.77	517.94	490.75	469.09	451.55	437.18	425.28
34000	569.52	533.64	505.62	483.30	465.24	450.43	438.16
35000	586.27	549.33	520.49	497.52	478.92	463.68	451.05
36000	603.02	565.03	535.36	511.73	492.60	476.93	463.94
37000	619.77	580.72	550.23	525.95	506.29	490.17	476.82
38000	636.52	596.42	565.11	540.16	519.97	503.42	489.71
39000	653.27	612.11	579.98	554.38	533.66	516.67	502.60
40000	670.02	627.81	594.85	568.59	547.34	529.92	515.49
41000	686.77	643.50	609.72	582.80	561.02	543.17	528.37
42000	703.52	659.20	624.59	597.02	574.71	556.41	541.26
43000	720.27	674.90	639.46	611.23	588.39	569.66	554.15
44000	737.02	690.59	654.33	625.45	602.07	582.91	567.03
45000	753.77	706.29	669.20	639.66	615.76	596.16	579.92
46000	770.52	721.98	684.08	653.88	629.44	609.40	592.81
47000	787.27	737.68	698.95	668.09	643.12	622.65	605.70
48000	804.02	753.37	713.82	682.31	656.81	635.90	618.58
49000	820.77	769.07	728.69	696.52	670.49	649.15	631.47
50000	837.52	784.76	743.56	710.74	684.17	662.40	644.36
51000	854.27	800.46	758.43	724.95	697.86	675.64	657.24
52000	871.02	816.15	773.30	739.17	711.54	688.89	670.13
53000	887.77	831.85	788.17	753.38	725.22	702.14	683.02
54000	904.53	847.54	803.04	767.60	738.91	715.39	695.90
55000	921.28	863.24	817.92	781.81	752.59	728.64	708.79
56000	938.03	878.93	832.79	796.03	766.27	741.88	721.68
57000	954.78	894.63	847.66	810.24	779.96	755.13	734.57
58000	971.53	910.32	862.53	824.46	793.64	768.38	747.45
59000	988.28	926.02	877.40	838.67	807.32	781.63	760.34
60000	1005.03	941.71	892.27	852.89	821.01	794.88	773.23
65000	1088.78	1020.19	966.63	923.96	889.43	861.12	837.66
70000	1172.53	1098.67	1040.98	995.03	957.84	927.35	902.10
75000	1256.29	1177.14	1115.34	1066.11	1026.26	993.59	966.53
80000	1340.04	1255.62	1189.70	1137.18	1094.68	1059.83	1030.97
85000	1423.79	1334.10	1264.05	1208.25	1163.09	1126.07	1095.41
90000	1507.54	1412.57	1338.41	1279.33	1231.51	1192.31	1159.84
95000	1591.29	1491.05	1412.76	1350.40	1299.93	1258.55	1224.28
100000	1675.05	1569.52	1487.12	1421.48	1368.35	1324.79	1288.71
105000	1758.80	1648.00	1561.48	1492.55	1436.76	1391.03	1353.15
110000	1842.55	1726.48	1635.83	1563.62	1505.18	1457.27	1417.58
120000	2010.06	1883.43	1784.54	1705.77	1642.02	1589.75	1546.46
130000	2177.56	2040.38	1933.26	1847.92	1778.85	1722.23	1675.33
140000	2345.07	2197.33	2081.97	1990.07	1915.68	1854.71	1804.20
150000	2512.57	2354.29	2230.68	2132.21	2052.52	1987.19	1933.07
160000	2680.08	2511.24	2379.39	2274.36	2189.35	2119.67	2061.94
170000	2847.58	2668.19	2528.10	2416.51	2326.19	2252.15	2190.81
180000	3015.08	2825.14	2676.82	2558.66	2463.02	2384.63	2319.68
190000	3182.59	2982.10	2825.53	2700.80	2599.86	2517.11	2448.55
200000	3350.09	3139.05	2974.24	2842.95	2736.69	2649.59	2577.43
210000	3517.60	3296.00	3122.95	2985.10	2873.53	2782.06	2706.30
220000	3685.10	3452.95	3271.66	3127.25	3010.36	2914.54	2835.17
230000	3852.61	3609.91	3420.38	3269.39	3147.20	3047.02	2964.04
240000	4020.11	3766.86	3569.09	3411.54	3284.03	3179.50	3092.91
250000	4187.62	3923.81	3717.80	3553.69	3420.87	3311.98	3221.78

13.25 % Monthly Payments

LOAN AMOUNT	15	16	17	18	19	20	21
				YEARS			
100	1.26	1.23	1.21	1.19	1.18	1.16	1.1
200	2.52	2.47	2.42	2.39	2.36	2.33	2.3
500	6.29	6.17	6.06	5.97	5.89	5.82	5.7
1000	12.59	12.33	12.12	11.93	11.78	11.64	11.5
2000	25.17	24.66	24.23	23.87	23.56	23.29	23.0
5000	62.93	61.66	60.58	59.67	58.89	58.22	57.6
6000	75.51	73.99	72.70	71.60	70.67	69.86	69.1
7000	88.10	86.32	84.82	83.54	82.44	81.50	80.7
8000	100.69	98.65	96.94	95.47	94.22	93.15	92.2
9000	113.27	110.99	109.05	107.41	106.00	104.79	103.7
10000	125.86	123.32	121.17	119.34	117.78	116.43	115.2
12000	151.03	147.98	145.40	143.21	141.33	139.72	138.3
15000	188.78	184.98	181.75	179.01	176.66	174.65	172.9
20000	251.71	246.64	242.34	238.68	235.55	232.87	230.5
25000	314.64	308.30	302.92	298.35	294.44	291.09	288.2
30000	377.57	369.96	363.51	358.02	353.33	349.30	345.8
31000	390.15	382.29	375.63	369.96	365.11	360.95	357.3
32000	402.74	394.62	387.74	381.89	376.89	372.59	368.8
33000	415.33	406.95	399.86	393.82	388.66	384.23	380.4
34000	427.91	419.28	411.98	405.76	400.44	395.88	391.9
35000	440.50	431.62	424.09	417.69	412.22	407.52	403.4
36000	453.08	443.95	436.21	429.63	424.00	419.16	415.0
37000	465.67	456.28	448.33	441.56	435.77	430.81	426.5
38000	478.25	468.61	460.45	453.49	447.55	442.45	438.0
39000	490.84	480.94	472.56	465.43	459.33	454.09	449.5
40000	503.43	493.27	484.68	477.36	471.11	465.74	461.1
41000	516.01	505.61	496.80	489.30	482.88	477.38	472.6
42000	528.60	517.94	508.91	501.23	494.66	489.02	484.1
43000	541.18	530.27	521.03	513.16	506.44	500.67	495.7
44000	553.77	542.60	533.15	525.10	518.22	512.31	507.2
45000	566.35	554.93	545.26	537.03	529.99	523.96	518.7
46000	578.94	567.27	557.38	548.97	541.77	535.60	530.2
47000	591.52	579.60	569.50	560.90	553.55	547.24	541.8
48000	604.11	591.93	581.61	572.83	565.33	558.89	553.3
49000	616.70	604.26	593.73	584.77	577.11	570.53	564.8
50000	629.28	616.59	605.85	596.70	588.88	582.17	576.3
51000	641.87	628.93	617.97	608.64	600.66	593.82	587.9
52000	654.45	641.26	630.08	620.57	612.44	605.46	599.4
53000	667.04	653.59	642.20	632.50	624.22	617.10	610.9
54000	679.62	665.92	654.32	644.44	635.99	628.75	622.5
55000	692.21	678.25	666.43	656.37	647.77	640.39	634.0
56000	704.80	690.58	678.55	668.31	659.55	652.03	645.5
57000	717.38	702.92	690.67	680.24	671.33	663.68	657.0
58000	729.97	715.25	702.78	692.18	683.10	675.32	668.6
59000	742.55	727.58	714.90	704.11	694.88	686.96	680.1
60000	755.14	739.91	727.02	716.04	706.66	698.61	691.6
65000	818.07	801.57	787.60	775.71	765.55	756.82	749.3
70000	880.99	863.23	848.19	835.38	824.44	815.04	806.9
75000	943.92	924.89	908.77	895.05	883.32	873.26	864.5
80000	1006.85	986.55	969.36	954.72	942.21	931.48	922.2
85000	1069.78	1048.21	1029.94	1014.39	1001.10	989.69	979.8
90000	1132.71	1109.87	1090.53	1074.06	1059.99	1047.91	1037.5
95000	1195.64	1171.53	1151.11	1133.73	1118.88	1106.13	1095.1
100000	1258.56	1233.19	1211.70	1193.41	1177.77	1164.34	1152.7
105000	1321.49	1294.85	1272.28	1253.08	1236.65	1222.56	1210.4
110000	1384.42	1356.51	1332.87	1312.75	1295.54	1280.78	1268.0
120000	1510.28	1479.82	1454.04	1432.09	1413.32	1397.21	1383.3
130000	1636.13	1603.14	1575.21	1551.43	1531.10	1513.65	1498.6
140000	1761.99	1726.46	1696.38	1670.77	1648.87	1630.08	1613.9
150000	1887.85	1849.78	1817.55	1790.11	1766.65	1746.52	1729.1
160000	2013.70	1973.10	1938.72	1909.45	1884.43	1862.95	1844.4
170000	2139.56	2096.42	2059.89	2028.79	2002.20	1979.39	1959.7
180000	2265.41	2219.74	2181.06	2148.13	2119.98	2095.82	2075.0
190000	2391.27	2343.06	2302.23	2267.47	2237.76	2212.25	2190.3
200000	2517.13	2466.37	2423.40	2386.81	2355.53	2328.69	2305.5
210000	2642.98	2589.69	2544.57	2506.15	2473.31	2445.12	2420.8
220000	2768.84	2713.01	2665.73	2625.49	2591.09	2561.56	2536.1
230000	2894.70	2836.33	2786.90	2744.83	2708.86	2677.99	2651.4
240000	3020.55	2959.65	2908.07	2864.17	2826.64	2794.43	2766.7
250000	3146.41	3082.97	3029.24	2983.51	2944.41	2910.86	2881.9

Monthly Payments 13.25 %

LOAN AMOUNT	22	23	24	25	30	35	40
				YEARS			
100	1.14	1.13	1.13	1.12	1.10	1.09	1.08
200	2.29	2.27	2.25	2.24	2.20	2.17	2.16
500	5.71	5.67	5.63	5.60	5.49	5.44	5.41
1000	11.43	11.34	11.27	11.20	10.98	10.87	10.81
2000	22.86	22.68	22.53	22.40	21.97	21.74	21.63
5000	57.14	56.71	56.33	56.01	54.91	54.35	54.06
6000	68.57	68.05	67.60	67.21	65.90	65.22	64.88
7000	80.00	79.39	78.87	78.41	76.88	76.09	75.69
8000	91.43	90.73	90.14	89.62	87.86	86.96	86.50
9000	102.85	102.08	101.40	100.82	98.84	97.84	97.31
10000	114.28	113.42	112.67	112.02	109.83	108.71	108.13
12000	137.14	136.10	135.20	134.42	131.79	130.45	129.75
15000	171.42	170.13	169.00	168.03	164.74	163.06	162.19
20000	228.56	226.84	225.34	224.04	219.65	217.41	216.25
25000	285.70	283.55	281.67	280.05	274.57	271.76	270.31
30000	342.84	340.25	338.01	336.06	329.48	326.12	324.38
31000	354.27	351.60	349.28	347.26	340.46	336.99	335.19
32000	365.70	362.94	360.54	358.46	351.44	347.86	346.00
33000	377.13	374.28	371.81	369.66	362.43	358.73	356.81
34000	388.56	385.62	383.08	380.86	373.41	369.60	367.63
35000	399.98	396.96	394.34	392.07	384.39	380.47	378.44
36000	411.41	408.31	405.61	403.27	395.37	391.34	389.25
37000	422.84	419.65	416.88	414.47	406.36	402.21	400.06
38000	434.27	430.99	428.14	425.67	417.34	413.08	410.88
39000	445.70	442.33	439.41	436.87	428.32	423.95	421.69
40000	457.13	453.67	450.68	448.08	439.31	434.82	432.50
41000	468.55	465.01	461.94	459.28	450.29	445.69	443.31
42000	479.98	476.36	473.21	470.48	461.27	456.56	454.13
43000	491.41	487.70	484.48	481.68	472.25	467.44	464.94
44000	502.84	499.04	495.75	492.88	483.24	478.31	475.75
45000	514.27	510.38	507.01	504.09	494.22	489.18	486.56
46000	525.69	521.72	518.28	515.29	505.20	500.05	497.38
47000	537.12	533.07	529.55	526.49	516.18	510.92	508.19
48000	548.55	544.41	540.81	537.69	527.17	521.79	519.00
49000	559.98	555.75	552.08	548.89	538.15	532.66	529.81
50000	571.41	567.09	563.35	560.10	549.13	543.53	540.63
51000	582.84	578.43	574.61	571.30	560.11	554.40	551.44
52000	594.26	589.77	585.88	582.50	571.10	565.27	562.25
53000	605.69	601.12	597.15	593.70	582.08	576.14	573.06
54000	617.12	612.46	608.42	604.90	593.06	587.01	583.88
55000	628.55	623.80	619.68	616.11	604.04	597.88	594.69
56000	639.98	635.14	630.95	627.31	615.03	608.75	605.50
57000	651.40	646.48	642.22	638.51	626.01	619.62	616.31
58000	662.83	657.83	653.48	649.71	636.99	630.49	627.13
59000	674.26	669.17	664.75	660.91	647.98	641.36	637.94
60000	685.69	680.51	676.02	672.11	658.96	652.24	648.75
65000	742.83	737.22	732.35	728.12	713.87	706.59	702.81
70000	799.97	793.93	788.69	784.13	768.78	760.94	756.88
75000	857.11	850.64	845.02	840.14	823.70	815.29	810.94
80000	914.25	907.34	901.36	896.15	878.61	869.65	865.00
85000	971.39	964.05	957.69	952.16	933.52	924.00	919.06
90000	1028.53	1020.76	1014.03	1008.17	988.44	978.35	973.13
95000	1085.67	1077.47	1070.36	1064.18	1043.35	1032.71	1027.19
100000	1142.81	1134.18	1126.69	1120.19	1098.26	1087.06	1081.25
105000	1199.95	1190.89	1183.03	1176.20	1153.18	1141.41	1135.31
110000	1257.10	1247.60	1239.36	1232.21	1208.09	1195.77	1189.38
120000	1371.38	1361.02	1352.03	1344.23	1317.92	1304.47	1297.50
130000	1485.66	1474.44	1464.70	1456.25	1427.74	1413.18	1405.63
140000	1599.94	1587.85	1577.37	1568.27	1537.57	1521.88	1513.75
150000	1714.22	1701.27	1690.04	1680.29	1647.39	1630.59	1621.88
160000	1828.50	1814.69	1802.71	1792.31	1757.22	1739.29	1730.00
170000	1942.78	1928.11	1915.38	1904.32	1867.05	1848.00	1838.13
180000	2057.07	2041.53	2028.05	2016.34	1976.87	1956.71	1946.25
190000	2171.35	2154.94	2140.72	2128.36	2086.70	2065.41	2054.38
200000	2285.63	2268.36	2253.39	2240.38	2196.53	2174.12	2162.50
210000	2399.91	2381.78	2366.06	2352.40	2306.35	2282.82	2270.63
220000	2514.19	2495.20	2478.73	2464.42	2416.18	2391.53	2378.75
230000	2628.47	2608.62	2591.40	2576.44	2526.01	2500.24	2486.88
240000	2742.75	2722.03	2704.07	2688.46	2635.83	2608.94	2595.00
250000	2857.04	2835.45	2816.74	2800.48	2745.66	2717.65	2703.13

13.50 %   Monthly Payments

LOAN AMOUNT	1	2	3	4	5	6	7
			YEARS				
100	8.94	4.76	3.38	2.69	2.28	2.01	1.8
200	17.88	9.52	6.75	5.38	4.56	4.03	3.6
500	44.69	23.80	16.88	13.45	11.41	10.07	9.1
1000	89.38	47.61	33.76	26.89	22.82	20.15	18.2
2000	178.76	95.21	67.52	53.79	45.64	40.29	36.5
5000	446.90	238.03	168.80	134.47	114.11	100.73	91.3
6000	536.28	285.63	202.55	161.37	136.93	120.87	109.5
7000	625.67	333.24	236.31	188.26	159.76	141.02	127.8
8000	715.05	380.84	270.07	215.16	182.58	161.16	146.1
9000	804.43	428.45	303.83	242.05	205.40	181.31	164.3
10000	893.81	476.05	337.59	268.95	228.22	201.46	182.6
12000	1072.57	571.26	405.11	322.74	273.87	241.75	219.1
15000	1340.71	714.08	506.39	403.42	342.34	302.18	273.9
20000	1787.61	952.11	675.18	537.89	456.45	402.91	365.3
25000	2234.52	1190.13	843.98	672.37	570.56	503.64	456.6
30000	2681.42	1428.16	1012.77	806.84	684.67	604.37	547.9
31000	2770.80	1475.77	1046.53	833.74	707.49	624.51	566.2
32000	2860.18	1523.37	1080.29	860.63	730.32	644.66	584.5
33000	2949.56	1570.98	1114.05	887.52	753.14	664.80	602.7
34000	3038.95	1618.58	1147.81	914.42	775.96	684.95	621.0
35000	3128.33	1666.19	1181.57	941.31	798.78	705.09	639.3
36000	3217.71	1713.79	1215.33	968.21	821.61	725.24	657.5
37000	3307.09	1761.40	1249.09	995.10	844.43	745.39	675.8
38000	3396.47	1809.00	1282.85	1022.00	867.25	765.53	694.0
39000	3485.85	1856.61	1316.61	1048.89	890.07	785.68	712.3
40000	3575.23	1904.22	1350.37	1075.79	912.90	805.82	730.6
41000	3664.61	1951.82	1384.12	1102.68	935.72	825.97	748.8
42000	3753.99	1999.43	1417.88	1129.58	958.54	846.11	767.1
43000	3843.37	2047.03	1451.64	1156.47	981.36	866.26	785.4
44000	3932.75	2094.64	1485.40	1183.37	1004.18	886.40	803.6
45000	4022.13	2142.24	1519.16	1210.26	1027.01	906.55	821.9
46000	4111.51	2189.85	1552.92	1237.16	1049.83	926.70	840.2
47000	4200.90	2237.45	1586.68	1264.05	1072.65	946.84	858.4
48000	4290.28	2285.06	1620.44	1290.94	1095.47	966.99	876.7
49000	4379.66	2332.66	1654.20	1317.84	1118.30	987.13	895.
50000	4469.04	2380.27	1687.96	1344.73	1141.12	1007.28	913.2
51000	4558.42	2427.87	1721.72	1371.63	1163.94	1027.42	931.5
52000	4647.80	2475.48	1755.48	1398.52	1186.76	1047.57	949.8
53000	4737.18	2523.09	1789.23	1425.42	1209.59	1067.71	968.
54000	4826.56	2570.69	1822.99	1452.31	1232.41	1087.86	986.
55000	4915.94	2618.30	1856.75	1479.21	1255.23	1108.01	1004.6
56000	5005.32	2665.90	1890.51	1506.10	1278.05	1128.15	1022.8
57000	5094.70	2713.51	1924.27	1533.00	1300.88	1148.30	1041.1
58000	5184.08	2761.11	1958.03	1559.89	1323.70	1168.44	1059.4
59000	5273.46	2808.72	1991.79	1586.79	1346.52	1188.59	1077.
60000	5362.84	2856.32	2025.55	1613.68	1369.34	1208.73	1095.9
65000	5809.75	3094.35	2194.34	1748.15	1483.45	1309.46	1187.2
70000	6256.65	3332.38	2363.14	1882.63	1597.57	1410.19	1278.5
75000	6703.56	3570.40	2531.94	2017.10	1711.68	1510.92	1369.
80000	7150.46	3808.43	2700.73	2151.57	1825.79	1611.65	1461.2
85000	7597.36	4046.46	2869.53	2286.05	1939.90	1712.37	1552.5
90000	8044.27	4284.48	3038.32	2420.52	2054.01	1813.10	1643.9
95000	8491.17	4522.51	3207.12	2554.99	2168.13	1913.83	1735.2
100000	8938.07	4760.54	3375.91	2689.47	2282.24	2014.56	1826.5
105000	9384.98	4998.57	3544.71	2823.94	2396.35	2115.28	1917.8
110000	9831.88	5236.59	3713.51	2958.41	2510.46	2216.01	2009.2
120000	10725.69	5712.65	4051.10	3227.36	2738.69	2417.47	2191.8
130000	11619.50	6188.70	4388.69	3496.31	2966.91	2618.92	2374.5
140000	12513.30	6664.75	4726.28	3765.26	3195.13	2820.38	2557.
150000	13407.11	7140.81	5063.87	4034.20	3423.36	3021.83	2739.8
160000	14300.92	7616.86	5401.46	4303.15	3651.58	3223.29	2922.4
170000	15194.73	8092.91	5739.05	4572.10	3879.80	3424.75	3105.
180000	16088.53	8568.97	6076.65	4841.04	4108.03	3626.20	3287.
190000	16982.34	9045.02	6414.24	5109.99	4336.25	3827.66	3470.
200000	17876.15	9521.08	6751.83	5378.94	4564.48	4029.11	3653.
210000	18769.96	9997.13	7089.42	5647.88	4792.70	4230.57	3835.
220000	19663.76	10473.18	7427.01	5916.83	5020.92	4432.02	4018.4
230000	20557.57	10949.24	7764.60	6185.78	5249.15	4633.48	4201.0
240000	21451.38	11425.29	8102.19	6454.72	5477.37	4834.94	4383.
250000	22345.19	11901.35	8439.78	6723.67	5705.59	5036.39	4566.

Monthly Payments 13.50 %

LOAN AMOUNT	8	9	10	11	12	13	14
				YEARS			
100	1.69	1.58	1.50	1.44	1.38	1.34	1.30
200	3.38	3.17	3.00	2.87	2.77	2.68	2.61
500	8.44	7.92	7.51	7.18	6.92	6.70	6.52
1000	16.88	15.83	15.01	14.36	13.83	13.40	13.04
2000	33.77	31.66	30.02	28.72	27.66	26.80	26.08
5000	84.42	79.16	75.05	71.79	69.15	66.99	65.20
6000	101.30	94.99	90.07	86.15	82.98	80.39	78.24
7000	118.18	110.82	105.08	100.51	96.81	93.78	91.28
8000	135.06	126.65	120.09	114.86	110.64	107.18	104.32
9000	151.95	142.48	135.10	129.22	124.47	120.58	117.36
10000	168.83	158.31	150.11	143.58	138.30	133.98	130.40
12000	202.60	189.98	180.13	172.30	165.96	160.77	156.48
15000	253.25	237.47	225.16	215.37	207.45	200.97	195.60
20000	337.66	316.63	300.22	287.16	276.60	267.95	260.80
25000	422.08	395.79	375.27	358.95	345.75	334.94	326.00
30000	506.49	474.94	450.33	430.74	414.90	401.93	391.20
31000	523.37	490.77	465.34	445.10	428.73	415.33	404.24
32000	540.26	506.61	480.35	459.46	442.56	428.73	417.28
33000	557.14	522.44	495.36	473.81	456.39	442.13	430.32
34000	574.02	538.27	510.37	488.17	470.22	455.52	443.36
35000	590.91	554.10	525.38	502.53	484.05	468.92	456.40
36000	607.79	569.93	540.39	516.89	497.88	482.32	469.44
37000	624.67	585.76	555.41	531.25	511.71	495.72	482.48
38000	641.55	601.59	570.42	545.60	525.54	509.11	495.52
39000	658.44	617.43	585.43	559.96	539.37	522.51	508.56
40000	675.32	633.26	600.44	574.32	553.20	535.91	521.60
41000	692.20	649.09	615.45	588.68	567.03	549.31	534.64
42000	709.09	664.92	630.46	603.04	580.86	562.71	547.68
43000	725.97	680.75	645.47	617.39	594.69	576.10	560.72
44000	742.85	696.58	660.48	631.75	608.52	589.50	573.76
45000	759.74	712.41	675.49	646.11	622.35	602.90	586.80
46000	776.62	728.25	690.50	660.47	636.18	616.30	599.84
47000	793.50	744.08	705.52	674.83	650.01	629.69	612.88
48000	810.38	759.91	720.53	689.18	663.84	643.09	625.92
49000	827.27	775.74	735.54	703.54	677.67	656.49	638.96
50000	844.15	791.57	750.55	717.90	691.50	669.89	652.00
51000	861.03	807.40	765.56	732.26	705.33	683.29	665.04
52000	877.92	823.23	780.57	746.61	719.16	696.68	678.08
53000	894.80	839.07	795.58	760.97	732.99	710.08	691.12
54000	911.68	854.90	810.59	775.33	746.82	723.48	704.16
55000	928.57	870.73	825.60	789.69	760.65	736.88	717.20
56000	945.45	886.56	840.61	804.05	774.48	750.27	730.24
57000	962.33	902.39	855.62	818.40	788.31	763.67	743.28
58000	979.21	918.22	870.64	832.76	802.14	777.07	756.32
59000	996.10	934.05	885.65	847.12	815.97	790.47	769.36
60000	1012.98	949.89	900.66	861.48	829.80	803.86	782.40
65000	1097.40	1029.04	975.71	933.27	898.95	870.85	847.60
70000	1181.81	1108.20	1050.77	1005.06	968.10	937.84	912.80
75000	1266.23	1187.36	1125.82	1076.85	1037.25	1004.83	978.00
80000	1350.64	1266.51	1200.88	1148.64	1106.40	1071.82	1043.21
85000	1435.06	1345.67	1275.93	1220.43	1175.55	1138.81	1108.41
90000	1519.47	1424.83	1350.99	1292.22	1244.70	1205.80	1173.61
95000	1603.89	1503.99	1426.04	1364.01	1313.85	1272.79	1238.81
100000	1688.30	1583.14	1501.10	1435.80	1383.00	1339.77	1304.01
105000	1772.72	1662.30	1576.15	1507.59	1452.15	1406.76	1369.21
110000	1857.13	1741.46	1651.21	1579.38	1521.31	1473.75	1434.41
120000	2025.96	1899.77	1801.32	1722.96	1659.61	1607.73	1564.81
130000	2194.79	2058.09	1951.42	1866.54	1797.91	1741.71	1695.21
140000	2363.62	2216.40	2101.53	2010.12	1936.21	1875.68	1825.61
150000	2532.45	2374.71	2251.64	2153.70	2074.51	2009.66	1956.01
160000	2701.28	2533.03	2401.75	2297.28	2212.81	2143.64	2086.41
170000	2870.11	2691.34	2551.86	2440.86	2351.11	2277.62	2216.81
180000	3038.94	2849.66	2701.97	2584.44	2489.41	2411.59	2347.21
190000	3207.77	3007.97	2852.08	2728.02	2627.71	2545.57	2477.61
200000	3376.60	3166.29	3002.19	2871.60	2766.01	2679.55	2608.01
210000	3545.43	3324.60	3152.30	3015.18	2904.31	2813.53	2738.41
220000	3714.26	3482.91	3302.41	3158.76	3042.61	2947.50	2868.81
230000	3883.09	3641.23	3452.52	3302.34	3180.91	3081.48	2999.21
240000	4051.92	3799.54	3602.63	3445.92	3319.21	3215.46	3129.62
250000	4220.75	3957.86	3752.74	3589.50	3457.51	3349.44	3260.02

13.50 % Monthly Payments

LOAN AMOUNT	15	16	17	18	19	20	21
				YEARS			
100	1.27	1.25	1.23	1.21	1.19	1.18	1.17
200	2.55	2.50	2.46	2.42	2.39	2.36	2.34
500	6.37	6.25	6.14	6.05	5.97	5.91	5.85
1000	12.74	12.49	12.28	12.10	11.94	11.81	11.70
2000	25.48	24.98	24.56	24.20	23.89	23.62	23.40
5000	63.71	62.45	61.39	60.49	59.72	59.06	58.49
6000	76.45	74.94	73.67	72.59	71.66	70.87	70.19
7000	89.19	87.43	85.95	84.69	83.61	82.69	81.89
8000	101.93	99.93	98.23	96.78	95.55	94.50	93.59
9000	114.67	112.42	110.51	108.88	107.50	106.31	105.29
10000	127.42	124.91	122.78	120.98	119.44	118.12	116.99
12000	152.90	149.89	147.34	145.18	143.33	141.75	140.39
15000	191.12	187.36	184.18	181.47	179.16	177.18	175.48
20000	254.83	249.81	245.57	241.96	238.88	236.25	233.98
25000	318.54	312.27	306.96	302.45	298.60	295.31	292.47
30000	382.25	374.72	368.35	362.94	358.32	354.37	350.97
31000	394.99	387.21	380.63	375.04	370.27	366.18	362.67
32000	407.73	399.70	392.91	387.14	382.21	377.99	374.36
33000	420.47	412.19	405.19	399.24	394.16	389.80	386.06
34000	433.21	424.68	417.47	411.34	406.10	401.62	397.76
35000	445.95	437.17	429.75	423.43	418.05	413.43	409.46
36000	458.70	449.66	442.02	435.53	429.99	425.24	421.16
37000	471.44	462.15	454.30	447.63	441.93	437.05	432.86
38000	484.18	474.64	466.58	459.73	453.88	448.87	444.56
39000	496.92	487.13	478.86	471.83	465.82	460.68	456.26
40000	509.66	499.63	491.14	483.92	477.77	472.49	467.96
41000	522.40	512.12	503.42	496.02	489.71	484.30	479.65
42000	535.15	524.61	515.70	508.12	501.65	496.11	491.35
43000	547.89	537.10	527.97	520.22	513.60	507.93	503.05
44000	560.63	549.59	540.25	532.32	525.54	519.74	514.75
45000	573.37	562.08	552.53	544.41	537.49	531.55	526.45
46000	586.11	574.57	564.81	556.51	549.43	543.36	538.15
47000	598.85	587.06	577.09	568.61	561.38	555.18	549.85
48000	611.59	599.55	589.37	580.71	573.32	566.99	561.55
49000	624.34	612.04	601.64	592.81	585.26	578.80	573.24
50000	637.08	624.53	613.92	604.91	597.21	590.61	584.94
51000	649.82	637.02	626.20	617.00	609.15	602.42	596.64
52000	662.56	649.51	638.48	629.10	621.10	614.24	608.34
53000	675.30	662.00	650.76	641.20	633.04	626.05	620.04
54000	688.04	674.49	663.04	653.30	644.98	637.86	631.74
55000	700.79	686.99	675.32	665.40	656.93	649.67	643.44
56000	713.53	699.48	687.59	677.49	668.87	661.49	655.14
57000	726.27	711.97	699.87	689.59	680.82	673.30	666.84
58000	739.01	724.46	712.15	701.69	692.76	685.11	678.53
59000	751.75	736.95	724.43	713.79	704.71	696.92	690.23
60000	764.49	749.44	736.71	725.89	716.65	708.74	701.93
65000	828.20	811.89	798.10	786.38	776.37	767.80	760.43
70000	891.91	874.34	859.49	846.87	836.09	826.86	818.92
75000	955.62	936.80	920.88	907.36	895.81	885.92	877.42
80000	1019.32	999.25	982.28	967.85	955.53	944.98	935.91
85000	1083.03	1061.70	1043.67	1028.34	1015.25	1004.04	994.40
90000	1146.74	1124.16	1105.06	1088.83	1074.97	1063.10	1052.90
95000	1210.45	1186.61	1166.45	1149.32	1134.69	1122.16	1111.39
100000	1274.16	1249.06	1227.85	1209.81	1194.42	1181.23	1169.89
105000	1337.86	1311.52	1289.24	1270.30	1254.14	1240.29	1228.38
110000	1401.57	1373.97	1350.63	1330.79	1313.86	1299.35	1286.88
120000	1528.99	1498.88	1473.41	1451.77	1433.30	1417.47	1403.87
130000	1656.40	1623.78	1596.20	1572.75	1552.74	1535.59	1520.85
140000	1783.82	1748.69	1718.98	1693.74	1672.18	1653.72	1637.84
150000	1911.23	1873.60	1841.77	1814.72	1791.62	1771.84	1754.83
160000	2038.65	1998.50	1964.55	1935.70	1911.07	1889.96	1871.82
170000	2166.06	2123.41	2087.34	2056.68	2030.51	2008.08	1988.81
180000	2293.48	2248.32	2210.12	2177.66	2149.95	2126.21	2105.80
190000	2420.90	2373.22	2332.91	2298.64	2269.39	2244.33	2222.79
200000	2548.31	2498.13	2455.69	2419.62	2388.83	2362.45	2339.78
210000	2675.73	2623.03	2578.48	2540.60	2508.27	2480.57	2456.76
220000	2803.14	2747.94	2701.26	2661.58	2627.71	2598.70	2573.75
230000	2930.56	2872.85	2824.04	2782.56	2747.16	2716.82	2690.74
240000	3057.97	2997.75	2946.83	2903.55	2866.60	2834.94	2807.73
250000	3185.39	3122.66	3069.61	3024.53	2986.04	2953.06	2924.72

Monthly Payments 13.50 %

LOAN AMOUNT	22	23	24	25	30	35	40
	YEARS						
100	1.16	1.15	1.14	1.14	1.12	1.11	1.10
200	2.32	2.30	2.29	2.28	2.23	2.21	2.20
500	5.80	5.76	5.72	5.69	5.58	5.53	5.50
1000	11.60	11.52	11.44	11.38	11.17	11.06	11.01
2000	23.20	23.03	22.89	22.76	22.34	22.12	22.01
5000	58.01	57.58	57.22	56.90	55.84	55.30	55.03
6000	69.61	69.10	68.66	68.28	67.01	66.36	66.03
7000	81.21	80.62	80.11	79.66	78.17	77.42	77.04
8000	92.81	92.13	91.55	91.04	89.34	88.48	88.04
9000	104.41	103.65	102.99	102.42	100.51	99.54	99.05
10000	116.01	115.17	114.44	113.80	111.68	110.60	110.05
12000	139.21	138.20	137.32	136.56	134.01	132.72	132.06
15000	174.02	172.75	171.66	170.70	167.52	165.91	165.08
20000	232.02	230.34	228.87	227.61	223.36	221.21	220.10
25000	290.03	287.92	286.09	284.51	279.20	276.51	275.13
30000	348.03	345.50	343.31	341.41	335.03	331.81	330.16
31000	359.64	357.02	354.75	352.79	346.20	342.87	341.16
32000	371.24	368.54	366.20	364.17	357.37	353.93	352.17
33000	382.84	380.05	377.64	375.55	368.54	364.99	363.17
34000	394.44	391.57	389.09	386.93	379.71	376.05	374.18
35000	406.04	403.09	400.53	398.31	390.87	387.11	385.18
36000	417.64	414.60	411.97	409.69	402.04	398.17	396.19
37000	429.24	426.12	423.42	421.07	413.21	409.23	407.19
38000	440.84	437.64	434.86	432.45	424.38	420.29	418.20
39000	452.45	449.15	446.30	443.83	435.54	431.35	429.20
40000	464.05	460.67	457.75	455.21	446.71	442.41	440.21
41000	475.65	472.19	469.19	466.59	457.88	453.47	451.21
42000	487.25	483.70	480.63	477.97	469.05	464.53	462.22
43000	498.85	495.22	492.08	489.35	480.22	475.59	473.22
44000	510.45	506.74	503.52	500.73	491.38	486.66	484.23
45000	522.05	518.25	514.97	512.11	502.55	497.72	495.24
46000	533.65	529.77	526.41	523.49	513.72	508.78	506.24
47000	545.25	541.29	537.85	534.88	524.89	519.84	517.25
48000	556.86	552.80	549.30	546.26	536.06	530.90	528.25
49000	568.46	564.32	560.74	557.64	547.22	541.96	539.26
50000	580.06	575.84	572.18	569.02	558.39	553.02	550.26
51000	591.66	587.35	583.63	580.40	569.56	564.08	561.27
52000	603.26	598.87	595.07	591.78	580.73	575.14	572.27
53000	614.86	610.39	606.52	603.16	591.89	586.20	583.28
54000	626.46	621.90	617.96	614.54	603.06	597.26	594.28
55000	638.06	633.42	629.40	625.92	614.23	608.32	605.29
56000	649.67	644.94	640.85	637.30	625.40	619.38	616.29
57000	661.27	656.45	652.29	648.68	636.57	630.44	627.30
58000	672.87	667.97	663.73	660.06	647.73	641.50	638.30
59000	684.47	679.49	675.18	671.44	658.90	652.56	649.31
60000	696.07	691.01	686.62	682.82	670.07	663.62	660.31
65000	754.08	748.59	743.84	739.72	725.91	718.92	715.34
70000	812.08	806.17	801.06	796.62	781.75	774.22	770.37
75000	870.09	863.76	858.28	853.52	837.59	829.53	825.39
80000	928.09	921.34	915.49	910.43	893.43	884.83	880.42
85000	986.10	978.92	972.71	967.33	949.26	940.13	935.44
90000	1044.10	1036.51	1029.93	1024.23	1005.10	995.43	990.47
95000	1102.11	1094.09	1087.15	1081.13	1060.94	1050.73	1045.50
100000	1160.12	1151.68	1144.37	1138.03	1116.78	1106.03	1100.52
105000	1218.12	1209.26	1201.59	1194.93	1172.62	1161.34	1155.55
110000	1276.13	1266.84	1258.81	1251.84	1228.46	1216.64	1210.58
120000	1392.14	1382.01	1373.24	1365.64	1340.14	1327.24	1320.63
130000	1508.15	1497.18	1487.68	1479.44	1451.82	1437.84	1430.68
140000	1624.16	1612.35	1602.12	1593.25	1563.49	1548.45	1540.73
150000	1740.17	1727.51	1716.55	1707.05	1675.17	1659.05	1650.78
160000	1856.19	1842.68	1830.99	1820.85	1786.85	1769.66	1760.84
170000	1972.20	1957.85	1945.43	1934.65	1898.53	1880.26	1870.89
180000	2088.21	2073.02	2059.86	2048.46	2010.21	1990.86	1980.94
190000	2204.22	2188.18	2174.30	2162.26	2121.89	2101.47	2090.99
200000	2320.23	2303.35	2288.74	2276.06	2233.56	2212.07	2201.05
210000	2436.24	2418.52	2403.17	2389.87	2345.24	2322.67	2311.10
220000	2552.26	2533.69	2517.61	2503.67	2456.92	2433.28	2421.15
230000	2668.27	2648.85	2632.05	2617.47	2568.60	2543.88	2531.20
240000	2784.28	2764.02	2746.48	2731.28	2680.28	2654.48	2641.26
250000	2900.29	2879.19	2860.92	2845.08	2791.95	2765.09	2751.31

13.75 % Monthly Payments

LOAN AMOUNT	YEARS 1	2	3	4	5	6	7
100	8.95	4.77	3.39	2.70	2.29	2.03	1.84
200	17.90	9.54	6.77	5.40	4.59	4.05	3.68
500	44.75	23.86	16.94	13.51	11.47	10.14	9.20
1000	89.49	47.72	33.87	27.01	22.94	20.27	18.39
2000	178.98	95.43	67.75	54.02	45.89	40.54	36.79
5000	447.46	238.58	169.37	135.06	114.72	101.35	91.97
6000	536.95	286.30	203.24	162.07	137.66	121.63	110.37
7000	626.44	334.02	237.11	189.09	160.61	141.90	128.76
8000	715.93	381.73	270.99	216.10	183.55	162.17	147.16
9000	805.43	429.45	304.86	243.11	206.50	182.44	165.55
10000	894.92	477.17	338.73	270.12	229.44	202.71	183.95
12000	1073.90	572.60	406.48	324.15	275.33	243.25	220.74
15000	1342.38	715.75	508.10	405.19	344.16	304.06	275.92
20000	1789.84	954.33	677.47	540.25	458.88	405.42	367.90
25000	2237.30	1192.92	846.83	675.31	573.60	506.77	459.87
30000	2684.76	1431.50	1016.20	810.37	688.32	608.13	551.84
31000	2774.25	1479.22	1050.07	837.39	711.26	628.40	570.24
32000	2863.74	1526.93	1083.95	864.40	734.21	648.67	588.63
33000	2953.23	1574.65	1117.82	891.41	757.15	668.94	607.03
34000	3042.72	1622.37	1151.69	918.42	780.09	689.21	625.42
35000	3132.21	1670.08	1185.57	945.44	803.04	709.48	643.82
36000	3221.71	1717.80	1219.44	972.45	825.98	729.75	662.21
37000	3311.20	1765.52	1253.31	999.46	848.92	750.02	680.61
38000	3400.69	1813.23	1287.19	1026.47	871.87	770.30	699.00
39000	3490.18	1860.95	1321.06	1053.49	894.81	790.57	717.40
40000	3579.67	1908.67	1354.93	1080.50	917.76	810.84	735.79
41000	3669.17	1956.38	1388.81	1107.51	940.70	831.11	754.19
42000	3758.66	2004.10	1422.68	1134.52	963.64	851.38	772.58
43000	3848.15	2051.82	1456.55	1161.54	986.59	871.65	790.97
44000	3937.64	2099.53	1490.43	1188.55	1009.53	891.92	809.37
45000	4027.13	2147.25	1524.30	1215.56	1032.48	912.19	827.76
46000	4116.63	2194.97	1558.17	1242.57	1055.42	932.46	846.16
47000	4206.12	2242.68	1592.05	1269.59	1078.36	952.73	864.55
48000	4295.61	2290.40	1625.92	1296.60	1101.31	973.00	882.95
49000	4385.10	2338.12	1659.79	1323.61	1124.25	993.28	901.34
50000	4474.59	2385.83	1693.67	1350.62	1147.20	1013.55	919.74
51000	4564.08	2433.55	1727.54	1377.63	1170.14	1033.82	938.13
52000	4653.58	2481.27	1761.41	1404.65	1193.08	1054.09	956.53
53000	4743.07	2528.98	1795.29	1431.66	1216.03	1074.36	974.92
54000	4832.56	2576.70	1829.16	1458.67	1238.97	1094.63	993.32
55000	4922.05	2624.42	1863.03	1485.68	1261.91	1114.90	1011.71
56000	5011.54	2672.13	1896.91	1512.70	1284.86	1135.17	1030.11
57000	5101.04	2719.85	1930.78	1539.71	1307.80	1155.44	1048.50
58000	5190.53	2767.57	1964.66	1566.72	1330.75	1175.71	1066.90
59000	5280.02	2815.29	1998.53	1593.73	1353.69	1195.98	1085.29
60000	5369.51	2863.00	2032.40	1620.75	1376.63	1216.26	1103.69
65000	5816.97	3101.59	2201.77	1755.81	1491.35	1317.61	1195.66
70000	6264.43	3340.17	2371.14	1890.87	1606.07	1418.96	1287.63
75000	6711.89	3578.75	2540.50	2025.93	1720.79	1520.32	1379.61
80000	7159.35	3817.34	2709.87	2161.00	1835.51	1621.67	1471.58
85000	7606.81	4055.92	2879.24	2296.06	1950.23	1723.03	1563.55
90000	8054.27	4294.50	3048.60	2431.12	2064.95	1824.38	1655.53
95000	8501.73	4533.09	3217.97	2566.18	2179.67	1925.74	1747.50
100000	8949.19	4771.67	3387.34	2701.24	2294.39	2027.09	1839.48
105000	9396.64	5010.25	3556.70	2836.31	2409.11	2128.45	1931.45
110000	9844.10	5248.84	3726.07	2971.37	2523.83	2229.80	2023.42
120000	10739.02	5726.00	4064.80	3241.49	2753.27	2432.51	2207.37
130000	11633.94	6203.17	4403.54	3511.62	2982.71	2635.22	2391.32
140000	12528.86	6680.34	4742.27	3781.74	3212.15	2837.93	2575.27
150000	13423.78	7157.50	5081.00	4051.87	3441.59	3040.64	2759.21
160000	14318.70	7634.67	5419.74	4321.99	3671.03	3243.35	2943.16
170000	15213.62	8111.84	5758.47	4592.12	3900.46	3446.06	3127.11
180000	16108.53	8589.01	6097.21	4862.24	4129.90	3648.77	3311.06
190000	17003.45	9066.17	6435.94	5132.37	4359.34	3851.48	3495.00
200000	17898.37	9543.34	6774.67	5402.49	4588.78	4054.18	3678.95
210000	18793.29	10020.51	7113.41	5672.61	4818.22	4256.89	3862.90
220000	19688.21	10497.67	7452.14	5942.74	5047.66	4459.60	4046.85
230000	20583.13	10974.84	7790.87	6212.86	5277.10	4662.31	4230.79
240000	21478.04	11452.01	8129.61	6482.99	5506.54	4865.02	4414.74
250000	22372.96	11929.17	8468.34	6753.11	5735.98	5067.73	4598.69

Monthly Payments 13.75 %

LOAN	YEARS						
AMOUNT	8	9	10	11	12	13	14
100	1.70	1.60	1.52	1.45	1.40	1.35	1.32
200	3.40	3.19	3.03	2.90	2.80	2.71	2.64
500	8.51	7.98	7.58	7.25	6.99	6.77	6.60
1000	17.02	15.97	15.15	14.50	13.98	13.55	13.19
2000	34.03	31.94	30.30	29.00	27.95	27.10	26.39
5000	85.08	79.84	75.76	72.51	69.89	67.74	65.97
6000	102.10	95.81	90.91	87.01	83.86	81.29	79.16
7000	119.11	111.78	106.06	101.51	97.84	94.84	92.36
8000	136.13	127.74	121.21	116.01	111.82	108.39	105.55
9000	153.14	143.71	136.36	130.52	125.79	121.93	118.74
10000	170.16	159.68	151.51	145.02	139.77	135.48	131.94
12000	204.19	191.62	181.81	174.02	167.73	162.58	158.32
15000	255.24	239.52	227.27	217.53	209.66	203.22	197.90
20000	340.32	319.36	303.02	290.04	279.54	270.96	263.87
25000	425.40	399.20	378.78	362.54	349.43	338.70	329.84
30000	510.48	479.04	454.54	435.05	419.32	406.45	395.81
31000	527.49	495.01	469.69	449.55	433.29	419.99	409.00
32000	544.51	510.98	484.84	464.06	447.27	433.54	422.20
33000	561.53	526.95	499.99	478.56	461.25	447.09	435.39
34000	578.54	542.92	515.14	493.06	475.23	460.64	448.58
35000	595.56	558.88	530.29	507.56	489.20	474.19	461.78
36000	612.57	574.85	545.44	522.06	503.18	487.73	474.97
37000	629.59	590.82	560.60	536.56	517.16	501.28	488.16
38000	646.61	606.79	575.75	551.07	531.13	514.83	501.36
39000	663.62	622.76	590.90	565.57	545.11	528.38	514.55
40000	680.64	638.72	606.05	580.07	559.09	541.93	527.74
41000	697.65	654.69	621.20	594.57	573.07	555.48	540.94
42000	714.67	670.66	636.35	609.07	587.04	569.02	554.13
43000	731.69	686.63	651.50	623.58	601.02	582.57	567.33
44000	748.70	702.60	666.65	638.08	615.00	596.12	580.52
45000	765.72	718.56	681.81	652.58	628.97	609.67	593.71
46000	782.73	734.53	696.96	667.08	642.95	623.22	606.91
47000	799.75	750.50	712.11	681.58	656.93	636.76	620.10
48000	816.77	766.47	727.26	696.08	670.91	650.31	633.29
49000	833.78	782.44	742.41	710.59	684.88	663.86	646.49
50000	850.80	798.40	757.56	725.09	698.86	677.41	659.68
51000	867.81	814.37	772.71	739.59	712.84	690.96	672.87
52000	884.83	830.34	787.86	754.09	726.81	704.51	686.07
53000	901.85	846.31	803.02	768.59	740.79	718.05	699.26
54000	918.86	862.28	818.17	783.09	754.77	731.60	712.46
55000	935.88	878.24	833.32	797.60	768.75	745.15	725.65
56000	952.89	894.21	848.47	812.10	782.72	758.70	738.84
57000	969.91	910.18	863.62	826.60	796.70	772.25	752.04
58000	986.93	926.15	878.77	841.10	810.68	785.79	765.23
59000	1003.94	942.12	893.92	855.60	824.66	799.34	778.42
60000	1020.96	958.09	909.07	870.11	838.63	812.89	791.62
65000	1106.04	1037.93	984.83	942.61	908.52	880.63	857.59
70000	1191.12	1117.77	1060.59	1015.12	978.40	948.37	923.55
75000	1276.20	1197.61	1136.34	1087.63	1048.29	1016.11	989.52
80000	1361.28	1277.45	1212.10	1160.14	1118.18	1083.85	1055.49
85000	1446.36	1357.29	1287.85	1232.65	1188.06	1151.60	1121.46
90000	1531.44	1437.13	1363.61	1305.16	1257.95	1219.34	1187.43
95000	1616.52	1516.97	1439.37	1377.67	1327.83	1287.08	1253.39
100000	1701.60	1596.81	1515.12	1450.18	1397.72	1354.82	1319.36
105000	1786.68	1676.65	1590.88	1522.68	1467.61	1422.56	1385.33
110000	1871.76	1756.49	1666.64	1595.19	1537.49	1490.30	1451.30
120000	2041.92	1916.17	1818.15	1740.21	1677.27	1625.78	1583.23
130000	2212.07	2075.85	1969.66	1885.23	1817.04	1761.26	1715.17
140000	2382.23	2235.53	2121.17	2030.25	1956.81	1896.74	1847.11
150000	2552.39	2395.21	2272.68	2175.26	2096.58	2032.23	1979.04
160000	2722.55	2554.89	2424.20	2320.28	2236.35	2167.71	2110.98
170000	2892.71	2714.58	2575.71	2465.30	2376.13	2303.19	2242.92
180000	3062.87	2874.26	2727.22	2610.32	2515.90	2438.67	2374.85
190000	3233.03	3033.94	2878.73	2755.33	2655.67	2574.15	2506.79
200000	3403.19	3193.62	3030.25	2900.35	2795.44	2709.64	2638.72
210000	3573.35	3353.30	3181.76	3045.37	2935.21	2845.12	2770.66
220000	3743.51	3512.98	3333.27	3190.39	3074.99	2980.60	2902.60
230000	3913.67	3672.66	3484.78	3335.40	3214.76	3116.08	3034.53
240000	4083.83	3832.34	3636.30	3480.42	3354.53	3251.56	3166.47
250000	4253.99	3992.02	3787.81	3625.44	3494.30	3387.04	3298.41

13.75 % Monthly Payments

LOAN AMOUNT	15	16	17	18	19	20	21
				YEARS			
100	1.29	1.27	1.24	1.23	1.21	1.20	1.19
200	2.58	2.53	2.49	2.45	2.42	2.40	2.37
500	6.45	6.33	6.22	6.13	6.06	5.99	5.94
1000	12.90	12.65	12.44	12.26	12.11	11.98	11.87
2000	25.80	25.30	24.88	24.53	24.22	23.96	23.74
5000	64.49	63.25	62.20	61.31	60.56	59.91	59.35
6000	77.39	75.90	74.64	73.58	72.67	71.89	71.22
7000	90.29	88.55	87.08	85.84	84.78	83.87	83.09
8000	103.18	101.20	99.52	98.10	96.89	95.85	94.96
9000	116.08	113.85	111.97	110.37	109.00	107.84	106.83
10000	128.98	126.50	124.41	122.63	121.11	119.82	118.70
12000	154.78	151.80	149.29	147.15	145.34	143.78	142.45
15000	193.47	189.75	186.61	183.94	181.67	179.73	178.06
20000	257.96	253.00	248.81	245.26	242.23	239.63	237.41
25000	322.45	316.25	311.01	306.57	302.78	299.54	296.76
30000	386.94	379.50	373.22	367.88	363.34	359.45	356.11
31000	399.84	392.15	385.66	380.15	375.45	371.43	367.98
32000	412.74	404.80	398.10	392.41	387.56	383.41	379.86
33000	425.64	417.45	410.54	404.67	399.67	395.40	391.73
34000	438.54	430.10	422.98	416.94	411.78	407.38	403.60
35000	451.43	442.75	435.42	429.20	423.90	419.36	415.47
36000	464.33	455.40	447.86	441.46	436.01	431.34	427.34
37000	477.23	468.05	460.30	453.72	448.12	443.32	439.21
38000	490.13	480.70	472.74	465.99	460.23	455.30	451.08
39000	503.03	493.35	485.18	478.25	472.34	467.29	462.95
40000	515.92	506.00	497.62	490.51	484.45	479.27	474.82
41000	528.82	518.65	510.06	502.78	496.56	491.25	486.69
42000	541.72	531.30	522.50	515.04	508.67	503.23	498.56
43000	554.62	543.95	534.95	527.30	520.79	515.21	510.43
44000	567.52	556.60	547.39	539.56	532.90	527.19	522.30
45000	580.42	569.25	559.83	551.83	545.01	539.18	534.17
46000	593.31	581.90	572.27	564.09	557.12	551.16	546.04
47000	606.21	594.55	584.71	576.35	569.23	563.14	557.91
48000	619.11	607.20	597.15	588.62	581.34	575.12	569.78
49000	632.01	619.85	609.59	600.88	593.45	587.10	581.65
50000	644.91	632.50	622.03	613.14	605.57	599.08	593.52
51000	657.80	645.15	634.47	625.40	617.68	611.07	605.39
52000	670.70	657.80	646.91	637.67	629.79	623.05	617.26
53000	683.60	670.45	659.35	649.93	641.90	635.03	629.14
54000	696.50	683.10	671.79	662.19	654.01	647.01	641.01
55000	709.40	695.75	684.23	674.45	666.12	658.99	652.88
56000	722.29	708.40	696.67	686.72	678.23	670.97	664.75
57000	735.19	721.05	709.11	698.98	690.34	682.96	676.62
58000	748.09	733.70	721.55	711.24	702.46	694.94	688.49
59000	760.99	746.35	733.99	723.51	714.57	706.92	700.36
60000	773.89	759.00	746.44	735.77	726.68	718.90	712.23
65000	838.38	822.25	808.64	797.08	787.23	778.81	771.58
70000	902.87	885.50	870.84	858.40	847.79	838.72	830.93
75000	967.36	948.75	933.04	919.71	908.35	898.63	890.29
80000	1031.85	1012.00	995.25	981.03	968.90	958.54	949.64
85000	1096.34	1075.25	1057.45	1042.34	1029.46	1018.44	1008.99
90000	1160.83	1138.50	1119.65	1103.65	1090.02	1078.35	1068.34
95000	1225.32	1201.76	1181.86	1164.97	1150.57	1138.26	1127.70
100000	1289.81	1265.01	1244.06	1226.28	1211.13	1198.17	1187.05
105000	1354.30	1328.26	1306.26	1287.60	1271.69	1258.08	1246.40
110000	1418.79	1391.51	1368.46	1348.91	1332.24	1317.99	1305.75
120000	1547.77	1518.01	1492.87	1471.54	1453.36	1437.80	1424.46
130000	1676.75	1644.51	1617.28	1594.17	1574.47	1557.62	1543.16
140000	1805.74	1771.01	1741.68	1716.79	1695.58	1677.44	1661.87
150000	1934.72	1897.51	1866.09	1839.42	1816.70	1797.25	1780.57
160000	2063.70	2024.01	1990.49	1962.05	1937.81	1917.07	1899.28
170000	2192.68	2150.51	2114.90	2084.68	2058.92	2036.89	2017.98
180000	2321.66	2277.01	2239.31	2207.31	2180.03	2156.70	2136.69
190000	2450.64	2403.51	2363.71	2329.94	2301.15	2276.52	2255.39
200000	2579.62	2530.01	2488.12	2452.56	2422.26	2396.34	2374.10
210000	2708.60	2656.51	2612.52	2575.19	2543.37	2516.16	2492.80
220000	2837.58	2783.01	2736.93	2697.82	2664.49	2635.97	2611.51
230000	2966.57	2909.51	2861.34	2820.45	2785.60	2755.79	2730.21
240000	3095.55	3036.01	2985.74	2943.08	2906.71	2875.61	2848.92
250000	3224.53	3162.51	3110.15	3065.70	3027.83	2995.42	2967.62

Monthly Payments 13.75 %

LOAN AMOUNT	22	23	24	25	30	35	40
				YEARS			
100	1.18	1.17	1.16	1.16	1.14	1.13	1.12
200	2.35	2.34	2.32	2.31	2.27	2.25	2.24
500	5.89	5.85	5.81	5.78	5.68	5.63	5.60
1000	11.77	11.69	11.62	11.56	11.35	11.25	11.20
2000	23.55	23.38	23.24	23.12	22.71	22.50	22.40
5000	58.87	58.46	58.10	57.80	56.77	56.25	55.99
6000	70.65	70.15	69.73	69.36	68.12	67.50	67.19
7000	82.42	81.85	81.35	80.91	79.47	78.75	78.39
8000	94.20	93.54	92.97	92.47	90.83	90.00	89.58
9000	105.97	105.23	104.59	104.03	102.18	101.25	100.78
10000	117.75	116.92	116.21	115.59	113.53	112.50	111.98
12000	141.30	140.31	139.45	138.71	136.24	135.00	134.38
15000	176.62	175.38	174.31	173.39	170.30	168.76	167.97
20000	235.50	233.85	232.42	231.19	227.07	225.01	223.96
25000	294.37	292.31	290.52	288.98	283.84	281.26	279.95
30000	353.24	350.77	348.63	346.78	340.60	337.51	335.94
31000	365.02	362.46	360.25	358.34	351.96	348.76	347.14
32000	376.79	374.15	371.87	369.90	363.31	360.01	358.34
33000	388.57	385.85	383.49	381.46	374.66	371.26	369.54
34000	400.34	397.54	395.11	393.02	386.02	382.51	380.73
35000	412.12	409.23	406.73	404.57	397.37	393.76	391.93
36000	423.89	420.92	418.36	416.13	408.72	405.01	403.13
37000	435.67	432.61	429.98	427.69	420.08	416.26	414.33
38000	447.44	444.31	441.60	439.25	431.43	427.51	425.53
39000	459.22	456.00	453.22	450.81	442.78	438.76	436.73
40000	470.99	467.69	464.84	462.37	454.14	450.01	447.92
41000	482.77	479.38	476.46	473.93	465.49	461.26	459.12
42000	494.54	491.08	488.08	485.49	476.84	472.52	470.32
43000	506.32	502.77	499.70	497.05	488.20	483.77	481.52
44000	518.09	514.46	511.32	508.61	499.55	495.02	492.72
45000	529.87	526.15	522.94	520.17	510.90	506.27	503.91
46000	541.64	537.85	534.57	531.73	522.26	517.52	515.11
47000	553.42	549.54	546.19	543.29	533.61	528.77	526.31
48000	565.19	561.23	557.81	554.85	544.96	540.02	537.51
49000	576.97	572.92	569.43	566.40	556.32	551.27	548.71
50000	588.74	584.61	581.05	577.96	567.67	562.52	559.90
51000	600.51	596.31	592.67	589.52	579.02	573.77	571.10
52000	612.29	608.00	604.29	601.08	590.38	585.02	582.30
53000	624.06	619.69	615.91	612.64	601.73	596.27	593.50
54000	635.84	631.38	627.53	624.20	613.08	607.52	604.70
55000	647.61	643.08	639.15	635.76	624.44	618.77	615.89
56000	659.39	654.77	650.78	647.32	635.79	630.02	627.09
57000	671.16	666.46	662.40	658.88	647.14	641.27	638.29
58000	682.94	678.15	674.02	670.44	658.50	652.52	649.49
59000	694.71	689.84	685.64	682.00	669.85	663.77	660.69
60000	706.49	701.54	697.26	693.56	681.20	675.02	671.89
65000	765.36	760.00	755.36	751.35	737.97	731.27	727.88
70000	824.24	818.46	813.47	809.15	794.74	787.53	783.87
75000	883.11	876.92	871.57	866.95	851.51	843.78	839.86
80000	941.98	935.38	929.68	924.74	908.27	900.03	895.85
85000	1000.86	993.84	987.78	982.54	965.04	956.28	951.84
90000	1059.73	1052.31	1045.89	1040.34	1021.81	1012.53	1007.83
95000	1118.61	1110.77	1103.99	1098.13	1078.57	1068.78	1063.82
100000	1177.48	1169.23	1162.10	1155.93	1135.34	1125.04	1119.81
105000	1236.35	1227.69	1220.20	1213.72	1192.11	1181.29	1175.80
110000	1295.23	1286.15	1278.31	1271.52	1248.88	1237.54	1231.79
120000	1412.98	1403.07	1394.52	1387.11	1362.41	1350.04	1343.77
130000	1530.72	1520.00	1510.73	1502.71	1475.94	1462.55	1455.75
140000	1648.47	1636.92	1626.94	1618.30	1589.48	1575.05	1567.73
150000	1766.22	1753.84	1743.15	1733.89	1703.01	1687.55	1679.71
160000	1883.97	1870.77	1859.36	1849.49	1816.55	1800.06	1791.69
170000	2001.72	1987.69	1975.57	1965.08	1930.08	1912.56	1903.67
180000	2119.46	2104.61	2091.78	2080.67	2043.61	2025.07	2015.66
190000	2237.21	2221.53	2207.99	2196.26	2157.15	2137.57	2127.64
200000	2354.96	2338.46	2324.20	2311.86	2270.68	2250.07	2239.62
210000	2472.71	2455.38	2440.41	2427.45	2384.22	2362.58	2351.60
220000	2590.46	2572.30	2556.62	2543.04	2497.75	2475.08	2463.58
230000	2708.20	2689.23	2672.83	2658.63	2611.29	2587.58	2575.56
240000	2825.95	2806.15	2789.04	2774.23	2724.82	2700.09	2687.54
250000	2943.70	2923.07	2905.25	2889.82	2838.35	2812.59	2799.52

14.00 % Monthly Payments

LOAN AMOUNT	1	2	3	4	5	6	7
	YEARS						
100	8.96	4.78	3.40	2.71	2.31	2.04	1.85
200	17.92	9.57	6.80	5.43	4.61	4.08	3.70
500	44.80	23.91	16.99	13.57	11.53	10.20	9.26
1000	89.60	47.83	33.99	27.13	23.07	20.40	18.52
2000	179.21	95.66	67.98	54.26	46.13	40.79	37.05
5000	448.01	239.14	169.94	135.65	115.33	101.98	92.62
6000	537.62	286.97	203.93	162.78	138.39	122.38	111.15
7000	627.22	334.80	237.91	189.91	161.46	142.78	129.67
8000	716.82	382.62	271.90	217.04	184.53	163.17	148.19
9000	806.43	430.45	305.89	244.17	207.59	183.57	166.72
10000	896.03	478.28	339.88	271.30	230.66	203.97	185.24
12000	1075.24	573.94	407.85	325.56	276.79	244.76	222.29
15000	1344.04	717.42	509.82	406.96	345.99	305.95	277.86
20000	1792.06	956.56	679.75	542.61	461.31	407.93	370.49
25000	2240.07	1195.70	849.69	678.26	576.64	509.91	463.11
30000	2688.09	1434.84	1019.63	813.91	691.97	611.90	555.73
31000	2777.69	1482.67	1053.62	841.04	715.04	632.29	574.25
32000	2867.29	1530.50	1087.61	868.17	738.10	652.69	592.78
33000	2956.90	1578.33	1121.59	895.30	761.17	673.09	611.30
34000	3046.50	1626.15	1155.58	922.43	784.23	693.48	629.83
35000	3136.10	1673.98	1189.57	949.56	807.30	713.88	648.35
36000	3225.71	1721.81	1223.56	976.69	830.36	734.28	666.87
37000	3315.31	1769.64	1257.54	1003.82	853.43	754.67	685.40
38000	3404.91	1817.47	1291.53	1030.96	876.50	775.07	703.92
39000	3494.51	1865.29	1325.52	1058.09	899.56	795.47	722.45
40000	3584.12	1913.12	1359.51	1085.22	922.63	815.86	740.97
41000	3673.72	1960.95	1393.50	1112.35	945.69	836.26	759.50
42000	3763.32	2008.78	1427.48	1139.48	968.76	856.66	778.02
43000	3852.93	2056.61	1461.47	1166.61	991.82	877.05	796.55
44000	3942.53	2104.43	1495.46	1193.74	1014.89	897.45	815.07
45000	4032.13	2152.26	1529.45	1220.87	1037.96	917.85	833.59
46000	4121.73	2200.09	1563.43	1248.00	1061.02	938.24	852.12
47000	4211.34	2247.92	1597.42	1275.13	1084.09	958.64	870.64
48000	4300.94	2295.75	1631.41	1302.26	1107.15	979.04	889.17
49000	4390.54	2343.57	1665.40	1329.39	1130.22	999.43	907.69
50000	4480.15	2391.40	1699.38	1356.52	1153.28	1019.83	926.22
51000	4569.75	2439.23	1733.37	1383.65	1176.35	1040.23	944.74
52000	4659.35	2487.06	1767.36	1410.78	1199.42	1060.62	963.26
53000	4748.96	2534.89	1801.35	1437.91	1222.48	1081.02	981.79
54000	4838.56	2582.71	1835.34	1465.04	1245.55	1101.42	1000.31
55000	4928.16	2630.54	1869.32	1492.17	1268.61	1121.81	1018.84
56000	5017.76	2678.37	1903.31	1519.30	1291.68	1142.21	1037.36
57000	5107.37	2726.20	1937.30	1546.43	1314.74	1162.61	1055.89
58000	5196.97	2774.03	1971.29	1573.56	1337.81	1183.00	1074.41
59000	5286.57	2821.86	2005.27	1600.69	1360.88	1203.40	1092.93
60000	5376.18	2869.68	2039.26	1627.82	1383.94	1223.80	1111.46
65000	5824.19	3108.82	2209.20	1763.48	1499.27	1325.78	1204.08
70000	6272.20	3347.96	2379.14	1899.13	1614.60	1427.76	1296.70
75000	6720.22	3587.10	2549.08	2034.78	1729.93	1529.74	1389.32
80000	7168.23	3826.24	2719.02	2170.43	1845.25	1631.73	1481.94
85000	7616.25	4065.38	2888.95	2306.08	1960.58	1733.71	1574.57
90000	8064.26	4304.52	3058.89	2441.74	2075.91	1835.69	1667.19
95000	8512.28	4543.66	3228.83	2577.39	2191.24	1937.68	1759.81
100000	8960.29	4782.81	3398.77	2713.04	2306.57	2039.66	1852.43
105000	9408.31	5021.95	3568.71	2848.69	2421.90	2141.64	1945.05
110000	9856.32	5261.09	3738.65	2984.34	2537.23	2243.62	2037.67
120000	10752.35	5739.37	4078.52	3255.65	2767.88	2447.59	2222.92
130000	11648.38	6217.65	4418.40	3526.95	2998.54	2651.56	2408.16
140000	12544.41	6695.93	4758.28	3798.26	3229.20	2855.52	2593.40
150000	13440.44	7174.21	5098.15	4069.56	3459.85	3059.49	2778.65
160000	14336.47	7652.49	5438.03	4340.86	3690.51	3263.45	2963.89
170000	15232.50	8130.77	5777.91	4612.17	3921.17	3467.42	3149.13
180000	16128.53	8609.05	6117.79	4883.47	4151.82	3671.39	3334.37
190000	17024.56	9087.33	6457.66	5154.78	4382.48	3875.35	3519.62
200000	17920.58	9565.61	6797.54	5426.08	4613.14	4079.32	3704.86
210000	18816.61	10043.89	7137.42	5697.38	4843.79	4283.28	3890.10
220000	19712.64	10522.17	7477.29	5968.69	5074.45	4487.25	4075.35
230000	20608.67	11000.45	7817.17	6239.99	5305.11	4691.22	4260.59
240000	21504.70	11478.73	8157.05	6511.30	5535.76	4895.18	4445.83
250000	22400.73	11957.01	8496.92	6782.60	5766.42	5099.15	4631.08

Monthly Payments 14.00 %

LOAN AMOUNT	8	9	10	11	12	13	14
			YEARS				
100	1.71	1.61	1.53	1.46	1.41	1.37	1.33
200	3.43	3.22	3.06	2.93	2.82	2.74	2.67
500	8.57	8.05	7.65	7.32	7.06	6.85	6.67
1000	17.15	16.11	15.29	14.65	14.12	13.70	13.35
2000	34.30	32.21	30.58	29.29	28.25	27.40	26.70
5000	85.75	80.53	76.46	73.23	70.62	68.50	66.74
6000	102.90	96.63	91.75	87.88	84.75	82.20	80.09
7000	120.05	112.74	107.04	102.52	98.87	95.89	93.43
8000	137.19	128.84	122.34	117.17	113.00	109.59	106.78
9000	154.34	144.95	137.63	131.81	127.12	123.29	120.13
10000	171.49	161.05	152.92	146.46	141.25	136.99	133.48
12000	205.79	193.26	183.50	175.75	169.50	164.39	160.17
15000	257.24	241.58	229.38	219.69	211.87	205.49	200.22
20000	342.99	322.10	305.84	292.92	282.50	273.98	266.96
25000	428.73	402.63	382.30	366.15	353.12	342.48	333.69
30000	514.48	483.16	458.76	439.38	423.75	410.98	400.43
31000	531.63	499.26	474.05	454.03	437.87	424.68	413.78
32000	548.78	515.37	489.34	468.67	452.00	438.37	427.13
33000	565.93	531.47	504.64	483.32	466.12	452.07	440.48
34000	583.08	547.58	519.93	497.97	480.25	465.77	453.83
35000	600.23	563.68	535.22	512.61	494.37	479.47	467.17
36000	617.38	579.79	550.51	527.26	508.50	493.17	480.52
37000	634.53	595.89	565.80	541.90	522.62	506.87	493.87
38000	651.67	612.00	581.10	556.55	536.75	520.57	507.22
39000	668.82	628.10	596.39	571.20	550.87	534.27	520.56
40000	685.97	644.21	611.68	585.84	565.00	547.97	533.91
41000	703.12	660.31	626.97	600.49	579.12	561.67	547.26
42000	720.27	676.42	642.26	615.13	593.25	575.37	560.61
43000	737.42	692.52	657.56	629.78	607.37	589.07	573.96
44000	754.57	708.63	672.85	644.43	621.50	602.76	587.30
45000	771.72	724.73	688.14	659.07	635.62	616.46	600.65
46000	788.87	740.84	703.43	673.72	649.75	630.16	614.00
47000	806.02	756.94	718.72	688.37	663.87	643.86	627.35
48000	823.17	773.05	734.02	703.01	678.00	657.56	640.69
49000	840.32	789.16	749.31	717.66	692.12	671.26	654.04
50000	857.47	805.26	764.60	732.30	706.25	684.96	667.39
51000	874.62	821.37	779.89	746.95	720.37	698.66	680.74
52000	891.77	837.47	795.18	761.60	734.50	712.36	694.09
53000	908.91	853.58	810.48	776.24	748.62	726.06	707.43
54000	926.06	869.68	825.77	790.89	762.75	739.76	720.78
55000	943.21	885.79	841.06	805.53	776.87	753.46	734.13
56000	960.36	901.89	856.35	820.18	791.00	767.16	747.48
57000	977.51	918.00	871.64	834.83	805.12	780.85	760.82
58000	994.66	934.10	886.94	849.47	819.25	794.55	774.17
59000	1011.81	950.21	902.23	864.12	833.37	808.25	787.52
60000	1028.96	966.31	917.52	878.76	847.50	821.95	800.87
65000	1114.71	1046.84	993.98	951.99	918.12	890.45	867.61
70000	1200.45	1127.36	1070.44	1025.22	988.75	958.94	934.35
75000	1286.20	1207.89	1146.90	1098.46	1059.37	1027.44	1001.08
80000	1371.95	1288.42	1223.36	1171.69	1130.00	1095.94	1067.82
85000	1457.69	1368.94	1299.82	1244.92	1200.62	1164.43	1134.56
90000	1543.44	1449.47	1376.28	1318.15	1271.25	1232.93	1201.30
95000	1629.19	1530.00	1452.74	1391.38	1341.87	1301.42	1268.04
100000	1714.93	1610.52	1529.20	1464.61	1412.49	1369.92	1334.78
105000	1800.68	1691.05	1605.66	1537.84	1483.12	1438.42	1401.52
110000	1886.43	1771.57	1682.12	1611.07	1553.74	1506.91	1468.26
120000	2057.92	1932.63	1835.04	1757.53	1694.99	1643.90	1601.74
130000	2229.41	2093.68	1987.96	1903.99	1836.24	1780.90	1735.21
140000	2400.91	2254.73	2140.88	2050.45	1977.49	1917.89	1868.69
150000	2572.40	2415.78	2293.80	2196.91	2118.74	2054.88	2002.17
160000	2743.89	2576.83	2446.72	2343.37	2259.99	2191.87	2135.65
170000	2915.39	2737.89	2599.64	2489.83	2401.24	2328.86	2269.13
180000	3086.88	2898.94	2752.56	2636.29	2542.49	2465.86	2402.60
190000	3258.37	3059.99	2905.48	2782.75	2683.74	2602.85	2536.08
200000	3429.87	3221.04	3058.40	2929.21	2824.99	2739.84	2669.56
210000	3601.36	3382.09	3211.32	3075.67	2966.24	2876.83	2803.04
220000	3772.85	3543.15	3364.24	3222.14	3107.49	3013.82	2936.52
230000	3944.35	3704.20	3517.16	3368.60	3248.74	3150.82	3069.99
240000	4115.84	3865.25	3670.08	3515.06	3389.99	3287.81	3203.47
250000	4287.33	4026.30	3823.00	3661.52	3531.24	3424.80	3336.95

14.00 % Monthly Payments

LOAN AMOUNT	15	16	17	18	19	20	21
				YEARS			
100	1.31	1.28	1.26	1.24	1.23	1.22	1.20
200	2.61	2.56	2.52	2.49	2.46	2.43	2.41
500	6.53	6.41	6.30	6.21	6.14	6.08	6.02
1000	13.06	12.81	12.60	12.43	12.28	12.15	12.04
2000	26.11	25.62	25.21	24.86	24.56	24.30	24.09
5000	65.28	64.05	63.02	62.14	61.40	60.76	60.21
6000	78.33	76.86	75.62	74.57	73.67	72.91	72.26
7000	91.39	89.67	88.22	87.00	85.95	85.06	84.30
8000	104.44	102.48	100.83	99.43	98.23	97.21	96.34
9000	117.50	115.29	113.43	111.85	110.51	109.37	108.38
10000	130.55	128.10	126.03	124.28	122.79	121.52	120.43
12000	156.66	153.72	151.24	149.14	147.35	145.82	144.51
15000	195.83	192.15	189.05	186.42	184.19	182.28	180.64
20000	261.11	256.20	252.07	248.56	245.58	243.04	240.85
25000	326.38	320.25	315.08	310.70	306.98	303.79	301.07
30000	391.66	384.30	378.10	372.84	368.37	364.55	361.28
31000	404.71	397.11	390.70	385.27	380.65	376.70	373.32
32000	417.77	409.92	403.31	397.70	392.93	388.86	385.37
33000	430.82	422.73	415.91	410.13	405.21	401.01	397.41
34000	443.88	435.54	428.51	422.56	417.49	413.16	409.45
35000	456.94	448.35	441.12	434.99	429.77	425.31	421.49
36000	469.99	461.16	453.72	447.41	442.05	437.46	433.54
37000	483.05	473.97	466.32	459.84	454.33	449.62	445.58
38000	496.10	486.78	478.93	472.27	466.61	461.77	457.62
39000	509.16	499.59	491.53	484.70	478.88	473.92	469.67
40000	522.21	512.40	504.13	497.13	491.16	486.07	481.71
41000	535.27	525.21	516.74	509.55	503.44	498.22	493.75
42000	548.32	538.02	529.34	521.98	515.72	510.37	505.79
43000	561.38	550.83	541.94	534.41	528.00	522.53	517.84
44000	574.43	563.64	554.55	546.84	540.28	534.68	529.88
45000	587.49	576.45	567.15	559.27	552.56	546.83	541.92
46000	600.54	589.26	579.75	571.70	564.84	558.98	553.96
47000	613.60	602.07	592.36	584.12	577.12	571.13	566.01
48000	626.65	614.89	604.96	596.55	589.40	583.28	578.05
49000	639.71	627.70	617.56	608.98	601.67	595.44	590.09
50000	652.76	640.51	630.17	621.41	613.95	607.59	602.13
51000	665.82	653.32	642.77	633.84	626.23	619.74	614.18
52000	678.88	666.13	655.37	646.26	638.51	631.89	626.22
53000	691.93	678.94	667.98	658.69	650.79	644.04	638.26
54000	704.99	691.75	680.58	671.12	663.07	656.19	650.31
55000	718.04	704.56	693.18	683.55	675.35	668.35	662.35
56000	731.10	717.37	705.79	695.98	687.63	680.50	674.39
57000	744.15	730.18	718.39	708.41	699.91	692.65	686.43
58000	757.21	742.99	730.99	720.83	712.19	704.80	698.48
59000	770.26	755.80	743.60	733.26	724.47	716.95	710.52
60000	783.32	768.61	756.20	745.69	736.74	729.11	722.56
65000	848.59	832.66	819.22	807.83	798.14	789.86	782.78
70000	913.87	896.71	882.24	869.97	859.54	850.62	842.99
75000	979.15	960.76	945.25	932.11	920.93	911.38	903.20
80000	1044.42	1024.81	1008.27	994.25	982.33	972.14	963.42
85000	1109.70	1088.86	1071.29	1056.39	1043.72	1032.90	1023.63
90000	1174.98	1152.91	1134.30	1118.53	1105.12	1093.66	1083.84
95000	1240.25	1216.96	1197.32	1180.68	1166.51	1154.42	1144.06
100000	1305.53	1281.01	1260.34	1242.82	1227.91	1215.18	1204.27
105000	1370.81	1345.06	1323.35	1304.96	1289.30	1275.93	1264.48
110000	1436.08	1409.11	1386.37	1367.10	1350.70	1336.69	1324.70
120000	1566.64	1537.21	1512.40	1491.38	1473.49	1458.21	1445.12
130000	1697.19	1665.31	1638.44	1615.66	1596.28	1579.73	1565.55
140000	1827.74	1793.41	1764.47	1739.94	1719.07	1701.25	1685.98
150000	1958.29	1921.52	1890.50	1864.22	1841.86	1822.76	1806.40
160000	2088.85	2049.62	2016.54	1988.51	1964.65	1944.28	1926.83
170000	2219.40	2177.72	2142.57	2112.79	2087.44	2065.80	2047.26
180000	2349.95	2305.82	2268.60	2237.07	2210.23	2187.32	2167.68
190000	2480.51	2433.92	2394.64	2361.35	2333.03	2308.83	2288.11
200000	2611.06	2562.02	2520.67	2485.63	2455.82	2430.35	2408.54
210000	2741.61	2690.12	2646.71	2609.91	2578.61	2551.87	2528.97
220000	2872.17	2818.22	2772.74	2734.20	2701.40	2673.39	2649.39
230000	3002.72	2946.32	2898.77	2858.48	2824.19	2794.90	2769.82
240000	3133.27	3074.43	3024.81	2982.76	2946.98	2916.42	2890.25
250000	3263.82	3202.53	3150.84	3107.04	3069.77	3037.94	3010.67

Monthly Payments 14.00 %

LOAN AMOUNT	22	23	24	25	30	35	40
				YEARS			
100	1.19	1.19	1.18	1.17	1.15	1.14	1.14
200	2.39	2.37	2.36	2.35	2.31	2.29	2.28
500	5.97	5.93	5.90	5.87	5.77	5.72	5.70
1000	11.95	11.87	11.80	11.74	11.54	11.44	11.39
2000	23.90	23.74	23.60	23.48	23.08	22.88	22.78
5000	59.75	59.34	58.99	58.69	57.70	57.20	56.96
6000	71.69	71.21	70.79	70.43	69.24	68.64	68.35
7000	83.64	83.08	82.59	82.17	80.78	80.08	79.74
8000	95.59	94.95	94.39	93.91	92.32	91.53	91.13
9000	107.54	106.82	106.19	105.65	103.85	102.97	102.52
10000	119.49	118.68	117.99	117.39	115.39	114.41	113.91
12000	143.39	142.42	141.59	140.87	138.47	137.29	136.69
15000	179.24	178.03	176.98	176.08	173.09	171.61	170.87
20000	238.98	237.37	235.98	234.78	230.79	228.81	227.82
25000	298.73	296.71	294.97	293.47	288.48	286.02	284.78
30000	358.47	356.05	353.97	352.16	346.18	343.22	341.73
31000	370.42	367.92	365.76	363.90	357.72	354.66	353.12
32000	382.37	379.79	377.56	375.64	369.26	366.10	364.51
33000	394.32	391.66	389.36	387.38	380.80	377.54	375.90
34000	406.27	403.53	401.16	399.12	392.34	388.98	387.30
35000	418.22	415.39	412.96	410.86	403.88	400.42	398.69
36000	430.16	427.26	424.76	422.60	415.42	411.86	410.08
37000	442.11	439.13	436.56	434.33	426.96	423.30	421.47
38000	454.06	451.00	448.36	446.07	438.50	434.74	432.86
39000	466.01	462.87	460.15	457.81	450.04	446.18	444.25
40000	477.96	474.74	471.95	469.55	461.58	457.63	455.64
41000	489.91	486.60	483.75	481.29	473.12	469.07	467.03
42000	501.86	498.47	495.55	493.03	484.65	480.51	478.42
43000	513.81	510.34	507.35	504.77	496.19	491.95	489.82
44000	525.76	522.21	519.15	516.51	507.73	503.39	501.21
45000	537.71	534.08	530.95	528.24	519.27	514.83	512.60
46000	549.65	545.95	542.75	539.98	530.81	526.27	523.99
47000	561.60	557.81	554.55	551.72	542.35	537.71	535.38
48000	573.55	569.68	566.34	563.46	553.89	549.15	546.77
49000	585.50	581.55	578.14	575.20	565.43	560.59	558.16
50000	597.45	593.42	589.94	586.94	576.97	572.03	569.55
51000	609.40	605.29	601.74	598.68	588.51	583.47	580.94
52000	621.35	617.16	613.54	610.42	600.05	594.91	592.34
53000	633.30	629.02	625.34	622.15	611.59	606.35	603.73
54000	645.25	640.89	637.14	633.89	623.13	617.79	615.12
55000	657.20	652.76	648.94	645.63	634.67	629.23	626.51
56000	669.15	664.63	660.74	657.37	646.21	640.68	637.90
57000	681.09	676.50	672.53	669.11	657.75	652.12	649.29
58000	693.04	688.37	684.33	680.85	669.29	663.56	660.68
59000	704.99	700.23	696.13	692.59	680.82	675.00	672.07
60000	716.94	712.10	707.93	704.33	692.36	686.44	683.46
65000	776.69	771.45	766.92	763.02	750.06	743.64	740.42
70000	836.43	830.79	825.92	821.71	807.76	800.84	797.37
75000	896.18	890.13	884.91	880.41	865.45	858.05	854.33
80000	955.92	949.47	943.91	939.10	923.15	915.25	911.28
85000	1015.67	1008.81	1002.90	997.80	980.85	972.45	968.24
90000	1075.41	1068.15	1061.90	1056.49	1038.55	1029.66	1025.20
95000	1135.16	1127.50	1120.89	1115.18	1096.24	1086.86	1082.15
100000	1194.90	1186.84	1179.88	1173.88	1153.94	1144.06	1139.11
105000	1254.65	1246.18	1238.88	1232.57	1211.64	1201.27	1196.06
110000	1314.39	1305.52	1297.87	1291.26	1269.33	1258.47	1253.02
120000	1433.88	1424.21	1415.86	1408.65	1384.73	1372.88	1366.93
130000	1553.37	1542.89	1533.85	1526.04	1500.12	1487.28	1480.84
140000	1672.86	1661.57	1651.84	1643.43	1615.52	1601.69	1594.75
150000	1792.35	1780.26	1769.83	1760.81	1730.91	1716.09	1708.66
160000	1911.84	1898.94	1887.81	1878.20	1846.30	1830.50	1822.57
170000	2031.33	2017.63	2005.80	1995.59	1961.70	1944.91	1936.48
180000	2150.82	2136.31	2123.79	2112.98	2077.09	2059.31	2050.39
190000	2270.31	2254.99	2241.78	2230.37	2192.49	2173.72	2164.30
200000	2389.80	2373.68	2359.77	2347.75	2307.88	2288.13	2278.21
210000	2509.29	2492.36	2477.76	2465.14	2423.27	2402.53	2392.12
220000	2628.78	2611.05	2595.75	2582.53	2538.67	2516.94	2506.03
230000	2748.27	2729.73	2713.73	2699.92	2654.06	2631.34	2619.94
240000	2867.76	2848.41	2831.72	2817.30	2769.46	2745.75	2733.85
250000	2987.26	2967.10	2949.71	2934.69	2884.85	2860.16	2847.76

14.25 % Monthly Payments

LOAN AMOUNT	YEARS 1	2	3	4	5	6	7
100	8.97	4.79	3.41	2.72	2.32	2.05	1.87
200	17.94	9.59	6.82	5.45	4.64	4.10	3.73
500	44.86	23.97	17.05	13.62	11.59	10.26	9.33
1000	89.71	47.94	34.10	27.25	23.19	20.52	18.65
2000	179.43	95.88	68.20	54.50	46.38	41.05	37.31
5000	448.57	239.70	170.51	136.24	115.94	102.61	93.27
6000	538.28	287.64	204.61	163.49	139.13	123.14	111.93
7000	628.00	335.58	238.72	190.74	162.31	143.66	130.58
8000	717.71	383.52	272.82	217.99	185.50	164.18	149.23
9000	807.43	431.46	306.92	245.24	208.69	184.70	167.89
10000	897.14	479.39	341.02	272.49	231.88	205.23	186.54
12000	1076.57	575.27	409.23	326.98	278.25	246.27	223.85
15000	1345.71	719.09	511.53	408.73	347.82	307.84	279.81
20000	1794.28	958.79	682.04	544.97	463.75	410.45	373.08
25000	2242.85	1198.49	852.55	681.21	579.69	513.06	466.36
30000	2691.42	1438.18	1023.06	817.46	695.63	615.68	559.63
31000	2781.13	1486.12	1057.17	844.70	718.82	636.20	578.28
32000	2870.85	1534.06	1091.27	871.95	742.01	656.72	596.93
33000	2960.56	1582.00	1125.37	899.20	765.19	677.24	615.59
34000	3050.27	1629.94	1159.47	926.45	788.38	697.77	634.24
35000	3139.99	1677.88	1193.58	953.70	811.57	718.29	652.90
36000	3229.70	1725.82	1227.68	980.95	834.76	738.81	671.55
37000	3319.42	1773.76	1261.78	1008.20	857.95	759.33	690.21
38000	3409.13	1821.70	1295.88	1035.44	881.13	779.86	708.86
39000	3498.84	1869.64	1329.98	1062.69	904.32	800.38	727.51
40000	3588.56	1917.58	1364.09	1089.94	927.51	820.90	746.17
41000	3678.27	1965.52	1398.19	1117.19	950.70	841.43	764.82
42000	3767.99	2013.46	1432.29	1144.44	973.88	861.95	783.48
43000	3857.70	2061.40	1466.39	1171.69	997.07	882.47	802.13
44000	3947.41	2109.34	1500.49	1198.94	1020.26	902.99	820.79
45000	4037.13	2157.28	1534.60	1226.18	1043.45	923.52	839.44
46000	4126.84	2205.21	1568.70	1253.43	1066.63	944.04	858.09
47000	4216.56	2253.15	1602.80	1280.68	1089.82	964.56	876.75
48000	4306.27	2301.09	1636.90	1307.93	1113.01	985.08	895.40
49000	4395.98	2349.03	1671.01	1335.18	1136.20	1005.61	914.06
50000	4485.70	2396.97	1705.11	1362.43	1159.39	1026.13	932.71
51000	4575.41	2444.91	1739.21	1389.68	1182.57	1046.65	951.36
52000	4665.13	2492.85	1773.31	1416.92	1205.76	1067.17	970.02
53000	4754.84	2540.79	1807.41	1444.17	1228.95	1087.70	988.67
54000	4844.55	2588.73	1841.52	1471.42	1252.14	1108.22	1007.33
55000	4934.27	2636.67	1875.62	1498.67	1275.32	1128.74	1025.98
56000	5023.98	2684.61	1909.72	1525.92	1298.51	1149.26	1044.64
57000	5113.70	2732.55	1943.82	1553.17	1321.70	1169.79	1063.29
58000	5203.41	2780.49	1977.92	1580.41	1344.89	1190.31	1081.94
59000	5293.12	2828.43	2012.03	1607.66	1368.07	1210.83	1100.60
60000	5382.84	2876.37	2046.13	1634.91	1391.26	1231.35	1119.25
65000	5831.41	3116.06	2216.64	1771.15	1507.20	1333.97	1212.52
70000	6279.98	3355.76	2387.15	1907.40	1623.14	1436.58	1305.79
75000	6728.55	3595.46	2557.66	2043.64	1739.08	1539.19	1399.07
80000	7177.12	3835.16	2728.17	2179.88	1855.02	1641.80	1492.34
85000	7625.69	4074.85	2898.68	2316.13	1970.96	1744.42	1585.61
90000	8074.26	4314.55	3069.19	2452.37	2086.89	1847.03	1678.88
95000	8522.83	4554.25	3239.70	2588.61	2202.83	1949.64	1772.15
100000	8971.40	4793.95	3410.21	2724.85	2318.77	2052.26	1865.42
105000	9419.97	5033.64	3580.73	2861.10	2434.71	2154.87	1958.69
110000	9868.54	5273.34	3751.24	2997.34	2550.65	2257.48	2051.96
120000	10765.68	5752.73	4092.26	3269.82	2782.52	2462.71	2238.51
130000	11662.82	6232.13	4433.28	3542.31	3014.40	2667.93	2425.05
140000	12559.96	6711.52	4774.30	3814.79	3246.28	2873.16	2611.59
150000	13457.09	7190.92	5115.32	4087.28	3478.16	3078.38	2798.13
160000	14354.23	7670.31	5456.34	4359.77	3710.03	3283.61	2984.67
170000	15251.37	8149.71	5797.37	4632.25	3941.91	3488.84	3171.22
180000	16148.51	8629.10	6138.39	4904.74	4173.79	3694.06	3357.76
190000	17045.65	9108.50	6479.41	5177.22	4405.66	3899.29	3544.30
200000	17942.79	9587.89	6820.43	5449.71	4637.54	4104.51	3730.84
210000	18839.93	10067.28	7161.45	5722.19	4869.42	4309.74	3917.38
220000	19737.07	10546.68	7502.47	5994.68	5101.30	4514.96	4103.93
230000	20634.21	11026.07	7843.49	6267.16	5333.17	4720.19	4290.47
240000	21531.35	11505.47	8184.52	6539.65	5565.05	4925.41	4477.01
250000	22428.49	11984.86	8525.54	6812.13	5796.93	5130.64	4663.55

Monthly Payments 14.25 %

LOAN AMOUNT	8	9	10	11	12	13	14
				YEARS			
100	1.73	1.62	1.54	1.48	1.43	1.39	1.35
200	3.46	3.25	3.09	2.96	2.85	2.77	2.70
500	8.64	8.12	7.72	7.40	7.14	6.93	6.75
1000	17.28	16.24	15.43	14.79	14.27	13.85	13.50
2000	34.57	32.49	30.87	29.58	28.55	27.70	27.01
5000	86.42	81.21	77.17	73.95	71.37	69.25	67.51
6000	103.70	97.46	92.60	88.75	85.64	83.10	81.02
7000	120.98	113.70	108.03	103.54	99.91	96.96	94.52
8000	138.26	129.94	123.47	118.33	114.19	110.81	108.02
9000	155.55	146.19	138.90	133.12	128.46	124.66	121.52
10000	172.83	162.43	154.33	147.91	142.73	138.51	135.03
12000	207.40	194.91	185.20	177.49	171.28	166.21	162.03
15000	259.25	243.64	231.50	221.86	214.10	207.76	202.54
20000	345.66	324.86	308.67	295.82	285.46	277.02	270.05
25000	432.08	406.07	385.83	369.77	356.83	346.27	337.56
30000	518.49	487.28	463.00	443.73	428.20	415.52	405.08
31000	535.78	503.53	478.43	458.52	442.47	429.38	418.58
32000	553.06	519.77	493.86	473.31	456.74	443.23	432.08
33000	570.34	536.01	509.30	488.10	471.02	457.08	445.59
34000	587.63	552.25	524.73	502.89	485.29	470.93	459.09
35000	604.91	568.50	540.16	517.68	499.56	484.78	472.59
36000	622.19	584.74	555.60	532.47	513.84	498.63	486.09
37000	639.48	600.98	571.03	547.26	528.11	512.48	499.60
38000	656.76	617.23	586.46	562.06	542.38	526.33	513.10
39000	674.04	633.47	601.90	576.85	556.66	540.18	526.60
40000	691.32	649.71	617.33	591.64	570.93	554.03	540.10
41000	708.61	665.95	632.76	606.43	585.20	567.88	553.61
42000	725.89	682.20	648.20	621.22	599.48	581.73	567.11
43000	743.17	698.44	663.63	636.01	613.75	595.58	580.61
44000	760.46	714.68	679.06	650.80	628.02	609.44	594.11
45000	777.74	730.93	694.50	665.59	642.30	623.29	607.62
46000	795.02	747.17	709.93	680.38	656.57	637.14	621.12
47000	812.31	763.41	725.36	695.17	670.84	650.99	634.62
48000	829.59	779.65	740.80	709.96	685.12	664.84	648.12
49000	846.87	795.90	756.23	724.76	699.39	678.69	661.63
50000	864.16	812.14	771.66	739.55	713.66	692.54	675.13
51000	881.44	828.38	787.10	754.34	727.94	706.39	688.63
52000	898.72	844.63	802.53	769.13	742.21	720.24	702.13
53000	916.01	860.87	817.96	783.92	756.48	734.09	715.64
54000	933.29	877.11	833.40	798.71	770.76	747.94	729.14
55000	950.57	893.35	848.83	813.50	785.03	761.79	742.64
56000	967.85	909.60	864.26	828.29	799.30	775.65	756.14
57000	985.14	925.84	879.70	843.08	813.57	789.50	769.65
58000	1002.42	942.08	895.13	857.87	827.85	803.35	783.15
59000	1019.70	958.32	910.56	872.66	842.12	817.20	796.65
60000	1036.99	974.57	926.00	887.46	856.39	831.05	810.15
65000	1123.40	1055.78	1003.16	961.41	927.76	900.30	877.67
70000	1209.82	1137.00	1080.33	1035.36	999.13	969.56	945.18
75000	1296.23	1218.21	1157.50	1109.32	1070.49	1038.81	1012.69
80000	1382.65	1299.42	1234.66	1183.27	1141.86	1108.06	1080.21
85000	1469.06	1380.64	1311.83	1257.23	1213.23	1177.32	1147.72
90000	1555.48	1461.85	1389.00	1331.18	1284.59	1246.57	1215.23
95000	1641.90	1543.07	1466.16	1405.14	1355.96	1315.83	1282.74
100000	1728.31	1624.28	1543.33	1479.09	1427.32	1385.08	1350.26
105000	1814.73	1705.49	1620.49	1553.05	1498.69	1454.34	1417.77
110000	1901.14	1786.71	1697.66	1627.00	1570.06	1523.59	1485.28
120000	2073.97	1949.13	1851.99	1774.91	1712.79	1662.10	1620.31
130000	2246.81	2111.56	2006.33	1922.82	1855.52	1800.61	1755.34
140000	2419.64	2273.99	2160.66	2070.73	1998.25	1939.11	1890.36
150000	2592.47	2436.42	2314.99	2218.64	2140.99	2077.62	2025.39
160000	2765.30	2598.85	2469.32	2366.55	2283.72	2216.13	2160.41
170000	2938.13	2761.27	2623.66	2514.46	2426.45	2354.64	2295.44
180000	3110.96	2923.70	2777.99	2662.37	2569.18	2493.15	2430.46
190000	3283.79	3086.13	2932.32	2810.28	2711.92	2631.65	2565.49
200000	3456.62	3248.56	3086.66	2958.18	2854.65	2770.16	2700.52
210000	3629.45	3410.99	3240.99	3106.09	2997.38	2908.67	2835.54
220000	3802.29	3573.41	3395.32	3254.00	3140.11	3047.18	2970.57
230000	3975.12	3735.84	3549.65	3401.91	3282.85	3185.69	3105.59
240000	4147.95	3898.27	3703.99	3549.82	3425.58	3324.19	3240.62
250000	4320.78	4060.70	3858.32	3697.73	3568.31	3462.70	3375.64

14.25 % Monthly Payments

LOAN AMOUNT	YEARS 15	16	17	18	19	20	21
100	1.32	1.30	1.28	1.26	1.24	1.23	1.22
200	2.64	2.59	2.55	2.52	2.49	2.46	2.44
500	6.61	6.49	6.38	6.30	6.22	6.16	6.11
1000	13.21	12.97	12.77	12.59	12.45	12.32	12.22
2000	26.43	25.94	25.53	25.19	24.89	24.64	24.43
5000	66.07	64.85	63.83	62.97	62.24	61.61	61.08
6000	79.28	77.82	76.60	75.56	74.68	73.93	73.29
7000	92.49	90.80	89.37	88.16	87.13	86.26	85.51
8000	105.70	103.77	102.13	100.75	99.58	98.58	97.72
9000	118.92	116.74	114.90	113.35	112.03	110.90	109.94
10000	132.13	129.71	127.67	125.94	124.47	123.22	122.15
12000	158.56	155.65	153.20	151.13	149.37	147.87	146.59
15000	198.20	194.56	191.50	188.91	186.71	184.84	183.23
20000	264.26	259.42	255.34	251.88	248.95	246.45	244.31
25000	330.33	324.27	319.17	314.85	311.19	308.06	305.39
30000	396.39	389.12	383.00	377.82	373.42	369.67	366.46
31000	409.61	402.09	395.77	390.42	385.87	382.00	378.68
32000	422.82	415.06	408.54	403.01	398.32	394.32	390.90
33000	436.03	428.04	421.30	415.61	410.77	406.64	403.11
34000	449.25	441.01	434.07	428.20	423.21	418.96	415.33
35000	462.46	453.98	446.84	440.79	435.66	431.28	427.54
36000	475.67	466.95	459.60	453.39	448.11	443.61	439.76
37000	488.88	479.92	472.37	465.98	460.56	455.93	451.97
38000	502.10	492.89	485.14	478.58	473.00	468.25	464.19
39000	515.31	505.86	497.90	491.17	485.45	480.57	476.40
40000	528.52	518.83	510.67	503.77	497.90	492.90	488.62
41000	541.74	531.80	523.44	516.36	510.35	505.22	500.84
42000	554.95	544.77	536.20	528.95	522.79	517.54	513.05
43000	568.16	557.74	548.97	541.55	535.24	529.86	525.27
44000	581.38	570.71	561.74	554.14	547.69	542.19	537.48
45000	594.59	583.69	574.50	566.74	560.14	554.51	549.70
46000	607.80	596.66	587.27	579.33	572.58	566.83	561.91
47000	621.02	609.63	600.04	591.92	585.03	579.15	574.13
48000	634.23	622.60	612.80	604.52	597.48	591.48	586.34
49000	647.44	635.57	625.57	617.11	609.93	603.80	598.56
50000	660.65	648.54	638.34	629.71	622.37	616.12	610.77
51000	673.87	661.51	651.10	642.30	634.82	628.44	622.99
52000	687.08	674.48	663.87	654.89	647.27	640.77	635.21
53000	700.29	687.45	676.64	667.49	659.72	653.09	647.42
54000	713.51	700.42	689.40	680.08	672.16	665.41	659.64
55000	726.72	713.39	702.17	692.68	684.61	677.73	671.85
56000	739.93	726.36	714.94	705.27	697.06	690.06	684.07
57000	753.15	739.33	727.71	717.87	709.51	702.38	696.28
58000	766.36	752.31	740.47	730.46	721.95	714.70	708.50
59000	779.57	765.28	753.24	743.05	734.40	727.02	720.71
60000	792.79	778.25	766.01	755.65	746.85	739.35	732.93
65000	858.85	843.10	829.84	818.62	809.09	800.96	794.01
70000	924.92	907.95	893.67	881.59	871.32	862.57	855.08
75000	990.98	972.81	957.51	944.56	933.56	924.18	916.16
80000	1057.05	1037.66	1021.34	1007.53	995.80	985.79	977.24
85000	1123.11	1102.52	1085.17	1070.50	1058.03	1047.41	1038.32
90000	1189.18	1167.37	1149.01	1133.47	1120.27	1109.02	1099.39
95000	1255.24	1232.22	1212.84	1196.44	1182.51	1170.63	1160.47
100000	1321.31	1297.08	1276.68	1259.41	1244.75	1232.24	1221.55
105000	1387.38	1361.93	1340.51	1322.38	1306.98	1293.85	1282.63
110000	1453.44	1426.79	1404.34	1385.35	1369.22	1355.47	1343.70
120000	1585.57	1556.49	1532.01	1511.30	1493.70	1478.69	1465.86
130000	1717.70	1686.20	1659.68	1637.24	1618.17	1601.92	1588.01
140000	1849.83	1815.91	1787.35	1763.18	1742.65	1725.14	1710.17
150000	1981.96	1945.62	1915.01	1889.12	1867.12	1848.36	1832.32
160000	2114.10	2075.32	2042.68	2015.06	1991.60	1971.59	1954.48
170000	2246.23	2205.03	2170.35	2141.00	2116.07	2094.81	2076.63
180000	2378.36	2334.74	2298.02	2266.94	2240.54	2218.04	2198.79
190000	2510.49	2464.45	2425.68	2392.89	2365.02	2341.26	2320.94
200000	2642.62	2594.16	2553.35	2518.83	2489.49	2464.49	2443.10
210000	2774.75	2723.86	2681.02	2644.77	2613.97	2587.71	2565.25
220000	2906.88	2853.57	2808.69	2770.71	2738.44	2710.93	2687.41
230000	3039.01	2983.28	2936.35	2896.65	2862.92	2834.16	2809.56
240000	3171.14	3112.99	3064.02	3022.59	2987.39	2957.38	2931.72
250000	3303.27	3242.69	3191.69	3148.53	3111.87	3080.61	3053.87

Monthly Payments 14.25 %

LOAN AMOUNT	22	23	24	25	30	35	40
				YEARS			
100	1.21	1.20	1.20	1.19	1.17	1.16	1.16
200	2.42	2.41	2.40	2.38	2.35	2.33	2.32
500	6.06	6.02	5.99	5.96	5.86	5.82	5.79
1000	12.12	12.05	11.98	11.92	11.73	11.63	11.58
2000	24.25	24.09	23.95	23.84	23.45	23.26	23.17
5000	60.62	60.23	59.89	59.59	58.63	58.16	57.92
6000	72.74	72.27	71.86	71.51	70.35	69.79	69.50
7000	84.87	84.32	83.84	83.43	82.08	81.42	81.09
8000	96.99	96.36	95.82	95.35	93.81	93.05	92.67
9000	109.11	108.41	107.79	107.27	105.53	104.68	104.26
10000	121.24	120.45	119.77	119.19	117.26	116.31	115.84
12000	145.49	144.54	143.73	143.02	140.71	139.57	139.01
15000	181.86	180.68	179.66	178.78	175.89	174.47	173.76
20000	242.48	240.90	239.54	238.37	234.51	232.62	231.68
25000	303.10	301.13	299.43	297.97	293.14	290.78	289.60
30000	363.71	361.35	359.32	357.56	351.77	348.93	347.52
31000	375.84	373.40	371.29	369.48	363.50	360.56	359.11
32000	387.96	385.44	383.27	381.40	375.22	372.20	370.69
33000	400.09	397.49	395.25	393.32	386.95	383.83	382.28
34000	412.21	409.53	407.23	405.24	398.68	395.46	393.86
35000	424.33	421.58	419.20	417.16	410.40	407.09	405.44
36000	436.46	433.62	431.18	429.07	422.13	418.72	417.03
37000	448.58	445.67	443.16	440.99	433.85	430.35	428.61
38000	460.70	457.71	455.13	452.91	445.58	441.98	440.20
39000	472.83	469.76	467.11	464.83	457.30	453.61	451.78
40000	484.95	481.80	479.09	476.75	469.03	465.24	463.37
41000	497.08	493.85	491.07	488.67	480.76	476.88	474.95
42000	509.20	505.89	503.04	500.59	492.48	488.51	486.53
43000	521.32	517.94	515.02	512.51	504.21	500.14	498.12
44000	533.45	529.98	527.00	524.42	515.93	511.77	509.70
45000	545.57	542.03	538.97	536.34	527.66	523.40	521.29
46000	557.70	554.07	550.95	548.26	539.38	535.03	532.87
47000	569.82	566.12	562.93	560.18	551.11	546.66	544.45
48000	581.94	578.16	574.91	572.10	562.84	558.29	556.04
49000	594.07	590.21	586.88	584.02	574.56	569.92	567.62
50000	606.19	602.25	598.86	595.94	586.29	581.56	579.21
51000	618.31	614.30	610.84	607.86	598.01	593.19	590.79
52000	630.44	626.34	622.82	619.77	609.74	604.82	602.37
53000	642.56	638.39	634.79	631.69	621.46	616.45	613.96
54000	654.69	650.43	646.77	643.61	633.19	628.08	625.54
55000	666.81	662.48	658.75	655.53	644.92	639.71	637.13
56000	678.93	674.52	670.72	667.45	656.64	651.34	648.71
57000	691.06	686.57	682.70	679.37	668.37	662.97	660.30
58000	703.18	698.61	694.68	691.29	680.09	674.60	671.88
59000	715.30	710.66	706.66	703.21	691.82	686.24	683.46
60000	727.43	722.70	718.63	715.12	703.54	697.87	695.05
65000	788.05	782.93	778.52	774.72	762.17	756.02	752.97
70000	848.67	843.15	838.41	834.31	820.80	814.18	810.89
75000	909.29	903.38	898.29	893.91	879.43	872.33	868.81
80000	969.90	963.60	958.18	953.50	938.06	930.49	926.73
85000	1030.52	1023.83	1018.06	1013.09	996.69	988.64	984.65
90000	1091.14	1084.05	1077.95	1072.69	1055.32	1046.80	1042.57
95000	1151.76	1144.28	1137.84	1132.28	1113.95	1104.96	1100.49
100000	1212.38	1204.50	1197.72	1191.87	1172.57	1163.11	1158.41
105000	1273.00	1264.73	1257.61	1251.47	1231.20	1221.27	1216.33
110000	1333.62	1324.95	1317.49	1311.06	1289.83	1279.42	1274.25
120000	1454.86	1445.40	1437.27	1430.25	1407.09	1395.73	1390.10
130000	1576.10	1565.85	1557.04	1549.44	1524.35	1512.04	1505.94
140000	1697.33	1686.31	1676.81	1668.62	1641.60	1628.35	1621.78
150000	1818.57	1806.76	1796.58	1787.81	1758.86	1744.67	1737.62
160000	1939.81	1927.21	1916.36	1907.00	1876.12	1860.98	1853.46
170000	2061.05	2047.66	2036.13	2026.19	1993.38	1977.29	1969.30
180000	2182.29	2168.11	2155.90	2145.37	2110.63	2093.60	2085.14
190000	2303.52	2288.56	2275.67	2264.56	2227.89	2209.91	2200.98
200000	2424.76	2409.01	2395.44	2383.75	2345.15	2326.22	2316.83
210000	2546.00	2529.46	2515.22	2502.94	2462.41	2442.53	2432.67
220000	2667.24	2649.91	2634.99	2622.12	2579.66	2558.84	2548.51
230000	2788.48	2770.36	2754.76	2741.31	2696.92	2675.15	2664.35
240000	2909.71	2890.81	2874.53	2860.50	2814.18	2791.47	2780.19
250000	3030.95	3011.26	2994.31	2979.69	2931.44	2907.78	2896.03

14.50 % Monthly Payments

LOAN AMOUNT	1	2	3	4	5	6	7
	YEARS						
100	8.98	4.81	3.42	2.74	2.33	2.06	1.88
200	17.96	9.61	6.84	5.47	4.66	4.13	3.76
500	44.91	24.03	17.11	13.68	11.65	10.32	9.39
1000	89.82	48.05	34.22	27.37	23.31	20.65	18.78
2000	179.65	96.10	68.43	54.73	46.62	41.30	37.57
5000	449.12	240.25	171.08	136.83	116.55	103.24	93.92
6000	538.95	288.31	205.30	164.20	139.86	123.89	112.71
7000	628.77	336.36	239.52	191.57	163.17	144.54	131.49
8000	718.60	384.41	273.73	218.93	186.48	165.19	150.28
9000	808.42	432.46	307.95	246.30	209.79	185.84	169.06
10000	898.25	480.51	342.17	273.67	233.10	206.49	187.84
12000	1077.90	576.61	410.60	328.40	279.72	247.79	225.41
15000	1347.37	720.76	513.25	410.50	349.65	309.73	281.77
20000	1796.50	961.02	684.33	547.34	466.20	412.98	375.69
25000	2245.62	1201.27	855.42	684.17	582.75	516.22	469.61
30000	2694.75	1441.53	1026.50	821.01	699.30	619.47	563.53
31000	2784.57	1489.58	1060.72	848.37	722.61	640.11	582.32
32000	2874.40	1537.63	1094.93	875.74	745.92	660.76	601.10
33000	2964.22	1585.68	1129.15	903.11	769.23	681.41	619.89
34000	3054.05	1633.73	1163.37	930.47	792.54	702.06	638.67
35000	3143.87	1681.78	1197.58	957.84	815.85	722.71	657.46
36000	3233.70	1729.83	1231.80	985.21	839.16	743.36	676.24
37000	3323.52	1777.88	1266.02	1012.57	862.47	764.01	695.03
38000	3413.35	1825.93	1300.24	1039.94	885.78	784.66	713.81
39000	3503.17	1873.98	1334.45	1067.31	909.09	805.30	732.59
40000	3593.00	1922.04	1368.67	1094.67	932.40	825.95	751.38
41000	3682.82	1970.09	1402.89	1122.04	955.71	846.60	770.16
42000	3772.65	2018.14	1437.10	1149.41	979.02	867.25	788.95
43000	3862.47	2066.19	1471.32	1176.77	1002.33	887.90	807.73
44000	3952.30	2114.24	1505.54	1204.14	1025.64	908.55	826.52
45000	4042.12	2162.29	1539.75	1231.51	1048.95	929.20	845.30
46000	4131.95	2210.34	1573.97	1258.87	1072.26	949.85	864.09
47000	4221.77	2258.39	1608.19	1286.24	1095.57	970.50	882.87
48000	4311.60	2306.44	1642.40	1313.61	1118.88	991.14	901.65
49000	4401.42	2354.49	1676.62	1340.98	1142.19	1011.79	920.44
50000	4491.25	2402.54	1710.84	1368.34	1165.50	1032.44	939.22
51000	4581.07	2450.60	1745.05	1395.71	1188.81	1053.09	958.01
52000	4670.90	2498.65	1779.27	1423.08	1212.12	1073.74	976.79
53000	4760.72	2546.70	1813.49	1450.44	1235.43	1094.39	995.58
54000	4850.55	2594.75	1847.70	1477.81	1258.74	1115.04	1014.36
55000	4940.37	2642.80	1881.92	1505.18	1282.05	1135.69	1033.15
56000	5030.20	2690.85	1916.14	1532.54	1305.36	1156.33	1051.93
57000	5120.02	2738.90	1950.35	1559.91	1328.67	1176.98	1070.72
58000	5209.85	2786.95	1984.57	1587.28	1351.98	1197.63	1089.50
59000	5299.67	2835.00	2018.79	1614.64	1375.29	1218.28	1108.28
60000	5389.50	2883.05	2053.00	1642.01	1398.60	1238.93	1127.07
65000	5838.62	3123.31	2224.09	1778.84	1515.15	1342.17	1220.99
70000	6287.75	3363.56	2395.17	1915.68	1631.70	1445.42	1314.91
75000	6736.87	3603.82	2566.25	2052.51	1748.25	1548.66	1408.84
80000	7186.00	3844.07	2737.34	2189.35	1864.80	1651.91	1502.76
85000	7635.12	4084.33	2908.42	2326.18	1981.35	1755.15	1596.68
90000	8084.25	4324.58	3079.50	2463.02	2097.90	1858.40	1690.60
95000	8533.37	4564.83	3250.59	2599.85	2214.45	1961.64	1784.53
100000	8982.50	4805.09	3421.67	2736.68	2331.00	2064.88	1878.45
105000	9431.62	5045.34	3592.75	2873.52	2447.55	2168.13	1972.37
110000	9880.75	5285.60	3763.84	3010.35	2564.10	2271.37	2066.29
120000	10779.00	5766.11	4106.01	3284.02	2797.20	2477.86	2254.14
130000	11677.25	6246.62	4448.17	3557.69	3030.30	2684.35	2441.98
140000	12575.50	6727.13	4790.34	3831.36	3263.40	2890.84	2629.83
150000	13473.75	7207.63	5132.51	4105.03	3496.50	3097.33	2817.67
160000	14372.00	7688.14	5474.67	4378.70	3729.60	3303.81	3005.52
170000	15270.25	8168.65	5816.84	4652.36	3962.70	3510.30	3193.36
180000	16168.49	8649.16	6159.01	4926.03	4195.80	3716.79	3381.21
190000	17066.74	9129.67	6501.18	5199.70	4428.90	3923.28	3569.05
200000	17964.99	9610.18	6843.34	5473.37	4662.00	4129.77	3756.90
210000	18863.24	10090.69	7185.51	5747.04	4895.09	4336.26	3944.74
220000	19761.49	10571.20	7527.68	6020.71	5128.19	4542.74	4132.59
230000	20659.74	11051.71	7869.84	6294.37	5361.29	4749.23	4320.43
240000	21557.99	11532.21	8212.01	6568.04	5594.39	4955.72	4508.27
250000	22456.24	12012.72	8554.18	6841.71	5827.49	5162.21	4696.12

Monthly Payments 14.50 %

LOAN AMOUNT	8	9	10	11	12	13	14
			YEARS				
100	1.74	1.64	1.56	1.49	1.44	1.40	1.37
200	3.48	3.28	3.12	2.99	2.88	2.80	2.73
500	8.71	8.19	7.79	7.47	7.21	7.00	6.83
1000	17.42	16.38	15.58	14.94	14.42	14.00	13.66
2000	34.83	32.76	31.15	29.87	28.84	28.01	27.32
5000	87.09	81.90	77.88	74.68	72.11	70.01	68.29
6000	104.50	98.28	93.45	89.62	86.53	84.02	81.95
7000	121.92	114.67	109.03	104.55	100.95	98.02	95.61
8000	139.34	131.05	124.60	119.49	115.38	112.02	109.26
9000	156.76	147.43	140.18	134.43	129.80	126.03	122.92
10000	174.17	163.81	155.75	149.36	144.22	140.03	136.58
12000	209.01	196.57	186.90	179.24	173.07	168.04	163.90
15000	261.26	245.71	233.63	224.04	216.33	210.04	204.87
20000	348.35	327.62	311.50	298.73	288.44	280.06	273.16
25000	435.43	409.52	389.38	373.41	360.55	350.07	341.45
30000	522.52	491.42	467.25	448.09	432.66	420.09	409.74
31000	539.94	507.81	482.83	463.03	447.09	434.09	423.40
32000	557.35	524.19	498.40	477.96	461.51	448.10	437.05
33000	574.77	540.57	513.98	492.90	475.93	462.10	450.71
34000	592.19	556.95	529.55	507.83	490.35	476.10	464.37
35000	609.61	573.33	545.13	522.77	504.77	490.10	478.03
36000	627.02	589.71	560.70	537.71	519.20	504.11	491.69
37000	644.44	606.09	576.28	552.64	533.62	518.11	505.34
38000	661.86	622.47	591.85	567.58	548.04	532.11	519.00
39000	679.28	638.85	607.43	582.52	562.46	546.12	532.66
40000	696.69	655.23	623.00	597.45	576.88	560.12	546.32
41000	714.11	671.61	638.58	612.39	591.31	574.12	559.98
42000	731.53	687.99	654.15	627.32	605.73	588.13	573.63
43000	748.94	704.38	669.73	642.26	620.15	602.13	587.29
44000	766.36	720.76	685.30	657.20	634.57	616.13	600.95
45000	783.78	737.14	700.88	672.13	648.99	630.13	614.61
46000	801.20	753.52	716.45	687.07	663.42	644.14	628.27
47000	818.61	769.90	732.03	702.01	677.84	658.14	641.92
48000	836.03	786.28	747.60	716.94	692.26	672.14	655.58
49000	853.45	802.66	763.18	731.88	706.68	686.15	669.24
50000	870.87	819.04	778.75	746.81	721.10	700.15	682.90
51000	888.28	835.42	794.33	761.75	735.53	714.15	696.56
52000	905.70	851.80	809.90	776.69	749.95	728.16	710.21
53000	923.12	868.18	825.48	791.62	764.37	742.16	723.87
54000	940.53	884.56	841.05	806.56	778.79	756.16	737.53
55000	957.95	900.95	856.63	821.50	793.22	770.16	751.19
56000	975.37	917.33	872.20	836.43	807.64	784.17	764.85
57000	992.79	933.71	887.78	851.37	822.06	798.17	778.50
58000	1010.20	950.09	903.35	866.31	836.48	812.17	792.16
59000	1027.62	966.47	918.93	881.24	850.90	826.18	805.82
60000	1045.04	982.85	934.50	896.18	865.33	840.18	819.48
65000	1132.13	1064.75	1012.38	970.86	937.44	910.19	887.77
70000	1219.21	1146.66	1090.25	1045.54	1009.55	980.21	956.06
75000	1306.30	1228.56	1168.13	1120.22	1081.66	1050.22	1024.35
80000	1393.38	1310.47	1246.00	1194.90	1153.77	1120.24	1092.64
85000	1480.47	1392.37	1323.88	1269.59	1225.88	1190.25	1160.93
90000	1567.56	1474.27	1401.75	1344.27	1297.99	1260.27	1229.22
95000	1654.64	1556.18	1479.63	1418.95	1370.10	1330.28	1297.51
100000	1741.73	1638.08	1557.50	1493.63	1442.21	1400.30	1365.79
105000	1828.82	1719.99	1635.38	1568.31	1514.32	1470.31	1434.08
110000	1915.90	1801.89	1713.26	1642.99	1586.43	1540.33	1502.37
120000	2090.08	1965.70	1869.01	1792.36	1730.65	1680.36	1638.95
130000	2264.25	2129.51	2024.76	1941.72	1874.87	1820.39	1775.53
140000	2438.42	2293.32	2180.51	2091.08	2019.09	1960.42	1912.11
150000	2612.60	2457.12	2336.26	2240.44	2163.31	2100.45	2048.69
160000	2786.77	2620.93	2492.01	2389.81	2307.54	2240.48	2185.27
170000	2960.94	2784.74	2647.76	2539.17	2451.76	2380.51	2321.85
180000	3135.12	2948.55	2803.51	2688.53	2595.98	2520.54	2458.43
190000	3309.29	3112.36	2959.26	2837.90	2740.20	2660.57	2595.01
200000	3483.46	3276.17	3115.01	2987.26	2884.42	2800.60	2731.59
210000	3657.64	3439.97	3270.76	3136.62	3028.64	2940.63	2868.17
220000	3831.81	3603.78	3426.51	3285.99	3172.86	3080.66	3004.75
230000	4005.98	3767.59	3582.26	3435.35	3317.08	3220.69	3141.33
240000	4180.15	3931.40	3738.01	3584.71	3461.30	3360.72	3277.91
250000	4354.33	4095.21	3893.76	3734.07	3605.52	3500.75	3414.49

14.50 % Monthly Payments

LOAN AMOUNT	15	16	17	18	19	20	21
100	1.34	1.31	1.29	1.28	1.26	1.25	1.24
200	2.67	2.63	2.59	2.55	2.52	2.50	2.48
500	6.69	6.57	6.47	6.38	6.31	6.25	6.19
1000	13.37	13.13	12.93	12.76	12.62	12.49	12.39
2000	26.74	26.26	25.86	25.52	25.23	24.99	24.78
5000	66.86	65.66	64.65	63.80	63.08	62.47	61.94
6000	80.23	78.79	77.58	76.56	75.70	74.96	74.33
7000	93.60	91.92	90.52	89.32	88.32	87.46	86.72
8000	106.97	105.06	103.45	102.09	100.93	99.95	99.11
9000	120.34	118.19	116.38	114.85	113.55	112.44	111.50
10000	133.72	131.32	129.31	127.61	126.16	124.94	123.89
12000	160.46	157.58	155.17	153.13	151.40	149.92	148.67
15000	200.57	196.98	193.96	191.41	189.25	187.41	185.83
20000	267.43	262.64	258.62	255.21	252.33	249.87	247.78
25000	334.29	328.30	323.27	319.02	315.41	312.34	309.72
30000	401.15	393.96	387.92	382.82	378.49	374.81	371.67
31000	414.52	407.09	400.85	395.58	391.11	387.30	384.05
32000	427.89	420.23	413.78	408.34	403.73	399.80	396.44
33000	441.26	433.36	426.72	421.10	416.34	412.29	408.83
34000	454.63	446.49	439.65	433.86	428.96	424.78	421.22
35000	468.00	459.62	452.58	446.62	441.58	437.28	433.61
36000	481.37	472.75	465.51	459.39	454.19	449.77	446.00
37000	494.75	485.89	478.44	472.15	466.81	462.27	458.39
38000	508.12	499.02	491.37	484.91	479.43	474.76	470.78
39000	521.49	512.15	504.30	497.67	492.04	487.25	483.17
40000	534.86	525.28	517.23	510.43	504.66	499.75	495.55
41000	548.23	538.41	530.16	523.19	517.27	512.24	507.94
42000	561.60	551.55	543.09	535.95	529.89	524.73	520.33
43000	574.97	564.68	556.02	548.71	542.51	537.23	532.72
44000	588.35	577.81	568.95	561.47	555.12	549.72	545.11
45000	601.72	590.94	581.88	574.23	567.74	562.22	557.50
46000	615.09	604.07	594.82	586.99	580.36	574.71	569.89
47000	628.46	617.21	607.75	599.75	592.97	587.20	582.28
48000	641.83	630.34	620.68	612.51	605.59	599.70	594.67
49000	655.20	643.47	633.61	625.27	618.21	612.19	607.05
50000	668.58	656.60	646.54	638.04	630.82	624.68	619.44
51000	681.95	669.74	659.47	650.80	643.44	637.18	631.83
52000	695.32	682.87	672.40	663.56	656.06	649.67	644.22
53000	708.69	696.00	685.33	676.32	668.67	662.16	656.61
54000	722.06	709.13	698.26	689.08	681.29	674.66	669.00
55000	735.43	722.26	711.19	701.84	693.91	687.15	681.39
56000	748.80	735.40	724.12	714.60	706.52	699.65	693.78
57000	762.18	748.53	737.05	727.36	719.14	712.14	706.16
58000	775.55	761.66	749.98	740.12	731.75	724.63	718.55
59000	788.92	774.79	762.91	752.88	744.37	737.13	730.94
60000	802.29	787.92	775.85	765.64	756.99	749.62	743.33
65000	869.15	853.58	840.50	829.45	820.07	812.09	805.28
70000	936.01	919.24	905.15	893.25	883.15	874.56	867.22
75000	1002.86	984.90	969.81	957.05	946.23	937.03	929.16
80000	1069.72	1050.56	1034.46	1020.86	1009.32	999.49	991.11
85000	1136.58	1116.23	1099.11	1084.66	1072.40	1061.96	1053.05
90000	1203.44	1181.89	1163.77	1148.46	1135.48	1124.43	1115.00
95000	1270.29	1247.55	1228.42	1212.27	1198.56	1186.90	1176.94
100000	1337.15	1313.21	1293.08	1276.07	1261.65	1249.37	1238.89
105000	1404.01	1378.87	1357.73	1339.87	1324.73	1311.84	1300.83
110000	1470.87	1444.53	1422.38	1403.68	1387.81	1374.30	1362.77
120000	1604.58	1575.85	1551.69	1531.28	1513.97	1499.24	1486.66
130000	1738.30	1707.17	1681.00	1658.89	1640.14	1624.18	1610.55
140000	1872.01	1838.49	1810.31	1786.50	1766.30	1749.11	1734.44
150000	2005.73	1969.81	1939.61	1914.11	1892.47	1874.05	1858.33
160000	2139.44	2101.13	2068.92	2041.71	2018.63	1998.99	1982.22
170000	2273.16	2232.45	2198.23	2169.32	2144.80	2123.92	2106.11
180000	2406.87	2363.77	2327.54	2296.93	2270.96	2248.86	2229.99
190000	2540.59	2495.09	2456.84	2424.53	2397.13	2373.80	2353.88
200000	2674.30	2626.41	2586.15	2552.14	2523.29	2498.73	2477.77
210000	2808.02	2757.73	2715.46	2679.75	2649.46	2623.67	2601.66
220000	2941.73	2889.05	2844.77	2807.36	2775.62	2748.61	2725.55
230000	3075.45	3020.37	2974.08	2934.96	2901.78	2873.55	2849.44
240000	3209.16	3151.69	3103.38	3062.57	3027.95	2998.48	2973.33
250000	3342.88	3283.02	3232.69	3190.18	3154.11	3123.42	3097.21

Monthly Payments 14.50 %

LOAN AMOUNT	22	23	24	25	30	35	40
	YEARS						
100	1.23	1.22	1.22	1.21	1.19	1.18	1.18
200	2.46	2.44	2.43	2.42	2.38	2.36	2.36
500	6.15	6.11	6.08	6.05	5.96	5.91	5.89
1000	12.30	12.22	12.16	12.10	11.91	11.82	11.78
2000	24.60	24.44	24.31	24.20	23.82	23.64	23.55
5000	61.50	61.11	60.78	60.50	59.56	59.11	58.89
6000	73.79	73.33	72.94	72.60	71.47	70.93	70.66
7000	86.09	85.56	85.09	84.69	83.39	82.75	82.44
8000	98.39	97.78	97.25	96.79	95.30	94.57	94.22
9000	110.69	110.00	109.40	108.89	107.21	106.40	106.00
10000	122.99	122.22	121.56	120.99	119.12	118.22	117.77
12000	147.59	146.67	145.87	145.19	142.95	141.86	141.33
15000	184.49	183.33	182.34	181.49	178.69	177.33	176.66
20000	245.98	244.44	243.12	241.98	238.25	236.44	235.55
25000	307.48	305.56	303.90	302.48	297.81	295.54	294.43
30000	368.97	366.67	364.68	362.98	357.37	354.65	353.32
31000	381.27	378.89	376.84	375.08	369.28	366.48	365.10
32000	393.57	391.11	389.00	387.17	381.20	378.30	376.87
33000	405.87	403.33	401.15	399.27	393.11	390.12	388.65
34000	418.17	415.56	413.31	411.37	405.02	401.94	400.43
35000	430.47	427.78	425.46	423.47	416.93	413.76	412.20
36000	442.77	440.00	437.62	435.57	428.85	425.58	423.98
37000	455.07	452.22	449.78	447.67	440.76	437.41	435.76
38000	467.37	464.44	461.93	459.77	452.67	449.23	447.54
39000	479.67	476.67	474.09	471.87	464.58	461.05	459.31
40000	491.97	488.89	486.24	483.97	476.50	472.87	471.09
41000	504.27	501.11	498.40	496.07	488.41	484.69	482.87
42000	516.56	513.33	510.56	508.17	500.32	496.51	494.65
43000	528.86	525.56	522.71	520.27	512.23	508.34	506.42
44000	541.16	537.78	534.87	532.37	524.15	520.16	518.20
45000	553.46	550.00	547.02	544.46	536.06	531.98	529.98
46000	565.76	562.22	559.18	556.56	547.97	543.80	541.75
47000	578.06	574.44	571.34	568.66	559.88	555.62	553.53
48000	590.36	586.67	583.49	580.76	571.80	567.45	565.31
49000	602.66	598.89	595.65	592.86	583.71	579.27	577.09
50000	614.96	611.11	607.81	604.96	595.62	591.09	588.86
51000	627.26	623.33	619.96	617.06	607.53	602.91	600.64
52000	639.56	635.56	632.12	629.16	619.45	614.73	612.42
53000	651.86	647.78	644.27	641.26	631.36	626.55	624.20
54000	664.15	660.00	656.43	653.36	643.27	638.38	635.97
55000	676.45	672.22	668.59	665.46	655.18	650.20	647.75
56000	688.75	684.44	680.74	677.56	667.10	662.02	659.53
57000	701.05	696.67	692.90	689.65	679.01	673.84	671.30
58000	713.35	708.89	705.05	701.75	690.92	685.66	683.08
59000	725.65	721.11	717.21	713.85	702.83	697.49	694.86
60000	737.95	733.33	729.37	725.95	714.75	709.31	706.64
65000	799.44	794.44	790.15	786.45	774.31	768.42	765.52
70000	860.94	855.55	850.93	846.94	833.87	827.52	824.41
75000	922.44	916.67	911.71	907.44	893.43	886.63	883.30
80000	983.93	977.78	972.49	967.94	952.99	945.74	942.18
85000	1045.43	1038.89	1033.27	1028.43	1012.56	1004.85	1001.07
90000	1106.92	1100.00	1094.05	1088.93	1072.12	1063.96	1059.96
95000	1168.42	1161.11	1154.83	1149.42	1131.68	1123.07	1118.84
100000	1229.92	1222.22	1215.61	1209.92	1191.24	1182.18	1177.73
105000	1291.41	1283.33	1276.39	1270.42	1250.80	1241.29	1236.61
110000	1352.91	1344.44	1337.17	1330.91	1310.37	1300.40	1295.50
120000	1475.90	1466.67	1458.73	1451.90	1429.49	1418.61	1413.27
130000	1598.89	1588.89	1580.29	1572.90	1548.61	1536.83	1531.05
140000	1721.88	1711.11	1701.85	1693.89	1667.74	1655.05	1648.82
150000	1844.87	1833.33	1823.42	1814.88	1786.86	1773.27	1766.59
160000	1967.86	1955.55	1944.98	1935.87	1905.99	1891.48	1884.36
170000	2090.86	2077.78	2066.54	2056.86	2025.11	2009.70	2002.14
180000	2213.85	2200.00	2188.10	2177.86	2144.24	2127.92	2119.91
190000	2336.84	2322.22	2309.66	2298.85	2263.36	2246.14	2237.68
200000	2459.83	2444.44	2431.22	2419.84	2382.48	2364.36	2355.46
210000	2582.82	2566.66	2552.78	2540.83	2501.61	2482.57	2473.23
220000	2705.81	2688.89	2674.34	2661.83	2620.73	2600.79	2591.00
230000	2828.80	2811.11	2795.90	2782.82	2739.86	2719.01	2708.77
240000	2951.80	2933.33	2917.46	2903.81	2858.98	2837.23	2826.55
250000	3074.79	3055.55	3039.03	3024.80	2978.10	2955.45	2944.32

14.75 % Monthly Payments

LOAN AMOUNT	1	2	3	4	5	6	7
			YEARS				
100	8.99	4.82	3.43	2.75	2.34	2.08	1.89
200	17.99	9.63	6.87	5.50	4.69	4.16	3.78
500	44.97	24.08	17.17	13.74	11.72	10.39	9.46
1000	89.94	48.16	34.33	27.49	23.43	20.78	18.92
2000	179.87	96.32	68.66	54.97	46.86	41.55	37.83
5000	449.68	240.81	171.66	137.43	117.16	103.88	94.58
6000	539.62	288.97	205.99	164.91	140.59	124.65	113.49
7000	629.55	337.14	240.32	192.40	164.03	145.43	132.41
8000	719.49	385.30	274.65	219.88	187.46	166.20	151.32
9000	809.42	433.46	308.98	247.37	210.89	186.98	170.24
10000	899.36	481.62	343.31	274.85	234.32	207.75	189.15
12000	1079.23	577.95	411.98	329.82	281.19	249.30	226.98
15000	1349.04	722.44	514.97	412.28	351.49	311.63	283.73
20000	1798.72	963.25	686.63	549.71	468.65	415.51	378.30
25000	2248.40	1204.06	858.28	687.13	585.81	519.39	472.88
30000	2698.08	1444.87	1029.94	824.56	702.97	623.26	567.45
31000	2788.01	1493.03	1064.27	852.05	726.41	644.04	586.37
32000	2877.95	1541.20	1098.60	879.53	749.84	664.81	605.28
33000	2967.89	1589.36	1132.94	907.02	773.27	685.59	624.20
34000	3057.82	1637.52	1167.27	934.50	796.70	706.36	643.11
35000	3147.76	1685.68	1201.60	961.99	820.14	727.14	662.03
36000	3237.69	1733.85	1235.93	989.47	843.57	747.91	680.94
37000	3327.63	1782.01	1270.26	1016.96	867.00	768.69	699.86
38000	3417.57	1830.17	1304.59	1044.44	890.43	789.47	718.77
39000	3507.50	1878.33	1338.92	1071.93	913.87	810.24	737.69
40000	3597.44	1926.50	1373.26	1099.41	937.30	831.02	756.60
41000	3687.37	1974.66	1407.59	1126.90	960.73	851.79	775.52
42000	3777.31	2022.82	1441.92	1154.38	984.16	872.57	794.43
43000	3867.25	2070.98	1476.25	1181.87	1007.60	893.34	813.35
44000	3957.18	2119.14	1510.58	1209.35	1031.03	914.12	832.26
45000	4047.12	2167.31	1544.91	1236.84	1054.46	934.89	851.18
46000	4137.05	2215.47	1579.24	1264.33	1077.89	955.67	870.09
47000	4226.99	2263.63	1613.58	1291.81	1101.33	976.44	889.01
48000	4316.93	2311.79	1647.91	1319.30	1124.76	997.22	907.92
49000	4406.86	2359.96	1682.24	1346.78	1148.19	1018.00	926.84
50000	4496.80	2408.12	1716.57	1374.27	1171.62	1038.77	945.75
51000	4586.73	2456.28	1750.90	1401.75	1195.06	1059.55	964.67
52000	4676.67	2504.44	1785.23	1429.24	1218.49	1080.32	983.59
53000	4766.61	2552.61	1819.56	1456.72	1241.92	1101.10	1002.50
54000	4856.54	2600.77	1853.89	1484.21	1265.35	1121.87	1021.42
55000	4946.48	2648.93	1888.23	1511.69	1288.79	1142.65	1040.33
56000	5036.41	2697.09	1922.56	1539.18	1312.22	1163.42	1059.25
57000	5126.35	2745.26	1956.89	1566.66	1335.65	1184.20	1078.16
58000	5216.28	2793.42	1991.22	1594.15	1359.08	1204.97	1097.08
59000	5306.22	2841.58	2025.55	1621.63	1382.52	1225.75	1115.99
60000	5396.16	2889.74	2059.88	1649.12	1405.95	1246.52	1134.91
65000	5845.84	3130.55	2231.54	1786.55	1523.11	1350.40	1229.48
70000	6295.52	3371.37	2403.20	1923.97	1640.27	1454.28	1324.06
75000	6745.20	3612.18	2574.85	2061.40	1757.44	1558.16	1418.63
80000	7194.88	3852.99	2746.51	2198.83	1874.60	1662.03	1513.21
85000	7644.56	4093.80	2918.17	2336.25	1991.76	1765.91	1607.78
90000	8094.24	4334.61	3089.82	2473.68	2108.92	1869.79	1702.36
95000	8543.91	4575.43	3261.48	2611.11	2226.09	1973.66	1796.93
100000	8993.59	4816.24	3433.14	2748.53	2343.25	2077.54	1891.51
105000	9443.27	5057.05	3604.80	2885.96	2460.41	2181.42	1986.09
110000	9892.95	5297.86	3776.45	3023.39	2577.57	2285.30	2080.66
120000	10792.31	5779.49	4119.77	3298.24	2811.90	2493.05	2269.81
130000	11691.67	6261.11	4463.08	3573.09	3046.22	2700.80	2458.96
140000	12591.03	6742.73	4806.39	3847.95	3280.55	2908.56	2648.11
150000	13490.39	7224.36	5149.71	4122.80	3514.87	3116.31	2837.26
160000	14389.75	7705.98	5493.02	4397.65	3749.20	3324.07	3026.42
170000	15289.11	8187.60	5836.34	4672.51	3983.52	3531.82	3215.57
180000	16188.47	8669.23	6179.65	4947.36	4217.85	3739.57	3404.72
190000	17087.83	9150.85	6522.96	5222.21	4452.17	3947.33	3593.87
200000	17987.19	9632.48	6866.28	5497.07	4686.50	4155.08	3783.02
210000	18886.55	10114.10	7209.59	5771.92	4920.82	4362.84	3972.17
220000	19785.91	10595.72	7552.91	6046.77	5155.15	4570.59	4161.32
230000	20685.27	11077.35	7896.22	6321.63	5389.47	4778.35	4350.47
240000	21584.63	11558.97	8239.53	6596.48	5623.80	4986.10	4539.62
250000	22483.99	12040.59	8582.85	6871.33	5858.12	5193.85	4728.77

Monthly Payments 14.75 %

LOAN AMOUNT	8	9	10	11	12	13	14
			YEARS				
100	1.76	1.65	1.57	1.51	1.46	1.42	1.38
200	3.51	3.30	3.14	3.02	2.91	2.83	2.76
500	8.78	8.26	7.86	7.54	7.29	7.08	6.91
1000	17.55	16.52	15.72	15.08	14.57	14.16	13.81
2000	35.10	33.04	31.43	30.16	29.14	28.31	27.63
5000	87.76	82.60	78.59	75.41	72.86	70.78	69.07
6000	105.31	99.12	94.30	90.49	87.43	84.93	82.88
7000	122.86	115.64	110.02	105.58	102.00	99.09	96.70
8000	140.42	132.15	125.74	120.66	116.57	113.25	110.51
9000	157.97	148.67	141.46	135.74	131.14	127.40	124.33
10000	175.52	165.19	157.17	150.82	145.71	141.56	138.14
12000	210.62	198.23	188.61	180.99	174.86	169.87	165.77
15000	263.28	247.79	235.76	226.23	218.57	212.34	207.21
20000	351.04	330.39	314.35	301.64	291.43	283.12	276.28
25000	438.80	412.98	392.93	377.05	364.29	353.89	345.35
30000	526.56	495.58	471.52	452.47	437.14	424.67	414.42
31000	544.11	512.10	487.24	467.55	451.72	438.83	428.23
32000	561.66	528.62	502.95	482.63	466.29	452.98	442.04
33000	579.21	545.14	518.67	497.71	480.86	467.14	455.86
34000	596.77	561.66	534.39	512.79	495.43	481.30	469.67
35000	614.32	578.18	550.11	527.88	510.00	495.45	483.49
36000	631.87	594.70	565.82	542.96	524.57	509.61	497.30
37000	649.42	611.21	581.54	558.04	539.15	523.76	511.11
38000	666.97	627.73	597.26	573.12	553.72	537.92	524.93
39000	684.52	644.25	612.97	588.21	568.29	552.07	538.74
40000	702.08	660.77	628.69	603.29	582.86	566.23	552.56
41000	719.63	677.29	644.41	618.37	597.43	580.39	566.37
42000	737.18	693.81	660.13	633.45	612.00	594.54	580.18
43000	754.73	710.33	675.84	648.53	626.57	608.70	594.00
44000	772.28	726.85	691.56	663.62	641.15	622.85	607.81
45000	789.84	743.37	707.28	678.70	655.72	637.01	621.63
46000	807.39	759.89	723.00	693.78	670.29	651.16	635.44
47000	824.94	776.41	738.71	708.86	684.86	665.32	649.25
48000	842.49	792.93	754.43	723.95	699.43	679.48	663.07
49000	860.04	809.45	770.15	739.03	714.00	693.63	676.88
50000	877.60	825.97	785.87	754.11	728.57	707.79	690.70
51000	895.15	842.48	801.58	769.19	743.15	721.94	704.51
52000	912.70	859.00	817.30	784.27	757.72	736.10	718.32
53000	930.25	875.52	833.02	799.36	772.29	750.25	732.14
54000	947.80	892.04	848.73	814.44	786.86	764.41	745.95
55000	965.36	908.56	864.45	829.52	801.43	778.57	759.76
56000	982.91	925.08	880.17	844.60	816.00	792.72	773.58
57000	1000.46	941.60	895.89	859.69	830.58	806.88	787.39
58000	1018.01	958.12	911.60	874.77	845.15	821.03	801.21
59000	1035.56	974.64	927.32	889.85	859.72	835.19	815.02
60000	1053.11	991.16	943.04	904.93	874.29	849.35	828.83
65000	1140.87	1073.76	1021.62	980.34	947.15	920.12	897.90
70000	1228.63	1156.35	1100.21	1055.75	1020.00	990.90	966.97
75000	1316.39	1238.95	1178.80	1131.16	1092.86	1061.68	1036.04
80000	1404.15	1321.54	1257.38	1206.58	1165.72	1132.46	1105.11
85000	1491.91	1404.14	1335.97	1281.99	1238.58	1203.24	1174.18
90000	1579.67	1486.74	1414.56	1357.40	1311.43	1274.02	1243.25
95000	1667.43	1569.33	1493.14	1432.81	1384.29	1344.80	1312.32
100000	1755.19	1651.93	1571.73	1508.22	1457.15	1415.58	1381.39
105000	1842.95	1734.53	1650.32	1583.63	1530.01	1486.35	1450.46
110000	1930.71	1817.12	1728.90	1659.04	1602.86	1557.13	1519.53
120000	2106.23	1982.32	1886.08	1809.86	1748.58	1698.69	1657.67
130000	2281.75	2147.51	2043.25	1960.69	1894.29	1840.25	1795.81
140000	2457.27	2312.70	2200.42	2111.51	2040.01	1981.81	1933.95
150000	2632.79	2477.90	2357.60	2262.33	2185.72	2123.36	2072.09
160000	2808.31	2643.09	2514.77	2413.15	2331.44	2264.92	2210.22
170000	2983.83	2808.28	2671.94	2563.97	2477.15	2406.48	2348.36
180000	3159.34	2973.48	2829.11	2714.80	2622.87	2548.04	2486.50
190000	3334.86	3138.67	2986.29	2865.62	2768.58	2689.59	2624.64
200000	3510.38	3303.86	3143.46	3016.44	2914.30	2831.15	2762.78
210000	3685.90	3469.06	3300.63	3167.26	3060.01	2972.71	2900.92
220000	3861.42	3634.25	3457.81	3318.08	3205.73	3114.27	3039.06
230000	4036.94	3799.44	3614.98	3468.91	3351.44	3255.82	3177.20
240000	4212.46	3964.63	3772.15	3619.73	3497.16	3397.38	3315.34
250000	4387.98	4129.83	3929.33	3770.55	3642.87	3538.94	3453.48

14.75 % Monthly Payments

LOAN AMOUNT	15	16	17	18	19	20	21
				YEARS			
100	1.35	1.33	1.31	1.29	1.28	1.27	1.2
200	2.71	2.66	2.62	2.59	2.56	2.53	2.5
500	6.77	6.65	6.55	6.46	6.39	6.33	6.2
1000	13.53	13.29	13.10	12.93	12.79	12.67	12.5
2000	27.06	26.59	26.19	25.86	25.57	25.33	25.1
5000	67.65	66.47	65.48	64.64	63.93	63.33	62.8
6000	81.18	79.76	78.57	77.57	76.72	75.99	75.3
7000	94.71	93.06	91.67	90.50	89.50	88.66	87.9
8000	108.24	106.35	104.76	103.42	102.29	101.32	100.5
9000	121.77	119.65	117.86	116.35	115.07	113.99	113.0
10000	135.30	132.94	130.95	129.28	127.86	126.65	125.6
12000	162.37	159.53	157.14	155.13	153.43	151.99	150.7
15000	202.96	199.41	196.43	193.92	191.79	189.98	188.4
20000	270.61	265.88	261.91	258.56	255.72	253.31	251.2
25000	338.26	332.35	327.38	323.20	319.65	316.64	314.0
30000	405.91	398.82	392.86	387.84	383.58	379.96	376.8
31000	419.45	412.11	405.96	400.76	396.37	392.63	389.4
32000	432.98	425.41	419.05	413.69	409.15	405.30	402.0
33000	446.51	438.70	432.15	426.62	421.94	417.96	414.5
34000	460.04	451.99	445.24	439.55	434.72	430.63	427.1
35000	473.57	465.29	458.34	452.48	447.51	443.29	439.7
36000	487.10	478.58	471.43	465.40	460.30	455.96	452.2
37000	500.63	491.88	484.53	478.33	473.08	468.62	464.8
38000	514.16	505.17	497.62	491.26	485.87	481.29	477.3
39000	527.69	518.46	510.72	504.19	498.65	493.95	489.9
40000	541.22	531.76	523.81	517.11	511.44	506.62	502.5
41000	554.75	545.05	536.91	530.04	524.23	519.28	515.0
42000	568.28	558.35	550.01	542.97	537.01	531.95	527.6
43000	581.81	571.64	563.10	555.90	549.80	544.62	540.2
44000	595.34	584.93	576.20	568.83	562.58	557.28	552.7
45000	608.87	598.23	589.29	581.75	575.37	569.95	565.3
46000	622.40	611.52	602.39	594.68	588.16	582.61	577.8
47000	635.93	624.82	615.48	607.61	600.94	595.28	590.4
48000	649.46	638.11	628.58	620.54	613.73	607.94	603.0
49000	662.99	651.40	641.67	633.47	626.51	620.61	615.5
50000	676.52	664.70	654.77	646.39	639.30	633.27	628.1
51000	690.06	677.99	667.86	659.32	652.09	645.94	640.7
52000	703.59	691.28	680.96	672.25	664.87	658.61	653.2
53000	717.12	704.58	694.05	685.18	677.66	671.27	665.8
54000	730.65	717.87	707.15	698.10	690.45	683.94	678.3
55000	744.18	731.17	720.24	711.03	703.23	696.60	690.9
56000	757.71	744.46	733.34	723.96	716.02	709.27	703.5
57000	771.24	757.75	746.44	736.89	728.80	721.93	716.0
58000	784.77	771.05	759.53	749.82	741.59	734.60	728.6
59000	798.30	784.34	772.63	762.74	754.38	747.26	741.2
60000	811.83	797.64	785.72	775.67	767.16	759.93	753.7
65000	879.48	864.11	851.20	840.31	831.09	823.26	816.5
70000	947.13	930.58	916.68	904.95	895.02	886.58	879.3
75000	1014.79	997.05	982.15	969.59	958.95	949.91	942.2
80000	1082.44	1063.52	1047.63	1034.23	1022.88	1013.24	1005.0
85000	1150.09	1129.98	1113.11	1098.87	1086.81	1076.57	1067.8
90000	1217.74	1196.45	1178.58	1163.51	1150.74	1139.89	1130.6
95000	1285.40	1262.92	1244.06	1228.15	1214.67	1203.22	1193.4
100000	1353.05	1329.39	1309.54	1292.79	1278.60	1266.55	1256.2
105000	1420.70	1395.86	1375.01	1357.43	1342.53	1329.88	1319.0
110000	1488.35	1462.33	1440.49	1422.07	1406.46	1393.20	1381.9
120000	1623.66	1595.27	1571.44	1551.34	1534.32	1519.86	1507.5
130000	1758.96	1728.21	1702.40	1680.62	1662.18	1646.51	1633.1
140000	1894.27	1861.15	1833.35	1809.90	1790.04	1773.17	1758.7
150000	2029.57	1994.09	1964.30	1939.18	1917.90	1899.82	1884.4
160000	2164.88	2127.03	2095.26	2068.46	2045.76	2026.48	2010.0
170000	2300.18	2259.97	2226.21	2197.74	2173.62	2153.13	2135.6
180000	2435.49	2392.91	2357.16	2327.02	2301.48	2279.79	2261.3
190000	2570.79	2525.85	2488.12	2456.29	2429.34	2406.44	2386.9
200000	2706.10	2658.79	2619.07	2585.57	2557.20	2533.10	2512.5
210000	2841.40	2791.73	2750.03	2714.85	2685.06	2659.75	2638.1
220000	2976.71	2924.67	2880.98	2844.13	2812.92	2786.41	2763.8
230000	3112.01	3057.61	3011.93	2973.41	2940.78	2913.06	2889.4
240000	3247.32	3190.55	3142.89	3102.69	3068.64	3039.72	3015.0
250000	3382.62	3323.48	3273.84	3231.97	3196.50	3166.37	3140.6

Monthly Payments 14.75 %

LOAN AMOUNT	YEARS 22	23	24	25	30	35	40
100	1.25	1.24	1.23	1.23	1.21	1.20	1.20
200	2.50	2.48	2.47	2.46	2.42	2.40	2.39
500	6.24	6.20	6.17	6.14	6.05	6.01	5.99
1000	12.48	12.40	12.34	12.28	12.10	12.01	11.97
2000	24.95	24.80	24.67	24.56	24.20	24.03	23.94
5000	62.38	62.00	61.68	61.40	60.50	60.06	59.85
6000	74.85	74.40	74.01	73.68	72.60	72.08	71.82
7000	87.33	86.80	86.35	85.96	84.70	84.09	83.79
8000	99.80	99.20	98.68	98.24	96.80	96.10	95.76
9000	112.28	111.60	111.02	110.52	108.89	108.11	107.73
10000	124.75	124.00	123.35	122.80	120.99	120.13	119.70
12000	149.70	148.80	148.03	147.36	145.19	144.15	143.65
15000	187.13	186.00	185.03	184.20	181.49	180.19	179.56
20000	249.50	248.00	246.71	245.60	241.99	240.25	239.41
25000	311.88	310.00	308.39	307.00	302.49	300.32	299.26
30000	374.25	372.00	370.06	368.40	362.98	360.38	359.11
31000	386.73	384.40	382.40	380.68	375.08	372.39	371.09
32000	399.20	396.80	394.73	392.96	387.18	384.40	383.06
33000	411.68	409.20	407.07	405.24	399.28	396.42	395.03
34000	424.15	421.60	419.41	417.52	411.38	408.43	407.00
35000	436.63	434.00	431.74	429.80	423.48	420.44	418.97
36000	449.10	446.40	444.08	442.08	435.58	432.45	430.94
37000	461.58	458.80	456.41	454.36	447.68	444.47	442.91
38000	474.05	471.20	468.75	466.64	459.78	456.48	454.88
39000	486.53	483.60	481.08	478.92	471.88	468.49	466.85
40000	499.00	496.00	493.42	491.20	483.98	480.51	478.82
41000	511.48	508.40	505.75	503.48	496.08	492.52	490.79
42000	523.95	520.80	518.09	515.76	508.17	504.53	502.76
43000	536.43	533.20	530.42	528.04	520.27	516.54	514.73
44000	548.90	545.60	542.76	540.33	532.37	528.56	526.70
45000	561.38	558.00	555.10	552.61	544.47	540.57	538.67
46000	573.85	570.39	567.43	564.89	556.57	552.58	550.64
47000	586.33	582.79	579.77	577.17	568.67	564.59	562.61
48000	598.80	595.19	592.10	589.45	580.77	576.61	574.58
49000	611.28	607.59	604.44	601.73	592.87	588.62	586.55
50000	623.75	619.99	616.77	614.01	604.97	600.63	598.52
51000	636.23	632.39	629.11	626.29	617.07	612.64	610.49
52000	648.70	644.79	641.44	638.57	629.17	624.66	622.47
53000	661.18	657.19	653.78	650.85	641.27	636.67	634.44
54000	673.65	669.59	666.11	663.13	653.37	648.68	646.41
55000	686.13	681.99	678.45	675.41	665.47	660.69	658.38
56000	698.60	694.39	690.79	687.69	677.57	672.71	670.35
57000	711.08	706.79	703.12	699.97	689.67	684.72	682.32
58000	723.55	719.19	715.46	712.25	701.77	696.73	694.29
59000	736.03	731.59	727.79	724.53	713.86	708.75	706.26
60000	748.50	743.99	740.13	736.81	725.96	720.76	718.23
65000	810.88	805.99	801.80	798.21	786.46	780.82	778.08
70000	873.25	867.99	863.48	859.61	846.96	840.88	837.93
75000	935.63	929.99	925.16	921.01	907.46	900.95	897.79
80000	998.00	991.99	986.84	982.41	967.95	961.01	957.64
85000	1060.38	1053.99	1048.51	1043.81	1028.45	1021.07	1017.49
90000	1122.75	1115.99	1110.19	1105.21	1088.95	1081.14	1077.34
95000	1185.13	1177.99	1171.87	1166.61	1149.44	1141.20	1137.20
100000	1247.50	1239.99	1233.55	1228.01	1209.94	1201.26	1197.05
105000	1309.88	1301.99	1295.22	1289.41	1270.44	1261.33	1256.90
110000	1372.25	1363.99	1356.90	1350.81	1330.93	1321.39	1316.75
120000	1497.00	1487.99	1480.26	1473.61	1451.93	1441.52	1436.46
130000	1621.75	1611.99	1603.61	1596.42	1572.92	1561.64	1556.16
140000	1746.50	1735.98	1726.96	1719.22	1693.92	1681.77	1675.87
150000	1871.25	1859.98	1850.32	1842.02	1814.91	1801.89	1795.57
160000	1996.00	1983.98	1973.67	1964.82	1935.90	1922.02	1915.28
170000	2120.75	2107.98	2097.03	2087.62	2056.90	2042.15	2034.98
180000	2245.50	2231.98	2220.38	2210.42	2177.89	2162.27	2154.69
190000	2370.25	2355.98	2343.74	2333.22	2298.89	2282.40	2274.39
200000	2495.00	2479.98	2467.09	2456.02	2419.88	2402.53	2394.10
210000	2619.75	2603.98	2590.45	2578.82	2540.87	2522.65	2513.80
220000	2744.50	2727.98	2713.80	2701.63	2661.87	2642.78	2633.51
230000	2869.25	2851.97	2837.16	2824.43	2782.86	2762.90	2753.21
240000	2994.00	2975.97	2960.51	2947.23	2903.86	2883.03	2872.92
250000	3118.75	3099.97	3083.86	3070.03	3024.85	3003.16	2992.62

15.00 % Monthly Payments

LOAN AMOUNT	YEARS 1	2	3	4	5	6	7
100	9.00	4.83	3.44	2.76	2.36	2.09	1.90
200	18.01	9.65	6.89	5.52	4.71	4.18	3.81
500	45.02	24.14	17.22	13.80	11.78	10.45	9.52
1000	90.05	48.27	34.45	27.60	23.56	20.90	19.05
2000	180.09	96.55	68.89	55.21	47.11	41.80	38.09
5000	450.23	241.37	172.23	138.02	117.78	104.51	95.23
6000	540.28	289.64	206.68	165.62	141.33	125.41	114.28
7000	630.33	337.92	241.12	193.23	164.89	146.32	133.32
8000	720.38	386.19	275.57	220.83	188.44	167.22	152.37
9000	810.42	434.47	310.02	248.44	212.00	188.12	171.41
10000	900.47	482.74	344.46	276.04	235.55	209.02	190.46
12000	1080.56	579.29	413.35	331.25	282.66	250.83	228.55
15000	1350.70	724.11	516.69	414.06	353.33	313.53	285.69
20000	1800.94	965.48	688.92	552.08	471.10	418.05	380.92
25000	2251.17	1206.85	861.15	690.10	588.88	522.56	476.15
30000	2701.41	1448.22	1033.39	828.12	706.66	627.07	571.38
31000	2791.45	1496.49	1067.83	855.72	730.21	647.97	590.43
32000	2881.50	1544.76	1102.28	883.33	753.77	668.87	609.47
33000	2971.55	1593.04	1136.72	910.93	777.32	689.78	628.52
34000	3061.59	1641.31	1171.17	938.54	800.88	710.68	647.57
35000	3151.64	1689.59	1205.62	966.14	824.43	731.58	666.61
36000	3241.69	1737.86	1240.06	993.74	847.99	752.48	685.66
37000	3331.73	1786.13	1274.51	1021.35	871.54	773.38	704.70
38000	3421.78	1834.41	1308.95	1048.95	895.10	794.29	723.75
39000	3511.83	1882.68	1343.40	1076.56	918.65	815.19	742.80
40000	3601.88	1930.96	1377.85	1104.16	942.21	836.09	761.84
41000	3691.92	1979.23	1412.29	1131.76	965.76	856.99	780.89
42000	3781.97	2027.50	1446.74	1159.37	989.32	877.90	799.94
43000	3872.02	2075.78	1481.19	1186.97	1012.88	898.80	818.98
44000	3962.06	2124.05	1515.63	1214.58	1036.43	919.70	838.03
45000	4052.11	2172.33	1550.08	1242.18	1059.99	940.60	857.07
46000	4142.16	2220.60	1584.52	1269.78	1083.54	961.51	876.12
47000	4232.20	2268.87	1618.97	1297.39	1107.10	982.41	895.17
48000	4322.25	2317.15	1653.42	1324.99	1130.65	1003.31	914.21
49000	4412.30	2365.42	1687.86	1352.60	1154.21	1024.21	933.26
50000	4502.34	2413.70	1722.31	1380.20	1177.76	1045.11	952.30
51000	4592.39	2461.97	1756.75	1407.80	1201.32	1066.02	971.35
52000	4682.44	2510.24	1791.20	1435.41	1224.87	1086.92	990.40
53000	4772.49	2558.52	1825.65	1463.01	1248.43	1107.82	1009.44
54000	4862.53	2606.79	1860.09	1490.62	1271.98	1128.72	1028.49
55000	4952.58	2655.06	1894.54	1518.22	1295.54	1149.63	1047.53
56000	5042.63	2703.34	1928.99	1545.82	1319.09	1170.53	1066.58
57000	5132.67	2751.61	1963.43	1573.43	1342.65	1191.43	1085.63
58000	5222.72	2799.89	1997.88	1601.03	1366.20	1212.33	1104.67
59000	5312.77	2848.16	2032.32	1628.64	1389.76	1233.24	1123.72
60000	5402.81	2896.43	2066.77	1656.24	1413.31	1254.14	1142.76
65000	5853.05	3137.80	2239.00	1794.26	1531.09	1358.65	1237.99
70000	6303.28	3379.17	2411.23	1932.28	1648.87	1463.16	1333.23
75000	6753.52	3620.54	2583.46	2070.30	1766.64	1567.67	1428.46
80000	7203.75	3861.91	2755.69	2208.32	1884.42	1672.18	1523.69
85000	7653.99	4103.28	2927.92	2346.34	2002.20	1776.69	1618.92
90000	8104.22	4344.65	3100.16	2484.36	2119.97	1881.21	1714.15
95000	8554.45	4586.02	3272.39	2622.38	2237.75	1985.72	1809.38
100000	9004.69	4827.39	3444.62	2760.40	2355.52	2090.23	1904.61
105000	9454.92	5068.76	3616.85	2898.42	2473.30	2194.74	1999.84
110000	9905.16	5310.13	3789.08	3036.44	2591.08	2299.25	2095.07
120000	10805.63	5792.87	4133.54	3312.48	2826.63	2508.28	2285.53
130000	11706.10	6275.61	4478.00	3588.52	3062.18	2717.30	2475.99
140000	12606.56	6758.35	4822.46	3864.56	3297.73	2926.32	2666.45
150000	13507.03	7241.09	5166.93	4140.60	3533.29	3135.34	2856.91
160000	14407.50	7723.82	5511.39	4416.64	3768.84	3344.37	3047.37
170000	15307.97	8206.56	5855.85	4692.68	4004.39	3553.39	3237.83
180000	16208.44	8689.30	6200.31	4968.72	4239.94	3762.41	3428.29
190000	17108.91	9172.04	6544.77	5244.76	4475.50	3971.44	3618.75
200000	18009.38	9654.78	6889.23	5520.80	4711.05	4180.46	3809.21
210000	18909.85	10137.52	7233.70	5796.84	4946.60	4389.48	3999.68
220000	19810.32	10620.26	7578.16	6072.88	5182.15	4598.50	4190.14
230000	20710.78	11103.00	7922.62	6348.92	5417.70	4807.53	4380.60
240000	21611.25	11585.74	8267.08	6624.96	5653.26	5016.55	4571.06
250000	22511.72	12068.48	8611.54	6901.00	5888.81	5225.57	4761.52

Monthly Payments 15.00 %

LOAN AMOUNT	8	9	10	11	12	13	14
			YEARS				
100	1.77	1.67	1.59	1.52	1.47	1.43	1.40
200	3.54	3.33	3.17	3.05	2.94	2.86	2.79
500	8.84	8.33	7.93	7.61	7.36	7.15	6.99
1000	17.69	16.66	15.86	15.23	14.72	14.31	13.97
2000	35.37	33.32	31.72	30.46	29.44	28.62	27.94
5000	88.43	83.29	79.30	76.14	73.61	71.55	69.85
6000	106.12	99.95	95.16	91.37	88.33	85.85	83.82
7000	123.81	116.61	111.02	106.60	103.05	100.16	97.79
8000	141.50	133.27	126.88	121.83	117.77	114.47	111.76
9000	159.18	149.92	142.74	137.06	132.49	128.78	125.73
10000	176.87	166.58	158.60	152.29	147.21	143.09	139.70
12000	212.24	199.90	190.32	182.74	176.66	171.71	167.65
15000	265.30	249.87	237.90	228.43	220.82	214.64	209.56
20000	353.74	333.16	317.20	304.57	294.43	286.18	279.41
25000	442.17	416.46	396.50	380.72	368.04	357.73	349.26
30000	530.61	499.75	475.80	456.86	441.64	429.27	419.11
31000	548.29	516.41	491.66	472.09	456.36	443.58	433.08
32000	565.98	533.06	507.52	487.32	471.09	457.89	447.05
33000	583.67	549.72	523.38	502.54	485.81	472.20	461.02
34000	601.36	566.38	539.24	517.77	500.53	486.51	474.99
35000	619.04	583.04	555.10	533.00	515.25	500.82	488.97
36000	636.73	599.70	570.96	548.23	529.97	515.13	502.94
37000	654.42	616.35	586.82	563.46	544.69	529.44	516.91
38000	672.10	633.01	602.68	578.69	559.41	543.74	530.88
39000	689.79	649.67	618.54	593.92	574.14	558.05	544.85
40000	707.48	666.33	634.40	609.14	588.86	572.36	558.82
41000	725.16	682.99	650.26	624.37	603.58	586.67	572.79
42000	742.85	699.65	666.12	639.60	618.30	600.98	586.76
43000	760.54	716.30	681.98	654.83	633.02	615.29	600.73
44000	778.22	732.96	697.84	670.06	647.74	629.60	614.70
45000	795.91	749.62	713.70	685.29	662.46	643.91	628.67
46000	813.60	766.28	729.56	700.52	677.19	658.22	642.64
47000	831.29	782.94	745.42	715.74	691.91	672.53	656.61
48000	848.97	799.60	761.28	730.97	706.63	686.84	670.58
49000	866.66	816.25	777.14	746.20	721.35	701.14	684.55
50000	884.35	832.91	793.00	761.43	736.07	715.45	698.52
51000	902.03	849.57	808.86	776.66	750.79	729.76	712.49
52000	919.72	866.23	824.72	791.89	765.51	744.07	726.46
53000	937.41	882.89	840.58	807.12	780.24	758.38	740.43
54000	955.09	899.55	856.44	822.34	794.96	772.69	754.40
55000	972.78	916.20	872.30	837.57	809.68	787.00	768.37
56000	990.47	932.86	888.16	852.80	824.40	801.31	782.34
57000	1008.15	949.52	904.02	868.03	839.12	815.62	796.31
58000	1025.84	966.18	919.88	883.26	853.84	829.93	810.28
59000	1043.53	982.84	935.74	898.49	868.56	844.23	824.26
60000	1061.21	999.49	951.60	913.72	883.29	858.54	838.23
65000	1149.65	1082.79	1030.90	989.86	956.89	930.09	908.08
70000	1238.08	1166.08	1110.20	1066.00	1030.50	1001.63	977.93
75000	1326.52	1249.37	1189.50	1142.15	1104.11	1073.18	1047.78
80000	1414.95	1332.66	1268.80	1218.29	1177.71	1144.73	1117.63
85000	1503.39	1415.95	1348.10	1294.43	1251.32	1216.27	1187.49
90000	1591.82	1499.24	1427.40	1370.57	1324.93	1287.82	1257.34
95000	1680.26	1582.53	1506.70	1446.72	1398.54	1359.36	1327.19
100000	1768.69	1665.82	1586.00	1522.86	1472.14	1430.91	1397.04
105000	1857.13	1749.12	1665.30	1599.00	1545.75	1502.45	1466.90
110000	1945.56	1832.41	1744.60	1675.15	1619.36	1574.00	1536.75
120000	2122.43	1998.99	1903.20	1827.43	1766.57	1717.09	1676.45
130000	2299.30	2165.57	2061.81	1979.72	1913.79	1860.18	1816.16
140000	2476.17	2332.15	2220.41	2132.01	2061.00	2003.27	1955.86
150000	2653.04	2498.74	2379.01	2284.29	2208.22	2146.36	2095.56
160000	2829.91	2665.32	2537.61	2436.58	2355.43	2289.45	2235.27
170000	3006.78	2831.90	2696.21	2588.86	2502.64	2432.54	2374.97
180000	3183.64	2998.48	2854.81	2741.15	2649.86	2575.63	2514.68
190000	3360.51	3165.07	3013.41	2893.44	2797.07	2718.72	2654.38
200000	3537.38	3331.65	3172.01	3045.72	2944.29	2861.81	2794.09
210000	3714.25	3498.23	3330.61	3198.01	3091.50	3004.90	2933.79
220000	3891.12	3664.81	3489.21	3350.29	3238.72	3147.99	3073.49
230000	4067.99	3831.40	3647.81	3502.58	3385.93	3291.08	3213.20
240000	4244.86	3997.98	3806.41	3654.87	3533.14	3434.18	3352.90
250000	4421.73	4164.56	3965.01	3807.15	3680.36	3577.27	3492.61

15.00 % Monthly Payments

LOAN AMOUNT	15	16	17	18	19	20	21
				YEARS			
100	1.37	1.35	1.33	1.31	1.30	1.28	1.27
200	2.74	2.69	2.65	2.62	2.59	2.57	2.55
500	6.85	6.73	6.63	6.55	6.48	6.42	6.37
1000	13.69	13.46	13.26	13.10	12.96	12.84	12.74
2000	27.38	26.91	26.52	26.19	25.91	25.68	25.47
5000	68.45	67.28	66.30	65.48	64.78	64.19	63.69
6000	82.14	80.74	79.56	78.57	77.74	77.03	76.42
7000	95.83	94.19	92.82	91.67	90.69	89.86	89.16
8000	109.52	107.65	106.08	104.76	103.65	102.70	101.90
9000	123.21	121.11	119.34	117.86	116.61	115.54	114.63
10000	136.90	134.56	132.61	130.96	129.56	128.38	127.37
12000	164.28	161.48	159.13	157.15	155.47	154.05	152.85
15000	205.35	201.85	198.91	196.43	194.34	192.57	191.06
20000	273.80	269.13	265.21	261.91	259.12	256.76	254.74
25000	342.25	336.41	331.51	327.39	323.90	320.95	318.43
30000	410.70	403.69	397.82	392.87	388.68	385.14	382.12
31000	424.39	417.15	411.08	405.96	401.64	397.97	394.85
32000	438.08	430.60	424.34	419.06	414.60	410.81	407.59
33000	451.77	444.06	437.60	432.15	427.55	423.65	420.33
34000	465.46	457.52	450.86	445.25	440.51	436.49	433.07
35000	479.15	470.97	464.12	458.35	453.46	449.32	445.80
36000	492.84	484.43	477.38	471.44	466.42	462.16	458.54
37000	506.53	497.89	490.64	484.54	479.38	475.00	471.28
38000	520.22	511.34	503.90	497.63	492.33	487.84	484.01
39000	533.91	524.80	517.16	510.73	505.29	500.68	496.75
40000	547.60	538.26	530.42	523.82	518.25	513.51	509.49
41000	561.29	551.71	543.68	536.92	531.20	526.35	522.23
42000	574.98	565.17	556.94	550.01	544.16	539.19	534.96
43000	588.67	578.63	570.20	563.11	557.11	552.03	547.70
44000	602.36	592.08	583.46	576.21	570.07	564.87	560.44
45000	616.05	605.54	596.72	589.30	583.03	577.70	573.17
46000	629.74	618.99	609.98	602.40	595.98	590.54	585.91
47000	643.43	632.45	623.25	615.49	608.94	603.38	598.65
48000	657.12	645.91	636.51	628.59	621.89	616.22	611.39
49000	670.81	659.36	649.77	641.68	634.85	629.05	624.12
50000	684.50	672.82	663.03	654.78	647.81	641.89	636.86
51000	698.19	686.28	676.29	667.88	660.76	654.73	649.60
52000	711.88	699.73	689.55	680.97	673.72	667.57	662.33
53000	725.57	713.19	702.81	694.07	686.68	680.41	675.07
54000	739.26	726.65	716.07	707.16	699.63	693.24	687.81
55000	752.95	740.10	729.33	720.26	712.59	706.08	700.55
56000	766.64	753.56	742.59	733.35	725.54	718.92	713.28
57000	780.33	767.01	755.85	746.45	738.50	731.76	726.02
58000	794.02	780.47	769.11	759.54	751.46	744.59	738.76
59000	807.71	793.93	782.37	772.64	764.41	757.43	751.50
60000	821.40	807.38	795.63	785.74	777.37	770.27	764.23
65000	889.85	874.67	861.93	851.21	842.15	834.46	827.92
70000	958.31	941.95	928.24	916.69	906.93	898.65	891.60
75000	1026.76	1009.23	994.54	982.17	971.71	962.84	955.29
80000	1095.21	1076.51	1060.84	1047.65	1036.49	1027.03	1018.98
85000	1163.66	1143.79	1127.15	1113.13	1101.27	1091.22	1082.66
90000	1232.11	1211.08	1193.45	1178.60	1166.05	1155.41	1146.35
95000	1300.56	1278.36	1259.75	1244.08	1230.83	1219.60	1210.03
100000	1369.01	1345.64	1326.05	1309.56	1295.61	1283.78	1273.72
105000	1437.46	1412.92	1392.36	1375.04	1360.39	1347.97	1337.41
110000	1505.91	1480.20	1458.66	1440.52	1425.18	1412.16	1401.09
120000	1642.81	1614.77	1591.26	1571.47	1554.74	1540.54	1528.46
130000	1779.71	1749.33	1723.87	1702.43	1684.30	1668.92	1655.84
140000	1916.61	1883.90	1856.48	1833.38	1813.86	1797.30	1783.21
150000	2053.51	2018.46	1989.08	1964.34	1943.42	1925.68	1910.58
160000	2190.41	2153.02	2121.69	2095.30	2072.98	2054.06	2037.95
170000	2327.31	2287.59	2254.29	2226.25	2202.54	2182.43	2165.33
180000	2464.21	2422.15	2386.90	2357.21	2332.11	2310.81	2292.70
190000	2601.11	2556.72	2519.50	2488.16	2461.67	2439.19	2420.07
200000	2738.01	2691.28	2652.11	2619.12	2591.23	2567.57	2547.44
210000	2874.92	2825.84	2784.71	2750.07	2720.79	2695.95	2674.81
220000	3011.82	2960.41	2917.32	2881.03	2850.35	2824.33	2802.19
230000	3148.72	3094.97	3049.92	3011.99	2979.91	2952.70	2929.56
240000	3285.62	3229.54	3182.53	3142.94	3109.47	3081.08	3056.93
250000	3422.52	3364.10	3315.13	3273.90	3239.04	3209.46	3184.30

Monthly Payments 15.00 %

LOAN AMOUNT	22	23	24	25	30	35	40
				YEARS			
100	1.27	1.26	1.25	1.25	1.23	1.22	1.22
200	2.53	2.52	2.50	2.49	2.46	2.44	2.43
500	6.33	6.29	6.26	6.23	6.14	6.10	6.08
1000	12.65	12.58	12.52	12.46	12.29	12.20	12.16
2000	25.30	25.16	25.03	24.92	24.57	24.41	24.33
5000	63.26	62.89	62.58	62.31	61.43	61.02	60.82
6000	75.91	75.47	75.09	74.77	73.72	73.22	72.98
7000	88.56	88.05	87.61	87.23	86.01	85.43	85.15
8000	101.21	100.62	100.12	99.69	98.29	97.63	97.31
9000	113.86	113.20	112.64	112.15	110.58	109.83	109.47
10000	126.51	125.78	125.15	124.61	122.87	122.04	121.64
12000	151.82	150.94	150.18	149.54	147.44	146.44	145.96
15000	189.77	188.67	187.73	186.92	184.30	183.05	182.46
20000	253.03	251.56	250.31	249.23	245.73	244.07	243.27
25000	316.28	314.45	312.88	311.54	307.17	305.09	304.09
30000	379.54	377.34	375.46	373.84	368.60	366.11	364.91
31000	392.19	389.92	387.97	386.31	380.89	378.31	377.08
32000	404.84	402.50	400.49	398.77	393.17	390.52	389.24
33000	417.50	415.08	413.00	411.23	405.46	402.72	401.40
34000	430.15	427.65	425.52	423.69	417.75	414.92	413.57
35000	442.80	440.23	438.03	436.15	430.03	427.13	425.73
36000	455.45	452.81	450.55	448.61	442.32	439.33	437.89
37000	468.10	465.39	463.07	461.07	454.61	451.53	450.06
38000	480.75	477.97	475.58	473.54	466.89	463.74	462.22
39000	493.40	490.54	488.10	486.00	479.18	475.94	474.39
40000	506.06	503.12	500.61	498.46	491.47	488.15	486.55
41000	518.71	515.70	513.13	510.92	503.75	500.35	498.71
42000	531.36	528.28	525.64	523.38	516.04	512.55	510.88
43000	544.01	540.86	538.16	535.84	528.33	524.76	523.04
44000	556.66	553.43	550.67	548.30	540.61	536.96	535.20
45000	569.31	566.01	563.19	560.77	552.90	549.16	547.37
46000	581.96	578.59	575.70	573.23	565.19	561.37	559.53
47000	594.62	591.17	588.22	585.69	577.47	573.57	571.70
48000	607.27	603.75	600.73	598.15	589.76	585.77	583.86
49000	619.92	616.32	613.25	610.61	602.05	597.98	596.02
50000	632.57	628.90	625.76	623.07	614.33	610.18	608.19
51000	645.22	641.48	638.28	635.53	626.62	622.39	620.35
52000	657.87	654.06	650.79	648.00	638.91	634.59	632.51
53000	670.52	666.64	663.31	660.46	651.19	646.79	644.68
54000	683.17	679.21	675.82	672.92	663.48	659.00	656.84
55000	695.83	691.79	688.34	685.38	675.77	671.20	669.01
56000	708.48	704.37	700.86	697.84	688.05	683.40	681.17
57000	721.13	716.95	713.37	710.30	700.34	695.61	693.33
58000	733.78	729.53	725.89	722.76	712.63	707.81	705.50
59000	746.43	742.11	738.40	735.23	724.91	720.01	717.66
60000	759.08	754.68	750.92	747.69	737.20	732.22	729.82
65000	822.34	817.57	813.49	809.99	798.63	793.24	790.64
70000	885.60	880.46	876.07	872.30	860.07	854.25	851.46
75000	948.85	943.35	938.65	934.61	921.50	915.27	912.28
80000	1012.11	1006.24	1001.22	996.92	982.93	976.29	973.10
85000	1075.37	1069.13	1063.80	1059.22	1044.37	1037.31	1033.92
90000	1138.62	1132.02	1126.37	1121.53	1105.80	1098.33	1094.74
95000	1201.88	1194.91	1188.95	1183.84	1167.23	1159.34	1155.56
100000	1265.14	1257.81	1251.53	1246.15	1228.67	1220.36	1216.37
105000	1328.40	1320.70	1314.10	1308.45	1290.10	1281.38	1277.19
110000	1391.65	1383.59	1376.68	1370.76	1351.53	1342.40	1338.01
120000	1518.17	1509.37	1501.83	1495.37	1474.40	1464.44	1459.65
130000	1644.68	1635.15	1626.99	1619.99	1597.27	1586.47	1581.29
140000	1771.19	1760.93	1752.14	1744.60	1720.13	1708.51	1702.92
150000	1897.71	1886.71	1877.29	1869.22	1843.00	1830.54	1824.56
160000	2024.22	2012.49	2002.44	1993.83	1965.87	1952.58	1946.20
170000	2150.74	2138.27	2127.60	2118.45	2088.74	2074.62	2067.84
180000	2277.25	2264.05	2252.75	2243.06	2211.60	2196.65	2189.47
190000	2403.76	2389.83	2377.90	2367.68	2334.47	2318.69	2311.11
200000	2530.28	2515.61	2503.06	2492.29	2457.34	2440.73	2432.75
210000	2656.79	2641.39	2628.21	2616.91	2580.20	2562.76	2554.38
220000	2783.31	2767.17	2753.36	2741.52	2703.07	2684.80	2676.02
230000	2909.82	2892.95	2878.51	2866.14	2825.94	2806.83	2797.66
240000	3036.33	3018.73	3003.67	2990.75	2948.80	2928.87	2919.30
250000	3162.85	3144.51	3128.82	3115.36	3071.67	3050.91	3040.93

15.25 % Monthly Payments

LOAN AMOUNT	1	2	3	4	5	6	7
				YEARS			
100	9.02	4.84	3.46	2.77	2.37	2.10	1.92
200	18.03	9.68	6.91	5.54	4.74	4.21	3.84
500	45.08	24.19	17.28	13.86	11.84	10.51	9.59
1000	90.16	48.39	34.56	27.72	23.68	21.03	19.18
2000	180.32	96.77	69.12	55.45	47.36	42.06	38.35
5000	450.79	241.93	172.81	138.61	118.39	105.15	95.89
6000	540.95	290.31	207.37	166.34	142.07	126.18	115.06
7000	631.10	338.70	241.93	194.06	165.75	147.21	134.24
8000	721.26	387.08	276.49	221.78	189.43	168.24	153.42
9000	811.42	435.47	311.05	249.51	213.10	189.27	172.60
10000	901.58	483.85	345.61	277.23	236.78	210.29	191.77
12000	1081.89	580.63	414.73	332.67	284.14	252.35	230.13
15000	1352.37	725.78	518.42	415.84	355.17	315.44	287.66
20000	1803.16	967.71	691.22	554.46	473.56	420.59	383.55
25000	2253.94	1209.64	864.03	693.07	591.96	525.74	479.44
30000	2704.73	1451.56	1036.83	831.69	710.35	630.88	575.32
31000	2794.89	1499.95	1071.39	859.41	734.03	651.91	594.50
32000	2885.05	1548.34	1105.95	887.13	757.70	672.94	613.68
33000	2975.21	1596.72	1140.52	914.85	781.38	693.97	632.85
34000	3065.37	1645.11	1175.08	942.58	805.06	715.00	652.03
35000	3155.52	1693.49	1209.64	970.30	828.74	736.03	671.21
36000	3245.68	1741.88	1244.20	998.02	852.42	757.06	690.39
37000	3335.84	1790.26	1278.76	1025.75	876.09	778.09	709.56
38000	3426.00	1838.65	1313.32	1053.47	899.77	799.12	728.74
39000	3516.15	1887.03	1347.88	1081.19	923.45	820.15	747.92
40000	3606.31	1935.42	1382.44	1108.91	947.13	841.18	767.10
41000	3696.47	1983.80	1417.00	1136.64	970.81	862.21	786.27
42000	3786.63	2032.19	1451.57	1164.36	994.49	883.24	805.45
43000	3876.79	2080.58	1486.13	1192.08	1018.16	904.27	824.63
44000	3966.94	2128.96	1520.69	1219.81	1041.84	925.30	843.81
45000	4057.10	2177.35	1555.25	1247.53	1065.52	946.33	862.98
46000	4147.26	2225.73	1589.81	1275.25	1089.20	967.36	882.16
47000	4237.42	2274.12	1624.37	1302.97	1112.88	988.39	901.34
48000	4327.57	2322.50	1658.93	1330.70	1136.55	1009.41	920.52
49000	4417.73	2370.89	1693.49	1358.42	1160.23	1030.44	939.69
50000	4507.89	2419.27	1728.05	1386.14	1183.91	1051.47	958.87
51000	4598.05	2467.66	1762.61	1413.87	1207.59	1072.50	978.05
52000	4688.21	2516.04	1797.18	1441.59	1231.27	1093.53	997.22
53000	4778.36	2564.43	1831.74	1469.31	1254.95	1114.56	1016.40
54000	4868.52	2612.82	1866.30	1497.03	1278.62	1135.59	1035.58
55000	4958.68	2661.20	1900.86	1524.76	1302.30	1156.62	1054.76
56000	5048.84	2709.59	1935.42	1552.48	1325.98	1177.65	1073.93
57000	5138.99	2757.97	1969.98	1580.20	1349.66	1198.68	1093.11
58000	5229.15	2806.36	2004.54	1607.93	1373.34	1219.71	1112.29
59000	5319.31	2854.74	2039.10	1635.65	1397.02	1240.74	1131.47
60000	5409.47	2903.13	2073.66	1663.37	1420.69	1261.77	1150.64
65000	5860.26	3145.06	2246.47	1801.99	1539.08	1366.92	1246.53
70000	6311.05	3386.98	2419.28	1940.60	1657.48	1472.06	1342.42
75000	6761.83	3628.91	2592.08	2079.21	1775.87	1577.21	1438.31
80000	7212.62	3870.84	2764.89	2217.83	1894.26	1682.36	1534.19
85000	7663.41	4112.77	2937.69	2356.44	2012.65	1787.50	1630.08
90000	8114.20	4354.69	3110.50	2495.06	2131.04	1892.65	1725.97
95000	8564.99	4596.62	3283.30	2633.67	2249.43	1997.80	1821.85
100000	9015.78	4838.55	3456.11	2772.29	2367.82	2102.95	1917.74
105000	9466.57	5080.47	3628.91	2910.90	2486.21	2208.09	2013.63
110000	9917.36	5322.40	3801.72	3049.51	2604.61	2313.24	2109.51
120000	10818.94	5806.26	4147.33	3326.74	2841.39	2523.54	2301.29
130000	11720.51	6290.11	4492.94	3603.97	3078.17	2733.83	2493.06
140000	12622.09	6773.97	4838.55	3881.20	3314.95	2944.13	2684.84
150000	13523.67	7257.82	5184.16	4158.43	3551.73	3154.42	2876.61
160000	14425.25	7741.68	5529.77	4435.66	3788.52	3364.71	3068.38
170000	15326.83	8225.53	5875.38	4712.89	4025.30	3575.01	3260.16
180000	16228.40	8709.38	6220.99	4990.11	4262.08	3785.30	3451.93
190000	17129.98	9193.24	6566.60	5267.34	4498.86	3995.60	3643.71
200000	18031.56	9677.09	6912.21	5544.57	4735.65	4205.89	3835.48
210000	18933.14	10160.95	7257.83	5821.80	4972.43	4416.19	4027.25
220000	19834.72	10644.80	7603.44	6099.03	5209.21	4626.48	4219.03
230000	20736.29	11128.66	7949.05	6376.26	5445.99	4836.78	4410.80
240000	21637.87	11612.51	8294.66	6653.49	5682.77	5047.07	4602.58
250000	22539.45	12096.37	8640.27	6930.71	5919.56	5257.37	4794.35

Monthly Payments 15.25 %

LOAN AMOUNT	8	9	10	11	12	13	14
				YEARS			
100	1.78	1.68	1.60	1.54	1.49	1.45	1.41
200	3.56	3.36	3.20	3.08	2.97	2.89	2.83
500	8.91	8.40	8.00	7.69	7.44	7.23	7.06
1000	17.82	16.80	16.00	15.38	14.87	14.46	14.13
2000	35.64	33.60	32.01	30.75	29.74	28.93	28.26
5000	89.11	83.99	80.02	76.88	74.36	72.31	70.64
6000	106.93	100.79	96.02	92.25	89.23	86.78	84.77
7000	124.76	117.58	112.02	107.63	104.10	101.24	98.89
8000	142.58	134.38	128.03	123.00	118.98	115.70	113.02
9000	160.40	151.18	144.03	138.38	133.85	130.17	127.15
10000	178.22	167.98	160.03	153.76	148.72	144.63	141.28
12000	213.87	201.57	192.04	184.51	178.46	173.56	169.53
15000	267.33	251.96	240.05	230.63	223.08	216.94	211.91
20000	356.45	335.95	320.07	307.51	297.44	289.26	282.55
25000	445.56	419.94	400.08	384.39	371.80	361.57	353.19
30000	534.67	503.93	480.10	461.27	446.16	433.89	423.83
31000	552.49	520.73	496.10	476.64	461.03	448.35	437.95
32000	570.31	537.52	512.10	492.02	475.90	462.81	452.08
33000	588.14	554.32	528.11	507.39	490.77	477.28	466.21
34000	605.96	571.12	544.11	522.77	505.64	491.74	480.34
35000	623.78	587.92	560.11	538.14	520.52	506.20	494.46
36000	641.60	604.71	576.12	553.52	535.39	520.67	508.59
37000	659.43	621.51	592.12	568.89	550.26	535.13	522.72
38000	677.25	638.31	608.12	584.27	565.13	549.59	536.85
39000	695.07	655.11	624.13	599.65	580.00	564.05	550.97
40000	712.89	671.90	640.13	615.02	594.88	578.52	565.10
41000	730.71	688.70	656.13	630.40	609.75	592.98	579.23
42000	748.54	705.50	672.14	645.77	624.62	607.44	593.36
43000	766.36	722.30	688.14	661.15	639.49	621.91	607.48
44000	784.18	739.10	704.14	676.52	654.36	636.37	621.61
45000	802.00	755.89	720.15	691.90	669.24	650.83	635.74
46000	819.83	772.69	736.15	707.27	684.11	665.29	649.87
47000	837.65	789.49	752.15	722.65	698.98	679.76	663.99
48000	855.47	806.29	768.16	738.03	713.85	694.22	678.12
49000	873.29	823.08	784.16	753.40	728.72	708.68	692.25
50000	891.12	839.88	800.16	768.78	743.60	723.15	706.38
51000	908.94	856.68	816.17	784.15	758.47	737.61	720.50
52000	926.76	873.48	832.17	799.53	773.34	752.07	734.63
53000	944.58	890.27	848.17	814.90	788.21	766.54	748.76
54000	962.41	907.07	864.18	830.28	803.08	781.00	762.89
55000	980.23	923.87	880.18	845.65	817.95	795.46	777.01
56000	998.05	940.67	896.18	861.03	832.83	809.92	791.14
57000	1015.87	957.46	912.19	876.41	847.70	824.39	805.27
58000	1033.69	974.26	928.19	891.78	862.57	838.85	819.40
59000	1051.52	991.06	944.19	907.16	877.44	853.31	833.52
60000	1069.34	1007.86	960.20	922.53	892.31	867.78	847.65
65000	1158.45	1091.84	1040.21	999.41	966.67	940.09	918.29
70000	1247.56	1175.83	1120.23	1076.29	1041.03	1012.40	988.93
75000	1336.67	1259.82	1200.24	1153.16	1115.39	1084.72	1059.56
80000	1425.79	1343.81	1280.26	1230.04	1189.75	1157.03	1130.20
85000	1514.90	1427.80	1360.28	1306.92	1264.11	1229.35	1200.84
90000	1604.01	1511.79	1440.29	1383.80	1338.47	1301.66	1271.48
95000	1693.12	1595.77	1520.31	1460.68	1412.83	1373.98	1342.11
100000	1782.23	1679.76	1600.33	1537.55	1487.19	1446.29	1412.75
105000	1871.34	1763.75	1680.34	1614.43	1561.55	1518.61	1483.39
110000	1960.45	1847.74	1760.36	1691.31	1635.91	1590.92	1554.03
120000	2138.68	2015.71	1920.39	1845.06	1784.63	1735.55	1695.30
130000	2316.90	2183.69	2080.42	1998.82	1933.35	1880.18	1836.58
140000	2495.12	2351.67	2240.46	2152.57	2082.07	2024.81	1977.85
150000	2673.35	2519.64	2400.49	2306.33	2230.79	2169.44	2119.13
160000	2851.57	2687.62	2560.52	2460.08	2379.51	2314.07	2260.40
170000	3029.79	2855.59	2720.55	2613.84	2528.22	2458.70	2401.68
180000	3208.02	3023.57	2880.59	2767.60	2676.94	2603.33	2542.95
190000	3386.24	3191.55	3040.62	2921.35	2825.66	2747.96	2684.23
200000	3564.46	3359.52	3200.65	3075.11	2974.38	2892.59	2825.50
210000	3742.69	3527.50	3360.68	3228.86	3123.10	3037.21	2966.78
220000	3920.91	3695.48	3520.72	3382.62	3271.82	3181.84	3108.05
230000	4099.13	3863.45	3680.75	3536.37	3420.54	3326.47	3249.33
240000	4277.36	4031.43	3840.78	3690.13	3569.26	3471.10	3390.60
250000	4455.58	4199.40	4000.81	3843.88	3717.98	3615.73	3531.88

15.25 % Monthly Payments

LOAN AMOUNT	15	16	17	18	19	20	21
	YEARS						
100	1.39	1.36	1.34	1.33	1.31	1.30	1.2
200	2.77	2.72	2.69	2.65	2.63	2.60	2.5
500	6.93	6.81	6.71	6.63	6.56	6.51	6.4
1000	13.85	13.62	13.43	13.26	13.13	13.01	12.9
2000	27.70	27.24	26.85	26.53	26.25	26.02	25.8
5000	69.25	68.10	67.13	66.32	65.63	65.05	64.5
6000	83.10	81.72	80.56	79.58	78.76	78.06	77.4
7000	96.95	95.34	93.98	92.85	91.89	91.08	90.3
8000	110.80	108.96	107.41	106.11	105.01	104.09	103.3
9000	124.65	122.57	120.84	119.37	118.14	117.10	116.2
10000	138.50	136.19	134.26	132.64	131.27	130.11	129.1
12000	166.20	163.43	161.12	159.17	157.52	156.13	154.9
15000	207.75	204.29	201.39	198.96	196.90	195.16	193.6
20000	277.00	272.39	268.53	265.28	262.54	260.21	258.2
25000	346.26	340.49	335.66	331.60	328.17	325.27	322.8
30000	415.51	408.58	402.79	397.92	393.80	390.32	387.3
31000	429.36	422.20	416.21	411.18	406.93	403.33	400.2
32000	443.21	435.82	429.64	424.44	420.06	416.34	413.1
33000	457.06	449.44	443.07	437.71	433.18	429.35	426.1
34000	470.91	463.06	456.49	450.97	446.31	442.36	439.0
35000	484.76	476.68	469.92	464.24	459.44	455.38	451.9
36000	498.61	490.30	483.35	477.50	472.57	468.39	464.8
37000	512.46	503.92	496.77	490.76	485.69	481.40	477.7
38000	526.31	517.54	510.20	504.03	498.82	494.41	490.6
39000	540.16	531.16	523.62	517.29	511.95	507.42	503.5
40000	554.01	544.78	537.05	530.56	525.07	520.43	516.4
41000	567.86	558.40	550.48	543.82	538.20	533.44	529.4
42000	581.71	572.02	563.90	557.08	551.33	546.45	542.3
43000	595.56	585.64	577.33	570.35	564.45	559.46	555.2
44000	609.41	599.25	590.76	583.61	577.58	572.47	568.1
45000	623.26	612.87	604.18	596.87	590.71	585.48	581.0
46000	637.11	626.49	617.61	610.14	603.83	598.49	593.9
47000	650.96	640.11	631.04	623.40	616.96	611.50	606.8
48000	664.81	653.73	644.46	636.67	630.09	624.51	619.7
49000	678.66	667.35	657.89	649.93	643.21	637.53	632.7
50000	692.51	680.97	671.31	663.19	656.34	650.54	645.6
51000	706.36	694.59	684.74	676.46	669.47	663.55	658.5
52000	720.21	708.21	698.17	689.72	682.59	676.56	671.4
53000	734.06	721.83	711.59	702.99	695.72	689.57	684.3
54000	747.91	735.45	725.02	716.25	708.85	702.58	697.2
55000	761.76	749.07	738.45	729.51	721.97	715.59	710.1
56000	775.61	762.69	751.87	742.78	735.10	728.60	723.0
57000	789.46	776.31	765.30	756.04	748.23	741.61	735.9
58000	803.31	789.93	778.72	769.31	761.35	754.62	748.9
59000	817.16	803.55	792.15	782.57	774.48	767.63	761.8
60000	831.01	817.17	805.58	795.83	787.61	780.64	774.7
65000	900.26	885.26	872.71	862.15	853.24	845.70	839.2
70000	969.52	953.36	939.84	928.47	918.88	910.75	903.8
75000	1038.77	1021.46	1006.97	994.79	984.51	975.80	968.4
80000	1108.02	1089.55	1074.10	1061.11	1050.14	1040.86	1032.9
85000	1177.27	1157.65	1141.23	1127.43	1115.78	1105.91	1097.5
90000	1246.52	1225.75	1208.36	1193.75	1181.41	1170.97	1162.0
95000	1315.77	1293.85	1275.50	1260.07	1247.05	1236.02	1226.6
100000	1385.02	1361.94	1342.63	1326.39	1312.68	1301.07	1291.2
105000	1454.27	1430.04	1409.76	1392.71	1378.31	1366.13	1355.7
110000	1523.52	1498.14	1476.89	1459.03	1443.95	1431.18	1420.3
120000	1662.03	1634.33	1611.15	1591.67	1575.22	1561.29	1549.4
130000	1800.53	1770.53	1745.42	1724.30	1706.49	1691.39	1678.5
140000	1939.03	1906.72	1879.68	1856.94	1837.75	1821.50	1807.7
150000	2077.53	2042.91	2013.94	1989.58	1969.02	1951.61	1936.8
160000	2216.03	2179.11	2148.20	2122.22	2100.29	2081.72	2065.9
170000	2354.54	2315.30	2282.47	2254.86	2231.56	2211.82	2195.0
180000	2493.04	2451.50	2416.73	2387.50	2362.83	2341.93	2324.1
190000	2631.54	2587.69	2550.99	2520.14	2494.09	2472.04	2453.3
200000	2770.04	2723.89	2685.26	2652.78	2625.36	2602.15	2582.4
210000	2908.55	2860.08	2819.52	2785.42	2756.63	2732.25	2711.5
220000	3047.05	2996.27	2953.78	2918.05	2887.90	2862.36	2840.6
230000	3185.55	3132.47	3088.04	3050.69	3019.17	2992.47	2969.8
240000	3324.05	3268.66	3222.31	3183.33	3150.43	3122.57	3098.9
250000	3462.55	3404.86	3356.57	3315.97	3281.70	3252.68	3228.0

Monthly Payments 15.25 %

LOAN AMOUNT	22	23	24	25	30	35	40
100	1.28	1.28	1.27	1.26	1.25	1.24	1.24
200	2.57	2.55	2.54	2.53	2.49	2.48	2.47
500	6.41	6.38	6.35	6.32	6.24	6.20	6.18
1000	12.83	12.76	12.70	12.64	12.47	12.39	12.36
2000	25.66	25.51	25.39	25.29	24.95	24.79	24.71
5000	64.14	63.78	63.48	63.22	62.37	61.97	61.79
6000	76.97	76.54	76.17	75.86	74.85	74.37	74.14
7000	89.80	89.30	88.87	88.50	87.32	86.76	86.50
8000	102.63	102.05	101.56	101.15	99.79	99.16	98.86
9000	115.45	114.81	114.26	113.79	112.27	111.55	111.21
10000	128.28	127.57	126.96	126.43	124.74	123.95	123.57
12000	153.94	153.08	152.35	151.72	149.69	148.74	148.28
15000	192.42	191.35	190.43	189.65	187.11	185.92	185.36
20000	256.56	255.13	253.91	252.86	249.48	247.90	247.14
25000	320.71	318.92	317.39	316.08	311.86	309.87	308.93
30000	384.85	382.70	380.87	379.30	374.23	371.84	370.71
31000	397.68	395.46	393.56	391.94	386.70	384.24	383.07
32000	410.50	408.21	406.26	404.58	399.17	396.63	395.42
33000	423.33	420.97	418.95	417.23	411.65	409.03	407.78
34000	436.16	433.73	431.65	429.87	424.12	421.42	420.14
35000	448.99	446.48	444.34	442.51	436.60	433.82	432.50
36000	461.82	459.24	457.04	455.16	449.07	446.21	444.85
37000	474.65	472.00	469.73	467.80	461.55	458.61	457.21
38000	487.47	484.75	482.43	480.44	474.02	471.00	469.57
39000	500.30	497.51	495.13	493.09	486.49	483.40	481.92
40000	513.13	510.27	507.82	505.73	498.97	495.79	494.28
41000	525.96	523.02	520.52	518.37	511.44	508.19	506.64
42000	538.79	535.78	533.21	531.01	523.92	520.58	518.99
43000	551.61	548.54	545.91	543.66	536.39	532.97	531.35
44000	564.44	561.29	558.60	556.30	548.87	545.37	543.71
45000	577.27	574.05	571.30	568.94	561.34	557.76	556.07
46000	590.10	586.81	583.99	581.59	573.81	570.16	568.42
47000	602.93	599.56	596.69	594.23	586.29	582.55	580.78
48000	615.76	612.32	609.39	606.87	598.76	594.95	593.14
49000	628.58	625.08	622.08	619.52	611.24	607.34	605.49
50000	641.41	637.83	634.78	632.16	623.71	619.74	617.85
51000	654.24	650.59	647.47	644.80	636.19	632.13	630.21
52000	667.07	663.35	660.17	657.45	648.66	644.53	642.56
53000	679.90	676.10	672.86	670.09	661.13	656.92	654.92
54000	692.73	688.86	685.56	682.73	673.61	669.32	667.28
55000	705.55	701.62	698.25	695.38	686.08	681.71	679.64
56000	718.38	714.37	710.95	708.02	698.56	694.11	691.99
57000	731.21	727.13	723.65	720.66	711.03	706.50	704.35
58000	744.04	739.89	736.34	733.31	723.50	718.90	716.71
59000	756.87	752.64	749.04	745.95	735.98	731.29	729.06
60000	769.69	765.40	761.73	758.59	748.45	743.69	741.42
65000	833.84	829.18	825.21	821.81	810.82	805.66	803.21
70000	897.98	892.97	888.69	885.02	873.20	867.63	864.99
75000	962.12	956.75	952.16	948.24	935.57	929.61	926.78
80000	1026.26	1020.53	1015.64	1011.46	997.94	991.58	988.56
85000	1090.40	1084.32	1079.12	1074.67	1060.31	1053.55	1050.35
90000	1154.54	1148.10	1142.60	1137.89	1122.68	1115.53	1112.13
95000	1218.68	1211.88	1206.08	1201.10	1185.05	1177.50	1173.92
100000	1282.82	1275.67	1269.55	1264.32	1247.42	1239.48	1235.70
105000	1346.97	1339.45	1333.03	1327.54	1309.79	1301.45	1297.49
110000	1411.11	1403.23	1396.51	1390.75	1372.16	1363.42	1359.27
120000	1539.39	1530.80	1523.46	1517.18	1496.91	1487.37	1482.84
130000	1667.67	1658.37	1650.42	1643.62	1621.65	1611.32	1606.41
140000	1795.95	1785.93	1777.37	1770.05	1746.39	1735.27	1729.98
150000	1924.24	1913.50	1904.33	1896.48	1871.13	1859.21	1853.55
160000	2052.52	2041.07	2031.28	2022.91	1995.87	1983.16	1977.12
170000	2180.80	2168.63	2158.24	2149.35	2120.62	2107.11	2100.69
180000	2309.08	2296.20	2285.19	2275.78	2245.36	2231.06	2224.26
190000	2437.37	2423.77	2412.15	2402.21	2370.10	2355.00	2347.83
200000	2565.65	2551.33	2539.11	2528.64	2494.84	2478.95	2471.40
210000	2693.93	2678.90	2666.06	2655.07	2619.59	2602.90	2594.97
220000	2822.21	2806.47	2793.02	2781.51	2744.33	2726.85	2718.54
230000	2950.50	2934.04	2919.97	2907.94	2869.07	2850.80	2842.11
240000	3078.78	3061.60	3046.93	3034.37	2993.81	2974.74	2965.68
250000	3207.06	3189.17	3173.88	3160.80	3118.55	3098.69	3089.25

15.50 % Monthly Payments

LOAN AMOUNT	YEARS 1	2	3	4	5	6	7
100	9.03	4.85	3.47	2.78	2.38	2.12	1.93
200	18.05	9.70	6.94	5.57	4.76	4.23	3.86
500	45.13	24.25	17.34	13.92	11.90	10.58	9.65
1000	90.27	48.50	34.68	27.84	23.80	21.16	19.31
2000	180.54	96.99	69.35	55.68	47.60	42.31	38.62
5000	451.34	242.49	173.38	139.21	119.01	105.78	96.55
6000	541.61	290.98	208.06	167.05	142.81	126.94	115.85
7000	631.88	339.48	242.73	194.89	166.61	148.10	135.16
8000	722.15	387.98	277.41	222.74	190.41	169.26	154.47
9000	812.42	436.47	312.08	250.58	214.21	190.41	173.78
10000	902.69	484.97	346.76	278.42	238.01	211.57	193.09
12000	1083.22	581.96	416.11	334.10	285.62	253.88	231.71
15000	1354.03	727.46	520.14	417.63	357.02	317.35	289.64
20000	1805.37	969.94	693.52	556.84	476.03	423.14	386.18
25000	2256.72	1212.43	866.90	696.05	595.04	528.92	482.73
30000	2708.06	1454.91	1040.28	835.26	714.04	634.71	579.27
31000	2798.33	1503.41	1074.96	863.10	737.85	655.87	598.58
32000	2888.60	1551.91	1109.63	890.94	761.65	677.02	617.89
33000	2978.87	1600.40	1144.31	918.78	785.45	698.18	637.20
34000	3069.13	1648.90	1178.99	946.62	809.25	719.34	656.51
35000	3159.40	1697.40	1213.66	974.47	833.05	740.49	675.82
36000	3249.67	1745.89	1248.34	1002.31	856.85	761.65	695.13
37000	3339.94	1794.39	1283.02	1030.15	880.65	782.81	714.44
38000	3430.21	1842.89	1317.69	1057.99	904.46	803.96	733.74
39000	3520.48	1891.39	1352.37	1085.83	928.26	825.12	753.05
40000	3610.75	1939.88	1387.04	1113.68	952.06	846.28	772.36
41000	3701.02	1988.38	1421.72	1141.52	975.86	867.43	791.67
42000	3791.28	2036.88	1456.40	1169.36	999.66	888.59	810.98
43000	3881.55	2085.37	1491.07	1197.20	1023.46	909.75	830.29
44000	3971.82	2133.87	1525.75	1225.04	1047.26	930.91	849.60
45000	4062.09	2182.37	1560.42	1252.88	1071.07	952.06	868.91
46000	4152.36	2230.87	1595.10	1280.73	1094.87	973.22	888.22
47000	4242.63	2279.36	1629.78	1308.57	1118.67	994.38	907.53
48000	4332.90	2327.86	1664.45	1336.41	1142.47	1015.53	926.84
49000	4423.16	2376.36	1699.13	1364.25	1166.27	1036.69	946.14
50000	4513.43	2424.85	1733.80	1392.09	1190.07	1057.85	965.45
51000	4603.70	2473.35	1768.48	1419.94	1213.87	1079.00	984.76
52000	4693.97	2521.85	1803.16	1447.78	1237.68	1100.16	1004.07
53000	4784.24	2570.35	1837.83	1475.62	1261.48	1121.32	1023.38
54000	4874.51	2618.84	1872.51	1503.46	1285.28	1142.47	1042.69
55000	4964.78	2667.34	1907.18	1531.30	1309.08	1163.63	1062.00
56000	5055.05	2715.84	1941.86	1559.15	1332.88	1184.79	1081.31
57000	5145.31	2764.33	1976.54	1586.99	1356.68	1205.95	1100.62
58000	5235.58	2812.83	2011.21	1614.83	1380.48	1227.10	1119.93
59000	5325.85	2861.33	2045.89	1642.67	1404.29	1248.26	1139.24
60000	5416.12	2909.82	2080.56	1670.51	1428.09	1269.42	1158.54
65000	5867.46	3152.31	2253.95	1809.72	1547.09	1375.20	1255.09
70000	6318.81	3394.80	2427.33	1948.93	1666.10	1480.99	1351.64
75000	6770.15	3637.28	2600.71	2088.14	1785.11	1586.77	1448.18
80000	7221.49	3879.77	2774.09	2227.35	1904.12	1692.56	1544.73
85000	7672.84	4122.25	2947.47	2366.56	2023.12	1798.34	1641.27
90000	8124.18	4364.74	3120.85	2505.77	2142.13	1904.12	1737.82
95000	8575.52	4607.22	3294.23	2644.98	2261.14	2009.91	1834.36
100000	9026.87	4849.71	3467.61	2784.19	2380.15	2115.69	1930.91
105000	9478.21	5092.19	3640.99	2923.40	2499.15	2221.48	2027.45
110000	9929.55	5334.68	3814.37	3062.61	2618.16	2327.26	2124.00
120000	10832.24	5819.65	4161.13	3341.03	2856.17	2538.83	2317.09
130000	11734.93	6304.62	4507.89	3619.44	3094.19	2750.40	2510.18
140000	12637.61	6789.59	4854.65	3897.86	3332.20	2961.97	2703.27
150000	13540.30	7274.56	5201.41	4176.28	3570.22	3173.54	2896.36
160000	14442.99	7759.53	5548.17	4454.70	3808.23	3385.11	3089.45
170000	15345.67	8244.50	5894.93	4733.12	4046.25	3596.68	3282.54
180000	16248.36	8729.47	6241.69	5011.54	4284.26	3808.25	3475.63
190000	17151.05	9214.45	6588.46	5289.96	4522.28	4019.82	3668.72
200000	18053.73	9699.42	6935.22	5568.38	4760.29	4231.39	3861.82
210000	18956.42	10184.39	7281.98	5846.79	4998.31	4442.96	4054.91
220000	19859.11	10669.36	7628.74	6125.21	5236.32	4654.53	4248.00
230000	20761.79	11154.33	7975.50	6403.63	5474.34	4866.10	4441.09
240000	21664.48	11639.30	8322.26	6682.05	5712.35	5077.67	4634.18
250000	22567.17	12124.27	8669.02	6960.47	5950.36	5289.23	4827.27

Monthly Payments 15.50 %

LOAN AMOUNT	8	9	10	11	12	13	14
100	1.80	1.69	1.61	1.55	1.50	1.46	1.43
200	3.59	3.39	3.23	3.10	3.00	2.92	2.86
500	8.98	8.47	8.07	7.76	7.51	7.31	7.14
1000	17.96	16.94	16.15	15.52	15.02	14.62	14.29
2000	35.92	33.87	32.29	31.05	30.05	29.23	28.57
5000	89.79	84.69	80.73	77.61	75.11	73.09	71.43
6000	107.75	101.62	96.88	93.14	90.14	87.70	85.71
7000	125.71	118.56	113.03	108.66	105.16	102.32	100.00
8000	143.66	135.50	129.18	124.18	120.18	116.94	114.28
9000	161.62	152.44	145.32	139.71	135.21	131.56	128.57
10000	179.58	169.37	161.47	155.23	150.23	146.17	142.85
12000	215.50	203.25	193.76	186.28	180.27	175.41	171.42
15000	269.37	254.06	242.20	232.84	225.34	219.26	214.28
20000	359.16	338.75	322.94	310.46	300.46	292.35	285.70
25000	448.95	423.44	403.67	388.07	375.57	365.43	357.13
30000	538.74	508.12	484.41	465.69	450.69	438.52	428.55
31000	556.70	525.06	500.56	481.21	465.71	453.14	442.84
32000	574.66	542.00	516.70	496.73	480.73	467.75	457.12
33000	592.62	558.93	532.85	512.26	495.76	482.37	471.41
34000	610.58	575.87	549.00	527.78	510.78	496.99	485.70
35000	628.53	592.81	565.14	543.30	525.80	511.61	499.98
36000	646.49	609.75	581.29	558.83	540.82	526.22	514.27
37000	664.45	626.68	597.44	574.35	555.85	540.84	528.55
38000	682.41	643.62	613.58	589.87	570.87	555.46	542.84
39000	700.37	660.56	629.73	605.39	585.89	570.08	557.12
40000	718.32	677.50	645.88	620.92	600.92	584.69	571.41
41000	736.28	694.43	662.02	636.44	615.94	599.31	585.69
42000	754.24	711.37	678.17	651.96	630.96	613.93	599.98
43000	772.20	728.31	694.32	667.49	645.98	628.55	614.26
44000	790.16	745.25	710.47	683.01	661.01	643.16	628.55
45000	808.12	762.18	726.61	698.53	676.03	657.78	642.83
46000	826.07	779.12	742.76	714.06	691.05	672.40	657.12
47000	844.03	796.06	758.91	729.58	706.08	687.01	671.40
48000	861.99	813.00	775.05	745.10	721.10	701.63	685.69
49000	879.95	829.93	791.20	760.62	736.12	716.25	699.97
50000	897.91	846.87	807.35	776.15	751.15	730.87	714.26
51000	915.86	863.81	823.49	791.67	766.17	745.48	728.54
52000	933.82	880.75	839.64	807.19	781.19	760.10	742.83
53000	951.78	897.68	855.79	822.72	796.21	774.72	757.11
54000	969.74	914.62	871.93	838.24	811.24	789.34	771.40
55000	987.70	931.56	888.08	853.76	826.26	803.95	785.68
56000	1005.65	948.50	904.23	869.29	841.28	818.57	799.97
57000	1023.61	965.43	920.38	884.81	856.31	833.19	814.25
58000	1041.57	982.37	936.52	900.33	871.33	847.80	828.54
59000	1059.53	999.31	952.67	915.85	886.35	862.42	842.82
60000	1077.49	1016.25	968.82	931.38	901.37	877.04	857.11
65000	1167.28	1100.93	1049.55	1008.99	976.49	950.13	928.53
70000	1257.07	1185.62	1130.29	1086.61	1051.60	1023.21	999.96
75000	1346.86	1270.31	1211.02	1164.22	1126.72	1096.30	1071.39
80000	1436.65	1354.99	1291.76	1241.84	1201.83	1169.39	1142.81
85000	1526.44	1439.68	1372.49	1319.45	1276.95	1242.47	1214.24
90000	1616.23	1524.37	1453.22	1397.07	1352.06	1315.56	1285.66
95000	1706.02	1609.06	1533.96	1474.68	1427.18	1388.65	1357.09
100000	1795.81	1693.74	1614.69	1552.29	1502.29	1461.73	1428.52
105000	1885.60	1778.43	1695.43	1629.91	1577.40	1534.82	1499.94
110000	1975.39	1863.12	1776.16	1707.52	1652.52	1607.91	1571.37
120000	2154.97	2032.49	1937.63	1862.75	1802.75	1754.08	1714.22
130000	2334.55	2201.86	2099.10	2017.98	1952.98	1900.25	1857.07
140000	2514.14	2371.24	2260.57	2173.21	2103.21	2046.43	1999.92
150000	2693.72	2540.61	2422.04	2328.44	2253.44	2192.60	2142.77
160000	2873.30	2709.99	2583.51	2483.67	2403.66	2338.77	2285.62
170000	3052.88	2879.36	2744.98	2638.90	2553.89	2484.95	2428.48
180000	3232.46	3048.74	2906.45	2794.13	2704.12	2631.12	2571.33
190000	3412.04	3218.11	3067.92	2949.36	2854.35	2777.29	2714.18
200000	3591.62	3387.48	3229.39	3104.59	3004.58	2923.47	2857.03
210000	3771.20	3556.86	3390.86	3259.82	3154.81	3069.64	2999.88
220000	3950.78	3726.23	3552.33	3415.05	3305.04	3215.81	3142.73
230000	4130.37	3895.61	3713.80	3570.28	3455.27	3361.99	3285.58
240000	4309.95	4064.98	3875.27	3725.51	3605.50	3508.16	3428.44
250000	4489.53	4234.36	4036.74	3880.74	3755.73	3654.33	3571.29

15.50 % Monthly Payments

LOAN AMOUNT	YEARS 15	16	17	18	19	20	21
100	1.40	1.38	1.36	1.34	1.33	1.32	1.31
200	2.80	2.76	2.72	2.69	2.66	2.64	2.62
500	7.01	6.89	6.80	6.72	6.65	6.59	6.54
1000	14.01	13.78	13.59	13.43	13.30	13.18	13.09
2000	28.02	27.57	27.19	26.87	26.60	26.37	26.18
5000	70.05	68.92	67.96	67.16	66.49	65.92	65.44
6000	84.07	82.70	81.56	80.60	79.79	79.10	78.53
7000	98.08	96.48	95.15	94.03	93.09	92.29	91.61
8000	112.09	110.26	108.74	107.46	106.38	105.47	104.70
9000	126.10	124.05	122.33	120.89	119.68	118.66	117.79
10000	140.11	137.83	135.93	134.33	132.98	131.84	130.88
12000	168.13	165.40	163.11	161.19	159.58	158.21	157.05
15000	210.16	206.75	203.89	201.49	199.47	197.76	196.31
20000	280.22	275.66	271.85	268.65	265.96	263.68	261.75
25000	350.27	344.58	339.81	335.82	332.45	329.60	327.19
30000	420.33	413.49	407.78	402.98	398.94	395.52	392.63
31000	434.34	427.27	421.37	416.41	412.24	408.71	405.72
32000	448.35	441.06	434.96	429.85	425.54	421.89	418.80
33000	462.36	454.84	448.55	443.28	438.83	435.08	431.89
34000	476.37	468.62	462.15	456.71	452.13	448.26	444.98
35000	490.38	482.41	475.74	470.14	465.43	461.44	458.07
36000	504.39	496.19	489.33	483.58	478.73	474.63	471.15
37000	518.40	509.97	502.93	497.01	492.03	487.81	484.24
38000	532.41	523.75	516.52	510.44	505.32	501.00	497.33
39000	546.43	537.54	530.11	523.88	518.62	514.18	510.42
40000	560.44	551.32	543.70	537.31	531.92	527.36	523.50
41000	574.45	565.10	557.30	550.74	545.22	540.55	536.59
42000	588.46	578.89	570.89	564.17	558.52	553.73	549.68
43000	602.47	592.67	584.48	577.61	571.81	566.92	562.77
44000	616.48	606.45	598.07	591.04	585.11	580.10	575.85
45000	630.49	620.24	611.67	604.47	598.41	593.29	588.94
46000	644.50	634.02	625.26	617.90	611.71	606.47	602.03
47000	658.51	647.80	638.85	631.34	625.01	619.65	615.12
48000	672.52	661.58	652.44	644.77	638.30	632.84	628.20
49000	686.53	675.37	666.04	658.20	651.60	646.02	641.29
50000	700.55	689.15	679.63	671.64	664.90	659.21	654.38
51000	714.56	702.93	693.22	685.07	678.20	672.39	667.47
52000	728.57	716.72	706.81	698.50	691.50	685.57	680.55
53000	742.58	730.50	720.41	711.93	704.79	698.76	693.64
54000	756.59	744.28	734.00	725.37	718.09	711.94	706.73
55000	770.60	758.07	747.59	738.80	731.39	725.13	719.82
56000	784.61	771.85	761.18	752.23	744.69	738.31	732.90
57000	798.62	785.63	774.78	765.66	757.99	751.49	745.99
58000	812.63	799.41	788.37	779.10	771.28	764.68	759.08
59000	826.64	813.20	801.96	792.53	784.58	777.86	772.17
60000	840.65	826.98	815.55	805.96	797.88	791.05	785.26
65000	910.71	895.90	883.52	873.13	864.37	856.97	850.69
70000	980.76	964.81	951.48	940.29	930.86	922.89	916.13
75000	1050.82	1033.73	1019.44	1007.45	997.35	988.81	981.57
80000	1120.87	1102.64	1087.41	1074.62	1063.84	1054.73	1047.01
85000	1190.93	1171.56	1155.37	1141.78	1130.33	1120.65	1112.44
90000	1260.98	1240.47	1223.33	1208.94	1196.82	1186.57	1177.88
95000	1331.04	1309.39	1291.29	1276.11	1263.31	1252.49	1243.32
100000	1401.09	1378.30	1359.26	1343.27	1329.80	1318.41	1308.76
105000	1471.15	1447.22	1427.22	1410.43	1396.29	1384.33	1374.20
110000	1541.20	1516.13	1495.18	1477.60	1462.78	1450.25	1439.63
120000	1681.31	1653.96	1631.11	1611.92	1595.76	1582.09	1570.51
130000	1821.42	1791.79	1767.03	1746.25	1728.74	1713.94	1701.39
140000	1961.53	1929.62	1902.96	1880.58	1861.72	1845.78	1832.26
150000	2101.64	2067.45	2038.89	2014.91	1994.70	1977.62	1963.14
160000	2241.75	2205.28	2174.81	2149.23	2127.68	2109.46	2094.01
170000	2381.86	2343.11	2310.74	2283.56	2260.66	2241.30	2224.89
180000	2521.96	2480.94	2446.66	2417.89	2393.64	2373.14	2355.77
190000	2662.07	2618.77	2582.59	2552.21	2526.62	2504.98	2486.64
200000	2802.18	2756.60	2718.51	2686.54	2659.60	2636.82	2617.52
210000	2942.29	2894.43	2854.44	2820.87	2792.58	2768.67	2748.39
220000	3082.40	3032.26	2990.36	2955.20	2925.56	2900.51	2879.27
230000	3222.51	3170.09	3126.29	3089.52	3058.54	3032.35	3010.15
240000	3362.62	3307.92	3262.22	3223.85	3191.52	3164.19	3141.02
250000	3502.73	3445.75	3398.14	3358.18	3324.50	3296.03	3271.90

Monthly Payments 15.50 %

LOAN AMOUNT	22	23	24	25	30	35	40
	YEARS						
100	1.30	1.29	1.29	1.28	1.27	1.26	1.26
200	2.60	2.59	2.58	2.57	2.53	2.52	2.51
500	6.50	6.47	6.44	6.41	6.33	6.29	6.28
1000	13.01	12.94	12.88	12.83	12.66	12.59	12.55
2000	26.01	25.87	25.75	25.65	25.32	25.17	25.10
5000	65.03	64.68	64.38	64.13	63.31	62.93	62.75
6000	78.03	77.61	77.26	76.95	75.97	75.52	75.30
7000	91.04	90.55	90.13	89.78	88.63	88.10	87.85
8000	104.04	103.49	103.01	102.60	101.30	100.69	100.40
9000	117.05	116.42	115.89	115.43	113.96	113.27	112.95
10000	130.06	129.36	128.76	128.25	126.62	125.86	125.50
12000	156.07	155.23	154.51	153.90	151.94	151.03	150.60
15000	195.08	194.04	193.14	192.38	189.93	188.79	188.25
20000	260.11	258.71	257.52	256.51	253.24	251.72	251.01
25000	325.14	323.39	321.90	320.63	316.55	314.65	313.76
30000	390.17	388.07	386.29	384.76	379.86	377.58	376.51
31000	403.17	401.01	399.16	397.59	392.52	390.17	389.06
32000	416.18	413.94	412.04	410.41	405.18	402.75	401.61
33000	429.18	426.88	424.91	423.24	417.85	415.34	414.16
34000	442.19	439.82	437.79	436.06	430.51	427.92	426.71
35000	455.19	452.75	450.67	448.89	443.17	440.51	439.26
36000	468.20	465.69	463.54	461.71	455.83	453.10	451.81
37000	481.21	478.62	476.42	474.54	468.49	465.68	464.36
38000	494.21	491.56	489.30	487.36	481.16	478.27	476.91
39000	507.22	504.49	502.17	500.19	493.82	490.85	489.46
40000	520.22	517.43	515.05	513.01	506.48	503.44	502.01
41000	533.23	530.37	527.92	525.84	519.14	516.03	514.56
42000	546.23	543.30	540.80	538.66	531.80	528.61	527.11
43000	559.24	556.24	553.68	551.49	544.47	541.20	539.66
44000	572.24	569.17	566.55	564.32	557.13	553.78	552.21
45000	585.25	582.11	579.43	577.14	569.79	566.37	564.76
46000	598.26	595.04	592.30	589.97	582.45	578.96	577.31
47000	611.26	607.98	605.18	602.79	595.11	591.54	589.86
48000	624.27	620.92	618.06	615.62	607.78	604.13	602.41
49000	637.27	633.85	630.93	628.44	620.44	616.71	614.96
50000	650.28	646.79	643.81	641.27	633.10	629.30	627.52
51000	663.28	659.72	656.69	654.09	645.76	641.89	640.07
52000	676.29	672.66	669.56	666.92	658.42	654.47	652.62
53000	689.29	685.59	682.44	679.74	671.09	667.06	665.17
54000	702.30	698.53	695.31	692.57	683.75	679.64	677.72
55000	715.31	711.47	708.19	705.39	696.41	692.23	690.27
56000	728.31	724.40	721.07	718.22	709.07	704.82	702.82
57000	741.32	737.34	733.94	731.04	721.73	717.40	715.37
58000	754.32	750.27	746.82	743.87	734.40	729.99	727.92
59000	767.33	763.21	759.70	756.70	747.06	742.57	740.47
60000	780.33	776.14	772.57	769.52	759.72	755.16	753.02
65000	845.36	840.82	836.95	833.65	823.03	818.09	815.77
70000	910.39	905.50	901.33	897.77	886.34	881.02	878.52
75000	975.42	970.18	965.71	961.90	949.65	943.95	941.27
80000	1040.45	1034.86	1030.10	1026.03	1012.96	1006.88	1004.02
85000	1105.47	1099.54	1094.48	1090.15	1076.27	1069.81	1066.78
90000	1170.50	1164.22	1158.86	1154.28	1139.58	1132.74	1129.53
95000	1235.53	1228.90	1223.24	1218.41	1202.89	1195.67	1192.28
100000	1300.56	1293.57	1287.62	1282.53	1266.20	1258.60	1255.03
105000	1365.58	1358.25	1352.00	1346.66	1329.51	1321.53	1317.78
110000	1430.61	1422.93	1416.38	1410.79	1392.82	1384.46	1380.53
120000	1560.67	1552.29	1545.14	1539.04	1519.44	1510.32	1506.04
130000	1690.72	1681.65	1673.91	1667.29	1646.06	1636.18	1631.54
140000	1820.78	1811.00	1802.67	1795.55	1772.68	1762.04	1757.04
150000	1950.83	1940.36	1931.43	1923.80	1899.30	1887.90	1882.55
160000	2080.89	2069.72	2060.19	2052.05	2025.92	2013.76	2008.05
170000	2210.95	2199.08	2188.95	2180.31	2152.54	2139.62	2133.55
180000	2341.00	2328.43	2317.71	2308.56	2279.16	2265.48	2259.05
190000	2471.06	2457.79	2446.48	2436.82	2405.78	2391.34	2384.56
200000	2601.11	2587.15	2575.24	2565.07	2532.40	2517.20	2510.06
210000	2731.17	2716.51	2704.00	2693.32	2659.02	2643.06	2635.56
220000	2861.22	2845.86	2832.76	2821.58	2785.64	2768.92	2761.07
230000	2991.28	2975.22	2961.52	2949.83	2912.26	2894.78	2886.57
240000	3121.34	3104.58	3090.29	3078.08	3038.88	3020.64	3012.07
250000	3251.39	3233.93	3219.05	3206.34	3165.50	3146.50	3137.58

15.75 % Monthly Payments

LOAN AMOUNT	YEARS 1	2	3	4	5	6	7
100	9.04	4.86	3.48	2.80	2.39	2.13	1.94
200	18.08	9.72	6.96	5.59	4.78	4.26	3.89
500	45.19	24.30	17.40	13.98	11.96	10.64	9.72
1000	90.38	48.61	34.79	27.96	23.92	21.28	19.44
2000	180.76	97.22	69.58	55.92	47.85	42.57	38.88
5000	451.90	243.04	173.96	139.81	119.62	106.42	97.21
6000	542.28	291.65	208.75	167.77	143.55	127.71	116.65
7000	632.66	340.26	243.54	195.73	167.47	148.99	136.09
8000	723.04	388.87	278.33	223.69	191.40	170.28	155.53
9000	813.42	437.48	313.12	251.65	215.32	191.56	174.97
10000	903.80	486.09	347.91	279.61	239.25	212.85	194.41
12000	1084.55	583.30	417.49	335.53	287.10	255.42	233.29
15000	1355.69	729.13	521.87	419.42	358.87	319.27	291.62
20000	1807.59	972.17	695.82	559.22	478.50	425.69	388.82
25000	2259.49	1215.22	869.78	699.03	598.12	532.12	486.03
30000	2711.39	1458.26	1043.74	838.83	717.75	638.54	583.23
31000	2801.77	1506.87	1078.53	866.79	741.67	659.83	602.67
32000	2892.14	1555.48	1113.32	894.75	765.60	681.11	622.12
33000	2982.52	1604.09	1148.11	922.72	789.52	702.40	641.56
34000	3072.90	1652.70	1182.90	950.68	813.45	723.68	661.00
35000	3163.28	1701.31	1217.69	978.64	837.37	744.96	680.44
36000	3253.66	1749.91	1252.48	1006.60	861.30	766.25	699.88
37000	3344.04	1798.52	1287.27	1034.56	885.22	787.53	719.32
38000	3434.42	1847.13	1322.07	1062.52	909.15	808.82	738.76
39000	3524.80	1895.74	1356.86	1090.48	933.07	830.10	758.20
40000	3615.18	1944.35	1391.65	1118.44	957.00	851.39	777.64
41000	3705.56	1992.96	1426.44	1146.40	980.92	872.67	797.08
42000	3795.94	2041.57	1461.23	1174.37	1004.85	893.96	816.53
43000	3886.32	2090.18	1496.02	1202.33	1028.77	915.24	835.97
44000	3976.70	2138.78	1530.81	1230.29	1052.70	936.53	855.41
45000	4067.08	2187.39	1565.60	1258.25	1076.62	957.81	874.85
46000	4157.46	2236.00	1600.40	1286.21	1100.55	979.10	894.29
47000	4247.84	2284.61	1635.19	1314.17	1124.47	1000.38	913.73
48000	4338.22	2333.22	1669.98	1342.13	1148.40	1021.67	933.17
49000	4428.60	2381.83	1704.77	1370.09	1172.32	1042.95	952.61
50000	4518.98	2430.44	1739.56	1398.05	1196.25	1064.24	972.05
51000	4609.36	2479.05	1774.35	1426.01	1220.17	1085.52	991.50
52000	4699.73	2527.65	1809.14	1453.98	1244.10	1106.80	1010.94
53000	4790.11	2576.26	1843.93	1481.94	1268.02	1128.09	1030.38
54000	4880.49	2624.87	1878.72	1509.90	1291.95	1149.37	1049.82
55000	4970.87	2673.48	1913.52	1537.86	1315.87	1170.66	1069.26
56000	5061.25	2722.09	1948.31	1565.82	1339.80	1191.94	1088.70
57000	5151.63	2770.70	1983.10	1593.78	1363.72	1213.23	1108.14
58000	5242.01	2819.31	2017.89	1621.74	1387.65	1234.51	1127.58
59000	5332.39	2867.92	2052.68	1649.70	1411.57	1255.80	1147.02
60000	5422.77	2916.52	2087.47	1677.66	1435.50	1277.08	1166.47
65000	5874.67	3159.57	2261.43	1817.47	1555.12	1383.51	1263.67
70000	6326.57	3402.61	2435.38	1957.28	1674.74	1489.93	1360.88
75000	6778.46	3645.65	2609.34	2097.08	1794.37	1596.35	1458.08
80000	7230.36	3888.70	2783.30	2236.89	1913.99	1702.78	1555.29
85000	7682.26	4131.74	2957.25	2376.69	2033.62	1809.20	1652.49
90000	8134.16	4374.79	3131.21	2516.50	2153.24	1915.62	1749.70
95000	8586.05	4617.83	3305.16	2656.30	2272.87	2022.05	1846.90
100000	9037.95	4860.87	3479.12	2796.11	2392.49	2128.47	1944.11
105000	9489.85	5103.92	3653.08	2935.91	2512.12	2234.89	2041.31
110000	9941.75	5346.96	3827.03	3075.72	2631.74	2341.32	2138.52
120000	10845.54	5833.05	4174.94	3355.33	2870.99	2554.16	2332.93
130000	11749.34	6319.13	4522.86	3634.94	3110.24	2767.01	2527.34
140000	12653.13	6805.22	4870.77	3914.55	3349.49	2979.86	2721.75
150000	13556.93	7291.31	5218.68	4194.16	3588.74	3192.71	2916.16
160000	14460.72	7777.40	5566.59	4473.77	3827.99	3405.55	3110.58
170000	15364.52	8263.48	5914.50	4753.38	4067.24	3618.40	3304.99
180000	16268.31	8749.57	6262.42	5032.99	4306.49	3831.25	3499.40
190000	17172.11	9235.66	6610.33	5312.60	4545.74	4044.09	3693.81
200000	18075.90	9721.75	6958.24	5592.22	4784.98	4256.94	3888.22
210000	18979.70	10207.83	7306.15	5871.83	5024.23	4469.79	4082.63
220000	19883.49	10693.92	7654.06	6151.44	5263.48	4682.63	4277.04
230000	20787.29	11180.01	8001.98	6431.05	5502.73	4895.48	4471.45
240000	21691.08	11666.10	8349.89	6710.66	5741.98	5108.33	4665.86
250000	22594.88	12152.18	8697.80	6990.27	5981.23	5321.18	4860.27

Monthly Payments 15.75 %

LOAN AMOUNT	8	9	10	11	12	13	14
				YEARS			
100	1.81	1.71	1.63	1.57	1.52	1.48	1.44
200	3.62	3.42	3.26	3.13	3.03	2.95	2.89
500	9.05	8.54	8.15	7.84	7.59	7.39	7.22
1000	18.09	17.08	16.29	15.67	15.17	14.77	14.44
2000	36.19	34.16	32.58	31.34	30.35	29.54	28.89
5000	90.47	85.39	81.46	78.35	75.87	73.86	72.22
6000	108.57	102.47	97.75	94.03	91.05	88.63	86.66
7000	126.66	119.54	114.04	109.70	106.22	103.41	101.10
8000	144.75	136.62	130.33	125.37	121.40	118.18	115.55
9000	162.85	153.70	146.62	141.04	136.57	132.95	129.99
10000	180.94	170.78	162.91	156.71	151.74	147.72	144.43
12000	217.13	204.93	195.49	188.05	182.09	177.27	173.32
15000	271.41	256.16	244.37	235.06	227.62	221.58	216.65
20000	361.89	341.55	325.82	313.42	303.49	295.45	288.87
25000	452.36	426.94	407.28	391.77	379.36	369.31	361.08
30000	542.83	512.33	488.73	470.13	455.23	443.17	433.30
31000	560.92	529.41	505.02	485.80	470.41	457.94	447.74
32000	579.02	546.49	521.32	501.47	485.58	472.71	462.19
33000	597.11	563.56	537.61	517.14	500.76	487.48	476.63
34000	615.21	580.64	553.90	532.81	515.93	502.26	491.07
35000	633.30	597.72	570.19	548.48	531.10	517.03	505.52
36000	651.39	614.80	586.48	564.15	546.28	531.80	519.96
37000	669.49	631.87	602.77	579.82	561.45	546.57	534.40
38000	687.58	648.95	619.06	595.49	576.63	561.35	548.85
39000	705.68	666.03	635.35	611.16	591.80	576.12	563.29
40000	723.77	683.11	651.64	626.83	606.98	590.89	577.73
41000	741.87	700.18	667.93	642.51	622.15	605.66	592.18
42000	759.96	717.26	684.23	658.18	637.33	620.43	606.62
43000	778.05	734.34	700.52	673.85	652.50	635.21	621.06
44000	796.15	751.42	716.81	689.52	667.67	649.98	635.51
45000	814.24	768.49	733.10	705.19	682.85	664.75	649.95
46000	832.34	785.57	749.39	720.86	698.02	679.52	664.39
47000	850.43	802.65	765.68	736.53	713.20	694.30	678.84
48000	868.53	819.73	781.97	752.20	728.37	709.07	693.28
49000	886.62	836.81	798.26	767.87	743.55	723.84	707.72
50000	904.72	853.88	814.55	783.54	758.72	738.61	722.17
51000	922.81	870.96	830.85	799.21	773.89	753.39	736.61
52000	940.90	888.04	847.14	814.88	789.07	768.16	751.05
53000	959.00	905.12	863.43	830.56	804.24	782.93	765.50
54000	977.09	922.19	879.72	846.23	819.42	797.70	779.94
55000	995.19	939.27	896.01	861.90	834.59	812.47	794.38
56000	1013.28	956.35	912.30	877.57	849.77	827.25	808.83
57000	1031.38	973.43	928.59	893.24	864.94	842.02	823.27
58000	1049.47	990.50	944.88	908.91	880.12	856.79	837.71
59000	1067.56	1007.58	961.17	924.58	895.29	871.56	852.16
60000	1085.66	1024.66	977.47	940.25	910.46	886.34	866.60
65000	1176.13	1110.05	1058.92	1018.61	986.34	960.20	938.82
70000	1266.60	1195.44	1140.38	1096.96	1062.21	1034.06	1011.03
75000	1357.07	1280.82	1221.83	1175.31	1138.08	1107.92	1083.25
80000	1447.54	1366.21	1303.29	1253.67	1213.95	1181.78	1155.47
85000	1538.02	1451.60	1384.74	1332.02	1289.82	1255.64	1227.68
90000	1628.49	1536.99	1466.20	1410.38	1365.70	1329.50	1299.90
95000	1718.96	1622.38	1547.65	1488.73	1441.57	1403.36	1372.12
100000	1809.43	1707.77	1629.11	1567.09	1517.44	1477.23	1444.33
105000	1899.90	1793.15	1710.57	1645.44	1593.31	1551.09	1516.55
110000	1990.37	1878.54	1792.02	1723.79	1669.18	1624.95	1588.77
120000	2171.32	2049.32	1954.93	1880.50	1820.93	1772.67	1733.20
130000	2352.26	2220.10	2117.84	2037.21	1972.67	1920.39	1877.63
140000	2533.20	2390.87	2280.75	2193.92	2124.42	2068.12	2022.07
150000	2714.15	2561.65	2443.66	2350.63	2276.16	2215.84	2166.50
160000	2895.09	2732.43	2606.58	2507.34	2427.91	2363.56	2310.93
170000	3076.03	2903.20	2769.49	2664.05	2579.65	2511.28	2455.37
180000	3256.97	3073.98	2932.40	2820.75	2731.39	2659.01	2599.80
190000	3437.92	3244.76	3095.31	2977.46	2883.14	2806.73	2744.23
200000	3618.86	3415.53	3258.22	3134.17	3034.88	2954.45	2888.67
210000	3799.80	3586.31	3421.13	3290.88	3186.63	3102.17	3033.10
220000	3980.75	3757.09	3584.04	3447.59	3338.37	3249.90	3177.53
230000	4161.69	3927.86	3746.95	3604.30	3490.11	3397.62	3321.97
240000	4342.63	4098.64	3909.86	3761.01	3641.86	3545.34	3466.40
250000	4523.58	4269.42	4072.77	3917.72	3793.60	3693.06	3610.83

15.75 % Monthly Payments

LOAN AMOUNT	YEARS 15	16	17	18	19	20	21
100	1.42	1.39	1.38	1.36	1.35	1.34	1.33
200	2.83	2.79	2.75	2.72	2.69	2.67	2.65
500	7.09	6.97	6.88	6.80	6.73	6.68	6.63
1000	14.17	13.95	13.76	13.60	13.47	13.36	13.26
2000	28.34	27.89	27.52	27.20	26.94	26.72	26.53
5000	70.86	69.74	68.80	68.01	67.35	66.79	66.32
6000	85.03	83.68	82.56	81.61	80.82	80.15	79.58
7000	99.21	97.63	96.32	95.21	94.29	93.51	92.84
8000	113.38	111.58	110.08	108.82	107.76	106.86	106.11
9000	127.55	125.52	123.83	122.42	121.23	120.22	119.37
10000	141.72	139.47	137.59	136.02	134.70	133.58	132.63
12000	170.07	167.37	165.11	163.22	161.64	160.30	159.16
15000	212.58	209.21	206.39	204.03	202.05	200.37	198.95
20000	283.44	278.94	275.19	272.04	269.39	267.16	265.27
25000	354.30	348.68	343.98	340.05	336.74	333.95	331.59
30000	425.16	418.41	412.78	408.06	404.09	400.74	397.90
31000	439.34	432.36	426.54	421.66	417.56	414.10	411.17
32000	453.51	446.31	440.30	435.27	431.03	427.46	424.43
33000	467.68	460.26	454.06	448.87	444.50	440.81	437.70
34000	481.85	474.20	467.82	462.47	457.97	454.17	450.96
35000	496.03	488.15	481.58	476.07	471.44	467.53	464.22
36000	510.20	502.10	495.34	489.67	484.91	480.89	477.49
37000	524.37	516.04	509.10	503.28	498.38	494.25	490.75
38000	538.54	529.99	522.86	516.88	511.85	507.60	504.01
39000	552.71	543.94	536.62	530.48	525.32	520.96	517.28
40000	566.89	557.89	550.38	544.08	538.79	534.32	530.54
41000	581.06	571.83	564.14	557.68	552.26	547.68	543.80
42000	595.23	585.78	577.89	571.29	565.73	561.04	557.07
43000	609.40	599.73	591.65	584.89	579.20	574.39	570.33
44000	623.57	613.67	605.41	598.49	592.67	587.75	583.59
45000	637.75	627.62	619.17	612.09	606.14	601.11	596.86
46000	651.92	641.57	632.93	625.69	619.61	614.47	610.12
47000	666.09	655.52	646.69	639.30	633.08	627.83	623.38
48000	680.26	669.46	660.45	652.90	646.55	641.18	636.65
49000	694.44	683.41	674.21	666.50	660.02	654.54	649.91
50000	708.61	697.36	687.97	680.10	673.49	667.90	663.17
51000	722.78	711.30	701.73	693.70	686.95	681.26	676.44
52000	736.95	725.25	715.49	707.31	700.42	694.62	689.70
53000	751.12	739.20	729.25	720.91	713.89	707.97	702.97
54000	765.30	753.15	743.01	734.51	727.36	721.33	716.23
55000	779.47	767.09	756.77	748.11	740.83	734.69	729.49
56000	793.64	781.04	770.53	761.72	754.30	748.05	742.76
57000	807.81	794.99	784.29	775.32	767.77	761.41	756.02
58000	821.98	808.93	798.04	788.92	781.24	774.76	769.28
59000	836.16	822.88	811.80	802.52	794.71	788.12	782.55
60000	850.33	836.83	825.56	816.12	808.18	801.48	795.81
65000	921.19	906.56	894.36	884.13	875.53	868.27	862.13
70000	992.05	976.30	963.16	952.14	942.88	935.06	928.44
75000	1062.91	1046.03	1031.95	1020.15	1010.23	1001.85	994.76
80000	1133.77	1115.77	1100.75	1088.16	1077.58	1068.64	1061.08
85000	1204.63	1185.51	1169.55	1156.17	1144.92	1135.43	1127.40
90000	1275.49	1255.24	1238.35	1224.19	1212.27	1202.22	1193.71
95000	1346.35	1324.98	1307.14	1292.20	1279.62	1269.01	1260.03
100000	1417.22	1394.71	1375.94	1360.21	1346.97	1335.80	1326.35
105000	1488.08	1464.45	1444.74	1428.22	1414.32	1402.59	1392.67
110000	1558.94	1534.18	1513.53	1496.23	1481.67	1469.38	1458.98
120000	1700.66	1673.66	1651.13	1632.25	1616.36	1602.96	1591.62
130000	1842.38	1813.13	1788.72	1768.27	1751.06	1736.54	1724.25
140000	1984.10	1952.60	1926.32	1904.29	1885.76	1870.12	1856.89
150000	2125.82	2092.07	2063.91	2040.31	2020.46	2003.70	1989.52
160000	2267.54	2231.54	2201.50	2176.33	2155.15	2137.28	2122.16
170000	2409.27	2371.01	2339.10	2312.35	2289.85	2270.86	2254.79
180000	2550.99	2510.48	2476.69	2448.37	2424.55	2404.44	2387.43
190000	2692.71	2649.95	2614.28	2584.39	2559.24	2538.02	2520.06
200000	2834.43	2789.43	2751.88	2720.41	2693.94	2671.60	2652.70
210000	2976.15	2928.90	2889.47	2856.43	2828.64	2805.18	2785.33
220000	3117.87	3068.37	3027.07	2992.45	2963.33	2938.76	2917.97
230000	3259.60	3207.84	3164.66	3128.47	3098.03	3072.34	3050.60
240000	3401.32	3347.31	3302.25	3264.49	3232.73	3205.92	3183.24
250000	3543.04	3486.78	3439.85	3400.51	3367.43	3339.50	3315.87

Monthly Payments 15.75 %

LOAN AMOUNT	22	23	24	25	30	35	40
				YEARS			
100	1.32	1.31	1.31	1.30	1.29	1.28	1.27
200	2.64	2.62	2.61	2.60	2.57	2.56	2.55
500	6.59	6.56	6.53	6.50	6.43	6.39	6.37
1000	13.18	13.12	13.06	13.01	12.85	12.78	12.74
2000	26.37	26.23	26.11	26.02	25.70	25.55	25.49
5000	65.92	65.58	65.29	65.04	64.25	63.89	63.72
6000	79.10	78.69	78.34	78.05	77.10	76.66	76.46
7000	92.28	91.81	91.40	91.05	89.95	89.44	89.21
8000	105.47	104.92	104.46	104.06	102.80	102.22	101.95
9000	118.65	118.04	117.52	117.07	115.65	115.00	114.69
10000	131.83	131.15	130.57	130.08	128.50	127.77	127.44
12000	158.20	157.38	156.69	156.09	154.20	153.33	152.92
15000	197.75	196.73	195.86	195.12	192.75	191.66	191.15
20000	263.67	262.30	261.15	260.16	257.00	255.55	254.87
25000	329.58	327.88	326.43	325.20	321.25	319.43	318.59
30000	395.50	393.46	391.72	390.24	385.50	383.32	382.31
31000	408.68	406.57	404.77	403.24	398.35	396.10	395.05
32000	421.87	419.69	417.83	416.25	411.20	408.88	407.80
33000	435.05	432.80	430.89	429.26	424.05	421.65	420.54
34000	448.23	445.92	443.95	442.27	436.90	434.43	433.28
35000	461.42	459.03	457.00	455.27	449.75	447.21	446.03
36000	474.60	472.15	470.06	468.28	462.60	459.98	458.77
37000	487.78	485.26	483.12	481.29	475.45	472.76	471.51
38000	500.97	498.38	496.18	494.30	488.30	485.54	484.26
39000	514.15	511.49	509.23	507.31	501.15	498.32	497.00
40000	527.33	524.61	522.29	520.31	514.00	511.09	509.74
41000	540.52	537.72	535.35	533.32	526.85	523.87	522.49
42000	553.70	550.84	548.40	546.33	539.70	536.65	535.23
43000	566.88	563.95	561.46	559.34	552.55	549.43	547.97
44000	580.07	577.07	574.52	572.35	565.40	562.20	560.72
45000	593.25	590.19	587.58	585.35	578.25	574.98	573.46
46000	606.43	603.30	600.63	598.36	591.10	587.76	586.21
47000	619.62	616.42	613.69	611.37	603.95	600.54	598.95
48000	632.80	629.53	626.75	624.38	616.80	613.31	611.69
49000	645.98	642.65	639.81	637.38	629.65	626.09	624.44
50000	659.17	655.76	652.86	650.39	642.50	638.87	637.18
51000	672.35	668.88	665.92	663.40	655.35	651.65	649.92
52000	685.53	681.99	678.98	676.41	668.20	664.42	662.67
53000	698.72	695.11	692.03	689.42	681.05	677.20	675.41
54000	711.90	708.22	705.09	702.42	693.90	689.98	688.15
55000	725.08	721.34	718.15	715.43	706.75	702.75	700.90
56000	738.27	734.45	731.21	728.44	719.60	715.53	713.64
57000	751.45	747.57	744.26	741.45	732.45	728.31	726.38
58000	764.63	760.68	757.32	754.46	745.30	741.09	739.13
59000	777.82	773.80	770.38	767.46	758.15	753.86	751.87
60000	791.00	786.91	783.44	780.47	771.00	766.64	764.62
65000	856.92	852.49	848.72	845.51	835.25	830.53	828.33
70000	922.83	918.07	914.01	910.55	899.50	894.41	892.05
75000	988.75	983.64	979.29	975.59	963.75	958.30	955.77
80000	1054.67	1049.22	1044.58	1040.63	1028.00	1022.19	1019.49
85000	1120.58	1114.79	1109.87	1105.67	1092.25	1086.08	1083.21
90000	1186.50	1180.37	1175.15	1170.71	1156.50	1149.96	1146.92
95000	1252.42	1245.95	1240.44	1235.75	1220.75	1213.85	1210.64
100000	1318.33	1311.52	1305.73	1300.78	1285.00	1277.74	1274.36
105000	1384.25	1377.10	1371.01	1365.82	1349.25	1341.62	1338.08
110000	1450.17	1442.67	1436.30	1430.86	1413.50	1405.51	1401.80
120000	1582.00	1573.83	1566.87	1560.94	1542.00	1533.28	1529.23
130000	1713.83	1704.98	1697.44	1691.02	1670.50	1661.06	1656.67
140000	1845.67	1836.13	1828.02	1821.10	1799.00	1788.83	1784.10
150000	1977.50	1967.28	1958.59	1951.18	1927.50	1916.60	1911.54
160000	2109.33	2098.44	2089.16	2081.26	2056.00	2044.38	2038.98
170000	2241.17	2229.59	2219.73	2211.33	2184.50	2172.15	2166.41
180000	2373.00	2360.74	2350.31	2341.41	2313.00	2299.92	2293.85
190000	2504.83	2491.89	2480.88	2471.49	2441.50	2427.70	2421.28
200000	2636.67	2623.04	2611.45	2601.57	2570.00	2555.47	2548.72
210000	2768.50	2754.20	2742.02	2731.65	2698.50	2683.24	2676.15
220000	2900.33	2885.35	2872.60	2861.73	2827.00	2811.02	2803.59
230000	3032.17	3016.50	3003.17	2991.80	2955.50	2938.79	2931.03
240000	3164.00	3147.65	3133.74	3121.88	3084.00	3066.57	3058.46
250000	3295.83	3278.81	3264.31	3251.96	3212.50	3194.34	3185.90

16.00 % Monthly Payments

LOAN AMOUNT	YEARS 1	2	3	4	5	6	7
100	9.05	4.87	3.49	2.81	2.40	2.14	1.96
200	18.10	9.74	6.98	5.62	4.81	4.28	3.91
500	45.25	24.36	17.45	14.04	12.02	10.71	9.79
1000	90.49	48.72	34.91	28.08	24.05	21.41	19.57
2000	180.98	97.44	69.81	56.16	48.10	42.83	39.15
5000	452.45	243.60	174.53	140.40	120.24	107.06	97.87
6000	542.94	292.32	209.44	168.48	144.29	128.48	117.44
7000	633.43	341.04	244.34	196.56	168.34	149.89	137.01
8000	723.92	389.76	279.25	224.64	192.39	171.30	156.59
9000	814.41	438.48	314.16	252.72	216.44	192.71	176.16
10000	904.90	487.20	349.06	280.80	240.49	214.13	195.73
12000	1085.88	584.65	418.88	336.97	288.58	256.95	234.88
15000	1357.35	730.81	523.60	421.21	360.73	321.19	293.60
20000	1809.81	974.41	698.13	561.61	480.97	428.26	391.47
25000	2262.26	1218.01	872.66	702.01	601.22	535.32	489.34
30000	2714.71	1461.61	1047.19	842.41	721.46	642.38	587.20
31000	2805.20	1510.33	1082.10	870.49	745.51	663.80	606.78
32000	2895.69	1559.05	1117.01	898.57	769.56	685.21	626.35
33000	2986.18	1607.77	1151.91	926.65	793.60	706.62	645.92
34000	3076.67	1656.49	1186.82	954.74	817.65	728.03	665.50
35000	3167.16	1705.21	1221.72	982.82	841.70	749.45	685.07
36000	3257.65	1753.94	1256.63	1010.90	865.75	770.86	704.64
37000	3348.14	1802.66	1291.54	1038.98	889.80	792.27	724.22
38000	3438.63	1851.38	1326.44	1067.06	913.85	813.68	743.79
39000	3529.12	1900.10	1361.35	1095.14	937.90	835.10	763.36
40000	3619.61	1948.82	1396.26	1123.22	961.94	856.51	782.94
41000	3710.10	1997.54	1431.16	1151.30	985.99	877.92	802.51
42000	3800.59	2046.26	1466.07	1179.38	1010.04	899.34	822.09
43000	3891.08	2094.98	1500.98	1207.46	1034.09	920.75	841.66
44000	3981.57	2143.70	1535.88	1235.54	1058.14	942.16	861.23
45000	4072.06	2192.42	1570.79	1263.62	1082.19	963.57	880.81
46000	4162.56	2241.14	1605.70	1291.70	1106.24	984.99	900.38
47000	4253.05	2289.86	1640.60	1319.78	1130.29	1006.40	919.95
48000	4343.54	2338.58	1675.51	1347.86	1154.33	1027.81	939.53
49000	4434.03	2387.30	1710.41	1375.94	1178.38	1049.23	959.10
50000	4524.52	2436.02	1745.32	1404.02	1202.43	1070.64	978.67
51000	4615.01	2484.74	1780.23	1432.10	1226.48	1092.05	998.25
52000	4705.50	2533.46	1815.13	1460.18	1250.53	1113.46	1017.82
53000	4795.99	2582.18	1850.04	1488.26	1274.58	1134.88	1037.39
54000	4886.48	2630.90	1884.95	1516.34	1298.63	1156.29	1056.97
55000	4976.97	2679.62	1919.85	1544.42	1322.67	1177.70	1076.54
56000	5067.46	2728.34	1954.76	1572.51	1346.72	1199.11	1096.11
57000	5157.95	2777.06	1989.67	1600.59	1370.77	1220.53	1115.69
58000	5248.44	2825.78	2024.57	1628.67	1394.82	1241.94	1135.26
59000	5338.93	2874.50	2059.48	1656.75	1418.87	1263.35	1154.83
60000	5429.42	2923.23	2094.39	1684.83	1442.92	1284.77	1174.41
65000	5881.87	3166.83	2268.92	1825.23	1563.16	1391.83	1272.27
70000	6334.32	3410.43	2443.45	1965.63	1683.40	1498.89	1370.14
75000	6786.77	3654.03	2617.98	2106.03	1803.65	1605.96	1468.01
80000	7239.23	3897.63	2792.51	2246.44	1923.89	1713.02	1565.88
85000	7691.68	4141.24	2967.05	2386.84	2044.13	1820.08	1663.74
90000	8144.13	4384.84	3141.58	2527.24	2164.38	1927.15	1761.61
95000	8596.58	4628.44	3316.11	2667.64	2284.62	2034.21	1859.48
100000	9049.03	4872.04	3490.64	2808.05	2404.86	2141.28	1957.35
105000	9501.48	5115.64	3665.17	2948.45	2525.11	2248.34	2055.21
110000	9953.94	5359.25	3839.71	3088.85	2645.35	2355.40	2153.08
120000	10858.84	5846.45	4188.77	3369.65	2885.83	2569.53	2348.81
130000	11763.74	6333.65	4537.84	3650.46	3126.32	2783.66	2544.55
140000	12668.65	6820.86	4886.90	3931.26	3366.81	2997.79	2740.28
150000	13573.55	7308.06	5235.96	4212.07	3607.29	3211.91	2936.02
160000	14478.45	7795.27	5585.03	4492.87	3847.78	3426.04	3131.75
170000	15383.36	8282.47	5934.09	4773.68	4088.27	3640.17	3327.49
180000	16288.26	8769.68	6283.16	5054.48	4328.75	3854.30	3523.22
190000	17193.16	9256.88	6632.22	5335.29	4569.24	4068.42	3718.96
200000	18098.07	9744.08	6981.29	5616.09	4809.72	4282.55	3914.69
210000	19002.97	10231.29	7330.35	5896.89	5050.21	4496.68	4110.43
220000	19907.87	10718.49	7679.41	6177.70	5290.70	4710.81	4306.16
230000	20812.78	11205.70	8028.48	6458.50	5531.18	4924.93	4501.89
240000	21717.68	11692.90	8377.54	6739.31	5771.67	5139.06	4697.63
250000	22622.58	12180.11	8726.61	7020.11	6012.16	5353.19	4893.36

Monthly Payments 16.00 %

LOAN AMOUNT	8	9	10	11	12	13	14
			YEARS				
100	1.82	1.72	1.64	1.58	1.53	1.49	1.46
200	3.65	3.44	3.29	3.16	3.07	2.99	2.92
500	9.12	8.61	8.22	7.91	7.66	7.46	7.30
1000	18.23	17.22	16.44	15.82	15.33	14.93	14.60
2000	36.46	34.44	32.87	31.64	30.65	29.86	29.20
5000	91.15	86.09	82.18	79.10	76.63	74.64	73.01
6000	109.39	103.31	98.61	94.92	91.96	89.57	87.61
7000	127.62	120.53	115.05	110.73	107.28	104.49	102.21
8000	145.85	137.75	131.49	126.55	122.61	119.42	116.82
9000	164.08	154.96	147.92	142.37	137.94	134.35	131.42
10000	182.31	172.18	164.36	158.19	153.26	149.28	146.02
12000	218.77	206.62	197.23	189.83	183.92	179.13	175.22
15000	273.46	258.27	246.54	237.29	229.90	223.92	219.03
20000	364.62	344.37	328.71	316.39	306.53	298.55	292.04
25000	455.77	430.46	410.89	395.48	383.16	373.19	365.05
30000	546.93	516.55	493.07	474.58	459.79	447.83	438.06
31000	565.16	533.77	509.51	490.40	475.12	462.76	452.66
32000	583.39	550.99	525.94	506.22	490.45	477.69	467.27
33000	601.62	568.20	542.38	522.04	505.77	492.61	481.87
34000	619.85	585.42	558.81	537.85	521.10	507.54	496.47
35000	638.08	602.64	575.25	553.67	536.42	522.47	511.07
36000	656.31	619.86	591.69	569.49	551.75	537.40	525.67
37000	674.54	637.08	608.12	585.31	567.08	552.33	540.28
38000	692.77	654.30	624.56	601.13	582.40	567.25	554.88
39000	711.00	671.51	640.99	616.95	597.73	582.18	569.48
40000	729.24	688.73	657.43	632.77	613.06	597.11	584.08
41000	747.47	705.95	673.86	648.59	628.38	612.04	598.68
42000	765.70	723.17	690.30	664.41	643.71	626.96	613.29
43000	783.93	740.39	706.74	680.23	659.04	641.89	627.89
44000	802.16	757.61	723.17	696.05	674.36	656.82	642.49
45000	820.39	774.82	739.61	711.87	689.69	671.75	657.09
46000	838.62	792.04	756.04	727.69	705.02	686.67	671.69
47000	856.85	809.26	772.48	743.51	720.34	701.60	686.30
48000	875.08	826.48	788.91	759.32	735.67	716.53	700.90
49000	893.31	843.70	805.35	775.14	750.99	731.46	715.50
50000	911.54	860.92	821.79	790.96	766.32	746.39	730.10
51000	929.77	878.13	838.22	806.78	781.65	761.31	744.70
52000	948.01	895.35	854.66	822.60	796.97	776.24	759.31
53000	966.24	912.57	871.09	838.42	812.30	791.17	773.91
54000	984.47	929.79	887.53	854.24	827.63	806.10	788.51
55000	1002.70	947.01	903.96	870.06	842.95	821.02	803.11
56000	1020.93	964.23	920.40	885.88	858.28	835.95	817.71
57000	1039.16	981.44	936.84	901.70	873.61	850.88	832.32
58000	1057.39	998.66	953.27	917.52	888.93	865.81	846.92
59000	1075.62	1015.88	969.71	933.34	904.26	880.73	861.52
60000	1093.85	1033.10	986.14	949.16	919.59	895.66	876.12
65000	1185.01	1119.19	1068.32	1028.25	996.22	970.30	949.13
70000	1276.16	1205.28	1150.50	1107.35	1072.85	1044.94	1022.14
75000	1367.32	1291.37	1232.68	1186.44	1149.48	1119.58	1095.15
80000	1458.47	1377.47	1314.86	1265.54	1226.11	1194.22	1168.16
85000	1549.62	1463.56	1397.04	1344.64	1302.75	1268.86	1241.17
90000	1640.78	1549.65	1479.21	1423.73	1379.38	1343.49	1314.18
95000	1731.93	1635.74	1561.39	1502.83	1456.01	1418.13	1387.19
100000	1823.09	1721.83	1643.57	1581.93	1532.64	1492.77	1460.20
105000	1914.24	1807.92	1725.75	1661.02	1609.27	1567.41	1533.21
110000	2005.40	1894.02	1807.93	1740.12	1685.91	1642.05	1606.22
120000	2187.71	2066.20	1972.29	1898.31	1839.17	1791.33	1752.24
130000	2370.01	2238.38	2136.64	2056.50	1992.44	1940.60	1898.26
140000	2552.32	2410.57	2301.00	2214.70	2145.70	2089.88	2044.28
150000	2734.63	2582.75	2465.36	2372.89	2298.96	2239.16	2190.30
160000	2916.94	2754.93	2629.71	2531.08	2452.23	2388.43	2336.33
170000	3099.25	2927.12	2794.07	2689.27	2605.49	2537.71	2482.35
180000	3281.56	3099.30	2958.43	2847.47	2758.76	2686.99	2628.37
190000	3463.87	3271.48	3122.78	3005.66	2912.02	2836.26	2774.39
200000	3646.18	3443.67	3287.14	3163.85	3065.28	2985.54	2920.41
210000	3828.48	3615.85	3451.50	3322.04	3218.55	3134.82	3066.43
220000	4010.79	3788.03	3615.86	3480.24	3371.81	3284.10	3212.45
230000	4193.10	3960.22	3780.21	3638.43	3525.08	3433.37	3358.47
240000	4375.41	4132.40	3944.57	3796.62	3678.34	3582.65	3504.49
250000	4557.72	4304.58	4108.93	3954.81	3831.61	3731.93	3650.51

16.00 % Monthly Payments

LOAN AMOUNT	15	16	17	18	19	20	21
100	1.43	1.41	1.39	1.38	1.36	1.35	1.34
200	2.87	2.82	2.79	2.75	2.73	2.71	2.69
500	7.17	7.06	6.96	6.89	6.82	6.77	6.72
1000	14.33	14.11	13.93	13.77	13.64	13.53	13.44
2000	28.67	28.22	27.85	27.54	27.28	27.06	26.88
5000	71.67	70.56	69.63	68.86	68.21	67.66	67.20
6000	86.00	84.67	83.56	82.63	81.85	81.19	80.64
7000	100.34	98.78	97.49	96.40	95.49	94.73	94.08
8000	114.67	112.89	111.41	110.18	109.14	108.26	107.52
9000	129.01	127.01	125.34	123.95	122.78	121.79	120.96
10000	143.34	141.12	139.27	137.72	136.42	135.32	134.40
12000	172.01	169.34	167.12	165.26	163.70	162.39	161.28
15000	215.01	211.68	208.90	206.58	204.63	202.99	201.60
20000	286.68	282.24	278.53	275.44	272.84	270.65	268.80
25000	358.35	352.79	348.17	344.30	341.05	338.31	336.00
30000	430.02	423.35	417.80	413.16	409.26	405.97	403.20
31000	444.35	437.47	431.73	426.93	422.90	419.50	416.64
32000	458.69	451.58	445.66	440.70	436.54	433.04	430.08
33000	473.02	465.69	459.58	454.47	450.18	446.57	443.52
34000	487.35	479.80	473.51	468.25	463.82	460.10	456.95
35000	501.69	493.91	487.44	482.02	477.47	473.63	470.39
36000	516.02	508.02	501.36	495.79	491.11	487.17	483.83
37000	530.36	522.14	515.29	509.56	504.75	500.70	497.27
38000	544.69	536.25	529.22	523.33	518.39	514.23	510.71
39000	559.02	550.36	543.14	537.10	532.03	527.76	524.15
40000	573.36	564.47	557.07	550.88	545.68	541.29	537.59
41000	587.69	578.58	571.00	564.65	559.32	554.83	551.03
42000	602.02	592.69	584.92	578.42	572.96	568.36	564.47
43000	616.36	606.81	598.85	592.19	586.60	581.89	577.91
44000	630.69	620.92	612.78	605.96	600.24	595.42	591.35
45000	645.03	635.03	626.70	619.74	613.89	608.96	604.79
46000	659.36	649.14	640.63	633.51	627.53	622.49	618.23
47000	673.69	663.25	654.56	647.28	641.17	636.02	631.67
48000	688.03	677.37	668.48	661.05	654.81	649.55	645.11
49000	702.36	691.48	682.41	674.82	668.45	663.09	658.55
50000	716.70	705.59	696.34	688.60	682.09	676.62	671.99
51000	731.03	719.70	710.26	702.37	695.74	690.15	685.43
52000	745.36	733.81	724.19	716.14	709.38	703.68	698.87
53000	759.70	747.92	738.12	729.91	723.02	717.22	712.31
54000	774.03	762.04	752.04	743.68	736.66	730.75	725.75
55000	788.37	776.15	765.97	757.46	750.30	744.28	739.19
56000	802.70	790.26	779.90	771.23	763.95	757.81	752.63
57000	817.03	804.37	793.82	785.00	777.59	771.34	766.07
58000	831.37	818.48	807.75	798.77	791.23	784.88	779.51
59000	845.70	832.60	821.68	812.54	804.87	798.41	792.95
60000	860.04	846.71	835.60	826.32	818.51	811.94	806.39
65000	931.71	917.27	905.24	895.17	886.72	879.60	873.59
70000	1003.37	987.82	974.87	964.03	954.93	947.27	940.79
75000	1075.04	1058.38	1044.51	1032.89	1023.14	1014.93	1007.99
80000	1146.71	1128.94	1114.14	1101.75	1091.35	1082.59	1075.19
85000	1218.38	1199.50	1183.77	1170.61	1159.56	1150.25	1142.39
90000	1290.05	1270.06	1253.41	1239.47	1227.77	1217.91	1209.59
95000	1361.72	1340.62	1323.04	1308.33	1295.98	1285.57	1276.79
100000	1433.39	1411.18	1392.67	1377.19	1364.19	1353.24	1343.98
105000	1505.06	1481.74	1462.31	1446.05	1432.40	1420.90	1411.18
110000	1576.73	1552.30	1531.94	1514.91	1500.61	1488.56	1478.38
120000	1720.07	1693.41	1671.21	1652.63	1637.03	1623.88	1612.78
130000	1863.41	1834.53	1810.48	1790.35	1773.45	1759.21	1747.18
140000	2006.75	1975.65	1949.74	1928.07	1909.87	1894.53	1881.58
150000	2150.09	2116.77	2089.01	2065.79	2046.28	2029.85	2015.98
160000	2293.43	2257.89	2228.28	2203.51	2182.70	2165.18	2150.38
170000	2436.77	2399.00	2367.55	2341.23	2319.12	2300.50	2284.77
180000	2580.11	2540.12	2506.81	2478.95	2455.54	2435.83	2419.17
190000	2723.45	2681.24	2646.08	2616.66	2591.96	2571.15	2553.57
200000	2866.78	2822.36	2785.35	2754.38	2728.38	2706.47	2687.97
210000	3010.12	2963.47	2924.62	2892.10	2864.80	2841.80	2822.37
220000	3153.46	3104.59	3063.88	3029.82	3001.22	2977.12	2956.77
230000	3296.80	3245.71	3203.15	3167.54	3137.64	3112.44	3091.17
240000	3440.14	3386.83	3342.42	3305.26	3274.06	3247.77	3225.56
250000	3583.48	3527.95	3481.68	3442.98	3410.47	3383.09	3359.96

Monthly Payments 16.00 %

LOAN AMOUNT	22	23	24	25	30	35	40
100	1.34	1.33	1.32	1.32	1.30	1.30	1.29
200	2.67	2.66	2.65	2.64	2.61	2.59	2.59
500	6.68	6.65	6.62	6.60	6.52	6.48	6.47
1000	13.36	13.30	13.24	13.19	13.04	12.97	12.94
2000	26.72	26.59	26.48	26.38	26.08	25.94	25.87
5000	66.81	66.48	66.19	65.95	65.19	64.84	64.68
6000	80.17	79.77	79.43	79.14	78.23	77.81	77.62
7000	93.53	93.07	92.67	92.33	91.27	90.78	90.56
8000	106.89	106.36	105.91	105.53	104.31	103.75	103.49
9000	120.25	119.66	119.15	118.72	117.34	116.72	116.43
10000	133.62	132.95	132.39	131.91	130.38	129.69	129.37
12000	160.34	159.54	158.86	158.29	156.46	155.63	155.24
15000	200.42	199.43	198.58	197.86	195.57	194.53	194.05
20000	267.23	265.90	264.77	263.81	260.76	259.38	258.74
25000	334.04	332.38	330.97	329.77	325.96	324.22	323.42
30000	400.85	398.85	397.16	395.72	391.15	389.06	388.11
31000	414.21	412.15	410.40	408.91	404.18	402.03	401.04
32000	427.57	425.44	423.64	422.10	417.22	415.00	413.98
33000	440.93	438.74	436.88	435.29	430.26	427.97	426.92
34000	454.29	452.03	450.12	448.48	443.30	440.94	439.85
35000	467.65	465.33	463.35	461.67	456.34	453.91	452.79
36000	481.02	478.62	476.59	474.87	469.38	466.88	465.73
37000	494.38	491.92	489.83	488.06	482.41	479.84	478.66
38000	507.74	505.21	503.07	501.25	495.45	492.81	491.60
39000	521.10	518.51	516.31	514.44	508.49	505.78	504.54
40000	534.46	531.80	529.55	527.63	521.53	518.75	517.47
41000	547.82	545.10	542.79	540.82	534.57	531.72	530.41
42000	561.18	558.39	556.03	554.01	547.61	544.69	543.35
43000	574.55	571.69	569.26	567.20	560.64	557.66	556.29
44000	587.91	584.98	582.50	580.39	573.68	570.63	569.22
45000	601.27	598.28	595.74	593.58	586.72	583.60	582.16
46000	614.63	611.58	608.98	606.77	599.76	596.56	595.10
47000	627.99	624.87	622.22	619.96	612.80	609.53	608.03
48000	641.35	638.17	635.46	633.15	625.83	622.50	620.97
49000	654.72	651.46	648.70	646.34	638.87	635.47	633.91
50000	668.08	664.76	661.93	659.53	651.91	648.44	646.84
51000	681.44	678.05	675.17	672.73	664.95	661.41	659.78
52000	694.80	691.35	688.41	685.92	677.99	674.38	672.72
53000	708.16	704.64	701.65	699.11	691.03	687.35	685.65
54000	721.52	717.94	714.89	712.30	704.06	700.31	698.59
55000	734.88	731.23	728.13	725.49	717.10	713.28	711.53
56000	748.25	744.53	741.37	738.68	730.14	726.25	724.46
57000	761.61	757.82	754.61	751.87	743.18	739.22	737.40
58000	774.97	771.12	767.84	765.06	756.22	752.19	750.34
59000	788.33	784.41	781.08	778.25	769.26	765.16	763.28
60000	801.69	797.71	794.32	791.44	782.29	778.13	776.21
65000	868.50	864.18	860.51	857.40	847.48	842.97	840.90
70000	935.31	930.66	926.71	923.35	912.68	907.81	905.58
75000	1002.11	997.13	992.90	989.30	977.87	972.66	970.27
80000	1068.92	1063.61	1059.10	1055.26	1043.06	1037.50	1034.95
85000	1135.73	1130.08	1125.29	1121.21	1108.25	1102.35	1099.63
90000	1202.54	1196.56	1191.48	1187.16	1173.44	1167.19	1164.32
95000	1269.35	1263.04	1257.68	1253.12	1238.63	1232.03	1229.00
100000	1336.15	1329.51	1323.87	1319.07	1303.82	1296.88	1293.69
105000	1402.96	1395.99	1390.06	1385.02	1369.01	1361.72	1358.37
110000	1469.77	1462.46	1456.26	1450.98	1434.20	1426.57	1423.06
120000	1603.38	1595.41	1588.64	1582.88	1564.59	1556.25	1552.42
130000	1737.00	1728.36	1721.03	1714.79	1694.97	1685.94	1681.79
140000	1870.61	1861.32	1853.42	1846.70	1825.35	1815.63	1811.16
150000	2004.23	1994.27	1985.80	1978.60	1955.73	1945.32	1940.53
160000	2137.85	2127.22	2118.19	2110.51	2086.12	2075.01	2069.90
170000	2271.46	2260.17	2250.58	2242.42	2216.50	2204.69	2199.27
180000	2405.08	2393.12	2382.96	2374.33	2346.88	2334.38	2328.64
190000	2538.69	2526.07	2515.35	2506.23	2477.26	2464.07	2458.00
200000	2672.31	2659.02	2647.74	2638.14	2607.64	2593.76	2587.37
210000	2805.92	2791.97	2780.13	2770.05	2738.03	2723.44	2716.74
220000	2939.54	2924.92	2912.51	2901.95	2868.41	2853.13	2846.11
230000	3073.15	3057.88	3044.90	3033.86	2998.79	2982.82	2975.48
240000	3206.77	3190.83	3177.29	3165.77	3129.17	3112.51	3104.85
250000	3340.38	3323.78	3309.67	3297.67	3259.56	3242.20	3234.22

16.25 % Monthly Payments

LOAN AMOUNT	YEARS 1	2	3	4	5	6	7
100	9.06	4.88	3.50	2.82	2.42	2.15	1.97
200	18.12	9.77	7.00	5.64	4.83	4.31	3.94
500	45.30	24.42	17.51	14.10	12.09	10.77	9.85
1000	90.60	48.83	35.02	28.20	24.17	21.54	19.71
2000	181.20	97.66	70.04	56.40	48.35	43.08	39.41
5000	453.01	244.16	175.11	141.00	120.86	107.71	98.53
6000	543.61	292.99	210.13	169.20	145.04	129.25	118.24
7000	634.21	341.83	245.15	197.40	169.21	150.79	137.94
8000	724.81	390.66	280.17	225.60	193.38	172.33	157.65
9000	815.41	439.49	315.20	253.80	217.55	193.87	177.36
10000	906.01	488.32	350.22	282.00	241.73	215.41	197.06
12000	1087.21	585.99	420.26	338.40	290.07	258.49	236.47
15000	1359.02	732.48	525.33	423.00	362.59	323.12	295.59
20000	1812.02	976.64	700.44	564.00	483.45	430.82	394.12
25000	2265.03	1220.80	875.54	705.00	604.31	538.53	492.65
30000	2718.03	1464.96	1050.65	846.00	725.18	646.23	591.18
31000	2808.63	1513.80	1085.67	874.20	749.35	667.77	610.89
32000	2899.24	1562.63	1120.70	902.40	773.52	689.32	630.60
33000	2989.84	1611.46	1155.72	930.60	797.69	710.86	650.30
34000	3080.44	1660.29	1190.74	958.80	821.87	732.40	670.01
35000	3171.04	1709.13	1225.76	987.00	846.04	753.94	689.72
36000	3261.64	1757.96	1260.78	1015.20	870.21	775.48	709.42
37000	3352.24	1806.79	1295.81	1043.40	894.38	797.02	729.13
38000	3442.84	1855.62	1330.83	1071.60	918.56	818.56	748.83
39000	3533.44	1904.45	1365.85	1099.80	942.73	840.10	768.54
40000	3624.04	1953.29	1400.87	1128.00	966.90	861.64	788.25
41000	3714.65	2002.12	1435.89	1156.20	991.07	883.19	807.95
42000	3805.25	2050.95	1470.91	1184.40	1015.25	904.73	827.66
43000	3895.85	2099.78	1505.94	1212.60	1039.42	926.27	847.36
44000	3986.45	2148.61	1540.96	1240.80	1063.59	947.81	867.07
45000	4077.05	2197.45	1575.98	1269.00	1087.77	969.35	886.78
46000	4167.65	2246.28	1611.00	1297.20	1111.94	990.89	906.48
47000	4258.25	2295.11	1646.02	1325.40	1136.11	1012.43	926.19
48000	4348.85	2343.94	1681.04	1353.60	1160.28	1033.97	945.90
49000	4439.45	2392.78	1716.07	1381.80	1184.46	1055.51	965.60
50000	4530.06	2441.61	1751.09	1410.00	1208.63	1077.06	985.31
51000	4620.66	2490.44	1786.11	1438.20	1232.80	1098.60	1005.01
52000	4711.26	2539.27	1821.13	1466.40	1256.97	1120.14	1024.72
53000	4801.86	2588.10	1856.15	1494.60	1281.15	1141.68	1044.43
54000	4892.46	2636.94	1891.18	1522.80	1305.32	1163.22	1064.13
55000	4983.06	2685.77	1926.20	1551.00	1329.49	1184.76	1083.84
56000	5073.66	2734.60	1961.22	1579.20	1353.66	1206.30	1103.54
57000	5164.26	2783.43	1996.24	1607.40	1377.84	1227.84	1123.25
58000	5254.86	2832.26	2031.26	1635.60	1402.01	1249.38	1142.96
59000	5345.47	2881.10	2066.28	1663.80	1426.18	1270.93	1162.66
60000	5436.07	2929.93	2101.31	1692.00	1450.35	1292.47	1182.37
65000	5889.07	3174.09	2276.41	1833.00	1571.22	1400.17	1280.90
70000	6342.08	3418.25	2451.52	1974.00	1692.08	1507.88	1379.43
75000	6795.08	3662.41	2626.63	2115.00	1812.94	1615.58	1477.96
80000	7248.09	3906.57	2801.74	2256.00	1933.80	1723.29	1576.49
85000	7701.09	4150.73	2976.85	2397.00	2054.67	1830.99	1675.02
90000	8154.10	4394.89	3151.96	2538.00	2175.53	1938.70	1773.55
95000	8607.11	4639.05	3327.07	2679.00	2296.39	2046.40	1872.08
100000	9060.11	4883.22	3502.18	2820.00	2417.26	2154.11	1970.62
105000	9513.12	5127.38	3677.29	2961.00	2538.12	2261.82	2069.15
110000	9966.12	5371.54	3852.39	3102.00	2658.98	2369.52	2167.68
120000	10872.13	5859.86	4202.61	3384.00	2900.71	2584.93	2364.74
130000	11778.14	6348.18	4552.83	3666.00	3142.43	2800.34	2561.80
140000	12684.15	6836.50	4903.05	3948.00	3384.16	3015.75	2758.86
150000	13590.17	7324.82	5253.26	4230.00	3625.88	3231.17	2955.92
160000	14496.18	7813.14	5603.48	4512.00	3867.61	3446.58	3152.99
170000	15402.19	8301.47	5953.70	4794.00	4109.33	3661.99	3350.05
180000	16308.20	8789.79	6303.92	5076.00	4351.06	3877.40	3547.11
190000	17214.21	9278.11	6654.14	5358.00	4592.79	4092.81	3744.17
200000	18120.22	9766.43	7004.35	5640.00	4834.51	4308.22	3941.23
210000	19026.23	10254.75	7354.57	5922.00	5076.24	4523.63	4138.29
220000	19932.24	10743.07	7704.79	6204.00	5317.96	4739.04	4335.35
230000	20838.25	11231.39	8055.01	6486.00	5559.69	4954.45	4532.42
240000	21744.27	11719.72	8405.22	6768.00	5801.41	5169.86	4729.48
250000	22650.28	12208.04	8755.44	7050.00	6043.14	5385.28	4926.54

Monthly Payments 16.25 %

LOAN AMOUNT	8	9	10	11	12	13	14
				YEARS			
100	1.84	1.74	1.66	1.60	1.55	1.51	1.48
200	3.67	3.47	3.32	3.19	3.10	3.02	2.95
500	9.18	8.68	8.29	7.98	7.74	7.54	7.38
1000	18.37	17.36	16.58	15.97	15.48	15.08	14.76
2000	36.74	34.72	33.16	31.94	30.96	30.17	29.52
5000	91.84	86.80	82.90	79.84	77.39	75.42	73.81
6000	110.21	104.16	99.48	95.81	92.87	90.50	88.57
7000	128.57	121.52	116.07	111.78	108.35	105.59	103.33
8000	146.94	138.88	132.65	127.75	123.83	120.67	118.09
9000	165.31	156.23	149.23	143.71	139.31	135.75	132.85
10000	183.68	173.59	165.81	159.68	154.79	150.84	147.61
12000	220.41	208.31	198.97	191.62	185.75	181.00	177.14
15000	275.52	260.39	248.71	239.52	232.18	226.26	221.42
20000	367.36	347.19	331.62	319.36	309.58	301.67	295.23
25000	459.20	433.99	414.52	399.20	386.97	377.09	369.03
30000	551.04	520.78	497.42	479.04	464.37	452.51	442.84
31000	569.40	538.14	514.00	495.01	479.85	467.59	457.60
32000	587.77	555.50	530.58	510.98	495.33	482.68	472.36
33000	606.14	572.86	547.17	526.95	510.80	497.76	487.12
34000	624.51	590.22	563.75	542.92	526.28	512.84	501.88
35000	642.87	607.58	580.33	558.88	541.76	527.93	516.64
36000	661.24	624.94	596.91	574.85	557.24	543.01	531.41
37000	679.61	642.30	613.49	590.82	572.72	558.10	546.17
38000	697.98	659.66	630.07	606.79	588.20	573.18	560.93
39000	716.35	677.02	646.65	622.76	603.68	588.26	575.69
40000	734.71	694.38	663.23	638.73	619.16	603.35	590.45
41000	753.08	711.74	679.81	654.69	634.64	618.43	605.21
42000	771.45	729.10	696.39	670.66	650.12	633.51	619.97
43000	789.82	746.45	712.97	686.63	665.59	648.60	634.73
44000	808.18	763.81	729.55	702.60	681.07	663.68	649.50
45000	826.55	781.17	746.13	718.57	696.55	678.77	664.26
46000	844.92	798.53	762.72	734.53	712.03	693.85	679.02
47000	863.29	815.89	779.30	750.50	727.51	708.93	693.78
48000	881.66	833.25	795.88	766.47	742.99	724.02	708.54
49000	900.02	850.61	812.46	782.44	758.47	739.10	723.30
50000	918.39	867.97	829.04	798.41	773.95	754.18	738.06
51000	936.76	885.33	845.62	814.38	789.43	769.27	752.82
52000	955.13	902.69	862.20	830.34	804.90	784.35	767.59
53000	973.50	920.05	878.78	846.31	820.38	799.43	782.35
54000	991.86	937.41	895.36	862.28	835.86	814.52	797.11
55000	1010.23	954.77	911.94	878.25	851.34	829.60	811.87
56000	1028.60	972.13	928.52	894.22	866.82	844.69	826.63
57000	1046.97	989.49	945.10	910.18	882.30	859.77	841.39
58000	1065.33	1006.85	961.68	926.15	897.78	874.85	856.15
59000	1083.70	1024.21	978.27	942.12	913.26	889.94	870.91
60000	1102.07	1041.56	994.85	958.09	928.74	905.02	885.68
65000	1193.91	1128.36	1077.75	1037.93	1006.13	980.44	959.48
70000	1285.75	1215.16	1160.65	1117.77	1083.53	1055.86	1033.29
75000	1377.59	1301.96	1243.56	1197.61	1160.92	1131.28	1107.09
80000	1469.43	1388.75	1326.46	1277.45	1238.32	1206.69	1180.90
85000	1561.27	1475.55	1409.37	1357.29	1315.71	1282.11	1254.71
90000	1653.11	1562.35	1492.27	1437.13	1393.10	1357.53	1328.51
95000	1744.94	1649.14	1575.17	1516.97	1470.50	1432.95	1402.32
100000	1836.78	1735.94	1658.08	1596.81	1547.89	1508.37	1476.13
105000	1928.62	1822.74	1740.98	1676.65	1625.29	1583.79	1549.93
110000	2020.46	1909.54	1823.89	1756.50	1702.68	1659.20	1623.74
120000	2204.14	2083.13	1989.69	1916.18	1857.47	1810.04	1771.35
130000	2387.82	2256.72	2155.50	2075.86	2012.26	1960.88	1918.96
140000	2571.50	2430.32	2321.31	2235.54	2167.05	2111.71	2066.58
150000	2755.18	2603.91	2487.12	2395.22	2321.84	2262.55	2214.19
160000	2938.85	2777.51	2652.92	2554.90	2476.63	2413.39	2361.80
170000	3122.53	2951.10	2818.73	2714.58	2631.42	2564.22	2509.41
180000	3306.21	3124.69	2984.54	2874.26	2786.21	2715.06	2657.03
190000	3489.89	3298.29	3150.35	3033.95	2941.00	2865.90	2804.64
200000	3673.57	3471.88	3316.16	3193.63	3095.79	3016.73	2952.25
210000	3857.25	3645.48	3481.96	3353.31	3250.58	3167.57	3099.86
220000	4040.92	3819.07	3647.77	3512.99	3405.37	3318.41	3247.48
230000	4224.60	3992.67	3813.58	3672.67	3560.16	3469.24	3395.09
240000	4408.28	4166.26	3979.39	3832.35	3714.95	3620.08	3542.70
250000	4591.96	4339.85	4145.19	3992.03	3869.73	3770.92	3690.31

16.25 % Monthly Payments

LOAN AMOUNT	15	16	17	18	19	20	21
				YEARS			
100	1.45	1.43	1.41	1.39	1.38	1.37	1.36
200	2.90	2.86	2.82	2.79	2.76	2.74	2.72
500	7.25	7.14	7.05	6.97	6.91	6.85	6.81
1000	14.50	14.28	14.09	13.94	13.81	13.71	13.62
2000	28.99	28.55	28.19	27.88	27.63	27.41	27.23
5000	72.48	71.38	70.47	69.71	69.07	68.54	68.08
6000	86.98	85.66	84.57	83.65	82.89	82.24	81.70
7000	101.47	99.94	98.66	97.60	96.70	95.95	95.32
8000	115.97	114.22	112.76	111.54	110.52	109.66	108.93
9000	130.47	128.49	126.85	125.48	124.33	123.36	122.55
10000	144.96	142.77	140.95	139.42	138.15	137.07	136.17
12000	173.95	171.32	169.14	167.31	165.77	164.49	163.40
15000	217.44	214.15	211.42	209.13	207.22	205.61	204.25
20000	289.92	285.54	281.89	278.85	276.29	274.14	272.33
25000	362.41	356.92	352.36	348.56	345.36	342.68	340.42
30000	434.89	428.31	422.84	418.27	414.44	411.22	408.50
31000	449.38	442.59	436.93	432.21	428.25	424.92	422.12
32000	463.88	456.86	451.03	446.15	442.07	438.63	435.73
33000	478.38	471.14	465.12	460.09	455.88	452.34	449.35
34000	492.87	485.42	479.22	474.04	469.70	466.04	462.97
35000	507.37	499.69	493.31	487.98	483.51	479.75	476.58
36000	521.86	513.97	507.41	501.92	497.32	493.46	490.20
37000	536.36	528.25	521.50	515.86	511.14	507.17	503.82
38000	550.86	542.52	535.59	529.81	524.95	520.87	517.43
39000	565.35	556.80	549.69	543.75	538.77	534.58	531.05
40000	579.85	571.08	563.78	557.69	552.58	548.29	544.67
41000	594.34	585.35	577.88	571.63	566.40	561.99	558.28
42000	608.84	599.63	591.97	585.58	580.21	575.70	571.90
43000	623.34	613.91	606.07	599.52	594.03	589.41	585.52
44000	637.83	628.19	620.16	613.46	607.84	603.12	599.13
45000	652.33	642.46	634.26	627.40	621.66	616.82	612.75
46000	666.83	656.74	648.35	641.34	635.47	630.53	626.37
47000	681.32	671.02	662.45	655.29	649.28	644.24	639.98
48000	695.82	685.29	676.54	669.23	663.10	657.94	653.60
49000	710.31	699.57	690.64	683.17	676.91	671.65	667.22
50000	724.81	713.85	704.73	697.11	690.73	685.36	680.83
51000	739.31	728.12	718.82	711.06	704.54	699.07	694.45
52000	753.80	742.40	732.92	725.00	718.36	712.77	708.07
53000	768.30	756.68	747.01	738.94	732.17	726.48	721.68
54000	782.80	770.96	761.11	752.88	745.99	740.19	735.30
55000	797.29	785.23	775.20	766.82	759.80	753.89	748.92
56000	811.79	799.51	789.30	780.77	773.62	767.60	762.53
57000	826.28	813.79	803.39	794.71	787.43	781.31	776.15
58000	840.78	828.06	817.49	808.65	801.24	795.02	789.77
59000	855.28	842.34	831.58	822.59	815.06	808.72	803.38
60000	869.77	856.62	845.68	836.54	828.87	822.43	817.00
65000	942.25	928.00	916.15	906.25	897.95	890.97	885.08
70000	1014.74	999.39	986.62	975.96	967.02	959.50	953.16
75000	1087.22	1070.77	1057.09	1045.67	1036.09	1028.04	1021.25
80000	1159.70	1142.16	1127.57	1115.38	1105.17	1096.57	1089.33
85000	1232.18	1213.54	1198.04	1185.09	1174.24	1165.11	1157.41
90000	1304.66	1284.93	1268.51	1254.80	1243.31	1233.65	1225.50
95000	1377.14	1356.31	1338.99	1324.52	1312.38	1302.18	1293.58
100000	1449.62	1427.69	1409.46	1394.23	1381.46	1370.72	1361.66
105000	1522.10	1499.08	1479.93	1463.94	1450.53	1439.25	1429.75
110000	1594.58	1570.46	1550.41	1533.65	1519.60	1507.79	1497.83
120000	1739.55	1713.23	1691.35	1673.07	1657.75	1644.86	1634.00
130000	1884.51	1856.00	1832.30	1812.50	1795.89	1781.93	1770.16
140000	2029.47	1998.77	1973.24	1951.92	1934.04	1919.01	1906.33
150000	2174.43	2141.54	2114.19	2091.34	2072.19	2056.08	2042.50
160000	2319.39	2284.31	2255.13	2230.76	2210.33	2193.15	2178.66
170000	2464.36	2427.08	2396.08	2370.19	2348.48	2330.22	2314.83
180000	2609.32	2569.85	2537.03	2509.61	2486.62	2467.29	2451.00
190000	2754.28	2712.62	2677.97	2649.03	2624.77	2604.36	2587.16
200000	2899.24	2855.39	2818.92	2788.45	2762.91	2741.44	2723.33
210000	3044.21	2998.16	2959.86	2927.88	2901.06	2878.51	2859.49
220000	3189.17	3140.93	3100.81	3067.30	3039.21	3015.58	2995.66
230000	3334.13	3283.70	3241.76	3206.72	3177.35	3152.65	3131.83
240000	3479.09	3426.47	3382.70	3346.14	3315.50	3289.72	3267.99
250000	3624.05	3569.24	3523.65	3485.57	3453.64	3426.79	3404.16

Monthly Payments 16.25 %

LOAN AMOUNT	YEARS 22	23	24	25	30	35	40
100	1.35	1.35	1.34	1.34	1.32	1.32	1.31
200	2.71	2.70	2.68	2.67	2.65	2.63	2.63
500	6.77	6.74	6.71	6.69	6.61	6.58	6.57
1000	13.54	13.48	13.42	13.37	13.23	13.16	13.13
2000	27.08	26.95	26.84	26.75	26.45	26.32	26.26
5000	67.70	67.38	67.10	66.87	66.13	65.80	65.65
6000	81.24	80.85	80.52	80.24	79.36	78.96	78.78
7000	94.78	94.33	93.94	93.62	92.59	92.12	91.91
8000	108.32	107.80	107.36	106.99	105.81	105.28	105.04
9000	121.86	121.28	120.78	120.36	119.04	118.44	118.17
10000	135.40	134.75	134.20	133.74	132.27	131.60	131.30
12000	162.48	161.70	161.05	160.49	158.72	157.92	157.56
15000	203.10	202.13	201.31	200.61	198.40	197.40	196.95
20000	270.80	269.51	268.41	267.48	264.53	263.21	262.60
25000	338.50	336.88	335.51	334.35	330.67	329.01	328.25
30000	406.20	404.26	402.61	401.22	396.80	394.81	393.90
31000	419.74	417.74	416.03	414.59	410.03	407.97	407.03
32000	433.28	431.21	429.46	427.96	423.25	421.13	420.16
33000	446.82	444.69	442.88	441.34	436.48	434.29	433.29
34000	460.36	458.16	456.30	454.71	449.71	447.45	446.42
35000	473.90	471.64	469.72	468.09	462.93	460.61	459.55
36000	487.45	485.11	483.14	481.46	476.16	473.77	472.68
37000	500.99	498.59	496.56	494.83	489.38	486.93	485.81
38000	514.53	512.06	509.98	508.21	502.61	500.09	498.94
39000	528.07	525.54	523.40	521.58	515.84	513.25	512.07
40000	541.61	539.02	536.82	534.96	529.06	526.41	525.20
41000	555.15	552.49	550.24	548.33	542.29	539.57	538.33
42000	568.69	565.97	563.66	561.70	555.52	552.73	551.46
43000	582.23	579.44	577.08	575.08	568.74	565.89	564.59
44000	595.77	592.92	590.50	588.45	581.97	579.05	577.73
45000	609.31	606.39	603.92	601.82	595.20	592.21	590.86
46000	622.85	619.87	617.34	615.20	608.42	605.37	603.99
47000	636.39	633.34	630.76	628.57	621.65	618.53	617.12
48000	649.93	646.82	644.18	641.95	634.88	631.69	630.25
49000	663.47	660.29	657.60	655.32	648.10	644.85	643.38
50000	677.01	673.77	671.02	668.69	661.33	658.01	656.51
51000	690.55	687.24	684.44	682.07	674.56	671.17	669.64
52000	704.09	700.72	697.87	695.44	687.78	684.33	682.77
53000	717.63	714.20	711.29	708.82	701.01	697.49	695.90
54000	731.17	727.67	724.71	722.19	714.24	710.65	709.03
55000	744.71	741.15	738.13	735.56	727.46	723.81	722.16
56000	758.25	754.62	751.55	748.94	740.69	736.98	735.29
57000	771.79	768.10	764.97	762.31	753.92	750.14	748.42
58000	785.33	781.57	778.39	775.68	767.14	763.30	761.55
59000	798.87	795.05	791.81	789.06	780.37	776.46	774.68
60000	812.41	808.52	805.23	802.43	793.60	789.62	787.81
65000	880.11	875.90	872.33	869.30	859.73	855.42	853.46
70000	947.81	943.28	939.43	936.17	925.86	921.22	919.11
75000	1015.51	1010.65	1006.54	1003.04	992.00	987.02	984.76
80000	1083.21	1078.03	1073.64	1069.91	1058.13	1052.82	1050.41
85000	1150.91	1145.41	1140.74	1136.78	1124.26	1118.62	1116.06
90000	1218.61	1212.78	1207.84	1203.65	1190.40	1184.42	1181.71
95000	1286.31	1280.16	1274.95	1270.52	1256.53	1250.23	1247.36
100000	1354.01	1347.54	1342.05	1337.39	1322.66	1316.03	1313.01
105000	1421.71	1414.92	1409.15	1404.26	1388.80	1381.83	1378.66
110000	1489.42	1482.29	1476.25	1471.13	1454.93	1447.63	1444.31
120000	1624.82	1617.05	1610.46	1604.87	1587.19	1579.23	1575.61
130000	1760.22	1751.80	1744.66	1738.60	1719.46	1710.84	1706.92
140000	1895.62	1886.55	1878.87	1872.34	1851.73	1842.44	1838.22
150000	2031.02	2021.31	2013.07	2006.08	1983.99	1974.04	1969.52
160000	2166.42	2156.06	2147.28	2139.82	2116.26	2105.64	2100.82
170000	2301.82	2290.82	2281.48	2273.56	2248.53	2237.25	2232.12
180000	2437.23	2425.57	2415.69	2407.30	2380.79	2368.85	2363.42
190000	2572.63	2560.32	2549.89	2541.04	2513.06	2500.45	2494.72
200000	2708.03	2695.08	2684.10	2674.78	2645.32	2632.05	2626.02
210000	2843.43	2829.83	2818.30	2808.51	2777.59	2763.66	2757.32
220000	2978.83	2964.58	2952.51	2942.25	2909.86	2895.26	2888.63
230000	3114.23	3099.34	3086.71	3075.99	3042.12	3026.86	3019.93
240000	3249.63	3234.09	3220.92	3209.73	3174.39	3158.47	3151.23
250000	3385.03	3368.85	3355.12	3343.47	3306.66	3290.07	3282.53

16.50 % Monthly Payments

LOAN AMOUNT	1	2	3	4	5	6	7
	YEARS						
100	9.07	4.89	3.51	2.83	2.43	2.17	1.98
200	18.14	9.79	7.03	5.66	4.86	4.33	3.97
500	45.36	24.47	17.57	14.16	12.15	10.83	9.92
1000	90.71	48.94	35.14	28.32	24.30	21.67	19.84
2000	181.42	97.89	70.27	56.64	48.59	43.34	39.68
5000	453.56	244.72	175.69	141.60	121.48	108.35	99.20
6000	544.27	293.66	210.82	169.92	145.78	130.02	119.04
7000	634.98	342.61	245.96	198.24	170.08	151.69	138.87
8000	725.69	391.55	281.10	226.56	194.37	173.36	158.71
9000	816.41	440.50	316.23	254.88	218.67	195.03	178.55
10000	907.12	489.44	351.37	283.20	242.97	216.70	198.39
12000	1088.54	587.33	421.65	339.84	291.56	260.04	238.07
15000	1360.68	734.16	527.06	424.80	364.45	325.05	297.59
20000	1814.24	978.88	702.74	566.39	485.93	433.39	396.78
25000	2267.80	1223.60	878.43	707.99	607.42	541.74	495.98
30000	2721.36	1468.32	1054.12	849.59	728.90	650.09	595.18
31000	2812.07	1517.26	1089.25	877.91	753.20	671.76	615.02
32000	2902.78	1566.21	1124.39	906.23	777.50	693.43	634.85
33000	2993.49	1615.15	1159.53	934.55	801.79	715.10	654.69
34000	3084.20	1664.09	1194.67	962.87	826.09	736.77	674.53
35000	3174.91	1713.04	1229.80	991.19	850.39	758.44	694.37
36000	3265.63	1761.98	1264.94	1019.51	874.68	780.11	714.21
37000	3356.34	1810.93	1300.08	1047.83	898.98	801.78	734.05
38000	3447.05	1859.87	1335.21	1076.15	923.28	823.45	753.89
39000	3537.76	1908.81	1370.35	1104.47	947.57	845.12	773.73
40000	3628.47	1957.76	1405.49	1132.79	971.87	866.79	793.57
41000	3719.19	2006.70	1440.63	1161.11	996.17	888.46	813.41
42000	3809.90	2055.64	1475.76	1189.43	1020.46	910.13	833.25
43000	3900.61	2104.59	1510.90	1217.75	1044.76	931.80	853.09
44000	3991.32	2153.53	1546.04	1246.07	1069.06	953.47	872.92
45000	4082.03	2202.48	1581.17	1274.39	1093.35	975.14	892.76
46000	4172.75	2251.42	1616.31	1302.71	1117.65	996.81	912.60
47000	4263.46	2300.36	1651.45	1331.03	1141.95	1018.48	932.44
48000	4354.17	2349.31	1686.59	1359.35	1166.24	1040.15	952.28
49000	4444.88	2398.25	1721.72	1387.67	1190.54	1061.82	972.12
50000	4535.59	2447.20	1756.86	1415.99	1214.84	1083.49	991.96
51000	4626.30	2496.14	1792.00	1444.31	1239.13	1105.16	1011.80
52000	4717.02	2545.08	1827.13	1472.63	1263.43	1126.83	1031.64
53000	4807.73	2594.03	1862.27	1500.94	1287.73	1148.50	1051.48
54000	4898.44	2642.97	1897.41	1529.26	1312.02	1170.17	1071.32
55000	4989.15	2691.92	1932.55	1557.58	1336.32	1191.84	1091.16
56000	5079.86	2740.86	1967.68	1585.90	1360.62	1213.51	1110.99
57000	5170.58	2789.80	2002.82	1614.22	1384.91	1235.17	1130.83
58000	5261.29	2838.75	2037.96	1642.54	1409.21	1256.84	1150.67
59000	5352.00	2887.69	2073.10	1670.86	1433.51	1278.51	1170.51
60000	5442.71	2936.64	2108.23	1699.18	1457.80	1300.18	1190.35
65000	5896.27	3181.35	2283.92	1840.78	1579.29	1408.53	1289.55
70000	6349.83	3426.07	2459.60	1982.38	1700.77	1516.88	1388.74
75000	6803.39	3670.79	2635.29	2123.98	1822.25	1625.23	1487.94
80000	7256.95	3915.51	2810.98	2265.58	1943.74	1733.58	1587.14
85000	7710.51	4160.23	2986.66	2407.18	2065.22	1841.93	1686.33
90000	8164.07	4404.95	3162.35	2548.77	2186.70	1950.28	1785.53
95000	8617.63	4649.67	3338.03	2690.37	2308.19	2058.62	1884.72
100000	9071.19	4894.39	3513.72	2831.97	2429.67	2166.97	1983.92
105000	9524.74	5139.11	3689.41	2973.57	2551.16	2275.32	2083.12
110000	9978.30	5383.83	3865.09	3115.17	2672.64	2383.67	2182.31
120000	10885.42	5873.27	4216.46	3398.37	2915.61	2600.37	2380.70
130000	11792.54	6362.71	4567.84	3681.56	3158.57	2817.07	2579.10
140000	12699.66	6852.15	4919.21	3964.76	3401.54	3033.76	2777.49
150000	13606.78	7341.59	5270.58	4247.96	3644.51	3250.46	2975.88
160000	14513.90	7831.03	5621.95	4531.15	3887.48	3467.16	3174.27
170000	15421.01	8320.47	5973.33	4814.35	4130.44	3683.85	3372.66
180000	16328.13	8809.91	6324.70	5097.55	4373.41	3900.55	3571.06
190000	17235.25	9299.35	6676.07	5380.75	4616.38	4117.25	3769.45
200000	18142.37	9788.78	7027.44	5663.94	4859.34	4333.95	3967.84
210000	19049.49	10278.22	7378.81	5947.14	5102.31	4550.64	4166.23
220000	19956.61	10767.66	7730.19	6230.34	5345.28	4767.34	4364.62
230000	20863.73	11257.10	8081.56	6513.53	5588.25	4984.04	4563.01
240000	21770.84	11746.54	8432.93	6796.73	5831.21	5200.74	4761.41
250000	22677.96	12235.98	8784.30	7079.93	6074.18	5417.43	4959.80

Monthly Payments 16.50 %

LOAN AMOUNT	8	9	10	11	12	13	14
				YEARS			
100	1.85	1.75	1.67	1.61	1.56	1.52	1.49
200	3.70	3.50	3.35	3.22	3.13	3.05	2.98
500	9.25	8.75	8.36	8.06	7.82	7.62	7.46
1000	18.51	17.50	16.73	16.12	15.63	15.24	14.92
2000	37.01	35.00	33.45	32.23	31.26	30.48	29.84
5000	92.53	87.50	83.63	80.59	78.16	76.20	74.60
6000	111.03	105.01	100.36	96.70	93.79	91.44	89.53
7000	129.54	122.51	117.08	112.82	109.42	106.68	104.45
8000	148.04	140.01	133.81	128.94	125.06	121.92	119.37
9000	166.55	157.51	150.54	145.06	140.69	137.16	134.29
10000	185.05	175.01	167.26	161.17	156.32	152.40	149.21
12000	222.06	210.01	200.72	193.41	187.58	182.88	179.05
15000	277.58	262.51	250.89	241.76	234.48	228.60	223.81
20000	370.10	350.02	334.53	322.35	312.64	304.80	298.42
25000	462.63	437.52	418.16	402.94	390.80	381.00	373.02
30000	555.16	525.03	501.79	483.52	468.96	457.20	447.63
31000	573.66	542.53	518.52	499.64	484.59	472.44	462.55
32000	592.17	560.03	535.24	515.76	500.22	487.68	477.47
33000	610.67	577.53	551.97	531.88	515.85	502.92	492.39
34000	629.18	595.03	568.69	547.99	531.49	518.16	507.31
35000	647.68	612.53	585.42	564.11	547.12	533.40	522.23
36000	666.19	630.03	602.15	580.23	562.75	548.65	537.16
37000	684.69	647.53	618.87	596.35	578.38	563.89	552.08
38000	703.20	665.03	635.60	612.46	594.01	579.13	567.00
39000	721.70	682.54	652.33	628.58	609.65	594.37	581.92
40000	740.21	700.04	669.05	644.70	625.28	609.61	596.84
41000	758.71	717.54	685.78	660.82	640.91	624.85	611.76
42000	777.22	735.04	702.50	676.93	656.54	640.09	626.68
43000	795.72	752.54	719.23	693.05	672.17	655.33	641.60
44000	814.23	770.04	735.96	709.17	687.81	670.57	656.52
45000	832.73	787.54	752.68	725.29	703.44	685.81	671.44
46000	851.24	805.04	769.41	741.40	719.07	701.05	686.37
47000	869.74	822.54	786.14	757.52	734.70	716.29	701.29
48000	888.25	840.04	802.86	773.64	750.33	731.53	716.21
49000	906.75	857.55	819.59	789.76	765.97	746.77	731.13
50000	925.26	875.05	836.31	805.87	781.60	762.01	746.05
51000	943.76	892.55	853.04	821.99	797.23	777.25	760.97
52000	962.27	910.05	869.77	838.11	812.86	792.49	775.89
53000	980.77	927.55	886.49	854.23	828.49	807.73	790.81
54000	999.28	945.05	903.22	870.34	844.12	822.97	805.73
55000	1017.78	962.55	919.95	886.46	859.76	838.21	820.65
56000	1036.29	980.05	936.67	902.58	875.39	853.45	835.58
57000	1054.79	997.55	953.40	918.70	891.02	868.69	850.50
58000	1073.30	1015.05	970.12	934.81	906.65	883.93	865.42
59000	1091.81	1032.55	986.85	950.93	922.28	899.17	880.34
60000	1110.31	1050.06	1003.58	967.05	937.92	914.41	895.26
65000	1202.84	1137.56	1087.21	1047.64	1016.08	990.61	969.86
70000	1295.36	1225.06	1170.84	1128.22	1094.24	1066.81	1044.47
75000	1387.89	1312.57	1254.47	1208.81	1172.40	1143.01	1119.07
80000	1480.41	1400.07	1338.10	1289.40	1250.56	1219.21	1193.68
85000	1572.94	1487.58	1421.73	1369.99	1328.72	1295.41	1268.28
90000	1665.47	1575.08	1505.37	1450.57	1406.87	1371.61	1342.89
95000	1757.99	1662.59	1589.00	1531.16	1485.03	1447.81	1417.49
100000	1850.52	1750.09	1672.63	1611.75	1563.19	1524.01	1492.10
105000	1943.04	1837.60	1756.26	1692.34	1641.35	1600.21	1566.70
110000	2035.57	1925.10	1839.89	1772.92	1719.51	1676.42	1641.31
120000	2220.62	2100.11	2007.15	1934.10	1875.83	1828.82	1790.52
130000	2405.67	2275.12	2174.42	2095.27	2032.15	1981.22	1939.73
140000	2590.72	2450.13	2341.68	2256.45	2188.47	2133.62	2088.94
150000	2775.78	2625.14	2508.94	2417.62	2344.79	2286.02	2238.15
160000	2960.83	2800.15	2676.21	2578.80	2501.11	2438.42	2387.36
170000	3145.88	2975.16	2843.47	2739.97	2657.43	2590.82	2536.57
180000	3330.93	3150.17	3010.73	2901.15	2813.75	2743.23	2685.78
190000	3515.98	3325.17	3178.00	3062.32	2970.07	2895.63	2834.99
200000	3701.03	3500.18	3345.26	3223.50	3126.39	3048.03	2984.20
210000	3886.09	3675.19	3512.52	3384.67	3282.71	3200.43	3133.41
220000	4071.14	3850.20	3679.78	3545.85	3439.03	3352.83	3282.62
230000	4256.19	4025.21	3847.05	3707.02	3595.35	3505.23	3431.83
240000	4441.24	4200.22	4014.31	3868.20	3751.67	3657.63	3581.04
250000	4626.29	4375.23	4181.57	4029.37	3907.99	3810.03	3730.25

16.50 % Monthly Payments

LOAN AMOUNT	15	16	17	18	19	20	21
100	1.47	1.44	1.43	1.41	1.40	1.39	1.38
200	2.93	2.89	2.85	2.82	2.80	2.78	2.76
500	7.33	7.22	7.13	7.06	6.99	6.94	6.90
1000	14.66	14.44	14.26	14.11	13.99	13.88	13.79
2000	29.32	28.89	28.53	28.23	27.98	27.76	27.59
5000	73.30	72.21	71.31	70.57	69.94	69.41	68.97
6000	87.95	86.66	85.58	84.68	83.93	83.29	82.76
7000	102.61	101.10	99.84	98.79	97.91	97.18	96.56
8000	117.27	115.54	114.10	112.90	111.90	111.06	110.35
9000	131.93	129.98	128.37	127.02	125.89	124.94	124.14
10000	146.59	144.43	142.63	141.13	139.88	138.82	137.94
12000	175.91	173.31	171.16	169.36	167.85	166.59	165.53
15000	219.89	216.64	213.94	211.70	209.82	208.24	206.91
20000	293.18	288.85	285.26	282.26	279.75	277.65	275.88
25000	366.48	361.07	356.57	352.83	349.69	347.06	344.85
30000	439.77	433.28	427.89	423.39	419.63	416.47	413.82
31000	454.43	447.72	442.15	437.51	433.62	430.36	427.61
32000	469.09	462.16	456.41	451.62	447.61	444.24	441.40
33000	483.75	476.61	470.68	465.73	461.59	458.12	455.20
34000	498.41	491.05	484.94	479.85	475.58	472.00	468.99
35000	513.07	505.49	499.20	493.96	489.57	485.89	482.78
36000	527.72	519.93	513.47	508.07	503.56	499.77	496.58
37000	542.38	534.38	527.73	522.18	517.54	513.65	510.37
38000	557.04	548.82	541.99	536.30	531.53	527.53	524.17
39000	571.70	563.26	556.25	550.41	545.52	541.41	537.96
40000	586.36	577.70	570.52	564.52	559.51	555.30	551.75
41000	601.02	592.15	584.78	578.64	573.50	569.18	565.55
42000	615.68	606.59	599.04	592.75	587.48	583.06	579.34
43000	630.34	621.03	613.31	606.86	601.47	596.94	593.14
44000	645.00	635.48	627.57	620.98	615.46	610.83	606.93
45000	659.66	649.92	641.83	635.09	629.45	624.71	620.72
46000	674.31	664.36	656.10	649.20	643.43	638.59	634.52
47000	688.97	678.80	670.36	663.32	657.42	652.47	648.31
48000	703.63	693.25	684.62	677.43	671.41	666.36	662.10
49000	718.29	707.69	698.88	691.54	685.40	680.24	675.90
50000	732.95	722.13	713.15	705.66	699.39	694.12	689.69
51000	747.61	736.57	727.41	719.77	713.37	708.00	703.49
52000	762.27	751.02	741.67	733.88	727.36	721.89	717.28
53000	776.93	765.46	755.94	747.99	741.35	735.77	731.07
54000	791.59	779.90	770.20	762.11	755.34	749.65	744.87
55000	806.25	794.34	784.46	776.22	769.32	763.53	758.66
56000	820.90	808.79	798.72	790.33	783.31	777.42	772.46
57000	835.56	823.23	812.99	804.45	797.30	791.30	786.25
58000	850.22	837.67	827.25	818.56	811.29	805.18	800.04
59000	864.88	852.11	841.51	832.67	825.27	819.06	813.84
60000	879.54	866.56	855.78	846.79	839.26	832.95	827.63
65000	952.84	938.77	927.09	917.35	909.20	902.36	896.60
70000	1026.13	1010.98	998.41	987.92	979.14	971.77	965.57
75000	1099.43	1083.20	1069.72	1058.48	1049.08	1041.18	1034.54
80000	1172.72	1155.41	1141.04	1129.05	1119.02	1110.59	1103.51
85000	1246.02	1227.62	1212.35	1199.61	1188.95	1180.01	1172.48
90000	1319.31	1299.84	1283.66	1270.18	1258.89	1249.42	1241.45
95000	1392.61	1372.05	1354.98	1340.74	1328.83	1318.83	1310.42
100000	1465.90	1444.26	1426.29	1411.31	1398.77	1388.24	1379.38
105000	1539.20	1516.47	1497.61	1481.88	1468.71	1457.66	1448.35
110000	1612.49	1588.69	1568.92	1552.44	1538.65	1527.07	1517.32
120000	1759.08	1733.11	1711.55	1693.57	1678.52	1665.89	1655.26
130000	1905.67	1877.54	1854.18	1834.70	1818.40	1804.72	1793.20
140000	2052.26	2021.97	1996.81	1975.83	1958.28	1943.54	1931.14
150000	2198.85	2166.39	2139.44	2116.97	2098.16	2082.37	2069.08
160000	2345.44	2310.82	2282.07	2258.10	2238.03	2221.19	2207.02
170000	2492.03	2455.25	2424.70	2399.23	2377.91	2360.01	2344.95
180000	2638.62	2599.67	2567.33	2540.36	2517.79	2498.84	2482.89
190000	2785.21	2744.10	2709.96	2681.49	2657.66	2637.66	2620.83
200000	2931.80	2888.52	2852.59	2822.62	2797.54	2776.49	2758.77
210000	3078.39	3032.95	2995.22	2963.75	2937.42	2915.31	2896.71
220000	3224.98	3177.38	3137.85	3104.88	3077.29	3054.14	3034.65
230000	3371.57	3321.80	3280.48	3246.01	3217.17	3192.96	3172.59
240000	3518.16	3466.23	3423.11	3387.14	3357.05	3331.78	3310.52
250000	3664.75	3610.65	3565.73	3528.28	3496.93	3470.61	3448.46

16.75 % Monthly Payments

LOAN AMOUNT	1	2	3	4	5	6	7
			YEARS				
100	9.08	4.91	3.53	2.84	2.44	2.18	2.00
200	18.16	9.81	7.05	5.69	4.88	4.36	3.99
500	45.41	24.53	17.63	14.22	12.21	10.90	9.99
1000	90.82	49.06	35.25	28.44	24.42	21.80	19.97
2000	181.65	98.11	70.51	56.88	48.84	43.60	39.95
5000	454.11	245.28	176.26	142.20	122.11	108.99	99.86
6000	544.94	294.33	211.52	170.64	146.53	130.79	119.84
7000	635.76	343.39	246.77	199.08	170.95	152.59	139.81
8000	726.58	392.45	282.02	227.52	195.37	174.39	159.78
9000	817.40	441.50	317.27	255.96	219.79	196.19	179.75
10000	908.23	490.56	352.53	284.40	244.21	217.99	199.73
12000	1089.87	588.67	423.03	341.28	293.05	261.58	239.67
15000	1362.34	735.84	528.79	426.59	366.32	326.98	299.59
20000	1816.45	981.11	705.06	568.79	488.42	435.97	399.45
25000	2270.56	1226.39	881.32	710.99	610.53	544.97	499.31
30000	2724.68	1471.67	1057.58	853.19	732.63	653.96	599.18
31000	2815.50	1520.73	1092.84	881.63	757.05	675.76	619.15
32000	2906.32	1569.78	1128.09	910.07	781.48	697.56	639.12
33000	2997.14	1618.84	1163.34	938.51	805.90	719.36	659.09
34000	3087.97	1667.89	1198.59	966.95	830.32	741.15	679.07
35000	3178.79	1716.95	1233.85	995.39	854.74	762.95	699.04
36000	3269.61	1766.01	1269.10	1023.83	879.16	784.75	719.01
37000	3360.43	1815.06	1304.35	1052.27	903.58	806.55	738.98
38000	3451.26	1864.12	1339.60	1080.70	928.00	828.35	758.96
39000	3542.08	1913.17	1374.86	1109.14	952.42	850.15	778.93
40000	3632.90	1962.23	1410.11	1137.58	976.84	871.95	798.90
41000	3723.73	2011.29	1445.36	1166.02	1001.27	893.74	818.88
42000	3814.55	2060.34	1480.62	1194.46	1025.69	915.54	838.85
43000	3905.37	2109.40	1515.87	1222.90	1050.11	937.34	858.82
44000	3996.19	2158.45	1551.12	1251.34	1074.53	959.14	878.79
45000	4087.02	2207.51	1586.37	1279.78	1098.95	980.94	898.77
46000	4177.84	2256.56	1621.63	1308.22	1123.37	1002.74	918.74
47000	4268.66	2305.62	1656.88	1336.66	1147.79	1024.54	938.71
48000	4359.48	2354.68	1692.13	1365.10	1172.21	1046.34	958.68
49000	4450.31	2403.73	1727.39	1393.54	1196.63	1068.13	978.66
50000	4541.13	2452.79	1762.64	1421.98	1221.06	1089.93	998.63
51000	4631.95	2501.84	1797.89	1450.42	1245.48	1111.73	1018.60
52000	4722.77	2550.90	1833.14	1478.86	1269.90	1133.53	1038.57
53000	4813.60	2599.95	1868.40	1507.30	1294.32	1155.33	1058.55
54000	4904.42	2649.01	1903.65	1535.74	1318.74	1177.13	1078.52
55000	4995.24	2698.07	1938.90	1564.18	1343.16	1198.93	1098.49
56000	5086.06	2747.12	1974.15	1592.62	1367.58	1220.72	1118.46
57000	5176.89	2796.18	2009.41	1621.06	1392.00	1242.52	1138.44
58000	5267.71	2845.23	2044.66	1649.50	1416.42	1264.32	1158.41
59000	5358.53	2894.29	2079.91	1677.94	1440.85	1286.12	1178.38
60000	5449.35	2943.34	2115.17	1706.38	1465.27	1307.92	1198.35
65000	5903.47	3188.62	2291.43	1848.57	1587.37	1416.91	1298.22
70000	6357.58	3433.90	2467.69	1990.77	1709.48	1525.91	1398.08
75000	6811.69	3679.18	2643.96	2132.97	1831.58	1634.90	1497.94
80000	7265.81	3924.46	2820.22	2275.17	1953.69	1743.89	1597.81
85000	7719.92	4169.74	2996.48	2417.37	2075.80	1852.89	1697.67
90000	8174.03	4415.02	3172.75	2559.56	2197.90	1961.88	1797.53
95000	8628.14	4660.29	3349.01	2701.76	2320.01	2070.87	1897.39
100000	9082.26	4905.57	3525.28	2843.96	2442.11	2179.87	1997.26
105000	9536.37	5150.85	3701.54	2986.16	2564.22	2288.86	2097.12
110000	9990.48	5396.13	3877.80	3128.36	2686.32	2397.85	2196.98
120000	10898.71	5886.69	4230.33	3412.75	2930.53	2615.84	2396.71
130000	11806.93	6377.25	4582.86	3697.15	3174.75	2833.82	2596.43
140000	12715.16	6867.80	4935.39	3981.54	3418.96	3051.81	2796.16
150000	13623.38	7358.36	5287.91	4265.94	3663.17	3269.80	2995.89
160000	14531.61	7848.92	5640.44	4550.34	3907.38	3487.78	3195.61
170000	15439.84	8339.47	5992.97	4834.73	4151.59	3705.77	3395.34
180000	16348.06	8830.03	6345.50	5119.13	4395.80	3923.76	3595.06
190000	17256.29	9320.59	6698.02	5403.52	4640.01	4141.74	3794.79
200000	18164.51	9811.15	7050.55	5687.92	4884.22	4359.73	3994.51
210000	19072.74	10301.70	7403.08	5972.32	5128.43	4577.72	4194.24
220000	19980.96	10792.26	7755.61	6256.71	5372.65	4795.70	4393.96
230000	20889.19	11282.82	8108.13	6541.11	5616.86	5013.69	4593.69
240000	21797.42	11773.38	8460.66	6825.51	5861.07	5231.68	4793.42
250000	22705.64	12263.93	8813.19	7109.90	6105.28	5449.66	4993.14

Monthly Payments 16.75 %

LOAN AMOUNT	8	9	10	11	12	13	14
				YEARS			
100	1.86	1.76	1.69	1.63	1.58	1.54	1.51
200	3.73	3.53	3.37	3.25	3.16	3.08	3.02
500	9.32	8.82	8.44	8.13	7.89	7.70	7.54
1000	18.64	17.64	16.87	16.27	15.79	15.40	15.08
2000	37.29	35.29	33.74	32.53	31.57	30.79	30.16
5000	93.21	88.21	84.36	81.34	78.93	76.99	75.41
6000	111.86	105.86	101.23	97.60	94.71	92.38	90.49
7000	130.50	123.50	118.11	113.87	110.50	107.78	105.57
8000	149.14	141.14	134.98	130.14	126.28	123.18	120.65
9000	167.79	158.79	151.85	146.41	142.07	138.57	135.73
10000	186.43	176.43	168.72	162.67	157.85	153.97	150.81
12000	223.71	211.71	202.47	195.21	189.43	184.77	180.97
15000	279.64	264.64	253.08	244.01	236.78	230.96	226.22
20000	372.86	352.86	337.44	325.35	315.71	307.94	301.62
25000	466.07	441.07	421.81	406.68	394.64	384.93	377.03
30000	559.29	529.29	506.17	488.02	473.56	461.91	452.44
31000	577.93	546.93	523.04	504.29	489.35	477.31	467.52
32000	596.57	564.57	539.91	520.55	505.13	492.71	482.60
33000	615.22	582.21	556.78	536.82	520.92	508.10	497.68
34000	633.86	599.86	573.66	553.09	536.70	523.50	512.76
35000	652.50	617.50	590.53	569.36	552.49	538.90	527.84
36000	671.14	635.14	607.40	585.62	568.28	554.30	542.92
37000	689.79	652.79	624.27	601.89	584.06	569.69	558.01
38000	708.43	670.43	641.15	618.16	599.85	585.09	573.09
39000	727.07	688.07	658.02	634.43	615.63	600.49	588.17
40000	745.72	705.71	674.89	650.69	631.42	615.88	603.25
41000	764.36	723.36	691.76	666.96	647.20	631.28	618.33
42000	783.00	741.00	708.63	683.23	662.99	646.68	633.41
43000	801.64	758.64	725.51	699.49	678.77	662.08	648.49
44000	820.29	776.28	742.38	715.76	694.56	677.47	663.57
45000	838.93	793.93	759.25	732.03	710.34	692.87	678.65
46000	857.57	811.57	776.12	748.30	726.13	708.27	693.74
47000	876.22	829.21	793.00	764.56	741.92	723.66	708.82
48000	894.86	846.86	809.87	780.83	757.70	739.06	723.90
49000	913.50	864.50	826.74	797.10	773.49	754.46	738.98
50000	932.14	882.14	843.61	813.37	789.27	769.85	754.06
51000	950.79	899.78	860.48	829.63	805.06	785.25	769.14
52000	969.43	917.43	877.36	845.90	820.84	800.65	784.22
53000	988.07	935.07	894.23	862.17	836.63	816.05	799.30
54000	1006.72	952.71	911.10	878.43	852.41	831.44	814.39
55000	1025.36	970.36	927.97	894.70	868.20	846.84	829.47
56000	1044.00	988.00	944.85	910.97	883.98	862.24	844.55
57000	1062.64	1005.64	961.72	927.24	899.77	877.63	859.63
58000	1081.29	1023.28	978.59	943.50	915.55	893.03	874.71
59000	1099.93	1040.93	995.46	959.77	931.34	908.43	889.79
60000	1118.57	1058.57	1012.33	976.04	947.13	923.83	904.87
65000	1211.79	1146.78	1096.70	1057.38	1026.05	1000.81	980.28
70000	1305.00	1235.00	1181.06	1138.71	1104.98	1077.80	1055.69
75000	1398.22	1323.21	1265.42	1220.05	1183.91	1154.78	1131.09
80000	1491.43	1411.43	1349.78	1301.38	1262.83	1231.77	1206.50
85000	1584.65	1499.64	1434.14	1382.72	1341.76	1308.75	1281.90
90000	1677.86	1587.86	1518.50	1464.06	1420.69	1385.74	1357.31
95000	1771.07	1676.07	1602.86	1545.39	1499.62	1462.72	1432.72
100000	1864.29	1764.28	1687.22	1626.73	1578.54	1539.71	1508.12
105000	1957.50	1852.50	1771.59	1708.07	1657.47	1616.70	1583.53
110000	2050.72	1940.71	1855.95	1789.40	1736.40	1693.68	1658.93
120000	2237.15	2117.14	2024.67	1952.08	1894.25	1847.65	1809.75
130000	2423.58	2293.57	2193.39	2114.75	2052.11	2001.62	1960.56
140000	2610.00	2470.00	2362.11	2277.42	2209.96	2155.59	2111.37
150000	2796.43	2646.43	2530.84	2440.10	2367.81	2309.56	2262.18
160000	2982.86	2822.85	2699.56	2602.77	2525.67	2463.54	2412.99
170000	3169.29	2999.28	2868.28	2765.44	2683.52	2617.51	2563.81
180000	3355.72	3175.71	3037.00	2928.12	2841.38	2771.48	2714.62
190000	3542.15	3352.14	3205.73	3090.79	2999.23	2925.45	2865.43
200000	3728.58	3528.57	3374.45	3253.46	3157.09	3079.42	3016.24
210000	3915.01	3705.00	3543.17	3416.13	3314.94	3233.39	3167.06
220000	4101.44	3881.42	3711.89	3578.81	3472.79	3387.36	3317.87
230000	4287.87	4057.85	3880.62	3741.48	3630.65	3541.33	3468.68
240000	4474.29	4234.28	4049.34	3904.15	3788.50	3695.30	3619.49
250000	4660.72	4410.71	4218.06	4066.83	3946.36	3849.27	3770.30

16.75 % Monthly Payments

LOAN AMOUNT	15	16	17	18	19	20	21
				YEARS			
100	1.48	1.46	1.44	1.43	1.42	1.41	1.40
200	2.96	2.92	2.89	2.86	2.83	2.81	2.79
500	7.41	7.30	7.22	7.14	7.08	7.03	6.99
1000	14.82	14.61	14.43	14.28	14.16	14.06	13.97
2000	29.64	29.22	28.86	28.57	28.32	28.12	27.94
5000	74.11	73.04	72.16	71.42	70.81	70.29	69.86
6000	88.93	87.65	86.59	85.71	84.97	84.35	83.83
7000	103.76	102.26	101.02	99.99	99.13	98.41	97.80
8000	118.58	116.87	115.45	114.28	113.29	112.46	111.77
9000	133.40	131.48	129.89	128.56	127.45	126.52	125.74
10000	148.22	146.09	144.32	142.84	141.61	140.58	139.71
12000	177.87	175.31	173.18	171.41	169.94	168.70	167.66
15000	222.33	219.13	216.48	214.27	212.42	210.87	209.57
20000	296.45	292.18	288.64	285.69	283.23	281.16	279.43
25000	370.56	365.22	360.79	357.11	354.03	351.45	349.29
30000	444.67	438.26	432.95	428.53	424.84	421.74	419.14
31000	459.49	452.87	447.38	442.82	439.00	435.80	433.12
32000	474.31	467.48	461.82	457.10	453.16	449.86	447.09
33000	489.14	482.09	476.25	471.39	467.32	463.92	461.06
34000	503.96	496.70	490.68	485.67	481.48	477.98	475.03
35000	518.78	511.31	505.11	499.95	495.64	492.03	489.00
36000	533.60	525.92	519.54	514.24	509.81	506.09	502.97
37000	548.43	540.52	533.98	528.52	523.97	520.15	516.94
38000	563.25	555.13	548.41	542.81	538.13	534.21	530.92
39000	578.07	569.74	562.84	557.09	552.29	548.27	544.89
40000	592.89	584.35	577.27	571.38	566.45	562.32	558.86
41000	607.71	598.96	591.70	585.66	580.61	576.38	572.83
42000	622.54	613.57	606.13	599.94	594.77	590.44	586.80
43000	637.36	628.18	620.57	614.23	608.94	604.50	600.77
44000	652.18	642.79	635.00	628.51	623.10	618.56	614.74
45000	667.00	657.40	649.43	642.80	637.26	632.62	628.72
46000	681.83	672.00	663.86	657.08	651.42	646.67	642.69
47000	696.65	686.61	678.29	671.37	665.58	660.73	656.66
48000	711.47	701.22	692.72	685.65	679.74	674.79	670.63
49000	726.29	715.83	707.16	699.94	693.90	688.85	684.60
50000	741.12	730.44	721.59	714.22	708.06	702.91	698.57
51000	755.94	745.05	736.02	728.50	722.23	716.96	712.54
52000	770.76	759.66	750.45	742.79	736.39	731.02	726.52
53000	785.58	774.27	764.88	757.07	750.55	745.08	740.49
54000	800.40	788.87	779.32	771.36	764.71	759.14	754.46
55000	815.23	803.48	793.75	785.64	778.87	773.20	768.43
56000	830.05	818.09	808.18	799.93	793.03	787.25	782.40
57000	844.87	832.70	822.61	814.21	807.19	801.31	796.37
58000	859.69	847.31	837.04	828.50	821.35	815.37	810.34
59000	874.52	861.92	851.47	842.78	835.52	829.43	824.32
60000	889.34	876.53	865.91	857.06	849.68	843.49	838.29
65000	963.45	949.57	938.06	928.49	920.48	913.78	908.14
70000	1037.56	1022.61	1010.22	999.91	991.29	984.07	978.00
75000	1111.67	1095.66	1082.38	1071.33	1062.10	1054.36	1047.86
80000	1185.78	1168.70	1154.54	1142.75	1132.90	1124.65	1117.72
85000	1259.90	1241.75	1226.70	1214.17	1203.71	1194.94	1187.57
90000	1334.01	1314.79	1298.86	1285.60	1274.52	1265.23	1257.43
95000	1408.12	1387.83	1371.02	1357.02	1345.32	1335.52	1327.29
100000	1482.23	1460.88	1443.18	1428.44	1416.13	1405.81	1397.15
105000	1556.34	1533.92	1515.34	1499.86	1486.93	1476.10	1467.00
110000	1630.45	1606.97	1587.49	1571.28	1557.74	1546.39	1536.86
120000	1778.68	1753.05	1731.81	1714.13	1699.35	1686.97	1676.57
130000	1926.90	1899.14	1876.13	1856.97	1840.97	1827.55	1816.29
140000	2075.12	2045.23	2020.45	1999.82	1982.58	1968.14	1956.00
150000	2223.35	2191.32	2164.76	2142.66	2124.19	2108.72	2095.72
160000	2371.57	2337.40	2309.08	2285.50	2265.80	2249.30	2235.43
170000	2519.79	2483.49	2453.40	2428.35	2407.42	2389.88	2375.15
180000	2668.02	2629.58	2597.72	2571.19	2549.03	2530.46	2514.86
190000	2816.24	2775.67	2742.04	2714.04	2690.64	2671.04	2654.58
200000	2964.46	2921.76	2886.35	2856.88	2832.26	2811.62	2794.29
210000	3112.69	3067.84	3030.67	2999.72	2973.87	2952.20	2934.01
220000	3260.91	3213.93	3174.99	3142.57	3115.48	3092.79	3073.72
230000	3409.13	3360.02	3319.31	3285.41	3257.09	3233.37	3213.43
240000	3557.35	3506.11	3463.62	3428.26	3398.71	3373.95	3353.15
250000	3705.58	3652.19	3607.94	3571.10	3540.32	3514.53	3492.86

Monthly Payments 16.75 %

LOAN AMOUNT	22	23	24	25	30	35	40
				YEARS			
100	1.39	1.38	1.38	1.37	1.36	1.35	1.35
200	2.78	2.77	2.76	2.75	2.72	2.71	2.70
500	6.95	6.92	6.89	6.87	6.80	6.77	6.76
1000	13.90	13.84	13.79	13.74	13.60	13.54	13.52
2000	27.80	27.67	27.57	27.48	27.21	27.09	27.03
5000	69.49	69.19	68.93	68.71	68.02	67.72	67.58
6000	83.39	83.02	82.71	82.45	81.62	81.26	81.10
7000	97.29	96.86	96.50	96.19	95.23	94.80	94.62
8000	111.19	110.70	110.28	109.93	108.83	108.35	108.13
9000	125.09	124.53	124.07	123.67	122.44	121.89	121.65
10000	138.99	138.37	137.85	137.41	136.04	135.43	135.16
12000	166.78	166.04	165.42	164.89	163.25	162.52	162.20
15000	208.48	207.56	206.78	206.12	204.06	203.15	202.75
20000	277.97	276.74	275.70	274.82	272.08	270.87	270.33
25000	347.46	345.93	344.63	343.53	340.10	338.58	337.91
30000	416.96	415.11	413.55	412.23	408.12	406.30	405.49
31000	430.85	428.95	427.34	425.98	421.72	419.85	419.01
32000	444.75	442.78	441.12	439.72	435.33	433.39	432.53
33000	458.65	456.62	454.91	453.46	448.93	446.93	446.04
34000	472.55	470.46	468.69	467.20	462.53	460.48	459.56
35000	486.45	484.30	482.48	480.94	476.14	474.02	473.08
36000	500.35	498.13	496.26	494.68	489.74	487.56	486.59
37000	514.24	511.97	510.05	508.42	503.34	501.11	500.11
38000	528.14	525.81	523.83	522.16	516.95	514.65	513.63
39000	542.04	539.64	537.62	535.90	530.55	528.19	527.14
40000	555.94	553.48	551.40	549.65	544.16	541.74	540.66
41000	569.84	567.32	565.19	563.39	557.76	555.28	554.18
42000	583.74	581.15	578.97	577.13	571.36	568.82	567.69
43000	597.64	594.99	592.76	590.87	584.97	582.37	581.21
44000	611.53	608.83	606.54	604.61	598.57	595.91	594.73
45000	625.43	622.67	620.33	618.35	612.18	609.45	608.24
46000	639.33	636.50	634.11	632.09	625.78	623.00	621.76
47000	653.23	650.34	647.90	645.83	639.38	636.54	635.27
48000	667.13	664.18	661.68	659.57	652.99	650.08	648.79
49000	681.03	678.01	675.47	673.32	666.59	663.63	662.31
50000	694.93	691.85	689.25	687.06	680.20	677.17	675.82
51000	708.82	705.69	703.04	700.80	693.80	690.71	689.34
52000	722.72	719.52	716.82	714.54	707.40	704.26	702.86
53000	736.62	733.36	730.61	728.28	721.01	717.80	716.37
54000	750.52	747.20	744.39	742.02	734.61	731.34	729.89
55000	764.42	761.04	758.18	755.76	748.21	744.89	743.41
56000	778.32	774.87	771.96	769.50	761.82	758.43	756.92
57000	792.22	788.71	785.75	783.25	775.42	771.97	770.44
58000	806.11	802.55	799.53	796.99	789.03	785.52	783.96
59000	820.01	816.38	813.32	810.73	802.63	799.06	797.47
60000	833.91	830.22	827.10	824.47	816.23	812.60	810.99
65000	903.40	899.41	896.03	893.17	884.25	880.32	878.57
70000	972.90	968.59	964.95	961.88	952.27	948.04	946.15
75000	1042.39	1037.78	1033.88	1030.59	1020.29	1015.75	1013.74
80000	1111.88	1106.96	1102.80	1099.29	1088.31	1083.47	1081.32
85000	1181.37	1176.15	1171.73	1168.00	1156.33	1151.19	1148.90
90000	1250.87	1245.33	1240.66	1236.70	1224.35	1218.91	1216.48
95000	1320.36	1314.52	1309.58	1305.41	1292.37	1286.62	1284.07
100000	1389.85	1383.70	1378.51	1374.11	1360.39	1354.34	1351.65
105000	1459.34	1452.89	1447.43	1442.82	1428.41	1422.06	1419.23
110000	1528.84	1522.07	1516.36	1511.53	1496.43	1489.77	1486.81
120000	1667.82	1660.44	1654.21	1648.94	1632.47	1625.21	1621.98
130000	1806.81	1798.81	1792.06	1786.35	1768.51	1760.64	1757.14
140000	1945.79	1937.18	1929.91	1923.76	1904.55	1896.07	1892.31
150000	2084.78	2075.55	2067.76	2061.17	2040.59	2031.51	2027.47
160000	2223.76	2213.92	2205.61	2198.58	2176.63	2166.94	2162.64
170000	2362.75	2352.29	2343.46	2335.99	2312.66	2302.38	2297.80
180000	2501.73	2490.66	2481.31	2473.41	2448.70	2437.81	2432.97
190000	2640.72	2629.03	2619.16	2610.82	2584.74	2573.24	2568.13
200000	2779.70	2767.40	2757.01	2748.23	2720.78	2708.68	2703.30
210000	2918.69	2905.77	2894.86	2885.64	2856.82	2844.11	2838.46
220000	3057.67	3044.14	3032.71	3023.05	2992.86	2979.55	2973.63
230000	3196.66	3182.51	3170.56	3160.46	3128.90	3114.98	3108.79
240000	3335.64	3320.88	3308.41	3297.87	3264.94	3250.41	3243.96
250000	3474.63	3459.25	3446.27	3435.29	3400.98	3385.85	3379.12

17.00 % Monthly Payments

LOAN AMOUNT	1	2	3	4	5	6	7
				YEARS			
100	9.09	4.92	3.54	2.86	2.45	2.19	2.01
200	18.19	9.83	7.07	5.71	4.91	4.39	4.02
500	45.47	24.58	17.68	14.28	12.27	10.96	10.05
1000	90.93	49.17	35.37	28.56	24.55	21.93	20.11
2000	181.87	98.34	70.74	57.12	49.09	43.86	40.21
5000	454.67	245.84	176.84	142.80	122.73	109.64	100.53
6000	545.60	295.01	212.21	171.36	147.27	131.57	120.64
7000	636.53	344.17	247.58	199.92	171.82	153.49	140.74
8000	727.47	393.34	282.95	228.48	196.37	175.42	160.85
9000	818.40	442.51	318.32	257.04	220.91	197.35	180.96
10000	909.33	491.68	353.68	285.60	245.46	219.28	201.06
12000	1091.20	590.01	424.42	342.72	294.55	263.13	241.28
15000	1364.00	737.51	530.53	428.39	368.19	328.92	301.59
20000	1818.66	983.35	707.37	571.19	490.91	438.56	402.13
25000	2273.33	1229.19	884.21	713.99	613.64	548.20	502.66
30000	2728.00	1475.03	1061.05	856.79	736.37	657.84	603.19
31000	2818.93	1524.20	1096.42	885.35	760.92	679.76	623.29
32000	2909.86	1573.36	1131.79	913.91	785.46	701.69	643.40
33000	3000.80	1622.53	1167.16	942.47	810.01	723.62	663.51
34000	3091.73	1671.70	1202.53	971.03	834.56	745.55	683.61
35000	3182.66	1720.87	1237.89	999.59	859.10	767.47	703.72
36000	3273.60	1770.03	1273.26	1028.15	883.65	789.40	723.83
37000	3364.53	1819.20	1308.63	1056.71	908.19	811.33	743.93
38000	3455.46	1868.37	1344.00	1085.27	932.74	833.26	764.04
39000	3546.40	1917.54	1379.37	1113.83	957.28	855.19	784.14
40000	3637.33	1966.70	1414.74	1142.39	981.83	877.11	804.25
41000	3728.26	2015.87	1450.11	1170.95	1006.38	899.04	824.36
42000	3819.20	2065.04	1485.47	1199.51	1030.92	920.97	844.46
43000	3910.13	2114.21	1520.84	1228.07	1055.47	942.90	864.57
44000	4001.06	2163.37	1556.21	1256.63	1080.01	964.83	884.68
45000	4092.00	2212.54	1591.58	1285.18	1104.56	986.75	904.78
46000	4182.93	2261.71	1626.95	1313.74	1129.10	1008.68	924.89
47000	4273.86	2310.88	1662.32	1342.30	1153.65	1030.61	944.99
48000	4364.80	2360.04	1697.68	1370.86	1178.20	1052.54	965.10
49000	4455.73	2409.21	1733.05	1399.42	1202.74	1074.46	985.21
50000	4546.66	2458.38	1768.42	1427.98	1227.29	1096.39	1005.31
51000	4637.60	2507.55	1803.79	1456.54	1251.83	1118.32	1025.42
52000	4728.53	2556.71	1839.16	1485.10	1276.38	1140.25	1045.53
53000	4819.46	2605.88	1874.53	1513.66	1300.92	1162.18	1065.63
54000	4910.40	2655.05	1909.89	1542.22	1325.47	1184.10	1085.74
55000	5001.33	2704.22	1945.26	1570.78	1350.02	1206.03	1105.84
56000	5092.26	2753.38	1980.63	1599.34	1374.56	1227.96	1125.95
57000	5183.20	2802.55	2016.00	1627.90	1399.11	1249.89	1146.06
58000	5274.13	2851.72	2051.37	1656.46	1423.65	1271.82	1166.16
59000	5365.06	2900.89	2086.74	1685.02	1448.20	1293.74	1186.27
60000	5455.99	2950.05	2122.11	1713.58	1472.74	1315.67	1206.38
65000	5910.66	3195.89	2298.95	1856.38	1595.47	1425.31	1306.91
70000	6365.33	3441.73	2475.79	1999.18	1718.20	1534.95	1407.44
75000	6819.99	3687.57	2652.63	2141.97	1840.93	1644.59	1507.97
80000	7274.66	3933.41	2829.47	2284.77	1963.66	1754.23	1608.50
85000	7729.33	4179.24	3006.32	2427.57	2086.39	1863.87	1709.03
90000	8183.99	4425.08	3183.16	2570.37	2209.12	1973.51	1809.56
95000	8638.66	4670.92	3360.00	2713.17	2331.85	2083.15	1910.10
100000	9093.32	4916.76	3536.84	2855.97	2454.57	2192.78	2010.63
105000	9547.99	5162.60	3713.68	2998.76	2577.30	2302.42	2111.16
110000	10002.66	5408.43	3890.53	3141.56	2700.03	2412.06	2211.69
120000	10911.99	5900.11	4244.21	3427.16	2945.49	2631.34	2412.75
130000	11821.32	6391.79	4597.89	3712.76	3190.95	2850.62	2613.82
140000	12730.65	6883.46	4951.58	3998.35	3436.40	3069.90	2814.88
150000	13639.99	7375.14	5305.26	4283.95	3681.86	3289.18	3015.94
160000	14549.32	7866.81	5658.95	4569.55	3927.32	3508.46	3217.00
170000	15458.65	8358.49	6012.63	4855.14	4172.78	3727.73	3418.07
180000	16367.98	8850.16	6366.32	5140.74	4418.23	3947.01	3619.13
190000	17277.32	9341.84	6720.00	5426.34	4663.69	4166.29	3820.19
200000	18186.65	9833.52	7073.68	5711.93	4909.15	4385.57	4021.25
210000	19095.98	10325.19	7427.37	5997.53	5154.61	4604.85	4222.32
220000	20005.31	10816.87	7781.05	6283.13	5400.06	4824.13	4423.38
230000	20914.65	11308.54	8134.74	6568.72	5645.52	5043.41	4624.44
240000	21823.98	11800.22	8488.42	6854.32	5890.98	5262.68	4825.50
250000	22733.31	12291.90	8842.10	7139.92	6136.44	5481.96	5026.57

Monthly Payments 17.00 %

LOAN AMOUNT	YEARS 8	9	10	11	12	13	14
100	1.88	1.78	1.70	1.64	1.59	1.56	1.52
200	3.76	3.56	3.40	3.28	3.19	3.11	3.05
500	9.39	8.89	8.51	8.21	7.97	7.78	7.62
1000	18.78	17.79	17.02	16.42	15.94	15.55	15.24
2000	37.56	35.57	34.04	32.84	31.88	31.11	30.48
5000	93.90	88.93	85.09	82.09	79.70	77.77	76.21
6000	112.69	106.71	102.11	98.51	95.64	93.33	91.45
7000	131.47	124.50	119.13	114.92	111.58	108.88	106.69
8000	150.25	142.28	136.15	131.34	127.52	124.44	121.94
9000	169.03	160.07	153.17	147.76	143.45	139.99	137.18
10000	187.81	177.85	170.19	164.18	159.39	155.55	152.42
12000	225.37	213.42	204.22	197.01	191.27	186.65	182.90
15000	281.71	266.78	255.28	246.26	239.09	233.32	228.63
20000	375.62	355.70	340.37	328.35	318.79	311.09	304.84
25000	469.52	444.63	425.47	410.44	398.48	388.86	381.05
30000	563.43	533.56	510.56	492.53	478.18	466.64	457.26
31000	582.21	551.34	527.58	508.95	494.12	482.19	472.50
32000	600.99	569.13	544.60	525.36	510.06	497.75	487.74
33000	619.77	586.91	561.62	541.78	526.00	513.30	502.98
34000	638.55	604.70	578.63	558.20	541.94	528.85	518.23
35000	657.33	622.48	595.65	574.62	557.88	544.41	533.47
36000	676.12	640.27	612.67	591.03	573.82	559.96	548.71
37000	694.90	658.05	629.69	607.45	589.76	575.52	563.95
38000	713.68	675.84	646.71	623.87	605.70	591.07	579.19
39000	732.46	693.62	663.73	640.29	621.64	606.63	594.44
40000	751.24	711.41	680.75	656.70	637.58	622.18	609.68
41000	770.02	729.19	697.76	673.12	653.52	637.74	624.92
42000	788.80	746.98	714.78	689.54	669.45	653.29	640.16
43000	807.58	764.76	731.80	705.96	685.39	668.85	655.40
44000	826.36	782.55	748.82	722.37	701.33	684.40	670.65
45000	845.14	800.33	765.84	738.79	717.27	699.95	685.89
46000	863.93	818.12	782.86	755.21	733.21	715.51	701.13
47000	882.71	835.90	799.88	771.63	749.15	731.06	716.37
48000	901.49	853.69	816.89	788.04	765.09	746.62	731.61
49000	920.27	871.47	833.91	804.46	781.03	762.17	746.85
50000	939.05	889.26	850.93	820.88	796.97	777.73	762.10
51000	957.83	907.04	867.95	837.30	812.91	793.28	777.34
52000	976.61	924.83	884.97	853.71	828.85	808.84	792.58
53000	995.39	942.61	901.99	870.13	844.79	824.39	807.82
54000	1014.17	960.40	919.01	886.55	860.73	839.95	823.06
55000	1032.95	978.18	936.03	902.97	876.67	855.50	838.31
56000	1051.73	995.97	953.04	919.38	892.61	871.05	853.55
57000	1070.52	1013.75	970.06	935.80	908.55	886.61	868.79
58000	1089.30	1031.54	987.08	952.22	924.48	902.16	884.03
59000	1108.08	1049.32	1004.10	968.64	940.42	917.72	899.27
60000	1126.86	1067.11	1021.12	985.06	956.36	933.27	914.52
65000	1220.76	1156.04	1106.21	1067.14	1036.06	1011.05	990.73
70000	1314.67	1244.96	1191.31	1149.23	1115.76	1088.82	1066.94
75000	1408.57	1333.89	1276.40	1231.32	1195.45	1166.59	1143.14
80000	1502.48	1422.81	1361.49	1313.41	1275.15	1244.36	1219.35
85000	1596.38	1511.74	1446.58	1395.49	1354.85	1322.14	1295.56
90000	1690.29	1600.67	1531.68	1477.58	1434.55	1399.91	1371.77
95000	1784.19	1689.59	1616.77	1559.67	1514.24	1477.68	1447.98
100000	1878.10	1778.52	1701.86	1641.76	1593.94	1555.45	1524.19
105000	1972.00	1867.44	1786.96	1723.85	1673.64	1633.23	1600.40
110000	2065.91	1956.37	1872.05	1805.93	1753.33	1711.00	1676.61
120000	2253.72	2134.22	2042.24	1970.11	1912.73	1866.55	1829.03
130000	2441.53	2312.07	2212.42	2134.29	2072.12	2022.09	1981.45
140000	2629.34	2489.92	2382.61	2298.46	2231.51	2177.64	2133.87
150000	2817.15	2667.78	2552.80	2462.64	2390.91	2333.18	2286.29
160000	3004.96	2845.63	2722.98	2626.81	2550.30	2488.73	2438.71
170000	3192.77	3023.48	2893.17	2790.99	2709.70	2644.27	2591.13
180000	3380.58	3201.33	3063.36	2955.17	2869.09	2799.82	2743.55
190000	3568.39	3379.18	3233.54	3119.34	3028.48	2955.36	2895.97
200000	3756.20	3557.03	3403.73	3283.52	3187.88	3110.91	3048.39
210000	3944.01	3734.89	3573.92	3447.69	3347.27	3266.45	3200.81
220000	4131.82	3912.74	3744.10	3611.87	3506.67	3422.00	3353.23
230000	4319.63	4090.59	3914.29	3776.04	3666.06	3577.54	3505.64
240000	4507.44	4268.44	4084.47	3940.22	3825.45	3733.09	3658.06
250000	4695.25	4446.29	4254.66	4104.40	3984.85	3888.64	3810.48

17.00 % Monthly Payments

LOAN AMOUNT	15	16	17	18	19	20	21
100	1.50	1.48	1.46	1.45	1.43	1.42	1.41
200	3.00	2.96	2.92	2.89	2.87	2.85	2.83
500	7.49	7.39	7.30	7.23	7.17	7.12	7.07
1000	14.99	14.78	14.60	14.46	14.34	14.23	14.15
2000	29.97	29.55	29.20	28.91	28.67	28.47	28.30
5000	74.93	73.88	73.01	72.28	71.68	71.17	70.75
6000	89.92	88.65	87.61	86.74	86.01	85.41	84.90
7000	104.90	103.43	102.21	101.19	100.35	99.64	99.05
8000	119.89	118.20	116.81	115.65	114.68	113.87	113.20
9000	134.87	132.98	131.41	130.11	129.02	128.11	127.35
10000	149.86	147.75	146.01	144.56	143.35	142.34	141.49
12000	179.83	177.30	175.21	173.47	172.02	170.81	169.79
15000	224.79	221.63	219.02	216.84	215.03	213.51	212.24
20000	299.72	295.51	292.02	289.12	286.71	284.68	282.99
25000	374.65	369.39	365.03	361.40	358.38	355.86	353.74
30000	449.58	443.26	438.03	433.68	430.06	427.03	424.48
31000	464.57	458.04	452.63	448.14	444.39	441.26	438.63
32000	479.55	472.81	467.23	462.60	458.73	455.49	452.78
33000	494.54	487.59	481.83	477.05	473.06	469.73	466.93
34000	509.53	502.36	496.44	491.51	487.40	483.96	481.08
35000	524.51	517.14	511.04	505.96	501.74	498.20	495.23
36000	539.50	531.91	525.64	520.42	516.07	512.43	509.38
37000	554.49	546.69	540.24	534.88	530.41	526.67	523.53
38000	569.47	561.47	554.84	549.33	544.74	540.90	537.68
39000	584.46	576.24	569.44	563.79	559.08	555.13	551.83
40000	599.44	591.02	584.04	578.25	573.41	569.37	565.98
41000	614.43	605.79	598.64	592.70	587.75	583.60	580.13
42000	629.42	620.57	613.24	607.16	602.08	597.84	594.28
43000	644.40	635.34	627.85	621.61	616.42	612.07	608.43
44000	659.39	650.12	642.45	636.07	630.75	626.30	622.58
45000	674.37	664.89	657.05	650.53	645.09	640.54	636.73
46000	689.36	679.67	671.65	664.98	659.42	654.77	650.87
47000	704.35	694.44	686.25	679.44	673.76	669.01	665.02
48000	719.33	709.22	700.85	693.89	688.09	683.24	679.17
49000	734.32	724.00	715.45	708.35	702.43	697.48	693.32
50000	749.30	738.77	730.05	722.81	716.76	711.71	707.47
51000	764.29	753.55	744.65	737.26	731.10	725.94	721.62
52000	779.28	768.32	759.25	751.72	745.43	740.18	735.77
53000	794.26	783.10	773.86	766.18	759.77	754.41	749.92
54000	809.25	797.87	788.46	780.63	774.11	768.65	764.07
55000	824.23	812.65	803.06	795.09	788.44	782.88	778.22
56000	839.22	827.42	817.66	809.54	802.78	797.12	792.37
57000	854.21	842.20	832.26	824.00	817.11	811.35	806.52
58000	869.19	856.97	846.86	838.46	831.45	825.58	820.67
59000	884.18	871.75	861.46	852.91	845.78	839.82	834.82
60000	899.17	886.52	876.06	867.37	860.12	854.05	848.97
65000	974.10	960.40	949.07	939.65	931.79	925.22	919.71
70000	1049.03	1034.28	1022.07	1011.93	1003.47	996.39	990.46
75000	1123.96	1108.16	1095.08	1084.21	1075.15	1067.57	1061.21
80000	1198.89	1182.03	1168.08	1156.49	1146.82	1138.74	1131.96
85000	1273.82	1255.91	1241.09	1228.77	1218.50	1209.91	1202.70
90000	1348.75	1329.79	1314.09	1301.05	1290.18	1281.08	1273.45
95000	1423.68	1403.66	1387.10	1373.33	1361.85	1352.25	1344.20
100000	1498.61	1477.54	1460.11	1445.61	1433.53	1423.42	1414.94
105000	1573.54	1551.42	1533.11	1517.89	1505.21	1494.59	1485.69
110000	1648.47	1625.30	1606.12	1590.18	1576.88	1565.76	1556.44
120000	1798.33	1773.05	1752.13	1734.74	1720.23	1708.10	1697.93
130000	1948.19	1920.80	1898.14	1879.30	1863.59	1850.45	1839.43
140000	2098.05	2068.56	2044.15	2023.86	2006.94	1992.79	1980.92
150000	2247.91	2216.31	2190.16	2168.42	2150.29	2135.13	2122.42
160000	2397.77	2364.07	2336.17	2312.98	2293.65	2277.47	2263.91
170000	2547.64	2511.82	2482.18	2457.54	2437.00	2419.81	2405.41
180000	2697.50	2659.57	2628.19	2602.11	2580.35	2562.16	2546.90
190000	2847.36	2807.33	2774.20	2746.67	2723.70	2704.50	2688.40
200000	2997.22	2955.08	2920.21	2891.23	2867.06	2846.84	2829.89
210000	3147.08	3102.84	3066.22	3035.79	3010.41	2989.18	2971.38
220000	3296.94	3250.59	3212.23	3180.35	3153.76	3131.52	3112.88
230000	3446.80	3398.35	3358.24	3324.91	3297.12	3273.87	3254.37
240000	3596.66	3546.10	3504.25	3469.47	3440.47	3416.21	3395.87
250000	3746.52	3693.85	3650.26	3614.04	3583.82	3558.55	3537.36

Monthly Payments 17.00 %

LOAN AMOUNT	22	23	24	25	30	35	40
				YEARS			
100	1.41	1.40	1.40	1.39	1.38	1.37	1.37
200	2.82	2.80	2.79	2.79	2.76	2.75	2.74
500	7.04	7.01	6.98	6.96	6.90	6.87	6.85
1000	14.08	14.02	13.97	13.93	13.79	13.73	13.71
2000	28.16	28.04	27.94	27.85	27.59	27.47	27.42
5000	70.39	70.09	69.84	69.63	68.96	68.67	68.55
6000	84.47	84.11	83.81	83.55	82.76	82.41	82.26
7000	98.55	98.13	97.77	97.48	96.55	96.14	95.97
8000	112.63	112.15	111.74	111.40	110.34	109.88	109.68
9000	126.70	126.16	125.71	125.33	124.13	123.61	123.39
10000	140.78	140.18	139.68	139.25	137.93	137.35	137.10
12000	168.94	168.22	167.61	167.10	165.51	164.82	164.52
15000	211.17	210.27	209.52	208.88	206.89	206.02	205.64
20000	281.56	280.37	279.36	278.50	275.86	274.70	274.19
25000	351.96	350.46	349.20	348.13	344.82	343.37	342.74
30000	422.35	420.55	419.03	417.76	413.78	412.05	411.29
31000	436.43	434.57	433.00	431.68	427.58	425.78	425.00
32000	450.50	448.59	446.97	445.61	441.37	439.52	438.71
33000	464.58	462.60	460.94	459.53	455.16	453.25	452.42
34000	478.66	476.62	474.91	473.46	468.95	466.99	466.13
35000	492.74	490.64	488.87	487.38	482.75	480.72	479.84
36000	506.82	504.66	502.84	501.31	496.54	494.46	493.55
37000	520.89	518.68	516.81	515.23	510.33	508.19	507.25
38000	534.97	532.70	530.78	529.16	524.13	521.93	520.96
39000	549.05	546.71	544.74	543.08	537.92	535.66	534.67
40000	563.13	560.73	558.71	557.01	551.71	549.40	548.38
41000	577.21	574.75	572.68	570.93	565.50	563.13	562.09
42000	591.29	588.77	586.65	584.86	579.30	576.87	575.80
43000	605.36	602.79	600.62	598.78	593.09	590.60	589.51
44000	619.44	616.81	614.58	612.71	606.88	604.34	603.22
45000	633.52	630.82	628.55	626.63	620.67	618.07	616.93
46000	647.60	644.84	642.52	640.56	634.47	631.81	630.64
47000	661.68	658.86	656.49	654.48	648.26	645.54	644.35
48000	675.76	672.88	670.45	668.41	662.05	659.28	658.06
49000	689.83	686.90	684.42	682.33	675.85	673.01	671.77
50000	703.91	700.92	698.39	696.26	689.64	686.75	685.48
51000	717.99	714.93	712.36	710.18	703.43	700.48	699.19
52000	732.07	728.95	726.33	724.11	717.22	714.22	712.90
53000	746.15	742.97	740.29	738.04	731.02	727.95	726.61
54000	760.23	756.99	754.26	751.96	744.81	741.69	740.32
55000	774.30	771.01	768.23	765.89	758.60	755.42	754.03
56000	788.38	785.03	782.20	779.81	772.39	769.16	767.74
57000	802.46	799.04	796.17	793.74	786.19	782.89	781.45
58000	816.54	813.06	810.13	807.66	799.98	796.63	795.16
59000	830.62	827.08	824.10	821.59	813.77	810.36	808.87
60000	844.69	841.10	838.07	835.51	827.57	824.10	822.58
65000	915.09	911.19	907.91	905.14	896.53	892.77	891.12
70000	985.48	981.28	977.75	974.76	965.49	961.45	959.67
75000	1055.87	1051.37	1047.59	1044.39	1034.46	1030.12	1028.22
80000	1126.26	1121.47	1117.42	1114.02	1103.42	1098.80	1096.77
85000	1196.65	1191.56	1187.26	1183.64	1172.38	1167.47	1165.32
90000	1267.04	1261.65	1257.10	1253.27	1241.35	1236.15	1233.86
95000	1337.43	1331.74	1326.94	1322.89	1310.31	1304.82	1302.41
100000	1407.82	1401.83	1396.78	1392.52	1379.28	1373.50	1370.96
105000	1478.22	1471.92	1466.62	1462.15	1448.24	1442.17	1439.51
110000	1548.61	1542.01	1536.46	1531.77	1517.20	1510.85	1508.06
120000	1689.39	1682.20	1676.14	1671.02	1655.13	1648.20	1645.15
130000	1830.17	1822.38	1815.82	1810.28	1793.06	1785.55	1782.25
140000	1970.95	1962.56	1955.49	1949.53	1930.99	1922.90	1919.34
150000	2111.74	2102.75	2095.17	2088.78	2068.91	2060.25	2056.44
160000	2252.52	2242.93	2234.85	2228.03	2206.84	2197.60	2193.54
170000	2393.30	2383.11	2374.53	2367.28	2344.77	2334.95	2330.63
180000	2534.08	2523.30	2514.21	2506.54	2482.70	2472.30	2467.73
190000	2674.87	2663.48	2653.88	2645.79	2620.63	2609.65	2604.82
200000	2815.65	2803.66	2793.56	2785.04	2758.55	2747.00	2741.92
210000	2956.43	2943.85	2933.24	2924.29	2896.48	2884.35	2879.01
220000	3097.21	3084.03	3072.92	3063.54	3034.41	3021.70	3016.11
230000	3238.00	3224.21	3212.60	3202.79	3172.34	3159.05	3153.21
240000	3378.78	3364.40	3352.27	3342.05	3310.26	3296.40	3290.30
250000	3519.56	3504.58	3491.95	3481.30	3448.19	3433.75	3427.40

17.25 % Monthly Payments

LOAN AMOUNT	YEARS 1	2	3	4	5	6	7
100	9.10	4.93	3.55	2.87	2.47	2.21	2.02
200	18.21	9.86	7.10	5.74	4.93	4.41	4.05
500	45.52	24.64	17.74	14.34	12.34	11.03	10.12
1000	91.04	49.28	35.48	28.68	24.67	22.06	20.24
2000	182.09	98.56	70.97	57.36	49.34	44.11	40.48
5000	455.22	246.40	177.42	143.40	123.35	110.29	101.20
6000	546.26	295.68	212.91	172.08	148.02	132.34	121.44
7000	637.31	344.96	248.39	200.76	172.69	154.40	141.68
8000	728.35	394.24	283.87	229.44	197.36	176.46	161.92
9000	819.40	443.52	319.36	258.12	222.04	198.52	182.16
10000	910.44	492.79	354.84	286.80	246.71	220.57	202.40
12000	1092.53	591.35	425.81	344.16	296.05	264.69	242.88
15000	1365.66	739.19	532.26	430.20	370.06	330.86	303.60
20000	1820.88	985.59	709.68	573.60	493.41	441.15	404.81
25000	2276.10	1231.99	887.10	717.00	616.76	551.43	506.01
30000	2731.32	1478.38	1064.53	860.40	740.12	661.72	607.21
31000	2822.36	1527.66	1100.01	889.08	764.79	683.78	627.45
32000	2913.40	1576.94	1135.49	917.76	789.46	705.83	647.69
33000	3004.45	1626.22	1170.98	946.44	814.13	727.89	667.93
34000	3095.49	1675.50	1206.46	975.12	838.80	749.95	688.17
35000	3186.54	1724.78	1241.95	1003.80	863.47	772.01	708.41
36000	3277.58	1774.06	1277.43	1032.48	888.14	794.06	728.65
37000	3368.62	1823.34	1312.91	1061.16	912.81	816.12	769.13
38000	3459.67	1872.62	1348.40	1089.84	937.48	838.18	767.13
39000	3550.71	1921.90	1383.88	1118.52	962.15	860.24	789.37
40000	3641.76	1971.18	1419.37	1147.20	986.82	882.29	809.61
41000	3732.80	2020.46	1454.85	1175.88	1011.49	904.35	829.85
42000	3823.84	2069.74	1490.34	1204.56	1036.17	926.41	850.09
43000	3914.89	2119.02	1525.82	1233.24	1060.84	948.47	870.33
44000	4005.93	2168.30	1561.30	1261.92	1085.51	970.52	890.57
45000	4096.98	2217.58	1596.79	1290.60	1110.18	992.58	910.81
46000	4188.02	2266.86	1632.27	1319.28	1134.85	1014.64	931.05
47000	4279.06	2316.14	1667.76	1347.95	1159.52	1036.69	951.29
48000	4370.11	2365.41	1703.24	1376.63	1184.19	1058.75	971.53
49000	4461.15	2414.69	1738.72	1405.31	1208.86	1080.81	991.77
50000	4552.19	2463.97	1774.21	1433.99	1233.53	1102.87	1012.02
51000	4643.24	2513.25	1809.69	1462.67	1258.20	1124.92	1032.26
52000	4734.28	2562.53	1845.18	1491.35	1282.87	1146.98	1052.50
53000	4825.33	2611.81	1880.66	1520.03	1307.54	1169.04	1072.74
54000	4916.37	2661.09	1916.15	1548.71	1332.21	1191.10	1092.98
55000	5007.41	2710.37	1951.63	1577.39	1356.88	1213.15	1113.22
56000	5098.46	2759.65	1987.11	1606.07	1381.55	1235.21	1133.46
57000	5189.50	2808.93	2022.60	1634.75	1406.22	1257.27	1153.70
58000	5280.55	2858.21	2058.08	1663.43	1430.89	1279.33	1173.94
59000	5371.59	2907.49	2093.57	1692.11	1455.57	1301.38	1194.18
60000	5462.63	2956.77	2129.05	1720.79	1480.24	1323.44	1214.42
65000	5917.85	3203.17	2306.47	1864.19	1603.59	1433.73	1315.62
70000	6373.07	3449.56	2483.89	2007.59	1726.94	1544.01	1416.82
75000	6828.29	3695.96	2661.31	2150.99	1850.29	1654.30	1518.02
80000	7283.51	3942.36	2838.73	2294.39	1973.65	1764.59	1619.22
85000	7738.73	4188.76	3016.16	2437.79	2097.00	1874.87	1720.43
90000	8193.95	4435.15	3193.58	2581.19	2220.35	1985.16	1821.63
95000	8649.17	4681.55	3371.00	2724.59	2343.71	2095.45	1922.83
100000	9104.39	4927.95	3548.42	2867.99	2467.06	2205.73	2024.03
105000	9559.61	5174.34	3725.84	3011.39	2590.41	2316.02	2125.23
110000	10014.83	5420.74	3903.26	3154.79	2713.77	2426.31	2226.43
120000	10925.27	5913.54	4258.10	3441.59	2960.47	2646.88	2428.84
130000	11835.71	6406.33	4612.94	3728.39	3207.18	2867.45	2631.24
140000	12746.15	6899.13	4967.79	4015.18	3453.88	3088.03	2833.64
150000	13656.58	7391.92	5322.63	4301.98	3700.59	3308.60	3036.05
160000	14567.02	7884.72	5677.47	4588.78	3947.30	3529.17	3238.45
170000	15477.46	8377.51	6032.31	4875.58	4194.00	3749.75	3440.85
180000	16387.90	8870.31	6387.15	5162.38	4440.71	3970.32	3643.25
190000	17298.34	9363.10	6741.99	5449.18	4687.41	4190.89	3845.66
200000	18208.78	9855.89	7096.84	5735.98	4934.12	4411.47	4048.06
210000	19119.22	10348.69	7451.68	6022.78	5180.83	4632.04	4250.46
220000	20029.66	10841.48	7806.52	6309.58	5427.53	4852.61	4452.87
230000	20940.10	11334.28	8161.36	6596.38	5674.24	5073.19	4655.27
240000	21850.53	11827.07	8516.20	6883.17	5920.94	5293.76	4857.67
250000	22760.97	12319.87	8871.05	7169.97	6167.65	5514.33	5060.08

Monthly Payments 17.25 %

LOAN AMOUNT	8	9	10	11	12	13	14
			YEARS				
100	1.89	1.79	1.72	1.66	1.61	1.57	1.54
200	3.78	3.59	3.43	3.31	3.22	3.14	3.08
500	9.46	8.96	8.58	8.28	8.05	7.86	7.70
1000	18.92	17.93	17.17	16.57	16.09	15.71	15.40
2000	37.84	35.86	34.33	33.14	32.19	31.42	30.81
5000	94.60	89.64	85.83	82.84	80.47	78.56	77.02
6000	113.52	107.57	102.99	99.41	96.56	94.27	92.42
7000	132.44	125.50	120.16	115.98	112.66	109.99	107.82
8000	151.36	143.42	137.32	132.55	128.75	125.70	123.23
9000	170.27	161.35	154.49	149.11	144.84	141.41	138.63
10000	189.19	179.28	171.65	165.68	160.94	157.12	154.03
12000	227.03	215.13	205.99	198.82	193.13	188.55	184.84
15000	283.79	268.92	257.48	248.52	241.41	235.69	231.05
20000	378.39	358.56	343.31	331.37	321.88	314.25	308.06
25000	472.99	448.20	429.14	414.21	402.35	392.81	385.08
30000	567.58	537.84	514.96	497.05	482.81	471.37	462.09
31000	586.50	555.76	532.13	513.62	498.91	487.09	477.50
32000	605.42	573.69	549.30	530.19	515.00	502.80	492.90
33000	624.34	591.62	566.46	546.75	531.10	518.51	508.30
34000	643.26	609.55	583.63	563.32	547.19	534.22	523.71
35000	662.18	627.48	600.79	579.89	563.28	549.94	539.11
36000	681.10	645.40	617.96	596.46	579.38	565.65	554.51
37000	700.02	663.33	635.12	613.03	595.47	581.36	569.92
38000	718.94	681.26	652.29	629.60	611.57	597.07	585.32
39000	737.86	699.19	669.45	646.16	627.66	612.79	600.72
40000	756.78	717.12	686.62	662.73	643.75	628.50	616.13
41000	775.70	735.04	703.78	679.30	659.85	644.21	631.53
42000	794.62	752.97	720.95	695.87	675.94	659.92	646.93
43000	813.54	770.90	738.12	712.44	692.03	675.64	662.33
44000	832.46	788.83	755.28	729.01	708.13	691.35	677.74
45000	851.37	806.76	772.45	745.57	724.22	707.06	693.14
46000	870.29	824.68	789.61	762.14	740.32	722.77	708.54
47000	889.21	842.61	806.78	778.71	756.41	738.49	723.95
48000	908.13	860.54	823.94	795.28	772.50	754.20	739.35
49000	927.05	878.47	841.11	811.85	788.60	769.91	754.75
50000	945.97	896.39	858.27	828.42	804.69	785.62	770.16
51000	964.89	914.32	875.44	844.98	820.78	801.34	785.56
52000	983.81	932.25	892.60	861.55	836.88	817.05	800.96
53000	1002.73	950.18	909.77	878.12	852.97	832.76	816.37
54000	1021.65	968.11	926.94	894.69	869.07	848.47	831.77
55000	1040.57	986.03	944.10	911.26	885.16	864.19	847.17
56000	1059.49	1003.96	961.27	927.83	901.25	879.90	862.58
57000	1078.41	1021.89	978.43	944.39	917.35	895.61	877.98
58000	1097.33	1039.82	995.60	960.96	933.44	911.32	893.38
59000	1116.25	1057.75	1012.76	977.53	949.54	927.04	908.78
60000	1135.17	1075.67	1029.93	994.10	965.63	942.75	924.19
65000	1229.76	1165.31	1115.76	1076.94	1046.10	1021.31	1001.20
70000	1324.36	1254.95	1201.58	1159.78	1126.57	1099.87	1078.22
75000	1418.96	1344.59	1287.41	1242.62	1207.04	1178.43	1155.23
80000	1513.56	1434.23	1373.24	1325.47	1287.51	1257.00	1232.25
85000	1608.15	1523.87	1459.07	1408.31	1367.97	1335.56	1309.27
90000	1702.75	1613.51	1544.89	1491.15	1448.44	1414.12	1386.28
95000	1797.35	1703.15	1630.72	1573.99	1528.91	1492.68	1463.30
100000	1891.94	1792.79	1716.55	1656.83	1609.38	1571.25	1540.31
105000	1986.54	1882.43	1802.37	1739.67	1689.85	1649.81	1617.33
110000	2081.14	1972.07	1888.20	1822.51	1770.32	1728.37	1694.34
120000	2270.33	2151.35	2059.86	1988.20	1931.26	1885.50	1848.38
130000	2459.53	2330.63	2231.51	2153.88	2092.20	2042.62	2002.41
140000	2648.72	2509.91	2403.17	2319.56	2253.14	2199.74	2156.44
150000	2837.92	2689.18	2574.82	2485.25	2414.07	2356.87	2310.47
160000	3027.11	2868.46	2746.48	2650.93	2575.01	2513.99	2464.50
170000	3216.30	3047.74	2918.13	2816.61	2735.95	2671.12	2618.53
180000	3405.50	3227.02	3089.79	2982.30	2896.89	2828.24	2772.56
190000	3594.69	3406.30	3261.44	3147.98	3057.83	2985.37	2926.59
200000	3783.89	3585.58	3433.09	3313.66	3218.76	3142.49	3080.63
210000	3973.08	3764.86	3604.75	3479.35	3379.70	3299.62	3234.66
220000	4162.28	3944.14	3776.40	3645.03	3540.64	3456.74	3388.69
230000	4351.47	4123.42	3948.06	3810.71	3701.58	3613.87	3542.72
240000	4540.67	4302.70	4119.71	3976.40	3862.52	3770.99	3696.75
250000	4729.86	4481.97	4291.37	4142.08	4023.46	3928.12	3850.78

17.25 % Monthly Payments

LOAN AMOUNT	15	16	17	18	19	20	21
100	1.52	1.49	1.48	1.46	1.45	1.44	1.43
200	3.03	2.99	2.95	2.93	2.90	2.88	2.87
500	7.58	7.47	7.39	7.31	7.25	7.21	7.16
1000	15.15	14.94	14.77	14.63	14.51	14.41	14.33
2000	30.30	29.89	29.54	29.26	29.02	28.82	28.66
5000	75.75	74.71	73.85	73.14	72.55	72.05	71.64
6000	90.90	89.66	88.62	87.77	87.06	86.46	85.97
7000	106.05	104.60	103.40	102.40	101.57	100.87	100.29
8000	121.20	119.54	118.17	117.03	116.08	115.29	114.62
9000	136.35	134.48	132.94	131.65	130.59	129.70	128.95
10000	151.50	149.43	147.71	146.28	145.10	144.11	143.28
12000	181.80	179.31	177.25	175.54	174.12	172.93	171.93
15000	227.26	224.14	221.56	219.42	217.65	216.16	214.92
20000	303.01	298.85	295.42	292.57	290.19	288.21	286.56
25000	378.76	373.56	369.27	365.71	362.74	360.27	358.20
30000	454.51	448.28	443.12	438.85	435.29	432.32	429.83
31000	469.66	463.22	457.89	453.48	449.80	446.73	444.16
32000	484.81	478.16	472.67	468.11	464.31	461.14	458.49
33000	499.96	493.10	487.44	482.73	478.82	475.55	472.82
34000	515.11	508.05	502.21	497.36	493.33	489.96	487.15
35000	530.26	522.99	516.98	511.99	507.84	504.37	501.47
36000	545.41	537.93	531.75	526.62	522.35	518.78	515.80
37000	560.56	552.87	546.52	541.25	536.86	533.20	530.13
38000	575.71	567.82	561.29	555.88	551.37	547.61	544.46
39000	590.86	582.76	576.06	570.50	565.88	562.02	558.78
40000	606.01	597.70	590.83	585.13	580.39	576.43	573.11
41000	621.16	612.64	605.60	599.76	594.90	590.84	587.44
42000	636.31	627.59	620.37	614.39	609.41	605.25	601.77
43000	651.46	642.53	635.14	629.02	623.92	619.66	616.10
44000	666.62	657.47	649.92	643.65	638.43	634.07	630.42
45000	681.77	672.41	664.69	658.27	652.94	648.48	644.75
46000	696.92	687.36	679.46	672.90	667.45	662.89	659.08
47000	712.07	702.30	694.23	687.53	681.96	677.30	673.41
48000	727.22	717.24	709.00	702.16	696.47	691.71	687.73
49000	742.37	732.18	723.77	716.79	710.98	706.12	702.06
50000	757.52	747.13	738.54	731.42	725.49	720.53	716.39
51000	772.67	762.07	753.31	746.04	740.00	734.94	730.72
52000	787.82	777.01	768.08	760.67	754.50	749.36	745.05
53000	802.97	791.95	782.85	775.30	769.01	763.77	759.37
54000	818.12	806.90	797.62	789.93	783.52	778.18	773.70
55000	833.27	821.84	812.39	804.56	798.03	792.59	788.03
56000	848.42	836.78	827.16	819.19	812.54	807.00	802.36
57000	863.57	851.72	841.94	833.81	827.05	821.41	816.68
58000	878.72	866.67	856.71	848.44	841.56	835.82	831.01
59000	893.87	881.61	871.48	863.07	856.07	850.23	845.34
60000	909.02	896.55	886.25	877.70	870.58	864.64	859.67
65000	984.77	971.26	960.10	950.84	943.13	936.69	931.31
70000	1060.52	1045.98	1033.96	1023.98	1015.68	1008.75	1002.95
75000	1136.28	1120.69	1107.81	1097.12	1088.23	1080.80	1074.59
80000	1212.03	1195.40	1181.66	1170.27	1160.78	1152.85	1146.22
85000	1287.78	1270.11	1255.52	1243.41	1233.33	1224.91	1217.86
90000	1363.53	1344.83	1329.37	1316.55	1305.87	1296.96	1289.50
95000	1439.28	1419.54	1403.23	1389.69	1378.42	1369.01	1361.14
100000	1515.03	1494.25	1477.08	1462.83	1450.97	1441.07	1432.78
105000	1590.79	1568.96	1550.93	1535.97	1523.52	1513.12	1504.42
110000	1666.54	1643.68	1624.79	1609.12	1596.07	1585.17	1576.06
120000	1818.04	1793.10	1772.50	1755.40	1741.17	1729.28	1719.34
130000	1969.54	1942.53	1920.20	1901.68	1886.26	1873.39	1862.61
140000	2121.05	2091.95	2067.91	2047.97	2031.36	2017.50	2005.89
150000	2272.55	2241.38	2215.62	2194.25	2176.46	2161.60	2149.17
160000	2424.06	2390.80	2363.33	2340.53	2321.55	2305.71	2292.45
170000	2575.56	2540.23	2511.04	2486.81	2466.65	2449.82	2435.73
180000	2727.06	2689.65	2658.74	2633.10	2611.75	2593.92	2579.01
190000	2878.57	2839.08	2806.45	2779.38	2756.84	2738.03	2722.28
200000	3030.07	2988.50	2954.16	2925.66	2901.94	2882.14	2865.56
210000	3181.57	3137.93	3101.87	3071.95	3047.04	3026.24	3008.84
220000	3333.08	3287.35	3249.58	3218.23	3192.14	3170.35	3152.12
230000	3484.58	3436.78	3397.28	3364.51	3337.23	3314.46	3295.40
240000	3636.08	3586.20	3544.99	3510.80	3482.33	3458.56	3438.67
250000	3787.59	3735.63	3692.70	3657.08	3627.43	3602.67	3581.95

Monthly Payments 16.50 %

LOAN AMOUNT	22	23	24	25	30	35	40
100	1.37	1.37	1.36	1.36	1.34	1.34	1.33
200	2.74	2.73	2.72	2.71	2.68	2.67	2.66
500	6.86	6.83	6.80	6.78	6.71	6.68	6.66
1000	13.72	13.66	13.60	13.56	13.42	13.35	13.32
2000	27.44	27.31	27.21	27.11	26.83	26.70	26.65
5000	68.60	68.28	68.01	67.79	67.08	66.76	66.62
6000	82.31	81.94	81.62	81.34	80.49	80.11	79.94
7000	96.03	95.59	95.22	94.90	93.91	93.46	93.26
8000	109.75	109.25	108.82	108.46	107.32	106.81	106.59
9000	123.47	122.90	122.42	122.02	120.74	120.17	119.91
10000	137.19	136.56	136.03	135.57	134.15	133.52	133.23
12000	164.63	163.87	163.23	162.69	160.98	160.22	159.88
15000	205.79	204.84	204.04	203.36	201.23	200.28	199.85
20000	274.38	273.12	272.05	271.15	268.30	267.04	266.47
25000	342.98	341.40	340.07	338.93	335.38	333.80	333.08
30000	411.57	409.68	408.08	406.72	402.46	400.55	399.70
31000	425.29	423.34	421.68	420.28	415.87	413.91	413.02
32000	439.01	436.99	435.28	433.84	429.29	427.26	426.35
33000	452.73	450.65	448.89	447.39	442.70	440.61	439.67
34000	466.45	464.30	462.49	460.95	456.12	453.96	452.99
35000	480.17	477.96	476.09	474.51	469.53	467.31	466.32
36000	493.89	491.62	489.69	488.07	482.95	480.67	479.64
37000	507.61	505.27	503.30	501.62	496.36	494.02	492.96
38000	521.33	518.93	516.90	515.18	509.78	507.37	506.29
39000	535.05	532.58	530.50	528.74	523.19	520.72	519.61
40000	548.77	546.24	544.10	542.29	536.61	534.07	532.93
41000	562.48	559.90	557.71	555.85	550.02	547.42	546.26
42000	576.20	573.55	571.31	569.41	563.44	560.78	559.58
43000	589.92	587.21	584.91	582.97	576.85	574.13	572.90
44000	603.64	600.86	598.51	596.52	590.27	587.48	586.23
45000	617.36	614.52	612.12	610.08	603.68	600.83	599.55
46000	631.08	628.18	625.72	623.64	617.10	614.18	612.87
47000	644.80	641.83	639.32	637.20	630.51	627.54	626.20
48000	658.52	655.49	652.93	650.75	643.93	640.89	639.52
49000	672.24	669.14	666.53	664.31	657.34	654.24	652.84
50000	685.96	682.80	680.13	677.87	670.76	667.59	666.17
51000	699.68	696.46	693.73	691.43	684.17	680.94	679.49
52000	713.40	710.11	707.34	704.98	697.59	694.29	692.81
53000	727.11	723.77	720.94	718.54	711.00	707.65	706.14
54000	740.83	737.43	734.54	732.10	724.42	721.00	719.46
55000	754.55	751.08	748.14	745.66	737.84	734.35	732.78
56000	768.27	764.74	761.75	759.21	751.25	747.70	746.11
57000	781.99	778.39	775.35	772.77	764.67	761.05	759.43
58000	795.71	792.05	788.95	786.33	778.08	774.41	772.75
59000	809.43	805.71	802.55	799.88	791.50	787.76	786.08
60000	823.15	819.36	816.16	813.44	804.91	801.11	799.40
65000	891.74	887.64	884.17	881.23	871.99	867.87	866.02
70000	960.34	955.92	952.18	949.02	939.06	934.63	932.63
75000	1028.94	1024.20	1020.20	1016.80	1006.14	1001.39	999.25
80000	1097.53	1092.48	1088.21	1084.59	1073.22	1068.15	1065.87
85000	1166.13	1160.76	1156.22	1152.38	1140.29	1134.90	1132.48
90000	1234.72	1229.04	1224.24	1220.16	1207.37	1201.66	1199.10
95000	1303.32	1297.32	1292.25	1287.95	1274.44	1268.42	1265.72
100000	1371.91	1365.60	1360.26	1355.74	1341.52	1335.18	1332.33
105000	1440.51	1433.88	1428.27	1423.52	1408.59	1401.94	1398.95
110000	1509.11	1502.16	1496.29	1491.31	1475.67	1468.70	1465.57
120000	1646.30	1638.72	1632.31	1626.88	1609.82	1602.22	1598.80
130000	1783.49	1775.28	1768.34	1762.46	1743.97	1735.74	1732.03
140000	1920.68	1911.84	1904.37	1898.03	1878.13	1869.25	1865.27
150000	2057.87	2048.40	2040.39	2033.60	2012.28	2002.77	1998.50
160000	2195.06	2184.96	2176.42	2169.18	2146.43	2136.29	2131.73
170000	2332.25	2321.52	2312.44	2304.75	2280.58	2269.81	2264.97
180000	2469.44	2458.08	2448.47	2440.33	2414.73	2403.33	2398.20
190000	2606.64	2594.64	2584.50	2575.90	2548.89	2536.84	2531.43
200000	2743.83	2731.20	2720.52	2711.47	2683.04	2670.36	2664.67
210000	2881.02	2867.76	2856.55	2847.05	2817.19	2803.88	2797.90
220000	3018.21	3004.32	2992.57	2982.62	2951.34	2937.40	2931.13
230000	3155.40	3140.88	3128.60	3118.19	3085.49	3070.92	3064.37
240000	3292.59	3277.44	3264.63	3253.77	3219.65	3204.44	3197.60
250000	3429.78	3414.00	3400.65	3389.34	3353.80	3337.95	3330.83

Monthly Payments 17.25 %

LOAN AMOUNT	22	23	24	25	30	35	40
				YEARS			
100	1.43	1.42	1.42	1.41	1.40	1.39	1.39
200	2.85	2.84	2.83	2.82	2.80	2.79	2.78
500	7.13	7.10	7.08	7.05	6.99	6.96	6.95
1000	14.26	14.20	14.15	14.11	13.98	13.93	13.90
2000	28.52	28.40	28.30	28.22	27.96	27.85	27.81
5000	71.29	71.00	70.75	70.55	69.91	69.63	69.51
6000	85.55	85.20	84.91	84.66	83.89	83.56	83.42
7000	99.81	99.40	99.06	98.77	97.87	97.49	97.32
8000	114.07	113.60	113.21	112.88	111.85	111.41	111.22
9000	128.32	127.80	127.36	126.99	125.84	125.34	125.12
10000	142.58	142.00	141.51	141.10	139.82	139.27	139.03
12000	171.10	170.40	169.81	169.31	167.78	167.12	166.83
15000	213.87	213.00	212.26	211.64	209.73	208.90	208.54
20000	285.17	284.00	283.02	282.19	279.63	278.53	278.05
25000	356.46	355.00	353.77	352.74	349.54	348.17	347.57
30000	427.75	426.00	424.53	423.29	419.45	417.80	417.08
31000	442.01	440.20	438.68	437.39	433.43	431.72	430.98
32000	456.27	454.40	452.83	451.50	447.42	445.65	444.88
33000	470.52	468.60	466.98	465.61	461.40	459.58	458.79
34000	484.78	482.80	481.13	479.72	475.38	473.50	472.69
35000	499.04	497.00	495.28	493.83	489.36	487.43	486.59
36000	513.30	511.20	509.43	507.94	503.34	501.36	500.49
37000	527.56	525.40	523.58	522.05	517.32	515.28	514.40
38000	541.82	539.60	537.73	536.16	531.31	529.21	528.30
39000	556.07	553.80	551.88	550.27	545.29	543.14	542.20
40000	570.33	568.00	566.03	564.38	559.27	557.06	556.11
41000	584.59	582.20	580.18	578.49	573.25	570.99	570.01
42000	598.85	596.40	594.34	592.60	587.23	584.92	583.91
43000	613.11	610.60	608.49	606.71	601.21	598.84	597.81
44000	627.37	624.80	622.64	620.82	615.20	612.77	611.72
45000	641.62	639.00	636.79	634.93	629.18	626.70	625.62
46000	655.88	653.20	650.94	649.04	643.16	640.62	639.52
47000	670.14	667.40	665.09	663.15	657.14	654.55	653.42
48000	684.40	681.60	679.24	677.26	671.12	668.48	667.33
49000	698.66	695.80	693.39	691.37	685.11	682.40	681.23
50000	712.92	710.00	707.54	705.48	699.09	696.33	695.13
51000	727.17	724.20	721.69	719.58	713.07	710.26	709.03
52000	741.43	738.40	735.84	733.69	727.05	724.18	722.94
53000	755.69	752.60	749.99	747.80	741.03	738.11	736.84
54000	769.95	766.80	764.15	761.91	755.01	752.04	750.74
55000	784.21	781.00	778.30	776.02	769.00	765.96	764.64
56000	798.47	795.20	792.45	790.13	782.98	779.89	778.55
57000	812.72	809.40	806.60	804.24	796.96	793.82	792.45
58000	826.98	823.60	820.75	818.35	810.94	807.74	806.35
59000	841.24	837.80	834.90	832.46	824.92	821.67	820.26
60000	855.50	852.00	849.05	846.57	838.90	835.60	834.16
65000	926.79	923.00	919.81	917.12	908.81	905.23	903.67
70000	998.08	994.00	990.56	987.67	978.72	974.86	973.18
75000	1069.37	1065.00	1061.31	1058.21	1048.63	1044.50	1042.70
80000	1140.67	1136.00	1132.07	1128.76	1118.54	1114.13	1112.21
85000	1211.96	1207.00	1202.82	1199.31	1188.45	1183.76	1181.72
90000	1283.25	1277.99	1273.58	1269.86	1258.36	1253.39	1251.24
95000	1354.54	1348.99	1344.33	1340.40	1328.27	1323.03	1320.75
100000	1425.83	1419.99	1415.08	1410.95	1398.17	1392.66	1390.26
105000	1497.12	1490.99	1485.84	1481.50	1468.08	1462.29	1459.78
110000	1568.41	1561.99	1556.59	1552.05	1537.99	1531.93	1529.29
120000	1711.00	1703.99	1698.10	1693.14	1677.81	1671.19	1668.32
130000	1853.58	1845.99	1839.61	1834.24	1817.63	1810.46	1807.34
140000	1996.16	1987.99	1981.12	1975.33	1957.44	1949.72	1946.37
150000	2138.75	2129.99	2122.63	2116.43	2097.26	2088.99	2085.39
160000	2281.33	2271.99	2264.14	2257.52	2237.08	2228.26	2224.42
170000	2423.91	2413.99	2405.64	2398.62	2376.90	2367.52	2363.45
180000	2566.50	2555.99	2547.15	2539.71	2516.71	2506.79	2502.47
190000	2709.08	2697.99	2688.66	2680.81	2656.53	2646.05	2641.50
200000	2851.66	2839.99	2830.17	2821.90	2796.35	2785.32	2780.53
210000	2994.25	2981.99	2971.68	2963.00	2936.17	2924.59	2919.55
220000	3136.83	3123.99	3113.19	3104.09	3075.98	3063.85	3058.58
230000	3279.41	3265.99	3254.69	3245.19	3215.80	3203.12	3197.61
240000	3422.00	3407.99	3396.20	3386.28	3355.62	3342.38	3336.63
250000	3564.58	3549.99	3537.71	3527.38	3495.43	3481.65	3475.66

17.50 % Monthly Payments

LOAN AMOUNT	1	2	3	4	5	6	7
				YEARS			
100	9.12	4.94	3.56	2.88	2.48	2.22	2.04
200	18.23	9.88	7.12	5.76	4.96	4.44	4.07
500	45.58	24.70	17.80	14.40	12.40	11.09	10.19
1000	91.15	49.39	35.60	28.80	24.80	22.19	20.37
2000	182.31	98.78	71.20	57.60	49.59	44.37	40.75
5000	455.77	246.96	178.00	144.00	123.98	110.94	101.87
6000	546.93	296.35	213.60	172.80	148.77	133.12	122.25
7000	638.08	345.74	249.20	201.60	173.57	155.31	142.62
8000	729.24	395.13	284.80	230.40	198.37	177.50	163.00
9000	820.39	444.52	320.40	259.20	223.16	199.68	183.37
10000	911.55	493.91	356.00	288.00	247.96	221.87	203.75
12000	1093.85	592.70	427.20	345.60	297.55	266.25	244.50
15000	1367.32	740.87	534.00	432.00	371.94	332.81	305.62
20000	1823.09	987.83	712.00	576.01	495.91	443.74	407.49
25000	2278.86	1234.79	890.00	720.01	619.89	554.68	509.37
30000	2734.64	1481.74	1068.00	864.01	743.87	665.61	611.24
31000	2825.79	1531.13	1103.60	892.81	768.67	687.80	631.61
32000	2916.94	1580.52	1139.20	921.61	793.46	709.99	651.99
33000	3008.10	1629.92	1174.80	950.41	818.26	732.17	672.36
34000	3099.25	1679.31	1210.40	979.21	843.05	754.36	692.74
35000	3190.41	1728.70	1246.00	1008.01	867.85	776.55	713.11
36000	3281.56	1778.09	1281.60	1036.81	892.64	798.74	733.49
37000	3372.72	1827.48	1317.20	1065.61	917.44	820.92	753.86
38000	3463.87	1876.87	1352.80	1094.41	942.24	843.11	774.24
39000	3555.03	1926.26	1388.40	1123.21	967.03	865.30	794.61
40000	3646.18	1975.66	1424.00	1152.01	991.83	887.48	814.99
41000	3737.33	2025.05	1459.60	1180.81	1016.62	909.67	835.36
42000	3828.49	2074.44	1495.20	1209.61	1041.42	931.86	855.74
43000	3919.64	2123.83	1530.80	1238.41	1066.21	954.04	876.11
44000	4010.80	2173.22	1566.40	1267.21	1091.01	976.23	896.48
45000	4101.95	2222.61	1602.00	1296.01	1115.81	998.42	916.86
46000	4193.11	2272.00	1637.60	1324.81	1140.60	1020.61	937.23
47000	4284.26	2321.40	1673.20	1353.61	1165.40	1042.79	957.61
48000	4375.42	2370.79	1708.80	1382.41	1190.19	1064.98	977.98
49000	4466.57	2420.18	1744.40	1411.21	1214.99	1087.17	998.36
50000	4557.73	2469.57	1780.00	1440.01	1239.78	1109.35	1018.73
51000	4648.88	2518.96	1815.60	1468.81	1264.58	1131.54	1039.11
52000	4740.03	2568.35	1851.20	1497.62	1289.38	1153.73	1059.48
53000	4831.19	2617.74	1886.80	1526.42	1314.17	1175.92	1079.86
54000	4922.34	2667.14	1922.40	1555.22	1338.97	1198.10	1100.23
55000	5013.50	2716.53	1958.00	1584.02	1363.76	1220.29	1120.61
56000	5104.65	2765.92	1993.60	1612.82	1388.56	1242.48	1140.98
57000	5195.81	2815.31	2029.20	1641.62	1413.35	1264.66	1161.36
58000	5286.96	2864.70	2064.80	1670.42	1438.15	1286.85	1181.73
59000	5378.12	2914.09	2100.40	1699.22	1462.94	1309.04	1202.10
60000	5469.27	2963.48	2136.00	1728.02	1487.74	1331.23	1222.48
65000	5925.04	3210.44	2314.00	1872.02	1611.72	1442.16	1324.35
70000	6380.82	3457.40	2492.00	2016.02	1735.70	1553.10	1426.23
75000	6836.59	3704.36	2670.00	2160.02	1859.68	1664.03	1528.10
80000	7292.36	3951.31	2848.00	2304.02	1983.65	1774.97	1629.97
85000	7748.13	4198.27	3026.00	2448.02	2107.63	1885.90	1731.85
90000	8203.91	4445.23	3204.00	2592.03	2231.61	1996.84	1833.72
95000	8659.68	4692.18	3382.00	2736.03	2355.59	2107.77	1935.59
100000	9115.45	4939.14	3560.01	2880.03	2479.57	2218.71	2037.47
105000	9571.22	5186.10	3738.01	3024.03	2603.55	2329.64	2139.34
110000	10027.00	5433.05	3916.01	3168.03	2727.52	2440.58	2241.21
120000	10938.54	5926.97	4272.01	3456.03	2975.48	2662.45	2444.96
130000	11850.09	6420.88	4628.01	3744.04	3223.44	2884.32	2648.71
140000	12761.63	6914.80	4984.01	4032.04	3471.39	3106.19	2852.45
150000	13673.18	7408.71	5340.01	4320.04	3719.35	3328.06	3056.20
160000	14584.72	7902.62	5696.01	4608.05	3967.31	3549.93	3259.95
170000	15496.27	8396.54	6052.01	4896.05	4215.27	3771.81	3463.69
180000	16407.81	8890.45	6408.01	5184.05	4463.22	3993.68	3667.44
190000	17319.36	9384.37	6764.01	5472.06	4711.18	4215.55	3871.19
200000	18230.90	9878.28	7120.01	5760.06	4959.14	4437.42	4074.93
210000	19142.45	10372.19	7476.01	6048.06	5207.09	4659.29	4278.68
220000	20053.99	10866.11	7832.01	6336.06	5455.05	4881.16	4482.42
230000	20965.54	11360.02	8188.01	6624.07	5703.01	5103.03	4686.17
240000	21877.08	11853.94	8544.01	6912.07	5950.96	5324.90	4889.92
250000	22788.63	12347.85	8900.01	7200.07	6198.92	5546.77	5093.66

Monthly Payments 17.50 %

LOAN AMOUNT	YEARS 8	9	10	11	12	13	14
100	1.91	1.81	1.73	1.67	1.62	1.59	1.56
200	3.81	3.61	3.46	3.34	3.25	3.17	3.11
500	9.53	9.04	8.66	8.36	8.12	7.94	7.78
1000	19.06	18.07	17.31	16.72	16.25	15.87	15.56
2000	38.12	36.14	34.63	33.44	32.50	31.74	31.13
5000	95.29	90.36	86.56	83.60	81.24	79.35	77.82
6000	114.35	108.43	103.88	100.32	97.49	95.23	93.39
7000	133.41	126.50	121.19	117.04	113.74	111.10	108.95
8000	152.47	144.57	138.50	133.76	129.99	126.97	124.52
9000	171.52	162.64	155.81	150.48	146.24	142.84	140.08
10000	190.58	180.71	173.13	167.19	162.49	158.71	155.65
12000	228.70	216.85	207.75	200.63	194.98	190.45	186.78
15000	285.87	271.07	259.69	250.79	243.73	238.06	233.47
20000	381.17	361.42	346.25	334.39	324.97	317.42	311.30
25000	476.46	451.78	432.82	417.99	406.22	396.77	389.12
30000	571.75	542.13	519.38	501.58	487.46	476.13	466.94
31000	590.81	560.20	536.69	518.30	503.71	492.00	482.51
32000	609.86	578.27	554.01	535.02	519.96	507.87	498.07
33000	628.92	596.34	571.32	551.74	536.21	523.74	513.64
34000	647.98	614.42	588.63	568.46	552.46	539.61	529.20
35000	667.04	632.49	605.95	585.18	568.70	555.48	544.77
36000	686.10	650.56	623.26	601.90	584.95	571.35	560.33
37000	705.16	668.63	640.57	618.62	601.20	587.22	575.90
38000	724.21	686.70	657.88	635.34	617.45	603.09	591.46
39000	743.27	704.77	675.20	652.06	633.70	618.96	607.03
40000	762.33	722.84	692.51	668.78	649.95	634.83	622.59
41000	781.39	740.91	709.82	685.50	666.20	650.70	638.16
42000	800.45	758.98	727.13	702.22	682.45	666.58	653.72
43000	819.51	777.05	744.45	718.94	698.69	682.45	669.29
44000	838.56	795.13	761.76	735.66	714.94	698.32	684.85
45000	857.62	813.20	779.07	752.38	731.19	714.19	700.42
46000	876.68	831.27	796.39	769.10	747.44	730.06	715.98
47000	895.74	849.34	813.70	785.82	763.69	745.93	731.54
48000	914.80	867.41	831.01	802.54	779.94	761.80	747.11
49000	933.85	885.48	848.32	819.26	796.19	777.67	762.67
50000	952.91	903.55	865.64	835.97	812.44	793.54	778.24
51000	971.97	921.62	882.95	852.69	828.68	809.41	793.80
52000	991.03	939.69	900.26	869.41	844.93	825.28	809.37
53000	1010.09	957.76	917.57	886.13	861.18	841.15	824.93
54000	1029.15	975.84	934.89	902.85	877.43	857.03	840.50
55000	1048.20	993.91	952.20	919.57	893.68	872.90	856.06
56000	1067.26	1011.98	969.51	936.29	909.93	888.77	871.63
57000	1086.32	1030.05	986.83	953.01	926.18	904.64	887.19
58000	1105.38	1048.12	1004.14	969.73	942.43	920.51	902.76
59000	1124.44	1066.19	1021.45	986.45	958.67	936.38	918.32
60000	1143.50	1084.26	1038.76	1003.17	974.92	952.25	933.89
65000	1238.79	1174.62	1125.33	1086.77	1056.17	1031.60	1011.71
70000	1334.08	1264.97	1211.89	1170.36	1137.41	1110.96	1089.54
75000	1429.37	1355.33	1298.45	1253.96	1218.65	1190.31	1167.36
80000	1524.66	1445.68	1385.02	1337.56	1299.90	1269.67	1245.18
85000	1619.95	1536.04	1471.58	1421.16	1381.14	1349.02	1323.01
90000	1715.24	1626.39	1558.15	1504.75	1462.38	1428.38	1400.83
95000	1810.54	1716.75	1644.71	1588.35	1543.63	1507.73	1478.65
100000	1905.83	1807.10	1731.27	1671.95	1624.87	1587.08	1556.48
105000	2001.12	1897.46	1817.84	1755.55	1706.11	1666.44	1634.30
110000	2096.41	1987.81	1904.40	1839.14	1787.36	1745.79	1712.13
120000	2286.99	2168.52	2077.53	2006.34	1949.85	1904.50	1867.77
130000	2477.57	2349.23	2250.65	2173.53	2112.33	2063.21	2023.42
140000	2668.16	2529.94	2423.78	2340.73	2274.82	2221.92	2179.07
150000	2858.74	2710.65	2596.91	2507.92	2437.31	2380.63	2334.72
160000	3049.32	2891.36	2770.04	2675.12	2599.79	2539.34	2490.37
170000	3239.91	3072.08	2943.16	2842.31	2762.28	2698.04	2646.01
180000	3430.49	3252.79	3116.29	3009.51	2924.77	2856.75	2801.66
190000	3621.07	3433.50	3289.42	3176.70	3087.26	3015.46	2957.31
200000	3811.65	3614.21	3462.55	3343.90	3249.74	3174.17	3112.96
210000	4002.24	3794.92	3635.67	3511.09	3412.23	3332.88	3268.61
220000	4192.82	3975.63	3808.80	3678.29	3574.72	3491.59	3424.25
230000	4383.40	4156.34	3981.93	3845.48	3737.20	3650.29	3579.90
240000	4573.98	4337.05	4155.05	4012.68	3899.69	3809.00	3735.55
250000	4764.57	4517.76	4328.18	4179.87	4062.18	3967.71	3891.20

17.50 % Monthly Payments

LOAN AMOUNT	15	16	17	18	19	20	21
100	1.53	1.51	1.49	1.48	1.47	1.46	1.45
200	3.06	3.02	2.99	2.96	2.94	2.92	2.90
500	7.66	7.56	7.47	7.40	7.34	7.29	7.25
1000	15.32	15.11	14.94	14.80	14.68	14.59	14.51
2000	30.63	30.22	29.88	29.60	29.37	29.18	29.01
5000	76.58	75.55	74.70	74.00	73.42	72.94	72.53
6000	91.89	90.66	89.65	88.81	88.11	87.53	87.04
7000	107.21	105.77	104.59	103.61	102.79	102.11	101.55
8000	122.52	120.88	119.53	118.41	117.48	116.70	116.05
9000	137.84	135.99	134.47	133.21	132.16	131.29	130.56
10000	153.15	151.10	149.41	148.01	146.85	145.88	145.07
12000	183.78	181.32	179.29	177.61	176.21	175.05	174.08
15000	229.73	226.65	224.11	222.01	220.27	218.81	217.60
20000	306.30	302.20	298.82	296.02	293.69	291.75	290.13
25000	382.88	377.75	373.52	370.02	367.11	364.69	362.66
30000	459.45	453.30	448.23	444.03	440.54	437.63	435.20
31000	474.77	468.41	463.17	458.83	455.22	452.21	449.70
32000	490.08	483.52	478.11	473.63	469.91	466.80	464.21
33000	505.40	498.63	493.05	488.43	484.59	481.39	478.72
34000	520.71	513.74	507.99	503.23	499.27	495.98	493.22
35000	536.03	528.85	522.93	518.03	513.96	510.56	507.73
36000	551.34	543.96	537.88	532.83	528.64	525.15	522.23
37000	566.66	559.07	552.82	547.63	543.33	539.74	536.74
38000	581.97	574.18	567.76	562.44	558.01	554.33	551.25
39000	597.29	589.29	582.70	577.24	572.70	568.91	565.75
40000	612.60	604.40	597.64	592.04	587.38	583.50	580.26
41000	627.92	619.51	612.58	606.84	602.07	598.09	594.77
42000	643.23	634.62	627.52	621.64	616.75	612.68	609.27
43000	658.55	649.73	642.46	636.44	631.43	627.26	623.78
44000	673.86	664.84	657.40	651.24	646.12	641.85	638.29
45000	689.18	679.95	672.34	666.04	660.80	656.44	652.79
46000	704.49	695.06	687.28	680.84	675.49	671.03	667.30
47000	719.81	710.17	702.23	695.64	690.17	685.61	681.81
48000	735.12	725.28	717.17	710.44	704.86	700.20	696.31
49000	750.44	740.39	732.11	725.25	719.54	714.79	710.82
50000	765.75	755.50	747.05	740.05	734.23	729.38	725.33
51000	781.07	770.61	761.99	754.85	748.91	743.96	739.83
52000	796.38	785.72	776.93	769.65	763.60	758.55	754.34
53000	811.70	800.83	791.87	784.45	778.28	773.14	768.85
54000	827.01	815.94	806.81	799.25	792.96	787.73	783.35
55000	842.33	831.05	821.75	814.05	807.65	802.31	797.86
56000	857.64	846.16	836.69	828.85	822.33	816.90	812.36
57000	872.96	861.27	851.64	843.65	837.02	831.49	826.87
58000	888.27	876.38	866.58	858.45	851.70	846.08	841.38
59000	903.59	891.49	881.52	873.25	866.39	860.66	855.88
60000	918.90	906.60	896.46	888.06	881.07	875.25	870.39
65000	995.48	982.15	971.16	962.06	954.49	948.19	942.92
70000	1072.05	1057.71	1045.87	1036.06	1027.92	1021.13	1015.46
75000	1148.63	1133.26	1120.57	1110.07	1101.34	1094.07	1087.99
80000	1225.20	1208.81	1195.28	1184.07	1174.76	1167.00	1160.52
85000	1301.78	1284.36	1269.98	1258.08	1248.19	1239.94	1233.05
90000	1378.36	1359.91	1344.69	1332.08	1321.61	1312.88	1305.59
95000	1454.93	1435.46	1419.39	1406.09	1395.03	1385.82	1378.12
100000	1531.51	1511.01	1494.10	1480.09	1468.45	1458.75	1450.65
105000	1608.08	1586.56	1568.80	1554.10	1541.88	1531.69	1523.18
110000	1684.66	1662.11	1643.51	1628.10	1615.30	1604.63	1595.72
120000	1837.81	1813.21	1792.92	1776.11	1762.14	1750.50	1740.78
130000	1990.96	1964.31	1942.33	1924.12	1908.99	1896.38	1885.85
140000	2144.11	2115.41	2091.74	2072.13	2055.83	2042.26	2030.91
150000	2297.26	2266.51	2241.15	2220.14	2202.68	2188.13	2175.98
160000	2450.41	2417.61	2390.56	2368.15	2349.53	2334.01	2321.04
170000	2603.56	2568.71	2539.97	2516.16	2496.37	2479.88	2466.11
180000	2756.71	2719.81	2689.38	2664.17	2643.22	2625.76	2611.17
190000	2909.86	2870.91	2838.79	2812.18	2790.06	2771.63	2756.24
200000	3063.01	3022.01	2988.20	2960.18	2936.91	2917.51	2901.30
210000	3216.16	3173.12	3137.61	3108.19	3083.75	3063.38	3046.37
220000	3369.31	3324.22	3287.02	3256.20	3230.60	3209.26	3191.43
230000	3522.46	3475.32	3436.42	3404.21	3377.44	3355.13	3336.50
240000	3675.61	3626.42	3585.83	3552.22	3524.29	3501.01	3481.56
250000	3828.77	3777.52	3735.24	3700.23	3671.13	3646.88	3626.63

Monthly Payments 17.50 %

LOAN AMOUNT	22	23	24	25	30	35	40
100	1.44	1.44	1.43	1.43	1.42	1.41	1.41
200	2.89	2.88	2.87	2.86	2.83	2.82	2.82
500	7.22	7.19	7.17	7.15	7.09	7.06	7.05
1000	14.44	14.38	14.33	14.29	14.17	14.12	14.10
2000	28.88	28.76	28.67	28.59	28.34	28.24	28.19
5000	72.19	71.91	71.67	71.47	70.85	70.59	70.48
6000	86.63	86.29	86.00	85.76	85.02	84.71	84.57
7000	101.07	100.67	100.34	100.06	99.20	98.83	98.67
8000	115.51	115.05	114.67	114.35	113.37	112.95	112.76
9000	129.95	129.44	129.01	128.65	127.54	127.06	126.86
10000	144.39	143.82	143.34	142.94	141.71	141.18	140.96
12000	173.26	172.58	172.01	171.53	170.05	169.42	169.15
15000	216.58	215.73	215.01	214.41	212.56	211.77	211.43
20000	288.77	287.64	286.68	285.88	283.42	282.36	281.91
25000	360.97	359.55	358.35	357.35	354.27	352.96	352.39
30000	433.16	431.46	430.02	428.82	425.12	423.55	422.87
31000	447.60	445.84	444.36	443.12	439.30	437.66	436.96
32000	462.04	460.22	458.69	457.41	453.47	451.78	451.06
33000	476.48	474.60	473.03	471.70	467.64	465.90	465.15
34000	490.92	488.98	487.36	486.00	481.81	480.02	479.25
35000	505.35	503.37	501.70	500.29	495.98	494.14	493.35
36000	519.79	517.75	516.03	514.59	510.15	508.26	507.44
37000	534.23	532.13	530.36	528.88	524.32	522.37	521.54
38000	548.67	546.51	544.70	543.17	538.49	536.49	535.63
39000	563.11	560.89	559.03	557.47	552.66	550.61	549.73
40000	577.55	575.27	573.37	571.76	566.83	564.73	563.82
41000	591.99	589.66	587.70	586.06	581.00	578.85	577.92
42000	606.43	604.04	602.03	600.35	595.17	592.96	592.02
43000	620.86	618.42	616.37	614.64	609.35	607.08	606.11
44000	635.30	632.80	630.70	628.94	623.52	621.20	620.21
45000	649.74	647.18	645.04	643.23	637.69	635.32	634.30
46000	664.18	661.57	659.37	657.53	651.86	649.44	648.40
47000	678.62	675.95	673.71	671.82	666.03	663.56	662.49
48000	693.06	690.33	688.04	686.11	680.20	677.67	676.59
49000	707.50	704.71	702.37	700.41	694.37	691.79	690.68
50000	721.94	719.09	716.71	714.70	708.54	705.91	704.78
51000	736.37	733.48	731.04	729.00	722.71	720.03	718.88
52000	750.81	747.86	745.38	743.29	736.88	734.15	732.97
53000	765.25	762.24	759.71	757.58	751.05	748.27	747.07
54000	779.69	776.62	774.04	771.88	765.22	762.38	761.16
55000	794.13	791.00	788.38	786.17	779.40	776.50	775.26
56000	808.57	805.38	802.71	800.47	793.57	790.62	789.35
57000	823.01	819.77	817.05	814.76	807.74	804.74	803.45
58000	837.45	834.15	831.38	829.05	821.91	818.86	817.54
59000	851.88	848.53	845.71	843.35	836.08	832.97	831.64
60000	866.32	862.91	860.05	857.64	850.25	847.09	845.74
65000	938.52	934.82	931.72	929.11	921.10	917.68	916.21
70000	1010.71	1006.73	1003.39	1000.58	991.96	988.27	986.69
75000	1082.90	1078.64	1075.06	1072.05	1062.81	1058.87	1057.17
80000	1155.10	1150.55	1146.73	1143.52	1133.67	1129.46	1127.65
85000	1227.29	1222.46	1218.40	1214.99	1204.52	1200.05	1198.13
90000	1299.48	1294.37	1290.07	1286.46	1275.37	1270.64	1268.60
95000	1371.68	1366.28	1361.74	1357.93	1346.23	1341.23	1339.08
100000	1443.87	1438.19	1433.41	1429.40	1417.08	1411.82	1409.56
105000	1516.06	1510.10	1505.09	1500.88	1487.94	1482.41	1480.04
110000	1588.26	1582.01	1576.76	1572.35	1558.79	1553.00	1550.52
120000	1732.65	1725.82	1720.10	1715.29	1700.50	1694.19	1691.47
130000	1877.03	1869.64	1863.44	1858.23	1842.21	1835.37	1832.43
140000	2021.42	2013.46	2006.78	2001.17	1983.91	1976.55	1973.38
150000	2165.81	2157.28	2150.12	2144.11	2125.62	2117.73	2114.34
160000	2310.19	2301.10	2293.46	2287.05	2267.33	2258.91	2255.30
170000	2454.58	2444.92	2436.81	2429.99	2409.04	2400.10	2396.25
180000	2598.97	2588.74	2580.15	2572.93	2550.75	2541.28	2537.21
190000	2743.35	2732.55	2723.49	2715.87	2692.46	2682.46	2678.16
200000	2887.74	2876.37	2866.83	2858.81	2834.16	2823.64	2819.12
210000	3032.13	3020.19	3010.17	3001.75	2975.87	2964.82	2960.08
220000	3176.52	3164.01	3153.51	3144.69	3117.58	3106.01	3101.03
230000	3320.90	3307.83	3296.85	3287.63	3259.29	3247.19	3241.99
240000	3465.29	3451.65	3440.20	3430.57	3401.00	3388.37	3382.94
250000	3609.68	3595.47	3583.54	3573.51	3542.71	3529.55	3523.90

17.75 % Monthly Payments

LOAN AMOUNT	YEARS 1	2	3	4	5	6	7
100	9.13	4.95	3.57	2.89	2.49	2.23	2.05
200	18.25	9.90	7.14	5.78	4.98	4.46	4.10
500	45.63	24.75	17.86	14.46	12.46	11.16	10.25
1000	91.27	49.50	35.72	28.92	24.92	22.32	20.51
2000	182.53	99.01	71.43	57.84	49.84	44.63	41.02
5000	456.33	247.52	178.58	144.60	124.60	111.59	102.55
6000	547.59	297.02	214.30	173.53	149.53	133.90	123.06
7000	638.86	346.52	250.01	202.45	174.45	156.22	143.57
8000	730.12	396.03	285.73	231.37	199.37	178.54	164.07
9000	821.39	445.53	321.44	260.29	224.29	200.85	184.58
10000	912.65	495.03	357.16	289.21	249.21	223.17	205.09
12000	1095.18	594.04	428.59	347.05	299.05	267.81	246.11
15000	1368.98	742.55	535.74	433.81	373.81	334.76	307.64
20000	1825.30	990.07	714.32	578.42	498.42	446.34	410.19
25000	2281.63	1237.58	892.90	723.02	623.02	557.93	512.73
30000	2737.95	1485.10	1071.48	867.63	747.63	669.51	615.28
31000	2829.22	1534.60	1107.20	896.55	772.55	691.83	635.79
32000	2920.48	1584.11	1142.91	925.47	797.47	714.15	656.30
33000	3011.75	1633.61	1178.63	954.39	822.39	736.47	676.81
34000	3103.01	1683.11	1214.34	983.31	847.31	758.78	697.32
35000	3194.28	1732.62	1250.06	1012.23	872.23	781.10	717.83
36000	3285.54	1782.12	1285.78	1041.15	897.16	803.42	738.34
37000	3376.81	1831.62	1321.49	1070.07	922.08	825.73	758.85
38000	3468.07	1881.13	1357.21	1098.99	947.00	848.05	779.35
39000	3559.34	1930.63	1392.93	1127.91	971.92	870.37	799.86
40000	3650.60	1980.13	1428.64	1156.83	996.84	892.68	820.37
41000	3741.87	2029.64	1464.36	1185.75	1021.76	915.00	840.88
42000	3833.13	2079.14	1500.07	1214.68	1046.68	937.32	861.39
43000	3924.40	2128.64	1535.79	1243.60	1071.60	959.64	881.90
44000	4015.66	2178.15	1571.51	1272.52	1096.52	981.95	902.41
45000	4106.93	2227.65	1607.22	1301.44	1121.44	1004.27	922.92
46000	4198.19	2277.15	1642.94	1330.36	1146.37	1026.59	943.43
47000	4289.46	2326.66	1678.65	1359.28	1171.29	1048.90	963.94
48000	4380.72	2376.16	1714.37	1388.20	1196.21	1071.22	984.45
49000	4471.99	2425.67	1750.09	1417.12	1221.13	1093.54	1004.96
50000	4563.25	2475.17	1785.80	1446.04	1246.05	1115.86	1025.47
51000	4654.52	2524.67	1821.52	1474.96	1270.97	1138.17	1045.98
52000	4745.78	2574.18	1857.23	1503.88	1295.89	1160.49	1066.49
53000	4837.05	2623.68	1892.95	1532.81	1320.81	1182.81	1086.99
54000	4928.31	2673.18	1928.67	1561.73	1345.73	1205.12	1107.50
55000	5019.58	2722.69	1964.38	1590.65	1370.65	1227.44	1128.01
56000	5110.85	2772.19	2000.10	1619.57	1395.57	1249.76	1148.52
57000	5202.11	2821.69	2035.81	1648.49	1420.50	1272.08	1169.03
58000	5293.38	2871.20	2071.53	1677.41	1445.42	1294.39	1189.54
59000	5384.64	2920.70	2107.25	1706.33	1470.34	1316.71	1210.05
60000	5475.91	2970.20	2142.96	1735.25	1495.26	1339.03	1230.56
65000	5932.23	3217.72	2321.54	1879.86	1619.86	1450.61	1333.11
70000	6388.56	3465.24	2500.12	2024.46	1744.47	1562.20	1435.65
75000	6844.88	3712.75	2678.70	2169.06	1869.07	1673.78	1538.20
80000	7301.21	3960.27	2857.28	2313.67	1993.68	1785.37	1640.75
85000	7757.53	4207.79	3035.86	2458.27	2118.28	1896.96	1743.29
90000	8213.86	4455.30	3214.44	2602.88	2242.89	2008.54	1845.84
95000	8670.18	4702.82	3393.02	2747.48	2367.49	2120.13	1948.39
100000	9126.51	4950.34	3571.60	2892.09	2492.10	2231.71	2050.93
105000	9582.83	5197.85	3750.18	3036.69	2616.70	2343.30	2153.48
110000	10039.16	5445.37	3928.76	3181.29	2741.31	2454.88	2256.03
120000	10951.81	5940.40	4285.92	3470.50	2990.52	2678.05	2461.12
130000	11864.46	6435.44	4643.08	3759.71	3239.73	2901.23	2666.21
140000	12777.11	6930.47	5000.24	4048.92	3488.94	3124.40	2871.31
150000	13689.76	7425.51	5357.40	4338.13	3738.15	3347.57	3076.40
160000	14602.41	7920.54	5714.56	4627.34	3987.36	3570.74	3281.49
170000	15515.07	8415.57	6071.72	4916.55	4236.57	3793.91	3486.59
180000	16427.72	8910.61	6428.88	5205.75	4485.78	4017.08	3691.68
190000	17340.37	9405.64	6786.05	5494.96	4734.99	4240.25	3896.77
200000	18253.02	9900.67	7143.21	5784.17	4984.20	4463.42	4101.87
210000	19165.67	10395.71	7500.37	6073.38	5233.41	4686.60	4306.96
220000	20078.32	10890.74	7857.53	6362.59	5482.62	4909.77	4512.05
230000	20990.97	11385.77	8214.69	6651.80	5731.83	5132.94	4717.15
240000	21903.62	11880.81	8571.85	6941.00	5981.04	5356.11	4922.24
250000	22816.27	12375.84	8929.01	7230.21	6230.25	5579.28	5127.33

Monthly Payments 17.75 %

LOAN AMOUNT	8	9	10	11	12	13	14
100	1.92	1.82	1.75	1.69	1.64	1.60	1.57
200	3.84	3.64	3.49	3.37	3.28	3.21	3.15
500	9.60	9.11	8.73	8.44	8.20	8.01	7.86
1000	19.20	18.21	17.46	16.87	16.40	16.03	15.73
2000	38.39	36.43	34.92	33.74	32.81	32.06	31.45
5000	95.99	91.07	87.30	84.36	82.02	80.15	78.63
6000	115.18	109.29	104.76	101.23	98.42	96.18	94.36
7000	134.38	127.50	122.22	118.10	114.83	112.21	110.09
8000	153.58	145.72	139.68	134.97	131.23	128.24	125.82
9000	172.78	163.93	157.14	151.84	147.64	144.27	141.54
10000	191.97	182.15	174.60	168.71	164.04	160.30	157.27
12000	230.37	218.57	209.52	202.45	196.85	192.36	188.72
15000	287.96	273.22	261.91	253.07	246.06	240.45	235.90
20000	383.95	364.29	349.21	337.42	328.08	320.59	314.54
25000	479.94	455.36	436.51	421.78	410.10	400.74	393.17
30000	575.92	546.44	523.81	506.13	492.12	480.89	471.81
31000	595.12	564.65	541.27	523.00	508.53	496.92	487.53
32000	614.32	582.87	558.73	539.88	524.93	512.95	503.26
33000	633.52	601.08	576.19	556.75	541.33	528.98	518.99
34000	652.71	619.29	593.65	573.62	557.74	545.01	534.71
35000	671.91	637.51	611.11	590.49	574.14	561.04	550.44
36000	691.11	655.72	628.57	607.36	590.55	577.07	566.17
37000	710.31	673.94	646.03	624.23	606.95	593.10	581.90
38000	729.50	692.15	663.50	641.10	623.35	609.13	597.62
39000	748.70	710.37	680.96	657.97	639.76	625.16	613.35
40000	767.90	728.58	698.42	674.84	656.16	641.19	629.08
41000	787.10	746.80	715.88	691.72	672.57	657.22	644.80
42000	806.29	765.01	733.34	708.59	688.97	673.25	660.53
43000	825.49	783.23	750.80	725.46	705.37	689.28	676.26
44000	844.69	801.44	768.26	742.33	721.78	705.31	691.98
45000	863.89	819.66	785.72	759.20	738.18	721.34	707.71
46000	883.08	837.87	803.18	776.07	754.59	737.37	723.44
47000	902.28	856.08	820.64	792.94	770.99	753.40	739.16
48000	921.48	874.30	838.10	809.81	787.39	769.43	754.89
49000	940.68	892.51	855.56	826.68	803.80	785.45	770.62
50000	959.87	910.73	873.02	843.56	820.20	801.48	786.35
51000	979.07	928.94	890.48	860.43	836.61	817.51	802.07
52000	998.27	947.16	907.94	877.30	853.01	833.54	817.80
53000	1017.46	965.37	925.40	894.17	869.41	849.57	833.53
54000	1036.66	983.59	942.86	911.04	885.82	865.60	849.25
55000	1055.86	1001.80	960.32	927.91	902.22	881.63	864.98
56000	1075.06	1020.02	977.78	944.78	918.63	897.66	880.71
57000	1094.25	1038.23	995.24	961.65	935.03	913.69	896.43
58000	1113.45	1056.44	1012.70	978.52	951.44	929.72	912.16
59000	1132.65	1074.66	1030.16	995.40	967.84	945.75	927.89
60000	1151.85	1092.87	1047.62	1012.27	984.24	961.78	943.61
65000	1247.83	1183.95	1134.93	1096.62	1066.26	1041.93	1022.25
70000	1343.82	1275.02	1222.23	1180.98	1148.28	1122.08	1100.88
75000	1439.81	1366.09	1309.53	1265.33	1230.30	1202.23	1179.52
80000	1535.80	1457.16	1396.83	1349.69	1312.32	1282.38	1258.15
85000	1631.78	1548.24	1484.13	1434.04	1394.34	1362.52	1336.79
90000	1727.77	1639.31	1571.44	1518.40	1476.36	1442.67	1415.42
95000	1823.76	1730.38	1658.74	1602.76	1558.39	1522.82	1494.06
100000	1919.75	1821.46	1746.04	1687.11	1640.41	1602.97	1572.69
105000	2015.73	1912.53	1833.34	1771.47	1722.43	1683.12	1651.32
110000	2111.72	2003.60	1920.64	1855.82	1804.45	1763.27	1729.96
120000	2303.69	2185.75	2095.25	2024.53	1968.49	1923.56	1887.23
130000	2495.67	2367.89	2269.85	2193.24	2132.53	2083.86	2044.50
140000	2687.64	2550.04	2444.46	2361.96	2296.57	2244.16	2201.77
150000	2879.62	2732.18	2619.06	2530.67	2460.61	2404.45	2359.04
160000	3071.59	2914.33	2793.66	2699.38	2624.65	2564.75	2516.30
170000	3263.57	3096.47	2968.27	2868.09	2788.69	2725.05	2673.57
180000	3455.54	3278.62	3142.87	3036.80	2952.73	2885.34	2830.84
190000	3647.52	3460.77	3317.48	3205.51	3116.77	3045.64	2988.11
200000	3839.49	3642.91	3492.08	3374.22	3280.81	3205.94	3145.38
210000	4031.46	3825.06	3666.68	3542.93	3444.85	3366.23	3302.65
220000	4223.44	4007.20	3841.29	3711.64	3608.89	3526.53	3459.92
230000	4415.41	4189.35	4015.89	3880.36	3772.93	3686.83	3617.19
240000	4607.39	4371.49	4190.50	4049.07	3936.97	3847.13	3774.46
250000	4799.36	4553.64	4365.10	4217.78	4101.01	4007.42	3931.73

17.75 % Monthly Payments

LOAN AMOUNT	YEARS 15	16	17	18	19	20	21
100	1.55	1.53	1.51	1.50	1.49	1.48	1.47
200	3.10	3.06	3.02	2.99	2.97	2.95	2.94
500	7.74	7.64	7.56	7.49	7.43	7.38	7.34
1000	15.48	15.28	15.11	14.97	14.86	14.76	14.69
2000	30.96	30.56	30.22	29.95	29.72	29.53	29.37
5000	77.40	76.39	75.56	74.87	74.30	73.82	73.43
6000	92.88	91.67	90.67	89.84	89.16	88.59	88.11
7000	108.36	106.95	105.78	104.82	104.02	103.35	102.80
8000	123.84	122.22	120.89	119.79	118.88	118.12	117.48
9000	139.32	137.50	136.00	134.77	133.74	132.88	132.17
10000	154.80	152.78	151.12	149.74	148.60	147.65	146.86
12000	185.76	183.34	181.34	179.69	178.32	177.18	176.23
15000	232.20	229.17	226.67	224.61	222.90	221.47	220.28
20000	309.60	305.56	302.23	299.48	297.19	295.30	293.71
25000	387.01	381.95	377.79	374.35	371.49	369.12	367.14
30000	464.41	458.34	453.35	449.22	445.79	442.94	440.57
31000	479.89	473.62	468.46	464.19	460.65	457.71	455.25
32000	495.37	488.90	483.57	479.17	475.51	472.47	469.94
33000	510.85	504.18	498.68	494.14	490.37	487.24	484.62
34000	526.33	519.45	513.79	509.11	505.23	502.00	499.31
35000	541.81	534.73	528.91	524.09	520.09	516.77	513.99
36000	557.29	550.01	544.02	539.06	534.95	531.53	528.68
37000	572.77	565.29	559.13	554.04	549.81	546.30	543.37
38000	588.25	580.57	574.24	569.01	564.67	561.06	558.05
39000	603.73	595.84	589.35	583.98	579.53	575.83	572.74
40000	619.21	611.12	604.46	598.96	594.39	590.59	587.42
41000	634.69	626.40	619.57	613.93	609.25	605.35	602.11
42000	650.17	641.68	634.69	628.91	624.11	620.12	616.79
43000	665.65	656.96	649.80	643.88	638.97	634.88	631.48
44000	681.13	672.23	664.91	658.85	653.83	649.65	646.16
45000	696.61	687.51	680.02	673.83	668.69	664.41	660.85
46000	712.09	702.79	695.13	688.80	683.55	679.18	675.54
47000	727.57	718.07	710.24	703.77	698.41	693.94	690.22
48000	743.05	733.35	725.36	718.75	713.27	708.71	704.91
49000	758.53	748.63	740.47	733.72	728.13	723.47	719.59
50000	774.01	763.90	755.58	748.70	742.99	738.24	734.28
51000	789.49	779.18	770.69	763.67	757.85	753.00	748.96
52000	804.97	794.46	785.80	778.64	772.71	767.77	763.65
53000	820.45	809.74	800.91	793.62	787.57	782.53	778.33
54000	835.93	825.02	816.03	808.59	802.43	797.30	793.02
55000	851.41	840.29	831.14	823.57	817.29	812.06	807.71
56000	866.89	855.57	846.25	838.54	832.15	826.83	822.39
57000	882.37	870.85	861.36	853.51	847.01	841.59	837.08
58000	897.85	886.13	876.47	868.49	861.87	856.36	851.76
59000	913.33	901.41	891.58	883.46	876.72	871.12	866.45
60000	928.81	916.68	906.70	898.44	891.58	885.89	881.13
65000	1006.21	993.07	982.25	973.31	965.88	959.71	954.56
70000	1083.62	1069.46	1057.81	1048.18	1040.18	1033.53	1027.99
75000	1161.02	1145.86	1133.37	1123.04	1114.48	1107.36	1101.42
80000	1238.42	1222.25	1208.93	1197.91	1188.78	1181.18	1174.84
85000	1315.82	1298.64	1284.48	1272.78	1263.08	1255.00	1248.27
90000	1393.22	1375.03	1360.04	1347.65	1337.38	1328.83	1321.70
95000	1470.62	1451.42	1435.60	1422.52	1411.68	1402.65	1395.13
100000	1548.02	1527.81	1511.16	1497.39	1485.97	1476.48	1468.56
105000	1625.42	1604.20	1586.72	1572.26	1560.27	1550.30	1541.98
110000	1702.83	1680.59	1662.27	1647.13	1634.57	1624.12	1615.41
120000	1857.63	1833.37	1813.39	1796.87	1783.17	1771.77	1762.27
130000	2012.43	1986.15	1964.51	1946.61	1931.77	1919.42	1909.12
140000	2167.23	2138.93	2115.62	2096.35	2080.36	2067.07	2055.98
150000	2322.03	2291.71	2266.74	2246.09	2228.96	2214.71	2202.83
160000	2476.84	2444.49	2417.85	2395.83	2377.56	2362.36	2349.69
170000	2631.64	2597.27	2568.97	2545.57	2526.16	2510.01	2496.55
180000	2786.44	2750.05	2720.09	2695.31	2674.75	2657.66	2643.40
190000	2941.24	2902.83	2871.20	2845.05	2823.35	2805.30	2790.26
200000	3096.05	3055.61	3022.32	2994.79	2971.95	2952.95	2937.11
210000	3250.85	3208.39	3173.43	3144.53	3120.55	3100.60	3083.97
220000	3405.65	3361.17	3324.55	3294.27	3269.14	3248.25	3230.82
230000	3560.45	3513.96	3475.66	3444.00	3417.74	3395.89	3377.68
240000	3715.25	3666.74	3626.78	3593.74	3566.34	3543.54	3524.53
250000	3870.06	3819.52	3777.90	3743.48	3714.94	3691.19	3671.39

Monthly Payments 17.75 %

LOAN AMOUNT	22	23	24	25	30	35	40
100	1.46	1.46	1.45	1.45	1.44	1.43	1.43
200	2.92	2.91	2.90	2.90	2.87	2.86	2.86
500	7.31	7.28	7.26	7.24	7.18	7.15	7.14
1000	14.62	14.56	14.52	14.48	14.36	14.31	14.29
2000	29.24	29.13	29.04	28.96	28.72	28.62	28.58
5000	73.10	72.82	72.59	72.39	71.80	71.55	71.44
6000	87.72	87.38	87.11	86.87	86.16	85.86	85.73
7000	102.34	101.95	101.62	101.35	100.52	100.17	100.02
8000	116.96	116.51	116.14	115.83	114.88	114.48	114.31
9000	131.57	131.08	130.66	130.31	129.24	128.79	128.60
10000	146.19	145.64	145.18	144.79	143.60	143.10	142.88
12000	175.43	174.77	174.21	173.75	172.32	171.72	171.46
15000	219.29	218.46	217.77	217.18	215.40	214.65	214.33
20000	292.39	291.28	290.35	289.58	287.20	286.20	285.77
25000	365.49	364.10	362.94	361.97	359.00	357.75	357.21
30000	438.58	436.92	435.53	434.36	430.80	429.29	428.65
31000	453.20	451.49	450.05	448.84	445.16	443.60	442.94
32000	467.82	466.05	464.57	463.32	459.52	457.91	457.23
33000	482.44	480.61	479.08	477.80	473.88	472.22	471.52
34000	497.06	495.18	493.60	492.28	488.24	486.53	485.81
35000	511.68	509.74	508.12	506.76	502.60	500.84	500.10
36000	526.30	524.31	522.64	521.24	516.96	515.15	514.39
37000	540.92	538.87	537.16	535.72	531.32	529.46	528.67
38000	555.54	553.43	551.67	550.20	545.68	543.77	542.96
39000	570.16	568.00	566.19	564.67	560.04	558.08	557.25
40000	584.78	582.56	580.71	579.15	574.40	572.39	571.54
41000	599.40	597.13	595.23	593.63	588.76	586.70	585.83
42000	614.02	611.69	609.74	608.11	603.12	601.01	600.12
43000	628.63	626.25	624.26	622.59	617.48	615.32	614.40
44000	643.25	640.82	638.78	637.07	631.84	629.63	628.69
45000	657.87	655.38	653.30	651.55	646.20	643.94	642.98
46000	672.49	669.95	667.81	666.03	660.56	658.25	657.27
47000	687.11	684.51	682.33	680.50	674.92	672.56	671.56
48000	701.73	699.08	696.85	694.98	689.28	686.87	685.85
49000	716.35	713.64	711.37	709.46	703.64	701.18	700.14
50000	730.97	728.20	725.89	723.94	718.00	715.49	714.42
51000	745.59	742.77	740.40	738.42	732.36	729.80	728.71
52000	760.21	757.33	754.92	752.90	746.72	744.11	743.00
53000	774.83	771.90	769.44	767.38	761.08	758.42	757.29
54000	789.45	786.46	783.96	781.86	775.44	772.73	771.58
55000	804.07	801.02	798.47	796.34	789.80	787.04	785.87
56000	818.69	815.59	812.99	810.81	804.16	801.35	800.15
57000	833.31	830.15	827.51	825.29	818.52	815.66	814.44
58000	847.93	844.72	842.03	839.77	832.88	829.97	828.73
59000	862.55	859.28	856.54	854.25	847.24	844.28	843.02
60000	877.16	873.84	871.06	868.73	861.60	858.59	857.31
65000	950.26	946.66	943.65	941.12	933.40	930.14	928.75
70000	1023.36	1019.48	1016.24	1013.52	1005.20	1001.69	1000.19
75000	1096.46	1092.31	1088.83	1085.91	1077.00	1073.24	1071.64
80000	1169.55	1165.13	1161.42	1158.31	1148.80	1144.79	1143.08
85000	1242.65	1237.95	1234.00	1230.70	1220.60	1216.33	1214.52
90000	1315.75	1310.77	1306.59	1303.09	1292.40	1287.88	1285.96
95000	1388.84	1383.59	1379.18	1375.49	1364.20	1359.43	1357.41
100000	1461.94	1456.41	1451.77	1447.88	1436.00	1430.98	1428.85
105000	1535.04	1529.23	1524.36	1520.28	1507.80	1502.53	1500.29
110000	1608.14	1602.05	1596.95	1592.67	1579.60	1574.08	1571.73
120000	1754.33	1747.69	1742.12	1737.46	1723.20	1717.18	1714.62
130000	1900.52	1893.33	1887.30	1882.25	1866.80	1860.28	1857.50
140000	2046.72	2038.97	2032.48	2027.03	2010.40	2003.37	2000.39
150000	2192.91	2184.61	2177.66	2171.82	2154.00	2146.47	2143.27
160000	2339.11	2330.25	2322.83	2316.61	2297.60	2289.57	2286.16
170000	2485.30	2475.89	2468.01	2461.40	2441.20	2432.67	2429.04
180000	2631.49	2621.53	2613.19	2606.19	2584.80	2575.77	2571.93
190000	2777.69	2767.17	2758.36	2750.98	2728.40	2718.86	2714.81
200000	2923.88	2912.81	2903.54	2895.76	2872.00	2861.96	2857.70
210000	3070.08	3058.45	3048.72	3040.55	3015.60	3005.06	3000.58
220000	3216.27	3204.10	3193.89	3185.34	3159.20	3148.16	3143.47
230000	3362.46	3349.74	3339.07	3330.13	3302.80	3291.26	3286.35
240000	3508.66	3495.38	3484.25	3474.92	3446.40	3434.36	3429.23
250000	3654.85	3641.02	3629.43	3619.71	3590.00	3577.45	3572.12

18.00 % Monthly Payments

LOAN AMOUNT	YEARS 1	2	3	4	5	6	7
100	9.14	4.96	3.58	2.90	2.50	2.24	2.06
200	18.28	9.92	7.17	5.81	5.01	4.49	4.13
500	45.69	24.81	17.92	14.52	12.52	11.22	10.32
1000	91.38	49.62	35.83	29.04	25.05	22.45	20.64
2000	182.75	99.23	71.66	58.08	50.09	44.89	41.29
5000	456.88	248.08	179.16	145.21	125.23	112.24	103.22
6000	548.25	297.69	214.99	174.25	150.28	134.68	123.87
7000	639.63	347.31	250.82	203.29	175.33	157.13	144.51
8000	731.01	396.92	286.66	232.33	200.37	179.58	165.15
9000	822.38	446.54	322.49	261.37	225.42	202.03	185.80
10000	913.76	496.15	358.32	290.42	250.47	224.47	206.44
12000	1096.51	595.38	429.99	348.50	300.56	269.37	247.73
15000	1370.63	744.23	537.48	435.62	375.70	336.71	309.67
20000	1827.51	992.31	716.64	580.83	500.93	448.95	412.89
25000	2284.39	1240.38	895.80	726.04	626.16	561.19	516.11
30000	2741.27	1488.46	1074.96	871.25	751.40	673.42	619.33
31000	2832.64	1538.08	1110.80	900.29	776.44	695.87	639.97
32000	2924.02	1587.69	1146.63	929.33	801.49	718.32	660.62
33000	3015.40	1637.31	1182.46	958.37	826.53	740.77	681.26
34000	3106.77	1686.92	1218.29	987.41	851.58	763.21	701.91
35000	3198.15	1736.54	1254.12	1016.46	876.63	785.66	722.55
36000	3289.52	1786.15	1289.96	1045.50	901.67	808.11	743.20
37000	3380.90	1835.77	1325.79	1074.54	926.72	830.56	763.84
38000	3472.27	1885.38	1361.62	1103.58	951.77	853.00	784.48
39000	3563.65	1935.00	1397.45	1132.62	976.81	875.45	805.13
40000	3655.03	1984.61	1433.28	1161.66	1001.86	897.90	825.77
41000	3746.40	2034.23	1469.12	1190.70	1026.91	920.34	846.42
42000	3837.78	2083.85	1504.95	1219.75	1051.95	942.79	867.06
43000	3929.15	2133.46	1540.78	1248.79	1077.00	965.24	887.71
44000	4020.53	2183.08	1576.61	1277.83	1102.05	987.69	908.35
45000	4111.90	2232.69	1612.44	1306.87	1127.09	1010.13	929.00
46000	4203.28	2282.31	1648.28	1335.91	1152.14	1032.58	949.64
47000	4294.66	2331.92	1684.11	1364.95	1177.19	1055.03	970.28
48000	4386.03	2381.54	1719.94	1394.00	1202.23	1077.48	990.93
49000	4477.41	2431.15	1755.77	1423.04	1227.28	1099.92	1011.57
50000	4568.78	2480.77	1791.61	1452.08	1252.33	1122.37	1032.22
51000	4660.16	2530.38	1827.44	1481.12	1277.37	1144.82	1052.86
52000	4751.53	2580.00	1863.27	1510.16	1302.42	1167.27	1073.51
53000	4842.91	2629.61	1899.10	1539.20	1327.46	1189.71	1094.15
54000	4934.28	2679.23	1934.93	1568.25	1352.51	1212.16	1114.79
55000	5025.66	2728.85	1970.77	1597.29	1377.56	1234.61	1135.44
56000	5117.04	2778.46	2006.60	1626.33	1402.60	1257.06	1156.08
57000	5208.41	2828.08	2042.43	1655.37	1427.65	1279.50	1176.73
58000	5299.79	2877.69	2078.26	1684.41	1452.70	1301.95	1197.37
59000	5391.16	2927.31	2114.09	1713.45	1477.74	1324.40	1218.02
60000	5482.54	2976.92	2149.93	1742.50	1502.79	1346.85	1238.66
65000	5939.42	3225.00	2329.09	1887.70	1628.02	1459.08	1341.88
70000	6396.29	3473.08	2508.25	2032.91	1753.26	1571.32	1445.10
75000	6853.17	3721.15	2687.41	2178.12	1878.49	1683.56	1548.33
80000	7310.05	3969.23	2866.57	2323.33	2003.72	1795.79	1651.55
85000	7766.93	4217.31	3045.73	2468.53	2128.95	1908.03	1754.77
90000	8223.81	4465.38	3224.89	2613.74	2254.19	2020.27	1857.99
95000	8680.69	4713.46	3404.05	2758.95	2379.42	2132.51	1961.21
100000	9137.56	4961.54	3583.21	2904.16	2504.65	2244.74	2064.43
105000	9594.44	5209.61	3762.37	3049.37	2629.88	2356.98	2167.66
110000	10051.32	5457.69	3941.53	3194.57	2755.12	2469.22	2270.88
120000	10965.08	5953.84	4299.85	3484.99	3005.58	2693.69	2477.32
130000	11878.83	6450.00	4658.17	3775.41	3256.05	2918.17	2683.76
140000	12792.59	6946.15	5016.49	4065.82	3506.51	3142.64	2890.21
150000	13706.35	7442.31	5374.82	4356.24	3756.98	3367.12	3096.65
160000	14620.10	7938.46	5733.14	4646.65	4007.44	3591.59	3303.09
170000	15533.86	8434.61	6091.46	4937.07	4257.91	3816.06	3509.54
180000	16447.62	8930.77	6449.78	5227.49	4508.37	4040.54	3715.98
190000	17361.37	9426.92	6808.10	5517.90	4758.84	4265.01	3922.42
200000	18275.13	9923.07	7166.42	5808.32	5009.30	4489.49	4128.87
210000	19188.88	10419.23	7524.74	6098.73	5259.77	4713.96	4335.31
220000	20102.64	10915.38	7883.06	6389.15	5510.23	4938.44	4541.75
230000	21016.40	11411.54	8241.38	6679.56	5760.70	5162.91	4748.20
240000	21930.15	11907.69	8599.71	6969.98	6011.16	5387.38	4954.64
250000	22843.91	12403.84	8958.03	7260.40	6261.63	5611.86	5161.08

Monthly Payments 18.00 %

LOAN MOUNT	8	9	10	11	12	13	14
100	1.93	1.84	1.76	1.70	1.66	1.62	1.59
200	3.87	3.67	3.52	3.40	3.31	3.24	3.18
500	9.67	9.18	8.80	8.51	8.28	8.09	7.94
1000	19.34	18.36	17.61	17.02	16.56	16.19	15.89
2000	38.67	36.72	35.22	34.05	33.12	32.38	31.78
5000	96.68	91.79	88.04	85.12	82.80	80.94	79.45
6000	116.02	110.15	105.65	102.14	99.36	97.13	95.34
7000	135.36	128.51	123.26	119.16	115.92	113.32	111.23
8000	154.70	146.87	140.87	136.19	132.48	129.51	127.12
9000	174.03	165.23	158.48	153.21	149.04	145.70	143.01
10000	193.37	183.58	176.08	170.23	165.60	161.89	158.89
12000	232.04	220.30	211.30	204.28	198.72	194.27	190.67
15000	290.05	275.38	264.13	255.35	248.40	242.83	238.34
20000	386.74	367.17	352.17	340.46	331.20	323.78	317.79
25000	483.42	458.96	440.21	425.58	414.00	404.72	397.24
30000	580.11	550.75	528.25	510.69	496.80	485.67	476.68
31000	599.45	569.11	545.86	527.72	513.35	501.86	492.57
32000	618.78	587.47	563.47	544.74	529.91	518.05	508.46
33000	638.12	605.83	581.08	561.76	546.47	534.24	524.35
34000	657.46	624.19	598.69	578.79	563.03	550.43	540.24
35000	676.79	642.55	616.30	595.81	579.59	566.61	556.13
36000	696.13	660.91	633.91	612.83	596.15	582.80	572.02
37000	715.47	679.26	651.51	629.86	612.71	598.99	587.91
38000	734.81	697.62	669.12	646.88	629.27	615.18	603.80
39000	754.14	715.98	686.73	663.90	645.83	631.37	619.69
40000	773.48	734.34	704.34	680.93	662.39	647.56	635.58
41000	792.82	752.70	721.95	697.95	678.95	663.75	651.47
42000	812.15	771.06	739.56	714.97	695.51	679.94	667.36
43000	831.49	789.41	757.17	732.00	712.07	696.13	683.25
44000	850.83	807.77	774.77	749.02	728.63	712.32	699.14
45000	870.16	826.13	792.38	766.04	745.19	728.50	715.03
46000	889.50	844.49	809.99	783.07	761.75	744.69	730.92
47000	908.84	862.85	827.60	800.09	778.31	760.88	746.81
48000	928.18	881.21	845.21	817.11	794.87	777.07	762.69
49000	947.51	899.57	862.82	834.13	811.43	793.26	778.58
50000	966.85	917.92	880.42	851.16	827.99	809.45	794.47
51000	986.19	936.28	898.03	868.18	844.55	825.64	810.36
52000	1005.52	954.64	915.64	885.20	861.11	841.83	826.25
53000	1024.86	973.00	933.25	902.23	877.67	858.02	842.14
54000	1044.20	991.36	950.86	919.25	894.23	874.20	858.03
55000	1063.53	1009.72	968.47	936.27	910.79	890.39	873.92
56000	1082.87	1028.07	986.08	953.30	927.35	906.58	889.81
57000	1102.21	1046.43	1003.68	970.32	943.91	922.77	905.70
58000	1121.55	1064.79	1021.29	987.34	960.47	938.96	921.59
59000	1140.88	1083.15	1038.90	1004.37	977.03	955.15	937.48
60000	1160.22	1101.51	1056.51	1021.39	993.59	971.34	953.37
65000	1256.90	1193.30	1144.55	1106.51	1076.39	1052.28	1032.82
70000	1353.59	1285.09	1232.59	1191.62	1159.19	1133.23	1112.26
75000	1450.27	1376.89	1320.64	1276.74	1241.99	1214.17	1191.71
80000	1546.96	1468.68	1408.68	1361.85	1324.79	1295.12	1271.16
85000	1643.64	1560.47	1496.72	1446.97	1407.59	1376.06	1350.60
90000	1740.33	1652.26	1584.76	1532.08	1490.39	1457.01	1430.05
95000	1837.01	1744.05	1672.81	1617.20	1573.18	1537.95	1509.50
100000	1933.70	1835.85	1760.85	1702.32	1655.98	1618.90	1588.95
105000	2030.38	1927.64	1848.89	1787.43	1738.78	1699.84	1668.39
110000	2127.07	2019.43	1936.93	1872.55	1821.58	1780.79	1747.84
120000	2320.44	2203.02	2113.02	2042.78	1987.18	1942.68	1906.74
130000	2513.81	2386.60	2289.10	2213.01	2152.78	2104.57	2065.63
140000	2707.18	2570.19	2465.19	2383.24	2318.38	2266.46	2224.53
150000	2900.55	2753.77	2641.27	2553.47	2483.98	2428.35	2383.42
160000	3093.92	2937.36	2817.36	2723.71	2649.57	2590.24	2542.32
170000	3287.29	3120.94	2993.44	2893.94	2815.17	2752.13	2701.21
180000	3480.66	3304.53	3169.53	3064.17	2980.77	2914.02	2860.10
190000	3674.03	3488.11	3345.61	3234.40	3146.37	3075.91	3019.00
200000	3867.40	3671.69	3521.70	3404.63	3311.97	3237.80	3177.89
210000	4060.77	3855.28	3697.78	3574.86	3477.57	3399.69	3336.79
220000	4254.14	4038.86	3873.87	3745.10	3643.16	3561.58	3495.68
230000	4447.51	4222.45	4049.95	3915.33	3808.76	3723.46	3654.58
240000	4640.88	4406.03	4226.04	4085.56	3974.36	3885.35	3813.47
250000	4834.25	4589.62	4402.12	4255.79	4139.96	4047.24	3972.37

18.00 % Monthly Payments

LOAN AMOUNT	15	16	17	18	19	20	21
				YEARS			
100	1.56	1.54	1.53	1.51	1.50	1.49	1.4
200	3.13	3.09	3.06	3.03	3.01	2.99	2.9
500	7.82	7.72	7.64	7.57	7.52	7.47	7.4
1000	15.65	15.45	15.28	15.15	15.04	14.94	14.8
2000	31.29	30.89	30.57	30.29	30.07	29.88	29.7
5000	78.23	77.23	76.41	75.74	75.18	74.71	74.3
6000	93.88	92.68	91.70	90.88	90.21	89.65	89.1
7000	109.52	108.13	106.98	106.03	105.25	104.60	104.0
8000	125.17	123.57	122.26	121.18	120.28	119.54	118.9
9000	140.81	139.02	137.54	136.33	135.32	134.48	133.7
10000	156.46	154.46	152.83	151.47	150.35	149.42	148.6
12000	187.75	185.36	183.39	181.77	180.42	179.31	178.3
15000	234.69	231.70	229.24	227.21	225.53	224.13	222.9
20000	312.92	308.93	305.65	302.95	300.71	298.85	297.3
25000	391.15	386.16	382.07	378.68	375.88	373.56	371.6
30000	469.38	463.39	458.48	454.42	451.06	448.27	445.9
31000	485.02	478.84	473.76	469.57	466.09	463.21	460.8
32000	500.67	494.29	489.04	484.71	481.13	478.15	475.6
33000	516.31	509.73	504.33	499.86	496.17	493.10	490.5
34000	531.96	525.18	519.61	515.01	511.20	508.04	505.4
35000	547.60	540.63	534.89	530.16	526.24	522.98	520.2
36000	563.25	556.07	550.17	545.30	541.27	537.92	535.1
37000	578.90	571.52	565.46	560.45	556.31	552.87	550.0
38000	594.54	586.97	580.74	575.60	571.34	567.81	564.8
39000	610.19	602.41	596.02	590.75	586.38	582.75	579.7
40000	625.83	617.86	611.30	605.89	601.41	597.69	594.6
41000	641.48	633.31	626.59	621.04	616.45	612.64	609.4
42000	657.13	648.75	641.87	636.19	631.48	627.58	624.3
43000	672.77	664.20	657.15	651.34	646.52	642.52	639.1
44000	688.42	679.65	672.43	666.48	661.55	657.46	654.0
45000	704.06	695.09	687.72	681.63	676.59	672.40	668.9
46000	719.71	710.54	703.00	696.78	691.62	687.35	683.7
47000	735.35	725.99	718.28	711.92	706.66	702.29	698.6
48000	751.00	741.43	733.56	727.07	721.70	717.23	713.5
49000	766.65	756.88	748.85	742.22	736.73	732.17	728.3
50000	782.29	772.32	764.13	757.37	751.77	747.12	743.2
51000	797.94	787.77	779.41	772.51	766.80	762.06	758.1
52000	813.58	803.22	794.70	787.66	781.84	777.00	772.9
53000	829.23	818.66	809.98	802.81	796.87	791.94	787.8
54000	844.88	834.11	825.26	817.96	811.91	806.89	802.7
55000	860.52	849.56	840.54	833.10	826.94	821.83	817.5
56000	876.17	865.00	855.83	848.25	841.98	836.77	832.4
57000	891.81	880.45	871.11	863.40	857.01	851.71	847.3
58000	907.46	895.90	886.39	878.55	872.05	866.65	862.1
59000	923.10	911.34	901.67	893.69	887.08	881.60	877.0
60000	938.75	926.79	916.96	908.84	902.12	896.54	891.9
65000	1016.98	1004.02	993.37	984.58	977.30	971.25	966.2
70000	1095.21	1081.25	1069.78	1060.31	1052.47	1045.96	1040.5
75000	1173.44	1158.49	1146.20	1136.05	1127.65	1120.67	1114.8
80000	1251.67	1235.72	1222.61	1211.79	1202.83	1195.39	1189.1
85000	1329.90	1312.95	1299.02	1287.52	1278.00	1270.10	1263.5
90000	1408.13	1390.18	1375.43	1363.26	1353.18	1344.81	1337.8
95000	1486.35	1467.42	1451.85	1439.00	1428.36	1419.52	1412.1
100000	1564.58	1544.65	1528.26	1514.73	1503.53	1494.23	1486.4
105000	1642.81	1621.88	1604.67	1590.47	1578.71	1568.94	1560.8
110000	1721.04	1699.11	1681.09	1666.21	1653.89	1643.66	1635.1
120000	1877.50	1853.58	1833.91	1817.68	1804.24	1793.08	1783.7
130000	2033.96	2008.04	1986.74	1969.15	1954.59	1942.50	1932.4
140000	2190.42	2162.51	2139.56	2120.63	2104.95	2091.92	2081.0
150000	2346.88	2316.97	2292.39	2272.10	2255.30	2241.35	2229.7
160000	2503.33	2471.44	2445.22	2423.57	2405.65	2390.77	2378.3
170000	2659.79	2625.90	2598.04	2575.05	2556.00	2540.19	2527.0
180000	2816.25	2780.37	2750.87	2726.52	2706.36	2689.62	2675.6
190000	2972.71	2934.83	2903.69	2877.99	2856.71	2839.04	2824.3
200000	3129.17	3089.30	3056.52	3029.47	3007.06	2988.46	2972.9
210000	3285.63	3243.76	3209.35	3180.94	3157.42	3137.89	3121.6
220000	3442.08	3398.23	3362.17	3332.41	3307.77	3287.31	3270.2
230000	3598.54	3552.69	3515.00	3483.89	3458.12	3436.73	3418.9
240000	3755.00	3707.16	3667.82	3635.36	3608.48	3586.16	3567.5
250000	3911.46	3861.62	3820.65	3786.83	3758.83	3735.58	3716.2

Monthly Payments 18.00 %

LOAN MOUNT	YEARS 22	23	24	25	30	35	40
100	1.48	1.47	1.47	1.47	1.45	1.45	1.45
200	2.96	2.95	2.94	2.93	2.91	2.90	2.90
500	7.40	7.37	7.35	7.33	7.27	7.25	7.24
1000	14.80	14.75	14.70	14.66	14.55	14.50	14.48
2000	29.60	29.49	29.40	29.33	29.10	29.00	28.96
5000	74.00	73.73	73.51	73.32	72.75	72.51	72.41
6000	88.80	88.48	88.21	87.98	87.30	87.01	86.89
7000	103.60	103.23	102.91	102.65	101.84	101.51	101.37
8000	118.40	117.97	117.61	117.31	116.39	116.01	115.85
9000	133.20	132.72	132.31	131.97	130.94	130.51	130.33
10000	148.00	147.47	147.01	146.64	145.49	145.01	144.81
12000	177.60	176.96	176.42	175.97	174.59	174.02	173.78
15000	222.01	221.20	220.52	219.96	218.24	217.52	217.22
20000	296.01	294.93	294.03	293.28	290.98	290.03	289.63
25000	370.01	368.66	367.54	366.59	363.73	362.53	362.03
30000	444.01	442.40	441.04	439.91	436.48	435.04	434.44
31000	458.81	457.14	455.75	454.58	451.03	449.54	448.92
32000	473.61	471.89	470.45	469.24	465.58	464.04	463.40
33000	488.41	486.64	485.15	483.91	480.13	478.55	477.88
34000	503.21	501.38	499.85	498.57	494.67	493.05	492.36
35000	518.01	516.13	514.55	513.23	509.22	507.55	506.84
36000	532.81	530.88	529.25	527.90	523.77	522.05	521.33
37000	547.62	545.62	543.96	542.56	538.32	536.55	535.81
38000	562.42	560.37	558.66	557.22	552.87	551.05	550.29
39000	577.22	575.11	573.36	571.89	567.42	565.55	564.77
40000	592.02	589.86	588.06	586.55	581.97	580.06	579.25
41000	606.82	604.61	602.76	601.22	596.52	594.56	593.73
42000	621.62	619.35	617.46	615.88	611.07	609.06	608.21
43000	636.42	634.10	632.16	630.54	625.62	623.56	622.69
44000	651.22	648.85	646.87	645.21	640.17	638.06	637.18
45000	666.02	663.59	661.57	659.87	654.72	652.56	651.66
46000	680.82	678.34	676.27	674.53	669.27	667.06	666.14
47000	695.62	693.09	690.97	689.20	683.81	681.57	680.62
48000	710.42	707.83	705.67	703.86	698.36	696.07	695.10
49000	725.22	722.58	720.37	718.53	712.91	710.57	709.58
50000	740.02	737.33	735.07	733.19	727.46	725.07	724.06
51000	754.82	752.07	749.78	747.85	742.01	739.57	738.54
52000	769.62	766.82	764.48	762.52	756.56	754.07	753.03
53000	784.42	781.57	779.18	777.18	771.11	768.57	767.51
54000	799.22	796.31	793.88	791.85	785.66	783.08	781.99
55000	814.02	811.06	808.58	806.51	800.21	797.58	796.47
56000	828.82	825.81	823.28	821.17	814.76	812.08	810.95
57000	843.62	840.55	837.99	835.84	829.31	826.58	825.43
58000	858.42	855.30	852.69	850.50	843.86	841.08	839.91
59000	873.22	870.05	867.39	865.16	858.41	855.58	854.39
60000	888.02	884.79	882.09	879.83	872.95	870.08	868.88
65000	962.03	958.52	955.60	953.15	945.70	942.59	941.28
70000	1036.03	1032.26	1029.10	1026.47	1018.45	1015.10	1013.69
75000	1110.03	1105.99	1102.61	1099.78	1091.19	1087.60	1086.10
80000	1184.03	1179.72	1176.12	1173.10	1163.94	1160.11	1158.50
85000	1258.03	1253.46	1249.63	1246.42	1236.69	1232.62	1230.91
90000	1332.04	1327.19	1323.13	1319.74	1309.43	1305.13	1303.31
95000	1406.04	1400.92	1396.64	1393.06	1382.18	1377.63	1375.72
100000	1480.04	1474.65	1470.15	1466.38	1454.92	1450.14	1448.13
105000	1554.04	1548.39	1543.66	1539.70	1527.67	1522.65	1520.53
110000	1628.04	1622.12	1617.16	1613.02	1600.42	1595.15	1592.94
120000	1776.05	1769.58	1764.18	1759.66	1745.91	1740.17	1737.75
130000	1924.05	1917.05	1911.19	1906.29	1891.40	1885.18	1882.57
140000	2072.06	2064.52	2058.21	2052.93	2036.89	2030.19	2027.38
150000	2220.06	2211.98	2205.22	2199.57	2182.39	2175.21	2172.19
160000	2368.07	2359.45	2352.24	2346.21	2327.88	2320.22	2317.00
170000	2516.07	2506.91	2499.25	2492.85	2473.37	2465.24	2461.82
180000	2664.07	2654.38	2646.27	2639.48	2618.86	2610.25	2606.63
190000	2812.08	2801.84	2793.28	2786.12	2764.36	2755.26	2751.44
200000	2960.08	2949.31	2940.30	2932.76	2909.85	2900.28	2896.25
210000	3108.09	3096.77	3087.31	3079.40	3055.34	3045.29	3041.07
220000	3256.09	3244.24	3234.33	3226.04	3200.83	3190.31	3185.88
230000	3404.09	3391.70	3381.34	3372.67	3346.33	3335.32	3330.69
240000	3552.10	3539.17	3528.36	3519.31	3491.82	3480.33	3475.50
250000	3700.10	3686.63	3675.37	3665.95	3637.31	3625.35	3620.32

18.25 % Monthly Payments

LOAN AMOUNT	YEARS 1	2	3	4	5	6	7
100	9.15	4.97	3.59	2.92	2.52	2.26	2.08
200	18.30	9.95	7.19	5.83	5.03	4.52	4.16
500	45.74	24.86	17.97	14.58	12.59	11.29	10.39
1000	91.49	49.73	35.95	29.16	25.17	22.58	20.78
2000	182.97	99.45	71.90	58.32	50.34	45.16	41.56
5000	457.43	248.64	179.74	145.81	125.86	112.89	103.90
6000	548.92	298.36	215.69	174.97	151.03	135.47	124.68
7000	640.40	348.09	251.64	204.14	176.21	158.05	145.46
8000	731.89	397.82	287.59	233.30	201.38	180.62	166.24
9000	823.38	447.55	323.53	262.46	226.55	203.20	187.02
10000	914.86	497.27	359.48	291.62	251.72	225.78	207.80
12000	1097.83	596.73	431.38	349.95	302.07	270.94	249.36
15000	1372.29	745.91	539.22	437.44	377.58	338.67	311.69
20000	1829.72	994.55	718.97	583.25	503.45	451.56	415.59
25000	2287.15	1243.19	898.71	729.06	629.31	564.45	519.49
30000	2744.58	1491.82	1078.45	874.87	755.17	677.34	623.39
31000	2836.07	1541.55	1114.40	904.04	780.34	699.92	644.17
32000	2927.56	1591.28	1150.35	933.20	805.51	722.50	664.95
33000	3019.04	1641.00	1186.29	962.36	830.68	745.07	685.73
34000	3110.53	1690.73	1222.24	991.52	855.86	767.65	706.51
35000	3202.02	1740.46	1258.19	1020.69	881.03	790.23	727.29
36000	3293.50	1790.19	1294.14	1049.85	906.20	812.81	748.07
37000	3384.99	1839.91	1330.09	1079.01	931.37	835.39	768.85
38000	3476.47	1889.64	1366.04	1108.17	956.55	857.96	789.63
39000	3567.96	1939.37	1401.98	1137.34	981.72	880.54	810.41
40000	3659.45	1989.10	1437.93	1166.50	1006.89	903.12	831.19
41000	3750.93	2038.82	1473.88	1195.66	1032.06	925.70	851.97
42000	3842.42	2088.55	1509.83	1224.82	1057.23	948.28	872.75
43000	3933.90	2138.28	1545.78	1253.99	1082.41	970.85	893.53
44000	4025.39	2188.01	1581.72	1283.15	1107.58	993.43	914.30
45000	4116.88	2237.73	1617.67	1312.31	1132.75	1016.01	935.08
46000	4208.36	2287.46	1653.62	1341.47	1157.92	1038.59	955.86
47000	4299.85	2337.19	1689.57	1370.64	1183.10	1061.17	976.64
48000	4391.34	2386.92	1725.52	1399.80	1208.27	1083.74	997.42
49000	4482.82	2436.64	1761.47	1428.96	1233.44	1106.32	1018.20
50000	4574.31	2486.37	1797.41	1458.12	1258.61	1128.90	1038.98
51000	4665.79	2536.10	1833.36	1487.29	1283.79	1151.48	1059.76
52000	4757.28	2585.83	1869.31	1516.45	1308.96	1174.06	1080.54
53000	4848.77	2635.55	1905.26	1545.61	1334.13	1196.63	1101.32
54000	4940.25	2685.28	1941.21	1574.77	1359.30	1219.21	1122.10
55000	5031.74	2735.01	1977.16	1603.94	1384.47	1241.79	1142.88
56000	5123.22	2784.74	2013.10	1633.10	1409.65	1264.37	1163.66
57000	5214.71	2834.46	2049.05	1662.26	1434.82	1286.95	1184.44
58000	5306.20	2884.19	2085.00	1691.42	1459.99	1309.53	1205.22
59000	5397.68	2933.92	2120.95	1720.59	1485.16	1332.10	1226.00
60000	5489.17	2983.65	2156.90	1749.75	1510.34	1354.68	1246.78
65000	5946.60	3232.28	2336.64	1895.56	1636.20	1467.57	1350.68
70000	6404.03	3480.92	2516.38	2041.37	1762.06	1580.46	1454.58
75000	6861.46	3729.56	2696.12	2187.19	1887.92	1693.35	1558.47
80000	7318.89	3978.19	2875.86	2333.00	2013.78	1806.24	1662.37
85000	7776.32	4226.83	3055.60	2478.81	2139.64	1919.13	1766.27
90000	8233.75	4475.47	3235.35	2624.62	2265.50	2032.02	1870.17
95000	8691.19	4724.10	3415.09	2770.44	2391.36	2144.91	1974.07
100000	9148.62	4972.74	3594.83	2916.25	2517.23	2257.80	2077.97
105000	9606.05	5221.38	3774.57	3062.06	2643.09	2370.69	2181.8[illegible]
110000	10063.48	5470.02	3954.31	3207.87	2768.95	2483.58	2285.76
120000	10978.34	5967.29	4313.79	3499.50	3020.67	2709.36	2493.56
130000	11893.20	6464.56	4673.28	3791.12	3272.39	2935.14	2701.35
140000	12808.06	6961.84	5032.76	4082.75	3524.12	3160.92	2909.15
150000	13722.92	7459.11	5392.24	4374.37	3775.84	3386.70	3116.95
160000	14637.79	7956.39	5751.73	4666.00	4027.56	3612.48	3324.74
170000	15552.65	8453.66	6111.21	4957.62	4279.28	3838.26	3532.54
180000	16467.51	8950.94	6470.69	5249.25	4531.01	4064.04	3740.34
190000	17382.37	9448.21	6830.18	5540.87	4782.73	4289.82	3948.13
200000	18297.23	9945.48	7189.66	5832.50	5034.45	4515.60	4155.93
210000	19212.09	10442.76	7549.14	6124.12	5286.17	4741.38	4363.73
220000	20126.95	10940.03	7908.62	6415.75	5537.90	4967.16	4571.52
230000	21041.82	11437.31	8268.11	6707.37	5789.62	5192.94	4779.32
240000	21956.68	11934.58	8627.59	6998.99	6041.34	5418.72	4987.12
250000	22871.54	12431.85	8987.07	7290.62	6293.06	5644.50	5194.91

Monthly Payments 18.25 %

LOAN AMOUNT	8	9	10	11	12	13	14
				YEARS			
100	1.95	1.85	1.78	1.72	1.67	1.63	1.61
200	3.90	3.70	3.55	3.44	3.34	3.27	3.21
500	9.74	9.25	8.88	8.59	8.36	8.17	8.03
1000	19.48	18.50	17.76	17.18	16.72	16.35	16.05
2000	38.95	37.01	35.51	34.35	33.43	32.70	32.10
5000	97.38	92.51	88.78	85.88	83.58	81.74	80.26
6000	116.86	111.02	106.54	103.05	100.30	98.09	96.31
7000	136.34	129.52	124.30	120.23	117.01	114.44	112.37
8000	155.82	148.02	142.06	137.41	133.73	130.79	128.42
9000	175.29	166.52	159.81	154.58	150.44	147.14	144.47
10000	194.77	185.03	177.57	171.76	167.16	163.49	160.52
12000	233.72	222.03	213.08	206.11	200.59	196.18	192.63
15000	292.15	277.54	266.35	257.63	250.74	245.23	240.79
20000	389.54	370.06	355.14	343.51	334.32	326.97	321.05
25000	486.92	462.57	443.92	429.39	417.90	408.72	401.31
30000	584.31	555.08	532.71	515.27	501.48	490.46	481.57
31000	603.78	573.59	550.47	532.44	518.20	506.81	497.63
32000	623.26	592.09	568.22	549.62	534.91	523.16	513.68
33000	642.74	610.59	585.98	566.80	551.63	539.51	529.73
34000	662.21	629.09	603.74	583.97	568.35	555.86	545.78
35000	681.69	647.60	621.49	601.15	585.06	572.20	561.84
36000	701.17	666.10	639.25	618.32	601.78	588.55	577.89
37000	720.65	684.60	657.01	635.50	618.49	604.90	593.94
38000	740.12	703.11	674.77	652.67	635.21	621.25	609.99
39000	759.60	721.61	692.52	669.85	651.93	637.60	626.05
40000	779.08	740.11	710.28	687.03	668.64	653.95	642.10
41000	798.55	758.61	728.04	704.20	685.36	670.30	658.15
42000	818.03	777.12	745.79	721.38	702.07	686.65	674.20
43000	837.51	795.62	763.55	738.55	718.79	702.99	690.26
44000	856.98	814.12	781.31	755.73	735.51	719.34	706.31
45000	876.46	832.62	799.06	772.90	752.22	735.69	722.36
46000	895.94	851.13	816.82	790.08	768.94	752.04	738.41
47000	915.41	869.63	834.58	807.25	785.65	768.39	754.47
48000	934.89	888.13	852.34	824.43	802.37	784.74	770.52
49000	954.37	906.64	870.09	841.61	819.09	801.09	786.57
50000	973.84	925.14	887.85	858.78	835.80	817.44	802.62
51000	993.32	943.64	905.61	875.96	852.52	833.78	818.68
52000	1012.80	962.14	923.36	893.13	869.24	850.13	834.73
53000	1032.28	980.65	941.12	910.31	885.95	866.48	850.78
54000	1051.75	999.15	958.88	927.48	902.67	882.83	866.83
55000	1071.23	1017.65	976.63	944.66	919.38	899.18	882.89
56000	1090.71	1036.16	994.39	961.84	936.10	915.53	898.94
57000	1110.18	1054.66	1012.15	979.01	952.82	931.88	914.99
58000	1129.66	1073.16	1029.91	996.19	969.53	948.23	931.04
59000	1149.14	1091.66	1047.66	1013.36	986.25	964.57	947.10
60000	1168.61	1110.17	1065.42	1030.54	1002.96	980.92	963.15
65000	1266.00	1202.68	1154.20	1116.42	1086.54	1062.67	1043.41
70000	1363.38	1295.19	1242.99	1202.29	1170.12	1144.41	1123.67
75000	1460.77	1387.71	1331.77	1288.17	1253.70	1226.15	1203.94
80000	1558.15	1480.22	1420.56	1374.05	1337.28	1307.90	1284.20
85000	1655.54	1572.74	1509.34	1459.93	1420.86	1389.64	1364.46
90000	1752.92	1665.25	1598.13	1545.81	1504.45	1471.38	1444.72
95000	1850.31	1757.76	1686.91	1631.69	1588.03	1553.13	1524.98
100000	1947.69	1850.28	1775.70	1717.56	1671.61	1634.87	1605.25
105000	2045.07	1942.79	1864.48	1803.44	1755.19	1716.61	1685.51
110000	2142.46	2035.31	1953.27	1889.32	1838.77	1798.36	1765.77
120000	2337.23	2220.33	2130.84	2061.08	2005.93	1961.84	1926.30
130000	2532.00	2405.36	2308.41	2232.83	2173.09	2125.33	2086.82
140000	2726.77	2590.39	2485.98	2404.59	2340.25	2288.82	2247.35
150000	2921.53	2775.42	2663.55	2576.35	2507.41	2452.31	2407.87
160000	3116.30	2960.44	2841.12	2748.10	2674.57	2615.79	2568.40
170000	3311.07	3145.47	3018.69	2919.86	2841.73	2779.28	2728.92
180000	3505.84	3330.50	3196.26	3091.61	3008.89	2942.77	2889.44
190000	3700.61	3515.53	3373.83	3263.37	3176.05	3106.25	3049.97
200000	3895.38	3700.56	3551.40	3435.13	3343.21	3269.74	3210.49
210000	4090.15	3885.58	3728.97	3606.88	3510.37	3433.23	3371.02
220000	4284.92	4070.61	3906.54	3778.64	3677.53	3596.72	3531.54
230000	4479.69	4255.64	4084.11	3950.40	3844.69	3760.20	3692.07
240000	4674.46	4440.67	4261.68	4122.15	4011.85	3923.69	3852.59
250000	4869.22	4625.69	4439.25	4293.91	4179.01	4087.18	4013.12

18.25 % Monthly Payments

LOAN AMOUNT	15	16	17	18	19	20	21
				YEARS			
100	1.58	1.56	1.55	1.53	1.52	1.51	1.5
200	3.16	3.12	3.09	3.06	3.04	3.02	3.0
500	7.91	7.81	7.73	7.66	7.61	7.56	7.5
1000	15.81	15.62	15.45	15.32	15.21	15.12	15.0
2000	31.62	31.23	30.91	30.64	30.42	30.24	30.0
5000	79.06	78.08	77.27	76.61	76.06	75.60	75.2
6000	94.87	93.69	92.72	91.93	91.27	90.72	90.2
7000	110.68	109.31	108.18	107.25	106.48	105.84	105.3
8000	126.49	124.92	123.63	122.57	121.69	120.96	120.3
9000	142.31	140.54	139.09	137.89	136.90	136.08	135.4
10000	158.12	156.15	154.54	153.21	152.11	151.20	150.4
12000	189.74	187.38	185.45	183.85	182.54	181.44	180.5
15000	237.18	234.23	231.81	229.82	228.17	226.80	225.6
20000	316.24	312.31	309.08	306.42	304.23	302.40	300.8
25000	395.30	390.38	386.35	383.03	380.28	378.01	376.1
30000	474.36	468.46	463.62	459.63	456.34	453.61	451.3
31000	490.17	484.08	479.07	474.95	471.55	468.73	466.3
32000	505.98	499.69	494.53	490.28	486.76	483.85	481.4
33000	521.79	515.31	509.98	505.60	501.97	498.97	496.4
34000	537.60	530.92	525.44	520.92	517.18	514.09	511.5
35000	553.42	546.54	540.89	536.24	532.39	529.21	526.5
36000	569.23	562.15	556.34	551.56	547.61	544.33	541.6
37000	585.04	577.77	571.80	566.88	562.82	559.45	556.6
38000	600.85	593.38	587.25	582.20	578.03	574.57	571.6
39000	616.66	609.00	602.71	597.52	593.24	589.69	586.7
40000	632.47	624.61	618.16	612.84	608.45	604.81	601.7
41000	648.29	640.23	633.61	628.17	623.66	619.93	616.8
42000	664.10	655.84	649.07	643.49	638.87	635.05	631.8
43000	679.91	671.46	664.52	658.81	654.08	650.17	646.9
44000	695.72	687.07	679.98	674.13	669.30	665.29	661.9
45000	711.53	702.69	695.43	689.45	684.51	680.41	677.0
46000	727.35	718.31	710.89	704.77	699.72	695.53	692.0
47000	743.16	733.92	726.34	720.09	714.93	710.65	707.1
48000	758.97	749.54	741.79	735.41	730.14	725.77	722.1
49000	774.78	765.15	757.25	750.73	745.35	740.89	737.1
50000	790.59	780.77	772.70	766.06	760.56	756.01	752.2
51000	806.41	796.38	788.16	781.38	775.77	771.13	767.2
52000	822.22	812.00	803.61	796.70	790.99	786.25	782.3
53000	838.03	827.61	819.06	812.02	806.20	801.37	797.3
54000	853.84	843.23	834.52	827.34	821.41	816.49	812.4
55000	869.65	858.84	849.97	842.66	836.62	831.61	827.4
56000	885.46	874.46	865.43	857.98	851.83	846.73	842.5
57000	901.28	890.07	880.88	873.30	867.04	861.85	857.5
58000	917.09	905.69	896.33	888.62	882.25	876.97	872.5
59000	932.90	921.30	911.79	903.95	897.46	892.09	887.6
60000	948.71	936.92	927.24	919.27	912.68	907.21	902.6
65000	1027.77	1015.00	1004.51	995.87	988.73	982.81	977.9
70000	1106.83	1093.07	1081.78	1072.48	1064.79	1058.42	1053.1
75000	1185.89	1171.15	1159.05	1149.08	1140.84	1134.02	1128.3
80000	1264.95	1249.23	1236.32	1225.69	1216.90	1209.62	1203.5
85000	1344.01	1327.30	1313.59	1302.29	1292.96	1285.22	1278.7
90000	1423.07	1405.38	1390.86	1378.90	1369.01	1360.82	1354.0
95000	1502.13	1483.46	1468.13	1455.51	1445.07	1436.42	1429.2
100000	1581.19	1561.53	1545.40	1532.11	1521.13	1512.02	1504.4
105000	1660.25	1639.61	1622.67	1608.72	1597.18	1587.62	1579.6
110000	1739.31	1717.69	1699.94	1685.32	1673.24	1663.22	1654.9
120000	1897.42	1873.84	1854.48	1838.53	1825.35	1814.43	1805.3
130000	2055.54	2029.99	2009.02	1991.75	1977.46	1965.63	1955.8
140000	2213.66	2186.15	2163.56	2144.96	2129.58	2116.83	2106.2
150000	2371.78	2342.30	2318.10	2298.17	2281.69	2268.03	2256.6
160000	2529.90	2498.45	2472.64	2451.38	2433.80	2419.23	2407.1
170000	2688.02	2654.61	2627.18	2604.59	2585.91	2570.44	2557.5
180000	2846.14	2810.76	2781.72	2757.80	2738.03	2721.64	2708.0
190000	3004.26	2966.91	2936.26	2911.01	2890.14	2872.84	2858.4
200000	3162.37	3123.07	3090.80	3064.22	3042.25	3024.04	3008.9
210000	3320.49	3279.22	3245.35	3217.43	3194.36	3175.25	3159.3
220000	3478.61	3435.37	3399.89	3370.65	3346.48	3326.45	3309.8
230000	3636.73	3591.53	3554.43	3523.86	3498.59	3477.65	3460.2
240000	3794.85	3747.68	3708.97	3677.07	3650.70	3628.85	3610.7
250000	3952.97	3903.83	3863.51	3830.28	3802.81	3780.05	3761.1

Monthly Payments 18.25 %

LOAN AMOUNT	22	23	24	25	30	35	40
			YEARS				
100	1.50	1.49	1.49	1.48	1.47	1.47	1.47
200	3.00	2.99	2.98	2.97	2.95	2.94	2.93
500	7.49	7.46	7.44	7.42	7.37	7.35	7.34
1000	14.98	14.93	14.89	14.85	14.74	14.69	14.67
2000	29.96	29.86	29.77	29.70	29.48	29.39	29.35
5000	74.91	74.65	74.43	74.24	73.69	73.46	73.37
6000	89.89	89.58	89.31	89.09	88.43	88.16	88.04
7000	104.87	104.50	104.20	103.94	103.17	102.85	102.72
8000	119.85	119.43	119.08	118.79	117.91	117.54	117.39
9000	134.84	134.36	133.97	133.64	132.65	132.24	132.07
10000	149.82	149.29	148.86	148.49	147.39	146.93	146.74
12000	179.78	179.15	178.63	178.19	176.86	176.32	176.09
15000	224.73	223.94	223.28	222.73	221.08	220.39	220.11
20000	299.63	298.59	297.71	296.98	294.77	293.86	293.48
25000	374.54	373.23	3[illegible]2.14	371.22	368.46	367.32	366.85
30000	449.45	447.88	446.57	445.47	442.16	440.79	440.22
31000	464.43	462.81	461.45	460.32	456.90	455.48	454.89
32000	479.41	477.74	476.34	475.17	471.63	470.17	469.57
33000	494.40	492.67	491.22	490.02	486.37	484.87	484.24
34000	509.38	507.59	506.11	504.87	501.11	499.56	498.91
35000	524.36	522.52	520.99	519.71	515.85	514.25	513.59
36000	539.34	537.45	535.88	534.56	530.59	528.95	528.26
37000	554.32	552.38	550.76	549.41	545.33	543.64	542.94
38000	569.30	567.31	565.65	564.26	560.07	558.33	557.61
39000	584.29	582.24	580.53	579.11	574.80	573.02	572.28
40000	599.27	597.17	595.42	593.96	589.54	587.72	586.96
41000	614.25	612.10	610.31	608.81	604.28	602.41	601.63
42000	629.23	627.03	625.19	623.66	619.02	617.10	616.31
43000	644.21	641.96	640.08	638.51	633.76	631.80	630.98
44000	659.19	656.89	654.96	653.35	648.50	646.49	645.65
45000	674.18	671.82	669.85	668.20	663.24	661.18	660.33
46000	689.16	686.75	684.73	683.05	677.97	675.88	675.00
47000	704.14	701.67	699.62	697.90	692.71	690.57	689.68
48000	719.12	716.60	714.50	712.75	707.45	705.26	704.35
49000	734.10	731.53	729.39	727.60	722.19	719.95	719.02
50000	749.08	746.46	744.28	742.45	736.93	734.65	733.70
51000	764.07	761.39	759.16	757.30	751.67	749.34	748.37
52000	779.05	776.32	774.05	772.15	766.41	764.03	763.05
53000	794.03	791.25	788.93	787.00	781.14	778.73	777.72
54000	809.01	806.18	803.82	801.84	795.88	793.42	792.39
55000	823.99	821.11	818.70	816.69	810.62	808.11	807.07
56000	838.97	836.04	833.59	831.54	825.36	822.80	821.74
57000	853.96	850.97	848.47	846.39	840.10	837.50	836.42
58000	868.94	865.90	863.36	861.24	854.84	852.19	851.09
59000	883.92	880.83	878.24	876.09	869.57	866.88	865.76
60000	898.90	895.76	893.13	890.94	884.31	881.58	880.44
65000	973.81	970.40	967.56	965.18	958.01	955.04	953.81
70000	1048.72	1045.05	1041.99	1039.43	1031.70	1028.51	1027.18
75000	1123.63	1119.69	1116.41	1113.67	1105.39	1101.97	1100.55
80000	1198.53	1194.34	1190.84	1187.92	1179.08	1175.43	1173.92
85000	1273.44	1268.99	1265.27	1262.16	1252.78	1248.90	1247.29
90000	1348.35	1343.63	1339.70	1336.41	1326.47	1322.36	1320.66
95000	1423.26	1418.28	1414.12	1410.65	1400.16	1395.83	1394.03
100000	1498.17	1492.93	1488.55	1484.90	1473.86	1469.29	1467.40
105000	1573.08	1567.57	1562.98	1559.14	1547.55	1542.76	1540.77
110000	1647.99	1642.22	1637.41	1633.39	1621.24	1616.22	1614.14
120000	1797.80	1791.51	1786.26	1781.88	1768.63	1763.15	1760.88
130000	1947.62	1940.80	1935.12	1930.37	1916.01	1910.08	1907.62
140000	2097.44	2090.10	2083.97	2078.86	2063.40	2057.01	2054.36
150000	2247.25	2239.39	2232.83	2227.35	2210.78	2203.94	2201.10
160000	2397.07	2388.68	2381.68	2375.84	2358.17	2350.87	2347.83
170000	2546.89	2537.97	2530.54	2524.33	2505.55	2497.80	2494.57
180000	2696.70	2687.27	2679.39	2672.81	2652.94	2644.73	2641.31
190000	2846.52	2836.56	2828.25	2821.30	2800.33	2791.66	2788.05
200000	2996.34	2985.85	2977.10	2969.79	2947.71	2938.59	2934.79
210000	3146.15	3135.14	3125.96	3118.28	3095.10	3085.52	3081.53
220000	3295.97	3284.44	3274.81	3266.77	3242.48	3232.45	3228.27
230000	3445.79	3433.73	3423.67	3415.26	3389.87	3379.38	3375.01
240000	3595.60	3583.02	3572.52	3563.75	3537.25	3526.30	3521.75
250000	3745.42	3732.31	3721.38	3712.24	3684.64	3673.23	3668.49

18.50 % Monthly Payments

LOAN AMOUNT	YEARS 1	2	3	4	5	6	7
100	9.16	4.98	3.61	2.93	2.53	2.27	2.09
200	18.32	9.97	7.21	5.86	5.06	4.54	4.18
500	45.80	24.92	18.03	14.64	12.65	11.35	10.46
1000	91.60	49.84	36.06	29.28	25.30	22.71	20.92
2000	183.19	99.68	72.13	58.57	50.60	45.42	41.83
5000	457.98	249.20	180.32	146.42	126.49	113.54	104.58
6000	549.58	299.04	216.39	175.70	151.79	136.25	125.49
7000	641.18	348.88	252.45	204.98	177.09	158.96	146.41
8000	732.77	398.72	288.52	234.27	202.39	181.67	167.32
9000	824.37	448.56	324.58	263.55	227.68	204.38	188.24
10000	915.97	498.39	360.65	292.84	252.98	227.09	209.15
12000	1099.16	598.07	432.77	351.40	303.58	272.51	250.98
15000	1373.95	747.59	540.97	439.25	379.47	340.63	313.73
20000	1831.93	996.79	721.29	585.67	505.96	454.18	418.31
25000	2289.92	1245.99	901.61	732.09	632.46	567.72	522.88
30000	2747.90	1495.18	1081.94	878.51	758.95	681.27	627.46
31000	2839.50	1545.02	1118.00	907.79	784.24	703.97	648.37
32000	2931.09	1594.86	1154.07	937.07	809.54	726.68	669.29
33000	3022.69	1644.70	1190.13	966.36	834.84	749.39	690.20
34000	3114.29	1694.54	1226.20	995.64	860.14	772.10	711.12
35000	3205.88	1744.38	1262.26	1024.92	885.44	794.81	732.03
36000	3297.48	1794.22	1298.32	1054.21	910.74	817.52	752.95
37000	3389.08	1844.06	1334.39	1083.49	936.03	840.23	773.87
38000	3480.67	1893.90	1370.45	1112.77	961.33	862.94	794.78
39000	3572.27	1943.74	1406.52	1142.06	986.63	885.65	815.70
40000	3663.87	1993.58	1442.58	1171.34	1011.93	908.35	836.61
41000	3755.46	2043.42	1478.65	1200.63	1037.23	931.06	857.53
42000	3847.06	2093.26	1514.71	1229.91	1062.53	953.77	878.44
43000	3938.66	2143.10	1550.78	1259.19	1087.82	976.48	899.36
44000	4030.25	2192.94	1586.84	1288.48	1113.12	999.19	920.27
45000	4121.85	2242.78	1622.91	1317.76	1138.42	1021.90	941.19
46000	4213.45	2292.62	1658.97	1347.04	1163.72	1044.61	962.10
47000	4305.04	2342.46	1695.04	1376.33	1189.02	1067.32	983.02
48000	4396.64	2392.30	1731.10	1405.61	1214.31	1090.03	1003.93
49000	4488.24	2442.14	1767.16	1434.89	1239.61	1112.73	1024.85
50000	4579.83	2491.97	1803.23	1464.18	1264.91	1135.44	1045.76
51000	4671.43	2541.81	1839.29	1493.46	1290.21	1158.15	1066.68
52000	4763.03	2591.65	1875.36	1522.74	1315.51	1180.86	1087.59
53000	4854.62	2641.49	1911.42	1552.03	1340.81	1203.57	1108.51
54000	4946.22	2691.33	1947.49	1581.31	1366.10	1226.28	1129.43
55000	5037.82	2741.17	1983.55	1610.59	1391.40	1248.99	1150.34
56000	5129.41	2791.01	2019.62	1639.88	1416.70	1271.70	1171.26
57000	5221.01	2840.85	2055.68	1669.16	1442.00	1294.41	1192.17
58000	5312.61	2890.69	2091.75	1698.45	1467.30	1317.11	1213.09
59000	5404.20	2940.53	2127.81	1727.73	1492.60	1339.82	1234.00
60000	5495.80	2990.37	2163.87	1757.01	1517.89	1362.53	1254.92
65000	5953.78	3239.57	2344.20	1903.43	1644.38	1476.08	1359.49
70000	6411.76	3488.76	2524.52	2049.85	1770.88	1589.62	1464.07
75000	6869.75	3737.96	2704.84	2196.27	1897.37	1703.17	1568.65
80000	7327.73	3987.16	2885.17	2342.68	2023.86	1816.71	1673.22
85000	7785.71	4236.36	3065.49	2489.10	2150.35	1930.25	1777.80
90000	8243.70	4485.55	3245.81	2635.52	2276.84	2043.80	1882.38
95000	8701.68	4734.75	3426.13	2781.94	2403.33	2157.34	1986.95
100000	9159.66	4983.95	3606.46	2928.35	2529.82	2270.89	2091.53
105000	9617.65	5233.15	3786.78	3074.77	2656.31	2384.43	2196.10
110000	10075.63	5482.34	3967.10	3221.19	2782.80	2497.98	2300.68
120000	10991.60	5980.74	4327.75	3514.02	3035.79	2725.06	2509.83
130000	11907.56	6479.13	4688.39	3806.86	3288.77	2952.15	2718.99
140000	12823.53	6977.53	5049.04	4099.70	3541.75	3179.24	2928.14
150000	13739.50	7475.92	5409.69	4392.53	3794.73	3406.33	3137.29
160000	14655.46	7974.32	5770.33	4685.37	4047.72	3633.42	3346.45
170000	15571.43	8472.71	6130.98	4978.20	4300.70	3860.51	3555.60
180000	16487.40	8971.11	6491.62	5271.04	4553.68	4087.60	3764.75
190000	17403.36	9469.50	6852.27	5563.87	4806.66	4314.69	3973.90
200000	18319.33	9967.90	7212.92	5856.71	5059.65	4541.77	4183.06
210000	19235.29	10466.29	7573.56	6149.54	5312.63	4768.86	4392.21
220000	20151.26	10964.69	7934.21	6442.38	5565.61	4995.95	4601.36
230000	21067.23	11463.08	8294.85	6735.21	5818.59	5223.04	4810.52
240000	21983.19	11961.48	8655.50	7028.05	6071.57	5450.13	5019.67
250000	22899.16	12459.87	9016.14	7320.88	6324.56	5677.22	5228.82

Monthly Payments 18.50 %

LOAN AMOUNT	8	9	10	11	12	13	14
				YEARS			
100	1.96	1.86	1.79	1.73	1.69	1.65	1.62
200	3.92	3.73	3.58	3.47	3.37	3.30	3.24
500	9.81	9.32	8.95	8.66	8.44	8.25	8.11
1000	19.62	18.65	17.91	17.33	16.87	16.51	16.22
2000	39.23	37.29	35.81	34.66	33.75	33.02	32.43
5000	98.09	93.24	89.53	86.64	84.36	82.54	81.08
6000	117.70	111.88	107.44	103.97	101.24	99.05	97.30
7000	137.32	130.53	125.34	121.30	118.11	115.56	113.51
8000	156.94	149.18	143.25	138.63	134.98	132.07	129.73
9000	176.55	167.83	161.15	155.96	151.85	148.58	145.94
10000	196.17	186.47	179.06	173.29	168.73	165.09	162.16
12000	235.41	223.77	214.87	207.94	202.47	198.11	194.59
15000	294.26	279.71	268.59	259.93	253.09	247.63	243.24
20000	392.34	372.95	358.12	346.57	337.45	330.18	324.32
25000	490.43	466.19	447.65	433.21	421.82	412.72	405.40
30000	588.51	559.42	537.18	519.86	506.18	495.27	486.48
31000	608.13	578.07	555.08	537.18	523.05	511.77	502.69
32000	627.75	596.72	572.99	554.51	539.93	528.28	518.91
33000	647.37	615.37	590.89	571.84	556.80	544.79	535.12
34000	666.98	634.01	608.80	589.17	573.67	561.30	551.34
35000	686.60	652.66	626.71	606.50	590.54	577.81	567.56
36000	706.22	671.31	644.61	623.83	607.42	594.32	583.77
37000	725.83	689.96	662.52	641.16	624.29	610.83	599.99
38000	745.45	708.60	680.42	658.48	641.16	627.34	616.20
39000	765.07	727.25	698.33	675.81	658.04	643.85	632.42
40000	784.69	745.90	716.24	693.14	674.91	660.35	648.64
41000	804.30	764.55	734.14	710.47	691.78	676.86	664.85
42000	823.92	783.19	752.05	727.80	708.65	693.37	681.07
43000	843.54	801.84	769.95	745.13	725.53	709.88	697.28
44000	863.15	820.49	787.86	762.46	742.40	726.39	713.50
45000	882.77	839.14	805.77	779.78	759.27	742.90	729.72
46000	902.39	857.78	823.67	797.11	776.14	759.41	745.93
47000	922.01	876.43	841.58	814.44	793.02	775.92	762.15
48000	941.62	895.08	859.48	831.77	809.89	792.43	778.36
49000	961.24	913.73	877.39	849.10	826.76	808.93	794.58
50000	980.86	932.37	895.29	866.43	843.64	825.44	810.80
51000	1000.47	951.02	913.20	883.75	860.51	841.95	827.01
52000	1020.09	969.67	931.11	901.08	877.38	858.46	843.23
53000	1039.71	988.32	949.01	918.41	894.25	874.97	859.44
54000	1059.33	1006.96	966.92	935.74	911.13	891.48	875.66
55000	1078.94	1025.61	984.82	953.07	928.00	907.99	891.87
56000	1098.56	1044.26	1002.73	970.40	944.87	924.50	908.09
57000	1118.18	1062.91	1020.64	987.73	961.74	941.01	924.31
58000	1137.79	1081.55	1038.54	1005.05	978.62	957.51	940.52
59000	1157.41	1100.20	1056.45	1022.38	995.49	974.02	956.74
60000	1177.03	1118.85	1074.35	1039.71	1012.36	990.53	972.95
65000	1275.11	1212.08	1163.88	1126.35	1096.73	1073.08	1054.03
70000	1373.20	1305.32	1253.41	1213.00	1181.09	1155.62	1135.11
75000	1471.29	1398.56	1342.94	1299.64	1265.45	1238.17	1216.19
80000	1569.37	1491.80	1432.47	1386.28	1349.82	1320.71	1297.27
85000	1667.46	1585.03	1522.00	1472.92	1434.18	1403.25	1378.35
90000	1765.54	1678.27	1611.53	1559.57	1518.54	1485.80	1459.43
95000	1863.63	1771.51	1701.06	1646.21	1602.91	1568.34	1540.51
100000	1961.71	1864.75	1790.59	1732.85	1687.27	1650.89	1621.59
105000	2059.80	1957.98	1880.12	1819.50	1771.63	1733.43	1702.67
110000	2157.89	2051.22	1969.65	1906.14	1856.00	1815.98	1783.75
120000	2354.06	2237.70	2148.71	2079.42	2024.72	1981.06	1945.91
130000	2550.23	2424.17	2327.77	2252.71	2193.45	2146.15	2108.07
140000	2746.40	2610.64	2506.82	2425.99	2362.18	2311.24	2270.23
150000	2942.57	2797.12	2685.88	2599.28	2530.91	2476.33	2432.39
160000	3138.74	2983.59	2864.94	2772.56	2699.63	2641.42	2594.54
170000	3334.92	3170.07	3044.00	2945.85	2868.36	2806.51	2756.70
180000	3531.09	3356.54	3223.06	3119.14	3037.09	2971.60	2918.86
190000	3727.26	3543.02	3402.12	3292.42	3205.81	3136.69	3081.02
200000	3923.43	3729.49	3581.18	3465.71	3374.54	3301.77	3243.18
210000	4119.60	3915.97	3760.24	3638.99	3543.27	3466.86	3405.34
220000	4315.77	4102.44	3939.30	3812.28	3712.00	3631.95	3567.50
230000	4511.94	4288.92	4118.36	3985.56	3880.72	3797.04	3729.66
240000	4708.12	4475.39	4297.41	4158.85	4049.45	3962.13	3891.82
250000	4904.29	4661.86	4476.47	4332.13	4218.18	4127.22	4053.98

18.50 % Monthly Payments

LOAN AMOUNT	15	16	17	18	19	20	21
				YEARS			
100	1.60	1.58	1.56	1.55	1.54	1.53	1.52
200	3.20	3.16	3.13	3.10	3.08	3.06	3.04
500	7.99	7.89	7.81	7.75	7.69	7.65	7.61
1000	15.98	15.78	15.63	15.50	15.39	15.30	15.22
2000	31.96	31.57	31.25	30.99	30.78	30.60	30.45
5000	79.89	78.92	78.13	77.48	76.94	76.49	76.12
6000	95.87	94.71	93.75	92.97	92.33	91.79	91.35
7000	111.85	110.49	109.38	108.47	107.71	107.09	106.57
8000	127.83	126.28	125.01	123.96	123.10	122.39	121.80
9000	143.80	142.06	140.63	139.46	138.49	137.69	137.02
10000	159.78	157.85	156.26	154.95	153.88	152.98	152.25
12000	191.74	189.41	187.51	185.94	184.65	183.58	182.69
15000	239.67	236.77	234.39	232.43	230.81	229.48	228.37
20000	319.57	315.69	312.52	309.91	307.75	305.97	304.49
25000	399.46	394.61	390.65	387.38	384.69	382.46	380.61
30000	479.35	473.54	468.77	464.86	461.63	458.95	456.74
31000	495.33	489.32	484.40	480.35	477.01	474.25	471.96
32000	511.31	505.11	500.03	495.85	492.40	489.55	487.19
33000	527.28	520.89	515.65	511.34	507.79	504.85	502.41
34000	543.26	536.68	531.28	526.84	523.18	520.15	517.64
35000	559.24	552.46	546.90	542.33	538.56	535.45	532.86
36000	575.22	568.24	562.53	557.83	553.95	550.74	548.08
37000	591.20	584.03	578.16	573.32	569.34	566.04	563.31
38000	607.18	599.81	593.78	588.82	584.73	581.34	578.53
39000	623.15	615.60	609.41	604.32	600.11	596.64	593.76
40000	639.13	631.38	625.03	619.81	615.50	611.94	608.98
41000	655.11	647.17	640.66	635.31	630.89	627.24	624.21
42000	671.09	662.95	656.28	650.80	646.28	642.53	639.43
43000	687.07	678.74	671.91	666.30	661.66	657.83	654.66
44000	703.05	694.52	687.54	681.79	677.05	673.13	669.88
45000	719.02	710.31	703.16	697.29	692.44	688.43	685.11
46000	735.00	726.09	718.79	712.78	707.83	703.73	700.33
47000	750.98	741.88	734.41	728.28	723.21	719.03	715.55
48000	766.96	757.66	750.04	743.77	738.60	734.32	730.78
49000	782.94	773.44	765.67	759.27	753.99	749.62	746.00
50000	798.92	789.23	781.29	774.76	769.38	764.92	761.23
51000	814.89	805.01	796.92	790.26	784.76	780.22	776.45
52000	830.87	820.80	812.54	805.75	800.15	795.52	791.68
53000	846.85	836.58	828.17	821.25	815.54	810.82	806.90
54000	862.83	852.37	843.79	836.74	830.93	826.12	822.13
55000	878.81	868.15	859.42	852.24	846.31	841.41	837.35
56000	894.79	883.94	875.05	867.73	861.70	856.71	852.58
57000	910.76	899.72	890.67	883.23	877.09	872.01	867.80
58000	926.74	915.51	906.30	898.73	892.48	887.31	883.02
59000	942.72	931.29	921.92	914.22	907.86	902.61	898.25
60000	958.70	947.07	937.55	929.72	923.25	917.91	913.47
65000	1038.59	1026.00	1015.68	1007.19	1000.19	994.40	989.60
70000	1118.48	1104.92	1093.81	1084.67	1077.13	1070.89	1065.72
75000	1198.37	1183.84	1171.94	1162.14	1154.07	1147.38	1141.84
80000	1278.27	1262.77	1250.07	1239.62	1231.00	1223.87	1217.97
85000	1358.16	1341.69	1328.20	1317.10	1307.94	1300.37	1294.09
90000	1438.05	1420.61	1406.32	1394.57	1384.88	1376.86	1370.21
95000	1517.94	1499.54	1484.45	1472.05	1461.82	1453.35	1446.33
100000	1597.83	1578.46	1562.58	1549.53	1538.75	1529.84	1522.46
105000	1677.72	1657.38	1640.71	1627.00	1615.69	1606.34	1598.58
110000	1757.62	1736.30	1718.84	1704.48	1692.63	1682.83	1674.70
120000	1917.40	1894.15	1875.10	1859.43	1846.50	1835.81	1826.95
130000	2077.18	2052.00	2031.36	2014.38	2000.38	1988.80	1979.19
140000	2236.97	2209.84	2187.62	2169.34	2154.26	2141.78	2131.44
150000	2396.75	2367.69	2343.87	2324.29	2308.13	2294.76	2283.68
160000	2556.53	2525.53	2500.13	2479.24	2462.01	2447.75	2435.93
170000	2716.32	2683.38	2656.39	2634.19	2615.88	2600.73	2588.18
180000	2876.10	2841.22	2812.65	2789.15	2769.76	2753.72	2740.42
190000	3035.88	2999.07	2968.91	2944.10	2923.63	2906.70	2892.67
200000	3195.67	3156.92	3125.17	3099.05	3077.51	3059.69	3044.91
210000	3355.45	3314.76	3281.42	3254.01	3231.38	3212.67	3197.16
220000	3515.23	3472.61	3437.68	3408.96	3385.26	3365.65	3349.40
230000	3675.02	3630.45	3593.94	3563.91	3539.13	3518.64	3501.65
240000	3834.80	3788.30	3750.20	3718.86	3693.01	3671.62	3653.90
250000	3994.58	3946.15	3906.46	3873.82	3846.88	3824.61	3806.14

Monthly Payments 18.50 %

LOAN AMOUNT	22	23	24	25	30	35	40
100	1.52	1.51	1.51	1.50	1.49	1.49	1.49
200	3.03	3.02	3.01	3.01	2.99	2.98	2.97
500	7.58	7.56	7.53	7.52	7.46	7.44	7.43
1000	15.16	15.11	15.07	15.03	14.93	14.88	14.87
2000	30.33	30.22	30.14	30.07	29.86	29.77	29.73
5000	75.82	75.56	75.35	75.17	74.64	74.42	74.33
6000	90.98	90.67	90.42	90.21	89.57	89.31	89.20
7000	106.14	105.79	105.49	105.24	104.50	104.19	104.07
8000	121.31	120.90	120.56	120.27	119.42	119.08	118.93
9000	136.47	136.01	135.63	135.31	134.35	133.96	133.80
10000	151.63	151.12	150.70	150.34	149.28	148.84	148.67
12000	181.96	181.35	180.84	180.41	179.14	178.61	178.40
15000	227.45	226.68	226.05	225.51	223.92	223.27	223.00
20000	303.26	302.24	301.39	300.69	298.56	297.69	297.33
25000	379.08	377.81	376.74	375.86	373.20	372.11	371.66
30000	454.90	453.37	452.09	451.03	447.84	446.53	446.00
31000	470.06	468.48	467.16	466.06	462.77	461.42	460.86
32000	485.22	483.59	482.23	481.10	477.69	476.30	475.73
33000	500.39	498.70	497.30	496.13	492.62	491.19	490.60
34000	515.55	513.82	512.37	511.17	507.55	506.07	505.46
35000	530.71	528.93	527.44	526.20	522.48	520.96	520.33
36000	545.88	544.04	542.51	541.24	537.41	535.84	535.20
37000	561.04	559.15	557.58	556.27	552.33	550.72	550.06
38000	576.20	574.26	572.65	571.30	567.26	565.61	564.93
39000	591.37	589.38	587.72	586.34	582.19	580.49	579.80
40000	606.53	604.49	602.79	601.37	597.12	595.38	594.66
41000	621.69	619.60	617.86	616.41	612.04	610.26	609.53
42000	636.86	634.71	632.93	631.44	626.97	625.15	624.40
43000	652.02	649.82	648.00	646.48	641.90	640.03	639.26
44000	667.18	664.94	663.07	661.51	656.83	654.92	654.13
45000	682.34	680.05	678.14	676.54	671.76	669.80	669.00
46000	697.51	695.16	693.21	691.58	686.68	684.68	683.86
47000	712.67	710.27	708.28	706.61	701.61	699.57	698.73
48000	727.83	725.39	723.35	721.65	716.54	714.45	713.59
49000	743.00	740.50	738.42	736.68	731.47	729.34	728.46
50000	758.16	755.61	753.49	751.72	746.40	744.22	743.33
51000	773.32	770.72	768.56	766.75	761.32	759.11	758.19
52000	788.49	785.83	783.63	781.78	776.25	773.99	773.06
53000	803.65	800.95	798.70	796.82	791.18	788.88	787.93
54000	818.81	816.06	813.77	811.85	806.11	803.76	802.79
55000	833.98	831.17	828.84	826.89	821.04	818.64	817.66
56000	849.14	846.28	843.90	841.92	835.96	833.53	832.53
57000	864.30	861.40	858.97	856.96	850.89	848.41	847.39
58000	879.47	876.51	874.04	871.99	865.82	863.30	862.26
59000	894.63	891.62	889.11	887.02	880.75	878.18	877.13
60000	909.79	906.73	904.18	902.06	895.68	893.07	891.99
65000	985.61	982.29	979.53	977.23	970.32	967.49	966.33
70000	1061.43	1057.85	1054.88	1052.40	1044.95	1041.91	1040.66
75000	1137.24	1133.42	1130.23	1127.57	1119.59	1116.33	1114.99
80000	1213.06	1208.98	1205.58	1202.75	1194.23	1190.76	1189.32
85000	1288.87	1284.54	1280.93	1277.92	1268.87	1265.18	1263.66
90000	1364.69	1360.10	1356.28	1353.09	1343.51	1339.60	1337.99
95000	1440.51	1435.66	1431.62	1428.26	1418.15	1414.02	1412.32
100000	1516.32	1511.22	1506.97	1503.43	1492.79	1488.44	1486.66
105000	1592.14	1586.78	1582.32	1578.60	1567.43	1562.87	1560.99
110000	1667.95	1662.34	1657.67	1653.78	1642.07	1637.29	1635.32
120000	1819.59	1813.46	1808.37	1804.12	1791.35	1786.13	1783.99
130000	1971.22	1964.59	1959.06	1954.46	1940.63	1934.98	1932.65
140000	2122.85	2115.71	2109.76	2104.81	2089.91	2083.82	2081.32
150000	2274.48	2266.83	2260.46	2255.15	2239.19	2232.67	2229.98
160000	2426.12	2417.95	2411.16	2405.49	2388.47	2381.51	2378.65
170000	2577.75	2569.08	2561.85	2555.83	2537.75	2530.35	2527.32
180000	2729.38	2720.20	2712.55	2706.18	2687.03	2679.20	2675.98
190000	2881.01	2871.32	2863.25	2856.52	2836.31	2828.04	2824.65
200000	3032.64	3022.44	3013.95	3006.86	2985.59	2976.89	2973.31
210000	3184.28	3173.56	3164.64	3157.21	3134.86	3125.73	3121.98
220000	3335.91	3324.69	3315.34	3307.55	3284.14	3274.58	3270.64
230000	3487.54	3475.81	3466.04	3457.89	3433.42	3423.42	3419.31
240000	3639.17	3626.93	3616.73	3608.24	3582.70	3572.27	3567.97
250000	3790.81	3778.05	3767.43	3758.58	3731.98	3721.11	3716.64

18.75 % Monthly Payments

LOAN AMOUNT	1	2	3	4	5	6	7
				YEARS			
100	9.17	5.00	3.62	2.94	2.54	2.28	2.11
200	18.34	9.99	7.24	5.88	5.08	4.57	4.21
500	45.85	24.98	18.09	14.70	12.71	11.42	10.53
1000	91.71	49.95	36.18	29.40	25.42	22.84	21.05
2000	183.41	99.90	72.36	58.81	50.85	45.68	42.10
5000	458.54	249.76	180.90	147.02	127.12	114.20	105.26
6000	550.24	299.71	217.09	176.43	152.55	137.04	126.31
7000	641.95	349.66	253.27	205.83	177.97	159.88	147.36
8000	733.66	399.61	289.45	235.24	203.40	182.72	168.41
9000	825.36	449.56	325.63	264.64	228.82	205.56	189.46
10000	917.07	499.52	361.81	294.05	254.24	228.40	210.51
12000	1100.49	599.42	434.17	352.86	305.09	274.08	252.61
15000	1375.61	749.27	542.71	441.07	381.37	342.60	315.77
20000	1834.14	999.03	723.62	588.10	508.49	456.80	421.02
25000	2292.68	1248.79	904.52	735.12	635.61	571.00	526.28
30000	2751.21	1498.55	1085.43	882.14	762.73	685.20	631.54
31000	2842.92	1548.50	1121.61	911.55	788.16	708.04	652.59
32000	2934.63	1598.45	1157.79	940.95	813.58	730.88	673.64
33000	3026.33	1648.40	1193.97	970.36	839.01	753.72	694.69
34000	3118.04	1698.36	1230.15	999.76	864.43	776.56	715.74
35000	3209.75	1748.31	1266.33	1029.17	889.85	799.40	736.79
36000	3301.46	1798.26	1302.51	1058.57	915.28	822.24	757.84
37000	3393.16	1848.21	1338.70	1087.98	940.70	845.08	778.90
38000	3484.87	1898.16	1374.88	1117.38	966.13	867.92	799.95
39000	3576.58	1948.11	1411.06	1146.79	991.55	890.76	821.00
40000	3668.28	1998.06	1447.24	1176.19	1016.98	913.60	842.05
41000	3759.99	2048.02	1483.42	1205.60	1042.40	936.44	863.10
42000	3851.70	2097.97	1519.60	1235.00	1067.83	959.28	884.15
43000	3943.41	2147.92	1555.78	1264.40	1093.25	982.12	905.20
44000	4035.11	2197.87	1591.96	1293.81	1118.67	1004.96	926.25
45000	4126.82	2247.82	1628.14	1323.21	1144.10	1027.80	947.31
46000	4218.53	2297.77	1664.32	1352.62	1169.52	1050.64	968.36
47000	4310.23	2347.73	1700.51	1382.02	1194.95	1073.48	989.41
48000	4401.94	2397.68	1736.69	1411.43	1220.37	1096.32	1010.46
49000	4493.65	2447.63	1772.87	1440.83	1245.80	1119.16	1031.51
50000	4585.35	2497.58	1809.05	1470.24	1271.22	1142.00	1052.56
51000	4677.06	2547.53	1845.23	1499.64	1296.65	1164.84	1073.61
52000	4768.77	2597.48	1881.41	1529.05	1322.07	1187.68	1094.66
53000	4860.48	2647.44	1917.59	1558.45	1347.49	1210.52	1115.71
54000	4952.18	2697.39	1953.77	1587.86	1372.92	1233.36	1136.77
55000	5043.89	2747.34	1989.95	1617.26	1398.34	1256.20	1157.82
56000	5135.60	2797.29	2026.13	1646.67	1423.77	1279.04	1178.87
57000	5227.30	2847.24	2062.32	1676.07	1449.19	1301.88	1199.92
58000	5319.01	2897.19	2098.50	1705.48	1474.62	1324.72	1220.97
59000	5410.72	2947.15	2134.68	1734.88	1500.04	1347.56	1242.02
60000	5502.43	2997.10	2170.86	1764.29	1525.46	1370.40	1263.07
65000	5960.96	3246.86	2351.76	1911.31	1652.59	1484.60	1368.33
70000	6419.50	3496.61	2532.67	2058.33	1779.71	1598.80	1473.59
75000	6878.03	3746.37	2713.57	2205.36	1906.83	1713.00	1578.84
80000	7336.57	3996.13	2894.48	2352.38	2033.95	1827.20	1684.10
85000	7795.10	4245.89	3075.38	2499.40	2161.08	1941.40	1789.35
90000	8253.64	4495.65	3256.29	2646.43	2288.20	2055.60	1894.61
95000	8712.17	4745.40	3437.19	2793.45	2415.32	2169.80	1999.87
100000	9170.71	4995.16	3618.10	2940.48	2542.44	2284.00	2105.12
105000	9629.24	5244.92	3799.00	3087.50	2669.56	2398.20	2210.38
110000	10087.78	5494.68	3979.91	3234.52	2796.69	2512.40	2315.63
120000	11004.85	5994.19	4341.72	3528.57	3050.93	2740.80	2526.15
130000	11921.92	6493.71	4703.53	3822.62	3305.17	2969.20	2736.66
140000	12838.99	6993.23	5065.34	4116.67	3559.42	3197.60	2947.17
150000	13756.06	7492.74	5427.14	4410.71	3813.66	3426.00	3157.68
160000	14673.13	7992.26	5788.95	4704.76	4067.91	3654.40	3368.20
170000	15590.21	8491.78	6150.76	4998.81	4322.15	3882.80	3578.71
180000	16507.28	8991.29	6512.57	5292.86	4576.39	4111.20	3789.22
190000	17424.35	9490.81	6874.38	5586.90	4830.64	4339.60	3999.73
200000	18341.42	9990.32	7236.19	5880.95	5084.88	4568.00	4210.25
210000	19258.49	10489.84	7598.00	6175.00	5339.13	4796.40	4420.76
220000	20175.56	10989.36	7959.81	6469.05	5593.37	5024.80	4631.27
230000	21092.63	11488.87	8321.62	6763.10	5847.61	5253.20	4841.78
240000	22009.70	11988.39	8683.43	7057.14	6101.86	5481.60	5052.29
250000	22926.77	12487.90	9045.24	7351.19	6356.10	5710.00	5262.81

Monthly Payments 18.75 %

LOAN AMOUNT	YEARS 8	9	10	11	12	13	14
100	1.98	1.88	1.81	1.75	1.70	1.67	1.64
200	3.95	3.76	3.61	3.50	3.41	3.33	3.28
500	9.88	9.40	9.03	8.74	8.51	8.33	8.19
1000	19.76	18.79	18.06	17.48	17.03	16.67	16.38
2000	39.52	37.59	36.11	34.96	34.06	33.34	32.76
5000	98.79	93.96	90.28	87.41	85.15	83.35	81.90
6000	118.55	112.76	108.33	104.89	102.18	100.02	98.28
7000	138.30	131.55	126.39	122.37	119.21	116.69	114.66
8000	158.06	150.34	144.44	139.85	136.24	133.36	131.04
9000	177.82	169.13	162.50	157.34	153.27	150.03	147.42
10000	197.58	187.93	180.55	174.82	170.30	166.69	163.80
12000	237.09	225.51	216.66	209.78	204.36	200.03	196.56
15000	296.37	281.89	270.83	262.23	255.45	250.04	245.70
20000	395.15	375.85	361.10	349.64	340.60	333.39	327.59
25000	493.94	469.81	451.38	437.05	425.74	416.74	409.49
30000	592.73	563.78	541.66	524.46	510.89	500.08	491.39
31000	612.49	582.57	559.71	541.94	527.92	516.75	507.77
32000	632.25	601.36	577.77	559.42	544.95	533.42	524.15
33000	652.01	620.15	595.82	576.90	561.98	550.09	540.53
34000	671.76	638.95	613.88	594.38	579.01	566.76	556.91
35000	691.52	657.74	631.93	611.86	596.04	583.43	573.29
36000	711.28	676.53	649.99	629.35	613.07	600.10	589.67
37000	731.04	695.32	668.04	646.83	630.10	616.77	606.05
38000	750.79	714.12	686.10	664.31	647.13	633.44	622.43
39000	770.55	732.91	704.15	681.79	664.16	650.11	638.81
40000	790.31	751.70	722.21	699.27	681.19	666.78	655.19
41000	810.07	770.49	740.26	716.76	698.22	683.45	671.57
42000	829.83	789.29	758.32	734.24	715.25	700.12	687.95
43000	849.58	808.08	776.37	751.72	732.28	716.79	704.33
44000	869.34	826.87	794.43	769.20	749.31	733.46	720.71
45000	889.10	845.66	812.48	786.68	766.34	750.13	737.09
46000	908.86	864.46	830.54	804.16	783.37	766.79	753.47
47000	928.61	883.25	848.59	821.65	800.40	783.46	769.85
48000	948.37	902.04	866.65	839.13	817.43	800.13	786.23
49000	968.13	920.83	884.70	856.61	834.46	816.80	802.61
50000	987.89	939.63	902.76	874.09	851.49	833.47	818.99
51000	1007.65	958.42	920.81	891.57	868.52	850.14	835.37
52000	1027.40	977.21	938.87	909.06	885.55	866.81	851.75
53000	1047.16	996.00	956.93	926.54	902.58	883.48	868.13
54000	1066.92	1014.80	974.98	944.02	919.61	900.15	884.51
55000	1086.68	1033.59	993.04	961.50	936.64	916.82	900.89
56000	1106.43	1052.38	1011.09	978.98	953.67	933.49	917.27
57000	1126.19	1071.17	1029.15	996.46	970.70	950.16	933.65
58000	1145.95	1089.97	1047.20	1013.95	987.73	966.83	950.03
59000	1165.71	1108.76	1065.26	1031.43	1004.76	983.50	966.41
60000	1185.46	1127.55	1083.31	1048.91	1021.79	1000.17	982.78
65000	1284.25	1221.51	1173.59	1136.32	1106.94	1083.51	1064.68
70000	1383.04	1315.48	1263.86	1223.73	1192.08	1166.86	1146.58
75000	1481.83	1409.44	1354.14	1311.14	1277.23	1250.21	1228.48
80000	1580.62	1503.40	1444.42	1398.55	1362.38	1333.56	1310.38
85000	1679.41	1597.36	1534.69	1485.96	1447.53	1416.90	1392.28
90000	1778.20	1691.33	1624.97	1573.37	1532.68	1500.25	1474.18
95000	1876.99	1785.29	1715.24	1660.77	1617.83	1583.60	1556.08
100000	1975.77	1879.25	1805.52	1748.18	1702.98	1666.95	1637.97
105000	2074.56	1973.21	1895.80	1835.59	1788.13	1750.29	1719.87
110000	2173.35	2067.18	1986.07	1923.00	1873.28	1833.64	1801.77
120000	2370.93	2255.10	2166.62	2097.82	2043.57	2000.33	1965.57
130000	2568.51	2443.03	2347.18	2272.64	2213.87	2167.03	2129.37
140000	2766.08	2630.95	2527.73	2447.46	2384.17	2333.72	2293.16
150000	2963.66	2818.88	2708.28	2622.28	2554.47	2500.42	2456.96
160000	3161.24	3006.80	2888.83	2797.09	2724.76	2667.11	2620.76
170000	3358.82	3194.73	3069.38	2971.91	2895.06	2833.81	2784.56
180000	3556.39	3382.65	3249.93	3146.73	3065.36	3000.50	2948.35
190000	3753.97	3570.58	3430.49	3321.55	3235.66	3167.20	3112.15
200000	3951.55	3758.50	3611.04	3496.37	3405.96	3333.89	3275.95
210000	4149.13	3946.43	3791.59	3671.19	3576.25	3500.59	3439.75
220000	4346.70	4134.35	3972.14	3846.00	3746.55	3667.28	3603.54
230000	4544.28	4322.28	4152.69	4020.82	3916.85	3833.97	3767.34
240000	4741.86	4510.20	4333.25	4195.64	4087.15	4000.67	3931.14
250000	4939.44	4698.13	4513.80	4370.46	4257.44	4167.36	4094.94

18.75 % Monthly Payments

LOAN AMOUNT	15	16	17	18	19	20	21
100	1.61	1.60	1.58	1.57	1.56	1.55	1.54
200	3.23	3.19	3.16	3.13	3.11	3.10	3.08
500	8.07	7.98	7.90	7.83	7.78	7.74	7.70
1000	16.15	15.95	15.80	15.67	15.56	15.48	15.40
2000	32.29	31.91	31.60	31.34	31.13	30.95	30.81
5000	80.73	79.77	78.99	78.35	77.82	77.38	77.02
6000	96.87	95.73	94.79	94.02	93.38	92.86	92.43
7000	113.02	111.68	110.59	109.69	108.95	108.34	107.83
8000	129.16	127.63	126.38	125.36	124.51	123.82	123.24
9000	145.31	143.59	142.18	141.03	140.08	139.29	138.64
10000	161.45	159.54	157.98	156.70	155.64	154.77	154.05
12000	193.74	191.45	189.58	188.04	186.77	185.72	184.86
15000	242.18	239.31	236.97	235.05	233.46	232.15	231.07
20000	322.90	319.08	315.96	313.40	311.28	309.54	308.10
25000	403.63	398.86	394.95	391.74	389.10	386.92	385.12
30000	484.36	478.63	473.94	470.09	466.92	464.31	462.14
31000	500.50	494.58	489.74	485.76	482.49	479.79	477.55
32000	516.65	510.54	505.54	501.43	498.05	495.26	492.95
33000	532.79	526.49	521.33	517.10	513.62	510.74	508.36
34000	548.94	542.44	537.13	532.77	529.18	526.22	523.76
35000	565.08	558.40	552.93	548.44	544.75	541.69	539.17
36000	581.23	574.35	568.73	564.11	560.31	557.17	554.57
37000	597.37	590.31	584.53	579.78	575.87	572.65	569.98
38000	613.52	606.26	600.32	595.45	591.44	588.12	585.38
39000	629.66	622.21	616.12	611.12	607.00	603.60	600.79
40000	645.81	638.17	631.92	626.79	622.57	619.08	616.19
41000	661.95	654.12	647.72	642.46	638.13	634.55	631.60
42000	678.10	670.08	663.52	658.13	653.69	650.03	647.00
43000	694.24	686.03	679.31	673.80	669.26	665.51	662.41
44000	710.39	701.99	695.11	689.47	684.82	680.99	677.81
45000	726.53	717.94	710.91	705.14	700.39	696.46	693.22
46000	742.68	733.89	726.71	720.81	715.95	711.94	708.62
47000	758.82	749.85	742.51	736.48	731.52	727.42	724.03
48000	774.97	765.80	758.30	752.15	747.08	742.89	739.43
49000	791.11	781.76	774.10	767.82	762.64	758.37	754.84
50000	807.26	797.71	789.90	783.49	778.21	773.85	770.24
51000	823.40	813.67	805.70	799.16	793.77	789.32	785.64
52000	839.55	829.62	821.50	814.83	809.34	804.80	801.05
53000	855.70	845.57	837.29	830.50	824.90	820.28	816.45
54000	871.84	861.53	853.09	846.17	840.46	835.76	831.86
55000	887.99	877.48	868.89	861.84	856.03	851.23	847.26
56000	904.13	893.44	884.69	877.51	871.59	866.71	862.67
57000	920.28	909.39	900.49	893.18	887.16	882.19	878.07
58000	936.42	925.34	916.28	908.85	902.72	897.66	893.48
59000	952.57	941.30	932.08	924.52	918.28	913.14	908.88
60000	968.71	957.25	947.88	940.19	933.85	928.62	924.29
65000	1049.44	1037.02	1026.87	1018.53	1011.67	1006.00	1001.31
70000	1130.16	1116.80	1105.86	1096.88	1089.49	1083.39	1078.34
75000	1210.89	1196.57	1184.85	1175.23	1167.31	1160.77	1155.36
80000	1291.62	1276.34	1263.84	1253.58	1245.13	1238.16	1232.38
85000	1372.34	1356.11	1342.83	1331.93	1322.95	1315.54	1309.41
90000	1453.07	1435.88	1421.82	1410.28	1400.77	1392.93	1386.43
95000	1533.79	1515.65	1500.81	1488.63	1478.59	1470.31	1463.46
100000	1614.52	1595.42	1579.80	1566.98	1556.42	1547.69	1540.48
105000	1695.25	1675.19	1658.79	1645.33	1634.24	1625.08	1617.50
110000	1775.97	1754.96	1737.78	1723.67	1712.06	1702.46	1694.53
120000	1937.42	1914.51	1895.76	1880.37	1867.70	1857.23	1848.58
130000	2098.88	2074.05	2053.74	2037.07	2023.34	2012.00	2002.62
140000	2260.33	2233.59	2211.72	2193.77	2178.98	2166.77	2156.67
150000	2421.78	2393.13	2369.70	2350.47	2334.62	2321.54	2310.72
160000	2583.23	2552.68	2527.68	2507.16	2490.26	2476.31	2464.77
170000	2744.68	2712.22	2685.66	2663.86	2645.91	2631.08	2618.82
180000	2906.13	2871.76	2843.64	2820.56	2801.55	2785.85	2772.86
190000	3067.59	3031.30	3001.62	2977.26	2957.19	2940.62	2926.91
200000	3229.04	3190.84	3159.60	3133.95	3112.83	3095.39	3080.96
210000	3390.49	3350.39	3317.58	3290.65	3268.47	3250.16	3235.01
220000	3551.94	3509.93	3475.56	3447.35	3424.11	3404.93	3389.06
230000	3713.39	3669.47	3633.54	3604.05	3579.75	3559.70	3543.10
240000	3874.85	3829.01	3791.52	3760.74	3735.40	3714.47	3697.15
250000	4036.30	3988.56	3949.50	3917.44	3891.04	3869.24	3851.20

Monthly Payments 18.75 %

LOAN AMOUNT	22	23	24	25	30	35	40
100	1.53	1.53	1.53	1.52	1.51	1.51	1.51
200	3.07	3.06	3.05	3.04	3.02	3.02	3.01
500	7.67	7.65	7.63	7.61	7.56	7.54	7.53
1000	15.35	15.30	15.25	15.22	15.12	15.08	15.06
2000	30.69	30.59	30.51	30.44	30.23	30.15	30.12
5000	76.73	76.48	76.27	76.10	75.59	75.38	75.30
6000	92.07	91.77	91.52	91.32	90.70	90.46	90.35
7000	107.42	107.07	106.78	106.54	105.82	105.53	105.41
8000	122.76	122.36	122.03	121.76	120.94	120.61	120.47
9000	138.11	137.66	137.29	136.98	136.06	135.68	135.53
10000	153.45	152.95	152.54	152.20	151.17	150.76	150.59
12000	184.14	183.54	183.05	182.64	181.41	180.91	180.71
15000	230.18	229.43	228.81	228.30	226.76	226.14	225.89
20000	306.90	305.91	305.08	304.40	302.35	301.52	301.18
25000	383.63	382.38	381.35	380.50	377.93	376.90	376.48
30000	460.35	458.86	457.62	456.60	453.52	452.28	451.77
31000	475.70	474.16	472.88	471.81	468.64	467.35	466.83
32000	491.04	489.45	488.13	487.03	483.75	482.43	481.89
33000	506.39	504.75	503.39	502.25	498.87	497.50	496.95
34000	521.73	520.04	518.64	517.47	513.99	512.58	512.01
35000	537.08	535.34	533.89	532.69	529.11	527.66	527.07
36000	552.42	550.63	549.15	547.91	544.22	542.73	542.13
37000	567.77	565.93	564.40	563.13	559.34	557.81	557.18
38000	583.11	581.22	579.66	578.35	574.46	572.88	572.24
39000	598.46	596.52	594.91	593.57	589.58	587.96	587.30
40000	613.80	611.82	610.17	608.79	604.69	603.04	602.36
41000	629.15	627.11	625.42	624.01	619.81	618.11	617.42
42000	644.49	642.41	640.67	639.23	634.93	633.19	632.48
43000	659.84	657.70	655.93	654.45	650.05	648.26	647.54
44000	675.18	673.00	671.18	669.67	665.16	663.34	662.60
45000	690.53	688.29	686.44	684.89	680.28	678.42	677.66
46000	705.87	703.59	701.69	700.11	695.40	693.49	692.72
47000	721.22	718.88	716.94	715.33	710.51	708.57	707.78
48000	736.56	734.18	732.20	730.55	725.63	723.64	722.83
49000	751.91	749.47	747.45	745.77	740.75	738.72	737.89
50000	767.25	764.77	762.71	760.99	755.87	753.79	752.95
51000	782.60	780.06	777.96	776.21	770.98	768.87	768.01
52000	797.94	795.36	793.22	791.43	786.10	783.95	783.07
53000	813.29	810.66	808.47	806.65	801.22	799.02	798.13
54000	828.63	825.95	823.72	821.87	816.34	814.10	813.19
55000	843.98	841.25	838.98	837.09	831.45	829.17	828.25
56000	859.32	856.54	854.23	852.31	846.57	844.25	843.31
57000	874.67	871.84	869.49	867.53	861.69	859.33	858.37
58000	890.01	887.13	884.74	882.75	876.81	874.40	873.42
59000	905.36	902.43	899.99	897.97	891.92	889.48	888.48
60000	920.70	917.72	915.25	913.19	907.04	904.55	903.54
65000	997.43	994.20	991.52	989.29	982.63	979.93	978.84
70000	1074.15	1070.68	1067.79	1065.39	1058.21	1055.31	1054.13
75000	1150.88	1147.15	1144.06	1141.49	1133.80	1130.69	1129.43
80000	1227.60	1223.63	1220.33	1217.59	1209.39	1206.07	1204.72
85000	1304.33	1300.11	1296.60	1293.69	1284.97	1281.45	1280.02
90000	1381.05	1376.58	1372.87	1369.79	1360.56	1356.83	1355.31
95000	1457.78	1453.06	1449.14	1445.88	1436.15	1432.21	1430.61
100000	1534.50	1529.54	1525.41	1521.98	1511.73	1507.59	1505.90
105000	1611.23	1606.01	1601.68	1598.08	1587.32	1582.97	1581.20
110000	1687.95	1682.49	1677.96	1674.18	1662.91	1658.35	1656.50
120000	1841.40	1835.45	1830.50	1826.38	1814.08	1809.11	1807.09
130000	1994.85	1988.40	1983.04	1978.58	1965.25	1959.87	1957.68
140000	2148.30	2141.35	2135.58	2130.78	2116.43	2110.63	2108.27
150000	2301.75	2294.31	2288.12	2282.98	2267.60	2261.38	2258.86
160000	2455.20	2447.26	2440.66	2435.17	2418.77	2412.14	2409.45
170000	2608.65	2600.21	2593.20	2587.37	2569.95	2562.90	2560.04
180000	2762.10	2753.17	2745.75	2739.57	2721.12	2713.66	2710.63
190000	2915.55	2906.12	2898.29	2891.77	2872.29	2864.42	2861.22
200000	3069.00	3059.08	3050.83	3043.97	3023.47	3015.18	3011.81
210000	3222.45	3212.03	3203.37	3196.17	3174.64	3165.94	3162.40
220000	3375.90	3364.98	3355.91	3348.36	3325.81	3316.70	3312.99
230000	3529.35	3517.94	3508.45	3500.56	3476.99	3467.46	3463.58
240000	3682.80	3670.89	3660.99	3652.76	3628.16	3618.21	3614.17
250000	3836.25	3823.84	3813.54	3804.96	3779.33	3768.97	3764.76

19.00 % Monthly Payments

LOAN AMOUNT	YEARS 1	2	3	4	5	6	7
100	9.18	5.01	3.63	2.95	2.56	2.30	2.12
200	18.36	10.01	7.26	5.91	5.11	4.59	4.24
500	45.91	25.03	18.15	14.76	12.78	11.49	10.59
1000	91.82	50.06	36.30	29.53	25.55	22.97	21.19
2000	183.64	100.13	72.59	59.05	51.10	45.94	42.37
5000	459.09	250.32	181.49	147.63	127.75	114.86	105.94
6000	550.91	300.38	217.78	177.16	153.30	137.83	127.12
7000	642.72	350.45	254.08	206.68	178.86	160.80	148.31
8000	734.54	400.51	290.38	236.21	204.41	183.77	169.50
9000	826.36	450.57	326.68	265.74	229.96	206.74	190.69
10000	918.18	500.64	362.97	295.26	255.51	229.71	211.87
12000	1101.81	600.77	435.57	354.31	306.61	275.66	254.25
15000	1377.26	750.96	544.46	442.89	383.26	344.57	317.81
20000	1836.35	1001.28	725.95	590.52	511.02	459.43	423.75
25000	2295.44	1251.59	907.44	738.15	638.77	574.28	529.69
30000	2754.53	1501.91	1088.92	885.78	766.52	689.14	635.62
31000	2846.34	1551.98	1125.22	915.31	792.08	712.11	656.81
32000	2938.16	1602.04	1161.52	944.84	817.63	735.08	678.00
33000	3029.98	1652.10	1197.82	974.36	843.18	758.06	699.19
34000	3121.80	1702.17	1234.11	1003.89	868.73	781.03	720.37
35000	3213.61	1752.23	1270.41	1033.42	894.28	804.00	741.56
36000	3305.43	1802.30	1306.71	1062.94	919.83	826.97	762.75
37000	3397.25	1852.36	1343.01	1092.47	945.38	849.94	783.94
38000	3489.07	1902.42	1379.30	1121.99	970.93	872.91	805.12
39000	3580.88	1952.49	1415.60	1151.52	996.48	895.88	826.31
40000	3672.70	2002.55	1451.90	1181.05	1022.03	918.86	847.50
41000	3764.52	2052.61	1488.20	1210.57	1047.58	941.83	868.69
42000	3856.34	2102.68	1524.49	1240.10	1073.13	964.80	889.87
43000	3948.15	2152.74	1560.79	1269.62	1098.69	987.77	911.06
44000	4039.97	2202.81	1597.09	1299.15	1124.24	1010.74	932.25
45000	4131.79	2252.87	1633.39	1328.68	1149.79	1033.71	953.44
46000	4223.61	2302.93	1669.68	1358.20	1175.34	1056.68	974.62
47000	4315.42	2353.00	1705.98	1387.73	1200.89	1079.65	995.81
48000	4407.24	2403.06	1742.28	1417.26	1226.44	1102.63	1017.00
49000	4499.06	2453.12	1778.58	1446.78	1251.99	1125.60	1038.19
50000	4590.88	2503.19	1814.87	1476.31	1277.54	1148.57	1059.37
51000	4682.69	2553.25	1851.17	1505.83	1303.09	1171.54	1080.56
52000	4774.51	2603.32	1887.47	1535.36	1328.64	1194.51	1101.75
53000	4866.33	2653.38	1923.77	1564.89	1354.19	1217.48	1122.94
54000	4958.15	2703.44	1960.06	1594.41	1379.74	1240.45	1144.12
55000	5049.96	2753.51	1996.36	1623.94	1405.29	1263.43	1165.31
56000	5141.78	2803.57	2032.66	1653.46	1430.85	1286.40	1186.50
57000	5233.60	2853.64	2068.96	1682.99	1456.40	1309.37	1207.69
58000	5325.42	2903.70	2105.25	1712.52	1481.95	1332.34	1228.87
59000	5417.23	2953.76	2141.55	1742.04	1507.50	1355.31	1250.06
60000	5509.05	3003.83	2177.85	1771.57	1533.05	1378.28	1271.25
65000	5968.14	3254.15	2359.33	1919.20	1660.80	1493.14	1377.19
70000	6427.23	3504.46	2540.82	2066.83	1788.56	1608.00	1483.12
75000	6886.31	3754.78	2722.31	2214.46	1916.31	1722.85	1589.06
80000	7345.40	4005.10	2903.80	2362.09	2044.07	1837.71	1695.00
85000	7804.49	4255.42	3085.28	2509.72	2171.82	1952.57	1800.94
90000	8263.58	4505.74	3266.77	2657.35	2299.57	2067.42	1906.87
95000	8722.66	4756.06	3448.26	2804.98	2427.33	2182.28	2012.81
100000	9181.75	5006.38	3629.75	2952.61	2555.08	2297.14	2118.75
105000	9640.84	5256.70	3811.23	3100.25	2682.84	2411.99	2224.68
110000	10099.93	5507.02	3992.72	3247.88	2810.59	2526.85	2330.62
120000	11018.10	6007.65	4355.69	3543.14	3066.10	2756.57	2542.50
130000	11936.28	6508.29	4718.67	3838.40	3321.61	2986.28	2754.37
140000	12854.45	7008.93	5081.64	4133.66	3577.11	3215.99	2966.25
150000	13772.63	7509.57	5444.62	4428.92	3832.62	3445.71	3178.12
160000	14690.80	8010.20	5807.59	4724.18	4088.13	3675.42	3390.00
170000	15608.98	8510.84	6170.57	5019.44	4343.64	3905.13	3601.87
180000	16527.15	9011.48	6533.54	5314.71	4599.15	4134.85	3813.75
190000	17445.33	9512.12	6896.52	5609.97	4854.66	4364.56	4025.62
200000	18363.50	10012.75	7259.49	5905.23	5110.16	4594.28	4237.50
210000	19281.68	10513.39	7622.47	6200.49	5365.67	4823.99	4449.37
220000	20199.85	11014.03	7985.44	6495.75	5621.18	5053.70	4661.24
230000	21118.03	11514.67	8348.42	6791.01	5876.69	5283.42	4873.12
240000	22036.20	12015.31	8711.39	7086.28	6132.20	5513.13	5084.99
250000	22954.38	12515.94	9074.36	7381.54	6387.70	5742.84	5296.87

Monthly Payments 19.00 %

LOAN AMOUNT	8	9	10	11	12	13	14
	YEARS						
100	1.99	1.89	1.82	1.76	1.72	1.68	1.65
200	3.98	3.79	3.64	3.53	3.44	3.37	3.31
500	9.95	9.47	9.10	8.82	8.59	8.42	8.27
1000	19.90	18.94	18.20	17.64	17.19	16.83	16.54
2000	39.80	37.88	36.41	35.27	34.37	33.66	33.09
5000	99.49	94.69	91.02	88.18	85.94	84.15	82.72
6000	119.39	113.63	109.23	105.81	103.12	100.98	99.26
7000	139.29	132.57	127.43	123.45	120.31	117.81	115.81
8000	159.19	151.50	145.64	141.08	137.50	134.64	132.35
9000	179.09	170.44	163.84	158.72	154.69	151.47	148.90
10000	198.99	189.38	182.05	176.36	171.87	168.30	165.44
12000	238.78	227.26	218.46	211.63	206.25	201.97	198.53
15000	298.48	284.07	273.07	264.53	257.81	252.46	248.16
20000	397.97	378.76	364.10	352.71	343.75	336.61	330.88
25000	497.47	473.45	455.12	440.89	429.68	420.76	413.60
30000	596.96	568.14	546.15	529.07	515.62	504.91	496.32
31000	616.86	587.08	564.35	546.70	532.81	521.74	512.86
32000	636.76	606.01	582.56	564.34	549.99	538.57	529.41
33000	656.66	624.95	600.76	581.97	567.18	555.40	545.95
34000	676.56	643.89	618.97	599.61	584.37	572.24	562.50
35000	696.45	662.83	637.17	617.24	601.55	589.07	579.04
36000	716.35	681.77	655.38	634.88	618.74	605.90	595.58
37000	736.25	700.70	673.58	652.52	635.93	622.73	612.13
38000	756.15	719.64	691.79	670.15	653.12	639.56	628.67
39000	776.05	738.58	709.99	687.79	670.30	656.39	645.22
40000	795.95	757.52	728.20	705.42	687.49	673.22	661.76
41000	815.85	776.46	746.40	723.06	704.68	690.05	678.30
42000	835.74	795.39	764.61	740.69	721.86	706.88	694.85
43000	855.64	814.33	782.81	758.33	739.05	723.71	711.39
44000	875.54	833.27	801.02	775.96	756.24	740.54	727.94
45000	895.44	852.21	819.22	793.60	773.43	757.37	744.48
46000	915.34	871.15	837.42	811.24	790.61	774.20	761.02
47000	935.24	890.08	855.63	828.87	807.80	791.03	777.57
48000	955.14	909.02	873.83	846.51	824.99	807.86	794.11
49000	975.04	927.96	892.04	864.14	842.18	824.69	810.66
50000	994.93	946.90	910.24	881.78	859.36	841.52	827.20
51000	1014.83	965.84	928.45	899.41	876.55	858.35	843.74
52000	1034.73	984.77	946.65	917.05	893.74	875.18	860.29
53000	1054.63	1003.71	964.86	934.68	910.92	892.01	876.83
54000	1074.53	1022.65	983.06	952.32	928.11	908.84	893.38
55000	1094.43	1041.59	1001.27	969.96	945.30	925.67	909.92
56000	1114.33	1060.53	1019.47	987.59	962.49	942.51	926.46
57000	1134.23	1079.46	1037.68	1005.23	979.67	959.34	943.01
58000	1154.12	1098.40	1055.88	1022.86	996.86	976.17	959.55
59000	1174.02	1117.34	1074.09	1040.50	1014.05	993.00	976.10
60000	1193.92	1136.28	1092.29	1058.13	1031.24	1009.83	992.64
65000	1293.41	1230.97	1183.32	1146.31	1117.17	1093.98	1075.36
70000	1392.91	1325.66	1274.34	1234.49	1203.11	1178.13	1158.08
75000	1492.40	1420.35	1365.37	1322.67	1289.04	1262.28	1240.80
80000	1591.90	1515.04	1456.39	1410.84	1374.98	1346.44	1323.52
85000	1691.39	1609.73	1547.42	1499.02	1460.92	1430.59	1406.24
90000	1790.88	1704.42	1638.44	1587.20	1546.85	1514.74	1488.96
95000	1890.38	1799.11	1729.46	1675.38	1632.79	1598.89	1571.68
100000	1989.87	1893.79	1820.49	1763.56	1718.73	1683.04	1654.40
105000	2089.36	1988.48	1911.51	1851.73	1804.66	1767.20	1737.12
110000	2188.86	2083.17	2002.54	1939.91	1890.60	1851.35	1819.84
120000	2387.84	2272.55	2184.59	2116.27	2062.47	2019.65	1985.28
130000	2586.83	2461.93	2366.64	2292.62	2234.34	2187.96	2150.72
140000	2785.82	2651.31	2548.68	2468.98	2406.22	2356.26	2316.16
150000	2984.80	2840.69	2730.73	2645.33	2578.09	2524.57	2481.60
160000	3183.79	3030.07	2912.78	2821.69	2749.96	2692.87	2647.04
170000	3382.78	3219.45	3094.83	2998.04	2921.83	2861.18	2812.48
180000	3581.76	3408.83	3276.88	3174.40	3093.71	3029.48	2977.92
190000	3780.75	3598.21	3458.93	3350.75	3265.58	3197.79	3143.36
200000	3979.74	3787.59	3640.98	3527.11	3437.45	3366.09	3308.80
210000	4178.72	3976.97	3823.03	3703.47	3609.32	3534.39	3474.24
220000	4377.71	4166.35	4005.08	3879.82	3781.20	3702.70	3639.68
230000	4576.70	4355.73	4187.12	4056.18	3953.07	3871.00	3805.12
240000	4775.69	4545.11	4369.17	4232.53	4124.94	4039.31	3970.56
250000	4974.67	4734.49	4551.22	4408.89	4296.81	4207.61	4136.00

19.00 % Monthly Payments

LOAN AMOUNT	15	16	17	18	19	20	21
100	1.63	1.61	1.60	1.58	1.57	1.57	1.56
200	3.26	3.22	3.19	3.17	3.15	3.13	3.12
500	8.16	8.06	7.99	7.92	7.87	7.83	7.79
1000	16.31	16.12	15.97	15.84	15.74	15.66	15.59
2000	32.62	32.25	31.94	31.69	31.48	31.31	31.17
5000	81.56	80.62	79.85	79.22	78.71	78.28	77.93
6000	97.87	96.75	95.82	95.07	94.45	93.93	93.51
7000	114.19	112.87	111.79	110.91	110.19	109.59	109.10
8000	130.50	128.99	127.76	126.76	125.93	125.25	124.68
9000	146.81	145.12	143.74	142.60	141.67	140.90	140.27
10000	163.12	161.24	159.71	158.45	157.41	156.56	155.85
12000	195.75	193.49	191.65	190.14	188.89	187.87	187.02
15000	244.69	241.86	239.56	237.67	236.12	234.84	233.78
20000	326.25	322.48	319.41	316.89	314.82	313.12	311.71
25000	407.81	403.11	399.26	396.12	393.53	391.39	389.63
30000	489.37	483.73	479.12	475.34	472.23	469.67	467.56
31000	505.69	499.85	495.09	491.18	487.97	485.33	483.14
32000	522.00	515.98	511.06	507.03	503.71	500.98	498.73
33000	538.31	532.10	527.03	522.87	519.46	516.64	514.32
34000	554.62	548.22	543.00	538.72	535.20	532.30	529.90
35000	570.94	564.35	558.97	554.56	550.94	547.95	545.49
36000	587.25	580.47	574.94	570.41	566.68	563.61	561.07
37000	603.56	596.60	590.91	586.25	582.42	579.26	576.66
38000	619.87	612.72	606.88	602.10	598.16	594.92	592.24
39000	636.19	628.85	622.85	617.94	613.90	610.57	607.83
40000	652.50	644.97	638.82	633.78	629.64	626.23	623.41
41000	668.81	661.09	654.79	649.63	645.38	641.89	639.0
42000	685.12	677.22	670.76	665.47	661.13	657.54	654.58
43000	701.44	693.34	686.73	681.32	676.87	673.20	670.17
44000	717.75	709.47	702.70	697.16	692.61	688.85	685.75
45000	734.06	725.59	718.68	713.01	708.35	704.51	701.34
46000	750.37	741.72	734.65	728.85	724.09	720.16	716.9
47000	766.69	757.84	750.62	744.70	739.83	735.82	732.51
48000	783.00	773.96	766.59	760.54	755.57	751.48	748.09
49000	799.31	790.09	782.56	776.39	771.31	767.13	763.68
50000	815.62	806.21	798.53	792.23	787.05	782.79	779.27
51000	831.94	822.34	814.50	808.08	802.79	798.44	794.85
52000	848.25	838.46	830.47	823.92	818.54	814.10	810.4
53000	864.56	854.58	846.44	839.76	834.28	829.76	826.0
54000	880.87	870.71	862.41	855.61	850.02	845.41	841.6
55000	897.19	886.83	878.38	871.45	865.76	861.07	857.1
56000	913.50	902.96	894.35	887.30	881.50	876.72	872.78
57000	929.81	919.08	910.32	903.14	897.24	892.38	888.36
58000	946.12	935.21	926.29	918.99	912.98	908.03	903.95
59000	962.43	951.33	942.26	934.83	928.72	923.69	919.5
60000	978.75	967.45	958.23	950.68	944.46	939.35	935.1
65000	1060.31	1048.08	1038.09	1029.90	1023.17	1017.62	1013.0
70000	1141.87	1128.70	1117.94	1109.12	1101.88	1095.90	1090.9
75000	1223.43	1209.32	1197.79	1188.35	1180.58	1174.18	1168.9
80000	1305.00	1289.94	1277.64	1267.57	1259.29	1252.46	1246.8
85000	1386.56	1370.56	1357.50	1346.79	1337.99	1330.74	1324.7
90000	1468.12	1451.18	1437.35	1426.02	1416.70	1409.02	1402.6
95000	1549.68	1531.80	1517.20	1505.24	1495.40	1487.30	1480.6
100000	1631.25	1612.42	1597.06	1584.46	1574.11	1565.58	1558.5
105000	1712.81	1693.05	1676.91	1663.68	1652.81	1643.85	1636.4
110000	1794.37	1773.67	1756.76	1742.91	1731.52	1722.13	1714.3
120000	1957.49	1934.91	1916.47	1901.35	1888.93	1878.69	1870.2
130000	2120.62	2096.15	2076.17	2059.80	2046.34	2035.25	2026.0
140000	2283.74	2257.39	2235.88	2218.25	2203.75	2191.81	2181.9
150000	2446.87	2418.64	2395.58	2376.69	2361.16	2348.36	2337.8
160000	2609.99	2579.88	2555.29	2535.14	2518.57	2504.92	2493.6
170000	2773.12	2741.12	2715.00	2693.58	2675.98	2661.48	2649.5
180000	2936.24	2902.36	2874.70	2852.03	2833.39	2818.04	2805.3
190000	3099.37	3063.61	3034.41	3010.48	2990.80	2974.59	2961.2
200000	3262.49	3224.85	3194.11	3168.92	3148.22	3131.15	3117.0
210000	3425.62	3386.09	3353.82	3327.37	3305.63	3287.71	3272.9
220000	3588.74	3547.33	3513.52	3485.81	3463.04	3444.27	3428.7
230000	3751.86	3708.58	3673.23	3644.26	3620.45	3600.82	3584.6
240000	3914.99	3869.82	3832.93	3802.71	3777.86	3757.38	3740.4
250000	4078.11	4031.06	3992.64	3961.15	3935.27	3913.94	3896.3

(Column headings 15–21: YEARS)

Monthly Payments 19.00 %

LOAN AMOUNT	22	23	24	25	30	35	40
				YEARS			
100	1.55	1.55	1.54	1.54	1.53	1.53	1.53
200	3.11	3.10	3.09	3.08	3.06	3.05	3.05
500	7.76	7.74	7.72	7.70	7.65	7.63	7.63
1000	15.53	15.48	15.44	15.41	15.31	15.27	15.25
2000	31.05	30.96	30.88	30.81	30.61	30.53	30.50
5000	77.64	77.39	77.19	77.03	76.53	76.34	76.26
6000	93.16	92.87	92.63	92.43	91.84	91.60	91.51
7000	108.69	108.35	108.07	107.84	107.15	106.87	106.76
8000	124.22	123.83	123.51	123.24	122.45	122.14	122.01
9000	139.74	139.31	138.95	138.65	137.76	137.41	137.26
10000	155.27	154.79	154.39	154.06	153.07	152.67	152.51
12000	186.32	185.75	185.26	184.87	183.68	183.21	183.02
15000	232.91	232.18	231.58	231.08	229.60	229.01	228.77
20000	310.54	309.58	308.77	308.11	306.14	305.35	305.03
25000	388.18	386.97	385.97	385.14	382.67	381.68	381.29
30000	465.81	464.36	463.16	462.17	459.20	458.02	457.54
31000	481.34	479.84	478.60	477.57	474.51	473.29	472.79
32000	496.86	495.32	494.04	492.98	489.82	488.55	488.05
33000	512.39	510.80	509.48	508.38	505.12	503.82	503.30
34000	527.92	526.28	524.92	523.79	520.43	519.09	518.55
35000	543.45	541.76	540.36	539.19	535.74	534.36	533.80
36000	558.97	557.24	555.79	554.60	551.04	549.62	549.05
37000	574.50	572.71	571.23	570.00	566.35	564.89	564.30
38000	590.03	588.19	586.67	585.41	581.66	580.16	579.55
39000	605.55	603.67	602.11	600.81	596.96	595.42	594.81
40000	621.08	619.15	617.55	616.22	612.27	610.69	610.06
41000	636.61	634.63	632.99	631.63	627.58	625.96	625.31
42000	652.14	650.11	648.43	647.03	642.88	641.23	640.56
43000	667.66	665.59	663.87	662.44	658.19	656.49	655.81
44000	683.19	681.07	679.30	677.84	673.50	671.76	671.06
45000	698.72	696.54	694.74	693.25	688.80	687.03	686.31
46000	714.24	712.02	710.18	708.65	704.11	702.30	701.57
47000	729.77	727.50	725.62	724.06	719.42	717.56	716.82
48000	745.30	742.98	741.06	739.46	734.73	732.83	732.07
49000	760.82	758.46	756.50	754.87	750.03	748.10	747.32
50000	776.35	773.94	771.94	770.28	765.34	763.36	762.57
51000	791.88	789.42	787.38	785.68	780.65	778.63	777.82
52000	807.41	804.90	802.81	801.09	795.95	793.90	793.07
53000	822.93	820.37	818.25	816.49	811.26	809.17	808.33
54000	838.46	835.85	833.69	831.90	826.57	824.43	823.58
55000	853.99	851.33	849.13	847.30	841.87	839.70	838.83
56000	869.51	866.81	864.57	862.71	857.18	854.97	854.08
57000	885.04	882.29	880.01	878.11	872.49	870.24	869.33
58000	900.57	897.77	895.45	893.52	887.79	885.50	884.58
59000	916.09	913.25	910.89	908.92	903.10	900.77	899.83
60000	931.62	928.73	926.32	924.33	918.41	916.04	915.09
65000	1009.26	1006.12	1003.52	1001.36	994.94	992.37	991.34
70000	1086.89	1083.51	1080.71	1078.39	1071.47	1068.71	1067.60
75000	1164.53	1160.91	1157.90	1155.41	1148.01	1145.05	1143.86
80000	1242.16	1238.30	1235.10	1232.44	1224.54	1221.38	1220.11
85000	1319.80	1315.69	1312.29	1309.47	1301.08	1297.72	1296.37
90000	1397.43	1393.09	1389.49	1386.50	1377.61	1374.06	1372.63
95000	1475.07	1470.48	1466.68	1463.52	1454.14	1450.39	1448.88
100000	1552.70	1547.88	1543.87	1540.55	1530.68	1526.73	1525.14
105000	1630.34	1625.27	1621.07	1617.58	1607.21	1603.07	1601.40
110000	1707.97	1702.66	1698.26	1694.61	1683.75	1679.40	1677.66
120000	1863.24	1857.45	1852.65	1848.66	1836.81	1832.08	1830.17
130000	2018.51	2012.24	2007.04	2002.72	1989.88	1984.75	1982.68
140000	2173.78	2167.03	2161.42	2156.77	2142.95	2137.42	2135.20
150000	2329.05	2321.81	2315.81	2310.83	2296.02	2290.09	2287.71
160000	2484.32	2476.60	2470.20	2464.88	2449.08	2442.77	2440.23
170000	2639.60	2631.39	2624.58	2618.94	2602.15	2595.44	2592.74
180000	2794.87	2786.18	2778.97	2772.99	2755.22	2748.11	2745.26
190000	2950.14	2940.96	2933.36	2927.05	2908.29	2900.79	2897.77
200000	3105.41	3095.75	3087.75	3081.10	3061.35	3053.46	3050.28
210000	3260.68	3250.54	3242.13	3235.16	3214.42	3206.13	3202.80
220000	3415.95	3405.33	3396.52	3389.21	3367.49	3358.80	3355.31
230000	3571.22	3560.11	3550.91	3543.27	3520.56	3511.48	3507.83
240000	3726.49	3714.90	3705.30	3697.32	3673.63	3664.15	3660.34
250000	3881.76	3869.69	3859.68	3851.38	3826.69	3816.82	3812.85

19.25 % Monthly Payments

LOAN AMOUNT	YEARS 1	2	3	4	5	6	7
100	9.19	5.02	3.64	2.96	2.57	2.31	2.13
200	18.39	10.04	7.28	5.93	5.14	4.62	4.26
500	45.96	25.09	18.21	14.82	12.84	11.55	10.66
1000	91.93	50.18	36.41	29.65	25.68	23.10	21.32
2000	183.86	100.35	72.83	59.30	51.35	46.21	42.65
5000	459.64	250.88	182.07	148.24	128.39	115.52	106.62
6000	551.57	301.06	218.48	177.89	154.06	138.62	127.94
7000	643.50	351.23	254.90	207.53	179.74	161.72	149.27
8000	735.42	401.41	291.31	237.18	205.42	184.82	170.59
9000	827.35	451.58	327.73	266.83	231.10	207.93	191.92
10000	919.28	501.76	364.14	296.48	256.77	231.03	213.24
12000	1103.13	602.11	436.97	355.77	308.13	277.24	255.89
15000	1378.92	752.64	546.21	444.72	385.16	346.55	319.86
20000	1838.56	1003.52	728.28	592.95	513.55	462.06	426.48
25000	2298.20	1254.40	910.35	741.19	641.94	577.58	533.10
30000	2757.84	1505.28	1092.42	889.43	770.32	693.09	639.72
31000	2849.76	1555.46	1128.84	919.08	796.00	716.19	661.04
32000	2941.69	1605.63	1165.25	948.73	821.68	739.30	682.37
33000	3033.62	1655.81	1201.66	978.37	847.36	762.40	703.69
34000	3125.55	1705.98	1238.08	1008.02	873.03	785.50	725.02
35000	3217.48	1756.16	1274.49	1037.67	898.71	808.61	746.34
36000	3309.40	1806.33	1310.91	1067.32	924.39	831.71	767.67
37000	3401.33	1856.51	1347.32	1096.96	950.07	854.81	788.99
38000	3493.26	1906.69	1383.73	1126.61	975.74	877.92	810.31
39000	3585.19	1956.86	1420.15	1156.26	1001.42	901.02	831.64
40000	3677.12	2007.04	1456.56	1185.91	1027.10	924.12	852.96
41000	3769.04	2057.21	1492.98	1215.56	1052.77	947.22	874.29
42000	3860.97	2107.39	1529.39	1245.20	1078.45	970.33	895.61
43000	3952.90	2157.57	1565.80	1274.85	1104.13	993.43	916.93
44000	4044.83	2207.74	1602.22	1304.50	1129.81	1016.53	938.26
45000	4136.76	2257.92	1638.63	1334.15	1155.48	1039.64	959.58
46000	4228.68	2308.09	1675.05	1363.79	1181.16	1062.74	980.9
47000	4320.61	2358.27	1711.46	1393.44	1206.84	1085.84	1002.2
48000	4412.54	2408.45	1747.87	1423.09	1232.52	1108.95	1023.5
49000	4504.47	2458.62	1784.29	1452.74	1258.19	1132.05	1044.8
50000	4596.39	2508.80	1820.70	1482.38	1283.87	1155.15	1066.2
51000	4688.32	2558.97	1857.12	1512.03	1309.55	1178.25	1087.5
52000	4780.25	2609.15	1893.53	1541.68	1335.23	1201.36	1108.8
53000	4872.18	2659.33	1929.94	1571.33	1360.90	1224.46	1130.1
54000	4964.11	2709.50	1966.36	1600.98	1386.58	1247.56	1151.5
55000	5056.03	2759.68	2002.77	1630.62	1412.26	1270.67	1172.8
56000	5147.96	2809.85	2039.19	1660.27	1437.94	1293.77	1194.1
57000	5239.89	2860.03	2075.60	1689.92	1463.61	1316.87	1215.4
58000	5331.82	2910.21	2112.01	1719.57	1489.29	1339.98	1236.7
59000	5423.75	2960.38	2148.43	1749.21	1514.97	1363.08	1258.1
60000	5515.67	3010.56	2184.84	1778.86	1540.65	1386.18	1279.4
65000	5975.31	3261.44	2366.91	1927.10	1669.03	1501.70	1386.0
70000	6434.95	3512.32	2548.98	2075.34	1797.42	1617.21	1492.6
75000	6894.59	3763.20	2731.05	2223.58	1925.81	1732.73	1599.3
80000	7354.23	4014.08	2913.12	2371.82	2054.19	1848.24	1705.9
85000	7813.87	4264.96	3095.19	2520.05	2182.58	1963.76	1812.5
90000	8273.51	4515.84	3277.26	2668.29	2310.97	2079.27	1919.1
95000	8733.15	4766.72	3459.33	2816.53	2439.36	2194.79	2025.7
100000	9192.79	5017.60	3641.40	2964.77	2567.74	2310.30	2132.4
105000	9652.43	5268.48	3823.48	3113.01	2696.13	2425.82	2239.0
110000	10112.07	5519.36	4005.55	3261.25	2824.52	2541.33	2345.6
120000	11031.35	6021.12	4369.69	3557.72	3081.29	2772.36	2558.8
130000	11950.63	6522.88	4733.83	3854.20	3338.07	3003.39	2772.1
140000	12869.91	7024.64	5097.97	4150.68	3594.84	3234.42	2985.3
150000	13789.18	7526.40	5462.11	4447.15	3851.62	3465.45	3198.6
160000	14708.46	8028.15	5826.25	4743.63	4108.39	3696.48	3411.8
170000	15627.74	8529.91	6190.39	5040.11	4365.16	3927.52	3625.0
180000	16547.02	9031.67	6554.53	5336.58	4621.94	4158.55	3838.3
190000	17466.30	9533.43	6918.67	5633.06	4878.71	4389.58	4051.5
200000	18385.58	10035.19	7282.81	5929.54	5135.49	4620.61	4264.8
210000	19304.86	10536.95	7646.95	6226.02	5392.26	4851.64	4478.0
220000	20224.14	11038.71	8011.09	6522.49	5649.04	5082.67	4691.2
230000	21143.42	11540.47	8375.23	6818.97	5905.81	5313.70	4904.5
240000	22062.70	12042.23	8739.37	7115.45	6162.58	5544.73	5117.7
250000	22981.97	12543.99	9103.51	7411.92	6419.36	5775.76	5331.0

Monthly Payments 19.25 %

LOAN AMOUNT	8	9	10	11	12	13	14
100	2.00	1.91	1.84	1.78	1.73	1.70	1.67
200	4.01	3.82	3.67	3.56	3.47	3.40	3.34
500	10.02	9.54	9.18	8.89	8.67	8.50	8.35
1000	20.04	19.08	18.35	17.79	17.35	16.99	16.71
2000	40.08	38.17	36.71	35.58	34.69	33.98	33.42
5000	100.20	95.42	91.77	88.95	86.73	84.96	83.54
6000	120.24	114.50	110.13	106.74	104.07	101.95	100.25
7000	140.28	133.59	128.48	124.53	121.42	118.94	116.96
8000	160.32	152.67	146.84	142.32	138.76	135.93	133.67
9000	180.36	171.75	165.19	160.11	156.11	152.93	150.38
10000	200.40	190.84	183.55	177.90	173.45	169.92	167.09
12000	240.48	229.00	220.26	213.48	208.14	203.90	200.50
15000	300.60	286.26	275.32	266.84	260.18	254.88	250.63
20000	400.80	381.67	367.10	355.79	346.90	339.84	334.17
25000	501.00	477.09	458.87	444.74	433.63	424.80	417.72
30000	601.20	572.51	550.65	533.69	520.35	509.76	501.26
31000	621.24	591.60	569.00	551.48	537.70	526.75	517.97
32000	641.28	610.68	587.36	569.27	555.04	543.74	534.68
33000	661.32	629.76	605.71	587.06	572.39	560.73	551.39
34000	681.36	648.85	624.07	604.85	589.74	577.72	568.09
35000	701.40	667.93	642.42	622.64	607.08	594.71	584.80
36000	721.44	687.01	660.78	640.43	624.43	611.71	601.51
37000	741.48	706.10	679.13	658.22	641.77	628.70	618.22
38000	761.52	725.18	697.49	676.01	659.12	645.69	634.93
39000	781.56	744.27	715.84	693.80	676.46	662.68	651.64
40000	801.60	763.35	734.20	711.59	693.81	679.67	668.35
41000	821.64	782.43	752.55	729.38	711.15	696.67	685.05
42000	841.68	801.52	770.91	747.17	728.50	713.66	701.76
43000	861.72	820.60	789.26	764.96	745.84	730.65	718.47
44000	881.76	839.68	807.62	782.75	763.19	747.64	735.18
45000	901.80	858.77	825.97	800.53	780.53	764.63	751.89
46000	921.84	877.85	844.33	818.32	797.88	781.63	768.60
47000	941.88	896.94	862.68	836.11	815.22	798.62	785.31
48000	961.92	916.02	881.04	853.90	832.57	815.61	802.02
49000	981.96	935.10	899.39	871.69	849.91	832.60	818.72
50000	1002.00	954.19	917.75	889.48	867.26	849.59	835.43
51000	1022.04	973.27	936.10	907.27	884.60	866.58	852.14
52000	1042.08	992.35	954.46	925.06	901.95	883.58	868.85
53000	1062.12	1011.44	972.81	942.85	919.29	900.57	885.56
54000	1082.16	1030.52	991.17	960.64	936.64	917.56	902.27
55000	1102.20	1049.61	1009.52	978.43	953.98	934.55	918.98
56000	1122.24	1068.69	1027.88	996.22	971.33	951.54	935.68
57000	1142.28	1087.77	1046.23	1014.01	988.67	968.54	952.39
58000	1162.32	1106.86	1064.59	1031.80	1006.02	985.53	969.10
59000	1182.36	1125.94	1082.94	1049.59	1023.36	1002.52	985.81
60000	1202.40	1145.02	1101.30	1067.38	1040.71	1019.51	1002.52
65000	1302.60	1240.44	1193.07	1156.33	1127.43	1104.47	1086.06
70000	1402.80	1335.86	1284.85	1245.28	1214.16	1189.43	1169.61
75000	1503.00	1431.28	1376.62	1334.22	1300.89	1274.39	1253.15
80000	1603.20	1526.70	1468.40	1423.17	1387.61	1359.35	1336.69
85000	1703.40	1622.12	1560.17	1512.12	1474.34	1444.31	1420.24
90000	1803.60	1717.54	1651.95	1601.07	1561.06	1529.27	1503.78
95000	1903.80	1812.96	1743.72	1690.02	1647.79	1614.23	1587.32
100000	2004.00	1908.37	1835.50	1778.97	1734.51	1699.19	1670.87
105000	2104.20	2003.79	1927.27	1867.91	1821.24	1784.14	1754.41
110000	2204.40	2099.21	2019.05	1956.86	1907.97	1869.10	1837.95
120000	2404.80	2290.05	2202.60	2134.76	2081.42	2039.02	2005.04
130000	2605.20	2480.89	2386.15	2312.66	2254.87	2208.94	2172.13
140000	2805.60	2671.72	2569.70	2490.55	2428.32	2378.86	2339.21
150000	3006.00	2862.56	2753.25	2668.45	2601.77	2548.78	2506.30
160000	3206.40	3053.40	2936.79	2846.35	2775.22	2718.70	2673.38
170000	3406.80	3244.24	3120.34	3024.24	2948.68	2888.61	2840.47
180000	3607.20	3435.07	3303.89	3202.14	3122.13	3058.53	3007.56
190000	3807.59	3625.91	3487.44	3380.04	3295.58	3228.45	3174.64
200000	4007.99	3816.75	3670.99	3557.93	3469.03	3398.37	3341.73
210000	4208.39	4007.59	3854.54	3735.83	3642.48	3568.29	3508.82
220000	4408.79	4198.42	4038.09	3913.73	3815.93	3738.21	3675.90
230000	4609.19	4389.26	4221.64	4091.62	3989.38	3908.13	3842.99
240000	4809.59	4580.10	4405.19	4269.52	4162.84	4078.04	4010.08
250000	5009.99	4770.94	4588.74	4447.42	4336.29	4247.96	4177.16

Columns 8–14: YEARS

19.25 % Monthly Payments

LOAN AMOUNT	YEARS 15	16	17	18	19	20	21
100	1.65	1.63	1.61	1.60	1.59	1.58	1.58
200	3.30	3.26	3.23	3.20	3.18	3.17	3.15
500	8.24	8.15	8.07	8.01	7.96	7.92	7.88
1000	16.48	16.29	16.14	16.02	15.92	15.83	15.77
2000	32.96	32.59	32.29	32.04	31.84	31.67	31.53
5000	82.40	81.47	80.72	80.10	79.59	79.17	78.83
6000	98.88	97.77	96.86	96.12	95.51	95.01	94.60
7000	115.36	114.06	113.00	112.14	111.43	110.84	110.36
8000	131.84	130.36	129.15	128.16	127.35	126.68	126.13
9000	148.32	146.65	145.29	144.18	143.26	142.51	141.89
10000	164.80	162.95	161.43	160.20	159.18	158.35	157.66
12000	197.76	195.54	193.72	192.24	191.02	190.02	189.19
15000	247.20	244.42	242.15	240.30	238.77	237.52	236.49
20000	329.60	325.89	322.87	320.40	318.37	316.70	315.32
25000	412.00	407.37	403.59	400.49	397.96	395.87	394.15
30000	494.40	488.84	484.30	480.59	477.55	475.05	472.98
31000	510.88	505.13	500.45	496.61	493.47	490.88	488.75
32000	527.36	521.43	516.59	512.63	509.39	506.72	504.51
33000	543.84	537.72	532.73	528.65	525.30	522.55	520.28
34000	560.32	554.02	548.88	544.67	541.22	538.38	536.05
35000	576.80	570.31	565.02	560.69	557.14	554.22	551.81
36000	593.28	586.61	581.16	576.71	573.06	570.05	567.58
37000	609.76	602.90	597.31	592.73	588.98	585.89	583.34
38000	626.24	619.20	613.45	608.75	604.90	601.72	599.11
39000	642.72	635.49	629.59	624.77	620.81	617.56	614.88
40000	659.20	651.79	645.74	640.79	636.73	633.39	630.64
41000	675.68	668.08	661.88	656.81	652.65	649.23	646.41
42000	692.16	684.37	678.03	672.83	668.57	665.06	662.17
43000	708.64	700.67	694.17	688.85	684.49	680.90	677.94
44000	725.12	716.96	710.31	704.87	700.41	696.73	693.71
45000	741.60	733.26	726.46	720.89	716.32	712.57	709.47
46000	758.08	749.55	742.60	736.91	732.24	728.40	725.24
47000	774.56	765.85	758.74	752.93	748.16	744.24	741.00
48000	791.04	782.14	774.89	768.95	764.08	760.07	756.77
49000	807.53	798.44	791.03	784.97	780.00	775.91	772.54
50000	824.01	814.73	807.17	800.99	795.92	791.74	788.30
51000	840.49	831.03	823.32	817.01	811.83	807.58	804.07
52000	856.97	847.32	839.46	833.03	827.75	823.41	819.84
53000	873.45	863.62	855.60	849.05	843.67	839.25	835.60
54000	889.93	879.91	871.75	865.07	859.59	855.08	851.37
55000	906.41	896.20	887.89	881.09	875.51	870.92	867.13
56000	922.89	912.50	904.03	897.11	891.43	886.75	882.90
57000	939.37	928.79	920.18	913.13	907.34	902.59	898.67
58000	955.85	945.09	936.32	929.15	923.26	918.42	914.43
59000	972.33	961.38	952.46	945.17	939.18	934.26	930.20
60000	988.81	977.68	968.61	961.19	955.10	950.09	945.96
65000	1071.21	1059.15	1049.32	1041.29	1034.69	1029.26	1024.79
70000	1153.61	1140.62	1130.04	1121.38	1114.28	1108.44	1103.62
75000	1236.01	1222.10	1210.76	1201.48	1193.87	1187.61	1182.45
80000	1318.41	1303.57	1291.48	1281.58	1273.46	1266.79	1261.28
85000	1400.81	1385.04	1372.19	1361.68	1353.06	1345.96	1340.11
90000	1483.21	1466.52	1452.91	1441.78	1432.65	1425.14	1418.95
95000	1565.61	1547.99	1533.63	1521.88	1512.24	1504.31	1497.78
100000	1648.01	1629.46	1614.35	1601.98	1591.83	1583.48	1576.61
105000	1730.41	1710.94	1695.06	1682.08	1671.42	1662.66	1655.44
110000	1812.81	1792.41	1775.78	1762.18	1751.01	1741.83	1734.27
120000	1977.61	1955.36	1937.22	1922.37	1910.20	1900.18	1891.93
130000	2142.41	2118.30	2098.65	2082.57	2069.38	2058.53	2049.59
140000	2307.21	2281.25	2260.08	2242.77	2228.56	2216.88	2207.25
150000	2472.02	2444.20	2421.52	2402.97	2387.75	2375.23	2364.91
160000	2636.82	2607.14	2582.95	2563.17	2546.93	2533.58	2522.57
170000	2801.62	2770.09	2744.39	2723.36	2706.11	2691.92	2680.23
180000	2966.42	2933.03	2905.82	2883.56	2865.30	2850.27	2837.89
190000	3131.22	3095.98	3067.26	3043.76	3024.48	3008.62	2995.55
200000	3296.02	3258.93	3228.69	3203.96	3183.66	3166.97	3153.21
210000	3460.82	3421.87	3390.13	3364.15	3342.84	3325.32	3310.87
220000	3625.62	3584.82	3551.56	3524.35	3502.03	3483.67	3468.53
230000	3790.42	3747.77	3713.00	3684.55	3661.21	3642.01	3626.19
240000	3955.22	3910.71	3874.43	3844.75	3820.39	3800.36	3783.85
250000	4120.03	4073.66	4035.86	4004.95	3979.58	3958.71	3941.51

Monthly Payments 19.25 %

LOAN AMOUNT	22	23	24	25	30	35	40
				YEARS			
100	1.57	1.57	1.56	1.56	1.55	1.55	1.54
200	3.14	3.13	3.12	3.12	3.10	3.09	3.09
500	7.85	7.83	7.81	7.80	7.75	7.73	7.72
1000	15.71	15.66	15.62	15.59	15.50	15.46	15.44
2000	31.42	31.32	31.25	31.18	30.99	30.92	30.89
5000	78.55	78.31	78.12	77.96	77.48	77.29	77.22
6000	94.26	93.97	93.74	93.55	92.98	92.75	92.66
7000	109.96	109.64	109.36	109.14	108.47	108.21	108.11
8000	125.67	125.30	124.99	124.73	123.97	123.67	123.55
9000	141.38	140.96	140.61	140.32	139.47	139.13	138.99
10000	157.09	156.62	156.23	155.91	154.96	154.59	154.44
12000	188.51	187.95	187.48	187.10	185.95	185.50	185.32
15000	235.64	234.94	234.35	233.87	232.44	231.88	231.66
20000	314.19	313.25	312.47	311.83	309.92	309.17	308.87
25000	392.73	391.56	390.59	389.78	387.41	386.47	386.09
30000	471.28	469.87	468.70	467.74	464.89	463.76	463.31
31000	486.99	485.53	484.33	483.33	480.38	479.22	478.75
32000	502.70	501.19	499.95	498.92	495.88	494.68	494.20
33000	518.41	516.86	515.58	514.51	511.38	510.13	509.64
34000	534.12	532.52	531.20	530.10	526.87	525.59	525.08
35000	549.82	548.18	546.82	545.70	542.37	541.05	540.53
36000	565.53	563.84	562.45	561.29	557.86	556.51	555.97
37000	581.24	579.51	578.07	576.88	573.36	571.97	571.42
38000	596.95	595.17	593.69	592.47	588.86	587.43	586.86
39000	612.66	610.83	609.32	608.06	604.35	602.89	602.30
40000	628.37	626.49	624.94	623.65	619.85	618.35	617.75
41000	644.08	642.16	640.56	639.24	635.35	633.80	633.19
42000	659.79	657.82	656.19	654.84	650.84	649.26	648.63
43000	675.50	673.48	671.81	670.43	666.34	664.72	664.08
44000	691.21	689.14	687.43	686.02	681.83	680.18	679.52
45000	706.92	704.81	703.06	701.61	697.33	695.64	694.97
46000	722.63	720.47	718.68	717.20	712.83	711.10	710.41
47000	738.34	736.13	734.30	732.79	728.32	726.56	725.85
48000	754.05	751.79	749.93	748.38	743.82	742.01	741.30
49000	769.75	767.45	765.55	763.97	759.32	757.47	756.74
50000	785.46	783.12	781.17	779.57	774.81	772.93	772.18
51000	801.17	798.78	796.80	795.16	790.31	788.39	787.63
52000	816.88	814.44	812.42	810.75	805.80	803.85	803.07
53000	832.59	830.10	828.04	826.34	821.30	819.31	818.51
54000	848.30	845.77	843.67	841.93	836.80	834.77	833.96
55000	864.01	861.43	859.29	857.52	852.29	850.22	849.40
56000	879.72	877.09	874.92	873.11	867.79	865.68	864.85
57000	895.43	892.75	890.54	888.70	883.29	881.14	880.29
58000	911.14	908.42	906.16	904.30	898.78	896.60	895.73
59000	926.85	924.08	921.79	919.89	914.28	912.06	911.18
60000	942.56	939.74	937.41	935.48	929.77	927.52	926.62
65000	1021.10	1018.05	1015.53	1013.44	1007.26	1004.81	1003.84
70000	1099.65	1096.36	1093.64	1091.39	1084.74	1082.10	1081.06
75000	1178.20	1174.68	1171.76	1169.35	1162.22	1159.40	1158.28
80000	1256.74	1252.99	1249.88	1247.30	1239.70	1236.69	1235.49
85000	1335.29	1331.30	1328.00	1325.26	1317.18	1313.98	1312.71
90000	1413.83	1409.61	1406.11	1403.22	1394.66	1391.28	1389.93
95000	1492.38	1487.92	1484.23	1481.17	1472.14	1468.57	1467.15
100000	1570.93	1566.23	1562.35	1559.13	1549.62	1545.86	1544.37
105000	1649.47	1644.55	1640.47	1637.09	1627.10	1623.16	1621.59
110000	1728.02	1722.86	1718.58	1715.04	1704.59	1700.45	1698.80
120000	1885.11	1879.48	1874.82	1870.96	1859.55	1855.04	1853.24
130000	2042.21	2036.10	2031.05	2026.87	2014.51	2009.62	2007.68
140000	2199.30	2192.73	2187.29	2182.78	2169.47	2164.21	2162.11
150000	2356.39	2349.35	2343.52	2338.70	2324.44	2318.79	2316.55
160000	2513.48	2505.97	2499.76	2494.61	2479.40	2473.38	2470.99
170000	2670.58	2662.60	2655.99	2650.52	2634.36	2627.97	2625.42
180000	2827.67	2819.22	2812.23	2806.44	2789.32	2782.55	2779.86
190000	2984.76	2975.84	2968.46	2962.35	2944.28	2937.14	2934.30
200000	3141.85	3132.47	3124.70	3118.26	3099.25	3091.73	3088.73
210000	3298.95	3289.09	3280.93	3274.18	3254.21	3246.31	3243.17
220000	3456.04	3445.71	3437.17	3430.09	3409.17	3400.90	3397.61
230000	3613.13	3602.34	3593.40	3586.00	3564.13	3555.48	3552.05
240000	3770.23	3758.96	3749.64	3741.91	3719.10	3710.07	3706.48
250000	3927.32	3915.58	3905.87	3897.83	3874.06	3864.66	3860.92

19.50 % Monthly Payments

LOAN AMOUNT	YEARS 1	2	3	4	5	6	7
100	9.20	5.03	3.65	2.98	2.58	2.32	2.15
200	18.41	10.06	7.31	5.95	5.16	4.65	4.29
500	46.02	25.14	18.27	14.88	12.90	11.62	10.73
1000	92.04	50.29	36.53	29.77	25.80	23.23	21.46
2000	184.08	100.58	73.06	59.54	51.61	46.47	42.92
5000	460.19	251.44	182.65	148.85	129.02	116.17	107.30
6000	552.23	301.73	219.18	178.62	154.83	139.41	128.77
7000	644.27	352.02	255.72	208.39	180.63	162.64	150.23
8000	736.31	402.31	292.25	238.16	206.43	185.88	171.69
9000	828.34	452.59	328.78	267.92	232.24	209.11	193.15
10000	920.38	502.88	365.31	297.69	258.04	232.35	214.61
12000	1104.46	603.46	438.37	357.23	309.65	278.82	257.53
15000	1380.57	754.32	547.96	446.54	387.06	348.52	321.91
20000	1840.77	1005.76	730.61	595.39	516.09	464.70	429.22
25000	2300.96	1257.20	913.27	744.23	645.11	580.87	536.52
30000	2761.15	1508.65	1095.92	893.08	774.13	697.05	643.83
31000	2853.19	1558.93	1132.45	922.85	799.93	720.28	665.29
32000	2945.22	1609.22	1168.98	952.62	825.74	743.52	686.75
33000	3037.26	1659.51	1205.51	982.39	851.54	766.75	708.21
34000	3129.30	1709.80	1242.05	1012.16	877.35	789.99	729.67
35000	3221.34	1760.09	1278.58	1041.93	903.15	813.22	751.13
36000	3313.38	1810.38	1315.11	1071.70	928.95	836.46	772.59
37000	3405.42	1860.66	1351.64	1101.47	954.76	859.69	794.05
38000	3497.45	1910.95	1388.17	1131.24	980.56	882.93	815.51
39000	3589.49	1961.24	1424.70	1161.01	1006.37	906.16	836.97
40000	3681.53	2011.53	1461.23	1190.78	1032.17	929.40	858.44
41000	3773.57	2061.82	1497.76	1220.55	1057.98	952.63	879.90
42000	3865.61	2112.10	1534.29	1250.31	1083.78	975.87	901.36
43000	3957.64	2162.39	1570.82	1280.08	1109.58	999.10	922.82
44000	4049.68	2212.68	1607.35	1309.85	1135.39	1022.34	944.28
45000	4141.72	2262.97	1643.88	1339.62	1161.19	1045.57	965.74
46000	4233.76	2313.26	1680.41	1369.39	1187.00	1068.81	987.20
47000	4325.80	2363.55	1716.94	1399.16	1212.80	1092.04	1008.66
48000	4417.84	2413.83	1753.48	1428.93	1238.61	1115.28	1030.12
49000	4509.87	2464.12	1790.01	1458.70	1264.41	1138.51	1051.58
50000	4601.91	2514.41	1826.54	1488.47	1290.21	1161.75	1073.04
51000	4693.95	2564.70	1863.07	1518.24	1316.02	1184.98	1094.51
52000	4785.99	2614.99	1899.60	1548.01	1341.82	1208.22	1115.97
53000	4878.03	2665.27	1936.13	1577.78	1367.63	1231.45	1137.43
54000	4970.07	2715.56	1972.66	1607.55	1393.43	1254.69	1158.89
55000	5062.10	2765.85	2009.19	1637.32	1419.23	1277.92	1180.35
56000	5154.14	2816.14	2045.72	1667.09	1445.04	1301.16	1201.81
57000	5246.18	2866.43	2082.25	1696.86	1470.84	1324.39	1223.27
58000	5338.22	2916.72	2118.78	1726.63	1496.65	1347.63	1244.73
59000	5430.26	2967.00	2155.31	1756.39	1522.45	1370.86	1266.19
60000	5522.30	3017.29	2191.84	1786.16	1548.26	1394.10	1287.65
65000	5982.49	3268.73	2374.50	1935.01	1677.28	1510.27	1394.96
70000	6442.68	3520.17	2557.15	2083.86	1806.30	1626.45	1502.26
75000	6902.87	3771.61	2739.81	2232.70	1935.32	1742.62	1609.57
80000	7363.06	4023.06	2922.46	2381.55	2064.34	1858.80	1716.87
85000	7823.25	4274.50	3105.11	2530.40	2193.36	1974.97	1824.18
90000	8283.44	4525.94	3287.77	2679.25	2322.38	2091.14	1931.48
95000	8743.63	4777.38	3470.42	2828.09	2451.41	2207.32	2038.78
100000	9203.83	5028.82	3653.07	2976.94	2580.43	2323.49	2146.09
105000	9664.02	5280.26	3835.73	3125.79	2709.45	2439.67	2253.39
110000	10124.21	5531.70	4018.38	3274.63	2838.47	2555.84	2360.70
120000	11044.59	6034.58	4383.69	3572.33	3096.51	2788.19	2575.31
130000	11964.97	6537.47	4749.00	3870.02	3354.56	3020.54	2789.92
140000	12885.36	7040.35	5114.30	4167.72	3612.60	3252.89	3004.52
150000	13805.74	7543.23	5479.61	4465.41	3870.64	3485.24	3219.13
160000	14726.12	8046.11	5844.92	4763.10	4128.68	3717.59	3433.74
170000	15646.50	8548.99	6210.23	5060.80	4386.73	3949.94	3648.35
180000	16566.89	9051.88	6575.53	5358.49	4644.77	4182.29	3862.96
190000	17487.27	9554.76	6940.84	5656.19	4902.81	4414.64	4077.57
200000	18407.65	10057.64	7306.15	5953.88	5160.85	4646.99	4292.18
210000	19328.03	10560.52	7671.46	6251.57	5418.90	4879.34	4506.79
220000	20248.42	11063.40	8036.76	6549.27	5676.94	5111.69	4721.40
230000	21168.80	11566.29	8402.07	6846.96	5934.98	5344.04	4936.00
240000	22089.18	12069.17	8767.38	7144.66	6193.03	5576.39	5150.61
250000	23009.56	12572.05	9132.69	7442.35	6451.07	5808.74	5365.22

Monthly Payments 19.50 %

LOAN AMOUNT	8	9	10	11	12	13	14
				YEARS			
100	2.02	1.92	1.85	1.79	1.75	1.72	1.69
200	4.04	3.85	3.70	3.59	3.50	3.43	3.37
500	10.09	9.61	9.25	8.97	8.75	8.58	8.44
1000	20.18	19.23	18.51	17.94	17.50	17.15	16.87
2000	40.36	38.46	37.01	35.89	35.01	34.31	33.75
5000	100.91	96.15	92.53	89.72	87.52	85.77	84.37
6000	121.09	115.38	111.03	107.67	105.02	102.92	101.24
7000	141.27	134.61	129.54	125.61	122.52	120.08	118.12
8000	161.45	153.84	148.04	143.55	140.03	137.23	134.99
9000	181.63	173.07	166.55	161.50	157.53	154.38	151.86
10000	201.82	192.30	185.05	179.44	175.03	171.54	168.74
12000	242.18	230.76	222.07	215.33	210.04	205.84	202.48
15000	302.72	288.45	277.58	269.16	262.55	257.30	253.11
20000	403.63	384.60	370.11	358.88	350.07	343.07	337.47
25000	504.54	480.75	462.64	448.60	437.59	428.84	421.84
30000	605.45	576.90	555.16	538.33	525.10	514.61	506.21
31000	625.63	596.13	573.67	556.27	542.61	531.76	523.08
32000	645.81	615.36	592.17	574.21	560.11	548.92	539.96
33000	665.99	634.59	610.68	592.16	577.61	566.07	556.83
34000	686.17	653.82	629.18	610.10	595.12	583.22	573.71
35000	706.36	673.05	647.69	628.05	612.62	600.38	590.58
36000	726.54	692.28	666.20	645.99	630.12	617.53	607.45
37000	746.72	711.51	684.70	663.93	647.63	634.69	624.33
38000	766.90	730.74	703.21	681.88	665.13	651.84	641.20
39000	787.08	749.97	721.71	699.82	682.63	668.99	658.07
40000	807.26	769.20	740.22	717.77	700.14	686.15	674.95
41000	827.45	788.43	758.72	735.71	717.64	703.30	691.82
42000	847.63	807.66	777.23	753.66	735.14	720.45	708.70
43000	867.81	826.89	795.73	771.60	752.65	737.61	725.57
44000	887.99	846.12	814.24	789.54	770.15	754.76	742.44
45000	908.17	865.35	832.74	807.49	787.65	771.91	759.32
46000	928.35	884.58	851.25	825.43	805.16	789.07	776.19
47000	948.53	903.81	869.76	843.38	822.66	806.22	793.06
48000	968.72	923.04	888.26	861.32	840.16	823.38	809.94
49000	988.90	942.27	906.77	879.26	857.67	840.53	826.81
50000	1009.08	961.50	925.27	897.21	875.17	857.68	843.68
51000	1029.26	980.73	943.78	915.15	892.68	874.84	860.56
52000	1049.44	999.96	962.28	933.10	910.18	891.99	877.43
53000	1069.62	1019.19	980.79	951.04	927.68	909.14	894.31
54000	1089.81	1038.42	999.29	968.99	945.19	926.30	911.18
55000	1109.99	1057.65	1017.80	986.93	962.69	943.45	928.05
56000	1130.17	1076.88	1036.30	1004.87	980.19	960.60	944.93
57000	1150.35	1096.10	1054.81	1022.82	997.70	977.76	961.80
58000	1170.53	1115.33	1073.31	1040.76	1015.20	994.91	978.67
59000	1190.71	1134.56	1091.82	1058.71	1032.70	1012.07	995.55
60000	1210.90	1153.79	1110.33	1076.65	1050.21	1029.22	1012.42
65000	1311.80	1249.94	1202.85	1166.37	1137.72	1114.99	1096.79
70000	1412.71	1346.09	1295.38	1256.09	1225.24	1200.76	1181.16
75000	1513.62	1442.24	1387.91	1345.81	1312.76	1286.52	1265.53
80000	1614.53	1538.39	1480.43	1435.53	1400.27	1372.29	1349.90
85000	1715.44	1634.54	1572.96	1525.25	1487.79	1458.06	1434.26
90000	1816.34	1730.69	1665.49	1614.98	1575.31	1543.83	1518.63
95000	1917.25	1826.84	1758.02	1704.70	1662.83	1629.60	1603.00
100000	2018.16	1922.99	1850.54	1794.42	1750.34	1715.36	1687.37
105000	2119.07	2019.14	1943.07	1884.14	1837.86	1801.13	1771.74
110000	2219.98	2115.29	2035.60	1973.86	1925.38	1886.90	1856.11
120000	2421.79	2307.59	2220.65	2153.30	2100.41	2058.44	2024.84
130000	2623.61	2499.89	2405.71	2332.74	2275.45	2229.97	2193.58
140000	2825.42	2692.19	2590.76	2512.18	2450.48	2401.51	2362.32
150000	3027.24	2884.49	2775.81	2691.63	2625.52	2573.05	2531.05
160000	3229.05	3076.79	2960.87	2871.07	2800.55	2744.58	2699.79
170000	3430.87	3269.08	3145.92	3050.51	2975.58	2916.12	2868.53
180000	3632.69	3461.38	3330.98	3229.95	3150.62	3087.66	3037.27
190000	3834.50	3653.68	3516.03	3409.39	3325.65	3259.19	3206.00
200000	4036.32	3845.98	3701.09	3588.83	3500.69	3430.73	3374.74
210000	4238.13	4038.28	3886.14	3768.28	3675.72	3602.27	3543.48
220000	4439.95	4230.58	4071.19	3947.72	3850.76	3773.80	3712.21
230000	4641.77	4422.88	4256.25	4127.16	4025.79	3945.34	3880.95
240000	4843.58	4615.18	4441.30	4306.60	4200.82	4116.88	4049.69
250000	5045.40	4807.48	4626.36	4486.04	4375.86	4288.41	4218.42

19.50 % Monthly Payments

LOAN AMOUNT	15	16	17	18	19	20	21
				YEARS			
100	1.66	1.65	1.63	1.62	1.61	1.60	1.59
200	3.33	3.29	3.26	3.24	3.22	3.20	3.19
500	8.32	8.23	8.16	8.10	8.05	8.01	7.97
1000	16.65	16.47	16.32	16.20	16.10	16.01	15.95
2000	33.30	32.93	32.63	32.39	32.19	32.03	31.89
5000	83.24	82.33	81.58	80.98	80.48	80.07	79.74
6000	99.89	98.79	97.90	97.17	96.57	96.09	95.68
7000	116.54	115.26	114.22	113.37	112.67	112.10	111.63
8000	133.19	131.72	130.53	129.56	128.77	128.11	127.58
9000	149.83	148.19	146.85	145.76	144.86	144.13	143.52
10000	166.48	164.65	163.17	161.95	160.96	160.14	159.47
12000	199.78	197.58	195.80	194.34	193.15	192.17	191.36
15000	249.72	246.98	244.75	242.93	241.44	240.21	239.21
20000	332.96	329.31	326.33	323.91	321.92	320.28	318.94
25000	416.20	411.63	407.92	404.88	402.40	400.35	398.68
30000	499.44	493.96	489.50	485.86	482.87	480.43	478.41
31000	516.09	510.43	505.82	502.05	498.97	496.44	494.36
32000	532.74	526.89	522.13	518.25	515.07	512.45	510.31
33000	549.39	543.36	538.45	534.44	531.16	528.47	526.25
34000	566.04	559.82	554.77	550.64	547.26	544.48	542.20
35000	582.68	576.29	571.08	566.83	563.35	560.50	558.15
36000	599.33	592.75	587.40	583.03	579.45	576.51	574.09
37000	615.98	609.22	603.72	599.23	595.55	592.53	590.04
38000	632.63	625.68	620.03	615.42	611.64	608.54	605.99
39000	649.28	642.15	636.35	631.62	627.74	624.55	621.93
40000	665.93	658.62	652.67	647.81	643.83	640.57	637.88
41000	682.57	675.08	668.98	664.01	659.93	656.58	653.83
42000	699.22	691.55	685.30	680.20	676.02	672.60	669.78
43000	715.87	708.01	701.62	696.40	692.12	688.61	685.72
44000	732.52	724.48	717.93	712.59	708.22	704.62	701.67
45000	749.17	740.94	734.25	728.79	724.31	720.64	717.62
46000	765.81	757.41	750.57	744.98	740.41	736.65	733.56
47000	782.46	773.87	766.88	761.18	756.50	752.67	749.51
48000	799.11	790.34	783.20	777.37	772.60	768.68	765.46
49000	815.76	806.80	799.52	793.57	788.70	784.70	781.41
50000	832.41	823.27	815.83	809.76	804.79	800.71	797.35
51000	849.05	839.73	832.15	825.96	820.89	816.72	813.30
52000	865.70	856.20	848.47	842.15	836.98	832.74	829.25
53000	882.35	872.67	864.78	858.35	853.08	848.75	845.19
54000	899.00	889.13	881.10	874.54	869.17	864.77	861.14
55000	915.65	905.60	897.42	890.74	885.27	880.78	877.09
56000	932.30	922.06	913.73	906.94	901.37	896.80	893.03
57000	948.94	938.53	930.05	923.13	917.46	912.81	908.98
58000	965.59	954.99	946.37	939.33	933.56	928.82	924.93
59000	982.24	971.46	962.69	955.52	949.65	944.84	940.88
60000	998.89	987.92	979.00	971.72	965.75	960.85	956.82
65000	1082.13	1070.25	1060.59	1052.69	1046.23	1040.92	1036.56
70000	1165.37	1152.58	1142.17	1133.67	1126.71	1120.99	1116.29
75000	1248.61	1234.90	1223.75	1214.65	1207.19	1201.06	1196.03
80000	1331.85	1317.23	1305.34	1295.62	1287.67	1281.14	1275.76
85000	1415.09	1399.56	1386.92	1376.60	1368.15	1361.21	1355.50
90000	1498.33	1481.89	1468.50	1457.57	1448.62	1441.28	1435.23
95000	1581.57	1564.21	1550.09	1538.55	1529.10	1521.35	1514.97
100000	1664.81	1646.54	1631.67	1619.53	1609.58	1601.42	1594.70
105000	1748.05	1728.87	1713.25	1700.50	1690.06	1681.49	1674.44
110000	1831.29	1811.19	1794.84	1781.48	1770.54	1761.56	1754.18
120000	1997.78	1975.85	1958.00	1943.43	1931.50	1921.70	1913.65
130000	2164.26	2140.50	2121.17	2105.39	2092.46	2081.85	2073.12
140000	2330.74	2305.15	2284.34	2267.34	2253.42	2241.99	2232.59
150000	2497.22	2469.81	2447.50	2429.29	2414.37	2402.13	2392.06
160000	2663.70	2634.46	2610.67	2591.24	2575.33	2562.27	2551.53
170000	2830.18	2799.12	2773.84	2753.20	2736.29	2722.41	2711.00
180000	2996.66	2963.77	2937.01	2915.15	2897.25	2882.56	2870.47
190000	3163.14	3128.42	3100.17	3077.10	3058.21	3042.70	3029.94
200000	3329.63	3293.08	3263.34	3239.05	3219.17	3202.84	3189.41
210000	3496.11	3457.73	3426.51	3401.01	3380.12	3362.98	3348.88
220000	3662.59	3622.39	3589.67	3562.96	3541.08	3523.12	3508.35
230000	3829.07	3787.04	3752.84	3724.91	3702.04	3683.27	3667.82
240000	3995.55	3951.69	3916.01	3886.87	3863.00	3843.41	3827.29
250000	4162.03	4116.35	4079.17	4048.82	4023.96	4003.55	3986.76

Monthly Payments 19.50 %

LOAN AMOUNT	22	23	24	25	30	35	40
				YEARS			
100	1.59	1.58	1.58	1.58	1.57	1.56	1.56
200	3.18	3.17	3.16	3.16	3.14	3.13	3.13
500	7.95	7.92	7.90	7.89	7.84	7.82	7.82
1000	15.89	15.85	15.81	15.78	15.69	15.65	15.64
2000	31.78	31.69	31.62	31.55	31.37	31.30	31.27
5000	79.46	79.23	79.04	78.89	78.43	78.25	78.18
6000	95.35	95.08	94.85	94.66	94.11	93.90	93.81
7000	111.24	110.92	110.66	110.44	109.80	109.55	109.45
8000	127.13	126.77	126.47	126.22	125.49	125.20	125.09
9000	143.03	142.61	142.28	142.00	141.17	140.85	140.72
10000	158.92	158.46	158.08	157.77	156.86	156.50	156.36
12000	190.70	190.15	189.70	189.33	188.23	187.80	187.63
15000	238.38	237.69	237.13	236.66	235.29	234.75	234.54
20000	317.83	316.92	316.17	315.54	313.71	313.00	312.72
25000	397.29	396.15	395.21	394.43	392.14	391.25	390.90
30000	476.75	475.38	474.25	473.32	470.57	469.50	469.07
31000	492.64	491.23	490.06	489.09	486.26	485.15	484.71
32000	508.54	507.07	505.87	504.87	501.94	500.80	500.35
33000	524.43	522.92	521.68	520.65	517.63	516.45	515.98
34000	540.32	538.77	537.49	536.43	533.31	532.10	531.62
35000	556.21	554.61	553.29	552.20	549.00	547.75	547.25
36000	572.10	570.46	569.10	567.98	564.69	563.40	562.89
37000	587.99	586.31	584.91	583.76	580.37	579.05	578.52
38000	603.89	602.15	600.72	599.54	596.06	594.70	594.16
39000	619.78	618.00	616.53	615.31	611.74	610.35	609.80
40000	635.67	633.84	632.34	631.09	627.43	626.00	625.43
41000	651.56	649.69	648.14	646.87	643.11	641.65	641.07
42000	667.45	665.54	663.95	662.64	658.80	657.30	656.70
43000	683.34	681.38	679.76	678.42	674.49	672.95	672.34
44000	699.24	697.23	695.57	694.20	690.17	688.60	687.98
45000	715.13	713.07	711.38	709.98	705.86	704.24	703.61
46000	731.02	728.92	727.19	725.75	721.54	719.89	719.25
47000	746.91	744.77	742.99	741.53	737.23	735.54	734.88
48000	762.80	760.61	758.80	757.31	752.91	751.19	750.52
49000	778.69	776.46	774.61	773.08	768.60	766.84	766.15
50000	794.59	792.30	790.42	788.86	784.29	782.49	781.79
51000	810.48	808.15	806.23	804.64	799.97	798.14	797.43
52000	826.37	824.00	822.04	820.42	815.66	813.79	813.06
53000	842.26	839.84	837.85	836.19	831.34	829.44	828.70
54000	858.15	855.69	853.65	851.97	847.03	845.09	844.33
55000	874.04	871.53	869.46	867.75	862.71	860.74	859.97
56000	889.94	887.38	885.27	883.53	878.40	876.39	875.61
57000	905.83	903.23	901.08	899.30	894.08	892.04	891.24
58000	921.72	919.07	916.89	915.08	909.77	907.69	906.88
59000	937.61	934.92	932.70	930.86	925.46	923.34	922.51
60000	953.50	950.77	948.50	946.63	941.14	938.99	938.15
65000	1032.96	1030.00	1027.55	1025.52	1019.57	1017.24	1016.33
70000	1112.42	1109.23	1106.59	1104.41	1098.00	1095.49	1094.51
75000	1191.88	1188.46	1185.63	1183.29	1176.43	1173.74	1172.69
80000	1271.34	1267.69	1264.67	1262.18	1254.86	1251.99	1250.86
85000	1350.80	1346.92	1343.71	1341.07	1333.28	1330.24	1329.04
90000	1430.26	1426.15	1422.76	1419.95	1411.71	1408.49	1407.22
95000	1509.71	1505.38	1501.80	1498.84	1490.14	1486.74	1485.40
100000	1589.17	1584.61	1580.84	1577.72	1568.57	1564.99	1563.58
105000	1668.63	1663.84	1659.88	1656.61	1647.00	1643.24	1641.76
110000	1748.09	1743.07	1738.92	1735.50	1725.43	1721.49	1719.94
120000	1907.01	1901.53	1897.01	1893.27	1882.28	1877.99	1876.30
130000	2065.92	2059.99	2055.09	2051.04	2039.14	2034.49	2032.65
140000	2224.84	2218.45	2213.18	2208.81	2196.00	2190.98	2189.01
150000	2383.76	2376.91	2371.26	2366.59	2352.86	2347.48	2345.37
160000	2542.68	2535.37	2529.34	2524.36	2509.71	2503.98	2501.73
170000	2701.59	2693.84	2687.43	2682.13	2666.57	2660.48	2658.09
180000	2860.51	2852.30	2845.51	2839.90	2823.43	2816.98	2814.45
190000	3019.43	3010.76	3003.60	2997.68	2980.28	2973.48	2970.80
200000	3178.35	3169.22	3161.68	3155.45	3137.14	3129.98	3127.16
210000	3337.26	3327.68	3319.76	3313.22	3294.00	3286.48	3283.52
220000	3496.18	3486.14	3477.85	3470.99	3450.85	3442.98	3439.88
230000	3655.10	3644.60	3635.93	3628.77	3607.71	3599.47	3596.24
240000	3814.01	3803.06	3794.02	3786.54	3764.57	3755.97	3752.59
250000	3972.93	3961.52	3952.10	3944.31	3921.43	3912.47	3908.95

19.75 % Monthly Payments

LOAN AMOUNT	YEARS 1	2	3	4	5	6	7
100	9.21	5.04	3.66	2.99	2.59	2.34	2.16
200	18.43	10.08	7.33	5.98	5.19	4.67	4.32
500	46.07	25.20	18.32	14.95	12.97	11.68	10.80
1000	92.15	50.40	36.65	29.89	25.93	23.37	21.60
2000	184.30	100.80	73.30	59.78	51.86	46.73	43.20
5000	460.74	252.00	183.24	149.46	129.66	116.84	107.99
6000	552.89	302.40	219.89	179.35	155.59	140.20	129.59
7000	645.04	352.80	256.53	209.24	181.52	163.57	151.19
8000	737.19	403.20	293.18	239.13	207.45	186.94	172.78
9000	829.34	453.60	329.83	269.02	233.38	210.30	194.38
10000	921.49	504.00	366.48	298.91	259.31	233.67	215.98
12000	1105.78	604.81	439.77	358.70	311.18	280.41	259.18
15000	1382.23	756.01	549.71	448.37	388.97	350.51	323.97
20000	1842.97	1008.01	732.95	597.83	518.63	467.34	431.96
25000	2303.71	1260.01	916.19	747.28	648.28	584.18	539.95
30000	2764.46	1512.01	1099.43	896.74	777.94	701.01	647.94
31000	2856.61	1562.41	1136.07	926.63	803.87	724.38	669.54
32000	2948.75	1612.81	1172.72	956.52	829.80	747.75	691.14
33000	3040.90	1663.22	1209.37	986.41	855.73	771.11	712.74
34000	3133.05	1713.62	1246.02	1016.30	881.66	794.48	734.33
35000	3225.20	1764.02	1282.66	1046.19	907.60	817.85	755.93
36000	3317.35	1814.42	1319.31	1076.09	933.53	841.22	777.53
37000	3409.50	1864.82	1355.96	1105.98	959.46	864.58	799.13
38000	3501.65	1915.22	1392.61	1135.87	985.39	887.95	820.73
39000	3593.79	1965.62	1429.25	1165.76	1011.32	911.32	842.32
40000	3685.94	2016.02	1465.90	1195.65	1037.25	934.68	863.92
41000	3778.09	2066.42	1502.55	1225.54	1063.18	958.05	885.52
42000	3870.24	2116.82	1539.20	1255.43	1089.12	981.42	907.12
43000	3962.39	2167.22	1575.84	1285.32	1115.05	1004.79	928.72
44000	4054.54	2217.62	1612.49	1315.22	1140.98	1028.15	950.31
45000	4146.69	2268.02	1649.14	1345.11	1166.91	1051.52	971.91
46000	4238.83	2318.42	1685.79	1375.00	1192.84	1074.89	993.51
47000	4330.98	2368.82	1722.43	1404.89	1218.77	1098.25	1015.11
48000	4423.13	2419.22	1759.08	1434.78	1244.70	1121.62	1036.71
49000	4515.28	2469.62	1795.73	1464.67	1270.63	1144.99	1058.30
50000	4607.43	2520.02	1832.38	1494.56	1296.57	1168.36	1079.90
51000	4699.58	2570.42	1869.02	1524.45	1322.50	1191.72	1101.50
52000	4791.73	2620.82	1905.67	1554.35	1348.43	1215.09	1123.10
53000	4883.87	2671.22	1942.32	1584.24	1374.36	1238.46	1144.70
54000	4976.02	2721.63	1978.97	1614.13	1400.29	1261.82	1166.29
55000	5068.17	2772.03	2015.61	1644.02	1426.22	1285.19	1187.89
56000	5160.32	2822.43	2052.26	1673.91	1452.15	1308.56	1209.49
57000	5252.47	2872.83	2088.91	1703.80	1478.09	1331.93	1231.09
58000	5344.62	2923.23	2125.56	1733.69	1504.02	1355.29	1252.69
59000	5436.77	2973.63	2162.20	1763.58	1529.95	1378.66	1274.28
60000	5528.91	3024.03	2198.85	1793.48	1555.88	1402.03	1295.88
65000	5989.66	3276.03	2382.09	1942.93	1685.54	1518.86	1403.87
70000	6450.40	3528.03	2565.33	2092.39	1815.19	1635.70	1511.86
75000	6911.14	3780.03	2748.57	2241.84	1944.85	1752.53	1619.85
80000	7371.89	4032.04	2931.80	2391.30	2074.51	1869.37	1727.84
85000	7832.63	4284.04	3115.04	2540.76	2204.16	1986.20	1835.83
90000	8293.37	4536.04	3298.28	2690.21	2333.82	2103.04	1943.82
95000	8754.11	4788.04	3481.52	2839.67	2463.48	2219.88	2051.81
100000	9214.86	5040.05	3664.75	2989.13	2593.13	2336.71	2159.80
105000	9675.60	5292.05	3847.99	3138.58	2722.79	2453.55	2267.80
110000	10136.34	5544.05	4031.23	3288.04	2852.45	2570.38	2375.79
120000	11057.83	6048.06	4397.70	3586.95	3111.76	2804.05	2591.77
130000	11979.31	6552.06	4764.18	3885.86	3371.07	3037.73	2807.75
140000	12900.80	7056.07	5130.66	4184.78	3630.38	3271.40	3023.73
150000	13822.29	7560.07	5497.13	4483.69	3889.70	3505.07	3239.71
160000	14743.77	8064.07	5863.61	4782.60	4149.01	3738.74	3455.69
170000	15665.26	8568.08	6230.08	5081.51	4408.32	3972.41	3671.67
180000	16586.74	9072.08	6596.56	5380.43	4667.64	4206.08	3887.65
190000	17508.23	9576.09	6963.03	5679.34	4926.95	4439.75	4103.63
200000	18429.71	10080.09	7329.51	5978.25	5186.26	4673.42	4319.61
210000	19351.20	10584.10	7695.98	6277.17	5445.58	4907.09	4535.59
220000	20272.69	11088.10	8062.46	6576.08	5704.89	5140.77	4751.57
230000	21194.17	11592.11	8428.93	6874.99	5964.20	5374.44	4967.55
240000	22115.66	12096.11	8795.41	7173.90	6223.52	5608.11	5183.53
250000	23037.14	12600.12	9161.88	7472.82	6482.83	5841.78	5399.51

Monthly Payments 19.75 %

LOAN AMOUNT	8	9	10	11	12	13	14
				YEARS			
100	2.03	1.94	1.87	1.81	1.77	1.73	1.70
200	4.06	3.88	3.73	3.62	3.53	3.46	3.41
500	10.16	9.69	9.33	9.05	8.83	8.66	8.52
1000	20.32	19.38	18.66	18.10	17.66	17.32	17.04
2000	40.65	38.75	37.31	36.20	35.32	34.63	34.08
5000	101.62	96.88	93.28	90.50	88.31	86.58	85.20
6000	121.94	116.26	111.94	108.59	105.97	103.90	102.23
7000	142.26	135.64	130.59	126.69	123.63	121.21	119.27
8000	162.59	155.01	149.25	144.79	141.30	138.53	136.31
9000	182.91	174.39	167.91	162.89	158.96	155.84	153.35
10000	203.24	193.76	186.56	180.99	176.62	173.16	170.39
12000	243.88	232.52	223.88	217.19	211.95	207.79	204.47
15000	304.85	290.65	279.84	271.49	264.93	259.74	255.59
20000	406.47	387.53	373.13	361.98	353.24	346.32	340.78
25000	508.09	484.41	466.41	452.48	441.55	432.90	425.98
30000	609.71	581.29	559.69	542.97	529.86	519.48	511.17
31000	630.03	600.67	578.34	561.07	547.53	536.79	528.21
32000	650.35	620.05	597.00	579.17	565.19	554.11	545.25
33000	670.68	639.42	615.66	597.27	582.85	571.42	562.29
34000	691.00	658.80	634.31	615.37	600.51	588.74	579.33
35000	711.32	678.18	652.97	633.47	618.17	606.05	596.37
36000	731.65	697.55	671.63	651.57	635.84	623.37	613.41
37000	751.97	716.93	690.28	669.67	653.50	640.69	630.45
38000	772.29	736.30	708.94	687.76	671.16	658.00	647.49
39000	792.62	755.68	727.59	705.86	688.82	675.32	664.53
40000	812.94	775.06	746.25	723.96	706.48	692.63	681.56
41000	833.27	794.43	764.91	742.06	724.15	709.95	698.60
42000	853.59	813.81	783.56	760.16	741.81	727.27	715.64
43000	873.91	833.19	802.22	778.26	759.47	744.58	732.68
44000	894.24	852.56	820.88	796.36	777.13	761.90	749.72
45000	914.56	871.94	839.53	814.46	794.80	779.21	766.76
46000	934.88	891.32	858.19	832.56	812.46	796.53	783.80
47000	955.21	910.69	876.84	850.66	830.12	813.84	800.84
48000	975.53	930.07	895.50	868.76	847.78	831.16	817.88
49000	995.85	949.45	914.16	886.85	865.44	848.48	834.92
50000	1016.18	968.82	932.81	904.95	883.11	865.79	851.96
51000	1036.50	988.20	951.47	923.05	900.77	883.11	869.00
52000	1056.82	1007.57	970.13	941.15	918.43	900.42	886.03
53000	1077.15	1026.95	988.78	959.25	936.09	917.74	903.07
54000	1097.47	1046.33	1007.44	977.35	953.75	935.06	920.11
55000	1117.80	1065.70	1026.09	995.45	971.42	952.37	937.15
56000	1138.12	1085.08	1044.75	1013.55	989.08	969.69	954.19
57000	1158.44	1104.46	1063.41	1031.65	1006.74	987.00	971.23
58000	1178.77	1123.83	1082.06	1049.75	1024.40	1004.32	988.27
59000	1199.09	1143.21	1100.72	1067.84	1042.06	1021.63	1005.31
60000	1219.41	1162.59	1119.38	1085.94	1059.73	1038.95	1022.35
65000	1321.03	1259.47	1212.66	1176.44	1148.04	1125.53	1107.54
70000	1422.65	1356.35	1305.94	1266.93	1236.35	1212.11	1192.74
75000	1524.27	1453.23	1399.22	1357.43	1324.66	1298.69	1277.93
80000	1625.88	1550.11	1492.50	1447.93	1412.97	1385.27	1363.13
85000	1727.50	1647.00	1585.78	1538.42	1501.28	1471.85	1448.33
90000	1829.12	1743.88	1679.06	1628.92	1589.59	1558.43	1533.52
95000	1930.74	1840.76	1772.35	1719.41	1677.90	1645.00	1618.72
100000	2032.35	1937.64	1865.63	1809.91	1766.21	1731.58	1703.91
105000	2133.97	2034.53	1958.91	1900.40	1854.52	1818.16	1789.11
110000	2235.59	2131.41	2052.19	1990.90	1942.83	1904.74	1874.30
120000	2438.83	2325.17	2238.75	2171.89	2119.45	2077.90	2044.69
130000	2642.06	2518.94	2425.32	2352.88	2296.07	2251.06	2215.09
140000	2845.30	2712.70	2611.88	2533.87	2472.70	2424.22	2385.48
150000	3048.53	2906.46	2798.44	2714.86	2649.32	2597.38	2555.87
160000	3251.77	3100.23	2985.00	2895.85	2825.94	2770.53	2726.26
170000	3455.00	3293.99	3171.57	3076.84	3002.56	2943.69	2896.65
180000	3658.24	3487.76	3358.13	3257.83	3179.18	3116.85	3067.04
190000	3861.47	3681.52	3544.69	3438.82	3355.80	3290.01	3237.43
200000	4064.71	3875.29	3731.25	3619.81	3532.42	3463.17	3407.82
210000	4267.94	4069.05	3917.82	3800.80	3709.04	3636.33	3578.22
220000	4471.18	4262.81	4104.38	3981.79	3885.66	3809.48	3748.61
230000	4674.42	4456.58	4290.94	4162.79	4062.29	3982.64	3919.00
240000	4877.65	4650.34	4477.50	4343.78	4238.91	4155.80	4089.39
250000	5080.89	4844.11	4664.07	4524.77	4415.53	4328.96	4259.78

19.75 % Monthly Payments

LOAN AMOUNT	YEARS 15	16	17	18	19	20	21
100	1.68	1.66	1.65	1.64	1.63	1.62	1.61
200	3.36	3.33	3.30	3.27	3.25	3.24	3.23
500	8.41	8.32	8.25	8.19	8.14	8.10	8.06
1000	16.82	16.64	16.49	16.37	16.27	16.19	16.13
2000	33.63	33.27	32.98	32.74	32.55	32.39	32.26
5000	84.08	83.18	82.45	81.86	81.37	80.97	80.64
6000	100.90	99.82	98.94	98.23	97.64	97.16	96.77
7000	117.72	116.46	115.43	114.60	113.92	113.36	112.90
8000	134.53	133.09	131.92	130.97	130.19	129.55	129.03
9000	151.35	149.73	148.41	147.34	146.46	145.74	145.15
10000	168.17	166.36	164.90	163.71	162.74	161.94	161.28
12000	201.80	199.64	197.88	196.45	195.28	194.33	193.54
15000	252.25	249.55	247.35	245.57	244.10	242.91	241.92
20000	336.33	332.73	329.81	327.42	325.47	323.88	322.57
25000	420.41	415.91	412.26	409.28	406.84	404.84	403.21
30000	504.50	499.09	494.71	491.13	488.21	485.81	483.85
31000	521.31	515.73	511.20	507.50	504.48	502.01	499.98
32000	538.13	532.37	527.69	523.87	520.76	518.20	516.10
33000	554.95	549.00	544.18	540.25	537.03	534.40	532.23
34000	571.76	565.64	560.67	556.62	553.30	550.59	548.36
35000	588.58	582.28	577.16	572.99	569.58	566.78	564.49
36000	605.39	598.91	593.65	589.36	585.85	582.98	580.62
37000	622.21	615.55	610.14	605.73	602.12	599.17	596.75
38000	639.03	632.19	626.63	622.10	618.40	615.36	612.87
39000	655.84	648.82	643.12	638.47	634.67	631.56	629.00
40000	672.66	665.46	659.61	654.84	650.95	647.75	645.13
41000	689.48	682.10	676.10	671.21	667.22	663.95	661.26
42000	706.29	698.73	692.59	687.58	683.49	680.14	677.39
43000	723.11	715.37	709.08	703.96	699.77	696.33	693.52
44000	739.93	732.01	725.57	720.33	716.04	712.53	709.64
45000	756.74	748.64	742.06	736.70	732.31	728.72	725.77
46000	773.56	765.28	758.55	753.07	748.59	744.91	741.90
47000	790.38	781.92	775.04	769.44	764.86	761.11	758.03
48000	807.19	798.55	791.53	785.81	781.13	777.30	774.16
49000	824.01	815.19	808.02	802.18	797.41	793.50	790.28
50000	840.83	831.82	824.51	818.55	813.68	809.69	806.41
51000	857.64	848.46	841.00	834.92	829.96	825.88	822.54
52000	874.46	865.10	857.49	851.30	846.23	842.08	838.67
53000	891.28	881.73	873.98	867.67	862.50	858.27	854.80
54000	908.09	898.37	890.47	884.04	878.78	874.47	870.93
55000	924.91	915.01	906.96	900.41	895.05	890.66	887.05
56000	941.73	931.64	923.45	916.78	911.32	906.85	903.18
57000	958.54	948.28	939.94	933.15	927.60	923.05	919.31
58000	975.36	964.92	956.44	949.52	943.87	939.24	935.44
59000	992.17	981.55	972.93	965.89	960.14	955.43	951.57
60000	1008.99	998.19	989.42	982.26	976.42	971.63	967.70
65000	1093.07	1081.37	1071.87	1064.12	1057.79	1052.60	1048.34
70000	1177.16	1164.55	1154.32	1145.97	1139.15	1133.57	1128.98
75000	1261.24	1247.74	1236.77	1227.83	1220.52	1214.53	1209.62
80000	1345.32	1330.92	1319.22	1309.69	1301.89	1295.50	1290.26
85000	1429.40	1414.10	1401.67	1391.54	1383.26	1376.47	1370.90
90000	1513.49	1497.28	1484.12	1473.40	1464.63	1457.44	1451.54
95000	1597.57	1580.47	1566.57	1555.25	1546.00	1538.41	1532.18
100000	1681.65	1663.65	1649.03	1637.11	1627.36	1619.38	1612.83
105000	1765.73	1746.83	1731.48	1718.96	1708.73	1700.35	1693.47
110000	1849.82	1830.01	1813.93	1800.82	1790.10	1781.32	1774.11
120000	2017.98	1996.38	1978.83	1964.53	1952.84	1943.26	1935.39
130000	2186.15	2162.74	2143.73	2128.24	2115.57	2105.19	2096.67
140000	2354.31	2329.11	2308.64	2291.95	2278.31	2267.13	2257.96
150000	2522.48	2495.47	2473.54	2455.66	2441.05	2429.07	2419.24
160000	2690.64	2661.84	2638.44	2619.37	2603.78	2591.01	2580.52
170000	2858.81	2828.20	2803.34	2783.08	2766.52	2752.95	2741.80
180000	3026.97	2994.57	2968.25	2946.79	2929.25	2914.88	2903.09
190000	3195.14	3160.93	3133.15	3110.50	3091.99	3076.82	3064.37
200000	3363.30	3327.30	3298.05	3274.21	3254.73	3238.76	3225.65
210000	3531.47	3493.66	3462.95	3437.92	3417.46	3400.70	3386.93
220000	3699.63	3660.03	3627.86	3601.63	3580.20	3562.64	3548.22
230000	3867.80	3826.39	3792.76	3765.35	3742.94	3724.57	3709.50
240000	4035.96	3992.76	3957.66	3929.06	3905.67	3886.51	3870.78
250000	4204.13	4159.12	4122.57	4092.77	4068.41	4048.45	4032.07

Monthly Payments 19.75 %

LOAN AMOUNT	22	23	24	25	30	35	40
100	1.61	1.60	1.60	1.60	1.59	1.58	1.58
200	3.21	3.21	3.20	3.19	3.18	3.17	3.17
500	8.04	8.02	8.00	7.98	7.94	7.92	7.91
1000	16.07	16.03	15.99	15.96	15.88	15.84	15.83
2000	32.15	32.06	31.99	31.93	31.75	31.68	31.66
5000	80.37	80.15	79.97	79.82	79.38	79.21	79.14
6000	96.45	96.18	95.96	95.78	95.25	95.05	94.97
7000	112.52	112.21	111.95	111.74	111.13	110.89	110.79
8000	128.60	128.24	127.95	127.71	127.00	126.73	126.62
9000	144.67	144.27	143.94	143.67	142.88	142.57	142.45
10000	160.74	160.30	159.93	159.63	158.75	158.41	158.28
12000	192.89	192.36	191.92	191.56	190.50	190.09	189.93
15000	241.12	240.45	239.90	239.45	238.13	237.62	237.42
20000	321.49	320.60	319.87	319.27	317.50	316.82	316.56
25000	401.86	400.75	399.84	399.08	396.88	396.03	395.70
30000	482.23	480.90	479.80	478.90	476.26	475.23	474.83
31000	498.31	496.93	495.80	494.86	492.13	491.07	490.66
32000	514.38	512.96	511.79	510.83	508.01	506.91	506.49
33000	530.45	528.99	527.78	526.79	523.88	522.76	522.32
34000	546.53	545.02	543.78	542.75	539.76	538.60	538.15
35000	562.60	561.05	559.77	558.72	555.63	554.44	553.97
36000	578.68	577.08	575.76	574.68	571.51	570.28	569.80
37000	594.75	593.11	591.76	590.64	587.38	586.12	585.63
38000	610.83	609.14	607.75	606.60	603.26	601.96	601.46
39000	626.90	625.17	623.74	622.57	619.13	617.80	617.28
40000	642.98	641.20	639.74	638.53	635.01	633.64	633.11
41000	659.05	657.23	655.73	654.49	650.88	649.48	648.94
42000	675.12	673.26	671.72	670.46	666.76	665.32	664.77
43000	691.20	689.29	687.72	686.42	682.63	681.17	680.60
44000	707.27	705.32	703.71	702.38	698.51	697.01	696.42
45000	723.35	721.35	719.71	718.35	714.38	712.85	712.25
46000	739.42	737.38	735.70	734.31	730.26	728.69	728.08
47000	755.50	753.41	751.69	750.27	746.13	744.53	743.91
48000	771.57	769.44	767.69	766.24	762.01	760.37	759.74
49000	787.64	785.47	783.68	782.20	777.88	776.21	775.56
50000	803.72	801.50	799.67	798.16	793.76	792.05	791.39
51000	819.79	817.53	815.67	814.13	809.63	807.89	807.22
52000	835.87	833.56	831.66	830.09	825.51	823.74	823.05
53000	851.94	849.59	847.65	846.05	841.38	839.58	838.87
54000	868.02	865.62	863.65	862.02	857.26	855.42	854.70
55000	884.09	881.65	879.64	877.98	873.13	871.26	870.53
56000	900.17	897.68	895.63	893.94	889.01	887.10	886.36
57000	916.24	913.71	911.63	909.91	904.88	902.94	902.19
58000	932.31	929.74	927.62	925.87	920.76	918.78	918.01
59000	948.39	945.77	943.61	941.83	936.64	934.62	933.84
60000	964.46	961.80	959.61	957.80	952.51	950.46	949.67
65000	1044.83	1041.95	1039.57	1037.61	1031.89	1029.67	1028.81
70000	1125.21	1122.10	1119.54	1117.43	1111.26	1108.87	1107.95
75000	1205.58	1202.25	1199.51	1197.25	1190.64	1188.08	1187.09
80000	1285.95	1282.40	1279.48	1277.06	1270.01	1267.29	1266.23
85000	1366.32	1362.55	1359.44	1356.88	1349.39	1346.49	1345.36
90000	1446.69	1442.70	1439.41	1436.70	1428.77	1425.70	1424.50
95000	1527.07	1522.85	1519.38	1516.51	1508.14	1504.90	1503.64
100000	1607.44	1603.00	1599.34	1596.33	1587.52	1584.11	1582.78
105000	1687.81	1683.15	1679.31	1676.15	1666.89	1663.31	1661.92
110000	1768.18	1763.30	1759.28	1755.96	1746.27	1742.52	1741.06
120000	1928.93	1923.60	1919.21	1915.59	1905.02	1900.93	1899.34
130000	2089.67	2083.90	2079.15	2075.23	2063.77	2059.34	2057.62
140000	2250.41	2244.20	2239.08	2234.86	2222.52	2217.75	2215.89
150000	2411.16	2404.50	2399.02	2394.49	2381.28	2376.16	2374.17
160000	2571.90	2564.80	2558.95	2554.13	2540.03	2534.57	2532.45
170000	2732.64	2725.10	2718.89	2713.76	2698.78	2692.98	2690.73
180000	2893.39	2885.40	2878.82	2873.39	2857.53	2851.39	2849.01
190000	3054.13	3045.70	3038.76	3033.02	3016.28	3009.80	3007.28
200000	3214.88	3206.00	3198.69	3192.66	3175.03	3168.21	3165.56
210000	3375.62	3366.30	3358.62	3352.29	3333.79	3326.62	3323.84
220000	3536.36	3526.60	3518.56	3511.92	3492.54	3485.04	3482.12
230000	3697.11	3686.90	3678.49	3671.56	3651.29	3643.45	3640.40
240000	3857.85	3847.20	3838.43	3831.19	3810.04	3801.86	3798.68
250000	4018.59	4007.50	3998.36	3990.82	3968.79	3960.27	3956.95

20.00 % Monthly Payments

LOAN AMOUNT	1	2	3	4	5	6	7
100	9.23	5.05	3.68	3.00	2.61	2.35	2.17
200	18.45	10.10	7.35	6.00	5.21	4.70	4.35
500	46.13	25.26	18.38	15.01	13.03	11.75	10.87
1000	92.26	50.51	36.76	30.01	26.06	23.50	21.74
2000	184.52	101.03	73.53	60.03	52.12	47.00	43.47
5000	461.29	252.56	183.82	150.07	130.29	117.50	108.68
6000	553.55	303.08	220.59	180.08	156.35	141.00	130.41
7000	645.81	353.59	257.35	210.09	182.41	164.50	152.15
8000	738.07	404.10	294.12	240.11	208.47	188.00	173.88
9000	830.33	454.61	330.88	270.12	234.53	211.50	195.62
10000	922.59	505.13	367.64	300.13	260.59	235.00	217.36
12000	1107.11	606.15	441.17	360.16	312.70	281.99	260.83
15000	1383.88	757.69	551.47	450.20	390.88	352.49	326.03
20000	1845.18	1010.26	735.29	600.27	521.17	469.99	434.71
25000	2306.47	1262.82	919.11	750.33	651.46	587.49	543.39
30000	2767.77	1515.38	1102.93	900.40	781.76	704.99	652.07
31000	2860.02	1565.90	1139.70	930.41	807.82	728.49	673.80
32000	2952.28	1616.41	1176.46	960.43	833.87	751.99	695.54
33000	3044.54	1666.92	1213.23	990.44	859.93	775.49	717.27
34000	3136.80	1717.43	1249.99	1020.45	885.99	798.98	739.01
35000	3229.06	1767.95	1286.76	1050.47	912.05	822.48	760.74
36000	3321.32	1818.46	1323.52	1080.48	938.11	845.98	782.48
37000	3413.58	1868.97	1360.28	1110.49	964.17	869.48	804.21
38000	3505.84	1919.49	1397.05	1140.50	990.23	892.98	825.95
39000	3598.10	1970.00	1433.81	1170.52	1016.28	916.48	847.68
40000	3690.35	2020.51	1470.58	1200.53	1042.34	939.98	869.42
41000	3782.61	2071.02	1507.34	1230.54	1068.40	963.48	891.16
42000	3874.87	2121.54	1544.11	1260.56	1094.46	986.98	912.89
43000	3967.13	2172.05	1580.87	1290.57	1120.52	1010.48	934.63
44000	4059.39	2222.56	1617.63	1320.58	1146.58	1033.98	956.36
45000	4151.65	2273.07	1654.40	1350.60	1172.64	1057.48	978.10
46000	4243.91	2323.59	1691.16	1380.61	1198.69	1080.98	999.83
47000	4336.17	2374.10	1727.93	1410.62	1224.75	1104.48	1021.57
48000	4428.43	2424.61	1764.69	1440.64	1250.81	1127.98	1043.30
49000	4520.68	2475.13	1801.46	1470.65	1276.87	1151.48	1065.04
50000	4612.94	2525.64	1838.22	1500.66	1302.93	1174.98	1086.78
51000	4705.20	2576.15	1874.99	1530.68	1328.99	1198.48	1108.51
52000	4797.46	2626.66	1911.75	1560.69	1355.05	1221.98	1130.25
53000	4889.72	2677.18	1948.51	1590.70	1381.10	1245.48	1151.98
54000	4981.98	2727.69	1985.28	1620.72	1407.16	1268.98	1173.72
55000	5074.24	2778.20	2022.04	1650.73	1433.22	1292.48	1195.45
56000	5166.50	2828.72	2058.81	1680.74	1459.28	1315.97	1217.19
57000	5258.75	2879.23	2095.57	1710.76	1485.34	1339.47	1238.92
58000	5351.01	2929.74	2132.34	1740.77	1511.40	1362.97	1260.66
59000	5443.27	2980.25	2169.10	1770.78	1537.46	1386.47	1282.39
60000	5535.53	3030.77	2205.87	1800.80	1563.51	1409.97	1304.13
65000	5996.83	3283.33	2389.69	1950.86	1693.81	1527.47	1412.81
70000	6458.12	3535.89	2573.51	2100.93	1824.10	1644.97	1521.49
75000	6919.41	3788.46	2757.33	2251.00	1954.39	1762.47	1630.16
80000	7380.71	4041.02	2941.15	2401.06	2084.69	1879.96	1738.84
85000	7842.00	4293.59	3124.98	2551.13	2214.98	1997.46	1847.52
90000	8303.30	4546.15	3308.80	2701.20	2345.27	2114.96	1956.20
95000	8764.59	4798.71	3492.62	2851.26	2475.56	2232.46	2064.87
100000	9225.89	5051.28	3676.44	3001.33	2605.86	2349.95	2173.55
105000	9687.18	5303.84	3860.27	3151.40	2736.15	2467.45	2282.23
110000	10148.47	5556.40	4044.09	3301.46	2866.44	2584.95	2390.91
120000	11071.06	6061.53	4411.73	3601.59	3127.03	2819.95	2608.26
130000	11993.65	6566.66	4779.38	3901.73	3387.62	3054.94	2825.62
140000	12916.24	7071.79	5147.02	4201.86	3648.20	3289.94	3042.97
150000	13838.83	7576.92	5514.66	4501.99	3908.79	3524.93	3260.33
160000	14761.42	8082.04	5882.31	4802.13	4169.37	3759.93	3477.68
170000	15684.01	8587.17	6249.95	5102.26	4429.96	3994.92	3695.04
180000	16606.59	9092.30	6617.60	5402.39	4690.54	4229.92	3912.39
190000	17529.18	9597.43	6985.24	5702.52	4951.13	4464.91	4129.75
200000	18451.77	10102.55	7352.89	6002.66	5211.72	4699.91	4347.10
210000	19374.36	10607.68	7720.53	6302.79	5472.30	4934.91	4564.46
220000	20296.95	11112.81	8088.17	6602.92	5732.89	5169.90	4781.81
230000	21219.54	11617.94	8455.82	6903.06	5993.47	5404.90	4999.17
240000	22142.13	12123.06	8823.46	7203.19	6254.06	5639.89	5216.52
250000	23064.71	12628.19	9191.11	7503.32	6514.64	5874.89	5433.88

Monthly Payments 20.00 %

LOAN AMOUNT	YEARS 8	9	10	11	12	13	14
100	2.05	1.95	1.88	1.83	1.78	1.75	1.72
200	4.09	3.90	3.76	3.65	3.56	3.50	3.44
500	10.23	9.76	9.40	9.13	8.91	8.74	8.60
1000	20.47	19.52	18.81	18.25	17.82	17.48	17.20
2000	40.93	39.05	37.61	36.51	35.64	34.96	34.41
5000	102.33	97.62	94.04	91.27	89.11	87.39	86.02
6000	122.79	117.14	112.84	109.53	106.93	104.87	103.23
7000	143.26	136.66	131.65	127.78	124.75	122.35	120.43
8000	163.73	156.19	150.46	146.03	142.57	139.83	137.64
9000	184.19	175.71	169.27	164.29	160.39	157.31	154.84
10000	204.66	195.23	188.07	182.54	178.21	174.78	172.05
12000	245.59	234.28	225.69	219.05	213.85	209.74	206.46
15000	306.99	292.85	282.11	273.82	267.32	262.18	258.07
20000	409.32	390.47	376.15	365.09	356.42	349.57	344.10
25000	511.65	488.08	470.19	456.36	445.53	436.96	430.12
30000	613.97	585.70	564.22	547.63	534.64	524.35	516.15
31000	634.44	605.22	583.03	565.88	552.46	541.83	533.35
32000	654.91	624.75	601.84	584.14	570.28	559.31	550.56
33000	675.37	644.27	620.65	602.39	588.10	576.79	567.76
34000	695.84	663.79	639.45	620.65	605.92	594.27	584.97
35000	716.30	683.32	658.26	638.90	623.74	611.74	602.17
36000	736.77	702.84	677.07	657.16	641.56	629.22	619.38
37000	757.24	722.36	695.88	675.41	659.38	646.70	636.58
38000	777.70	741.89	714.68	693.66	677.20	664.18	653.79
39000	798.17	761.41	733.49	711.92	695.03	681.66	670.99
40000	818.63	780.93	752.30	730.17	712.85	699.14	688.20
41000	839.10	800.46	771.11	748.43	730.67	716.61	705.40
42000	859.56	819.98	789.91	766.68	748.49	734.09	722.61
43000	880.03	839.50	808.72	784.94	766.31	751.57	739.81
44000	900.50	859.03	827.53	803.19	784.13	769.05	757.02
45000	920.96	878.55	846.34	821.45	801.95	786.53	774.22
46000	941.43	898.07	865.14	839.70	819.77	804.01	791.43
47000	961.89	917.60	883.95	857.95	837.60	821.48	808.63
48000	982.36	937.12	902.76	876.21	855.42	838.96	825.84
49000	1002.83	956.64	921.57	894.46	873.24	856.44	843.04
50000	1023.29	976.17	940.37	912.72	891.06	873.92	860.25
51000	1043.76	995.69	959.18	930.97	908.88	891.40	877.45
52000	1064.22	1015.21	977.99	949.23	926.70	908.88	894.66
53000	1084.69	1034.74	996.80	967.48	944.52	926.36	911.86
54000	1105.15	1054.26	1015.60	985.73	962.34	943.83	929.07
55000	1125.62	1073.78	1034.41	1003.99	980.16	961.31	946.27
56000	1146.09	1093.31	1053.22	1022.24	997.99	978.79	963.48
57000	1166.55	1112.83	1072.03	1040.50	1015.81	996.27	980.68
58000	1187.02	1132.35	1090.83	1058.75	1033.63	1013.75	997.89
59000	1207.48	1151.88	1109.64	1077.01	1051.45	1031.23	1015.09
60000	1227.95	1171.40	1128.45	1095.26	1069.27	1048.70	1032.29
65000	1330.28	1269.01	1222.49	1186.53	1158.38	1136.10	1118.32
70000	1432.61	1366.63	1316.52	1277.80	1247.48	1223.49	1204.34
75000	1534.94	1464.25	1410.56	1369.08	1336.59	1310.88	1290.37
80000	1637.27	1561.86	1504.60	1460.35	1425.69	1398.27	1376.39
85000	1739.60	1659.48	1598.64	1551.62	1514.80	1485.66	1462.42
90000	1841.92	1757.10	1692.67	1642.89	1603.91	1573.06	1548.44
95000	1944.25	1854.71	1786.71	1734.16	1693.01	1660.45	1634.47
100000	2046.58	1952.33	1880.75	1825.43	1782.12	1747.84	1720.49
105000	2148.91	2049.95	1974.79	1916.71	1871.22	1835.23	1806.52
110000	2251.24	2147.56	2068.82	2007.98	1960.33	1922.62	1892.54
120000	2455.90	2342.80	2256.90	2190.52	2138.54	2097.41	2064.59
130000	2660.56	2538.03	2444.97	2373.06	2316.75	2272.19	2236.64
140000	2865.22	2733.26	2633.05	2555.61	2494.96	2446.98	2408.69
150000	3069.87	2928.50	2821.12	2738.15	2673.18	2621.76	2580.74
160000	3274.53	3123.73	3009.20	2920.69	2851.39	2796.54	2752.79
170000	3479.19	3318.96	3197.27	3103.24	3029.60	2971.33	2924.84
180000	3683.85	3514.20	3385.35	3285.78	3207.81	3146.11	3096.88
190000	3888.51	3709.43	3573.42	3468.32	3386.02	3320.90	3268.93
200000	4093.17	3904.66	3761.50	3650.87	3564.23	3495.68	3440.98
210000	4297.82	4099.89	3949.57	3833.41	3742.45	3670.46	3613.03
220000	4502.48	4295.13	4137.65	4015.95	3920.66	3845.25	3785.08
230000	4707.14	4490.36	4325.72	4198.50	4098.87	4020.03	3957.13
240000	4911.80	4685.59	4513.80	4381.04	4277.08	4194.82	4129.18
250000	5116.46	4880.83	4701.87	4563.58	4455.29	4369.60	4301.23

20.00 % Monthly Payments

LOAN AMOUNT	15	16	17	18	19	20	21
	YEARS						
100	1.70	1.68	1.67	1.65	1.65	1.64	1.63
200	3.40	3.36	3.33	3.31	3.29	3.27	3.26
500	8.49	8.40	8.33	8.27	8.23	8.19	8.15
1000	16.99	16.81	16.66	16.55	16.45	16.37	16.31
2000	33.97	33.62	33.33	33.09	32.90	32.75	32.62
5000	84.93	84.04	83.32	82.74	82.26	81.87	81.55
6000	101.91	100.85	99.98	99.28	98.71	98.24	97.86
7000	118.90	117.66	116.65	115.83	115.16	114.62	114.17
8000	135.88	134.46	133.31	132.38	131.61	130.99	130.48
9000	152.87	151.27	149.98	148.92	148.07	147.36	146.79
10000	169.85	168.08	166.64	165.47	164.52	163.74	163.10
12000	203.82	201.70	199.97	198.57	197.42	196.48	195.72
15000	254.78	252.12	249.96	248.21	246.78	245.60	244.65
20000	339.71	336.16	333.28	330.94	329.03	327.47	326.19
25000	424.63	420.20	416.60	413.68	411.29	409.34	407.74
30000	509.56	504.24	499.92	496.41	493.55	491.21	489.29
31000	526.54	521.05	516.59	512.96	510.00	507.58	505.60
32000	543.53	537.85	533.25	529.51	526.45	523.96	521.91
33000	560.51	554.66	549.92	546.06	542.91	540.33	538.22
34000	577.50	571.47	566.58	562.60	559.36	556.70	554.53
35000	594.48	588.28	583.25	579.15	575.81	573.08	570.84
36000	611.47	605.09	599.91	595.70	592.26	589.45	587.15
37000	628.45	621.89	616.57	612.24	608.71	605.82	603.46
38000	645.44	638.70	633.24	628.79	625.16	622.20	619.77
39000	662.43	655.51	649.90	645.34	641.62	638.57	636.08
40000	679.41	672.32	666.57	661.89	658.07	654.95	652.39
41000	696.40	689.13	683.23	678.43	674.52	671.32	668.70
42000	713.38	705.93	699.89	694.98	690.97	687.69	685.01
43000	730.37	722.74	716.56	711.53	707.42	704.07	701.32
44000	747.35	739.55	733.22	728.07	723.87	720.44	717.63
45000	764.34	756.36	749.89	744.62	740.33	736.81	733.94
46000	781.32	773.16	766.55	761.17	756.78	753.19	750.25
47000	798.31	789.97	783.21	777.72	773.23	769.56	766.56
48000	815.29	806.78	799.88	794.26	789.68	785.93	782.86
49000	832.28	823.59	816.54	810.81	806.13	802.31	799.17
50000	849.26	840.40	833.21	827.36	822.59	818.68	815.48
51000	866.25	857.20	849.87	843.90	839.04	835.06	831.79
52000	883.23	874.01	866.54	860.45	855.49	851.43	848.10
53000	900.22	890.82	883.20	877.00	871.94	867.80	864.41
54000	917.20	907.63	899.86	893.55	888.39	884.18	880.72
55000	934.19	924.44	916.53	910.09	904.84	900.55	897.03
56000	951.18	941.24	933.19	926.64	921.30	916.92	913.34
57000	968.16	958.05	949.86	943.19	937.75	933.30	929.65
58000	985.15	974.86	966.52	959.73	954.20	949.67	945.96
59000	1002.13	991.67	983.18	976.28	970.65	966.04	962.27
60000	1019.12	1008.48	999.85	992.83	987.10	982.42	978.58
65000	1104.04	1092.52	1083.17	1075.57	1069.36	1064.29	1060.13
70000	1188.97	1176.56	1166.49	1158.30	1151.62	1146.15	1141.68
75000	1273.90	1260.59	1249.81	1241.04	1233.88	1228.02	1223.23
80000	1358.82	1344.63	1333.13	1323.77	1316.14	1309.89	1304.77
85000	1443.75	1428.67	1416.45	1406.51	1398.39	1391.76	1386.32
90000	1528.67	1512.71	1499.77	1489.24	1480.65	1473.63	1467.87
95000	1613.60	1596.75	1583.09	1571.98	1562.91	1555.50	1549.42
100000	1698.53	1680.79	1666.41	1654.72	1645.17	1637.36	1630.97
105000	1783.45	1764.83	1749.74	1737.45	1727.43	1719.23	1712.52
110000	1868.38	1848.87	1833.06	1820.19	1809.69	1801.10	1794.07
120000	2038.23	2016.95	1999.70	1985.66	1974.20	1964.84	1957.16
130000	2208.08	2185.03	2166.34	2151.13	2138.72	2128.57	2120.26
140000	2377.94	2353.11	2332.98	2316.60	2303.24	2292.31	2283.36
150000	2547.79	2521.19	2499.62	2482.07	2467.76	2456.05	2446.45
160000	2717.64	2689.27	2666.26	2647.54	2632.27	2619.78	2609.55
170000	2887.50	2857.35	2832.90	2813.02	2796.79	2783.52	2772.65
180000	3057.35	3025.43	2999.55	2978.49	2961.31	2947.26	2935.74
190000	3227.20	3193.51	3166.19	3143.96	3125.82	3110.99	3098.84
200000	3397.05	3361.59	3332.83	3309.43	3290.34	3274.73	3261.94
210000	3566.91	3529.67	3499.47	3474.90	3454.86	3438.46	3425.03
220000	3736.76	3697.75	3666.11	3640.37	3619.37	3602.20	3588.13
230000	3906.61	3865.82	3832.75	3805.85	3783.89	3765.94	3751.23
240000	4076.46	4033.90	3999.39	3971.32	3948.41	3929.67	3914.32
250000	4246.32	4201.98	4166.04	4136.79	4112.93	4093.41	4077.42

Monthly Payments 20.00 %

LOAN AMOUNT	22	23	24	25	30	35	40
				YEARS			
100	1.63	1.62	1.62	1.61	1.61	1.60	1.60
200	3.25	3.24	3.24	3.23	3.21	3.21	3.20
500	8.13	8.11	8.09	8.07	8.03	8.02	8.01
1000	16.26	16.21	16.18	16.15	16.06	16.03	16.02
2000	32.51	32.43	32.36	32.30	32.13	32.06	32.04
5000	81.29	81.07	80.89	80.75	80.32	80.16	80.10
6000	97.54	97.28	97.07	96.90	96.39	96.19	96.12
7000	113.80	113.50	113.25	113.05	112.45	112.23	112.14
8000	130.06	129.71	129.43	129.20	128.52	128.26	128.16
9000	146.31	145.93	145.61	145.34	144.58	144.29	144.18
10000	162.57	162.14	161.79	161.49	160.65	160.32	160.20
12000	195.09	194.57	194.14	193.79	192.78	192.39	192.24
15000	243.86	243.21	242.68	242.24	240.97	240.48	240.30
20000	325.14	324.28	323.57	322.99	321.29	320.64	320.39
25000	406.43	405.35	404.47	403.74	401.62	400.80	400.49
30000	487.72	486.42	485.36	484.48	481.94	480.97	480.59
31000	503.97	502.64	501.54	500.63	498.00	497.00	496.61
32000	520.23	518.85	517.72	516.78	514.07	513.03	512.63
33000	536.49	535.06	533.89	532.93	530.13	529.06	528.65
34000	552.75	551.28	550.07	549.08	546.20	545.09	544.67
35000	569.00	567.49	566.25	565.23	562.26	561.13	560.69
36000	585.26	583.71	582.43	581.38	578.33	577.16	576.71
37000	601.52	599.92	598.61	597.53	594.39	593.19	592.73
38000	617.77	616.14	614.79	613.68	610.46	609.22	608.75
39000	634.03	632.35	630.97	629.83	626.52	625.25	624.77
40000	650.29	648.56	647.15	645.98	642.59	641.29	640.79
41000	666.55	664.78	663.32	662.13	658.65	657.32	656.81
42000	682.80	680.99	679.50	678.28	674.71	673.35	672.83
43000	699.06	697.21	695.68	694.43	690.78	689.38	688.85
44000	715.32	713.42	711.86	710.58	706.84	705.42	704.87
45000	731.57	729.63	728.04	726.72	722.91	721.45	720.89
46000	747.83	745.85	744.22	742.87	738.97	737.48	736.91
47000	764.09	762.06	760.40	759.02	755.04	753.51	752.93
48000	780.35	778.28	776.57	775.17	771.10	769.54	768.95
49000	796.60	794.49	792.75	791.32	787.17	785.58	784.96
50000	812.86	810.70	808.93	807.47	803.23	801.61	800.98
51000	829.12	826.92	825.11	823.62	819.30	817.64	817.00
52000	845.37	843.13	841.29	839.77	835.36	833.67	833.02
53000	861.63	859.35	857.47	855.92	851.43	849.70	849.04
54000	877.89	875.56	873.65	872.07	867.49	865.74	865.06
55000	894.15	891.77	889.82	888.22	883.55	881.77	881.08
56000	910.40	907.99	906.00	904.37	899.62	897.80	897.10
57000	926.66	924.20	922.18	920.52	915.68	913.83	913.12
58000	942.92	940.42	938.36	936.67	931.75	929.87	929.14
59000	959.18	956.63	954.54	952.82	947.81	945.90	945.16
60000	975.43	972.85	970.72	968.97	963.88	961.93	961.18
65000	1056.72	1053.92	1051.61	1049.71	1044.20	1042.09	1041.28
70000	1138.00	1134.99	1132.50	1130.46	1124.52	1122.25	1121.38
75000	1219.29	1216.06	1213.40	1211.21	1204.85	1202.41	1201.48
80000	1300.58	1297.13	1294.29	1291.96	1285.17	1282.57	1281.58
85000	1381.86	1378.20	1375.18	1372.70	1365.49	1362.73	1361.67
90000	1463.15	1459.27	1456.08	1453.45	1445.82	1442.90	1441.77
95000	1544.43	1540.34	1536.97	1534.20	1526.14	1523.06	1521.87
100000	1625.72	1621.41	1617.86	1614.94	1606.46	1603.22	1601.97
105000	1707.01	1702.48	1698.76	1695.69	1686.79	1683.38	1682.07
110000	1788.29	1783.55	1779.65	1776.44	1767.11	1763.54	1762.17
120000	1950.86	1945.69	1941.44	1937.93	1927.76	1923.86	1922.36
130000	2113.44	2107.83	2103.22	2099.43	2088.40	2084.18	2082.56
140000	2276.01	2269.97	2265.01	2260.92	2249.05	2244.50	2242.76
150000	2438.58	2432.11	2426.79	2422.42	2409.69	2404.83	2402.95
160000	2601.15	2594.25	2588.58	2583.91	2570.34	2565.15	2563.15
170000	2763.73	2756.40	2750.37	2745.40	2730.99	2725.47	2723.35
180000	2926.30	2918.54	2912.15	2906.90	2891.63	2885.79	2883.54
190000	3088.87	3080.68	3073.94	3068.39	3052.28	3046.11	3043.74
200000	3251.44	3242.82	3235.73	3229.89	3212.93	3206.43	3203.94
210000	3414.01	3404.96	3397.51	3391.38	3373.57	3366.76	3364.13
220000	3576.59	3567.10	3559.30	3552.88	3534.22	3527.08	3524.33
230000	3739.16	3729.24	3721.08	3714.37	3694.86	3687.40	3684.53
240000	3901.73	3891.38	3882.87	3875.87	3855.51	3847.72	3844.73
250000	4064.30	4053.52	4044.66	4037.36	4016.16	4008.04	4004.92

20.25 % Monthly Payments

LOAN AMOUNT	1	2	3	4	5	6	7
				YEARS			
100	9.24	5.06	3.69	3.01	2.62	2.36	2.19
200	18.47	10.13	7.38	6.03	5.24	4.73	4.37
500	46.18	25.31	18.44	15.07	13.09	11.82	10.94
1000	92.37	50.63	36.88	30.14	26.19	23.63	21.87
2000	184.74	101.25	73.76	60.27	52.37	47.26	43.75
5000	461.85	253.13	184.41	150.68	130.93	118.16	109.37
6000	554.21	303.75	221.29	180.81	157.12	141.79	131.24
7000	646.58	354.38	258.17	210.95	183.30	165.43	153.11
8000	738.95	405.00	295.05	241.08	209.49	189.06	174.99
9000	831.32	455.63	331.93	271.22	235.67	212.69	196.86
10000	923.69	506.25	368.81	301.35	261.86	236.32	218.73
12000	1108.43	607.50	442.58	361.63	314.23	283.59	262.48
15000	1385.54	759.38	553.22	452.03	392.79	354.48	328.10
20000	1847.38	1012.50	737.63	602.71	523.72	472.64	437.47
25000	2309.23	1265.63	922.04	753.39	654.65	590.81	546.83
30000	2771.07	1518.75	1106.44	904.06	785.58	708.97	656.20
31000	2863.44	1569.38	1143.32	934.20	811.77	732.60	678.07
32000	2955.81	1620.00	1180.21	964.34	837.95	756.23	699.94
33000	3048.18	1670.63	1217.09	994.47	864.14	779.86	721.82
34000	3140.55	1721.25	1253.97	1024.61	890.33	803.50	743.69
35000	3232.92	1771.88	1290.85	1054.74	916.51	827.13	765.56
36000	3325.29	1822.50	1327.73	1084.88	942.70	850.76	787.44
37000	3417.66	1873.13	1364.61	1115.01	968.88	874.39	809.31
38000	3510.03	1923.75	1401.49	1145.15	995.07	898.02	831.18
39000	3602.40	1974.38	1438.38	1175.28	1021.26	921.66	853.06
40000	3694.76	2025.00	1475.26	1205.42	1047.44	945.29	874.93
41000	3787.13	2075.63	1512.14	1235.55	1073.63	968.92	896.80
42000	3879.50	2126.25	1549.02	1265.69	1099.81	992.55	918.68
43000	3971.87	2176.88	1585.90	1295.83	1126.00	1016.19	940.55
44000	4064.24	2227.50	1622.78	1325.96	1152.19	1039.82	962.42
45000	4156.61	2278.13	1659.66	1356.10	1178.37	1063.45	984.30
46000	4248.98	2328.75	1696.55	1386.23	1204.56	1087.08	1006.17
47000	4341.35	2379.38	1733.43	1416.37	1230.74	1110.72	1028.04
48000	4433.72	2430.01	1770.31	1446.50	1256.93	1134.35	1049.92
49000	4526.09	2480.63	1807.19	1476.64	1283.12	1157.98	1071.79
50000	4618.46	2531.26	1844.07	1506.77	1309.30	1181.61	1093.66
51000	4710.82	2581.88	1880.95	1536.91	1335.49	1205.24	1115.54
52000	4803.19	2632.51	1917.83	1567.04	1361.67	1228.88	1137.41
53000	4895.56	2683.13	1954.72	1597.18	1387.86	1252.51	1159.28
54000	4987.93	2733.76	1991.60	1627.32	1414.05	1276.14	1181.16
55000	5080.30	2784.38	2028.48	1657.45	1440.23	1299.77	1203.03
56000	5172.67	2835.01	2065.36	1687.59	1466.42	1323.41	1224.90
57000	5265.04	2885.63	2102.24	1717.72	1492.60	1347.04	1246.78
58000	5357.41	2936.26	2139.12	1747.86	1518.79	1370.67	1268.65
59000	5449.78	2986.88	2176.00	1777.99	1544.98	1394.30	1290.52
60000	5542.15	3037.51	2212.89	1808.13	1571.16	1417.93	1312.40
65000	6003.99	3290.63	2397.29	1958.81	1702.09	1536.10	1421.76
70000	6465.84	3543.76	2581.70	2109.48	1833.02	1654.26	1531.13
75000	6927.68	3796.88	2766.11	2260.16	1963.95	1772.42	1640.49
80000	7389.53	4050.01	2950.51	2410.84	2094.88	1890.58	1749.86
85000	7851.37	4303.13	3134.92	2561.51	2225.81	2008.74	1859.23
90000	8313.22	4556.26	3319.33	2712.19	2356.74	2126.90	1968.59
95000	8775.07	4809.39	3503.74	2862.87	2487.67	2245.06	2077.96
100000	9236.91	5062.51	3688.14	3013.55	2618.60	2363.22	2187.33
105000	9698.76	5315.64	3872.55	3164.22	2749.53	2481.38	2296.69
110000	10160.60	5568.76	4056.96	3314.90	2880.47	2599.55	2406.06
120000	11084.29	6075.01	4425.77	3616.26	3142.33	2835.87	2624.79
130000	12007.98	6581.26	4794.58	3917.61	3404.19	3072.19	2843.52
140000	12931.68	7087.51	5163.40	4218.97	3666.05	3308.51	3062.26
150000	13855.37	7593.77	5532.21	4520.32	3927.91	3544.84	3280.99
160000	14779.06	8100.02	5901.03	4821.68	4189.77	3781.16	3499.72
170000	15702.75	8606.27	6269.84	5123.03	4451.63	4017.48	3718.45
180000	16626.44	9112.52	6638.66	5424.38	4713.49	4253.80	3937.19
190000	17550.13	9618.77	7007.47	5725.74	4975.35	4490.12	4155.92
200000	18473.82	10125.02	7376.28	6027.09	5237.21	4726.45	4374.65
210000	19397.51	10631.27	7745.10	6328.45	5499.07	4962.77	4593.38
220000	20321.20	11137.52	8113.91	6629.80	5760.93	5199.09	4812.12
230000	21244.90	11643.77	8482.73	6931.16	6022.79	5435.41	5030.85
240000	22168.59	12150.03	8851.54	7232.51	6284.65	5671.74	5249.58
250000	23092.28	12656.28	9220.36	7533.87	6546.51	5908.06	5468.31

Monthly Payments 20.25 %

LOAN AMOUNT	8	9	10	11	12	13	14
				YEARS			
100	2.06	1.97	1.90	1.84	1.80	1.76	1.74
200	4.12	3.93	3.79	3.68	3.60	3.53	3.47
500	10.30	9.84	9.48	9.20	8.99	8.82	8.69
1000	20.61	19.67	18.96	18.41	17.98	17.64	17.37
2000	41.22	39.34	37.92	36.82	35.96	35.28	34.74
5000	103.04	98.35	94.80	92.05	89.90	88.21	86.86
6000	123.65	118.02	113.75	110.46	107.88	105.85	104.23
7000	144.26	137.69	132.71	128.87	125.86	123.49	121.60
8000	164.87	157.36	151.67	147.28	143.84	141.13	138.97
9000	185.48	177.03	170.63	165.69	161.83	158.77	156.34
10000	206.08	196.71	189.59	184.10	179.81	176.41	173.71
12000	247.30	236.05	227.51	220.92	215.77	211.70	208.45
15000	309.13	295.06	284.39	276.15	269.71	264.62	260.57
20000	412.17	393.41	379.18	368.20	359.61	352.83	347.42
25000	515.21	491.76	473.98	460.25	449.52	441.03	434.28
30000	618.25	590.12	568.77	552.30	539.42	529.24	521.13
31000	638.86	609.79	587.73	570.71	557.40	546.88	538.50
32000	659.47	629.46	606.69	589.12	575.38	564.52	555.87
33000	680.08	649.13	625.65	607.53	593.36	582.16	573.25
34000	700.69	668.80	644.61	625.94	611.34	599.81	590.62
35000	721.30	688.47	663.57	644.35	629.32	617.45	607.99
36000	741.90	708.14	682.53	662.76	647.30	635.09	625.36
37000	762.51	727.81	701.49	681.17	665.28	652.73	642.73
38000	783.12	747.48	720.44	699.58	683.26	670.37	660.10
39000	803.73	767.15	739.40	717.99	701.24	688.01	677.47
40000	824.34	786.82	758.36	736.40	719.22	705.65	694.84
41000	844.95	806.49	777.32	754.81	737.20	723.29	712.21
42000	865.55	826.16	796.28	773.22	755.19	740.94	729.58
43000	886.16	845.83	815.24	791.63	773.17	758.58	746.96
44000	906.77	865.50	834.20	810.04	791.15	776.22	764.33
45000	927.38	885.17	853.16	828.45	809.13	793.86	781.70
46000	947.99	904.84	872.12	846.86	827.11	811.50	799.07
47000	968.60	924.51	891.08	865.27	845.09	829.14	816.44
48000	989.20	944.19	910.03	883.68	863.07	846.78	833.81
49000	1009.81	963.86	928.99	902.09	881.05	864.43	851.18
50000	1030.42	983.53	947.95	920.50	899.03	882.07	868.55
51000	1051.03	1003.20	966.91	938.91	917.01	899.71	885.92
52000	1071.64	1022.87	985.87	957.32	934.99	917.35	903.30
53000	1092.25	1042.54	1004.83	975.73	952.97	934.99	920.67
54000	1112.86	1062.21	1023.79	994.14	970.95	952.63	938.04
55000	1133.46	1081.88	1042.75	1012.55	988.93	970.27	955.41
56000	1154.07	1101.55	1061.71	1030.96	1006.91	987.91	972.78
57000	1174.68	1121.22	1080.67	1049.37	1024.89	1005.56	990.15
58000	1195.29	1140.89	1099.63	1067.78	1042.88	1023.20	1007.52
59000	1215.90	1160.56	1118.58	1086.19	1060.86	1040.84	1024.89
60000	1236.51	1180.23	1137.54	1104.60	1078.84	1058.48	1042.26
65000	1339.55	1278.58	1232.34	1196.65	1168.74	1146.69	1129.12
70000	1442.59	1376.94	1327.13	1288.70	1258.64	1234.89	1215.97
75000	1545.63	1475.29	1421.93	1380.75	1348.55	1323.10	1302.83
80000	1648.67	1573.64	1516.72	1472.80	1438.45	1411.31	1389.69
85000	1751.72	1672.00	1611.52	1564.85	1528.35	1499.51	1476.54
90000	1854.76	1770.35	1706.31	1656.90	1618.25	1587.72	1563.40
95000	1957.80	1868.70	1801.11	1748.95	1708.16	1675.93	1650.25
100000	2060.84	1967.05	1895.91	1841.00	1798.06	1764.13	1737.11
105000	2163.89	2065.41	1990.70	1933.05	1887.96	1852.34	1823.96
110000	2266.93	2163.76	2085.50	2025.10	1977.87	1940.55	1910.82
120000	2473.01	2360.46	2275.09	2209.20	2157.67	2116.96	2084.53
130000	2679.10	2557.17	2464.68	2393.30	2337.48	2293.37	2258.24
140000	2885.18	2753.87	2654.27	2577.40	2517.29	2469.79	2431.95
150000	3091.27	2950.58	2843.86	2761.50	2697.09	2646.20	2605.66
160000	3297.35	3147.28	3033.45	2945.60	2876.90	2822.61	2779.37
170000	3503.43	3343.99	3223.04	3129.70	3056.70	2999.03	2953.08
180000	3709.52	3540.70	3412.63	3313.80	3236.51	3175.44	3126.79
190000	3915.60	3737.40	3602.22	3497.90	3416.32	3351.85	3300.50
200000	4121.69	3934.11	3791.81	3682.00	3596.12	3528.27	3474.21
210000	4327.77	4130.81	3981.40	3866.10	3775.93	3704.68	3647.92
220000	4533.86	4327.52	4170.99	4050.20	3955.73	3881.09	3821.64
230000	4739.94	4524.22	4360.58	4234.30	4135.54	4057.51	3995.35
240000	4946.02	4720.93	4550.17	4418.40	4315.35	4233.92	4169.06
250000	5152.11	4917.63	4739.76	4602.50	4495.15	4410.33	4342.77

20.25 % Monthly Payments

LOAN AMOUNT	15	16	17	18	19	20	21
100	1.72	1.70	1.68	1.67	1.66	1.66	1.65
200	3.43	3.40	3.37	3.34	3.33	3.31	3.30
500	8.58	8.49	8.42	8.36	8.32	8.28	8.25
1000	17.15	16.98	16.84	16.72	16.63	16.55	16.49
2000	34.31	33.96	33.68	33.45	33.26	33.11	32.98
5000	85.77	84.90	84.19	83.62	83.15	82.77	82.46
6000	102.93	101.88	101.03	100.34	99.78	99.32	98.95
7000	120.08	118.86	117.87	117.06	116.41	115.88	115.44
8000	137.23	135.84	134.71	133.79	133.04	132.43	131.93
9000	154.39	152.82	151.54	150.51	149.67	148.98	148.42
10000	171.54	169.80	168.38	167.24	166.30	165.54	164.91
12000	205.85	203.76	202.06	200.68	199.56	198.64	197.90
15000	257.32	254.70	252.57	250.85	249.45	248.31	247.37
20000	343.09	339.59	336.77	334.47	332.60	331.07	329.83
25000	428.86	424.49	420.96	418.09	415.75	413.84	412.28
30000	514.63	509.39	505.15	501.71	498.90	496.61	494.74
31000	531.79	526.37	521.99	518.43	515.53	513.17	511.23
32000	548.94	543.35	538.83	535.15	532.16	529.72	527.72
33000	566.09	560.33	555.66	551.88	548.79	546.27	544.21
34000	583.25	577.31	572.50	568.60	565.42	562.83	560.70
35000	600.40	594.29	589.34	585.32	582.05	579.38	577.20
36000	617.56	611.27	606.18	602.05	598.68	595.93	593.69
37000	634.71	628.25	623.02	618.77	615.31	612.49	610.18
38000	651.87	645.23	639.86	635.49	631.94	629.04	626.67
39000	669.02	662.21	656.69	652.22	648.57	645.59	643.16
40000	686.17	679.19	673.53	668.94	665.20	662.15	659.65
41000	703.33	696.17	690.37	685.66	681.83	678.70	676.14
42000	720.48	713.15	707.21	702.39	698.46	695.26	692.64
43000	737.64	730.13	724.05	719.11	715.09	711.81	709.13
44000	754.79	747.11	740.89	735.83	731.72	728.36	725.62
45000	771.95	764.09	757.72	752.56	748.35	744.92	742.11
46000	789.10	781.07	774.56	769.28	764.98	761.47	758.60
47000	806.26	798.05	791.40	786.01	781.61	778.02	775.09
48000	823.41	815.03	808.24	802.73	798.24	794.58	791.58
49000	840.56	832.01	825.08	819.45	814.87	811.13	808.07
50000	857.72	848.99	841.92	836.18	831.50	827.69	824.57
51000	874.87	865.96	858.75	852.90	848.13	844.24	841.06
52000	892.03	882.94	875.59	869.62	864.76	860.79	857.55
53000	909.18	899.92	892.43	886.35	881.39	877.35	874.04
54000	926.34	916.90	909.27	903.07	898.02	893.90	890.53
55000	943.49	933.88	926.11	919.79	914.65	910.45	907.02
56000	960.64	950.86	942.95	936.52	931.28	927.01	923.51
57000	977.80	967.84	959.78	953.24	947.91	943.56	940.00
58000	994.95	984.82	976.62	969.96	964.54	960.12	956.50
59000	1012.11	1001.80	993.46	986.69	981.17	976.67	972.99
60000	1029.26	1018.78	1010.30	1003.41	997.80	993.22	989.48
65000	1115.03	1103.68	1094.49	1087.03	1080.95	1075.99	1071.94
70000	1200.81	1188.58	1178.68	1170.65	1164.10	1158.76	1154.39
75000	1286.58	1273.48	1262.87	1254.26	1247.25	1241.53	1236.85
80000	1372.35	1358.38	1347.07	1337.88	1330.40	1324.30	1319.30
85000	1458.12	1443.27	1431.26	1421.50	1413.55	1407.07	1401.76
90000	1543.89	1528.17	1515.45	1505.12	1496.70	1489.83	1484.22
95000	1629.66	1613.07	1599.64	1588.73	1579.85	1572.60	1566.67
100000	1715.44	1697.97	1683.83	1672.35	1663.00	1655.37	1649.13
105000	1801.21	1782.87	1768.02	1755.97	1746.15	1738.14	1731.59
110000	1886.98	1867.77	1852.22	1839.59	1829.30	1820.91	1814.04
120000	2058.52	2037.56	2020.60	2006.82	1995.60	1986.45	1978.96
130000	2230.07	2207.36	2188.98	2174.06	2161.90	2151.98	2143.87
140000	2401.61	2377.16	2357.37	2341.29	2328.20	2317.52	2308.78
150000	2573.15	2546.96	2525.75	2508.53	2494.50	2483.06	2473.70
160000	2744.70	2716.75	2694.13	2675.76	2660.80	2648.59	2638.61
170000	2916.24	2886.55	2862.52	2843.00	2827.10	2814.13	2803.52
180000	3087.79	3056.35	3030.90	3010.23	2993.40	2979.67	2968.44
190000	3259.33	3226.14	3199.28	3177.47	3159.70	3145.21	3133.35
200000	3430.87	3395.94	3367.67	3344.70	3326.01	3310.74	3298.26
210000	3602.42	3565.74	3536.05	3511.94	3492.31	3476.28	3463.18
220000	3773.96	3735.53	3704.43	3679.17	3658.61	3641.82	3628.09
230000	3945.50	3905.33	3872.82	3846.41	3824.91	3807.35	3793.00
240000	4117.05	4075.13	4041.20	4013.65	3991.21	3972.89	3957.91
250000	4288.59	4244.93	4209.58	4180.88	4157.51	4138.43	4122.83

Monthly Payments 20.25 %

LOAN AMOUNT	22	23	24	25	30	35	40
100	1.64	1.64	1.64	1.63	1.63	1.62	1.62
200	3.29	3.28	3.27	3.27	3.25	3.24	3.24
500	8.22	8.20	8.18	8.17	8.13	8.11	8.11
1000	16.44	16.40	16.36	16.34	16.25	16.22	16.21
2000	32.88	32.80	32.73	32.67	32.51	32.45	32.42
5000	82.20	81.99	81.82	81.68	81.27	81.12	81.06
6000	98.64	98.39	98.18	98.01	97.52	97.34	97.27
7000	115.08	114.79	114.55	114.35	113.78	113.56	113.48
8000	131.52	131.19	130.91	130.69	130.03	129.79	129.69
9000	147.96	147.58	147.28	147.02	146.29	146.01	145.90
10000	164.40	163.98	163.64	163.36	162.54	162.23	162.11
12000	197.28	196.78	196.37	196.03	195.05	194.68	194.54
15000	246.60	245.97	245.46	245.04	243.81	243.35	243.17
20000	328.80	327.97	327.28	326.71	325.08	324.46	324.23
25000	411.01	409.96	409.10	408.39	406.35	405.58	405.29
30000	493.21	491.95	490.92	490.07	487.62	486.70	486.34
31000	509.65	508.35	507.28	506.41	503.88	502.92	502.55
32000	526.09	524.75	523.65	522.74	520.13	519.14	518.77
33000	542.53	541.14	540.01	539.08	536.38	535.36	534.98
34000	558.97	557.54	556.37	555.41	552.64	551.59	551.19
35000	575.41	573.94	572.74	571.75	568.89	567.81	567.40
36000	591.85	590.34	589.10	588.08	585.15	584.03	583.61
37000	608.29	606.74	605.47	604.42	601.40	600.26	599.82
38000	624.73	623.14	621.83	620.76	617.65	616.48	616.03
39000	641.17	639.53	638.19	637.09	633.91	632.70	632.25
40000	657.61	655.93	654.56	653.43	650.16	648.93	648.46
41000	674.05	672.33	670.92	669.76	666.42	665.15	664.67
42000	690.49	688.73	687.28	686.10	682.67	681.37	680.88
43000	706.93	705.13	703.65	702.43	698.92	697.60	697.09
44000	723.37	721.53	720.01	718.77	715.18	713.82	713.30
45000	739.81	737.92	736.38	735.11	731.43	730.04	729.51
46000	756.25	754.32	752.74	751.44	747.69	746.27	745.73
47000	772.69	770.72	769.10	767.78	763.94	762.49	761.94
48000	789.13	787.12	785.47	784.11	780.20	778.71	778.15
49000	805.57	803.52	801.83	800.45	796.45	794.94	794.36
50000	822.01	819.92	818.20	816.78	812.70	811.16	810.57
51000	838.45	836.31	834.56	833.12	828.96	827.38	826.78
52000	854.89	852.71	850.92	849.46	845.21	843.61	842.99
53000	871.33	869.11	867.29	865.79	861.47	859.83	859.21
54000	887.77	885.51	883.65	882.13	877.72	876.05	875.42
55000	904.21	901.91	900.02	898.46	893.97	892.27	891.63
56000	920.65	918.31	916.38	914.80	910.23	908.50	907.84
57000	937.09	934.70	932.74	931.13	926.48	924.72	924.05
58000	953.53	951.10	949.11	947.47	942.74	940.94	940.26
59000	969.97	967.50	965.47	963.80	958.99	957.17	956.47
60000	986.41	983.90	981.84	980.14	975.24	973.39	972.69
65000	1068.61	1065.89	1063.66	1061.82	1056.51	1054.51	1053.74
70000	1150.81	1147.88	1145.47	1143.50	1137.78	1135.62	1134.80
75000	1233.02	1229.87	1227.29	1225.18	1219.06	1216.74	1215.86
80000	1315.22	1311.87	1309.11	1306.85	1300.33	1297.85	1296.91
85000	1397.42	1393.86	1390.93	1388.53	1381.60	1378.97	1377.97
90000	1479.62	1475.85	1472.75	1470.21	1462.87	1460.09	1459.03
95000	1561.82	1557.84	1554.57	1551.89	1544.14	1541.20	1540.09
100000	1644.02	1639.83	1636.39	1633.57	1625.41	1622.32	1621.14
105000	1726.22	1721.82	1718.21	1715.25	1706.68	1703.43	1702.20
110000	1808.42	1803.81	1800.03	1796.92	1787.95	1784.55	1783.26
120000	1972.83	1967.80	1963.67	1960.28	1950.49	1946.78	1945.37
130000	2137.23	2131.78	2127.31	2123.64	2113.03	2109.01	2107.49
140000	2301.63	2295.76	2290.95	2286.99	2275.57	2271.24	2269.60
150000	2466.03	2459.75	2454.59	2450.35	2438.11	2433.48	2431.71
160000	2630.43	2623.73	2618.23	2613.71	2600.65	2595.71	2593.83
170000	2794.84	2787.71	2781.87	2777.07	2763.19	2757.94	2755.94
180000	2959.24	2951.70	2945.51	2940.42	2925.73	2920.17	2918.06
190000	3123.64	3115.68	3109.15	3103.78	3088.27	3082.40	3080.17
200000	3288.04	3279.66	3272.78	3267.14	3250.81	3244.64	3242.29
210000	3452.44	3443.65	3436.42	3430.49	3413.35	3406.87	3404.40
220000	3616.85	3607.63	3600.06	3593.85	3575.90	3569.10	3566.51
230000	3781.25	3771.61	3763.70	3757.21	3738.44	3731.33	3728.63
240000	3945.65	3935.60	3927.34	3920.56	3900.98	3893.56	3890.74
250000	4110.05	4099.58	4090.98	4083.92	4063.52	4055.79	4052.86

20.50 % Monthly Payments

LOAN AMOUNT	1	2	3	4	5	6	7
				YEARS			
100	9.25	5.07	3.70	3.03	2.63	2.38	2.20
200	18.50	10.15	7.40	6.05	5.26	4.75	4.40
500	46.24	25.37	18.50	15.13	13.16	11.88	11.01
1000	92.48	50.74	37.00	30.26	26.31	23.77	22.01
2000	184.96	101.47	74.00	60.52	52.63	47.53	44.02
5000	462.40	253.69	184.99	151.29	131.57	118.83	110.06
6000	554.88	304.42	221.99	181.55	157.88	142.59	132.07
7000	647.36	355.16	258.99	211.80	184.20	166.36	154.08
8000	739.83	405.90	295.99	242.06	210.51	190.12	176.09
9000	832.31	456.64	332.99	272.32	236.82	213.89	198.10
10000	924.79	507.37	369.99	302.58	263.14	237.65	220.11
12000	1109.75	608.85	443.98	363.09	315.76	285.18	264.14
15000	1387.19	761.06	554.98	453.87	394.71	356.48	330.17
20000	1849.59	1014.75	739.97	605.16	526.27	475.30	440.23
25000	2311.98	1268.44	924.96	756.45	657.84	594.13	550.28
30000	2774.38	1522.12	1109.96	907.73	789.41	712.96	660.34
31000	2866.86	1572.86	1146.95	937.99	815.73	736.72	682.35
32000	2959.34	1623.60	1183.95	968.25	842.04	760.49	704.36
33000	3051.82	1674.34	1220.95	998.51	868.35	784.25	726.37
34000	3144.30	1725.07	1257.95	1028.77	894.67	808.02	748.38
35000	3236.78	1775.81	1294.95	1059.02	920.98	831.78	770.40
36000	3329.26	1826.55	1331.95	1089.28	947.29	855.55	792.41
37000	3421.74	1877.29	1368.95	1119.54	973.61	879.31	814.42
38000	3514.21	1928.02	1405.94	1149.80	999.92	903.08	836.43
39000	3606.69	1978.76	1442.94	1180.05	1026.24	926.84	858.44
40000	3699.17	2029.50	1479.94	1210.31	1052.55	950.61	880.45
41000	3791.65	2080.24	1516.94	1240.57	1078.86	974.37	902.46
42000	3884.13	2130.97	1553.94	1270.83	1105.18	998.14	924.47
43000	3976.61	2181.71	1590.94	1301.09	1131.49	1021.90	946.49
44000	4069.09	2232.45	1627.93	1331.34	1157.80	1045.67	968.50
45000	4161.57	2283.19	1664.93	1361.60	1184.12	1069.43	990.51
46000	4254.05	2333.92	1701.93	1391.86	1210.43	1093.20	1012.52
47000	4346.53	2384.66	1738.93	1422.12	1236.74	1116.96	1034.53
48000	4439.01	2435.40	1775.93	1452.37	1263.06	1140.73	1056.54
49000	4531.49	2486.14	1812.93	1482.63	1289.37	1164.49	1078.55
50000	4623.97	2536.87	1849.93	1512.89	1315.69	1188.26	1100.56
51000	4716.45	2587.61	1886.92	1543.15	1342.00	1212.02	1122.58
52000	4808.93	2638.35	1923.92	1573.41	1368.31	1235.79	1144.59
53000	4901.40	2689.09	1960.92	1603.66	1394.63	1259.55	1166.60
54000	4993.88	2739.82	1997.92	1633.92	1420.94	1283.32	1188.61
55000	5086.36	2790.56	2034.92	1664.18	1447.25	1307.08	1210.62
56000	5178.84	2841.30	2071.92	1694.44	1473.57	1330.85	1232.63
57000	5271.32	2892.04	2108.92	1724.69	1499.88	1354.61	1254.64
58000	5363.80	2942.77	2145.91	1754.95	1526.20	1378.38	1276.66
59000	5456.28	2993.51	2182.91	1785.21	1552.51	1402.15	1298.67
60000	5548.76	3044.25	2219.91	1815.47	1578.82	1425.91	1320.68
65000	6011.16	3297.94	2404.90	1966.76	1710.39	1544.74	1430.73
70000	6473.55	3551.62	2589.90	2118.05	1841.96	1663.56	1540.79
75000	6935.95	3805.31	2774.89	2269.34	1973.53	1782.39	1650.85
80000	7398.35	4059.00	2959.88	2420.62	2105.10	1901.21	1760.90
85000	7860.74	4312.69	3144.87	2571.91	2236.67	2020.04	1870.96
90000	8323.14	4566.37	3329.87	2723.20	2368.23	2138.87	1981.02
95000	8785.54	4820.06	3514.86	2874.49	2499.80	2257.69	2091.07
100000	9247.93	5073.75	3699.85	3025.78	2631.37	2376.52	2201.13
105000	9710.33	5327.44	3884.84	3177.07	2762.94	2495.34	2311.19
110000	10172.73	5581.12	4069.84	3328.36	2894.51	2614.17	2421.24
120000	11097.52	6088.50	4439.82	3630.94	3157.65	2851.82	2641.36
130000	12022.31	6595.87	4809.81	3933.51	3420.78	3089.47	2861.47
140000	12947.11	7103.25	5179.79	4236.09	3683.92	3327.12	3081.58
150000	13871.90	7610.62	5549.78	4538.67	3947.06	3564.78	3301.69
160000	14796.69	8118.00	5919.76	4841.25	4210.20	3802.43	3521.81
170000	15721.49	8625.37	6289.75	5143.83	4473.33	4040.08	3741.92
180000	16646.28	9132.75	6659.73	5446.41	4736.47	4277.73	3962.03
190000	17571.07	9640.12	7029.72	5748.98	4999.61	4515.38	4182.15
200000	18495.87	10147.50	7399.70	6051.56	5262.74	4753.03	4402.26
210000	19420.66	10654.87	7769.69	6354.14	5525.88	4990.69	4622.37
220000	20345.45	11162.25	8139.67	6656.72	5789.02	5228.34	4842.49
230000	21270.25	11669.62	8509.66	6959.30	6052.16	5465.99	5062.60
240000	22195.04	12177.00	8879.64	7261.87	6315.29	5703.64	5282.71
250000	23119.83	12684.37	9249.63	7564.45	6578.43	5941.29	5502.82

Monthly Payments 20.50 %

LOAN AMOUNT	8	9	10	11	12	13	14
100	2.08	1.98	1.91	1.86	1.81	1.78	1.75
200	4.15	3.96	3.82	3.71	3.63	3.56	3.51
500	10.38	9.91	9.56	9.28	9.07	8.90	8.77
1000	20.75	19.82	19.11	18.57	18.14	17.80	17.54
2000	41.50	39.64	38.22	37.13	36.28	35.61	35.08
5000	103.76	99.09	95.55	92.83	90.70	89.02	87.69
6000	124.51	118.91	114.67	111.40	108.84	106.83	105.23
7000	145.26	138.73	133.78	129.96	126.98	124.63	122.76
8000	166.01	158.54	152.89	148.53	145.12	142.44	140.30
9000	186.76	178.36	172.00	167.09	163.26	160.24	157.84
10000	207.51	198.18	191.11	185.66	181.40	178.05	175.38
12000	249.02	237.82	229.33	222.79	217.68	213.66	210.45
15000	311.27	297.27	286.66	278.49	272.11	267.07	263.06
20000	415.03	396.36	382.22	371.32	362.81	356.09	350.75
25000	518.78	495.45	477.77	464.15	453.51	445.12	438.44
30000	622.54	594.54	573.33	556.98	544.21	534.14	526.13
31000	643.29	614.36	592.44	575.55	562.35	551.94	543.66
32000	664.04	634.18	611.55	594.11	580.49	569.75	561.20
33000	684.80	654.00	630.66	612.68	598.63	587.55	578.74
34000	705.55	673.82	649.77	631.24	616.77	605.36	596.28
35000	726.30	693.63	668.88	649.81	634.91	623.16	613.82
36000	747.05	713.45	688.00	668.38	653.05	640.97	631.35
37000	767.80	733.27	707.11	686.94	671.20	658.77	648.89
38000	788.55	753.09	726.22	705.51	689.34	676.58	666.43
39000	809.30	772.91	745.33	724.07	707.48	694.38	683.97
40000	830.05	792.72	764.44	742.64	725.62	712.19	701.50
41000	850.81	812.54	783.55	761.21	743.76	729.99	719.04
42000	871.56	832.36	802.66	779.77	761.90	747.79	736.58
43000	892.31	852.18	821.77	798.34	780.04	765.60	754.12
44000	913.06	872.00	840.88	816.90	798.18	783.40	771.65
45000	933.81	891.81	859.99	835.47	816.32	801.21	789.19
46000	954.56	911.63	879.11	854.04	834.46	819.01	806.73
47000	975.31	931.45	898.22	872.60	852.60	836.82	824.27
48000	996.07	951.27	917.33	891.17	870.74	854.62	841.80
49000	1016.82	971.09	936.44	909.73	888.88	872.43	859.34
50000	1037.57	990.90	955.55	928.30	907.02	890.23	876.88
51000	1058.32	1010.72	974.66	946.87	925.16	908.04	894.42
52000	1079.07	1030.54	993.77	965.43	943.30	925.84	911.95
53000	1099.82	1050.36	1012.88	984.00	961.44	943.65	929.49
54000	1120.57	1070.18	1031.99	1002.56	979.58	961.45	947.03
55000	1141.33	1090.00	1051.10	1021.13	997.72	979.26	964.57
56000	1162.08	1109.81	1070.22	1039.70	1015.86	997.06	982.10
57000	1182.83	1129.63	1089.33	1058.26	1034.00	1014.86	999.64
58000	1203.58	1149.45	1108.44	1076.83	1052.14	1032.67	1017.18
59000	1224.33	1169.27	1127.55	1095.39	1070.28	1050.47	1034.72
60000	1245.08	1189.09	1146.66	1113.96	1088.42	1068.28	1052.25
65000	1348.84	1288.18	1242.21	1206.79	1179.13	1157.30	1139.94
70000	1452.60	1387.27	1337.77	1299.62	1269.83	1246.32	1227.63
75000	1556.35	1486.36	1433.32	1392.45	1360.53	1335.35	1315.32
80000	1660.11	1585.45	1528.88	1485.28	1451.23	1424.37	1403.01
85000	1763.87	1684.54	1624.43	1578.11	1541.94	1513.39	1490.69
90000	1867.62	1783.63	1719.99	1670.94	1632.64	1602.42	1578.38
95000	1971.38	1882.72	1815.54	1763.77	1723.34	1691.44	1666.07
100000	2075.14	1981.81	1911.10	1856.60	1814.04	1780.46	1753.76
105000	2178.89	2080.90	2006.65	1949.43	1904.74	1869.49	1841.45
110000	2282.65	2179.99	2102.21	2042.26	1995.45	1958.51	1929.13
120000	2490.16	2378.17	2293.32	2227.92	2176.85	2136.56	2104.51
130000	2697.68	2576.35	2484.43	2413.58	2358.25	2314.60	2279.88
140000	2905.19	2774.53	2675.54	2599.24	2539.66	2492.65	2455.26
150000	3112.70	2972.71	2866.65	2784.90	2721.06	2670.70	2630.64
160000	3320.22	3170.90	3057.76	2970.56	2902.47	2848.74	2806.01
170000	3527.73	3369.08	3248.87	3156.22	3083.87	3026.79	2981.39
180000	3735.25	3567.26	3439.98	3341.88	3265.27	3204.83	3156.76
190000	3942.76	3765.44	3631.09	3527.54	3446.68	3382.88	3332.14
200000	4150.27	3963.62	3822.20	3713.20	3628.08	3560.93	3507.52
210000	4357.79	4161.80	4013.31	3898.86	3809.49	3738.97	3682.89
220000	4565.30	4359.98	4204.42	4084.52	3990.89	3917.02	3858.27
230000	4772.81	4558.16	4395.53	4270.18	4172.30	4095.07	4033.64
240000	4980.33	4756.34	4586.64	4455.84	4353.70	4273.11	4209.02
250000	5187.84	4954.52	4777.75	4641.50	4535.10	4451.16	4384.39

20.50 % Monthly Payments

LOAN AMOUNT	15	16	17	18	19	20	21
100	1.73	1.72	1.70	1.69	1.68	1.67	1.67
200	3.46	3.43	3.40	3.38	3.36	3.35	3.33
500	8.66	8.58	8.51	8.45	8.40	8.37	8.34
1000	17.32	17.15	17.01	16.90	16.81	16.73	16.67
2000	34.65	34.30	34.03	33.80	33.62	33.47	33.35
5000	86.62	85.76	85.06	84.50	84.04	83.67	83.37
6000	103.94	102.91	102.08	101.40	100.85	100.40	100.04
7000	121.27	120.06	119.09	118.30	117.66	117.14	116.71
8000	138.59	137.21	136.10	135.20	134.47	133.87	133.38
9000	155.91	154.37	153.12	152.10	151.28	150.61	150.06
10000	173.24	171.52	170.13	169.00	168.09	167.34	166.73
12000	207.89	205.82	204.15	202.80	201.70	200.81	200.08
15000	259.86	257.28	255.19	253.50	252.13	251.01	250.10
20000	346.48	343.04	340.26	338.00	336.17	334.68	333.46
25000	433.09	428.79	425.32	422.50	420.21	418.35	416.83
30000	519.71	514.55	510.38	507.00	504.26	502.02	500.19
31000	537.04	531.71	527.40	523.90	521.07	518.75	516.87
32000	554.36	548.86	544.41	540.81	537.87	535.49	533.54
33000	571.69	566.01	561.42	557.71	554.68	552.22	550.21
34000	589.01	583.16	578.44	574.61	571.49	568.96	566.89
35000	606.33	600.31	595.45	591.51	588.30	585.69	583.56
36000	623.66	617.46	612.46	608.41	605.11	602.42	600.23
37000	640.98	634.62	629.47	625.31	621.92	619.16	616.91
38000	658.30	651.77	646.49	642.21	638.73	635.89	633.58
39000	675.63	668.92	663.50	659.11	655.54	652.63	650.25
40000	692.95	686.07	680.51	676.01	672.34	669.36	666.92
41000	710.28	703.22	697.53	692.91	689.15	686.09	683.60
42000	727.60	720.38	714.54	709.81	705.96	702.83	700.27
43000	744.92	737.53	731.55	726.71	722.77	719.56	716.94
44000	762.25	754.68	748.56	743.61	739.58	736.30	733.62
45000	779.57	771.83	765.58	760.51	756.39	753.03	750.29
46000	796.89	788.98	782.59	777.41	773.20	769.76	766.96
47000	814.22	806.13	799.60	794.31	790.00	786.50	783.64
48000	831.54	823.29	816.62	811.21	806.81	803.23	800.31
49000	848.87	840.44	833.63	828.11	823.62	819.97	816.98
50000	866.19	857.59	850.64	845.01	840.43	836.70	833.6
51000	883.51	874.74	867.65	861.91	857.24	853.43	850.3
52000	900.84	891.89	884.67	878.81	874.05	870.17	867.0
53000	918.16	909.04	901.68	895.71	890.86	886.90	883.6
54000	935.48	926.20	918.69	912.61	907.66	903.64	900.3
55000	952.81	943.35	935.70	929.51	924.47	920.37	917.0
56000	970.13	960.50	952.72	946.41	941.28	937.10	933.6
57000	987.46	977.65	969.73	963.31	958.09	953.84	950.3
58000	1004.78	994.80	986.74	980.21	974.90	970.57	967.0
59000	1022.10	1011.96	1003.76	997.11	991.71	987.31	983.7
60000	1039.43	1029.11	1020.77	1014.01	1008.52	1004.04	1000.3
65000	1126.05	1114.87	1105.83	1098.51	1092.56	1087.71	1083.7
70000	1212.67	1200.63	1190.90	1183.01	1176.60	1171.38	1167.1
75000	1299.28	1286.38	1275.96	1267.51	1260.64	1255.05	1250.4
80000	1385.90	1372.14	1361.03	1352.01	1344.69	1338.72	1333.8
85000	1472.52	1457.90	1446.09	1436.51	1428.73	1422.39	1417.2
90000	1559.14	1543.66	1531.15	1521.01	1512.77	1506.06	1500.5
95000	1645.76	1629.42	1616.22	1605.52	1596.82	1589.73	1583.9
100000	1732.38	1715.18	1701.28	1690.02	1680.86	1673.40	1667.3
105000	1819.00	1800.94	1786.35	1774.52	1764.90	1757.07	1750.6
110000	1905.62	1886.70	1871.41	1859.02	1848.95	1840.74	1834.0
120000	2078.86	2058.21	2041.54	2028.02	2017.03	2008.08	2000.7
130000	2252.09	2229.73	2211.67	2197.02	2185.12	2175.42	2167.5
140000	2425.33	2401.25	2381.79	2366.02	2353.20	2342.76	2334.2
150000	2598.57	2572.77	2551.92	2535.02	2521.29	2510.10	2500.9
160000	2771.81	2744.29	2722.05	2704.03	2689.37	2677.44	2667.7
170000	2945.05	2915.80	2892.18	2873.03	2857.46	2844.78	2834.4
180000	3118.28	3087.32	3062.31	3042.03	3025.55	3012.12	3001.1
190000	3291.52	3258.84	3232.43	3211.03	3193.63	3179.46	3167.8
200000	3464.76	3430.36	3402.56	3380.03	3361.72	3346.80	3334.6
210000	3638.00	3601.88	3572.69	3549.03	3529.80	3514.14	3501.3
220000	3811.23	3773.39	3742.82	3718.04	3697.89	3681.48	3668.0
230000	3984.47	3944.91	3912.95	3887.04	3865.98	3848.82	3834.8
240000	4157.71	4116.43	4083.08	4056.04	4034.06	4016.16	4001.5
250000	4330.95	4287.95	4253.20	4225.04	4202.15	4183.50	4168.2

Monthly Payments 20.50 %

LOAN AMOUNT	22	23	24	25	30	35	40
100	1.66	1.66	1.65	1.65	1.64	1.64	1.64
200	3.32	3.32	3.31	3.30	3.29	3.28	3.28
500	8.31	8.29	8.27	8.26	8.22	8.21	8.20
1000	16.62	16.58	16.55	16.52	16.44	16.41	16.40
2000	33.25	33.17	33.10	33.04	32.89	32.83	32.81
5000	83.12	82.91	82.75	82.61	82.22	82.07	82.02
6000	99.74	99.50	99.30	99.13	98.66	98.48	98.42
7000	116.36	116.08	115.85	115.65	115.10	114.90	114.82
8000	132.99	132.66	132.39	132.18	131.55	131.31	131.22
9000	149.61	149.24	148.94	148.70	147.99	147.73	147.63
10000	166.23	165.83	165.49	165.22	164.43	164.14	164.03
12000	199.48	198.99	198.59	198.26	197.32	196.97	196.84
15000	249.35	248.74	248.24	247.83	246.65	246.21	246.05
20000	332.47	331.65	330.99	330.44	328.87	328.28	328.06
25000	415.58	414.57	413.73	413.05	411.09	410.35	410.08
30000	498.70	497.48	496.48	495.66	493.30	492.42	492.09
31000	515.32	514.06	513.03	512.18	509.75	508.84	508.49
32000	531.95	530.65	529.58	528.70	526.19	525.25	524.90
33000	548.57	547.23	546.13	545.23	542.63	541.66	541.30
34000	565.19	563.81	562.68	561.75	559.08	558.08	557.70
35000	581.82	580.39	579.23	578.27	575.52	574.49	574.11
36000	598.44	596.98	595.78	594.79	591.97	590.91	590.51
37000	615.06	613.56	612.33	611.31	608.41	607.32	606.91
38000	631.69	630.14	628.87	627.84	624.85	623.74	623.32
39000	648.31	646.72	645.42	644.36	641.30	640.15	639.72
40000	664.94	663.31	661.97	660.88	657.74	656.56	656.12
41000	681.56	679.89	678.52	677.40	674.18	672.98	672.52
42000	698.18	696.47	695.07	693.92	690.63	689.39	688.93
43000	714.81	713.05	711.62	710.45	707.07	705.81	705.33
44000	731.43	729.64	728.17	726.97	723.51	722.22	721.73
45000	748.05	746.22	744.72	743.49	739.96	738.63	738.14
46000	764.68	762.80	761.27	760.01	756.40	755.05	754.54
47000	781.30	779.39	777.82	776.53	772.84	771.46	770.94
48000	797.92	795.97	794.37	793.06	789.29	787.88	787.35
49000	814.55	812.55	810.92	809.58	805.73	804.29	803.75
50000	831.17	829.13	827.47	826.10	822.17	820.70	820.15
51000	847.79	845.72	844.02	842.62	838.62	837.12	836.55
52000	864.42	862.30	860.57	859.14	855.06	853.53	852.96
53000	881.04	878.88	877.11	875.67	871.50	869.95	869.36
54000	897.66	895.46	893.66	892.19	887.95	886.36	885.76
55000	914.29	912.05	910.21	908.71	904.39	902.77	902.17
56000	930.91	928.63	926.76	925.23	920.84	919.19	918.57
57000	947.53	945.21	943.31	941.75	937.28	935.60	934.97
58000	964.16	961.79	959.86	958.28	953.72	952.02	951.38
59000	980.78	978.38	976.41	974.80	970.17	968.43	967.78
60000	997.40	994.96	992.96	991.32	986.61	984.85	984.18
65000	1080.52	1077.87	1075.71	1073.93	1068.83	1066.92	1066.20
70000	1163.64	1160.79	1158.45	1156.54	1151.04	1148.99	1148.21
75000	1246.75	1243.70	1241.20	1239.15	1233.26	1231.06	1230.23
80000	1329.87	1326.61	1323.95	1321.76	1315.48	1313.13	1312.24
85000	1412.99	1409.53	1406.69	1404.37	1397.70	1395.20	1394.26
90000	1496.10	1492.44	1489.44	1486.98	1479.91	1477.27	1476.27
95000	1579.22	1575.35	1572.19	1569.59	1562.13	1559.34	1558.29
100000	1662.34	1658.27	1654.93	1652.20	1644.35	1641.41	1640.30
105000	1745.45	1741.18	1737.68	1734.81	1726.57	1723.48	1722.32
110000	1828.57	1824.09	1820.43	1817.42	1808.78	1805.55	1804.33
120000	1994.81	1989.92	1985.92	1982.64	1973.22	1969.69	1968.36
130000	2161.04	2155.75	2151.41	2147.86	2137.65	2133.83	2132.39
140000	2327.27	2321.57	2316.91	2313.08	2302.09	2297.97	2296.42
150000	2493.51	2487.40	2482.40	2478.30	2466.52	2462.11	2460.46
160000	2659.74	2653.23	2647.89	2643.52	2630.96	2626.25	2624.49
170000	2825.97	2819.05	2813.39	2808.74	2795.39	2790.39	2788.52
180000	2992.21	2984.88	2978.88	2973.96	2959.83	2954.54	2952.55
190000	3158.44	3150.71	3144.37	3139.18	3124.26	3118.68	3116.58
200000	3324.68	3316.53	3309.87	3304.40	3288.70	3282.82	3280.61
210000	3490.91	3482.36	3475.36	3469.62	3453.13	3446.96	3444.64
220000	3657.14	3648.19	3640.85	3634.84	3617.57	3611.10	3608.67
230000	3823.38	3814.01	3806.35	3800.06	3782.00	3775.24	3772.70
240000	3989.61	3979.84	3971.84	3965.28	3946.44	3939.38	3936.73
250000	4155.84	4145.67	4137.33	4130.50	4110.87	4103.52	4100.76

20.75 % Monthly Payments

LOAN AMOUNT	YEARS 1	2	3	4	5	6	7
100	9.26	5.08	3.71	3.04	2.64	2.39	2.21
200	18.52	10.17	7.42	6.08	5.29	4.78	4.43
500	46.29	25.42	18.56	15.19	13.22	11.95	11.07
1000	92.59	50.85	37.12	30.38	26.44	23.90	22.15
2000	185.18	101.70	74.23	60.76	52.88	47.80	44.30
5000	462.95	254.25	185.58	151.90	132.21	119.49	110.75
6000	555.54	305.10	222.69	182.28	158.65	143.39	132.90
7000	648.13	355.95	259.81	212.66	185.09	167.29	155.05
8000	740.72	406.80	296.93	243.04	211.53	191.19	177.20
9000	833.31	457.65	334.04	273.42	237.97	215.09	199.35
10000	925.90	508.50	371.16	303.80	264.42	238.98	221.50
12000	1111.07	610.20	445.39	364.56	317.30	286.78	265.80
15000	1388.84	762.75	556.74	455.70	396.62	358.48	332.24
20000	1851.79	1017.00	742.31	607.61	528.83	477.97	442.99
25000	2314.74	1271.25	927.89	759.51	661.04	597.46	553.74
30000	2777.69	1525.50	1113.47	911.41	793.25	716.95	664.49
31000	2870.28	1576.35	1150.59	941.79	819.69	740.85	686.64
32000	2962.86	1627.20	1187.70	972.17	846.13	764.75	708.79
33000	3055.45	1678.05	1224.82	1002.55	872.57	788.65	730.94
34000	3148.04	1728.90	1261.93	1032.93	899.01	812.54	753.09
35000	3240.63	1779.75	1299.05	1063.31	925.46	836.44	775.24
36000	3333.22	1830.60	1336.17	1093.69	951.90	860.34	797.39
37000	3425.81	1881.45	1373.28	1124.07	978.34	884.24	819.54
38000	3518.40	1932.30	1410.40	1154.45	1004.78	908.14	841.69
39000	3610.99	1983.15	1447.51	1184.83	1031.22	932.04	863.84
40000	3703.58	2034.00	1484.63	1215.21	1057.66	955.93	885.99
41000	3796.17	2084.85	1521.74	1245.59	1084.11	979.83	908.13
42000	3888.76	2135.70	1558.86	1275.97	1110.55	1003.73	930.28
43000	3981.35	2186.55	1595.98	1306.35	1136.99	1027.63	952.43
44000	4073.94	2237.40	1633.09	1336.73	1163.43	1051.53	974.58
45000	4166.53	2288.25	1670.21	1367.11	1189.87	1075.43	996.73
46000	4259.12	2339.09	1707.32	1397.49	1216.31	1099.32	1018.88
47000	4351.71	2389.94	1744.44	1427.87	1242.76	1123.22	1041.03
48000	4444.30	2440.79	1781.55	1458.25	1269.20	1147.12	1063.18
49000	4536.89	2491.64	1818.67	1488.63	1295.64	1171.02	1085.33
50000	4629.48	2542.49	1855.79	1519.01	1322.08	1194.92	1107.48
51000	4722.07	2593.34	1892.90	1549.40	1348.52	1218.82	1129.63
52000	4814.66	2644.19	1930.02	1579.78	1374.96	1242.72	1151.78
53000	4907.24	2695.04	1967.13	1610.16	1401.41	1266.61	1173.93
54000	4999.83	2745.89	2004.25	1640.54	1427.85	1290.51	1196.08
55000	5092.42	2796.74	2041.36	1670.92	1454.29	1314.41	1218.23
56000	5185.01	2847.59	2078.48	1701.30	1480.73	1338.31	1240.38
57000	5277.60	2898.44	2115.60	1731.68	1507.17	1362.21	1262.53
58000	5370.19	2949.29	2152.71	1762.06	1533.61	1386.11	1284.68
59000	5462.78	3000.14	2189.83	1792.44	1560.05	1410.00	1306.83
60000	5555.37	3050.99	2226.94	1822.82	1586.50	1433.90	1328.98
65000	6018.32	3305.24	2412.52	1974.72	1718.70	1553.39	1439.73
70000	6481.27	3559.49	2598.10	2126.62	1850.91	1672.89	1550.47
75000	6944.21	3813.74	2783.68	2278.52	1983.12	1792.38	1661.22
80000	7407.16	4067.99	2969.26	2430.42	2115.33	1911.87	1771.97
85000	7870.11	4322.24	3154.83	2582.33	2247.54	2031.36	1882.72
90000	8333.06	4576.49	3340.41	2734.23	2379.74	2150.85	1993.47
95000	8796.00	4830.74	3525.99	2886.13	2511.95	2270.34	2104.21
100000	9258.95	5084.99	3711.57	3038.03	2644.16	2389.84	2214.96
105000	9721.90	5339.24	3897.15	3189.93	2776.37	2509.33	2325.71
110000	10184.85	5593.49	4082.73	3341.83	2908.58	2628.82	2436.4
120000	11110.74	6101.99	4453.88	3645.64	3172.99	2867.80	2657.9
130000	12036.64	6610.49	4825.04	3949.44	3437.41	3106.79	2879.45
140000	12962.53	7118.98	5196.20	4253.24	3701.82	3345.77	3100.95
150000	13888.43	7627.48	5567.36	4557.04	3966.24	3584.76	3322.44
160000	14814.32	8135.98	5938.51	4860.85	4230.66	3823.74	3543.94
170000	15740.22	8644.48	6309.67	5164.65	4495.07	4062.72	3765.44
180000	16666.11	9152.98	6680.83	5468.45	4759.49	4301.71	3986.93
190000	17592.01	9661.48	7051.98	5772.26	5023.90	4540.69	4208.43
200000	18517.90	10169.98	7423.14	6076.06	5288.32	4779.67	4429.93
210000	19443.80	10678.48	7794.30	6379.86	5552.74	5018.66	4651.4
220000	20369.69	11186.98	8165.45	6683.67	5817.15	5257.64	4872.9
230000	21295.59	11695.47	8536.61	6987.47	6081.57	5496.62	5094.4
240000	22221.49	12203.97	8907.77	7291.27	6345.99	5735.61	5315.9
250000	23147.38	12712.47	9278.93	7595.07	6610.40	5974.59	5537.4

Monthly Payments 20.75 %

LOAN AMOUNT	8	9	10	11	12	13	14
				YEARS			
100	2.09	2.00	1.93	1.87	1.83	1.80	1.77
200	4.18	3.99	3.85	3.74	3.66	3.59	3.54
500	10.45	9.98	9.63	9.36	9.15	8.98	8.85
1000	20.89	19.97	19.26	18.72	18.30	17.97	17.70
2000	41.79	39.93	38.53	37.44	36.60	35.94	35.41
5000	104.47	99.83	96.32	93.61	91.50	89.84	88.52
6000	125.37	119.80	115.58	112.33	109.80	107.81	106.23
7000	146.26	139.76	134.84	131.06	128.10	125.78	123.93
8000	167.16	159.73	154.11	149.78	146.40	143.75	141.64
9000	188.05	179.69	173.37	168.50	164.71	161.71	159.34
10000	208.95	199.66	192.63	187.22	183.01	179.68	177.04
12000	250.74	239.59	231.16	224.67	219.61	215.62	212.45
15000	313.42	299.49	288.95	280.84	274.51	269.52	265.57
20000	417.89	399.32	385.27	374.45	366.01	359.37	354.09
25000	522.37	499.15	481.58	468.06	457.51	449.21	442.61
30000	626.84	598.98	577.90	561.67	549.02	539.05	531.13
31000	647.73	618.95	597.16	580.39	567.32	557.02	548.84
32000	668.63	638.91	616.42	599.12	585.62	574.99	566.54
33000	689.52	658.88	635.69	617.84	603.92	592.95	584.25
34000	710.42	678.84	654.95	636.56	622.22	610.92	601.95
35000	731.31	698.81	674.21	655.28	640.52	628.89	619.65
36000	752.21	718.78	693.48	674.01	658.82	646.86	637.36
37000	773.10	738.74	712.74	692.73	677.12	664.83	655.06
38000	794.00	758.71	732.00	711.45	695.42	682.80	672.77
39000	814.89	778.67	751.27	730.17	713.72	700.76	690.47
40000	835.78	798.64	770.53	748.90	732.02	718.73	708.18
41000	856.68	818.61	789.79	767.62	750.32	736.70	725.88
42000	877.57	838.57	809.06	786.34	768.62	754.67	743.59
43000	898.47	858.54	828.32	805.06	786.92	772.64	761.29
44000	919.36	878.50	847.58	823.78	805.23	790.60	778.99
45000	940.26	898.47	866.85	842.51	823.53	808.57	796.70
46000	961.15	918.44	886.11	861.23	841.83	826.54	814.40
47000	982.05	938.40	905.37	879.95	860.13	844.51	832.11
48000	1002.94	958.37	924.64	898.67	878.43	862.48	849.81
49000	1023.84	978.33	943.90	917.40	896.73	880.45	867.52
50000	1044.73	998.30	963.16	936.12	915.03	898.41	885.22
51000	1065.63	1018.27	982.43	954.84	933.33	916.38	902.93
52000	1086.52	1038.23	1001.69	973.56	951.63	934.35	920.63
53000	1107.41	1058.20	1020.95	992.29	969.93	952.32	938.33
54000	1128.31	1078.16	1040.22	1011.01	988.23	970.29	956.04
55000	1149.20	1098.13	1059.48	1029.73	1006.53	988.26	973.74
56000	1170.10	1118.10	1078.74	1048.45	1024.83	1006.22	991.45
57000	1190.99	1138.06	1098.01	1067.18	1043.13	1024.19	1009.15
58000	1211.89	1158.03	1117.27	1085.90	1061.43	1042.16	1026.86
59000	1232.78	1177.99	1136.53	1104.62	1079.73	1060.13	1044.56
60000	1253.68	1197.96	1155.80	1123.34	1098.03	1078.10	1062.27
65000	1358.15	1297.79	1252.11	1216.95	1189.54	1167.94	1150.79
70000	1462.62	1397.62	1348.43	1310.57	1281.04	1257.78	1239.31
75000	1567.10	1497.45	1444.75	1404.18	1372.54	1347.62	1327.83
80000	1671.57	1597.28	1541.06	1497.79	1464.05	1437.46	1416.35
85000	1776.04	1697.11	1637.38	1591.40	1555.55	1527.31	1504.88
90000	1880.52	1796.94	1733.70	1685.01	1647.05	1617.15	1593.40
95000	1984.99	1896.77	1830.01	1778.63	1738.56	1706.99	1681.92
100000	2089.46	1996.60	1926.33	1872.24	1830.06	1796.83	1770.44
105000	2193.93	2096.43	2022.64	1965.85	1921.56	1886.67	1858.96
110000	2298.41	2196.26	2118.96	2059.46	2013.06	1976.51	1947.49
120000	2507.35	2395.92	2311.59	2246.69	2196.07	2156.20	2124.53
130000	2716.30	2595.58	2504.23	2433.91	2379.08	2335.88	2301.58
140000	2925.25	2795.24	2696.86	2621.13	2562.08	2515.56	2478.62
150000	3134.19	2994.90	2889.49	2808.36	2745.09	2695.24	2655.66
160000	3343.14	3194.56	3082.12	2995.58	2928.09	2874.93	2832.71
170000	3552.08	3394.22	3274.76	3182.81	3111.10	3054.61	3009.75
180000	3761.03	3593.88	3467.39	3370.03	3294.10	3234.29	3186.80
190000	3969.98	3793.54	3660.02	3557.25	3477.11	3413.98	3363.84
200000	4178.92	3993.20	3852.66	3744.48	3660.12	3593.66	3540.89
210000	4387.87	4192.86	4045.29	3931.70	3843.12	3773.34	3717.93
220000	4596.82	4392.52	4237.92	4118.92	4026.13	3953.02	3894.97
230000	4805.76	4592.18	4430.55	4306.15	4209.13	4132.71	4072.02
240000	5014.71	4791.84	4623.19	4493.37	4392.14	4312.39	4249.06
250000	5223.65	4991.50	4815.82	4680.60	4575.15	4492.07	4426.11

20.75 % Monthly Payments

LOAN AMOUNT	15	16	17	18	19	20	21
				YEARS			
100	1.75	1.73	1.72	1.71	1.70	1.69	1.69
200	3.50	3.46	3.44	3.42	3.40	3.38	3.37
500	8.75	8.66	8.59	8.54	8.49	8.46	8.43
1000	17.49	17.32	17.19	17.08	16.99	16.91	16.86
2000	34.99	34.65	34.38	34.15	33.97	33.83	33.71
5000	87.47	86.62	85.94	85.39	84.94	84.57	84.28
6000	104.96	103.95	103.13	102.46	101.92	101.49	101.13
7000	122.45	121.27	120.31	119.54	118.91	118.40	117.99
8000	139.95	138.59	137.50	136.62	135.90	135.32	134.84
9000	157.44	155.92	154.69	153.69	152.89	152.23	151.70
10000	174.94	173.24	171.88	170.77	169.87	169.14	168.55
12000	209.92	207.89	206.25	204.92	203.85	202.97	202.26
15000	262.40	259.86	257.81	256.16	254.81	253.72	252.83
20000	349.87	346.48	343.75	341.54	339.75	338.29	337.10
25000	437.34	433.10	429.69	426.93	424.68	422.86	421.38
30000	524.81	519.73	515.63	512.31	509.62	507.43	505.65
31000	542.30	537.05	532.82	529.39	526.61	524.35	522.51
32000	559.79	554.37	550.00	546.47	543.60	541.26	539.36
33000	577.29	571.70	567.19	563.54	560.58	558.18	556.22
34000	594.78	589.02	584.38	580.62	577.57	575.09	573.07
35000	612.27	606.35	601.57	597.70	594.56	592.01	589.93
36000	629.77	623.67	618.75	614.77	611.55	608.92	606.78
37000	647.26	640.99	635.94	631.85	628.53	625.84	623.64
38000	664.76	658.32	653.13	648.93	645.52	642.75	640.49
39000	682.25	675.64	670.32	666.01	662.51	659.67	657.35
40000	699.74	692.97	687.50	683.08	679.50	676.58	674.20
41000	717.24	710.29	704.69	700.16	696.48	693.49	691.06
42000	734.73	727.62	721.88	717.24	713.47	710.41	707.91
43000	752.22	744.94	739.07	734.31	730.46	727.32	724.77
44000	769.72	762.26	756.25	751.39	747.45	744.24	741.63
45000	787.21	779.59	773.44	768.47	764.43	761.15	758.48
46000	804.70	796.91	790.63	785.54	781.42	778.07	775.34
47000	822.20	814.24	807.82	802.62	798.41	794.98	792.19
48000	839.69	831.56	825.00	819.70	815.39	811.90	809.05
49000	857.18	848.88	842.19	836.78	832.38	828.81	825.90
50000	874.68	866.21	859.38	853.85	849.37	845.72	842.76
51000	892.17	883.53	876.57	870.93	866.36	862.64	859.61
52000	909.66	900.86	893.75	888.01	883.34	879.55	876.47
53000	927.16	918.18	910.94	905.08	900.33	896.47	893.32
54000	944.65	935.51	928.13	922.16	917.32	913.38	910.18
55000	962.15	952.83	945.32	939.24	934.31	930.30	927.03
56000	979.64	970.15	962.50	956.32	951.29	947.21	943.89
57000	997.13	987.48	979.69	973.39	968.28	964.13	960.74
58000	1014.63	1004.80	996.88	990.47	985.27	981.04	977.60
59000	1032.12	1022.13	1014.07	1007.55	1002.26	997.95	994.45
60000	1049.61	1039.45	1031.25	1024.62	1019.24	1014.87	1011.31
65000	1137.08	1126.07	1117.19	1110.01	1104.18	1099.44	1095.58
70000	1224.55	1212.69	1203.13	1195.39	1189.12	1184.01	1179.86
75000	1312.02	1299.31	1289.07	1280.78	1274.05	1268.59	1264.13
80000	1399.48	1385.93	1375.01	1366.16	1358.99	1353.16	1348.41
85000	1486.95	1472.56	1460.94	1451.55	1443.93	1437.73	1432.68
90000	1574.42	1559.18	1546.88	1536.94	1528.87	1522.30	1516.96
95000	1661.89	1645.80	1632.82	1622.32	1613.80	1606.88	1601.24
100000	1749.36	1732.42	1718.76	1707.71	1698.74	1691.45	1685.51
105000	1836.82	1819.04	1804.70	1793.09	1783.68	1776.02	1769.79
110000	1924.29	1905.66	1890.63	1878.48	1868.61	1860.59	1854.06
120000	2099.23	2078.90	2062.51	2049.25	2038.49	2029.74	2022.61
130000	2274.16	2252.14	2234.39	2220.02	2208.36	2198.88	2191.16
140000	2449.10	2425.39	2406.26	2390.79	2378.23	2368.03	2359.72
150000	2624.03	2598.63	2578.14	2561.56	2548.11	2537.17	2528.27
160000	2798.97	2771.87	2750.01	2732.33	2717.98	2706.32	2696.82
170000	2973.90	2945.11	2921.89	2903.10	2887.86	2875.46	2865.37
180000	3148.84	3118.35	3093.76	3073.87	3057.73	3044.61	3033.92
190000	3323.78	3291.59	3265.64	3244.64	3227.60	3213.75	3202.47
200000	3498.71	3464.84	3437.52	3415.41	3397.48	3382.90	3371.02
210000	3673.65	3638.08	3609.39	3586.18	3567.35	3552.04	3539.57
220000	3848.58	3811.32	3781.27	3756.95	3737.23	3721.19	3708.13
230000	4023.52	3984.56	3953.14	3927.72	3907.10	3890.33	3876.68
240000	4198.45	4157.80	4125.02	4098.49	4076.97	4059.48	4045.23
250000	4373.39	4331.04	4296.90	4269.26	4246.85	4228.62	4213.78

Monthly Payments 20.75 %

LOAN AMOUNT	22	23	24	25	30	35	40
100	1.68	1.68	1.67	1.67	1.66	1.66	1.66
200	3.36	3.35	3.35	3.34	3.33	3.32	3.32
500	8.40	8.38	8.37	8.35	8.32	8.30	8.30
1000	16.81	16.77	16.73	16.71	16.63	16.60	16.59
2000	33.61	33.53	33.47	33.42	33.27	33.21	33.19
5000	84.03	83.84	83.67	83.54	83.16	83.02	82.97
6000	100.84	100.60	100.41	100.25	99.80	99.63	99.57
7000	117.65	117.37	117.14	116.96	116.43	116.23	116.16
8000	134.45	134.14	133.88	133.67	133.06	132.84	132.76
9000	151.26	150.90	150.61	150.38	149.70	149.44	149.35
10000	168.07	167.67	167.35	167.08	166.33	166.05	165.94
12000	201.68	201.21	200.82	200.50	199.59	199.26	199.13
15000	252.10	251.51	251.02	250.63	249.49	249.07	248.92
20000	336.13	335.34	334.70	334.17	332.66	332.10	331.89
25000	420.17	419.18	418.37	417.71	415.82	415.12	414.86
30000	504.20	503.01	502.04	501.25	498.99	498.15	497.83
31000	521.01	519.78	518.78	517.96	515.62	514.75	514.43
32000	537.81	536.55	535.51	534.67	532.25	531.36	531.02
33000	554.62	553.32	552.25	551.38	548.88	547.96	547.62
34000	571.43	570.08	568.98	568.09	565.52	564.57	564.21
35000	588.23	586.85	585.72	584.79	582.15	581.17	580.81
36000	605.04	603.62	602.45	601.50	598.78	597.78	597.40
37000	621.85	620.38	619.19	618.21	615.42	614.38	614.00
38000	638.65	637.15	635.92	634.92	632.05	630.99	630.59
39000	655.46	653.92	652.66	651.63	648.68	647.59	647.19
40000	672.27	670.69	669.39	668.34	665.31	664.20	663.78
41000	689.07	687.45	686.13	685.04	681.95	680.80	680.37
42000	705.88	704.22	702.86	701.75	698.58	697.41	696.97
43000	722.69	720.99	719.60	718.46	715.21	714.01	713.56
44000	739.49	737.75	736.33	735.17	731.85	730.62	730.16
45000	756.30	754.52	753.07	751.88	748.48	747.22	746.75
46000	773.11	771.29	769.80	768.59	765.11	763.83	763.35
47000	789.91	788.06	786.54	785.29	781.74	780.43	779.94
48000	806.72	804.82	803.27	802.00	798.38	797.04	796.54
49000	823.53	821.59	820.01	818.71	815.01	813.64	813.13
50000	840.33	838.36	836.74	835.42	831.64	830.24	829.72
51000	857.14	855.12	853.48	852.13	848.28	846.85	846.32
52000	873.95	871.89	870.21	868.84	864.91	863.45	862.91
53000	890.75	888.66	886.95	885.54	881.54	880.06	879.51
54000	907.56	905.43	903.68	902.25	898.17	896.66	896.10
55000	924.37	922.19	920.42	918.96	914.81	913.27	912.70
56000	941.17	938.96	937.15	935.67	931.44	929.87	929.29
57000	957.98	955.73	953.89	952.38	948.07	946.48	945.89
58000	974.79	972.49	970.62	969.09	964.71	963.08	962.48
59000	991.59	989.26	987.35	985.79	981.34	979.69	979.08
60000	1008.40	1006.03	1004.09	1002.50	997.97	996.29	995.67
65000	1092.43	1089.86	1087.76	1086.05	1081.14	1079.32	1078.64
70000	1176.47	1173.70	1171.44	1169.59	1164.30	1162.34	1161.61
75000	1260.50	1257.54	1255.11	1253.13	1247.46	1245.37	1244.59
80000	1344.54	1341.37	1338.79	1336.67	1330.63	1328.39	1327.56
85000	1428.57	1425.21	1422.46	1420.21	1413.79	1411.42	1410.53
90000	1512.60	1509.04	1506.13	1503.76	1496.96	1494.44	1493.50
95000	1596.64	1592.88	1589.81	1587.30	1580.12	1577.47	1576.48
100000	1680.67	1676.71	1673.48	1670.84	1663.29	1660.49	1659.45
105000	1764.70	1760.55	1757.16	1754.38	1746.45	1743.51	1742.42
110000	1848.74	1844.39	1840.83	1837.92	1829.62	1826.54	1825.39
120000	2016.80	2012.06	2008.18	2005.01	1995.94	1992.59	1991.34
130000	2184.87	2179.73	2175.53	2172.09	2162.27	2158.64	2157.28
140000	2352.94	2347.40	2342.88	2339.17	2328.60	2324.69	2323.23
150000	2521.00	2515.07	2510.22	2506.26	2494.93	2490.73	2489.17
160000	2689.07	2682.74	2677.57	2673.34	2661.26	2656.78	2655.12
170000	2857.14	2850.41	2844.92	2840.43	2827.59	2822.83	2821.06
180000	3025.20	3018.09	3012.27	3007.51	2993.92	2988.88	2987.01
190000	3193.27	3185.76	3179.62	3174.59	3160.24	3154.93	3152.95
200000	3361.34	3353.43	3346.97	3341.68	3326.57	3320.98	3318.90
210000	3529.40	3521.10	3514.31	3508.76	3492.90	3487.03	3484.84
220000	3697.47	3688.77	3681.66	3675.85	3659.23	3653.08	3650.79
230000	3865.54	3856.44	3849.01	3842.93	3825.56	3819.13	3816.73
240000	4033.61	4024.11	4016.36	4010.01	3991.89	3985.18	3982.68
250000	4201.67	4191.79	4183.71	4177.10	4158.22	4151.22	4148.62

21.00 % Monthly Payments

LOAN AMOUNT	1	2	3	4	5	6	7
				YEARS			
100	9.27	5.10	3.72	3.05	2.66	2.40	2.23
200	18.54	10.19	7.45	6.10	5.31	4.81	4.46
500	46.35	25.48	18.62	15.25	13.28	12.02	11.14
1000	92.70	50.96	37.23	30.50	26.57	24.03	22.29
2000	185.40	101.92	74.47	61.01	53.14	48.06	44.58
5000	463.50	254.81	186.16	152.51	132.85	120.16	111.44
6000	556.20	305.77	223.40	183.02	159.42	144.19	133.73
7000	648.90	356.74	260.63	213.52	185.99	168.22	156.02
8000	741.60	407.70	297.86	244.02	212.56	192.25	178.31
9000	834.30	458.66	335.10	274.53	239.13	216.29	200.59
10000	927.00	509.62	372.33	305.03	265.70	240.32	222.88
12000	1112.40	611.55	446.80	366.04	318.84	288.38	267.46
15000	1390.50	764.44	558.49	457.54	398.55	360.48	334.32
20000	1853.99	1019.25	744.66	610.06	531.39	480.64	445.76
25000	2317.49	1274.06	930.82	762.57	664.24	600.80	557.21
30000	2780.99	1528.87	1116.99	915.09	797.09	720.95	668.65
31000	2873.69	1579.83	1154.22	945.59	823.66	744.99	690.94
32000	2966.39	1630.79	1191.46	976.09	850.23	769.02	713.22
33000	3059.09	1681.76	1228.69	1006.60	876.80	793.05	735.51
34000	3151.79	1732.72	1265.92	1037.10	903.37	817.08	757.80
35000	3244.49	1783.68	1303.15	1067.60	929.94	841.11	780.09
36000	3337.19	1834.64	1340.39	1098.11	956.51	865.15	802.38
37000	3429.89	1885.61	1377.62	1128.61	983.08	889.18	824.67
38000	3522.59	1936.57	1414.85	1159.11	1009.65	913.21	846.95
39000	3615.29	1987.53	1452.09	1189.61	1036.22	937.24	869.24
40000	3707.99	2038.49	1489.32	1220.12	1062.79	961.27	891.53
41000	3800.69	2089.46	1526.55	1250.62	1089.36	985.30	913.82
42000	3893.39	2140.42	1563.79	1281.12	1115.93	1009.34	936.11
43000	3986.09	2191.38	1601.02	1311.63	1142.50	1033.37	958.39
44000	4078.79	2242.34	1638.25	1342.13	1169.07	1057.40	980.68
45000	4171.49	2293.31	1675.48	1372.63	1195.64	1081.43	1002.97
46000	4264.19	2344.27	1712.72	1403.14	1222.21	1105.46	1025.26
47000	4356.88	2395.23	1749.95	1433.64	1248.78	1129.49	1047.55
48000	4449.58	2446.19	1787.18	1464.14	1275.35	1153.53	1069.84
49000	4542.28	2497.15	1824.42	1494.64	1301.91	1177.56	1092.12
50000	4634.98	2548.12	1861.65	1525.15	1328.48	1201.59	1114.41
51000	4727.68	2599.08	1898.88	1555.65	1355.05	1225.62	1136.70
52000	4820.38	2650.04	1936.12	1586.15	1381.62	1249.65	1158.99
53000	4913.08	2701.00	1973.35	1616.66	1408.19	1273.69	1181.28
54000	5005.78	2751.97	2010.58	1647.16	1434.76	1297.72	1203.57
55000	5098.48	2802.93	2047.81	1677.66	1461.33	1321.75	1225.85
56000	5191.18	2853.89	2085.05	1708.16	1487.90	1345.78	1248.14
57000	5283.88	2904.85	2122.28	1738.67	1514.47	1369.81	1270.43
58000	5376.58	2955.82	2159.51	1769.17	1541.04	1393.84	1292.72
59000	5469.28	3006.78	2196.75	1799.67	1567.61	1417.88	1315.01
60000	5561.98	3057.74	2233.98	1830.18	1594.18	1441.91	1337.29
65000	6025.48	3312.55	2420.14	1982.69	1727.03	1562.07	1448.74
70000	6488.98	3567.36	2606.31	2135.21	1859.88	1682.23	1560.18
75000	6952.48	3822.18	2792.47	2287.72	1992.73	1802.39	1671.62
80000	7415.97	4076.99	2978.64	2440.24	2125.58	1922.54	1783.06
85000	7879.47	4331.80	3164.80	2592.75	2258.42	2042.70	1894.50
90000	8342.97	4586.61	3350.97	2745.27	2391.27	2162.86	2005.94
95000	8806.47	4841.42	3537.13	2897.78	2524.12	2283.02	2117.38
100000	9269.97	5096.23	3723.30	3050.29	2656.97	2403.18	2228.82
105000	9733.47	5351.05	3909.46	3202.81	2789.82	2523.34	2340.27
110000	10196.96	5605.86	4095.63	3355.32	2922.67	2643.50	2451.71
120000	11123.96	6115.48	4467.96	3660.35	3188.36	2883.82	2674.59
130000	12050.96	6625.10	4840.29	3965.38	3454.06	3124.14	2897.47
140000	12977.95	7134.73	5212.62	4270.41	3719.76	3364.45	3120.35
150000	13904.95	7644.35	5584.95	4575.44	3985.45	3604.77	3343.24
160000	14831.95	8153.97	5957.28	4880.47	4251.15	3845.09	3566.12
170000	15758.95	8663.60	6329.61	5185.50	4516.85	4085.41	3789.00
180000	16685.94	9173.22	6701.94	5490.53	4782.54	4325.73	4011.88
190000	17612.94	9682.84	7074.27	5795.56	5048.24	4566.04	4234.77
200000	18539.94	10192.47	7446.60	6100.59	5313.94	4806.36	4457.65
210000	19466.93	10702.09	7818.93	6405.62	5579.64	5046.68	4680.53
220000	20393.93	11211.71	8191.26	6710.65	5845.33	5287.00	4903.41
230000	21320.93	11721.34	8563.59	7015.68	6111.03	5527.32	5126.30
240000	22247.92	12230.96	8935.92	7320.71	6376.73	5767.63	5349.18
250000	23174.92	12740.58	9308.25	7625.74	6642.42	6007.95	5572.06

Monthly Payments 21.00 %

LOAN AMOUNT	8	9	10	11	12	13	14
			YEARS				
100	2.10	2.01	1.94	1.89	1.85	1.81	1.79
200	4.21	4.02	3.88	3.78	3.69	3.63	3.57
500	10.52	10.06	9.71	9.44	9.23	9.07	8.94
1000	21.04	20.11	19.42	18.88	18.46	18.13	17.87
2000	42.08	40.23	38.83	37.76	36.92	36.26	35.74
5000	105.19	100.57	97.08	94.40	92.31	90.66	89.36
6000	126.23	120.69	116.50	113.27	110.77	108.79	107.23
7000	147.27	140.80	135.91	132.15	129.23	126.93	125.10
8000	168.31	160.91	155.33	151.03	147.69	145.06	142.97
9000	189.34	181.03	174.74	169.91	166.15	163.19	160.84
10000	210.38	201.14	194.16	188.79	184.61	181.32	178.72
12000	252.46	241.37	232.99	226.55	221.53	217.59	214.46
15000	315.57	301.71	291.24	283.19	276.92	271.98	268.07
20000	420.76	402.29	388.32	377.58	369.22	362.65	357.43
25000	525.95	502.86	485.40	471.98	461.53	453.31	446.79
30000	631.15	603.43	582.48	566.37	553.83	543.97	536.15
31000	652.18	623.54	601.89	585.25	572.29	562.10	554.02
32000	673.22	643.66	621.31	604.13	590.76	580.23	571.89
33000	694.26	663.77	640.73	623.01	609.22	598.37	589.76
34000	715.30	683.88	660.14	641.89	627.68	616.50	607.63
35000	736.34	704.00	679.56	660.77	646.14	634.63	625.51
36000	757.37	724.11	698.97	679.65	664.60	652.76	643.38
37000	778.41	744.23	718.39	698.53	683.06	670.89	661.25
38000	799.45	764.34	737.80	717.41	701.52	689.03	679.12
39000	820.49	784.46	757.22	736.29	719.98	707.16	696.99
40000	841.53	804.57	776.64	755.16	738.44	725.29	714.86
41000	862.57	824.68	796.05	774.04	756.91	743.42	732.74
42000	883.60	844.80	815.47	792.92	775.37	761.56	750.61
43000	904.64	864.91	834.88	811.80	793.83	779.69	768.48
44000	925.68	885.03	854.30	830.68	812.29	797.82	786.35
45000	946.72	905.14	873.72	849.56	830.75	815.95	804.22
46000	967.76	925.26	893.13	868.44	849.21	834.09	822.09
47000	988.79	945.37	912.55	887.32	867.67	852.22	839.97
48000	1009.83	965.48	931.96	906.20	886.13	870.35	857.84
49000	1030.87	985.60	951.38	925.08	904.59	888.48	875.71
50000	1051.91	1005.71	970.80	943.96	923.06	906.61	893.58
51000	1072.95	1025.83	990.21	962.83	941.52	924.75	911.45
52000	1093.99	1045.94	1009.63	981.71	959.98	942.88	929.32
53000	1115.02	1066.06	1029.04	1000.59	978.44	961.01	947.20
54000	1136.06	1086.17	1048.46	1019.47	996.90	979.14	965.07
55000	1157.10	1106.28	1067.88	1038.35	1015.36	997.28	982.94
56000	1178.14	1126.40	1087.29	1057.23	1033.82	1015.41	1000.81
57000	1199.18	1146.51	1106.71	1076.11	1052.28	1033.54	1018.68
58000	1220.21	1166.63	1126.12	1094.99	1070.74	1051.67	1036.55
59000	1241.25	1186.74	1145.54	1113.87	1089.20	1069.81	1054.43
60000	1262.29	1206.86	1164.96	1132.75	1107.67	1087.94	1072.30
65000	1367.48	1307.43	1262.03	1227.14	1199.97	1178.60	1161.65
70000	1472.67	1408.00	1359.11	1321.54	1292.28	1269.26	1251.01
75000	1577.86	1508.57	1456.19	1415.93	1384.58	1359.92	1340.37
80000	1683.05	1609.14	1553.27	1510.33	1476.89	1450.58	1429.73
85000	1788.25	1709.71	1650.35	1604.72	1569.19	1541.25	1519.09
90000	1893.44	1810.28	1747.43	1699.12	1661.50	1631.91	1608.44
95000	1998.63	1910.85	1844.51	1793.52	1753.80	1722.57	1697.80
100000	2103.82	2011.43	1941.59	1887.91	1846.11	1813.23	1787.16
105000	2209.01	2112.00	2038.67	1982.31	1938.42	1903.89	1876.52
110000	2314.20	2212.57	2135.75	2076.70	2030.72	1994.55	1965.88
120000	2524.58	2413.71	2329.91	2265.49	2215.33	2175.88	2144.59
130000	2734.96	2614.85	2524.07	2454.29	2399.94	2357.20	2323.31
140000	2945.35	2816.00	2718.23	2643.08	2584.55	2538.52	2502.03
150000	3155.73	3017.14	2912.39	2831.87	2769.17	2719.84	2680.74
160000	3366.11	3218.28	3106.55	3020.66	2953.78	2901.17	2859.46
170000	3576.49	3419.42	3300.71	3209.45	3138.39	3082.49	3038.17
180000	3786.87	3620.57	3494.87	3398.24	3323.00	3263.81	3216.89
190000	3997.25	3821.71	3689.02	3587.03	3507.61	3445.14	3395.61
200000	4207.64	4022.85	3883.18	3775.82	3692.22	3626.46	3574.32
210000	4418.02	4223.99	4077.34	3964.61	3876.83	3807.78	3753.04
220000	4628.40	4425.14	4271.50	4153.41	4061.44	3989.11	3931.75
230000	4838.78	4626.28	4465.66	4342.20	4246.05	4170.43	4110.47
240000	5049.16	4827.42	4659.82	4530.99	4430.66	4351.75	4289.19
250000	5259.54	5028.56	4853.98	4719.78	4615.28	4533.07	4467.90

21.00 % Monthly Payments

LOAN AMOUNT	15	16	17	18	19	20	21
	YEARS						
100	1.77	1.75	1.74	1.73	1.72	1.71	1.70
200	3.53	3.50	3.47	3.45	3.43	3.42	3.41
500	8.83	8.75	8.68	8.63	8.58	8.55	8.52
1000	17.66	17.50	17.36	17.25	17.17	17.10	17.04
2000	35.33	34.99	34.73	34.51	34.33	34.19	34.07
5000	88.32	87.48	86.81	86.27	85.83	85.48	85.19
6000	105.98	104.98	104.18	103.53	103.00	102.57	102.22
7000	123.65	122.48	121.54	120.78	120.16	119.67	119.26
8000	141.31	139.97	138.90	138.03	137.33	136.76	136.30
9000	158.97	157.47	156.26	155.29	154.50	153.86	153.34
10000	176.64	174.97	173.63	172.54	171.66	170.95	170.37
12000	211.96	209.96	208.35	207.05	206.00	205.14	204.45
15000	264.95	262.45	260.44	258.81	257.50	256.43	255.56
20000	353.27	349.94	347.25	345.08	343.33	341.90	340.75
25000	441.59	437.42	434.07	431.36	429.16	427.38	425.93
30000	529.91	524.91	520.88	517.63	514.99	512.86	511.12
31000	547.57	542.40	538.24	534.88	532.16	529.95	528.16
32000	565.24	559.90	555.60	552.13	549.33	547.05	545.19
33000	582.90	577.40	572.97	569.39	566.49	564.14	562.23
34000	600.56	594.89	590.33	586.64	583.66	581.24	579.27
35000	618.23	612.39	607.69	603.90	600.82	598.33	596.30
36000	635.89	629.89	625.05	621.15	617.99	615.43	613.34
37000	653.55	647.38	642.42	638.41	635.16	632.52	630.38
38000	671.22	664.88	659.78	655.66	652.32	649.62	647.42
39000	688.88	682.38	677.14	672.91	669.49	666.71	664.45
40000	706.55	699.87	694.50	690.17	686.66	683.81	681.49
41000	724.21	717.37	711.87	707.42	703.82	700.90	698.53
42000	741.87	734.87	729.23	724.68	720.99	718.00	715.57
43000	759.54	752.37	746.59	741.93	738.16	735.09	732.60
44000	777.20	769.86	763.96	759.18	755.32	752.19	749.64
45000	794.86	787.36	781.32	776.44	772.49	769.28	766.68
46000	812.53	804.86	798.68	793.69	789.65	786.38	783.71
47000	830.19	822.35	816.04	810.95	806.82	803.47	800.75
48000	847.85	839.85	833.41	828.20	823.99	820.57	817.79
49000	865.52	857.35	850.77	845.46	841.15	837.66	834.83
50000	883.18	874.84	868.13	862.71	858.32	854.76	851.86
51000	900.85	892.34	885.49	879.96	875.49	871.85	868.90
52000	918.51	909.84	902.86	897.22	892.65	888.95	885.94
53000	936.17	927.33	920.22	914.47	909.82	906.04	902.98
54000	953.84	944.83	937.58	931.73	926.99	923.14	920.01
55000	971.50	962.33	954.94	948.98	944.15	940.23	937.05
56000	989.16	979.82	972.31	966.24	961.32	957.33	954.09
57000	1006.83	997.32	989.67	983.49	978.49	974.42	971.12
58000	1024.49	1014.82	1007.03	1000.74	995.65	991.52	988.16
59000	1042.15	1032.32	1024.39	1018.00	1012.82	1008.62	1005.20
60000	1059.82	1049.81	1041.76	1035.25	1029.98	1025.71	1022.24
65000	1148.14	1137.30	1128.57	1121.52	1115.82	1111.19	1107.42
70000	1236.45	1224.78	1215.38	1207.79	1201.65	1196.66	1192.61
75000	1324.77	1312.27	1302.20	1294.07	1287.48	1282.14	1277.80
80000	1413.09	1399.75	1389.01	1380.34	1373.31	1367.61	1362.98
85000	1501.41	1487.23	1475.82	1466.61	1459.14	1453.09	1448.17
90000	1589.73	1574.72	1562.64	1552.88	1544.98	1538.57	1533.35
95000	1678.04	1662.20	1649.45	1639.15	1630.81	1624.04	1618.54
100000	1766.36	1749.69	1736.26	1725.42	1716.64	1709.52	1703.73
105000	1854.68	1837.17	1823.08	1811.69	1802.47	1794.99	1788.91
110000	1943.00	1924.66	1909.89	1897.96	1888.31	1880.47	1874.10
120000	2119.64	2099.62	2083.51	2070.50	2059.97	2051.42	2044.47
130000	2296.27	2274.59	2257.14	2243.05	2231.63	2222.37	2214.84
140000	2472.91	2449.56	2430.77	2415.59	2403.30	2393.32	2385.22
150000	2649.54	2624.53	2604.39	2588.13	2574.96	2564.28	2555.59
160000	2826.18	2799.50	2778.02	2760.67	2746.63	2735.23	2725.96
170000	3002.82	2974.47	2951.65	2933.21	2918.29	2906.18	2896.34
180000	3179.45	3149.44	3125.27	3105.76	3089.95	3077.13	3066.71
190000	3356.09	3324.41	3298.90	3278.30	3261.62	3248.08	3237.08
200000	3532.73	3499.37	3472.52	3450.84	3433.28	3419.03	3407.45
210000	3709.36	3674.34	3646.15	3623.38	3604.95	3589.99	3577.83
220000	3886.00	3849.31	3819.78	3795.92	3776.61	3760.94	3748.20
230000	4062.63	4024.28	3993.40	3968.47	3948.27	3931.89	3918.57
240000	4239.27	4199.25	4167.03	4141.01	4119.94	4102.84	4088.94
250000	4415.91	4374.22	4340.66	4313.55	4291.60	4273.79	4259.32

Monthly Payments 21.00 %

LOAN AMOUNT	22	23	24	25	30	35	40
100	1.70	1.70	1.69	1.69	1.68	1.68	1.68
200	3.40	3.39	3.38	3.38	3.36	3.36	3.36
500	8.50	8.48	8.46	8.45	8.41	8.40	8.39
1000	16.99	16.95	16.92	16.89	16.82	16.80	16.79
2000	33.98	33.90	33.84	33.79	33.64	33.59	33.57
5000	84.95	84.76	84.60	84.47	84.11	83.98	83.93
6000	101.94	101.71	101.52	101.37	100.93	100.77	100.71
7000	118.93	118.66	118.44	118.26	117.76	117.57	117.50
8000	135.92	135.61	135.36	135.16	134.58	134.36	134.29
9000	152.91	152.57	152.28	152.05	151.40	151.16	151.07
10000	169.90	169.52	169.20	168.95	168.22	167.96	167.86
12000	203.88	203.42	203.04	202.74	201.87	201.55	201.43
15000	254.85	254.28	253.81	253.42	252.33	251.93	251.79
20000	339.80	339.03	338.41	337.90	336.44	335.91	335.72
25000	424.75	423.79	423.01	422.37	420.56	419.89	419.65
30000	509.70	508.55	507.61	506.85	504.67	503.87	503.57
31000	526.69	525.50	524.53	523.74	521.49	520.66	520.36
32000	543.68	542.46	541.45	540.63	538.31	537.46	537.15
33000	560.67	559.41	558.37	557.53	555.13	554.25	553.93
34000	577.66	576.36	575.29	574.42	571.96	571.05	570.72
35000	594.65	593.31	592.21	591.32	588.78	587.85	587.50
36000	611.64	610.26	609.13	608.21	605.60	604.64	604.29
37000	628.64	627.21	626.06	625.11	622.42	621.44	621.08
38000	645.63	644.17	642.98	642.00	639.24	638.23	637.86
39000	662.62	661.12	659.90	658.90	656.07	655.03	654.65
40000	679.61	678.07	676.82	675.79	672.89	671.82	671.43
41000	696.60	695.02	693.74	692.69	689.71	688.62	688.22
42000	713.59	711.97	710.66	709.58	706.53	705.42	705.00
43000	730.58	728.92	727.58	726.48	723.35	722.21	721.79
44000	747.57	745.88	744.50	743.37	740.18	739.01	738.58
45000	764.56	762.83	761.42	760.27	757.00	755.80	755.36
46000	781.55	779.78	778.34	777.16	773.82	772.60	772.15
47000	798.54	796.73	795.26	794.06	790.64	789.39	788.93
48000	815.53	813.68	812.18	810.95	807.47	806.19	805.72
49000	832.52	830.63	829.10	827.85	824.29	822.98	822.51
50000	849.51	847.59	846.02	844.74	841.11	839.78	839.29
51000	866.50	864.54	862.94	861.64	857.93	856.58	856.08
52000	883.49	881.49	879.86	878.53	874.75	873.37	872.86
53000	900.48	898.44	896.78	895.43	891.58	890.17	889.65
54000	917.47	915.39	913.70	912.32	908.40	906.96	906.43
55000	934.46	932.35	930.62	929.22	925.22	923.76	923.22
56000	951.45	949.30	947.54	946.11	942.04	940.55	940.01
57000	968.44	966.25	964.46	963.01	958.87	957.35	956.79
58000	985.43	983.20	981.38	979.90	975.69	974.14	973.58
59000	1002.42	1000.15	998.30	996.80	992.51	990.94	990.36
60000	1019.41	1017.10	1015.22	1013.69	1009.33	1007.74	1007.15
65000	1104.36	1101.86	1099.83	1098.16	1093.44	1091.71	1091.08
70000	1189.31	1186.62	1184.43	1182.64	1177.55	1175.69	1175.01
75000	1274.26	1271.38	1269.03	1267.11	1261.67	1259.67	1258.94
80000	1359.21	1356.14	1353.63	1351.59	1345.78	1343.65	1342.87
85000	1444.16	1440.90	1438.23	1436.06	1429.89	1427.63	1426.79
90000	1529.11	1525.66	1522.84	1520.54	1514.00	1511.60	1510.72
95000	1614.06	1610.41	1607.44	1605.01	1598.11	1595.58	1594.65
100000	1699.01	1695.17	1692.04	1689.48	1682.22	1679.56	1678.58
105000	1783.96	1779.93	1776.64	1773.96	1766.33	1763.54	1762.51
110000	1868.92	1864.69	1861.24	1858.43	1850.44	1847.52	1846.44
120000	2038.82	2034.21	2030.45	2027.38	2018.66	2015.47	2014.30
130000	2208.72	2203.73	2199.65	2196.33	2186.89	2183.43	2182.16
140000	2378.62	2373.24	2368.86	2365.28	2355.11	2351.38	2350.01
150000	2548.52	2542.76	2538.06	2534.23	2523.33	2519.34	2517.87
160000	2718.42	2712.28	2707.27	2703.17	2691.55	2687.30	2685.73
170000	2888.32	2881.79	2876.47	2872.12	2859.78	2855.25	2853.59
180000	3058.22	3051.31	3045.67	3041.07	3028.00	3023.21	3021.45
190000	3228.13	3220.83	3214.88	3210.02	3196.22	3191.16	3189.31
200000	3398.03	3390.35	3384.08	3378.97	3364.44	3359.12	3357.16
210000	3567.93	3559.86	3553.29	3547.92	3532.66	3527.08	3525.02
220000	3737.83	3729.38	3722.49	3716.86	3700.89	3695.03	3692.88
230000	3907.73	3898.90	3891.69	3885.81	3869.11	3862.99	3860.74
240000	4077.63	4068.42	4060.90	4054.76	4037.33	4030.94	4028.60
250000	4247.53	4237.93	4230.10	4223.71	4205.55	4198.90	4196.46

21.25 % Monthly Payments

LOAN AMOUNT	YEARS 1	2	3	4	5	6	7
100	9.28	5.11	3.74	3.06	2.67	2.42	2.24
200	18.56	10.21	7.47	6.13	5.34	4.83	4.49
500	46.40	25.54	18.68	15.31	13.35	12.08	11.21
1000	92.81	51.07	37.35	30.63	26.70	24.17	22.43
2000	185.62	102.15	74.70	61.25	53.40	48.33	44.85
5000	464.05	255.37	186.75	153.13	133.49	120.83	112.14
6000	556.86	306.45	224.10	183.75	160.19	144.99	134.56
7000	649.67	357.52	261.45	214.38	186.89	169.16	156.99
8000	742.48	408.60	298.80	245.01	213.58	193.32	179.42
9000	835.29	459.67	336.15	275.63	240.28	217.49	201.84
10000	928.10	510.75	373.50	306.26	266.98	241.65	224.27
12000	1113.72	612.90	448.20	367.51	320.38	289.99	269.13
15000	1392.15	766.12	560.26	459.39	400.47	362.48	336.41
20000	1856.20	1021.50	747.01	612.51	533.96	483.31	448.54
25000	2320.24	1276.87	933.76	765.64	667.45	604.14	560.68
30000	2784.29	1532.24	1120.51	918.77	800.94	724.96	672.81
31000	2877.10	1583.32	1157.86	949.40	827.64	749.13	695.24
32000	2969.91	1634.39	1195.21	980.02	854.34	773.30	717.67
33000	3062.72	1685.47	1232.56	1010.65	881.03	797.46	740.10
34000	3155.53	1736.54	1269.91	1041.28	907.73	821.63	762.52
35000	3248.34	1787.62	1307.26	1071.90	934.43	845.79	784.95
36000	3341.15	1838.69	1344.61	1102.53	961.13	869.96	807.38
37000	3433.96	1889.77	1381.96	1133.15	987.83	894.12	829.80
38000	3526.77	1940.84	1419.31	1163.78	1014.52	918.29	852.23
39000	3619.58	1991.92	1456.66	1194.40	1041.22	942.45	874.66
40000	3712.39	2042.99	1494.01	1225.03	1067.92	966.62	897.09
41000	3805.20	2094.07	1531.37	1255.66	1094.62	990.79	919.51
42000	3898.01	2145.14	1568.72	1286.28	1121.32	1014.95	941.94
43000	3990.82	2196.22	1606.07	1316.91	1148.01	1039.12	964.37
44000	4083.63	2247.29	1643.42	1347.53	1174.71	1063.28	986.79
45000	4176.44	2298.37	1680.77	1378.16	1201.41	1087.45	1009.22
46000	4269.25	2349.44	1718.12	1408.78	1228.11	1111.61	1031.65
47000	4362.06	2400.52	1755.47	1439.41	1254.81	1135.78	1054.08
48000	4454.87	2451.59	1792.82	1470.04	1281.50	1159.94	1076.50
49000	4547.68	2502.67	1830.17	1500.66	1308.20	1184.11	1098.93
50000	4640.49	2553.74	1867.52	1531.29	1334.90	1208.27	1121.36
51000	4733.30	2604.82	1904.87	1561.91	1361.60	1232.44	1143.78
52000	4826.11	2655.89	1942.22	1592.54	1388.30	1256.61	1166.21
53000	4918.92	2706.97	1979.57	1623.16	1414.99	1280.77	1188.64
54000	5011.73	2758.04	2016.92	1653.79	1441.69	1304.94	1211.07
55000	5104.54	2809.11	2054.27	1684.42	1468.39	1329.10	1233.49
56000	5197.35	2860.19	2091.62	1715.04	1495.09	1353.27	1255.92
57000	5290.16	2911.26	2128.97	1745.67	1521.79	1377.43	1278.35
58000	5382.97	2962.34	2166.32	1776.29	1548.48	1401.60	1300.77
59000	5475.78	3013.41	2203.67	1806.92	1575.18	1425.76	1323.20
60000	5568.59	3064.49	2241.02	1837.54	1601.88	1449.93	1345.63
65000	6032.64	3319.86	2427.77	1990.67	1735.37	1570.76	1457.76
70000	6496.69	3575.24	2614.53	2143.80	1868.86	1691.58	1569.90
75000	6960.73	3830.61	2801.28	2296.93	2002.35	1812.41	1682.04
80000	7424.78	4085.99	2988.03	2450.06	2135.84	1933.24	1794.17
85000	7888.83	4341.36	3174.78	2603.19	2269.33	2054.07	1906.31
90000	8352.88	4596.73	3361.53	2756.32	2402.82	2174.89	2018.44
95000	8816.93	4852.11	3548.29	2909.45	2536.31	2295.72	2130.58
100000	9280.98	5107.48	3735.04	3062.57	2669.80	2416.55	2242.71
105000	9745.03	5362.86	3921.79	3215.70	2803.29	2537.38	2354.85
110000	10209.08	5618.23	4108.54	3368.83	2936.78	2658.20	2466.99
120000	11137.18	6128.98	4482.04	3675.09	3203.76	2899.86	2691.26
130000	12065.27	6639.73	4855.55	3981.35	3470.74	3141.51	2915.53
140000	12993.37	7150.47	5229.05	4287.60	3737.72	3383.17	3139.80
150000	13921.47	7661.22	5602.56	4593.86	4004.70	3624.82	3364.07
160000	14849.57	8171.97	5976.06	4900.12	4271.68	3866.48	3588.34
170000	15777.67	8682.72	6349.56	5206.38	4538.66	4108.13	3812.62
180000	16705.76	9193.47	6723.07	5512.63	4805.64	4349.79	4036.89
190000	17633.86	9704.22	7096.57	5818.89	5072.62	4591.44	4261.16
200000	18561.96	10214.96	7470.07	6125.15	5339.60	4833.10	4485.43
210000	19490.06	10725.71	7843.58	6431.41	5606.58	5074.75	4709.70
220000	20418.16	11236.46	8217.08	6737.66	5873.56	5316.41	4933.97
230000	21346.25	11747.21	8590.59	7043.92	6140.54	5558.06	5158.24
240000	22274.35	12257.96	8964.09	7350.18	6407.52	5799.72	5382.52
250000	23202.45	12768.70	9337.59	7656.44	6674.50	6041.37	5606.79

Monthly Payments 21.25 %

LOAN AMOUNT	8	9	10	11	12	13	14
	YEARS						
100	2.12	2.03	1.96	1.90	1.86	1.83	1.80
200	4.24	4.05	3.91	3.81	3.72	3.66	3.61
500	10.59	10.13	9.78	9.52	9.31	9.15	9.02
1000	21.18	20.26	19.57	19.04	18.62	18.30	18.04
2000	42.36	40.53	39.14	38.07	37.24	36.59	36.08
5000	105.91	101.31	97.84	95.18	93.11	91.48	90.20
6000	127.09	121.58	117.41	114.22	111.73	109.78	108.23
7000	148.27	141.84	136.98	133.25	130.35	128.08	126.27
8000	169.46	162.10	156.55	152.29	148.98	146.37	144.31
9000	190.64	182.37	176.12	171.33	167.60	164.67	162.35
10000	211.82	202.63	195.69	190.36	186.22	182.97	180.39
12000	254.18	243.15	234.83	228.43	223.46	219.56	216.47
15000	317.73	303.94	293.53	285.54	279.33	274.45	270.59
20000	423.64	405.26	391.38	380.72	372.44	365.93	360.78
25000	529.55	506.57	489.22	475.90	465.55	457.42	450.98
30000	635.46	607.88	587.07	571.09	558.66	548.90	541.17
31000	656.64	628.15	606.64	590.12	577.28	567.20	559.21
32000	677.83	648.41	626.20	609.16	595.90	585.49	577.25
33000	699.01	668.67	645.77	628.19	614.52	603.79	595.29
34000	720.19	688.94	665.34	647.23	633.15	622.09	613.33
35000	741.37	709.20	684.91	666.27	651.77	640.38	631.37
36000	762.55	729.46	704.48	685.30	670.39	658.68	649.41
37000	783.74	749.72	724.05	704.34	689.01	676.98	667.45
38000	804.92	769.99	743.62	723.38	707.63	695.27	685.49
39000	826.10	790.25	763.19	742.41	726.26	713.57	703.53
40000	847.28	810.51	782.76	761.45	744.88	731.87	721.56
41000	868.46	830.78	802.33	780.48	763.50	750.16	739.60
42000	889.65	851.04	821.89	799.52	782.12	768.46	757.64
43000	910.83	871.30	841.46	818.56	800.74	786.76	775.68
44000	932.01	891.56	861.03	837.59	819.37	805.05	793.72
45000	953.19	911.83	880.60	856.63	837.99	823.35	811.76
46000	974.37	932.09	900.17	875.67	856.61	841.65	829.80
47000	995.56	952.35	919.74	894.70	875.23	859.94	847.84
48000	1016.74	972.62	939.31	913.74	893.85	878.24	865.88
49000	1037.92	992.88	958.88	932.77	912.48	896.54	883.92
50000	1059.10	1013.14	978.45	951.81	931.10	914.83	901.96
51000	1080.28	1033.40	998.01	970.85	949.72	933.13	920.00
52000	1101.47	1053.67	1017.58	989.88	968.34	951.43	938.03
53000	1122.65	1073.93	1037.15	1008.92	986.96	969.72	956.07
54000	1143.83	1094.19	1056.72	1027.95	1005.59	988.02	974.11
55000	1165.01	1114.46	1076.29	1046.99	1024.21	1006.32	992.15
56000	1186.20	1134.72	1095.86	1066.03	1042.83	1024.61	1010.19
57000	1207.38	1154.98	1115.43	1085.06	1061.45	1042.91	1028.23
58000	1228.56	1175.24	1135.00	1104.10	1080.07	1061.21	1046.27
59000	1249.74	1195.51	1154.57	1123.14	1098.70	1079.50	1064.31
60000	1270.92	1215.77	1174.13	1142.17	1117.32	1097.80	1082.35
65000	1376.83	1317.08	1271.98	1237.35	1210.43	1189.28	1172.54
70000	1482.74	1418.40	1369.82	1332.53	1303.54	1280.76	1262.74
75000	1588.65	1519.71	1467.67	1427.71	1396.65	1372.25	1352.93
80000	1694.56	1621.03	1565.51	1522.90	1489.76	1463.73	1443.13
85000	1800.47	1722.34	1663.36	1618.08	1582.87	1555.21	1533.33
90000	1906.38	1823.65	1761.20	1713.26	1675.98	1646.70	1623.52
95000	2012.30	1924.97	1859.05	1808.44	1769.09	1738.18	1713.72
100000	2118.21	2026.28	1956.89	1903.62	1862.20	1829.66	1803.91
105000	2224.12	2127.60	2054.73	1998.80	1955.31	1921.15	1894.11
110000	2330.03	2228.91	2152.58	2093.98	2048.42	2012.63	1984.30
120000	2541.85	2431.54	2348.27	2284.34	2234.64	2195.60	2164.69
130000	2753.67	2634.17	2543.96	2474.71	2420.86	2378.56	2345.09
140000	2965.49	2836.80	2739.65	2665.07	2607.08	2561.53	2525.48
150000	3177.31	3039.42	2935.34	2855.43	2793.30	2744.50	2705.87
160000	3389.13	3242.05	3131.02	3045.79	2979.52	2927.46	2886.26
170000	3600.95	3444.68	3326.71	3236.15	3165.73	3110.43	3066.65
180000	3812.77	3647.31	3522.40	3426.52	3351.95	3293.40	3247.04
190000	4024.59	3849.94	3718.09	3616.88	3538.17	3476.36	3427.43
200000	4236.41	4052.57	3913.78	3807.24	3724.39	3659.33	3607.82
210000	4448.23	4255.19	4109.47	3997.60	3910.61	3842.29	3788.22
220000	4660.05	4457.82	4305.16	4187.96	4096.83	4025.26	3968.61
230000	4871.87	4660.45	4500.85	4378.33	4283.05	4208.23	4149.00
240000	5083.69	4863.08	4696.54	4568.69	4469.27	4391.19	4329.39
250000	5295.51	5065.71	4892.23	4759.05	4655.49	4574.16	4509.78

21.25 % Monthly Payments

LOAN AMOUNT	15	16	17	18	19	20	21
				YEARS			
100	1.78	1.77	1.75	1.74	1.73	1.73	1.72
200	3.57	3.53	3.51	3.49	3.47	3.46	3.44
500	8.92	8.83	8.77	8.72	8.67	8.64	8.61
1000	17.83	17.67	17.54	17.43	17.35	17.28	17.22
2000	35.67	35.34	35.08	34.86	34.69	34.55	34.44
5000	89.17	88.35	87.69	87.16	86.73	86.38	86.10
6000	107.00	106.02	105.23	104.59	104.07	103.66	103.32
7000	124.84	123.69	122.77	122.02	121.42	120.93	120.54
8000	142.67	141.36	140.30	139.45	138.77	138.21	137.76
9000	160.51	159.03	157.84	156.88	156.11	155.48	154.98
10000	178.34	176.70	175.38	174.32	173.46	172.76	172.20
12000	214.01	212.04	210.46	209.18	208.15	207.31	206.63
15000	267.51	265.05	263.07	261.47	260.18	259.14	258.29
20000	356.68	353.40	350.76	348.63	346.91	345.52	344.39
25000	445.85	441.75	438.45	435.79	433.64	431.90	430.49
30000	535.02	530.10	526.14	522.95	520.37	518.28	516.59
31000	552.85	547.77	543.68	540.38	537.71	535.56	533.81
32000	570.69	565.44	561.21	557.81	555.06	552.83	551.03
33000	588.52	583.10	578.75	575.24	572.41	570.11	568.25
34000	606.36	600.77	596.29	592.67	589.75	587.39	585.47
35000	624.19	618.44	613.83	610.11	607.10	604.66	602.69
36000	642.02	636.11	631.37	627.54	624.44	621.94	619.90
37000	659.86	653.78	648.90	644.97	641.79	639.21	637.12
38000	677.69	671.45	666.44	662.40	659.13	656.49	654.34
39000	695.53	689.12	683.98	679.83	676.48	673.77	671.56
40000	713.36	706.79	701.52	697.26	693.83	691.04	688.78
41000	731.19	724.46	719.05	714.69	711.17	708.32	706.00
42000	749.03	742.13	736.59	732.13	728.52	725.59	723.22
43000	766.86	759.80	754.13	749.56	745.86	742.87	740.44
44000	784.70	777.47	771.67	766.99	763.21	760.15	757.66
45000	802.53	795.14	789.21	784.42	780.55	777.42	774.88
46000	820.36	812.81	806.74	801.85	797.90	794.70	792.10
47000	838.20	830.48	824.28	819.28	815.25	811.97	809.32
48000	856.03	848.15	841.82	836.72	832.59	829.25	826.54
49000	873.87	865.82	859.36	854.15	849.94	846.53	843.76
50000	891.70	883.49	876.90	871.58	867.28	863.80	860.98
51000	909.53	901.16	894.43	889.01	884.63	881.08	878.20
52000	927.37	918.83	911.97	906.44	901.97	898.35	895.42
53000	945.20	936.50	929.51	923.87	919.32	915.63	912.64
54000	963.04	954.17	947.05	941.31	936.66	932.91	929.86
55000	980.87	971.84	964.59	958.74	954.01	950.18	947.08
56000	998.70	989.51	982.12	976.17	971.36	967.46	964.30
57000	1016.54	1007.18	999.66	993.60	988.70	984.73	981.52
58000	1034.37	1024.85	1017.20	1011.03	1006.05	1002.01	998.74
59000	1052.21	1042.52	1034.74	1028.46	1023.39	1019.29	1015.96
60000	1070.04	1060.19	1052.28	1045.89	1040.74	1036.56	1033.17
65000	1159.21	1148.54	1139.97	1133.05	1127.47	1122.94	1119.27
70000	1248.38	1236.89	1227.65	1220.21	1214.19	1209.32	1205.37
75000	1337.55	1325.24	1315.34	1307.37	1300.92	1295.70	1291.47
80000	1426.72	1413.59	1403.03	1394.53	1387.65	1382.08	1377.57
85000	1515.89	1501.94	1490.72	1481.68	1474.38	1468.46	1463.66
90000	1605.06	1590.29	1578.41	1568.84	1561.11	1554.84	1549.76
95000	1694.23	1678.64	1666.10	1656.00	1647.84	1641.22	1635.86
100000	1783.40	1766.98	1753.79	1743.16	1734.56	1727.60	1721.96
105000	1872.57	1855.33	1841.48	1830.32	1821.29	1813.98	1808.06
110000	1961.74	1943.68	1929.17	1917.47	1908.02	1900.36	1894.15
120000	2140.08	2120.38	2104.55	2091.79	2081.48	2073.12	2066.35
130000	2318.42	2297.08	2279.93	2266.11	2254.93	2245.88	2238.55
140000	2496.76	2473.78	2455.31	2440.42	2428.39	2418.65	2410.74
150000	2675.10	2650.48	2630.69	2614.74	2601.85	2591.41	2582.94
160000	2853.44	2827.18	2806.07	2789.05	2775.30	2764.17	2755.13
170000	3031.78	3003.87	2981.45	2963.37	2948.76	2936.93	2927.33
180000	3210.12	3180.57	3156.83	3137.68	3122.22	3109.69	3099.52
190000	3388.46	3357.27	3332.21	3312.00	3295.67	3282.45	3271.72
200000	3566.80	3533.97	3507.59	3486.32	3469.13	3455.21	3443.92
210000	3745.14	3710.67	3682.96	3660.63	3642.58	3627.97	3616.11
220000	3923.48	3887.37	3858.34	3834.95	3816.04	3800.73	3788.31
230000	4101.82	4064.06	4033.72	4009.26	3989.50	3973.49	3960.50
240000	4280.16	4240.76	4209.10	4183.58	4162.95	4146.25	4132.70
250000	4458.50	4417.46	4384.48	4357.90	4336.41	4319.01	4304.89

Monthly Payments 21.25 %

LOAN AMOUNT	22	23	24	25	30	35	40
100	1.72	1.71	1.71	1.71	1.70	1.70	1.70
200	3.43	3.43	3.42	3.42	3.40	3.40	3.40
500	8.59	8.57	8.55	8.54	8.51	8.49	8.49
1000	17.17	17.14	17.11	17.08	17.01	16.99	16.98
2000	34.35	34.27	34.21	34.16	34.02	33.97	33.95
5000	85.87	85.68	85.53	85.41	85.06	84.93	84.88
6000	103.04	102.82	102.64	102.49	102.07	101.92	101.86
7000	120.22	119.95	119.74	119.57	119.08	118.90	118.84
8000	137.39	137.09	136.85	136.65	136.09	135.89	135.82
9000	154.56	154.23	153.95	153.73	153.10	152.88	152.79
10000	171.74	171.36	171.06	170.81	170.11	169.86	169.77
12000	206.08	205.64	205.27	204.98	204.14	203.83	203.72
15000	257.61	257.05	256.59	256.22	255.17	254.79	254.65
20000	343.47	342.73	342.12	341.63	340.23	339.72	339.54
25000	429.34	428.41	427.65	427.03	425.29	424.65	424.42
30000	515.21	514.09	513.18	512.44	510.34	509.59	509.31
31000	532.39	531.23	530.29	529.52	527.36	526.57	526.29
32000	549.56	548.37	547.39	546.60	544.37	543.56	543.26
33000	566.73	565.50	564.50	563.68	561.38	560.54	560.24
34000	583.91	582.64	581.61	580.77	578.39	577.53	577.22
35000	601.08	599.77	598.71	597.85	595.40	594.52	594.19
36000	618.25	616.91	615.82	614.93	612.41	611.50	611.17
37000	635.43	634.05	632.92	632.01	629.43	628.49	628.15
38000	652.60	651.18	650.03	649.09	646.44	645.48	645.13
39000	669.77	668.32	667.14	666.17	663.45	662.46	662.10
40000	686.95	685.46	684.24	683.25	680.46	679.45	679.08
41000	704.12	702.59	701.35	700.34	697.47	696.43	696.06
42000	721.30	719.73	718.45	717.42	714.48	713.42	713.03
43000	738.47	736.87	735.56	734.50	731.49	730.41	730.01
44000	755.64	754.00	752.67	751.58	748.51	747.39	746.99
45000	772.82	771.14	769.77	768.66	765.52	764.38	763.96
46000	789.99	788.28	786.88	785.74	782.53	781.37	780.94
47000	807.16	805.41	803.99	802.82	799.54	798.35	797.92
48000	824.34	822.55	821.09	819.90	816.55	815.34	814.90
49000	841.51	839.68	838.20	836.99	833.56	832.32	831.87
50000	858.69	856.82	855.30	854.07	850.57	849.31	848.85
51000	875.86	873.96	872.41	871.15	867.59	866.30	865.83
52000	893.03	891.09	889.52	888.23	884.60	883.28	882.80
53000	910.21	908.23	906.62	905.31	901.61	900.27	899.78
54000	927.38	925.37	923.73	922.39	918.62	917.25	916.76
55000	944.55	942.50	940.83	939.47	935.63	934.24	933.73
56000	961.73	959.64	957.94	956.56	952.64	951.23	950.71
57000	978.90	976.78	975.05	973.64	969.66	968.21	967.69
58000	996.08	993.91	992.15	990.72	986.67	985.20	984.67
59000	1013.25	1011.05	1009.26	1007.80	1003.68	1002.19	1001.64
60000	1030.42	1028.19	1026.36	1024.88	1020.69	1019.17	1018.62
65000	1116.29	1113.87	1111.89	1110.29	1105.75	1104.10	1103.50
70000	1202.16	1199.55	1197.42	1195.69	1190.80	1189.03	1188.39
75000	1288.03	1285.23	1282.95	1281.10	1275.86	1273.96	1273.27
80000	1373.90	1370.91	1368.49	1366.51	1360.92	1358.90	1358.16
85000	1459.77	1456.60	1454.02	1451.91	1445.98	1443.83	1443.04
90000	1545.63	1542.28	1539.55	1537.32	1531.03	1528.76	1527.93
95000	1631.50	1627.96	1625.08	1622.73	1616.09	1613.69	1612.81
100000	1717.37	1713.64	1710.61	1708.13	1701.15	1698.62	1697.70
105000	1803.24	1799.32	1796.14	1793.54	1786.21	1783.55	1782.58
110000	1889.11	1885.01	1881.67	1878.95	1871.26	1868.48	1867.47
120000	2060.85	2056.37	2052.73	2049.76	2041.38	2038.34	2037.24
130000	2232.58	2227.73	2223.79	2220.57	2211.49	2208.21	2207.01
140000	2404.32	2399.10	2394.85	2391.39	2381.61	2378.07	2376.78
150000	2576.06	2570.46	2565.91	2562.20	2551.72	2547.93	2546.55
160000	2747.79	2741.83	2736.97	2733.01	2721.84	2717.79	2716.32
170000	2919.53	2913.19	2908.03	2903.83	2891.95	2887.65	2886.09
180000	3091.27	3084.56	3079.09	3074.64	3062.07	3057.52	3055.86
190000	3263.01	3255.92	3250.15	3245.46	3232.18	3227.38	3225.63
200000	3434.74	3427.28	3421.21	3416.27	3402.30	3397.24	3395.40
210000	3606.48	3598.65	3592.27	3587.08	3572.41	3567.10	3565.17
220000	3778.22	3770.01	3763.33	3757.90	3742.53	3736.96	3734.94
230000	3949.95	3941.38	3934.40	3928.71	3912.64	3906.83	3904.71
240000	4121.69	4112.74	4105.46	4099.52	4082.76	4076.69	4074.48
250000	4293.43	4284.11	4276.52	4270.34	4252.87	4246.55	4244.25

21.50 % Monthly Payments

LOAN AMOUNT	YEARS 1	2	3	4	5	6	7
100	9.29	5.12	3.75	3.07	2.68	2.43	2.26
200	18.58	10.24	7.49	6.15	5.37	4.86	4.51
500	46.46	25.59	18.73	15.37	13.41	12.15	11.28
1000	92.92	51.19	37.47	30.75	26.83	24.30	22.57
2000	185.84	102.37	74.94	61.50	53.65	48.60	45.13
5000	464.60	255.94	187.34	153.74	134.13	121.50	112.83
6000	557.52	307.12	224.81	184.49	160.96	145.80	135.40
7000	650.44	358.31	262.27	215.24	187.79	170.10	157.96
8000	743.36	409.50	299.74	245.99	214.61	194.40	180.53
9000	836.28	460.69	337.21	276.74	241.44	218.69	203.10
10000	929.20	511.87	374.68	307.49	268.26	242.99	225.66
12000	1115.04	614.25	449.61	368.98	321.92	291.59	270.80
15000	1393.80	767.81	562.02	461.23	402.40	364.49	338.49
20000	1858.40	1023.75	749.36	614.97	536.53	485.99	451.33
25000	2323.00	1279.68	936.70	768.72	670.66	607.49	564.16
30000	2787.60	1535.62	1124.04	922.46	804.79	728.98	676.99
31000	2880.52	1586.81	1161.50	953.21	831.62	753.28	699.56
32000	2973.44	1637.99	1198.97	983.96	858.45	777.58	722.12
33000	3066.36	1689.18	1236.44	1014.71	885.27	801.88	744.69
34000	3159.28	1740.37	1273.91	1045.46	912.10	826.18	767.26
35000	3252.20	1791.56	1311.37	1076.20	938.93	850.48	789.82
36000	3345.12	1842.74	1348.84	1106.95	965.75	874.78	812.39
37000	3438.04	1893.93	1386.31	1137.70	992.58	899.08	834.95
38000	3530.96	1945.12	1423.78	1168.45	1019.41	923.38	857.52
39000	3623.88	1996.31	1461.25	1199.20	1046.23	947.68	880.09
40000	3716.80	2047.49	1498.71	1229.95	1073.06	971.98	902.65
41000	3809.72	2098.68	1536.18	1260.70	1099.89	996.28	925.22
42000	3902.64	2149.87	1573.65	1291.45	1126.71	1020.58	947.79
43000	3995.56	2201.06	1611.12	1322.19	1153.54	1044.88	970.35
44000	4088.48	2252.24	1648.59	1352.94	1180.37	1069.17	992.92
45000	4181.39	2303.43	1686.05	1383.69	1207.19	1093.47	1015.48
46000	4274.31	2354.62	1723.52	1414.44	1234.02	1117.77	1038.05
47000	4367.23	2405.80	1760.99	1445.19	1260.84	1142.07	1060.62
48000	4460.15	2456.99	1798.46	1475.94	1287.67	1166.37	1083.18
49000	4553.07	2508.18	1835.92	1506.69	1314.50	1190.67	1105.75
50000	4645.99	2559.37	1873.39	1537.43	1341.32	1214.97	1128.32
51000	4738.91	2610.55	1910.86	1568.18	1368.15	1239.27	1150.88
52000	4831.83	2661.74	1948.33	1598.93	1394.98	1263.57	1173.45
53000	4924.75	2712.93	1985.80	1629.68	1421.80	1287.87	1196.02
54000	5017.67	2764.12	2023.26	1660.43	1448.63	1312.17	1218.58
55000	5110.59	2815.30	2060.73	1691.18	1475.46	1336.47	1241.15
56000	5203.51	2866.49	2098.20	1721.93	1502.28	1360.77	1263.71
57000	5296.43	2917.68	2135.67	1752.68	1529.11	1385.07	1286.28
58000	5389.35	2968.87	2173.14	1783.42	1555.94	1409.37	1308.85
59000	5482.27	3020.05	2210.60	1814.17	1582.76	1433.67	1331.41
60000	5575.19	3071.24	2248.07	1844.92	1609.59	1457.97	1353.98
65000	6039.79	3327.18	2435.41	1998.67	1743.72	1579.46	1466.81
70000	6504.39	3583.11	2622.75	2152.41	1877.85	1700.96	1579.64
75000	6968.99	3839.05	2810.09	2306.15	2011.99	1822.46	1692.47
80000	7433.59	4094.99	2997.43	2459.90	2146.12	1943.95	1805.31
85000	7898.19	4350.92	3184.77	2613.64	2280.25	2065.45	1918.14
90000	8362.79	4606.86	3372.11	2767.38	2414.38	2186.95	2030.97
95000	8827.39	4862.80	3559.45	2921.13	2548.52	2308.45	2143.80
100000	9291.99	5118.73	3746.79	3074.87	2682.65	2429.94	2256.63
105000	9756.59	5374.67	3934.12	3228.61	2816.78	2551.44	2369.46
110000	10221.19	5630.61	4121.46	3382.36	2950.91	2672.94	2482.30
120000	11150.39	6142.48	4496.14	3689.84	3219.18	2915.93	2707.96
130000	12079.59	6654.35	4870.82	3997.33	3487.44	3158.93	2933.62
140000	13008.78	7166.23	5245.50	4304.82	3755.71	3401.92	3159.29
150000	13937.98	7678.10	5620.18	4612.30	4023.97	3644.91	3384.95
160000	14867.18	8189.97	5994.86	4919.79	4292.24	3887.91	3610.61
170000	15796.38	8701.85	6369.53	5227.28	4560.50	4130.90	3836.28
180000	16725.58	9213.72	6744.21	5534.77	4828.77	4373.90	4061.94
190000	17654.78	9725.59	7118.89	5842.25	5097.03	4616.89	4287.60
200000	18583.98	10237.47	7493.57	6149.74	5365.30	4859.89	4513.27
210000	19513.18	10749.34	7868.25	6457.23	5633.56	5102.88	4738.93
220000	20442.38	11261.21	8242.93	6764.71	5901.83	5345.87	4964.59
230000	21371.57	11773.09	8617.61	7072.20	6170.09	5588.87	5190.26
240000	22300.77	12284.96	8992.28	7379.69	6438.36	5831.86	5415.92
250000	23229.97	12796.83	9366.96	7687.17	6706.62	6074.86	5641.58

Monthly Payments 21.50 %

LOAN AMOUNT	8	9	10	11	12	13	14
100	2.13	2.04	1.97	1.92	1.88	1.85	1.82
200	4.27	4.08	3.94	3.84	3.76	3.69	3.64
500	10.66	10.21	9.86	9.60	9.39	9.23	9.10
1000	21.33	20.41	19.72	19.19	18.78	18.46	18.21
2000	42.65	40.82	39.44	38.39	37.57	36.92	36.41
5000	106.63	102.06	98.61	95.97	93.92	92.31	91.03
6000	127.96	122.47	118.33	115.16	112.70	110.77	109.24
7000	149.28	142.88	138.06	134.36	131.48	129.23	127.45
8000	170.61	163.29	157.78	153.55	150.27	147.69	145.66
9000	191.94	183.71	177.50	172.74	169.05	166.15	163.86
10000	213.26	204.12	197.22	191.94	187.83	184.61	182.07
12000	255.91	244.94	236.67	230.32	225.40	221.54	218.48
15000	319.89	306.18	295.83	287.90	281.75	276.92	273.10
20000	426.52	408.23	394.44	383.87	375.66	369.23	364.14
25000	533.16	510.29	493.06	479.84	469.58	461.53	455.17
30000	639.79	612.35	591.67	575.81	563.50	553.84	546.21
31000	661.11	632.76	611.39	595.00	582.28	572.30	564.42
32000	682.44	653.18	631.11	614.20	601.06	590.76	582.62
33000	703.77	673.59	650.83	633.39	619.84	609.22	600.83
34000	725.09	694.00	670.56	652.58	638.63	627.68	619.04
35000	746.42	714.41	690.28	671.78	657.41	646.15	637.24
36000	767.74	734.82	710.00	690.97	676.19	664.61	655.45
37000	789.07	755.23	729.72	710.16	694.98	683.07	673.66
38000	810.40	775.65	749.44	729.36	713.76	701.53	691.86
39000	831.72	796.06	769.17	748.55	732.54	719.99	710.07
40000	853.05	816.47	788.89	767.74	751.33	738.45	728.28
41000	874.38	836.88	808.61	786.94	770.11	756.91	746.48
42000	895.70	857.29	828.33	806.13	788.89	775.38	764.69
43000	917.03	877.70	848.06	825.33	807.68	793.84	782.90
44000	938.35	898.12	867.78	844.52	826.46	812.30	801.11
45000	959.68	918.53	887.50	863.71	845.24	830.76	819.31
46000	981.01	938.94	907.22	882.91	864.03	849.22	837.52
47000	1002.33	959.35	926.94	902.10	882.81	867.68	855.73
48000	1023.66	979.76	946.67	921.29	901.59	886.14	873.93
49000	1044.99	1000.17	966.39	940.49	920.38	904.60	892.14
50000	1066.31	1020.59	986.11	959.68	939.16	923.07	910.35
51000	1087.64	1041.00	1005.83	978.87	957.94	941.53	928.55
52000	1108.96	1061.41	1025.56	998.07	976.73	959.99	946.76
53000	1130.29	1081.82	1045.28	1017.26	995.51	978.45	964.97
54000	1151.62	1102.23	1065.00	1036.46	1014.29	996.91	983.18
55000	1172.94	1122.65	1084.72	1055.65	1033.07	1015.37	1001.38
56000	1194.27	1143.06	1104.44	1074.84	1051.86	1033.83	1019.59
57000	1215.60	1163.47	1124.17	1094.04	1070.64	1052.29	1037.80
58000	1236.92	1183.88	1143.89	1113.23	1089.42	1070.76	1056.00
59000	1258.25	1204.29	1163.61	1132.42	1108.21	1089.22	1074.21
60000	1279.57	1224.70	1183.33	1151.62	1126.99	1107.68	1092.42
65000	1386.21	1326.76	1281.94	1247.59	1220.91	1199.99	1183.45
70000	1492.84	1428.82	1380.56	1343.55	1314.82	1292.29	1274.49
75000	1599.47	1530.88	1479.17	1439.52	1408.74	1384.60	1365.52
80000	1706.10	1632.94	1577.78	1535.49	1502.65	1476.90	1456.56
85000	1812.73	1735.00	1676.39	1631.46	1596.57	1569.21	1547.59
90000	1919.36	1837.06	1775.00	1727.43	1690.49	1661.52	1638.63
95000	2025.99	1939.11	1873.61	1823.39	1784.40	1753.82	1729.66
100000	2132.62	2041.17	1972.22	1919.36	1878.32	1846.13	1820.69
105000	2239.25	2143.23	2070.83	2015.33	1972.23	1938.44	1911.73
110000	2345.89	2245.29	2169.44	2111.30	2066.15	2030.74	2002.76
120000	2559.15	2449.41	2366.67	2303.23	2253.98	2215.36	2184.83
130000	2772.41	2653.53	2563.89	2495.17	2441.81	2399.97	2366.90
140000	2985.67	2857.64	2761.11	2687.11	2629.64	2584.58	2548.97
150000	3198.94	3061.76	2958.33	2879.04	2817.48	2769.20	2731.04
160000	3412.20	3265.88	3155.56	3070.98	3005.31	2953.81	2913.11
170000	3625.46	3469.99	3352.78	3262.92	3193.14	3138.42	3095.18
180000	3838.72	3674.11	3550.00	3454.85	3380.97	3323.04	3277.25
190000	4051.99	3878.23	3747.22	3646.79	3568.80	3507.65	3459.32
200000	4265.25	4082.35	3944.44	3838.72	3756.64	3692.26	3641.39
210000	4478.51	4286.46	4141.67	4030.66	3944.47	3876.88	3823.46
220000	4691.77	4490.58	4338.89	4222.60	4132.30	4061.49	4005.53
230000	4905.03	4694.70	4536.11	4414.53	4320.13	4246.10	4187.60
240000	5118.30	4898.82	4733.33	4606.47	4507.96	4430.71	4369.67
250000	5331.56	5102.93	4930.56	4798.41	4695.79	4615.33	4551.74

21.50 % Monthly Payments

LOAN AMOUNT	YEARS 15	16	17	18	19	20	21
100	1.80	1.78	1.77	1.76	1.75	1.75	1.74
200	3.60	3.57	3.54	3.52	3.51	3.49	3.48
500	9.00	8.92	8.86	8.80	8.76	8.73	8.70
1000	18.00	17.84	17.71	17.61	17.53	17.46	17.40
2000	36.01	35.69	35.43	35.22	35.05	34.91	34.80
5000	90.02	89.22	88.57	88.05	87.63	87.29	87.01
6000	108.03	107.06	106.28	105.66	105.15	104.74	104.41
7000	126.03	124.90	123.99	123.26	122.68	122.20	121.81
8000	144.04	142.74	141.71	140.87	140.20	139.66	139.22
9000	162.04	160.59	159.42	158.48	157.73	157.11	156.62
10000	180.05	178.43	177.13	176.09	175.25	174.57	174.02
12000	216.06	214.12	212.56	211.31	210.30	209.48	208.82
15000	270.07	267.65	265.70	264.14	262.88	261.86	261.03
20000	360.09	356.86	354.27	352.18	350.50	349.14	348.04
25000	450.12	446.08	442.84	440.23	438.13	436.43	435.05
30000	540.14	535.29	531.40	528.28	525.75	523.71	522.06
31000	558.15	553.14	549.12	545.88	543.28	541.17	539.46
32000	576.15	570.98	566.83	563.49	560.80	558.63	556.86
33000	594.16	588.82	584.54	581.10	578.33	576.08	574.27
34000	612.16	606.67	602.26	598.71	595.85	593.54	591.67
35000	630.16	624.51	619.97	616.32	613.38	611.00	609.07
36000	648.17	642.35	637.69	633.93	630.90	628.45	626.47
37000	666.17	660.19	655.40	651.54	648.43	645.91	643.88
38000	684.18	678.04	673.11	669.15	665.95	663.37	661.28
39000	702.18	695.88	690.83	686.76	683.48	680.83	678.68
40000	720.19	713.72	708.54	704.37	701.00	698.28	696.08
41000	738.19	731.57	726.25	721.98	718.53	715.74	713.48
42000	756.20	749.41	743.97	739.59	736.05	733.20	730.89
43000	774.20	767.25	761.68	757.20	753.58	750.65	748.29
44000	792.21	785.10	779.39	774.80	771.10	768.11	765.69
45000	810.21	802.94	797.11	792.41	788.63	785.57	783.09
46000	828.22	820.78	814.82	810.02	806.15	803.03	800.49
47000	846.22	838.63	832.53	827.63	823.68	820.48	817.90
48000	864.23	856.47	850.25	845.24	841.20	837.94	835.30
49000	882.23	874.31	867.96	862.85	858.73	855.40	852.70
50000	900.23	892.16	885.67	880.46	876.25	872.85	870.10
51000	918.24	910.00	903.39	898.07	893.78	890.31	887.50
52000	936.24	927.84	921.10	915.68	911.30	907.77	904.91
53000	954.25	945.68	938.81	933.29	928.83	925.23	922.31
54000	972.25	963.53	956.53	950.90	946.35	942.68	939.71
55000	990.26	981.37	974.24	968.51	963.88	960.14	957.11
56000	1008.26	999.21	991.96	986.11	981.40	977.60	974.51
57000	1026.27	1017.06	1009.67	1003.72	998.93	995.05	991.92
58000	1044.27	1034.90	1027.38	1021.33	1016.45	1012.51	1009.32
59000	1062.28	1052.74	1045.10	1038.94	1033.98	1029.97	1026.72
60000	1080.28	1070.59	1062.81	1056.55	1051.50	1047.42	1044.12
65000	1170.31	1159.80	1151.38	1144.60	1139.13	1134.71	1131.13
70000	1260.33	1249.02	1239.94	1232.64	1226.75	1222.00	1218.14
75000	1350.35	1338.23	1328.51	1320.69	1314.38	1309.28	1305.15
80000	1440.38	1427.45	1417.08	1408.74	1402.01	1396.57	1392.16
85000	1530.40	1516.66	1505.65	1496.78	1489.63	1483.85	1479.17
90000	1620.42	1605.88	1594.21	1584.83	1577.26	1571.14	1566.18
95000	1710.45	1695.09	1682.78	1672.87	1664.88	1658.42	1653.19
100000	1800.47	1784.31	1771.35	1760.92	1752.51	1745.71	1740.20
105000	1890.49	1873.53	1859.92	1848.97	1840.13	1832.99	1827.21
110000	1980.52	1962.74	1948.48	1937.01	1927.76	1920.28	1914.22
120000	2160.56	2141.17	2125.62	2113.10	2103.01	2094.85	2088.24
130000	2340.61	2319.60	2302.75	2289.19	2278.26	2269.42	2262.26
140000	2520.66	2498.03	2479.89	2465.29	2453.51	2443.99	2436.28
150000	2700.70	2676.47	2657.02	2641.38	2628.76	2618.56	2610.30
160000	2880.75	2854.90	2834.16	2817.47	2804.01	2793.13	2784.32
170000	3060.80	3033.33	3011.29	2993.56	2979.26	2967.70	2958.35
180000	3240.85	3211.76	3188.43	3169.65	3154.51	3142.27	3132.37
190000	3420.89	3390.19	3365.56	3345.75	3329.76	3316.84	3306.39
200000	3600.94	3568.62	3542.70	3521.84	3505.01	3491.42	3480.41
210000	3780.99	3747.05	3719.83	3697.93	3680.26	3665.99	3654.43
220000	3961.03	3925.48	3896.97	3874.02	3855.51	3840.56	3828.45
230000	4141.08	4103.91	4074.10	4050.11	4030.77	4015.13	4002.47
240000	4321.13	4282.34	4251.24	4226.21	4206.02	4189.70	4176.49
250000	4501.17	4460.78	4428.37	4402.30	4381.27	4364.27	4350.51

Monthly Payments 21.50 %

LOAN AMOUNT	22	23	24	25	30	35	40
100	1.74	1.73	1.73	1.73	1.72	1.72	1.72
200	3.47	3.46	3.46	3.45	3.44	3.44	3.43
500	8.68	8.66	8.65	8.63	8.60	8.59	8.58
1000	17.36	17.32	17.29	17.27	17.20	17.18	17.17
2000	34.71	34.64	34.58	34.54	34.40	34.35	34.34
5000	86.79	86.61	86.46	86.34	86.00	85.88	85.84
6000	104.14	103.93	103.75	103.61	103.20	103.06	103.01
7000	121.50	121.25	121.04	120.88	120.41	120.24	120.18
8000	138.86	138.57	138.33	138.14	137.61	137.41	137.34
9000	156.22	155.89	155.63	155.41	154.81	154.59	154.51
10000	173.57	173.21	172.92	172.68	172.01	171.77	171.68
12000	208.29	207.85	207.50	207.21	206.41	206.12	206.02
15000	260.36	259.82	259.38	259.02	258.01	257.65	257.52
20000	347.15	346.42	345.84	345.36	344.01	343.53	343.36
25000	433.94	433.03	432.29	431.70	430.02	429.42	429.20
30000	520.72	519.64	518.75	518.04	516.02	515.30	515.04
31000	538.08	536.96	536.05	535.30	533.22	532.48	532.21
32000	555.44	554.28	553.34	552.57	550.42	549.65	549.38
33000	572.79	571.60	570.63	569.84	567.62	566.83	566.54
34000	590.15	588.92	587.92	587.11	584.83	584.01	583.71
35000	607.51	606.24	605.21	604.38	602.03	601.18	600.88
36000	624.87	623.56	622.50	621.64	619.23	618.36	618.05
37000	642.22	640.88	639.80	638.91	636.43	635.54	635.22
38000	659.58	658.21	657.09	656.18	653.63	652.71	652.39
39000	676.94	675.53	674.38	673.45	670.83	669.89	669.55
40000	694.30	692.85	691.67	690.72	688.03	687.07	686.72
41000	711.65	710.17	708.96	707.98	705.23	704.24	703.89
42000	729.01	727.49	726.26	725.25	722.43	721.42	721.06
43000	746.37	744.81	743.55	742.52	739.63	738.60	738.23
44000	763.73	762.13	760.84	759.79	756.83	755.77	755.39
45000	781.08	779.45	778.13	777.05	774.03	772.95	772.56
46000	798.44	796.78	795.42	794.32	791.23	790.13	789.73
47000	815.80	814.10	812.71	811.59	808.43	807.30	806.90
48000	833.16	831.42	830.01	828.86	825.64	824.48	824.07
49000	850.51	848.74	847.30	846.13	842.84	841.66	841.23
50000	867.87	866.06	864.59	863.39	860.04	858.83	858.40
51000	885.23	883.38	881.88	880.66	877.24	876.01	875.57
52000	902.59	900.70	899.17	897.93	894.44	893.19	892.74
53000	919.94	918.02	916.46	915.20	911.64	910.36	909.91
54000	937.30	935.34	933.76	932.47	928.84	927.54	927.07
55000	954.66	952.67	951.05	949.73	946.04	944.72	944.24
56000	972.01	969.99	968.34	967.00	963.24	961.89	961.41
57000	989.37	987.31	985.63	984.27	980.44	979.07	978.58
58000	1006.73	1004.63	1002.92	1001.54	997.64	996.25	995.75
59000	1024.09	1021.95	1020.22	1018.81	1014.84	1013.42	1012.91
60000	1041.44	1039.27	1037.51	1036.07	1032.04	1030.60	1030.08
65000	1128.23	1125.88	1123.97	1122.41	1118.05	1116.48	1115.92
70000	1215.02	1212.48	1210.43	1208.75	1204.05	1202.37	1201.76
75000	1301.81	1299.09	1296.88	1295.09	1290.06	1288.25	1287.60
80000	1388.59	1385.70	1383.34	1381.43	1376.06	1374.13	1373.44
85000	1475.38	1472.30	1469.80	1467.77	1462.06	1460.02	1459.28
90000	1562.17	1558.91	1556.26	1554.11	1548.07	1545.90	1545.12
95000	1648.95	1645.51	1642.72	1640.45	1634.07	1631.78	1630.96
100000	1735.74	1732.12	1729.18	1726.79	1720.07	1717.67	1716.80
105000	1822.53	1818.73	1815.64	1813.13	1806.08	1803.55	1802.64
110000	1909.32	1905.33	1902.10	1899.47	1892.08	1889.43	1888.48
120000	2082.89	2078.54	2075.01	2072.15	2064.09	2061.20	2060.16
130000	2256.46	2251.76	2247.93	2244.83	2236.10	2232.97	2231.84
140000	2430.04	2424.97	2420.85	2417.50	2408.10	2404.73	2403.52
150000	2603.61	2598.18	2593.77	2590.18	2580.11	2576.50	2575.20
160000	2777.19	2771.39	2766.69	2762.86	2752.12	2748.27	2746.88
170000	2950.76	2944.60	2939.60	2935.54	2924.13	2920.04	2918.56
180000	3124.33	3117.82	3112.52	3108.22	3096.13	3091.80	3090.24
190000	3297.91	3291.03	3285.44	3280.90	3268.14	3263.57	3261.93
200000	3471.48	3464.24	3458.36	3453.58	3440.15	3435.34	3433.61
210000	3645.06	3637.45	3631.28	3626.26	3612.15	3607.10	3605.29
220000	3818.63	3810.66	3804.19	3798.93	3784.16	3778.87	3776.97
230000	3992.20	3983.88	3977.11	3971.61	3956.17	3950.64	3948.65
240000	4165.78	4157.09	4150.03	4144.29	4128.18	4122.40	4120.33
250000	4339.35	4330.30	4322.95	4316.97	4300.18	4294.17	4292.01

21.75 % Monthly Payments

LOAN AMOUNT	1	2	3	4	5	6	7
100	9.30	5.13	3.76	3.09	2.70	2.44	2.27
200	18.61	10.26	7.52	6.17	5.39	4.89	4.54
500	46.51	25.65	18.79	15.44	13.48	12.22	11.35
1000	93.03	51.30	37.59	30.87	26.96	24.43	22.71
2000	186.06	102.60	75.17	61.74	53.91	48.87	45.41
5000	465.15	256.50	187.93	154.36	134.78	122.17	113.53
6000	558.18	307.80	225.51	185.23	161.73	146.60	136.23
7000	651.21	359.10	263.10	216.10	188.69	171.04	158.94
8000	744.24	410.40	300.68	246.97	215.64	195.47	181.65
9000	837.27	461.70	338.27	277.85	242.60	219.90	204.35
10000	930.30	513.00	375.85	308.72	269.55	244.34	227.06
12000	1116.36	615.60	451.03	370.46	323.46	293.20	272.47
15000	1395.45	769.50	563.78	463.08	404.33	366.50	340.59
20000	1860.60	1026.00	751.71	617.44	539.10	488.67	454.12
25000	2325.75	1282.50	939.64	771.80	673.88	610.84	567.64
30000	2790.90	1539.00	1127.56	926.15	808.66	733.01	681.17
31000	2883.93	1590.30	1165.15	957.03	835.61	757.44	703.88
32000	2976.96	1641.60	1202.73	987.90	862.57	781.88	726.59
33000	3069.99	1692.90	1240.32	1018.77	889.52	806.31	749.29
34000	3163.02	1744.20	1277.90	1049.64	916.48	830.74	772.00
35000	3256.05	1795.50	1315.49	1080.51	943.43	855.18	794.70
36000	3349.08	1846.80	1353.08	1111.38	970.39	879.61	817.41
37000	3442.11	1898.10	1390.66	1142.26	997.34	904.04	840.11
38000	3535.14	1949.40	1428.25	1173.13	1024.30	928.48	862.82
39000	3628.17	2000.70	1465.83	1204.00	1051.25	952.91	885.53
40000	3721.20	2052.00	1503.42	1234.87	1078.21	977.34	908.23
41000	3814.23	2103.30	1541.00	1265.74	1105.16	1001.78	930.94
42000	3907.26	2154.59	1578.59	1296.62	1132.12	1026.21	953.64
43000	4000.29	2205.89	1616.17	1327.49	1159.07	1050.65	976.35
44000	4093.32	2257.19	1653.76	1358.36	1186.03	1075.08	999.05
45000	4186.35	2308.49	1691.34	1389.23	1212.98	1099.51	1021.76
46000	4279.38	2359.79	1728.93	1420.10	1239.94	1123.95	1044.47
47000	4372.41	2411.09	1766.51	1450.97	1266.89	1148.38	1067.17
48000	4465.44	2462.39	1804.10	1481.85	1293.85	1172.81	1089.88
49000	4558.47	2513.69	1841.69	1512.72	1320.80	1197.25	1112.58
50000	4651.50	2564.99	1879.27	1543.59	1347.76	1221.68	1135.29
51000	4744.53	2616.29	1916.86	1574.46	1374.71	1246.11	1158.00
52000	4837.56	2667.59	1954.44	1605.33	1401.67	1270.55	1180.70
53000	4930.59	2718.89	1992.03	1636.21	1428.62	1294.98	1203.41
54000	5023.62	2770.19	2029.61	1667.08	1455.58	1319.41	1226.11
55000	5116.65	2821.49	2067.20	1697.95	1482.53	1343.85	1248.82
56000	5209.68	2872.79	2104.78	1728.82	1509.49	1368.28	1271.52
57000	5302.71	2924.09	2142.37	1759.69	1536.44	1392.72	1294.23
58000	5395.74	2975.39	2179.95	1790.56	1563.40	1417.15	1316.94
59000	5488.77	3026.69	2217.54	1821.44	1590.36	1441.58	1339.64
60000	5581.80	3077.99	2255.13	1852.31	1617.31	1466.02	1362.35
65000	6046.95	3334.49	2443.05	2006.67	1752.09	1588.18	1475.88
70000	6512.10	3590.99	2630.98	2161.03	1886.86	1710.35	1589.41
75000	6977.25	3847.49	2818.91	2315.39	2021.64	1832.52	1702.93
80000	7442.40	4103.99	3006.83	2469.74	2156.41	1954.69	1816.46
85000	7907.55	4360.49	3194.76	2624.10	2291.19	2076.86	1929.99
90000	8372.70	4616.99	3382.69	2778.46	2425.97	2199.02	2043.52
95000	8837.84	4873.49	3570.62	2932.82	2560.74	2321.19	2157.05
100000	9302.99	5129.99	3758.54	3087.18	2695.52	2443.36	2270.58
105000	9768.14	5386.49	3946.47	3241.54	2830.29	2565.53	2384.11
110000	10233.29	5642.99	4134.40	3395.90	2965.07	2687.70	2497.64
120000	11163.59	6155.99	4510.25	3704.62	3234.62	2932.03	2724.69
130000	12093.89	6668.98	4886.11	4013.33	3504.17	3176.37	2951.75
140000	13024.19	7181.98	5261.96	4322.05	3773.72	3420.71	3178.81
150000	13954.49	7694.98	5637.81	4630.77	4043.28	3665.04	3405.87
160000	14884.79	8207.98	6013.67	4939.49	4312.83	3909.38	3632.93
170000	15815.09	8720.98	6389.52	5248.21	4582.38	4153.71	3859.98
180000	16745.39	9233.98	6765.38	5556.92	4851.93	4398.05	4087.04
190000	17675.69	9746.98	7141.23	5865.64	5121.48	4642.39	4314.10
200000	18605.99	10259.98	7517.09	6174.36	5391.04	4886.72	4541.16
210000	19536.29	10772.97	7892.94	6483.08	5660.59	5131.06	4768.22
220000	20466.59	11285.97	8268.79	6791.80	5930.14	5375.39	4995.27
230000	21396.89	11798.97	8644.65	7100.51	6199.69	5619.73	5222.33
240000	22327.19	12311.97	9020.50	7409.23	6469.24	5864.07	5449.39
250000	23257.49	12824.97	9396.36	7717.95	6738.79	6108.40	5676.45

Monthly Payments 21.75 %

LOAN AMOUNT	8	9	10	11	12	13	14
	YEARS						
100	2.15	2.06	1.99	1.94	1.89	1.86	1.84
200	4.29	4.11	3.98	3.87	3.79	3.73	3.68
500	10.74	10.28	9.94	9.68	9.47	9.31	9.19
1000	21.47	20.56	19.88	19.35	18.94	18.63	18.38
2000	42.94	41.12	39.75	38.70	37.89	37.25	36.75
5000	107.35	102.80	99.38	96.76	94.72	93.13	91.88
6000	128.82	123.37	119.26	116.11	113.67	111.76	110.25
7000	150.30	143.93	139.13	135.46	132.61	130.38	128.63
8000	171.77	164.49	159.01	154.81	151.56	149.01	147.00
9000	193.24	185.05	178.88	174.16	170.50	167.64	165.38
10000	214.71	205.61	198.76	193.51	189.45	186.26	183.75
12000	257.65	246.73	238.51	232.22	227.34	223.52	220.50
15000	322.06	308.41	298.14	290.27	284.17	279.39	275.63
20000	429.41	411.22	397.52	387.03	378.89	372.53	367.50
25000	536.77	514.02	496.90	483.78	473.62	465.66	459.38
30000	644.12	616.83	596.28	580.54	568.34	558.79	551.25
31000	665.59	637.39	616.15	599.89	587.29	577.42	569.63
32000	687.06	657.95	636.03	619.24	606.23	596.04	588.00
33000	708.53	678.51	655.90	638.60	625.18	614.67	606.38
34000	730.00	699.07	675.78	657.95	644.12	633.29	624.75
35000	751.48	719.63	695.66	677.30	663.07	651.92	643.13
36000	772.95	740.19	715.53	696.65	682.01	670.55	661.50
37000	794.42	760.76	735.41	716.00	700.95	689.17	679.88
38000	815.89	781.32	755.28	735.35	719.90	707.80	698.25
39000	837.36	801.88	775.16	754.70	738.84	726.43	716.63
40000	858.83	822.44	795.04	774.06	757.79	745.05	735.00
41000	880.30	843.00	814.91	793.41	776.73	763.68	753.38
42000	901.77	863.56	834.79	812.76	795.68	782.30	771.75
43000	923.24	884.12	854.66	832.11	814.62	800.93	790.13
44000	944.71	904.68	874.54	851.46	833.57	819.56	808.50
45000	966.18	925.24	894.41	870.81	852.51	838.18	826.88
46000	987.65	945.80	914.29	890.16	871.46	856.81	845.25
47000	1009.12	966.37	934.17	909.51	890.40	875.44	863.63
48000	1030.59	986.93	954.04	928.87	909.35	894.06	882.00
49000	1052.07	1007.49	973.92	948.22	928.29	912.69	900.38
50000	1073.54	1028.05	993.79	967.57	947.24	931.32	918.75
51000	1095.01	1048.61	1013.67	986.92	966.18	949.94	937.13
52000	1116.48	1069.17	1033.55	1006.27	985.13	968.57	955.50
53000	1137.95	1089.73	1053.42	1025.62	1004.07	987.19	973.88
54000	1159.42	1110.29	1073.30	1044.97	1023.01	1005.82	992.25
55000	1180.89	1130.85	1093.17	1064.33	1041.96	1024.45	1010.63
56000	1202.36	1151.41	1113.05	1083.68	1060.90	1043.07	1029.00
57000	1223.83	1171.97	1132.93	1103.03	1079.85	1061.70	1047.38
58000	1245.30	1192.54	1152.80	1122.38	1098.79	1080.33	1065.75
59000	1266.77	1213.10	1172.68	1141.73	1117.74	1098.95	1084.13
60000	1288.24	1233.66	1192.55	1161.08	1136.68	1117.58	1102.51
65000	1395.60	1336.46	1291.93	1257.84	1231.41	1210.71	1194.38
70000	1502.95	1439.27	1391.31	1354.60	1326.13	1303.84	1286.26
75000	1610.30	1542.07	1490.69	1451.35	1420.85	1396.97	1378.13
80000	1717.66	1644.88	1590.07	1548.11	1515.58	1490.10	1470.01
85000	1825.01	1747.68	1689.45	1644.87	1610.30	1583.24	1561.88
90000	1932.37	1850.49	1788.83	1741.62	1705.02	1676.37	1653.76
95000	2039.72	1953.29	1888.21	1838.38	1799.75	1769.50	1745.63
100000	2147.07	2056.10	1987.59	1935.14	1894.47	1862.63	1837.51
105000	2254.43	2158.90	2086.97	2031.90	1989.20	1955.76	1929.38
110000	2361.78	2261.71	2186.35	2128.65	2083.92	2048.89	2021.26
120000	2576.49	2467.32	2385.11	2322.17	2273.37	2235.16	2205.01
130000	2791.19	2672.92	2583.86	2515.68	2462.81	2421.42	2388.76
140000	3005.90	2878.53	2782.62	2709.19	2652.26	2607.68	2572.51
150000	3220.61	3084.14	2981.38	2902.71	2841.71	2793.95	2756.26
160000	3435.32	3289.75	3180.14	3096.22	3031.15	2980.21	2940.01
170000	3650.02	3495.36	3378.90	3289.74	3220.60	3166.47	3123.76
180000	3864.73	3700.97	3577.66	3483.25	3410.05	3352.74	3307.52
190000	4079.44	3906.58	3776.42	3676.76	3599.50	3539.00	3491.27
200000	4294.15	4112.19	3975.18	3870.28	3788.94	3725.26	3675.02
210000	4508.85	4317.80	4173.93	4063.79	3978.39	3911.52	3858.77
220000	4723.56	4523.41	4372.69	4257.30	4167.84	4097.79	4042.52
230000	4938.27	4729.02	4571.45	4450.82	4357.28	4284.05	4226.27
240000	5152.97	4934.63	4770.21	4644.33	4546.73	4470.31	4410.02
250000	5367.68	5140.24	4968.97	4837.85	4736.18	4656.58	4593.77

21.75 % Monthly Payments

LOAN AMOUNT	YEARS 15	16	17	18	19	20	21
100	1.82	1.80	1.79	1.78	1.77	1.76	1.76
200	3.64	3.60	3.58	3.56	3.54	3.53	3.52
500	9.09	9.01	8.94	8.89	8.85	8.82	8.79
1000	18.18	18.02	17.89	17.79	17.70	17.64	17.58
2000	36.35	36.03	35.78	35.57	35.41	35.28	35.17
5000	90.88	90.08	89.45	88.94	88.52	88.19	87.92
6000	109.05	108.10	107.34	106.72	106.23	105.83	105.51
7000	127.23	126.12	125.22	124.51	123.93	123.47	123.09
8000	145.41	144.13	143.11	142.30	141.64	141.11	140.68
9000	163.58	162.15	161.00	160.08	159.34	158.74	158.26
10000	181.76	180.17	178.89	177.87	177.05	176.38	175.85
12000	218.11	216.20	214.67	213.44	212.46	211.66	211.02
15000	272.64	270.25	268.34	266.81	265.57	264.57	263.77
20000	363.51	360.33	357.79	355.74	354.09	352.77	351.69
25000	454.39	450.42	447.23	444.68	442.62	440.96	439.62
30000	545.27	540.50	536.68	533.61	531.14	529.15	527.54
31000	563.45	558.52	554.57	551.40	548.85	546.79	545.12
32000	581.62	576.53	572.46	569.18	566.55	564.42	562.71
33000	599.80	594.55	590.35	586.97	584.25	582.06	580.29
34000	617.97	612.57	608.24	604.76	601.96	599.70	597.88
35000	636.15	630.58	626.12	622.55	619.66	617.34	615.46
36000	654.32	648.60	644.01	640.33	637.37	634.98	633.05
37000	672.50	666.62	661.90	658.12	655.07	652.62	650.63
38000	690.68	684.63	679.79	675.91	672.78	670.25	668.22
39000	708.85	702.65	697.68	693.69	690.48	687.89	685.80
40000	727.03	720.66	715.57	711.48	708.19	705.53	703.38
41000	745.20	738.68	733.46	729.27	725.89	723.17	720.97
42000	763.38	756.70	751.35	747.05	743.60	740.81	738.55
43000	781.55	774.71	769.24	764.84	761.30	758.45	756.14
44000	799.73	792.73	787.13	782.63	779.01	776.08	773.72
45000	817.91	810.75	805.02	800.42	796.71	793.72	791.31
46000	836.08	828.76	822.91	818.20	814.42	811.36	808.89
47000	854.26	846.78	840.80	835.99	832.12	829.00	826.48
48000	872.43	864.80	858.69	853.78	849.82	846.64	844.06
49000	890.61	882.81	876.57	871.56	867.53	864.28	861.65
50000	908.78	900.83	894.46	889.35	885.23	881.91	879.23
51000	926.96	918.85	912.35	907.14	902.94	899.55	896.82
52000	945.13	936.86	930.24	924.92	920.64	917.19	914.40
53000	963.31	954.88	948.13	942.71	938.35	934.83	931.98
54000	981.49	972.90	966.02	960.50	956.05	952.47	949.57
55000	999.66	990.91	983.91	978.29	973.76	970.11	967.15
56000	1017.84	1008.93	1001.80	996.07	991.46	987.74	984.74
57000	1036.01	1026.95	1019.69	1013.86	1009.17	1005.38	1002.32
58000	1054.19	1044.96	1037.58	1031.65	1026.87	1023.02	1019.91
59000	1072.36	1062.98	1055.47	1049.43	1044.58	1040.66	1037.49
60000	1090.54	1081.00	1073.36	1067.22	1062.28	1058.30	1055.08
65000	1181.42	1171.08	1162.80	1156.16	1150.80	1146.49	1143.00
70000	1272.30	1261.16	1252.25	1245.09	1239.33	1234.68	1230.92
75000	1363.18	1351.25	1341.70	1334.03	1327.85	1322.87	1318.85
80000	1454.05	1441.33	1431.14	1422.96	1416.37	1411.06	1406.77
85000	1544.93	1531.41	1520.59	1511.90	1504.90	1499.25	1494.69
90000	1635.81	1621.50	1610.04	1600.83	1593.42	1587.44	1582.62
95000	1726.69	1711.58	1699.48	1689.77	1681.95	1675.64	1670.54
100000	1817.57	1801.66	1788.93	1778.70	1770.47	1763.83	1758.46
105000	1908.45	1891.75	1878.37	1867.64	1858.99	1852.02	1846.38
110000	1999.32	1981.83	1967.82	1956.57	1947.52	1940.21	1934.31
120000	2181.08	2161.99	2146.71	2134.44	2124.56	2116.59	2110.15
130000	2362.84	2342.16	2325.61	2312.31	2301.61	2292.98	2286.00
140000	2544.59	2522.33	2504.50	2490.18	2478.66	2469.36	2461.85
150000	2726.35	2702.49	2683.39	2668.05	2655.70	2645.74	2637.69
160000	2908.11	2882.66	2862.29	2845.92	2832.75	2822.12	2813.54
170000	3089.86	3062.83	3041.18	3023.79	3009.80	2998.51	2989.39
180000	3271.62	3242.99	3220.07	3201.66	3186.84	3174.89	3165.23
190000	3453.38	3423.16	3398.96	3379.53	3363.89	3351.27	3341.08
200000	3635.13	3603.32	3577.86	3557.40	3540.94	3527.65	3516.92
210000	3816.89	3783.49	3756.75	3735.27	3717.98	3704.04	3692.77
220000	3998.65	3963.66	3935.64	3913.14	3895.03	3880.42	3868.62
230000	4180.40	4143.82	4114.53	4091.01	4072.08	4056.80	4044.46
240000	4362.16	4323.99	4293.43	4268.88	4249.12	4233.19	4220.31
250000	4543.92	4504.16	4472.32	4446.75	4426.17	4409.57	4396.15

Monthly Payments 21.75 %

LOAN AMOUNT	22	23	24	25	30	35	40
				YEARS			
100	1.75	1.75	1.75	1.75	1.74	1.74	1.74
200	3.51	3.50	3.50	3.49	3.48	3.47	3.47
500	8.77	8.75	8.74	8.73	8.69	8.68	8.68
1000	17.54	17.51	17.48	17.45	17.39	17.37	17.36
2000	35.08	35.01	34.96	34.91	34.78	34.73	34.72
5000	87.71	87.53	87.39	87.27	86.95	86.84	86.79
6000	105.25	105.04	104.87	104.73	104.34	104.20	104.15
7000	122.79	122.54	122.34	122.18	121.73	121.57	121.51
8000	140.33	140.05	139.82	139.64	139.12	138.94	138.87
9000	157.87	157.55	157.30	157.09	156.51	156.30	156.23
10000	175.41	175.06	174.78	174.54	173.90	173.67	173.59
12000	210.49	210.07	209.73	209.45	208.68	208.40	208.31
15000	263.12	262.59	262.16	261.82	260.85	260.51	260.38
20000	350.82	350.12	349.55	349.09	347.80	347.34	347.18
25000	438.53	437.65	436.94	436.36	434.75	434.18	433.97
30000	526.24	525.18	524.33	523.63	521.70	521.01	520.77
31000	543.78	542.69	541.80	541.09	539.09	538.38	538.13
32000	561.32	560.19	559.28	558.54	556.48	555.75	555.49
33000	578.86	577.70	576.76	576.00	573.87	573.11	572.84
34000	596.40	595.21	594.24	593.45	591.26	590.48	590.20
35000	613.94	612.71	611.71	610.91	608.65	607.85	607.56
36000	631.48	630.22	629.19	628.36	626.04	625.21	624.92
37000	649.02	647.72	646.67	645.82	643.43	642.58	642.28
38000	666.57	665.23	664.15	663.27	660.82	659.95	659.64
39000	684.11	682.74	681.63	680.72	678.21	677.31	677.00
40000	701.65	700.24	699.10	698.18	695.60	694.68	694.36
41000	719.19	717.75	716.58	715.63	712.99	712.05	711.72
42000	736.73	735.25	734.06	733.09	730.38	729.42	729.07
43000	754.27	752.76	751.54	750.54	747.77	746.78	746.43
44000	771.81	770.27	769.01	768.00	765.16	764.15	763.79
45000	789.35	787.77	786.49	785.45	782.55	781.52	781.15
46000	806.90	805.28	803.97	802.91	799.94	798.88	798.51
47000	824.44	822.78	821.45	820.36	817.33	816.25	815.87
48000	841.98	840.29	838.92	837.81	834.72	833.62	833.23
49000	859.52	857.80	856.40	855.27	852.11	850.98	850.59
50000	877.06	875.30	873.88	872.72	869.50	868.35	867.95
51000	894.60	892.81	891.36	890.18	886.89	885.72	885.30
52000	912.14	910.32	908.83	907.63	904.28	903.09	902.66
53000	929.68	927.82	926.31	925.09	921.67	920.45	920.02
54000	947.23	945.33	943.79	942.54	939.06	937.82	937.38
55000	964.77	962.83	961.27	960.00	956.45	955.19	954.74
56000	982.31	980.34	978.74	977.45	973.84	972.55	972.10
57000	999.85	997.85	996.22	994.90	991.23	989.92	989.46
58000	1017.39	1015.35	1013.70	1012.36	1008.62	1007.29	1006.82
59000	1034.93	1032.86	1031.18	1029.81	1026.00	1024.66	1024.18
60000	1052.47	1050.36	1048.65	1047.27	1043.39	1042.02	1041.53
65000	1140.18	1137.89	1136.04	1134.54	1130.34	1128.86	1128.33
70000	1227.88	1225.42	1223.43	1221.81	1217.29	1215.69	1215.12
75000	1315.59	1312.95	1310.82	1309.08	1304.24	1302.53	1301.92
80000	1403.30	1400.48	1398.21	1396.36	1391.19	1389.36	1388.71
85000	1491.00	1488.02	1485.59	1483.63	1478.14	1476.20	1475.51
90000	1578.71	1575.55	1572.98	1570.90	1565.09	1563.03	1562.30
95000	1666.42	1663.08	1660.37	1658.17	1652.04	1649.87	1649.10
100000	1754.12	1750.61	1747.76	1745.45	1738.99	1736.70	1735.89
105000	1841.83	1838.14	1835.14	1832.72	1825.94	1823.54	1822.69
110000	1929.53	1925.67	1922.53	1919.99	1912.89	1910.37	1909.48
120000	2104.95	2100.73	2097.31	2094.54	2086.79	2084.04	2083.07
130000	2280.36	2275.79	2272.08	2269.08	2260.69	2257.72	2256.66
140000	2455.77	2450.85	2446.86	2443.62	2434.59	2431.39	2430.25
150000	2631.18	2625.91	2621.64	2618.17	2608.49	2605.06	2603.84
160000	2806.59	2800.97	2796.41	2792.71	2782.39	2778.73	2777.43
170000	2982.01	2976.03	2971.19	2967.26	2956.29	2952.40	2951.01
180000	3157.42	3151.09	3145.96	3141.80	3130.18	3126.07	3124.60
190000	3332.83	3326.15	3320.74	3316.35	3304.08	3299.74	3298.19
200000	3508.24	3501.21	3495.51	3490.89	3477.98	3473.41	3471.78
210000	3683.65	3676.27	3670.29	3665.44	3651.88	3647.08	3645.37
220000	3859.07	3851.33	3845.07	3839.98	3825.78	3820.75	3818.96
230000	4034.48	4026.39	4019.84	4014.53	3999.68	3994.42	3992.55
240000	4209.89	4201.45	4194.62	4189.07	4173.58	4168.09	4166.14
250000	4385.30	4376.51	4369.39	4363.62	4347.48	4341.76	4339.73

22.00 % Monthly Payments

LOAN AMOUNT	YEARS 1	2	3	4	5	6	7
100	9.31	5.14	3.77	3.10	2.71	2.46	2.28
200	18.63	10.28	7.54	6.20	5.42	4.91	4.57
500	46.57	25.71	18.85	15.50	13.54	12.28	11.42
1000	93.14	51.41	37.70	31.00	27.08	24.57	22.85
2000	186.28	102.82	75.41	61.99	54.17	49.14	45.69
5000	465.70	257.06	188.52	154.98	135.42	122.84	114.23
6000	558.84	308.47	226.22	185.97	162.50	147.41	137.07
7000	651.98	359.89	263.92	216.97	189.59	171.98	159.92
8000	745.12	411.30	301.62	247.96	216.67	196.54	182.76
9000	838.26	462.71	339.33	278.96	243.76	221.11	205.61
10000	931.40	514.12	377.03	309.95	270.84	245.68	228.46
12000	1117.68	616.95	452.44	371.94	325.01	294.82	274.15
15000	1397.10	771.19	565.55	464.93	406.26	368.52	342.68
20000	1862.80	1028.25	754.06	619.90	541.68	491.36	456.91
25000	2328.50	1285.31	942.58	774.88	677.10	614.20	571.14
30000	2794.20	1542.37	1131.09	929.85	812.52	737.04	685.37
31000	2887.34	1593.79	1168.80	960.85	839.61	761.61	708.21
32000	2980.48	1645.20	1206.50	991.84	866.69	786.18	731.06
33000	3073.62	1696.61	1244.20	1022.84	893.77	810.74	753.90
34000	3166.76	1748.02	1281.91	1053.83	920.86	835.31	776.75
35000	3259.90	1799.44	1319.61	1084.83	947.94	859.88	799.59
36000	3353.04	1850.85	1357.31	1115.82	975.03	884.45	822.44
37000	3446.18	1902.26	1395.01	1146.82	1002.11	909.02	845.28
38000	3539.32	1953.67	1432.72	1177.81	1029.19	933.58	868.13
39000	3632.46	2005.09	1470.42	1208.81	1056.28	958.15	890.98
40000	3725.60	2056.50	1508.12	1239.80	1083.36	982.72	913.82
41000	3818.74	2107.91	1545.83	1270.80	1110.45	1007.29	936.67
42000	3911.88	2159.32	1583.53	1301.79	1137.53	1031.86	959.51
43000	4005.02	2210.74	1621.23	1332.79	1164.62	1056.43	982.36
44000	4098.16	2262.15	1658.94	1363.78	1191.70	1080.99	1005.20
45000	4191.30	2313.56	1696.64	1394.78	1218.78	1105.56	1028.05
46000	4284.44	2364.97	1734.34	1425.77	1245.87	1130.13	1050.89
47000	4377.58	2416.39	1772.05	1456.77	1272.95	1154.70	1073.74
48000	4470.72	2467.80	1809.75	1487.76	1300.04	1179.27	1096.59
49000	4563.86	2519.21	1847.45	1518.76	1327.12	1203.83	1119.43
50000	4657.00	2570.62	1885.15	1549.75	1354.20	1228.40	1142.28
51000	4750.14	2622.04	1922.86	1580.75	1381.29	1252.97	1165.12
52000	4843.28	2673.45	1960.56	1611.74	1408.37	1277.54	1187.97
53000	4936.42	2724.86	1998.26	1642.74	1435.46	1302.11	1210.81
54000	5029.56	2776.27	2035.97	1673.73	1462.54	1326.67	1233.66
55000	5122.70	2827.69	2073.67	1704.73	1489.62	1351.24	1256.50
56000	5215.84	2879.10	2111.37	1735.72	1516.71	1375.81	1279.35
57000	5308.98	2930.51	2149.08	1766.72	1543.79	1400.38	1302.19
58000	5402.12	2981.92	2186.78	1797.71	1570.88	1424.95	1325.04
59000	5495.26	3033.34	2224.48	1828.71	1597.96	1449.51	1347.89
60000	5588.40	3084.75	2262.19	1859.70	1625.04	1474.08	1370.73
65000	6054.10	3341.81	2450.70	2014.68	1760.46	1596.92	1484.96
70000	6519.80	3598.87	2639.22	2169.65	1895.88	1719.76	1599.19
75000	6985.50	3855.93	2827.73	2324.63	2031.31	1842.60	1713.41
80000	7451.20	4113.00	3016.25	2479.60	2166.73	1965.44	1827.64
85000	7916.90	4370.06	3204.76	2634.58	2302.15	2088.28	1941.87
90000	8382.60	4627.12	3393.28	2789.56	2437.57	2211.12	2056.10
95000	8848.30	4884.18	3581.79	2944.53	2572.99	2333.96	2170.32
100000	9314.00	5141.25	3770.31	3099.51	2708.41	2456.80	2284.55
105000	9779.70	5398.31	3958.82	3254.48	2843.83	2579.64	2398.78
110000	10245.40	5655.37	4147.34	3409.46	2979.25	2702.48	2513.01
120000	11176.80	6169.50	4524.37	3719.41	3250.09	2948.16	2741.46
130000	12108.20	6683.62	4901.40	4029.36	3520.93	3193.84	2969.92
140000	13039.60	7197.74	5278.43	4339.31	3791.77	3439.52	3198.37
150000	13971.00	7711.87	5655.46	4649.26	4062.61	3685.20	3426.83
160000	14902.40	8225.99	6032.50	4959.21	4333.45	3930.88	3655.28
170000	15833.79	8740.12	6409.53	5269.16	4604.29	4176.56	3883.74
180000	16765.19	9254.24	6786.56	5579.11	4875.13	4422.24	4112.19
190000	17696.59	9768.37	7163.59	5889.06	5145.97	4667.92	4340.65
200000	18627.99	10282.49	7540.62	6199.01	5416.81	4913.61	4569.10
210000	19559.39	10796.62	7917.65	6508.96	5687.65	5159.29	4797.56
220000	20490.79	11310.74	8294.68	6818.91	5958.50	5404.97	5026.02
230000	21422.19	11824.87	8671.71	7128.86	6229.34	5650.65	5254.47
240000	22353.59	12338.99	9048.74	7438.81	6500.18	5896.33	5482.93
250000	23284.99	12853.12	9425.77	7748.76	6771.02	6142.01	5711.38

Monthly Payments 22.00 %

LOAN AMOUNT	8	9	10	11	12	13	14
100	2.16	2.07	2.00	1.95	1.91	1.88	1.85
200	4.32	4.14	4.01	3.90	3.82	3.76	3.71
500	10.81	10.36	10.01	9.75	9.55	9.40	9.27
1000	21.62	20.71	20.03	19.51	19.11	18.79	18.54
2000	43.23	41.42	40.06	39.02	38.21	37.58	37.09
5000	108.08	103.55	100.15	97.55	95.53	93.96	92.72
6000	129.69	124.26	120.18	117.06	114.64	112.75	111.26
7000	151.31	144.97	140.21	136.57	133.75	131.54	129.80
8000	172.92	165.68	160.24	156.08	152.85	150.33	148.35
9000	194.54	186.39	180.27	175.59	171.96	169.12	166.89
10000	216.16	207.11	200.30	195.09	191.07	187.92	185.44
12000	259.39	248.53	240.36	234.11	229.28	225.50	222.52
15000	324.23	310.66	300.45	292.64	286.60	281.87	278.15
20000	432.31	414.21	400.60	390.19	382.13	375.83	370.87
25000	540.39	517.76	500.75	487.74	477.66	469.79	463.59
30000	648.47	621.32	600.90	585.28	573.20	563.75	556.31
31000	670.08	642.03	620.93	604.79	592.30	582.54	574.85
32000	691.70	662.74	640.96	624.30	611.41	601.33	593.39
33000	713.31	683.45	660.99	643.81	630.52	620.12	611.94
34000	734.93	704.16	681.02	663.32	649.62	638.92	630.48
35000	756.54	724.87	701.05	682.83	668.73	657.71	649.02
36000	778.16	745.58	721.08	702.34	687.84	676.50	667.57
37000	799.77	766.29	741.10	721.85	706.94	695.29	686.11
38000	821.39	787.00	761.13	741.36	726.05	714.08	704.65
39000	843.01	807.71	781.16	760.87	745.16	732.87	723.20
40000	864.62	828.42	801.19	780.38	764.26	751.66	741.74
41000	886.24	849.13	821.22	799.89	783.37	770.46	760.28
42000	907.85	869.84	841.25	819.40	802.48	789.25	778.83
43000	929.47	890.55	861.28	838.91	821.58	808.04	797.37
44000	951.08	911.26	881.31	858.42	840.69	826.83	815.92
45000	972.70	931.97	901.34	877.93	859.80	845.62	834.46
46000	994.31	952.68	921.37	897.44	878.90	864.41	853.00
47000	1015.93	973.39	941.40	916.95	898.01	883.21	871.55
48000	1037.54	994.10	961.43	936.45	917.12	902.00	890.09
49000	1059.16	1014.81	981.46	955.96	936.22	920.79	908.63
50000	1080.78	1035.53	1001.49	975.47	955.33	939.58	927.18
51000	1102.39	1056.24	1021.52	994.98	974.44	958.37	945.72
52000	1124.01	1076.95	1041.55	1014.49	993.54	977.16	964.26
53000	1145.62	1097.66	1061.58	1034.00	1012.65	995.96	982.81
54000	1167.24	1118.37	1081.61	1053.51	1031.76	1014.75	1001.35
55000	1188.85	1139.08	1101.64	1073.02	1050.86	1033.54	1019.89
56000	1210.47	1159.79	1121.67	1092.53	1069.97	1052.33	1038.44
57000	1232.08	1180.50	1141.70	1112.04	1089.08	1071.12	1056.98
58000	1253.70	1201.21	1161.73	1131.55	1108.18	1089.91	1075.52
59000	1275.32	1221.92	1181.76	1151.06	1127.29	1108.71	1094.07
60000	1296.93	1242.63	1201.79	1170.57	1146.40	1127.50	1112.61
65000	1405.01	1346.18	1301.94	1268.12	1241.93	1221.46	1205.33
70000	1513.09	1449.74	1402.09	1365.66	1337.46	1315.41	1298.05
75000	1621.16	1553.29	1502.24	1463.21	1432.99	1409.37	1390.76
80000	1729.24	1656.84	1602.39	1560.76	1528.53	1503.33	1483.48
85000	1837.32	1760.39	1702.54	1658.31	1624.06	1597.29	1576.20
90000	1945.40	1863.95	1802.69	1755.85	1719.59	1691.25	1668.92
95000	2053.47	1967.50	1902.84	1853.40	1815.13	1785.20	1761.63
100000	2161.55	2071.05	2002.99	1950.95	1910.66	1879.16	1854.35
105000	2269.63	2174.60	2103.14	2048.49	2006.19	1973.12	1947.07
110000	2377.71	2278.16	2203.28	2146.04	2101.72	2067.08	2039.79
120000	2593.86	2485.26	2403.58	2341.14	2292.79	2254.99	2225.22
130000	2810.02	2692.37	2603.88	2536.23	2483.86	2442.91	2410.66
140000	3026.17	2899.47	2804.18	2731.33	2674.92	2630.83	2596.09
150000	3242.33	3106.58	3004.48	2926.42	2865.99	2818.74	2781.53
160000	3458.48	3313.68	3204.78	3121.52	3057.05	3006.66	2966.96
170000	3674.64	3520.79	3405.08	3316.61	3248.12	3194.58	3152.40
180000	3890.79	3727.89	3605.38	3511.71	3439.19	3382.49	3337.83
190000	4106.95	3935.00	3805.67	3706.80	3630.25	3570.41	3523.27
200000	4323.10	4142.10	4005.97	3901.89	3821.32	3758.32	3708.70
210000	4539.26	4349.21	4206.27	4096.99	4012.38	3946.24	3894.14
220000	4755.41	4556.31	4406.57	4292.08	4203.45	4134.16	4079.58
230000	4971.57	4763.42	4606.87	4487.18	4394.51	4322.07	4265.01
240000	5187.72	4970.52	4807.17	4682.27	4585.58	4509.99	4450.45
250000	5403.88	5177.63	5007.47	4877.37	4776.65	4697.91	4635.88

Column headings 8–14 are YEARS.

22.00 % Monthly Payments

LOAN AMOUNT	15	16	17	18	19	20	21
	YEARS						
100	1.83	1.82	1.81	1.80	1.79	1.78	1.78
200	3.67	3.64	3.61	3.59	3.58	3.56	3.55
500	9.17	9.10	9.03	8.98	8.94	8.91	8.88
1000	18.35	18.19	18.07	17.97	17.88	17.82	17.77
2000	36.69	36.38	36.13	35.93	35.77	35.64	35.53
5000	91.73	90.95	90.33	89.83	89.42	89.10	88.84
6000	110.08	109.14	108.39	107.79	107.31	106.92	106.60
7000	128.43	127.33	126.46	125.76	125.19	124.74	124.37
8000	146.78	145.52	144.52	143.72	143.08	142.56	142.14
9000	165.12	163.71	162.59	161.69	160.96	160.38	159.91
10000	183.47	181.90	180.65	179.65	178.84	178.20	177.67
12000	220.16	218.28	216.78	215.58	214.61	213.84	213.21
15000	275.20	272.86	270.98	269.48	268.27	267.29	266.51
20000	366.94	363.81	361.31	359.30	357.69	356.39	355.35
25000	458.67	454.76	451.63	449.13	447.11	445.49	444.18
30000	550.41	545.71	541.96	538.95	536.53	534.59	533.02
31000	568.75	563.90	560.02	556.92	554.42	552.41	550.79
32000	587.10	582.09	578.09	574.88	572.30	570.23	568.55
33000	605.45	600.28	596.16	592.85	590.19	588.05	586.32
34000	623.80	618.47	614.22	610.81	608.07	605.87	604.09
35000	642.14	636.66	632.29	628.78	625.96	623.69	621.86
36000	660.49	654.85	650.35	646.74	643.84	641.51	639.62
37000	678.84	673.04	668.42	664.71	661.73	659.33	657.39
38000	697.18	691.24	686.48	682.67	679.61	677.15	675.16
39000	715.53	709.43	704.55	700.64	697.49	694.97	692.93
40000	733.88	727.62	722.61	718.60	715.38	712.79	710.69
41000	752.22	745.81	740.68	736.57	733.26	730.60	728.46
42000	770.57	764.00	758.74	754.53	751.15	748.42	746.23
43000	788.92	782.19	776.81	772.50	769.03	766.24	764.00
44000	807.26	800.38	794.87	790.46	786.92	784.06	781.76
45000	825.61	818.57	812.94	808.43	804.80	801.88	799.53
46000	843.96	836.76	831.00	826.39	822.69	819.70	817.30
47000	862.31	854.95	849.07	844.36	840.57	837.52	835.06
48000	880.65	873.14	867.14	862.32	858.46	855.34	852.83
49000	899.00	891.33	885.20	880.29	876.34	873.16	870.60
50000	917.35	909.52	903.27	898.25	894.22	890.98	888.37
51000	935.69	927.71	921.33	916.22	912.11	908.80	906.13
52000	954.04	945.90	939.40	934.18	929.99	926.62	923.90
53000	972.39	964.09	957.46	952.15	947.88	944.44	941.67
54000	990.73	982.28	975.53	970.11	965.76	962.26	959.44
55000	1009.08	1000.47	993.59	988.08	983.65	980.08	977.20
56000	1027.43	1018.66	1011.66	1006.04	1001.53	997.90	994.97
57000	1045.77	1036.85	1029.72	1024.01	1019.42	1015.72	1012.74
58000	1064.12	1055.04	1047.79	1041.97	1037.30	1033.54	1030.51
59000	1082.47	1073.23	1065.85	1059.94	1055.18	1051.36	1048.27
60000	1100.82	1091.42	1083.92	1077.90	1073.07	1069.18	1066.04
65000	1192.55	1182.38	1174.25	1167.73	1162.49	1158.28	1154.88
70000	1284.28	1273.33	1264.57	1257.55	1251.91	1247.37	1243.71
75000	1376.02	1364.28	1354.90	1347.38	1341.34	1336.47	1332.55
80000	1467.75	1455.23	1445.23	1437.20	1430.76	1425.57	1421.39
85000	1559.49	1546.18	1535.55	1527.03	1520.18	1514.67	1510.22
90000	1651.22	1637.14	1625.88	1616.85	1609.60	1603.77	1599.06
95000	1742.96	1728.09	1716.20	1706.68	1699.03	1692.86	1687.90
100000	1834.69	1819.04	1806.53	1796.50	1788.45	1781.96	1776.7
105000	1926.43	1909.99	1896.86	1886.33	1877.87	1871.06	1865.57
110000	2018.16	2000.94	1987.18	1976.16	1967.29	1960.16	1954.41
120000	2201.63	2182.85	2167.84	2155.81	2146.14	2138.36	2132.08
130000	2385.10	2364.75	2348.49	2335.46	2324.98	2316.55	2309.75
140000	2568.57	2546.66	2529.14	2515.11	2503.83	2494.75	2487.43
150000	2752.04	2728.56	2709.80	2694.76	2682.67	2672.94	2665.10
160000	2935.51	2910.46	2890.45	2874.41	2861.52	2851.14	2842.77
170000	3118.98	3092.37	3071.10	3054.06	3040.36	3029.34	3020.45
180000	3302.45	3274.27	3251.76	3233.71	3219.21	3207.53	3198.12
190000	3485.92	3456.18	3432.41	3413.36	3398.05	3385.73	3375.79
200000	3669.39	3638.08	3613.06	3593.01	3576.90	3563.93	3553.4
210000	3852.85	3819.98	3793.72	3772.66	3755.74	3742.12	3731.14
220000	4036.32	4001.89	3974.37	3952.31	3934.59	3920.32	3908.81
230000	4219.79	4183.79	4155.02	4131.96	4113.43	4098.51	4086.49
240000	4403.26	4365.70	4335.68	4311.61	4292.28	4276.71	4264.16
250000	4586.73	4547.60	4516.33	4491.26	4471.12	4454.91	4441.83

Monthly Payments 22.00 %

LOAN AMOUNT	22	23	24	25	30	35	40
	YEARS						
100	1.77	1.77	1.77	1.76	1.76	1.76	1.75
200	3.55	3.54	3.53	3.53	3.52	3.51	3.51
500	8.86	8.85	8.83	8.82	8.79	8.78	8.77
1000	17.73	17.69	17.66	17.64	17.58	17.56	17.55
2000	35.45	35.38	35.33	35.28	35.16	35.11	35.10
5000	88.63	88.45	88.32	88.21	87.90	87.79	87.75
6000	106.35	106.15	105.98	105.85	105.47	105.34	105.30
7000	124.08	123.84	123.64	123.49	123.05	122.90	122.85
8000	141.80	141.53	141.31	141.13	140.63	140.46	140.40
9000	159.53	159.22	158.97	158.77	158.21	158.02	157.95
10000	177.25	176.91	176.63	176.41	175.79	175.57	175.50
12000	212.70	212.29	211.96	211.69	210.95	210.69	210.60
15000	265.88	265.36	264.95	264.62	263.69	263.36	263.24
20000	354.50	353.82	353.27	352.82	351.58	351.15	350.99
25000	443.13	442.27	441.58	441.03	439.48	438.93	438.74
30000	531.75	530.73	529.90	529.23	527.37	526.72	526.49
31000	549.48	548.42	547.57	546.87	544.95	544.28	544.04
32000	567.20	566.11	565.23	564.51	562.53	561.83	561.59
33000	584.93	583.80	582.89	582.16	580.11	579.39	579.14
34000	602.65	601.49	600.56	599.80	597.69	596.95	596.69
35000	620.38	619.18	618.22	617.44	615.27	614.50	614.24
36000	638.10	636.88	635.88	635.08	632.84	632.06	631.79
37000	655.83	654.57	653.55	652.72	650.42	649.62	649.34
38000	673.55	672.26	671.21	670.36	668.00	667.18	666.89
39000	691.28	689.95	688.87	688.00	685.58	684.73	684.44
40000	709.00	707.64	706.54	705.64	703.16	702.29	701.99
41000	726.73	725.33	724.20	723.28	720.74	719.85	719.54
42000	744.45	743.02	741.86	740.92	738.32	737.41	737.08
43000	762.18	760.71	759.53	758.57	755.90	754.96	754.63
44000	779.90	778.40	777.19	776.21	773.48	772.52	772.18
45000	797.63	796.09	794.85	793.85	791.06	790.08	789.73
46000	815.36	813.79	812.52	811.49	808.64	807.63	807.28
47000	833.08	831.48	830.18	829.13	826.21	825.19	824.83
48000	850.81	849.17	847.84	846.77	843.79	842.75	842.38
49000	868.53	866.86	865.51	864.41	861.37	860.31	859.93
50000	886.26	884.55	883.17	882.05	878.95	877.86	877.48
51000	903.98	902.24	900.83	899.69	896.53	895.42	895.03
52000	921.71	919.93	918.50	917.34	914.11	912.98	912.58
53000	939.43	937.62	936.16	934.98	931.69	930.54	930.13
54000	957.16	955.31	953.82	952.62	949.27	948.09	947.68
55000	974.88	973.00	971.49	970.26	966.85	965.65	965.23
56000	992.61	990.70	989.15	987.90	984.43	983.21	982.78
57000	1010.33	1008.39	1006.81	1005.54	1002.00	1000.76	1000.33
58000	1028.06	1026.08	1024.48	1023.18	1019.58	1018.32	1017.88
59000	1045.78	1043.77	1042.14	1040.82	1037.16	1035.88	1035.43
60000	1063.51	1061.46	1059.80	1058.46	1054.74	1053.44	1052.98
65000	1152.13	1149.91	1148.12	1146.67	1142.64	1141.22	1140.73
70000	1240.76	1238.37	1236.44	1234.87	1230.53	1229.01	1228.47
75000	1329.38	1326.82	1324.75	1323.08	1318.43	1316.80	1316.22
80000	1418.01	1415.28	1413.07	1411.29	1406.32	1404.58	1403.97
85000	1506.63	1503.73	1501.39	1499.49	1494.22	1492.37	1491.72
90000	1595.26	1592.19	1589.71	1587.70	1582.11	1580.16	1579.47
95000	1683.89	1680.64	1678.02	1675.90	1670.01	1667.94	1667.22
100000	1772.51	1769.10	1766.34	1764.11	1757.90	1755.73	1754.96
105000	1861.14	1857.55	1854.66	1852.31	1845.80	1843.51	1842.71
110000	1949.76	1946.01	1942.97	1940.52	1933.69	1931.30	1930.46
120000	2127.01	2122.92	2119.61	2116.93	2109.48	2106.87	2105.96
130000	2304.26	2299.83	2296.24	2293.34	2285.27	2282.45	2281.45
140000	2481.52	2476.74	2472.88	2469.75	2461.06	2458.02	2456.95
150000	2658.77	2653.65	2649.51	2646.16	2636.85	2633.59	2632.45
160000	2836.02	2830.56	2826.14	2822.57	2812.64	2809.16	2807.94
170000	3013.27	3007.47	3002.78	2998.98	2988.43	2984.74	2983.44
180000	3190.52	3184.38	3179.41	3175.39	3164.22	3160.31	3158.93
190000	3367.77	3361.29	3356.05	3351.80	3340.01	3335.88	3334.43
200000	3545.02	3538.20	3532.68	3528.21	3515.80	3511.46	3509.93
210000	3722.27	3715.11	3709.31	3704.62	3691.60	3687.03	3685.42
220000	3899.52	3892.02	3885.95	3881.03	3867.39	3862.60	3860.92
230000	4076.78	4068.93	4062.58	4057.44	4043.18	4038.17	4036.42
240000	4254.03	4245.84	4239.22	4233.86	4218.97	4213.75	4211.91
250000	4431.28	4422.75	4415.85	4410.27	4394.76	4389.32	4387.41

22.25 % Monthly Payments

LOAN AMOUNT	YEARS 1	2	3	4	5	6	7
100	9.32	5.15	3.78	3.11	2.72	2.47	2.30
200	18.65	10.31	7.56	6.22	5.44	4.94	4.60
500	46.62	25.76	18.91	15.56	13.61	12.35	11.49
1000	93.25	51.53	37.82	31.12	27.21	24.70	22.99
2000	186.50	103.05	75.64	62.24	54.43	49.41	45.97
5000	466.25	257.63	189.10	155.59	136.07	123.51	114.93
6000	559.50	309.15	226.93	186.71	163.28	148.22	137.91
7000	652.75	360.68	264.75	217.83	190.49	172.92	160.90
8000	746.00	412.20	302.57	248.95	217.71	197.62	183.88
9000	839.25	463.73	340.39	280.07	244.92	222.32	206.87
10000	932.50	515.25	378.21	311.18	272.13	247.03	229.86
12000	1119.00	618.30	453.85	373.42	326.56	296.43	275.83
15000	1398.75	772.88	567.31	466.78	408.20	370.54	344.78
20000	1865.00	1030.50	756.42	622.37	544.26	494.05	459.71
25000	2331.25	1288.13	945.52	777.96	680.33	617.57	574.64
30000	2797.50	1545.75	1134.63	933.55	816.39	741.08	689.57
31000	2890.75	1597.28	1172.45	964.67	843.61	765.78	712.55
32000	2984.00	1648.80	1210.27	995.79	870.82	790.49	735.54
33000	3077.25	1700.33	1248.09	1026.91	898.03	815.19	758.52
34000	3170.50	1751.85	1285.91	1058.03	925.25	839.89	781.51
35000	3263.75	1803.38	1323.73	1089.15	952.46	864.59	804.49
36000	3357.00	1854.90	1361.55	1120.26	979.67	889.30	827.48
37000	3450.25	1906.43	1399.37	1151.38	1006.89	914.00	850.46
38000	3543.50	1957.95	1437.19	1182.50	1034.10	938.70	873.45
39000	3636.75	2009.48	1475.01	1213.62	1061.31	963.40	896.44
40000	3730.00	2061.00	1512.83	1244.74	1088.53	988.11	919.42
41000	3823.25	2112.53	1550.66	1275.86	1115.74	1012.81	942.41
42000	3916.50	2164.05	1588.48	1306.98	1142.95	1037.51	965.39
43000	4009.75	2215.58	1626.30	1338.09	1170.17	1062.22	988.38
44000	4103.00	2267.10	1664.12	1369.21	1197.38	1086.92	1011.36
45000	4196.25	2318.63	1701.94	1400.33	1224.59	1111.62	1034.35
46000	4289.50	2370.15	1739.76	1431.45	1251.81	1136.32	1057.33
47000	4382.75	2421.68	1777.58	1462.57	1279.02	1161.03	1080.32
48000	4476.00	2473.20	1815.40	1493.69	1306.23	1185.73	1103.31
49000	4569.25	2524.73	1853.22	1524.80	1333.44	1210.43	1126.29
50000	4662.50	2576.25	1891.04	1555.92	1360.66	1235.13	1149.28
51000	4755.75	2627.78	1928.86	1587.04	1387.87	1259.84	1172.26
52000	4849.00	2679.30	1966.68	1618.16	1415.08	1284.54	1195.25
53000	4942.25	2730.83	2004.51	1649.28	1442.30	1309.24	1218.23
54000	5035.50	2782.35	2042.33	1680.40	1469.51	1333.94	1241.22
55000	5128.75	2833.88	2080.15	1711.52	1496.72	1358.65	1264.20
56000	5222.00	2885.40	2117.97	1742.63	1523.94	1383.35	1287.19
57000	5315.25	2936.93	2155.79	1773.75	1551.15	1408.05	1310.18
58000	5408.50	2988.45	2193.61	1804.87	1578.36	1432.76	1333.16
59000	5501.75	3039.98	2231.43	1835.99	1605.58	1457.46	1356.15
60000	5595.00	3091.50	2269.25	1867.11	1632.79	1482.16	1379.13
65000	6061.25	3349.13	2458.36	2022.70	1768.86	1605.67	1494.06
70000	6527.50	3606.76	2647.46	2178.29	1904.92	1729.19	1608.99
75000	6993.75	3864.38	2836.56	2333.88	2040.99	1852.70	1723.91
80000	7460.00	4122.01	3025.67	2489.48	2177.05	1976.21	1838.84
85000	7926.25	4379.63	3214.77	2645.07	2313.12	2099.73	1953.77
90000	8392.50	4637.26	3403.88	2800.66	2449.18	2223.24	2068.70
95000	8858.75	4894.88	3592.98	2956.25	2585.25	2346.75	2183.63
100000	9325.00	5152.51	3782.09	3111.85	2721.32	2470.27	2298.55
105000	9791.25	5410.13	3971.19	3267.44	2857.38	2593.78	2413.48
110000	10257.50	5667.76	4160.29	3423.03	2993.45	2717.30	2528.41
120000	11190.00	6183.01	4538.50	3734.22	3265.58	2964.32	2758.26
130000	12122.49	6698.26	4916.71	4045.40	3537.71	3211.35	2988.12
140000	13054.99	7213.51	5294.92	4356.58	3809.84	3458.38	3217.97
150000	13987.49	7728.76	5673.13	4667.77	4081.97	3705.40	3447.83
160000	14919.99	8244.01	6051.34	4978.95	4354.11	3952.43	3677.68
170000	15852.49	8759.26	6429.55	5290.14	4626.24	4199.46	3907.54
180000	16784.99	9274.51	6807.75	5601.32	4898.37	4446.48	4137.40
190000	17717.49	9789.76	7185.96	5912.51	5170.50	4693.51	4367.25
200000	18649.99	10305.02	7564.17	6223.69	5442.63	4940.54	4597.11
210000	19582.49	10820.27	7942.38	6534.88	5714.76	5187.56	4826.96
220000	20514.99	11335.52	8320.59	6846.06	5986.90	5434.59	5056.82
230000	21447.49	11850.77	8698.80	7157.25	6259.03	5681.62	5286.67
240000	22379.99	12366.02	9077.01	7468.43	6531.16	5928.64	5516.53
250000	23312.49	12881.27	9455.21	7779.62	6803.29	6175.67	5746.38

Monthly Payments 22.25 %

LOAN AMOUNT	8	9	10	11	12	13	14
100	2.18	2.09	2.02	1.97	1.93	1.90	1.87
200	4.35	4.17	4.04	3.93	3.85	3.79	3.74
500	10.88	10.43	10.09	9.83	9.63	9.48	9.36
1000	21.76	20.86	20.18	19.67	19.27	18.96	18.71
2000	43.52	41.72	40.37	39.34	38.54	37.91	37.42
5000	108.80	104.30	100.92	98.34	96.34	94.79	93.56
6000	130.56	125.16	121.11	118.01	115.61	113.74	112.27
7000	152.32	146.02	141.29	137.68	134.88	132.70	130.99
8000	174.08	166.88	161.47	157.34	154.15	151.66	149.70
9000	195.85	187.74	181.66	177.01	173.42	170.62	168.41
10000	217.61	208.60	201.84	196.68	192.69	189.57	187.12
12000	261.13	250.32	242.21	236.01	231.23	227.49	224.55
15000	326.41	312.91	302.76	295.02	289.03	284.36	280.68
20000	435.21	417.21	403.68	393.36	385.38	379.14	374.25
25000	544.01	521.51	504.60	491.70	481.72	473.93	467.81
30000	652.82	625.81	605.53	590.04	578.06	568.72	561.37
31000	674.58	646.67	625.71	609.70	597.33	587.67	580.08
32000	696.34	667.53	645.89	629.37	616.60	606.63	598.79
33000	718.10	688.39	666.08	649.04	635.87	625.59	617.50
34000	739.86	709.25	686.26	668.71	655.14	644.55	636.22
35000	761.62	730.11	706.45	688.38	674.41	663.50	654.93
36000	783.38	750.97	726.63	708.04	693.68	682.46	673.64
37000	805.14	771.83	746.81	727.71	712.94	701.42	692.35
38000	826.90	792.69	767.00	747.38	732.21	720.38	711.07
39000	848.66	813.55	787.18	767.05	751.48	739.33	729.78
40000	870.42	834.41	807.37	786.72	770.75	758.29	748.49
41000	892.18	855.27	827.55	806.38	790.02	777.25	767.20
42000	913.95	876.14	847.74	826.05	809.29	796.20	785.91
43000	935.71	897.00	867.92	845.72	828.56	815.16	804.63
44000	957.47	917.86	888.10	865.39	847.83	834.12	823.34
45000	979.23	938.72	908.29	885.06	867.09	853.08	842.05
46000	1000.99	959.58	928.47	904.72	886.36	872.03	860.76
47000	1022.75	980.44	948.66	924.39	905.63	890.99	879.48
48000	1044.51	1001.30	968.84	944.06	924.90	909.95	898.19
49000	1066.27	1022.16	989.02	963.73	944.17	928.90	916.90
50000	1088.03	1043.02	1009.21	983.39	963.44	947.86	935.61
51000	1109.79	1063.88	1029.39	1003.06	982.71	966.82	954.32
52000	1131.55	1084.74	1049.58	1022.73	1001.98	985.78	973.04
53000	1153.31	1105.60	1069.76	1042.40	1021.24	1004.73	991.75
54000	1175.07	1126.46	1089.95	1062.07	1040.51	1023.69	1010.46
55000	1196.83	1147.32	1110.13	1081.73	1059.78	1042.65	1029.17
56000	1218.59	1168.18	1130.31	1101.40	1079.05	1061.61	1047.89
57000	1240.35	1189.04	1150.50	1121.07	1098.32	1080.56	1066.60
58000	1262.11	1209.90	1170.68	1140.74	1117.59	1099.52	1085.31
59000	1283.88	1230.76	1190.87	1160.41	1136.86	1118.48	1104.02
60000	1305.64	1251.62	1211.05	1180.07	1156.13	1137.43	1122.74
65000	1414.44	1355.92	1311.97	1278.41	1252.47	1232.22	1216.30
70000	1523.24	1460.23	1412.89	1376.75	1348.81	1327.01	1309.86
75000	1632.04	1564.53	1513.81	1475.09	1445.16	1421.79	1403.42
80000	1740.85	1668.83	1614.73	1573.43	1541.50	1516.58	1496.98
85000	1849.65	1773.13	1715.65	1671.77	1637.85	1611.37	1590.54
90000	1958.45	1877.43	1816.58	1770.11	1734.19	1706.15	1684.10
95000	2067.26	1981.73	1917.50	1868.45	1830.53	1800.94	1777.66
100000	2176.06	2086.04	2018.42	1966.79	1926.88	1895.72	1871.23
105000	2284.86	2190.34	2119.34	2065.13	2023.22	1990.51	1964.79
110000	2393.67	2294.64	2220.26	2163.47	2119.56	2085.30	2058.35
120000	2611.27	2503.24	2422.10	2360.15	2312.25	2274.87	2245.47
130000	2828.88	2711.85	2623.94	2556.83	2504.94	2464.44	2432.59
140000	3046.48	2920.45	2825.78	2753.50	2697.63	2654.01	2619.72
150000	3264.09	3129.05	3027.63	2950.18	2890.32	2843.59	2806.84
160000	3481.70	3337.66	3229.47	3146.86	3083.00	3033.16	2993.96
170000	3699.30	3546.26	3431.31	3343.54	3275.69	3222.73	3181.08
180000	3916.91	3754.87	3633.15	3540.22	3468.38	3412.30	3368.21
190000	4134.51	3963.47	3834.99	3736.90	3661.07	3601.88	3555.33
200000	4352.12	4172.07	4036.83	3933.58	3853.75	3791.45	3742.45
210000	4569.73	4380.68	4238.68	4130.26	4046.44	3981.02	3929.57
220000	4787.33	4589.28	4440.52	4326.94	4239.13	4170.59	4116.70
230000	5004.94	4797.88	4642.36	4523.61	4431.82	4360.17	4303.82
240000	5222.54	5006.49	4844.20	4720.29	4624.50	4549.74	4490.94
250000	5440.15	5215.09	5046.04	4916.97	4817.19	4739.31	4678.06

22.25 % Monthly Payments

LOAN AMOUNT	15	16	17	18	19	20	21
100	1.85	1.84	1.82	1.81	1.81	1.80	1.80
200	3.70	3.67	3.65	3.63	3.61	3.60	3.59
500	9.26	9.18	9.12	9.07	9.03	9.00	8.98
1000	18.52	18.36	18.24	18.14	18.06	18.00	17.95
2000	37.04	36.73	36.48	36.29	36.13	36.00	35.90
5000	92.59	91.82	91.21	90.72	90.32	90.01	89.75
6000	111.11	110.19	109.45	108.86	108.39	108.01	107.70
7000	129.63	128.55	127.69	127.00	126.45	126.01	125.65
8000	148.15	146.92	145.93	145.15	144.52	144.01	143.60
9000	166.67	165.28	164.17	163.29	162.58	162.01	161.55
10000	185.18	183.64	182.42	181.43	180.64	180.01	179.50
12000	222.22	220.37	218.90	217.72	216.77	216.01	215.40
15000	277.78	275.47	273.62	272.15	270.97	270.02	269.25
20000	370.37	367.29	364.83	362.87	361.29	360.02	359.00
25000	462.96	459.11	456.04	453.58	451.61	450.03	448.75
30000	555.55	550.93	547.25	544.30	541.93	540.03	538.50
31000	574.07	569.30	565.49	562.44	560.00	558.03	556.45
32000	592.59	587.66	583.73	580.58	578.06	576.04	574.40
33000	611.11	606.03	601.97	598.73	596.13	594.04	592.36
34000	629.63	624.39	620.21	616.87	614.19	612.04	610.31
35000	648.15	642.76	638.45	635.01	632.26	630.04	628.26
36000	666.66	661.12	656.70	653.16	650.32	648.04	646.21
37000	685.18	679.48	674.94	671.30	668.38	666.04	664.16
38000	703.70	697.85	693.18	689.44	686.45	684.04	682.11
39000	722.22	716.21	711.42	707.59	704.51	702.04	700.06
40000	740.74	734.58	729.66	725.73	722.58	720.04	718.01
41000	759.26	752.94	747.90	743.87	740.64	738.05	735.96
42000	777.78	771.31	766.15	762.02	758.71	756.05	753.91
43000	796.29	789.67	784.39	780.16	776.77	774.05	771.86
44000	814.81	808.03	802.63	798.30	794.84	792.05	789.81
45000	833.33	826.40	820.87	816.45	812.90	810.05	807.76
46000	851.85	844.76	839.11	834.59	830.96	828.05	825.71
47000	870.37	863.13	857.35	852.73	849.03	846.05	843.66
48000	888.89	881.49	875.60	870.88	867.09	864.05	861.61
49000	907.40	899.86	893.84	889.02	885.16	882.05	879.56
50000	925.92	918.22	912.08	907.16	903.22	900.06	897.51
51000	944.44	936.59	930.32	925.31	921.29	918.06	915.46
52000	962.96	954.95	948.56	943.45	939.35	936.06	933.41
53000	981.48	973.31	966.80	961.59	957.42	954.06	951.36
54000	1000.00	991.68	985.04	979.74	975.48	972.06	969.31
55000	1018.51	1010.04	1003.29	997.88	993.54	990.06	987.26
56000	1037.03	1028.41	1021.53	1016.02	1011.61	1008.06	1005.21
57000	1055.55	1046.77	1039.77	1034.17	1029.67	1026.06	1023.16
58000	1074.07	1065.14	1058.01	1052.31	1047.74	1044.06	1041.11
59000	1092.59	1083.50	1076.25	1070.45	1065.80	1062.07	1059.06
60000	1111.11	1101.87	1094.49	1088.60	1083.87	1080.07	1077.01
65000	1203.70	1193.69	1185.70	1179.31	1174.19	1170.07	1166.76
70000	1296.29	1285.51	1276.91	1270.03	1264.51	1260.08	1256.51
75000	1388.88	1377.33	1368.12	1360.75	1354.83	1350.08	1346.26
80000	1481.48	1469.15	1459.33	1451.46	1445.16	1440.09	1436.01
85000	1574.07	1560.98	1550.53	1542.18	1535.48	1530.09	1525.76
90000	1666.66	1652.80	1641.74	1632.89	1625.80	1620.10	1615.51
95000	1759.25	1744.62	1732.95	1723.61	1716.12	1710.11	1705.26
100000	1851.85	1836.44	1824.16	1814.33	1806.45	1800.11	1795.02
105000	1944.44	1928.27	1915.36	1905.04	1896.77	1890.12	1884.77
110000	2037.03	2020.09	2006.57	1995.76	1987.09	1980.12	1974.52
120000	2222.21	2203.73	2188.99	2177.19	2167.73	2160.13	2154.02
130000	2407.40	2387.38	2371.40	2358.63	2348.38	2340.15	2333.52
140000	2592.58	2571.02	2553.82	2540.06	2529.02	2520.16	2513.02
150000	2777.77	2754.66	2736.24	2721.49	2709.67	2700.17	2692.52
160000	2962.95	2938.31	2918.65	2902.92	2890.31	2880.18	2872.02
170000	3148.14	3121.95	3101.07	3084.36	3070.96	3060.19	3051.53
180000	3333.32	3305.60	3283.48	3265.79	3251.60	3240.20	3231.03
190000	3518.51	3489.24	3465.90	3447.22	3432.25	3420.21	3410.53
200000	3703.69	3672.89	3648.31	3628.66	3612.89	3600.22	3590.03
210000	3888.88	3856.53	3830.73	3810.09	3793.53	3780.23	3769.53
220000	4074.06	4040.17	4013.15	3991.52	3974.18	3960.25	3949.03
230000	4259.24	4223.82	4195.56	4172.95	4154.82	4140.26	4128.54
240000	4444.43	4407.46	4377.98	4354.39	4335.47	4320.27	4308.04
250000	4629.61	4591.11	4560.39	4535.82	4516.11	4500.28	4487.54

Monthly Payments 22.25 %

LOAN AMOUNT	22	23	24	25	30	35	40
			YEARS				
100	1.79	1.79	1.78	1.78	1.78	1.77	1.77
200	3.58	3.58	3.57	3.57	3.55	3.55	3.55
500	8.95	8.94	8.92	8.91	8.88	8.87	8.87
1000	17.91	17.88	17.85	17.83	17.77	17.75	17.74
2000	35.82	35.75	35.70	35.66	35.54	35.49	35.48
5000	89.55	89.38	89.25	89.14	88.84	88.74	88.70
6000	107.45	107.26	107.10	106.97	106.61	106.48	106.44
7000	125.36	125.13	124.94	124.79	124.38	124.23	124.18
8000	143.27	143.01	142.79	142.62	142.14	141.98	141.92
9000	161.18	160.88	160.64	160.45	159.91	159.73	159.66
10000	179.09	178.76	178.49	178.28	177.68	177.47	177.40
12000	214.91	214.51	214.19	213.93	213.22	212.97	212.88
15000	268.64	268.14	267.74	267.42	266.52	266.21	266.10
20000	358.18	357.52	356.99	356.55	355.36	354.95	354.80
25000	447.73	446.90	446.23	445.69	444.20	443.68	443.51
30000	537.27	536.28	535.48	534.83	533.04	532.42	532.21
31000	555.18	554.16	553.33	552.66	550.81	550.17	549.95
32000	573.09	572.03	571.18	570.49	568.58	567.92	567.69
33000	591.00	589.91	589.03	588.31	586.35	585.66	585.43
34000	608.91	607.78	606.87	606.14	604.11	603.41	603.17
35000	626.82	625.66	624.72	623.97	621.88	621.16	620.91
36000	644.73	643.54	642.57	641.80	639.65	638.91	638.65
37000	662.64	661.41	660.42	659.62	657.42	656.65	656.39
38000	680.55	679.29	678.27	677.45	675.19	674.40	674.13
39000	698.45	697.16	696.12	695.28	692.95	692.15	691.87
40000	716.36	715.04	713.97	713.11	710.72	709.90	709.61
41000	734.27	732.92	731.82	730.93	728.49	727.64	727.35
42000	752.18	750.79	749.67	748.76	746.26	745.39	745.09
43000	770.09	768.67	767.52	766.59	764.03	763.14	762.83
44000	788.00	786.54	785.37	784.42	781.79	780.89	780.57
45000	805.91	804.42	803.22	802.25	799.56	798.63	798.31
46000	823.82	822.30	821.07	820.07	817.33	816.38	816.05
47000	841.73	840.17	838.92	837.90	835.10	834.13	833.79
48000	859.64	858.05	856.76	855.73	852.87	851.87	851.53
49000	877.55	875.92	874.61	873.56	870.64	869.62	869.27
50000	895.45	893.80	892.46	891.38	888.40	887.37	887.01
51000	913.36	911.68	910.31	909.21	906.17	905.12	904.75
52000	931.27	929.55	928.16	927.04	923.94	922.86	922.49
53000	949.18	947.43	946.01	944.87	941.71	940.61	940.23
54000	967.09	965.30	963.86	962.69	959.48	958.36	957.97
55000	985.00	983.18	981.71	980.52	977.24	976.11	975.71
56000	1002.91	1001.06	999.56	998.35	995.01	993.85	993.45
57000	1020.82	1018.93	1017.41	1016.18	1012.78	1011.60	1011.19
58000	1038.73	1036.81	1035.26	1034.01	1030.55	1029.35	1028.93
59000	1056.64	1054.68	1053.11	1051.83	1048.32	1047.10	1046.67
60000	1074.55	1072.56	1070.96	1069.66	1066.08	1064.84	1064.41
65000	1164.09	1161.94	1160.20	1158.80	1154.92	1153.58	1153.11
70000	1253.64	1251.32	1249.45	1247.94	1243.76	1242.32	1241.81
75000	1343.18	1340.70	1338.69	1337.08	1332.60	1331.05	1330.52
80000	1432.73	1430.08	1427.94	1426.21	1421.45	1419.79	1419.22
85000	1522.27	1519.46	1517.19	1515.35	1510.29	1508.53	1507.92
90000	1611.82	1608.84	1606.43	1604.49	1599.13	1597.27	1596.62
95000	1701.36	1698.22	1695.68	1693.63	1687.97	1686.00	1685.32
100000	1790.91	1787.60	1784.93	1782.77	1776.81	1774.74	1774.02
105000	1880.46	1876.98	1874.17	1871.91	1865.65	1863.48	1862.72
110000	1970.00	1966.36	1963.42	1961.04	1954.49	1952.21	1951.42
120000	2149.09	2145.12	2141.91	2139.32	2132.17	2129.69	2128.83
130000	2328.18	2323.88	2320.40	2317.60	2309.85	2307.16	2306.23
140000	2507.27	2502.64	2498.90	2495.88	2487.53	2484.64	2483.63
150000	2686.36	2681.40	2677.39	2674.15	2665.21	2662.11	2661.03
160000	2865.46	2860.16	2855.88	2852.43	2842.89	2839.58	2838.43
170000	3044.55	3038.92	3034.37	3030.71	3020.57	3017.06	3015.84
180000	3223.64	3217.68	3212.87	3208.98	3198.25	3194.53	3193.24
190000	3402.73	3396.44	3391.36	3387.26	3375.93	3372.01	3370.64
200000	3581.82	3575.20	3569.85	3565.54	3553.61	3549.48	3548.04
210000	3760.91	3753.96	3748.34	3743.81	3731.29	3726.95	3725.44
220000	3940.00	3932.72	3926.84	3922.09	3908.97	3904.43	3902.85
230000	4119.09	4111.48	4105.33	4100.37	4086.65	4081.90	4080.25
240000	4298.18	4290.24	4283.82	4278.64	4264.34	4259.37	4257.65
250000	4477.27	4469.00	4462.32	4456.92	4442.02	4436.85	4435.05

22.50 % Monthly Payments

LOAN AMOUNT	1	2	3	4	5	6	7
	YEARS						
100	9.34	5.16	3.79	3.12	2.73	2.48	2.31
200	18.67	10.33	7.59	6.25	5.47	4.97	4.63
500	46.68	25.82	18.97	15.62	13.67	12.42	11.56
1000	93.36	51.64	37.94	31.24	27.34	24.84	23.13
2000	186.72	103.28	75.88	62.48	54.68	49.68	46.25
5000	466.80	258.19	189.69	156.21	136.71	124.19	115.63
6000	560.16	309.83	227.63	187.45	164.05	149.03	138.75
7000	653.52	361.46	265.57	218.69	191.40	173.86	161.88
8000	746.88	413.10	303.51	249.94	218.74	198.70	185.01
9000	840.24	464.74	341.45	281.18	246.08	223.54	208.13
10000	933.60	516.38	379.39	312.42	273.42	248.38	231.26
12000	1120.32	619.65	455.26	374.90	328.11	298.05	277.51
15000	1400.40	774.57	569.08	468.63	410.14	372.56	346.89
20000	1867.20	1032.75	758.77	624.84	546.85	496.75	462.52
25000	2334.00	1290.94	948.47	781.05	683.56	620.94	578.15
30000	2800.80	1549.13	1138.16	937.26	820.27	745.13	693.77
31000	2894.16	1600.77	1176.10	968.50	847.62	769.96	716.90
32000	2987.52	1652.41	1214.04	999.74	874.96	794.80	740.03
33000	3080.88	1704.05	1251.98	1030.99	902.30	819.64	763.15
34000	3174.24	1755.68	1289.92	1062.23	929.64	844.48	786.28
35000	3267.60	1807.32	1327.86	1093.47	956.99	869.32	809.40
36000	3360.96	1858.96	1365.79	1124.71	984.33	894.15	832.53
37000	3454.32	1910.60	1403.73	1155.95	1011.67	918.99	855.65
38000	3547.68	1962.23	1441.67	1187.20	1039.01	943.83	878.78
39000	3641.04	2013.87	1479.61	1218.44	1066.36	968.67	901.91
40000	3734.40	2065.51	1517.55	1249.68	1093.70	993.50	925.03
41000	3827.76	2117.15	1555.49	1280.92	1121.04	1018.34	948.16
42000	3921.12	2168.78	1593.43	1312.16	1148.38	1043.18	971.28
43000	4014.48	2220.42	1631.36	1343.41	1175.73	1068.02	994.41
44000	4107.84	2272.06	1669.30	1374.65	1203.07	1092.85	1017.54
45000	4201.20	2323.70	1707.24	1405.89	1230.41	1117.69	1040.66
46000	4294.56	2375.34	1745.18	1437.13	1257.75	1142.53	1063.79
47000	4387.92	2426.97	1783.12	1468.37	1285.10	1167.37	1086.91
48000	4481.28	2478.61	1821.06	1499.62	1312.44	1192.20	1110.04
49000	4574.64	2530.25	1859.00	1530.86	1339.78	1217.04	1133.16
50000	4668.00	2581.89	1896.94	1562.10	1367.12	1241.88	1156.29
51000	4761.36	2633.52	1934.87	1593.34	1394.47	1266.72	1179.42
52000	4854.72	2685.16	1972.81	1624.58	1421.81	1291.55	1202.54
53000	4948.08	2736.80	2010.75	1655.83	1449.15	1316.39	1225.67
54000	5041.44	2788.44	2048.69	1687.07	1476.49	1341.23	1248.79
55000	5134.80	2840.08	2086.63	1718.31	1503.83	1366.07	1271.92
56000	5228.16	2891.71	2124.57	1749.55	1531.18	1390.90	1295.05
57000	5321.52	2943.35	2162.51	1780.79	1558.52	1415.74	1318.17
58000	5414.88	2994.99	2200.45	1812.04	1585.86	1440.58	1341.30
59000	5508.24	3046.63	2238.38	1843.28	1613.20	1465.42	1364.42
60000	5601.60	3098.26	2276.32	1874.52	1640.55	1490.25	1387.55
65000	6068.39	3356.45	2466.02	2030.73	1777.26	1614.44	1503.18
70000	6535.19	3614.64	2655.71	2186.94	1913.97	1738.63	1618.81
75000	7001.99	3872.83	2845.40	2343.15	2050.68	1862.82	1734.44
80000	7468.79	4131.02	3035.10	2499.36	2187.40	1987.01	1850.06
85000	7935.59	4389.21	3224.79	2655.57	2324.11	2111.19	1965.69
90000	8402.39	4647.40	3414.48	2811.78	2460.82	2235.38	2081.32
95000	8869.19	4905.58	3604.18	2967.99	2597.53	2359.57	2196.95
100000	9335.99	5163.77	3793.87	3124.20	2734.25	2483.76	2312.58
105000	9802.79	5421.96	3983.57	3280.41	2870.96	2607.95	2428.21
110000	10269.59	5680.15	4173.26	3436.62	3007.67	2732.13	2543.84
120000	11203.19	6196.53	4552.65	3749.04	3281.09	2980.51	2775.10
130000	12136.79	6712.90	4932.03	4061.46	3554.52	3228.88	3006.35
140000	13070.39	7229.28	5311.42	4373.88	3827.94	3477.26	3237.61
150000	14003.99	7745.66	5690.81	4686.30	4101.37	3725.64	3468.87
160000	14937.59	8262.04	6070.19	4998.72	4374.79	3974.01	3700.13
170000	15871.19	8778.41	6449.58	5311.14	4648.22	4222.39	3931.39
180000	16804.79	9294.79	6828.97	5623.56	4921.64	4470.76	4162.65
190000	17738.38	9811.17	7208.36	5935.98	5195.07	4719.14	4393.90
200000	18671.98	10327.55	7587.74	6248.40	5468.49	4967.52	4625.16
210000	19605.58	10843.92	7967.13	6560.82	5741.91	5215.89	4856.42
220000	20539.18	11360.30	8346.52	6873.24	6015.34	5464.27	5087.68
230000	21472.78	11876.68	8725.90	7185.66	6288.76	5712.64	5318.94
240000	22406.38	12393.05	9105.29	7498.08	6562.19	5961.02	5550.19
250000	23339.98	12909.43	9484.68	7810.50	6835.61	6209.39	5781.45

Monthly Payments 22.50 %

LOAN AMOUNT	8	9	10	11	12	13	14
				YEARS			
100	2.19	2.10	2.03	1.98	1.94	1.91	1.89
200	4.38	4.20	4.07	3.97	3.89	3.82	3.78
500	10.95	10.51	10.17	9.91	9.72	9.56	9.44
1000	21.91	21.01	20.34	19.83	19.43	19.12	18.88
2000	43.81	42.02	40.68	39.65	38.86	38.25	37.76
5000	109.53	105.05	101.69	99.13	97.16	95.62	94.41
6000	131.44	126.06	122.03	118.96	116.59	114.74	113.29
7000	153.34	147.07	142.37	138.79	136.02	133.86	132.17
8000	175.25	168.08	162.71	158.61	155.45	152.99	151.05
9000	197.15	189.09	183.05	178.44	174.88	172.11	169.93
10000	219.06	210.11	203.39	198.27	194.31	191.23	188.81
12000	262.87	252.13	244.07	237.92	233.18	229.48	226.58
15000	328.59	315.16	305.08	297.40	291.47	286.85	283.22
20000	438.12	420.21	406.78	396.53	388.63	382.46	377.63
25000	547.65	525.26	508.47	495.67	485.78	478.08	472.03
30000	657.18	630.32	610.16	594.80	582.94	573.69	566.44
31000	679.09	651.33	630.50	614.63	602.37	592.82	585.32
32000	700.99	672.34	650.84	634.45	621.80	611.94	604.20
33000	722.90	693.35	671.18	654.28	641.23	631.06	623.08
34000	744.80	714.36	691.52	674.11	660.66	650.19	641.96
35000	766.71	735.37	711.86	693.93	680.09	669.31	660.84
36000	788.62	756.38	732.20	713.76	699.53	688.43	679.73
37000	810.52	777.39	752.54	733.59	718.96	707.56	698.61
38000	832.43	798.40	772.87	753.41	738.39	726.68	717.49
39000	854.33	819.41	793.21	773.24	757.82	745.80	736.37
40000	876.24	840.42	813.55	793.06	777.25	764.93	755.25
41000	898.15	861.43	833.89	812.89	796.68	784.05	774.13
42000	920.05	882.44	854.23	832.72	816.11	803.17	793.01
43000	941.96	903.45	874.57	852.54	835.54	822.30	811.89
44000	963.86	924.46	894.91	872.37	854.98	841.42	830.78
45000	985.77	945.47	915.25	892.20	874.41	860.54	849.66
46000	1007.67	966.48	935.58	912.02	893.84	879.67	868.54
47000	1029.58	987.50	955.92	931.85	913.27	898.79	887.42
48000	1051.49	1008.51	976.26	951.68	932.70	917.91	906.30
49000	1073.39	1029.52	996.60	971.50	952.13	937.03	925.18
50000	1095.30	1050.53	1016.94	991.33	971.56	956.16	944.06
51000	1117.20	1071.54	1037.28	1011.16	990.99	975.28	962.94
52000	1139.11	1092.55	1057.62	1030.98	1010.43	994.40	981.83
53000	1161.02	1113.56	1077.96	1050.81	1029.86	1013.53	1000.71
54000	1182.92	1134.57	1098.29	1070.64	1049.29	1032.65	1019.59
55000	1204.83	1155.58	1118.63	1090.46	1068.72	1051.77	1038.47
56000	1226.73	1176.59	1138.97	1110.29	1088.15	1070.90	1057.35
57000	1248.64	1197.60	1159.31	1130.12	1107.58	1090.02	1076.23
58000	1270.55	1218.61	1179.65	1149.94	1127.01	1109.14	1095.11
59000	1292.45	1239.62	1199.99	1169.77	1146.44	1128.27	1113.99
60000	1314.36	1260.63	1220.33	1189.60	1165.88	1147.39	1132.88
65000	1423.89	1365.68	1322.02	1288.73	1263.03	1243.01	1227.28
70000	1533.42	1470.74	1423.72	1387.86	1360.19	1338.62	1321.69
75000	1642.95	1575.79	1525.41	1487.00	1457.35	1434.24	1416.09
80000	1752.48	1680.84	1627.10	1586.13	1554.50	1529.85	1510.50
85000	1862.01	1785.90	1728.80	1685.26	1651.66	1625.47	1604.91
90000	1971.54	1890.95	1830.49	1784.40	1748.81	1721.08	1699.31
95000	2081.07	1996.00	1932.19	1883.53	1845.97	1816.70	1793.72
100000	2190.60	2101.05	2033.88	1982.66	1943.13	1912.32	1888.13
105000	2300.13	2206.11	2135.57	2081.80	2040.28	2007.93	1982.53
110000	2409.66	2311.16	2237.27	2180.93	2137.44	2103.55	2076.94
120000	2628.72	2521.26	2440.66	2379.19	2331.75	2294.78	2265.75
130000	2847.78	2731.37	2644.04	2577.46	2526.06	2486.01	2454.56
140000	3066.84	2941.47	2847.43	2775.73	2720.38	2677.24	2643.38
150000	3285.90	3151.58	3050.82	2973.99	2914.69	2868.47	2832.19
160000	3504.96	3361.69	3254.21	3172.26	3109.00	3059.71	3021.00
170000	3724.02	3571.79	3457.59	3370.53	3303.32	3250.94	3209.82
180000	3943.08	3781.90	3660.98	3568.79	3497.63	3442.17	3398.63
190000	4162.14	3992.00	3864.37	3767.06	3691.94	3633.40	3587.44
200000	4381.20	4202.11	4067.76	3965.32	3886.25	3824.63	3776.25
210000	4600.26	4412.21	4271.15	4163.59	4080.57	4015.86	3965.07
220000	4819.32	4622.32	4474.53	4361.86	4274.88	4207.10	4153.88
230000	5038.37	4832.42	4677.92	4560.12	4469.19	4398.33	4342.69
240000	5257.43	5042.53	4881.31	4758.39	4663.50	4589.56	4531.50
250000	5476.49	5252.63	5084.70	4956.66	4857.82	4780.79	4720.32

22.50 % Monthly Payments

LOAN AMOUNT	15	16	17	18	19	20	21
100	1.87	1.85	1.84	1.83	1.82	1.82	1.8
200	3.74	3.71	3.68	3.66	3.65	3.64	3.6
500	9.35	9.27	9.21	9.16	9.12	9.09	9.0
1000	18.69	18.54	18.42	18.32	18.24	18.18	18.1
2000	37.38	37.08	36.84	36.64	36.49	36.37	36.2
5000	93.45	92.69	92.09	91.61	91.22	90.91	90.6
6000	112.14	111.23	110.51	109.93	109.47	109.10	108.8
7000	130.83	129.77	128.93	128.25	127.71	127.28	126.9
8000	149.52	148.31	147.34	146.57	145.96	145.46	145.0
9000	168.21	166.85	165.76	164.90	164.20	163.64	163.2
10000	186.90	185.39	184.18	183.22	182.45	181.83	181.3
12000	224.28	222.46	221.02	219.86	218.93	218.19	217.6
15000	280.35	278.08	276.27	274.83	273.67	272.74	272.0
20000	373.80	370.77	368.36	366.43	364.89	363.65	362.6
25000	467.26	463.47	460.45	458.04	456.11	454.57	453.3
30000	560.71	556.16	552.54	549.65	547.34	545.48	543.9
31000	579.40	574.70	570.96	567.97	565.58	563.66	562.1
32000	598.09	593.24	589.38	586.29	583.83	581.85	580.2
33000	616.78	611.78	607.80	604.62	602.07	600.03	598.3
34000	635.47	630.32	626.21	622.94	620.32	618.21	616.5
35000	654.16	648.85	644.63	641.26	638.56	636.40	634.6
36000	672.85	667.39	663.05	659.58	656.80	654.58	652.7
37000	691.54	685.93	681.47	677.90	675.05	672.76	670.9
38000	710.23	704.47	699.89	696.22	693.29	690.94	689.0
39000	728.92	723.01	718.30	714.55	711.54	709.13	707.1
40000	747.61	741.55	736.72	732.87	729.78	727.31	725.3
41000	766.30	760.09	755.14	751.19	748.03	745.49	743.4
42000	784.99	778.63	773.56	769.51	766.27	763.68	761.5
43000	803.68	797.16	791.98	787.83	784.52	781.86	779.7
44000	822.37	815.70	810.39	806.15	802.76	800.04	797.8
45000	841.06	834.24	828.81	824.48	821.01	818.22	815.9
46000	859.75	852.78	847.23	842.80	839.25	836.41	834.1
47000	878.44	871.32	865.65	861.12	857.50	854.59	852.2
48000	897.13	889.86	884.07	879.44	875.74	872.77	870.3
49000	915.82	908.40	902.48	897.76	893.98	890.95	888.5
50000	934.51	926.94	920.90	916.08	912.23	909.14	906.6
51000	953.20	945.47	939.32	934.41	930.47	927.32	924.7
52000	971.89	964.01	957.74	952.73	948.72	945.50	942.9
53000	990.58	982.55	976.16	971.05	966.96	963.69	961.0
54000	1009.27	1001.09	994.57	989.37	985.21	981.87	979.1
55000	1027.96	1019.63	1012.99	1007.69	1003.45	1000.05	997.3
56000	1046.65	1038.17	1031.41	1026.01	1021.70	1018.23	1015.4
57000	1065.34	1056.71	1049.83	1044.34	1039.94	1036.42	1033.5
58000	1084.03	1075.24	1068.25	1062.66	1058.19	1054.60	1051.7
59000	1102.72	1093.78	1086.66	1080.98	1076.43	1072.78	1069.8
60000	1121.41	1112.32	1105.08	1099.30	1094.67	1090.96	1087.9
65000	1214.87	1205.02	1197.17	1190.91	1185.90	1181.88	1178.6
70000	1308.32	1297.71	1289.26	1282.52	1277.12	1272.79	1269.3
75000	1401.77	1390.40	1381.35	1374.13	1368.34	1363.71	1359.9
80000	1495.22	1483.10	1473.44	1465.74	1459.57	1454.62	1450.6
85000	1588.67	1575.79	1565.53	1557.34	1550.79	1545.53	1541.3
90000	1682.12	1668.48	1657.62	1648.95	1642.01	1636.45	1631.9
95000	1775.57	1761.18	1749.71	1740.56	1733.23	1727.36	1722.6
100000	1869.02	1853.87	1841.80	1832.17	1824.46	1818.27	1813.3
105000	1962.48	1946.56	1933.89	1923.78	1915.68	1909.19	1903.9
110000	2055.93	2039.26	2025.98	2015.39	2006.90	2000.10	1994.6
120000	2242.83	2224.64	2210.16	2198.60	2189.35	2181.93	2175.9
130000	2429.73	2410.03	2394.35	2381.82	2371.79	2363.76	2357.3
140000	2616.63	2595.42	2578.53	2565.04	2554.24	2545.58	2538.6
150000	2803.54	2780.81	2762.71	2748.25	2736.69	2727.41	2719.9
160000	2990.44	2966.19	2946.89	2931.47	2919.13	2909.24	2901.2
170000	3177.34	3151.58	3131.07	3114.69	3101.58	3091.07	3082.6
180000	3364.24	3336.97	3315.25	3297.90	3284.02	3272.89	3263.9
190000	3551.15	3522.35	3499.43	3481.12	3466.47	3454.72	3445.2
200000	3738.05	3707.74	3683.61	3664.34	3648.92	3636.55	3626.6
210000	3924.95	3893.13	3867.79	3847.56	3831.36	3818.38	3807.9
220000	4111.85	4078.51	4051.97	4030.77	4013.81	4000.20	3989.2
230000	4298.76	4263.90	4236.15	4213.99	4196.25	4182.03	4170.6
240000	4485.66	4449.29	4420.33	4397.21	4378.70	4363.86	4351.9
250000	4672.56	4634.68	4604.51	4580.42	4561.14	4545.69	4533.2

Monthly Payments 22.50 %

LOAN AMOUNT	22	23	24	25	30	35	40
				YEARS			
100	1.81	1.81	1.80	1.80	1.80	1.79	1.79
200	3.62	3.61	3.61	3.60	3.59	3.59	3.59
500	9.05	9.03	9.02	9.01	8.98	8.97	8.97
1000	18.09	18.06	18.04	18.01	17.96	17.94	17.93
2000	36.19	36.12	36.07	36.03	35.91	35.87	35.86
5000	90.47	90.31	90.18	90.07	89.79	89.69	89.65
6000	108.56	108.37	108.21	108.09	107.74	107.62	107.58
7000	126.65	126.43	126.25	126.10	125.70	125.56	125.51
8000	144.75	144.49	144.28	144.11	143.66	143.50	143.45
9000	162.84	162.55	162.32	162.13	161.61	161.44	161.38
10000	180.93	180.61	180.35	180.14	179.57	179.37	179.31
12000	217.12	216.73	216.42	216.17	215.48	215.25	215.17
15000	271.40	270.92	270.53	270.21	269.36	269.06	268.96
20000	361.86	361.22	360.70	360.29	359.14	358.75	358.61
25000	452.33	451.53	450.88	450.36	448.93	448.43	448.27
30000	542.79	541.83	541.05	540.43	538.71	538.12	537.92
31000	560.89	559.89	559.09	558.44	556.67	556.06	555.85
32000	578.98	577.95	577.13	576.46	574.62	574.00	573.78
33000	597.07	596.01	595.16	594.47	592.58	591.93	591.71
34000	615.17	614.08	613.20	612.49	610.54	609.87	609.64
35000	633.26	632.14	631.23	630.50	628.50	627.81	627.57
36000	651.35	650.20	649.27	648.51	646.45	645.75	645.50
37000	669.45	668.26	667.30	666.53	664.41	663.68	663.43
38000	687.54	686.32	685.34	684.54	682.37	681.62	681.36
39000	705.63	704.38	703.37	702.56	700.32	699.56	699.29
40000	723.73	722.44	721.41	720.57	718.28	717.50	717.23
41000	741.82	740.50	739.44	738.59	736.24	735.43	735.16
42000	759.91	758.56	757.48	756.60	754.19	753.37	753.09
43000	778.01	776.62	775.51	774.62	772.15	771.31	771.02
44000	796.10	794.69	793.55	792.63	790.11	789.24	788.95
45000	814.19	812.75	811.58	810.64	808.07	807.18	806.88
46000	832.29	830.81	829.62	828.66	826.02	825.12	824.81
47000	850.38	848.87	847.65	846.67	843.98	843.06	842.74
48000	868.47	866.93	865.69	864.69	861.94	860.99	860.67
49000	886.56	884.99	883.72	882.70	879.89	878.93	878.60
50000	904.66	903.05	901.76	900.72	897.85	896.87	896.53
51000	922.75	921.11	919.79	918.73	915.81	914.81	914.46
52000	940.84	939.17	937.83	936.74	933.77	932.74	932.39
53000	958.94	957.23	955.86	954.76	951.72	950.68	950.32
54000	977.03	975.30	973.90	972.77	969.68	968.62	968.25
55000	995.12	993.36	991.93	990.79	987.64	986.56	986.18
56000	1013.22	1011.42	1009.97	1008.80	1005.59	1004.49	1004.12
57000	1031.31	1029.48	1028.00	1026.82	1023.55	1022.43	1022.05
58000	1049.40	1047.54	1046.04	1044.83	1041.51	1040.37	1039.98
59000	1067.50	1065.60	1064.07	1062.84	1059.46	1058.31	1057.91
60000	1085.59	1083.66	1082.11	1080.86	1077.42	1076.24	1075.84
65000	1176.06	1173.97	1172.29	1170.93	1167.21	1165.93	1165.49
70000	1266.52	1264.27	1262.46	1261.00	1256.99	1255.62	1255.14
75000	1356.99	1354.58	1352.64	1351.07	1346.78	1345.30	1344.80
80000	1447.45	1444.88	1442.81	1441.14	1436.56	1434.99	1434.45
85000	1537.92	1535.19	1532.99	1531.22	1526.35	1524.68	1524.10
90000	1628.38	1625.49	1623.16	1621.29	1616.13	1614.36	1613.76
95000	1718.85	1715.80	1713.34	1711.36	1705.92	1704.05	1703.41
100000	1809.32	1806.10	1803.52	1801.43	1795.70	1793.74	1793.06
105000	1899.78	1896.41	1893.69	1891.50	1885.49	1883.43	1882.72
110000	1990.25	1986.71	1983.87	1981.57	1975.27	1973.11	1972.37
120000	2171.18	2167.32	2164.22	2161.72	2154.84	2152.49	2151.68
130000	2352.11	2347.93	2344.57	2341.86	2334.41	2331.86	2330.98
140000	2533.04	2528.54	2524.92	2522.00	2513.98	2511.23	2510.29
150000	2713.97	2709.16	2705.27	2702.15	2693.55	2690.61	2689.59
160000	2894.91	2889.77	2885.63	2882.29	2873.12	2869.98	2868.90
170000	3075.84	3070.38	3065.98	3062.43	3052.69	3049.36	3048.21
180000	3256.77	3250.99	3246.33	3242.57	3232.26	3228.73	3227.51
190000	3437.70	3431.60	3426.68	3422.72	3411.83	3408.10	3406.82
200000	3618.63	3612.21	3607.03	3602.86	3591.40	3587.48	3586.13
210000	3799.56	3792.82	3787.38	3783.00	3770.97	3766.85	3765.43
220000	3980.50	3973.43	3967.73	3963.15	3950.55	3946.22	3944.74
230000	4161.43	4154.04	4148.09	4143.29	4130.12	4125.60	4124.04
240000	4342.36	4334.65	4328.44	4323.43	4309.69	4304.97	4303.35
250000	4523.29	4515.26	4508.79	4503.58	4489.26	4484.35	4482.66

22.75 % Monthly Payments

LOAN AMOUNT	YEARS 1	2	3	4	5	6	7
100	9.35	5.18	3.81	3.14	2.75	2.50	2.3
200	18.69	10.35	7.61	6.27	5.49	4.99	4.6
500	46.73	25.88	19.03	15.68	13.74	12.49	11.6
1000	93.47	51.75	38.06	31.37	27.47	24.97	23.2
2000	186.94	103.50	76.11	62.73	54.94	49.95	46.5
5000	467.35	258.75	190.28	156.83	137.36	124.86	116.3
6000	560.82	310.50	228.34	188.19	164.83	149.84	139.6
7000	654.29	362.25	266.40	219.56	192.30	174.81	162.8
8000	747.76	414.00	304.45	250.93	219.78	199.78	186.1
9000	841.23	465.75	342.51	282.29	247.25	224.75	209.4
10000	934.70	517.50	380.57	313.66	274.72	249.73	232.6
12000	1121.64	621.00	456.68	376.39	329.66	299.67	279.2
15000	1402.05	776.26	570.85	470.49	412.08	374.59	349.0
20000	1869.40	1035.01	761.13	627.31	549.44	499.45	465.3
25000	2336.75	1293.76	951.42	784.14	686.80	624.32	581.6
30000	2804.10	1552.51	1141.70	940.97	824.16	749.18	697.9
31000	2897.57	1604.26	1179.76	972.34	851.63	774.15	721.2
32000	2991.03	1656.01	1217.81	1003.70	879.10	799.13	744.5
33000	3084.50	1707.76	1255.87	1035.07	906.57	824.10	767.7
34000	3177.97	1759.51	1293.93	1066.43	934.05	849.07	791.0
35000	3271.44	1811.26	1331.98	1097.80	961.52	874.04	814.3
36000	3364.91	1863.01	1370.04	1129.17	988.99	899.02	837.5
37000	3458.38	1914.77	1408.10	1160.53	1016.46	923.99	860.8
38000	3551.85	1966.52	1446.15	1191.90	1043.93	948.96	884.1
39000	3645.32	2018.27	1484.21	1223.26	1071.41	973.94	907.3
40000	3738.79	2070.02	1522.27	1254.63	1098.88	998.91	930.6
41000	3832.26	2121.77	1560.32	1285.99	1126.35	1023.88	953.9
42000	3925.73	2173.52	1598.38	1317.36	1153.82	1048.85	977.1
43000	4019.20	2225.27	1636.44	1348.73	1181.29	1073.83	1000.4
44000	4112.67	2277.02	1674.49	1380.09	1208.77	1098.80	1023.7
45000	4206.14	2328.77	1712.55	1411.46	1236.24	1123.77	1046.9
46000	4299.61	2380.52	1750.61	1442.82	1263.71	1148.74	1070.2
47000	4393.08	2432.27	1788.66	1474.19	1291.18	1173.72	1093.5
48000	4486.55	2484.02	1826.72	1505.55	1318.65	1198.69	1116.7
49000	4580.02	2535.77	1864.78	1536.92	1346.12	1223.66	1140.0
50000	4673.49	2587.52	1902.83	1568.29	1373.60	1248.64	1163.3
51000	4766.96	2639.27	1940.89	1599.65	1401.07	1273.61	1186.5
52000	4860.43	2691.02	1978.95	1631.02	1428.54	1298.58	1209.8
53000	4953.90	2742.77	2017.00	1662.38	1456.01	1323.55	1233.1
54000	5047.37	2794.52	2055.06	1693.75	1483.48	1348.53	1256.3
55000	5140.84	2846.27	2093.12	1725.11	1510.96	1373.50	1279.6
56000	5234.31	2898.02	2131.17	1756.48	1538.43	1398.47	1302.9
57000	5327.78	2949.77	2169.23	1787.85	1565.90	1423.44	1326.1
58000	5421.25	3001.52	2207.29	1819.21	1593.37	1448.42	1349.4
59000	5514.72	3053.27	2245.34	1850.58	1620.84	1473.39	1372.7
60000	5608.19	3105.02	2283.40	1881.94	1648.32	1498.36	1395.9
65000	6075.54	3363.78	2473.68	2038.77	1785.68	1623.23	1512.3
70000	6542.89	3622.53	2663.97	2195.60	1923.04	1748.09	1628.6
75000	7010.24	3881.28	2854.25	2352.43	2060.40	1872.95	1744.9
80000	7477.59	4140.03	3044.53	2509.26	2197.75	1997.82	1861.3
85000	7944.94	4398.78	3234.82	2666.09	2335.11	2122.68	1977.6
90000	8412.29	4657.54	3425.10	2822.91	2472.47	2247.54	2093.9
95000	8879.64	4916.29	3615.38	2979.74	2609.83	2372.41	2210.3
100000	9346.98	5175.04	3805.67	3136.57	2747.19	2497.27	2326.6
105000	9814.33	5433.79	3995.95	3293.40	2884.55	2622.13	2442.9
110000	10281.68	5692.55	4186.23	3450.23	3021.91	2747.00	2559.3
120000	11216.38	6210.05	4566.80	3763.89	3296.63	2996.72	2791.9
130000	12151.08	6727.55	4947.37	4077.54	3571.35	3246.45	3024.6
140000	13085.78	7245.06	5327.93	4391.20	3846.07	3496.18	3257.2
150000	14020.48	7762.56	5708.50	4704.86	4120.79	3745.91	3489.9
160000	14955.17	8280.07	6089.07	5018.51	4395.51	3995.63	3722.6
170000	15889.87	8797.57	6469.63	5332.17	4670.23	4245.36	3955.2
180000	16824.57	9315.07	6850.20	5645.83	4944.95	4495.09	4187.9
190000	17759.27	9832.58	7230.77	5959.49	5219.67	4744.81	4420.6
200000	18693.97	10350.08	7611.33	6273.14	5494.39	4994.54	4653.2
210000	19628.67	10867.59	7991.90	6586.80	5769.11	5244.27	4885.9
220000	20563.37	11385.09	8372.47	6900.46	6043.83	5494.00	5118.6
230000	21498.06	11902.59	8753.03	7214.11	6318.55	5743.72	5351.2
240000	22432.76	12420.10	9133.60	7527.77	6593.26	5993.45	5583.9
250000	23367.46	12937.60	9514.17	7841.43	6867.98	6243.18	5816.5

Monthly Payments 22.75 %

LOAN AMOUNT	8	9	10	11	12	13	14
				YEARS			
100	2.21	2.12	2.05	2.00	1.96	1.93	1.91
200	4.41	4.23	4.10	4.00	3.92	3.86	3.81
500	11.03	10.58	10.25	9.99	9.80	9.64	9.53
1000	22.05	21.16	20.49	19.99	19.59	19.29	19.05
2000	44.10	42.32	40.99	39.97	39.19	38.58	38.10
5000	110.26	105.81	102.47	99.93	97.97	96.45	95.25
6000	132.31	126.97	122.96	119.91	117.56	115.74	114.30
7000	154.36	148.13	143.46	139.90	137.16	135.03	133.35
8000	176.41	169.29	163.95	159.89	156.75	154.32	152.40
9000	198.46	190.45	184.44	179.87	176.35	173.60	171.45
10000	220.52	211.61	204.94	199.86	195.94	192.89	190.51
12000	264.62	253.93	245.92	239.83	235.13	231.47	228.61
15000	330.77	317.42	307.41	299.79	293.91	289.34	285.76
20000	441.03	423.22	409.87	399.71	391.88	385.79	381.01
25000	551.29	529.03	512.34	499.64	489.85	482.23	476.26
30000	661.55	634.83	614.81	599.57	587.82	578.68	571.52
31000	683.60	655.99	635.31	619.56	607.42	597.97	590.57
32000	705.65	677.15	655.80	639.54	627.01	617.26	609.62
33000	727.70	698.31	676.29	659.53	646.60	636.55	628.67
34000	749.76	719.47	696.79	679.51	666.20	655.84	647.72
35000	771.81	740.64	717.28	699.50	685.79	675.13	666.77
36000	793.86	761.80	737.77	719.48	705.39	694.42	685.82
37000	815.91	782.96	758.27	739.47	724.98	713.71	704.87
38000	837.96	804.12	778.76	759.46	744.57	733.00	723.92
39000	860.01	825.28	799.26	779.44	764.17	752.29	742.97
40000	882.07	846.44	819.75	799.43	783.76	771.58	762.02
41000	904.12	867.60	840.24	819.41	803.36	790.86	781.07
42000	926.17	888.76	860.74	839.40	822.95	810.15	800.12
43000	948.22	909.92	881.23	859.38	842.55	829.44	819.17
44000	970.27	931.08	901.72	879.37	862.14	848.73	838.22
45000	992.32	952.25	922.22	899.36	881.73	868.02	857.27
46000	1014.38	973.41	942.71	919.34	901.33	887.31	876.33
47000	1036.43	994.57	963.21	939.33	920.92	906.60	895.38
48000	1058.48	1015.73	983.70	959.31	940.52	925.89	914.43
49000	1080.53	1036.89	1004.19	979.30	960.11	945.18	933.48
50000	1102.58	1058.05	1024.69	999.28	979.70	964.47	952.53
51000	1124.63	1079.21	1045.18	1019.27	999.30	983.76	971.58
52000	1146.69	1100.37	1065.67	1039.25	1018.89	1003.05	990.63
53000	1168.74	1121.53	1086.17	1059.24	1038.49	1022.34	1009.68
54000	1190.79	1142.69	1106.66	1079.23	1058.08	1041.63	1028.73
55000	1212.84	1163.86	1127.16	1099.21	1077.67	1060.92	1047.78
56000	1234.89	1185.02	1147.65	1119.20	1097.27	1080.21	1066.83
57000	1256.94	1206.18	1168.14	1139.18	1116.86	1099.49	1085.88
58000	1279.00	1227.34	1188.64	1159.17	1136.46	1118.78	1104.93
59000	1301.05	1248.50	1209.13	1179.15	1156.05	1138.07	1123.98
60000	1323.10	1269.66	1229.62	1199.14	1175.64	1157.36	1143.03
65000	1433.36	1375.47	1332.09	1299.07	1273.61	1253.81	1238.29
70000	1543.62	1481.27	1434.56	1399.00	1371.58	1350.26	1333.54
75000	1653.87	1587.08	1537.03	1498.93	1469.56	1446.70	1428.79
80000	1764.13	1692.88	1639.50	1598.85	1567.53	1543.15	1524.04
85000	1874.39	1798.69	1741.97	1698.78	1665.50	1639.60	1619.30
90000	1984.65	1904.49	1844.44	1798.71	1763.47	1736.04	1714.55
95000	2094.91	2010.30	1946.90	1898.64	1861.44	1832.49	1809.80
100000	2205.16	2116.10	2049.37	1998.57	1959.41	1928.94	1905.06
105000	2315.42	2221.91	2151.84	2098.50	2057.38	2025.38	2000.31
110000	2425.68	2327.71	2254.31	2198.42	2155.35	2121.83	2095.56
120000	2646.20	2539.32	2459.25	2398.28	2351.29	2314.73	2286.07
130000	2866.71	2750.93	2664.18	2598.14	2547.23	2507.62	2476.57
140000	3087.23	2962.54	2869.12	2797.99	2743.17	2700.51	2667.08
150000	3307.75	3174.15	3074.06	2997.85	2939.11	2893.41	2857.58
160000	3528.26	3385.76	3279.00	3197.71	3135.05	3086.30	3048.09
170000	3748.78	3597.37	3483.93	3397.56	3330.99	3279.19	3238.59
180000	3969.30	3808.98	3688.87	3597.42	3526.93	3472.09	3429.10
190000	4189.81	4020.59	3893.81	3797.28	3722.87	3664.98	3619.61
200000	4410.33	4232.20	4098.75	3997.13	3918.81	3857.88	3810.11
210000	4630.85	4443.81	4303.68	4196.99	4114.75	4050.77	4000.62
220000	4851.36	4655.42	4508.62	4396.85	4310.70	4243.66	4191.12
230000	5071.88	4867.03	4713.56	4596.70	4506.64	4436.56	4381.63
240000	5292.40	5078.64	4918.49	4796.56	4702.58	4629.45	4572.13
250000	5512.91	5290.25	5123.43	4996.42	4898.52	4822.34	4762.64

22.75 % Monthly Payments

LOAN AMOUNT	15	16	17	18	19	20	21
	YEARS						
100	1.89	1.87	1.86	1.85	1.84	1.84	1.83
200	3.77	3.74	3.72	3.70	3.68	3.67	3.66
500	9.43	9.36	9.30	9.25	9.21	9.18	9.16
1000	18.86	18.71	18.59	18.50	18.42	18.36	18.32
2000	37.72	37.43	37.19	37.00	36.85	36.73	36.63
5000	94.31	93.57	92.97	92.50	92.12	91.82	91.58
6000	113.17	112.28	111.57	111.00	110.55	110.19	109.90
7000	132.04	130.99	130.16	129.50	128.97	128.55	128.21
8000	150.90	149.71	148.76	148.00	147.40	146.92	146.53
9000	169.76	168.42	167.35	166.50	165.82	165.28	164.85
10000	188.62	187.13	185.95	185.00	184.25	183.64	183.16
12000	226.35	224.56	223.14	222.00	221.10	220.37	219.79
15000	282.93	280.70	278.92	277.50	276.37	275.47	274.74
20000	377.25	374.26	371.89	370.01	368.50	367.29	366.32
25000	471.56	467.83	464.87	462.51	460.62	459.11	457.90
30000	565.87	561.40	557.84	555.01	552.75	550.93	549.48
31000	584.73	580.11	576.44	573.51	571.17	569.30	567.80
32000	603.59	598.82	595.03	592.01	589.60	587.66	586.12
33000	622.46	617.54	613.63	610.51	608.02	606.03	604.43
34000	641.32	636.25	632.22	629.01	626.45	624.39	622.75
35000	660.18	654.96	650.82	647.51	644.87	642.76	641.06
36000	679.04	673.68	669.41	666.01	663.29	661.12	659.38
37000	697.90	692.39	688.00	684.51	681.72	679.49	677.70
38000	716.77	711.10	706.60	703.01	700.14	697.85	696.01
39000	735.63	729.81	725.19	721.51	718.57	716.22	714.33
40000	754.49	748.53	743.79	740.01	736.99	734.58	732.64
41000	773.35	767.24	762.38	758.51	755.42	752.94	750.96
42000	792.22	785.95	780.98	777.01	773.84	771.31	769.28
43000	811.08	804.67	799.57	795.51	792.27	789.67	787.59
44000	829.94	823.38	818.17	814.01	810.69	808.04	805.91
45000	848.80	842.09	836.76	832.51	829.12	826.40	824.23
46000	867.67	860.81	855.36	851.01	847.54	844.77	842.54
47000	886.53	879.52	873.95	869.51	865.97	863.13	860.86
48000	905.39	898.23	892.55	888.01	884.39	881.50	879.17
49000	924.25	916.95	911.14	906.51	902.82	899.86	897.49
50000	943.11	935.66	929.74	925.01	921.24	918.22	915.81
51000	961.98	954.37	948.33	943.51	939.67	936.59	934.12
52000	980.84	973.09	966.93	962.01	958.09	954.95	952.44
53000	999.70	991.80	985.52	980.52	976.52	973.32	970.75
54000	1018.56	1010.51	1004.11	999.02	994.94	991.68	989.07
55000	1037.43	1029.23	1022.71	1017.52	1013.37	1010.05	1007.39
56000	1056.29	1047.94	1041.30	1036.02	1031.79	1028.41	1025.70
57000	1075.15	1066.65	1059.90	1054.52	1050.22	1046.78	1044.02
58000	1094.01	1085.37	1078.49	1073.02	1068.64	1065.14	1062.33
59000	1112.87	1104.08	1097.09	1091.52	1087.07	1083.50	1080.65
60000	1131.74	1122.79	1115.68	1110.02	1105.49	1101.87	1098.97
65000	1226.05	1216.36	1208.66	1202.52	1197.62	1193.69	1190.55
70000	1320.36	1309.92	1301.63	1295.02	1289.74	1285.51	1282.13
75000	1414.67	1403.49	1394.60	1387.52	1381.86	1377.34	1373.71
80000	1508.98	1497.06	1487.58	1480.02	1473.99	1469.16	1465.29
85000	1603.29	1590.62	1580.55	1572.52	1566.11	1560.98	1556.87
90000	1697.61	1684.19	1673.52	1665.03	1658.24	1652.80	1648.45
95000	1791.92	1777.75	1766.50	1757.53	1750.36	1744.63	1740.03
100000	1886.23	1871.32	1859.47	1850.03	1842.49	1836.45	1831.61
105000	1980.54	1964.89	1952.45	1942.53	1934.61	1928.27	1923.19
110000	2074.85	2058.45	2045.42	2035.03	2026.73	2020.09	2014.77
120000	2263.47	2245.58	2231.37	2220.03	2210.98	2203.74	2197.93
130000	2452.10	2432.72	2417.31	2405.04	2395.23	2387.38	2381.09
140000	2640.72	2619.85	2603.26	2590.04	2579.48	2571.03	2564.26
150000	2829.34	2806.98	2789.21	2775.04	2763.73	2754.67	2747.42
160000	3017.97	2994.11	2975.15	2960.05	2947.98	2938.32	2930.58
170000	3206.59	3181.24	3161.10	3145.05	3132.23	3121.96	3113.74
180000	3395.21	3368.38	3347.05	3330.05	3316.47	3305.61	3296.90
190000	3583.83	3555.51	3533.00	3515.05	3500.72	3489.25	3480.06
200000	3772.46	3742.64	3718.94	3700.06	3684.97	3672.90	3663.22
210000	3961.08	3929.77	3904.89	3885.06	3869.22	3856.54	3846.38
220000	4149.70	4116.90	4090.84	4070.06	4053.47	4040.19	4029.54
230000	4338.33	4304.04	4276.78	4255.07	4237.72	4223.83	4212.71
240000	4526.95	4491.17	4462.73	4440.07	4421.96	4407.48	4395.87
250000	4715.57	4678.30	4648.68	4625.07	4606.21	4591.12	4579.03

Monthly Payments 22.75 %

LOAN AMOUNT	22	23	24	25	30	35	40
				YEARS			
100	1.83	1.82	1.82	1.82	1.81	1.81	1.81
200	3.66	3.65	3.64	3.64	3.63	3.63	3.62
500	9.14	9.12	9.11	9.10	9.07	9.06	9.06
1000	18.28	18.25	18.22	18.20	18.15	18.13	18.12
2000	36.55	36.49	36.44	36.40	36.29	36.25	36.24
5000	91.39	91.23	91.11	91.00	90.73	90.64	90.60
6000	109.66	109.48	109.33	109.21	108.88	108.76	108.73
7000	127.94	127.72	127.55	127.41	127.02	126.89	126.85
8000	146.22	145.97	145.77	145.61	145.17	145.02	144.97
9000	164.50	164.22	163.99	163.81	163.31	163.15	163.09
10000	182.77	182.46	182.21	182.01	181.46	181.27	181.21
12000	219.33	218.95	218.65	218.41	217.75	217.53	217.45
15000	274.16	273.69	273.32	273.01	272.19	271.91	271.81
20000	365.55	364.92	364.42	364.02	362.92	362.54	362.42
25000	456.93	456.15	455.53	455.02	453.65	453.18	453.02
30000	548.32	547.38	546.63	546.03	544.38	543.82	543.63
31000	566.60	565.63	564.85	564.23	562.52	561.94	561.75
32000	584.87	583.88	583.07	582.43	580.67	580.07	579.87
33000	603.15	602.12	601.30	600.63	598.81	598.20	597.99
34000	621.43	620.37	619.52	618.83	616.96	616.33	616.11
35000	639.71	638.61	637.74	637.03	635.11	634.45	634.23
36000	657.98	656.86	655.96	655.23	653.25	652.58	652.35
37000	676.26	675.11	674.18	673.43	671.40	670.71	670.47
38000	694.54	693.35	692.40	691.64	689.54	688.84	688.59
39000	712.81	711.60	710.62	709.84	707.69	706.96	706.71
40000	731.09	729.85	728.84	728.04	725.84	725.09	724.84
41000	749.37	748.09	747.06	746.24	743.98	743.22	742.96
42000	767.65	766.34	765.29	764.44	762.13	761.34	761.08
43000	785.92	784.58	783.51	782.64	780.27	779.47	779.20
44000	804.20	802.83	801.73	800.84	798.42	797.60	797.32
45000	822.48	821.08	819.95	819.04	816.57	815.73	815.44
46000	840.76	839.32	838.17	837.24	834.71	833.85	833.56
47000	859.03	857.57	856.39	855.44	852.86	851.98	851.68
48000	877.31	875.81	874.61	873.64	871.00	870.11	869.80
49000	895.59	894.06	892.83	891.85	889.15	888.23	887.92
50000	913.86	912.31	911.05	910.05	907.30	906.36	906.04
51000	932.14	930.55	929.27	928.25	925.44	924.49	924.17
52000	950.42	948.80	947.50	946.45	943.59	942.62	942.29
53000	968.70	967.04	965.72	964.65	961.73	960.74	960.41
54000	986.97	985.29	983.94	982.85	979.88	978.87	978.53
55000	1005.25	1003.54	1002.16	1001.05	998.02	997.00	996.65
56000	1023.53	1021.78	1020.38	1019.25	1016.17	1015.13	1014.77
57000	1041.81	1040.03	1038.60	1037.45	1034.32	1033.25	1032.89
58000	1060.08	1058.28	1056.82	1055.65	1052.46	1051.38	1051.01
59000	1078.36	1076.52	1075.04	1073.85	1070.61	1069.51	1069.13
60000	1096.64	1094.77	1093.26	1092.06	1088.75	1087.63	1087.25
65000	1188.02	1186.00	1184.37	1183.06	1179.48	1178.27	1177.86
70000	1279.41	1277.23	1275.48	1274.07	1270.21	1268.91	1268.46
75000	1370.80	1368.46	1366.58	1365.07	1360.94	1359.54	1359.07
80000	1462.18	1459.69	1457.69	1456.07	1451.67	1450.18	1449.67
85000	1553.57	1550.92	1548.79	1547.08	1542.40	1540.82	1540.28
90000	1644.96	1642.15	1639.90	1638.08	1633.13	1631.45	1630.88
95000	1736.34	1733.38	1731.00	1729.09	1723.86	1722.09	1721.48
100000	1827.73	1824.61	1822.11	1820.09	1814.59	1812.72	1812.09
105000	1919.12	1915.84	1913.21	1911.10	1905.32	1903.36	1902.69
110000	2010.50	2007.07	2004.32	2002.10	1996.05	1994.00	1993.30
120000	2193.28	2189.54	2186.53	2184.11	2177.51	2175.27	2174.51
130000	2376.05	2372.00	2368.74	2366.12	2358.97	2356.54	2355.72
140000	2558.82	2554.46	2550.95	2548.13	2540.43	2537.81	2536.92
150000	2741.59	2736.92	2733.16	2730.14	2721.89	2719.09	2718.13
160000	2924.37	2919.38	2915.37	2912.15	2903.34	2900.36	2899.34
170000	3107.14	3101.84	3097.58	3094.16	3084.80	3081.63	3080.55
180000	3289.91	3284.30	3279.79	3276.17	3266.26	3262.90	3261.76
190000	3472.69	3466.76	3462.00	3458.18	3447.72	3444.18	3442.97
200000	3655.46	3649.23	3644.22	3640.19	3629.18	3625.45	3624.18
210000	3838.23	3831.69	3826.43	3822.20	3810.64	3806.72	3805.39
220000	4021.01	4014.15	4008.64	4004.20	3992.10	3987.99	3986.60
230000	4203.78	4196.61	4190.85	4186.21	4173.56	4169.26	4167.81
240000	4386.55	4379.07	4373.06	4368.22	4355.02	4350.54	4349.01
250000	4569.32	4561.53	4555.27	4550.23	4536.48	4531.81	4530.22

23.00 % Monthly Payments

LOAN AMOUNT	YEARS 1	2	3	4	5	6	7
100	9.36	5.19	3.82	3.15	2.76	2.51	2.34
200	18.72	10.37	7.63	6.30	5.52	5.02	4.68
500	46.79	25.93	19.09	15.74	13.80	12.55	11.70
1000	93.58	51.86	38.17	31.49	27.60	25.11	23.41
2000	187.16	103.73	76.35	62.98	55.20	50.22	46.81
5000	467.90	259.32	190.87	157.45	138.01	125.54	117.04
6000	561.48	311.18	229.05	188.94	165.61	150.65	140.44
7000	655.06	363.04	267.22	220.43	193.21	175.76	163.85
8000	748.64	414.91	305.40	251.92	220.81	200.86	187.26
9000	842.22	466.77	343.57	283.41	248.41	225.97	210.66
10000	935.80	518.63	381.75	314.90	276.02	251.08	234.07
12000	1122.96	622.36	458.10	377.87	331.22	301.30	280.89
15000	1403.70	777.95	572.62	472.34	414.02	376.62	351.11
20000	1871.59	1037.26	763.49	629.79	552.03	502.16	468.14
25000	2339.49	1296.58	954.37	787.24	690.04	627.70	585.18
30000	2807.39	1555.89	1145.24	944.69	828.05	753.24	702.21
31000	2900.97	1607.76	1183.42	976.18	855.65	778.35	725.62
32000	2994.55	1659.62	1221.59	1007.67	883.25	803.46	749.03
33000	3088.13	1711.48	1259.77	1039.16	910.85	828.57	772.44
34000	3181.71	1763.35	1297.94	1070.65	938.45	853.67	795.84
35000	3275.29	1815.21	1336.11	1102.13	966.06	878.78	819.25
36000	3368.87	1867.07	1374.29	1133.62	993.66	903.89	842.66
37000	3462.45	1918.94	1412.46	1165.11	1021.26	929.00	866.06
38000	3556.03	1970.80	1450.64	1196.60	1048.86	954.11	889.47
39000	3649.61	2022.66	1488.81	1228.09	1076.46	979.21	912.88
40000	3743.19	2074.53	1526.99	1259.58	1104.06	1004.32	936.29
41000	3836.77	2126.39	1565.16	1291.07	1131.67	1029.43	959.69
42000	3930.35	2178.25	1603.34	1322.56	1159.27	1054.54	983.10
43000	4023.93	2230.11	1641.51	1354.05	1186.87	1079.65	1006.51
44000	4117.51	2281.98	1679.69	1385.54	1214.47	1104.75	1029.91
45000	4211.09	2333.84	1717.86	1417.03	1242.07	1129.86	1053.32
46000	4304.67	2385.70	1756.04	1448.52	1269.67	1154.97	1076.73
47000	4398.25	2437.57	1794.21	1480.01	1297.28	1180.08	1100.14
48000	4491.83	2489.43	1832.39	1511.50	1324.88	1205.19	1123.54
49000	4585.41	2541.29	1870.56	1542.99	1352.48	1230.30	1146.95
50000	4678.99	2593.16	1908.74	1574.48	1380.08	1255.40	1170.36
51000	4772.57	2645.02	1946.91	1605.97	1407.68	1280.51	1193.76
52000	4866.15	2696.88	1985.09	1637.46	1435.28	1305.62	1217.17
53000	4959.73	2748.75	2023.26	1668.95	1462.89	1330.73	1240.58
54000	5053.31	2800.61	2061.43	1700.44	1490.49	1355.84	1263.99
55000	5146.89	2852.47	2099.61	1731.93	1518.09	1380.94	1287.39
56000	5240.47	2904.34	2137.78	1763.42	1545.69	1406.05	1310.80
57000	5334.04	2956.20	2175.96	1794.90	1573.29	1431.16	1334.21
58000	5427.62	3008.06	2214.13	1826.39	1600.89	1456.27	1357.62
59000	5521.20	3059.92	2252.31	1857.88	1628.50	1481.38	1381.02
60000	5614.78	3111.79	2290.48	1889.37	1656.10	1506.48	1404.43
65000	6082.68	3371.10	2481.36	2046.82	1794.10	1632.02	1521.47
70000	6550.58	3630.42	2672.23	2204.27	1932.11	1757.56	1638.50
75000	7018.48	3889.73	2863.10	2361.72	2070.12	1883.11	1755.54
80000	7486.38	4149.05	3053.98	2519.16	2208.13	2008.65	1872.57
85000	7954.28	4408.37	3244.85	2676.61	2346.14	2134.19	1989.61
90000	8422.18	4667.68	3435.72	2834.06	2484.15	2259.73	2106.64
95000	8890.07	4927.00	3626.60	2991.51	2622.15	2385.27	2223.68
100000	9357.97	5186.31	3817.47	3148.96	2760.16	2510.81	2340.72
105000	9825.87	5445.63	4008.34	3306.40	2898.17	2636.35	2457.75
110000	10293.77	5704.94	4199.22	3463.85	3036.18	2761.89	2574.79
120000	11229.57	6223.58	4580.97	3778.75	3312.19	3012.97	2808.86
130000	12165.37	6742.21	4962.71	4093.64	3588.21	3264.05	3042.93
140000	13101.16	7260.84	5344.46	4408.54	3864.23	3515.13	3277.00
150000	14036.96	7779.47	5726.21	4723.43	4140.24	3766.21	3511.07
160000	14972.76	8298.10	6107.95	5038.33	4416.26	4017.29	3745.14
170000	15908.55	8816.73	6489.70	5353.23	4692.27	4268.37	3979.22
180000	16844.35	9335.36	6871.45	5668.12	4968.29	4519.45	4213.29
190000	17780.15	9853.99	7253.20	5983.02	5244.31	4770.53	4447.36
200000	18715.95	10372.63	7634.94	6297.91	5520.32	5021.61	4681.43
210000	19651.74	10891.26	8016.69	6612.81	5796.34	5272.69	4915.50
220000	20587.54	11409.89	8398.44	6927.70	6072.35	5523.77	5149.57
230000	21523.34	11928.52	8780.18	7242.60	6348.37	5774.86	5383.65
240000	22459.14	12447.15	9161.93	7557.49	6624.39	6025.94	5617.72
250000	23394.93	12965.78	9543.68	7872.39	6900.40	6277.02	5851.79

Monthly Payments 23.00 %

LOAN AMOUNT	8	9	10	11	12	13	14
	YEARS						
100	2.22	2.13	2.06	2.01	1.98	1.95	1.92
200	4.44	4.26	4.13	4.03	3.95	3.89	3.84
500	11.10	10.66	10.32	10.07	9.88	9.73	9.61
1000	22.20	21.31	20.65	20.15	19.76	19.46	19.22
2000	44.40	42.62	41.30	40.29	39.51	38.91	38.44
5000	110.99	106.56	103.24	100.73	98.79	97.28	96.10
6000	133.19	127.87	123.89	120.87	118.54	116.74	115.32
7000	155.38	149.18	144.54	141.02	138.30	136.19	134.54
8000	177.58	170.49	165.19	161.16	158.06	155.65	153.76
9000	199.78	191.81	185.84	181.31	177.81	175.10	172.98
10000	221.98	213.12	206.49	201.45	197.57	194.56	192.20
12000	266.37	255.74	247.79	241.74	237.09	233.47	230.64
15000	332.96	319.68	309.73	302.18	296.36	291.84	288.30
20000	443.95	426.24	412.98	402.90	395.14	389.12	384.40
25000	554.94	532.79	516.22	503.63	493.93	486.40	480.50
30000	665.93	639.35	619.47	604.35	592.72	583.68	576.60
31000	688.13	660.67	640.12	624.50	612.47	603.13	595.82
32000	710.32	681.98	660.77	644.64	632.23	622.59	615.04
33000	732.52	703.29	681.42	664.79	651.99	642.04	634.26
34000	754.72	724.60	702.07	684.93	671.74	661.50	653.48
35000	776.92	745.91	722.71	705.08	691.50	680.96	672.70
36000	799.11	767.22	743.36	725.22	711.26	700.41	691.92
37000	821.31	788.54	764.01	745.37	731.02	719.87	711.14
38000	843.51	809.85	784.66	765.51	750.77	739.32	730.36
39000	865.71	831.16	805.31	785.66	770.53	758.78	749.58
40000	887.90	852.47	825.96	805.80	790.29	778.23	768.80
41000	910.10	873.78	846.61	825.95	810.04	797.69	788.02
42000	932.30	895.09	867.26	846.09	829.80	817.15	807.24
43000	954.50	916.41	887.91	866.24	849.56	836.60	826.46
44000	976.69	937.72	908.55	886.38	869.32	856.06	845.68
45000	998.89	959.03	929.20	906.53	889.07	875.51	864.90
46000	1021.09	980.34	949.85	926.67	908.83	894.97	884.13
47000	1043.29	1001.65	970.50	946.82	928.59	914.43	903.35
48000	1065.48	1022.97	991.15	966.96	948.34	933.88	922.57
49000	1087.68	1044.28	1011.80	987.11	968.10	953.34	941.79
50000	1109.88	1065.59	1032.45	1007.25	987.86	972.79	961.01
51000	1132.08	1086.90	1053.10	1027.40	1007.62	992.25	980.23
52000	1154.28	1108.21	1073.75	1047.54	1027.37	1011.71	999.45
53000	1176.47	1129.52	1094.40	1067.69	1047.13	1031.16	1018.67
54000	1198.67	1150.84	1115.04	1087.83	1066.89	1050.62	1037.89
55000	1220.87	1172.15	1135.69	1107.98	1086.64	1070.07	1057.11
56000	1243.07	1193.46	1156.34	1128.12	1106.40	1089.53	1076.33
57000	1265.26	1214.77	1176.99	1148.27	1126.16	1108.98	1095.55
58000	1287.46	1236.08	1197.64	1168.41	1145.92	1128.44	1114.77
59000	1309.66	1257.40	1218.29	1188.56	1165.67	1147.90	1133.99
60000	1331.86	1278.71	1238.94	1208.70	1185.43	1167.35	1153.21
65000	1442.84	1385.27	1342.18	1309.43	1284.22	1264.63	1249.31
70000	1553.83	1491.82	1445.43	1410.15	1383.00	1361.91	1345.41
75000	1664.82	1598.38	1548.67	1510.88	1481.79	1459.19	1441.51
80000	1775.81	1704.94	1651.92	1611.60	1580.57	1556.47	1537.61
85000	1886.80	1811.50	1755.16	1712.33	1679.36	1653.75	1633.71
90000	1997.78	1918.06	1858.41	1813.05	1778.15	1751.03	1729.81
95000	2108.77	2024.62	1961.65	1913.78	1876.93	1848.31	1825.91
100000	2219.76	2131.18	2064.90	2014.50	1975.72	1945.59	1922.01
105000	2330.75	2237.74	2168.14	2115.23	2074.50	2042.87	2018.11
110000	2441.74	2344.30	2271.39	2215.95	2173.29	2140.15	2114.21
120000	2663.71	2557.41	2477.88	2417.40	2370.86	2334.70	2306.41
130000	2885.69	2770.53	2684.37	2618.85	2568.43	2529.26	2498.61
140000	3107.66	2983.65	2890.86	2820.30	2766.00	2723.82	2690.82
150000	3329.64	3196.77	3097.35	3021.75	2963.58	2918.38	2883.02
160000	3551.62	3409.89	3303.84	3223.20	3161.15	3112.94	3075.22
170000	3773.59	3623.00	3510.33	3424.65	3358.72	3307.50	3267.42
180000	3995.57	3836.12	3716.82	3626.10	3556.29	3502.06	3459.62
190000	4217.54	4049.24	3923.30	3827.55	3753.86	3696.62	3651.82
200000	4439.52	4262.36	4129.79	4029.00	3951.43	3891.17	3844.02
210000	4661.50	4475.47	4336.28	4230.45	4149.01	4085.73	4036.22
220000	4883.47	4688.59	4542.77	4431.90	4346.58	4280.29	4228.42
230000	5105.45	4901.71	4749.26	4633.36	4544.15	4474.85	4420.63
240000	5327.42	5114.83	4955.75	4834.81	4741.72	4669.41	4612.83
250000	5549.40	5327.95	5162.24	5036.26	4939.29	4863.97	4805.03

23.00 % Monthly Payments

LOAN AMOUNT	15	16	17	18	19	20	21
100	1.90	1.89	1.88	1.87	1.86	1.85	1.85
200	3.81	3.78	3.75	3.74	3.72	3.71	3.70
500	9.52	9.44	9.39	9.34	9.30	9.27	9.25
1000	19.03	18.89	18.77	18.68	18.61	18.55	18.50
2000	38.07	37.78	37.54	37.36	37.21	37.09	37.00
5000	95.17	94.44	93.86	93.40	93.03	92.73	92.50
6000	114.21	113.33	112.63	112.07	111.63	111.28	111.00
7000	133.24	132.22	131.40	130.75	130.24	129.82	129.49
8000	152.28	151.10	150.17	149.43	148.84	148.37	147.99
9000	171.31	169.99	168.94	168.11	167.45	166.92	166.49
10000	190.35	188.88	187.72	186.79	186.05	185.46	184.99
12000	228.41	226.66	225.26	224.15	223.26	222.56	221.99
15000	285.52	283.32	281.57	280.19	279.08	278.20	277.49
20000	380.69	377.76	375.43	373.58	372.11	370.93	369.98
25000	475.86	472.20	469.29	466.98	465.13	463.66	462.48
30000	571.04	566.64	563.15	560.37	558.16	556.39	554.98
31000	590.07	585.53	581.92	579.05	576.76	574.94	573.48
32000	609.11	604.41	600.69	597.73	595.37	593.48	591.98
33000	628.14	623.30	619.46	616.41	613.97	612.03	610.47
34000	647.18	642.19	638.23	635.09	632.58	630.58	628.97
35000	666.21	661.08	657.01	653.77	651.18	649.12	647.47
36000	685.24	679.97	675.78	672.45	669.79	667.67	665.97
37000	704.28	698.85	694.55	691.12	688.40	686.21	684.47
38000	723.31	717.74	713.32	709.80	707.00	704.76	702.97
39000	742.35	736.63	732.09	728.48	725.61	723.31	721.47
40000	761.38	755.52	750.86	747.16	744.21	741.85	739.97
41000	780.42	774.40	769.64	765.84	762.82	760.40	758.47
42000	799.45	793.29	788.41	784.52	781.42	778.95	776.97
43000	818.49	812.18	807.18	803.20	800.03	797.49	795.47
44000	837.52	831.07	825.95	821.88	818.63	816.04	813.97
45000	856.56	849.96	844.72	840.56	837.24	834.59	832.47
46000	875.59	868.84	863.49	859.24	855.84	853.13	850.96
47000	894.63	887.73	882.26	877.92	874.45	871.68	869.46
48000	913.66	906.62	901.04	896.59	893.05	890.22	887.96
49000	932.69	925.51	919.81	915.27	911.66	908.77	906.46
50000	951.73	944.40	938.58	933.95	930.26	927.32	924.96
51000	970.76	963.28	957.35	952.63	948.87	945.86	943.46
52000	989.80	982.17	976.12	971.31	967.47	964.41	961.96
53000	1008.83	1001.06	994.89	989.99	986.08	982.96	980.46
54000	1027.87	1019.95	1013.67	1008.67	1004.68	1001.50	998.96
55000	1046.90	1038.84	1032.44	1027.35	1023.29	1020.05	1017.46
56000	1065.94	1057.72	1051.21	1046.03	1041.90	1038.60	1035.96
57000	1084.97	1076.61	1069.98	1064.71	1060.50	1057.14	1054.46
58000	1104.01	1095.50	1088.75	1083.38	1079.11	1075.69	1072.96
59000	1123.04	1114.39	1107.52	1102.06	1097.71	1094.23	1091.45
60000	1142.07	1133.28	1126.30	1120.74	1116.32	1112.78	1109.95
65000	1237.25	1227.71	1220.15	1214.14	1209.34	1205.51	1202.45
70000	1332.42	1322.15	1314.01	1307.53	1302.37	1298.24	1294.95
75000	1427.59	1416.59	1407.87	1400.93	1395.40	1390.98	1387.44
80000	1522.77	1511.03	1501.73	1494.32	1488.42	1483.71	1479.94
85000	1617.94	1605.47	1595.58	1587.72	1581.45	1576.44	1572.43
90000	1713.11	1699.91	1689.44	1681.11	1674.47	1669.17	1664.93
95000	1808.28	1794.35	1783.30	1774.51	1767.50	1761.90	1757.43
100000	1903.46	1888.79	1877.16	1867.90	1860.53	1854.64	1849.92
105000	1998.63	1983.23	1971.02	1961.30	1953.55	1947.37	1942.42
110000	2093.80	2077.67	2064.87	2054.70	2046.58	2040.10	2034.92
120000	2284.15	2266.55	2252.59	2241.49	2232.63	2225.56	2219.91
130000	2474.50	2455.43	2440.31	2428.28	2418.69	2411.03	2404.90
140000	2664.84	2644.31	2628.02	2615.07	2604.74	2596.49	2589.89
150000	2855.19	2833.19	2815.74	2801.86	2790.79	2781.95	2774.88
160000	3045.53	3022.07	3003.45	2988.65	2976.84	2967.42	2959.88
170000	3235.88	3210.95	3191.17	3175.44	3162.90	3152.88	3144.87
180000	3426.22	3399.83	3378.89	3362.23	3348.95	3338.34	3329.86
190000	3616.57	3588.71	3566.60	3549.02	3535.00	3523.81	3514.85
200000	3806.92	3777.58	3754.32	3735.81	3721.05	3709.27	3699.85
210000	3997.26	3966.46	3942.03	3922.60	3907.11	3894.73	3884.84
220000	4187.61	4155.34	4129.75	4109.39	4093.16	4080.20	4069.83
230000	4377.95	4344.22	4317.46	4296.18	4279.21	4265.66	4254.82
240000	4568.30	4533.10	4505.18	4482.97	4465.27	4451.12	4439.81
250000	4758.64	4721.98	4692.90	4669.76	4651.32	4636.59	4624.81

Monthly Payments 23.00 %

LOAN AMOUNT	YEARS 22	23	24	25	30	35	40
100	1.85	1.84	1.84	1.84	1.83	1.83	1.83
200	3.69	3.69	3.68	3.68	3.67	3.66	3.66
500	9.23	9.22	9.20	9.19	9.17	9.16	9.16
1000	18.46	18.43	18.41	18.39	18.33	18.32	18.31
2000	36.92	36.86	36.81	36.78	36.67	36.63	36.62
5000	92.31	92.16	92.04	91.94	91.67	91.58	91.55
6000	110.77	110.59	110.44	110.33	110.01	109.90	109.87
7000	129.23	129.02	128.85	128.71	128.34	128.22	128.18
8000	147.69	147.45	147.26	147.10	146.68	146.54	146.49
9000	166.15	165.88	165.66	165.49	165.01	164.85	164.80
10000	184.61	184.31	184.07	183.88	183.35	183.17	183.11
12000	221.54	221.18	220.88	220.65	220.02	219.80	219.73
15000	276.92	276.47	276.11	275.81	275.02	274.75	274.66
20000	369.23	368.63	368.14	367.75	366.69	366.34	366.22
25000	461.54	460.78	460.18	459.69	458.37	457.92	457.77
30000	553.84	552.94	552.21	551.63	550.04	549.51	549.33
31000	572.31	571.37	570.62	570.01	568.38	567.83	567.64
32000	590.77	589.80	589.02	588.40	586.71	586.14	585.95
33000	609.23	608.23	607.43	606.79	605.04	604.46	604.26
34000	627.69	626.66	625.84	625.18	623.38	622.78	622.57
35000	646.15	645.09	644.25	643.56	641.71	641.09	640.88
36000	664.61	663.53	662.65	661.95	660.05	659.41	659.20
37000	683.08	681.96	681.06	680.34	678.38	677.73	677.51
38000	701.54	700.39	699.47	698.73	696.72	696.04	695.82
39000	720.00	718.82	717.87	717.11	715.05	714.36	714.13
40000	738.46	737.25	736.28	735.50	733.39	732.68	732.44
41000	756.92	755.68	754.69	753.89	751.72	751.00	750.75
42000	775.38	774.11	773.09	772.28	770.06	769.31	769.06
43000	793.84	792.54	791.50	790.66	788.39	787.63	787.37
44000	812.31	810.98	809.91	809.05	806.73	805.95	805.68
45000	830.77	829.41	828.32	827.44	825.06	824.26	823.99
46000	849.23	847.84	846.72	845.83	843.40	842.58	842.31
47000	867.69	866.27	865.13	864.21	861.73	860.90	860.62
48000	886.15	884.70	883.54	882.60	880.07	879.21	878.93
49000	904.61	903.13	901.94	900.99	898.40	897.53	897.24
50000	923.07	921.56	920.35	919.38	916.73	915.85	915.55
51000	941.54	939.99	938.76	937.77	935.07	934.17	933.86
52000	960.00	958.43	957.16	956.15	953.40	952.48	952.17
53000	978.46	976.86	975.57	974.54	971.74	970.80	970.48
54000	996.92	995.29	993.98	992.93	990.07	989.12	988.79
55000	1015.38	1013.72	1012.39	1011.32	1008.41	1007.43	1007.10
56000	1033.84	1032.15	1030.79	1029.70	1026.74	1025.75	1025.42
57000	1052.31	1050.58	1049.20	1048.09	1045.08	1044.07	1043.73
58000	1070.77	1069.01	1067.61	1066.48	1063.41	1062.38	1062.04
59000	1089.23	1087.44	1086.01	1084.87	1081.75	1080.70	1080.35
60000	1107.69	1105.88	1104.42	1103.25	1100.08	1099.02	1098.66
65000	1200.00	1198.03	1196.46	1195.19	1191.75	1190.60	1190.21
70000	1292.30	1290.19	1288.49	1287.13	1283.43	1282.19	1281.77
75000	1384.61	1382.34	1380.53	1379.07	1375.10	1373.77	1373.32
80000	1476.92	1474.50	1472.56	1471.00	1466.78	1465.36	1464.88
85000	1569.23	1566.66	1564.60	1562.94	1558.45	1556.94	1556.43
90000	1661.53	1658.81	1656.63	1654.88	1650.12	1648.53	1647.99
95000	1753.84	1750.97	1748.67	1746.82	1741.80	1740.11	1739.54
100000	1846.15	1843.13	1840.70	1838.75	1833.47	1831.70	1831.10
105000	1938.46	1935.28	1932.74	1930.69	1925.14	1923.28	1922.65
110000	2030.76	2027.44	2024.77	2022.63	2016.82	2014.87	2014.21
120000	2215.38	2211.75	2208.84	2206.51	2200.16	2198.04	2197.32
130000	2399.99	2396.06	2392.91	2390.38	2383.51	2381.20	2380.43
140000	2584.61	2580.38	2576.98	2574.26	2566.86	2564.37	2563.54
150000	2769.22	2764.69	2761.05	2758.13	2750.20	2747.54	2746.65
160000	2953.84	2949.00	2945.12	2942.01	2933.55	2930.71	2929.76
170000	3138.45	3133.31	3129.19	3125.88	3116.90	3113.88	3112.87
180000	3323.07	3317.63	3313.26	3309.76	3300.24	3297.05	3295.98
190000	3507.68	3501.94	3497.33	3493.63	3483.59	3480.22	3479.09
200000	3692.30	3686.25	3681.40	3677.51	3666.94	3663.39	3662.20
210000	3876.91	3870.56	3865.47	3861.39	3850.29	3846.56	3845.31
220000	4061.53	4054.88	4049.54	4045.26	4033.63	4029.73	4028.42
230000	4246.14	4239.19	4233.61	4229.14	4216.98	4212.90	4211.53
240000	4430.76	4423.50	4417.68	4413.01	4400.33	4396.07	4394.64
250000	4615.37	4607.81	4601.75	4596.89	4583.67	4579.24	4577.75

23.25 % Monthly Payments

LOAN AMOUNT	1	2	3	4	5	6	7
	YEARS						
100	9.37	5.20	3.83	3.16	2.77	2.52	2.35
200	18.74	10.40	7.66	6.32	5.55	5.05	4.71
500	46.84	25.99	19.15	15.81	13.87	12.62	11.77
1000	93.69	51.98	38.29	31.61	27.73	25.24	23.55
2000	187.38	103.95	76.59	63.23	55.46	50.49	47.10
5000	468.45	259.88	191.46	158.07	138.66	126.22	117.74
6000	562.14	311.86	229.76	189.68	166.39	151.46	141.29
7000	655.83	363.83	268.05	221.29	194.12	176.71	164.84
8000	749.52	415.81	306.34	252.91	221.85	201.95	188.39
9000	843.21	467.78	344.64	284.52	249.58	227.19	211.93
10000	936.90	519.76	382.93	316.14	277.31	252.44	235.48
12000	1124.28	623.71	459.51	379.36	332.78	302.92	282.58
15000	1405.34	779.64	574.39	474.20	415.97	378.65	353.22
20000	1873.79	1039.52	765.86	632.27	554.63	504.87	470.96
25000	2342.24	1299.40	957.32	790.34	693.29	631.09	588.71
30000	2810.69	1559.28	1148.79	948.41	831.94	757.31	706.45
31000	2904.38	1611.25	1187.08	980.02	859.68	782.55	729.99
32000	2998.07	1663.23	1225.37	1011.63	887.41	807.80	753.54
33000	3091.76	1715.20	1263.66	1043.25	915.14	833.04	777.09
34000	3185.45	1767.18	1301.96	1074.86	942.87	858.28	800.64
35000	3279.14	1819.16	1340.25	1106.47	970.60	883.53	824.19
36000	3372.83	1871.13	1378.54	1138.09	998.33	908.77	847.74
37000	3466.51	1923.11	1416.84	1169.70	1026.06	934.02	871.28
38000	3560.20	1975.08	1455.13	1201.31	1053.80	959.26	894.83
39000	3653.89	2027.06	1493.42	1232.93	1081.53	984.50	918.38
40000	3747.58	2079.04	1531.71	1264.54	1109.26	1009.75	941.93
41000	3841.27	2131.01	1570.01	1296.16	1136.99	1034.99	965.48
42000	3934.96	2182.99	1608.30	1327.77	1164.72	1060.23	989.03
43000	4028.65	2234.96	1646.59	1359.38	1192.45	1085.48	1012.57
44000	4122.34	2286.94	1684.89	1391.00	1220.19	1110.72	1036.12
45000	4216.03	2338.91	1723.18	1422.61	1247.92	1135.96	1059.67
46000	4309.72	2390.89	1761.47	1454.22	1275.65	1161.21	1083.22
47000	4403.41	2442.87	1799.76	1485.84	1303.38	1186.45	1106.77
48000	4497.10	2494.84	1838.06	1517.45	1331.11	1211.70	1130.31
49000	4590.79	2546.82	1876.35	1549.06	1358.84	1236.94	1153.86
50000	4684.48	2598.79	1914.64	1580.68	1386.57	1262.18	1177.41
51000	4778.17	2650.77	1952.94	1612.29	1414.31	1287.43	1200.96
52000	4871.86	2702.75	1991.23	1643.90	1442.04	1312.67	1224.51
53000	4965.55	2754.72	2029.52	1675.52	1469.77	1337.91	1248.06
54000	5059.24	2806.70	2067.81	1707.13	1497.50	1363.16	1271.60
55000	5152.93	2858.67	2106.11	1738.75	1525.23	1388.40	1295.15
56000	5246.62	2910.65	2144.40	1770.36	1552.96	1413.64	1318.70
57000	5340.31	2962.62	2182.69	1801.97	1580.69	1438.89	1342.25
58000	5434.00	3014.60	2220.99	1833.59	1608.43	1464.13	1365.80
59000	5527.69	3066.58	2259.28	1865.20	1636.16	1489.38	1389.35
60000	5621.38	3118.55	2297.57	1896.81	1663.89	1514.62	1412.89
65000	6089.82	3378.43	2489.04	2054.88	1802.55	1640.84	1530.63
70000	6558.27	3638.31	2680.50	2212.95	1941.20	1767.06	1648.38
75000	7026.72	3898.19	2871.96	2371.02	2079.86	1893.27	1766.12
80000	7495.17	4158.07	3063.43	2529.08	2218.52	2019.49	1883.86
85000	7963.62	4417.95	3254.89	2687.15	2357.18	2145.71	2001.60
90000	8432.06	4677.83	3446.36	2845.22	2495.83	2271.93	2119.34
95000	8900.51	4937.71	3637.82	3003.29	2634.49	2398.15	2237.08
100000	9368.96	5197.59	3829.28	3161.36	2773.15	2524.37	2354.82
105000	9837.41	5457.47	4020.75	3319.42	2911.81	2650.58	2472.56
110000	10305.86	5717.35	4212.21	3477.49	3050.46	2776.80	2590.30
120000	11242.75	6237.11	4595.14	3793.63	3327.78	3029.24	2825.79
130000	12179.65	6756.86	4978.07	4109.76	3605.09	3281.68	3061.27
140000	13116.54	7276.62	5361.00	4425.90	3882.41	3534.11	3296.75
150000	14053.44	7796.38	5743.93	4742.03	4159.72	3786.55	3532.23
160000	14990.33	8316.14	6126.86	5058.17	4437.04	4038.99	3767.72
170000	15927.23	8835.90	6509.78	5374.30	4714.35	4291.42	4003.20
180000	16864.13	9355.66	6892.71	5690.44	4991.67	4543.86	4238.68
190000	17801.02	9875.42	7275.64	6006.57	5268.98	4796.30	4474.16
200000	18737.92	10395.18	7658.57	6322.71	5546.30	5048.73	4709.64
210000	19674.81	10914.93	8041.50	6638.85	5823.61	5301.17	4945.13
220000	20611.71	11434.69	8424.43	6954.98	6100.93	5553.61	5180.61
230000	21548.61	11954.45	8807.36	7271.12	6378.24	5806.04	5416.09
240000	22485.50	12474.21	9190.28	7587.25	6655.56	6058.48	5651.57
250000	23422.40	12993.97	9573.21	7903.39	6932.87	6310.91	5887.06

Monthly Payments 23.25 %

LOAN AMOUNT	8	9	10	11	12	13	14
	YEARS						
100	2.23	2.15	2.08	2.03	1.99	1.96	1.94
200	4.47	4.29	4.16	4.06	3.98	3.92	3.88
500	11.17	10.73	10.40	10.15	9.96	9.81	9.69
1000	22.34	21.46	20.80	20.30	19.92	19.62	19.39
2000	44.69	42.93	41.61	40.61	39.84	39.25	38.78
5000	111.72	107.31	104.02	101.52	99.60	98.11	96.95
6000	134.06	128.78	124.83	121.83	119.52	117.74	116.34
7000	156.41	150.24	145.63	142.13	139.44	137.36	135.73
8000	178.75	171.70	166.44	162.44	159.36	156.98	155.12
9000	201.09	193.17	187.24	182.74	179.29	176.60	174.51
10000	223.44	214.63	208.05	203.05	199.21	196.23	193.90
12000	268.13	257.55	249.65	243.66	239.05	235.47	232.68
15000	335.16	321.94	312.07	304.57	298.81	294.34	290.85
20000	446.88	429.26	416.09	406.09	398.41	392.45	387.80
25000	558.60	536.57	520.11	507.62	498.01	490.57	484.75
30000	670.32	643.89	624.14	609.14	597.62	588.68	581.70
31000	692.66	665.35	644.94	629.44	617.54	608.30	601.09
32000	715.00	686.81	665.74	649.75	637.46	627.92	620.48
33000	737.35	708.27	686.55	670.05	657.38	647.55	639.87
34000	759.69	729.74	707.35	690.36	677.30	667.17	659.26
35000	782.03	751.20	728.16	710.66	697.22	686.79	678.65
36000	804.38	772.66	748.96	730.97	717.14	706.42	698.04
37000	826.72	794.13	769.77	751.27	737.06	726.04	717.43
38000	849.07	815.59	790.57	771.58	756.98	745.66	736.82
39000	871.41	837.05	811.38	791.88	776.90	765.28	756.21
40000	893.75	858.51	832.18	812.19	796.82	784.91	775.60
41000	916.10	879.98	852.99	832.49	816.74	804.53	794.99
42000	938.44	901.44	873.79	852.80	836.66	824.15	814.38
43000	960.79	922.90	894.59	873.10	856.58	843.77	833.77
44000	983.13	944.37	915.40	893.41	876.50	863.40	853.16
45000	1005.47	965.83	936.20	913.71	896.43	883.02	872.55
46000	1027.82	987.29	957.01	934.02	916.35	902.64	891.94
47000	1050.16	1008.75	977.81	954.32	936.27	922.26	911.33
48000	1072.50	1030.22	998.62	974.62	956.19	941.89	930.72
49000	1094.85	1051.68	1019.42	994.93	976.11	961.51	950.11
50000	1117.19	1073.14	1040.23	1015.23	996.03	981.13	969.50
51000	1139.54	1094.61	1061.03	1035.54	1015.95	1000.76	988.89
52000	1161.88	1116.07	1081.83	1055.84	1035.87	1020.38	1008.28
53000	1184.22	1137.53	1102.64	1076.15	1055.79	1040.00	1027.67
54000	1206.57	1158.99	1123.44	1096.45	1075.71	1059.62	1047.06
55000	1228.91	1180.46	1144.25	1116.76	1095.63	1079.25	1066.45
56000	1251.26	1201.92	1165.05	1137.06	1115.55	1098.87	1085.84
57000	1273.60	1223.38	1185.86	1157.37	1135.47	1118.49	1105.23
58000	1295.94	1244.85	1206.66	1177.67	1155.39	1138.11	1124.62
59000	1318.29	1266.31	1227.47	1197.98	1175.31	1157.74	1144.01
60000	1340.63	1287.77	1248.27	1218.28	1195.23	1177.36	1163.40
65000	1452.35	1395.09	1352.29	1319.80	1294.84	1275.47	1260.35
70000	1564.07	1502.40	1456.32	1421.33	1394.44	1373.59	1357.29
75000	1675.79	1609.71	1560.34	1522.85	1494.04	1471.70	1454.24
80000	1787.51	1717.03	1664.36	1624.37	1593.65	1569.81	1551.19
85000	1899.23	1824.34	1768.38	1725.90	1693.25	1667.93	1648.14
90000	2010.95	1931.66	1872.41	1827.42	1792.85	1766.04	1745.09
95000	2122.67	2038.97	1976.43	1928.94	1892.45	1864.15	1842.04
100000	2234.38	2146.29	2080.45	2030.47	1992.06	1962.27	1938.99
105000	2346.10	2253.60	2184.47	2131.99	2091.66	2060.38	2035.94
110000	2457.82	2360.91	2288.50	2233.51	2191.26	2158.49	2132.89
120000	2681.26	2575.54	2496.54	2436.56	2390.47	2354.72	2326.79
130000	2904.70	2790.17	2704.59	2639.61	2589.67	2550.94	2520.69
140000	3128.14	3004.80	2912.63	2842.65	2788.88	2747.17	2714.59
150000	3351.58	3219.43	3120.68	3045.70	2988.09	2943.40	2908.49
160000	3575.01	3434.06	3328.72	3248.75	3187.29	3139.62	3102.39
170000	3798.45	3648.69	3536.77	3451.79	3386.50	3335.85	3296.29
180000	4021.89	3863.31	3744.81	3654.84	3585.70	3532.08	3490.19
190000	4245.33	4077.94	3952.86	3857.89	3784.91	3728.30	3684.09
200000	4468.77	4292.57	4160.90	4060.94	3984.11	3924.53	3877.99
210000	4692.21	4507.20	4368.95	4263.98	4183.32	4120.76	4071.88
220000	4915.65	4721.83	4576.99	4467.03	4382.52	4316.98	4265.78
230000	5139.08	4936.46	4785.04	4670.08	4581.73	4513.21	4459.68
240000	5362.52	5151.08	4993.08	4873.12	4780.94	4709.44	4653.58
250000	5585.96	5365.71	5201.13	5076.17	4980.14	4905.66	4847.48

23.25 % Monthly Payments

LOAN AMOUNT	YEARS 15	16	17	18	19	20	21
100	1.92	1.91	1.89	1.89	1.88	1.87	1.87
200	3.84	3.81	3.79	3.77	3.76	3.75	3.74
500	9.60	9.53	9.47	9.43	9.39	9.36	9.34
1000	19.21	19.06	18.95	18.86	18.79	18.73	18.68
2000	38.41	38.13	37.90	37.72	37.57	37.46	37.36
5000	96.04	95.31	94.74	94.29	93.93	93.64	93.41
6000	115.24	114.38	113.69	113.15	112.71	112.37	112.09
7000	134.45	133.44	132.64	132.01	131.50	131.10	130.78
8000	153.66	152.50	151.59	150.86	150.29	149.83	149.46
9000	172.86	171.57	170.54	169.72	169.07	168.55	168.14
10000	192.07	190.63	189.49	188.58	187.86	187.28	186.82
12000	230.49	228.75	227.38	226.30	225.43	224.74	224.19
15000	288.11	285.94	284.23	282.87	281.79	280.92	280.24
20000	384.14	381.26	378.97	377.16	375.72	374.57	373.65
25000	480.18	476.57	473.72	471.45	469.65	468.21	467.06
30000	576.21	571.89	568.46	565.74	563.57	561.85	560.47
31000	595.42	590.95	587.41	584.60	582.36	580.58	579.16
32000	614.63	610.01	606.36	603.46	601.15	599.31	597.84
33000	633.83	629.07	625.31	622.31	619.93	618.03	616.52
34000	653.04	648.14	644.25	641.17	638.72	636.76	635.20
35000	672.25	667.20	663.20	660.03	657.50	655.49	653.88
36000	691.46	686.26	682.15	678.89	676.29	674.22	672.57
37000	710.66	705.33	701.10	697.74	695.08	692.95	691.25
38000	729.87	724.39	720.05	716.60	713.86	711.68	709.93
39000	749.08	743.45	739.00	735.46	732.65	730.40	728.61
40000	768.28	762.51	757.95	754.32	751.43	749.13	747.30
41000	787.49	781.58	776.89	773.18	770.22	767.86	765.98
42000	806.70	800.64	795.84	792.03	789.00	786.59	784.66
43000	825.91	819.70	814.79	810.89	807.79	805.32	803.34
44000	845.11	838.77	833.74	829.75	826.58	824.05	822.03
45000	864.32	857.83	852.69	848.61	845.36	842.77	840.71
46000	883.53	876.89	871.64	867.47	864.15	861.50	859.39
47000	902.73	895.95	890.59	886.32	882.93	880.23	878.07
48000	921.94	915.02	909.53	905.18	901.72	898.96	896.76
49000	941.15	934.08	928.48	924.04	920.51	917.69	915.44
50000	960.36	953.14	947.43	942.90	939.29	936.42	934.12
51000	979.56	972.21	966.38	961.76	958.08	955.14	952.80
52000	998.77	991.27	985.33	980.61	976.86	973.87	971.49
53000	1017.98	1010.33	1004.28	999.47	995.65	992.60	990.17
54000	1037.18	1029.39	1023.23	1018.33	1014.43	1011.33	1008.85
55000	1056.39	1048.46	1042.18	1037.19	1033.22	1030.06	1027.53
56000	1075.60	1067.52	1061.12	1056.05	1052.01	1048.79	1046.22
57000	1094.81	1086.58	1080.07	1074.90	1070.79	1067.51	1064.90
58000	1114.01	1105.65	1099.02	1093.76	1089.58	1086.24	1083.58
59000	1133.22	1124.71	1117.97	1112.62	1108.36	1104.97	1102.26
60000	1152.43	1143.77	1136.92	1131.48	1127.15	1123.70	1120.95
65000	1248.46	1239.09	1231.66	1225.77	1221.08	1217.34	1214.36
70000	1344.50	1334.40	1326.41	1320.06	1315.01	1310.98	1307.77
75000	1440.53	1429.71	1421.15	1414.35	1408.94	1404.62	1401.18
80000	1536.57	1525.03	1515.89	1508.64	1502.87	1498.27	1494.59
85000	1632.60	1620.34	1610.63	1602.93	1596.79	1591.91	1588.01
90000	1728.64	1715.66	1705.38	1697.22	1690.72	1685.55	1681.42
95000	1824.68	1810.97	1800.12	1791.51	1784.65	1779.19	1774.83
100000	1920.71	1906.29	1894.86	1885.80	1878.58	1872.83	1868.24
105000	2016.75	2001.60	1989.61	1980.09	1972.51	1966.47	1961.65
110000	2112.78	2096.91	2084.35	2074.38	2066.44	2060.11	2055.07
120000	2304.85	2287.54	2273.84	2262.96	2254.30	2247.40	2241.89
130000	2496.92	2478.17	2463.32	2451.54	2442.16	2434.68	2428.71
140000	2688.99	2668.80	2652.81	2640.12	2630.02	2621.96	2615.54
150000	2881.07	2859.43	2842.30	2828.70	2817.87	2809.25	2802.36
160000	3073.14	3050.06	3031.78	3017.28	3005.73	2996.53	2989.19
170000	3265.21	3240.69	3221.27	3205.85	3193.59	3183.81	3176.01
180000	3457.28	3431.31	3410.76	3394.43	3381.45	3371.10	3362.84
190000	3649.35	3621.94	3600.24	3583.01	3569.31	3558.38	3549.66
200000	3841.42	3812.57	3789.73	3771.59	3757.16	3745.66	3736.48
210000	4033.49	4003.20	3979.22	3960.17	3945.02	3932.95	3923.31
220000	4225.56	4193.83	4168.70	4148.75	4132.88	4120.23	4110.13
230000	4417.63	4384.46	4358.19	4337.33	4320.74	4307.51	4296.96
240000	4609.71	4575.09	4547.67	4525.91	4508.60	4494.80	4483.78
250000	4801.78	4765.71	4737.16	4714.49	4696.46	4682.08	4670.61

Monthly Payments 23.25 %

LOAN AMOUNT	22	23	24	25	30	35	40
100	1.86	1.86	1.86	1.86	1.85	1.85	1.85
200	3.73	3.72	3.72	3.71	3.70	3.70	3.70
500	9.32	9.31	9.30	9.29	9.26	9.25	9.25
1000	18.65	18.62	18.59	18.57	18.52	18.51	18.50
2000	37.29	37.23	37.19	37.15	37.05	37.01	37.00
5000	93.23	93.08	92.96	92.87	92.62	92.53	92.50
6000	111.87	111.70	111.56	111.44	111.14	111.04	111.01
7000	130.52	130.31	130.15	130.02	129.66	129.55	129.51
8000	149.17	148.93	148.74	148.59	148.19	148.05	148.01
9000	167.81	167.55	167.34	167.17	166.71	166.56	166.51
10000	186.46	186.16	185.93	185.74	185.23	185.07	185.01
12000	223.75	223.40	223.12	222.89	222.28	222.08	222.01
15000	279.69	279.25	278.89	278.61	277.85	277.60	277.51
20000	372.91	372.33	371.86	371.48	370.47	370.13	370.02
25000	466.14	465.41	464.82	464.35	463.08	462.66	462.52
30000	559.37	558.49	557.79	557.22	555.70	555.20	555.03
31000	578.02	577.11	576.38	575.80	574.23	573.70	573.53
32000	596.66	595.73	594.97	594.37	592.75	592.21	592.03
33000	615.31	614.34	613.57	612.95	611.27	610.72	610.53
34000	633.96	632.96	632.16	631.52	629.80	629.22	629.03
35000	652.60	651.57	650.75	650.10	648.32	647.73	647.53
36000	671.25	670.19	669.35	668.67	666.84	666.24	666.03
37000	689.89	688.81	687.94	687.24	685.37	684.74	684.54
38000	708.54	707.42	706.53	705.82	703.89	703.25	703.04
39000	727.18	726.04	725.13	724.39	722.41	721.76	721.54
40000	745.83	744.66	743.72	742.97	740.94	740.26	740.04
41000	764.48	763.27	762.31	761.54	759.46	758.77	758.54
42000	783.12	781.89	780.90	780.11	777.98	777.27	777.04
43000	801.77	800.51	799.50	798.69	796.51	795.78	795.54
44000	820.41	819.12	818.09	817.26	815.03	814.29	814.04
45000	839.06	837.74	836.68	835.84	833.55	832.79	832.54
46000	857.70	856.36	855.28	854.41	852.08	851.30	851.04
47000	876.35	874.97	873.87	872.99	870.60	869.81	869.54
48000	895.00	893.59	892.46	891.56	889.12	888.31	888.05
49000	913.64	912.20	911.05	910.13	907.65	906.82	906.55
50000	932.29	930.82	929.65	928.71	926.17	925.33	925.05
51000	950.93	949.44	948.24	947.28	944.69	943.83	943.55
52000	969.58	968.05	966.83	965.86	963.22	962.34	962.05
53000	988.22	986.67	985.43	984.43	981.74	980.85	980.55
54000	1006.87	1005.29	1004.02	1003.00	1000.26	999.35	999.05
55000	1025.52	1023.90	1022.61	1021.58	1018.79	1017.86	1017.55
56000	1044.16	1042.52	1041.21	1040.15	1037.31	1036.37	1036.05
57000	1062.81	1061.14	1059.80	1058.73	1055.83	1054.87	1054.55
58000	1081.45	1079.75	1078.39	1077.30	1074.36	1073.38	1073.05
59000	1100.10	1098.37	1096.98	1095.88	1092.88	1091.89	1091.56
60000	1118.74	1116.99	1115.58	1114.45	1111.40	1110.39	1110.06
65000	1211.97	1210.07	1208.54	1207.32	1204.02	1202.93	1202.56
70000	1305.20	1303.15	1301.51	1300.19	1296.64	1295.46	1295.07
75000	1398.43	1396.23	1394.47	1393.06	1389.25	1387.99	1387.57
80000	1491.66	1489.31	1487.44	1485.93	1481.87	1480.52	1480.08
85000	1584.89	1582.40	1580.40	1578.80	1574.49	1573.06	1572.58
90000	1678.12	1675.48	1673.37	1671.67	1667.10	1665.59	1665.09
95000	1771.35	1768.56	1766.33	1764.54	1759.72	1758.12	1757.59
100000	1864.57	1861.64	1859.29	1857.42	1852.34	1850.65	1850.09
105000	1957.80	1954.72	1952.26	1950.29	1944.96	1943.19	1942.60
110000	2051.03	2047.81	2045.22	2043.16	2037.57	2035.72	2035.10
120000	2237.49	2233.97	2231.15	2228.90	2222.81	2220.79	2220.11
130000	2423.95	2420.13	2417.08	2414.64	2408.04	2405.85	2405.12
140000	2610.40	2606.30	2603.01	2600.38	2593.27	2590.92	2590.13
150000	2796.86	2792.46	2788.94	2786.12	2778.51	2775.98	2775.14
160000	2983.32	2978.63	2974.87	2971.86	2963.74	2961.05	2960.15
170000	3169.78	3164.79	3160.80	3157.61	3148.98	3146.11	3145.16
180000	3356.23	3350.96	3346.73	3343.35	3334.21	3331.18	3330.17
190000	3542.69	3537.12	3532.66	3529.09	3519.44	3516.24	3515.18
200000	3729.15	3723.28	3718.59	3714.83	3704.68	3701.31	3700.19
210000	3915.61	3909.45	3904.52	3900.57	3889.91	3886.37	3885.20
220000	4102.06	4095.61	4090.45	4086.31	4075.15	4071.44	4070.21
230000	4288.52	4281.78	4276.38	4272.06	4260.38	4256.51	4255.22
240000	4474.98	4467.94	4462.31	4457.80	4445.61	4441.57	4440.23
250000	4661.44	4654.11	4648.24	4643.54	4630.85	4626.64	4625.24

(YEARS: 22, 23, 24, 25, 30, 35, 40)

23.50 % Monthly Payments

LOAN AMOUNT	1	2	3	4	5	6	7
100	9.38	5.21	3.84	3.17	2.79	2.54	2.37
200	18.76	10.42	7.68	6.35	5.57	5.08	4.74
500	46.90	26.04	19.21	15.87	13.93	12.69	11.84
1000	93.80	52.09	38.41	31.74	27.86	25.38	23.69
2000	187.60	104.18	76.82	63.48	55.72	50.76	47.38
5000	469.00	260.44	192.06	158.69	139.31	126.90	118.45
6000	562.80	312.53	230.47	190.43	167.17	152.28	142.14
7000	656.60	364.62	268.88	222.16	195.03	177.66	165.83
8000	750.40	416.71	307.29	253.90	222.89	203.04	189.52
9000	844.19	468.80	345.70	285.64	250.75	228.42	213.21
10000	937.99	520.89	384.11	317.38	278.62	253.79	236.90
12000	1125.59	625.06	460.93	380.85	334.34	304.55	284.27
15000	1406.99	781.33	576.17	476.07	417.92	380.69	355.34
20000	1875.99	1041.77	768.22	634.75	557.23	507.59	473.79
25000	2344.99	1302.22	960.28	793.44	696.54	634.49	592.24
30000	2813.98	1562.66	1152.33	952.13	835.85	761.38	710.69
31000	2907.78	1614.75	1190.74	983.87	863.71	786.76	734.38
32000	3001.58	1666.84	1229.15	1015.61	891.57	812.14	758.07
33000	3095.38	1718.93	1267.57	1047.34	919.43	837.52	781.76
34000	3189.18	1771.01	1305.98	1079.08	947.29	862.90	805.44
35000	3282.98	1823.10	1344.39	1110.82	975.15	888.28	829.13
36000	3376.78	1875.19	1382.80	1142.56	1003.02	913.66	852.82
37000	3470.58	1927.28	1421.21	1174.29	1030.88	939.04	876.51
38000	3564.38	1979.37	1459.62	1206.03	1058.74	964.42	900.20
39000	3658.18	2031.46	1498.03	1237.77	1086.60	989.80	923.89
40000	3751.98	2083.55	1536.44	1269.51	1114.46	1015.18	947.58
41000	3845.78	2135.63	1574.85	1301.25	1142.32	1040.56	971.27
42000	3939.58	2187.72	1613.27	1332.98	1170.18	1065.94	994.96
43000	4033.38	2239.81	1651.68	1364.72	1198.05	1091.32	1018.65
44000	4127.17	2291.90	1690.09	1396.46	1225.91	1116.70	1042.34
45000	4220.97	2343.99	1728.50	1428.20	1253.77	1142.08	1066.03
46000	4314.77	2396.08	1766.91	1459.93	1281.63	1167.46	1089.72
47000	4408.57	2448.17	1805.32	1491.67	1309.49	1192.84	1113.41
48000	4502.37	2500.26	1843.73	1523.41	1337.35	1218.22	1137.10
49000	4596.17	2552.34	1882.14	1555.15	1365.22	1243.59	1160.79
50000	4689.97	2604.43	1920.55	1586.88	1393.08	1268.97	1184.48
51000	4783.77	2656.52	1958.96	1618.62	1420.94	1294.35	1208.17
52000	4877.57	2708.61	1997.38	1650.36	1448.80	1319.73	1231.86
53000	4971.37	2760.70	2035.79	1682.10	1476.66	1345.11	1255.55
54000	5065.17	2812.79	2074.20	1713.84	1504.52	1370.49	1279.24
55000	5158.97	2864.88	2112.61	1745.57	1532.38	1395.87	1302.93
56000	5252.77	2916.96	2151.02	1777.31	1560.25	1421.25	1326.61
57000	5346.57	2969.05	2189.43	1809.05	1588.11	1446.63	1350.30
58000	5440.37	3021.14	2227.84	1840.79	1615.97	1472.01	1373.99
59000	5534.17	3073.23	2266.25	1872.52	1643.83	1497.39	1397.68
60000	5627.97	3125.32	2304.66	1904.26	1671.69	1522.77	1421.37
65000	6096.96	3385.76	2496.72	2062.95	1811.00	1649.67	1539.82
70000	6565.96	3646.21	2688.78	2221.64	1950.31	1776.56	1658.27
75000	7034.96	3906.65	2880.83	2380.33	2089.62	1903.46	1776.72
80000	7503.95	4167.09	3072.89	2539.01	2228.92	2030.36	1895.16
85000	7972.95	4427.54	3264.94	2697.70	2368.23	2157.26	2013.61
90000	8441.95	4687.98	3457.00	2856.39	2507.54	2284.15	2132.06
95000	8910.94	4948.42	3649.05	3015.08	2646.85	2411.05	2250.51
100000	9379.94	5208.87	3841.11	3173.77	2786.15	2537.95	2368.95
105000	9848.94	5469.31	4033.16	3332.46	2925.46	2664.85	2487.40
110000	10317.94	5729.75	4225.22	3491.15	3064.77	2791.74	2605.85
120000	11255.93	6250.64	4609.33	3808.52	3343.39	3045.54	2842.75
130000	12193.92	6771.53	4993.44	4125.90	3622.00	3299.33	3079.64
140000	13131.92	7292.41	5377.55	4443.28	3900.62	3553.13	3316.54
150000	14069.91	7813.30	5761.66	4760.65	4179.23	3806.92	3553.43
160000	15007.91	8334.19	6145.77	5078.03	4457.85	4060.72	3790.33
170000	15945.90	8855.07	6529.88	5395.41	4736.46	4314.51	4027.22
180000	16883.90	9375.96	6913.99	5712.78	5015.08	4568.31	4264.12
190000	17821.89	9896.85	7298.10	6030.16	5293.69	4822.10	4501.01
200000	18759.88	10417.73	7682.22	6347.54	5572.31	5075.90	4737.91
210000	19697.88	10938.62	8066.33	6664.91	5850.92	5329.69	4974.81
220000	20635.87	11459.50	8450.44	6982.29	6129.54	5583.49	5211.70
230000	21573.87	11980.39	8834.55	7299.67	6408.15	5837.28	5448.60
240000	22511.86	12501.28	9218.66	7617.04	6686.77	6091.08	5685.49
250000	23449.85	13022.16	9602.77	7934.42	6965.39	6344.87	5922.39

Monthly Payments 23.50 %

LOAN AMOUNT	8	9	10	11	12	13	14
100	2.25	2.16	2.10	2.05	2.01	1.98	1.96
200	4.50	4.32	4.19	4.09	4.02	3.96	3.91
500	11.25	10.81	10.48	10.23	10.04	9.89	9.78
1000	22.49	21.61	20.96	20.46	20.08	19.79	19.56
2000	44.98	43.23	41.92	40.93	40.17	39.58	39.12
5000	112.45	108.07	104.80	102.32	100.42	98.95	97.80
6000	134.94	129.69	125.76	122.79	120.51	118.74	117.36
7000	157.43	151.30	146.72	143.25	140.59	138.53	136.92
8000	179.92	172.91	167.68	163.72	160.67	158.32	156.48
9000	202.41	194.53	188.64	184.18	180.76	178.11	176.04
10000	224.90	216.14	209.60	204.65	200.84	197.90	195.60
12000	269.88	259.37	251.52	245.58	241.01	237.48	234.72
15000	337.36	324.21	314.41	306.97	301.26	296.85	293.40
20000	449.81	432.28	419.21	409.29	401.68	395.79	391.20
25000	562.26	540.36	524.01	511.62	502.11	494.74	489.00
30000	674.71	648.43	628.81	613.94	602.53	593.69	586.80
31000	697.20	670.04	649.77	634.40	622.61	613.48	606.36
32000	719.69	691.65	670.73	654.87	642.70	633.27	625.92
33000	742.18	713.27	691.69	675.33	662.78	653.06	645.48
34000	764.67	734.88	712.65	695.80	682.86	672.85	665.04
35000	787.16	756.50	733.61	716.26	702.95	692.64	684.60
36000	809.65	778.11	754.57	736.73	723.03	712.43	704.16
37000	832.14	799.73	775.53	757.19	743.12	732.22	723.72
38000	854.63	821.34	796.49	777.66	763.20	752.01	743.28
39000	877.12	842.95	817.45	798.12	783.29	771.80	762.84
40000	899.61	864.57	838.41	818.58	803.37	791.59	782.40
41000	922.10	886.18	859.37	839.05	823.45	811.38	801.96
42000	944.60	907.80	880.34	859.51	843.54	831.17	821.52
43000	967.09	929.41	901.30	879.98	863.62	850.96	841.08
44000	989.58	951.03	922.26	900.44	883.71	870.75	860.64
45000	1012.07	972.64	943.22	920.91	903.79	890.54	880.20
46000	1034.56	994.25	964.18	941.37	923.88	910.33	899.76
47000	1057.05	1015.87	985.14	961.84	943.96	930.12	919.32
48000	1079.54	1037.48	1006.10	982.30	964.04	949.91	938.88
49000	1102.03	1059.10	1027.06	1002.77	984.13	969.70	958.44
50000	1124.52	1080.71	1048.02	1023.23	1004.21	989.49	978.00
51000	1147.01	1102.33	1068.98	1043.70	1024.30	1009.27	997.56
52000	1169.50	1123.94	1089.94	1064.16	1044.38	1029.06	1017.12
53000	1191.99	1145.55	1110.90	1084.63	1064.47	1048.85	1036.68
54000	1214.48	1167.17	1131.86	1105.09	1084.55	1068.64	1056.24
55000	1236.97	1188.78	1152.82	1125.55	1104.63	1088.43	1075.80
56000	1259.46	1210.40	1173.78	1146.02	1124.72	1108.22	1095.36
57000	1281.95	1232.01	1194.74	1166.48	1144.80	1128.01	1114.92
58000	1304.44	1253.62	1215.70	1186.95	1164.89	1147.80	1134.48
59000	1326.93	1275.24	1236.66	1207.41	1184.97	1167.59	1154.04
60000	1349.42	1296.85	1257.62	1227.88	1205.05	1187.38	1173.60
65000	1461.87	1404.92	1362.42	1330.20	1305.48	1286.33	1271.40
70000	1574.33	1513.00	1467.23	1432.52	1405.90	1385.28	1369.20
75000	1686.78	1621.07	1572.03	1534.85	1506.32	1484.23	1467.00
80000	1799.23	1729.14	1676.83	1637.17	1606.74	1583.18	1564.80
85000	1911.68	1837.21	1781.63	1739.49	1707.16	1682.12	1662.60
90000	2024.13	1945.28	1886.43	1841.82	1807.58	1781.07	1760.40
95000	2136.58	2053.35	1991.23	1944.14	1908.00	1880.02	1858.20
100000	2249.04	2161.42	2096.04	2046.46	2008.42	1978.97	1956.00
105000	2361.49	2269.49	2200.84	2148.79	2108.85	2077.92	2053.80
110000	2473.94	2377.56	2305.64	2251.11	2209.27	2176.87	2151.60
120000	2698.84	2593.71	2515.24	2455.75	2410.11	2374.76	2347.20
130000	2923.75	2809.85	2724.85	2660.40	2610.95	2572.66	2542.80
140000	3148.65	3025.99	2934.45	2865.05	2811.79	2770.56	2738.40
150000	3373.55	3242.13	3144.05	3069.69	3012.64	2968.46	2934.00
160000	3598.46	3458.27	3353.66	3274.34	3213.48	3166.35	3129.60
170000	3823.36	3674.42	3563.26	3478.99	3414.32	3364.25	3325.20
180000	4048.26	3890.56	3772.86	3683.63	3615.16	3562.15	3520.80
190000	4273.17	4106.70	3982.47	3888.28	3816.01	3760.04	3716.40
200000	4498.07	4322.84	4192.07	4092.92	4016.85	3957.94	3912.00
210000	4722.98	4538.99	4401.68	4297.57	4217.69	4155.84	4107.60
220000	4947.88	4755.13	4611.28	4502.22	4418.53	4353.73	4303.20
230000	5172.78	4971.27	4820.88	4706.86	4619.38	4551.63	4498.80
240000	5397.69	5187.41	5030.49	4911.51	4820.22	4749.53	4694.40
250000	5622.59	5403.55	5240.09	5116.16	5021.06	4947.43	4890.00

23.50 % Monthly Payments

LOAN AMOUNT	15	16	17	18	19	20	21
100	1.94	1.92	1.91	1.90	1.90	1.89	1.89
200	3.88	3.85	3.83	3.81	3.79	3.78	3.77
500	9.69	9.62	9.56	9.52	9.48	9.46	9.43
1000	19.38	19.24	19.13	19.04	18.97	18.91	18.87
2000	38.76	38.48	38.25	38.07	37.93	37.82	37.73
5000	96.90	96.19	95.63	95.19	94.83	94.55	94.33
6000	116.28	115.43	114.76	114.22	113.80	113.46	113.19
7000	135.66	134.67	133.88	133.26	132.77	132.37	132.06
8000	155.04	153.90	153.01	152.30	151.73	151.28	150.93
9000	174.42	173.14	172.13	171.33	170.70	170.19	169.79
10000	193.80	192.38	191.26	190.37	189.66	189.10	188.66
12000	232.56	230.86	229.51	228.44	227.60	226.92	226.39
15000	290.70	288.57	286.89	285.56	284.50	283.66	282.99
20000	387.60	384.76	382.52	380.74	379.33	378.21	377.31
25000	484.50	480.95	478.15	475.93	474.16	472.76	471.64
30000	581.40	577.14	573.78	571.11	568.99	567.31	565.97
31000	600.78	596.38	592.90	590.15	587.96	586.22	584.84
32000	620.16	615.62	612.03	609.19	606.93	605.13	603.70
33000	639.54	634.85	631.15	628.22	625.89	624.04	622.57
34000	658.92	654.09	650.28	647.26	644.86	642.95	641.43
35000	678.30	673.33	669.41	666.30	663.83	661.86	660.30
36000	697.68	692.57	688.53	685.33	682.79	680.77	679.16
37000	717.05	711.81	707.66	704.37	701.76	699.68	698.03
38000	736.43	731.04	726.78	723.41	720.73	718.59	716.90
39000	755.81	750.28	745.91	742.44	739.69	737.50	735.76
40000	775.19	769.52	765.04	761.48	758.66	756.42	754.63
41000	794.57	788.76	784.16	780.52	777.63	775.33	773.49
42000	813.95	808.00	803.29	799.56	796.59	794.24	792.36
43000	833.33	827.23	822.41	818.59	815.56	813.15	811.22
44000	852.71	846.47	841.54	837.63	834.53	832.06	830.09
45000	872.09	865.71	860.66	856.67	853.49	850.97	848.96
46000	891.47	884.95	879.79	875.70	872.46	869.88	867.82
47000	910.85	904.19	898.92	894.74	891.43	888.79	886.69
48000	930.23	923.42	918.04	913.78	910.39	907.70	905.55
49000	949.61	942.66	937.17	932.82	929.36	926.61	924.42
50000	968.99	961.90	956.29	951.85	948.32	945.52	943.28
51000	988.37	981.14	975.42	970.89	967.29	964.43	962.15
52000	1007.75	1000.38	994.55	989.93	986.26	983.34	981.02
53000	1027.13	1019.61	1013.67	1008.96	1005.22	1002.25	999.88
54000	1046.51	1038.85	1032.80	1028.00	1024.19	1021.16	1018.75
55000	1065.89	1058.09	1051.92	1047.04	1043.16	1040.07	1037.61
56000	1085.27	1077.33	1071.05	1066.07	1062.12	1058.98	1056.48
57000	1104.65	1096.57	1090.18	1085.11	1081.09	1077.89	1075.34
58000	1124.03	1115.80	1109.30	1104.15	1100.06	1096.80	1094.21
59000	1143.41	1135.04	1128.43	1123.19	1119.02	1115.71	1113.08
60000	1162.79	1154.28	1147.55	1142.22	1137.99	1134.62	1131.94
65000	1259.69	1250.47	1243.18	1237.41	1232.82	1229.17	1226.27
70000	1356.59	1346.66	1338.81	1332.59	1327.65	1323.73	1320.60
75000	1453.49	1442.85	1434.44	1427.78	1422.49	1418.28	1414.93
80000	1550.39	1539.04	1530.07	1522.96	1517.32	1512.83	1509.25
85000	1647.29	1635.23	1625.70	1618.15	1612.15	1607.38	1603.58
90000	1744.19	1731.42	1721.33	1713.33	1706.98	1701.93	1697.91
95000	1841.09	1827.61	1816.96	1808.52	1801.82	1796.49	1792.24
100000	1937.99	1923.80	1912.59	1903.70	1896.65	1891.04	1886.57
105000	2034.89	2019.99	2008.22	1998.89	1991.48	1985.59	1980.90
110000	2131.79	2116.18	2103.85	2094.07	2086.31	2080.14	2075.23
120000	2325.58	2308.56	2295.11	2284.45	2275.98	2269.25	2263.88
130000	2519.38	2500.94	2486.36	2474.82	2465.64	2458.35	2452.54
140000	2713.18	2693.32	2677.62	2665.19	2655.31	2647.45	2641.20
150000	2906.98	2885.70	2868.88	2855.56	2844.97	2836.56	2829.85
160000	3100.78	3078.08	3060.14	3045.93	3034.64	3025.66	3018.51
170000	3294.58	3270.46	3251.40	3236.30	3224.30	3214.76	3207.17
180000	3488.38	3462.84	3442.66	3426.67	3413.97	3403.87	3395.82
190000	3682.17	3655.22	3633.92	3617.04	3603.63	3592.97	3584.48
200000	3875.97	3847.60	3825.18	3807.41	3793.30	3782.08	3773.14
210000	4069.77	4039.98	4016.44	3997.78	3982.96	3971.18	3961.79
220000	4263.57	4232.36	4207.69	4188.15	4172.63	4160.28	4150.45
230000	4457.37	4424.74	4398.95	4378.52	4362.29	4349.39	4339.11
240000	4651.17	4617.12	4590.21	4568.89	4551.96	4538.49	4527.76
250000	4844.97	4809.50	4781.47	4759.26	4741.62	4727.60	4716.42

Monthly Payments 23.50 %

LOAN AMOUNT	22	23	24	25	30	35	40
100	1.88	1.88	1.88	1.88	1.87	1.87	1.87
200	3.77	3.76	3.76	3.75	3.74	3.74	3.74
500	9.42	9.40	9.39	9.38	9.36	9.35	9.35
1000	18.83	18.80	18.78	18.76	18.71	18.70	18.69
2000	37.66	37.60	37.56	37.52	37.42	37.39	37.38
5000	94.15	94.01	93.89	93.80	93.56	93.48	93.45
6000	112.98	112.81	112.67	112.56	112.27	112.18	112.14
7000	131.81	131.61	131.45	131.33	130.98	130.87	130.84
8000	150.64	150.41	150.23	150.09	149.70	149.57	149.53
9000	169.47	169.21	169.01	168.85	168.41	168.26	168.22
10000	188.30	188.02	187.79	187.61	187.12	186.96	186.91
12000	225.96	225.62	225.35	225.13	224.54	224.35	224.29
15000	282.45	282.02	281.68	281.41	280.68	280.44	280.36
20000	376.60	376.03	375.58	375.21	374.24	373.92	373.81
25000	470.75	470.04	469.47	469.02	467.80	467.40	467.27
30000	564.90	564.05	563.37	562.82	561.36	560.88	560.72
31000	583.73	582.85	582.15	581.58	580.07	579.58	579.41
32000	602.56	601.65	600.92	600.34	598.78	598.27	598.10
33000	621.39	620.45	619.70	619.10	617.50	616.97	616.79
34000	640.22	639.25	638.48	637.87	636.21	635.66	635.48
35000	659.05	658.06	657.26	656.63	654.92	654.36	654.18
36000	677.88	676.86	676.04	675.39	673.63	673.06	672.87
37000	696.71	695.66	694.82	694.15	692.34	691.75	691.56
38000	715.54	714.46	713.60	712.91	711.06	710.45	710.25
39000	734.37	733.26	732.38	731.67	729.77	729.14	728.94
40000	753.20	752.06	751.16	750.43	748.48	747.84	747.63
41000	772.03	770.87	769.93	769.19	767.19	766.54	766.32
42000	790.86	789.67	788.71	787.95	785.90	785.23	785.01
43000	809.69	808.47	807.49	806.71	804.62	803.93	803.70
44000	828.52	827.27	826.27	825.47	823.33	822.62	822.39
45000	847.35	846.07	845.05	844.23	842.04	841.32	841.08
46000	866.18	864.87	863.83	862.99	860.75	860.02	859.77
47000	885.01	883.68	882.61	881.75	879.46	878.71	878.46
48000	903.84	902.48	901.39	900.52	898.18	897.41	897.16
49000	922.67	921.28	920.17	919.28	916.89	916.10	915.85
50000	941.50	940.08	938.94	938.04	935.60	934.80	934.54
51000	960.33	958.88	957.72	956.80	954.31	953.50	953.23
52000	979.16	977.68	976.50	975.56	973.02	972.19	971.92
53000	997.99	996.48	995.28	994.32	991.74	990.89	990.61
54000	1016.82	1015.29	1014.06	1013.08	1010.45	1009.58	1009.30
55000	1035.65	1034.09	1032.84	1031.84	1029.16	1028.28	1027.99
56000	1054.48	1052.89	1051.62	1050.60	1047.87	1046.98	1046.68
57000	1073.31	1071.69	1070.40	1069.36	1066.58	1065.67	1065.37
58000	1092.14	1090.49	1089.18	1088.12	1085.30	1084.37	1084.06
59000	1110.97	1109.29	1107.95	1106.88	1104.01	1103.06	1102.75
60000	1129.80	1128.10	1126.73	1125.64	1122.72	1121.76	1121.44
65000	1223.95	1222.10	1220.63	1219.45	1216.28	1215.24	1214.90
70000	1318.10	1316.11	1314.52	1313.25	1309.84	1308.72	1308.35
75000	1412.25	1410.12	1408.42	1407.06	1403.40	1402.20	1401.81
80000	1506.40	1504.13	1502.31	1500.86	1496.96	1495.68	1495.26
85000	1600.55	1598.14	1596.21	1594.66	1590.52	1589.16	1588.71
90000	1694.70	1692.14	1690.10	1688.47	1684.08	1682.64	1682.17
95000	1788.85	1786.15	1783.99	1782.27	1777.64	1776.12	1775.62
100000	1883.00	1880.16	1877.89	1876.07	1871.20	1869.60	1869.07
105000	1977.15	1974.17	1971.78	1969.88	1964.76	1963.08	1962.53
110000	2071.30	2068.18	2065.68	2063.68	2058.32	2056.56	2055.98
120000	2259.61	2256.19	2253.47	2251.29	2245.44	2243.52	2242.89
130000	2447.91	2444.21	2441.26	2438.90	2432.56	2430.48	2429.80
140000	2636.21	2632.22	2629.04	2626.50	2619.68	2617.44	2616.70
150000	2824.51	2820.24	2816.83	2814.11	2806.80	2804.40	2803.61
160000	3012.81	3008.26	3004.62	3001.72	2993.92	2991.36	2990.52
170000	3201.11	3196.27	3192.41	3189.33	3181.04	3178.32	3177.42
180000	3389.41	3384.29	3380.20	3376.93	3368.16	3365.28	3364.33
190000	3577.71	3572.30	3567.99	3564.54	3555.28	3552.24	3551.24
200000	3766.01	3760.32	3755.78	3752.15	3742.40	3739.20	3738.15
210000	3954.31	3948.34	3943.57	3939.76	3929.52	3926.16	3925.05
220000	4142.61	4136.35	4131.36	4127.36	4116.64	4113.12	4111.96
230000	4330.91	4324.37	4319.14	4314.97	4303.76	4300.08	4298.87
240000	4519.21	4512.38	4506.93	4502.58	4490.88	4487.04	4485.78
250000	4707.51	4700.40	4694.72	4690.19	4678.00	4674.00	4672.68

23.75 % Monthly Payments

LOAN AMOUNT	1	2	3	4	5	6	7
100	9.39	5.22	3.85	3.19	2.80	2.55	2.3
200	18.78	10.44	7.71	6.37	5.60	5.10	4.7
500	46.95	26.10	19.26	15.93	14.00	12.76	11.9
1000	93.91	52.20	38.53	31.86	27.99	25.52	23.8
2000	187.82	104.40	77.06	63.72	55.98	51.03	47.6
5000	469.55	261.01	192.65	159.31	139.96	127.58	119.1
6000	563.46	313.21	231.18	191.17	167.95	153.09	142.9
7000	657.36	365.41	269.71	223.03	195.94	178.61	166.8
8000	751.27	417.61	308.24	254.90	223.93	204.12	190.6
9000	845.18	469.81	346.76	286.76	251.93	229.64	214.4
10000	939.09	522.01	385.29	318.62	279.92	255.16	238.3
12000	1126.91	626.42	462.35	382.34	335.90	306.19	285.9
15000	1408.64	783.02	577.94	477.93	419.88	382.73	357.4
20000	1878.18	1044.03	770.59	637.24	559.84	510.31	476.6
25000	2347.73	1305.04	963.23	796.55	699.79	637.89	595.7
30000	2817.28	1566.04	1155.88	955.86	839.75	765.47	714.9
31000	2911.19	1618.25	1194.41	987.72	867.75	790.98	738.7
32000	3005.09	1670.45	1232.94	1019.58	895.74	816.50	762.6
33000	3099.00	1722.65	1271.47	1051.44	923.73	842.01	786.4
34000	3192.91	1774.85	1310.00	1083.31	951.72	867.53	810.2
35000	3286.82	1827.05	1348.53	1115.17	979.71	893.04	834.0
36000	3380.73	1879.25	1387.06	1147.03	1007.70	918.56	857.9
37000	3474.64	1931.45	1425.59	1178.89	1035.70	944.07	881.7
38000	3568.55	1983.66	1464.12	1210.75	1063.69	969.59	905.5
39000	3662.46	2035.86	1502.65	1242.62	1091.68	995.11	929.4
40000	3756.37	2088.06	1541.18	1274.48	1119.67	1020.62	953.2
41000	3850.28	2140.26	1579.71	1306.34	1147.66	1046.14	977.0
42000	3944.19	2192.46	1618.23	1338.20	1175.66	1071.65	1000.9
43000	4038.10	2244.66	1656.76	1370.06	1203.65	1097.17	1024.7
44000	4132.01	2296.86	1695.29	1401.93	1231.64	1122.68	1048.5
45000	4225.91	2349.07	1733.82	1433.79	1259.63	1148.20	1072.4
46000	4319.82	2401.27	1772.35	1465.65	1287.62	1173.71	1096.2
47000	4413.73	2453.47	1810.88	1497.51	1315.61	1199.23	1120.0
48000	4507.64	2505.67	1849.41	1529.37	1343.61	1224.75	1143.8
49000	4601.55	2557.87	1887.94	1561.24	1371.60	1250.26	1167.7
50000	4695.46	2610.07	1926.47	1593.10	1399.59	1275.78	1191.5
51000	4789.37	2662.28	1965.00	1624.96	1427.58	1301.29	1215.3
52000	4883.28	2714.48	2003.53	1656.82	1455.57	1326.81	1239.2
53000	4977.19	2766.68	2042.06	1688.68	1483.56	1352.32	1263.0
54000	5071.10	2818.88	2080.59	1720.55	1511.56	1377.84	1286.8
55000	5165.01	2871.08	2119.12	1752.41	1539.55	1403.35	1310.7
56000	5258.92	2923.28	2157.65	1784.27	1567.54	1428.87	1334.5
57000	5352.83	2975.48	2196.18	1816.13	1595.53	1454.39	1358.3
58000	5446.73	3027.69	2234.70	1847.99	1623.52	1479.90	1382.2
59000	5540.64	3079.89	2273.23	1879.86	1651.52	1505.42	1406.0
60000	5634.55	3132.09	2311.76	1911.72	1679.51	1530.93	1429.8
65000	6104.10	3393.10	2504.41	2071.03	1819.47	1658.51	1549.0
70000	6573.64	3654.10	2697.06	2230.34	1959.43	1786.09	1668.1
75000	7043.19	3915.11	2889.70	2389.65	2099.38	1913.66	1787.3
80000	7512.74	4176.12	3082.35	2548.96	2239.34	2041.24	1906.4
85000	7982.28	4437.13	3275.00	2708.27	2379.30	2168.82	2025.6
90000	8451.83	4698.13	3467.65	2867.58	2519.26	2296.40	2144.8
95000	8921.38	4959.14	3660.29	3026.89	2659.22	2423.98	2263.9
100000	9390.92	5220.15	3852.94	3186.20	2799.18	2551.55	2383.1
105000	9860.47	5481.15	4045.59	3345.51	2939.14	2679.13	2502.2
110000	10330.01	5742.16	4238.23	3504.82	3079.10	2806.71	2621.4
120000	11269.11	6264.18	4623.53	3823.44	3359.01	3061.86	2859.7
130000	12208.20	6786.19	5008.82	4142.06	3638.93	3317.02	3098.0
140000	13147.29	7308.21	5394.12	4460.68	3918.85	3572.17	3336.3
150000	14086.38	7830.22	5779.41	4779.30	4198.77	3827.33	3574.6
160000	15025.47	8352.24	6164.70	5097.91	4478.69	4082.48	3812.9
170000	15964.57	8874.25	6550.00	5416.53	4758.60	4337.64	4051.2
180000	16903.66	9396.26	6935.29	5735.15	5038.52	4592.80	4289.6
190000	17842.75	9918.28	7320.58	6053.77	5318.44	4847.95	4527.9
200000	18781.84	10440.29	7705.88	6372.39	5598.36	5103.11	4766.2
210000	19720.93	10962.31	8091.17	6691.01	5878.28	5358.26	5004.5
220000	20660.03	11484.32	8476.47	7009.63	6158.19	5613.42	5242.8
230000	21599.12	12006.34	8861.76	7328.25	6438.11	5868.57	5481.1
240000	22538.21	12528.35	9247.05	7646.87	6718.03	6123.73	5719.4
250000	23477.30	13050.37	9632.35	7965.49	6997.95	6378.88	5957.7

Monthly Payments 23.75 %

LOAN AMOUNT	8	9	10	11	12	13	14
	YEARS						
100	2.26	2.18	2.11	2.06	2.02	2.00	1.97
200	4.53	4.35	4.22	4.12	4.05	3.99	3.95
500	11.32	10.88	10.56	10.31	10.12	9.98	9.87
1000	22.64	21.77	21.12	20.62	20.25	19.96	19.73
2000	45.27	43.53	42.23	41.25	40.50	39.91	39.46
5000	113.19	108.83	105.58	103.12	101.24	99.79	98.65
6000	135.82	130.60	126.70	123.75	121.49	119.74	118.38
7000	158.46	152.36	147.82	144.37	141.74	139.70	138.11
8000	181.10	174.13	168.93	165.00	161.99	159.66	157.84
9000	203.73	195.89	190.05	185.62	182.23	179.61	177.57
10000	226.37	217.66	211.16	206.25	202.48	199.57	197.30
12000	271.65	261.19	253.40	247.50	242.98	239.48	236.76
15000	339.56	326.49	316.75	309.37	303.72	299.36	295.95
20000	452.74	435.32	422.33	412.50	404.96	399.14	394.61
25000	565.93	544.15	527.91	515.62	506.21	498.93	493.26
30000	679.11	652.98	633.49	618.75	607.45	598.71	591.91
31000	701.75	674.74	654.61	639.37	627.69	618.67	611.64
32000	724.39	696.51	675.73	660.00	647.94	638.62	631.37
33000	747.03	718.27	696.84	680.62	668.19	658.58	651.10
34000	769.66	740.04	717.96	701.25	688.44	678.54	670.83
35000	792.30	761.81	739.08	721.87	708.69	698.50	690.56
36000	814.94	783.57	760.19	742.49	728.94	718.45	710.29
37000	837.57	805.34	781.31	763.12	749.18	738.41	730.02
38000	860.21	827.10	802.43	783.74	769.43	758.37	749.75
39000	882.85	848.87	823.54	804.37	789.68	778.32	769.48
40000	905.49	870.63	844.66	824.99	809.93	798.28	789.21
41000	928.12	892.40	865.78	845.62	830.18	818.24	808.94
42000	950.76	914.17	886.89	866.24	850.42	838.19	828.67
43000	973.40	935.93	908.01	886.87	870.67	858.15	848.40
44000	996.03	957.70	929.13	907.49	890.92	878.11	868.13
45000	1018.67	979.46	950.24	928.12	911.17	898.07	887.86
46000	1041.31	1001.23	971.36	948.74	931.42	918.02	907.59
47000	1063.95	1023.00	992.48	969.37	951.67	937.98	927.32
48000	1086.58	1044.76	1013.59	989.99	971.91	957.94	947.05
49000	1109.22	1066.53	1034.71	1010.62	992.16	977.89	966.79
50000	1131.86	1088.29	1055.82	1031.24	1012.41	997.85	986.52
51000	1154.49	1110.06	1076.94	1051.87	1032.66	1017.81	1006.25
52000	1177.13	1131.83	1098.06	1072.49	1052.91	1037.76	1025.98
53000	1199.77	1153.59	1119.17	1093.12	1073.15	1057.72	1045.71
54000	1222.41	1175.36	1140.29	1113.74	1093.40	1077.68	1065.44
55000	1245.04	1197.12	1161.41	1134.37	1113.65	1097.64	1085.17
56000	1267.68	1218.89	1182.52	1154.99	1133.90	1117.59	1104.90
57000	1290.32	1240.65	1203.64	1175.62	1154.15	1137.55	1124.63
58000	1312.96	1262.42	1224.76	1196.24	1174.40	1157.51	1144.36
59000	1335.59	1284.19	1245.87	1216.87	1194.64	1177.46	1164.09
60000	1358.23	1305.95	1266.99	1237.49	1214.89	1197.42	1183.82
65000	1471.42	1414.78	1372.57	1340.62	1316.13	1297.21	1282.47
70000	1584.60	1523.61	1478.15	1443.74	1417.37	1396.99	1381.12
75000	1697.79	1632.44	1583.74	1546.86	1518.62	1496.78	1479.77
80000	1810.97	1741.27	1689.32	1649.99	1619.86	1596.56	1578.42
85000	1924.16	1850.10	1794.90	1753.11	1721.10	1696.35	1677.08
90000	2037.34	1958.93	1900.48	1856.24	1822.34	1796.13	1775.73
95000	2150.53	2067.76	2006.07	1959.36	1923.58	1895.92	1874.38
100000	2263.72	2176.59	2111.65	2062.49	2024.82	1995.70	1973.03
105000	2376.90	2285.42	2217.23	2165.61	2126.06	2095.49	2071.68
110000	2490.09	2394.25	2322.81	2268.73	2227.30	2195.27	2170.33
120000	2716.46	2611.90	2533.98	2474.98	2429.78	2394.84	2367.64
130000	2942.83	2829.56	2745.14	2681.23	2632.27	2594.41	2564.94
140000	3169.20	3047.22	2956.31	2887.48	2834.75	2793.98	2762.24
150000	3395.57	3264.88	3167.47	3093.73	3037.23	2993.55	2959.55
160000	3621.94	3482.54	3378.64	3299.98	3239.71	3193.12	3156.85
170000	3848.32	3700.20	3589.80	3506.23	3442.19	3392.69	3354.15
180000	4074.69	3917.86	3800.97	3712.47	3644.68	3592.26	3551.46
190000	4301.06	4135.52	4012.13	3918.72	3847.16	3791.83	3748.76
200000	4527.43	4353.17	4223.30	4124.97	4049.64	3991.40	3946.06
210000	4753.80	4570.83	4434.46	4331.22	4252.12	4190.97	4143.36
220000	4980.17	4788.49	4645.63	4537.47	4454.61	4390.54	4340.67
230000	5206.55	5006.15	4856.79	4743.72	4657.09	4590.11	4537.97
240000	5432.92	5223.81	5067.96	4949.97	4859.57	4789.68	4735.27
250000	5659.29	5441.47	5279.12	5156.21	5062.05	4989.25	4932.58

23.75 % Monthly Payments

LOAN AMOUNT	15	16	17	18	19	20	21
	YEARS						
100	1.96	1.94	1.93	1.92	1.91	1.91	1.90
200	3.91	3.88	3.86	3.84	3.83	3.82	3.81
500	9.78	9.71	9.65	9.61	9.57	9.55	9.52
1000	19.55	19.41	19.30	19.22	19.15	19.09	19.05
2000	39.11	38.83	38.61	38.43	38.29	38.19	38.10
5000	97.76	97.07	96.52	96.08	95.74	95.46	95.25
6000	117.32	116.48	115.82	115.30	114.88	114.56	114.29
7000	136.87	135.89	135.12	134.51	134.03	133.65	133.34
8000	156.42	155.31	154.43	153.73	153.18	152.74	152.39
9000	175.98	174.72	173.73	172.95	172.33	171.83	171.44
10000	195.53	194.13	193.03	192.16	191.47	190.93	190.49
12000	234.63	232.96	231.64	230.60	229.77	229.11	228.59
15000	293.29	291.20	289.55	288.24	287.21	286.39	285.74
20000	391.06	388.27	386.07	384.33	382.95	381.85	380.98
25000	488.82	485.33	482.58	480.41	478.68	477.31	476.23
30000	586.59	582.40	579.10	576.49	574.42	572.78	571.47
31000	606.14	601.81	598.40	595.70	593.57	591.87	590.52
32000	625.69	621.23	617.71	614.92	612.71	610.96	609.57
33000	645.24	640.64	637.01	634.14	631.86	630.05	628.62
34000	664.80	660.05	656.31	653.35	651.01	649.15	647.67
35000	684.35	679.47	675.62	672.57	670.15	668.24	666.72
36000	703.90	698.88	694.92	691.79	689.30	687.33	685.76
37000	723.46	718.29	714.22	711.00	708.45	706.42	704.81
38000	743.01	737.71	733.52	730.22	727.60	725.52	723.86
39000	762.56	757.12	752.83	749.43	746.74	744.61	742.91
40000	782.11	776.53	772.13	768.65	765.89	763.70	761.96
41000	801.67	795.95	791.43	787.87	785.04	782.79	781.01
42000	821.22	815.36	810.74	807.08	804.19	801.89	800.06
43000	840.77	834.77	830.04	826.30	823.33	820.98	819.11
44000	860.33	854.19	849.34	845.52	842.48	840.07	838.16
45000	879.88	873.60	868.65	864.73	861.63	859.16	857.21
46000	899.43	893.01	887.95	883.95	880.78	878.26	876.25
47000	918.98	912.43	907.25	903.16	899.92	897.35	895.30
48000	938.54	931.84	926.56	922.38	919.07	916.44	914.35
49000	958.09	951.25	945.86	941.60	938.22	935.53	933.40
50000	977.64	970.67	965.16	960.81	957.36	954.63	952.45
51000	997.20	990.08	984.47	980.03	976.51	973.72	971.50
52000	1016.75	1009.49	1003.77	999.25	995.66	992.81	990.55
53000	1036.30	1028.91	1023.07	1018.46	1014.81	1011.90	1009.60
54000	1055.85	1048.32	1042.38	1037.68	1033.95	1031.00	1028.65
55000	1075.41	1067.73	1061.68	1056.89	1053.10	1050.09	1047.70
56000	1094.96	1087.15	1080.98	1076.11	1072.25	1069.18	1066.74
57000	1114.51	1106.56	1100.29	1095.33	1091.40	1088.27	1085.79
58000	1134.06	1125.97	1119.59	1114.54	1110.54	1107.37	1104.84
59000	1153.62	1145.39	1138.89	1133.76	1129.69	1126.46	1123.89
60000	1173.17	1164.80	1158.20	1152.98	1148.84	1145.55	1142.94
65000	1270.93	1261.87	1254.71	1249.06	1244.57	1241.01	1238.19
70000	1368.70	1358.93	1351.23	1345.14	1340.31	1336.48	1333.43
75000	1466.46	1456.00	1447.75	1441.22	1436.05	1431.94	1428.68
80000	1564.23	1553.07	1544.26	1537.30	1531.78	1527.40	1523.92
85000	1661.99	1650.13	1640.78	1633.38	1627.52	1622.87	1619.17
90000	1759.76	1747.20	1737.30	1729.46	1723.26	1718.33	1714.41
95000	1857.52	1844.27	1833.81	1825.54	1818.99	1813.79	1809.66
100000	1955.28	1941.33	1930.33	1921.63	1914.73	1909.25	1904.90
105000	2053.05	2038.40	2026.85	2017.71	2010.46	2004.72	2000.15
110000	2150.81	2135.47	2123.36	2113.79	2106.20	2100.18	2095.39
120000	2346.34	2329.60	2316.39	2305.95	2297.67	2291.10	2285.88
130000	2541.87	2523.73	2509.43	2498.11	2489.15	2482.03	2476.37
140000	2737.40	2717.87	2702.46	2690.28	2680.62	2672.95	2666.86
150000	2932.93	2912.00	2895.49	2882.44	2872.09	2863.88	2857.35
160000	3128.45	3106.13	3088.53	3074.60	3063.57	3054.81	3047.84
170000	3323.98	3300.27	3281.56	3266.76	3255.04	3245.73	3238.33
180000	3519.51	3494.40	3474.59	3458.93	3446.51	3436.66	3428.82
190000	3715.04	3688.53	3667.62	3651.09	3637.98	3627.58	3619.31
200000	3910.57	3882.67	3860.66	3843.25	3829.46	3818.51	3809.80
210000	4106.10	4076.80	4053.69	4035.41	4020.93	4009.43	4000.29
220000	4301.63	4270.93	4246.72	4227.58	4212.40	4200.36	4190.78
230000	4497.15	4465.07	4439.76	4419.74	4403.88	4391.28	4381.27
240000	4692.68	4659.20	4632.79	4611.90	4595.35	4582.21	4571.76
250000	4888.21	4853.33	4825.82	4804.06	4786.82	4773.13	4762.25

Monthly Payments 23.75 %

LOAN AMOUNT	22	23	24	25	30	35	40
				YEARS			
100	1.90	1.90	1.90	1.89	1.89	1.89	1.89
200	3.80	3.80	3.79	3.79	3.78	3.78	3.78
500	9.51	9.49	9.48	9.47	9.45	9.44	9.44
1000	19.01	18.99	18.96	18.95	18.90	18.89	18.88
2000	38.03	37.97	37.93	37.89	37.80	37.77	37.76
5000	95.07	94.93	94.82	94.74	94.50	94.43	94.40
6000	114.09	113.92	113.79	113.68	113.40	113.31	113.28
7000	133.10	132.91	132.75	132.63	132.30	132.20	132.16
8000	152.12	151.89	151.72	151.58	151.20	151.08	151.04
9000	171.13	170.88	170.68	170.53	170.10	169.97	169.92
10000	190.14	189.87	189.65	189.47	189.00	188.85	188.80
12000	228.17	227.84	227.58	227.37	226.81	226.62	226.56
15000	285.22	284.80	284.47	284.21	283.51	283.28	283.21
20000	380.29	379.74	379.30	378.95	378.01	377.71	377.61
25000	475.36	474.67	474.12	473.68	472.51	472.13	472.01
30000	570.43	569.60	568.94	568.42	567.01	566.56	566.41
31000	589.45	588.59	587.91	587.37	585.92	585.44	585.29
32000	608.46	607.58	606.87	606.31	604.82	604.33	604.17
33000	627.47	626.56	625.84	625.26	623.72	623.21	623.05
34000	646.49	645.55	644.80	644.21	642.62	642.10	641.93
35000	665.50	664.54	663.77	663.16	661.52	660.99	660.81
36000	684.52	683.52	682.73	682.10	680.42	679.87	679.69
37000	703.53	702.51	701.70	701.05	699.32	698.76	698.57
38000	722.55	721.50	720.66	720.00	718.22	717.64	717.45
39000	741.56	740.49	739.63	738.94	737.12	736.53	736.33
40000	760.58	759.47	758.59	757.89	756.02	755.41	755.21
41000	779.59	778.46	777.56	776.84	774.92	774.30	774.09
42000	798.60	797.45	796.52	795.79	793.82	793.18	792.98
43000	817.62	816.43	815.49	814.73	812.72	812.07	811.86
44000	836.63	835.42	834.45	833.68	831.62	830.95	830.74
45000	855.65	854.41	853.42	852.63	850.52	849.84	849.62
46000	874.66	873.39	872.38	871.58	869.42	868.72	868.50
47000	893.68	892.38	891.35	890.52	888.32	887.61	887.38
48000	912.69	911.37	910.31	909.47	907.22	906.49	906.26
49000	931.70	930.35	929.28	928.42	926.12	925.38	925.14
50000	950.72	949.34	948.24	947.37	945.02	944.27	944.02
51000	969.73	968.33	967.21	966.31	963.93	963.15	962.90
52000	988.75	987.31	986.17	985.26	982.83	982.04	981.78
53000	1007.76	1006.30	1005.14	1004.21	1001.73	1000.92	1000.66
54000	1026.78	1025.29	1024.10	1023.15	1020.63	1019.81	1019.54
55000	1045.79	1044.27	1043.07	1042.10	1039.53	1038.69	1038.42
56000	1064.81	1063.26	1062.03	1061.05	1058.43	1057.58	1057.30
57000	1083.82	1082.25	1081.00	1080.00	1077.33	1076.46	1076.18
58000	1102.83	1101.23	1099.96	1098.94	1096.23	1095.35	1095.06
59000	1121.85	1120.22	1118.92	1117.89	1115.13	1114.23	1113.94
60000	1140.86	1139.21	1137.89	1136.84	1134.03	1133.12	1132.82
65000	1235.93	1234.14	1232.71	1231.57	1228.53	1227.54	1227.22
70000	1331.01	1329.08	1327.54	1326.31	1323.03	1321.97	1321.63
75000	1426.08	1424.01	1422.36	1421.05	1417.54	1416.40	1416.03
80000	1521.15	1518.94	1517.19	1515.78	1512.04	1510.82	1510.43
85000	1616.22	1613.88	1612.01	1610.52	1606.54	1605.25	1604.83
90000	1711.29	1708.81	1706.83	1705.26	1701.04	1699.68	1699.23
95000	1806.37	1803.75	1801.66	1799.99	1795.55	1794.10	1793.63
100000	1901.44	1898.68	1896.48	1894.73	1890.05	1888.53	1888.04
105000	1996.51	1993.61	1991.31	1989.47	1984.55	1982.96	1982.44
110000	2091.58	2088.55	2086.13	2084.20	2079.05	2077.38	2076.84
120000	2281.73	2278.42	2275.78	2273.68	2268.06	2266.24	2265.64
130000	2471.87	2468.28	2465.43	2463.15	2457.06	2455.09	2454.45
140000	2662.01	2658.15	2655.08	2652.62	2646.07	2643.94	2643.25
150000	2852.16	2848.02	2844.72	2842.10	2835.07	2832.80	2832.05
160000	3042.30	3037.89	3034.37	3031.57	3024.08	3021.65	3020.86
170000	3232.44	3227.76	3224.02	3221.04	3213.08	3210.50	3209.66
180000	3422.59	3417.62	3413.67	3410.51	3402.09	3399.35	3398.46
190000	3612.73	3607.49	3603.32	3599.99	3591.09	3588.21	3587.27
200000	3802.88	3797.36	3792.96	3789.46	3780.10	3777.06	3776.07
210000	3993.02	3987.23	3982.61	3978.93	3969.10	3965.91	3964.88
220000	4183.16	4177.10	4172.26	4168.41	4158.11	4154.77	4153.68
230000	4373.31	4366.96	4361.91	4357.88	4347.11	4343.62	4342.48
240000	4563.45	4556.83	4551.56	4547.35	4536.12	4532.47	4531.29
250000	4753.60	4746.70	4741.21	4736.83	4725.12	4721.33	4720.09

24.00 % Monthly Payments

LOAN AMOUNT	YEARS 1	2	3	4	5	6	7
100	9.40	5.23	3.86	3.20	2.81	2.57	2.40
200	18.80	10.46	7.73	6.40	5.62	5.13	4.79
500	47.01	26.16	19.32	15.99	14.06	12.83	11.99
1000	94.02	52.31	38.65	31.99	28.12	25.65	23.97
2000	188.04	104.63	77.30	63.97	56.24	51.30	47.95
5000	470.09	261.57	193.24	159.93	140.61	128.26	119.86
6000	564.11	313.89	231.89	191.92	168.73	153.91	143.84
7000	658.13	366.20	270.53	223.90	196.86	179.56	167.81
8000	752.15	418.51	309.18	255.89	224.98	205.21	191.78
9000	846.17	470.83	347.83	287.88	253.10	230.87	215.76
10000	940.19	523.14	386.48	319.86	281.22	256.52	239.73
12000	1128.23	627.77	463.77	383.84	337.47	307.82	287.68
15000	1410.28	784.71	579.72	479.80	421.83	384.78	359.59
20000	1880.38	1046.29	772.96	639.73	562.44	513.04	479.46
25000	2350.47	1307.86	966.20	799.66	703.06	641.30	599.32
30000	2820.57	1569.43	1159.43	959.59	843.67	769.55	719.19
31000	2914.59	1621.74	1198.08	991.58	871.79	795.21	743.16
32000	3008.61	1674.06	1236.73	1023.56	899.91	820.86	767.13
33000	3102.63	1726.37	1275.38	1055.55	928.03	846.51	791.11
34000	3196.65	1778.69	1314.03	1087.54	956.16	872.16	815.08
35000	3290.66	1831.00	1352.67	1119.52	984.28	897.81	839.05
36000	3384.68	1883.32	1391.32	1151.51	1012.40	923.46	863.03
37000	3478.70	1935.63	1429.97	1183.50	1040.52	949.12	887.00
38000	3572.72	1987.94	1468.62	1215.48	1068.64	974.77	910.97
39000	3666.74	2040.26	1507.26	1247.47	1096.77	1000.42	934.95
40000	3760.76	2092.57	1545.91	1279.46	1124.89	1026.07	958.92
41000	3854.78	2144.89	1584.56	1311.44	1153.01	1051.72	982.89
42000	3948.80	2197.20	1623.21	1343.43	1181.13	1077.38	1006.86
43000	4042.82	2249.52	1661.86	1375.41	1209.26	1103.03	1030.84
44000	4136.83	2301.83	1700.50	1407.40	1237.38	1128.68	1054.81
45000	4230.85	2354.14	1739.15	1439.39	1265.50	1154.33	1078.78
46000	4324.87	2406.46	1777.80	1471.37	1293.62	1179.98	1102.76
47000	4418.89	2458.77	1816.45	1503.36	1321.74	1205.63	1126.73
48000	4512.91	2511.09	1855.09	1535.35	1349.87	1231.29	1150.70
49000	4606.93	2563.40	1893.74	1567.33	1377.99	1256.94	1174.68
50000	4700.95	2615.72	1932.39	1599.32	1406.11	1282.59	1198.65
51000	4794.97	2668.03	1971.04	1631.31	1434.23	1308.24	1222.62
52000	4888.99	2720.34	2009.69	1663.29	1462.36	1333.89	1246.59
53000	4983.01	2772.66	2048.33	1695.28	1490.48	1359.55	1270.57
54000	5077.02	2824.97	2086.98	1727.27	1518.60	1385.20	1294.54
55000	5171.04	2877.29	2125.63	1759.25	1546.72	1410.85	1318.51
56000	5265.06	2929.60	2164.28	1791.24	1574.84	1436.50	1342.49
57000	5359.08	2981.92	2202.92	1823.22	1602.97	1462.15	1366.46
58000	5453.10	3034.23	2241.57	1855.21	1631.09	1487.80	1390.43
59000	5547.12	3086.54	2280.22	1887.20	1659.21	1513.46	1414.41
60000	5641.14	3138.86	2318.87	1919.18	1687.33	1539.11	1438.38
65000	6111.23	3400.43	2512.11	2079.12	1827.94	1667.37	1558.24
70000	6581.33	3662.00	2705.35	2239.05	1968.56	1795.63	1678.11
75000	7051.42	3923.57	2898.59	2398.98	2109.17	1923.89	1797.97
80000	7521.52	4185.15	3091.82	2558.91	2249.78	2052.14	1917.84
85000	7991.61	4446.72	3285.06	2718.84	2390.39	2180.40	2037.70
90000	8461.71	4708.29	3478.30	2878.78	2531.00	2308.66	2157.57
95000	8931.80	4969.86	3671.54	3038.71	2671.61	2436.92	2277.43
100000	9401.90	5231.43	3864.78	3198.64	2812.22	2565.18	2397.30
105000	9871.99	5493.00	4058.02	3358.57	2952.83	2693.44	2517.16
110000	10342.09	5754.57	4251.26	3518.50	3093.45	2821.70	2637.03
120000	11282.28	6277.72	4637.74	3838.37	3374.67	3078.22	2876.76
130000	12222.47	6800.86	5024.21	4158.23	3655.89	3334.73	3116.49
140000	13162.66	7324.00	5410.69	4478.09	3937.11	3591.25	3356.22
150000	14102.85	7847.15	5797.17	4797.96	4218.33	3847.77	3595.95
160000	15043.04	8370.29	6183.65	5117.82	4499.56	4104.29	3835.67
170000	15983.23	8893.43	6570.13	5437.69	4780.78	4360.81	4075.40
180000	16923.41	9416.58	6956.60	5757.55	5062.00	4617.32	4315.13
190000	17863.60	9939.72	7343.08	6077.41	5343.22	4873.84	4554.86
200000	18803.79	10462.86	7729.56	6397.28	5624.45	5130.36	4794.59
210000	19743.98	10986.01	8116.04	6717.14	5905.67	5386.88	5034.32
220000	20684.17	11509.15	8502.52	7037.01	6186.89	5643.40	5274.05
230000	21624.36	12032.29	8888.99	7356.87	6468.11	5899.91	5513.78
240000	22564.55	12555.44	9275.47	7676.73	6749.33	6156.43	5753.51
250000	23504.74	13078.58	9661.95	7996.60	7030.56	6412.95	5993.24

Monthly Payments 24.00 %

LOAN AMOUNT	YEARS 8	9	10	11	12	13	14
100	2.28	2.19	2.13	2.08	2.04	2.01	1.99
200	4.56	4.38	4.25	4.16	4.08	4.02	3.98
500	11.39	10.96	10.64	10.39	10.21	10.06	9.95
1000	22.78	21.92	21.27	20.79	20.41	20.12	19.90
2000	45.57	43.84	42.55	41.57	40.82	40.25	39.80
5000	113.92	109.59	106.36	103.93	102.06	100.62	99.50
6000	136.71	131.51	127.64	124.71	122.47	120.75	119.41
7000	159.49	153.42	148.91	145.50	142.89	140.87	139.31
8000	182.27	175.34	170.18	166.28	163.30	161.00	159.21
9000	205.06	197.26	191.46	187.07	183.71	181.12	179.11
10000	227.84	219.18	212.73	207.85	204.12	201.25	199.01
12000	273.41	263.01	255.28	249.42	244.95	241.49	238.81
15000	341.76	328.77	319.09	311.78	306.19	301.87	298.51
20000	455.68	438.36	425.46	415.71	408.25	402.49	398.02
25000	569.61	547.95	531.82	519.63	510.31	503.11	497.52
30000	683.53	657.53	638.19	623.56	612.37	603.74	597.03
31000	706.31	679.45	659.46	644.35	632.79	623.86	616.93
32000	729.10	701.37	680.73	665.13	653.20	643.99	636.83
33000	751.88	723.29	702.01	685.92	673.61	664.11	656.73
34000	774.66	745.21	723.28	706.70	694.02	684.24	676.63
35000	797.45	767.12	744.55	727.49	714.44	704.36	696.53
36000	820.23	789.04	765.83	748.27	734.85	724.48	716.43
37000	843.02	810.96	787.10	769.06	755.26	744.61	736.33
38000	865.80	832.88	808.37	789.84	775.67	764.73	756.23
39000	888.58	854.79	829.64	810.63	796.09	784.86	776.13
40000	911.37	876.71	850.92	831.42	816.50	804.98	796.03
41000	934.15	898.63	872.19	852.20	836.91	825.11	815.94
42000	956.94	920.55	893.46	872.99	857.32	845.23	835.84
43000	979.72	942.47	914.74	893.77	877.73	865.36	855.74
44000	1002.51	964.38	936.01	914.56	898.15	885.48	875.64
45000	1025.29	986.30	957.28	935.34	918.56	905.61	895.54
46000	1048.07	1008.22	978.55	956.13	938.97	925.73	915.44
47000	1070.86	1030.14	999.83	976.91	959.38	945.86	935.34
48000	1093.64	1052.05	1021.10	997.70	979.80	965.98	955.24
49000	1116.43	1073.97	1042.37	1018.48	1000.21	986.10	975.14
50000	1139.21	1095.89	1063.65	1039.27	1020.62	1006.23	995.04
51000	1162.00	1117.81	1084.92	1060.05	1041.03	1026.35	1014.94
52000	1184.78	1139.73	1106.19	1080.84	1061.45	1046.48	1034.84
53000	1207.56	1161.64	1127.46	1101.63	1081.86	1066.60	1054.75
54000	1230.35	1183.56	1148.74	1122.41	1102.27	1086.73	1074.65
55000	1253.13	1205.48	1170.01	1143.20	1122.68	1106.85	1094.55
56000	1275.92	1227.40	1191.28	1163.98	1143.10	1126.98	1114.45
57000	1298.70	1249.31	1212.56	1184.77	1163.51	1147.10	1134.35
58000	1321.48	1271.23	1233.83	1205.55	1183.92	1167.23	1154.25
59000	1344.27	1293.15	1255.10	1226.34	1204.33	1187.35	1174.15
60000	1367.05	1315.07	1276.38	1247.12	1224.75	1207.47	1194.05
65000	1480.97	1424.66	1382.74	1351.05	1326.81	1308.10	1293.56
70000	1594.90	1534.25	1489.10	1454.98	1428.87	1408.72	1393.06
75000	1708.82	1643.84	1595.47	1558.90	1530.93	1509.34	1492.56
80000	1822.74	1753.42	1701.83	1662.83	1632.99	1609.97	1592.07
85000	1936.66	1863.01	1808.20	1766.76	1735.06	1710.59	1691.57
90000	2050.58	1972.60	1914.56	1870.68	1837.12	1811.21	1791.08
95000	2164.50	2082.19	2020.93	1974.61	1939.18	1911.84	1890.58
100000	2278.42	2191.78	2127.29	2078.54	2041.24	2012.46	1990.09
105000	2392.34	2301.37	2233.66	2182.46	2143.31	2113.08	2089.59
110000	2506.26	2410.96	2340.02	2286.39	2245.37	2213.70	2189.09
120000	2734.11	2630.14	2552.75	2494.25	2449.49	2414.95	2388.10
130000	2961.95	2849.31	2765.48	2702.10	2653.62	2616.20	2587.11
140000	3189.79	3068.49	2978.21	2909.95	2857.74	2817.44	2786.12
150000	3417.63	3287.67	3190.94	3117.81	3061.87	3018.69	2985.13
160000	3645.48	3506.85	3403.67	3325.66	3265.99	3219.93	3184.14
170000	3873.32	3726.03	3616.40	3533.51	3470.11	3421.18	3383.15
180000	4101.16	3945.20	3829.13	3741.37	3674.24	3622.42	3582.15
190000	4329.00	4164.38	4041.85	3949.22	3878.36	3823.67	3781.16
200000	4556.84	4383.56	4254.58	4157.08	4082.49	4024.92	3980.17
210000	4784.69	4602.74	4467.31	4364.93	4286.61	4226.16	4179.18
220000	5012.53	4821.92	4680.04	4572.78	4490.74	4427.41	4378.19
230000	5240.37	5041.10	4892.77	4780.64	4694.86	4628.65	4577.20
240000	5468.21	5260.27	5105.50	4988.49	4898.98	4829.90	4776.21
250000	5696.06	5479.45	5318.23	5196.34	5103.11	5031.15	4975.21

24.00 % Monthly Payments

LOAN AMOUNT	15	16	17	18	19	20	21
100	1.97	1.96	1.95	1.94	1.93	1.93	1.92
200	3.95	3.92	3.90	3.88	3.87	3.85	3.85
500	9.86	9.79	9.74	9.70	9.66	9.64	9.62
1000	19.73	19.59	19.48	19.40	19.33	19.27	19.23
2000	39.45	39.18	38.96	38.79	38.66	38.55	38.46
5000	98.63	97.94	97.40	96.98	96.64	96.37	96.16
6000	118.36	117.53	116.89	116.37	115.97	115.65	115.39
7000	138.08	137.12	136.37	135.77	135.30	134.92	134.63
8000	157.81	156.71	155.85	155.16	154.63	154.20	153.86
9000	177.53	176.30	175.33	174.56	173.95	173.47	173.09
10000	197.26	195.89	194.81	193.96	193.28	192.75	192.32
12000	236.71	235.07	233.77	232.75	231.94	231.30	230.79
15000	295.89	293.83	292.21	290.93	289.92	289.12	288.49
20000	394.52	391.78	389.62	387.91	386.56	385.50	384.65
25000	493.15	489.72	487.02	484.89	483.20	481.87	480.81
30000	591.78	587.67	584.43	581.87	579.85	578.24	576.97
31000	611.51	607.25	603.91	601.26	599.17	597.52	596.20
32000	631.23	626.84	623.39	620.66	618.50	616.79	615.44
33000	650.96	646.43	642.87	640.06	637.83	636.07	634.67
34000	670.69	666.02	662.35	659.45	657.16	655.34	653.90
35000	690.41	685.61	681.83	678.85	676.49	674.62	673.13
36000	710.14	705.20	701.31	698.24	695.81	693.89	692.37
37000	729.86	724.79	720.79	717.64	715.14	713.17	711.60
38000	749.59	744.38	740.27	737.03	734.47	732.44	730.83
39000	769.32	763.97	759.75	756.43	753.80	751.72	750.06
40000	789.04	783.55	779.23	775.82	773.13	770.99	769.30
41000	808.77	803.14	798.72	795.22	792.46	790.27	788.53
42000	828.49	822.73	818.20	814.62	811.78	809.54	807.76
43000	848.22	842.32	837.68	834.01	831.11	828.81	826.99
44000	867.95	861.91	857.16	853.41	850.44	848.09	846.23
45000	887.67	881.50	876.64	872.80	869.77	867.36	865.46
46000	907.40	901.09	896.12	892.20	889.10	886.64	884.69
47000	927.12	920.68	915.60	911.59	908.42	905.91	903.92
48000	946.85	940.27	935.08	930.99	927.75	925.19	923.15
49000	966.58	959.85	954.56	950.38	947.08	944.46	942.39
50000	986.30	979.44	974.04	969.78	966.41	963.74	961.62
51000	1006.03	999.03	993.52	989.18	985.74	983.01	980.85
52000	1025.75	1018.62	1013.00	1008.57	1005.07	1002.29	1000.08
53000	1045.48	1038.21	1032.49	1027.97	1024.39	1021.56	1019.32
54000	1065.21	1057.80	1051.97	1047.36	1043.72	1040.84	1038.55
55000	1084.93	1077.39	1071.45	1066.76	1063.05	1060.11	1057.78
56000	1104.66	1096.98	1090.93	1086.15	1082.38	1079.39	1077.01
57000	1124.38	1116.56	1110.41	1105.55	1101.71	1098.66	1096.25
58000	1144.11	1136.15	1129.89	1124.95	1121.03	1117.94	1115.48
59000	1163.84	1155.74	1149.37	1144.34	1140.36	1137.21	1134.71
60000	1183.56	1175.33	1168.85	1163.74	1159.69	1156.49	1153.94
65000	1282.19	1273.28	1266.26	1260.71	1256.33	1252.86	1250.11
70000	1380.82	1371.22	1363.66	1357.69	1352.97	1349.23	1346.27
75000	1479.45	1469.16	1461.06	1454.67	1449.61	1445.61	1442.43
80000	1578.08	1567.11	1558.47	1551.65	1546.25	1541.98	1538.59
85000	1676.71	1665.05	1655.87	1648.63	1642.90	1638.36	1634.75
90000	1775.34	1763.00	1753.28	1745.60	1739.54	1734.73	1730.92
95000	1873.97	1860.94	1850.68	1842.58	1836.18	1831.10	1827.08
100000	1972.60	1958.89	1948.09	1939.56	1932.82	1927.48	1923.24
105000	2071.23	2056.83	2045.49	2036.54	2029.46	2023.85	2019.40
110000	2169.86	2154.77	2142.89	2133.52	2126.10	2120.22	2115.56
120000	2367.12	2350.66	2337.70	2327.47	2319.38	2312.97	2307.89
130000	2564.38	2546.55	2532.51	2521.43	2512.66	2505.72	2500.21
140000	2761.65	2742.44	2727.32	2715.39	2705.95	2698.47	2692.53
150000	2958.91	2938.33	2922.13	2909.34	2899.23	2891.21	2884.86
160000	3156.17	3134.22	3116.94	3103.30	3092.51	3083.96	3077.18
170000	3353.43	3330.11	3311.75	3297.25	3285.79	3276.71	3269.51
180000	3550.69	3525.99	3506.55	3491.21	3479.07	3469.46	3461.83
190000	3747.95	3721.88	3701.36	3685.17	3672.35	3662.21	3654.15
200000	3945.21	3917.77	3896.17	3879.12	3865.64	3854.95	3846.48
210000	4142.47	4113.66	4090.98	4073.08	4058.92	4047.70	4038.80
220000	4339.73	4309.55	4285.79	4267.03	4252.20	4240.45	4231.13
230000	4536.99	4505.44	4480.60	4460.99	4445.48	4433.20	4423.45
240000	4734.25	4701.33	4675.41	4654.95	4638.76	4625.94	4615.77
250000	4931.51	4897.21	4870.21	4848.90	4832.05	4818.69	4808.10

Monthly Payments 24.00 %

LOAN AMOUNT	22	23	24	25	30	35	40
				YEARS			
100	1.92	1.92	1.92	1.91	1.91	1.91	1.91
200	3.84	3.83	3.83	3.83	3.82	3.81	3.81
500	9.60	9.59	9.58	9.57	9.54	9.54	9.53
1000	19.20	19.17	19.15	19.13	19.09	19.07	19.07
2000	38.40	38.34	38.30	38.27	38.18	38.15	38.14
5000	95.99	95.86	95.75	95.67	95.44	95.37	95.35
6000	115.19	115.03	114.90	114.80	114.53	114.45	114.42
7000	134.39	134.20	134.06	133.94	133.62	133.52	133.49
8000	153.59	153.38	153.21	153.07	152.71	152.60	152.56
9000	172.79	172.55	172.36	172.20	171.80	171.67	171.63
10000	191.99	191.72	191.51	191.34	190.89	190.74	190.70
12000	230.38	230.06	229.81	229.61	229.07	228.89	228.84
15000	287.98	287.58	287.26	287.01	286.33	286.12	286.05
20000	383.97	383.44	383.01	382.68	381.78	381.49	381.40
25000	479.97	479.30	478.77	478.35	477.22	476.86	476.75
30000	575.96	575.16	574.52	574.01	572.67	572.23	572.09
31000	595.16	594.33	593.67	593.15	591.76	591.31	591.16
32000	614.36	613.50	612.82	612.28	610.84	610.38	610.23
33000	633.56	632.68	631.97	631.42	629.93	629.46	629.30
34000	652.76	651.85	651.13	650.55	649.02	648.53	648.37
35000	671.96	671.02	670.28	669.68	668.11	667.61	667.44
36000	691.15	690.19	689.43	688.82	687.20	686.68	686.51
37000	710.35	709.36	708.58	707.95	706.29	705.76	705.58
38000	729.55	728.54	727.73	727.09	725.38	724.83	724.65
39000	748.75	747.71	746.88	746.22	744.47	743.90	743.72
40000	767.95	766.88	766.03	765.35	763.56	762.98	762.79
41000	787.15	786.05	785.18	784.49	782.64	782.05	781.86
42000	806.35	805.22	804.33	803.62	801.73	801.13	800.93
43000	825.55	824.40	823.48	822.75	820.82	820.20	820.00
44000	844.74	843.57	842.63	841.89	839.91	839.28	839.07
45000	863.94	862.74	861.78	861.02	859.00	858.35	858.14
46000	883.14	881.91	880.93	880.16	878.09	877.43	877.21
47000	902.34	901.08	900.09	899.29	897.18	896.50	896.28
48000	921.54	920.26	919.24	918.42	916.27	915.57	915.35
49000	940.74	939.43	938.39	937.56	935.36	934.65	934.42
50000	959.94	958.60	957.54	956.69	954.44	953.72	953.49
51000	979.14	977.77	976.69	975.83	973.53	972.80	972.56
52000	998.33	996.94	995.84	994.96	992.62	991.87	991.63
53000	1017.53	1016.12	1014.99	1014.09	1011.71	1010.95	1010.70
54000	1036.73	1035.29	1034.14	1033.23	1030.80	1030.02	1029.77
55000	1055.93	1054.46	1053.29	1052.36	1049.89	1049.10	1048.84
56000	1075.13	1073.63	1072.44	1071.49	1068.98	1068.17	1067.91
57000	1094.33	1092.80	1091.59	1090.63	1088.07	1087.24	1086.98
58000	1113.53	1111.98	1110.74	1109.76	1107.16	1106.32	1106.05
59000	1132.73	1131.15	1129.89	1128.90	1126.24	1125.39	1125.12
60000	1151.92	1150.32	1149.04	1148.03	1145.33	1144.47	1144.19
65000	1247.92	1246.18	1244.80	1243.70	1240.78	1239.84	1239.54
70000	1343.91	1342.04	1340.55	1339.37	1336.22	1335.21	1334.89
75000	1439.91	1437.90	1436.31	1435.04	1431.67	1430.58	1430.24
80000	1535.90	1533.76	1532.06	1530.71	1527.11	1525.96	1525.59
85000	1631.89	1629.62	1627.81	1626.38	1622.56	1621.33	1620.94
90000	1727.89	1725.48	1723.57	1722.04	1718.00	1716.70	1716.28
95000	1823.88	1821.34	1819.32	1817.71	1813.44	1812.07	1811.63
100000	1919.87	1917.20	1915.07	1913.38	1908.89	1907.45	1906.98
105000	2015.87	2013.06	2010.83	2009.05	2004.33	2002.82	2002.33
110000	2111.86	2108.92	2106.58	2104.72	2099.78	2098.19	2097.68
120000	2303.85	2300.64	2298.09	2296.06	2290.67	2288.94	2288.38
130000	2495.84	2492.36	2489.60	2487.40	2481.56	2479.68	2479.08
140000	2687.82	2684.08	2681.10	2678.74	2672.44	2670.43	2669.78
150000	2879.81	2875.80	2872.61	2870.07	2863.33	2861.17	2860.47
160000	3071.80	3067.52	3064.12	3061.41	3054.22	3051.91	3051.17
170000	3263.79	3259.24	3255.63	3252.75	3245.11	3242.66	3241.87
180000	3455.77	3450.96	3447.13	3444.09	3436.00	3433.40	3432.57
190000	3647.76	3642.68	3638.64	3635.43	3626.89	3624.15	3623.27
200000	3839.75	3834.40	3830.15	3826.77	3817.78	3814.89	3813.97
210000	4031.74	4026.12	4021.66	4018.10	4008.67	4005.64	4004.66
220000	4223.72	4217.84	4213.16	4209.44	4199.56	4196.38	4195.36
230000	4415.71	4409.56	4404.67	4400.78	4390.44	4387.13	4386.06
240000	4607.70	4601.28	4596.18	4592.12	4581.33	4577.87	4576.76
250000	4799.69	4793.00	4787.69	4783.46	4772.22	4768.62	4767.46

Annual Amortization Schedules

Annual amortization schedules are rarely seen but are very important when a mortgage holder really wants to understand the underlying concepts of a mortgage loan. The schedules display (1) the progress made each year by a mortgage holder toward the repayment of the loan principal and (2) the interest charges that have been paid during any year. The schedules are based on a mortgage loan of $10,000 and on annual interest rates that vary from 5% to 24% in increments of ¼%. At every interest rate, schedules for both 25-year and 30-year mortgages are given.

Each schedule has three columns for each year. The first column shows the interest paid during the year and the second column shows the principal paid during the year. These two amounts add up to the annual payment (or the sum of twelve monthly payments). The third column in each schedule shows the remaining balance of the mortgage at the end of each year. Note that, at the end of the complete term on each schedule, the remaining balance is zero. You may also note that from the first year of payments to the last year the interest paid during the year decreases as the years go by. The payment toward the principal increases over the years.

Here are some illustrative situations to help you understand and use the schedules:

Situation 1

Mr. Brown holds a 30-year conventional mortgage for an original principal of $30,000.00 at an annual interest rate of 9%. He has just completed his tenth year of monthly payments. For tax and other reasons the following questions arise: What interest charges were paid during the tenth year? How much principal has been paid during the tenth year? What is left to be paid on the principal?

The answers are found by first locating, on the 9% page of the annual amortization schedules, the 30-year schedule. Note that the schedule is based on a principal of $10,000.00, and because Mr. Brown's original principal was $30,000.00, all amounts on this schedule must be multiplied by 3. Looking down the schedule to the 10-year line you will notice that (1) the interest paid during the tenth year is $795.35, (2) the amount paid toward the principal during the year is $156.01, and (3) the remaining balance of the principal at the end of the year is $8,916.35. Multiplying by 3 provides Mr. Brown with these answers:

$2,386.05	(interest charges paid during the tenth year)
$468.03	(principal paid during the tenth year)
$26.749.05	(portion of principal still to be paid)

Situation 2

Mrs. Jones holds a 25-year conventional mortgage for an original principal of $40,000.00 at an annual interest rate of 8% and has just completed her twentieth year of monthly payments. For comparative purposes she wants to know how much of the principal is left unpaid. To find the answer, she must first locate the page that shows the 8% schedules. Using the schedule for the 25-year mortgage, she must look down to the 20-year line and then across to the last column showing the mortgage balance at the end of the twentieth year. The amount shown, $3,775.64, is based on a mortgage principal of $10,000.00. Since Mrs. Jones' original mortgage was 4 times as great she must multiply this amount by 4 to get $15,102.56 as the answer.

Annual Amortization Schedules

Based on a Mortgage of $ 10,000.00

5.00 %

30 YEAR TERM:
Monthly Payment = 53.37
Annual Payment = 640.44

25 YEAR TERM:
Monthly Payment = 58.16
Annual Payment = 697.92

YR	30 YR: INTER PD DUR YEAR	30 YR: PRINCP PD DUR YEAR	30 YR: MORTG BAL END OF YR	25 YR: INTER PD DUR YEAR	25 YR: PRINCP PD DUR YEAR	25 YR: MORTG BAL END OF YR
1	491.53	148.91	9851.09	490.19	207.73	9792.27
2	484.00	156.44	9694.65	479.68	218.24	9574.03
3	476.08	164.36	9530.28	468.63	229.29	9344.74
4	467.75	172.69	9357.60	457.02	240.90	9103.84
5	459.01	181.43	9176.17	444.83	253.09	8850.75
6	449.83	190.61	8985.56	432.01	265.91	8584.84
7	440.18	200.26	8785.30	418.55	279.37	8305.48
8	430.04	210.40	8574.90	404.41	293.51	8011.97
9	419.39	221.05	8353.84	389.55	308.37	7703.60
10	408.20	232.24	8121.60	373.94	323.98	7379.61
11	396.44	244.00	7877.60	357.54	340.38	7039.23
12	384.09	256.35	7621.25	340.31	357.61	6681.62
13	371.11	269.33	7351.92	322.20	375.72	6305.90
14	357.47	282.97	7068.95	303.18	394.74	5911.16
15	343.15	297.29	6771.66	283.20	414.72	5496.44
16	328.10	312.34	6459.32	262.20	435.72	5060.72
17	312.29	328.15	6131.17	240.14	457.78	4602.94
18	295.67	344.77	5786.40	216.97	480.95	4121.99
19	278.22	362.22	5424.18	192.62	505.30	3616.69
20	259.88	380.56	5043.62	167.04	530.88	3085.81
21	240.62	399.82	4643.80	140.16	557.76	2528.05
22	220.38	420.06	4223.74	111.93	585.99	1942.06
23	199.11	441.33	3782.41	82.26	615.66	1326.40
24	176.77	463.67	3318.74	51.09	646.83	679.57
25	153.29	487.15	2831.59	18.35	679.57	0.00
26	128.63	511.81	2319.78			
27	102.72	537.72	1782.07			
28	75.50	564.94	1217.13			
29	46.90	593.54	623.59			
30	16.85	623.59	0.00			

5.25 %

30 YEAR TERM:
Monthly Payment = 54.87
Annual Payment = 658.44

25 YEAR TERM:
Monthly Payment = 59.59
Annual Payment = 715.08

YR	30 YR: INTER PD DUR YEAR	30 YR: PRINCP PD DUR YEAR	30 YR: MORTG BAL END OF YR	25 YR: INTER PD DUR YEAR	25 YR: PRINCP PD DUR YEAR	25 YR: MORTG BAL END OF YR
1	515.98	142.46	9857.54	514.60	200.48	9799.52
2	508.40	150.04	9707.50	503.94	211.14	9588.37
3	500.42	158.02	9549.48	492.71	222.37	9366.00
4	492.02	166.42	9383.06	480.88	234.20	9131.80
5	483.16	175.28	9207.78	468.42	246.66	8885.14
6	473.84	184.60	9023.18	455.30	259.78	8625.36
7	464.02	194.42	8828.77	441.48	273.60	8351.76
8	453.68	204.76	8624.01	426.93	288.15	8063.61
9	442.79	215.65	8408.36	411.60	303.48	7760.14
10	431.32	227.12	8181.24	395.46	319.62	7440.52
11	419.24	239.20	7942.04	378.46	336.62	7103.90
12	406.52	251.92	7690.12	360.56	354.52	6749.38
13	393.12	265.32	7424.80	341.70	373.38	6376.00
14	379.01	279.43	7145.36	321.84	393.24	5982.76
15	364.14	294.30	6851.07	300.93	414.15	5568.61
16	348.49	309.95	6541.12	278.90	436.18	5132.43
17	332.00	326.44	6214.68	255.70	459.38	4673.05
18	314.64	343.80	5870.88	231.26	483.82	4189.23
19	296.36	362.08	5508.80	205.53	509.55	3679.68
20	277.10	381.34	5127.46	178.43	536.65	3143.03
21	256.81	401.63	4725.83	149.88	565.20	2577.83
22	235.45	422.99	4302.84	119.82	595.26	1982.57
23	212.95	445.49	3857.35	88.16	626.92	1355.65
24	189.26	469.18	3388.17	54.81	660.27	695.38
25	164.30	494.14	2894.03	19.70	695.38	0.00
26	138.02	520.42	2373.61			
27	110.34	548.10	1825.51			
28	81.19	577.25	1248.25			
29	50.48	607.96	640.30			
30	18.14	640.30	0.00			

Annual Amortization Schedules

Based on a Mortgage of $ 10,000.00

5.50 %

30 YEAR TERM:
Monthly Payment = 56.39
Annual Payment = 676.68

25 YEAR TERM:
Monthly Payment = 61.04
Annual Payment = 732.48

YR	INTER PD DUR YEAR	PRINCP PD DUR YEAR	MORTG BAL END OF YR	INTER PD DUR YEAR	PRINCP PD DUR YEAR	MORTG BAL END OF YR
1	540.43	136.25	9863.75	539.04	193.44	9806.56
2	532.83	143.85	9719.91	528.25	204.23	9602.33
3	524.81	151.87	9568.04	516.87	215.61	9386.72
4	516.35	160.33	9407.71	504.84	227.64	9159.08
5	507.41	169.27	9238.44	492.15	240.33	8918.75
6	497.97	178.71	9059.73	478.75	253.73	8665.02
7	488.01	188.67	8871.05	464.60	267.88	8397.15
8	477.49	199.19	8671.86	449.67	282.81	8114.33
9	466.38	210.30	8461.56	433.90	298.58	7815.75
10	454.65	222.03	8239.53	417.25	315.23	7500.53
11	442.27	234.41	8005.12	399.68	332.80	7167.72
12	429.20	247.48	7757.65	381.12	351.36	6816.36
13	415.41	261.27	7496.38	361.53	370.95	6445.42
14	400.84	275.84	7220.54	340.85	391.63	6053.78
15	385.46	291.22	6929.31	319.01	413.47	5640.31
16	369.22	307.46	6621.86	295.96	436.52	5203.79
17	352.08	324.60	6297.26	271.62	460.86	4742.93
18	333.98	342.70	5954.56	245.92	486.56	4256.38
19	314.87	361.81	5592.75	218.79	513.69	3742.69
20	294.70	381.98	5210.77	190.15	542.33	3200.36
21	273.40	403.28	4807.49	159.92	572.56	2627.80
22	250.92	425.76	4381.73	127.99	604.49	2023.31
23	227.18	449.50	3932.22	94.29	638.19	1385.12
24	202.12	474.56	3457.66	58.70	673.78	711.34
25	175.66	501.02	2956.64	21.14	711.34	0.00
26	147.72	528.96	2427.68			
27	118.23	558.45	1869.22			
28	87.09	589.59	1279.63			
29	54.22	622.46	657.17			
30	19.51	657.17	0.00			

5.75 %

30 YEAR TERM:
Monthly Payment = 57.93
Annual Payment = 695.16

25 YEAR TERM:
Monthly Payment = 62.50
Annual Payment = 750.00

YR	INTER PD DUR YEAR	PRINCP PD DUR YEAR	MORTG BAL END OF YR	INTER PD DUR YEAR	PRINCP PD DUR YEAR	MORTG BAL END OF YR
1	564.90	130.26	9869.74	563.39	186.61	9813.39
2	557.30	137.86	9731.88	552.51	197.49	9615.90
3	549.26	145.90	9585.98	540.99	209.01	9406.89
4	540.75	154.41	9431.56	528.80	221.20	9185.69
5	531.74	163.42	9268.15	515.90	234.10	8951.59
6	522.21	172.95	9095.20	502.24	247.76	8703.84
7	512.12	183.04	8912.16	487.79	262.21	8441.63
8	501.45	193.71	8718.45	472.50	277.50	8164.13
9	490.15	205.01	8513.44	456.31	293.69	7870.44
10	478.19	216.97	8296.47	439.18	310.82	7559.63
11	465.54	229.62	8066.84	421.06	328.94	7230.68
12	452.14	243.02	7823.83	401.87	348.13	6882.55
13	437.97	257.19	7566.63	381.56	368.44	6514.11
14	422.97	272.19	7294.44	360.07	389.93	6124.19
15	407.09	288.07	7006.37	337.33	412.67	5711.52
16	390.29	304.87	6701.50	313.26	436.74	5274.78
17	372.51	322.65	6378.85	287.79	462.21	4812.57
18	353.69	341.47	6037.38	260.83	489.17	4323.40
19	333.77	361.39	5675.99	232.30	517.70	3805.70
20	312.69	382.47	5293.52	202.10	547.90	3257.80
21	290.38	404.78	4888.74	170.14	579.86	2677.94
22	266.78	428.38	4460.36	136.32	613.68	2064.26
23	241.79	453.37	4006.99	100.53	649.47	1414.79
24	215.35	479.81	3527.17	62.65	687.35	727.44
25	187.36	507.80	3019.37	22.56	727.44	0.00
26	157.74	537.42	2481.96			
27	126.40	568.76	1913.19			
28	93.22	601.94	1311.25			
29	58.11	637.05	674.20			
30	20.96	674.20	0.00			

Annual Amortization Schedules

Based on a Mortgage of $ 10,000.00

6.00 %

30 YEAR TERM:
Monthly Payment = 59.48
Annual Payment = 713.76

25 YEAR TERM:
Monthly Payment = 63.98
Annual Payment = 767.76

YR	30 YR INTER PD DUR YEAR	30 YR PRINCP PD DUR YEAR	30 YR MORTG BAL END OF YR	25 YR INTER PD DUR YEAR	25 YR PRINCP PD DUR YEAR	25 YR MORTG BAL END OF YR
1	589.26	124.50	9875.50	587.79	179.97	9820.03
2	581.68	132.08	9743.42	576.83	190.93	9629.10
3	573.64	140.12	9603.30	565.20	202.56	9426.54
4	565.10	148.66	9454.64	552.87	214.89	9211.65
5	556.05	157.71	9296.93	539.78	227.98	8983.67
6	546.44	167.32	9129.61	525.90	241.86	8741.81
7	536.25	177.51	8952.10	511.17	256.59	8485.21
8	525.44	188.32	8763.79	495.54	272.22	8212.99
9	513.98	199.78	8564.00	478.96	288.80	7924.19
10	501.81	211.95	8352.05	461.37	306.39	7617.81
11	488.90	224.86	8127.19	442.71	325.05	7292.76
12	475.21	238.55	7888.64	422.92	344.84	6947.92
13	460.68	253.08	7635.56	401.92	365.84	6582.08
14	445.27	268.49	7367.06	379.64	388.12	6193.96
15	428.92	284.84	7082.22	356.00	411.76	5782.20
16	411.57	302.19	6780.03	330.93	436.83	5345.37
17	393.16	320.60	6459.43	304.32	463.44	4881.93
18	373.64	340.12	6119.31	276.10	491.66	4390.27
19	352.93	360.83	5758.48	246.16	521.60	3868.67
20	330.95	382.81	5375.67	214.39	553.37	3315.31
21	307.64	406.12	4969.55	180.69	587.07	2728.24
22	282.91	430.85	4538.70	144.94	622.82	2105.42
23	256.67	457.09	4081.61	107.01	660.75	1444.67
24	228.83	484.93	3596.68	66.77	700.99	743.68
25	199.30	514.46	3082.21	24.08	743.68	0.00
26	167.97	545.79	2536.42			
27	134.73	579.03	1957.39			
28	99.47	614.29	1343.10			
29	62.06	651.70	691.39			
30	22.37	691.39	0.00			

6.25 %

30 YEAR TERM:
Monthly Payment = 61.05
Annual Payment = 732.60

25 YEAR TERM:
Monthly Payment = 65.47
Annual Payment = 785.64

YR	30 YR INTER PD DUR YEAR	30 YR PRINCP PD DUR YEAR	30 YR MORTG BAL END OF YR	25 YR INTER PD DUR YEAR	25 YR PRINCP PD DUR YEAR	25 YR MORTG BAL END OF YR
1	613.65	118.95	9881.05	612.11	173.53	9826.47
2	606.10	126.50	9754.55	601.10	184.54	9641.93
3	598.07	134.53	9620.01	589.38	196.26	9445.67
4	589.53	143.07	9476.94	576.92	208.72	9236.95
5	580.45	152.15	9324.79	563.68	221.96	9014.99
6	570.79	161.81	9162.98	549.59	236.05	8778.94
7	560.52	172.08	8990.89	534.60	251.04	8527.90
8	549.59	183.01	8807.89	518.67	266.97	8260.93
9	537.98	194.62	8613.26	501.72	283.92	7977.01
10	525.62	206.98	8406.29	483.70	301.94	7675.06
11	512.48	220.12	8186.17	464.53	321.11	7353.96
12	498.51	234.09	7952.08	444.15	341.49	7012.47
13	483.65	248.95	7703.14	422.47	363.17	6649.30
14	467.85	264.75	7438.39	399.42	386.22	6263.08
15	451.05	281.55	7156.83	374.90	410.74	5852.34
16	433.17	299.43	6857.41	348.83	436.81	5415.54
17	414.17	318.43	6538.98	321.11	464.53	4951.00
18	393.95	338.65	6200.33	291.62	494.02	4456.98
19	372.46	360.14	5840.19	260.26	525.38	3931.60
20	349.60	383.00	5457.19	226.91	558.73	3372.87
21	325.29	407.31	5049.87	191.44	594.20	2778.67
22	299.43	433.17	4616.70	153.73	631.91	2146.76
23	271.94	460.66	4156.04	113.61	672.03	1474.73
24	242.69	489.91	3666.13	70.96	714.68	760.05
25	211.60	521.00	3145.13	25.59	760.05	0.00
26	178.52	554.08	2591.05			
27	143.35	589.25	2001.81			
28	105.95	626.65	1375.16			
29	66.17	666.43	708.73			
30	23.87	708.73	0.00			

Annual Amortization Schedules

Based on a Mortgage of $ 10,000.00

6.50 %

30 YEAR TERM:
Monthly Payment = 62.64
Annual Payment = 751.68

25 YEAR TERM
Monthly Payment = 66.9
Annual Payment = 803.7

YR	INTER PD DUR YEAR	PRINCP PD DUR YEAR	MORTG BAL END OF YR	INTER PD DUR YEAR	PRINCP PD DUR YEAR	MORTG BAL END OF YR
1	638.06	113.62	9886.38	636.48	167.28	9832.72
2	630.56	121.12	9765.26	625.43	178.33	9654.39
3	622.56	129.12	9636.14	613.65	190.11	9464.28
4	614.03	137.65	9498.49	601.09	202.67	9261.61
5	604.94	146.74	9351.75	587.70	216.06	9045.56
6	595.24	156.44	9195.31	573.43	230.33	8815.23
7	584.91	166.77	9028.54	558.22	245.54	8569.69
8	573.89	177.79	8850.76	542.00	261.76	8307.93
9	562.15	189.53	8661.23	524.71	279.05	8028.87
10	549.63	202.05	8459.18	506.27	297.49	7731.39
11	536.28	215.40	8243.78	486.62	317.14	7414.25
12	522.06	229.62	8014.16	465.67	338.09	7076.17
13	506.89	244.79	7769.36	443.34	360.42	6715.75
14	490.72	260.96	7508.40	419.53	384.23	6331.52
15	473.48	278.20	7230.20	394.15	409.61	5921.92
16	455.10	296.58	6933.62	367.10	436.66	5485.25
17	435.51	316.17	6617.45	338.25	465.51	5019.74
18	414.63	337.05	6280.40	307.50	496.26	4523.49
19	392.36	359.32	5921.08	274.72	529.04	3994.45
20	368.63	383.05	5538.03	239.78	563.98	3430.46
21	343.32	408.36	5129.67	202.52	601.24	2829.23
22	316.35	435.33	4694.34	162.81	640.95	2188.27
23	287.59	464.09	4230.25	120.47	683.29	1504.98
24	256.94	494.74	3735.51	75.33	728.43	776.55
25	224.26	527.42	3208.08	27.21	776.55	0.00
26	189.42	562.26	2645.82			
27	152.28	599.40	2046.42			
28	112.68	639.00	1407.42			
29	70.47	681.21	726.21			
30	25.47	726.21	0.00			

6.75 %

30 YEAR TERM:
Monthly Payment = 64.24
Annual Payment = 770.88

25 YEAR TERM
Monthly Payment = 68.5
Annual Payment = 822.0

YR	INTER PD DUR YEAR	PRINCP PD DUR YEAR	MORTG BAL END OF YR	INTER PD DUR YEAR	PRINCP PD DUR YEAR	MORTG BAL END OF YR
1	662.40	108.48	9891.52	660.78	161.22	9838.78
2	654.95	115.93	9775.58	649.71	172.29	9666.49
3	646.99	123.89	9651.70	637.89	184.11	9482.38
4	638.49	132.39	9519.31	625.25	196.75	9285.63
5	629.40	141.48	9377.83	611.75	210.25	9075.38
6	619.69	151.19	9226.64	597.31	224.69	8850.69
7	609.31	161.57	9065.07	581.89	240.11	8610.58
8	598.22	172.66	8892.41	565.41	256.59	8353.99
9	586.37	184.51	8707.90	547.80	274.20	8079.79
10	573.71	197.17	8510.73	528.98	293.02	7786.77
11	560.17	210.71	8300.02	508.87	313.13	7473.64
12	545.71	225.17	8074.85	487.37	334.63	7139.01
13	530.26	240.62	7834.23	464.40	357.60	6781.41
14	513.74	257.14	7577.09	439.86	382.14	6399.27
15	496.09	274.79	7302.30	413.63	408.37	5990.90
16	477.23	293.65	7008.65	385.60	436.40	5554.50
17	457.07	313.81	6694.84	355.64	466.36	5088.14
18	435.53	335.35	6359.49	323.63	498.37	4589.78
19	412.51	358.37	6001.12	289.43	532.57	4057.20
20	387.92	382.96	5618.16	252.87	569.13	3488.07
21	361.63	409.25	5208.91	213.81	608.19	2879.88
22	333.54	437.34	4771.57	172.06	649.94	2229.94
23	303.52	467.36	4304.21	127.45	694.55	1535.39
24	271.44	499.44	3804.77	79.78	742.22	793.17
25	237.16	533.72	3271.06	28.83	793.17	0.00
26	200.53	570.35	2700.70			
27	161.38	609.50	2091.20			
28	119.54	651.34	1439.86			
29	74.84	696.04	743.82			
30	27.06	743.82	0.00			

Annual Amortization Schedules

Based on a Mortgage of $ 10,000.00

7.00 %

0 YEAR TERM:
lonthly Payment = 65.86
nnual Payment = 790.32

25 YEAR TERM:
Monthly Payment = 70.04
Annual Payment = 840.48

R	INTER PD DUR YEAR	PRINCP PD DUR YEAR	MORTG BAL END OF YR	INTER PD DUR YEAR	PRINCP PD DUR YEAR	MORTG BAL END OF YR
1	686.77	103.55	9896.45	685.13	155.35	9844.65
2	679.39	110.93	9785.52	674.07	166.41	9678.24
3	671.49	118.83	9666.69	662.22	178.26	9499.98
4	663.03	127.29	9539.39	649.52	190.96	9309.02
5	653.96	136.36	9403.03	635.92	204.56	9104.46
6	644.25	146.07	9256.96	621.35	219.13	8885.33
7	633.84	156.48	9100.49	605.74	234.74	8650.59
8	622.70	167.62	8932.86	589.02	251.46	8399.13
9	610.76	179.56	8753.30	571.11	269.37	8129.76
0	597.97	192.35	8560.95	551.93	288.55	7841.21
1	584.27	206.05	8354.90	531.37	309.11	7532.11
2	569.59	220.73	8134.18	509.36	331.12	7200.98
3	553.87	236.45	7897.73	485.77	354.71	6846.28
4	537.03	253.29	7644.45	460.51	379.97	6466.31
5	518.99	271.33	7373.12	433.45	407.03	6059.27
6	499.67	290.65	7082.46	404.46	436.02	5623.25
7	478.97	311.35	6771.11	373.40	467.08	5156.17
8	456.79	333.53	6437.58	340.13	500.35	4655.82
9	433.03	357.29	6080.29	304.50	535.99	4119.84
0	407.59	382.73	5697.56	266.32	574.16	3545.68
1	380.33	409.99	5287.56	225.42	615.06	2930.62
2	351.12	439.20	4848.36	181.62	658.86	2271.76
3	319.84	470.48	4377.89	134.69	705.79	1565.97
4	286.33	503.99	3873.90	84.42	756.06	809.91
5	250.43	539.89	3334.01	30.57	809.91	0.00
6	211.98	578.34	2755.67			
7	170.79	619.53	2136.14			
8	126.66	663.66	1472.49			
9	79.39	710.93	761.56			
0	28.76	761.56	0.00			

7.25 %

0 YEAR TERM:
lonthly Payment = 67.49
nnual Payment = 809.88

25 YEAR TERM:
Monthly Payment = 71.59
Annual Payment = 859.08

R	INTER PD DUR YEAR	PRINCP PD DUR YEAR	MORTG BAL END OF YR	INTER PD DUR YEAR	PRINCP PD DUR YEAR	MORTG BAL END OF YR
1	711.06	98.82	9901.18	709.43	149.65	9850.35
2	703.77	106.11	9795.07	698.38	160.70	9689.65
3	695.94	113.94	9681.13	686.52	172.56	9517.09
4	687.53	122.35	9558.78	673.78	185.30	9331.79
5	678.49	131.39	9427.39	660.10	198.98	9132.81
6	668.80	141.08	9286.31	645.42	213.66	8919.15
7	658.38	151.50	9134.81	629.65	229.43	8689.71
8	647.20	162.68	8972.13	612.71	246.37	8443.34
9	635.19	174.69	8797.44	594.52	264.56	8178.79
0	622.30	187.58	8609.86	575.00	284.08	7894.70
1	608.45	201.43	8408.43	554.03	305.05	7589.65
2	593.58	216.30	8192.13	531.51	327.57	7262.08
3	577.62	232.26	7959.87	507.33	351.75	6910.33
4	560.47	249.41	7710.46	481.37	377.71	6532.62
5	542.06	267.82	7442.65	453.49	405.59	6127.02
6	522.29	287.59	7155.06	423.55	435.53	5691.49
7	501.07	308.81	6846.25	391.40	467.68	5223.81
8	478.27	331.61	6514.64	356.88	502.20	4721.61
9	453.79	356.09	6158.55	319.81	539.27	4182.33
0	427.51	382.37	5776.18	280.00	579.08	3603.25
1	399.29	410.59	5365.59	237.26	621.82	2981.43
2	368.98	440.90	4924.69	191.36	667.72	2313.71
3	336.43	473.45	4451.24	142.07	717.01	1596.70
4	301.49	508.39	3942.85	89.15	769.93	826.77
5	263.96	545.92	3396.93	32.31	826.77	0.00
6	223.66	586.22	2810.71			
7	180.39	629.49	2181.22			
8	133.93	675.95	1505.27			
9	84.03	725.85	779.42			
0	30.46	779.42	0.00			

Annual Amortization Schedules

Based on a Mortgage of $ 10,000.00

7.50 %

30 YEAR TERM:
Monthly Payment = 69.14
Annual Payment = 829.68

25 YEAR TERM
Monthly Payment = 73.1
Annual Payment = 877.9

YR	INTER PD DUR YEAR	PRINCP PD DUR YEAR	MORTG BAL END OF YR	INTER PD DUR YEAR	PRINCP PD DUR YEAR	MORTG BA END OF YF
1	735.41	94.27	9905.73	733.78	144.14	9855.86
2	728.21	101.47	9804.26	722.77	155.15	9700.71
3	720.46	109.22	9695.03	710.92	167.00	9533.71
4	712.11	117.57	9577.46	698.16	179.76	9353.94
5	703.13	126.55	9450.91	684.42	193.50	9160.44
6	693.46	136.22	9314.69	669.64	208.28	8952.16
7	683.05	146.63	9168.06	653.72	224.20	8727.96
8	671.85	157.83	9010.22	636.59	241.33	8486.63
9	659.79	169.89	8840.33	618.15	259.77	8226.86
10	646.80	182.88	8657.45	598.30	279.62	7947.25
11	632.83	196.85	8460.61	576.94	300.98	7646.27
12	617.79	211.89	8248.72	553.94	323.98	7322.29
13	601.60	228.08	8020.64	529.19	348.73	6973.56
14	584.18	245.50	7775.13	502.54	375.38	6598.18
15	565.42	264.26	7510.87	473.86	404.06	6194.12
16	545.23	284.45	7226.42	442.99	434.93	5759.19
17	523.49	306.19	6920.23	409.76	468.16	5291.03
18	500.10	329.58	6590.65	373.99	503.93	4787.10
19	474.92	354.76	6235.88	335.48	542.44	4244.67
20	447.81	381.87	5854.01	294.04	583.88	3660.79
21	418.63	411.05	5442.96	249.43	628.49	3032.29
22	387.22	442.46	5000.51	201.41	676.51	2355.78
23	353.42	476.26	4524.25	149.72	728.20	1627.58
24	317.03	512.65	4011.60	94.08	783.84	843.73
25	277.86	551.82	3459.78	34.19	843.73	0.00
26	235.70	593.98	2865.79			
27	190.31	639.37	2226.43			
28	141.46	688.22	1538.21			
29	88.88	740.80	797.40			
30	32.28	797.40	0.00			

7.75 %

30 YEAR TERM:
Monthly Payment = 70.80
Annual Payment = 849.60

25 YEAR TERM
Monthly Payment = 74.7
Annual Payment = 896.7

YR	INTER PD DUR YEAR	PRINCP PD DUR YEAR	MORTG BAL END OF YR	INTER PD DUR YEAR	PRINCP PD DUR YEAR	MORTG BA END OF YF
1	759.70	89.90	9910.10	757.96	138.80	9861.20
2	752.59	97.01	9813.09	747.00	149.76	9711.44
3	744.93	104.67	9708.42	735.17	161.59	9549.85
4	736.66	112.94	9595.48	722.40	174.36	9375.49
5	727.74	121.86	9473.62	708.63	188.13	9187.36
6	718.11	131.49	9342.13	693.76	203.00	8984.37
7	707.72	141.88	9200.25	677.73	219.03	8765.33
8	696.51	153.09	9047.16	660.42	236.34	8529.00
9	684.42	165.18	8881.98	641.75	255.01	8273.99
10	671.37	178.23	8703.75	621.61	275.15	7998.84
11	657.29	192.31	8511.44	599.87	296.89	7701.95
12	642.10	207.50	8303.94	576.41	320.35	7381.60
13	625.70	223.90	8080.04	551.11	345.65	7035.95
14	608.02	241.58	7838.46	523.80	372.96	6662.99
15	588.93	260.67	7577.79	494.34	402.42	6260.56
16	568.34	281.26	7296.53	462.54	434.22	5826.35
17	546.12	303.48	6993.05	428.24	468.52	5357.83
18	522.14	327.46	6665.59	391.23	505.53	4852.29
19	496.27	353.33	6312.26	351.29	545.47	4306.82
20	468.36	381.24	5931.02	308.19	588.57	3718.25
21	438.24	411.36	5519.66	261.70	635.06	3083.19
22	405.74	443.86	5075.80	211.53	685.23	2397.96
23	370.68	478.92	4596.87	157.39	739.37	1658.59
24	332.84	516.76	4080.11	98.98	797.78	860.81
25	292.02	557.58	3522.53	35.95	860.81	0.00
26	247.97	601.63	2920.90			
27	200.44	649.16	2271.73			
28	149.15	700.45	1571.28			
29	93.81	755.79	815.49			
30	34.11	815.49	0.00			

Annual Amortization Schedules

Based on a Mortgage of $ 10,000.00

8.00 %

30 YEAR TERM:
Monthly Payment = 72.47
Annual Payment = 869.64

25 YEAR TERM:
Monthly Payment = 76.32
Annual Payment = 915.84

YR	INTER PD DUR YEAR	PRINCP PD DUR YEAR	MORTG BAL END OF YR	INTER PD DUR YEAR	PRINCP DUR YEAR	MORTG BAL END OF YR
1	783.92	85.72	9914.28	782.22	133.62	9866.38
2	776.93	92.71	9821.57	771.31	144.53	9721.85
3	769.36	100.28	9721.29	759.52	156.32	9565.53
4	761.18	108.46	9612.83	746.76	169.08	9396.45
5	752.33	117.31	9495.52	732.97	182.87	9213.58
6	742.76	126.88	9368.64	718.04	197.80	9015.78
7	732.40	137.24	9231.40	701.90	213.94	8801.84
8	721.20	148.44	9082.97	684.45	231.39	8570.45
9	709.09	160.55	8922.42	665.56	250.28	8320.17
10	695.99	173.65	8748.77	645.14	270.70	8049.48
11	681.82	187.82	8560.95	623.05	292.79	7756.69
12	666.50	203.14	8357.81	599.16	316.68	7440.01
13	649.92	219.72	8138.09	573.32	342.52	7097.49
14	631.99	237.65	7900.44	545.37	370.47	6727.02
15	612.60	257.04	7643.40	515.14	400.70	6326.32
16	591.62	278.02	7365.38	482.44	433.40	5892.93
17	568.94	300.70	7064.68	447.08	468.76	5424.17
18	544.40	325.24	6739.44	408.83	507.01	4917.15
19	517.86	351.78	6387.66	367.46	548.38	4368.77
20	489.16	380.48	6007.18	322.71	593.13	3775.64
21	458.11	411.53	5595.64	274.31	641.53	3134.11
22	424.53	445.11	5150.53	221.96	693.88	2440.23
23	388.21	481.43	4669.10	165.34	750.50	1689.72
24	348.92	520.72	4148.38	104.10	811.74	877.98
25	306.43	563.21	3585.17	37.86	877.98	0.00
26	260.47	609.17	2976.00			
27	210.76	658.88	2317.12			
28	157.00	712.64	1604.48			
29	98.85	770.79	833.69			
30	35.95	833.69	0.00			

8.25 %

30 YEAR TERM:
Monthly Payment = 74.16
Annual Payment = 889.92

25 YEAR TERM:
Monthly Payment = 77.92
Annual Payment = 935.04

YR	INTER PD DUR YEAR	PRINCP PD DUR YEAR	MORTG BAL END OF YR	INTER PD DUR YEAR	PRINCP PD DUR YEAR	MORTG BAL END OF YR
1	808.22	81.70	9918.30	806.42	128.62	9871.38
2	801.34	88.58	9829.71	795.59	139.45	9731.93
3	793.88	96.04	9733.67	783.85	151.19	9580.74
4	785.79	104.13	9629.54	771.12	163.92	9416.82
5	777.02	112.90	9516.65	757.32	177.72	9239.10
6	767.52	122.40	9394.25	742.35	192.69	9046.41
7	757.21	132.71	9261.54	726.13	208.91	8837.50
8	746.04	143.88	9117.65	708.54	226.50	8610.99
9	733.92	156.00	8961.66	689.46	245.58	8365.42
10	720.79	169.13	8792.52	668.79	266.25	8099.16
11	706.55	183.37	8609.15	646.37	288.67	7810.49
12	691.11	198.82	8410.33	622.06	312.98	7497.51
13	674.36	215.56	8194.78	595.71	339.33	7158.18
14	656.21	233.71	7961.07	567.14	367.90	6790.27
15	636.54	253.38	7707.69	536.16	398.88	6391.39
16	615.20	274.72	7432.97	502.57	432.47	5958.92
17	592.07	297.85	7135.12	466.16	468.88	5490.04
18	566.99	322.93	6812.19	426.68	508.36	4981.67
19	539.80	350.12	6462.06	383.87	551.17	4430.50
20	510.32	379.60	6082.46	337.46	597.58	3832.92
21	478.35	411.57	5670.90	287.14	647.90	3185.03
22	443.70	446.22	5224.68	232.59	702.45	2482.58
23	406.13	483.79	4740.88	173.44	761.60	1720.98
24	365.39	524.53	4216.35	109.31	825.73	895.25
25	321.22	568.70	3647.66	39.79	895.25	0.00
26	273.34	616.58	3031.08			
27	221.42	668.50	2362.58			
28	165.13	724.79	1637.79			
29	104.11	785.81	851.98			
30	37.94	851.98	0.00			

Annual Amortization Schedules

Based on a Mortgage of $ 10,000.00

8.50 %

30 YEAR TERM:
Monthly Payment = 75.85
Annual Payment = 910.20

25 YEAR TERM:
Monthly Payment = 79.54
Annual Payment = 954.48

YR	30 YR INTER PD DUR YEAR	30 YR PRINCP PD DUR YEAR	30 YR MORTG BAL END OF YR	25 YR INTER PD DUR YEAR	25 YR PRINCP PD DUR YEAR	25 YR MORTG BAL END OF YR
1	832.34	77.86	9922.14	830.70	123.78	9876.22
2	825.59	84.61	9837.53	819.96	134.52	9741.70
3	818.24	91.96	9745.57	808.28	146.20	9595.50
4	810.26	99.94	9645.63	795.59	158.89	9436.62
5	801.58	108.62	9537.01	781.80	172.68	9263.93
6	792.15	118.05	9418.97	766.81	187.67	9076.26
7	781.91	128.29	9290.67	750.52	203.96	8872.30
8	770.77	139.43	9151.24	732.81	221.67	8650.63
9	758.67	151.53	8999.71	713.57	240.91	8409.72
10	745.51	164.69	8835.03	692.66	261.82	8147.90
11	731.22	178.98	8656.04	669.93	284.55	7863.35
12	715.68	194.52	8461.52	645.23	309.25	7554.10
13	698.79	211.40	8250.12	618.38	336.10	7218.00
14	680.44	229.76	8020.36	589.21	365.27	6852.73
15	660.50	249.70	7770.66	557.50	396.98	6455.75
16	638.82	271.38	7499.29	523.04	431.44	6024.31
17	615.27	294.93	7204.35	485.59	468.89	5555.42
18	589.66	320.54	6883.82	444.89	509.59	5045.83
19	561.84	348.36	6535.46	400.65	553.83	4492.00
20	531.60	378.60	6156.86	352.57	601.91	3890.09
21	498.74	411.46	5745.39	300.33	654.15	3235.94
22	463.02	447.18	5298.21	243.54	710.94	2525.00
23	424.20	486.00	4812.21	181.83	772.65	1752.34
24	382.01	528.19	4284.02	114.76	839.72	912.62
25	336.16	574.04	3709.98	41.86	912.62	0.00
26	286.33	623.87	3086.12			
27	232.18	678.02	2408.09			
28	173.32	736.88	1671.21			
29	109.35	800.85	870.36			
30	39.83	870.36	0.00			

8.75 %

30 YEAR TERM:
Monthly Payment = 77.56
Annual Payment = 930.72

25 YEAR TERM:
Monthly Payment = 81.16
Annual Payment = 973.92

YR	30 YR INTER PD DUR YEAR	30 YR PRINCP PD DUR YEAR	30 YR MORTG BAL END OF YR	25 YR INTER PD DUR YEAR	25 YR PRINCP PD DUR YEAR	25 YR MORTG BAL END OF YR
1	856.55	74.17	9925.83	854.83	119.09	9880.91
2	849.92	80.80	9845.03	844.18	129.74	9751.17
3	842.69	88.03	9757.00	832.58	141.34	9609.82
4	834.82	95.90	9661.11	819.94	153.98	9455.84
5	826.25	104.47	9556.64	806.17	167.75	9288.10
6	816.91	113.81	9442.82	791.17	182.75	9105.35
7	806.73	123.99	9318.83	774.83	199.09	8906.26
8	795.64	135.08	9183.76	757.03	216.89	8689.37
9	783.57	147.15	9036.61	737.64	236.28	8453.09
10	770.41	160.31	8876.29	716.51	257.41	8195.69
11	756.08	174.64	8701.65	693.50	280.42	7915.26
12	740.46	190.26	8511.39	668.42	305.50	7609.76
13	723.45	207.27	8304.12	641.11	332.81	7276.95
14	704.91	225.81	8078.31	611.35	362.57	6914.38
15	684.72	246.00	7832.32	578.93	394.99	6519.39
16	662.73	267.99	7564.33	543.61	430.31	6089.08
17	638.77	291.95	7272.37	505.14	468.78	5620.30
18	612.66	318.06	6954.32	463.22	510.70	5109.60
19	584.22	346.50	6607.82	417.56	556.36	4553.23
20	553.24	377.48	6230.34	367.81	606.11	3947.12
21	519.49	411.23	5819.11	313.62	660.30	3286.82
22	482.72	448.00	5371.11	254.57	719.35	2567.47
23	442.66	488.06	4883.06	190.25	783.67	1783.81
24	399.02	531.70	4351.36	120.18	853.74	930.07
25	351.48	579.24	3772.12	43.85	930.07	0.00
26	299.69	631.03	3141.09			
27	243.27	687.45	2453.64			
28	181.80	748.92	1704.72			
29	114.84	815.88	888.84			
30	41.88	888.84	0.00			

Annual Amortization Schedules

Based on a Mortgage of $ 10,000.00

9.00 %

30 YEAR TERM:
Monthly Payment = 79.28
Annual Payment = 951.36

25 YEAR TERM:
Monthly Payment = 82.80
Annual Payment = 993.60

YR	30 YR INTER PD DUR YEAR	30 YR PRINCP PD DUR YEAR	30 YR MORTG BAL END OF YR	25 YR INTER PD DUR YEAR	25 YR PRINCP PD DUR YEAR	25 YR MORTG BAL END OF YR
1	880.72	70.64	9929.36	879.04	114.56	9885.44
2	874.22	77.14	9852.22	868.49	125.11	9760.33
3	867.12	84.24	9767.98	856.98	136.62	9623.71
4	859.37	91.99	9675.99	844.41	149.19	9474.52
5	850.90	100.46	9575.53	830.68	162.92	9311.60
6	841.66	109.70	9465.83	815.69	177.91	9133.68
7	831.56	119.80	9346.04	799.31	194.29	8939.40
8	820.54	130.82	9215.22	781.43	212.17	8727.23
9	808.50	142.86	9072.36	761.91	231.69	8495.54
10	795.35	156.01	8916.35	740.59	253.01	8242.53
11	781.00	170.36	8745.99	717.30	276.30	7966.23
12	765.32	186.04	8559.95	691.88	301.72	7664.51
13	748.20	203.16	8356.79	664.11	329.49	7335.02
14	729.50	221.86	8134.93	633.79	359.81	6975.21
15	709.09	242.27	7892.66	600.68	392.92	6582.29
16	686.79	264.57	7628.09	564.52	429.08	6153.22
17	662.45	288.91	7339.18	525.04	468.56	5684.65
18	635.86	315.50	7023.68	481.92	511.68	5172.97
19	606.82	344.54	6679.14	434.83	558.77	4614.20
20	575.12	376.24	6302.90	383.41	610.19	4004.01
21	540.49	410.87	5892.03	327.25	666.35	3337.66
22	502.68	448.68	5443.36	265.93	727.67	2609.99
23	461.40	489.96	4953.39	198.97	794.63	1815.36
24	416.31	535.05	4418.34	125.85	867.75	947.61
25	367.07	584.29	3834.05	45.99	947.61	0.00
26	313.30	638.06	3195.99			
27	254.58	696.78	2499.21			
28	190.46	760.90	1738.31			
29	120.44	830.92	907.39			
30	43.97	907.39	0.00			

9.25 %

30 YEAR TERM:
Monthly Payment = 81.01
Annual Payment = 972.12

25 YEAR TERM:
Monthly Payment = 84.44
Annual Payment = 1013.28

YR	30 YR INTER PD DUR YEAR	30 YR PRINCP PD DUR YEAR	30 YR MORTG BAL END OF YR	25 YR INTER PD DUR YEAR	25 YR PRINCP PD DUR YEAR	25 YR MORTG BAL END OF YR
1	904.86	67.26	9932.74	903.09	110.19	9889.81
2	898.49	73.63	9859.11	892.67	120.61	9769.20
3	891.53	80.59	9778.52	881.25	132.03	9637.17
4	883.90	88.22	9690.30	868.76	144.52	9492.65
5	875.55	96.57	9593.73	855.08	158.20	9334.44
6	866.41	105.71	9488.02	840.11	173.17	9161.27
7	856.41	115.71	9372.30	823.72	189.56	8971.71
8	845.45	126.67	9245.64	805.78	207.50	8764.20
9	833.47	138.65	9106.99	786.14	227.14	8537.06
10	820.35	151.77	8955.21	764.64	248.64	8288.43
11	805.98	166.14	8789.07	741.11	272.17	8016.26
12	790.26	181.86	8607.21	715.35	297.93	7718.33
13	773.05	199.07	8408.14	687.16	326.12	7392.21
14	754.21	217.91	8190.23	656.30	356.98	7035.23
15	733.58	238.54	7951.69	622.51	390.77	6644.46
16	711.01	261.11	7690.58	585.53	427.75	6216.71
17	686.30	285.82	7404.76	545.05	468.23	5748.47
18	659.25	312.87	7091.89	500.73	512.55	5235.93
19	629.64	342.48	6749.41	452.23	561.05	4674.87
20	597.23	374.89	6374.51	399.13	614.15	4060.72
21	561.75	410.37	5964.14	341.01	672.27	3388.45
22	522.91	449.21	5514.93	277.38	735.90	2652.55
23	480.40	491.72	5023.20	207.74	805.54	1847.01
24	433.86	538.26	4484.94	131.50	881.78	965.23
25	382.92	589.20	3895.74	48.05	965.23	0.00
26	327.16	644.96	3250.78			
27	266.12	706.00	2544.78			
28	199.30	772.82	1771.97			
29	126.17	845.95	926.01			
30	46.11	926.01	0.00			

Annual Amortization Schedules

Based on a Mortgage of $ 10,000.00

9.50 %

30 YEAR TERM:
Monthly Payment = 82.76
Annual Payment = 993.12

25 YEAR TERM:
Monthly Payment = 86.10
Annual Payment = 1033.20

YR	30 YR INTER PD DUR YEAR	30 YR PRINCP PD DUR YEAR	30 YR MORTG BAL END OF YR	25 YR INTER PD DUR YEAR	25 YR PRINCP PD DUR YEAR	25 YR MORTG BAL END OF YR
1	929.09	64.03	9935.97	927.24	105.96	9894.04
2	922.87	70.25	9865.72	916.94	116.26	9777.78
3	916.03	77.09	9788.63	905.63	127.57	9650.21
4	908.54	84.58	9704.05	893.23	139.97	9510.24
5	900.31	92.81	9611.24	879.61	153.59	9356.65
6	891.28	101.84	9509.40	864.67	168.53	9188.13
7	881.38	111.74	9397.66	848.28	184.92	9003.21
8	870.51	122.61	9275.05	830.30	202.90	8800.31
9	858.59	134.53	9140.52	810.57	222.63	8577.68
10	845.50	147.62	8992.90	788.91	244.29	8333.39
11	831.15	161.97	8830.92	765.16	268.04	8065.35
12	815.39	177.73	8653.20	739.09	294.11	7771.23
13	798.11	195.01	8458.19	710.48	322.72	7448.51
14	779.14	213.98	8244.21	679.10	354.10	7094.41
15	758.33	234.79	8009.42	644.66	388.54	6705.87
16	735.50	257.62	7751.79	606.87	426.33	6279.54
17	710.44	282.68	7469.12	565.41	467.79	5811.74
18	682.95	310.17	7158.94	519.91	513.29	5298.45
19	652.78	340.34	6818.61	469.99	563.21	4735.24
20	619.68	373.44	6445.17	415.21	617.99	4117.25
21	583.36	409.76	6035.41	355.11	678.09	3439.16
22	543.51	449.61	5585.80	289.16	744.04	2695.13
23	499.78	493.34	5092.47	216.80	816.40	1878.72
24	451.80	541.32	4551.15	137.40	895.80	982.92
25	399.16	593.96	3957.19	50.28	982.92	0.00
26	341.39	651.73	3305.46			
27	278.01	715.11	2590.35			
28	208.46	784.66	1805.69			
29	132.14	860.98	944.71			
30	48.41	944.71	0.00			

9.75 %

30 YEAR TERM:
Monthly Payment = 84.51
Annual Payment = 1014.12

25 YEAR TERM:
Monthly Payment = 87.77
Annual Payment = 1053.24

YR	30 YR INTER PD DUR YEAR	30 YR PRINCP PD DUR YEAR	30 YR MORTG BAL END OF YR	25 YR INTER PD DUR YEAR	25 YR PRINCP PD DUR YEAR	25 YR MORTG BAL END OF YR
1	953.19	60.93	9939.07	951.37	101.87	9898.13
2	947.10	67.02	9872.04	941.20	112.04	9786.09
3	940.41	73.71	9798.33	930.01	123.23	9662.85
4	933.04	81.08	9717.25	917.70	135.54	9527.31
5	924.95	89.17	9628.08	904.16	149.08	9378.23
6	916.04	98.08	9530.00	889.27	163.97	9214.26
7	906.24	107.88	9422.12	872.89	180.35	9033.91
8	895.47	118.65	9303.47	854.88	198.36	8835.55
9	883.62	130.50	9172.97	835.07	218.17	8617.38
10	870.58	143.54	9029.43	813.28	239.96	8377.42
11	856.25	157.87	8871.56	789.31	263.93	8113.49
12	840.48	173.64	8697.92	762.95	290.29	7823.21
13	823.14	190.98	8506.94	733.96	319.28	7503.93
14	804.06	210.06	8296.88	702.07	351.17	7152.76
15	783.08	231.04	8065.85	667.00	386.24	6766.51
16	760.01	254.11	7811.74	628.42	424.82	6341.70
17	734.63	279.49	7532.25	585.99	467.25	5874.45
18	706.71	307.41	7224.84	539.32	513.92	5360.53
19	676.01	338.11	6886.73	488.00	565.24	4795.29
20	642.24	371.88	6514.85	431.54	621.70	4173.59
21	605.10	409.02	6105.83	369.45	683.79	3489.80
22	564.25	449.87	5655.96	301.15	752.09	2737.71
23	519.32	494.80	5161.16	226.04	827.20	1910.51
24	469.90	544.22	4616.94	143.42	909.82	1000.69
25	415.54	598.58	4018.37	52.55	1000.69	0.00
26	355.76	658.36	3360.01			
27	290.01	724.11	2635.89			
28	217.68	796.44	1839.45			
29	138.14	875.98	963.47			
30	50.65	963.47	0.00			

Annual Amortization Schedules

Based on a Mortgage of $ 10,000.00

10.00 %

30 YEAR TERM:
Monthly Payment = 86.27
Annual Payment = 1035.24

25 YEAR TERM:
Monthly Payment = 89.45
Annual Payment = 1073.40

	30 YEAR TERM			25 YEAR TERM		
YR	INTER PD DUR YEAR	PRINCP PD DUR YEAR	MORTG BAL END OF YR	INTER PD DUR YEAR	PRINCP PD DUR YEAR	MORTG BAL END OF YR
1	977.26	57.98	9942.02	975.48	97.92	9902.08
2	971.32	63.92	9878.10	965.44	107.96	9794.12
3	964.77	70.47	9807.63	954.37	119.03	9675.09
4	957.54	77.70	9729.93	942.17	131.23	9543.86
5	949.58	85.66	9644.27	928.72	144.68	9399.19
6	940.80	94.44	9549.83	913.89	159.51	9239.68
7	931.12	104.12	9445.71	897.54	175.86	9063.83
8	920.45	114.79	9330.92	879.52	193.88	8869.94
9	908.68	126.56	9204.36	859.65	213.75	8656.19
10	895.71	139.53	9064.83	837.74	235.66	8420.53
11	881.41	153.83	8911.00	813.58	259.82	8160.71
12	865.64	169.60	8741.40	786.95	286.45	7874.26
13	848.26	186.98	8554.42	757.59	315.81	7558.45
14	829.09	206.15	8348.27	725.22	348.18	7210.26
15	807.96	227.28	8120.99	689.53	383.87	6826.39
16	784.66	250.58	7870.41	650.18	423.22	6403.17
17	758.98	276.26	7594.15	606.80	466.60	5936.58
18	730.66	304.58	7289.57	558.98	514.42	5422.15
19	699.44	335.80	6953.78	506.25	567.15	4855.00
20	665.02	370.22	6583.56	448.11	625.29	4229.71
21	627.08	408.16	6175.40	384.02	689.38	3540.34
22	585.24	450.00	5725.40	313.36	760.04	2780.30
23	539.12	496.12	5229.27	235.46	837.94	1942.36
24	488.26	546.98	4682.29	149.57	923.83	1018.52
25	432.20	603.04	4079.25	54.88	1018.52	0.00
26	370.39	664.85	3414.40			
27	302.24	733.00	2681.40			
28	227.11	808.13	1873.26			
29	144.27	890.97	982.29			
30	52.95	982.29	0.00			

10.25 %

30 YEAR TERM:
Monthly Payment = 88.04
Annual Payment = 1056.48

25 YEAR TERM:
Monthly Payment = 91.14
Annual Payment = 1093.68

	30 YEAR TERM			25 YEAR TERM		
YR	INTER PD DUR YEAR	PRINCP PD DUR YEAR	MORTG BAL END OF YR	INTER PD DUR YEAR	PRINCP PD DUR YEAR	MORTG BAL END OF YR
1	1001.33	55.15	9944.85	999.57	94.11	9905.89
2	995.53	60.95	9883.90	989.67	104.01	9801.88
3	989.12	67.36	9816.54	978.74	114.94	9686.94
4	982.04	74.44	9742.10	966.66	127.02	9559.92
5	974.22	82.26	9659.84	953.30	140.38	9419.54
6	965.57	90.91	9568.93	938.55	155.13	9264.40
7	956.01	100.47	9468.46	922.24	171.44	9092.96
8	945.45	111.03	9357.43	904.21	189.47	8903.49
9	933.78	122.70	9234.73	884.30	209.38	8694.11
10	920.88	135.60	9099.12	862.28	231.40	8462.71
11	906.62	149.86	8949.27	837.96	255.72	8206.99
12	890.87	165.61	8783.66	811.07	282.61	7924.39
13	873.46	183.02	8600.63	781.36	312.31	7612.07
14	854.22	202.26	8398.37	748.53	345.15	7266.92
15	832.95	223.53	8174.85	712.25	381.43	6885.49
16	809.46	247.02	7927.82	672.15	421.53	6463.96
17	783.49	272.99	7654.83	627.84	465.84	5998.12
18	754.79	301.69	7353.14	578.86	514.82	5483.30
19	723.07	333.41	7019.73	524.74	568.94	4914.36
20	688.02	368.46	6651.28	464.93	628.75	4285.61
21	649.29	407.19	6244.08	398.83	694.85	3590.77
22	606.48	450.00	5794.09	325.79	767.89	2822.87
23	559.18	497.30	5296.78	245.06	848.62	1974.25
24	506.90	549.58	4747.20	155.85	937.83	1036.42
25	449.12	607.36	4139.83	57.26	1036.42	0.00
26	385.27	671.21	3468.62			
27	314.71	741.77	2726.85			
28	236.73	819.75	1907.10			
29	150.55	905.93	1001.17			
30	55.31	1001.17	0.00			

Annual Amortization Schedules

Based on a Mortgage of $ 10,000.00

10.50 %

30 YEAR TERM:
Monthly Payment = 89.81
Annual Payment = 1077.72

25 YEAR TERM:
Monthly Payment = 92.83
Annual Payment = 1113.96

YR	30 YR INTER PD DUR YEAR	30 YR PRINCP PD DUR YEAR	30 YR MORTG BAL END OF YR	25 YR INTER PD DUR YEAR	25 YR PRINCP PD DUR YEAR	25 YR MORTG BAL END OF YR
1	1025.27	52.45	9947.55	1023.52	90.44	9909.56
2	1019.62	58.10	9889.45	1013.78	100.18	9809.38
3	1013.36	64.36	9825.08	1002.98	110.97	9698.41
4	1006.42	71.30	9753.78	991.03	122.93	9575.48
5	998.74	78.98	9674.80	977.78	136.18	9439.30
6	990.23	87.49	9587.30	963.11	150.85	9288.44
7	980.80	96.92	9490.38	946.85	167.11	9121.33
8	970.35	107.37	9383.02	928.84	185.12	8936.22
9	958.78	118.94	9264.08	908.90	205.06	8731.15
10	945.97	131.75	9132.33	886.80	227.16	8503.99
11	931.77	145.95	8986.38	862.32	251.64	8252.35
12	916.04	161.68	8824.70	835.20	278.76	7973.60
13	898.62	179.10	8645.61	805.17	308.79	7664.80
14	879.32	198.40	8447.21	771.89	342.07	7322.74
15	857.95	219.77	8227.44	735.03	378.93	6943.81
16	834.26	243.46	7983.98	694.20	419.76	6524.05
17	808.03	269.69	7714.29	648.97	464.99	6059.06
18	778.97	298.75	7415.54	598.86	515.10	5543.96
19	746.78	330.94	7084.60	543.36	570.60	4973.36
20	711.12	366.60	6717.99	481.87	632.09	4341.27
21	671.61	406.11	6311.89	413.76	700.20	3641.08
22	627.85	449.87	5862.02	338.31	775.65	2865.43
23	579.37	498.35	5363.67	254.73	859.23	2006.20
24	525.68	552.04	4811.63	162.14	951.82	1054.38
25	466.19	611.53	4200.10	59.58	1054.38	0.00
26	400.29	677.43	3522.67			
27	327.30	750.42	2772.24			
28	246.43	831.29	1940.96			
29	156.86	920.86	1020.09			
30	57.63	1020.09	0.00			

10.75 %

30 YEAR TERM:
Monthly Payment = 91.60
Annual Payment = 1099.20

25 YEAR TERM:
Monthly Payment = 94.54
Annual Payment = 1134.48

YR	30 YR INTER PD DUR YEAR	30 YR PRINCP PD DUR YEAR	30 YR MORTG BAL END OF YR	25 YR INTER PD DUR YEAR	25 YR PRINCP PD DUR YEAR	25 YR MORTG BAL END OF YR
1	1049.33	49.87	9950.13	1047.59	86.89	9913.11
2	1043.82	55.38	9894.75	1038.00	96.48	9816.64
3	1037.71	61.49	9833.26	1027.35	107.13	9709.51
4	1030.92	68.28	9764.98	1015.53	118.95	9590.56
5	1023.38	75.82	9689.16	1002.40	132.08	9458.47
6	1015.01	84.19	9604.98	987.81	146.67	9311.81
7	1005.72	93.48	9511.50	971.62	162.86	9148.95
8	995.40	103.80	9407.70	953.65	180.83	8968.12
9	983.94	115.26	9292.45	933.69	200.79	8767.32
10	971.22	127.98	9164.47	911.52	222.96	8544.36
11	957.09	142.11	9022.36	886.91	247.57	8296.79
12	941.41	157.79	8864.57	859.58	274.90	8021.89
13	923.99	175.21	8689.36	829.23	305.25	7716.64
14	904.65	194.55	8494.80	795.54	338.94	7377.70
15	883.17	216.03	8278.77	758.12	376.36	7001.34
16	859.32	239.88	8038.90	716.57	417.91	6583.43
17	832.84	266.36	7772.54	670.44	464.04	6119.39
18	803.44	295.76	7476.78	619.22	515.26	5604.13
19	770.79	328.41	7148.37	562.34	572.14	5031.99
20	734.54	364.66	6783.71	499.18	635.30	4396.68
21	694.28	404.92	6378.79	429.05	705.43	3691.25
22	649.59	449.61	5929.18	351.18	783.30	2907.95
23	599.95	499.25	5429.93	264.71	869.77	2038.18
24	544.84	554.36	4875.57	168.70	965.78	1072.40
25	483.65	615.55	4260.02	62.08	1072.40	0.00
26	415.70	683.50	3576.52			
27	340.25	758.95	2817.56			
28	256.46	842.74	1974.83			
29	163.44	935.76	1039.06			
30	60.14	1039.06	0.00			

Annual Amortization Schedules

Based on a Mortgage of $ 10,000.00

11.00 %

30 YEAR TERM:
Monthly Payment = 93.39
Annual Payment = 1120.68

25 YEAR TERM:
Monthly Payment = 96.25
Annual Payment = 1155.00

YR	30 YR INTER PD DUR YEAR	30 YR PRINCP PD DUR YEAR	30 YR MORTG BAL END OF YR	25 YR INTER PD DUR YEAR	25 YR PRINCP PD DUR YEAR	25 YR MORTG BAL END OF YR
1	1073.27	47.41	9952.59	1071.54	83.46	9916.54
2	1067.91	52.77	9899.82	1062.10	92.90	9823.64
3	1061.95	58.73	9841.09	1051.60	103.40	9720.25
4	1055.31	65.37	9775.72	1039.92	115.08	9605.16
5	1047.92	72.76	9702.96	1026.91	128.09	9477.07
6	1039.70	80.98	9621.97	1012.43	142.57	9334.51
7	1030.54	90.14	9531.84	996.32	158.68	9175.83
8	1020.36	100.32	9431.51	978.39	176.61	8999.21
9	1009.02	111.66	9319.85	958.42	196.58	8802.64
10	996.40	124.28	9195.56	936.21	218.79	8583.84
11	982.35	138.33	9057.23	911.48	243.52	8340.32
12	966.71	153.97	8903.27	883.95	271.05	8069.27
13	949.31	171.37	8731.90	853.32	301.68	7767.58
14	929.94	190.74	8541.16	819.22	335.78	7431.80
15	908.38	212.30	8328.86	781.27	373.73	7058.07
16	884.39	236.29	8092.57	739.03	415.97	6642.09
17	857.68	263.00	7829.58	692.01	462.99	6179.10
18	827.96	292.72	7536.85	639.68	515.32	5663.79
19	794.87	325.81	7211.05	581.44	573.56	5090.22
20	758.05	362.63	6848.41	516.61	638.39	4451.83
21	717.06	403.62	6444.80	444.46	710.54	3741.29
22	671.44	449.24	5995.56	364.15	790.85	2950.43
23	620.67	500.01	5495.55	274.76	880.24	2070.19
24	564.15	556.53	4939.02	175.27	979.73	1090.46
25	501.25	619.43	4319.59	64.54	1090.46	0.00
26	431.24	689.44	3630.15			
27	353.32	767.36	2862.79			
28	266.59	854.09	2008.70			
29	170.05	950.63	1058.07			
30	62.61	1058.07	0.00			

11.25 %

30 YEAR TERM:
Monthly Payment = 95.19
Annual Payment = 1142.28

25 YEAR TERM:
Monthly Payment = 97.98
Annual Payment = 1175.76

YR	30 YR INTER PD DUR YEAR	30 YR PRINCP PD DUR YEAR	30 YR MORTG BAL END OF YR	25 YR INTER PD DUR YEAR	25 YR PRINCP PD DUR YEAR	25 YR MORTG BAL END OF YR
1	1097.22	45.06	9954.94	1095.60	80.16	9919.84
2	1092.01	50.27	9904.67	1086.33	89.43	9830.41
3	1086.19	56.09	9848.58	1075.98	99.78	9730.63
4	1079.71	62.57	9786.01	1064.44	111.32	9619.31
5	1072.47	69.81	9716.20	1051.57	124.19	9495.12
6	1064.39	77.89	9638.31	1037.20	138.56	9356.56
7	1055.39	86.89	9551.41	1021.18	154.58	9201.98
8	1045.33	96.95	9454.47	1003.30	172.46	9029.51
9	1034.12	108.16	9346.31	983.35	192.41	8837.10
10	1021.61	120.67	9225.64	961.09	214.67	8622.43
11	1007.65	134.63	9091.02	936.26	239.50	8382.94
12	992.08	150.20	8940.82	908.56	267.20	8115.74
13	974.71	167.57	8773.25	877.66	298.10	7817.64
14	955.33	186.95	8586.30	843.18	332.58	7485.06
15	933.71	208.57	8377.73	804.71	371.05	7114.01
16	909.58	232.70	8145.03	761.79	413.97	6700.04
17	882.67	259.61	7885.41	713.91	461.85	6238.19
18	852.64	289.64	7595.77	660.49	515.27	5722.92
19	819.14	323.14	7272.63	600.89	574.87	5148.06
20	781.76	360.52	6912.11	534.40	641.36	4506.70
21	740.06	402.22	6509.89	460.22	715.54	3791.16
22	693.54	448.74	6061.15	377.46	798.30	2992.86
23	641.64	500.64	5560.50	285.12	890.64	2102.23
24	583.73	558.55	5001.95	182.11	993.65	1108.58
25	519.13	623.15	4378.80	67.18	1108.58	0.00
26	447.05	695.23	3683.57			
27	366.64	775.64	2907.92			
28	276.92	865.36	2042.57			
29	176.83	965.45	1077.12			
30	65.16	1077.12	0.00			

Annual Amortization Schedules

Based on a Mortgage of $ 10,000.00

11.50 %

30 YEAR TERM:
Monthly Payment = 97.00
Annual Payment = 1164.00

25 YEAR TERM:
Monthly Payment = 99.71
Annual Payment = 1196.52

YR	30 YR INTER PD DUR YEAR	30 YR PRINCP PD DUR YEAR	30 YR MORTG BAL END OF YR	25 YR INTER PD DUR YEAR	25 YR PRINCP PD DUR YEAR	25 YR MORTG BAL END OF YR
1	1121.18	42.82	9957.18	1119.54	76.98	9923.02
2	1116.12	47.88	9909.30	1110.44	86.08	9836.94
3	1110.45	53.55	9855.75	1100.25	96.27	9740.67
4	1104.12	59.88	9795.87	1088.86	107.66	9633.01
5	1097.03	66.97	9728.90	1076.12	120.40	9512.61
6	1089.11	74.89	9654.01	1061.88	134.64	9377.98
7	1080.25	83.75	9570.26	1045.95	150.57	9227.41
8	1070.34	93.66	9476.60	1028.14	168.38	9059.03
9	1059.26	104.74	9371.86	1008.22	188.30	8870.73
10	1046.87	117.13	9254.73	985.94	210.58	8660.15
11	1033.01	130.99	9123.74	961.03	235.49	8424.66
12	1017.51	146.49	8977.25	933.17	263.35	8161.31
13	1000.18	163.82	8813.44	902.01	294.51	7866.80
14	980.80	183.20	8630.24	867.17	329.35	7537.46
15	959.13	204.87	8425.37	828.21	368.31	7169.14
16	934.89	229.11	8196.27	784.63	411.89	6757.26
17	907.79	256.21	7940.06	735.91	460.61	6296.64
18	877.48	286.52	7653.53	681.41	515.11	5781.53
19	843.58	320.42	7333.11	620.47	576.05	5205.49
20	805.67	358.33	6974.79	552.32	644.20	4561.29
21	763.28	400.72	6574.07	476.11	720.41	3840.88
22	715.87	448.13	6125.94	390.88	805.64	3035.23
23	662.86	501.14	5624.80	295.57	900.95	2134.28
24	603.57	560.43	5064.36	188.98	1007.54	1126.74
25	537.27	626.73	4437.63	69.78	1126.74	0.00
26	463.12	700.88	3736.75			
27	380.20	783.80	2952.95			
28	287.47	876.53	2076.42			
29	183.77	980.23	1096.19			
30	67.81	1096.19	0.00			

11.75 %

30 YEAR TERM:
Monthly Payment = 98.82
Annual Payment = 1185.84

25 YEAR TERM:
Monthly Payment = 101.44
Annual Payment = 1217.28

YR	30 YR INTER PD DUR YEAR	30 YR PRINCP PD DUR YEAR	30 YR MORTG BAL END OF YR	25 YR INTER PD DUR YEAR	25 YR PRINCP PD DUR YEAR	25 YR MORTG BAL END OF YR
1	1145.16	40.68	9959.32	1143.37	73.91	9926.09
2	1140.24	45.60	9913.72	1134.43	82.85	9843.24
3	1134.73	51.11	9862.61	1124.41	92.87	9750.37
4	1128.54	57.30	9805.31	1113.18	104.10	9646.27
5	1121.61	64.23	9741.08	1100.59	116.69	9529.58
6	1113.84	72.00	9669.09	1086.47	130.81	9398.77
7	1105.14	80.70	9588.38	1070.65	146.63	9252.14
8	1095.38	90.46	9497.92	1052.92	164.36	9087.78
9	1084.43	101.41	9396.51	1033.04	184.24	8903.53
10	1072.17	113.67	9282.84	1010.75	206.53	8697.00
11	1058.42	127.42	9155.42	985.77	231.51	8465.49
12	1043.01	142.83	9012.59	957.77	259.51	8205.98
13	1025.73	160.11	8852.48	926.38	290.90	7915.08
14	1006.37	179.47	8673.00	891.20	326.08	7589.00
15	984.66	201.18	8471.82	851.76	365.52	7223.48
16	960.33	225.51	8246.31	807.55	409.73	6813.74
17	933.05	252.79	7993.52	757.99	459.29	6354.45
18	902.47	283.37	7710.15	702.44	514.84	5839.61
19	868.20	317.64	7392.51	640.16	577.12	5262.49
20	829.78	356.06	7036.45	570.36	646.92	4615.57
21	786.71	399.13	6637.32	492.12	725.16	3890.41
22	738.44	447.40	6189.92	404.41	812.87	3077.54
23	684.33	501.51	5688.41	306.09	911.19	2166.34
24	623.67	562.17	5126.24	195.88	1021.40	1144.94
25	555.67	630.17	4496.07	72.34	1144.94	0.00
26	479.45	706.39	3789.68			
27	394.01	791.83	2997.85			
28	298.24	887.60	2110.25			
29	190.88	994.96	1115.30			
30	70.54	1115.30	0.00			

Annual Amortization Schedules

Based on a Mortgage of $ 10,000.00

12.00 %

30 YEAR TERM:
Monthly Payment = 100.64
Annual Payment = 1207.68

25 YEAR TERM:
Monthly Payment = 103.19
Annual Payment = 1238.28

YR	INTER PD DUR YEAR (30 yr)	PRINCP PD DUR YEAR (30 yr)	MORTG BAL END OF YR (30 yr)	INTER PD DUR YEAR (25 yr)	PRINCP PD DUR YEAR (25 yr)	MORTG BAL END OF YR (25 yr)
1	1169.04	38.64	9961.36	1167.33	70.95	9929.05
2	1164.26	43.42	9917.94	1158.56	79.72	9849.33
3	1158.90	48.78	9869.16	1148.70	89.58	9759.75
4	1152.87	54.81	9814.35	1137.63	100.65	9659.10
5	1146.09	61.59	9752.76	1125.19	113.09	9546.02
6	1138.48	69.20	9683.57	1111.22	127.06	9418.95
7	1129.93	77.75	9605.82	1095.51	142.77	9276.18
8	1120.32	87.36	9518.45	1077.86	160.42	9115.76
9	1109.52	98.16	9420.30	1058.04	180.24	8935.52
10	1097.39	110.29	9310.00	1035.76	202.52	8733.00
11	1083.76	123.92	9186.08	1010.73	227.55	8505.45
12	1068.44	139.24	9046.84	982.60	255.68	8249.77
13	1051.23	156.45	8890.39	951.00	287.28	7962.48
14	1031.89	175.79	8714.60	915.49	322.79	7639.70
15	1010.17	197.51	8517.09	875.59	362.69	7277.01
16	985.75	221.93	8295.16	830.77	407.51	6869.50
17	958.32	249.36	8045.80	780.40	457.88	6411.61
18	927.50	280.18	7765.62	723.80	514.48	5897.14
19	892.87	314.81	7450.82	660.21	578.07	5319.07
20	853.96	353.72	7097.10	588.76	649.52	4669.55
21	810.24	397.44	6699.66	508.48	729.80	3939.76
22	761.12	446.56	6253.10	418.28	820.00	3119.76
23	705.92	501.76	5751.34	316.93	921.35	2198.41
24	643.91	563.77	5187.56	203.05	1035.23	1163.18
25	574.22	633.46	4554.11	75.10	1163.18	0.00
26	495.93	711.75	3842.35			
27	407.96	799.72	3042.63			
28	309.11	898.57	2144.06			
29	198.05	1009.63	1134.42			
30	73.25	1134.42	0.00			

12.25 %

30 YEAR TERM:
Monthly Payment = 102.47
Annual Payment = 1229.64

25 YEAR TERM:
Monthly Payment = 104.94
Annual Payment = 1259.28

YR	INTER PD DUR YEAR (30 yr)	PRINCP PD DUR YEAR (30 yr)	MORTG BAL END OF YR (30 yr)	INTER PD DUR YEAR (25 yr)	PRINCP PD DUR YEAR (25 yr)	MORTG BAL END OF YR (25 yr)
1	1192.94	36.70	9963.30	1191.18	68.10	9931.90
2	1188.31	41.33	9921.98	1182.58	76.70	9855.20
3	1183.09	46.55	9875.43	1172.89	86.39	9768.81
4	1177.22	52.42	9823.01	1161.99	97.29	9671.52
5	1170.60	59.04	9763.96	1149.71	109.57	9561.94
6	1163.14	66.50	9697.47	1135.87	123.41	9438.54
7	1154.75	74.89	9622.58	1120.29	138.99	9299.55
8	1145.29	84.35	9538.23	1102.74	156.54	9143.01
9	1134.64	95.00	9443.24	1082.98	176.30	8966.71
10	1122.65	106.99	9336.25	1060.72	198.56	8768.15
11	1109.14	120.50	9215.75	1035.65	223.63	8544.53
12	1093.93	135.71	9080.04	1007.42	251.86	8292.67
13	1076.80	152.84	8927.20	975.62	283.66	8009.01
14	1057.50	172.14	8755.06	939.81	319.47	7689.54
15	1035.77	193.87	8561.19	899.48	359.80	7329.74
16	1011.29	218.35	8342.84	854.05	405.23	6924.51
17	983.73	245.91	8096.93	802.89	456.39	6468.12
18	952.68	276.96	7819.97	745.27	514.01	5954.11
19	917.71	311.93	7508.04	680.38	578.90	5375.21
20	878.33	351.31	7156.73	607.29	651.99	4723.22
21	833.98	395.66	6761.07	524.97	734.31	3988.91
22	784.02	445.62	6315.45	432.27	827.01	3161.90
23	727.76	501.88	5813.57	327.86	931.42	2230.48
24	664.40	565.24	5248.33	210.26	1049.02	1181.46
25	593.04	636.60	4611.73	77.82	1181.46	0.00
26	512.67	716.97	3894.76			
27	422.15	807.49	3087.27			
28	320.20	909.44	2177.83			
29	205.38	1024.26	1153.57			
30	76.07	1153.57	0.00			

Annual Amortization Schedules

Based on a Mortgage of $ 10,000.00

12.50 %

30 YEAR TERM:
Monthly Payment = 104.30
Annual Payment = 1251.60

25 YEAR TERM:
Monthly Payment = 106.70
Annual Payment = 1280.40

YR	30 YR INTER PD DUR YEAR	30 YR PRINCP PD DUR YEAR	30 YR MORTG BAL END OF YR	25 YR INTER PD DUR YEAR	25 YR PRINCP PD DUR YEAR	25 YR MORTG BAL END OF YR
1	1216.76	34.84	9965.16	1215.04	65.36	9934.64
2	1212.27	39.33	9925.82	1206.62	73.78	9860.86
3	1207.19	44.41	9881.42	1197.10	83.30	9777.56
4	1201.47	50.13	9831.29	1186.37	94.03	9683.53
5	1195.01	56.59	9774.69	1174.25	106.15	9577.37
6	1187.71	63.89	9710.81	1160.56	119.84	9457.53
7	1179.48	72.12	9638.69	1145.11	135.29	9322.25
8	1170.18	81.42	9557.27	1127.67	152.73	9169.52
9	1159.69	91.91	9465.35	1107.99	172.41	8997.11
10	1147.84	103.76	9361.59	1085.76	194.64	8802.47
11	1134.46	117.14	9244.45	1060.67	219.73	8582.74
12	1119.36	132.24	9112.21	1032.35	248.05	8334.69
13	1102.32	149.28	8962.93	1000.37	280.03	8054.66
14	1083.07	168.53	8794.40	964.27	316.13	7738.54
15	1061.35	190.25	8604.15	923.52	356.88	7381.66
16	1036.82	214.78	8389.37	877.52	402.88	6978.78
17	1009.14	242.46	8146.91	825.59	454.81	6523.97
18	977.88	273.72	7873.19	766.96	513.44	6010.53
19	942.60	309.00	7564.18	700.77	579.63	5430.90
20	902.76	348.84	7215.35	626.06	654.34	4776.56
21	857.80	393.80	6821.55	541.71	738.69	4037.86
22	807.03	444.57	6376.98	446.48	833.92	3203.95
23	749.73	501.87	5875.11	338.99	941.41	2262.53
24	685.03	566.57	5308.54	217.63	1062.77	1199.76
25	612.00	639.60	4668.94	80.64	1199.76	0.00
26	529.55	722.05	3946.89			
27	436.47	815.13	3131.76			
28	331.40	920.20	2211.56			
29	212.78	1038.82	1172.73			
30	78.87	1172.73	0.00			

12.75 %

30 YEAR TERM:
Monthly Payment = 106.14
Annual Payment = 1273.68

25 YEAR TERM:
Monthly Payment = 108.47
Annual Payment = 1301.64

YR	30 YR INTER PD DUR YEAR	30 YR PRINCP PD DUR YEAR	30 YR MORTG BAL END OF YR	25 YR INTER PD DUR YEAR	25 YR PRINCP PD DUR YEAR	25 YR MORTG BAL END OF YR
1	1240.60	33.08	9966.92	1238.92	62.72	9937.28
2	1236.25	37.43	9929.49	1230.67	70.97	9866.32
3	1231.32	42.36	9887.14	1221.34	80.30	9786.01
4	1225.75	47.93	9839.21	1210.77	90.87	9695.14
5	1219.45	54.23	9784.98	1198.81	102.83	9592.32
6	1212.31	61.37	9723.61	1185.29	116.35	9475.96
7	1204.24	69.44	9654.17	1169.98	131.66	9344.30
8	1195.10	78.58	9575.59	1152.66	148.98	9195.32
9	1184.76	88.92	9486.67	1133.06	168.58	9026.73
10	1173.07	100.61	9386.06	1110.88	190.76	8835.97
11	1159.83	113.85	9272.21	1085.78	215.86	8620.11
12	1144.85	128.83	9143.38	1057.38	244.26	8375.85
13	1127.90	145.78	8997.60	1025.24	276.40	8099.45
14	1108.72	164.96	8832.64	988.88	312.76	7786.69
15	1087.02	186.66	8645.97	947.73	353.91	7432.78
16	1062.46	211.22	8434.76	901.17	400.47	7032.31
17	1034.67	239.01	8195.75	848.48	453.16	6579.15
18	1003.23	270.45	7925.29	788.86	512.78	6066.38
19	967.64	306.04	7619.26	721.40	580.24	5486.14
20	927.38	346.30	7272.96	645.06	656.58	4829.56
21	881.82	391.86	6881.10	558.68	742.96	4086.60
22	830.27	443.41	6437.69	460.93	840.71	3245.89
23	771.93	501.75	5935.93	350.32	951.32	2294.57
24	705.92	567.76	5368.17	225.17	1076.47	1218.10
25	631.22	642.46	4725.71	83.54	1218.10	0.00
26	546.69	726.99	3998.72			
27	451.05	822.63	3176.09			
28	342.82	930.86	2245.23			
29	220.35	1053.33	1191.91			
30	81.77	1191.91	0.00			

Annual Amortization Schedules

Based on a Mortgage of $ 10,000.00

13.00 %

30 YEAR TERM:
Monthly Payment = 107.98
Annual Payment = 1295.76

25 YEAR TERM:
Monthly Payment = 110.24
Annual Payment = 1322.88

YR	30 YR INTER PD DUR YEAR	30 YR PRINCP PD DUR YEAR	30 YR MORTG BAL END OF YR	25 YR INTER PD DUR YEAR	25 YR PRINCP PD DUR YEAR	25 YR MORTG BAL END OF YR
1	1264.36	31.40	9968.60	1262.71	60.17	9939.83
2	1260.15	35.61	9932.99	1254.63	68.25	9871.58
3	1255.37	40.39	9892.60	1245.47	77.41	9794.17
4	1249.95	45.81	9846.78	1235.08	87.80	9706.37
5	1243.80	51.96	9794.82	1223.29	99.59	9606.78
6	1236.82	58.94	9735.88	1209.93	112.95	9493.83
7	1228.91	66.85	9669.03	1194.77	128.11	9365.72
8	1219.94	75.82	9593.21	1177.57	145.31	9220.41
9	1209.76	86.00	9507.21	1158.07	164.81	9055.59
10	1198.22	97.54	9409.67	1135.94	186.94	8868.66
11	1185.13	110.63	9299.04	1110.85	212.03	8656.63
12	1170.28	125.48	9173.55	1082.39	240.49	8416.15
13	1153.43	142.33	9031.22	1050.11	272.77	8143.38
14	1134.33	161.43	8869.79	1013.50	309.38	7834.00
15	1112.66	183.10	8686.69	971.98	350.90	7483.10
16	1088.08	207.68	8479.02	924.88	398.00	7085.10
17	1060.21	235.55	8243.46	871.45	451.43	6633.67
18	1028.59	267.17	7976.30	810.86	512.02	6121.65
19	992.73	303.03	7673.27	742.14	580.74	5540.91
20	952.06	343.70	7329.56	664.19	658.69	4882.22
21	905.92	389.84	6939.73	575.77	747.11	4135.11
22	853.60	442.16	6497.56	475.49	847.39	3287.72
23	794.25	501.51	5996.05	361.75	961.13	2326.59
24	726.93	568.83	5427.22	232.74	1090.14	1236.46
25	650.58	645.18	4782.04	86.42	1236.46	0.00
26	563.98	731.78	4050.27			
27	465.76	830.00	3220.27			
28	354.35	941.41	2278.86			
29	227.99	1067.77	1211.09			
30	84.67	1211.09	0.00			

13.25 %

30 YEAR TERM:
Monthly Payment = 109.83
Annual Payment = 1317.96

25 YEAR TERM:
Monthly Payment = 112.02
Annual Payment = 1344.24

YR	30 YR INTER PD DUR YEAR	30 YR PRINCP PD DUR YEAR	30 YR MORTG BAL END OF YR	25 YR INTER PD DUR YEAR	25 YR PRINCP PD DUR YEAR	25 YR MORTG BAL END OF YR
1	1288.16	29.80	9970.20	1286.52	57.72	9942.28
2	1284.08	33.88	9936.33	1278.61	65.63	9876.65
3	1279.45	38.51	9897.81	1269.63	74.61	9802.04
4	1274.17	43.79	9854.03	1259.42	84.82	9717.22
5	1268.18	49.78	9804.25	1247.81	96.43	9620.79
6	1261.37	56.59	9747.65	1234.61	109.63	9511.15
7	1253.62	64.34	9683.31	1219.60	124.64	9386.51
8	1244.81	73.15	9610.16	1202.54	141.70	9244.81
9	1234.80	83.16	9527.00	1183.14	161.10	9083.71
10	1223.41	94.55	9432.46	1161.09	183.15	8900.55
11	1210.47	107.49	9324.97	1136.01	208.23	8692.33
12	1195.76	122.20	9202.77	1107.51	236.73	8455.60
13	1179.03	138.93	9063.84	1075.10	269.14	8186.46
14	1160.01	157.95	8905.89	1038.26	305.98	7880.48
15	1138.39	179.57	8726.32	996.38	347.86	7532.62
16	1113.81	204.15	8522.17	948.76	395.48	7137.14
17	1085.86	232.10	8290.08	894.62	449.62	6687.52
18	1054.09	263.87	8026.21	833.07	511.17	6176.35
19	1017.97	299.99	7726.22	763.10	581.14	5595.22
20	976.91	341.05	7385.17	683.55	660.69	4934.53
21	930.22	387.74	6997.43	593.11	751.13	4183.39
22	877.14	440.82	6556.61	490.29	853.95	3329.44
23	816.80	501.16	6055.45	373.39	970.85	2358.59
24	748.20	569.76	5485.69	240.49	1103.75	1254.84
25	670.20	647.76	4837.93	89.40	1254.84	0.00
26	581.53	736.43	4101.50			
27	480.72	837.24	3264.27			
28	366.11	951.85	2312.42			
29	235.82	1082.14	1230.28			
30	87.68	1230.28	0.00			

Annual Amortization Schedules

Based on a Mortgage of $ 10,000.00

13.50 %

30 YEAR TERM:
Monthly Payment = 111.68
Annual Payment = 1340.16

25 YEAR TERM:
Monthly Payment = 113.80
Annual Payment = 1365.60

	30 YEAR TERM			25 YEAR TERM		
YR	INTER PD DUR YEAR	PRINCP PD DUR YEAR	MORTG BAL END OF YR	INTER PD DUR YEAR	PRINCP PD DUR YEAR	MORTG BAL END OF YR
1	1311.89	28.27	9971.73	1310.23	55.37	9944.63
2	1307.94	32.22	9939.51	1302.51	63.09	9881.54
3	1303.44	36.72	9902.79	1293.70	71.90	9809.64
4	1298.32	41.84	9860.95	1283.67	81.93	9727.71
5	1292.48	47.68	9813.27	1272.23	93.37	9634.34
6	1285.83	54.33	9758.94	1259.20	106.40	9527.94
7	1278.24	61.92	9697.02	1244.35	121.25	9406.70
8	1269.60	70.56	9626.46	1227.43	138.17	9268.53
9	1259.76	80.40	9546.06	1208.15	157.45	9111.08
10	1248.54	91.62	9454.44	1186.18	179.42	8931.66
11	1235.75	104.41	9350.03	1161.14	204.46	8727.20
12	1221.18	118.98	9231.05	1132.61	232.99	8494.20
13	1204.57	135.59	9095.46	1100.09	265.51	8228.69
14	1185.65	154.51	8940.95	1063.04	302.56	7926.13
15	1164.09	176.07	8764.88	1020.81	344.79	7581.34
16	1139.52	200.64	8564.24	972.69	392.91	7188.44
17	1111.52	228.64	8335.59	917.86	447.74	6740.70
18	1079.61	260.55	8075.04	855.38	510.22	6230.47
19	1043.25	296.91	7778.13	784.17	581.43	5649.05
20	1001.81	338.35	7439.78	703.03	662.57	4986.48
21	954.59	385.57	7054.21	610.56	755.04	4231.44
22	900.78	439.38	6614.83	505.19	860.41	3371.03
23	839.46	500.70	6114.13	385.12	980.48	2390.55
24	769.59	570.57	5543.56	248.29	1117.31	1273.24
25	689.96	650.20	4893.36	92.36	1273.24	0.00
26	599.22	740.94	4152.43			
27	495.82	844.34	3308.09			
28	377.99	962.17	2345.92			
29	243.71	1096.45	1249.47			
30	90.69	1249.47	0.00			

13.75 %

30 YEAR TERM:
Monthly Payment = 113.53
Annual Payment = 1362.36

25 YEAR TERM:
Monthly Payment = 115.59
Annual Payment = 1387.08

	30 YEAR TERM			25 YEAR TERM		
YR	INTER PD DUR YEAR	PRINCP PD DUR YEAR	MORTG BAL END OF YR	INTER PD DUR YEAR	PRINCP PD DUR YEAR	MORTG BAL END OF YR
1	1335.54	26.82	9973.18	1333.98	53.10	9946.90
2	1331.72	30.64	9942.54	1326.43	60.65	9886.25
3	1327.36	35.00	9907.54	1317.80	69.28	9816.97
4	1322.39	39.97	9867.56	1307.95	79.13	9737.84
5	1316.70	45.66	9821.90	1296.69	90.39	9647.45
6	1310.21	52.15	9769.75	1283.84	103.24	9544.21
7	1302.79	59.57	9710.18	1269.15	117.93	9426.29
8	1294.32	68.04	9642.13	1252.38	134.70	9291.59
9	1284.64	77.72	9564.41	1233.23	153.85	9137.73
10	1273.58	88.78	9475.64	1211.34	175.74	8962.00
11	1260.96	101.40	9374.23	1186.35	200.73	8761.26
12	1246.53	115.83	9258.41	1157.80	229.28	8531.98
13	1230.06	132.30	9126.11	1125.19	261.89	8270.09
14	1211.25	151.11	8974.99	1087.94	299.14	7970.95
15	1189.75	172.61	8802.39	1045.40	341.68	7629.27
16	1165.20	197.16	8605.23	996.80	390.28	7238.99
17	1137.16	225.20	8380.03	941.29	445.79	6793.20
18	1105.13	257.23	8122.81	877.89	509.19	6284.01
19	1068.55	293.81	7828.99	805.47	581.61	5702.40
20	1026.76	335.60	7493.40	722.75	664.33	5038.06
21	979.03	383.33	7110.07	628.26	758.82	4279.24
22	924.51	437.85	6672.22	520.34	866.74	3412.50
23	862.24	500.12	6172.09	397.06	990.02	2422.48
24	791.11	571.25	5600.84	256.26	1130.82	1291.66
25	709.86	652.50	4948.34	95.42	1291.66	0.00
26	617.05	745.31	4203.03			
27	511.05	851.31	3351.72			
28	389.97	972.39	2379.34			
29	251.68	1110.68	1268.65			
30	93.71	1268.65	0.00			

Annual Amortization Schedules

Based on a Mortgage of $ 10,000.00

14.00 %

30 YEAR TERM:
Monthly Payment = 115.39
Annual Payment = 1384.68

25 YEAR TERM:
Monthly Payment = 117.39
Annual Payment = 1408.68

YR	30 YR INTER PD DUR YEAR	30 YR PRINCP PD DUR YEAR	30 YR MORTG BAL END OF YR	25 YR INTER PD DUR YEAR	25 YR PRINCP PD DUR YEAR	25 YR MORTG BAL END OF YR
1	1359.23	25.44	9974.56	1357.76	50.92	9949.08
2	1355.55	29.13	9945.42	1350.38	58.30	9890.78
3	1351.33	33.35	9912.07	1341.94	66.74	9824.04
4	1346.49	38.19	9873.88	1332.26	76.42	9747.62
5	1340.96	43.72	9830.16	1321.19	87.49	9660.14
6	1334.63	50.05	9780.11	1308.51	100.17	9559.97
7	1327.37	57.31	9722.80	1294.00	114.68	9445.29
8	1319.07	65.61	9657.19	1277.38	131.30	9314.00
9	1309.56	75.12	9582.08	1258.36	150.32	9163.67
10	1298.68	86.00	9496.07	1236.58	172.10	8991.57
11	1286.22	98.46	9397.61	1211.64	197.04	8794.53
12	1271.95	112.73	9284.88	1183.09	225.59	8568.94
13	1255.61	129.07	9155.81	1150.40	258.28	8310.66
14	1236.91	147.77	9008.04	1112.98	295.70	8014.96
15	1215.50	169.18	8838.86	1070.13	338.55	7676.41
16	1190.99	193.69	8645.17	1021.07	387.61	7288.80
17	1162.92	221.76	8423.41	964.91	443.77	6845.03
18	1130.79	253.89	8169.52	900.61	508.07	6336.95
19	1094.00	290.68	7878.84	826.99	581.69	5755.26
20	1051.88	332.80	7546.03	742.70	665.98	5089.28
21	1003.66	381.02	7165.01	646.20	762.48	4326.79
22	948.44	436.24	6728.77	535.71	872.97	3453.83
23	885.23	499.45	6229.33	409.22	999.46	2454.37
24	812.86	571.82	5657.51	264.40	1144.28	1310.09
25	730.01	654.67	5002.84	98.59	1310.09	0.00
26	635.15	749.53	4253.31			
27	526.54	858.14	3395.17			
28	402.19	982.48	2412.68			
29	259.83	1124.85	1287.84			
30	96.84	1287.84	0.00			

14.25 %

30 YEAR TERM:
Monthly Payment = 117.26
Annual Payment = 1407.12

25 YEAR TERM:
Monthly Payment = 119.19
Annual Payment = 1430.28

YR	30 YR INTER PD DUR YEAR	30 YR PRINCP PD DUR YEAR	30 YR MORTG BAL END OF YR	25 YR INTER PD DUR YEAR	25 YR PRINCP PD DUR YEAR	25 YR MORTG BAL END OF YR
1	1382.99	24.13	9975.87	1381.46	48.82	9951.18
2	1379.43	27.69	9948.17	1374.25	56.03	9895.15
3	1375.34	31.78	9916.39	1365.99	64.29	9830.86
4	1370.65	36.47	9879.92	1356.50	73.78	9757.07
5	1365.27	41.85	9838.07	1345.61	84.67	9672.40
6	1359.09	48.03	9790.03	1333.11	97.17	9575.24
7	1352.00	55.12	9734.92	1318.77	111.51	9463.73
8	1343.87	63.25	9671.66	1302.32	127.96	9335.77
9	1334.53	72.59	9599.07	1283.43	146.85	9188.92
10	1323.82	83.30	9515.77	1261.76	168.52	9020.40
11	1311.53	95.59	9420.18	1236.89	193.39	8827.02
12	1297.42	109.70	9310.48	1208.35	221.93	8605.09
13	1281.23	125.89	9184.59	1175.60	254.68	8350.41
14	1262.65	144.47	9040.12	1138.02	292.26	8058.15
15	1241.33	165.79	8874.33	1094.89	335.39	7722.76
16	1216.86	190.26	8684.08	1045.39	384.89	7337.87
17	1188.79	218.33	8465.74	988.59	441.69	6896.18
18	1156.57	250.55	8215.19	923.41	506.87	6389.31
19	1119.59	287.53	7927.66	848.60	581.68	5807.63
20	1077.16	329.96	7597.70	762.76	667.52	5140.11
21	1028.46	378.66	7219.04	664.25	766.03	4374.09
22	972.58	434.54	6784.51	551.21	879.07	3495.01
23	908.46	498.66	6285.84	421.48	1008.80	2486.21
24	834.86	572.26	5713.59	272.60	1157.68	1328.53
25	750.41	656.71	5056.88	101.75	1328.53	0.00
26	653.50	753.62	4303.26			
27	542.28	864.84	3438.42			
28	414.65	992.47	2445.95			
29	268.19	1138.93	1307.01			
30	100.11	1307.01	0.00			

Annual Amortization Schedules

Based on a Mortgage of $ 10,000.00

14.50 %

30 YEAR TERM:
Monthly Payment = 119.12
Annual Payment = 1429.44

25 YEAR TERM:
Monthly Payment = 120.99
Annual Payment = 1451.88

YR	INTER PD DUR YEAR	PRINCP PD DUR YEAR	MORTG BAL END OF YR	INTER PD DUR YEAR	PRINCP PD DUR YEAR	MORTG BAL END OF YR
1	1406.55	22.89	9977.11	1405.08	46.80	9953.20
2	1403.12	26.32	9950.79	1398.04	53.84	9899.36
3	1399.16	30.28	9920.51	1389.95	61.93	9837.43
4	1394.61	34.83	9885.68	1380.65	71.23	9766.20
5	1389.38	40.06	9845.62	1369.95	81.93	9684.26
6	1383.36	46.08	9799.54	1357.63	94.25	9590.02
7	1376.43	53.01	9746.53	1343.47	108.41	9481.61
8	1368.47	60.97	9685.56	1327.18	124.70	9356.92
9	1359.31	70.13	9615.43	1308.45	143.43	9213.48
10	1348.77	80.67	9534.76	1286.90	164.98	9048.50
11	1336.65	92.79	9441.97	1262.11	189.77	8858.73
12	1322.71	106.73	9335.23	1233.59	218.29	8640.44
13	1306.67	122.77	9212.46	1200.79	251.09	8389.35
14	1288.22	141.22	9071.25	1163.07	288.81	8100.54
15	1267.00	162.44	8908.81	1119.67	332.21	7768.33
16	1242.60	186.84	8721.97	1069.75	382.13	7386.20
17	1214.52	214.92	8507.05	1012.34	439.54	6946.65
18	1182.23	247.21	8259.84	946.29	505.59	6441.07
19	1145.08	284.36	7975.48	870.32	581.56	5859.51
20	1102.36	327.08	7648.40	782.94	668.94	5190.57
21	1053.21	376.23	7272.17	682.43	769.45	4421.12
22	996.68	432.76	6839.41	566.81	885.07	3536.05
23	931.66	497.78	6341.63	433.83	1018.05	2518.00
24	856.86	572.58	5769.05	280.86	1171.02	1346.98
25	770.83	658.61	5110.44	104.90	1346.98	0.00
26	671.87	757.57	4352.86			
27	558.04	871.40	3481.46			
28	427.10	1002.34	2479.12			
29	276.50	1152.94	1326.18			
30	103.26	1326.18	0.00			

14.75 %

30 YEAR TERM:
Monthly Payment = 120.99
Annual Payment = 1451.88

25 YEAR TERM:
Monthly Payment = 122.80
Annual Payment = 1473.60

YR	INTER PD DUR YEAR	PRINCP PD DUR YEAR	MORTG BAL END OF YR	INTER PD DUR YEAR	PRINCP PD DUR YEAR	MORTG BAL END OF YR
1	1430.18	21.70	9978.30	1428.73	44.87	9955.13
2	1426.86	25.02	9953.28	1421.87	51.73	9903.41
3	1423.04	28.84	9924.44	1413.96	59.64	9843.77
4	1418.62	33.26	9891.18	1404.84	68.76	9775.01
5	1413.54	38.34	9852.84	1394.32	79.28	9695.73
6	1407.67	44.21	9808.64	1382.20	91.40	9604.33
7	1400.91	50.97	9757.67	1368.22	105.38	9498.95
8	1393.12	58.76	9698.91	1352.10	121.50	9377.46
9	1384.13	67.75	9631.16	1333.52	140.08	9237.38
10	1373.77	78.11	9553.05	1312.10	161.50	9075.88
11	1361.82	90.06	9462.99	1287.40	186.20	8889.68
12	1348.05	103.83	9359.17	1258.92	214.68	8675.00
13	1332.17	119.71	9239.46	1226.09	247.51	8427.49
14	1313.86	138.02	9101.44	1188.24	285.36	8142.13
15	1292.76	159.12	8942.32	1144.59	329.01	7813.12
16	1268.42	183.46	8758.86	1094.27	379.33	7433.79
17	1240.36	211.52	8547.34	1036.26	437.34	6996.45
18	1208.01	243.87	8303.47	969.37	504.23	6492.23
19	1170.72	281.16	8022.31	892.26	581.34	5910.89
20	1127.71	324.17	7698.14	803.35	670.25	5240.64
21	1078.14	373.74	7324.40	700.84	772.76	4467.88
22	1020.98	430.90	6893.50	582.66	890.94	3576.94
23	955.07	496.81	6396.69	446.40	1027.20	2549.73
24	879.09	572.79	5823.90	289.30	1184.30	1365.43
25	791.49	660.39	5163.52	108.17	1365.43	0.00
26	690.49	761.39	4402.13			
27	574.05	877.83	3524.30			
28	439.79	1012.09	2512.21			
29	285.01	1166.87	1345.34			
30	106.54	1345.34	0.00			

Annual Amortization Schedules

Based on a Mortgage of $ 10,000.00

15.00 %

30 YEAR TERM:
Monthly Payment = 122.87
Annual Payment = 1474.44

25 YEAR TERM:
Monthly Payment = 124.61
Annual Payment = 1495.32

YR	30 YR INTER PD DUR YEAR	30 YR PRINCP PD DUR YEAR	30 YR MORTG BAL END OF YR	25 YR INTER PD DUR YEAR	25 YR PRINCP PD DUR YEAR	25 YR MORTG BAL END OF YR
1	1453.87	20.57	9979.43	1452.32	43.00	9957.00
2	1450.67	23.77	9955.65	1445.63	49.69	9907.30
3	1446.97	27.47	9928.18	1437.89	57.43	9849.87
4	1442.69	31.75	9896.43	1428.95	66.37	9783.51
5	1437.75	36.69	9859.74	1418.63	76.69	9706.81
6	1432.04	42.40	9817.34	1406.69	88.63	9618.18
7	1425.44	49.00	9768.35	1392.90	102.42	9515.76
8	1417.82	56.62	9711.72	1376.96	118.36	9397.40
9	1409.01	65.44	9646.29	1358.54	136.78	9260.62
10	1398.82	75.62	9570.67	1337.25	158.07	9102.55
11	1387.05	87.39	9483.28	1312.65	182.67	8919.88
12	1373.45	100.99	9382.30	1284.22	211.10	8708.79
13	1357.74	116.70	9265.60	1251.37	243.95	8464.84
14	1339.58	134.86	9130.73	1213.41	281.91	8182.93
15	1318.59	155.85	8974.88	1169.54	325.78	7857.14
16	1294.33	180.11	8794.77	1118.83	376.49	7480.66
17	1266.30	208.14	8586.64	1060.24	435.08	7045.58
18	1233.91	240.53	8346.11	992.54	502.78	6542.80
19	1196.48	277.96	8068.15	914.29	581.03	5961.77
20	1153.22	321.22	7746.94	823.87	671.45	5290.31
21	1103.24	371.20	7375.73	719.37	775.95	4514.37
22	1045.47	428.97	6946.76	598.62	896.70	3617.66
23	978.71	495.73	6451.03	459.07	1036.25	2581.41
24	901.56	572.88	5878.15	297.80	1197.52	1383.89
25	812.40	662.04	5216.11	111.43	1383.89	0.00
26	709.38	765.06	4451.05			
27	590.31	884.13	3566.92			
28	452.72	1021.72	2545.20			
29	293.71	1180.73	1364.48			
30	109.96	1364.48	0.00			

15.25 %

30 YEAR TERM:
Monthly Payment = 124.74
Annual Payment = 1496.88

25 YEAR TERM:
Monthly Payment = 126.43
Annual Payment = 1517.16

YR	30 YR INTER PD DUR YEAR	30 YR PRINCP PD DUR YEAR	30 YR MORTG BAL END OF YR	25 YR INTER PD DUR YEAR	25 YR PRINCP PD DUR YEAR	25 YR MORTG BAL END OF YR
1	1477.38	19.50	9980.50	1475.95	41.21	9958.79
2	1474.29	22.59	9957.91	1469.42	47.74	9911.05
3	1470.72	26.16	9931.75	1461.87	55.29	9855.76
4	1466.57	30.31	9901.44	1453.11	64.05	9791.71
5	1461.78	35.10	9866.34	1442.97	74.19	9717.52
6	1456.22	40.66	9825.68	1431.23	85.93	9631.59
7	1449.78	47.10	9778.58	1417.62	99.54	9532.06
8	1442.33	54.55	9724.02	1401.87	115.29	9416.76
9	1433.69	63.19	9660.83	1383.61	133.55	9283.22
10	1423.68	73.20	9587.64	1362.47	154.69	9128.53
11	1412.10	84.78	9502.86	1337.98	179.18	8949.35
12	1398.67	98.21	9404.65	1309.62	207.54	8741.80
13	1383.13	113.75	9290.90	1276.76	240.40	8501.40
14	1365.12	131.76	9159.14	1238.70	278.46	8222.94
15	1344.26	152.62	9006.51	1194.61	322.55	7900.40
16	1320.10	176.78	8829.73	1143.55	373.61	7526.79
17	1292.11	204.77	8624.96	1084.40	432.76	7094.03
18	1259.69	237.19	8387.77	1015.89	501.27	6592.76
19	1222.14	274.74	8113.03	936.53	580.63	6012.14
20	1178.65	318.23	7794.80	844.61	672.55	5339.59
21	1128.27	368.61	7426.18	738.14	779.02	4560.57
22	1069.91	426.97	6999.21	614.81	902.35	3658.22
23	1002.31	494.57	6504.64	471.96	1045.20	2613.02
24	924.02	572.86	5931.78	306.48	1210.68	1402.34
25	833.32	663.56	5268.22	114.82	1402.34	0.00
26	728.27	768.61	4499.61			
27	606.59	890.29	3609.33			
28	465.65	1031.23	2578.09			
29	302.39	1194.49	1383.60			
30	113.28	1383.60	0.00			

Annual Amortization Schedules

Based on a Mortgage of $ 10,000.00

15.50 %

30 YEAR TERM:
Monthly Payment = 126.62
Annual Payment = 1519.44

25 YEAR TERM:
Monthly Payment = 128.25
Annual Payment = 1539.00

YR	30 YR INTER PD DUR YEAR	30 YR PRINCP PD DUR YEAR	30 YR MORTG BAL END OF YR	25 YR INTER PD DUR YEAR	25 YR PRINCP PD DUR YEAR	25 YR MORTG BAL END OF YR
1	1500.96	18.48	9981.52	1499.51	39.49	9960.51
2	1497.98	21.46	9960.06	1493.15	45.85	9914.66
3	1494.53	24.91	9935.15	1485.77	53.23	9861.43
4	1490.52	28.92	9906.22	1477.20	61.80	9799.62
5	1485.86	33.58	9872.64	1467.25	71.75	9727.87
6	1480.45	38.99	9833.65	1455.69	83.31	9644.57
7	1474.17	45.27	9788.39	1442.28	96.72	9547.85
8	1466.89	52.55	9735.83	1426.71	112.29	9435.56
9	1458.42	61.02	9674.82	1408.63	130.37	9305.19
10	1448.60	70.84	9603.98	1387.64	151.36	9153.82
11	1437.20	82.24	9521.73	1363.27	175.73	8978.09
12	1423.95	95.49	9426.25	1334.98	204.02	8774.07
13	1408.58	110.86	9315.38	1302.13	236.87	8537.20
14	1390.73	128.71	9186.67	1263.99	275.01	8262.18
15	1370.01	149.43	9037.24	1219.71	319.29	7942.89
16	1345.95	173.49	8863.75	1168.30	370.70	7572.19
17	1318.01	201.43	8662.32	1108.62	430.38	7141.81
18	1285.58	233.86	8428.47	1039.32	499.68	6642.13
19	1247.93	271.51	8156.96	958.87	580.13	6062.00
20	1204.22	315.22	7841.73	865.47	673.53	5388.47
21	1153.46	365.98	7475.75	757.02	781.98	4606.49
22	1094.54	424.90	7050.85	631.12	907.88	3698.61
23	1026.13	493.31	6557.54	484.95	1054.05	2644.56
24	946.70	572.74	5984.80	315.24	1223.76	1420.80
25	854.48	664.96	5319.84	118.20	1420.80	0.00
26	747.42	772.02	4547.83			
27	623.12	896.32	3651.51			
28	478.81	1040.63	2610.88			
29	311.26	1208.18	1402.70			
30	116.74	1402.70	0.00			

15.75 %

30 YEAR TERM:
Monthly Payment = 128.50
Annual Payment = 1542.00

25 YEAR TERM:
Monthly Payment = 130.08
Annual Payment = 1560.96

YR	30 YR INTER PD DUR YEAR	30 YR PRINCP PD DUR YEAR	30 YR MORTG BAL END OF YR	25 YR INTER PD DUR YEAR	25 YR PRINCP PD DUR YEAR	25 YR MORTG BAL END OF YR
1	1524.48	17.52	9982.48	1523.12	37.84	9962.16
2	1521.62	20.38	9962.10	1516.93	44.03	9918.13
3	1518.28	23.72	9938.38	1509.72	51.24	9866.89
4	1514.40	27.60	9910.78	1501.33	59.63	9807.26
5	1509.88	32.12	9878.66	1491.57	69.39	9737.87
6	1504.62	37.38	9841.28	1480.21	80.75	9657.12
7	1498.50	43.50	9797.78	1466.99	93.97	9563.15
8	1491.38	50.62	9747.16	1451.61	109.35	9453.79
9	1483.09	58.91	9688.25	1433.71	127.25	9326.54
10	1473.45	68.55	9619.70	1412.87	148.09	9178.46
11	1462.23	79.77	9539.93	1388.63	172.33	9006.13
12	1449.17	92.83	9447.11	1360.42	200.54	8805.59
13	1433.97	108.03	9339.08	1327.59	233.37	8572.23
14	1416.29	125.71	9213.37	1289.39	271.57	8300.66
15	1395.71	146.29	9067.08	1244.94	316.02	7984.64
16	1371.76	170.24	8896.85	1193.20	367.76	7616.88
17	1343.90	198.10	8698.74	1133.00	427.96	7188.92
18	1311.47	230.53	8468.21	1062.94	498.02	6690.90
19	1273.73	268.27	8199.94	981.42	579.54	6111.36
20	1229.81	312.19	7887.75	886.54	674.42	5436.94
21	1178.71	363.29	7524.45	776.14	784.82	4652.13
22	1119.23	422.77	7101.69	647.67	913.29	3738.83
23	1050.03	491.97	6609.71	498.16	1062.80	2676.03
24	969.49	572.51	6037.20	324.18	1236.78	1439.25
25	875.77	666.23	5370.97	121.71	1439.25	0.00
26	766.71	775.29	4595.68			
27	639.79	902.21	3693.46			
28	492.09	1049.91	2643.56			
29	320.22	1221.78	1421.78			
30	120.22	1421.78	0.00			

Annual Amortization Schedules

Based on a Mortgage of $ 10,000.00

16.00 %

30 YEAR TERM: Monthly Payment = 130.38; Annual Payment = 1564.56

25 YEAR TERM: Monthly Payment = 131.91; Annual Payment = 1582.92

YR	30 YR INTER PD DUR YEAR	30 YR PRINCP PD DUR YEAR	30 YR MORTG BAL END OF YR	25 YR INTER PD DUR YEAR	25 YR PRINCP PD DUR YEAR	25 YR MORTG BAL END OF YR
1	1547.96	16.60	9983.40	1546.67	36.25	9963.75
2	1545.20	19.36	9964.04	1540.64	42.28	9921.46
3	1541.98	22.58	9941.46	1533.60	49.32	9872.15
4	1538.22	26.34	9915.13	1525.39	57.53	9814.62
5	1533.84	30.72	9884.40	1515.82	67.10	9747.52
6	1528.73	35.83	9848.57	1504.66	78.26	9669.26
7	1522.77	41.79	9806.78	1491.63	91.29	9577.97
8	1515.81	48.75	9758.03	1476.44	106.48	9471.49
9	1507.70	56.86	9701.17	1458.72	124.20	9347.30
10	1498.24	66.32	9634.84	1438.06	144.86	9202.43
11	1487.20	77.36	9557.48	1413.95	168.97	9033.47
12	1474.33	90.23	9467.25	1385.84	197.08	8836.38
13	1459.31	105.25	9362.00	1353.04	229.88	8606.51
14	1441.80	122.76	9239.24	1314.79	268.13	8338.38
15	1421.37	143.19	9096.06	1270.17	312.75	8025.63
16	1397.55	167.01	8929.04	1218.13	364.79	7660.85
17	1369.76	194.80	8734.24	1157.43	425.49	7235.36
18	1337.34	227.22	8507.02	1086.63	496.29	6739.07
19	1299.53	265.03	8241.99	1004.05	578.87	6160.21
20	1255.43	309.13	7932.86	907.73	675.19	5485.01
21	1203.99	360.57	7572.29	795.37	787.55	4697.47
22	1143.99	420.57	7151.72	664.33	918.59	3778.87
23	1074.01	490.55	6661.17	511.47	1071.45	2707.43
24	992.38	572.18	6089.00	333.18	1249.74	1457.69
25	897.17	667.39	5421.61	125.23	1457.69	0.00
26	786.12	778.44	4643.17			
27	656.59	907.97	3735.19			
28	505.50	1059.06	2676.13			
29	329.27	1235.29	1440.84			
30	123.72	1440.84	0.00			

16.25 %

30 YEAR TERM: Monthly Payment = 132.27; Annual Payment = 1587.24

25 YEAR TERM: Monthly Payment = 133.74; Annual Payment = 1604.88

YR	30 YR INTER PD DUR YEAR	30 YR PRINCP PD DUR YEAR	30 YR MORTG BAL END OF YR	25 YR INTER PD DUR YEAR	25 YR PRINCP PD DUR YEAR	25 YR MORTG BAL END OF YR
1	1571.51	15.73	9984.27	1570.15	34.73	9965.27
2	1568.86	18.38	9965.89	1564.28	40.60	9924.67
3	1565.75	21.49	9944.40	1557.42	47.47	9877.21
4	1562.11	25.13	9919.27	1549.39	55.49	9821.72
5	1557.86	29.38	9889.89	1540.00	64.88	9756.84
6	1552.90	34.34	9855.55	1529.03	75.85	9681.00
7	1547.09	40.15	9815.39	1516.21	88.67	9592.32
8	1540.30	46.94	9768.45	1501.21	103.67	9488.66
9	1532.36	54.88	9713.57	1483.68	121.20	9367.46
10	1523.08	64.16	9649.41	1463.19	141.69	9225.77
11	1512.23	75.01	9574.40	1439.23	165.65	9060.12
12	1499.54	87.70	9486.70	1411.22	193.66	8866.46
13	1484.72	102.52	9384.18	1378.47	226.41	8640.05
14	1467.38	119.86	9264.32	1340.18	264.70	8375.35
15	1447.11	140.13	9124.19	1295.42	309.46	8065.89
16	1423.41	163.83	8960.36	1243.09	361.79	7704.11
17	1395.71	191.53	8768.83	1181.91	422.97	7281.14
18	1363.32	223.92	8544.91	1110.39	494.49	6786.65
19	1325.46	261.78	8283.13	1026.77	578.11	6208.54
20	1281.19	306.05	7977.08	929.01	675.87	5532.67
21	1229.44	357.80	7619.28	814.72	790.16	4742.51
22	1168.93	418.31	7200.97	681.10	923.78	3818.73
23	1098.19	489.05	6711.92	524.89	1079.99	2738.74
24	1015.50	571.74	6140.18	342.26	1262.62	1476.13
25	918.81	668.43	5471.75	128.75	1476.13	0.00
26	805.78	781.46	4690.29			
27	673.63	913.61	3776.69			
28	519.14	1068.10	2708.59			
29	338.53	1248.71	1459.87			
30	127.37	1459.87	0.00			

Annual Amortization Schedules

Based on a Mortgage of $ 10,000.00

16.50 %

30 YEAR TERM:
Monthly Payment = 134.15
Annual Payment = 1609.80

25 YEAR TERM:
Monthly Payment = 135.57
Annual Payment = 1626.84

YR	INTER PD DUR YEAR	PRINCP PD DUR YEAR	MORTG BAL END OF YR	INTER PD DUR YEAR	PRINCP PD DUR YEAR	MORTG BAL END OF YR
1	1594.90	14.90	9985.10	1593.58	33.26	9966.74
2	1592.34	17.46	9967.65	1587.86	38.98	9927.76
3	1589.34	20.46	9947.19	1581.16	45.68	9882.08
4	1585.83	23.97	9923.22	1573.32	53.52	9828.56
5	1581.71	28.09	9895.13	1564.12	62.72	9765.84
6	1576.88	32.91	9862.21	1553.35	73.49	9692.35
7	1571.23	38.57	9823.64	1540.72	86.12	9606.23
8	1564.60	45.20	9778.45	1525.92	100.92	9505.31
9	1556.84	52.96	9725.49	1508.59	118.25	9387.06
10	1547.74	62.06	9663.43	1488.27	138.57	9248.48
11	1537.08	72.72	9590.70	1464.46	162.38	9086.10
12	1524.58	85.22	9505.49	1436.56	190.28	8895.83
13	1509.94	99.86	9405.63	1403.87	222.97	8672.86
14	1492.79	117.01	9288.61	1365.57	261.27	8411.59
15	1472.68	137.12	9151.49	1320.68	306.16	8105.42
16	1449.12	160.68	8990.82	1268.08	358.76	7746.66
17	1421.52	188.28	8802.54	1206.44	420.40	7326.26
18	1389.17	220.63	8581.91	1134.21	492.63	6833.63
19	1351.27	258.53	8323.37	1049.57	577.27	6256.36
20	1306.85	302.95	8020.42	950.40	676.44	5579.92
21	1254.80	355.00	7665.42	834.18	792.66	4787.25
22	1193.81	415.99	7249.43	697.99	928.85	3858.41
23	1122.34	487.46	6761.96	538.41	1088.43	2769.98
24	1038.59	571.21	6190.75	351.41	1275.43	1494.55
25	940.45	669.35	5521.40	132.29	1494.55	0.00
26	825.45	784.35	4737.05			
27	690.69	919.11	3817.94			
28	532.79	1077.01	2740.93			
29	347.75	1262.05	1478.88			
30	130.92	1478.88	0.00			

16.75 %

30 YEAR TERM:
Monthly Payment = 136.04
Annual Payment = 1632.48

25 YEAR TERM:
Monthly Payment = 137.41
Annual Payment = 1648.92

YR	INTER PD DUR YEAR	PRINCP PD DUR YEAR	MORTG BAL END OF YR	INTER PD DUR YEAR	PRINCP PD DUR YEAR	MORTG BAL END OF YR
1	1618.37	14.11	9985.89	1617.06	31.86	9968.14
2	1615.91	16.57	9969.31	1611.50	37.42	9930.72
3	1613.01	19.47	9949.85	1604.97	43.95	9886.77
4	1609.62	22.86	9926.98	1597.30	51.62	9835.15
5	1605.63	26.85	9900.13	1588.29	60.63	9774.53
6	1600.94	31.54	9868.59	1577.71	71.21	9703.32
7	1595.43	37.05	9831.54	1565.29	83.63	9619.69
8	1588.97	43.51	9788.03	1550.69	98.23	9521.46
9	1581.38	51.10	9736.93	1533.55	115.37	9406.09
10	1572.46	60.02	9676.91	1513.41	135.51	9270.58
11	1561.98	70.50	9606.41	1489.77	159.15	9111.43
12	1549.68	82.80	9523.61	1461.99	186.93	8924.50
13	1535.23	97.25	9426.37	1429.37	219.55	8704.95
14	1518.26	114.22	9312.15	1391.06	257.86	8447.09
15	1498.33	134.15	9177.99	1346.06	302.86	8144.23
16	1474.92	157.56	9020.43	1293.20	355.72	7788.51
17	1447.42	185.06	8835.37	1231.12	417.80	7370.71
18	1415.12	217.36	8618.02	1158.21	490.71	6880.01
19	1377.19	255.29	8362.73	1072.58	576.34	6303.67
20	1332.64	299.84	8062.89	972.00	676.92	5626.75
21	1280.32	352.16	7710.72	853.87	795.05	4831.69
22	1218.86	413.62	7297.10	715.12	933.80	3897.89
23	1146.67	485.81	6811.30	552.16	1096.76	2801.13
24	1061.89	570.59	6240.71	360.76	1288.16	1512.97
25	962.32	670.16	5570.55	135.95	1512.97	0.00
26	845.37	787.11	4783.44			
27	708.00	924.48	3858.96			
28	546.67	1085.81	2773.15			
29	357.18	1275.30	1497.86			
30	134.62	1497.86	0.00			

Annual Amortization Schedules

Based on a Mortgage of $ 10,000.00

17.00 %

30 YEAR TERM:
Monthly Payment = 137.93
Annual Payment = 1655.16

25 YEAR TERM:
Monthly Payment = 139.25
Annual Payment = 1671.00

YR	30 YR INTER PD DUR YEAR	30 YR PRINCP PD DUR YEAR	30 YR MORTG BAL END OF YR	25 YR INTER PD DUR YEAR	25 YR PRINCP PD DUR YEAR	25 YR MORTG BAL END OF YR
1	1641.79	13.37	9986.63	1640.49	30.51	9969.49
2	1639.43	15.73	9970.90	1635.08	35.92	9933.57
3	1636.64	18.52	9952.38	1628.72	42.28	9891.29
4	1633.35	21.81	9930.57	1621.22	49.78	9841.51
5	1629.49	25.67	9904.90	1612.40	58.60	9782.91
6	1624.94	30.22	9874.68	1602.02	68.98	9713.93
7	1619.58	35.58	9839.10	1589.79	81.21	9632.72
8	1613.28	41.88	9797.22	1575.40	95.60	9537.12
9	1605.86	49.30	9747.92	1558.45	112.55	9424.57
10	1597.12	58.04	9689.87	1538.51	132.49	9292.08
11	1586.83	68.33	9621.55	1515.03	155.97	9136.11
12	1574.72	80.44	9541.11	1487.39	183.61	8952.49
13	1560.47	94.69	9446.42	1454.85	216.15	8736.34
14	1543.69	111.47	9334.94	1416.54	254.46	8481.88
15	1523.93	131.23	9203.71	1371.44	299.56	8182.32
16	1500.67	154.49	9049.22	1318.35	352.65	7829.67
17	1473.29	181.87	8867.35	1255.85	415.15	7414.52
18	1441.06	214.10	8653.26	1182.28	488.72	6925.80
19	1403.12	252.04	8401.21	1095.66	575.34	6350.46
20	1358.45	296.71	8104.50	993.70	677.30	5673.16
21	1305.86	349.30	7755.21	873.67	797.33	4875.83
22	1243.96	411.20	7344.01	732.36	938.64	3937.18
23	1171.09	484.07	6859.93	566.01	1104.99	2832.19
24	1085.30	569.86	6290.07	370.17	1300.83	1531.36
25	984.30	670.86	5619.21	139.64	1531.36	0.00
26	865.41	789.75	4829.46			
27	725.44	929.72	3899.74			
28	560.68	1094.48	2805.26			
29	366.71	1288.45	1516.80			
30	138.36	1516.80	0.00			

17.25 %

30 YEAR TERM:
Monthly Payment = 139.82
Annual Payment = 1677.84

25 YEAR TERM:
Monthly Payment = 141.10
Annual Payment = 1693.20

YR	30 YR INTER PD DUR YEAR	30 YR PRINCP PD DUR YEAR	30 YR MORTG BAL END OF YR	25 YR INTER PD DUR YEAR	25 YR PRINCP PD DUR YEAR	25 YR MORTG BAL END OF YR
1	1665.18	12.66	9987.34	1663.98	29.22	9970.78
2	1662.90	14.94	9972.41	1658.73	34.47	9936.31
3	1660.22	17.62	9954.78	1652.52	40.68	9895.63
4	1657.04	20.80	9933.99	1645.20	48.00	9847.64
5	1653.30	24.54	9909.45	1636.57	56.63	9791.00
6	1648.89	28.95	9880.50	1626.38	66.82	9724.18
7	1643.68	34.16	9846.34	1614.35	78.85	9645.33
8	1637.53	40.31	9806.03	1600.16	93.04	9552.30
9	1630.28	47.56	9758.46	1583.42	109.78	9442.52
10	1621.72	56.12	9702.34	1563.67	129.53	9312.99
11	1611.62	66.22	9636.13	1540.36	152.84	9160.15
12	1599.71	78.13	9557.99	1512.86	180.34	8979.82
13	1585.65	92.19	9465.80	1480.41	212.79	8767.03
14	1569.06	108.78	9357.02	1442.12	251.08	8515.95
15	1549.48	128.36	9228.66	1396.95	296.25	8219.70
16	1526.39	151.45	9077.21	1343.64	349.56	7870.14
17	1499.14	178.70	8898.50	1280.74	412.46	7457.67
18	1466.98	210.86	8687.64	1206.52	486.68	6970.99
19	1429.04	248.80	8438.84	1118.95	574.25	6396.74
20	1384.27	293.57	8145.27	1015.62	677.58	5719.16
21	1331.44	346.40	7798.87	893.69	799.51	4919.65
22	1269.11	408.73	7390.14	749.83	943.37	3976.28
23	1195.57	482.27	6907.87	580.08	1113.12	2863.16
24	1108.79	569.05	6338.82	379.79	1313.41	1549.75
25	1006.39	671.45	5667.37	143.45	1549.75	0.00
26	885.57	792.27	4875.10			
27	743.01	934.83	3940.27			
28	574.80	1103.04	2837.23			
29	376.32	1301.52	1535.71			
30	142.13	1535.71	0.00			

Annual Amortization Schedules

Based on a Mortgage of $ 10,000.00

17.50 %

30 YEAR TERM:
Monthly Payment = 141.71
Annual Payment = 1700.52

25 YEAR TERM:
Monthly Payment = 142.94
Annual Payment = 1715.28

YR	30 YR INTER PD DUR YEAR	30 YR PRINCP PD DUR YEAR	30 YR MORTG BAL END OF YR	25 YR INTER PD DUR YEAR	25 YR PRINCP PD DUR YEAR	25 YR MORTG BAL END OF YR
1	1688.53	11.99	9988.01	1687.30	27.98	9972.02
2	1686.34	14.18	9973.84	1682.20	33.08	9938.94
3	1683.75	16.77	9957.07	1676.15	39.13	9899.81
4	1680.69	19.83	9937.24	1669.00	46.28	9853.54
5	1677.07	23.45	9913.79	1660.55	54.73	9798.81
6	1672.79	27.73	9886.06	1650.56	64.72	9734.08
7	1667.72	32.80	9853.26	1638.73	76.55	9657.54
8	1661.73	38.79	9814.47	1624.75	90.53	9567.01
9	1654.64	45.88	9768.59	1608.22	107.06	9459.95
10	1646.26	54.26	9714.33	1588.66	126.62	9333.33
11	1636.35	64.17	9650.17	1565.53	149.75	9183.58
12	1624.63	75.89	9574.28	1538.18	177.10	9006.48
13	1610.77	89.75	9484.53	1505.83	209.45	8797.04
14	1594.38	106.14	9378.39	1467.58	247.70	8549.33
15	1574.99	125.53	9252.87	1422.33	292.95	8256.38
16	1552.06	148.46	9104.41	1368.82	346.46	7909.92
17	1524.95	175.57	8928.84	1305.54	409.74	7500.18
18	1492.88	207.64	8721.20	1230.70	484.58	7015.60
19	1454.95	245.57	8475.63	1142.19	573.09	6442.51
20	1410.10	290.42	8185.20	1037.51	677.77	5764.73
21	1357.05	343.47	7841.73	913.71	801.57	4963.16
22	1294.31	406.21	7435.53	767.29	947.99	4015.18
23	1220.12	480.40	6955.12	594.14	1121.14	2894.04
24	1132.37	568.15	6386.97	389.36	1325.92	1568.11
25	1028.59	671.93	5715.04	147.17	1568.11	0.00
26	905.86	794.66	4920.37			
27	760.71	939.81	3980.56			
28	589.04	1111.48	2869.09			
29	386.03	1314.49	1554.59			
30	145.93	1554.59	0.00			

17.75 %

30 YEAR TERM:
Monthly Payment = 143.60
Annual Payment = 1723.20

25 YEAR TERM:
Monthly Payment = 144.79
Annual Payment = 1737.48

YR	30 YR INTER PD DUR YEAR	30 YR PRINCP PD DUR YEAR	30 YR MORTG BAL END OF YR	25 YR INTER PD DUR YEAR	25 YR PRINCP PD DUR YEAR	25 YR MORTG BAL END OF YR
1	1711.85	11.35	9988.65	1710.70	26.78	9973.22
2	1709.75	13.45	9975.19	1705.73	31.75	9941.47
3	1707.25	15.95	9959.25	1699.85	37.63	9903.83
4	1704.29	18.91	9940.34	1692.87	44.61	9859.22
5	1700.79	22.41	9917.93	1684.60	52.88	9806.34
6	1696.64	26.56	9891.37	1674.80	62.68	9743.66
7	1691.71	31.49	9859.88	1663.18	74.30	9669.35
8	1685.87	37.33	9822.55	1649.40	88.08	9581.27
9	1678.95	44.25	9778.31	1633.07	104.41	9476.87
10	1670.75	52.45	9725.86	1613.72	123.76	9353.10
11	1661.03	62.17	9663.69	1590.78	146.70	9206.40
12	1649.51	73.69	9590.00	1563.58	173.90	9032.50
13	1635.84	87.36	9502.64	1531.34	206.14	8826.37
14	1619.65	103.55	9399.09	1493.13	244.35	8582.02
15	1600.45	122.75	9276.34	1447.84	289.64	8292.38
16	1577.70	145.50	9130.85	1394.14	343.34	7949.04
17	1550.73	172.47	8958.37	1330.50	406.98	7542.05
18	1518.76	204.44	8753.93	1255.05	482.43	7059.62
19	1480.86	242.34	8511.59	1165.62	571.86	6487.76
20	1435.93	287.27	8224.32	1059.61	677.87	5809.89
21	1382.68	340.52	7883.80	933.95	803.53	5006.36
22	1319.56	403.64	7480.16	784.99	952.49	4053.87
23	1244.73	478.47	7001.69	608.42	1129.06	2924.82
24	1156.03	567.17	6434.52	399.12	1338.36	1586.46
25	1050.89	672.31	5762.21	151.02	1586.46	0.00
26	926.26	796.94	4965.27			
27	778.53	944.67	4020.60			
28	603.41	1119.79	2900.81			
29	395.83	1327.37	1573.44			
30	149.76	1573.44	0.00			

Annual Amortization Schedules

Based on a Mortgage of $ 10,000.00

18.00 %

30 YEAR TERM:
Monthly Payment = 145.49
Annual Payment = 1745.88

YR	INTER PD DUR YEAR	PRINCP PD DUR YEAR	MORTG BAL END OF YR
1	1735.13	10.75	9989.25
2	1733.11	12.77	9976.49
3	1730.71	15.17	9961.32
4	1727.86	18.02	9943.29
5	1724.47	21.41	9921.88
6	1720.44	25.44	9896.44
7	1715.65	30.23	9866.21
8	1709.97	35.91	9830.30
9	1703.21	42.67	9787.63
10	1695.19	50.69	9736.94
11	1685.65	60.23	9676.71
12	1674.32	71.56	9605.15
13	1660.86	85.02	9520.13
14	1644.87	101.01	9419.12
15	1625.87	120.01	9299.12
16	1603.30	142.58	9156.53
17	1576.48	169.40	8987.13
18	1544.61	201.27	8785.86
19	1506.75	239.13	8546.74
20	1461.77	284.11	8262.63
21	1408.33	337.55	7925.08
22	1344.84	401.04	7524.05
23	1269.41	476.47	7047.57
24	1179.78	566.10	6481.47
25	1073.30	672.58	5808.89
26	946.79	799.09	5009.80
27	796.48	949.40	4060.39
28	617.89	1127.99	2932.41
29	405.72	1340.16	1592.25
30	153.63	1592.25	0.00

25 YEAR TERM:
Monthly Payment = 146.64
Annual Payment = 1759.68

YR	INTER PD DUR YEAR	PRINCP PD DUR YEAR	MORTG BAL END OF YR
1	1734.04	25.64	9974.36
2	1729.22	30.46	9943.89
3	1723.48	36.20	9907.70
4	1716.68	43.00	9864.70
5	1708.59	51.09	9813.60
6	1698.98	60.70	9752.90
7	1687.56	72.12	9680.78
8	1673.99	85.69	9595.09
9	1657.88	101.80	9493.29
10	1638.73	120.95	9372.33
11	1615.97	143.71	9228.63
12	1588.94	170.74	9057.89
13	1556.83	202.85	8855.04
14	1518.67	241.01	8614.03
15	1473.34	286.34	8327.69
16	1419.48	340.20	7987.48
17	1355.48	404.20	7583.29
18	1279.45	480.23	7103.06
19	1189.12	570.56	6532.51
20	1081.80	677.88	5854.63
21	954.29	805.39	5049.24
22	802.80	956.88	4092.36
23	622.81	1136.87	2955.49
24	408.97	1350.71	1604.78
25	154.90	1604.78	0.00

18.25 %

30 YEAR TERM:
Monthly Payment = 147.39
Annual Payment = 1768.68

YR	INTER PD DUR YEAR	PRINCP PD DUR YEAR	MORTG BAL END OF YR
1	1758.51	10.17	9989.83
2	1756.56	12.12	9977.71
3	1754.25	14.43	9963.28
4	1751.50	17.18	9946.10
5	1748.22	20.46	9925.64
6	1744.32	24.36	9901.28
7	1739.67	29.01	9872.27
8	1734.13	34.55	9837.72
9	1727.54	41.14	9796.58
10	1719.69	48.99	9747.58
11	1710.34	58.34	9689.24
12	1699.21	69.47	9619.77
13	1685.95	82.73	9537.04
14	1670.16	98.52	9438.52
15	1651.36	117.32	9321.20
16	1628.97	139.71	9181.49
17	1602.31	166.37	9015.12
18	1570.56	198.12	8817.01
19	1532.76	235.92	8581.09
20	1487.74	280.94	8300.14
21	1434.13	334.55	7965.59
22	1370.29	398.39	7567.20
23	1294.26	474.42	7092.78
24	1203.73	564.95	6527.84
25	1095.92	672.76	5855.08
26	967.55	801.13	5053.95
27	814.67	954.01	4099.93
28	632.62	1136.06	2963.87
29	415.83	1352.85	1611.02
30	157.66	1611.02	0.00

25 YEAR TERM:
Monthly Payment = 148.49
Annual Payment = 1781.88

YR	INTER PD DUR YEAR	PRINCP PD DUR YEAR	MORTG BAL END OF YR
1	1757.33	24.55	9975.45
2	1752.65	29.23	9946.22
3	1747.07	34.81	9911.42
4	1740.43	41.45	9869.97
5	1732.52	49.36	9820.61
6	1723.10	58.78	9761.83
7	1711.89	70.00	9691.83
8	1698.53	83.35	9608.48
9	1682.62	99.26	9509.22
10	1663.68	118.20	9391.03
11	1641.13	140.75	9250.27
12	1614.27	167.61	9082.66
13	1582.28	199.60	8883.06
14	1544.19	237.69	8645.37
15	1498.83	283.05	8362.32
16	1444.82	337.06	8025.27
17	1380.50	401.38	7623.89
18	1303.91	477.97	7145.92
19	1212.70	569.18	6576.74
20	1104.09	677.80	5898.94
21	974.74	807.14	5091.81
22	820.72	961.16	4130.65
23	637.31	1144.57	2986.07
24	418.89	1362.99	1623.08
25	158.80	1623.08	0.00

Annual Amortization Schedules

Based on a Mortgage of $ 10,000.00

18.50 %

30 YEAR TERM:
Monthly Payment = 149.28
Annual Payment = 1791.36

25 YEAR TERM:
Monthly Payment = 150.34
Annual Payment = 1804.08

YR	30 YR INTER PD DUR YEAR	30 YR PRINCP PD DUR YEAR	30 YR MORTG BAL END OF YR	25 YR INTER PD DUR YEAR	25 YR PRINCP PD DUR YEAR	25 YR MORTG BAL END OF YR
1	1781.73	9.63	9990.37	1780.58	23.49	9976.51
2	1779.86	11.50	9978.87	1776.04	28.04	9948.46
3	1777.64	13.72	9965.15	1770.61	33.47	9914.99
4	1774.98	16.38	9948.78	1764.13	39.95	9875.04
5	1771.81	19.55	9929.23	1756.40	47.68	9827.36
6	1768.03	23.33	9905.90	1747.17	56.91	9770.45
7	1763.52	27.84	9878.06	1736.15	67.93	9702.53
8	1758.13	33.23	9844.83	1723.01	81.07	9621.45
9	1751.69	39.67	9805.16	1707.32	96.76	9524.69
10	1744.02	47.34	9757.82	1688.59	115.49	9409.19
11	1734.85	56.51	9701.31	1666.23	137.85	9271.35
12	1723.92	67.44	9633.86	1639.55	164.53	9106.81
13	1710.86	80.50	9553.36	1607.70	196.38	8910.44
14	1695.28	96.08	9457.28	1569.69	234.39	8676.05
15	1676.68	114.68	9342.61	1524.33	279.75	8396.30
16	1654.49	136.87	9205.73	1470.18	333.90	8062.40
17	1627.99	163.37	9042.37	1405.55	398.53	7663.87
18	1596.37	194.99	8847.38	1328.41	475.67	7188.20
19	1558.63	232.73	8614.65	1236.34	567.74	6620.46
20	1513.59	277.77	8336.88	1126.45	677.63	5942.84
21	1459.82	331.54	8005.34	995.30	808.78	5134.05
22	1395.65	395.71	7609.63	838.75	965.33	4168.72
23	1319.06	472.30	7137.33	651.90	1152.18	3016.55
24	1227.64	563.72	6573.61	428.89	1375.19	1641.36
25	1118.53	672.83	5900.78	162.72	1641.36	0.00
26	988.30	803.06	5097.72			
27	832.86	958.50	4139.22			
28	647.34	1144.02	2995.20			
29	425.91	1365.45	1629.75			
30	161.61	1629.75	0.00			

18.75 %

30 YEAR TERM:
Monthly Payment = 151.17
Annual Payment = 1814.04

25 YEAR TERM:
Monthly Payment = 152.20
Annual Payment = 1826.40

YR	30 YR INTER PD DUR YEAR	30 YR PRINCP PD DUR YEAR	30 YR MORTG BAL END OF YR	25 YR INTER PD DUR YEAR	25 YR PRINCP PD DUR YEAR	25 YR MORTG BAL END OF YR
1	1804.92	9.12	9990.88	1803.91	22.49	9977.51
2	1803.13	10.91	9979.98	1799.50	26.90	9950.61
3	1800.99	13.05	9966.93	1794.22	32.18	9918.43
4	1798.43	15.61	9951.32	1787.90	38.50	9879.93
5	1795.37	18.67	9932.65	1780.34	46.06	9833.87
6	1791.70	22.34	9910.32	1771.30	55.10	9778.78
7	1787.32	26.72	9883.60	1760.49	65.91	9712.87
8	1782.07	31.97	9851.63	1747.55	78.85	9634.02
9	1775.80	38.24	9813.39	1732.07	94.33	9539.69
10	1768.29	45.75	9767.65	1713.56	112.84	9426.85
11	1759.32	54.73	9712.92	1691.41	134.99	9291.86
12	1748.57	65.47	9647.45	1664.91	161.49	9130.38
13	1735.72	78.32	9569.14	1633.21	193.19	8937.19
14	1720.35	93.69	9475.45	1595.29	231.11	8706.09
15	1701.96	112.08	9363.37	1549.93	276.47	8429.62
16	1679.96	134.08	9229.28	1495.66	330.74	8098.88
17	1653.64	160.40	9068.89	1430.74	395.66	7703.23
18	1622.16	191.88	8877.00	1353.08	473.32	7229.91
19	1584.49	229.55	8647.45	1260.17	566.23	6663.68
20	1539.43	274.61	8372.85	1149.03	677.37	5986.31
21	1485.53	328.51	8044.34	1016.07	810.33	5175.98
22	1421.05	392.99	7651.35	857.01	969.39	4206.59
23	1343.91	470.13	7181.21	666.73	1159.67	3046.92
24	1251.63	562.41	6618.80	439.10	1387.30	1659.61
25	1141.23	672.81	5945.99	166.79	1659.61	0.00
26	1009.17	804.87	5141.12			
27	851.18	962.86	4178.26			
28	662.18	1151.86	3026.40			
29	436.08	1377.96	1648.44			
30	165.60	1648.44	0.00			

Annual Amortization Schedules

Based on a Mortgage of $ 10,000.00

19.00 %

30 YEAR TERM:
Monthly Payment = 153.07
Annual Payment = 1836.84

25 YEAR TERM:
Monthly Payment = 154.06
Annual Payment = 1848.72

YR	30 YR INTER PD DUR YEAR	30 YR PRINCP PD DUR YEAR	30 YR MORTG BAL END OF YR	25 YR INTER PD DUR YEAR	25 YR PRINCP PD DUR YEAR	25 YR MORTG BAL END OF YR
1	1828.21	8.63	9991.37	1827.20	21.52	9978.48
2	1826.49	10.35	9981.03	1822.92	25.80	9952.67
3	1824.44	12.40	9968.62	1817.78	30.94	9921.73
4	1821.97	14.87	9953.75	1811.62	37.10	9884.63
5	1819.01	17.83	9935.91	1804.24	44.48	9840.15
6	1815.46	21.38	9914.53	1795.38	53.34	9786.82
7	1811.20	25.64	9888.89	1784.77	63.95	9722.87
8	1806.10	30.74	9858.15	1772.04	76.68	9646.19
9	1799.98	36.86	9821.29	1756.78	91.94	9554.25
10	1792.64	44.20	9777.09	1738.48	110.24	9444.01
11	1783.85	52.99	9724.10	1716.54	132.18	9311.84
12	1773.30	63.54	9660.56	1690.24	158.48	9153.35
13	1760.65	76.19	9584.37	1658.69	190.03	8963.33
14	1745.49	91.35	9493.02	1620.87	227.85	8735.48
15	1727.31	109.53	9383.49	1575.53	273.19	8462.29
16	1705.51	131.33	9252.16	1521.16	327.56	8134.73
17	1679.37	157.47	9094.69	1455.96	392.76	7741.97
18	1648.03	188.81	8905.88	1377.79	470.93	7271.04
19	1610.46	226.38	8679.50	1284.07	564.65	6706.39
20	1565.40	271.44	8408.06	1171.69	677.03	6029.36
21	1511.38	325.46	8082.59	1036.94	811.78	5217.58
22	1446.60	390.24	7692.35	875.38	973.34	4244.24
23	1368.93	467.91	7224.44	681.66	1167.06	3077.18
24	1275.81	561.03	6663.41	449.38	1399.34	1677.84
25	1164.15	672.69	5990.72	170.88	1677.84	0.00
26	1030.26	806.58	5184.14			
27	869.74	967.10	4217.04			
28	677.26	1159.58	3057.46			
29	446.47	1390.37	1667.09			
30	169.75	1667.09	0.00			

19.25 %

30 YEAR TERM:
Monthly Payment = 154.96
Annual Payment = 1859.52

25 YEAR TERM:
Monthly Payment = 155.91
Annual Payment = 1870.92

YR	30 YR INTER PD DUR YEAR	30 YR PRINCP PD DUR YEAR	30 YR MORTG BAL END OF YR	25 YR INTER PD DUR YEAR	25 YR PRINCP PD DUR YEAR	25 YR MORTG BAL END OF YR
1	1851.35	8.17	9991.83	1850.32	20.60	9979.40
2	1849.71	9.81	9982.02	1846.17	24.75	9954.65
3	1847.73	11.79	9970.23	1841.18	29.74	9924.91
4	1845.35	14.17	9956.05	1835.17	35.75	9889.16
5	1842.49	17.03	9939.02	1827.96	42.96	9846.20
6	1839.05	20.47	9918.55	1819.29	51.63	9794.58
7	1834.92	24.60	9893.95	1808.88	62.04	9732.53
8	1829.96	29.56	9864.39	1796.36	74.56	9657.97
9	1823.99	35.53	9828.86	1781.32	89.60	9568.37
10	1816.82	42.70	9786.16	1763.24	107.68	9460.69
11	1808.21	51.31	9734.85	1741.51	129.41	9331.28
12	1797.86	61.66	9673.18	1715.40	155.52	9175.76
13	1785.41	74.11	9599.08	1684.02	186.90	8988.86
14	1770.46	89.06	9510.02	1646.31	224.61	8764.25
15	1752.49	107.03	9402.99	1601.00	269.93	8494.33
16	1730.90	128.62	9274.37	1546.53	324.39	8169.94
17	1704.95	154.57	9119.80	1481.08	389.84	7780.11
18	1673.76	185.76	8934.04	1402.43	468.49	7311.61
19	1636.28	223.24	8710.81	1307.90	563.02	6748.60
20	1591.24	268.28	8442.53	1194.31	676.61	6071.99
21	1537.11	322.41	8120.12	1057.79	813.13	5258.86
22	1472.06	387.46	7732.66	893.73	977.19	4281.67
23	1393.89	465.63	7267.03	696.57	1174.35	3107.33
24	1299.94	559.58	6707.45	459.63	1411.29	1696.04
25	1187.03	672.49	6034.96	174.88	1696.04	0.00
26	1051.35	808.17	5226.79			
27	888.29	971.23	4255.56			
28	692.33	1167.19	3088.38			
29	456.84	1402.68	1685.69			
30	173.83	1685.69	0.00			

Annual Amortization Schedules

Based on a Mortgage of $ 10,000.00

19.50 %

30 YEAR TERM:
Monthly Payment = 156.86
Annual Payment = 1882.32

25 YEAR TERM:
Monthly Payment = 157.77
Annual Payment = 1893.24

YR	INTER PD DUR YEAR (30 yr)	PRINCP PD DUR YEAR (30 yr)	MORTG BAL END OF YR (30 yr)	INTER PD DUR YEAR (25 yr)	PRINCP PD DUR YEAR (25 yr)	MORTG BAL END OF YR (25 yr)
1	1874.59	7.73	9992.27	1873.53	19.71	9980.29
2	1873.01	9.31	9982.96	1869.50	23.74	9956.55
3	1871.11	11.21	9971.75	1864.65	28.59	9927.96
4	1868.81	13.51	9958.25	1858.80	34.44	9893.52
5	1866.05	16.27	9941.98	1851.76	41.48	9852.04
6	1862.73	19.59	9922.39	1843.27	49.97	9802.07
7	1858.72	23.60	9898.78	1833.05	60.19	9741.88
8	1853.89	28.43	9870.36	1820.74	72.50	9669.39
9	1848.08	34.24	9836.12	1805.92	87.32	9582.06
10	1841.08	41.24	9794.87	1788.06	105.18	9476.89
11	1832.64	49.68	9745.19	1766.55	126.69	9350.20
12	1822.48	59.84	9685.36	1740.64	152.60	9197.60
13	1810.25	72.07	9613.28	1709.44	183.80	9013.80
14	1795.51	86.81	9526.47	1671.85	221.39	8792.41
15	1777.75	104.57	9421.90	1626.57	266.67	8525.74
16	1756.37	125.95	9295.95	1572.04	321.20	8204.53
17	1730.61	151.71	9144.24	1506.35	386.89	7817.64
18	1699.58	182.74	8961.50	1427.23	466.01	7351.63
19	1662.21	220.11	8741.39	1331.92	561.32	6790.31
20	1617.20	265.12	8476.27	1217.13	676.11	6114.20
21	1562.98	319.34	8156.93	1078.86	814.38	5299.82
22	1497.67	384.65	7772.28	912.32	980.92	4318.89
23	1419.01	463.31	7308.97	711.71	1181.53	3137.36
24	1324.26	558.06	6750.91	470.08	1423.16	1714.20
25	1210.13	672.19	6078.72	179.03	1714.20	0.00
26	1072.67	809.65	5269.07			
27	907.09	975.23	4293.84			
28	707.65	1174.67	3119.16			
29	467.42	1414.90	1704.26			
30	178.06	1704.26	0.00			

19.75 %

30 YEAR TERM:
Monthly Payment = 158.75
Annual Payment = 1905.00

25 YEAR TERM:
Monthly Payment = 159.63
Annual Payment = 1915.56

YR	INTER PD DUR YEAR (30 yr)	PRINCP PD DUR YEAR (30 yr)	MORTG BAL END OF YR (30 yr)	INTER PD DUR YEAR (25 yr)	PRINCP PD DUR YEAR (25 yr)	MORTG BAL END OF YR (25 yr)
1	1897.69	7.31	9992.69	1896.70	18.86	9981.14
2	1896.17	8.83	9983.86	1892.79	22.77	9958.38
3	1894.34	10.66	9973.20	1888.08	27.48	9930.89
4	1892.13	12.87	9960.33	1882.38	33.18	9897.71
5	1889.47	15.53	9944.80	1875.50	40.06	9857.65
6	1886.25	18.75	9926.05	1867.20	48.36	9809.30
7	1882.36	22.64	9903.40	1857.18	58.38	9750.91
8	1877.67	27.33	9876.07	1845.08	70.48	9680.43
9	1872.00	33.00	9843.08	1830.47	85.09	9595.35
10	1865.16	39.84	9803.24	1812.84	102.72	9492.62
11	1856.91	48.09	9755.15	1791.55	124.01	9368.61
12	1846.94	58.06	9697.09	1765.85	149.71	9218.90
13	1834.91	70.09	9627.00	1734.82	180.74	9038.15
14	1820.38	84.62	9542.38	1697.36	218.20	8819.95
15	1802.84	102.16	9440.22	1652.14	263.42	8556.53
16	1781.67	123.33	9316.89	1597.54	318.02	8238.51
17	1756.11	148.89	9168.01	1531.63	383.93	7854.58
18	1725.26	179.74	8988.26	1452.06	463.50	7391.08
19	1688.00	217.00	8771.26	1356.00	559.56	6831.52
20	1643.03	261.97	8509.29	1240.03	675.53	6155.99
21	1588.74	316.26	8193.03	1100.02	815.54	5340.45
22	1523.19	381.81	7811.22	931.00	984.56	4355.90
23	1444.06	460.94	7350.28	726.95	1188.61	3167.29
24	1348.53	556.47	6793.81	480.61	1434.95	1732.34
25	1233.20	671.80	6122.01	183.22	1732.34	0.00
26	1093.97	811.03	5310.97			
27	925.88	979.12	4331.85			
28	722.95	1182.05	3149.81			
29	477.97	1427.03	1722.78			
30	182.22	1722.78	0.00			

Annual Amortization Schedules

Based on a Mortgage of $ 10,000.00

20.00 %

30 YEAR TERM:
Monthly Payment = 160.65
Annual Payment = 1927.80

25 YEAR TERM:
Monthly Payment = 161.49
Annual Payment = 1937.88

YR	30 YR INTER PD DUR YEAR	30 YR PRINCP PD DUR YEAR	30 YR MORTG BAL END OF YR	25 YR INTER PD DUR YEAR	25 YR PRINCP PD DUR YEAR	25 YR MORTG BAL END OF YR
1	1920.88	6.92	9993.08	1919.84	18.04	9981.96
2	1919.43	8.37	9984.71	1916.05	21.83	9960.13
3	1917.67	10.13	9974.58	1911.46	26.42	9933.71
4	1915.54	12.26	9962.32	1905.92	31.96	9901.75
5	1912.97	14.83	9947.48	1899.20	38.68	9863.07
6	1909.85	17.95	9929.54	1891.08	46.80	9816.27
7	1906.08	21.72	9907.82	1881.25	56.63	9759.65
8	1901.52	26.28	9881.54	1869.36	68.52	9691.13
9	1896.00	31.80	9849.75	1854.97	82.91	9608.22
10	1889.33	38.47	9811.27	1837.56	100.32	9507.91
11	1881.25	46.55	9764.72	1816.50	121.38	9386.53
12	1871.47	56.33	9708.39	1791.01	146.87	9239.65
13	1859.64	68.16	9640.24	1760.16	177.72	9061.94
14	1845.33	82.47	9557.77	1722.84	215.04	8846.90
15	1828.01	99.79	9457.98	1677.69	260.19	8586.71
16	1807.06	120.74	9337.23	1623.05	314.83	8271.88
17	1781.70	146.10	9191.13	1556.93	380.95	7890.93
18	1751.02	176.78	9014.35	1476.93	460.95	7429.98
19	1713.89	213.91	8800.44	1380.13	557.75	6872.23
20	1668.97	258.83	8541.62	1263.01	674.87	6197.36
21	1614.62	313.18	8228.44	1121.28	816.60	5380.76
22	1548.85	378.95	7849.49	949.80	988.08	4392.68
23	1469.27	458.53	7390.96	742.30	1195.58	3197.10
24	1372.98	554.82	6836.14	491.23	1446.65	1750.45
25	1256.47	671.33	6164.81	187.43	1750.45	0.00
26	1115.49	812.31	5352.51			
27	944.91	982.89	4369.61			
28	738.50	1189.30	3180.31			
29	488.75	1439.05	1741.26			
30	186.54	1741.26	0.00			

20.25 %

30 YEAR TERM:
Monthly Payment = 162.54
Annual Payment = 1950.48

25 YEAR TERM:
Monthly Payment = 163.36
Annual Payment = 1960.32

YR	30 YR INTER PD DUR YEAR	30 YR PRINCP PD DUR YEAR	30 YR MORTG BAL END OF YR	25 YR INTER PD DUR YEAR	25 YR PRINCP PD DUR YEAR	25 YR MORTG BAL END OF YR
1	1943.93	6.55	9993.45	1943.06	17.26	9982.74
2	1942.54	7.94	9985.51	1939.39	20.93	9961.80
3	1940.85	9.63	9975.88	1934.93	25.39	9936.42
4	1938.80	11.68	9964.21	1929.53	30.79	9905.63
5	1936.32	14.16	9950.04	1922.98	37.34	9868.29
6	1933.30	17.18	9932.87	1915.04	45.28	9823.00
7	1929.65	20.83	9912.04	1905.40	54.92	9768.08
8	1925.22	25.26	9886.78	1893.72	66.60	9701.48
9	1919.84	30.64	9856.14	1879.55	80.77	9620.71
10	1913.33	37.15	9818.99	1862.36	97.96	9522.75
11	1905.42	45.06	9773.93	1841.52	118.80	9403.96
12	1895.84	54.64	9719.29	1816.25	144.07	9259.89
13	1884.21	66.27	9653.02	1785.60	174.72	9085.16
14	1870.11	80.37	9572.65	1748.43	211.89	8873.27
15	1853.01	97.47	9475.18	1703.34	256.98	8616.29
16	1832.28	118.20	9356.98	1648.67	311.65	8304.65
17	1807.13	143.35	9213.63	1582.37	377.95	7926.69
18	1776.63	173.85	9039.78	1501.96	458.36	7468.33
19	1739.64	210.84	8828.94	1404.44	555.88	6912.46
20	1694.79	255.69	8573.25	1286.18	674.14	6238.31
21	1640.39	310.09	8263.16	1142.75	817.57	5420.75
22	1574.42	376.06	7887.09	968.82	991.50	4429.24
23	1494.41	456.07	7431.02	757.87	1202.45	3226.79
24	1397.38	553.10	6877.92	502.05	1458.27	1768.52
25	1279.71	670.77	6207.15	191.80	1768.52	0.00
26	1137.00	813.48	5393.67			
27	963.93	986.55	4407.12			
28	754.04	1196.44	3210.67			
29	499.49	1450.99	1759.69			
30	190.79	1759.69	0.00			

Annual Amortization Schedules

Based on a Mortgage of $ 10,000.00

20.50 %

30 YEAR TERM: Monthly Payment = 164.43; Annual Payment = 1973.16

25 YEAR TERM: Monthly Payment = 165.22; Annual Payment = 1982.64

YR	30 YR INTER PD DUR YEAR	30 YR PRINCP PD DUR YEAR	30 YR MORTG BAL END OF YR	25 YR INTER PD DUR YEAR	25 YR PRINCP PD DUR YEAR	25 YR MORTG BAL END OF YR
1	1966.97	6.19	9993.81	1966.13	16.51	9983.49
2	1965.63	7.53	9986.28	1962.57	20.07	9963.41
3	1964.01	9.15	9977.12	1958.24	24.40	9939.02
4	1962.04	11.12	9966.00	1952.98	29.66	9909.36
5	1959.64	13.52	9952.48	1946.59	36.05	9873.31
6	1956.72	16.44	9936.04	1938.82	43.82	9829.50
7	1953.18	19.98	9916.07	1929.38	53.26	9776.24
8	1948.88	24.28	9891.78	1917.90	64.74	9711.50
9	1943.64	29.52	9862.27	1903.95	78.69	9632.81
10	1937.28	35.88	9826.39	1887.00	95.64	9537.17
11	1929.55	43.61	9782.79	1866.38	116.26	9420.91
12	1920.15	53.01	9729.78	1841.33	141.31	9279.60
13	1908.73	64.43	9665.35	1810.88	171.76	9107.84
14	1894.85	78.31	9587.04	1773.86	208.78	8899.06
15	1877.97	95.19	9491.85	1728.87	253.77	8645.29
16	1857.46	115.70	9376.14	1674.18	308.46	8336.82
17	1832.52	140.64	9235.51	1607.70	374.94	7961.88
18	1802.21	170.95	9064.56	1526.90	455.74	7506.14
19	1765.37	207.79	8856.77	1428.68	553.96	6952.19
20	1720.59	252.57	8604.20	1309.30	673.34	6278.85
21	1666.16	307.00	8297.21	1164.20	818.44	5460.41
22	1600.00	373.16	7924.05	987.82	994.82	4465.58
23	1519.59	453.57	7470.47	773.43	1209.21	3256.37
24	1421.84	551.32	6919.15	512.83	1469.81	1786.56
25	1303.02	670.14	6249.02	196.08	1786.56	0.00
26	1158.60	814.55	5434.46			
27	983.06	990.10	4444.36			
28	769.69	1203.47	3240.89			
29	510.34	1462.82	1778.07			
30	195.09	1778.07	0.00			

20.75 %

30 YEAR TERM: Monthly Payment = 166.33; Annual Payment = 1995.96

25 YEAR TERM: Monthly Payment = 167.08; Annual Payment = 2004.96

YR	30 YR INTER PD DUR YEAR	30 YR PRINCP PD DUR YEAR	30 YR MORTG BAL END OF YR	25 YR INTER PD DUR YEAR	25 YR PRINCP PD DUR YEAR	25 YR MORTG BAL END OF YR
1	1990.10	5.86	9994.14	1989.16	15.80	9984.20
2	1988.82	7.14	9987.00	1985.71	19.25	9964.96
3	1987.26	8.70	9978.30	1981.51	23.45	9941.51
4	1985.36	10.60	9967.71	1976.40	28.56	9912.95
5	1983.05	12.91	9954.80	1970.16	34.80	9878.15
6	1980.23	15.73	9939.07	1962.57	42.39	9835.76
7	1976.80	19.16	9919.92	1953.32	51.64	9784.12
8	1972.62	23.34	9896.58	1942.04	62.92	9721.20
9	1967.53	28.43	9868.14	1928.31	76.65	9644.55
10	1961.32	34.64	9833.50	1911.58	93.38	9551.17
11	1953.76	42.20	9791.30	1891.20	113.76	9437.41
12	1944.55	51.41	9739.89	1866.37	138.59	9298.82
13	1933.33	62.63	9677.26	1836.12	168.84	9129.98
14	1919.66	76.30	9600.95	1799.27	205.69	8924.29
15	1903.00	92.96	9508.00	1754.37	250.59	8673.70
16	1882.71	113.25	9394.75	1699.68	305.28	8368.42
17	1858.00	137.96	9256.79	1633.05	371.91	7996.50
18	1827.88	168.08	9088.71	1551.87	453.09	7543.42
19	1791.20	204.76	8883.95	1452.98	551.98	6991.44
20	1746.51	249.45	8634.49	1332.50	672.46	6318.98
21	1692.06	303.90	8330.59	1185.73	819.23	5499.74
22	1625.73	370.23	7960.36	1006.92	998.04	4501.70
23	1544.92	451.04	7509.32	789.08	1215.88	3285.83
24	1446.47	549.49	6959.83	523.70	1481.26	1804.57
25	1326.54	669.42	6290.41	200.39	1804.57	0.00
26	1180.43	815.53	5474.89			
27	1002.43	993.53	4481.36			
28	785.58	1210.38	3270.97			
29	521.40	1474.56	1796.41			
30	199.55	1796.41	0.00			

Annual Amortization Schedules
Based on a Mortgage of $ 10,000.00

21.00 %

30 YEAR TERM:
Monthly Payment = 168.22
Annual Payment = 2018.64

25 YEAR TERM:
Monthly Payment = 168.95
Annual Payment = 2027.40

YR	30 YR INTER PD DUR YEAR	30 YR PRINCP PD DUR YEAR	30 YR MORTG BAL END OF YR	25 YR INTER PD DUR YEAR	25 YR PRINCP PD DUR YEAR	25 YR MORTG BAL END OF YR
1	2013.10	5.54	9994.46	2012.29	15.11	9984.89
2	2011.87	6.77	9987.69	2008.95	18.45	9966.44
3	2010.38	8.26	9979.42	2004.87	22.53	9943.91
4	2008.55	10.09	9969.33	1999.89	27.51	9916.40
5	2006.32	12.32	9957.01	1993.81	33.59	9882.81
6	2003.59	15.05	9941.96	1986.39	41.01	9841.80
7	2000.27	18.37	9923.59	1977.32	50.08	9791.73
8	1996.21	22.43	9901.16	1966.26	61.14	9730.58
9	1991.25	27.39	9873.77	1952.74	74.66	9655.92
10	1985.20	33.44	9840.33	1936.24	91.16	9564.76
11	1977.80	40.84	9799.49	1916.09	111.31	9453.45
12	1968.78	49.86	9749.63	1891.49	135.91	9317.54
13	1957.76	60.88	9688.75	1861.45	165.95	9151.59
14	1944.30	74.34	9614.41	1824.77	202.63	8948.96
15	1927.87	90.77	9523.64	1779.98	247.42	8701.54
16	1907.81	110.83	9412.81	1725.30	302.10	8399.44
17	1883.31	135.33	9277.48	1658.52	368.88	8030.56
18	1853.40	165.24	9112.24	1576.99	450.41	7580.16
19	1816.88	201.76	8910.48	1477.44	549.96	7030.20
20	1772.29	246.35	8664.13	1355.89	671.51	6358.69
21	1717.84	300.80	8363.33	1207.47	819.93	5538.76
22	1651.35	367.29	7996.04	1026.24	1001.16	4537.60
23	1570.17	448.47	7547.57	804.96	1222.44	3315.16
24	1471.05	547.59	6999.98	534.77	1492.63	1822.53
25	1350.02	668.62	6331.35	204.86	1822.53	0.00
26	1202.23	816.41	5514.94			
27	1021.79	996.85	4518.09			
28	801.46	1217.18	3300.91			
29	532.43	1486.21	1814.70			
30	203.94	1814.70	0.00			

21.25 %

30 YEAR TERM:
Monthly Payment = 170.11
Annual Payment = 2041.32

25 YEAR TERM:
Monthly Payment = 170.81
Annual Payment = 2049.72

YR	30 YR INTER PD DUR YEAR	30 YR PRINCP PD DUR YEAR	30 YR MORTG BAL END OF YR	25 YR INTER PD DUR YEAR	25 YR PRINCP PD DUR YEAR	25 YR MORTG BAL END OF YR
1	2036.08	5.24	9994.76	2035.27	14.45	9985.55
2	2034.90	6.42	9988.34	2032.03	17.69	9967.86
3	2033.47	7.85	9980.48	2028.07	21.65	9946.21
4	2031.71	9.61	9970.87	2023.23	26.49	9919.72
5	2029.56	11.76	9959.11	2017.30	32.42	9887.30
6	2026.93	14.39	9944.72	2010.05	39.67	9847.63
7	2023.70	17.62	9927.10	2001.17	48.55	9799.08
8	2019.76	21.56	9905.54	1990.30	59.42	9739.66
9	2014.94	26.38	9879.16	1977.01	72.71	9666.94
10	2009.03	32.29	9846.88	1960.73	88.99	9577.96
11	2001.81	39.51	9807.36	1940.82	108.90	9469.05
12	1992.97	48.35	9759.01	1916.45	133.27	9335.78
13	1982.15	59.17	9699.84	1886.62	163.10	9172.68
14	1968.90	72.42	9627.42	1850.12	199.60	8973.09
15	1952.70	88.62	9538.79	1805.45	244.27	8728.82
16	1932.86	108.46	9430.34	1750.79	298.93	8429.89
17	1908.59	132.73	9297.61	1683.89	365.83	8064.06
18	1878.89	162.43	9135.18	1602.03	447.69	7616.37
19	1842.54	198.78	8936.40	1501.84	547.88	7068.48
20	1798.05	243.27	8693.13	1379.23	670.49	6397.99
21	1743.61	297.71	8395.42	1229.18	820.54	5577.45
22	1676.99	364.33	8031.09	1045.55	1004.17	4573.27
23	1595.46	445.86	7585.23	820.82	1228.90	3344.38
24	1495.68	545.64	7039.58	545.81	1503.91	1840.47
25	1373.57	667.75	6371.83	209.25	1840.47	0.00
26	1224.13	817.19	5554.64			
27	1041.25	1000.07	4554.57			
28	817.45	1223.87	3330.70			
29	543.56	1497.76	1832.94			
30	208.38	1832.94	0.00			

Annual Amortization Schedules

Based on a Mortgage of $ 10,000.00

21.50 %

30 YEAR TERM:
Monthly Payment = 172.01
Annual Payment = 2064.12

25 YEAR TERM:
Monthly Payment = 172.68
Annual Payment = 2072.16

YR	30 YR INTER PD DUR YEAR	30 YR PRINCP PD DUR YEAR	30 YR MORTG BAL END OF YR	25 YR INTER PD DUR YEAR	25 YR PRINCP PD DUR YEAR	25 YR MORTG BAL END OF YR
1	2059.16	4.96	9995.04	2058.34	13.82	9986.18
2	2058.04	6.08	9988.96	2055.20	16.96	9969.22
3	2056.66	7.46	9981.49	2051.36	20.80	9948.42
4	2054.97	9.15	9972.34	2046.65	25.51	9922.91
5	2052.89	11.23	9961.11	2040.87	31.29	9891.63
6	2050.35	13.77	9947.34	2033.78	38.38	9853.25
7	2047.23	16.89	9930.45	2025.09	47.07	9806.18
8	2043.40	20.72	9909.74	2014.42	57.74	9748.44
9	2038.71	25.41	9884.33	2001.34	70.82	9677.63
10	2032.95	31.17	9853.16	1985.30	86.86	9590.77
11	2025.89	38.23	9814.93	1965.62	106.54	9484.23
12	2017.23	46.89	9768.05	1941.48	130.68	9353.55
13	2006.61	57.51	9710.53	1911.88	160.28	9193.27
14	1993.58	70.54	9639.99	1875.57	196.59	8996.68
15	1977.60	86.52	9553.47	1831.03	241.13	8755.55
16	1958.00	106.12	9447.35	1776.40	295.76	8459.78
17	1933.95	130.17	9317.18	1709.39	362.77	8097.01
18	1904.46	159.66	9157.52	1627.20	444.96	7652.06
19	1868.29	195.83	8961.69	1526.39	545.76	7106.29
20	1823.93	240.19	8721.50	1402.75	669.41	6436.88
21	1769.51	294.61	8426.89	1251.09	821.07	5615.81
22	1702.76	361.36	8065.53	1065.07	1007.09	4608.72
23	1620.89	443.23	7622.30	836.91	1235.25	3373.47
24	1520.48	543.64	7078.66	557.05	1515.11	1858.36
25	1397.31	666.81	6411.85	213.80	1858.36	0.00
26	1246.24	817.88	5593.97			
27	1060.95	1003.17	4590.80			
28	833.67	1230.45	3360.35			
29	554.91	1509.21	1851.14			
30	212.98	1851.14	0.00			

21.75 %

30 YEAR TERM:
Monthly Payment = 173.90
Annual Payment = 2086.80

25 YEAR TERM:
Monthly Payment = 174.54
Annual Payment = 2094.48

YR	30 YR INTER PD DUR YEAR	30 YR PRINCP PD DUR YEAR	30 YR MORTG BAL END OF YR	25 YR INTER PD DUR YEAR	25 YR PRINCP PD DUR YEAR	25 YR MORTG BAL END OF YR
1	2082.11	4.69	9995.31	2081.26	13.22	9986.78
2	2081.03	5.77	9989.54	2078.23	16.25	9970.53
3	2079.71	7.09	9982.45	2074.50	19.98	9950.55
4	2078.08	8.72	9973.73	2069.92	24.56	9925.98
5	2076.08	10.72	9963.02	2064.28	30.20	9895.79
6	2073.63	13.17	9949.85	2057.36	37.12	9858.67
7	2070.61	16.19	9933.65	2048.85	45.63	9813.04
8	2066.89	19.91	9913.75	2038.38	56.10	9756.94
9	2062.33	24.47	9889.28	2025.52	68.96	9687.98
10	2056.72	30.08	9859.19	2009.70	84.78	9603.20
11	2049.82	36.98	9822.21	1990.26	104.22	9498.98
12	2041.34	45.46	9776.75	1966.36	128.12	9370.86
13	2030.91	55.89	9720.86	1936.98	157.50	9213.37
14	2018.09	68.71	9652.15	1900.86	193.62	9019.75
15	2002.34	84.46	9567.69	1856.46	238.02	8781.73
16	1982.97	103.83	9463.85	1801.88	292.60	8489.13
17	1959.16	127.64	9336.21	1734.78	359.70	8129.42
18	1929.88	156.92	9179.29	1652.29	442.19	7687.23
19	1893.90	192.90	8986.39	1550.88	543.60	7143.63
20	1849.66	237.14	8749.26	1426.22	668.26	6475.37
21	1795.28	291.52	8457.73	1272.97	821.51	5653.85
22	1728.43	358.37	8099.36	1084.57	1009.91	4643.94
23	1646.24	440.56	7658.80	852.97	1241.51	3402.44
24	1545.21	541.59	7117.21	568.26	1526.22	1876.22
25	1421.01	665.79	6451.42	218.26	1876.22	0.00
26	1268.32	818.48	5632.94			
27	1080.63	1006.17	4626.77			
28	849.88	1236.92	3389.85			
29	566.23	1520.57	1869.28			
30	217.52	1869.28	0.00			

Annual Amortization Schedules

Based on a Mortgage of $ 10,000.00

22.00 %

30 YEAR TERM: Monthly Payment = 175.79; Annual Payment = 2109.48

25 YEAR TERM: Monthly Payment = 176.41; Annual Payment = 2116.92

YR	INTER PD DUR YEAR	PRINCP PD DUR YEAR	MORTG BAL END OF YR	INTER PD DUR YEAR	PRINCP PD DUR YEAR	MORTG BAL END OF YR
1	2105.04	4.44	9995.56	2104.28	12.64	9987.36
2	2104.01	5.47	9990.10	2101.34	15.58	9971.78
3	2102.74	6.74	9983.36	2097.73	19.19	9952.58
4	2101.18	8.30	9975.06	2093.27	23.65	9928.93
5	2099.25	10.23	9964.83	2087.78	29.14	9899.79
6	2096.88	12.60	9952.23	2081.02	35.90	9863.89
7	2093.96	15.52	9936.71	2072.69	44.23	9819.66
8	2090.35	19.13	9917.58	2062.42	54.50	9765.16
9	2085.91	23.57	9894.02	2049.77	67.15	9698.01
10	2080.44	29.04	9864.98	2034.18	82.74	9615.27
11	2073.70	35.78	9829.20	2014.98	101.94	9513.33
12	2065.40	44.08	9785.13	1991.32	125.60	9387.73
13	2055.17	54.31	9730.82	1962.17	154.75	9232.98
14	2042.56	66.91	9663.90	1926.25	190.67	9042.31
15	2027.03	82.45	9581.46	1882.00	234.92	8807.38
16	2007.90	101.58	9479.87	1827.47	289.45	8517.93
17	1984.32	125.16	9354.71	1760.29	356.63	8161.30
18	1955.27	154.21	9200.51	1677.51	439.41	7721.89
19	1919.48	190.00	9010.51	1575.53	541.39	7180.50
20	1875.38	234.10	8776.41	1449.87	667.05	6513.45
21	1821.05	288.43	8487.97	1295.05	821.87	5691.57
22	1754.10	355.38	8132.60	1104.29	1012.63	4678.94
23	1671.62	437.86	7694.73	869.26	1247.66	3431.28
24	1569.99	539.49	7155.25	579.68	1537.24	1894.04
25	1444.78	664.70	6490.54	222.88	1894.04	0.00
26	1290.50	818.98	5671.56			
27	1100.41	1009.07	4662.49			
28	866.21	1243.27	3419.21			
29	577.64	1531.84	1887.38			
30	222.10	1887.38	0.00			

22.25 %

30 YEAR TERM: Monthly Payment = 177.68; Annual Payment = 2132.16

25 YEAR TERM: Monthly Payment = 178.28; Annual Payment = 2139.36

YR	INTER PD DUR YEAR	PRINCP PD DUR YEAR	MORTG BAL END OF YR	INTER PD DUR YEAR	PRINCP PD DUR YEAR	MORTG BAL END OF YR
1	2127.96	4.20	9995.80	2127.27	12.09	9987.91
2	2126.98	5.18	9990.62	2124.43	14.93	9972.98
3	2125.76	6.40	9984.22	2120.92	18.44	9954.54
4	2124.26	7.90	9976.32	2116.59	22.77	9931.77
5	2122.40	9.76	9966.56	2111.24	28.12	9903.65
6	2120.11	12.05	9954.51	2104.64	34.72	9868.93
7	2117.28	14.88	9939.63	2096.48	42.88	9826.05
8	2113.78	18.38	9921.25	2086.41	52.95	9773.11
9	2109.47	22.69	9898.56	2073.98	65.38	9707.72
10	2104.14	28.02	9870.53	2058.62	80.74	9626.98
11	2097.55	34.61	9835.93	2039.65	99.70	9527.28
12	2089.43	42.73	9793.19	2016.24	123.12	9404.15
13	2079.39	52.77	9740.42	1987.32	152.04	9252.11
14	2066.99	65.17	9675.26	1951.61	187.75	9064.36
15	2051.69	80.47	9594.79	1907.51	231.85	8832.51
16	2032.79	99.37	9495.42	1853.05	286.31	8546.20
17	2009.45	122.71	9372.71	1785.80	353.56	8192.64
18	1980.63	151.53	9221.17	1702.76	436.60	7756.04
19	1945.03	187.13	9034.05	1600.22	539.14	7216.90
20	1901.08	231.08	8802.97	1473.58	665.78	6551.12
21	1846.81	285.35	8517.62	1317.21	822.15	5728.97
22	1779.79	352.37	8165.25	1124.10	1015.26	4713.72
23	1697.02	435.14	7730.11	885.64	1253.72	3460.00
24	1594.82	537.34	7192.77	591.18	1548.18	1911.82
25	1468.61	663.55	6529.22	227.54	1911.82	0.00
26	1312.76	819.40	5709.81			
27	1120.30	1011.86	4697.95			
28	882.64	1249.52	3448.43			
29	589.15	1543.01	1905.42			
30	226.74	1905.42	0.00			

Annual Amortization Schedules

Based on a Mortgage of $ 10,000.00

22.50 %

30 YEAR TERM:
Monthly Payment = 179.57
Annual Payment = 2154.84

25 YEAR TERM:
Monthly Payment = 180.14
Annual Payment = 2161.68

YR	30 YR INTER PD DUR YEAR	30 YR PRINCP PD DUR YEAR	30 YR MORTG BAL END OF YR	25 YR INTER PD DUR YEAR	25 YR PRINCP PD DUR YEAR	25 YR MORTG BAL END OF YR
1	2150.87	3.97	9996.03	2150.12	11.56	9988.44
2	2149.93	4.91	9991.12	2147.37	14.31	9974.13
3	2148.76	6.08	9985.04	2143.97	17.71	9956.42
4	2147.32	7.52	9977.51	2139.76	21.92	9934.49
5	2145.53	9.31	9968.20	2134.55	27.13	9907.36
6	2143.31	11.53	9956.68	2128.10	33.58	9873.79
7	2140.58	14.27	9942.41	2120.12	41.56	9832.23
8	2137.18	17.66	9924.76	2110.25	51.43	9780.79
9	2132.99	21.85	9902.91	2098.02	63.66	9717.13
10	2127.80	27.04	9875.86	2082.89	78.79	9638.35
11	2121.37	33.47	9842.39	2064.17	97.51	9540.84
12	2113.41	41.43	9800.96	2040.99	120.69	9420.15
13	2103.57	51.27	9749.69	2012.31	149.37	9270.78
14	2091.38	63.46	9686.24	1976.81	184.87	9085.92
15	2076.30	78.54	9607.70	1932.88	228.80	8857.12
16	2057.64	97.20	9510.50	1878.50	283.18	8573.94
17	2034.54	120.30	9390.20	1811.21	350.47	8223.47
18	2005.95	148.89	9241.30	1727.91	433.77	7789.70
19	1970.56	184.28	9057.03	1624.83	536.85	7252.84
20	1926.77	228.07	8828.95	1497.24	664.44	6588.40
21	1872.56	282.28	8546.68	1339.33	822.35	5766.05
22	1805.48	349.36	8197.32	1143.89	1017.79	4748.26
23	1722.45	432.39	7764.93	902.01	1259.67	3488.59
24	1619.69	535.15	7229.78	602.64	1559.04	1929.55
25	1492.51	662.33	6567.45	232.13	1929.55	0.00
26	1335.10	819.74	5747.72			
27	1140.29	1014.55	4733.17			
28	899.18	1255.67	3477.50			
29	600.76	1554.08	1923.42			
30	231.42	1923.42	0.00			

22.75 %

30 YEAR TERM:
Monthly Payment = 181.46
Annual Payment = 2177.52

25 YEAR TERM:
Monthly Payment = 182.01
Annual Payment = 2184.12

YR	30 YR INTER PD DUR YEAR	30 YR PRINCP PD DUR YEAR	30 YR MORTG BAL END OF YR	25 YR INTER PD DUR YEAR	25 YR PRINCP PD DUR YEAR	25 YR MORTG BAL END OF YR
1	2173.77	3.75	9996.25	2173.06	11.06	9988.94
2	2172.86	4.66	9991.59	2170.41	13.71	9975.23
3	2171.74	5.78	9985.82	2167.11	17.01	9958.22
4	2170.36	7.16	9978.65	2163.02	21.10	9937.11
5	2168.63	8.89	9969.77	2157.94	26.18	9910.94
6	2166.50	11.02	9958.74	2151.65	32.47	9878.47
7	2163.85	13.67	9945.07	2143.84	40.28	9838.19
8	2160.56	16.96	9928.11	2134.16	49.96	9788.23
9	2156.48	21.04	9907.07	2122.15	61.97	9726.25
10	2151.42	26.10	9880.97	2107.24	76.88	9649.38
11	2145.15	32.37	9848.60	2088.76	95.36	9554.02
12	2137.36	40.16	9808.44	2065.83	118.29	9435.73
13	2127.71	49.81	9758.63	2037.39	146.73	9289.00
14	2115.73	61.79	9696.85	2002.11	182.01	9106.99
15	2100.88	76.64	9620.20	1958.35	225.77	8881.22
16	2082.45	95.07	9525.13	1904.06	280.05	8601.16
17	2059.59	117.93	9407.20	1836.73	347.39	8253.77
18	2031.23	146.29	9260.91	1753.20	430.92	7822.86
19	1996.06	181.46	9079.46	1649.59	534.53	7288.33
20	1952.43	225.09	8854.37	1521.07	663.05	6625.28
21	1898.31	279.21	8575.16	1361.65	822.47	5802.81
22	1831.18	346.34	8228.82	1163.90	1020.22	4782.59
23	1747.91	429.61	7799.20	918.59	1265.53	3517.06
24	1644.61	532.91	7266.29	614.31	1569.81	1947.25
25	1516.48	661.04	6605.25	236.87	1947.25	0.00
26	1357.54	819.98	5785.27			
27	1160.38	1017.14	4768.13			
28	915.82	1261.70	3506.43			
29	612.46	1565.06	1941.36			
30	236.16	1941.36	0.00			

Annual Amortization Schedules

Based on a Mortgage of $ 10,000.00

23.00 %

0 YEAR TERM
lonthly Payment = 183.35
nnual Payment =2200.20

R	INTER PD DUR YEAR	PRINCP PD DUR YEAR	MORTG BAL END OF YR
1	2196.65	3.55	9996.45
2	2195.79	4.41	9992.04
3	2194.71	5.49	9986.55
4	2193.38	6.82	9979.73
5	2191.72	8.48	9971.25
6	2189.66	10.54	9960.71
7	2187.09	13.11	9947.61
8	2183.91	16.29	9931.31
9	2179.94	20.26	9911.06
0	2175.02	25.18	9885.88
1	2168.89	31.31	9854.57
2	2161.28	38.92	9815.65
3	2151.81	48.39	9767.26
4	2140.04	60.16	9707.10
5	2125.41	74.79	9632.31
6	2107.22	92.98	9539.33
7	2084.60	115.60	9423.73
8	2056.49	143.71	9280.02
9	2021.53	178.67	9101.35
0	1978.08	222.12	8879.23
1	1924.05	276.15	8603.08
2	1856.88	343.32	8259.76
3	1773.38	426.82	7832.94
4	1669.57	530.63	7302.31
5	1540.51	659.69	6642.62
6	1380.05	820.15	5822.47
7	1180.57	1019.63	4802.84
8	932.57	1267.63	3535.21
9	624.25	1575.95	1959.26
0	240.94	1959.26	0.00

25 YEAR TERM
Monthly Payment = 183.88
Annual Payment =2206.56

INTER PD DUR YEAR	PRINCP PD DUR YEAR	MORTG BAL END OF YR
2195.99	10.57	9989.43
2193.42	13.14	9976.29
2190.22	16.34	9959.95
2186.25	20.31	9939.63
2181.31	25.25	9914.38
2175.16	31.40	9882.98
2167.53	39.03	9843.94
2158.03	48.53	9795.42
2146.23	60.33	9735.08
2131.55	75.01	9660.08
2113.31	93.25	9566.83
2090.63	115.93	9450.90
2062.43	144.13	9306.77
2027.38	179.18	9127.59
1983.80	222.76	8904.83
1929.61	276.95	8627.88
1862.25	344.31	8283.57
1778.51	428.05	7855.52
1674.40	532.16	7323.36
1544.96	661.60	6661.77
1384.05	822.51	5839.25
1183.99	1022.57	4816.68
935.28	1271.28	3545.40
626.07	1580.49	1964.91
241.65	1964.91	0.00

23.25 %

0 YEAR TERM:
lonthly Payment = 185.23
nnual Payment =2222.76

R	INTER PD DUR YEAR	PRINCP PD DUR YEAR	MORTG BAL END OF YR
1	2219.40	3.36	9996.64
2	2218.58	4.18	9992.46
3	2217.55	5.21	9987.25
4	2216.27	6.49	9980.76
5	2214.67	8.09	9972.67
6	2212.68	10.08	9962.59
7	2210.20	12.56	9950.03
8	2207.11	15.65	9934.38
9	2203.26	19.50	9914.88
0	2198.46	24.30	9890.58
1	2192.48	30.28	9860.30
2	2185.04	37.72	9822.58
3	2175.76	47.00	9775.57
4	2164.19	58.57	9717.01
5	2149.78	72.98	9644.03
6	2131.83	90.93	9553.10
7	2109.46	113.30	9439.80
8	2081.59	141.17	9298.63
9	2046.86	175.90	9122.72
0	2003.58	219.18	8903.54
1	1949.66	273.10	8630.44
2	1882.47	340.29	8290.15
3	1798.76	424.00	7866.15
4	1694.45	528.31	7337.84
5	1564.47	658.29	6679.55
6	1402.53	820.23	5859.32
7	1200.74	1022.02	4837.30
8	949.31	1273.45	3563.84
9	636.02	1586.74	1977.10
0	245.66	1977.10	0.00

25 YEAR TERM:
Monthly Payment = 185.74
Annual Payment =2228.88

INTER PD DUR YEAR	PRINCP PD DUR YEAR	MORTG BAL END OF YR
2218.77	10.11	9989.89
2216.29	12.59	9977.30
2213.19	15.69	9961.60
2209.33	19.55	9942.05
2204.52	24.36	9917.69
2198.52	30.36	9887.33
2191.05	37.83	9849.50
2181.75	47.13	9802.37
2170.15	58.73	9743.64
2155.70	73.18	9670.46
2137.70	91.18	9579.28
2115.27	113.61	9465.67
2087.32	141.56	9324.11
2052.49	176.39	9147.72
2009.10	219.78	8927.94
1955.03	273.85	8654.09
1887.66	341.22	8312.87
1803.72	425.16	7887.71
1699.12	529.76	7357.95
1568.79	660.09	6697.86
1406.40	822.48	5875.38
1204.06	1024.82	4850.55
951.94	1276.94	3573.61
637.79	1591.09	1982.52
246.36	1982.52	0.00

Annual Amortization Schedules

Based on a Mortgage of $ 10,000.00

23.50 %

30 YEAR TERM:
Monthly Payment = 187.12
Annual Payment = 2245.44

25 YEAR TERM
Monthly Payment = 187.6
Annual Payment = 2251.3

YR	30 YR INTER PD DUR YEAR	30 YR PRINCP PD DUR YEAR	30 YR MORTG BAL END OF YR	25 YR INTER PD DUR YEAR	25 YR PRINCP PD DUR YEAR	25 YR MORTG BAL END OF YR
1	2242.27	3.17	9996.83	2241.66	9.66	9990.34
2	2241.48	3.96	9992.86	2239.25	12.07	9978.27
3	2240.49	4.95	9987.91	2236.25	15.07	9963.20
4	2239.26	6.18	9981.73	2232.50	18.82	9944.37
5	2237.72	7.72	9974.01	2227.82	23.50	9920.87
6	2235.80	9.64	9964.37	2221.97	29.35	9891.52
7	2233.40	12.04	9952.34	2214.66	36.66	9854.86
8	2230.41	15.03	9937.31	2205.54	45.78	9809.09
9	2226.67	18.77	9918.53	2194.16	57.16	9751.92
10	2222.00	23.44	9895.09	2179.93	71.39	9680.53
11	2216.16	29.28	9865.81	2162.17	89.15	9591.38
12	2208.88	36.56	9829.25	2139.99	111.33	9480.05
13	2199.78	45.66	9783.60	2112.29	139.03	9341.02
14	2188.42	57.02	9726.58	2077.70	173.62	9167.40
15	2174.24	71.20	9655.38	2034.50	216.82	8950.58
16	2156.52	88.92	9566.46	1980.55	270.77	8679.82
17	2134.40	111.04	9455.42	1913.19	338.13	8341.68
18	2106.77	138.67	9316.75	1829.06	422.26	7919.42
19	2072.27	173.17	9143.58	1723.99	527.33	7392.09
20	2029.18	216.26	8927.32	1592.79	658.53	6733.56
21	1975.38	270.06	8657.26	1428.95	822.37	5911.19
22	1908.18	337.26	8320.00	1224.33	1026.99	4884.20
23	1824.27	421.17	7898.84	968.81	1282.51	3601.69
24	1719.48	525.96	7372.88	649.72	1601.60	2000.09
25	1588.62	656.82	6716.06	251.23	2000.09	0.00
26	1425.20	820.24	5895.83			
27	1221.12	1024.32	4871.51			
28	966.27	1279.17	3592.33			
29	648.00	1597.44	1994.89			
30	250.55	1994.89	0.00			

23.75 %

30 YEAR TERM:
Monthly Payment = 189.00
Annual Payment = 2268.00

25 YEAR TERM
Monthly Payment = 189.4
Annual Payment = 2273.6

YR	30 YR INTER PD DUR YEAR	30 YR PRINCP PD DUR YEAR	30 YR MORTG BAL END OF YR	25 YR INTER PD DUR YEAR	25 YR PRINCP PD DUR YEAR	25 YR MORTG BAL END OF YR
1	2265.00	3.00	9997.00	2264.40	9.24	9990.76
2	2264.24	3.76	9993.24	2262.08	11.56	9979.20
3	2263.30	4.70	9988.54	2259.17	14.47	9964.72
4	2262.12	5.88	9982.66	2255.52	18.12	9946.61
5	2260.64	7.36	9975.29	2250.97	22.67	9923.93
6	2258.78	9.22	9966.08	2245.26	28.38	9895.56
7	2256.46	11.54	9954.54	2238.12	35.52	9860.04
8	2253.56	14.44	9940.10	2229.19	44.45	9815.58
9	2249.93	18.07	9922.03	2218.00	55.64	9759.94
10	2245.38	22.62	9899.42	2204.00	69.64	9690.31
11	2239.69	28.31	9871.11	2186.48	87.16	9603.15
12	2232.57	35.43	9835.68	2164.55	109.09	9494.06
13	2223.66	44.34	9791.33	2137.10	136.54	9357.52
14	2212.50	55.50	9735.83	2102.75	170.89	9186.63
15	2198.53	69.47	9666.36	2059.76	213.88	8972.75
16	2181.06	86.94	9579.42	2005.94	267.70	8705.05
17	2159.18	108.82	9470.60	1938.59	335.05	8370.00
18	2131.80	136.20	9334.40	1854.29	419.35	7950.65
19	2097.53	170.47	9163.94	1748.78	524.86	7425.79
20	2054.64	213.36	8950.58	1616.73	656.91	6768.88
21	2000.96	267.04	8683.55	1451.45	822.19	5946.68
22	1933.78	334.22	8349.32	1244.58	1029.06	4917.62
23	1849.69	418.31	7931.01	985.67	1287.97	3629.65
24	1744.44	523.56	7407.45	661.61	1612.03	2017.62
25	1612.71	655.29	6752.16	256.02	2017.62	0.00
26	1447.84	820.16	5931.99			
27	1241.48	1026.52	4905.47			
28	983.21	1284.79	3620.68			
29	659.95	1608.05	2012.63			
30	255.37	2012.63	0.00			

Annual Amortization Schedules

Based on a Mortgage of $ 10,000.00

24.00 %

30 YEAR TERM:
Monthly Payment = 190.89
Annual Payment = 2290.68

25 YEAR TERM:
Monthly Payment = 191.34
Annual Payment = 2296.08

YR	30 YR INTER PD DUR YEAR	30 YR PRINCP PD DUR YEAR	30 YR MORTG BAL END OF YR	25 YR INTER PD DUR YEAR	25 YR PRINCP PD DUR YEAR	25 YR MORTG BAL END OF YR
1	2287.84	2.84	9997.16	2287.25	8.83	9991.17
2	2287.12	3.56	9993.60	2285.00	11.08	9980.09
3	2286.22	4.46	9989.14	2282.18	13.90	9966.19
4	2285.08	5.60	9983.54	2278.64	17.44	9948.75
5	2283.65	7.03	9976.51	2274.21	21.87	9926.88
6	2281.87	8.81	9967.70	2268.65	27.43	9899.45
7	2279.63	11.05	9956.65	2261.67	34.41	9865.03
8	2276.81	13.87	9942.78	2252.91	43.17	9821.86
9	2273.29	17.39	9925.38	2241.93	54.15	9767.71
10	2268.86	21.82	9903.57	2228.15	67.93	9699.78
11	2263.31	27.37	9876.20	2210.87	85.21	9614.58
12	2256.35	34.33	9841.86	2189.19	106.89	9507.69
13	2247.61	43.07	9798.79	2162.00	134.08	9373.61
14	2236.66	54.02	9744.77	2127.89	168.19	9205.43
15	2222.91	67.77	9677.00	2085.11	210.97	8994.45
16	2205.67	85.01	9591.99	2031.44	264.64	8729.81
17	2184.05	106.63	9485.36	1964.11	331.97	8397.84
18	2156.92	133.76	9351.60	1879.66	416.42	7981.42
19	2122.89	167.79	9183.81	1773.72	522.36	7459.06
20	2080.20	210.48	8973.33	1640.83	655.25	6803.81
21	2026.66	264.02	8709.31	1474.14	821.94	5981.87
22	1959.49	331.19	8378.12	1265.03	1031.05	4950.82
23	1875.24	415.44	7962.67	1002.74	1293.34	3657.47
24	1769.55	521.13	7441.54	673.71	1622.37	2035.10
25	1636.97	653.71	6787.83	260.98	2035.10	0.00
26	1470.67	820.01	5967.82			
27	1262.06	1028.62	4939.19			
28	1000.37	1290.31	3648.88			
29	672.12	1618.56	2030.32			
30	260.36	2030.32	0.00			

Glossary

acceleration clause A clause in a mortgage stipulating that, if certain defined conditions occur, any amount of money still outstanding is due and payable at once. Also called a *call-back clause*.

Adjustable Rate Mortgage (ARM) A mortgage, the interest rate of which varies during the term of the mortgage. Also called a *Variable Rate Mortgage*.

amortization The process of repaying a loan through a series of installment payments.

annual interest rate A percentage that, when multiplied by the principal, gives the amount of money that the principal will earn over the period of a year.

balloon note A note that usually calls for a final payment greater than the regular periodic payments.

blanket mortgage One mortgage that covers more than one parcel of real estate.

bridge loan A short-term loan in effect from the end of one loan to the beginning of another loan, or prior to permanent financing.

call-back clause *See* acceleration clause.

conventional mortgage A mortgage made by a bank or other private institution and not insured by a governmental agency.

discount points A charge, made by the lending institution to the borrower, that is based on the mortgage amount. A point is one percent of the principal mortgage amount.

first mortgage The primary mortgage on a property. If a foreclosure occurs, the first mortgage is repaid before any "junior" mortgages.

Flexible Payment Mortgage (FPM) A mortgage with payments that vary over the term of the mortgage. Usually the initial payments are lower than later payments.

Graduated Payment Mortgage (GPM) A mortgage with payments that increase in a specified manner over the term of the mortgage.

interest The amount of money earned by the principal during a specified period of time.

interest rate A percentage that, when multiplied by the principal, determines the amount of money that the principal earns over a period of time, usually one year.

junior mortgage A mortgage of lesser rank than the first mortgage. *See also* first mortgage.

mortgage A legal document that establishes real estate as the security for the loan which finances that real estate. Colloquially, the term *mortgage* is sometimes used to refer to the loan itself.

mortgage commitment A written offer of a mortgage loan by a lending institution. Often in the form of a letter, the commitment specifies the terms and conditions of the mortgage loan being offered to the prospective borrower.

mortgagee The institution or person who is the lender or creditor on a mortgage loan.

mortgagor The institution or person who is the borrower or debtor on a mortgage loan.

open-end mortgage A mortgage that provides for additional amounts to be loaned to the borrower without the need to create a new mortgage.

points *See* discount points.

prepayment clause A clause in a mortgage enabling the borrower to pay off the mortgage balance before the end of the mortgage term. This privilege sometimes involves a prepayment penalty.

Price Level Adjusted Mortgage (PLAM) A mortgage that provides for a periodic changing of the interest rate. A portion of the rate is determined by the contract rate, and an additional portion is determined by recalculating the mortgage balance based on a cost of living index.

principal Initial amount of money invested or borrowed.

Renegotiated Rate Mortgage (RRM) *See* Rollover Mortgage (ROM).

Reverse Annuity Mortgage (RAM) A type of mortgage that allows a borrower to draw on the current equity of the property.

Rollover Mortgage (ROM) A mortgage that provides for the renegotiation of the interest rate and the payment terms at specific intervals. Also called a *Renegotiated Rate Mortgage.*

Shared Appreciation Mortgage (SAM) A mortgage providing for the lender to receive a share in the appreciation of residential real estate. In return for this, the borrower is given an interest rate lower than the prevailing rate. Also called a *Shared Equity Mortgage.*

Shared Equity Mortgage (SEM) *See* Shared Appreciation Mortgage (SAM).

subject to mortgage A purchaser of mortgaged real estate having title but not being responsible for any of the mortgage debt beyond the value of his or her equity in the property.

Variable Rate Mortgage (VRM) *See* Adjustable Rate Mortgage.

Telephone No.

Telephone No.

Notes

Notes

Notes

Notes

ISBN PREFIX: 0-8120

BARRON'S

Barron's Educational Series, Inc.
250 Wireless Boulevard, Hauppauge, NY 11788
Call toll-free: 1-800-645-3476
In Canada: Georgetown Book Warehouse
34 Armstrong Ave., Georgetown, Ontario L7G 4R9
Call toll-free: 1-800-247-7160